International Directory of
COMPANY
HISTORIES

International Directory of

COMPANY

HISTORIES

VOLUME 114

Editor

Jay P. Pederson

ST. JAMES PRESS
A part of Gale, Cengage Learning

Detroit • New York • San Francisco • New Haven, Conn • Waterville, Maine • London

International Directory of Company Histories, Volume 114

Jay P. Pederson, Editor

Project Editor: Miranda H. Ferrara

Editorial: Virgil Burton, Donna Craft, Louise Gagné, Peggy Geeseman, Julie Gough, Sonya Hill, Keith Jones, Matthew Miskelly, Lynn Pearce, Laura Peterson, Holly Selden, Justine Ventimiglia

Production Technology Specialist: Mike Weaver

Imaging and Multimedia: John Watkins

Composition and Electronic Prepress: Gary Leach, Evi Seoud

Manufacturing: Rhonda Dover

Product Manager: Jenai Drouillard

Cover Photograph: Philadelphia Bourse, Philadelphia. Courtesy Library of Congress, Prints & Photographs Division, Detroit Publishing Company Collection.

For product information and technology assistance, contact us at **Gale Customer Support, 1-800-877-4253.** For permission to use material from this text or product, submit all requests online at **www.cengage.com/permissions.** Further permissions questions can be emailed to **permissionrequest@cengage.com**

Gale
27500 Drake Rd.
Farmington Hills, MI, 48331-3535

LIBRARY OF CONGRESS CATALOG NUMBER 89-190943
ISBN-13: 978-1-4144-4110-8
ISBN-10: 1-4144-4110-X

This title is also available as an e-book
ISBN-13: 978-1-55862-777-2   ISBN-10: 1-55862-777-4
Contact your Gale, a part of Cengage Learning sales representative for ordering information.

BRITISH LIBRARY CATALOGUING IN PUBLICATION DATA
International directory of company histories, Vol. 114
Jay P. Pederson
33.87409

Printed in the United States of America
1 2 3 4 5 6 7 14 13 12 11 10

Contents

Preface

The St. James Press series *The International Directory of Company Histories* (*IDCH*) is intended for reference use by students, business people, librarians, historians, economists, investors, job candidates, and others who seek to learn more about the historical development of the world's most important companies. To date, *IDCH* has profiled more than 10,930 companies in 114 volumes.

INCLUSION CRITERIA

Most companies chosen for inclusion in *IDCH* have achieved a minimum of US$25 million in annual sales and are leading influences in their industries or geographical locations. Companies may be publicly held, private, or nonprofit. State-owned companies that are important in their industries and that may operate much like public or private companies also are included. Wholly owned subsidiaries and divisions are profiled if they meet the requirements for inclusion. Entries on companies that have had major changes since they were last profiled may be selected for updating.

The *IDCH* series highlights 25% private and nonprofit companies, and features updated entries on approximately 35 companies per volume.

ENTRY FORMAT

Each entry begins with the company's legal name; the address of its headquarters; its telephone, toll-free, and fax numbers; and its web site. A statement of public, private, state, or parent ownership follows. A company with a legal name in both English and the language of its headquarters country is listed by the English name, with the native-language name in parentheses.

The company's founding or earliest incorporation date, the number of employees, and the most recent available sales figures follow. Sales figures are given in local currencies with equivalents in U.S. dollars. For some private companies, sales figures are estimates and indicated by the abbreviation *est*. The entry lists the exchanges on which the company's stock is traded and its ticker symbol, as well as the company's NAICS codes.

Entries generally contain a *Company Perspectives* box which provides a short summary of the company's mission, goals, and ideals; a *Key Dates* box highlighting milestones in the company's history; lists of *Principal Subsidiaries, Principal Divisions, Principal Operating Units, Principal Competitors*; and articles for *Further Reading*.

American spelling is used throughout *IDCH*, and the word "billion" is used in its U.S. sense of one thousand million.

SOURCES

Entries have been compiled from publicly accessible sources both in print and on the Internet such as general and academic periodicals, books, and annual reports, as well as material supplied by the companies themselves.

CUMULATIVE INDEXES

IDCH contains three indexes: the **Cumulative Index to Companies**, which provides an alphabetical index to companies profiled in the *IDCH* series, the **Index to Industries**, which allows researchers to locate companies by their principal industry, and the **Geographic Index**, which lists companies alphabetically by the country of their headquarters. The indexes are cumulative and specific instructions for using them are found immediately preceding each index.

SPECIAL TO THIS VOLUME

This volume of *IDCH* contains entries on two notable French champagne houses, Champagne Bollinger S.A. and Vranken Pommery Monopole S.A., as well as the Trinidad and Togabo-based producer of one of the world's most unique food and drink ingredients, Angostura Aromatic Bitters.

SUGGESTIONS WELCOME

Comments and suggestions from users of *IDCH* on any aspect of the product as well as suggestions for companies to be included or updated are cordially invited. Please write:

The Editor
International Directory of Company Histories
St. James Press
Gale, Cengage Learning
27500 Drake Rd.
Farmington Hills, Michigan 48331-3535

St. James Press does not endorse any of the companies or products mentioned in this series. Companies appearing in the *International Directory of Company Histories* were selected without reference to their wishes and have in no way endorsed their entries.

Notes on Contributors

M. L. Cohen
Novelist, business writer, and researcher living in Paris.

Jeffrey L. Covell
Seattle-based writer.

Ed Dinger
Writer and editor based in Bronx, New York.

Paul R. Greenland
Illinois-based writer and researcher; author of two books and former senior editor of a national business magazine; contributor to *The Encyclopedia of Chicago History, The Encyclopedia of Religion,* and the *Encyclopedia of American Industries.*

Robert Halasz
Former editor in chief of *World Progress* and *Funk & Wagnalls New Encyclopedia Yearbook*; author, *The U.S. Marines* (Millbrook Press, 1993).

Frederick C. Ingram
Writer based in South Carolina.

Kathleen Peippo
Minnesota-based writer.

Carrie Rothburd
Writer and editor specializing in corporate profiles, academic texts, and academic journal articles.

Roger Rouland
Writer and scholar specializing in company histories, literary criticism, literary essays, and poetry; freelance photographer specializing in nature photography.

Laura Rydberg
Minnesota-based writer specializing in company histories and creative nonfiction.

David E. Salamie
Part-owner of InfoWorks Development Group, a reference publication development and editorial services company.

Mary Tradii
Michigan-based writer.

Frank Uhle
Ann Arbor-based writer; movie projectionist, disc jockey, and staff member of *Psychotronic Video* magazine.

List of Abbreviations

€ European euro
¥ Japanese yen
£ United Kingdom pound
$ United States dollar

A

AB Aktiebolag (Finland, Sweden)
AB Oy Aktiebolag Osakeyhtiot (Finland)
A.E. Anonimos Eteria (Greece)
AED Emirati dirham
AG Aktiengesellschaft (Austria, Germany, Switzerland, Liechtenstein)
aG auf Gegenseitigkeit (Austria, Germany)
A.m.b.a. Andelsselskab med begraenset ansvar (Denmark)
A.O. Anonim Ortaklari/Ortakligi (Turkey)
ApS Amparteselskab (Denmark)
ARS Argentine peso
A.S. Anonim Sirketi (Turkey)
A/S Aksjeselskap (Norway)
A/S Aktieselskab (Denmark, Sweden)
Ay Avoinyhtio (Finland)
ATS Austrian shilling
AUD Australian dollar
Ay Avoinyhtio (Finland)

B

B.A. Buttengewone Aansprakeiijkheid (Netherlands)
BEF Belgian franc

BHD Bahraini dinar
Bhd. Berhad (Malaysia, Brunei)
BND Brunei dollar
BRL Brazilian real
B.V. Besloten Vennootschap (Belgium, Netherlands)

C

C. de R.L. Compania de Responsabilidad Limitada (Spain)
C. por A. Compania por Acciones (Dominican Republic)
C.A. Compania Anonima (Ecuador, Venezuela)
C.V. Commanditaire Vennootschap (Netherlands, Belgium)
CAD Canadian dollar
CEO Chief Executive Officer
CFO Chief Financial Officer
CHF Swiss franc
Cia. Compagnia (Italy)
Cia. Companhia (Brazil, Portugal)
Cia. Compania (Latin America [except Brazil], Spain)
Cie. Compagnie (Belgium, France, Luxembourg, Netherlands)
CIO Chief Information Officer
CLP Chilean peso
CNY Chinese yuan
Co. Company
COO Chief Operating Officer
Coop. Cooperative
COP Colombian peso

Corp. Corporation
CPT Cuideachta Phoibi Theoranta (Republic of Ireland)
CRL Companhia a Responsabilidao Limitida (Portugal, Spain)
CZK Czech koruna

D

D&B Dunn & Bradstreet
DEM German deutsche mark (W. Germany to 1990; unified Germany to 2002)
Div. Division (United States)
DKK Danish krone
DZD Algerian dinar

E

E.P.E. Etema Pemorismenis Evthynis (Greece)
EC Exempt Company (Arab countries)
Edms. Bpk. Eiendoms Beperk (South Africa)
EEK Estonian Kroon
eG eingetragene Genossenschaft (Germany)
EGMBH Eingetragene Genossenschaft mit beschraenkter Haftung (Austria, Germany)
EGP Egyptian pound
Ek For Ekonomisk Forening (Sweden)
EP Empresa Portuguesa (Portugal)

ESOP Employee Stock Options and Ownership
ESP Spanish peseta
Et(s). Etablissement(s) (Belgium, France, Luxembourg)
eV eingetragener Verein (Germany)
EUR European euro

F
FIM Finnish markka
FRF French franc

G
G.I.E. Groupement d'Interet Economique (France)
gGmbH gemeinnutzige Gesellschaft mit beschraenkter Haftung (Austria, Germany, Switzerland)
GmbH Gesellschaft mit beschraenkter Haftung (Austria, Germany, Switzerland)
GRD Greek drachma
GWA Gewerbte Amt (Austria, Germany)

H
HB Handelsbolag (Sweden)
HF Hlutafelag (Iceland)
HKD Hong Kong dollar
HUF Hungarian forint

I
IDR Indonesian rupiah
IEP Irish pound
ILS Israeli shekel (new)
Inc. Incorporated (United States, Canada)
INR Indian rupee
IPO Initial Public Offering
I/S Interesentselskap (Norway)
I/S Interessentselskab (Denmark)
ISK Icelandic krona
ITL Italian lira

J
JMD Jamaican dollar
JOD Jordanian dinar

K
KB Kommanditbolag (Sweden)
KES Kenyan schilling
Kft Korlatolt Felelossegu Tarsasag (Hungary)
KG Kommanditgesellschaft (Austria, Germany, Switzerland)

KGaA Kommanditgesellschaft auf Aktien (Austria, Germany, Switzerland)
KK Kabushiki Kaisha (Japan)
KPW North Korean won
KRW South Korean won
K/S Kommanditselskab (Denmark)
K/S Kommandittselskap (Norway)
KWD Kuwaiti dinar
Ky Kommandiitiyhtio (Finland)

L
L.L.C. Limited Liability Company (Arab countries, Egypt, Greece, United States)
L.L.P. Limited Liability Partnership (United States)
L.P. Limited Partnership (Canada, South Africa, United Kingdom, United States)
LBO Leveraged Buyout
Lda. Limitada (Spain)
Ltd. Limited
Ltda. Limitada (Brazil, Portugal)
Ltee. Limitee (Canada, France)
LUF Luxembourg franc

M
mbH mit beschraenkter Haftung (Austria, Germany)
Mij. Maatschappij (Netherlands)
MUR Mauritian rupee
MXN Mexican peso
MYR Malaysian ringgit

N
N.A. National Association (United States)
N.V. Naamloze Vennootschap (Belgium, Netherlands)
NGN Nigerian naira
NLG Netherlands guilder
NOK Norwegian krone
NZD New Zealand dollar

O
OAO Otkrytoe Aktsionernoe Obshchestve (Russia)
OHG Offene Handelsgesellschaft (Austria, Germany, Switzerland)
OMR Omani rial
OOO Obschestvo s Ogranichennoi Otvetstvennostiu (Russia)

OOUR Osnova Organizacija Udruzenog Rada (Yugoslavia)
Oy Osakeyhtiö (Finland)

P
P.C. Private Corp. (United States)
P.L.L.C. Professional Limited Liability Corporation (United States)
P.T. Perusahaan/Perseroan Terbatas (Indonesia)
PEN Peruvian Nuevo Sol
PHP Philippine peso
PKR Pakistani rupee
P/L Part Lag (Norway)
PLC Public Limited Co. (United Kingdom, Ireland)
PLN Polish zloty
PTE Portuguese escudo
Pte. Private (Singapore)
Pty. Proprietary (Australia, South Africa, United Kingdom)
Pvt. Private (India, Zimbabwe)
PVBA Personen Vennootschap met Beperkte Aansprakelijkheid (Belgium)
PYG Paraguay guarani

Q
QAR Qatar riyal

R
REIT Real Estate Investment Trust
RMB Chinese renminbi
Rt Reszvenytarsasag (Hungary)
RUB Russian ruble

S
S.A. Sociedad Anónima (Latin America [except Brazil], Spain, Mexico)
S.A. Sociedades Anônimas (Brazil, Portugal)
S.A. Société Anonyme (Arab countries, Belgium, France, Jordan, Luxembourg, Switzerland)
S.A. de C.V. Sociedad Anonima de Capital Variable (Mexico)
S.A.B. de C.V. Sociedad Anónima Bursátil de Capital Variable (Mexico)
S.A.C. Sociedad Anonima Comercial (Latin America [except Brazil])
S.A.C.I. Sociedad Anonima Comercial e Industrial (Latin America [except Brazil])

S.A.C.I.y.F. Sociedad Anonima Comercial e Industrial y Financiera (Latin America [except Brazil])

S.A.R.L. Sociedade Anonima de Responsabilidade Limitada (Brazil, Portugal)

S.A.R.L. Société à Responsabilité Limitée (France, Belgium, Luxembourg)

S.A.S. Societe Anonyme Syrienne (Arab countries)

S.A.S. Societá in Accomandita Semplice (Italy)

S.C. Societe en Commandite (Belgium, France, Luxembourg)

S.C.A. Societe Cooperativa Agricole (France, Italy, Luxembourg)

S.C.I. Sociedad Cooperativa Ilimitada (Spain)

S.C.L. Sociedad Cooperativa Limitada (Spain)

S.C.R.L. Societe Cooperative a Responsabilite Limitee (Belgium)

S.E. Societas Europaea (European Union Member states

S.L. Sociedad Limitada (Latin America [except Brazil], Portugal, Spain)

S.N.C. Société en Nom Collectif (France)

S.p.A. Società per Azioni (Italy)

S.R.L. Sociedad de Responsabilidad Limitada (Spain, Mexico, Latin America [except Brazil])

S.R.L. Società a Responsabilità Limitata (Italy)

S.R.O. Spolecnost s Rucenim Omezenym (Czechoslovakia

S.S.K. Sherkate Sahami Khass (Iran)

S.V. Samemwerkende Vennootschap (Belgium)

S.Z.R.L. Societe Zairoise a Responsabilite Limitee (Zaire)

SAA Societe Anonyme Arabienne (Arab countries)

SAK Societe Anonyme Kuweitienne (Arab countries)

SAL Societe Anonyme Libanaise (Arab countries)

SAO Societe Anonyme Omanienne (Arab countries)

SAQ Societe Anonyme Qatarienne (Arab countries)

SAR Saudi riyal

Sdn. Bhd. Sendirian Berhad (Malaysia)

SEK Swedish krona

SGD Singapore dollar

S/L Salgslag (Norway)

Soc. Sociedad (Latin America [except Brazil], Spain)

Soc. Sociedade (Brazil, Portugal)

Soc. Societa (Italy)

Sp. z.o.o. Spólka z ograniczona odpowiedzialnoscia (Poland)

Ste. Societe (France, Belgium, Luxembourg, Switzerland)

Ste. Cve. Societe Cooperative (Belgium)

T

THB Thai baht

TND Tunisian dinar

TRL Turkish lira

TTD Trinidad and Tobago dollar

TWD Taiwan dollar (new)

U

U.A. Uitgesloten Aansporakeiijkheid (Netherlands)

u.p.a. utan personligt ansvar (Sweden)

V

V.O.f. Vennootschap onder firma (Netherlands)

VAG Verein der Arbeitgeber (Austria, Germany)

VEB Venezuelan bolivar

VERTR Vertriebs (Austria, Germany)

VND Vietnamese dong

VVAG Versicherungsverein auf Gegenseitigkeit (Austria, Germany)

W–Z

WA Wettelika Aansprakalikhaed (Netherlands)

WLL With Limited Liability (Bahrain, Kuwait, Qatar, Saudi Arabia)

YK Yugen Kaisha (Japan)

ZAO Zakrytoe Aktsionernoe Obshchestve (Russia)

ZAR South African rand

ZMK Zambian kwacha

ZWD Zimbabwean dollar

Aaron's, Inc.

———————◼———————

309 East Paces Ferry Road, N.E.
Atlanta, Georgia 30305-2377
U.S.A.
Telephone: (404) 231-0011
Fax: (404) 240-6584
Web site: http://aaronrents.com

Public Company
Incorporated: 1962
Employees: 10,000
Sales: $1.75 billion (2009)
Stock Exchanges: New York
Ticker Symbol: AAN
NAICS: 337211 Wood Office Furniture Manufacturing;
442110 Furniture Stores; 442229 All Other Home
Furnishings Stores; 443111 Household Appliance
Stores; 443112 Radio, Television, and Other
Electronics Stores; 532299 All Other Consumer
Goods Rental

◼ ◼ ◼

Aaron's, Inc., rents and sells residential and office
furniture, household appliances, consumer electronics,
and accessories to both individual and corporate
customers. In addition to being one of the largest
companies in its industry, Aaron's is distinguished as the
only rental company that manufactures and reconditions
its own furniture. Aaron's Rental Purchase division
focuses on providing durable household goods to lower-
to middle-income consumers with limited or no access
to traditional credit sources such as bank financing,

installment credit, or credit cards. The company operates more than 1,694 company-owned and franchised
stores in 48 states, Canada, and Puerto Rico.

STEADY GROWTH FROM THE
LATE FIFTIES

Aaron Rents is the creation of entrepreneur R. Charles
Loudermilk. Loudermilk was born in Atlanta, Georgia,
in 1927—"on the wrong side of the tracks," by his
admission. He attended Georgia Tech, had a tour in the
Navy, and earned his business degree from the
University of North Carolina, before accepting a job
with Pet Milk Company and, later, the pharmaceutical
and chemical giant Pfizer. While working for Pfizer during the early 1950s, Loudermilk came across a small
North Carolina store that rented furniture and other
merchandise. Eager to strike out on his own, Loudermilk drew on the concept and started a rental business
in 1955, borrowing $500 from Trust Company Bank,
while a partner invested another $500.

Loudermilk's first order was for 300 chairs. He and
his partner rushed to an army surplus store and
purchased 500 chairs. They delivered 300 of them to an
auction in Atlanta and charged 10 cents per chair per
day. "It was a hot day and the chairs didn't stack well,"
Loudermilk recalled in company annals. "My partner
decided he didn't want to be in the rental business
anymore." After his partner bailed out, Loudermilk
stuck with his idea and continued to buy and rent
furniture. Because he had little money to invest in the
business, he worked at his mother's restaurant and
poured virtually every nickel back into his rental venture

for seven straight years. Later, Loudermilk was able to rent a small storefront and hire a woman to answer the telephone; he named the company Aaron Rents to ensure top billing in the Yellow Pages.

Loudermilk gave his receptionist a catalog from a California company and told her to buy rental equipment from it. When a customer called or came in to rent some item, she would simply let that person select pieces from the catalog. If an order came in for a table or bed, for example, Loudermilk would drive down to Sears, buy a piece similar to the one in the catalog, and deliver it himself. Thus Loudermilk got into renting party equipment and sickroom gear, later moving into office and residential furniture. "People said it was a gamble," Loudermilk recalled in the November 21, 1983 issue of *Forbes*. "It really wasn't. We never bought the second item until the first one was rented."

EXPANSION IN THE SIXTIES TO MID-SEVENTIES

Loudermilk spent the late 1950s nurturing the business at his original Buckhead area store before branching out in the 1960s with a second shop. A third store was opened in 1964 and rented only furniture. By that time, inventory had grown to include large outdoor tents. Loudermilk rented four tents to civil rights marchers when they made their famous trek from Selma to Montgomery, Alabama, in 1965. Two years later, the company opened an outlet in Baltimore, its first outside of Atlanta. By 1969, Aaron Rents was generating a healthy $2 million annually from an inventory of about $3 million.

Aside from furniture and party-related supplies, eventually Aaron Rents outlets were renting everything from corkscrews and pillowcases to sofas and executive desks. The business was relatively simple and straightforward. Loudermilk would purchase goods, rent

them out, and depreciate them down to a value of zero. Tax laws during the early 1970s allowed him to depreciate the entire value of the item over a period of three years; the depreciated value was written off against income to reduce taxes. Everything that he could get in rent or resale of the item after that was pure profit.

Aaron Rents prospered during the 1960s and 1970s. By the mid-1970s, the operation had expanded to include nearly 20 showrooms that were generating annual sales of about $10 million. That sales figure made Aaron the largest private company operating in the burgeoning U.S. furniture rental business. Although Aaron's steady growth prior to the 1980s was admirable, it was meager in comparison with the rampant expansion the company would achieve in the following 15 years. Several factors contributed to that expansion. Significantly, in the late 1970s, Loudermilk decided to focus his efforts on the residential and office markets, rather than his traditional party and sickroom segment. That decision resulted in a rapid climb in sales. Therefore, in 1982, Loudermilk sold off his party and sickroom equipment operations and dumped the proceeds into his residential and business division.

In addition to shifting the company's focus, Loudermilk achieved growth during the late 1970s and early 1980s through new financing strategies. Rather than waiting until his goods had depreciated to reap his profits, he began taking less depreciation during the rental period and then barely breaking even on the resale of the furniture. A $200 desk, for instance, would be depreciated down to $100 and then marked up to $130 for resale. Simply put, he found a way to take his profits earlier. When the furniture was no longer rentable, Loudermilk would sell it alongside value-oriented new furniture in warehouse-style stores, called Aaron Sells Furniture, next to his rental shops. That way, he was able to attract customers who did not want to rent but did not have cash for expensive new furniture.

The overall strategy helped to boost the company's net income to a record $4.7 million in 1983 from sales of $55.4 million. By the end of that year, Aaron Rents was operating a total of 92 stores in 14 mostly southern states. It was servicing 50,000 rental contracts worth an average of $48 monthly, giving Aaron roughly 15 percent of the $350 million furniture rental market. Loudermilk had become a multimillionaire. He spent his weekends on his 3,700-acre south Georgia plantation, where he tended his herd of purebred Limousin cattle and perused his corn and soybean fields. When not at the plantation, he might be found hunting geese in Alaska or Scotland. Otherwise, Loudermilk worked to enlarge his rental empire.

KEY DATES

1955: R. Charles Loudermilk starts Aaron Rents.

1964: Aaron Rents opens its first furniture rental store.

1971: Aaron Rents acquires MacTavish Furniture Industries.

1982: Aaron Rents goes public.

1983: Aaron Rents acquires Modern Furniture Rental.

1987: Company purchases Ball Stalker and enters the rent-to-own business.

1990: Aaron Rents begins to offer franchise options.

1998: Company acquires Lamps Forever.

2003: Annual revenue tops $1 billion.

2009: Aaron Rents changes its name to Aaron's, Inc.

GROWTH THROUGH ACQUISITIONS IN THE EIGHTIES

Another important factor in Aaron Rents' tremendous expansion during the early 1980s was Loudermilk's strategy to add to the company's growth through acquisition. Loudermilk took Aaron Rents public in 1982 to raise expansion capital (he retained 42 percent of the company's stock, valued then at about $38 million). He used part of the money from the public offering to buy a few of his largest private competitors. Most notable were the acquisitions of leading private rental companies Metrolease (Metropolitan Furniture Leasing), of North Carolina, and the Houston-based Modern Furniture Rental. Loudermilk bought Modern Furniture in July 1983 for $6.5 million in cash before plunking down $4.5 million for Metrolease the following summer. Meanwhile, the rental industry in general was expanding, adding fuel to Aaron Rents' growth. Aaron Rents' annual revenues surged to $84 million in 1984, making it the largest rental company in the nation. Aaron Rents surpassed the venerable industry leader GranTree, which had doubled its revenues from $41 million in 1977 to $82 million in 1984.

At the same time, Aaron Rents' bottom line was benefiting from in-house manufacturing operations. The company had started producing its furniture out of necessity in 1971 when Lockheed Corp. brought employees to Atlanta from all over the world to build a new plane.

Manufacturers simply could not meet Aaron's demand for furniture to rent to the influx of workers, so

Loudermilk decided to begin building the furniture himself. He purchased a local manufacturer called Mac-Tavish Furniture Industries and was instantly in the furniture-making business. The decision to manufacture proved fruitful, and Aaron became the only company in the rental industry to exclusively build its furniture. The benefits were multifold. Not only did Aaron benefit from a dependable, low-cost furniture source, but it also saved money and time related to the repair and reconditioning of its old furniture. In addition, Aaron was able to control both styling and price to suit the specific needs of its targeted customers.

Aaron continued to pursue acquisitions and to expand its furniture making operations during 1984 and 1985. By early 1986, the chain had grown to include 154 stores in 20 states and annual revenues were topping a fat $100 million. Despite sales gains, however, earnings growth had stalled. The problem was primarily the result of the fast store expansion. New stores typically took 12 to 18 months to achieve profitability. Many of Aaron's outlets were still dragging down the bottom line. Loudermilk decided to slow the company's expansion and to focus on consolidating and streamlining existing operations. During 1986 and 1987, the company closed some Aaron Sells outlets, beefed up its management team, and launched a drive to cut costs and improve profit margins. Loudermilk took a break from day-to-day management of the company during those years, devoting much of his time to his duties as chairman of the Metro Atlanta Rapid Transit Authority and to his political interests.

The effects of management efforts at Aaron seemed apparent by 1988. Sales rose to $119 million and $132 million in 1987 and 1988, respectively, while net earnings climbed to $4.79 million and $5.54 million. The sales gains, however, were partially the result of Loudermilk's October 1987 purchase of Ball Stalker Inc., an Atlanta-based manufacturer and distributor of upscale office furniture. Similarly, the profit increase was generated primarily by a cut in Aaron's effective corporate tax rate from 46 percent to 34 percent. The tax cut was ushered in with the renowned Tax Reform Act of 1986 (TRA). The TRA eliminated many of the depreciation benefits that Aaron had enjoyed previously, however. Thus, although earnings rose between 1987 and 1988, they were still low compared with previous projections, and the TRA promised to hurt future profits as well. Evidencing investor discontent with the situation, Aaron's stock price skidded from a high of $25.75 in 1984 to just $12 before the 1987 stock market crash, after which it plummeted to a low of $6.50.

Realizing that his company was struggling, Loudermilk returned to day-to-day control of the company in

1987. He renewed the company's efforts to overhaul operations, cut costs, and boost margins. At the same time, Loudermilk continued to expand the Aaron network of stores. Early in 1988, he purchased furniture rental operations in Florida from Furniture Enterprises and Powell Furniture Rental, as well as a Jackson, Mississippi, store from competitor Cort Furniture Rental Corp. By late 1988, the company was operating 183 stores in 31 states. Before the end of the year, however, that number would be reduced as a result of the consolidation of several Aaron Sells outlets with adjacent Aaron Rents stores.

Significantly, Aaron followed in the footsteps of its chief competitors, GranTree and the highly successful Rent-A-Center, in 1987 when it entered the rent-to-own business. Under that program, customers were allowed to make regular payments over a predetermined period, usually 18 or 24 months, to use furniture, appliances, electronics, and other goods. These payments differed from usual rent payments by being applied to the purchase price, and the consumer could own the item at the end of the rental period. By late 1988, Aaron was offering rent-to-own at 18 of its store locations, introducing a 12-month ownership plan, and Loudermilk was planning to expand the successful program throughout his network. The rent-to-own initiative was part of Loudermilk's push to focus on renting rather than selling furniture.

REORGANIZATION AND FRANCHISING IN THE LATE EIGHTIES AND NINETIES

Facing flat market growth in the furniture rental industry, Loudermilk stepped up reorganization efforts in 1989 by eliminating distinctions between the rental, sales, and combination-store divisions. He replaced them with six geographical regions, each with a vice president responsible for 10 to 20 outlets. Previously, a single manager had been placed in charge of about 60 stores. Similarly, the office furniture rental division, which consisted of about 47 stores going into 1990, was reorganized into six geographical regions, each of which was headed by a vice president. Finally, Loudermilk initiated a franchising campaign designed to increase Aaron's regional coverage with minimal capital cost to the company.

The reorganization was slow to take hold. In fact, Aaron suffered three consecutive years of declining sales and earnings beginning in 1989. Eventually, the company's financial performance recovered. Among Loudermilk's successful moves during the early 1990s was renting office equipment, not just office furniture. He had hesitated to rent equipment for several years

because he felt that Aaron lacked the management expertise to handle that market segment. That move contributed to Aaron's turnaround, however, which began in 1992. Although Aaron's sales for 1992 grew marginally to about $145 million, the company posted a profit of about $3.1 million, Aaron's first profit gain since 1988.

Encouraged by success with the Aaron Rental Purchase stores, which made up Aaron's rent-to-own business, Loudermilk began expanding the chain through both franchises and company-owned stores. As a result, revenues sailed to $158 million in 1993 before rocketing to about $186 million in 1994. Throughout fiscal 1994, the second-ranked company on *Franchise* magazine's Gold 100 list added rental-purchase stores to its chain at a rate of one per week. Growth continued during 1995.

By September 1995, Aaron was operating a total of 206 company-owned outlets and 33 franchised stores, and sales were booming. Revenues swelled 24 percent in fiscal 1995 to nearly $230 million as net income vaulted to a record $11.33 million. By 1998, the number of stores had increased to about 300 (368 by 1999) and revenues were at $380 million, $200 million of which came from the rental purchase business. Aaron also continued to benefit from its five furniture manufacturing plants in Georgia and Florida.

Aaron was selective regarding to whom it would sell franchise rights, and where its franchises would be located. "We don't want to be hidden in the middle of a shopping center. We want locations comparable to Blockbuster Video. You never see a Blockbuster store that is not very, very visible," Loudermilk was quoted as saying in the October/November 1995 issue of *Progressive Rentals*. Aaron's stores were on average 10,000 to 12,000 square feet, larger and more attractive than the competition, usually suburban in location, and serving customers with a higher income than other rent-to-own businesses. When he could not find a large enough store, Loudermilk would build a stand-alone unit marked by Aaron's unique design. Aaron's franchise support center provided assistance to franchisees in selecting store location and training in management and operation.

In the late 1990s, the company commanded approximately 30 percent of the estimated $600 rent-to-rent market in the United States and was branching out into the corporate relocation and small office/home office markets. Apartment management companies represented another expanding segment of its rent-to-rent customer base. Aaron Direct, the company's warehouse concept, had a presence in six markets serving national customers that provided interim housing for companies relocating employees. In 1998, the company acquired Lamps Forever, a manufacturer of designer lamps, tables, and matching accessories.

The following year, in a major expansion of its national advertising, Aaron acquired rights to the NASCAR Busch Grand National Car Race. Beginning in 2000, the "Aaron's 312" campaign played off the longest race of the season, a 312-mile run, while reminding sports fans, whose demographic profile exactly matched the company's target customer base, of Aaron's three forms of purchasing: cash or check, credit card, or its Lease Plus 12-month lease program.

In 1999, Aaron was also added to the S&P Small-Cap 600 Index. Also, for the second straight year, the company was named one of the 200 best small companies by *Forbes*. The company fixed its strategic focus on expansion for the years 2000 and beyond. Adding stores in established markets, targeting the growing office furniture rental segment, accelerating franchised rental purchase store openings, and adding company-operated stores in major markets, Aaron Rents sought to continue growing.

RECORD PROFITS AND UNPRECEDENTED GROWTH: 2000–09

During the next several years, Aaron's grew exponentially, expanding in all areas of its business from opening new stores and servicing new markets to manufacturing. In 2000 and 2001, Aaron's increased its office equipment offerings by partnering with CompUSA to market personal computers. It also acquired several furniture chains for conversion, including 10 rental purchase stores in Puerto Rico (Aaron's first expansion outside the United States) and 52 stores from a bankrupt furniture chain, Heilig-Meyers. Manufacturing capacity was also ramped up, with the company opening its 11th factory. In total, Aaron's added 92 stores in 2001. By the end of the year, the company had more than 650 stores in 42 states and Puerto Rico. Sales were booming. Revenues for the year increased dramatically to $546.7 million.

Loudermilk was credited largely for Aaron's fast-paced growth because he was not afraid to try new ideas. He was also adept at recognizing mistakes and correcting them quickly. In 2002, Aaron Rents experimented with operating a traditional retailer, acquiring 26 Sight 'n Sound Appliance Centers (a specialty retailer of furniture, appliances, and consumer electronics) and letting the company keep its name. A year later, Aaron Rents had learned the hard way that it could not compete such large electronics retailers as Best

Buy, and started converting all Sight 'n Sound stores to Aaron Rents stores.

In 2003, Aaron's ambitious expansion showed no signs of slowing down. Growth continued to come from a combination of acquisitions of independent and franchise operations and new store openings. Midyear, the company announced that it would acquire 15 franchise stores and that it was interested in buying as many as 50 more. By the end of 2003, it had also opened six stores in Ontario, Canada, and had entered into an agreement with Rosey Rentals to convert 31 of its stores to franchised Aaron Rents. At the end of 2003, Aaron had more than 850 company operated and franchised stores. It also hit a financial milestone, exceeding $1 billion in revenue for the year.

In the spring of 2004, Aaron confirmed it was on track to open even more stores than the year before. In June it acquired 26 rental purchase stores from Easy Way. In September it acquired 25 stores from Home Express. Franchise store acquisitions also peaked. By the end of the year, it had 147 more stores than the previous year, with 1,000 stores in 45 states, Canada, and Puerto Rico. From 2005 to 2007, Aaron's continued its spending spree. During the next several years it purchased 19 rental stores from Rent-A-Center (its top competitor), a chain of rental stores from Briley Investments and Alliance Rental Centers, and 33 stores from Prime Time Rentals. In tandem with these acquisitions Aaron's began a process of identifying, merging, and selling stores that were not achieving performance goals. This strategy enabled the company to continue to grow. In 2007, revenues totaled $1.4 billion.

In 2008, Loudermilk's son, Robert C. Loudermilk Jr., was elected the company's chief operating officer. That year, the company continued to follow a strategy of merging and closing stores. It sold its Aaron's Corporate Furnishings division to CORT Business Services Corporation for $72 million because it did not have the same growth rate or prospects of the company's highly successful Aaron's Sales & Lease Ownership division. With this sale, the company exited the rent-to-rent market. At the end of the year, Aaron's acquired Cleeks Lease, as well as all the Rosey Rentals franchise stores. The company finished the year with 1,535 stores earning revenues of $1.6 billion.

The downturn in the world economy in 2008 and 2009 proved to be a boon for Aaron's business, with more consumers turning to the rent-to-own option. First-quarter earnings for 2009 jumped 57 percent. Revenues for the year were up 10 percent from 2008 to total $1.75 billion. As a result, the company continued its pursuit of acquisition and expansion when many other stores were closing and going out of business. In

April 2009, it announced that it would be changing its name to Aaron's, Inc. Moving forward, it seemed there were few obstacles for the company's continued growth.

Dave Mote
Updated, Carrie Rothburd

PRINCIPAL SUBSIDIARIES

Aaron Investment Company.

PRINCIPAL DIVISIONS

Aaron's, Inc. Admin. Office; Aaron's Sales & Lease Ownership; Mac Tavish Furniture Industries; RIMCO; Aaron's, Inc. Distribution Center.

PRINCIPAL COMPETITORS

Bestway, Inc.; Brook Furniture Rental, Inc.; Rent-A-Center, Inc.; Best Buy Co., Inc.; W. S. Badcock Corporation; Sears, Roebuck and Co.

FURTHER READING

Bork, Robert H., "Money in the Mattress," *Forbes*, November 21, 1983, p. 108.

Gilligan, Gregory J., "Rent-to-Own Delivers to Aaron a New Direction, Higher Sales," *Richmond Times-Dispatch*, Bus. Sec., July 31, 1993.

Hallem, Jeanie Franco, "'Cooling It' Is New Motto for Aaron Rents," *Atlanta Business Chronicle*, February 24, 1986, p. 2B.

Kapner, Suzanne, "Rent-to-Own Makes a Comeback," *Fortune*, June 8, 2009, p. 22.

Massey, John, "Check Out Charlie," *Progressive Rentals*, October/November 1995, p. 23.

Miller, Matt, "To Rent in Full," *Daily Deal/The Deal*, October 6, 2003, p. 3.

Robertshaw, Nicky, "Aaron Rents Expanding with Six-Eight Stores," *Memphis Business Journal*, November 21, 1994, p. 3.

Schonbak, Judith, "Aaron Rents Bounces Back," *Business Atlanta*, September 1988, p. 32.

———, "Aaron Rents Launches New Venture," *Business Atlanta*, July 1992, p. 8.

Weiner, Daniel P., "Aaron Rents Inc.," *Fortune*, November 25, 1985, p. 40.

Welch, Mary, "'Radical' Shift for Aaron Rents," *Atlanta Business Chronicle*, December 19, 1988, p. 6.

Abu Dhabi National Oil Company

P.O. Box 898
Abu Dhabi,
United Arab Emirates
Telephone: (+971 02) 6020000
Fax: (+971 02) 6023389
Web site: http://www.adnoc.com
Government-Owned Company

Founded: 1971
Incorporated: 1998
Employees: 5,184
Sales: $38.79 billion (2007)
NAICS: 211111 Crude Petroleum and Natural Gas
Extraction; 211112 Natural Gas Liquid Extraction;
324110 Petroleum Refineries

■ ■ ■

Abu Dhabi National Oil Company (ADNOC) is one of the world's leading oil and gas companies. The government-owned company produces more than 2.9 million barrels of oil per day, and plans to increase its capacity to 3.5 million barrels per day by 2018. As the national oil company of Abu Dhabi, the largest of the United Arab Emirates (UAE), ADNOC also controls the world's fourth-largest oil reserve. ADNOC has also been developing its natural gas production operations, launching the exploitation of the Shah gas fields in 2010. ADNOC conducts its upstream operations through subsidiaries Abu Dhabi Company for Onshore Oil Operations (ADCO), Abu Dhabi Marine Operating Company (ADMA-OPCO), Zakum Development

Company (ZADCO), and Abu Dhabi Gas Industries Limited (GASCO). The company's downstream operations include Abu Dhabi Gas Liquefaction Company Ltd. (ADGAS) and Abu Dhabi Oil Refining Company (TAKREER).

Other subsidiaries provide exploration and production services, including National Drilling Company and ESNAAD. The group's Chemicals and Petrochemicals division is focused largely on Abu Dhabi Polymers Company Limited (Borouge), and includes a joint venture with Total, Ruwais Fertilizer Industries (FERTIL). ADNOC operates its own fleet of vessels through two transportation subsidiaries, Abu Dhabi National Tanker Company (ADNATCO) and National Gas Shipping Company (NGSCO). Lastly, the company's Distribution division, including its network of service stations, operates primarily through ADNOC Distribution. ADNOC is led by CEO Yousef Omair bin Yousef. The company operates under the auspices of the Supreme Petroleum Council, headed by UAE President Sheikh Khalifa bin Zayed Al-Nahyan. The company last reported revenues of $38.79 billion in 2007.

ROOTS IN FOREIGN OIL INTERESTS

Abu Dhabi was a latecomer to the Middle Eastern oil industry, only beginning production in 1962. The search for oil had begun nearly 30 years earlier, however. As elsewhere in the Middle East, this search was in the hands of foreign oil interests organized in a consortium. In 1928 a group of U.K., Anglo-Dutch, and U.S. international oil companies formed Iraq Petroleum

Company (IPC) with a concession that came to cover most of Iraq.

Once IPC was formed, each partner agreed that it would not hold concessions in any other part of the former territory of the Ottoman Empire except in association with all the other partners, and in the same proportions as IPC. Most of the Persian Gulf states, including Abu Dhabi but excluding Kuwait, were included in this nebulous area. The oil companies involved marked in red on a map the boundary of the area to which they intended the agreement to apply, and it became known as the Red Line Agreement. Thus when attention turned to searching for oil in the Trucial States (as the UAE was known until 1971), a consortium with exactly the same ownership structure as IPC was formed.

In 1935 a new U.K. company was established, Petroleum Development (Trucial States) Ltd., commonly referred to as PDTC. PDTC's ownership was identical to that of IPC, with the Anglo-Persian Oil Company (later British Petroleum), Shell, Compagnie Française des Pétroles, and two U.S. companies (Exxon and Mobil Oil) owning 23.75 percent each of the shares, and investor Calouste Gulbenkian's interests the remaining 5 percent. PDTC contacted all the sheikdoms offering arrangements for concession rights to explore for oil and to develop production should oil be found. In January 1939 Abu Dhabi granted PDTC such concessions for a period of 75 years.

Oil exploration in Abu Dhabi was slow to get started. It was delayed first by World War II. Thereafter,

the IPC group focused on the search for oil in Qatar, where oil exports began in 1949. Knowledge of the geology of the emirate was limited, and economic conditions there were very underdeveloped. The town of Abu Dhabi itself was no more than a tiny village, and there were no roads in the entire emirate in the 1950s.

FINDING OIL IN THE FIFTIES

Drilling finally began in 1950, but the search for oil proved a prolonged one. In July 1953 a well was drilled in the Bab field in Murban, south of Tarif, but mechanical difficulties led to its being abandoned despite evidence of the presence of oil. Further drilling at Bab finally established the potential of the field by 1960. The Bu Hasa field was proved soon after when oil was discovered in commercial quantities, and exports started in 1963. In the following years, PDTC relinquished its concessions in the other Trucial States to concentrate its efforts on Abu Dhabi. In 1963, PDTC was renamed Abu Dhabi Petroleum Company (ADPC).

Meanwhile, oil also had been discovered offshore by other companies. In 1951 Abu Dhabi had established that the concession granted to PDTC did not include the continental shelf belonging to the emirate. As a result, Abu Dhabi granted a concession to cover the offshore territory first to International Marine Oil Company, which failed to achieve results, and then, in 1954, to Abu Dhabi Marine Areas Ltd. (ADMA), a new company two-thirds owned by British Petroleum (BP) and one-third by Compagnie Française des Pétroles.

In 1959 ADMA's drilling barge struck oil at Umm Shaif, located 80 miles into the gulf near Das Island. In 1962 the first shipment of oil was loaded from Das Island. The onshore and offshore oil discoveries made Abu Dhabi a large-scale oil producer. Its oil production grew from zero in 1960 to 102.8 million barrels in 1965, and 253.7 million barrels in 1970. By that date its production was one of the largest in the Middle East, and about one-quarter that of Kuwait.

STATE-OWNED COMPANY IN 1971

During the late 1960s there was growing resentment in Abu Dhabi, as elsewhere in the Middle East, of foreign ownership of oil resources, and especially the consortium system. The government concluded a 50-50 profit-sharing agreement with ADPC and ADMA in 1965 and 1966, respectively. In 1971 the government established Abu Dhabi National Oil Company (ADNOC) as a wholly state-owned company. With the formation of the Organization of Petroleum Exporting

KEY DATES

1962: Oil production begins in Abu Dhabi.

1971: Government establishes Abu Dhabi National Oil Company (ADNOC).

1988: Company is restructured.

1998: Company is reorganized again; five new directorates are added.

2002: ADNOC completes the Borouge Petrochemical Complex.

2006: ADNOC launches development of two onshore and two offshore oilfields.

2010: ADNOC announces plans to award contracts of $40 billion in 2010 for its onshore oil development, and another $24 billion for offshore development over the next six years.

Countries (OPEC), Abu Dhabi followed the general policy of requesting participation in the foreign oil companies active in its territory.

ADNOC acquired, effective January 1, 1973, 25 percent of the assets of ADPC and ADMA. The finalization of the ADMA participation agreement was complicated by BP's announcement in December 1972 of the sale of a 30 percent interest in ADMA to Japan Oil Development Co. (Jadco), formed by a consortium of Japanese companies. The government withheld its approval of this deal until March 1973, when BP agreed to finance the construction of an ADNOC-owned refinery in Abu Dhabi. By a further agreement in December 1974, the ADNOC interest in the ADPC and ADMA concessions was raised to 60 percent. These two companies were reincorporated later as Abu Dhabi Company for Onshore Oil Operation and Abu Dhabi Marine Operating Company.

Abu Dhabi was distinctive among the OPEC members in the gulf in retaining the former concessionaire companies as equity holders in the operating enterprises. It did not, as elsewhere, seek to remove foreign ownership entirely. ADNOC, therefore, developed as a holding company with an intricate web of majority and minority equity stakes in other producing companies. The government was motivated in this strategy by a desire to pursue production and exploration as energetically as possible. As part of this aim, from the 1960s various new concessions were granted to mostly independent oil companies in areas relinquished by ADPC and ADMA, all of which included provisions

for ADNOC to have the option to take up to 60 percent interest in successful ventures.

ADNOC established subsidiary companies specialized in the various sectors of the oil industry. In 1973 Abu Dhabi National Oil Company for Distribution was created to take over the marketing of oil products within Abu Dhabi, which was formerly in the hands of the Western oil companies. Abu Dhabi National Tankers was founded in 1975 to operate a tanker fleet. In 1973 the Abu Dhabi Gas Liquefaction Company was formed, owned 51 percent by ADNOC, 22 percent by Mitsui, around 16 percent by BP, around 8 percent by Compagnie Française des Pétroles, and 2 percent by Bridgestone Liquefied Gas.

The gas liquefaction company opened a plant on Das Island in 1977 to process gas from the main offshore oilfields. ADNOC was also anxious that Abu Dhabi should have its own refinery capacity. ADNOC's first oil refinery, situated at Umm Al Nar, opened in 1976, and in 1981 the company opened a second refinery at Ruwais. These plants made the UAE self-sufficient in refined petroleum products, with a surplus to export. In 1990 the two refineries had a combined capacity of 180,000 barrels per day, while domestic UAE consumption was about 80,000 barrels per day of refined products.

NEW VENTURES IN THE EIGHTIES

ADNOC also diversified overseas, again favoring joint venture and mixed ownership structures. Together with the Pakistani government, ADNOC formed Pak Arab Fertilizers Ltd., which started producing chemical fertilizers in Pakistan in 1978 and, by 1983, was producing 290,000 tons of calcium ammonia nitrate, 350,000 tons of nitrophosphate, and 50,000 tons of urea. The Pak Arab Refinery, another joint venture between ADNOC and the Pakistani government, started production in 1981. By 1990, however, ADNOC's foreign ventures remained much less substantial than those of Kuwait Petroleum Corporation.

The 1980s was an unsettled period for the world oil industry, and Abu Dhabi could not isolate itself from the general problems. Demand for OPEC oil fell sharply by about 45 percent in the first half of the decade. Producer states such as Abu Dhabi found themselves, and their state oil companies, with large bureaucracies that were slow to respond to changing circumstances. In 1988 the UAE restructured its oil administration with the aim of cutting out some of this bureaucracy. The department of petroleum was abolished, and a new higher council of petroleum was created.

The organization of ADNOC was restructured as part of this process. ADNOC's board was replaced by an 11-member petroleum council, and Sohal Fares al-Mazrui was appointed as ADNOC general manager and secretary general to the higher council, chaired by UAE's president, Sheikh Zayed. The move was designed to improve relations between ADNOC and its foreign equity partners, as well as to bring the industry under closer government control. During 1989 Mazrui also was appointed head of Abu Dhabi National Oil Company for Distribution. During 1987 and 1988 oil exploration and development were virtually halted, but in 1989 a series of new projects was given the go-ahead.

ADNOC proved itself one of the better managed state oil companies. The strategy of alliances with Western oil companies gave it access to skills and technologies that would have been hard to generate internally. Abu Dhabi's huge oil reserves also placed ADNOC in a powerful competitive position. In terms of sheer production capacity, ADNOC in 1990 had entered the ranks of the world's 10 largest oil companies, with a sustainable output of around one million barrels per day, and sufficiently large oil reserves to enable it to keep operating for more than 100 years at 1990 production levels.

RESTRUCTURING FOR THE NINETIES

The 1988 restructuring had enhanced the efficiency of the operating affiliates, and ADNOC was able to claim that its cost of producing a barrel of oil was one of the lowest in the world. The enormous damage done to neighboring Kuwait's oil production and refining facilities during the Iraqi invasion and occupation of that country between August 1990 and February 1991 enhanced the competitive advantages of the Abu Dhabi oil industry, at least in the short term, but it also served as a reminder of the political uncertainties of the gulf region.

ADNOC worked on expanding its oil production capacity after the Persian Gulf War. The company increased production at its Upper Zakum offshore oil-field and at the onshore Bab field in the early 1990s. Some increased production went to foreign partners such as Tokyo Electric Power Co., a large customer for the company's natural gas products. Demand also increased domestically. ADNOC spent between $5 billion and $6 billion in the early 1990s on several major projects. Aside from upgrading facilities at key oilfields, the company spent close to $2 billion to increase its production of electrical power and fresh water. ADNOC also expanded the capacity of its two refineries, Umm Al Nar and Ruwais, in the early 1990s.

Expansion of the Ruwais refinery continued in 1996. ADNOC formed a joint venture with the Finnish-Norwegian company Borealis to put $1.1 billion toward development of a petrochemical plant at Ruwais. The plant was to produce high-density polyethylene and ethylene. In another joint venture, headed by the Japanese firm Sumitomo Trading, AD-NOC also began building a $1 billion plant at Ruwais that would produce benzene and other so-called aromatic chemicals. ADNOC also laid more than 100 miles of new pipeline in the mid-1990s.

In 1998, the company underwent a major reorganization. ADNOC aimed to continue its expansion, and it needed to revamp management to handle future growth. ADNOC's subsidiaries had been grouped into nine directorates. The company added five more directorates and around 200 management positions. The company formed some new subsidiaries at this time as well. The gas processing directorate was put in charge of a new subsidiary, Abu Dhabi Gas Processing & Pipelines (Gappco), and a new refining company, Abu Dhabi Refining Company (Refco), also launched that year. The next year the company created a new gas processing and pipeline company, Abu Dhabi Gas Co. (Atheer); Abu Dhabi Oil Refining Company (Takreer); and, to operate its ethylene and polyethylene plants, Borouge, or Abu Dhabi Polymers Company Ltd.

EXPANSION PLANS FROM 2001

Shortly after revamping the structure of the company, ADNOC focused on building the brand of its ADNOC-Fod subsidiary. ADNOC-Fod supplied fuel, gas, and lubricants to the UAE military and to commercial airlines, and ran more than 200 gas stations. The ADNOC-Fod gas stations had no competitors within Abu Dhabi, but the brand was not as strong in other parts of the Emirates. ADNOC developed a new logo for the stations, which was then applied throughout the company. The company also redesigned the stations themselves and began adding convenience stores.

ADNOC was still committed to major expansion by 2001. It planned to increase its oil capacity from 2.6 to 2.8 barrels a day in 2001 to 3.6 barrels a day by 2005. The company later revised the deadline for this expansion to 2010, and then again to later in the next decade. Meanwhile, ADNOC continued to export heavily, particularly to Japan and Southeast Asia. The company also poured more money into developing its natural gas business. Worldwide demand for natural gas was increasing rapidly, and the company invested in exploration and development. Its two main natural gas companies were Abu Dhabi Gas Liquefaction Company and Abu Dhabi Gas Industries Company.

ADNOC's efforts to develop fully integrated operations continued apace into the new century. In 2001, the company commissioned the Borouge complex's polyethylene plant and ethane cracker. The Borouge Petrochemical Complex was officially inaugurated in October 2002. ADNOC also opened the UAE region's first liquefied natural gas filling station in 2004, then launched construction of a $1.3 billion ethylene cracker in 2007. That facility, slated to have a total capacity of 1.5 million metric tons per year, was to become one of the largest and most modern in the world.

TARGETING 3.5 MILLION BARRELS BEFORE 2020

In the meantime, ADNOC's existing oilfields, some of which had launched production 40 years earlier, were aging rapidly. The company's youngest oilfield at the time dated back to 1995. In 2006, however, ADNOC began taking steps to develop a new series of oilfields, designed to help it meet its expansion targets. These included two onshore fields, Qusahwira and Bida al-Qemzan, and two offshore fields, Nasr and Umm al-Lulu. The company also earmarked $5 billion for these projects.

As the oil market boomed into the second half of the decade, with oil prices reaching their highest levels in history, ADNOC appeared at last prepared to launch its full-fledged capacity expansion. In 2008, the company announced its intention to spend more than $28 billion through 2009. The company's projects also included a move to exploit the massive Shah gas field, located 180 kilometers from Abu Dhabi city, through a joint venture with ConocoPhillips. That project, which was expected to cost at least $10 billion, had become necessary in order to meet the fast-growing gas consumption levels in the UAE.

Despite the economic crisis at the end of the decade, which also caused a sharp drop in global oil prices, ADNOC remained committed to its capacity investment program. The company was nonetheless forced to revise its forecasts for completion of this expansion, in part because of delays in getting a number of its projects underway. The company remained optimistic that it would reach its target of 3.5 million barrels of oil per day before 2020.

Part of this optimism came from ADNOC's continued investments. In 2010, the company announced plans to award another $40 billion in contracts for its onshore development operations before the end of March of that year. At the same time, the company announced its intention to spend another $24 billion developing Abu Dhabi's extensive offshore oil and gas fields, most of which had been explored but never exploited. As the state-owned company overseeing one of the world's largest oil and gas reserves, ADNOC appeared certain to remain a major player in the global market.

Geoffrey Jones
Updated, A. Woodward; M. L. Cohen

PRINCIPAL SUBSIDIARIES

Abu Dhabi Company for Onshore Oil Exploration; Abu Dhabi Gas; Abu Dhabi Gas Industries Ltd.; Abu Dhabi Marine Operating Company; Abu Dhabi National Tanker Company; Abu Dhabi Oil Refining Company; Abu Dhabi Petroleum Ports Operating Company; Abu Dhabi Polymers Company Ltd. (Borouge); ESNAAD; National Drilling Company; National Gas Shipping Company; National Petroleum Construction Company; Ruwais Fertilizer Industry; Zakum Development Company.

PRINCIPAL DIVISIONS

Exploration and Production of Oil and Gas; Oil and Gas Processing; Exploration and Production Services; Chemicals and Petrochemicals; Maritime Transportation; Refined Products Distribution.

PRINCIPAL OPERATING UNITS

Abu Dhabi Company for Onshore Oil Operations; Abu Dhabi Marine Operating Company; Zakum Development Company; Abu Dhabi Polymers Company Ltd. (Borouge).

PRINCIPAL COMPETITORS

Saudi Arabian Oil Co.; National Iranian Oil Co.; Kuwait Petroleum Corp.; Turkmengas; Société Nationale pour la Recherche, la Production, le Transport, la; Qatar Petroleum; Kuwait National Petroleum Co.; National Oil Corp.

FURTHER READING

"Abu Dhabi Key to U.A.E. Growth Upstream and Downstream," *Oil & Gas Journal*, August 15, 1994, p. 27.

"Abu Dhabi National Oil Company and Its Group of Companies," *Institutional Investor*, August 1999, p. 17.

Acton, Maurice, "The Falcon Rising," *NPN International*, May 2000, p. 18.

"ADNOC Is Setting Pace for Region," *MEED Middle East Economic Digest*, November 20, 2009, p. 7.

Amir, Ghazail, "The Middle East Moves with Refining Deals," *Chemical Market Reporter*, March 17, 1997, pp. SR10–SR11.

"Big Spending to Expand Capacity," *Middle East Economic Digest*, December 4, 1998, p. 48.

Drummond, James, "Abu Dhabi Set to Exploit Gas from Shah Field," *Financial Times*, July 9, 2008, p. 16.

Dutta, Ashok, "Entering a New Phase," *MEED Middle East Economic Digest*, July 19, 2002, p. 28.

———, "Entering New Territory," *MEED Middle East Economic Digest*, April 28, 2006.

———, "Raring to Go," *MEED Middle East Economic Digest*, March 10, 2006, p. 44.

Evans, John, *OPEC: Its Member States and the World Energy Markets*, London: Longmans, 1986.

Hille, Kathrin, "CPC, ADNOC Plans $1bn Joint Venture," *Financial Times*, August 10, 2006, p. 20.

James, Ed, "ADNOC: Meeting Its Ambitious Production Targets Is the Main Challenge for Abu Dhabi," *MEED Middle East Economic Digest*, July 4, 2008, p. 40.

Luciani, Giacomo, *The Oil Companies and the Arab World*, London: Croom Helm, 1984.

Mallakh, Ragaei El, *The Economic Development of the United Arab Emirates*, London: Croom Helm, 1981.

"The Role of State Oil Companies," *Oil & Gas Journal*, August 16, 1993, p. 62.

Salisbury, Peter, "Abu Dhabi Moves Offshore," *MEED Middle East Economic Digest*, February 19, 2010, p. S13.

———, "Abu Dhabi Prepares for the Upturn," *MEED Middle East Economic Digest*, November 20, 2009, p. 7.

Siddiqui, Moin A., "The United Arab Emirates: Financial Report," *Middle East*, March 2001, p. 35.

Tippee, Bob, "Gas Receives New Priority in Abu Dhabi's Onshore Work," *Oil & Gas Journal*, August 11, 1997, pp. 51–54.

"UAE Operations Step Up Oil, Gas Production," *Oil & Gas Journal*, August 14, 1995, p. 18.

ACT, Inc.

---

500 ACT Drive
Iowa City, Iowa 52243
U.S.A.
Telephone: (319) 337-1000
Fax: (319) 339-3021
Web site: http://www.act.org

Nonprofit Organization
Incorporated: 1960 as American College Testing Program, Inc.
Employees: 1,500
Sales: $250 million (2009 est.)
NAICS: 611710 Educational Support Services; 541612 Human Resources and Executive Search Consulting Services; 511130 Book Publishers; 511140 Database and Directory Publishers; 511210 Software Publishers

■■■

ACT, Inc., is a nonprofit organization that develops and administers educational and workforce development programs, most notably the ACT college entrance examination. Approximately one million high school students each year take the ACT exam, which is accepted by all four-year colleges and universities in the United States. The other major facet of the organization is its WorkKeys program, which helps businesses assess the capabilities of their employees. ACT offers its educational and workforce programs throughout the United States and internationally. The organization maintains international field offices in Australia, South Korea, China, Indonesia, Singapore, and Spain.

INFLUENCE OF E.F. LINDQUIST

ACT owes its creation to the vision of one of the 20th century's most renowned figures in achievement testing. Everett Franklin Lindquist gained his first experience in large-scale academic testing in 1929, two years after he became an assistant professor at the University of Iowa College of Education. His superior, the head of secondary education at the College of Education, had developed the idea for the Iowa Academic Meet, a competition meant to identify and publicize the brightest students in Iowa's secondary schools, and he turned to Lindquist to construct the tests and oversee their statewide administration.

Lindquist immersed himself in the project, although he had some misgivings about what became popularly known as the "Brain Derby." The Iowa Academic Meet strove to give academic accomplishments the same attention attracted by athletic accomplishments, becoming a highly competitive battle with the victors determined in a finals competition staged in Iowa City. Lindquist felt the program was too competitive (its name change to the Iowa Every-Pupil Achievement Testing Program occurred because of his efforts) but he used its popularity to develop his beliefs and skills in administering large-scale achievement testing.

Lindquist's dissatisfaction with extant testing procedures was the impetus for the formation of ACT. Before he helped found his most enduring creation, however, he used the Iowa Every-Pupil program to his advantage. The large number of testing sites and the larger number of students testing at the sites became the proving ground for ACT. He thought about the nature, purposes, and the uses of achievement tests, developed concerns about the emphasis on learning by rote, and became worried about teachers and school administrators "teaching the test," or slanting their instruction specifically to maximize scores on the Iowa Every-Pupil tests. Lindquist developed new procedures regarding test construction, scoring and reporting, and the interpretation of results, using all that he had learned to create new series of examinations.

In 1935 Lindquist and his associates developed the Iowa Tests of Basic Skills, an assessment for grades six through eight designed to test generalized abilities instead of emphasizing the memorization of subject matter. When the Iowa Every-Pupil program was shut down in 1942, Lindquist began administering the Iowa Tests of Educational Development, a new testing series for high school students that required problem solving and critical thinking. Meanwhile, his scholarly work in the field of achievement testing continued. Lindquist wrote books on testing and statistics, he helped develop the Armed Forces Tests of General Educational Development (the high school equivalency test known as the GED), and he helped develop a machine capable of scoring tests, pioneering the first practical optical-mark recognition system.

ACT ASSESSMENT DEBUTS, TAKES ON THE SAT: 1959

By the end of the 1950s Lindquist held sway as a national figure in large-scale achievement testing, possessing the expertise he would use to create ACT. Lindquist collaborated with Ted McCarrel, who had arrived at the University of Iowa in 1946 as director of admissions, and developed an achievement test for college admissions. When the first ACT Assessment was administered in Texas in November 1959, Lindquist

entered a fragmented market populated by numerous statewide and regional entities, but the market, nonetheless, was dominated by a single competitor, the College Entrance Examination Board (the College Board) and its college admissions test, the Scholastic Aptitude Test (SAT). From the start, Lindquist faced stiff opposition from those committed to the SAT, beginning his long battle to win support for his testing philosophies.

The roots of the College Board stretched to 1900, when a group of primarily elite institutions in the northeastern United States formed the organization to administer an examination for entry into College Board-member institutions. Critics of the College Board exam claimed it was biased toward students from private preparatory academies, a charge that persisted when the College Board exam was replaced by the SAT following World War II. The College Board handed the responsibility for administering the SAT to the Educational Testing Service in 1947, but it retained ownership and editorial control over the test.

Lindquist voiced his concerns about the SAT to both organizations at an Educational Testing Service-sponsored conference in November 1958. He advised that the test, which continued to be predominantly used in the Northeast, needed to be administered in every region in the country. He also argued for profound changes to its construction, criticizing it as a test of innate intelligence and insisting that it should emphasize problem solving and reasoning. Officials in charge of the College Board and the Educational Testing Service dismissed Lindquist's suggestions, prompting him to begin the basic organizational work for ACT the following March.

Although they intended the ACT Assessment to be administered throughout the country, Lindquist and McCarrel initially concentrated on marketing their program to institutions in the Midwest. Greater geographic coverage was achieved during the 1960s, a decade that also saw the organization devote considerable time to research, as Lindquist sought to improve the capability of the ACT Assessment to provide a more comprehensive profile of students that could be used in admission, placement, and guidance. The Standard Research Service Division was formed in 1961 and three years later became part of the more expansive Research and Development Division.

ACT diversified during the 1960s, expanding its program beyond sets of academic tests to include career guidance components and services related to financial aid. As participation in the ACT Assessment grew, increasing from the 75,000 students who took the first test to nearly one million students by the end of the 1960s, the organization matured physically. Initially

KEY DATES

1959: First ACT college entrance exam is administered in Texas.

1972: Passage of the Education Amendment Act fuels the growth of ACT's financial aid services business.

1985: ACT begins publishing preparation guides for its college entrance examination.

1990: WorkKeys is marketed to corporate clientele.

2005: Optional writing test is added to ACT's college entrance examination.

2009: ACT celebrates its 50th anniversary.

housed in offices at the University of Iowa, ACT purchased a parcel of land northeast of Iowa City and built its own headquarters, moving into the complex in 1968, when 1,425 colleges and universities participated in its program.

FINANCIAL AID SERVICES EXPAND: 1972–79

ACT expanded its services ambitiously during the 1970s, moving into new areas and deepening its involvement in career guidance and financial aid. The organization entered the adult education field during the decade, solidifying its position by taking over the administration of the Regents External Degree Examinations, a proficiency examination developed by the New York Board of Regents. In 1975 ACT took responsibility for administering the test to adults outside the state of New York. The organization's greatest growth occurred in the financial aid sector, growth that was fueled by the enactment of the Education Amendment Act in 1972, which, among other provisions, created the Basic Educational Opportunity Grant program and the Student Loan Marketing Association (Sallie Mae). ACT's Division of Student Assistance Programs became the organization's largest operating unit, fulfilling the federal government's Basic Educational Opportunity Grant contract by processing five million Family Financial Statement Forms by the end of the decade. When the U.S. Department of Education awarded the contract to another entity at the beginning of the 1980s, ACT lost one-third of its revenues and nearly 200 of its 558 employees.

The loss of the Basic Educational Opportunity Grant contract delivered a stinging blow to ACT, but the organization quickly recovered, finding new areas to compensate for the major reduction in its data-processing activities. ACT published its first preparation booklet during the 1980s, distributing *Preparing for the ACT Assessment* in 1985 along with the organization's registration materials. The organization also explored creating programs for students in grades 8 and 10, which led to the formation of the Educational Planning and Assessment System during the decade, an assessment system for students planning to attend college and those choosing a different path. At the end of the decade, the Enhanced Act Assessment was introduced, which featured a new Reading Test and Science Reasoning Test and subscores for English and mathematics that provided a more precise evaluation of achieved skills and remedial needs for course placement.

WORKKEYS COURTS CORPORATE CLIENTELE: 1990–99

Although the ACT Assessment Program remained the cornerstone of the organization, the diversification into other services and programs highlighted ACT's progress during its first decades in operation. The expansion and evolution of the organization continued in the 1990s, notably the development of the WorkKeys System, the largest and most ambitious project undertaken during the decade.

ACT began developing the WorkKeys system in the late 1980s, but the program reached fruition during the 1990s, extending ACT's involvement into the market for workforce skills. The assessment of knowledge, skills, and career goals became part of the organization's Center for Education and Work. WorkKeys consisted of numerous assessments, including Reading for Information, Mathematical Problem Solving, Locating Information, Teamwork, and Applied Technology. The assessments categorized test takers into five levels: Preparatory, Work-ready, Intermediate, Advanced, and Specialist.

ACT entered its fifth decade as a far more comprehensive and ambitious organization than at its inception. From college admissions assessments, ACT had broadened its scope considerably to include career guidance, financial aid, and corporate services, among a host of others, becoming along the way an international organization exporting its programs and services abroad. During the first decade of the 21st century, ACT reorganized itself, as it often had to do to bring cohesion to its ever-expanding roster of programs and services. The organization formed three new divisions: ACT Education, ACT Workplace, and ACT International, giving it the structure supporting its operations as it concluded its first half-century of operation.

One of the most significant developments of the decade was to its core college admissions test. In 2005, an optional writing test was added to the ACT Assessment, an addition also included in what had been renamed the SAT Reasoning Test. ACT continued to enjoy enviable success with its original college admissions product. A record high 1.3 million students took the ACT college entrance exam in 2007, but the mission first established by Lindquist had greatly expanded by the time ACT celebrated its 50th anniversary in 2009. Success in the years ahead would depend on the organization's ability to progress on numerous fronts, as it pursued a broadly defined agenda of "helping people achieve education and workplace success."

Jeffrey L. Covell

PRINCIPAL SUBSIDIARIES

ACT International, B.V.; ACT Education Solutions, Limited; ACT Business Solutions, B.V.

PRINCIPAL DIVISIONS

ACT Education; ACT Workplace; ACT International.

PRINCIPAL COMPETITORS

The College Board; Educational Testing Service; Questar Assessment, Inc.

FURTHER READING

ACT: The First Fifty Years, 1959–2009, Iowa City: ACT, Inc., 2009.

Toppo, Greg, "ACT Participation Reaches Record," *USA Today*, August 15, 2007, p. 7D.

AMC Entertainment Inc.

920 Main Street
Kansas City, Missouri 64105
U.S.A.
Telephone: (816) 221-4000
Fax: (816) 480-4617
Web site: http://www.amcentertainment.com

Private Company
Incorporated: 1968
Employees: 800
Sales: $2.26 billion (2009 est.)
NAICS: 512131 Motion Picture Theaters (Except Drive-In)

■ ■ ■

AMC Entertainment Inc., the pioneer of the suburban "multiplex" theater concept, operates the second-largest movie theater chain in the United States. Averaging 15 screens per theater, AMC owns or has interests in 294 theaters with 4,373 screens in 30 states and the District of Columbia. The company also operates more than 200 screens in Canada, Hong Kong, France, and the United Kingdom. Its greatest concentration of theaters in the United States is in California, home to 42 theaters and 651 screens. The company is controlled by CCMP Capital and Apollo Management.

KANSAS CITY BEGINNINGS

AMC was incorporated by Stanley H. Durwood (formerly Dubinsky) in 1968, but the business was actu-

ally started by Durwood's father in 1920. The elder Durwood had previously been a struggling actor working for a traveling tent show. In 1920, he bailed out of his acting career and leased a movie theater in downtown Kansas City. Also in 1920, Durwood's wife gave birth to Stanley, who would grow the start-up business into a small theater empire before the end of the century. During the 1920s and 1930s, Durwood was successful enough to open a few more theaters in the Kansas City area. He also did well enough to help send Stanley to Harvard University during the early 1940s.

Stanley Durwood graduated from Harvard in 1943 with a bachelor of arts degree. He joined the U.S. Air Force after college and served during World War II, eventually attaining the rank of lieutenant. After the war, Stanley returned to Kansas City and joined the family business, Durwood Theaters. During the 1950s, Stanley, along with his father and younger brother and sister, slowly expanded the business into a chain of 10 local movie houses and drive-in theaters. It was during this period that Stanley contrived an ingenious idea for a new kind of cinema, a single complex with multiple theater screens. Although he was never able to realize his vision while his father was in control of the operation, he kept the idea alive in his mind.

Stanley's father died in 1960, and Stanley and his siblings continued to run the business, with Stanley in charge of operations. By the time Stanley took control of the business, the theater industry was rapidly evolving into a regional, and even national, industry. Because they owned only 10 theaters, the Durwoods were under pressure from larger operators with more and bigger complexes. The market reach of such operations was often much greater, so they were usually able to lasso the choice releases, leaving the Durwoods to choose from the less popular motion pictures.

"I had to beg and plead for an Abbott and Costello picture," Durwood recalled in the March 25, 1994 *Kansas City Business Journal*. When Durwood finally got the comedy from the movie distributors, he hated it, but it was a big-name film, and his theaters were packed. Durwood noted, "I thought, what a crummy picture. Now if I could get two crummy pictures in here, I could double my gross and the rent would be the same." Seeking to boost attendance without increasing operating costs, Durwood believed that his multiscreen concept could be the solution.

BIRTH OF THE MULTIPLEX IN THE SIXTIES

In 1963 Durwood realized his vision when he built the first multiscreen theater. The concept was unheard of at the time and seemed extravagant. Critics wondered why anyone would need two different screens. However, the multiscreen theater, located in a suburban shopping mall, was a success. Durwood quickly began to reconfigure some of his existing facilities into multiple screen, or "multiplex," cinemas. In 1965 Durwood bought out his brother's and sister's ownership interests. Then, in 1968, he incorporated the business as American Multi-Cinema Inc. (the name was shortened in 1983 to AMC). At the time of incorporation, AMC consisted of a local chain of 12 theaters with a total of 22 screens. AMC boosted that figure in 1969 when it opened its first six-screen theater.

AMC took advantage of industry gains during the 1970s, but was also able to consistently strengthen its competitive position in relation to its peers. It achieved those market share gains mostly through construction of new multiscreen cinemas, many of which were adjoined to, or located near, shopping malls.

Despite AMC's success, many of the company's competitors sat on the sidelines during the popularization of multiplex theaters, failing to recognize the long-term nature of the trend. A few competitors, particularly General Cinemas, also built some multiscreen theaters. However, Durwood led the charge. The AMC chain included more than 500 screens in theaters scattered primarily around the Midwest by 1981. AMC's most rampant period of growth was yet to come.

DURWOOD'S STRATEGY BREEDS SUCCESS

The success of AMC's multiscreen concept was rooted in Durwood's penchant for efficiency. One prominent studio executive even referred to Durwood as the "father of modern theater exhibition" and the "inventor of professional theater management." Despite its novelty, the multiplex philosophy was relatively straightforward. By putting several screens under one roof, AMC was effectively combining several separate theater facilities. The chief benefit was that the theaters were able to share infrastructure and employees, thus spreading costs over a higher revenue base. For example, by staggering starting times of the movies, one (or a few) employees could staff the box office, while twice as many workers would be needed at two separate theaters. Likewise, only one or two concession stands were needed, parking area requirements were minimized, and costs related to air-conditioning, the lobby, and other infrastructure elements were significantly reduced.

A corollary benefit of multi-cinema theaters, which Durwood especially recognized when he began building complexes with more than two or three screens, was increased market reach. By offering different types of movies, one facility could simultaneously appeal to several segments of the moviegoing population. In addition, AMC could maximize profits on selected features by extending the run of movies that turned out to be very popular. Finally, multiple screens complemented other AMC technical and marketing innovations during the 1970s and 1980s. For example, the company was credited with introducing automated projection systems. AMC introduced the industry's first cupholder armrest in 1981.

EXPANSION IN THE EIGHTIES

AMC's biggest growth spurt occurred during the 1980s. Although annual movie attendance throughout the decade remained near the one billion mark, the theater industry in general succeeded in steadily boosting ticket prices faster than inflation, thus increasing margins. More importantly, AMC continued to parlay its multi-

KEY DATES

1920: Company's first theater is leased.
1963: First multiscreen theater is built.
1968: AMC is incorporated as American Multi-Cinema Inc.
1988: AMC's holdings reach 1,500 screens.
1995: First "megaplex" is built.
1999: Longtime Chairman and CEO Stanley H. Durwood dies.
2002: AMC acquires General Cinema Corp.
2004: In a $2 billion buyout, AMC is taken private.
2006: AMC acquires Loews Cineplex Entertainment, making it the second-largest movie theater operator in the country.
2009: Gerardo Lopez is named CEO and president.

screen concept into a competitive advantage and was able to significantly boost its share of box-office receipts. During 1982 and 1983, AMC increased its total number of screens by more than 200, to about 700. Still eager to speed up expansion, the 63-year-old Durwood took his company public in 1983. Until that year, the company had been 100 percent owned by Durwood and his family. He reluctantly sold about 12 percent of AMC's stock in 1983 in a bid to raise expansion capital.

By 1986, AMC's total number of theater complexes had bolted past 200 with more than 1,100 screens in the United States. Furthermore, Durwood stepped up expansion in Western Europe, Australia, and Singapore. By 1990, he planned to be operating 2,500 screens in the United States and 1,500 more overseas.

AMC's strategy represented a slight departure from, or perhaps an amplification of, the growth tactics it had utilized in the past. Instead of building complexes with five or six screens, most of its new facilities during the early and mid-1980s housed 8 to 12 screens. Furthermore, Durwood was targeting smaller cities in Sun Belt states, especially Florida, Texas, and California. However, to achieve the stellar growth, Durwood was forced to take on a massive load of debt. He hoped to pay the debt off in the long term from strong profit gains.

CRITICISM DIRECTED TOWARD AMC

As the U.S. theater industry expanded unchecked during the mid- and late 1980s, some critics feared that the market was becoming increasingly overbuilt as theater

demand was declining. AMC's holdings, alone, had reached 1,500 screens by 1988, and a lot more construction was on the design boards. Furthermore, several of its competitors were hurriedly adding more screens to their existing complexes in what became a trend to "add value" to their theaters. In AMC's case, critics also cited a lack of a market presence in key metropolitan areas like New York, Chicago, and Boston. Moreover, some observers felt that AMC, unlike other theater industry leaders, had made a mistake by not diversifying into movie-related industries during the 1980s.

The criticism about AMC's lack of diversification was prompted by the fact that the theater industry had felt increasing pressure from an onslaught of other channels for movie viewing since the 1970s. Home videos and cable television, particularly, had been vying for consumer entertainment dollars. In response, AMC's competitors had diversified out of the theater business. United Artists, the industry leader, had invested heavily in cable television and telecommunications. Similarly, General Cinemas had become active in soft-drink and retail industries. However, to AMC's delight, the movie industry continued to raise ticket and concession prices throughout the 1980s. AMC boosted both its ticket and concession revenues during 1988 and 1989 to bring its gross sales to more than $456 million during 1989. Part of that growth was attributable to specific blockbuster releases that buoyed earnings during the period.

Despite record sales during the late 1980s, AMC was having financial trouble that intensified during the early 1990s. Notwithstanding a history of extremely sound management of its theaters (Durwood himself was known for always flying coach class, buying his suits off the rack, and driving an economical Honda Civic), AMC had let its operating costs escalate during its rapid expansion. Furthermore, the company's cash flow was being devoured by a crushing debt load. AMC lost money every year between 1988 and 1992, with the exception of one year in which it gleaned $567,000 in earnings from its operations.

To combat slumping profits, AMC reined in its growth efforts beginning in the late 1980s and concentrated on whipping existing operations into shape. The company added a string of new theaters in 1988, bringing its total number of screens to nearly 1,700, but then stopped expanding and started slashing costs. Of its 276 theaters, AMC closed 40 of the least profitable, reducing its total number of screens to about 1,600 by 1994. It also cut its workforce by about 1,000. As it scrambled to meet its debt obligations, industry revenues picked up. Although AMC's sales wavered barely above the $400 million mark, its operating costs declined and the company posted a $1.3 million net profit in 1993. Although the company was more than $300 million in debt, analysts were optimistic, and it appeared as though Durwood's long-term strategy might pay off after all.

Having overseen a period of great expansion, Stanley Durwood's son Edward left the presidency of AMC in 1995, and Philip M. Singleton, chief operating officer, moved into the post. A former Marine Corps captain and fighter pilot, Singleton had been with AMC since 1974. He was joined by Peter C. Brown, who was appointed chief financial officer.

BIRTH OF THE MEGAPLEX IN THE NINETIES

In the mid-1990s, founder Stanley Durwood was laying new plans to begin building a string of vast complexes with as many as 24 screens under the same roof. This concept was realized in Dallas in 1995 and quickly duplicated in other major markets. As with the multiplex, megaplexes consolidated operations costs and broadened the company's reach across more market sectors. Moreover, such tremendous spaces also permitted other revenue-generating efforts to flourish, such as restaurants, video-game parlors, and CD and book sales. Despite the million-dollar price tag for the construction of every megaplex, AMC was generally able to recoup its losses. The company did curtail its ambitions slightly by the end of the century, though, building more 20-plexes than 30-plexes. The comforts ushered in by megaplexes made any venues constructed before the 1990s seem old-fashioned.

Durwood died in 1999 of esophageal cancer, and Brown took over as CEO and president. Meanwhile, AMC was busy going international, with a 13-plex in Fukuoka, Japan, and a 20-plex in Portugal, among other locations in Canada, England, and Spain. A joint venture with the Planet Hollywood theme restaurants, Planet Movie, was also planned, but stalled amid the restaurant company's ongoing financial troubles. More promising, AMC and Hollywood.com, Inc., a Web site for movies and entertainment, joined forces to sell movie tickets over MovieTickets.com in 2000.

INDUSTRY BUCKLES

Brown ascended to the top of AMC's management ranks just as the movie theater industry plunged into a period of despair. Consumers spent a record $7.5 billion at the box office the year Brown was named CEO, but the nation's theater chains did not reap financial rewards from the increase in business. Throughout the country, theater operators had spent lavishly on constructing new megaplexes in an attempt to lure customers and they began to suffer the consequences of saturating markets with expensive properties. "The whole industry just got way ahead of their customer base," an analyst explained in the January 17, 2000 issue of *Business Week*. "There's no way to raise the prices for tickets or Cokes fast enough to offset it."

A spate of bankruptcies spread throughout the industry during the first years of the 21st century, as one large chain after another paid the price for overexpansion. Although AMC, the pioneer of the megaplex concept, felt the sting of investing in expansion, the company emerged from the torturous period occupying an enviable position. AMC was the largest chain to avoid Chapter 11, which enabled it to assume an aggressive posture when the flurry of bankruptcies sparked an industry trend toward consolidation. Brown vowed to complete strategic acquisitions to turn AMC into a larger company and he followed through on his promise, orchestrating a period of expansion that turned his company from the fourth-largest cinema operator in the United States into the second-largest chain.

ACQUISITIONS BOOST STATURE

Brown made his first substantial move in a surprise courtroom announcement during General Cinema's bankruptcy hearing in 2001. He announced AMC was willing to acquire the more than 600 screens operated by General Cinema, which led to a monthlong auction at the end of the year that saw AMC prevail in its attempt to purchase the troubled chain. The deal, valued at $167.3 million, closed in March 2002, giving AMC roughly 3,500 screens worldwide.

Next, after completing several relatively small acquisitions, Brown set his sights on the nation's fifth-largest chain, Loews Cineplex Entertainment. AMC began discussing a merger in November 2003 with Loews's owner, Onex Corp., a diversified Canadian conglomerate. The merger promised to give AMC more than 5,600 screens worldwide, but the merger talks ended in early 2004. Several months later, AMC agreed to sell itself to Marquee Holdings, an investment company owned by JPMorgan Partners and Apollo Investments. The deal, worth an estimated $2 billion, was completed in December 2004, a transaction that took AMC private.

After the conversion to private ownership, Brown revisited the prospect of acquiring Loews. Merger discussions with Onex had failed to reach a successful conclusion, but after the chain was sold to affiliates of Bain Capital Partners, The Carlyle Group, and Spectrum Equity Investors in 2004, hopes for a corporate marriage were renewed. The second round of negotiations, begun in late 2005, gave Brown what he wanted. In January 2006, AMC merged with Loews, giving AMC 4,431 screens in the United States and 1,241 screens in 11 foreign countries. AMC emerged from the merger with nearly 5,700 screens, making it the second-largest cinema operator in the country, trailing only Regal Entertainment, the owner of 6,100 screens.

NEW LEADERSHIP

At the end of the decade, a rare event in the history of AMC occurred. Brown, who had more than doubled AMC's annual revenues during his decade-long leadership, retired in 2009. Gerardo "Gerry" Lopez was named Brown's replacement in March 2009, becoming only the fourth CEO in the history of AMC. Lopez, formerly the executive vice president of Starbucks Coffee Company, inherited a dominant competitor in the exhibition industry, a company that he intended to lead toward a profitable future.

Dave Mote
Updated, Mark Swartz; Jeffrey L. Covell

PRINCIPAL SUBSIDIARIES

American Multi-Cinema, Inc.; Movietickets.com, Inc.; AMC Europe S.A. (France); LCE AcquisitionSub, Inc.; LCE Mexican Holdings, Inc.; LCE Lux HoldCo S.a.r.l. (Luxembourg); AMC Netherlands Holdo B.V. (Netherlands); Club Cinema of Mazza, Inc.; AMC License Services, Inc.; Premium Theater of Framingham, Inc.; Loews Theatre Management Corp.; Loews Citywalk Theatre Corporation; Loews Cineplex U.S. Callco,

LLC; AMC Card Processing Services, Inc.; Centertainment Development, Inc.; AMC International, Inc.; AMC Theatres of Canada, Inc.; AMC Theatres of U.K. Limited.

PRINCIPAL COMPETITORS

Cinemark Holdings, Inc.; Carmike Cinemas, Inc.; Regal Entertainment Group.

FURTHER READING

"AMC's New Chief Fine-Tunes Theater Chain's Strategy," *Wall Street Journal*, July 23, 1999, p. B6.

Bacha, Sarah Mills, "Movie Theater with 24 Screens Part of Project," *Columbus Dispatch*, August 10, 1994, p. G1.

Block, A. B., "What Makes Stanley Borrow? Stan Durwood's AMC Entertainment Is Loaded with Debt and Costly Leases. So Why Does the Stock Sell for 27 Times Earnings?" *Forbes*, September 22, 1986.

Cardenas, Gina, "Movie Theater Economics," *New Miami*, September 1993, p. 18.

Gold, Howard, "Screen Gem?" *Forbes*, September 10, 1984, p. 194.

Graham, Sandy, "From Multi to Mega," *Colorado Bizz*, January 2000, p. 50.

Grove, Christopher, "Durwood Legacy Packs 'Em In," *Variety*, May 16–22, 1999, p. 42.

Harris, Kathryn, "AMC Theater Empire Playing Real-Life Drama," *Los Angeles Times*, March 27, 1988, Sec. 4, p. 1.

Henderson, Barry, "AMC Bets on Theater Allure over Couch," *Kansas City Business Journal*, March 25, 1994, p. 3.

Snyder, Gabriel, "AMC, Loews Toast Merger Completion," *Daily Variety*, January 27, 2006, p. 6.

"Trouble in Cinema Paradise," *Business Week*, January 17, 2000, p. 98.

American Booksellers Association, Inc.

———————■———————

200 White Plains Road, Suite 600
Tarrytown, New York 10591
U.S.A.
Telephone: (914) 591-2665
Toll Free: (800) 637-0037
Fax: (914) 591-2720
Web site: http://www.bookweb.org

Nonprofit Organization
Incorporated: 1900
Employees: 52
Operating Revenues: $5 million (2008 est.)
NAICS: 813910 Business Associations

■ ■ ■

American Booksellers Association, Inc., (ABA) is a trade organization that represents independent bookstores. Its services include education, advocacy, marketing, and sales assistance via the Indiebound.org Web site. The organization also publishes the online member newsletter *Bookselling This Week*, sponsors annual meetings, distributes lists of top-selling titles, and oversees the Indies Choice book awards. The nonprofit group is funded by membership fees as well as an endowment.

EARLY YEARS

ABA got its start on November 15, 1900, when a group of six booksellers sent a letter to other members of the trade announcing a new organization to advocate for their mutual interests. The effort was not the first of its type, similar attempts in 1802 and 1874 having fizzled, but booksellers were facing new challenges as publishers had recently begun opening their own retail stores, offering national chains large discounts, and selling books by mail.

The newly formed group quickly signed up nearly 750 members, who would pay dues of $2 per year. An advisory board of 50 was appointed, representing all U.S. states except North Dakota, and Henry T. Coates of Philadelphia was named president, with John W. Nichols hired as manager for a small stipend. Local and state organizations were also created.

On July 24, 1901, the ABA held its first annual convention in New York. The group's members passed a resolution stating that they would buy books only from publishers who participated in a "net price" plan, which required they refuse to serve booksellers who did not respect an established list price. Schoolbooks, adult fiction, and new editions were excepted.

In 1902 department store Macy's sued the American Publishers Association under the Sherman Antitrust Act to stop publishers from boycotting retailers who did not abide by the net price plan. The suit (to which the ABA lent its support) went to the U.S. Supreme Court, which in 1913 found the net price requirement illegal. Although the American Publishers Association disbanded the following year, the ABA soldiered on, continuing to fight against price-cutting by chains.

COMPANY PERSPECTIVES

ABA's Mission: Provide advocacy, education, opportunities for peer interaction, support services, and new business models to independent, professional booksellers.

ADDING EDUCATION PROGRAMS: 1913

In 1913 the ABA formed a committee to start a booksellers' school, and the following year its first course, for store clerks, was offered in conjunction with the Booksellers League of New York. A joint publisher and bookseller board of trade was also created around this time, the first of many such liaison groups.

The first annual meeting outside New York was held in 1916 in Chicago, and during that year the monthly *ABA Bulletin* was launched. Its subjects would range from news to sales and service techniques. Various promotional ideas including Children's Book Week and the Year-Round Bookselling Campaign were being promoted, with thousands of letters, posters, and flyers sent out to stores, libraries, schools, churches, and other parties.

In 1925 a Cooperative Clearing House was established to consolidate orders that members made to New York publishers, saving shipping costs by sending them together in one package. To facilitate this effort, a warehouse operation called American Booksellers Service Co. was founded. A year later the ABA was incorporated, in part to reduce liability in case of a lawsuit.

In 1927 the organization began targeting the new threat posed by the Literary Guild and Book-of-the-Month-Club, which sold books by subscription through the mail. The ABA's efforts to compete by creating its own Bookselection Plan proved unsuccessful, however. Book sales fell during the Great Depression, and membership dropped to 507 by 1937 before starting to pick up again. During World War II the ABA helped collect books for members of the armed forces, and after the war it sold the Service Co. warehouse unit, although the organization continued to offer its members order consolidation services.

ABA CONVENTION ADDS TRADE SHOW IN 1947

The 1947 ABA convention in New York was the first to feature a trade show, which offered publishers and other vendors the chance to display their wares to booksellers. This part of the event would grow to become one of its major components in future years.

In the late 1940s the ABA asked several publishers to lease the printing plates of popular new books so they could reprint them in the same way that book clubs did. After being rebuffed, the organization complained to the Federal Trade Commission alleging discrimination. The case was resolved in the 1950s through legislation and other measures, with publishers required to allow booksellers to offer discounted prices if book clubs could do the same.

The ABA's annual convention was growing, with attendance reaching 3,500 by 1967 and then doubling again over the next seven years. A tradition of celebrity speakers that had begun with the 1902 appearance of Mark Twain was continued with such guests as the Rev. Dr. Martin Luther King Jr., former President Dwight D. Eisenhower, and Attorney General Robert Kennedy.

During the 1970s the organization started the monthly *American Bookseller* magazine and the weekly *ABA Newswire*. The latter gave booksellers advance information about which authors would be on television or touring the country, allowing them time to stock up on titles.

ABA HELPS FOUND "BANNED BOOKS WEEK" IN 1982

A display of 500 banned books at the 1982 ABA convention led to the creation of Banned Books Week, which became an annual event. Although it would primarily be sponsored by the American Library Association, the organization would continue to support it along with groups such as the National Association of College Stores.

In January 1984 ABA Executive Director G. Roysce Smith stepped down after a 12-year tenure, and Bernie Rath took his place. The 34-year-old Rath had been a book salesman before heading the Canadian Booksellers Association. The organization now had 5,000 members, 25 employees, and an annual budget of $1.4 million. Twenty-one regional associations were also in operation.

The organization was now facing new threats to its members' prosperity. In the 1960s national chains including Waldenbooks and B. Dalton had begun putting stores in malls and other high-traffic locations around the United States, and during the late 1970s discount chains such as Crown Books had appeared, which sold titles at up to 40 percent below publishers' retail prices. In August 1984 the ABA's online Book Ordering System (BOS) debuted. It would consolidate

KEY DATES

1900: American Booksellers Association is founded.
1947: ABA's annual convention adds trade show component.
1996: ABA sells convention to Reed Association Expositions & Services.
1997: Penguin USA pays ABA $25 million for violating pricing consent decree.
1999: Book Sense promotional campaign is launched.
2008: Organization rebrands promotional effort, e-commerce Web site as IndieBound.

orders among independent bookstores to get a greater discount from publishers, bringing them closer parity with chains. The ABA invested $350,000 to establish BOS, which would cost $150,000 per year to operate. In the first six months 150 stores signed on for the $70-per-month service, as did 15 publishers, but it was not enough to subsidize the operation.

In 1986 the ABA joined *Playboy* magazine and the Council for Periodical Distributors Association to sue Attorney General Edwin Meese III and the Attorney General's Commission on Pornography, charging them with harassment and creating a "blacklist" of stores that sold pornographic magazines. A letter sent by the panel to retailers had led major chains including 7-Eleven to stop selling *Playboy* and *Penthouse*, which filed a separate suit.

SUCCESS WITH BOOK DISTRIBUTION IN 1987

In 1987 the ABA began a new venture, distributing Chronicle Publications' 1,360-page *Chronicle of the 20th Century*, which by year's end had sold more than 250,000 copies at a list price of $49.50. The profits were used to fund an expansion that added several executive positions, launched centralized buying services for items such as shopping bags, and facilitated the purchasing of insurance, as well as boosting the organization's profile by sponsoring author/humorist Garrison Keillor's radio program. In 1990 the American Booksellers Foundation for Free Expression was also founded to combat censorship.

The ABA's annual convention was continuing to grow, with some 1,000 exhibitors now renting over 2,000 booths, which cost between $350 and $1,600 each. In addition to serving booksellers, the convention

(which was the largest of its type in the English-speaking world) had become a marketplace for publishers, with deals for foreign rights often consummated on-site.

The ABA now had 8,000 members, which operated 4,500 bookstores. The total number of bookstores in the United States had grown by 76 percent during the 1980s, to 17,620, with chain outlets comprising 24 percent of this figure, although they sold 39 percent of the books. A new trend was the book "superstore," which might have 150,000 titles and 20,000 square feet, about four times the average store's size.

On the heels of its successful run as a distributor, in 1991 the ABA tried its hand at publishing with the *American Spectrum Encyclopedia*, which retailed for $85 and had a first printing of 100,000. Sales were weak, however, and many copies were returned unsold. During the year an annual award, the ABBY, was begun for several categories of books, which highlighted the more eclectic nature of ABA members' offerings. Revenues now stood at $8.2 million, of which $4.6 million was from the annual convention, whose attendance had recently topped 35,000.

STAKE IN CONVENTION SOLD TO REED PUBLISHING IN 1993

In early 1993 the ABA sold a 49 percent stake in its annual convention to the exhibition services unit of Reed Publishing for $17 million. The latter firm would begin managing the convention the following year.

In the spring the ABA bought three buildings in Tarrytown, New York, from Kraft General Foods for $2.8 million, which included a mansion and carriage house dating to 1858 and a 30,000-square-foot office building. After extensive renovations the organization's headquarters were moved there the following year. In 1994 the ABA also hired public relations firm the Wallis Group to create an ad campaign to support independent booksellers, and reformatted its weekly *Newswire* as *Bookselling This Week*, which would include more news stories and photographs.

In May 1994, just before its annual convention was to begin, the ABA filed suit against five major publishers including Houghton Mifflin and Penguin USA, alleging that they had violated the Robinson-Patman Act by giving chain stores secret discounts and promotional deals, and asking that all booksellers be given the same treatment. The Federal Trade Commission had been investigating similar claims since the early 1980s, but no action had been taken.

In February 1995 Hugh Lauter Levin, one of the five publishers named in the ABA suit, settled out of court, and in the fall Houghton Mifflin and Penguin did as well. Each would pay the ABA a lump sum, ostensibly to cover legal costs, and simplify its discount policies so that all customers were given the same pricing schedules.

PUBLISHERS SETTLE LAWSUITS IN 1996

In January 1996 the emboldened ABA filed a similar suit against publishing giant Random House. Although the latter offered to make some pricing changes, the suit was not dropped and Random House pulled out of the ABA convention's trade exhibition. In August, the last two publishers named in the original suit, Rutledge Hill Press and St. Martin's, settled.

In September 1996, with more major publishers including Simon and Schuster vowing to pull out of the annual ABA convention, the organization sold its remaining stake to Reed Association Expositions & Services for an estimated $20 million, after which the event's name was changed to BookExpo America. The ABA would continue to serve as a sponsor, with the American Association of Publishers later also joining.

In the fall the Federal Trade Commission ended its 17-year investigation of book pricing without taking action, after which Random House settled with the ABA, agreeing to maintain the pricing policies it had recently established without admitting wrongdoing or paying a fine. The recent settlements with publishers meant that some 40 percent of the trade book market was now covered by legally binding consent decrees, while many other publishers had also changed their discount policies in ways that were acceptable to ABA members.

PENGUIN PAYS ABA $25 MILLION FOR VIOLATING AGREEMENT

In September 1997 Penguin USA agreed to pay the ABA $25 million for violating the consent decree, the largest amount in the history of the Robinson-Patman Act, which the publisher blamed on the actions of a rogue employee. Half of the total would be distributed to booksellers who had purchased Penguin titles, with the rest going to the ABA. In November former bookseller and ABA President Avin Mark Domnitz took the post of executive director, replacing Bernie Rath.

Major bookstore chain operators Borders and Barnes & Noble had recently quit the ABA, in part motivated by its vigorous defense of smaller stores. During the year the organization established a new strategic focus that defined a core member as "the independent bookstore with a storefront location operated by professional independent booksellers according to sound business principles."

In March 1998 the ABA and a group of booksellers sued Borders and Barnes & Noble, alleging that both chains had secured illegal deals and preferential treatment from publishers, in part by threatening to return large numbers of books. In June the ABA also began a restructuring of its operations, canceling the monthly *American Bookseller* while boosting the content of *Bookselling This Week* and creating new information, marketing, and communications units. The group's membership committee was also realigned, and several staff positions were eliminated, leaving the ABA's payroll at about 50.

LAUNCH OF BOOK SENSE: 1999

In the spring of 1999 the ABA introduced a new national marketing campaign called Book Sense, which would encompass an e-commerce Web site so its members could compete with the likes of Amazon.com. The campaign and site each cost about $2 million, largely funded by the Penguin settlement.

After several delays, in the summer of 2000 BookSense.com came online in test form, before officially being launched the following January. More than 1,200 booksellers participated, with some having their own co-branded Web sites containing unique content, such as title recommendations and events listings. The national BookSense.com fed customers searching for books to local stores, combining their sales efforts via a database of 2.4 million titles.

In January 2001 the ABA doubled its membership dues and raised other fees it charged, in part to avoid using its endowment for operating costs. The organization now had $45 million in assets, including $35 million in cash and securities. Dues were based on a store's sales, and would now start at $350 per year (up from $175) and top out at just over $1,000 for the largest stores. The ABA cited rising costs of advocacy programs.

RESOLUTION OF BORDERS, BARNES & NOBLE SUIT: 2001

The suit against Barnes & Noble and Borders Group came to trial in the spring, but after six days of testimony it was settled for $4.7 million, which was intended to reimburse a quarter of the ABA's legal costs. The chains proclaimed victory, as they did not agree to change any of their practices, while the ABA countered that it had exposed the industry's bias toward chains and had forced a halt to many of the worst practices prior to the settlement.

The U.S. economy was once again in a rough patch, and between May 2000 and May 2001 the number of member stores fell by more than 10 percent, from 2,830 to 2,461. In the preceding decade the percentage of book sales at independent bookstores had dropped by more than half, from 33 percent to 15 percent.

In 2001 the ABA signed an agreement with Book-scan, which compiled sales data from booksellers around the United States including the major chains, so that its members' input could be better represented. The following year the organization made *Bookselling This Week* an online-only publication. The USA Patriot Act of 2003 allowed searches of booksellers' records, and the ABA and a host of other groups protested, seeking an amendment that would reduce the law's reach.

BOOKSENSE SHOWS RESULTS IN 2003

Booksellers' hardships now seemed to be easing, and during 2003 independent store sales rose to 16 percent of the total market, while dollar share increased to 18 percent. The BookSense online store and promotional program were given major credit. It now encompassed a national advertising campaign, the BookSense awards (formerly the ABBYs), weekly best-seller and special category lists, a list of "Booksellers Picks," and an electronic gift card program.

Many BookSense services were free to members, with a fee charged for the 200-plus stores that participated in the Web site ($350 for setup, $175 per month, and 4.5 percent of orders filled by wholesalers Ingram and Baker & Taylor). The cost of operating BookSense.com was underwritten in part by nearly $2 million in advertising annually purchased by publishers. Other services provided to ABA members at this time included mailings of galley copies of books, catalogs, and in-store promotional materials (much of it supplied by publishers).

The ABA was now seeking to cut costs and in 2004 sold its Tarrytown headquarters for $5.75 million. In 2004 the organization also formed a marketing partnership with trade magazine *Publishers Weekly*, which would offer it promotional consideration in print and online. Membership stood at just over 1,800, although the number of provisional members considering starting bookshops grew by a third during the year to 119.

In the fall of 2005 the ABA and the National Grocers Association filed class-action lawsuits against Visa USA, MasterCard, Inc., and numerous banks, alleging collusion in the setting of transaction fees, which were rapidly rising. Like booksellers, grocers typically

had a profit margin of around 1 to 2 percent, and such fees were a significant hardship. During the year the organization also established the Winter Institute, a free two-day educational and social gathering.

In 2008 the ABA formed a strategic partnership with distribution giant Ingram, which would help underwrite bookseller education programs for three years, starting at BookExpo. Other education events were held throughout the year at regional book shows and ABA forums, while much useful information was also made available on the ABA Web site, including in-depth articles, financial worksheets, and videos.

BOOKSENSE.COM BECOMES INDIEBOUND.ORG IN 2008

The 2008 BookExpo saw the rebranding of BookSense.com as IndieBound.org, which was intended to emphasize its link to the growing interest in supporting local businesses and sustainable business practices. ABA members were also encouraged to seek other local independent firms for cross-marketing efforts. The ABBY awards, which had become the BookSense awards in 2000, would become the Indie Choice awards.

The ABA continued to pursue new promotional vehicles, including using Twitter and Facebook, and in 2009 introduced an iPhone application. In June of that year longtime ABA Chief Operating Officer Oren Teicher, 59, succeeded Avin Domnitz as CEO of the organization. He answered to a board of nine booksellers who were elected by ABA members.

With the U.S. economy in the worst downturn in decades, the ABA cut its membership dues in half and offered members free admission to BookExpo. Revenues, which had hit $7.5 million in 2007, were expected to drop significantly.

In August 2009 the ABA announced a deal with Sony for member stores to sell digital content in the open EPUB format, as well as the Reader device, although implementation of the plan hit several snags. October saw another legal challenge as the ABA wrote a letter to the U.S. Department of Justice asking for an investigation of "predatory pricing" by Wal-Mart, Amazon.com, and Target. The retail giants were engaged in a pre-Christmas price war that made 10 popular books available for as little as $8.98, despite suggested prices of three or four times that amount. The number of ABA member bookstores stood at just 1,700.

More than a century after it was founded to act as the voice of independent bookstore owners, the American Booksellers Association had broadened its offerings to include education, marketing, online sales, and more. Although its ranks had thinned in the face of superstore chains and online discounters, the survivors were a determined lot who believed in the value of printed books and face-to-face customer service. As long as they were willing to carry on, the ABA was committed to being there for them.

Frank Uhle

PRINCIPAL DIVISIONS

ABA IndieCommerce.

PRINCIPAL COMPETITORS

Barnes & Noble, Inc.; Borders Group, Inc.; Amazon. com, Inc.; Wal-Mart Stores, Inc.; Booksite.com.

FURTHER READING

"ABA Rolls Out New Campaign," *Publishers Weekly*, June 2, 2008, p. 9.

Anderson, Charles B., ed., *Bookselling in America and the World*, New York: Quadrangle/The New York Times Book Co., 1975.

Baker, John F., and Jim Milliot, "AES Buys Annual Show from the ABA," *Publishers Weekly*, September 16, 1996, p. 10.

Carvajal, Doreen, "Booksellers Getting $25 Million Settlement from Penguin," *New York Times*, October 6, 1997, p. D10.

———, "Independent Booksellers Plan to Open On-Line Store," *New York Times*, March 15, 1999, p. C1.

Cox, Meg, "Publishing: Booksellers Say Five Publishers Play Favorites," *Wall Street Journal*, May 27, 1994, p. B1.

French, William, "Rath's New Job Is One of Epic Proportions," *Globe and Mail*, November 1, 1984, p. E1.

Holt, Patricia, "ABA Gets Fired Up to 'Win,'" *San Francisco Chronicle*, February 1, 1998, p. 2.

Maul, Kimberly, "ABA Utilizes Readers to Enhance Its Story," *PR Week US*, January 26, 2009, p. 5.

Milliot, Jim, "Looking for the Peace Dividend: With Lawsuits Settled, the Industry Hopes for Business Pickup, and Debates Future of BookExpo," *Publishers Weekly*, January 6, 1997, p. 43.

Mutter, John, "ABA at a Crossroads," *Publishers Weekly*, March 2, 1992, p. 9.

———, "BookSense Turns Five," *Publishers Weekly*, May 31, 2004, p. 26.

Rosen, Judith, "ABA Grapples with E-Commerce Services," *Publishers Weekly*, November 23, 2009, p. 4.

Zeitchuk, Steven, "ABA Reaches Settlement with B&N, Borders," *Publishers Weekly*, April 23, 2001, p. 9.

American Heart Association, Inc.

———■———

7272 Greenville Avenue
Dallas, Texas 75231
U.S.A.
Telephone: (214) 373-6300
Toll Free: (800) 242-8721
Fax: (214) 706-1191
Web site: http://www.americanheart.org

Nonprofit Organization
Incorporated: 1924
Employees: 3,500
Operating Revenues: $469.4 million (2009)
NAICS: 541710 Research and Development in the
    Physical, Engineering, and Life Sciences

■ ■ ■

American Heart Association, Inc., (AHA) is a nonprofit organization dedicated to reducing deaths and disability caused by cardiovascular disease. An affiliate, the American Stroke Association, focuses on the prevention of strokes. AHA provides funding for research, serves as a clearinghouse for information on cardiovascular diseases, and acts as a public policy advocate. In addition to its headquarters in Dallas, Texas, AHA maintains eight regional offices covering the United States and Puerto Rico. The organization's activities are further supported by local chapters.

NEW YORK CITY ORIGINS: 1916

The American Heart Association traces its heritage to a New York City organization, the Association for the

Prevention and Relief of Heart Disease, established in 1916. At the time, it was determined that as many as 20,000 city schoolchildren and a large number of industrial workers were suffering from organic heart disease. Because little was known about treatment, patients were essentially confined to bed and they all too often died. In fact, there were now more deaths caused by cardiac problems than tuberculosis. To address this reality, the new association was formed by prominent physicians, educators, social workers, municipal officials, and public-spirited citizens. A major foundation provided much of the initial funding, but to carry on the work of the association, annual memberships were sold for $3. Lifetime members paid $200 and were designated as patrons.

Serving as president was Dr. Lewis Atterbury Conner who founded the association with Dr. Robert H. Halsey, John Wyckoff, Haven Emerson, and other colleagues. The goal was to coordinate the activities of the city agencies that were separately helping patients who suffered from heart disease. Further objectives were to gather information about heart disease, develop and apply measures to prevent heart disease, find suitable jobs for heart disease patients, advocate for the development of institutions to care for cardiac patients who were unable to support themselves, and foster the establishment of similar organizations in other cities.

FORMATION OF AMERICAN
HEART ASSOCIATION: 1924

The New York organization made quick strides. By the end of 1920 there were 30 clinics in the city providing free examinations and advice. Progress was also made in the organization's mandate to urge the creation of similar organizations in other cities in the United States. Associations were established in Boston, Philadelphia, and Chicago. At the annual American Medical Association meeting in 1922, 41 physicians met to discuss forming a national organization. Two years later Drs. Conner and Halsey met with leaders of other local organizations to establish the American Heart Association. The other founding members were Drs. Paul D. White of Boston, Joseph Sailer of Philadelphia, Robert B. Preble of Chicago, and Hugh D. McCulloch of St. Louis. Dr. Conner, who spent 50 years on the staff of the New York Hospital and Cornell University Medical College, would also found the *American Heart Journal* in 1925, the first medical subspecialty journal and the official publication of AHA for the next 25 years. Dr. Conner served as its editor until 1938.

Because so little was known about cardiovascular diseases, much of the early years of AHA, then based in New York City, was simply devoted to understanding the problem. Working with physicians and researchers to learn more about the subject, AHA was very much an association of physicians run by physicians. By 1932 the organization had 1,277 members. AHA expanded its purview in 1935 when George Brown of the Mayo Clinic and Irving Wright of New York persuaded AHA's leaders to form a "Section for the Study of Peripheral Circulation." It was the first of many special interest groups that would later become known as "councils" within the AHA organization.

CHANGING EMPHASIS: 1939–46

An organization run by physicians had its drawbacks, however. The country was in the midst of the Great Depression and AHA was not adept at raising the money it needed to pursue its original goals, and it could not hope to fund research as well. In 1939, AHA spent more than it raised, resulting in a deficit of nearly $2,000. In that year Boston cardiologist Jack Marvin suggested that the organization needed to be restructured. In 1942 New Haven cardiologist Howard

Sprague took the suggestion further by presenting a proposal that called for a national fundraising campaign to sponsor both research and public health and lay education programs.

Rather than appeal to the public, Marvin and Sprague attempted to raise money from major insurance companies to support 22 projects. The results were disappointing. It became exceedingly clear that a reorganization was needed, albeit the physician membership was uncomfortable with the publicity that would attend the change. Of some help in spurring a change in AHA was the creation of "The Council on Heart Diseases, Inc." Although informally tied to the New York AHA chapter, it clearly held the potential to become a separate national organization and a potential competitor.

In 1946 Sprague presented a white paper at the annual AHA board of directors meeting that detailed a two-year plan to transform the association from a professional society into a voluntary health organization. The plan called for half of the governing board to include laypeople. Because many AHA members feared that interest in research would diminish under such an arrangement, the reformers proposed a "Scientific Council," which would become a power group dominated by physicians and scientists within the AHA structure. It also served as the natural home for special interests groups, such as the one focused on Peripheral Circulation established in the 1930s.

REORGANIZATION: 1948

The reformer's plan was accepted, and in 1948 the AHA made the transition to a voluntary health agency. Thus, more non-medical people were brought into leadership, including those with backgrounds in education, business management, community organization, public relations, and fundraising. In that same year, AHA introduced itself to the general public while launching a major fundraising campaign. A contest was held on the popular radio game show *Truth or Consequences*, in which listeners were asked to write 25 words about the American Heart Association and guess the identity of the "Walking Man." Along with their guesses, listeners made contributions, $1.75 million in all, before the identity of the mystery person was revealed to be popular entertainer Jack Benny.

To further its fundraising abilities, later in 1948 AHA appointed a fundraising director, E. J. Ade, who had served as the technical director for war fund drives during World War II. He spearheaded the Association's first national fundraising campaign. In February 1949 AHA raised $2.65 million, 72 percent of which

```
┌─────────────────────────────────────────────┐
│                                             │
│             KEY DATES                       │
│                  ■                          │
│  ─────────────────────────────────────────  │
│                                             │
│  1916: Association for the Prevention and   │
│        Relief of Heart Disease is founded   │
│        in New York City.                    │
│  1924: American Heart Association (AHA) is  │
│        founded as a scientific society.     │
│  1948: AHA becomes a voluntary health       │
│        organization.                        │
│  1975: National Center relocates to Dallas, │
│        Texas.                               │
│  2003: AHA conducts first paid advertising  │
│        campaign.                            │
│                                             │
└─────────────────────────────────────────────┘
```

remained with the local chapters. The national organization reaped nearly $750,000, of which half was allocated to research.

Another goal of the reorganized AHA was to expand the number of local heart associations and strengthen ties with existing ones. States and cities from around the country requested help in developing associations. AHA encouraged the formation of state heart associations, which could then coordinate local chapter programs. As had been the case since the days of the original New York City organization, local chapters were encouraged to promote proper hospital and follow-up care, the establishment of cardiac clinics, and the development of vocational training and employment opportunities for cardiac patients. AHA also forged a merger with another national heart group in 1949. The American Foundation of High Blood Pressure was folded into AHA's Scientific Council and became known as the Council for High Blood Pressure Research.

In the quarter-century following the reorganization, AHA enjoyed strong growth on every front. Local chapters spread across the United States, helping the association to raise increasing amounts of funds. Much of that money supported advances in the study and treatment of cardiovascular diseases. As a result, AHA increased its influence both nationally and internationally and it became an important health care advocate. Also of note, in 1950 *Circulation* magazine was launched and succeeded *American Heart Journal* as AHA's official publication, while its predecessor continued to act as a noteworthy medical publication serving a scientific audience. In addition, AHA began promoting a healthy diet to prevent cardiovascular disease. As early as 1961 it recommended a diet low in salt, fat, and cholesterol. The period also saw the election of the first woman to head the organization. In 1964, Dr. Helen B. Taussig was elected president at

AHA's annual meeting in Atlantic City. She was well known for her work related to inborn heart defects and was the co-developer of the blue baby operation.

NATIONAL CENTER MOVES TO DALLAS: 1975

Because of the increased importance of its state and local chapters, AHA moved its National Center to a more central location, settling in Dallas, Texas, in 1975. More changes were in store in the 1980s. Research efforts had traditionally focused on heart disease in white men. AHA now began to study heart disease in women and minorities. It was also in the 1980s that AHA introduced the "heart healthy" seal of approval that, for a fee, it permitted to be displayed on processed foods that met dietary guidelines related to salt, cholesterol, and fat content. The first "HeartCheck" foods were introduced in 1990, but several states and two major nutrition societies complained to the Food and Drug Administration that claiming health benefits from single foods was misleading.

The "HeartCheck" program was shelved and the fees returned to manufacturers, but it reemerged in 1994 in a slightly altered form. Some of the foods that were considered "heart healthy" included such products as Frosted Flakes, Fruity Marshmallow Krispies, and Low-Fat Pop-Tarts. Some critics were also concerned about the AHA logo adorning medicines. Nevertheless, the AHA continued to make the transition from scientific society to public health agency. In June 1997 it was reorganized into a single corporation under the auspices of new CEO M. Cass Wheeler.

Rather than focus on serving the need of affiliates, AHA's National Center devoted more attention to individuals. It dedicated more resources toward outreach efforts to prevent heart disease and stroke. Under the leadership of Wheeler, the AHA became more adept at publicizing its scientific findings and more forceful in taking positions on health care issues. Affiliate research programs were also better coordinated. AHA's publishing efforts were revamped. Scientific journals were published online and, to lower costs, the work was outsourced.

Changes continued into the new century. The American Stroke Association division was formed. To address the problem of heart disease in women, the "Go Red for Women" program was introduced. In 2003 the AHA launched the first paid advertising campaign in its history, budgeting $36 million for three years to pay for a national branding campaign. The public's unaided awareness of the association had reached a plateau of 19 percent, a far cry from the 40 percent recognition enjoyed by the American Cancer Society, which had experienced a surge in recent years. The AHA also sought to reach individuals through the workplace. It launched the Start! corporate wellness program. Companies with high compliance would then be recognized as a "Fit Friendly Company," a designation that could be used in employee recruitment advertising.

After 11 years at the helm, Wheeler announced his retirement in 2008. He was succeeded as CEO by Nancy Brown, who had served as his chief operating officer for the previous seven years. She was well prepared to lead the association into the second decade of the new century, the challenge of its mission undiminished.

Ed Dinger

PRINCIPAL OPERATING UNITS

Advocacy; Corporate Operations; Field Operations and Development; Healthcare Markets; Science Operations; Technology and Customer Strategies.

FURTHER READING

"Dr. L. Conner Dies; Heart Specialist," *New York Times*, December 4, 1950.

"Expansion Is Planned by Heart Association," *New York Times*, September 25, 1948.

Fye, W. Bruce, "A History of the American Heart Association's Council on Clinical Cardiology," *Circulation*, March 1983, p. 1057.

Gordon, Jennifer, "Heart Association Wellness Program Gains Traction," *Dallas Business Journal*, February 16, 2007.

"Heart Association Set Fund Record," *New York Times*, February 18, 1950.

Moore, W. M., *Fighting for Life: The Story of the American Heart Association 1911–1975*, Dallas: American Heart Association, 1983.

Morris, Stephanie, "Dialogue: The Heart of the Matter," *Texas Lawyer*, January 29, 2007.

"Move to Combat Heart Disease," *New York Times*, November 18, 1916.

Patrick, Stephanie, "Heart Association to Tap Paid Advertising," *Dallas Business Journal*, April 11, 2003.

American Physicians Service Group, Inc.

1301 Capital of Texas Highway, Suite C300
Austin, Texas 78746-7304
U.S.A.
Telephone: (512) 328-0888
Toll Free: (800) 252-3628
Fax: (512) 314-4398
Web site: http://www.amph.com

Public Company
Incorporated: 1974
Employees: 99
Total Assets: $299.8 million (2009)
Stock Exchanges: NASDAQ
Ticker Symbol: AMPH
NAICS: 523110 Investment Banking and Securities Dealing; 524126 Direct Property and Casualty Insurance Carriers; 524128 Other Direct Insurance (Except Life, Health, and Medical) Carriers

■ ■ ■

American Physicians Service Group, Inc., is the holding company for insurance and investment businesses operating primarily in the state of Texas. APS Insurance Company, Inc. is the leading underwriter for professional medical liability insurance in Texas, with additional operations in Arkansas and Oklahoma. APS Insurance operates on a "claims made" basis, providing coverage claims lodged over the duration of the policy period. APS Insurance offers malpractice insurance through independent sales agents and its own sales representatives.

American Physicians Service Group offers several financial products and services through APS Financial Corporation. Serving insurance companies, investment institutions, and wealthy individuals as a licensed broker, subsidiaries of APS Financial offer high-yield bonds, securities trading, management of fixed income and equity assets, proprietary investment research, portfolio accounting and analysis, and management of syndicated bank loans, including clearing of trade claims and distressed private debt.

NEED LEADS TO NEW ORGANIZATION

An alarming rate of medical malpractice claims during the late 1960s and early 1970s preceded the formation of American Physicians Service Group (APS). In 1972 Dr. Jack Chandler formed a physicians union through which doctors could seek ways to cope with an unprecedented number of lawsuits. This group of physicians decided to form their own reciprocal insurance exchange for the purpose of providing themselves and other Texas physicians with low-cost professional medical liability insurance. The doctors established a nonprofit entity to underwrite the insurance, the physician-owned American Physicians Insurance Exchange (APIE), and businessman Jack Murphy established APS Insurance Services, Inc., in 1975 to manage APIE.

A subsidiary of APS Insurance Services, APS Facilities Management, Inc. (FMI), handled the actual office administration. FMI sold and issued insurance policies and, as "attorney-in-fact," handled all aspects of claims

COMPANY PERSPECTIVES

We will provide superior service to our clients with uncompromising commitment to integrity, excellence and value creations.

Our clients will receive the highest level of commitment and service with an attitude reflecting total dedication to relationships, innovation, responsiveness and efficiency.

management, including investigation, legal defense, and claims settlements. FMI paid all expenses related to daily operations, such as payroll, office leasing, information technology, and supplies and equipment. APIE paid all claims and related expenses. APS received a fee based on a percentage of earned premiums before reinsurance, plus a percentage of profits. The contract automatically renewed on an annual basis unless a majority of subscribers voted to change management firms.

Having fulfilled the need for low-cost insurance in Texas, APS sought other business opportunities. In 1980 the company began offering medical malpractice insurance in Arkansas, and in 1981 the company established APS Financial Corporation, a securities brokerage serving insurance companies, institutions, and wealthy individuals. APS Financial extended APS's existing investment portfolio management activities by offering investment portfolio accounting and analysis to insurance companies as well. By 1982 APS revenues reached $4.87 million, and the company found itself in the position to offer other services to physicians.

DEVELOPMENT OF PRACTICE MANAGEMENT SYSTEMS: EIGHTIES

A public offering of over-the-counter stock in 1983 provided APS with the funds it needed to expand in new areas of business. Paul Koether, a New Jersey investor and the chief executive officer of APS, brought his knowledge of investment opportunities to a strategy of acquisition in office computer information systems. In February 1984 APS completed the acquisition of Comtrol Systems, a computer systems developer that catered to the needs of the health care industry. Other acquisitions included Great Western Business Forms, Inc.

APS obtained funds for further expansion the following April when American Continental Corporation purchased a minority interest in APS for $6 million. Lincoln Savings & Loan Association, a subsidiary of American Continental, purchased new shares of APS stock for $6.25 each, more than $2.00 less than the over-the-counter trading price. However, in addition to acquiring an interest in APS, Lincoln Savings provided APS with a $20 million credit facility.

In June APS purchased two California medical services companies. Databill, Inc., with $3.2 million in annual revenues, provided computer-based management services, such as patient billing, to dental groups in the western United States. The acquisition involved issuance of $4 million in common stock and a stock exchange. The second acquisition, of Hagy & Hagy, Inc., added operations in office management for hospital-based physicians. APS purchased the company for approximately $2 million, the equivalent to a year's revenue.

Computer systems development improved through further acquisitions. In November 1984 APS purchased Computer Information Architects, Inc., and Intellectron, Inc. The acquisition of CMS Medical Billing Systems, Inc. in 1985 and Physicians Office Systems, Inc. and Data Terminal Corporation in 1986 contributed revenues and knowledge to software development. All computer software operations were combined as APS Systems, Inc.

The combined capabilities of these companies led to the development of APS BULLET-3000, a medical practice management software. The software eased handling of insurance company billing, patient medical records, and patient appointment scheduling. In addition to physicians' offices, APS licensed the software to university medical schools. In 1987 University of Arkansas Medical Sciences became the first such organization to install the BULLET-3000.

By early 1988 APS decided to exit data systems business unrelated to its office management services. The company sold some operations, including Databill, for $11.6 million. APS continued to gain revenue from CyCare, the acquiring company, until the end of 1990.

In March 1989 Paul Koether resigned as chairman and chief executive officer, causing a sudden change in executive leadership. Murphy took the chairman position, and Kenneth Shifrin, who previously held the positions of senior vice president of finance and chief operating officer, became chief executive officer in March 1989. Shifrin became chairman of the board in March 1990.

KEY DATES

1981: American Physicians Service Group (APS) establishes brokerage and financial services subsidiary, APS Financial.

1984: APS begins series of acquisitions in medical office management computer software.

1998: APS Asset Management is formed.

2005: APS enters distressed debt investment market with formation of APS Clearing.

2007: APS completes merger with American Physicians Exchange Insurance.

NEW BUSINESSES AND SHIFTING FORTUNES

Shifrin led APS as the company further developed its office management business. For $5 million, APS acquired a 42 percent interest in Prime Medical Services in 1989. Prime Medical provided office management for cardiac rehabilitation clinics and diagnostic imaging centers. Prime Medical operated at a loss, but APS expected that application of its management systems would make the company profitable. With a controlling interest in Prime Medical, APS took four of the five seats on the board of directors.

The acquisition of Prime Medical temporarily affected earnings at APS, which had been increasing steadily. APS reported $2.3 million in net earnings in 1988, the latter derived from revenues of $12.5 million. Prime Medical revenues of $13.8 million resulted in a $3 million loss for the fiscal year ending June 30, 1989, giving APS a $640,000 loss for its fiscal year. Shifrin closed units that could not be made profitable, and by the end of 1991, Prime Medical became a profitable part of the APS enterprise. That year APS recorded revenues of $17.32 million and garnered net earnings of $496,000.

APS succeeded by obtaining new business in providing computer software systems to university medical schools. Also, APS hired a new president of insurance services, who contained and improved business retention. Record earnings at APS Financial contributed to profitability at APS as well.

APS sought further expansion of its practice management capabilities in April 1992, when the company purchased a $2 million interest in Ronald Luke & Associates, Inc. (RLA). Another Austin-based health care management company, RLA's utilization review, medical bill review, and case management services complemented APS's third party administration for medical and dental insurance claims. APS expected the two companies to find new opportunities in combining these administrative services.

APS benefited from a 1994 partnership with AIH Systems, provider of software to the managed care industry. The two companies combined their complementary computer software, BULLET 3000 and AIH's AMISYS, a comprehensive package of 22 software applications. Swedish Medical Services, Inc., of Seattle, which recently formed as a physician hospital organization, purchased the combined package for implementation across its health care network.

As more effective computer software competition increased during the mid-1990s, APS Systems struggled to compete. By 1996 the subsidiary operated at a loss. In an attempt to sustain the business, APS invested $1 million in a joint venture with International Software Solutions, Inc. However, the high cost of software development hindered adequate advances. APS Systems discontinued operations in 1997.

LATE NINETIES INVOLVEMENT IN MEDICAL AND NONMEDICAL BUSINESSES

APS invested in both medical and nonmedical businesses during the late 1990s. In 1996 APS acquired Exsorbet Industries, Inc., renamed Consolidated Eco-Systems, an environmental consulting and engineering company, renamed APS Consulting. New health care operations involved a $2 million investment in Uncommon Care, Inc., which specialized in developing and operating facilities dealing exclusively with care for people with Alzheimer's.

Medical management activities included the formation of APS Practice Management, which specialized in office management for OB/GYN medical practices. Renamed Syntera Healthcare, in 1999 the company merged with FemPartners, Inc., the leading OB/GYN practice management firm in Texas. Afterward APS retained a 12 percent equity ownership. A merger between Prime Medical and HealthTronics, Inc., a urology services provider, expanded Prime Medical's activities. However, it reduced APS's ownership interest to 15 percent.

By 2002, APS decided to focus on malpractice insurance and investment business only. APS sold APS Consulting, Inc., to its managers. Also, the company sold most of its interest in PrimeMedia and all of its interest in Uncommon Care. By this time, APS had exited the office management business as well.

FINANCIAL & INSURANCE ACTIVITIES

Concurrent with its diversification activities, APS continued to develop its core insurance and financial services businesses. APS formed a joint venture with Florida Physicians Insurance Company, Inc., in April 1997. FPIC acquired a 20 percent interest in APS Insurance Services in order to gain access to the Texas medical malpractice insurance market. FPIC's investment lent APS the strength and geographic range based on FPIC's $100 million equity and A- credit rating from AM Best.

Expansion at APS Financial in 1998 included the formation of APS Asset Management to offer fixed income and equity assets investment services. Also, APS Financial began to trade in high-yield corporate bonds. This area of investment included development of proprietary research and analysis on corporations in order to support clients' purchasing decisions.

APS expanded its financial services offerings through a $5.7 million investment in Financial Industries Corporation (FIC) in June 2003. An underwriter of individual life insurance and annuity products, FIC failed to meet its performance targets, however, resulting in a $1.6 million write-down for APS in 2004.

APS Clearing Corporation, later APS Capital Corporation, was formed in 2005 to take advantage of new investment opportunities created by subprime lending. Distressed debt acquisitions included syndicated bank loans and private loan portfolios. New, more efficient handling processes enabled APS to clear and settle debt in-house. Marketed to hedge funds and institutional investors, the distressed credit market offered liquidity to companies selling debt maintenance while APS expanded investment opportunities without competing with its clients.

2003 TEXAS TORT REFORM & APIE-APS MERGER

The Texas professional liability insurance industry underwent dramatic changes as claims increased during the late 1990s. Most of the insurance carriers left the Texas market, resulting in a decline from 17 underwriters in the state in 1999 to only four in 2002. Although APS profited by its relationship with FPIC, FPIC decided to exit the Texas market, and APS repurchased its shares in 2003. While the situation allowed APIE to provide coverage to more doctors, the increased risk led to premium increases. Rates increased about 85 percent between 1999 and 2003, and the industry experienced substantial losses.

These conditions led to tort reform in Texas, which took effect in September 2003. Tort reform restricted noneconomic medical malpractice damages to $250,000 and less. Hence, American Physicians Insurance Exchange reduced insurance premiums in February and August 2005, averaging 5 percent and 13 percent, respectively. The reductions saved doctors more than $12 million, and the number of claims declined significantly, prompting insurance carriers to reduce rates. The changes increased competition in the state of Texas, as risk of carrying malpractice insurance declined.

These changes led to a discussion about APS purchasing APIE, and in June 2006 APS announced a plan to merge with APIE. The transaction required regulatory approval and approval of APIE's subscribers, the physician owners who held insurance policies with the organization. Through the merger, the subscribers would gain greater liquidity, at $115 million, and APS gained a stronger financial standing through combined assets of $280 million. The transition involved converting APIE from a nonprofit organization to a for-profit company. Hence, American Physicians Insurance Exchange became American Physicians Insurance Company (API). APS completed the acquisition in April 2007, paying $39 million for API, including 2.1 million shares of stock and the assumption of $10.4 million in debt. A secondary offering of stock followed in May.

The merger of APS and API supported expansion into the Oklahoma professional liability insurance market. In August 2007 API obtained approval to sell insurance in Oklahoma, and the company underwrote more than $4 million in policies there over the next two years.

Before the merger with APIE, management services accounted for less than half of revenues, at $33.56 million in 2006. After the merger insurance premiums accounted for almost all revenues, especially as the Wall Street crisis of late 2008 greatly impacted financial services revenues. New opportunities in financial advising and mergers and acquisitions helped to sustain APS Financial. Overall, APS operated profitably through this period, with net income of $22.86 million from total revenues of $84.01 million in 2009.

Mary Tradii

PRINCIPAL SUBSIDIARIES

American Physicians Insurance Company; APS Asset Management, Inc.; APS Capital Corporation; APS Investment Services, Inc.

PRINCIPAL OPERATING UNITS

APS Insurance Services; APS Investment Services.

PRINCIPAL COMPETITORS

Advocate MD Insurance of the Southwest, Inc.; The Doctors Company; Medical Protective Insurance Services, Inc.; Physicians Liability Insurance Company of Oklahoma; ProAssurance Corporation; State Volunteer Mutual Insurance Company (Arkansas); Texas Medical Liability Insurance Underwriting Association; Texas Medical Liability Trust.

FURTHER READING

"American Physicians Service Group, Inc. Announces Strategic Merger with Medical Malpractice Partner," *Internet Wire*, June 5, 2006.

Belli, Anne, "Tort Reform: Two Insurers Cut Malpractice Rates," *Houston Chronicle*, March 3, 2005, p. 1.

Green, Tim, "Shifrin Sees APS Rebound from 1989 Slowdown," *Austin Business Journal*, April 9, 1990, p. 1.

AMETEK, Inc.

AMETEK, Inc.

———————— ■ ————————

37 North Valley Road, Building 4
P.O. Box 1764
Paoli, Pennsylvania 19301
U.S.A.
Telephone: (610) 647-2121
Fax: (215) 323-9337
Web site: http://www.ametek.com

Public Company
Incorporated: 1930 as American Machine and Metals,
    Inc.
Employees: 10,100
Sales: $2.1 billion (2009)
Stock Exchanges: New York
Ticker Symbol: AME
NAICS: 335312 Motor and Generator Manufacturing;
    333319 Other Commercial and Service Industry
    Machinery Manufacturing; 333412 Industrial and
    Commercial Fan and Blower Manufacturing;
    334417 Electronic Connector Manufacturing;
    334513 Instruments and Related Product
    Manufacturing for Measuring, Displaying, and
    Controlling Industrial Process Variables; 334515
    Instrument Manufacturing for Measuring and Test-
    ing Electricity and Electrical Signals; 334516
    Analytical Laboratory Instrument Manufacturing;
    334519 Other Measuring and Controlling Device
    Manufacturing; 488190 Other Support Activities
    for Air Transportation

■ ■ ■

AMETEK, Inc., is a global manufacturer and marketer
of specialized electronic instruments and electromechanical devices such as air-moving motors. A small
regional firm at the outset, AMETEK over the years has
directed its operations into the global market, acquiring
plants in North America, Europe, Asia, and South
America. It has 80 manufacturing facilities and 80 sales
and service centers around the world. The United States
accounts for about one-half of revenues. Acquisitive
throughout its history, AMETEK reached $1 billion in
sales in 2000 and passed the $2 billion mark seven years
later.

NEW YORK ORIGINS

By March 1930, several months after the stock market
crash, AMETEK's predecessor, the publicly traded
Manhattan Electrical Supply Company, had fallen into
bankruptcy, and stockholders decided to establish a new
company in which Manhattan Electrical would be
included. The new firm, American Machine and Metals,
Inc., was listed on the New York Stock Exchange as
AME.

AME consisted of several companies, including the
Troy Laundry Machinery division in East Moline, Il-
linois, Haliwell Electric in New York City, and the Trout
Mining Company in Phillipsburg, Montana. One year
after AME's formation, Manhattan Electrical Supply
Co. proved to be ill-fitted to the group and was sold by
the end of 1931. In its place, the Tolhurst Machine
Works of Troy, New York, which showed a small profit
despite the national economic conditions, was brought
into the AME fold. AME headquarters were located on
Wall Street, and the company's first president was Philip
G. Mumford, under whose leadership the company

COMPANY PERSPECTIVES

AMETEK's Corporate Growth Plan is founded on four key strategies: Operational Excellence, Strategic Acquisitions & Alliances, Global & Market Expansion, and New Products. Its objectives are double-digit annual percentage growth in earnings per share and a superior return on total capital.

managed to survive the Great Depression years, although it operated in the red for well over a year.

By 1932, the worst year of the Depression, AME began to show a slight profit, reporting overall assets of nearly $5 million. With the New Deal inaugurated the following year and massive government orders flowing into the economy, AME's business showed marked improvement. By 1935, AME was profitable. Perhaps because the firm was born of the Depression, the company took its social responsibilities seriously. Its 900 employees received benefits and incentives and were a factor in the company's rapid recovery. At the end of fiscal 1935, AME was able to pay its stockholders their first dividends.

The onset of war in Europe in 1939 brought about significant growth for AME. During this time, the U.S. government began looking for businesses that could be transformed rapidly into manufacturers of critical war materiel should the country become involved in the war. One of those selected was the East Moline branch of AME, which in 1941 converted its production towards the war effort, turning out laundries for ships and fans for tanks. By war's end, the company's Tolhurst division was manufacturing centrifuges that helped produce the new miracle medicines of the war, penicillin and sulfa drugs.

ACQUISITION OF U.S. GAUGE: 1944

Like many U.S. companies, AME's growth during the war years was phenomenal, enabling stockholders to consider further acquisitions. Their choice in terms of future growth proved excellent: the United States Gauge Company in New York. The purchase was finalized in 1944 for the price of $3 million in cash. This division employed 1,450 people, almost twice the number that had begun work at AME in 1930. Considering the importance of U.S. Gauge in the postwar years, this purchase marked a turning point in the history of the

company that would contribute to a transformation in its identity.

After a period of impressive growth and sales, AME experienced a slump during the immediate postwar years. Mumford, having guided the company through tough times, stepped down as president in 1948 and was replaced by the energetic, younger John C. Vander Pyl. Soon thereafter, the company's business increased, chiefly because of the demands of the Cold War. Tensions turned into open hostilities in Korea in 1950, and for the next several years the demands of confronting communism kept the U.S. economy almost as prosperous as during the World War II years.

Annual sales for AME in 1955 stood at $30 million, making the company a comparably small player among the giants of U.S. industry. Nevertheless, stockholders' dividends had increased annually, and in 1955, they once again approved a worthy acquisition: the purchase of Lamb Electric for $34 million. Like U.S. Gauge, Lamb Electric would become one of the most important components of AME and would enable the company to make the transition from the manufacture of simple machinery to technologically more advanced products.

By the early 1960s, AME's principal operations had changed significantly from the traditional manufacture of heavy machinery and mining ventures. Trout Mining of Montana had been divested in 1958, and with the additions of U.S. Gauge and Lamb Electric, the company was producing a wide variety of precision components and electric motors for small appliances. In recognition of the company's new focus on smaller, more technologically refined products, stockholders approved the company's name change in 1961 from American Machine and Metals to AMETEK, Inc., a changeover that allowed the firm to retain AME as its stock trading symbol.

Rapid expansion followed, and new plants, among the first to boast central air conditioning, were constructed. In 1965, with the acquisition of Mansfield and Green, Inc., AMETEK was launched into the lab instruments business. The accession of Dr. John H. Lux as president of the firm in 1966 also vitalized the company. Under Lux, managers were required to visit company plants and get to know the employees and business firsthand, a strategy that boosted employee morale and contributed to company growth. In 1967, the first water filtration equipment business of the company, Plymouth Industrial Products, Inc., was acquired. Furthermore, Lamb Electric branched out into the manufacture of computer and photocopier motors. By 1980, sales had reached $400 million, and three years later, AMETEK for the first time made it into the

KEY DATES

■

1930: Manhattan Electrical Supply Company reorganizes as American Machine and Metals, Inc.

1961: American Machine and Metals is renamed AMETEK, Inc.

1993: Industry downturn prompts restructuring.

2000: Total revenues exceed $1 billion.

2006: AMETEK builds its aerospace maintenance repair business.

2007: Total revenues exceed $2 billion.

rankings of the *Fortune* 500 companies, with a reputation as a manufacturer of highly advanced products and materials.

KETEMA, INC., SPINOFF IN 1988

In 1988, stockholders approved a major restructuring of AMETEK, which resulted in the divestment of 14 lower-growth subsidiaries. As a result, AMETEK became much more streamlined with a sharper focus. Henceforth, the company consisted of three principal segments: Electromechanical, Precision Instruments, and Industrial Materials. Moreover, AMETEK expanded its markets globally, with exports accounting for an increasingly larger proportion of sales revenues. These changes proved timely as trade barriers were collapsing in much of the world, and free market economies were on the rise in Eastern Europe, Russia, and China. With a diverse array of products, the company would not suffer should any one of them fail in the marketplace.

In 1993, under Chairman and CEO Walter E. Blankley, AMETEK consisted of 33 manufacturing facilities and 14 divisions across the country and abroad. Of its three principal operating segments, the Electromechanical Group, which included Lamb Electric, represented more than 40 percent of company sales. Its market was global, with over 25 percent of its sales derived from overseas.

To enhance this division, AMETEK acquired three Italian electric motor companies that gave the company a base on the European continent. The Electromechanical group produced a wide variety of electric motors, chiefly for floor care appliances, computers, copiers, medical equipment, and high efficiency heating units. As a producer of small appliances, the Electromechanical Group became a global leader in the early 1990s,

increasing its sales 24 percent in 1992, despite an economic recession in the United States.

The second principal segment of AMETEK was the Precision Instruments Group, to which U.S. Gauge belonged as did Aerospace Products, Inc., acquired by AMETEK in 1989. Manufacturing advanced measuring and monitoring devices for the aerospace industry, this group of companies generated nearly 40 percent of company sales in 1993. However, of all AMETEK's operations, Precision Instruments suffered the most from the 1990s recession, primarily due to cutbacks in military spending and financial difficulties in the commercial airlines industry, areas on which Precision Instruments relied for nearly half of its sales. Nevertheless, the division manufactured a wide variety of products and expected to make up for its losses by exploring new markets.

For example, demand for instrument panels for the heavy truck industry increased as did the need for measuring and monitoring devices in Europe, where air pollution standards had become increasingly stringent. Furthermore, industry analysts projected that by 2000, most airplanes would need modernization and repair, renewing business opportunities in the airline industry. AMETEK's acquisitions of Debro Messtechnik GmbH in Germany and AMETEK Denmark A/S testified to the broadening of the market for precision instruments.

AMETEK's third major segment, Industrial Materials, contributed approximately 20 percent of sales in 1993. Among the great variety of items produced by this group were specialty metals, heat exchangers, featherweight foam sheet packaging material, drinking water filters and treatment systems, and high-temperature-resistant plastics and textiles. Plymouth Products, in Sheboygan, Wisconsin, was a leading producer of kitchen and bathroom water filtration products, demand for which was expanding rapidly. Such important acquisitions as the Kleen Plus Company in Milwaukee and AMETEK Filters (formerly Euro-filtec) in Billingham, England, were expected to position AMETEK as a global leader in the water filtration enterprise. Furthermore, Industrial Materials was the only producer in the world of low-density polypropylene foam packing material and a leader in heat exchanger technology, aimed at recovering waste energy from boilers more efficiently.

Growing concern for the environment at home and abroad prompted AMETEK to produce and market environmentally safe products. In addition, the Haveg manufacturing facility, in the Industrial Materials group, became the world's largest producer of silica yarn, a suitable replacement for asbestos. The Microfoam division of Industrial Materials produced plastic furniture packing that not only was recyclable but was made without chlorofluorocarbons, another first for AMETEK. High-efficiency furnaces that use the type of high-temperature motor blowers produced by AMETEK were increasing in popularity in the early 1990s.

RESTRUCTURING AFTER 1993

A broad range of products, attention to international marketing opportunities, and new product development for a safer environment were regarded as AMETEK's strengths and seemed assured to provide growth and profitability in the future. Nevertheless, an industry slowdown ended AMETEK's 54-year string of quarterly dividends in 1993. The company subsequently began a restructuring. The Precision Instruments Group consolidated some of its operations in New York and Florida at the Mansfield & Green and U.S. Gauge subsidiaries.

In 1996 the company folded its $24 million Westchester Plastics business in with its Haveg textiles and heat exchangers unit to form the Chemical Products Division. Three years later, the chemicals business was put up for sale as the company sought to focus on motors and instruments. However, AMETEK ultimately retained the unit, expanding the Westchester Plastics operation in 2003.

ACQUISITION DRIVE UNDERWAY IN 1995

While AMETEK maintained significant research and development activities through the downturn, the company's main driver of growth was building product lines through complementary acquisitions. In June 1995 the company added Dixson Inc., a Grand Junction, Colorado, supplier of instrumentation for heavy trucks.

In 1997 AMETEK bought Rotron Inc. from EG&G Inc. for $103 million. Rotron made brushless electric motors controlled by microprocessors, a specialty perceived to be in high demand in the future. Rotron, based in Woodstock, New York, had annual revenues of $70 million. There was also a significant divestiture during the year, with the sale of AMETEK's water-filtration line to Culligan Water Technologies for $155 million.

Frank Hermance succeeded Walter Blankley in 1997 to become AMETEK's CEO after serving as president and chief operating officer for three years. He stated the goal of doubling the company in size within five years, largely through acquisitions.

In January 1999 the company acquired National Controls Corp., a Chicago-area provider of instruments and controls for restaurant equipment. AMETEK

bought Gulton-Statham Transducers Inc., based in Costa Mesa, California, in May 1999 for $23 million. It made pressure sensors for aerospace and industrial use. Detroit's Patriot Sensors & Controls Corp. was added in August 1999 for $70 million. It had plants in Michigan and California and revenues of $40 million a year.

$1 BILLION COMPANY IN 2000

By the end of 1999, AMETEK had 12 divisions and operations in seven countries. There were 7,500 employees in all. The company had the previous year begun to consolidate some of its plants and shift some production to lower-wage countries. AMETEK's annual revenues exceeded $1 billion in 2000. They would double within seven years.

EDAX Inc., a Mahwah, New Jersey, manufacturer of electron microscope analysis equipment, was bought for $37 million in 2001. Its previous owner, Panta Electronics Group, had acquired it from Philips Electronics NV three years earlier. This purchase, noted *Instrument Business Outlook*, brought AMETEK into lab equipment and the life sciences.

Later in the year AMETEK added Instruments for Research and Applied Science (IRAS) from PerkinElmer for $63 million. This buy brought the company into other new laboratory areas. One of the IRAS businesses, ORTEC, made nuclear spectroscopes. Another, Princeton Applied Research, supplied electrical instruments. These became the basis of AMETEK's Advanced Measurement Technology unit.

AMETEK continued to shop for new acquisitions, with an annual budget of $150 million funded through its own cash flow and a $300 million line of credit. The analytical instruments industry remained highly fragmented, offering many candidates. The company sought complementary businesses in "differentiated" niches.

In March 2003 the company bought Solidstate Controls Inc. for $36 million. During the year it also acquired Tulsa, Oklahoma's Chandler Instruments Company, L.L.C., paying about $50 million. Chandler made analytical equipment used by the petroleum industry.

In June 2004 AMETEK acquired Taylor Hobson Holdings for $95 million. This was a pioneer in the field of ultra-precise surface-measurement instruments used in the electronics and optics industries. Its annual revenues were about $70 million.

Hughes-Treitler Manufacturing Corporation, a maker of heat exchangers used in military helicopters and fixed-wing aircraft, was acquired for $48 million in

July 2004. Based in Garden City, New York, the company had revenues of about $32 million.

NEW SPECIALTIES AFTER 2005

PennEngineering Motion Technologies (PMT) was purchased for $64 million in 2006. It was a motor manufacturer with operations in the United States and Italy. Another acquisition during the year was Land Instruments International, a U.K. supplier of thermal analytical instrumentation.

In June 2005 the company bought Spectro Analytical Instruments GmbH and Company KG, which made instruments to determine the composition of materials. The 2006 acquisition of Umeco plc's repair and overhaul division for $74 million bolstered the growing maintenance, repair, and operations business with operations in the United Kingdom and France. Related acquisitions during the year included Southern Aeroparts and B&S Aircraft Parts.

Tulsa, Oklahoma's Drake Air, a repairer of heat-transfer equipment used in commercial aircraft, was added in February 2008. It had annual revenues of $15 million. Britain's Muirhead Aerospace was also added in November 2008. Two months later, AMETEK added aerospace repair firm High Standard Aviation. AMETEK's total revenues exceeded $2 billion in fiscal 2007. During the year the company acquired CAMECA SAS, a maker of spectrometry systems, for EUR 82 million.

In July 2008 Canada's Xantrex Technology Inc., which was being acquired by Schneider Electric of France, announced the sale of its San Diego-based programmable power business to AMETEK for $120 million. It had annual revenues of $80 million selling power supplies used in testing electronics in a variety of industries.

Pennsylvania's Reading Alloys Inc., acquired in April 2008, produced titanium alloys for the aerospace industry. It had sales of $80 million a year. One of the first suppliers of titanium, the company was formed in 1953 by Fred Perfect and had been owned by nearby KB Alloys Inc. for 10 years before AMETEK bought it.

AMETEK boosted its materials testing lines with the June 2008 purchase of Newage Testing Instruments, a supplier of hardness testing equipment. Other companies acquired in 2008 included Motion Control Group and Vision Research Inc., a specialist in high-speed digital imaging.

The United States accounted for about one-half of 2008 revenues of $2.53 billion. Europe was its next largest market. With 55 percent of revenues, the Electronic Instruments operating group was slightly larger than the Electromechanical side of the business.

In 2009 AMETEK opened an instruments subsidiary in India and soon made several complementary acquisitions there, of Unispec Marketing Pvt. Ltd. and Thelsha Technical Services Pvt. Ltd. During the year the company also acquired Ameron Global, which made components for pressurized gas systems.

Revenues slipped to $2.1 billion for 2009, but the company was able to maintain a roughly 10 percent net profit. AMETEK had about 10,000 employees in all. AMETEK continued to make strategic acquisitions. In early 2010 the company bought Sterling Ultra Precision, a distributor of tools for making ophthalmic lenses. In April it added Imago Scientific Instruments, a Madison, Wisconsin, provider of atomic level imaging technology used in advanced materials science.

Sina Dubovoj
Updated, Frederick C. Ingram

PRINCIPAL SUBSIDIARIES

Advanced Measurement Technology, Inc.; AMETEK (Bermuda), Ltd.; AMETEK Canada, LLC; AMETEK Canada 2 ULC; AMETEK Lamb Motores de Mexico, S.A. de C.V.; AMETEK Motors Holding, Inc.; AMETEK Receivables Corp.; AMETEK Thermal Systems, Inc.; Chandler Instruments Company, L.L.C.; Controls Holding Corporation; Drake Air, Inc.; EDAX Inc.; Elgar Holdings, Inc.; EMA Corp.; HCC Industries, Inc.; HP Acquisitions Corp.; KBA Holding, Inc.; NCC Holdings, Inc.; NewAge Testing Instruments, Inc.; PowerTest Group, Ltd. (Hong Kong); Rotron Incorporated; SCPH Holdings, Inc.; Seiko EG&G Co. Ltd. (Japan; 49%); Solidstate Controls, LLC; Vision Research, Inc.; AMETEK Singapore Private Ltd.; EMA Holdings UK Limited.

PRINCIPAL DIVISIONS

AMETEK Advanced Measurement Technology; AMETEK Aerospace & Defense; AMETEK Chemical Products; AMETEK Engineered Materials, Interconnects & Packaging; AMETEK Floorcare & Specialty Motors; AMETEK Instrumentation & Specialty Controls; AMETEK Materials Analysis; AMETEK Measurement & Calibration Technologies; AMETEK Power Systems & Instruments; AMETEK Process & Analytical Instruments; AMETEK Programmable Power; AMETEK Technical & Industrial Products; AMETEK Ultra Precision Technologies.

PRINCIPAL OPERATING UNITS

Electronic Instruments; Electromechanical.

PRINCIPAL COMPETITORS

General Electric Company; Agilent Technologies, Inc.; Thermo Fisher Scientific Inc.; Tektronix, Inc.; Emerson Electric Co.

FURTHER READING

"Ametek Expands to Fill Niches," *Instrument Business Outlook*, September 15, 2003, pp. 4, 11.

Eginton, William, "AMETEK Acquires Taylor Hobson Holdings," *Mergers & Acquisitions*, January 1, 2005.

"Gauging the Last 100 Years," *Oil, Gas, & Petrochem Equipment*, October 1, 2004, p. 30.

Haflich, Frank, and Maria Guzzo, "Ametek's Buy of Reading Nice Fit for Both Firms," *American Metal Market*, April 17, 2008, pp. 1–2.

Irving, Robert R., "Ametek Trading New Plant, Cash for GE Facility," *Metalworking News*, June 12, 1989, pp. 5+.

"Ketema: A New M&A Player," *Mergers & Acquisitions*, March/April 1990, p. 240.

Khermouch, Gerry, "John Dandalides Steps Down as Ametek Chief," *Metalworking News*, February 5, 1990, pp. 6+.

McLaughlin, Paul, "Communication: The Key to Successful Due Diligence," *Philadelphia Business Journal*, September 14, 2001, p. 1.

Piotrowski, Michael A., "Manufacturer Reorganizes Largo Unit," *South Florida Business Journal*, August 4, 1995, pp. 3+.

Reisch, Marc, "Environmental Push Pays Off for Packaging Firm," *Chemical & Engineering News*, February 3, 1992, pp. 14–15.

"Unique Recycling Idea Could Save Millions," *Modern Materials*, December 1992, p. 12.

"Woodbridge Heads Re-Formed Concern; Manhattan Electrical Supply Reorganized as American Machine and Metals," *New York Times*, Bus. Sec., July 2, 1930, p. 46.

Angostura Holdings Ltd.

P.O. Box 62
Eastern Main Road and Angostura Street
Laventille,
Trinidad and Tobago
Telephone: (+868) 623 1841
Fax: (+868) 623 1847
Web site: http://www.angostura.com

Public Company
Founded: 1824
Incorporated: 1867 as Dr. J.G.B. Siegert & Hijo
Employees: 414
Sales: TTD 840 million ($134.6 million) (2007)
Stock Exchanges: Trinidad and Tobago
Ticker Symbol: AHL
NAICS: 312140 Distilleries

■ ■ ■

Angostura Holdings Ltd. is the producer and distributor of one of Trinidad and Tobago's most iconic products, Angostura Aromatic Bitters, used throughout the world as an ingredient in cocktails and food recipes. The recipe behind Angostura's bitters, invented in 1824, is said to be one of the world's oldest and most jealously guarded trade secrets. In addition to its aromatic bitters, the company also produces its LLB brand of lemon, lime bitters, and Angostura Orange Bitters, introduced in 2007.

Angostura Holdings is also Trinidad and Tobago's leading rum distillery, producing a variety of labels under the Angostura and Fernandes brands. The company also produces Blu vodka and Mokatika, a coffee liqueur. Angostura's international operations include a distillery in Scotland, where it produces its Angostura Single Barrel scotch whiskey, and the Medleys bourbon distillery in Kentucky, acquired in 2007. That distillery, which had been shut down in the early 1990s, is expected to resume production some time after 2010.

Angostura Holdings, although listed on the Trinidad and Tobago Stock Exchange, had been controlled by the country's largest private conglomerate, CL Financial, which collapsed at the beginning of 2009. The Trinidad and Tobago government took over as Angostura Holding's majority shareholder in August of that year. Wayne Yip Choy was named chief executive of subsidiary Angostura Limited in November 2009, and then became CEO and managing director of Angostura Holdings in January 2010. Amid the unraveling of CL Financial, Angostura has not reported its annual revenues since 2007, when its sales reached TTD 840 million ($134.6 million).

REMEDY RECIPE IN 1824

The history of Angostura Bitters began in the early decades of the 19th century when Johann Gottlieb Benjamin Siegert traveled to Venezuela where he became surgeon general of the military hospital under Simon Bolívar. Born in 1796, Siegert had studied medicine in Berlin, then was deployed as a physician to the Prussian army during the Battle of Waterloo in 1815. Siegert soon joined a number of former Prussian and British veterans of the Napoleonic wars to aid Bolívar's effort to liberate the Spanish colonies in South America. Siegert

KEY DATES

1824: J. G. B. Siegert invents the recipe for Angostura Bitters.

1875: Siegert's sons move the company to Trinidad.

1909: Company goes public as Angostura Bitters.

1982: Company lists on the Trinidad and Tobago Stock Exchange as Angostura Holdings.

1999: CL Financial becomes the company's majority shareholder.

2010: Angostura temporarily suspends production of its bitters due to a bottle shortage.

arrived in the port town of Angostura (later Ciudad Bolívar), then the headquarters for Bolívar's revolutionary government, in 1820.

Siegert sought to develop medicines to alleviate the ailments and discomfort experienced by the European troops as they adjusted to the region's tropical climate. His interest soon turned to chemistry as he began to explore the properties of the many plants, spices, and herbs of the region's rain forests. By 1824, Siegert had concocted his remedy, the recipe of which was based on gentian, with alcohol as a solvent, but otherwise kept a strict secret. Siegert called his tonic *amargos aromáticos*, or aromatic bitters.

The Angostura bitters quickly developed a following among Siegert's patients, who, returning to Europe, brought bottles of the tonic with them. By 1830, Siegert had begun making his first shipments of tonic to England. He also began supplying the nearby British colony in Trinidad. Over the next decades, Siegert extended his sales to a number of markets, setting up a network of sales agents. Siegert's production remained at the artisan level, however, and into the 1850s his exports amounted to little more than 240 cases per year. In 1850, however, as demand for the tonic began to grow, Siegert retired from his military commission to take up manufacturing of the tonic full time.

MOVING TO TRINIDAD IN 1875

Siegert was joined by his oldest son, Carlos, and in 1867 the company incorporated as Dr. J.G.B. Siegert & Hijo. Siegert died just three years later. In 1872, Carlos brought younger brother Alfredo into the business, which then became known as Dr. J.G.B. Siegert & Hijos. By then, however, Venezuela was in the midst of a civil war. This led the Siegerts to move their opera-

tions to the more politically stable Trinidad in 1875, where a third brother, Luis, joined the company as well.

Angostura Bitters had by then built a significant international reputation not only for its curative properties as a tonic, but also as an important ingredient in cocktails and other recipes. Carlos Siegert played a major role in building the product's reputation, traveling the world as its ambassador. Through Siegert's efforts, Angostura Bitters soon became something of a mainstay among the prize winners at the world's international exhibitions.

Among the first of the company's awards was that received at the London Exhibition in 1862. This was followed by an award in Paris in 1867, and then Vienna in 1873. Through the end of the century, Angostura Bitters received numerous other awards, ranging from Philadelphia in 1878 and Amsterdam in 1883, to Chicago in 1893. In 1900, the company received the Gold Medal at the Paris Exhibition. Four years later, the bitters were awarded the Grand Prize at the St. Louis Exhibition, followed by a Gold Medal in London in 1905.

Carlos Siegert died in 1903, and Luis Siegert died just two years later. By then Alfredo Siegert had taken over as the head of the company, and helped establish it as a leading supplier to Europe's royal families. This started in 1904, when the company was named a supplier to the king of Prussia. In 1907, the company added a warrant to supply the Spanish royal family. Finally, in 1910, the company received the royal warrant as a supplier to the British royal family under George V. By then, Siegert had taken the company public, listing it as Angostura Bitters (Dr. J.G.B. Siegert & Sons) Limited in 1909.

BATTLING IMITATORS DURING WORLD WAR I

Alfredo Siegert launched the company into a number of investments over the next several years. When these failed, the family was forced to give up control of the company to their creditors. Angostura soon regained its footing, however, and managed to remain profitable despite losing much of its trade in continental Europe due to World War I. The rising strength of the temperance movement in England and elsewhere also created difficulties for the company, which saw a drop-off in England following the imposition of restrictions on the purchase and consumption of alcoholic beverages.

At the same time, Angostura was confronted by another problem caused by its own success, a growing number of imitators. The company had already faced this problem in the final years of the previous century, when a business in the United States attempted to produce and market its own bitters using the Angostura name. The company managed to win an injunction against that business, affirming its trademark.

During World War I, as Angostura Bitters became unavailable to the European continent, a number of German companies attempted to launch their own imitations of the original recipe. This helped fuel a misconception among drinkers in England that the company itself was a German company, despite its long presence in the British colony of Trinidad.

DISTILLING EXTENSION IN 1936

Following the war, the company's fortunes rose again as it recovered its continental European business. In the United States, Angostura Bitters won classification as an ingredient, despite its alcoholic base, preserving its sales there during the Prohibition Era. By then, Angostura Bitters had long found its way into many popular recipes, including for cakes, jams, and jellies.

Robert Siegert, great-grandson of the company's founder, took over as head of the business in the 1930s, and set the stage for the company's transition into Trinidad and Tobago's leading drinks group. Under Siegert's direction, the company began to develop modern production methods, establishing new quality control standards. This effort in turn led Angostura to launch its own distilling operations in order to ensure the quality and supply of the alcohol used as a base for its bitters.

At the same time, the company used its distillery to begin producing its own rums, which had become one of the major exports of Trinidad and other Caribbean markets. Angostura's rum appeared to meet the standards of Trinidad's population, and the company's rum soon became a leading seller on that island, before becoming a well-respected rum brand on the international market as well.

REGAINING CONTROL IN 1958

While Angostura's rum sales grew strongly through the middle of the century, its Angostura Bitters continued to attract new challengers. Throughout its existence, Angostura had jealously guarded the secret to the recipe behind its world-famous product. For much of the company's history, that recipe had been kept within the Siegert family, helping to maintain their position at the head of the company, despite loss of ownership control.

Shortly before the start of World War II, however, the company faced a new competitor: one of its own employees, a foreman who, after watching the arrival of ingredients at the warehouse over a period of two years, managed to compile a complete list of the bitters'

ingredients. He then set up his own company to produce a variant of the bitters. That company quickly closed down, however, in large part because he proved unable to work out the proportions used for each ingredient.

A more serious challenge to the company's survival in Trinidad came in the late 1950s. In 1958, the company was approached by its U.S. distributor, which sought to acquire the company and move its operations to the United States. Angostura successfully fought off that bid, only to be confronted by a new takeover offer from J.C.B. Limited, based in Bermuda, that same year. This time the Trinidad and Tobago government stepped in, launching a successful counteroffer. The government then agreed to provide a loan to the Siegert family, through a holding company, so that they could buy back control of the company.

Angostura continued to boost its international profile into the new decade. By 1960, the company's products reached more than 140 countries worldwide. Angostura's distillery operations also produced more than 1.3 million liters per year by then.

EXPANDING IN THE SEVENTIES

Angostura itself attempted to get acquisitive in the late 1960s. Angostura sought to diversify its operations beyond its rum and bitters production. In this way, the company hoped to protect itself against the downswings in the increasingly fickle global alcoholic beverages sector. Angostura began planning an extension into spices and other products. For this, the company formed a new subsidiary, A1 Holdings, bringing in Canada's John Labatt as a minority partner. In 1969, Angostura launched a takeover bid for West Indies general merchant Alston. When another company launched a higher counterbid, however, Angostura was forced to withdraw.

Instead, Angostura revised its strategy in the 1970s. By then, Robert Siegert, who remained chairman of the company, had turned over its direction to Deputy Chairman Albert Gomez and Managing Director Thomas Gatcliffe. Both were taught the recipe to Angostura Bitters, and, as according to company tradition, took turns personally supervising the mixture several times per year. Gatcliffe in particular became a major figure in Angostura's growth over the next decades, remaining at the head of the company until the late 1990s.

Angostura faced another takeover threat at the beginning of the 1970s from a Canadian company. Again, the group's suitor threatened to move the company's operations outside of Trinidad and Tobago.

As one of the country's major employers, Angostura remained too important to the country's economy. This led the government to step in a second time to rescue the group. In the process, Angostura received a new majority shareholder, Bermuda-based Bacardi Ltd., which acquired a 45 percent stake in the company in 1971. Bacardi's investment in Angostura was strategic, providing the company with access to Angostura's rum production for its own export operations.

With Angostura's ownership questions settled, the company under Gatcliffe's leadership, Angostura once again refocused its business around its core operations of rum and bitters. In 1973, the group bought out the brand name and recipe for one of its chief rum rivals, the Fernandes distillery, located across the street from its own. Angostura thus expanded its portfolio of rums, while also tightening its grip on the domestic rum market with control of Trinidad and Tobago's two leading brands.

NEW SHAREHOLDERS IN 1999

Angostura returned to the public market in 1982, when it listed its shares on the Trinidad and Tobago Stock Exchange. At that time the company adopted its new name, Angostura Holdings Limited. In 1985, the Trinidad and Tobago government awarded the company its first National Award for its contribution to the country's economy and international reputation. In that year, also, Angostura completed an expansion of its distillery, boosting its production capacity. The expansion of the distillery continued through the 1990s, reaching 20 million liters by 1998.

The 1990s were also marked by a new extension of Angostura's operations, as it sought to leverage its famous brand into a line of sauces. For this, the company launched Angostura-branded Worcestershire, teriyaki, and soy sauces, largely for export markets. These were initially produced in the United States by a third-party manufacturer. In 1997, the company built its own production facility in Trinidad. Angostura also extended the range to include drink mixes, included a Bloody Mary mix.

In the meantime, Angostura had caught the attention of fast-rising CL Financial, founded in 1993 by Lawrence Duprey, owner of Colonial Life Insurance Company. Duprey, who later acquired several other drinks companies, planned to transform Angostura into an international drinks player. By 1999, Duprey had reached an agreement to acquire Bacardi's stake in the company for $28 million.

As part of CL Financial, Angostura began its drive to achieve a stronger international presence. This led the company to purchase nearly 19 percent of Scotland's Burn Stewart Distillers in 1999, adding that company's whiskey to its portfolio. The company also picked up a 20 percent stake in U.S. Virgin Islands-based group Todhunter International that year, adding its Cruzan rum brand. Angostura later gained full control of Burn Stewart, and increased its share of Todhunter to nearly 68 percent.

SURVIVING THE COLLAPSE IN 2010

Angostura's expansion remained relatively modest, however. The company later added a vodka brand, Blu, as well as a coffee liqueur called Mokatika. Angostura's expansion plans hit a snag in 2002, when it failed in its bid to acquire Ireland's Cooley Distillery. Another takeover for Jamaica-based Wray & Nephew in 2007 also failed. By then, the company had sold off its stake in Todhunter to V&S, for $122 million in 2005.

Sales of the group's core Angostura brand remained strong through the decade, as the company boosted capacity at its distillery operation to 50 million liters. The company remained on the lookout for growth opportunities. In 2004, for example, it announced its intention to spend $11 million to build an ethanol-production plant in the United States. The company returned to the United States in 2007 with the purchase of the Medley bourbon distillery in Kentucky. That business had shut down its distillery operations in the early 1990s. Angostura, however, announced plans to spend $25 million to modernize the distillery ahead of relaunching its production some time after 2010.

By then, however, Angostura had been caught up in the financial collapse of parent company CL Financial at the beginning of 2009. CL Financial had grown to a TTD 8 billion giant equivalent to roughly 18 percent of Trinidad and Tobago's total economy, but had been caught off-guard by the global economic recession at the end of the decade. Angostura itself was burdened with a debt load of more than TTD 600 million ($95 million). Amid the unraveling of CL Financial's own financial situation, Angostura failed to provide financial details for its 2008 and 2009 years, leading to the temporary suspension on trading of its shares. By August 2009, the Trinidad and Tobago government was forced to step in to rescue the company, taking over CL Financial's share. The company then dismissed its CEO, Patrick Patel, who later was criticized for leading an extravagant lifestyle at the company's expense.

Wayne Yip Choy was named chief executive at subsidiary Angostura Ltd. in November 2009, before being named CEO of Angostura Holdings itself. By then,

Angostura faced a new difficulty. In late 2009, the company turned to a Chinese manufacturer for the supply of the iconic Angostura Bitters bottle. The new supplier failed to deliver on time, however, and early in 2010 the company was forced to suspend production of Angostura Bitters temporarily. The move sent a shockwave through the international bartending industry, as barkeepers scrambled to ensure their supply of what had become one of the cocktail world's most well-known and essential ingredients.

M. L. Cohen

PRINCIPAL SUBSIDIARIES

Trinidad Distillers Limited; Fernandes Distillers Limited; Angostura Limited.

PRINCIPAL DIVISIONS

Angostura Bitters; Angostura Sauces.

PRINCIPAL OPERATING UNITS

Distillery; Bottling.

PRINCIPAL COMPETITORS

Asahi Kasei Corp.; Diageo PLC; Asahi Breweries Ltd.; Suntory Holdings Ltd.; Fortune Brands Inc.; Bacardi Bottling Corp.; Brown-Forman Corporation; Maxxium Worldwide B.V.

FURTHER READING

"Angostura Brand Boosts Rum Sector," *Grocer*, June 21, 2008, p. 67.

Bentley, Stephanie, "Rum Approach Warms Up Burn," *Daily Mail*, April 24, 2002, p. 65.

"Bitters Shortage Causes Panic in New York Bars," *Philippines News Agency*, January 14, 2010.

Conaway, Janelle, "An Aroma of Mystery," *Americas*, September–October 2009, p. 58.

Marajh, Camini, "Living Large: Cash-Strapped Angostura's Culture of Executive Excess," *Trinidad & Tobago Express*, November 15, 2009.

"Mizkan Americas Acquires US Angostura Rights," *just-drinks. com*, January 12, 2010.

Wilson, Anthony, "Can Angostura Survive (the Silence)?" *Trinidad & Tobago Guardian*, February 25, 2010.

———, "Govt. Moves to Take Control of Angostura," *Trinidad & Tobago Guardian*, August 27, 2009.

Applied Materials, Inc.

3050 Bowers Avenue
Santa Clara, California 95054-3299
U.S.A.
Telephone: (408) 727-5555
Fax: (408) 748-9943
Web site: http://www.appliedmaterials.com

Public Company
Incorporated: 1967
Employees: 13,032
Sales: $5.01 billion (2009)
Stock Exchanges: NASDAQ
Ticker Symbol: AMAT
NAICS: 333295 Semiconductor Machinery Manufacturing; 334413 Semiconductor and Related Device Manufacturing

■ ■ ■

Based in Santa Clara, California, Applied Materials, Inc., is a leading nanomanufacturing firm. The company's offerings include a wide range of equipment, service, and software. Applied Materials' technology is used to produce most of the world's semiconductor chips and flat-panel displays. In addition, the company's products also are used in the production of solar photovoltaic panels. In 2009, the company posted sales of just over $5 billion.

ORIGINS & RAPID GROWTH

Applied Materials was founded in 1967 to manufacture chemical vapor deposition systems for semiconductor wafer fabrication. The semiconductor industry itself, however, which makes the microcircuitry used in all electronics products, dates back to the invention of the first transistor during the early 1950s by scientists working at Bell Telephone Laboratories. With the advent of the transistor, it was possible to make electronic circuitry smaller and this, in turn, led to the manufacture of products that were lighter weight, more compact, and more energy efficient.

During the late 1950s semiconductor chip makers who initially both designed and built their own production equipment began to contract with vendors that supplied the equipment used to make their miniaturized devices. This trend helped to develop the semiconductor equipment industry. In the modern world, semiconductor manufacturing technology revolutionized the industrialized nations, providing the basis for all electronic products ranging from advanced fighter aircraft instrumentation to consumer goods such as radios and digital clocks.

Within this historical context, Applied Materials' place in the development of the semiconductor manufacturing industry was unique. From 1967 to 1973 company revenues grew at a pace of more than 40 percent annually, and its total market share of the semiconductor equipment industry reached 6.5 percent. With such rapid market expansion and such enviable financial success, in 1972 the company decided to go public. In 1974 management decided to acquire Galamar Industries, a manufacturer of silicon wafers. During the mid-1970s, however, a severe recession had a very negative effect on the entire semiconductor industry. Applied Materials was hit especially hard, suf-

COMPANY PERSPECTIVES

With more than 40 years of commitment to facilitating positive change through technological innovation, Applied has improved the way people learn, work and play. Technology is at the heart and soul of our DNA.

fering a 45 percent drop in sales in 1975. Despite the drop in sales, management pursued prospects for growth, entering into a joint venture with Fairchild Camera and Instrument Corporation to construct a silicon production site in the same year.

Persistent financial problems related to non-semiconductor areas throughout 1976 and 1977 necessitated both organizational and management changes. James C. Morgan, formerly a partner in a private venture-capital firm and with extensive experience in management at Textron's high-technology divisions, became president and chief executive officer. Morgan immediately shut down the unprofitable Galamar Industries, sold its share in the silicon manufacturing center, and concentrated on improving its area of expertise in the semiconductor industry. In 1978 Applied Materials reported an increase in sales of approximately 17 percent, and in 1979 sales grew by a phenomenal 51 percent over the previous year.

EXPANSION AMID INDUSTRY DOWNTURNS

Applied Materials, under the guidance of Morgan, continued its expansion strategy and acquired the ion implantation division of British-based Lintott Engineering, Ltd., in 1979. The company also formed Applied Materials Japan, Inc., a joint venture created to increase the company's share of the growing Japanese semiconductor equipment market. Sales reached $69.3 million in 1980, but by 1982 the company was once again hit hard by a worldwide recession in the semiconductor industry. At the end of that year, Applied Materials reported a loss of $9.4 million on total sales of $88.2 million.

The company's commitment to research and development, however, helped it weather the recession much better than many other vendors. The introduction of the AME 8100 Series Plasma Etch Systems revolutionized the dry etching of semiconductors. The quick market acceptance of this product and an agreement reached with the General Electric Venture Capital Corporation supplying a $20 million investment helped

the company ride out the remainder of the recession.

By 1983 the company was financially healthy once again; sales broke the $100 million mark. With 30 percent of its total sales originating from Japan, management steered a course to increase participation in the Japanese semiconductor market and started construction of a technology facility which would not only include a state-of-the-art research and development laboratory but also incorporate the most advanced technology for processing semiconductor wafers.

In 1984 increased demand for semiconductors pushed worldwide sales up a record 45 percent to approximately $26 billion, and Applied Materials benefited from this strong upturn to report sales of $168.4 million, a 60 percent surge over 1983. In 1985, though, the cyclical nature of the semiconductor industry was again apparent when worldwide sales decreased by almost 20 percent. This downturn led to the worst recession ever for the semiconductor equipment industry and, as the recession deepened in 1986, many of the company's major customers began to reduce their equipment budgets. As a result, revenues continued to decline although Applied Materials was still performing better than most other companies in the semiconductor equipment market.

ADVANCES IN TECHNOLOGY

A large part of Applied Materials' success during the recession was due to the development of leading-edge technology. In 1986, the company introduced the Precision Etch 8300A, featuring major improvements in contamination control and higher than previous levels of automation. In 1987, the company introduced the Precision 5000 CVD, a new system that met the industry's need for significant improvements in the low-temperature deposition of dielectric materials.

Orders for this new technology helped Applied Materials improve its financial position, as did a public stock offering which brought in an additional $54.7 million. In the same year, James W. Bagley, Applied Materials senior vice president of operations since 1981, with over 15 years of previous experience in engineering and project management at Texas Instruments, was appointed president and chief operating officer. Morgan, after serving 12 years as president, remained chief executive officer and chairman of the company's board of directors.

The combination of Applied Materials' commitment to new product introduction and a renewed demand in the worldwide semiconductor equipment market made 1988 a record year for the company. Net sales of $362.8 million more than doubled the previous

KEY DATES

1967: Applied Materials is established.
1972: Firm goes public.
1993: Sales exceed $1 billion.
2003: James Morgan retires as CEO, remains chairman, and is succeeded by Michael R. Splinter.
2009: Chairman Morgan announces his retirement and is succeeded by President and CEO Splinter.
2010: Two company executives are arrested by prosecutors in Korea over allegations of stealing chip-making technology from Samsung Electronics Company Ltd.

year's sales figures. By continuing to introduce new products and by improving the technology and applications in its existing product lines, revenues jumped to $501.8 million in 1989. With the previous addition of a service center in Beijing, China, and a regional office in Seoul, Korea, during the mid-1980s, in 1989 the company continued to build upon its presence in the Pacific Rim with the construction of new facilities in Japan. After 10 years, over 40 percent of the company's revenues were coming from the Asia/Pacific market.

NEW PRODUCT DEVELOPMENT

New product development was the cornerstone of management's strategy for improving the company's market position in the early 1990s. In 1990 the company introduced the Endura 5500 PVD in order to enter a new market, physical vapor deposition. In 1991 the firm announced its intention to enter the market for thin-film transistor liquid crystal display manufacturing equipment. Shipments for systems that manufacture these flat-panel displays (FPDs) started in 1993. In 1992 Applied Materials was beginning to reap the benefits of its strategy for product introduction and its expansion in Japan and the Pacific Rim. Total revenues were reported at $751.4 million, backlog orders at $254 million, and net income at $39.5 million. The geographical distribution of sales broke down as follows: 40 percent in the United States, 30 percent in Japan, 18 percent in Europe, and 12 percent in the Pacific Rim.

In 1993 Applied Materials entered into an agreement with Komatsu, Ltd., a Japanese firm, to form a new company named Applied Komatsu Technology, Inc. The company was created in order to develop,

manufacture, and market systems that were employed in producing FPDs. Operating with facilities in both the United States and Japan, it was agreed upon that company headquarters were to be established in Japan. In October 1993, the company announced its first product, the AKT 1600 PECVD, for chemical vapor deposition of thin films employed in manufacturing thin-film transistor structures in FPDs. The development of this technology had broad applications ranging from desktop and laptop computers to any electronic products that use high-quality, color displays.

The strategy of Applied Materials in establishing partnerships such as the one with Komatsu proved extremely profitable for the firm. Joint ventures increased the company's market share in Japan because the new operation functioned like a Japanese firm and relied on Japanese employees to provide the manufacturing base, marketing skills, and sales techniques required to do business in that country. In addition, the intimate relationships created with valued Japanese customers helped to sell Applied Materials' products when the customer decided to open a plant in the United States or somewhere overseas. The success of this strategy was the reason why nearly one-third of all Applied Materials sales involved Japanese semiconductor customers in the early 1990s.

Applied Materials continued to focus on establishing long-term relationships with users of semiconductor equipment in the 1990s and also took advantage of foreseeable trends in manufacturing technology. For example, as the semiconductor industry produced more and more circuits with smaller geometries, particulate contamination in what is called the "cleanroom" became a major concern requiring contaminant-free manufacturing environments. One solution to this problem of particulate contamination was the trend toward through-the-wall equipment design, where manufacturing equipment was completely encased in an airtight shell (a "cleanroom" environment) with only one access port which connects the equipment to the wafer fabrication facility. Applied Materials focused on developing new and highly reliable equipment for semiconductor customers to use within this "cleanroom" manufacturing environment.

In 1993 Applied Materials reached one of its long-term goals: It became the first company within the semiconductor equipment industry to hit the $1 billion mark in revenues. Total sales in 1993 amounted to $1.08 billion. One critical element in the company's financial success was the 13 percent of total revenue, or $140.2 million in fiscal 1993, invested in research and development. The commitment of a significant portion of its revenue to developing new technology historically provided stability and helped the company weather the cyclical periods of growth and recession in the semiconductor industry. This commitment was also recognized throughout the industry. In 1996 Morgan was awarded the National Medal of Technology by President Bill Clinton.

CONTINUING GROWTH

During the mid- to late 1990s, Applied Materials continued to focus on developing new technology and creating close working partnerships with customers by means of global expansion. The company also made several key acquisitions that secured its position as the number one semiconductor equipment manufacturer in the world. In early 1997 the firm completed the purchase of Opal Inc. and Orbot Instruments Ltd., both Israel-based companies involved in inspection equipment and metrology. Morgan commented on the acquisitions in a 1996 *Electronic News* article, stating, "Our entry into the market for metrology and inspection equipment is consistent with our long-term standing strategy of serving our global customers with a broader array of enabling technology required to economically manufacture new generations of advanced semiconductor devices."

Meanwhile however, the semiconductor industry found itself embroiled in a downturn related to an economic crisis in Asia and oversupply and falling prices in several key industries including the personal computer market. While Applied Materials was forced to cut jobs, it continued to forge ahead. In 1998 the company opened its Equipment and Process Integration Center in Santa Clara, which was used to launch new products and services that supported the Copper Interconnect Equipment Set Solution. During the 1990s copper began to replace aluminum as the main electrical conductor for the interconnect circuitry in chips. As chips became increasingly smaller, copper became more effective in carrying current through the circuitry, mainly because it had a lower resistance than aluminum and could carry more current to a smaller area.

That same year, Applied Materials also acquired Consilium Inc., a supplier of manufacturing execution system software used by the semiconductor industry. In 1999 the firm purchased the remaining interest in its joint venture with Komatsu Ltd. and also acquired Obsidian Inc., a firm whose chemical mechanical planarization technology fit into Applied Materials' burgeoning product line. That year, revenue surpassed $5 billion.

A NEW MILLENNIUM

Applied Materials entered the new millennium on solid ground. It made a significant purchase at the start of 2000, announcing its intent to acquire Etec Systems Inc. for nearly $1.8 billion. Upon completion of the deal, Applied Materials stood as the leader in the mask pattern generation market. The company defined a mask pattern generation system as one that uses a laser or electron beam to write each layer of a semiconductor chip's design onto a piece of chrome-coated quartz glass, which is called the mask or photomask. A series of completed masks were then used to transfer the chip's design onto the semiconductor wafer.

During that time, 300 millimeters (mm) became the new standard wafer size in the semiconductor industry, replacing 200mm wafers. As the industry shifted to manufacturing chips on 300mm wafers (these new wafers had a larger surface area and could hold 2.5 more chips), the company launched its 300mm wafer systems product line, the broadest line in the industry. The firm expected that it would be key in the firm's growth over the next five years.

The year 2000 proved to be a record year for Applied Materials. Fueled by the growth of the Internet and communications industries, the company secured $12.3 billion in new orders. Revenue reached $9.6 billion, nearly doubling over the previous year. However, the industry entered into another downturn and chip makers cut back on investments in new technology. As such, Applied Materials announced that it anticipated a decline in worldwide semiconductor capital spending during 2001. The firm itself cut back on spending and began company-wide layoffs.

Applied Materials historically weathered downturns well, and continued to prepare for the next upswing. During 2001 it began a $30 million advertising campaign titled "Information for Everyone." Management eyeballed the campaign as crucial to building name recognition outside of the semiconductor industry. The firm also set plans in motion to acquire Global Knowledge Services Inc. in late 2001. Global's data mining services were expected to go hand-in-hand with Applied Materials' inspection and defect reduction products. New orders for 2001 declined to $6.1 billion while sales fell to $7.34 billion.

While the slowdown in the semiconductor industry continued into early 2002, Applied Materials remained optimistic. The worldwide semiconductor market was expected to exceed $312 billion in 2003. In addition, the market for semiconductor fabrication equipment was slated to reach $38 billion by 2004. Nevertheless, the immediate situation caused the company to announce the elimination of 1,750 jobs (11 percent of its workforce) in November 2002.

LEADERSHIP CHANGES

A major development took place at Applied Materials in April 2003 when CEO James Morgan announced he would retire after 27 years with the company, ending his tenure as the longest-running CEO of a major technology company. Under Morgan, Applied Materials had evolved from a struggling start-up to the largest chipmaking equipment manufacturer in the world. Michael R. Splinter, a former Intel executive with more than 30 years of industry experience, was named CEO, and Morgan remained with the company as chairman. That year, the company lost $149.1 million on sales of $4.47 billion.

Conditions improved significantly in 2004. That year the company saw its revenues increase 80 percent, surpassing $8 billion, and profits totaled $1.3 billion. In addition, Applied Materials established a commodity consumable services joint venture with Praxair Electronics, and expanded its services business by agreeing to acquire Metron Technology for $85 million. At the end of the year Joseph Bronson resigned as chief financial officer and was succeeded by Nancy Handel.

China came to the forefront during mid-decade. In 2005 Applied Materials announced plans to build a development center in Xi'an for the purpose of offering global engineering and software support services. By this time Shanghai-based Semiconductor Manufacturing International Corp., then the third-largest contract chip manufacturer in the world, had been trying to place a $1 billion equipment order with Applied Materials for nine months. However, due to resistance from Micron Technology Inc. and Idaho Senator Michael D. Crapo, the purchase was deadlocked at the Export-Import Bank of the United States, which was needed to provide loan guarantees.

GROWTH IN SOLAR TECHNOLOGY

In early 2006 Applied Materials invested in the Hillsboro, Oregon-based stationary fuel cell manufacturer ClearEdge Power Inc. Midway through the year the company furthered its growth in the solar market by acquiring Longmont, Colorado-based Applied Films Corp. in a $464 million stock deal. Around the same time, Applied Materials also established a track technologies joint venture with Japan-based Dainippon Screen Mfg. Co. Ltd.

In September 2006 Applied Materials repurchased 145 million shares of its common stock for approximately $2.5 billion, and the company's board of directors approved a three-year, $5 billion stock buyback initiative. Upon the retirement of Nancy Handel in October, Applied Materials named George S. Davis as its chief financial officer. Finally, in November the company continued to strengthen its position in the solar sector via an investment in Solaicx, a manufacturer of silicon wafers for the photovoltaic market.

In early 2007 Applied Materials completed the acquisition of Brooks Software from Brooks Automation Inc. in a $125 million cash deal. China continued to be an important part of the company's strategy. This was evident by the opening of the company's 106,000-square-foot Xi'an China Global Development and Technology Support Center.

During the second half of 2007 Applied Materials acquired BOC Edwards Inc.'s Kachina semiconductor equipment parts cleaning and refurbishment operations, and parted with about $483 million to acquire Switzerland-based HCT Shaping Systems SA. Growth also continued in the company's solar business. In October Applied Materials established the SunFab Technology Center in Alzenau, Germany, to research next-generation solar technology. In early 2008 the company agreed to acquire the Treviso, Italy-based photovoltaic cell manufacturer Baccini S.p.A. for $334 million in cash.

CHALLENGING TIMES

By the end of the decade Applied Materials was operating in difficult economic conditions. In November 2008 the company trimmed 1,800 jobs from its workforce, in order to realize savings of approximately $400 million per year. Difficulties continued into 2009. During the third quarter alone, revenues fell 39 percent and the company recorded a $54.9 million net loss.

A significant leadership change took place in early 2009. At that time Chairman James Morgan announced plans to retire after holding the position for more than 20 years and serving on the company's board for more than 31 years. President and CEO Mike Splinter was named Morgan's successor.

China and solar technology continued to be of great importance to Applied Materials in 2009. That year the company celebrated its 25th anniversary in China, and it had become one of the world's largest photovoltaic equipment suppliers. In August Applied Materials revealed plans to invest in a spin-off of the Singapore Agency for Science, Technology and Research, in order to develop technology intended to increase the life span of organic solar cells and related devices.

Solar-related developments continued during the latter part of the year. In October the Solar Technology Center, an advanced solar research and customer demonstration facility, opened its doors in Xi'an, China. In November Applied Materials acquired the assets of Albuquerque, New Mexico-based Advent Solar Inc. The company ended the year with a net loss of $305.3 million on sales of $5.01 billion, a 38 percent decrease from 2008. In November plans were made to eliminate up to 1,500 jobs from Applied Materials' workforce.

UNDER INVESTIGATION IN 2010

Applied Materials faced a difficult situation in early 2010 when two of its executives were arrested by prosecutors in Korea, over allegations of stealing chip-making technology from Samsung Electronics Company Ltd. Also arrested was an executive from Hynix Semiconductor Inc. In addition, 14 individuals from both companies were under investigation.

On a more positive note, in March Applied Materials' board approved a $2 billion, three-year stock buy-back program. In addition, the company announced plans to increase its quarterly cash dividend by 17 percent. Despite difficult economic conditions, Applied Materials enjoyed a position of industry leadership during the 21st century's second decade, and appeared to have good chances for continued success.

Thomas Derdak
Updated, Christina M. Stansell; Paul R. Greenland

PRINCIPAL SUBSIDIARIES

1325949 Ontario Inc. (Canada); AFCO C.V. (Netherlands); AFCO GP, LLC; AKT Japan, LLC; AKT, Inc. (Japan); Applied Films Asia Pacific Limited (Hong Kong); Applied Films Taiwan Co., Ltd.; Applied Materials (Chennai) Private Limited (India); Applied Materials (China) Holdings, Ltd.; Applied Materials (Holdings); Applied Materials Asia-Pacific, Ltd.; Applied Materials Belgium N.V.; Applied Materials China, Ltd.; Applied Materials Deutschland Holding GmbH (Germany); Applied Materials France SARL; Applied Materials GmbH (Germany); Applied Materials India Private Limited; Applied Materials Ireland Ltd.; Applied Materials Israel, Ltd.; Applied Materials Italy Srl; Applied Materials Japan, Inc.; Applied Materials South East Asia Pte. Ltd. (Malaysia); Applied Materials Spain S.L.; Applied Materials SPV1, Inc.; Applied Materials SPV2, Inc.; Applied Materials Switzerland SA; Applied Ventures, LLC; Display Products Group, Inc.; Etec Systems, Inc.; Metron Technology (Asia) Ltd.; Metron Technology (Europa) Ltd. (Scotland); Metron Technology, Inc.; PT Applied Materials Indonesia.

PRINCIPAL COMPETITORS

KLA-Tencor Corporation; Lam Research Corporation; Tokyo Electron Limited.

FURTHER READING

Chappell, Jeff, "AMAT Sets Record Quarter and Year," *Electronic News*, November 20, 2000, p. 10.

"Chipmaking: 'Long-Term Opportunity Is So Vivid Today,'" *Business Week Online*, July 16, 2001.

Erkanat, Judy, "Applied Buys Opal, Orbot," *Electronic News*, December 2, 1996, p. 1.

———, "Applied Moves on 3 Product Fronts," *Electronic News*, June 24, 1996, p. 46.

Lineback, Robert J., "Applied Cuts Growth, Spending Projections," *Electronic Engineering Times*, February 19, 2001, p. 43.

Nam, Inn-Soo, and Jerry A. DiColo, "Korean Prosecutors Arrest Chip Executives," *Wall Street Journal Eastern Edition*, February 4, 2010, p. B2.

Ristelhueber, Robert, "Applied Rides Acquisition Route to Dominance," *Engineering Electronic Times*, January 24, 2000, p. 45.

Serwer, Andy, "An End to Morgan's Record Run: Big Tech's Longest-Tenured CEO Bows Out at Applied Materials," *Fortune*, May 26, 2003, p. 172.

Ardent Health Services LLC

---■---

1 Burton Hills Boulevard, Suite 250
Nashville, Tennessee 37215
U.S.A.
Telephone: (615) 296-3000
Fax: (615) 296-6351
Web site: http://www.ardenthealth.com

Private Company
Incorporated: 1992 as Behavioral Healthcare Corporation
Employees: 7,745
Operating Revenues: $1.8 billion (2009 est.)
NAICS: 6222110 General Medical and Surgical
Hospitals

■ ■ ■

A private company based in Nashville, Tennessee, Ardent Health Services LLC owns and operates a network of seven acute care hospitals and related facilities in Tulsa, Oklahoma, and Albuquerque, New Mexico. Tulsa operations include the Hillcrest Medical Center, the Oklahoma Heart Institute, the Bailey Medical Center, the Utica Park Clinic, the Cushing Regional Hospital, and the Henryetta Medical Center. In Albuquerque, Ardent operates four facilities under the Lovelace name as well as the Lovelace Health Plan insurance unit with 220,000 members and S.E.D. Medical Laboratories. Since 2001 Ardent has been majority-owned by Welsh, Carson, Anderson & Stowe, a New York private-equity firm that is the largest private-equity investor in the health care sector.

EARLY YEARS: 1992–96

Ardent Health Services was founded in Nashville in December 1992 as Behavioral Healthcare Corporation (BHC) by Edward A. Stack to own and operate psychiatric hospitals. Stack was the former Western Group president of HCA Psychiatric Company, a unit of Hospital Corporation of America (HCA). When HCA elected to sell 22 of its 48 psychiatric hospitals, Stack struck out on his own and reached an agreement in early 1993 to buy six of the hospitals in Nevada and Texas to launch BHC. They included 231-bed Shoal Creek Hospital in Austin, Texas; 87-bed Richland Hospital in North Richland Hills, Texas; 70-bed Cedar Crest Residential Treatment Center for adolescents; 95-bed West Hills Hospital in Reno, Nevada; 80-bed Montevista Hospital in Las Vegas, Nevada; and 74-bed Willow Springs Residential Treatment Center in Reno, Nevada. The new company was owned by Stack and other members of senior management as well as individual and institutional investors.

BHC soon expanded its operations. In January 1994 the company acquired two more psychiatric hospitals owned by HCA subsidiaries. They were the 59-bed Canyon Ridge Hospital in Chino, California, and the 61-bed Cedar Vista Hospital in Fresno, California. Two years later five more hospitals were brought into the fold, acquired for $10 million in cash plus working capital from McLean, Virginia-based Mental Health Management, Inc. The five psychiatric and substance abuse facilities were Aspen Hill Hospital in Flagstaff, Arizona; Pacific Shores Hospital in Oxnard, California; Pinion Hills Hospital in Santa Fe, New Mexico; Pinon Hills Residential Treatment Center in

Valdere, New Mexico; and Windsor Hospital in Chagrin Falls, Ohio.

A much larger transaction followed later in 1996 when BHC acquired the U.S. and Puerto Rico psychiatric operations of Las Vegas-based Community Psychiatric Centers (CPC) for $60 million in cash, and stock and stock equivalents valued at $70 million to $105 million. The addition of the CPC operations brought the total number of BHC facilities to 38 hospitals and four residential treatment centers, and increased annual revenues to more than $300 million. The plan was now to take BHC public, but it was never brought to fruition.

FAILED TRANSACTIONS: 1997–98

The end of the 1990s was marked by a pair of ill-fated transactions. In September 1997 BHC reached an agreement to merge with a subsidiary of Atlanta-based Charter Behavioral Health Systems, the United States' largest provider of behavioral health care services with 93 facilities in 33 states. Two months later, however, the merger was terminated by mutual agreement. In July 1998 BHC reached another agreement to be acquired by a publicly traded San Diego-based mental health services provider, PMR Corp. The deal, regarded as a merger, called for PMR to pay $94 million in cash plus 2.6 million shares of stock and the assumption of $90 million in debt for a total value at $209 million. The merger was slated to close by November 1998. Market conditions changed in the meantime, however, as the cost of credit for the bonds that were to finance the deal soared from 9 percent to about 13 percent. As a result, this transaction was also canceled.

Instead of expanding, difficult conditions forced BHC to contract, so that by 2001 the company was reduced to 24 hospitals. The majority owner of the company, with a 61 percent interest, was Louisville-based Vencor, Inc., while the New York firm of Welsh,

Carson, Anderson & Stowe (WCAS) held a 17 percent stake. Experiencing some financial troubles, Vencor soon filed for Chapter 11 bankruptcy protection and reorganized as Kindred Healthcare. Vencor was interested in selling its stake in BHC and approached WCAS about buying it. WCAS then hired veteran health care executive David T. Vandewater as a consultant to study BHC and make a recommendation.

Vandewater was a somewhat controversial figure. Prior to joining Ardent, he had served as president and chief operating officer of Nashville-based Columbia/HCA Healthcare Corporation. Under his leadership HCA had experienced tremendous growth, increasing annual revenues to $20 billion, making it the largest health care organization in the world. His tenure was not without incident, however. In 1997 federal agents raided the HCA offices, the start of a criminal and civil Medicare fraud investigation that led to the resignation of Vandewater and HCA's CEO, Richard Scott. Little had been heard of Vandewater since July 1997, but he remained in Nashville and was clearly interested in resuming his career, a desire he shared with WCAS principal Russ Carson.

After analyzing BHC, Vandewater concluded that it was a strong behavioral health company that required only some tweaks to take advantage of a market in which a large number of behavioral hospitals had gone out of business in recent years. Moreover, he believed that the company's infrastructure could be leveraged to add a new line of business. Vandewater's experience was medical-surgical, making it an obvious choice for such a line should he expand his consulting role and assume a leadership role.

WCAS ACQUIRES MAJORITY CONTROL: 2001

In early 2001 WCAS bought out Kindred to take control of BHC with the intent of expanding it into the acute care business. Because of the shift in focus, a name change was in order and BHC became Ardent Health Services LLC. The new owners also changed chief executives. In February 2001 Stack resigned and at the same time Vandewater became chairman. In May 2001 he became CEO as well. With $145 million in pledged funding from WCAS, he wasted no time in taking Ardent in a new direction. In August 2001 the company acquired its first medical-surgical hospital, the 201-bed Summit Hospital in Baton Rouge, Louisiana. In November Ardent acquired an acute hospital in Lexington, Kentucky, the 336-bed Samaritan Hospital.

In 2002 Ardent moved into the Albuquerque, New Mexico, market by acquiring St. Joseph Health Care

```
┌─────────────────────────────────────────────┐
│                                             │
│              KEY DATES                      │
│                  ■                          │
│  ─────────────────────────────────────────  │
│                                             │
│  1992:  Edward Stack forms Behavioral       │
│         Healthcare Corporation.             │
│  1993:  Company acquires six psychiatric    │
│         hospitals from Hospital Corporation │
│         of America.                         │
│  2001:  Welsh, Carson, Anderson & Stowe     │
│         acquires majority control and       │
│         changes name to Ardent Health       │
│         Services LLC.                       │
│  2002:  Ardent enters Albuquerque, New      │
│         Mexico, market.                     │
│  2005:  Psychiatric Hospital division is    │
│         sold.                               │
│                                             │
└─────────────────────────────────────────────┘
```

System, which included four hospitals. It was an attractive market given that the city was fast growing and listed among the top five U.S. cities in which businesses wanted to locate. Ardent quickly furthered its commitment to Albuquerque by paying $211 million to acquire Lovelace Sandia Health Systems, an integrated operation that included the 225-bed Lovelace Hospital, the 235,000-member Lovelace Health Plan, a multispecialty physician group practice, and a network of family practice clinics.

More acquisitions were to follow elsewhere in the country. In October 2003 Ardent bought the Northwestern Institute of Psychiatry to gain access to the Philadelphia, Pennsylvania, market. A year later Ardent established itself in Tulsa, Oklahoma, in a $281 million purchase of Hillcrest HealthCare System. HHS included six metropolitan Tulsa hospitals, including the 557-bed medical center, as well as 10 regional hospitals, and two long-term care facilities. To complete the deal, Ardent agreed to invest approximately $100 million in improvements over the next five years, including new equipment, upgraded information systems, and new facilities.

SALE OF PSYCHIATRIC HOSPITALS: 2005

Ardent elected in 2005 to focus on its acute care, medical-surgical assets. The company sold its 20-facility behavioral health division to another Nashville concern, Psychiatric Solutions Inc., for $500 million in cash and $60 million in stock. Ardent would be left with 14 hospitals in Tulsa, Albuquerque, and Baton Rouge, and annual revenues of $1.8 billion. With the money it received, Ardent redeemed $225 million in principal notes, thus exiting the public markets and freeing itself of the burden of financial disclosures. Proceeds of the

sale were also earmarked for the building of the Bailey Medical Center in Owasso, Oklahoma, at a cost of $50 million, as well as to expand cardiovascular services at Hillcrest Medical Center and in Albuquerque, estimated to cost $45 million.

Ardent now had a tighter focus, but it also had some work to do to bring cohesion to its operating units. In Albuquerque the company had to contend with differing cultures that existed between Lovelace and St. Joseph. A number of top executives at Lovelace soon departed. Although they said their leaving was unrelated to the merger, it had the same effect of replacing the old with the new to impact the overall culture. In addition, Ardent announced the closing of a hospital on the city's southeast side. Albuquerque residents, as a result, were also confused by the changes, uncertain what was now included in the Lovelace Sandia network.

To redress these concerns, Ardent undertook a rebranding campaign in 2006. The Lovelace Sandia name was reduced to just Lovelace and supported by a new slogan, "You're going to love Lovelace." In addition to advertising, Lovelace's facilities were upgraded to present a consistent look, down to lab coats and letterhead.

There were more than just surface changes at work at Lovelace. In 2007 the system's doctors formed an independent group called ABQ Health Partners. Although they would continue to see the same patients at the same offices, accept the same insurance, and receive the same compensation and benefits, there was a distinct difference in the new arrangement. The system had suffered from low morale among practitioners, leading to an annual doctor turnover rate of 20 percent, twice the usual rate. By going independent, the doctors now had control over how their practices were run and improvements could be made to patient care. The prospect of such a change prompted 180 doctors to agree to become co-owners of ABQ Health Partners.

LOUISIANA MARKET EXIT: 2008

Changes were made elsewhere in Ardent's two other markets, Baton Rouge and Tulsa. Since 2004 Ardent had operated the Summit Hospital in Baton Rouge in a 50/50 partnership with Ochsner Health System as the Ochsner Medical Center. In November 2007 Ardent agreed to sell its half-interest, and in early 2008 Ardent exited the Louisiana market. In Tulsa, in the meantime, Ardent divested some underperforming hospitals. It also reached an agreement to preserve the long-term stability of the 304-bed Oklahoma State University Center, the primary teaching hospital for the school's medical college that was owned by Hillcrest HealthCare System.

In addition, Ardent provided uncompensated health care to underserved Oklahoma residents while helping to train physicians. In April 2008 an arrangement was made for Ardent to sell the hospital to a new public trust for a nominal $5 million. In this way, the needs of Ardent, the medical college, and the patients were met.

After 10 years of owning Ardent, WCAS had yet to receive a significant dividend from its investment. In 2010, Ardent made plans to issue a $400 million term loan to fund a distribution to WCAS, as much as $277 million. The balance of the loan was slated for the retirement of existing debt as well as corporate purposes. Whether those corporate purposes included additional acquisitions remained to be seen.

Ed Dinger

PRINCIPAL SUBSIDIARIES

Hillcrest Medical Group, Inc.; Lovelace Health System, Inc.

PRINCIPAL COMPETITORS

Presbyterian Healthcare Services; Saint Francis Health System; St. John Health System.

FURTHER READING

"Ardent Completes Hillcrest Purchase," *Nashville Business Journal*, August 16, 2004.

"Ardent to Buy Tulsa Health System for $281 Million," *Nashville Business Journal*, May 11, 2004.

Cate, Molly, "Welsh Carson Puts $145 Million into Venture," *Nashville Business Journal*, July 6, 2001.

Domrzalski, Dennis, "Ardent to Buy New Mexico Health System," *Nashville Business Journal*, March 20, 2002.

Galloro, Vince, "Ardent Distribution Coming," *Modern Healthcare*, March 1, 2010.

"HCA Exec Buys 6 Psych Facilities," *Modern Healthcare*, February 22, 1993.

Moore, Roy, "Psych Solutions Buying Ardent Behavioral Sites," *Nashville Business Journal*, March 11, 2005.

Nascenzi, Nicole, "Ardent Health Sells Division," *Tulsa World*, March 12, 2005, p. A15.

Raifor, Dave, "Ardent Buys Second Hospital in New Mexico," *Nashville Business Journal*, July 5, 2002.

———, "Ardent Growing Up Quickly," *Nashville Business Journal*, October 4, 2002.

———, "Vandewater Leading Ardent onto Health Care's Main Stage," *Nashville Business Journal*, September 20, 2002.

Rose, Craig D., "2 Mental Services Units Fail to Merge," *San Diego Union-Tribune*, November 6, 1998, p. C1.

Ascension Health

———————■———————

4600 Edmundson Road
St. Louis, Missouri 63136
U.S.A.
Telephone: (314) 733-8000
Fax: (314) 733-8013
Web site: http://www.ascensionhealth.org

Nonprofit Organization
Incorporated: 1999
Employees: 113,000
Operating Revenues: $14.27 billion (2009)
NAICS: 622110 General Medical and Surgical
Hospitals; 623110 Nursing Care Facilities

■ ■ ■

Ascension Health is the largest Catholic health care system in the United States, with operating revenue of more than $14.2 billion. A 113,000-strong workforce of medical and other professionals serves the system's 72 hospitals, nursing care centers, and related facilities throughout 19 states and the District of Columbia. Ascension Health is especially dedicated to serving the poor and vulnerable, and providing holistic care to its patients. In 2008, Ascension Health spent nearly $870 million on community benefits and care for the poor.

Additionally, Ascension Health runs a market-savvy and profitable venture corporation, Ascension Health Ventures (AHV). AHV specializes in investments of expansion- to late-stage health care companies. These investments, which began in 2001 with a commitment of $125 million, provide Ascension with early insight into developments in health care, health technology, and medical information.

FAR-REACHING ROOTS

Although a relatively new contender in the health care arena, Ascension Health likes to trace its roots much further back. Ascension Health was formally incorporated in November 1999 with the gathering of four provinces of the Daughters of Charity, whose own roots can be traced to 17th-century France and St. Vincent de Paul, founder of the congregation of the Daughters of Charity. The Daughters of Charity first came to the United States with Elizabeth Ann Seton in 1809, and many more waves were to follow. In 1828, religious sisters first came to St. Louis with the express intention of opening a hospital, albeit a primitive three-room cabin hospital. They quickly expanded, however, and within the next 150 years opened hospitals in California, Michigan, and the District of Columbia. Their work, especially their efforts in pooling resources for the sake of bettering hospital efficiency, laid the groundwork for the Daughters of Charity National Health System.

Two other congregations assisted as well: the Sisters of St. Joseph of Carondelet and the Congregation of St. Joseph. The sisters of St. Joseph of Carondelet also had roots stretching back to 17th-century France, although they split from France upon coming to the States. This congregation provided a crucial step toward health care efficiency in its formation of Carondelet Health Care Systems in 1981, which brought together 13 different health care systems. The Congregation of St. Joseph was

COMPANY PERSPECTIVES

Rooted in the loving ministry of Jesus as healer, we commit ourselves to serving all persons with special attention to those who are poor and vulnerable. Our Catholic health ministry is dedicated to spiritually centered, holistic care which sustains and improves the health of individuals and communities. We are advocates for a compassionate and just society through our actions and our words.

formed in 2007 with the merger of seven previously separated congregations dedicated to St. Joseph. Roots from these congregations, too, reached back to 17th-century France. Like the other orders associated with Ascension Health, the St. Joseph congregations came to the United States for the purpose of running schools and hospitals. One congregation's health care ministry, the Sisters of St. Joseph of Nazareth, grew primarily throughout Kansas, and in 1999 merged with the Daughters of Charity to form Ascension Health.

FLEXIBLE, VOCAL LEADERSHIP MODEL

Within 10 years of its inception, Ascension Health had created a strong organizational framework in which all components of the corporation (the congregations, the business managers, and the board of trustees) had a voice. For instance, the sisters' involvement in the corporation did not stop at its formation. Rather, Ascension chose to use the sisters' experience and advice through the creation of the Sponsors Council. The Sponsors Council was designed to be a group composed of representatives from each of the sponsoring congregations. The council also included the president of Marian College in Indiana, as well as the former vice president of St. Vincent's Healthcare of Jacksonville, Florida. The board of trustees also used sisters from varying provinces, as well as laymen and laywomen.

Finally, the Leadership Team was responsible for the day-to-day management of Ascension Health, as well as promoting its growth. The team was composed of financial, medical, advocacy, legal, and marketing components. The role of CEO was first held by Douglas French who, during his tenure, oversaw the 2002 merger of Ascension Health with Carondelet Health System, as well as the launch of Ascension Health Ventures. When French went on sabbatical two years later, Anthony Tersigni was named interim CEO. Ter-

signi ascended to the position of CEO when French decided not to return to Ascension at the end of his sabbatical.

MISSION AND ACTION

One of the first goals established by the organization was outlined in 2003. The target was to decrease the number of preventable deaths (deaths due to falls, hospital-acquired infections, and errors) by 900. By December 2006, the goal had been exceeded, with an estimated 2,000 deaths prevented, thanks to higher safety standards. To reach the goal, the corporation spent over $50 million on new bed frames and surfaces. This was done to decrease severe pressure ulcers, a common culprit of hospital injuries.

HEALTH CARE THAT WORKS

This success gave credence to a larger and more difficult goal of the corporation. In 2002, Ascension Health revised its vision statement to give greater emphasis to the fight for health care reform. The new campaign homed in on the goal of providing "[h]ealthcare that works, healthcare that is safe, healthcare that leaves no one behind." This new "Strategic Direction" was designated for completion by 2020.

"Healthcare That Works," according to Ascension Health's Web site, was focused on providing health care that "achieves absolute satisfaction" for both the patients and the staff, with an aim of creating a "consistent, exceptional experience." "Healthcare That Is Safe" built on the past successes Ascension Health made toward patient safety, and worked to decrease even more the number of preventable deaths within its hospital settings. Finally, the goal of achieving health care that leaves no one behind was intended so that "all persons, particularly those who are uninsured or underinsured, receive health care services and health care insurance that creates ... improved health outcomes."

Ascension's leadership board cooperated with legislators in Washington, D.C., and also reached out to communities to create local systems that encouraged coverage for all. Ascension Health also practiced what it preached. In 2008, Ascension hospitals and care centers received and treated an uninsured or underinsured patient every 34 seconds, at a cost of $783 million.

INVESTMENTS

It would not be true to call Ascension Health a "charity-run" organization, however. Ascension Health boasted a healthy profit of $371 million in 2009 and had earned

KEY DATES

17th century: Religious orders responsible for formation of Ascension Health are founded in France.
1999: Ascension Health is created.
2002: Carondelet Health System becomes part of Ascension Health.
2004: Ascension Health is recognized as the largest Catholic health care system in the United States.

high esteem in the corporate world. According to the *Modern Healthcare* article "Ascending in Healthcare," Ascension had positioned itself behind only two other health care organizations, and was listed at 220th in the *Fortune* 500.

Part of the organization's success had been because of the investment venture begun under former CEO Douglas French. Ascension Health Ventures (AHV), begun in 2001 as a wholly owned subsidiary, signified a way for the corporation to both invest in future medical procedures and technology, as well as provide the corporation with insight into new developments. AHV specialized in investments for expansion- to late-stage health care companies, and enabled limited partners to earn venture capital. The subsidiary started with capital of $125 million, and netted more than $29 million in its first five years.

The success of AHV enabled Ascension Health to initiate another venture fund in 2007 with a limited partnership consisting of Ascension Health, Catholic Health Initiatives, Catholic Health East, and Catholic Healthcare West. The $200 million Catholic Health Ventures II (CHV II) fund, as the venture operation was named, looked into expansion- to late-stage health care companies that specialized in medical devices, medical information, or technological services. CHV II invested approximately $5 million to $10 million in each company. AHV served as a general partner and offered management services to CHV II.

TROUBLING FUTURE FOR CATHOLIC INSTITUTIONS

These successes bode well for Ascension Health, especially as other Catholic institutions in the United States failed. In New York City alone, seven out of eight Catholic hospitals closed in 2007. The future for the remaining hospital, St. Vincent's, also looked grim. According to the *America* article "Then There Was One:

The Unraveling of Catholic Health Care," there were a few primary reasons surrounding the rapid failure of these Catholic health care institutions, reasons that could easily pertain to Ascension Health as well. These included a "harsh" market environment for faith-based institutions, a frail Catholic philanthropy, an increasing trend toward secular values among American Catholics, and poor political connections.

There was also pressure from the United States Conference of Catholic Bishops (USCCB) to conform to moral and ethical demands. The USCCB placed strict ethical and moral demands on hospitals, and refused certain procedures that were common in protestant or secular hospitals. Although Ascension focused its ethics on a primarily "Catholic perspective," outside pressure from other health care organizations, patients, and even the courts was not easily countered. Examples of debate between Catholic hospitals and their more secular counterparts included abortion, contraception (especially "emergency contraception"), sterilization, and end-of-life issues. As pressures mounted, Catholic bishops were becoming increasingly emboldened. Already one hospital in Oregon had been stripped of its Catholic identity. Even though such a prospect was unlikely for Ascension Health in the near future, it was still a warning: Such a blow could do irrevocable harm to the mission and value system of a historically Catholic institution.

The most daunting prospect of all for Ascension Health, however, had more to do with the actions of Capitol Hill than the Vatican. Beginning in 2009 and continuing through the passage of the Patient Protection and Affordable Care Act in 2010, health care reform once again became a major political issue, and Ascension Health became one of its most forceful proponents. In *PR Newswire* Tersigni declared, "'At Ascension Health we believe Americans need health reform now. ... Now is the time for us to move forward, and we look forward to health reform becoming a reality."

Laura Rydberg

PRINCIPAL DIVISIONS

Sponsors Council; Board of Trustees; Leadership Council.

PRINCIPAL COMPETITORS

Catholic Healthcare East; Catholic Health West; Catholic Health Initiatives.

FURTHER READING

Browder, Sue Ellin, "Beginning of the End for Church-Backed Hospitals?" *National Catholic Register*, March 14–27, 2010.

DerGurahian, Jean, "Ascension: Work to Be Done: System Says Plan Prevents Deaths, Not All Mistakes," *Modern Healthcare*, July 21, 2008, p. 16.

Evans, Melanie, "Ascending in Healthcare; Roman Catholic Ascension Health Has Made a *Fortune* 500 Name for Itself with Business Acumen, Risk-Taking and Efficiency," *Modern Healthcare*, May 14, 2007, p. 6.

Reilly, Patrick, "Mass Exodus; Catholic System CEO 4th to Step Down in 2 Months," *Modern Healthcare*, May 10, 2004, p. 8.

Sulmasy, Daniel P. "Then There Was One: The Unraveling of Catholic Health Care," *America*, March 16, 2010, pp. 10–15.

AutoNation, Inc.

———■———

AutoNation Tower
110 S.E. Sixth Street
Fort Lauderdale, Florida 33301
U.S.A.
Telephone: (954) 769-6000
Fax: (954) 769-6537
Web site: http://corp.autonation.com

Public Company
Incorporated: 1998
Employees: 17,000
Sales: $10.8 billion (2009)
Stock Exchanges: New York
Ticker Symbol: AN
NAICS: 441110 New Car Dealers; 441120 Used Car
Dealers; 524210 Insurance Agencies and Broker-
ages; 811111 General Automotive Repair

■ ■ ■

Fort Lauderdale, Florida-based AutoNation, Inc., is the nation's largest automotive retailer. The company serves consumers via more than 200 dealerships. Since its establishment, AutoNation has sold more than seven million vehicles, a significant milestone that sets the company apart from its competitors. The typical Auto-Nation dealership generates 59 percent of its revenue from new-vehicle sales, 29 percent from used-vehicle sales, and 12 percent from automotive parts and service.

FROM WASTE DISPOSAL TO AUTOMOTIVE RETAIL

H. Wayne Huizenga was one of the best-known entrepreneurs in the United States due to his wild success in creating two mammoth companies: Waste Management and Blockbuster Video. In 1995, Huizenga and a partner began a new foray into business with the purchase of Republic Industries, a U.S. waste-disposal company. Huizenga hoped to build Republic Industries into a group with interests in security, rubbish collection, and used-car superstores. After a failed attempt at purchasing the ADT group (a Bermuda-based security and car auction company) in 1996, Republic succeeded in purchasing National Car Rental for $600 million in stock. The car rental company had 800 outlets in the United States and Canada, with a fleet of 100,000 vehicles. With National, as well as Alamo (acquired the previous year), Huizenga's dream of supplying his used-car superstores with quality rental cars had become reality.

At the same time that Republic was purchasing rental car companies to build a rental segment of Republic, it was also building AutoNation, a chain of used-car superstores. Huizenga merged AutoNation into Republic in April 1996. The used-car superstores offered customers a way to purchase used cars without the stress of bargaining or haggling. Automobile prices were set in advance to make for a more customer-friendly atmosphere. By December 1996, Republic had begun acquiring new-car dealerships in addition to building the AutoNation chain of used-car megastores.

TAKING OUT THE TRASH

Almost as soon as Huizenga's automobile chain was off the ground, he spun off the company's original waste business as Republic Services Inc. Huizenga sold all of the remaining interest in Republic Services in a public stock offering during the second quarter of 1997. The company continued to operate under the name Republic, but company officials began to take steps to make AutoNation the company's predominant national brand. The AutoNation brand began to be used at some of Republic's new-car dealerships. The first market tested was Denver, Colorado, where the company consolidated its 17 dealerships under the name John Elway AutoNation. Soon after, in 1998, the company took the definitive leap toward establishing AutoNation as a national brand, changing the company's name from Republic Industries Inc. to AutoNation, Inc.

Following the name change, the company was split into two operating groups: the AutoNation Retail Group and AutoNation Rental Group. The Retail Group oversaw the company's used-and-new car superstores and franchise, while the Rental Group oversaw the company's three automotive rental brands (National Car Rental Systems, Alamo Rent-A-Car Inc., and CarTemps USA). Each of the rental companies adopted AutoNation as its sub-brand, and the new-car franchises added the label "An AutoNation Company" to their dealerships.

LOW PROFITS AT USED-CAR MEGASTORES TRIGGER BIG CHANGES

AutoNation's used-car megastores did not turn the profits that the company had hoped for. The megastores fell victim to an increase in new-car sales and with that increase, the devaluation of used cars. When the company's stock started slipping, AutoNation decided to open new-car dealerships inside the used-car superstores.

Four of the used-new combination stores were AutoNation Dodge in Grand Prairie, Texas; Seminole Ford and AutoNation USA in Sanford, Florida; AutoNation Chrysler-Plymouth in Douglasville, Georgia; and AutoNation Nissan in Perrine, Florida. Regardless of AutoNation's positive outlook and statements surrounding the launching of the new-used stores, the integrated stores did not work the magic that AutoNation hoped they would.

The company's drooping profits and management's inability to turn those profits around caused AutoNation's founder and co-CEOs to step down from their positions to make room for fresh ideas in the form of a new chief executive. The new executive was Michael Jackson, who came to AutoNation with many years of automobile dealership experience. To take the chief executive position at AutoNation, it was necessary for Jackson to resign as president of Mercedes-Benz of North America. Only four months after Jackson had taken the reins at AutoNation, he faced the task of deciding the fate of the company's unprofitable used-car megastores. His decision was quick. On December 19, 1999, Jackson announced the closure of 23 of the company's 29 used-car megastores and the integration of the remaining megastores into new-car franchise outlets.

In an interview with *Knight-Ridder/Tribune Business News*, Jackson said, "I knew when I joined AutoNation of their announced plan to integrate used-car stores into our new-car stores, but after looking at it closer realized it would be difficult to do, would require that we invest an inordinate amount of capital into those stores and at the end of the day still end up losing money, which made no sense." He continued, "We decided to simply close the stores." In the same interview, Jackson went on to say, "Our focus now is on improving our operating margins and on creating a unique and branded customer experience in our new-vehicle franchises, which are now AutoNation's sole business focus. By closing the megastores, we have taken the necessary steps to ensure the long-term success of AutoNation."

SUCCESS ON THE WORLD WIDE WEB

When AutoNation decided to expand its customer reach through an online presence, it did not waste years developing the idea and Web site. AutoNationDirect.com and Web sites for 270 of AutoNation's dealers were developed in a quick 18 months, by a four-person information technology team and several vendors. The AutoNationDirect.com Web site enabled customers to buy vehicles from all of AutoNation's 400 new-and-used car stores without ever needing to visit the dealership.

KEY DATES

1995: H. Wayne Huizenga purchases Republic Industries Inc.
1996: Republic purchases National Car Rental and begins acquiring new-car dealerships.
1997: Republic spins off its waste business as Republic Services Inc.
1998: Republic changes its name to AutoNation, Inc.
2002: Chairman Huizenga steps down.
2003: Mike Jackson begins serving as chairman on January 1; AutoNation becomes part of the S&P 500 Index.
2004: Huizenga severs ties with the organization when he relinquishes his board seat.
2005: AutoNation sells its five millionth vehicle.
2006: Huizenga is named to the Automotive Hall of Fame.
2008: Billionaire Edward Lampert increases his stake in AutoNation to 36 percent.
2009: Lampert's ownership interest exceeds 45 percent.

Although AutoNation's Web site was slated to be used as a marketing platform, the company did not expect the Web site itself to generate a large amount of profits because it believed that few customers would be willing to buy a vehicle sight unseen. Instead, the company used the Web sites to build traffic to send out to its dealerships. In May 1999, AutoNation President John Costello discussed with *Automotive News'* Donna Harris the Web advantage as AutoNation saw it. He explained that promoting a Web site could expand a dealership's territory from the typical 10-mile radius to a 30-mile radius. He said, "The Internet provides an opportunity to generate greater traffic and revenue. The physical dealership will play an important role in the sales and ownership experience."

AUTONATION SPINS OFF ANC RENTAL

On April 4, 2000, AutoNation announced that it expected to spin off ANC Rental Corp. ANC Rental Corp. included Alamo, National, and CarTemps rental operations. The announcement was long-awaited, due to the fact that ANC Rental lost $71 million in 1999. AutoNation reasoned that it was spinning ANC off in order to focus more completely on its new-car

dealerships. The spinoff was completed in early June.

Due to the upheaval that AutoNation underwent in 1999 and the beginning months of 2000, it came as no surprise that the company announced a large loss for the first quarter of 2000. The spin-off of ANC and the closure of the company's 23 used-vehicle megastores contributed to the reported $403 million loss. CEO Michael Jackson told *Automotive News*, in January 2000, that AutoNation intended to concentrate on becoming a new-vehicle retailer now that it was free of its rental business.

In July 2000, AutoNation decided to capitalize on brand recognition by changing the names of 28 of its 30 car dealerships in Florida to Maroone (after successful dealership owner Michael E. Maroone, who joined AutoNation in 1997). Although the company renamed existing dealerships, the AutoNation name was displayed underneath the Maroone and AutoWay names.

INTERNET PARTNERSHIPS

Developing the online AutoNation brand and partnering up with well-known and well-connected Internet companies was an important next step in AutoNation's reach for new-vehicle sales success. In May 2000, AutoNation and AOL announced their intention to ally and build the world's largest "virtual auto dealership." The companies built a co-branded Web site called, "AOL AutosDirect, Powered by http://AutoNation.com." The deal allowed AutoNation to be the exclusive retailer of new-and-used vehicles to AOL members who purchased a car or truck through the new co-branded site. AOL members who purchased vehicles through this site were eligible to receive a slew of exclusive benefits.

During the same month, AutoNation acquired AutoVantage, a car-buying service from Cendant Corporation. AutoVantage was ranked by J.D. Power & Associates as one of the most popular automotive lead providers, and had a network of approximately 900 dealers throughout the country. The purchase of AutoVantage gave AutoNation the reach it would need to serve AOL's geographically diverse customer base.

AutoVantage and AOL were not the only two Internet partnerships that AutoNation had in the works. In October 2000, the company reached an agreement with Autoweb.com to allow AutoNation to use the content and technology platform of the Autoweb Web site. Then, in February 2001, the company entered into a three-year partnership with MSN CarPoint. Under their agreement, CarPoint would send Internet sales leads to AutoNation's dealerships and affiliated dealerships.

NEW DEVELOPMENTS, LEADERSHIP CHANGES

Shortly after AutoNation spun off ANC Rental, ANC filed for Chapter 11 bankruptcy (November 13, 2001). When AutoNation spun off ANC, the company continued to guarantee its former unit's credit, as well as the six- to nine-month leases of a large amount of vehicles from Mitsubishi Motor Sales of America Inc. In an AutoNation filing with the U.S. Securities and Exchange Commission, the company reported that the Mitsubishi leases held by AutoNation were a $4 million to $5 million monthly obligation, which could potentially increase to $8 million. AutoNation feared that it could end up paying upward of $150 million if it had to cover ANC's credit obligations.

Midway through 2002, *Automotive News* named AutoNation as the nation's top seller of both new and used cars. Significant leadership changes took place in September of that year. H. Wayne Huizenga announced that he would step down as chairman at the end of the year, in order to concentrate on other businesses. Following his departure, Mike Jackson began serving as chairman on January 1, 2003.

In February 2003, Huizenga sold four million shares of his stock in AutoNation, generating $55 million. Around the same time, the company became part of the S&P 500 Index. In addition, *Fortune* named AutoNation as America's Most Admired Automotive Retailing & Services Company for the second consecutive year. Midway through the year, AutoNation signed an agreement that resolved potential claims in connection with ANC's bankruptcy, and capped its total obligation at $29.6 million. That year, the company's 287 dealerships generated sales of $18.9 billion.

In May 2004, Huizenga severed ties with the organization when he relinquished his board seat. Major changes were made to AutoNation's regional management structure that September when the company consolidated operations into five regions, down from 10 districts.

ACCOMPLISHMENTS AND RECOGNITION

AutoNation continued to garner national recognition during the middle of the decade. In early 2005 *Fortune* named the company as America's Most Admired Automotive Retailing & Services Company for the fourth consecutive year. In late February, AutoNation sold its five millionth vehicle. The achievement was unprecedented in the history of the industry. It also was in 2005 that the company established LiveDealAutos. com, a new Web site through which it planned to sell 20,000 used vehicles through its dealership network.

In April 2006, ESL investments, the Greenwich, Connecticut-based hedge fund owned by billionaire Edward S. Lampert, sold 20.3 million AutoNation shares back to the company. The $468 million deal reduced ESL's ownership interest to 26.7 percent, down from 29.4 percent. It also was in 2006 that AutoNation CEO Mike Jackson revealed plans to begin focusing on dealership acquisitions within the premium luxury automotive market category. Late in the year, H. Wayne Huizenga was named to the Automotive Hall of Fame.

Several significant milestones were reached in 2007. That year, AutoNation sold its six millionth vehicle and was again named the nation's most admired auto retailer. In April, the company unveiled its Fuel Efficient E-Vehicle Program. At this time, AutoNation was negatively impacted by slumps in the Florida and California housing markets, which affected purchases of big-ticket items. Subsequently, the company began divesting underperforming dealerships. Compared to 257 dealerships at the end of 2006, AutoNation's portfolio numbered 246 dealerships in late 2007. In addition, it began buying back stock. In the third quarter alone, AutoNation repurchased 8.2 million shares of its stock for $341 million.

By 2008 Mike Maroone was serving as president of AutoNation. In January, the company's stock dipped to $11.72 per share, down from an all-time high of approximately $40 a decade earlier. Edward Lampert capitalized on this situation by acquiring $323 million worth of AutoNation shares between November 2007 and March 2008, bringing his total ownership interest to 36 percent. Later in the year, Microsoft's Bill Gates upped his stake in the company to about 12 percent. Activity continued in early 2009 when Lampert increased his stake to more than 45 percent.

ONLINE SALES FOCUS

Approaching the 21st century's second decade, AutoNation began focusing on online sales. In November 2009 AutoNation Direct (a service the company had begun piloting in 2008) was available at more than 100 locations in Colorado, California, and Florida. At that time, the company revealed plans to begin hiring additional staff, paving the way for a nationwide rollout by late 2010. Moving forward, CEO Mike Jackson indicated AutoNation would ramp up its investments in technology and make online sales a major priority.

Tammy Weisberger
Updated, Paul R. Greenland

PRINCIPAL OPERATING UNITS

Domestic; Import; Premium Luxury.

PRINCIPAL COMPETITORS

Group 1 Automotive, Inc.; Penske Automotive Group, Inc.; Sonic Automotive, Inc.

FURTHER READING

Altaner, David, "South Florida AutoNation Car Dealerships to Change Their Name," *Knight-Ridder/Tribune Business News*, May 8, 2000.

"AutoNation, Autoweb.com Make a Deal," *Automotive News*, October 23, 2000, p. 4.

"AutoNation Plans Big Push in Online Sales," *Automotive News*, November 30, 2009, p. 4.

Gale, Kevin, "AutoNation Drives into Future with Tighter Operational Focus," *South Florida Business Journal*, June 16, 2000, p. 1.

Harris, Donna, "AutoNation Overpowers Its Web Buying-Service Rivals," *Automotive News*, October 29, 2001, p. 33.

———, "AutoNation Puts Checkbook Away," *Automotive News*, November 22, 1999, p. 4.

———, "AutoNation Sees Big Net Sales," *Automotive News*, May 10, 1999, p. 8.

———, "AutoNation Trims Regional Management," *Automotive News*, September 13, 2004, p. 53.

———, "Chain Sees Megastore Rebound: New-Used Combos Fuel Comeback," *Automotive News*, October 18, 1999, p. 26.

———, "Pager Speeds Up Response to Internet Leads," *Automotive News*, May 10, 1999, p. 20.

———, "School Bell Chimes at AutoNation," *Automotive News*, August 27, 2001, p. 4.

Henry, Jim, "AutoNation to Get Sales Leads from CarPoint," *Automotive News*, February 3, 2001, p. 1.

Mateja, Jim, "Its Out with Old, In with New at Florida-Based AutoNation," *Knight-Ridder/Tribune Business News*, December 19, 1999.

Miller, Joe, "Fresh Phase: Republic Becomes AutoNation," *Automotive News*, April 12, 1998, p. 4.

Sawyers, Arlene, "AutoNation Reports $403.1 Million Loss for Quarter," *Automotive News*, January 31, 2000, p. 8.

———, "Top 100 Groups Add Sales in 2001; 10 Biggest Win More Than 50 Percent of Used-Vehicle Volume," *Automotive News*, May 20, 2002, p. 32.

Seemuth, Mike, "AutoNation Buyback Plan Has Billionaire among Takers," *Miami Daily Business Review*, April 26, 2006.

———, "Billionaire Boosts Stake in AutoNation," *Miami Daily Business Review*, November 7, 2007.

———, "Huizenga Sells AutoNation Block Worth $55 Million," *Miami Daily Business Review*, March 6, 2003, p. A1.

Shuldiner, Herbert, "The Wal-Mart of Auto Sales? AutoNation's Mike Jackson Has Big Plans for the Car Retailer," *Chief Executive*, July 2004, p. 38.

Thompson, Chrissie, "Lampert nears 50% Stake in AutoNation; CEO Jackson: It's a 'Vote of Confidence,' Not a Coup," *Automotive News*, February 23, 2009, p. 8.

Waters, Richard, "The Americas: Republic Industries Acquires Car Rental Concern," *Financial Times*, January 7, 1997, p. 17.

Wernle, Bradford, "AutoNation Goal: Buy Luxury-Brand Stores," *Automotive News*, October 9, 2006.

AXA Group

25, avenue Matignon
Paris, 75008
France
Telephone: (33 1) 40 75 57 00
Fax: (33 1) 40 75 57 95
Web site: http://www.axa.com

Mutual Company
Incorporated: 1817 as Compagnie d'assurances Mutuelles contre l'incendie dans les départements de la Seine et de l'Eure
Employees: 214,044
Total Assets: EUR 673.44 billion (2008)
Stock Exchanges: Euronext Paris
Ticker Symbol: CS
NAICS: 524113 Direct Life Insurance Carriers

■ ■ ■

AXA Group is a global leader in financial protection, ranking among the world's largest insurance groups and the world's largest asset managers. Primary operations are in Europe, North America, and the Asia-Pacific region, but AXA also has a presence in the Middle East, Africa, and Latin America. The company's diversified operating businesses include Life & Savings, Property & Casualty, International Insurance, Asset Management, and Banking. AXA claims 80 million clients worldwide and total assets of EUR 673.44 billion.

NORMANDY ROOTS: 19TH CENTURY

The first company in the history of the AXA Group was created in 1817. This company was responsible for the two main characteristics of the group before the 1970s: its location in Normandy and its legal status as a mutual company. Jacques-Théodore le Carpentier, with 17 other property owners, established Compagnie d'assurances Mutuelles contre l'incendie dans les départements de la Seine et de l'Eure, a fire insurance company situated at Rouen. In the company's legal documents it was stated that every shareholder was to be both insurer and insured party for five years, the basic principle of mutuality, where the insured parties own the company. On the properties insured was a plaque bearing the letters P.A.C.L. (*propriété assurée contre l'incendie*), indicating that they were insured against fire loss.

The first damage for which the company had to pay occurred in 1819, amounting to FRF 7.5. Realizing the impossibility of sharing this cost among 1,264 shareholders, the company invented the reserve fund. Soon afterward in 1822, the famous fire of Rouen Cathedral required shareholders to pay for a more important claim, an event not easily forgotten.

Great changes following the Industrial Revolution, as well as increasing competition from companies such as La Providence and La Paternelle, created in 1838 and 1843, respectively, required the company to expand and diversify its activities. Adolphe Lanne, manager since 1832, decided to create two companies. The first one, Mutualité mobilière, replaced the original company. The second, Mutualité Immobilière, was to insure movables risks. The people of Rouen called the former Ancienne Mutuelle to distinguish it from the latter, which began conducting business in 1847.

In 1852 a major quarrel occurred between insurance companies and the French government. Concerned about the dangers associated with the recent invention of the match, insurers tried for more than 20 years to have its production restricted or even forbidden. The government held on, and eventually established a state monopoly for the making and selling of matches. In the meantime the board made two decisions. They would extend activities to cover the whole of France, and Mutualité Mobilière would now also cover real estate risks. In 1881, Mutualité Immobilière and Mutualité Mobilière merged under the name of Ancienne Mutuelle, which it retained until 1977. At this time the new chairman, M. Masselin, decided to offer life insurance. In this way Mutuelle Vie life insurance company was born.

WAR SURVIVOR

The beginning of the 20th century and World War I did not bring any great change for Ancienne Mutuelle (AM). After moving offices in Rouen in 1902, the first important step was undertaken just after the war when in 1922 Anciennes Mutuelles Accidents, an automobile insurance branch, was established. It developed quickly and would make a major contribution to the company's profits.

In World War II, the company did not escape so lightly. In April 1944 its new offices were bombed by U.S. forces. This loss was followed by the death of Gaston de Payenneville, chairman since 1913. AM emerged from the war in poor shape generally, although the accident and life divisions were less severely afflicted. Soon the necessity of a tighter group structure became apparent. This change was accomplished in 1946 with

the constitution of Groupe Ancienne Mutuelle under the leadership of André Sahut d'Izarn.

In 1948 the Groupe was thriving once more, proving the validity of its motto: "E cinere suo re divide" (rising again from its ashes). From the mid-1940s until the 1970s the Groupe experienced steady though unspectacular growth achieved by a succession of mergers with other insurance mutual companies. The first, in 1946, was with Ancienne Mutuelle du Calvados, created in 1819 and a longtime collaborator of AM. Then in 1950 Mutuelle d'Orléans asked to join the Groupe, via Mutuelle Vie, since it was a life insurance company. Next came Mutualité Générale life insurance company, also known for insuring the French *communes*, cities, or parts of cities, with individual legal status. Finally in 1954 La Participation, created in 1899 as a non-life insurance company, entered AM.

In 1955, before the Groupe began to expand abroad, André Sahut d'Izarn could count within his company eight mutuals and additional nonmutual companies that were 100 percent subsidiaries. Among the latter was Ancienne Mutuelle Transport de Bétail, created in 1939 in order to insure rail transport of livestock. It soon became a public company, after which it was acquired by AM. In 1977 it became the AMRE, the reinsurance company of AM.

PIVOTAL LEADERSHIP

In 1955 AM went into business in Canada, focusing particularly on Quebec. This step, together with the arrival at AM of a young graduate, Claude Bébéar, the son of a schoolteacher, marked the beginning of a great phase of expansion at AM. In the midst of the political events of May 1968 in Paris, André Sahut d'Izarn celebrated in fitting style the 150th anniversary of the Groupe. The party in Belbeuf, Normandy, was said to have been particularly lavish and welcomed a very special guest: a computer, recently acquired.

After this phase of development, AM experienced a crisis. The death of Chairman André Sahut d'Izarn in June 1972 may have been a contributing factor. In April 1974, the longest strike known in insurance history began. It lasted for more than two months and totally paralyzed Groupe AM. Eventually it ended in June with the nomination of Claude Bébéar as chairman and the establishment of an innovative social policy.

From this point, the history of AXA, at that stage Groupe Ancienne Mutuelle, cannot be separated from the story of Claude Bébéar's ambition and rise to power. In the French insurance world, Bébéar was known as the cowboy of insurance, also described by *Nouvel Economiste*, October 21, 1988, as the "avant-garde insurer"

KEY DATES

1817: Mutual fire insurance company is created in Rouen.
1881: Merger creates Ancienne Mutuelle.
1946: Aftermath of World War II necessitates tightened structure.
1982: Drouot Group is taken over; AXA name is adopted two years later.
1992: AXA acquires majority interest in The Equitable.
1996: UAP merges into AXA, creating the world's second-largest insurance group and largest asset manager.
2006: Winterthur Group acquisition strengthens European market.
2008: Global financial crisis cuts into earnings.
2010: AXA looks to emerging markets for expansion.

and elected by his peers in 1988 as Manager of the Year.

He started by changing the name of the group, with its old-fashioned connotations, replacing the adjective *ancienne* with *unies*, or "united." By 1978, Mutuelles Unies had taken control of the Compagnie Parisienne de Garantie. Mutuelle de l'Quest, specializing in legal protection, also joined the group. Two years later, Mutuelles Unies and its subsidiaries achieved total revenue of FRF 2.4 million with 2,300 employees around the world and more than 700 sole agents working for the group.

The first major opportunity for Bébéar to expand through acquisition occurred in 1982 with the spectacular purchase of the Drouot Group. Established in 1948 as a public company listed on the Paris Stock Exchange, the Drouot Group began operating under this name only from 1977, although its history went back to the 19th century. At the time of its purchase, the results of its automobile insurance division were poor and its financial policy was not very sound. Nevertheless, the takeover battle turned out to be fierce and highly publicized. Bébéar was trying to absorb a company at least as big as his own.

This takeover bid was also said to have been quite traumatic for the Drouot employees. According to the *Expansion*, May 31, 1990, other companies began to fear what they called "other drouotisations." Trying to justify himself, Bébéar explained in the same paper: "We may be upsetting people but we are also cutting out the

dead wood." Not only did he achieve the latter, but he soon took further significant steps, transforming Mutuelles Unies into AXA in 1984. He chose this name because it had no meaning whatsoever, was internationally pronounceable, and was an easily remembered palindrome.

The next stage occurred in 1986, with Drouot as the vehicle. Drouot made a takeover bid for La Providence, an old company owned by an ancient line of the French aristocracy. At that very moment La Providence was merging with Le Secours, another insurance company established in 1880. When AXA via Drouot took control of La Providence at the end of a long takeover battle, Bébéar killed two birds with one stone and acquired both La Providence and Le Secours.

The pair merged under the name of Présence. These were important life and non-life insurance companies with a large network of domestic and international branches, especially in Europe. They had also had, until the 1960s, considerable presence in the French colonies, La Providence in Algeria and Le Secours in Indochina. Although the purchases of Drouot and Presence were crucial points in AXA's development, AXA's last coup remained its most famous.

INTERNATIONAL CLOUT: LATE EIGHTIES

The events began in 1988 when Bernard Pagezy, chairman of the holding company la Compagnie du Midi, including the AGP (Assurances du Groupe de Paris), came to see Claude Bébéar. Threatened with absorption by the Italian insurers Generali, Pagezy asked AXA for protection. He proposed to give Bébéar Midi's insurance interests in exchange for participation and protection.

This happy marriage did not last very long, and the collaboration soon turned into a fight as AXA began to think seriously about buying Midi. It was through the proceedings of February 1989's general meeting that Bébéar, assisted by Generali, the very same company that Midi feared, eventually managed to take 100 percent control of la Compagnie du Midi. After a short period as AXA-Midi, the company's name reverted to AXA.

By acquiring Midi, not only had AXA taken over a major holding company but now as a result controlled Midi's enormous international network. Compagnie du Midi had had a significant presence abroad, especially in the United Kingdom. In 1982 it had taken possession of London & Hull, an airline, marine, and industrial insurance company. Five years later, it bought life insurers Equity & Law. Its U.K. interests alone achieved revenue in 1988 of FRF 5.5 million.

In February 1989 AXA could boast 42 companies around the world, 4,000 general agents, 16,000 employees, and revenue of FRF 45 million. Only nine years earlier, Mutuelles Unies had had 2,300 employees, 700 agents, and revenue of FRF 2.4 million. Claude Bébéar had definitely proved his business acumen. The structure of AXA, with mutual companies heading the group, protected the company from any kind of takeover bid.

Meanwhile, AXA embarked on a total restructuring of the group. The restructuring began in 1986 when Bébéar, for the first time in French insurance history, began the complete transformation of AXA's distribution network. Instead of a traditional system, whereby each company had its own general agents, insurance brokers, and other sales organizations, Bébéar chose to reorganize horizontally. He merged all group companies into three main units, each of them corresponding to a single channel of distribution.

As a result, AXA consisted of three entities. AXA Assurances included the company's general agents, Uni Europe the insurance brokers, and Franklin Assurances dealt with the remaining sales organizations. This structure was valid only for France. Foreign distribution was not affected. Bébéar was convinced of his system's efficiency and of its relevance to the market.

BUILDING MOMENTUM: 1991–96

Fortune magazine ranked AXA 16th among top diversified financial companies based on profits in 1991, although its asset-based standing fell from 22nd to 34th place. During the year AXA acquired a majority interest in the struggling U.S. insurer The Equitable Companies Incorporated. When The Equitable demutualized in 1992, AXA gained a controlling interest.

In 1994, AXA acquired businesses in Canada and Belgium. The company also launched its first worldwide institutional advertising campaign. The following year AXA made headway in the Pacific region. Japan Life began operations, and AXA acquired Australia's largest pension fund manager. National Mutual Fund Management was purchased for what the *Wall Street Journal* called a "bargain price." International efforts gave way to a big domestic deal in 1996.

Union des Assurances de Paris (UAP) was formed in 1968, when France reorganized state-run insurance companies into four large groups. At inception UAP ranked as the second-largest insurer in Europe behind Allianz of West Germany. A period of restructuring followed the amalgamation, including the creation of nonlife, life, assurance, and savings branches.

In the early 1970s UAP expanded through acquisitions but also contended with high costs and losses.

UAP gained a significant banking presence in 1984 with the acquisition of Banque Worms. That year international operations, which generated more than 40 percent of total income, reorganized. Internally the large insurer endured upheaval during the decade, changing presidents four times in a span of eight years.

In 1990 a law change permitted foreign investors to own shares in state controlled companies. UAP responded by selling interest in the company, thus increasing its capital. Allowed to float up to 25 percent of its shares publicly, UAP also engaged in share swaps with Banque Nationale de Paris and Banco Central of Spain. In 1996 UAP agreed to merge into AXA, creating the world's second-largest insurance group and largest asset manager, according to the *International Herald Tribune* (*IHT*).

AXA-UAP

The stock and cash deal was valued at more than $9 billion. Combined AXA-UAP 1995 revenue was FRF 313 billion with assets under management of FRF 2.29 trillion. AXA-UAP ranked just behind Nippon Life of Japan among insurers and ahead of Fidelity Investments among fund managers. Insurance industry consolidation perpetuated mergers by companies attempting to compete in the global market.

Bébéar was named president of the combined company, and Jacques Friedmann, UAP president, was designated chairman of the supervisory board. UAP was the larger in terms of sales but was less profitable. AXA's consolidated net profit was FRF 2.7 billion in 1995. UAP's real estate holdings and expensive "but lackluster" European investments added up to losses, according to *IHT*. Its stock had fallen off since its initial public offering. AXA had been on the rise during the months prior to the merger announcement. Combined AXA-UAP could claim status as the largest company on the Paris Stock Exchange with capitalization of more than FRF 100 billion.

Geographically the insurers' interests were complementary. AXA owned 60 percent of Equitable in the United States. National Mutual in Australia gave it a "substantial" Asia-Pacific presence, according to *IHT*. AXA generated more than 42 percent of its business in the United States with "slightly less" in Europe. UAP, on the other hand, produced 40 percent of its sales in France and more than 50 percent in the rest of Europe.

In 1999, AXA was the world's third-largest money manager behind FMR Corp.'s Fidelity Investments and UBS AG, according to the *Wall Street Journal*. AXA had succeeded in redefining itself as a savings company providing financial products, one of Europe's first insurers to do so. Boding well for AXA's future, European nations were moving savings and pensions from government to individual and employer control, to the benefit of money managers.

AXA acquired U.K.-based Guardian Royal Exchange PLC in 1999 for $5.6 billion, climbing to the number three slot in the United Kingdom's property and casualty insurance industry. The deal also enhanced its position in Germany. AXA gained a majority interest in Japan's 13th-largest domestic insurer, Nippon Dantai Life Insurance Company, during 2000. In the United States AXA sold its interest in Donaldson Lufkin & Jenrette (DLJ) to Credit Suisse Group, and its U.S. asset management subsidiary Alliance Capital acquired Sanford C. Bernstein. AXA followed up by acquiring all shares not already owned of the U.S.-based holding company AXA Financial, Inc., and the outstanding minority interest in Sun Life & Provincial Holdings in the United Kingdom.

TUMULTUOUS TIMES: 2001–06

AXA reported a big drop in profits for 2001. The company suffered elevated claims related to the September 11, 2001, terrorist attacks on the United States. AXA also posted losses linked to investments in U.S.-based Enron. Money manager Alliance had invested heavily in the energy trader just prior to its bankruptcy, according to *Barron's*. Adding to its woes, the French life insurance market slowed.

AXA sold some of its operations in the early 2000s, including Banque Worms in 2001. In Australia, AXA refocused its attention on core life insurance and financial advisory businesses, selling its health insurance business during 2002. AXA pulled back its insurance presence in South America during 2002 and 2003.

The resurgence of the insurance industry in Europe contributed to markedly improved sales and net income in 2003. AXA's profits continued to climb in 2004, rising to about EUR 4.6 billion. Nevertheless, the figure was about half that of competitor AIG. Insurance accounted for the bulk of AXA's business, with the remainder from financial management. During 2004 AXA had pursued growth in Asia via joint ventures and acquired The MONY Group Inc. The purchase expanded AXA's life insurance distribution capacity in the United States by 25 percent.

AXA bought out AXA Konzern minority interests in Germany in 2005. Then in 2006 AXA acquired Winterthur Group for EUR 7.9 billion from Credit Suisse Group, enhancing its presence in many markets. Winterthur operated in 17 countries, served 13 million clients, and was one of the top 10 multiline insurers in Europe, according to *A.M. Best Newswire*. The company also had operations in Asia.

For the year, three of AXA's four divisions produced double-digit gains in net income. Life and savings climbed 20 percent, asset management 28 percent, and international insurance operations 92 percent. Property and casualty climbed 8 percent. The two largest European insurers by premium income, AXA SA and Allianz SE, benefited from relative calm during 2006 in terms of weather and financial markets.

GLOBAL CRISIS: 2007–10

At the beginning of 2007, AXA ranked as Europe's second-largest insurer by market capitalization. "At the heart of AXA's business model are innovative financial products, multiple distribution channels and open architecture, which allows customers to invest in a range of funds," Andrea Felsted observed in a February *Financial Times* article. During 2007 AXA worked to integrate Winterthur affiliates in countries such as Spain, Japan, and Switzerland while disposing of operations in the United States and Taiwan. In other business, AXA sold its Dutch operations, acquired a leading South Korean niche insurer, and entered the Russian market.

Founder Claude Bébéar announced his departure as chairman of AXA in February 2008, complying with age-related company statutes. He had stepped aside as CEO in 2000, at the age of 65, succeeded at that time as well by Henri de Castries. Addressing the state of the global financial market, he told the *Financial Times*, "Banks have short memories. In the 1980s–90s they were hit by junk bonds. Now it's loans to individual housebuyers." The time was marked by a global economic crisis brought on by the collapse of the U.S. mortgage market.

AXA saw its 2008 earnings fall to EUR 0.9 billion, from a record EUR 5.7 billion during 2007. A decline in variable annuity sales and in assets under management, combined with write-downs, contributed to the drop-off in earnings. Alliance-Bernstein investments in entities such as Fannie Mae, Freddie Mac, Lehman, AIG, and Citigroup had soured. The smaller property and casualty business, largely in Europe, provided a semblance of stability during the tumultuous times.

Global acquisitions had changed the face of AXA. In 2008 France contributed just 24 percent of revenues, according to *Barron's*. Northern, Central, and Eastern Europe produced 26 percent and North America 18 percent. Asia Pacific added 10 percent as did the United Kingdom and Ireland. Southern Europe and Latin America produced the remainder. Moreover, AXA sought to increase the emerging markets' share of revenue to 25 percent by 2020.

Since taking the helm as CEO in 2000, de Castries had guided the company through the heavy claim losses of 2001, the early 2000s bear market, and then the global financial crisis. Along the way he faced his share of criticism, including retention of the low-margin property and casualty business and sale of investment bank DLJ. *Barron's* considered the nature of his tenure in late 2009: "His disciplined approach, de Castries learned from his predecessor and mentor Claude Bébéar, never wavered, and he was ultimately vindicated by events during the 2008 financial meltdown. ING and Fortis were badly damaged by their banking connections, as was AIG by its disastrous forays into derivatives insurance, securities lending speculation and residential mortgage origination. Even the formidable Allianz suffered acute indigestion from its 2001 purchase of Dresdner Bank—a company it has since sold." AXA's net income rebounded in 2009, climbing to EUR 3.6 billion.

Sonia Kronlund
Updated, Kathleen Peippo

PRINCIPAL SUBSIDIARIES

AXA Assistance SA; AXA Corporate Solutions Life Reinsurance Company; Colisee Re; AXA Financial, Inc. (USA); AXA Canada Inc.; AXA Holding Maroc (Morocco); AXA Holdings Belgium; AXA Bank Europe (Belgium); AXA France Assurance; Compagnie Financière de Paris; AXA Bank Europe SA Magyarorszagi Fioktelepe (Hungary); AXA Italia SpA (Italy); AXA Konzern AG (Germany); DBV-Winterthur Holding AG (Germany); AXA Versicherungen AG (Germany); AXA Leben AG (Germany); AXA Bank AG (Germany); AXA Luxembourg SA; Seguro Directo Gere (Portugal); AXA Mediterranean Holding SA (Spain); AXA Life Ltd (Switzerland); AXA Insurance Ltd (Switzerland); AXA Holding AS (Turkey).

PRINCIPAL COMPETITORS

Allianz SE; Assicurazioni Generali SpA; ING Groep N.V.

FURTHER READING

Alexandre, Roger, "Tu fusionneras dans la douleur," *L'Expansion*, May 31, 1990.

Amiel, Geraldine, and Jethro Mullen, "International Finance—Earnings: AXA's '09 Profit Quadruples," *Wall Street Journal*, February 19, 2010, p. C2.

Antoni, Marie Louise, "Claude Bébéar, un assureur d'avant-garde," *Nouvel Economiste*, November 21, 1988.

"Axa Financial's Alliance to Acquire Sanford Bernstein for $3.5 Billion," *A.M. Best Newswire*, June 22, 2000.

"Axa Profit More Than Triples When Converted from French to U.S. GAAP," *A.M. Best Newswire*, April 13, 2004.

Betts, Paul, "Bébéar Is Going by the Book He Wrote," *Financial Times*, February 29, 2008, p. 16.

Daneshkhu, Scheherazade, and Paul J. Davies, "Axa Gets Bullish and Busy on Acquisitions," *Financial Times*, November 10, 2009, p. 15.

Felsted, Andrea, "Axa Hopes Its Thoroughbred Credentials Will Help Net Top-Five Position in the UK," *Financial Times*, February 24, 2007, p. 17.

Gray, Simon, "Stakes Are Raised in PanEuroLife Case as Axa Chairman Is Grilled," *International Money Marketing*, July 2001, p. 1.

James, Barry, "A French Insurance Behemoth to Buy UAP and Create World's No. 2 Firm," *International Herald Tribune*, November 13, 1996, p. 16.

Klees, Dee, "AXA in Review: Global Insurer's Profits Rise, but Revenues Fall," *Syracuse (NY) Post-Standard*, June 20, 2005, p. 7.

Laing, Jonathan R., "*Tres Bien!*" *Barron's*, December 14, 2009, pp. 25+.

McDonald, Ian, "Earnings Digest—Insurance: Insurers Need Another Quiet Year," *Wall Street Journal*, February 23, 2007, p. C6.

McGee, Suzanne, "European Takeovers Offer Wealth of Trophies," *Wall Street Journal*, March 11, 1999, p. 13.

Pilla, David, "International Growth Spurs 18% Rise in Axa's 2006 Profit," *A.M. Best Newswire*, February 23, 2007.

"The Rediscovery of America," *Best's Review*, November 2006.

"U.S. Terrorist Attacks Knock Axa's Bottom Line," *Africa News Service*, March 15, 2002.

BANFI®

Banfi Products Corp.

———■———

1111 Cedar Swamp Road
Old Brookville, New York 11545
U.S.A.
Telephone: (516) 626-9200
Toll Free: (800) 645-6511
Fax: (516) 626-9218
Web site: http://www.banfi.com

Private Company
Incorporated: 1919 as House of Banfi
Employees: 150
Sales: $250 million (2009 est.)
NAICS: 312130 Wineries; 424820 Wine and Distilled
    Alcoholic Beverage Merchant Wholesalers

■ ■ ■

Banfi Products Corp. operates through two divisions, Banfi Vintners, the leading wine importer in North America, and Castello Banfi, which operates vineyard estates in Italy. Banfi Vintners is the sole U.S. importer of Castello Banfi wines as well as wines from other producers, notably Bolla, Riunite, and Fontana from Italy; Concha y Toro and Emiliana from Chile; Trivento from Argentina; Wisdom & Warter Sherries from Spain; and Stone's Ginger wine from England. Castello Banfi, based in Montalcino, Tuscany, produces wines from three properties, Castello Banfi, Banfi Tuscany, and Vigne Regali. The division also operates a 14-room luxury hotel named Il Borgo. Banfi is owned and managed by the Mariani family.

BANFI'S EARLY YEARS: 1919–67

Giovanni (John) Mariani and a brother founded the House of Banfi in 1919 to import medicinal bitters and Italian food products, naming it for Teodolinda Banfi, an aunt who was head of the household staff of the Milanese archbishop who later became Pope Pius XL. Located in the Little Italy area of Manhattan just below Greenwich Village, the firm began importing classic Italian wines after the end of Prohibition. World War II interrupted this trade, and after the war the firm turned to Bordeaux wines from France. Mariani's sons made annual visits to the vineyards and cellars of the Bordeaux region and also to other renowned wine-growing areas, such as France's Burgundy and Germany's Rhineland.

Over the objections of their father, John Mariani Jr. and his brother Harry went to Italy in 1967 to search for a low-alcohol, semisweet wine that could be chilled. While in the Emilia Romagna region of north central Italy, they were introduced to a fruity, fizzy Lambrusco grown from the grapes of a growers' cooperative federation named Cantine Cooperative Riunite. Over the next year John Mariani spent much of his time speaking to the cooperative managers and oenologists about making changes for the U.S. market. "We tried several blends based on different proportions of the grapes they used, and experimented with ways to bring out the fruit and body," he said in the November 30, 1981, issue of *Fortune.*

Mariani not only wanted Riunite Lambrusco to be sweeter, he wanted its natural effervescence to be reduced so that the wine would not be subject to a U.S.

COMPANY PERSPECTIVES

Our mission is to nurture Banfi's leadership position by offering wines of superior quality, and fostering the appreciation of wine through education, while maintaining family ownership, business ethics, and a culture of teamwork and pride in shared success.

tax aimed at imported champagne. Riunite's technicians solved the problem by stopping fermentation early, keeping sugar content high, alcohol low, and bubbly carbon dioxide below the tax level.

RELEASE OF RIUNITE: 1969

Banfi, which moved from New York City to Long Island in 1970, began test marketing Riunite in New York, Los Angeles, Chicago, and Miami in 1968, sponsoring tastings for consumer groups and pressing distributors for orders. The initial consignment of 100 cases grew to 20,000 in 1969 and 50,000 in 1970. The drink, packaged with a twist-off top rather than a cork, caught on with young people and showed great potential as an entry-level wine, but Banfi restricted it to the test areas until 1974. After going into nationwide distribution, Riunite reached second place among imported wine brands in 1975, with 1.2 million cases sold. The following year Banfi invested $4 million in promotion and advertising, and sales reached two million cases, putting Riunite into first place, displacing Portugal's Mateus.

During the 1970s Riunite rode the crest of a wave that saw table-wine imports grow by 500 percent in the United States and Lambrusco-type wines by an eye-popping 40-fold. "Somehow or other, in the 1970s, it became fashionable to drink wine," a Banfi executive explained in a 1984 *Marketing & Media Decisions* article. At the same time, he added, "wine became accessible to a broader group of people. The wine business went from being a specialty business to one that is on the cusp of being a mass appeal business."

Banfi's first advertisements were low-budget radio spots featuring Buffalo Bob Smith of the early TV show *Howdy Doody*, backed by a chorus, which included Harry Mariani, singing "It's Riunite time!" to the tune of the show's theme song. In 1974 the company switched its account to a firm that introduced award-winning television commercials typically suggesting a dose of Riunite to settle lovers' quarrels. Banfi switched to more upscale commercials in 1978, although still

with a hint of romance. At the same time the Marianis were encouraging the public to quaff Riunite casually, with ads that matched the words "nice" and "ice." By 1981 one ad showed a bottle of wine being tossed from hand to hand at a picnic, like a soft drink. In addition, like beer or soda, Riunite was as light on the pocketbook as on the palette, averaging just $3 a bottle.

DOMESTIC & FOREIGN VINEYARDS: 1980–84

By 1980 Banfi alone was importing more wine from Italy, some nine million cases a year, than France and Germany combined were exporting to the United States. Its Riunite imports now included a white (Bianco) and a rosé (Rosato) wine as well as Lambrusco red. The distributor, which had been renamed Villa Banfi, moved its headquarters in 1983 from Farmingdale, Long Island, to an estate, complete with a 60-room mansion, in Old Brookville. Adjacent to the 52-acre grounds, Banfi purchased 75 acres of rolling farmland for eventual planting of grapevines. It also took a half-interest in Villa Armando, a California winery.

Beyond these acquisitions, John Mariani sought to bring to fruition a long-standing dream to produce internationally acknowledged fine wines. Between 1978 and 1981 his company invested $40 million in Italian vineyards or acreage suitable for planting grapevines. By 1984, when company sales reached an estimated $225 million, Villa Banfi had not only purchased two wineries in the Piedmont region of northern Italy but 7,100 acres of prime wine-producing land just outside the medieval walled town of Montalcino, perched on a hilltop south of Siena. Here workers planted vines of cabernet sauvignon, chardonnay, pinot grigio, and brunello, the ancient grape of Tuscany, very similar to sangiovese. The company restored a 1,000-year-old fortress on the property (renamed Castello Banfi) and established one of the most technologically advanced wineries in Western Europe, including computer-monitored pressing and temperature-control systems and vats made of stainless steel rather than concrete.

RIUNITE SALES SOAR & DECLINE: 1983–87

Aided by $17 million worth of advertising, 90 percent on television, Villa Banfi sold about 11 million cases of Riunite in 1983, more than the next six imported brands combined. The following year the company topped this total with 11.2 million cases, but the boom ended in 1985 when Banfi had to recall 1.4 million cases of Riunite after the federal government found in samples trace amounts of a chemical normally used in

KEY DATES

1919: Company is founded to import Italian foods and medicinal bitters.

1969: Having diversified into wine distribution, Banfi imports 20,000 cases of Riunite.

1976: Riunite becomes top U.S. wine import, with two million cases sold.

1978: Banfi begins buying Italian vineyards and wineries.

1984: Riunite's U.S. sales peak at 11.2 million cases.

2007: A luxury hotel, Il Borgo, opens at the company's Tuscan estate in Montalcino, Italy.

2009: Banfi celebrates its 90th anniversary.

antifreeze. This debacle not only cost the company $34 million to recall and destroy the wine but left Riunite with a stigma that could not be erased, even though the U.S. Food and Drug Administration later acknowledged that the wine was safe to drink. Ironically John Mariani had told Jeanne Toomey of *Advertising Age* four years earlier that, after traces of asbestos had been found in his father during a postmortem examination, "I then became engrossed in the pure and natural aspect of our products. ... I ... made every effort to see that there were no additives." In 1986, in addition, sales of all Italian wines were rocked by a scandal arising from the addition of toxic wood alcohol to inexpensive bulk wines.

Villa Banfi had already taken a step to broaden its line by introducing D'Oro, a product of its Strevi winery in Piedmont fermented from the same muscat grape from which sparkling Asti Spumante is produced. To compensate for the drop in sales of its standard Riunite table wines, the company, in 1986, introduced fruit-flavored Riunite Peach and Riunite Raspberry as competitors in the wine-cooler category, adding a third, Sunny Apple, soon after. D'Oro and the standard Riunite red, rosé, and white wines were positioned against popular California table wines, while the company's own fine wines began to appear in the United States at prices ranging from $5 to $28 a bottle.

The switch to fruit-flavored Riunite came just in time for Villa Banfi, renamed Banfi Vintners, as sales of the company's standard table wines continued to drop in 1986 and 1987. Some 8.1 million cases of Riunite were sold in 1987, with the fruit-flavored brands accounting for more than 30 percent of sales. With wine-cooler sales stagnating the following year, however,

Banfi introduced its fourth Riunite table wine, Blush Bianco. Also in 1988, the company purchased Excelsior, a small company that was importing Concha y Toro, the leading wine brand in Chile. To exploit foreign markets, Banfi had signed agreements with companies as large and diverse as Mitsubishi in Japan, Hiram Walker in Canada, and Allied Breweries in Great Britain to act as its agents.

In 1991 the Excelsior operation became Excelsior Wines & Spirits, in order to emphasize that it was distributing a wide variety of alcoholic beverages other than the traditional Banfi products. Excelsior was carrying more than 100 wine lines in the New York metropolitan area and also had signed an agreement to distribute M.S. Walker's liquor brands. Excelsior, a subsidiary, grew in sales from $12 million in 1990 to $26 million in 1996 but sold its wholesale line the following year to Charmer Industries Inc., a larger wine and liquor wholesaler. Harry Mariani explained to Alan J. Wax of *Newsday* that it would have been "economically difficult" for Excelsior to compete with major national distributors.

WINE PRODUCTION IN LONG ISLAND AND TUSCANY: 1994–99

By 1994 Banfi was producing a wide range of wines at its estate in Tuscany, where 2,700 of the 7,100 acres now had been given to plantings. Brunello di Montalcino was selling for $50 a bottle. Another Brunello, Poggio all'Oro, was named best of show that year in a competition of 741 wines from 16 countries. Besides Castello Banfi's Brunellos, the estate was producing blends of sangiovese, cabernet sauvignon, syrah, pinot grigio, and chardonnay, and the Strevi winery operation was continuing to produce a sparkling red wine named Barchetto d'Acqui.

The company also had planted chardonnay grapes on about 47 acres of its Old Brookville property but sold the grapes to other vintners instead of making its own wine. North Shore Old Wealth, a chardonnay made at Chateau Frank from these grapes, was selling for about $12 a bottle in 1998. Banfi also had owned, since the 1980s, Jumby Bay, a 312-acre resort and vacation-home community on a private island north of Antigua in the West Indies. In 1997 the company brought suit against developer Homer G. Williams after reportedly losing in excess of $20 million of its $50 million investment on a failed business venture there.

BANFI BRANDS AT THE MILLENNIUM

By 1999 Banfi Vintners had spent $200 million on its Tuscan operation, which was producing 400,000 cases of wine per year, plus olive oil and balsamic vinegar. About one-tenth of the wine yield was Brunello di Montalcino, selling for between $25 and $250 a bottle. A British wine writer was quoted by Phyllis Berman of *Forbes* in these words, "The great wine estates of France have nothing to compare with it. In all of Europe, Castello Banfi is unique." The 16,000-member Association of Italian Sommeliers voted Castello Banfi Italy's "Best Wine Estate" in 1999, and in 2000 the Vinitaly Wine Competition voted Castello Banfi "International Winery of the Year" for an unprecedented fourth time. Vini Banfi of Strevi was continuing to produce premium sparkling wines, and Principessa Gavia of Gavi, also in Piedmont, was producing Principessa Gavia from the Cortese di Gavi grape. On Long Island, Banfi continued to maintain the only commercial vineyard in Long Island's Nassau County and the closest one to New York City, growing grapes for about 2,000 gallons a year of Old Brookville Chardonnay.

Riunite continued to be the leading imported wine brand in the United States in 1998, with 2.1 million cases sold at $5 a bottle. Some 60 percent of this volume consisted of Lambrusco. In second place was Concha y Toro, with two million cases sold, compared to only 90,000 in 1988, when Banfi purchased Excelsior. Created by Banfi, another Chilean brand, Walnut Crest, was in ninth place. In 1999 Banfi introduced the United States to BRL Hardy's Stonehaven brand, produced from a $13 million new winery on Australia's Limestone Coast. Other wines being carried by Banfi were those from the Borgogno, Cecchi, Florio, Placido, and Sartori wineries of Italy and the TriVento label from Argentina's Vina Patagonia winery.

THIRD GENERATION TAKES THE HELM

The second generation of the Mariani family led the company as it entered the 21st century. John Mariani served as chairman and CEO and Harry Mariani performed the duties of president and COO. The two leaders ceded their authority during the decade, passing the reins of command to the third generation of the family. Leadership responsibilities were split into co-CEO positions, with Harry Mariani's son, James W. Mariani, sharing control over the company with his cousin, Cristina Mariani-May, the youngest daughter of John Mariani. A graduate of Colgate University and Cornell University, James Mariani joined the family business on a full-time basis in the 1990s, as did Cristina Mariani-May, who earned degrees from Georgetown University and Columbia University.

Distribution expanded considerably under the guidance of the company's two new leaders. At the start of the decade, production from Castello Banfi could be purchased in 53 countries in Europe, Asia, the Middle East, North America, and South America, a true global presence that was fleshed out as the company secured agreements with distributors that deepened its market penetration. Castello Banfi entered India during the decade, launching its efforts with wine tastings in Mumbai and New Delhi. The division furthered its presence in Poland and Russia, using its contacts to develop new distribution agreements throughout Eastern Europe. By the end of the decade, Castello Banfi wines, the family's Poggio all'Oro, BelnerO, Brunello di Montalcino, and others, could be purchased in 85 countries.

The Mariani family added to the scope of Castello Banfi's operations later in the decade, completing a project spearheaded by Cristina Mariani-May. Near its winery in Montalcino, set amid more than 7,000 acres of vineyards and olive groves, Castello Banfi built a luxury hotel, Il Borgo. The hotel opened in 2007, featuring 14 suites and dining facilities. The Mariani family celebrated the 90th anniversary of their family business two years later, ending the decade as a notable vintner that possessed a powerful distribution arm. Nearly a century after the business was founded to import food and medicinal bitters, the modern version of Banfi represented far more than the original vision of Giovanni Mariani, holding sway as a producer, exporter, and importer of a large portfolio of wines.

Robert Halasz
Updated, Jeffrey L. Covell

PRINCIPAL DIVISIONS

Banfi Vintners; Castello Banfi.

PRINCIPAL COMPETITORS

Constellation Wines U.S., Inc.; E. & J. Gallo Winery; Southern Wine & Spirits of America, Inc.

FURTHER READING

"Builders of Brunello," *Wine Spectator*, July 2007.

Burck, Charles G., "The Toyota of the Wine Trade," *Fortune*, November 30, 1981, p. 154.

Durie, Elspeth, "Riunite Lambrusco: A Natural Sparkler Bubbling in Success," *Advertising Age*, September 26, 1977, p. 96.

Herman, Phyllis, "Up from Buffalo Bob," *Forbes*, April 19, 1999, p. 120.

Khermouch, Gerry, "Banfi's Beer Guy Rethinks Riunite," *Brandweek*, July 5, 1999, p. 12.

Thayer, Warren, "Riunite's Bubbly Rise to the Top of the Wine Market," *Marketing & Media Decisions*, Spring 1984, p. 85.

Bloomsbury Publishing PLC

36 Soho Square
London, W1D 3QY
United Kingdom
Telephone: (+44 020) 7494 2111
Fax: (+44 020) 7434 0151
Web site: http://www.bloomsbury.com

Public Company
Founded: 1986
Incorporated: 1994
Employees: 295
Sales: £99.95 million ($165 million) (2008)
Stock Exchanges: London
Ticker Symbol: BMY
NAICS: 511130 Book Publishers

∎ ∎ ∎

Bloomsbury Publishing PLC is one of the world's best-known midsize publishing companies, in large part due to the extraordinary success of the Harry Potter book series. While the Harry Potter series ended in 2007, Bloomsbury's Trade division continues to publish children's and literary fiction through its Bloomsbury, Berlin Verlag, Walker Publishing, and other imprints in the United Kingdom, the United States, and Germany. The company has also diversified into the specialist publishing field. Bloomsbury's Specialist division has a strong list of reference, academic, and business database titles and imprints, grouped under subsidiary A&C Black. The division manages such titles as *Who's Who* and *Whitaker's Almanac*; *Wisden Cricketers' Almanac*, published by John Wisden & Co; the *Arden Shakespeare*; *Bloomsbury Academic*, launched in 2008; and *Qatar Finance*, in partnership with Qatar Foundation. Bloomsbury Publishing is listed on the London Stock Exchange and is led by founder and CEO Nigel Newton. Approximately 70 percent of Bloomsbury's employees also hold shares in the company.

PUBLISHING ON A HUMAN SCALE IN 1986

Nigel Newton and partners Liz Calder, David Reynolds, and Alan Wherry founded Bloomsbury Publishing in London in 1986. Newton, born in the United States, was the son of Peter Newton, a British-born former *Financial Times* journalist and entrepreneur who also helped pioneer the Napa Valley wine industry. Nigel Newton, who held dual U.S.-British citizenship, studied English at Cambridge University, then joined Macmillan London as a sales director. In 1977, Newton joined another publishing house, Sidgwick & Jackson, rising to deputy managing director by the age of 27.

The 1980s represented a major period of consolidation for the publishing industry, marked by a series of mergers and acquisitions that resulted in the creation of a small number of large-scale publishing empires. Newton, however, spotted an opportunity in this market for a publishing company dedicated to remaining an independent, midsized firm able to operate on a human scale.

Newton soon recruited David Reynolds, who had also gained a reputation in the publishing world, to the project and the pair set about establishing a business

> ## COMPANY PERSPECTIVES
>
> Bloomsbury Publishing is one of Europe's leading independent publishing houses with a reputation for a high quality management team and a highly valuable portfolio of intellectual properties.

plan. They then added two other industry heavyweights, Liz Calder, the editor who had discovered Salman Rushdie and Julian Barnes, among others, and Alan Wherry, sales director of Penguin Books. By the middle of 1986, Newton had prepared a 50-page business plan that included allowing its authors to acquire shares of the company through a trust holding 5 percent of the company's shares. Newton named the company Bloomsbury, after the famous literary circle associated with Virginia Woolf.

Between the authors' trust and the Bloomsbury name, the company generated a great deal of interest, and by September 1986 had amassed nearly $3 million in start-up funding. The company also quickly lined up an impressive stable of writers, including Nadine Gordimer, John Irving, Scott Turow, and Jay McInerny. By the end of 1987, the company boasted nine best sellers.

PUBLIC OFFERING IN 1994

Literary fiction remained a company mainstay. From the start, however, Bloomsbury displayed a willingness to diversify its catalog into a variety of areas. Other company successes included Linda McCartney's *Home Cooking*, and a variety of other nonfiction titles. Into the early 1990s, half of the company's catalog consisted of nonfiction, with another 25 percent represented by reference works.

By 1990, the company's revenues had reached £6.7 million ($11 million). The company had also spread its operations into the United States, selling the print rights to many of its popular titles to other publishers there. By the beginning of the 1990s, these sales accounted for approximately 10 percent of the company's total revenues.

Bloomsbury had another major success in 2003 with Joanna Trollope's *A Spanish Lover*. For this, the company printed 1.3 million copies of the book's first chapter, partly funded by advertising, which were then included in the *Sunday Times* as a supplement. *Times* readers were also given a rebate coupon redeemable

within three days of the novel's publication. The campaign worked and the novel became a best seller for the company.

Bloomsbury's notoriety encouraged the company to go public with a listing on the London Stock Exchange in 1994. The listing, which included the 5 percent held by authors' trust, raised more than £27 million and provided the backing for the company's newest venture, the expansion of its operations into the children's literature sector. The company also launched paperback publishing that year.

HARRY POTTER MAGIC IN 1997

Bloomsbury continued to build on its reputation through the middle of the 1990s, signing on a number of notable authors including Margaret Atwood, Donna Tartt, and Michael Ondaatje, and becoming the first to publish a fully updated dictionary of synonyms since *Roget's Thesaurus*. At the same time, Bloomsbury had been building its presence in the United States, leading the company to create a dedicated subsidiary there in 1998. This move was accompanied by a new rights issue, raising an additional £6.1 million to fund the group's growing reference paperback and other operations. By 1999, the company's reference book division scored another major coup when it teamed up with Microsoft to develop and publish the *Encarta World English Dictionary* in print and CD form. Also in 1999, Bloomsbury formed a partnership with Macmillan to develop the English Language Teaching Database.

By then, Bloomsbury had become one of the world's most well-known publishing houses. In 1997, Newton reportedly asked his then eight-year-old daughter to read a manuscript for a children's book from an unknown writer, named J. K. Rowling. The book, which became the first in the Harry Potter series, sparked a global publishing phenomenon. By 2000, the release of the series' fourth book was accompanied by print runs of 1.5 million in the United Kingdom and nearly four million in the United States. These joined more than 35 million Harry Potter books already in print around the world, and quickly led to the first of several blockbuster films derived from the series.

Bloomsbury, which backed the launch of each Harry Potter title with increasingly lavish publicity campaigns, could claim credit for revolutionizing the market for children's and youth literature. The company's sales passed $20 million in 1998, and £21 million ($34 million) in 1999, then jumped to nearly £51 million ($71 million) in 2000. By mid-2001, the Harry Potter series had sold more than 105 million copies, and was responsible for more than half of Blooms-

KEY DATES

1986: Nigel Newton leads the founding of Bloomsbury Publishing in London.

1994: Bloomsbury goes public with a listing on the London Stock Exchange.

1997: Bloomsbury acquires the rights to the Harry Potter series.

2000: Bloomsbury acquires A&C Black in order to develop its specialist publishing division.

2007: Company releases the final volume in the Harry Potter series.

2010: Bloomsbury forms a science publishing joint venture based in Doha, Qatar.

bury's revenues. In that year, Bloomsbury launched a separate Bloomsbury Children's USA division to capitalize on the success of the Harry Potter series and other children's books in the United States.

ACQUISITION STRATEGY IN 2000

The success of the Harry Potter series provided Bloomsbury with the cash reserves to back a new expansion strategy. Rather than target further expansion in the children's literature market, Newton instead turned toward building the company's specialist publishing operations. The major part of this was accomplished with the acquisition of A&C Black PLC in 2000. That company had been founded at the beginning of the 19th century and had grown into a major British publishing house, producing *Black's Medical Dictionary* and the *Who's Who* series. A&C Black's imprints included noted ornithological publisher Christopher Helm, which published the *Helm Identification Guides*.

Bloomsbury also began building its Web presence, launching the Bloomsbury.com Web site in 2000. In 2001, the company also teamed up with the *Economist* to develop an online business database. The first part of this work, called *Business—The Ultimate Resource*, was released in 2002.

That year was marked by a flurry of acquisitions, starting with *Whitaker's Almanac*, in publication since 1868. Soon after, the group acquired the T&AD Poyser Natural History imprint, created in 1973 to publish ornithology works. T&AD Poyser was merged into A&C Black following its acquisition. In September 2002, A&C Black completed a new acquisition, of Thomas Reed Publications. Founded in 1768, this company focused on producing nautical guides and

other books, including *Reed's Nautical Almanac*, for the professional and leisure boating market. Next, Bloomsbury expanded its reference publishing operations with the purchase of Peter Collin Publishing, which specialized in publishing English and bilingual books, as well as *Bradford's Crossword Dictionary*, travel guides, and phrase books.

ENTERING GERMANY IN 2003

Bloomsbury took advantage of a slump in the German publishing industry to gain access to that market, the third largest after the U.S. and U.K. markets. In April 2003, the company acquired Berlin Verlag, founded by Arnulf Conradi in 1994. Berlin Verlag focused on adult fiction, and already published German-language editions of a number of Bloomsbury's books. Following the acquisition, Bloomsbury began developing a list of its children's titles under the Berlin Verlag imprint as well. The move into Germany became part of the group's policy of acquiring titles with international appeal, which then received simultaneous launches in the group's three markets. The company completed the year with another acquisition, of Nautical Data Ltd.

Bloomsbury's acquisitions helped broaden the company's revenue base, as its sales rose to £83 million ($133 million) by the end of 2003. The company continued to seek new purchases. This led to the December 2004 agreement to acquire Walker Publishing Company for $7 million. That company had been founded in 1959 and had built up a strong reputation for its list of children's titles, as well as nonfiction and adult fiction titles.

Bloomsbury's acquisition strategy continued to focus on building its specialist publishing division into the second half of the decade. The company's purchases included Methuen Drama, one of the United Kingdom's leading publishers of dramatic works, in 2006, and, in 2008, Featherstone Education, Oxford International Publishers, and its Berg Publishers imprints, John Wisden & Co, publisher of the famed *Wisden's Cricketers' Almanac*, and the *Arden Shakespeare*, the leading publisher of scholarly works and editions of the plays of Shakespeare.

POST-POTTER FROM 2007

Bloomsbury in the meantime had continued to set new records with the launches of the remaining titles in the Harry Potter series. In 2005, for example, the company sold more than two million copies of the sixth volume of the series in just 24 hours in the United Kingdom. The launch of the final volume in 2007 performed even better, selling more than 2.6 million copies in the United Kingdom on the first day of its release. In that week, the company claimed to have captured 88 percent of all U.K. book sales.

The Harry Potter series had continued to fuel Bloomsbury's sales growth into the second half of the decade, raising its revenues past £109 million ($160 million) in 2005, and then setting a new record of more than £151 million ($240 million) in 2007. While the company had developed a series of spin-off products based on the Harry Potter series to be rolled out over the next several years, it nonetheless braced itself for its post-Potter era.

Bloomsbury's sales inevitably slipped the following year, tumbling to £99.98 million for 1998. The company nonetheless celebrated a number of successes that year, including the release of the best-selling *A Thousand Splendid Suns* by Khaled Hosseini, and a new J. K. Rowling novel written for the Children's High Level Group charity. The company also maintained a strong treasury of nearly £50 million, built up through the success of the Harry Potter series.

Bloomsbury also faced difficult trading conditions brought on by the global economic downturn, which intensified through 2009. The company nonetheless continued to seek new opportunities. In July of that year, Bloomsbury completed the acquisition of Tottel Publishing, a noted publisher of legal and related books. That company was then renamed Bloomsbury Professional. Also in 2009, Bloomsbury launched Qfinance, developed in partnership with Qatar Financial Centre Authority, formed in 2007.

This partnership was complemented with an agreement with the Qatar Foundation in 2008 to develop Arabic- and English-language works. In January 2010, Bloomsbury extended this relationship, launching a new joint venture with Qatar Foundation and Qatar National Research Fund to launch a new publishing company focused on the science market, to be based in Doha. While best known for its association with Harry Potter, Bloomsbury hoped its focus on the specialist publishing sector would provide it with the magic formula for growth into the new decade.

M. L. Cohen

PRINCIPAL SUBSIDIARIES

A & C Black Plc; Bloomsbury Book Publishing Company Limited; Bloomsbury Information Limited; Blooms-bury Publishing Inc. (USA); BV Berlin Verlag GmbH (Germany); Peter Collin Publishing Limited; Walker Publishing Company, Inc. (USA); Writer's Café, Inc.

PRINCIPAL DIVISIONS

Specialist; Trade.

PRINCIPAL OPERATING UNITS

A&C Black; Bloomsbury.

PRINCIPAL COMPETITORS

Berkshire Hathaway Inc.; Bertelsmann AG; Thomson Reuters PLC; Reed Elsevier PLC; Wiley Publishing Inc.; McGraw-Hill Companies Inc.; Wolters Kluwer N.V.; Axel Springer Verlag AG.

FURTHER READING

"Bloomsbury Goes for 'Bendyback,'" *Bookseller*, January 15, 2010, p. 5.

Carvajal, Doreen, "If Harry Potter Vanishes, What's Next for British Publisher?" *New York Times*, July 18, 2005, p. C4.

Davoudi, Salamander, "Bloomsbury Pins Hopes on Blumenthal," *Financial Times*, August 28, 2009, p. 16.

Edgecliffe-Johnson, Andrew, "Bloomsbury Looks to Five Years of Potter," *Financial Times*, April 5, 2006, p. 20.

Fenton, Ben, "Bloomsbury Feels the Loss of Potter's Magic," *Financial Times*, April 1, 2009, p. 19.

———, "Bloomsbury Seeks Revenue Magic from Energy Database," *Financial Times*, October 5, 2009, p. 20.

Jones, Philip, "Tough First Half for Bloomsbury," *Bookseller*, September 4, 2009, p. 8.

Lawless, John, "Beyond Harry Potter," *Business Week*, May 30, 2005, p. 54.

Morais, Richard C., "Bloomsbury Blooms," *Forbes*, January 27, 1997, p. 58.

Tivnan, Tom, "My Noughties," *Bookseller*, December 18, 2009, p. 21.

Velaigam, Malar, "Bloomsbury Continues to Diversify," *Investors Chronicle*, October 19, 2009.

———, "Bloomsbury Presses On," *Investors Chronicle*, January 15, 2010.

Wylie, Ian, "Harry Potter's Corporate Parent," *Fast Company*, August 31, 2001.

Bravo Company

───────■───────

30 Rockefeller Plaza, 8th Floor East
New York, New York 10112
U.S.A.
Telephone: (212) 664-4444
Web site: http://www.bravotv.com

Wholly Owned Subsidiary of NBC Universal
Founded: 1980
Employees: 100
Sales: $370 million (2007 est.)
NAICS: 515210 Cable and Other Subscription Programming

■ ■ ■

Bravo Company operates the popular cable channel Bravo. Originally focused on fine arts and cultural programming, Bravo radically switched gears in 2003 after NBC acquired it. Most shows on the network are reality-based and feature competitions, celebrities, and assorted oddball characters. Popular programs have included *Queer Eye for the Straight Guy*, *Project Runway*, *Millionaire Matchmaker*, and the *Real Housewives* franchise. Bravo reaches 80 million U.S. households.

ESTABLISHING A NICHE: 1980–89

In December 1980, a Long Island-based cable company, Cablevision Systems, launched Bravo Company as a two-night-per-week cable programming service that featured performing arts programs such as opera and ballet. Bravo shared the channel with an R-rated adult movie service, Escapade, which aired on the other five nights. Bravo's addition to the channel was intended to make Escapade more acceptable to a mainstream audience. However, the combination of the two channels was not a success and they soon split. Escapade became the Playboy channel. Bravo filled its 12-hour schedule with an evolving mix of cultural programming.

By 1982 the network had approximately 75,000 monthly subscribers. It had also added films to the schedule. The network specialized in art films commonly shown in the film-repertory theaters of large cities: European works, American fringe productions, and neglected gems of times past from directors including Federico Fellini, François Truffaut, Jean-Luc Godard, and Akira Kurosawa. Bravo's devotion to these films represented a kind of network-wide counterprogramming. "We're looking for a niche to establish ourselves in," said Bravo's general manager, Robert Weisberg, in a 1985 *New York Times* article. In addition to being cost-effective for the network, the films were also crowd-pleasers. According to monthly questionnaires, Bravo had the highest viewer satisfaction levels in the cable industry. The remainder of the schedule was devoted to performing arts programs, including ballet, opera, dance, and jazz concerts.

Art films proved to be so successful that Bravo added more to the schedule in the following years, branching out to include independent U.S. productions, obscure foreign directors, and historically significant movies. Its subscriber base swelled, growing to 350,000 by 1985. That year, Bravo increased its partnerships with cable operators around the United States. It also began coproducing performing arts programs such as

Jazz Counterpoint, a documentary series featuring interviews and performances by famous jazz musicians.

Bravo underwent changes in 1987 when Josh Sapan was appointed president. To build popularity with viewers, he changed the network's programming, increasing films to 60 percent of the schedule. Additionally, Sapan began campaigning among cable operators to distribute Bravo as part of basic cable services. To do this, he changed the network's revenue model, lowering fees for cable operators and seeking new sources of revenue from sponsors including Texaco, Kodak, and Mercedes-Benz. Subsequently, Bravo began running public television-like sponsorship announcements pre- and post-program. By 1988, these sponsorships evolved into full-scale commercials between shows.

As a sponsor-supported network, Bravo had an upscale, high-income demographic that ranged in age from 25 to 54 and attracted high-end marketers including Saab, IBM, and American Express. Viewers tended to be affluent, educated, and lived in large cities, upscale suburbs, and college communities. Citing Nielsen Media Research figures, Bravo boasted it had the highest concentration of any ad-supported network, broadcast or cable, of upscale professional adults with an average household income of $60,000.

FLOURISHING AS AN ARTS NETWORK: 1990–94

By the early 1990s Bravo was growing rapidly. In 1990, its subscriber base increased by one million for a total of five million subscribers. The network passed the 10-million-subscriber mark in 1992, up 43 percent in one year. By 1993 the network was profitable for the first time since its launch 12 years earlier, making it the fastest-growing U.S. cable channel. As the only major television network without a cable arm, NBC became a shareholder of Bravo to gain a foothold in the cable market.

Bravo used the influx of revenue to further expand its market. In 1993 it launched several projects that

helped to establish Bravo as a highbrow yet accessible network that was relevant to local communities. *Community Cinema* showcased the work of local filmmakers; *Culture in the Classroom* provided commercial-free programming for teachers; *Unfinished Stories* featured documentaries and provided funding to AIDS care-giving organizations. Another original Bravo series, *Arts-Break*, was a news program that covered major arts events in U.S. communities, including film festivals, jazz concerts, and dance troupes. Of these new programs, Sapan said in a 1993 *Electronic Media* article, "We want to keep cultural television alive by making it more available to people who don't partake [in it] by not being snooty or elitist."

In 1994 Bravo subscribers topped 11.5 million, and the network increased its programming schedule from 12 to 24 hours per day. To capitalize on the popularity of its films, it launched a new premium cable service devoted to the types of movies that appealed to its audience, the Independent Film Channel, which was met with enthusiasm by famous filmmakers and prestigious universities. Additionally, Bravo expanded the scope of its original programming and debuted *Inside the Actors' Studio*. In the first several years, guests included Tom Hanks, Harrison Ford, Julia Roberts, Steven Spielberg, Robert De Niro, and Anthony Hopkins. The show went on to become the network's breakthrough program in terms of awareness and recognition. *Inside* helped define Bravo's brand and consistently drew more viewers than the network's prime-time average.

ADVERTISING AND ORIGINAL PROGRAMMING: 1995–2001

A year later, Bravo's audience had doubled to 22 million homes in 1995. However, about this time the cable market shifted dramatically, forcing Bravo executives to rethink their film-focused schedule. New networks flooded the cable market and competition for viewers became fierce. Moreover, Bravo had been largely alone in its arts-focused programming in the past, whereas now it competed with several new start-ups. Plus, the competitive market translated into skyrocketing prices for movie packages. To differentiate itself from its competitors, garner audience attention, and remain profitable, Bravo's programming strategy switched to original programming. The plan was to debut several new series and one or two big-scale specials per year.

In an effort to raise revenue for the original programming, in 1998 without warning, Bravo began selling traditional commercial spots that aired during programs. Immediately, Bravo was barraged with complaints and criticism from viewers and critics. Ratings took a nosedive and some viewers abandoned the network. The switch to commercial programming had been in the works for some time. Bravo had anticipated fallout and had specifically created its sister channel, the Independent Film Channel, for the viewers who jumped ship.

Advertising brought in a large influx of revenue and Bravo was able to double its programming budget. It invested $20 million into its first original eight-hour miniseries, *The Count of Monte Cristo*, which aired the summer of 1999. Starring French actor Gérard Depardieu and featuring English subtitles, *Monte Cristo* was the highest-rated original program in the network's history, scoring a 1.4 Nielsen Media Research rating. That year, Bravo also launched a weekly satirical news show created by controversial filmmaker Michael Moore, *The Awful Truth*, and a documentary on the world-famous circus group Cirque du Soleil.

In 1999 Bravo reached 50 million homes. That year, total revenues topped $68 million of which $33 million was spent on programming. The network's rapid growth was due in large part to its focus on advertising, rather than subscriber fees, to generate revenue. To take advantage of special advertising deals, more and more cable operators included it in their basic package. Bravo's distribution deals were huge.

Flush with cash from both ad revenue and new distribution deals, in 2001 Bravo splurged on big-ticket programming. It licensed two major shows, *The Larry Sanders Show* and *The West Wing*, in an effort to attract new viewers and broaden its subscriber base. These shows were a considerable departure from such past acquisitions as *Max Headroom*, *Twin Peaks*, and *Moonlighting*, which all had a cult following. There was concern at the time that this move would change

Bravo's audience, lowering its average total income bracket. That year, Cablevision invested $825 million in the network and sought additional partners. Metro-Goldwyn-Mayer purchased a 20 percent stake.

SHIFTING OWNERSHIP AND PRIORITIES: 2002–03

In 2002 NBC bought Bravo for $1.25 billion from Cablevision and Metro-Goldwyn-Mayer. At the time, Bravo ranked 11th among cable networks and reached 68 million households, well ahead of competitors A&E and Trio. Regarding the direction the network would go after acquisition, in a 2002 *Los Angeles Times* article NBC's chief executive, Bob Wright, said: "We'll continue it in the vein it is today." In 2003 NBC appointed Jeff Gaspin, a former programming executive at VH1, president of Bravo. Gaspin claimed that Bravo's schedule would not become heavily laden with repurposed NBC shows.

However, programming changes were in the works and Gaspin began stretching the definition of Bravo's artsy tradition. Several new programs slated for the network in 2003 diverged markedly from the past. A new series, *Queer Eye for the Straight Guy*, featured five gay men who remade the living space and fashion style of one straight guy. Planned specials included *Showbiz Moms*, a reality show about mothers in the entertainment industry, and *Significant Others*, a comedy series about couples in marriage counseling. Repurposed NBC content, *Kingpin* and *Boomtown*, were also on the schedule. Although the new shows were a significant departure from Bravo's past programming, Gaspin did not think they were a step down culturally. In a June 2003 *Advertising Age* article he said, "We don't want to become low rent with the programming that we do. ... We don't want to become common."

When *Queer Eye* launched in July 2003, Bravo became the most buzzed-about network on cable. Week-by-week Bravo's ratings grew exponentially. Signifying an audience shift, the network's median viewer age dropped from 50.8 to 45.3. By November 2003 *Queer Eye* mania had peaked, and NBC was eager to duplicate its success. Gaspin's spin on the network's goal had also significantly shifted. In a November 2003 *Television Week* interview, he said, "We want to come out next summer with a new look." He described Bravo as a "hip and cool network for a young, hip crowd." When Bravo's programming schedule for 2004 was announced, the lineup included a mixture of reality-based and pop culture performance shows. Programs included *Project Runway*, *Celebrity Poker Showdown*, and *Kathy Griffin: My Life on the D-List*.

REALITY SHOWS AND PRODUCT PLACEMENT: 2004–10

In 2004 Bravo's subscriber base topped 76 million households and the network had a new president, Lauren Zalaznick. In a 2004 *New York Times* article, Zalaznick explained Bravo's new strategy: "to produce programs that offer interesting and new perspectives, unique twists on popular trends, and that take viewers behind the scenes of the creative process in entertaining and compelling ways." A year later, Bravo spent $130 million on programming and there were more than 30 series and specials in development. New competitions and reality shows included *Top Chef, Real Housewives of Orange County, Being Bobby Brown,* and *Ex Wives Club.* Research indicated that the network's median age had dropped to 41 and that it still attracted upscale viewers. Bravo had undergone a complete transformation.

Bravo's abrupt change in direction confused many in the industry. At the time, industry pundits talked about how Bravo was indistinguishable from its competitors. "They're all over the map," said Robert Sawyer, a creative director and brand strategist in a 2004 *New York Times* article. "They don't have a position. … Couldn't the same shows be on E?" Due to increasing competition from other cable networks that also focused on reality programming, ratings lagged. According to a 2005 *Variety* article, to differentiate Bravo's reality shows from the competition, Zalaznick's approach was to make them "more upscale, hopefully hipper."

A few years later, in 2007, Bravo officials declared their target demographic had shifted to 18- to 49-year-olds. Of this switch, Bravo's vice president of ad sales, Susan Malfa, said in a 2007 *Multichannel News* article, "It's the best audience in cable. … They buy things. They set trends." Targeting an affluent audience interested in buying products became increasingly important. In 2007 Bravo began selling branded merchandise, including books, games, and gym clothes. Integrating sponsored products into shows, such as *Top Chef* and *Top Design,* became standard. Advertisers liked product placement because it offered a new way to market their goods. As the network ramped up its sales pitches for its show-branded and advertisers' merchandise, there was skepticism in the industry that viewers would respond well to outright sales pitches. Many viewers took note and complained. In 2008 several Web sites emerged, spoofing the blatant advertisements and suggesting drinking games for each time a brand name was mentioned.

In 2008 Bravo had the highest concentration of viewers in households making more than $125,000. Additionally, various studies showed that Bravo's audience was growing increasingly upscale, educated, trendy, and engaged—all characteristics of an audience that spent significantly and were highly attractive to advertisers. Its first-quarter ad sales that year were up 20 percent. The network had broken into cable's top 20 among adults 18 to 49. Seventy-five percent of its programming was original.

In 2009 Bravo added *The Fashion Show* to its lineup to replace *Project Runway,* which it lost when the show moved to the Lifetime network. It also debuted *NYC Prep,* a reality show focused on the lives of rich and entitled high schoolers. The network reached 80 million homes. However, doubts were growing in the industry about the wisdom of Bravo's fascination with the rich and famous during the worst economic downturn since the Great Depression. Viewers who were increasingly worried about their jobs might not respond well to programming about glamour and glitz.

Carrie Rothburd

PRINCIPAL COMPETITORS

A&E Television Networks, LLC; Discovery Communications, Inc.; E! Entertainment Television, Inc.; FX Networks, LLC; MTV Networks Company; TBS Superstation, Inc.; WE: Women's Entertainment, LLC.

FURTHER READING

Cleland, Kim, "Bravo Steps Up to Big Leagues," *Advertising Age,* May 15, 2000, p. S14.

Donlon, Brian, "Bravo Channels Culture through Cable," *USA Today,* December 26, 1990, p. 3D.

Ellin, Abby, "Bravo Learns to Make Noise and Have Fun," *New York Times,* July 5, 2004, p. C1.

Gubernick, Lisa, "Bravo!" *Forbes,* April 26, 1993, p. 197.

Hibberd, James, "Bravo's Gaspin Talks Content," *Television Week,* December 1, 2003, p. 3.

Jensen, Elizabeth, "A Bravo New World," *Los Angeles Times,* April 30, 1999, p. 2.

Lee, Will, "Bravo's Taste Shifts to Pricier Shows," *Cable World,* August 20, 2001, p. 16.

Martin, Denise, "Bravo Needs an Encore," *Variety,* July 25, 2005, p. 18.

Moss, Linda, "Bravo Trumpets Young, Affluent Audience," *Multichannel News,* April 16, 2007, p. 17.

Romano, Allison, "Bravo! NBC Has a Cable Net," *Broadcast Cable,* November 22, 2002, p. 12.

Schneider, Steve, "Cable TV Notes; Bravo Thrives on Culture," *New York Times,* December 15, 1985, p. 36.

Whitney, Daisy, "Bravo Stretches, Adds Viewers & Advertisers," *Advertising Age,* June 9, 2003, p. S14.

Brightstar Corp.

9725 NW 117th Avenue, Suite 300
Miami, Florida 33178
U.S.A.
Telephone: (305) 421-6000
Fax: (305) 513-3959
Web site: http://www.brightstarcorp.com

Private Company
Incorporated: 1997
Employees: 2,101
Sales: $3.6 billion (2008 est.)
NAICS: 423610 Electrical Apparatus and Equipment, Wiring Supplies, and Related Merchant Wholesalers; 517212 Cellular and Other Wireless Telecommunications

■ ■ ■

Brightstar Corp. is a Miami, Florida-based, private company that specializes in the global distribution of wireless communications products from more than 60 manufacturers, including such major brands of cellphones and smart phones as Motorola, Kyocera, Samsung, LG, and Sony Ericsson. Additionally, Brightstar distributes wireless modems, wireless broadband communication devices, and branded and aftermarket accessories. All told, the company customizes and ships products to more than 160,000 points of sale around the world. Brightstar's distribution business unit also includes the Idea to Consumer division, which develops fixed wireless phones for sale under its own brand as well as Tier 1 and Tier 2 brands, including Motorola and Kyocera.

Brightstar's second business unit, Integrated Supply Chain Solutions, provides retailers and wireless network operators with outsourced supply chain services, including the sourcing of products at a discounted price; estimation of product demand; sales and operations planning; inventory management; merchandising assistance; and customer care and repair services. The company employs about 2,100 people located in offices in more than 40 countries spread across Latin America, Europe, the Middle East and Africa, and Asia and the South Pacific. Brightstar is the largest Hispanic-owned business in the United States. One of the company's founders, R. Marcelo Claure, serves as chairman, president, and chief executive officer.

COFOUNDER, A WELL TRAVELED YOUTH

The son of a Bolivian diplomat, Marcelo Claure was born in Guatemala and lived in a number of other countries, including the Dominican Republic and Morocco. After completing high school in Bolivia, he earned a business degree from Bentley College in Waltham, Massachusetts, in the early 1990s. He was not an especially avid student, but possessed an entrepreneurial streak. In kindergarten he was known to sell marbles from a case to fellow students.

After college Claure served as a chief lieutenant in the successful bid of the notoriously poor Bolivia national soccer team to land a berth in the World Cup. He then returned to Boston and became involved in a gray-market business, buying and selling frequent-flier miles, with his best friend, Alan Mota. In order to receive sales calls night and day, they shopped for a cellphone and quickly realized that all of the Boston-area stores offered poor service. One store owner expressed his distaste for the business, prompting Claure to offer to buy the store, with no money down but payment in full within six months. Not only did Claure keep his end of the bargain, he and Mota quickly grew the business into a 134-store northeastern chain, USA Wireless, which became Bell Atlantic's largest dealer in the United States.

FORMATION OF BRIGHTSTAR: 1997

Claure sold USA Wireless and became president of Small World Communications, a struggling California-based cellphone chain that he turned around. Because of his roots, Claure recognized that wireless penetration was low in Latin America and that there was an opening for a distributor to dominate that market. Thus, in October 1997 Claure and partners sold assets and borrowed money, moved to Miami, and established a company to distribute cellphones in Latin American countries. Indicative of their ambitions, they combined the names of the top competitors in the market, Texas-based CellStar Corp. and Indiana-based Brightpoint Inc., to coin Brightstar Corp.

Because Brightstar was unable to attract bank financing in the beginning, it found a way to make money by purchasing Motorola phones through Bell Canada, which was able to receive a better volume discount by buying extra phones. Brightstar then sold the phones to retailers in the United States and Latin America for less than what Motorola charged. Brightstar had hoped to achieve $50,000 in sales for the final three months of 1997 but instead posted $14 million in sales. The company then scouted the Far East and secured sources of less-expensive Asian-assembled phones, and resold them at a hefty profit. Soon Brightstar had no problem arranging for bank financing.

In 1998 Brightstar opened offices in Bolivia and Brazil to provide the kind of localized support that became a key to its success. At the time, Nokia held a

60 percent market share. Ericsson had negligible sales and with little to lose made Brightstar its main Latin America distributor. Given that Ericsson phones were both expensive and unattractive, Brightstar elected to focus on the only aspect it could control, making doing business with them as easy as possible. While other manufacturers simply let the network carriers worry about how their products were brought into Latin American countries, Brightstar took care of all the problems when it came to supplying Ericsson phones to the carriers. There were no minimum orders, delivery was direct, and payment terms were generous. Carriers quickly grew dependent on Brightstar and as a result Ericsson's market share doubled within the year. Brightstar also saw its revenues soar to $73 million.

COMPANY AGREES TO BE ACQUIRED: 1998

Brightstar began to expand its service offerings in 1998. It provided value-added services to several wireless network carriers in Brazil, and in October 1998 Telecel, Bolivia's largest operator, contracted Brightstar to take over all of its handset and accessory distribution. The young company's rapid growth did not go unnoticed. Brightstar began receiving acquisition offers, and in October 1998 Brightstar agreed to be acquired by Miami-based CHS Electronics Inc., then one of the world's largest distributors of personal computers, peripherals, and software.

The global footprint of CHS held obvious advantages, and Brightstar took advantage of the pending acquisition to establish operations within CHS offices in all major Latin America markets. As a result, Ericsson expanded its relationship with Brightstar, signing a distribution and logistics contract with Brightstar, which now handled such in-country value-added services as customization, private labeling, and after-sales support. The CHS infrastructure also allowed Brightstar to forge relationships with all of the major operators in Latin America and by mid-1999 Brightstar was serving the major players.

The deal with CHS never came to fruition, however. In 1999, as the technology sector collapsed, publicly traded CHS began to experience severe financial problems, leading to a plummeting stock price. CHS sold assets, returned ownership to some of its acquisitions, and was still forced to seek Chapter 11 bankruptcy protection in 2000. The Brightstar acquisition had been slated to close in November 1999 with an initial purchase payment, but in October CHS declared it would be unable to comply and Brightstar's shares were returned to its founders.

KEY DATES

1997: Company is established in Miami.
1999: Sale of business to CHS Electronics Inc. is canceled.
2000: Supply Chain Solutions division is formed.
2004: Initial public offering of stock is shelved.
2007: Lindsay Goldberg invests $283 million in Brightstar.

Brightstar enjoyed benefits from the CHS interlude while, in the end, retaining its independence, but without the deep pockets of a corporate parent, Brightstar now had to focus on internal growth. The company proved more than capable of pursuing such a strategy. While others in the telecom field struggled, and in many cases went out of business, Brightstar continued to enjoy robust growth, providing a cost benefit to its customers that during lean times made its services more attractive than ever. As soon as the agreement with Ericsson expired in 2000, Motorola was quick to sign Brightstar as its master distributor in Latin America. It proved to be a wise decision. In a matter of three years Motorola doubled its market share in the region to 33 percent, mostly at the expense of Nokia, which was now reduced to a similar slice of the market.

SUPPLY CHAIN SOLUTIONS: 2000

Brightstar also drove growth through further diversification. In 2000 it formed the Supply Chain Solutions division, and soon signed its first supply chain contract with Codetel in the Dominican Republic. Brightstar also expanded its Latin America presence in 2000 by launching subsidiaries in Argentina, Ecuador, Uruguay, and Venezuela. For the year Brightstar doubled sales to $355 million.

While Latin America with its low penetration of cellphones and poorly developed supply chain infrastructure was an ideal market to crack, Brightstar was not afraid of doing business in the extremely competitive U.S. market, which the company entered along with Canada in 2001. It also added subsidiaries in Peru and El Salvador and launched a Global Wireless Data division to help drive revenues to $631 million in 2001.

Never complacent, Brightstar formed a division in 2002 to focus on smart phones, modems, and broadband products. It also opened a manufacturing division to develop fixed wireless phones for Latin America, and opened its first manufacturing facility in Mexico. Sales increased to $848 million in 2002 and $1.2 billion in 2003, as Brightstar became the third Hispanic-owned business to ever reach the $1 billion sales mark. Brightstar now eyed the European and Asian markets, and sought to build its own assembly plants and shipping facilities. To fund its aspirations, Brightstar turned to a private placement of stock, and in January 2004 sold a 27 percent stake in the company for $61.75 million to Falcon Investment Advisors, Prudential Capital Group, Ramius Capital Group, and Bill Gates-controlled Grandview Capital Management.

CANCELLATION OF IPO: 2004

Flush with cash, Brightstar opened subsidiaries in Australia and Hong Kong in 2004, and reentered the Brazilian market. The company filed for an initial public offering (IPO) of stock in hopes of raising an additional $115 million, but the offering was canceled due to poor market conditions. With $1.7 billion in revenues in 2004, however, Brightstar was hardly in desperate need of additional cash.

Internal growth increased further in 2005 when Brightstar became the authorized U.S. distributor for Verizon Wireless and the exclusive sourcing partner for Australia's market leader, Telstra. In that same year, Brightstar formed a subsidiary in Mumbai, India, a market that was more than twice as large as Latin America. Brightstar was especially interested in pursuing the fixed wireless business in India, offering traditional-looking desk phones that relied on wireless technology instead of landlines, especially popular in rural areas that lacked a telecommunications infrastructure. Brightstar sold devices under its Avvido brand developed for the market as well as products from other manufacturers.

After posting revenues of $2.25 billion in 2005, Brightstar became the world's largest wireless distribution and supply chain solutions company. On its way to $4.3 billion in gross revenues in 2006, the company entered northern Africa and the Middle East through a joint venture with Aptec Distribution FZ LLC, a major information technology distributor in the region, and opened new sales distributions centers in South Africa as well as Malaysia, the Philippines, and Singapore.

RAISING EXPANSION FUNDS: 2007

Brightstar received further financing in 2007. The Japanese conglomerate Mitsui & Co. bought $50 million in stock, the money earmarked for the expansion of Asia-Pacific operations. Later in the year Brightstar received $283 million in equity financing from Lindsay

Goldberg, a New York-based investment partnership, which became the second-largest shareholder after Claure. To expand its European business, Brightstar formed a joint venture with Tech Data, an information technology products distributor, in 2007. It also formed Brightstar Retail with WSA Distributing to add to the mix such consumer electronics products as cordless phones, two-way radios, flat screens, and MP3 players.

Brightstar, after just 10 years in operation, recorded gross revenues of $4.8 billion in 2007, representing a 5 percent global market share for wireless devices. The company expanded on a number of fronts in 2008. It entered Eastern Europe and signed an exclusive supply chain services contract in Turkey with the country's second-largest operator, Vodafone Turkey. A year later a similar deal was struck with Hong Kong's largest operator, CSL Limited, and Alegro in Ecuador. The Brightstar Europe joint venture expanded into Germany and Brightstar also signed a pan-European agreement to distribute BlackBerry products. Moreover, the company received several U.S. patents for wireless technology. As a result of its breadth, both in terms of market reach and capabilities, Brightstar was well-positioned for continued future growth.

Ed Dinger

PRINCIPAL DIVISIONS

Distribution; Integrated Supply Chain Solutions.

PRINCIPAL COMPETITORS

Brightpoint, Inc.; Ingram Micro Inc.; TESSCO Technologies Incorporated.

FURTHER READING

Garcia, Beatrice E., "Miami-Based Cell Phone Distributor Wants to Go Public," *Miami Herald*, August 11, 2004.

———, "Miami-Based Distributor of Mobile Phones, Services Enjoys Meteoric Rise," *Miami Herald*, January 19, 2004.

Hemlock, Doreen, "Brightstar to Tap Indian Market," *South Florida Sun-Sentinel*, December 31, 2005.

Jacobs, Daniel G., "How R. Marcelo Claure Diversified Brightstar from a Simple Distributor into a Dynamic Enterprise," *Smart Business*, July 2006.

McDougall, Christopher, "Closing the Deal," *Inc.*, March 1, 2004.

Reveron, Derek, "Shining Through," *Hispanic Business Magazine*, June 2007.

Russell, Joel, "Why Brightstar Shines," *Hispanic Business Magazine*, January/February 2004.

British American Tobacco PLC

---

4 Temple Pl., Globe House
London, WC2R 2PG
United Kingdom
Telephone: (+44 207) 845 1000
Fax: (+44 207) 845 2214
Web site: http://www.bat.com

Public Company
Incorporated: 1902
Employees: 95,710
Sales: £40.71 billion ($65.2 billion) (2009)
Stock Exchanges: London
Ticker Symbol: BATS
NAICS: 312221 Cigarette Manufacturing; 312229 Other Tobacco Product Manufacturing

■ ■ ■

British American Tobacco PLC (BAT) is one of the world's largest producers of cigarettes and other tobacco products. The company operates on a global basis through its Global Drive Brand (GDB) portfolio, which includes the Dunhill, Kent, Pall Mall, and Lucky Strike brands. BAT also markets Vogue, Viceroy, Rothmans, Kool, State 555, Peter Stuyvesant, John Player Gold Leaf, and Benson & Hedges brands to specific regional markets. In 2009, BAT sold more than 700 billion "sticks" (the industry term for individual cigarettes) directly, and another 183 billion sticks through its associate companies. The latter includes the group's 42 percent stake in Reynolds American Inc., which acquired BAT's U.S. operations in 2004.

In addition to cigarette sales, BAT also markets looseleaf tobacco for the roll-your-own market. The company has also been developing international sales of "snus," a Swedish variety of chewing tobacco. BAT reported gross sales of £40.7 billion ($65 million) in 2009, for net revenues of £14.2 billion ($22.7 billion). The company is listed on the London Stock Exchange and is led by CEO Paul Adams.

ORIGINS IN ANGLO-AMERICAN TRADE WAR

British American Tobacco originated from a compromise between two rival tobacco manufacturers, one American and one British. James Buchanan ("Buck") Duke, head of the highly successful American Tobacco Company, decided in 1901 to make a bid for the U.K. market. In response, several smaller independent British tobacco companies banded together to form the Imperial Tobacco Company Ltd. It was from these two tobacco companies that British American Tobacco was born.

Imperial Tobacco was able to resist American Tobacco's attempt to capture its native market but only after a prolonged trade war that proved expensive for both companies. After American Tobacco withdrew from the English marketplace, Imperial was in a stronger position and decided to press its advantage.

When Imperial started to make moves toward the U.S. market, Chairman Duke saw the need for a compromise. A truce was called, and the two rival merchants agreed not to conduct business in each other's domestic markets. Each company also assigned brand rights to the other so that consumers who had

```
┌─────────────────────────────────────────┐
│                                         │
│     COMPANY PERSPECTIVES                │
│     ────────────────■───────────        │
│                                         │
│     Our vision is to achieve leadership of the global │
│     tobacco industry in order to create shareholder value. │
│                                         │
└─────────────────────────────────────────┘
```

grown accustomed to a given brand would not be lost. This deal also initiated the creation of a new company, British American Tobacco (BAT), of which American Tobacco owned two-thirds and Duke was the first chairman.

BRITISH AMERICAN TOBACCO IN 1902

This new company, registered in London in 1902, acquired the recipes and trademarks of both originating companies. It also acquired all the export business and overseas production operations of each company. The new company's sales and growth potential seemed limited compared to the successes of Imperial and American. Nevertheless, the company grew slowly but steadily during the first decade of the century.

In 1911 the U.S. government sued many U.S. tobacco companies in an early application of antitrust law. Both British American Tobacco and American Tobacco were among the defendants. On appeal, the Supreme Court ruled that much of the domestic tobacco industry engaged in illegal practices in restraint of trade. The Court sent the case back to a special four-judge panel appointed to hear the case in the first instance to devise a remedy. The panel's disposition of the case harmed neither of Duke's companies. In an arrangement approved by the panel, American Tobacco canceled most of its covenants with British American Tobacco and Imperial and sold all of its shares in British American. Most of the sold shares were bought by British investors, and subsequently British American Tobacco was listed on the London Stock Exchange.

This left British American Tobacco, still chaired by Duke, able to sell its product independently all over the world, except in the United Kingdom where it was still bound by its covenant with Imperial. Imperial at this time also retained a one-third share of British American, but this did little to impair the company's success. Duke's operation began rapid expansion of British exports and overseas operations. Many new subsidiaries were established around the world during the brief period between the disentanglement from American Tobacco and World War I. Local sources of raw materi-

als were discovered and developed, and international sales grew steadily.

The war brought large numbers of women into the company for the first time. The women were employed primarily in the distribution of cigarettes to the troops abroad, most of whom had switched to cigarettes from the less convenient pipe. The switch, although initiated by soldiers during wartime, caught on with civilians internationally, and British American began selling cigarettes in increasing numbers.

The end of the war brought even greater fortunes to British American Tobacco. Historically, no commercial enterprise had been able to penetrate the huge Chinese market beyond the coastal government trading stations. British American, under Duke's leadership, was able to exploit this untapped interior market. It achieved record growth in the years immediately following this breakthrough, and maintained impressive sales levels throughout the rest of Duke's chairmanship. While chairman, Duke was the pioneer of British American's growth. The company's next chairman, Sir Hugo Cunliffe-Owen, was its pioneer of decentralization.

DECENTRALIZATION & GROWTH: 1923–62

Sir Hugo had been involved with British American Tobacco since its inception. Early involvement in the negotiations between American Tobacco and Imperial endeared him to Duke, who appointed Sir Hugo as director and secretary. Sir Hugo held those positions until Duke retired in 1923 (and died two years later) and then succeeded him as chairman. When Sir Hugo inherited the chair, British American's capitalization had quadrupled since 1902, and its sales had grown by nearly a factor of 40. By 1923 the company's world sales had grown to 50 billion cigarettes per year.

Sir Hugo visited China in 1923 to decentralize one of British American's largest operations. Chinese cigarette consumption had grown from 0.3 trillion in 1902 to 25 trillion in 1920 and to nearly 40 trillion by the time of his visit. Sir Hugo's plan was to restructure BAT China Ltd. into independent regional units that could continue to operate if local conditions deteriorated. Sir Hugo also spent a great deal of time and energy over the next two decades lobbying the Chinese government to minimize the taxation of tobacco.

Sir Hugo's decentralizing efforts spread from China to many of British American's other international operations. The chairman felt that increased local autonomy would lead to better decisions and improved group performance. This proved true despite skepticism

KEY DATES

1902: Company incorporates in England as British American Tobacco, Limited.

1927: Company acquires Brown and Williamson, a U.S. tobacco producer in North Carolina.

1962: Company makes its first moves toward diversification, acquiring Mardon Packaging International and Wiggins Teape Ltd., two paper companies.

1976: Company changes its name to BAT Industries Limited.

1989: Company begins selling nontobacco subsidiaries.

1998: BAT Industries Ltd. spins off remaining nontobacco businesses into an independent company and changes its name to British American Tobacco, PLC.

2004: BAT merges Brown and Williamson with R.J. Reynolds, creating Reynolds American.

2008: BAT acquires Tekel, in Turkey, and ST in Sweden.

2009: BAT acquires Bentoel in Indonesia.

that too much decentralization could produce an unwieldy corporate structure. In 1927, British American had the resources to enter the U.S. market, monopolized at one time by American Tobacco. Sir Hugo acquired Brown and Williamson, a small tobacco producer in North Carolina. With British American's help, this modest company became a major cigarette manufacturer in the United States. This pattern of rapid growth from modest beginnings was maintained through the Great Depression and steadily through World War II. At the end of the war, in 1945, Sir Hugo stepped down from the chairmanship and became titular president of the company.

Without Sir Hugo's active participation, the management of British American did little other than maintain the company's steady growth through the late 1940s and 1950s. Profitability remained undiminished and the company successfully weathered the storm of the Communist Revolution in China, at which time all of BAT China Ltd.'s assets were nationalized.

DIVERSIFICATION: 1962–88

By 1962, British American Tobacco's capitalization was such that it was able to begin major moves toward

diversification. During that year, British American acquired minority interest in two companies, neither of which was involved in tobacco production or sales. Mardon Packaging International handled cigarette packaging and was thus a logical choice for acquisition. Wiggins Teape Ltd., on the other hand, was a large specialty paper manufacturer. Mardon was not highly successful at first. It was formed from five smaller packaging companies in cooperation with Imperial Tobacco and its first-year sales were modest. It grew steadily, however, and by the end of the 1970s was advancing sales at a rate of 15 percent per annum.

DEPARTMENT STORES IN THE SEVENTIES

The success of these two enterprises, which later became wholly owned subsidiaries of British American Tobacco, paved the way for further and greater acquisitions. The groundwork was now laid for British American's transformation from a large tobacco company to an even larger conglomerate. While other major tobacco companies attempted to diversify into other packaged goods, British American wasted little time in moving into unrelated but profitable fields. During the 1960s and early 1970s, several major international fragrance and perfume houses were brought in to create a third segment of British American Tobacco's group. These companies included such internationally known concerns as Lentheric, Yardley, and Germaine Monteil.

Once these companies were thoroughly absorbed into British American's operations, the company turned its eye toward a West German department store chain called Horten. It first bought a minority share. Later it acquired the entire company. This led almost immediately to further department store chain acquisitions. Gimbels and Saks Fifth Avenue were acquired in the United States, Kohl's and Department Stores International in the United Kingdom, and Argos, the British catalog store, joined in 1979. Patrick Sheehy, before becoming British American's chairman, was involved in one more such acquisition. Marshall Field's department stores were the unwilling subject of a takeover bid conducted by the controversial team of Carl Icahn and Alan Clone. Sheehy was able to persuade BAT to make a friendly bid for the chain and managed to prevent Icahn from succeeding.

Many of these investments gave British American a good deal of trouble at first, just as Mardon had previously. While Saks Fifth Avenue, which appealed to the upper-middle-class consumer, maintained high profitability, Gimbels, despite efforts to bring in wealthier clientele, had a consistently poor showing. With the exception of Gimbels, the company absorbed and made a success of its retailing leg as well as its earlier expansion into paper.

BAT INDUSTRIES IN 1976

In 1972 the Treaty of Rome brought the United Kingdom into the European Economic Community (EEC) and terminated the agreements between British American Tobacco and Imperial Tobacco. New restraint of trade laws prohibited their arrangement. The companies exchanged brand rights once again, each retaining full ownership of its original brands in the United Kingdom and Western Europe only. British American kept its brand and trademark ownership in the rest of the world and in the duty-free trade outside Western Europe. Ties with Imperial Tobacco were finally severed in 1980 when that company sold its remaining few shares in BAT after having made major reductions over the preceding decade.

Due to the increasingly diversified nature of British American's interests, the name of the company was officially changed to BAT Industries Limited in 1976, and management was restructured for tighter control. BAT Industries became a holding company for several smaller operating companies organized according to industry. These operating companies in turn controlled the individual manufacturing and retailing enterprises.

Appleton Papers was added to the BAT operation in 1978. This U.S. company established BAT as the world leader in the manufacture of carbonless paper. That year BAT also acquired Pegulan, a large home-improvements company in West Germany, as well as two fruit juice companies in Brazil. Other purchases followed in pulp production in Brazil and Portugal.

Within two years of his 1982 accession to BAT's chairmanship, Patrick Sheehy decided to add a fourth leg to BAT's existing three supports. Eagle Star, a British insurance group, was involved in an unfriendly takeover struggle with the West German firm Allianz when Sheehy contacted its chairman, Sir Denis Mountain, with a friendly proposal. Eagle Star, which had rejected a low bid from Allianz as "grossly inadequate," accepted a similar bid from BAT as Sir Denis felt the two companies could work together well. In fact, BAT Industries saw a 26 percent rise in pretax profit during the first half of 1987, 45 percent of which was due to Eagle Star. Hambro Life Assurance, another large British firm, became Allied Dunbar when it was acquired by BAT in 1985. In 1988, BAT expanded its financial services group into the United States, with the acquisition of the insurance enterprise Farmer's Group Inc.

RESTRUCTURING IN THE EIGHTIES

After the addition of financial services to BAT's portfolio, Sheehy implemented a policy of "focusing and reshaping the business" rather than continuing to move into new areas. Sheehy believed that BAT should only be involved in companies able to maintain a leadership position in their markets. This led to some significant divestitures for BAT. In 1984, British American Cosmetics, International Stores, and Kohl's Food Stores were all sold. Mardon Packaging was sold to its own management in 1985, and in 1986, Gimbels and Kohl's (USA) department stores were put up for sale. That year 88 Batus retail stores were also divested in the United States along with the West German Pegulan.

With the increasing uncertainty of a long-term market in tobacco, Sheehy also took steps to decrease BAT's dependence on that industry. In 1986, only 50 percent of BAT's pretax profit came from its tobacco group. This was down from 57 percent in 1985 and 71 percent in 1982. This change did not result from a decrease in tobacco sales, however, but to overall growth in the other groups, most notably Eagle Star, which increased its contribution to BAT's profits from 11 percent in 1985 to 19 percent in 1986.

In July 1988, Sir James Goldsmith brought BAT's diversification strategy into question. A British billionaire, who had previously participated in a number of leveraged buyouts of U.S. companies, Sir James launched a hostile takeover of BAT. He proposed a buyout financed entirely by debt. Of the $21 billion Sir James offered for the company, $6.4 billion would have been raised through high-yield junk bonds and the remainder by a consortium of banks assembled by Bankers Trust. Current BAT shareholders would receive no cash for their shares. They would instead receive shares of Sir James's investment company, Hoylake Investments, and bonds from the loans.

Sir James planned to pay off the loans with the proceeds from selling BAT's nontobacco holdings. Sir James's proposed buyout failed in May 1990, when California insurance regulators refused to approve his acquisition of the insurance company, Farmer's Group. Nevertheless, this attempted buyout caused BAT to begin to reconsider its diversification strategy.

TOBACCO FOCUS IN THE NINETIES

In the United States and, to some extent in Europe, the 1990s were not good years for cigarette sales. The U.S. courts awarded multimillion-dollar verdicts to smokers who sued tobacco companies for severe illnesses that they claimed to be tobacco-related and to relatives of smokers who died from such illnesses. Governments at the federal, state, and local levels discouraged smoking through such means as bans on advertising, bans on smoking in public places, the imposition of significant taxes on tobacco products, and other measures. These initiatives substantially reduced tobacco consumption in the United States and, to a lesser extent, in Europe.

From a worldwide perspective, however, demand for tobacco products remained strong. Asia comprised many tobacco customers and offered even more potential customers. The end of the Soviet Union's dominance of the nations of Eastern Europe in 1989–90 opened promising new markets for tobacco products. Thus, BAT was in a good position to move its business back to the exclusive sale of tobacco. The company began to do so in 1990 when it sold or spun off parts or all of numerous nontobacco properties. These included Wiggins Teape Appleton, Breuners, Ivey, Marshall Field's, Saks Fifth Avenue, and 50 percent of Horten. In 1993 the company sold one of its financial properties, Eagle Star Levin N.V.

Using the cash proceeds from these sales, BAT began in 1994 to purchase numerous tobacco properties throughout the world. In that year, it acquired major interests in several Eastern European and Asian tobacco processors. It also bought 100 percent of American Tobacco. Between 1995 and 1997, BAT continued disposing of nontobacco properties and acquiring tobacco properties throughout the world.

In 1998 the company spun off its remaining nontobacco enterprises and consolidated its tobacco operations into the renamed British American Tobacco. At the time, CEO Martin Broughton expressed the company's determination to regain "world leadership in tobacco." This move was followed in 1999 by the acquisition of Rothman's, a significant player in tobacco markets in Asia and Africa. The company then acquired Canada's dominant tobacco company, Imasco, in 2000. In the meantime, the company's U.S. assets exposed it to the landmark $250 billion settlement made between the tobacco industry and the U.S. government in 1998.

NUMBER TWO IN 2000

Soon after the Imasco acquisition, BAT sold off all of its nontobacco operations. This refocused the Canadian company around its core of Imperial Tobacco, the leading cigarette company in that market. By then, BAT itself had grown to sales of more than $35 billion around the world, with profits of $1 billion. BAT had also claimed a 15 percent share of the global market, giving it the second place, behind Phillip Morris.

BAT began reshuffling its manufacturing network in the early years of the new decade. This led the company to close two of its Canadian factories and a site in the United Kingdom in 2003. In 2005, BAT announced its decision to shut down its remaining U.K. factory. This decision came in part because of new European Union (EU) legislation banning the sale and manufacture of cigarettes containing more than 10 milligrams of tar. Instead, the company shifted its production to non-EU markets, such as Poland, Romania, Serbia, and Switzerland. By then, the group's other EU holdings included Ente Tabacchi Italiano, acquired from the Italian government in 2003 for nearly $3.7 billion.

BAT found itself named in a new lawsuit brought by the U.S. Justice Department against the tobacco industry in 2004. In that year, the company decided to sell Brown and Williamson, then the third-largest player in the United States, to its number two rival, R.J. Reynolds. The newly merged company, called Reynolds American, also took over BAT's exposure to the 1998 settlement. In exchange, BAT took a minority share of 42 percent in the new company, in a deal worth nearly $7 billion.

Paul Adams took over as BAT's CEO at the beginning of 2004. BAT now deepened its focus on emerging markets, pursuing a two-pronged approach. The first part of the group's sales strategy targeted developing its Global Drive Brand (GDB) portfolio, which included four premium brands, Dunhill, Kent, Lucky Strike, and Pall Mall. The other part targeted the development of the group's regional and international brands portfolio, which included its Vogue, Viceroy, Rothmans, Kool, State 555, Peter Stuyvesant, John Player Gold Leaf, and Benson & Hedges brands.

ACQUIRING SCALE

Throughout the first decade of the new century, BAT had continued to expand its Asian manufacturing operations, adding a number of factories and processing plants in Vietnam, Turkey, and South Korea. In 2004, BAT made an attempt to break into the Chinese market, announcing that it had become the first foreign manufacturer to win authorization to build a factory there. The Chinese market, where smokers represented more than one-third of the total population, was already the world's largest single market. BAT's announcement prompted the Chinese government's State Tobacco Monopoly Administration to call for a ban on all joint ventures in order to keep foreign brands out of the market.

In 2005, the company sparked controversy when reports surfaced that it had been secretly operating a cigarette factory in North Korea since 2001. As Adams told *Forbes*, however: "Why shouldn't we sell there? We will sell where it's legal, where we can operate to our own international standards, and where we can make money."

The company's operations in the Western market, in the meantime, had come under steadily increasing pressure during the decade, as the number of smoking bans multiplied across Europe and North America. The implementation of bans on cigarette advertisements, as well as sharply raised taxes on tobacco products further cut into the group's sales in the West. As a result, the group continued to streamline its manufacturing operations in these markets, shutting down factories in New Zealand and the Netherlands in 2006.

BAT resumed its quest for acquisitions during the second half of the decade. This led the company to complete two major purchases in 2008. The first of these came in February of that year, when BAT agreed to pay $1.7 billion to acquire Tekel Cigarette from the Turkish government. This purchase gave the company the controlling share of the world's eighth-largest tobacco market. Just days later, BAT announced that it had reached an agreement for a second acquisition, the purchase of Skandinavisk Tobakskompagni (ST) in a deal worth nearly $4 billion. The ST acquisition gave BAT a 33 percent share of the Swedish tobacco market, including its four brands, North State, King's Original, Scotsman Original and Corner Red. ST also brought BAT a new product line, "snus," a Swedish form of chewing tobacco. BAT then began rolling out snus to other markets.

In 2009, BAT scored another major acquisition, when it paid $580 million to acquire Bentoel, the fourth-largest maker of kretek (tobacco and clove) cigarettes in Indonesia. These acquisitions helped boost the company's total gross sales (which includes the various duty, excise, and other taxes imposed on tobacco products) past £40 billion ($65 billion) by the beginning of 2010. The company, which offset the rising taxes on its products by raising its prices, also reported net revenues of £14.2 billion ($22.7 billion). BAT also remained highly profitable, posting adjusted profits of more than £4.6 billion ($7.4 million) for the year. With cigarette sales in the developing world showing few signs of slowing, BAT expected to remain at the top of the global tobacco industry.

Updated, Anne L. Potter; M. L. Cohen

PRINCIPAL SUBSIDIARIES

B.A.T. (U.K. and Export) Ltd.; B.A.T. Capital Corporation (USA); B.A.T. International Finance p.l.c.; BAT-Mark Ltd.; British American Tobacco (Brands) Inc. (USA); British American Tobacco (Brands) Ltd.; British American Tobacco (GLP) Ltd.; British American Tobacco (Investments) Ltd.; British American Tobacco Holdings (Netherlands) B.V.; British American Tobacco International Ltd. (Switzerland); British-American Tobacco (Holdings) Ltd.; Reynolds American Inc. (USA; 42%); Tobacco Insurance Company Ltd.

PRINCIPAL DIVISIONS

Africa and Middle East; Americas; Asia-Pacific; Associates; Eastern Europe; Western Europe.

PRINCIPAL OPERATING UNITS

Global Drive Brand (GDB) Portfolio–Dunhill, Kent, Lucky Strike and Pall Mall; Other International Brands.

PRINCIPAL COMPETITORS

Philip Morris International Management S.A.; Yunnan Yuxi Hongta Tobacco Company Ltd.; Loews Corporation; Zhangjiako Cigarette Factory; Japan Tobacco Inc.; Djarum, PT; Imperial Tobacco Group PLC; Altria Group Inc.

FURTHER READING

"Addicted to BAT," *Investors Chronicle*, August 6, 2009.

Boland, Vincent, and Pan Kwan Yuk, "BAT Tekel Deal to Draw Market Share from Turkey's Marlboro Men," *Financial Times*, February 23, 2008, p. 18.

"British American Tobacco Acquires STK," *Investors Chronicle*, March 5, 2008.

Cochran, Sherman, *Encountering Chinese Networks: Western, Japanese, and Chinese Corporations in China, 1880–1937*, Berkeley: University of California Press, 2000, 257 p.

Cookson, Clive, "BAT Puts 'Less Toxic' Tobacco to the Test," *Financial Times*, May 9, 2009, p. 12.

Cox, Howard, *The Global Cigarette: Origins and Evolution of British American Tobacco, 1880–1945*, New York: Oxford University Press, 2000, 401 p.

———, "Learning to Do Business in China: The Evolution of BAT's Cigarette Distribution Network, 1902–41," *Business History*, July 1997, pp. 30–65.

Freedman, Michael, "Smokin'," *Forbes*, June 18, 2007, p. 144.

Hughman, John, "Price Hikes Prop Up BAT," *Investors Chronicle*, February 25, 2010.

Killgren, Lucy, "Focus on Emerging Markets Sustains BAT," *Financial Times*, May 8, 2008, p. 20.

Kuchler, Hannah, "BAT Benefits from Increased Cigarette Prices," *Financial Times*, February 26, 2010, p. 22.

McGregor, Richard, "Chinese Wall of Resistance for BAT," *Financial Times*, July 26, 2004, p. 25.

Urquhart, Lisa, "BAT Ends Production of Cigarettes in the UK," *Financial Times*, July 14, 2005, p. 22.

———, "BAT Secures Some Breathing Space," *Financial Times*, February 28, 2005, p. 25.

———, "Smoke Clears to Reveal Acquisitive BAT Chief Martin Broughton," *Financial Times*, October 29, 2003, p. 31.

Yuk, Pan Kwan, "Innovation Fires Up BAT's Chief," *Financial Times*, May 9, 2009.

The Brock Group of Companies

3640 West 12th Street
Houston, Texas 77008
U.S.A.
Telephone: (713) 869-1935
Toll Free: (800) 818-5030
Fax: (713) 869-1937
Web site: http://www.brockgroup.com

Private Company
Incorporated: 1947 as Service Painting Company
Employees: 7,500
Sales: $650.9 million (2008)
NAICS: 238990 All Other Specialty Trade Contractors

■ ■ ■

The Brock Group of Companies is a Houston, Texas-based specialty contractor provider comprising about 14 subsidiaries that serve multiple industries in the United States, Canada, South America, and the Caribbean. They include refining, power, nuclear, food and beverage, manufacturing, chemical, pulp and paper, offshore, logistics, pipeline and transmission, and Canadian Oil Sands. Core services include painting and other coatings, scaffolding, lead and asbestos abatement, and insulation. Other services include grounds and facilities maintenance, janitorial services, fireproofing, tank linings, offsite blasting and painting, power washing, roofing, and general labor, cleanup, and hole watch. Brock also provides disaster response, emergency restoration, and mold and mildew remediation services. Moreover,

Brock offers engineering surveys, heat loss surveys, corrosion surveys, and heat tracing.

Important keys to Brock's success are the multiple skills of its personnel and the bundling of services that provides greater value to customers than merely serving as a labor contractor. Brock's varied slate of customers includes Anheuser Busch, Bayer, Citgo Refining, Conoco Phillips, Dow Chemical, Eastman Chemical, Exxon Corporation, Federal Express, Honeywell, Philip Morris, Shell Oil Corporation, and Weyerhaeuser. Brock is majority owned by New York investment firm Lindsay Goldberg & Bessemer but is still led by the Brock family. Brothers Brad and Todd Brock serve as the company's chairman and vice chairman, respectively.

POST-WORLD WAR II ORIGINS

The roots of the Brock Group reach back to Beaumont, Texas, where in 1947 Cecil Anderson was hired to paint a logo on a tank. It was the start of a small painting company called Service Painting Company. He was soon joined by his nephew, Jerry Brock, who became involved with Service Painting in 1953 and worked his way up through the ranks until he succeeded his uncle as the head of the business. Brock proved to be a gifted entrepreneur, launching a wide variety of businesses in addition to adding maintenance-oriented companies to complement Service Painting. He also established Brock Enterprises to provide in-house support for his slate of businesses.

It was in the early 1970s that Brock took advantage of the expertise possessed by his different service companies to offer bundled services to customers. The

COMPANY PERSPECTIVES

Brock is recognized throughout the industry as a leader among specialty craft providers. While simple in concept, our goal of Lowering Cost and Adding Value is no small task. Few have mastered the complex business of managing field work processes, engineering, training, metrics, and in-house resources. We set the pace, setting the standard for others to follow.

arrangement served the interests of both parties. Brock generated more business, essentially cross-selling services to customers of its subsidiaries. Customers, on the other hand, benefited in several ways. Using Brock as a single-source provider was not only convenient, but it also saved money because Brock could consolidate overhead costs and pass the savings onto the customer. Moreover, with a variety of maintenance tasks being handled by one provider, there was improved efficiency that cut down on delays as one group handed off work to another. Communication was also improved, as was performance, the quality of work, and safety, all of which provided customers with less obvious cost savings.

INTRODUCTION OF FLEX-CREWS: 1979

In 1979 the Brock operation evolved further when for the first time an industrial maintenance company used a "flex-crew" of workers with multiple skills to perform a multitask project. The benefits of employing workers with flexible skills were manifold. It was essentially a natural extension of the bundled services concept, further reducing handoffs of tasks, saving time and money for customers. With a versatile workforce that could readily adapt to needs in the marketplace, Brock was able to keep down headcounts and lower overhead costs. Additionally, employees trained in more than one craft found their work more engaging and satisfying. As a result they became more productive, again saving money in the long run.

Through bundling services and employing flex-crews, Brock became the leading specialty service provider to heavy industrial clients for painting, scaffolding, insulation, and asbestos and lead abatement. The next generation of the Brock family, the sons of Jerry Brock, became involved in the business in the 1980s. First, Brad Brock joined the company in 1980. He was followed in 1986 by Todd Brock. The brothers worked their way up through the organization and as-

sumed the top management positions in the 1990s, with Brad Brock succeeding his father as chief executive officer and Todd Brock serving as chief operating officer.

Brad and Todd Brock oversaw another growth spurt in the Brock Group of Companies, as new capabilities were added beyond coatings, scaffolding, insulation, and asbestos and lead abatement to create larger bundles of services the company could offer clients. New services included roofing, yard and grounds maintenance, facilities maintenance, janitorial, and labor support. In addition, Brock improved its operations in terms of technology, engineering, and project managing.

The addition of service capabilities offered new opportunities for Brock employees to add new skills, but the company found it increasingly difficult to find new employees. Crafts in general were becoming less attractive to a younger generation, and a shortage of workers developed as these skilled workers retired. In many parts of the country undocumented workers from other countries rushed in to take some of these available jobs and employers asked few questions. Following the September 11, 2001, terrorist attacks on the United States, security was tightened at critical infrastructure sites across the country, some of which were served by Brock.

In 2005, 60 undocumented workers from Guatemala, Honduras, and Mexico employed by a Brock Group contractor were arrested. Although there was no evidence they had any terrorist ties, they worked at what were considered sensitive sites, including power plants, petrochemical refineries, a national air cargo facility, and a pipeline company. Brock was not a target of the investigation and cooperated with federal investigators. The incident demonstrated, at the very least, the challenge maintenance service companies faced of securing suitable labor. It was a situation that was greatly magnified in the Gulf Coast region in 2004 and 2005, when rebuilding efforts after hurricanes devastated the region drained the labor pool from industrial maintenance and construction work.

SALE OF MAJORITY INTEREST: 2006

After nearly 60 years in business, Brock had enjoyed strong growth, but in order to expand further it needed to recapitalize. In 2006 it sold a controlling stake to the New York-based investment partnership Lindsay Goldberg & Bessemer LP that managed $5.1 billion of equity capital, investing across a wide range of industries. Lindsay Goldberg was a relatively new firm, formed in 2001, but its co-managing partners, Alan E. Goldberg and Robert D. Lindsay, were seasoned investors. Goldberg was the former chairman and CEO

```
┌─────────────────────────────────────────┐
│                                         │
│            KEY DATES                    │
│              ─────■─────                 │
│                                         │
│   1947:  Cecil Anderson forms Service Painting │
│          Company in Beaumont, Texas.    │
│   1953:  Jerry Brock joins uncle's company. │
│   1979:  Brock Group uses first flex-crew. │
│   1980:  First Brock son joins company. │
│   2006:  Lindsay Goldberg & Bessemer acquires │
│          controlling interest.          │
│                                         │
└─────────────────────────────────────────┘
```

of Morgan Stanley Private Equity, which Lindsay helped to found. Lindsay also played a key role in growing the global private-equity business of Bessemer Holdings.

Lindsay Goldberg acquired a majority stake in a company that employed 2,600 skilled workers serving 150 customers in 260 facilities. With Todd and Brad Brock remaining to run the company, Brock now had access to capital through its new owners to expand in its exiting markets. A few months later, in early 2007, Brock was able to complete a significant acquisition, purchasing another Houston company, XServ Inc., a major provider of industrial scaffolding and insulation services. XServ was formed in 1999 as a holding company for seven-year-old United Scaffolding. In addition to $250 million in annual revenues, XServ added operations in the Caribbean and South America.

Brock completed two other acquisitions in 2007. It added Kingsport, Tennessee-based A&L Industrial Construction and Maintenance Inc. in June. In business since 1985, A&L offered industrial sandblasting, painting, linings, fireproofing, and insulation services. Brock also acquired Steeplejack Industrial Group Inc. of Edmonton, Alberta, Canada, in September. With nine branches providing oil and gas, power generating, paper and pulp, mining, and other industrial and commercial customers in Alberta and Saskatchewan with project management, manpower, and equipment supply services, Steeplejack gave Brock entry to promising new markets in Canada.

FURTHER ACQUISITIONS: 2008

With the financial backing of Lindsay Goldberg, Brock pursued further acquisitions in 2008, despite a credit crunch that led to a decreased level of mergers and acquisitions. Sulphur, Louisiana-based Page Industries, Inc., and its subsidiaries (Thermal Manpower, Inc., Abatement Specialties, Inc., and Prefab, Inc.) were acquired in April 2008. They were regional players in industrial insulation, fireproofing, asbestos and lead

abatement, and other services. A month later, Brock added to its Canadian holdings with the acquisition of Vancouver-based Westcor Services Limited. Employing 450, Westcor provided insulation, fireproofing, and environmental services to the petrochemical, pulp and paper, utility, and marine industries. The company would be run under the auspices of Steeplejack's chief executive officer.

Later in 2008 Brock acquired Atlantic Industrial Inc. of Columbia, Maryland, doing business in 34 states. Atlantic provided industrial scaffolding, insulation, and complementary services. Formed in 1980, it was the holding company for two subsidiaries, La Porte, Texas-based Atlantic Scaffolding Company and Atlantic Plant Services, operating out of Joliet, Illinois. Although it was a fast-growing company, experiencing an increase in revenues from $57 million in 2005 to $137 million in 2006, it was one of the few small independent companies left in the rapidly consolidating scaffolding industry. Large oil companies, the major customers for scaffolding services, increasingly preferred to work with larger companies such as Brock, which they considered more reliable. As a result, Atlantic had little choice but to combine with a larger concern.

At the same time Brock acquired Atlantic it also purchased Clute, Texas-based Miken Specialties, Ltd. Established in 1996, Miken served industrial customers with scaffolding, insulation, roofing, vessel or steel structure painting, and other services along the Texas and Louisiana Gulf Coast. Miken added a slate of new customers and about 1,200 employees. Also of note in 2008, the Brock brothers turned over day-to-day control of the Brock Group of companies. Todd Brock became chairman and Brad Brock became vice chairman, while Jeff Davis was promoted to CEO and Michael E. McGinnis was named president.

Brock completed an add-on acquisition to its Atlantic Plant Services business in February 2009 with the purchase of Master Mechanical Insulation, Inc. (MMI). Founded in Huntington, West Virginia, in 1987, MMI was a regional provider of insulation on boilers, pumps, piping, valves, vessels, tanks, ductwork, and other mechanical system applications. It served industrial and commercial customers in West Virginia, southern Ohio, eastern Kentucky, northern Virginia, and western Pennsylvania. Another unit, Master Mechanical Sales, Inc., distributed insulation and asbestos abatement materials in the Ohio Valley market.

NEW HEADQUARTERS: 2009

Other changes were in store for Brock in 2009. It moved to a new corporate headquarters in Houston's

Sam Houston Crossing Business Park. In September 2009, Brock sought to simplify the company's structure by beginning the process of consolidating a number of operations under Brock Services, Ltd., including Brock Industries, Inc., Brock Maintenance, Inc., and Brock Specialty Services, Ltd. The changes positioned Brock for continued growth in the years to come.

Ed Dinger

PRINCIPAL SUBSIDIARIES

Brock Services, Ltd.; Brock Holdings III, Inc.

PRINCIPAL COMPETITORS

EMCOR Group, Inc.; KBR, Inc.; Turner Industries Group, L.L.C.

FURTHER READING

"The Brock Group Completes XServ Acquisition," *Chemical Business Newsbase*, February 26, 2007.

Dance, Scott, "Columbia Scaffolding Firm Sells," *Baltimore Business Journal*, June 6, 2008.

———, "M&A Activity Has Slowed, but 'Good Deals Will Get Done,'" *Baltimore Business Journal*, June 20, 2008.

Seper, Jerry, "ICE Arrests 60 Illegals Working in Sensitive Areas," *Washington Times*, May 21, 2005, p. A04.

"Southeast Texas Business in Brief," *Beaumont Enterprise*, July 23, 2006.

"Ultimate Success in Service Starts Here," *BIC Magazine*, May 2007.

Ybarra, Rose, "Undocumented Immigrants in SE Texas Live in Fear of Being Deported," *Beaumont Enterprise*, April 30, 2007.

Brown-Forman
Corporation

850 Dixie Highway
Louisville, Kentucky 40210-1038
U.S.A.
Telephone: (502) 585-1100
Fax: (502) 774-7876
Web site: http://www.brown-forman.com

Public Company
Founded: 1870 as J.T.S. Brown and Bro.
Incorporated: 1901 as Brown-Forman Co.
Employees: 3,850
Sales: $3.19 billion (2009)
Stock Exchanges: New York
Ticker Symbol: BFB
NAICS: 312130 Wineries; 312140 Distilleries

■ ■ ■

Brown-Forman Corporation is one of the world's 10 largest producers and marketers of spirits and wines. Among the full-line distiller's principal brands are Jack Daniel's whiskey, Southern Comfort liqueur, Canadian Mist Canadian whiskey, Old Forester bourbon, Finlandia vodka, el Jimador and Herradura tequilas, Chambord and Tuaca liqueurs, Korbel champagne, and Bonterra, Fetzer, and Sonoma-Cutrer wines. About half of Brown-Forman's sales are generated outside the United States, with Europe accounting for around 28 percent of overall revenues. The company's largest international markets include the United Kingdom, Australia, Mexico, Poland, Germany, France, Spain, Italy, South Africa, China, Japan, Canada, and Russia.

The founding Brown family remains firmly in control of Brown-Forman, owning about 67 percent of the common shares.

EARLY HISTORY

At the time of Brown-Forman's founding in 1870, bourbon was typically sold to taverns in barrels, and bartenders decanted the alcohol into special bottles with the name of the tavern on the label. With savings and borrowed money totaling $5,500, George Garvin Brown, a young pharmaceuticals salesman, and his half-brother, John Thompson Street Brown Jr., founded their own distillery in Louisville, Kentucky, under the name J.T.S. Brown and Bro. They too initially sold whiskeys in barrels under such names as Mellwood Bourbon, Atherton Bourbon, and Sidroc Bourbon. In 1873, however, the Browns shifted gears. They poured the bourbon into bottles at the distillery, corked and sealed the bottles, labeled them with the brand Old Forester, and warned taverns not to buy the bourbon if the seals were broken. As an additional innovation, all of the labels were handwritten and included a guarantee on the quality of the bourbon. Old Forester sold well as a result of these innovations.

Over the next two decades, the company went through a series of name changes as partners of George Garvin Brown came and went. In 1890 George Forman, a friend of Brown's who had joined the firm in 1872 and later became its bookkeeper, bought out the shares of one of these partners, and the company thus adopted the name Brown, Forman & Co. When Forman died in

COMPANY PERSPECTIVES

Brown-Forman's rich and lengthy experience as a company, coupled with our longstanding shareholders' enduring commitment, forms the basis of our long-term perspective. While we acknowledge the importance of short-term results, we do not obsess over them. Instead, we devote our energies and efforts to achieving consistent, sustainable results year after year.

That means we are willing to invest in anticipation of future profits, although the potential return may be years away. This practice allows us to dial back spending when consumers are less responsive. And this broad perspective extends to our philosophy of patiently building brands that will endure for generations.

1901, his widow sold his shares to Brown, who became sole owner. She also granted permission for Brown to continue to use the Forman name. Brown that same year incorporated the firm as Brown-Forman Co. The following year the name was changed to Brown-Forman Distillery Company after the purchase of Mattingly Distillery of St. Mary's, Kentucky.

In 1905 Brown-Forman continued its packaging innovations by bottling Old Forester in pear-shaped bottles. Old Forester's tavern sales increased significantly as a result. These increased sales led to a certain amount of bitterness among other distillers in Kentucky. Some competitors went so far as to slip iron nails into barrels of Brown-Forman whiskey to make it turn black.

Brown-Forman's bourbon was aged in barrels in large warehouses. At that time, warehouses were not heated, and labels on bourbon bore the expression "summers old," a reference to the fact that bourbon can age only in a warm climate. As a result, during the early decades of the 20th century it took many years for the bourbon to be prepared for the market. Consequently, the word "old" became a common prefix in any brand name of bourbon.

When George Garvin Brown died in 1917 at the age of 70, his oldest son, Owsley, took the helm. Owsley Brown led the company through a critical period that encompassed two world wars, Prohibition, and the Great Depression.

SURVIVING PROHIBITION

Old Forester, produced, marketed, and distributed by Brown-Forman, continued to be very successful under the private ownership of the Brown family, which had no plans to diversify. All the company's advertising concentrated on marketing Old Forester, which it promoted as a product that would restore health: "Many, many times a day, eminent physicians say, Old Forester will life prolong and make old age hale and strong." Although this advertising was effective, Prohibition threatened to close Brown-Forman. The pre-Prohibition advertising, however, had been valuable as Brown-Forman Distillery was one of 10 distillers permitted by the government to sell alcohol for medicinal purposes during Prohibition (1920–33). The marketing of Old Forester had saved the company from the kind of downfall that other distillers suffered as a result of Prohibition. The same year of Prohibition's appeal, Brown-Forman completed its first issue of public stock, although the Brown family maintained control of the majority of shares.

Brown-Forman spent the decade between the end of Prohibition and World War II adjusting to the fact that it could now legally sell Old Forester as bourbon. The bourbon now needed to be advertised as an alcoholic beverage rather than as a health tonic, in order to change the image it had acquired during Prohibition. The extensive advertising of the late 1930s and early 1940s, however, was largely futile; the production of alcoholic beverages was once again severely curtailed during World War II. This time Old Forester could not be advertised as a health tonic because even this type of alcohol had become illegal.

In spite of this development, the Brown family was not pessimistic about the future of their distillery. They investigated ways in which their alcohol could be used to help the war effort, and during the war Brown-Forman produced alcohol that was used in making both gunpowder and rubber. The Browns also continued to plan for the end of World War II and the future of Brown-Forman Distillers Corporation (the name the company adopted in 1940). They wanted their bourbon to have a head start in the postwar market.

During World War II Brown-Forman's executive committee considered the fact that it took at least four years to age a marketable bourbon. They attempted to predict when the war would end and correctly decided on 1945. By starting the aging in 1941, they could have Old Forester ready for sale immediately following the war. As the competition's bourbon would not be marketable until 1949, Brown-Forman could monopolize the bourbon market for the first four postwar years. Because the executive committee's predic-

KEY DATES

■

1870: George Garvin Brown and his half-brother found a whiskey distillery in Louisville, Kentucky, under the name J.T.S. Brown and Bro.

1901: Brown becomes sole owner; company is incorporated as Brown-Forman Co. but is soon renamed Brown-Forman Distillery Company.

1920: Prohibition is enacted; Brown-Forman receives a license to sell alcohol for medicinal purposes.

1933: Prohibition is repealed; company completes its first issue of public stock.

1956: Company purchases Jack Daniel Distillery.

1979: Company purchases Southern Comfort.

1983: Company acquires Lenox, maker of crystal, china, and giftware, as well as Hartmann luggage.

1984: Company's name is changed to Brown-Forman Corporation.

1991: Dansk International, maker of premium giftware, is acquired.

1992: Fetzer Vineyards is acquired.

1999: Brown-Forman purchases an 80 percent interest in Sonoma-Cutrer Vineyards.

2000: Company buys a 45 percent stake in Finlandia Vodka Worldwide; full control is later acquired.

2005-07: Sale of Lenox and other durable goods businesses leaves Brown-Forman fully focused on its global spirits and wine business.

tions were correct and resulted in impressive sales, Brown-Forman management decided to create a committee system of management. Finance, marketing, and production committees were created, in addition to the executive committee, to discuss and implement policies that could lead to the future success of the company.

In 1945 the management at Brown-Forman implemented an annual training course for 10 to 20 selected individuals from outside the firm. These individuals worked in all areas of the company, from the lowest to the highest positions. Approximately half of them were then hired by other companies, and half continued with Brown-Forman in management positions. In this way, Brown-Forman created for itself

an adequate supply of employees for management positions from outside the company itself. The remaining employees, however, were hired according to a policy of "planned nepotism."

Since George Garvin Brown founded Brown-Forman in 1870, the Browns supported this type of company nepotism. In 1945 the executives at Brown-Forman publicly stated that nepotism was good for their business and would be encouraged. They believed that if a father enjoyed working at Brown-Forman, his son would feel just as comfortable working there. Brown-Forman executives, as a policy, encouraged the children and grandchildren of good employees to work for the company. In the meantime, in concert with this policy, a member of the Brown family continued to serve as CEO, with W. L. Lyons Brown, a grandson of the founder, succeeding Owsley Brown in 1945, followed by Geo. Garvin Brown II, named to the top post in 1951.

POSTWAR DIVERSIFICATION

One of the effects of the limited production of alcohol during World War II was that postwar consumers favored whiskey blends that did not have a strong alcohol taste. The executives at Brown-Forman, however, did not pay attention to this new trend. They continued to sell bourbon with high alcohol content. In 1956 Brown-Forman diversified into the premium rye whiskey business by purchasing the Jack Daniel Distillery in Lynchburg, Tennessee. Jack Daniel's had been founded in 1866 and enjoyed a popular, "down-home" image. The label of the "Tennessee sipping whiskey" featured men in overalls, coonhounds, and scenes from Lynchburg. Brown-Forman's confidence in the value of the Jack Daniel's franchise was evinced by the fact that the acquisition cost $20 million, a debt that exceeded the company's net worth. The deal also confirmed Brown-Forman's movement away from being a company that produced only bourbon.

In another diversification move from 1956, Brown-Forman purchased the Joseph Garneau Company, Inc., an importer of scotch whiskeys and European wines. The company's expansion helped push sales over the $100 million mark by 1960. Although Brown-Forman had not followed consumer trends after World War II when blends were popular, the company succumbed to the high demand for scotch in the 1960s. By 1962 scotch held 9 percent of the liquor market, and the popularity of wine was increasing steadily.

Despite the diversifications, Brown-Forman portrayed itself as a medium-sized company. This stance worked in favor of the company during the 1960s. Before 1963, 80 percent of all hard liquor in the United

States was sold by the four largest distilling companies, and the remaining 20 percent was sold by Brown-Forman, Heublein, James B. Beam Distilling Co., and the American Distilling Co. In 1963, however, these smaller companies increased their sales by 70 percent, while the larger companies did not increase their sales at all. Consumer tastes during the 1960s favored the small, independent distilling companies. One reason for this change was that consumers in increasing numbers were switching from blended whiskey, popular after World War II, to straight whiskey.

In 1964, in order to continue its expansion in the broader market for alcoholic beverages, Brown-Forman purchased all outstanding stock of the Oertel Brewing Co., a small Louisville brewery. This company produced beer that was distributed in Kentucky, Tennessee, Indiana, Ohio, and Alabama. The brewery later became unprofitable, and Brown-Forman sold its interest in the company during the late 1960s. However, the purchase of Oertel was proof of Brown-Forman's willingness to diversify into new areas of the alcohol market.

In 1966 Daniel L. Street was appointed president of Brown-Forman, the first time that a person outside the Brown family had been president of the company. Street joined Brown-Forman as a lawyer in 1938 and advanced to the position of executive vice president in 1953. He continued Brown-Forman's program of diversification while president. In 1967 he authorized a merger with Quality Importers, which provided Brown-Forman with a "top scotch and good gin," according to Street. Quality Importers produced Ambassador scotch, Ambassador gin, and Old Bushmills Irish whiskey. By 1968 sales had risen to $180 million as Brown-Forman continued to expand under the direction of Street.

Although Street effectively diversified Brown-Forman, William F. Lucas replaced him as president in 1969. Lucas was also not part of the Brown family. He had joined Brown-Forman as an engineer in 1935 and advanced through the ranks. Lucas concentrated on marketing Brown-Forman's premium-priced products, namely, President's Choice, Jack Daniel's, Old Forester, and Early Times. Lucas did not spend large sums advertising Brown-Forman's low-profit brands, because he felt that, as higher quality whiskey could be made for pennies more per fifth, and could be sold at a much higher price, only the expensive brands merited increased advertising expenditures.

ADDING CANADIAN MIST AND SOUTHERN COMFORT

In 1969 Lucas purchased the Bols line of liqueurs and Korbel champagne and brandy. These purchases expanded Brown-Forman's premium product line. In the early 1970s, as the demand for wine soared, Lucas initiated the purchase of Bolla and Cella Italian wines. This purchase was followed by the company's development of another product called Gold Pennant Canadian Whiskey. This whiskey was marketed specifically to women. Each bottle sold was accompanied by a horoscope pamphlet with "love potion" recipes for each astrological sign.

Lucas then bought six-year-old barrel-stored whiskey from Publicker Industries Inc. In the 1960s Publicker had decided to make light whiskey but had later, when it was unsuccessful, reversed this decision. Lucas used Publicker's misfortune to Brown-Forman's advantage by purchasing their light whiskey, triple filtering it, and marketing the clear 80 proof product. Light whiskey is a clear beverage because it is aged in used barrels that have already given their color to the whiskey previously stored in them. The clear whiskey is then distilled at a higher proof so it is lighter in taste. The term "light whiskey" actually refers to the type or body of the whiskey and not to its color.

In December 1970 Schenley Industries, National Distillers and Chemical Corporation, and American Distilling Co. filed an injunction against Brown-Forman to bar introduction and further distribution of Brown-Forman's light whiskey called Frost 8/80. Under government restrictions light whiskey was not permitted to be marketed until July 1972. Although Brown-Forman's light whiskey was distributed before it was allowed to be, Brown-Forman's competition dropped its suit because Frost 8/80 was already on the market. As a result, Brown-Forman was free to advertise its new product as a "dry, white whiskey" with which "the possibilities are endless." By advertising the whiskey as easily combining with any mixers, Brown-Forman tried to capture a share of the vodka and lighter Canadian whiskey market. The difficulty was that consumers did not buy Frost 8/80. They were used to drinking whiskey with color and, moreover, they could not associate Frost 8/80 with identically colored vodka because the flavors were different.

By 1973, $6 million had been invested in Frost 8/80 without a profitable return. Brown-Forman had extensively researched the popularity of a white whiskey and had received positive consumer response in various areas of the United States. Consumers, however, were confused by the company's advertising promotions and did not purchase the product. The extensive market research that Lucas had consulted before distributing Frost 8/80 had been incorrect.

Although light whiskey was not successful, Lucas still believed that American tastes were turning to lighter alcoholic drinks. For this reason, in 1971, Lucas contacted Lester Abdson and Oscar Getz, who owned Barton Brands of Canada. Barton Brands bottled Canadian Mist, a blended whiskey. Brown-Forman could not purchase the entire company because of strict antitrust laws, so Lucas negotiated an agreement with Getz and Abdson to buy Canadian Mist and its distillery without buying the entire company. (This was the first time that a major brand of liquor was sold separately from the remainder of the company.) Lucas's determination to satisfy the American taste for lighter drinks was not diminished by the strict antitrust laws or the failure of Frost 8/80. By 1973 sales of such products had significantly increased.

In 1975 W. L. Lyons Brown Jr. was appointed president of Brown-Forman. He was a great-grandson of the company founder. After two presidents who were not related to the Brown family, W. L. Lyons Brown Jr. reestablished the tradition of a Brown at the head of the business. Unfortunately, Brown-Forman's success dwindled in the late 1970s as the bourbon market declined. The new leader moved aggressively to concentrate on faster-growing segments of the alcoholic beverage market. In 1979 Brown-Forman spent $35 million to advertise its full line of alcoholic products. Brown significantly increased Brown-Forman's wine and liqueur revenue to 22 percent of total sales. Most importantly, in 1979 the company purchased privately held Southern Comfort for $90 million. This purchase provided Brown-Forman with greater access to foreign markets because one-fifth of Southern Comfort sales were overseas.

The acquisitions of Southern Comfort and Jack Daniel's were similar because both companies were small and privately held. Also, each company had developed a distinctive character for their single product. Unlike Jack Daniel's, Southern Comfort is a liqueur and does not need to be aged. It can be produced and sold at a much faster rate. Before the Brown-Forman acquisition, Southern Comfort was already the number one selling liqueur. Brown-Forman simply enhanced its success. The company was equally successful with Jack Daniel's. From 1970 to 1979 Brown-Forman tripled Jack Daniel's sales to 1.7 million cases by popularizing the image of a quaint distillery nestled in a Tennessee hollow. Overall, by the end of the 1970s Brown-Forman had advanced to sixth place in the alcohol industry and become the fastest-growing full-line distiller.

EXPANDING BEYOND ALCOHOLIC BEVERAGES

Despite overall growth, the company experienced a setback with Southern Comfort in 1982. As competi-

tion increased, the share held by Southern Comfort in the market decreased. Brown-Forman responded to this weakening market share with another innovative idea, one- and three-quarter-liter plastic bottles to replace the half-gallon glass bottles. After petitioning the Bureau of Alcohol, Tobacco, and Firearms, the company was granted permission to begin using the plastic bottle in 1983. Later tests indicated, however, that a loose molecule of plastic could contaminate the alcohol, and the container was soon prohibited.

In 1983 Brown-Forman acquired Lenox Inc., even though Lenox fervently fought the acquisition. Lenox made crystal, china, and giftware, and Hartmann luggage, products that presented special problems for Brown-Forman. Drastically different methods of distribution were needed to market the Lenox products. Nonetheless management at Brown-Forman understood the need for a transition. This was apparent in the 1984 name change from Brown-Forman Distillers Corporation, under which it had been known since 1940, to Brown-Forman Corporation.

Subsidiary shuffling continued in the late 1980s and early 1990s, as the company worked to solidify its position in giftware. Brown-Forman sold Lenox's Art-Carved jewelry division to SGI Acquisition Corporation for $120 million cash in 1989, and sold the related Lenox Awards division to Jostens in 1990. The Lenox subsidiary acquired the Kirk-Stieff Co., a manufacturer and marketer of silver tableware, and Wings Luggage, Inc., in 1990 and 1991, respectively. Brown-Forman purchased Denver's Athalon Products Ltd., a manufacturer of travel and leisure products, in 1989, and supplemented its Lenox operations with the $70 million acquisition of premium giftware maker Dansk International Designs Ltd. in 1991.

Nevertheless, the company's realignment did not exclude the rearrangement of other alcoholic products. Brown-Forman bought California Cooler Inc. in 1985 for $63 million, and sold Cella Italian Wines to Cosorzio Interprovinciale Vini, an Italian firm, at the end of the decade.

Unfortunately, a recession in the early 1990s, in combination with price and tax hikes, brought a halt to a burgeoning trend toward premium liquors, as consumers traded down to less expensive brands. Unit sales in the liquor industry fell 5.6 percent in 1991, which was widely characterized as "one of the worst years since Prohibition." The decline continued in 1992, when total sales dropped about 3 percent.

Brown-Forman launched several ready-to-serve cocktails as extensions of its primary brands in the early 1990s. Jack Daniel's Country Cocktails, which were introduced nationally in 1992, soon became one of the nation's top 20 spirit brands. Southern Comfort Cocktails and Pepe Lopez Margaritas were introduced soon afterward. It was hoped that these products would serve as an alternative to beer, rather than erode or cannibalize their parent brands. In August 1992 Brown-Forman acquired Fetzer Vineyards, an important producer of premium California wines, for about $80 million. In the process, Brown-Forman became the fifth-largest player in the U.S. wine market.

W. L. Lyons Brown Jr. retired as CEO in 1993, and younger brother Owsley Brown II assumed the position. The new leader helped boost his company's stock through a Dutch auction whereby the company repurchased over 4.5 million shares.

LATE-CENTURY INTERNATIONAL EXPANSION

In the mid- to late 1990s, Brown-Forman made a concerted effort to bolster its non-U.S. sales. In 1994, Brown-Forman Beverages Worldwide was created through a reorganization that combined the previously separate U.S. and overseas divisions. Among the subsequent overseas initiatives was the 1995 formation of a joint venture with Jagatijit Industries, Limited, of India to distribute Brown-Forman alcoholic products in India. Southern Comfort was introduced into that country the following year. In South Africa, a blended whiskey called BlueGrass Kentucky Whiskey was successfully introduced. Worldwide sales of Jack Daniel's increased rapidly, with the brand becoming the world's seventh best-selling spirits brand by decade's end.

During this period, Brown-Forman also gained a presence in the hot superpremium vodka category through a 1996 agreement whereby it became the exclusive U.S. importer of the Finlandia brand. Brown-Forman helped increase U.S. sales of Finlandia by nearly 50 percent by 1999, and in August 2000 the company acquired a 45 percent stake in Finlandia Vodka Worldwide Ltd., with the balance of the ownership remaining with Altia Group Ltd., a distiller and marketer owned by the government of Finland. Also in 2000, Brown-Forman expanded its distribution of Glenmorangie Scotch, which the company had been marketing in the United States since 1991. Brown-Forman agreed to take over sales and marketing of the brand in continental Europe, the Far East, Australia, and South America. On the wine front, meantime, Brown-Forman acquired an 80 percent interest in Sonoma-Cutrer Vineyards, Inc., in April 1999, then one year later acquired most of the remaining stake. Sonoma-Cutrer was one of the leading U.S. makers of premium Chardonnay wine. Brown-Forman's net sales surpassed the

$2 billion mark for the first time in the fiscal year ending in April 1999.

While the spirits and wine operations were being steadily expanded, Brown-Forman's consumer durables business, the Lenox, Gorham, Dansk, Kirk Stieff, and Hartmann brands, were not performing as well. At the turn of the millennium, durables accounted for more than one-quarter of overall sales but only 10 percent of the profits. A number of analysts called for the divestment of these brands but Brown-Forman resisted such pleas and company officials pointed instead to such positives as the cash flow generated by the brands. The company also attempted to revive the brands' flagging fortunes through a number of initiatives. Lenox, known for its fine china, began selling lines of casual dinnerware. The same brand also found success with a number of millennium-themed products and, in a departure from its traditional department store sales, garnered increasing revenue from catalog, direct mail, and Internet channels. Dansk, meantime, was successfully reintroduced into department stores.

Consolidation in the global spirits business was a major trend of this time. Brown-Forman did not remain on the sideline, but ultimately came away empty-handed, when Vivendi Universal S.A. placed the Seagram spirits and wine group on the auction block. Brown-Forman partnered with Bermuda-based Bacardi Limited on a joint bid, but in late 2000 a competing joint bid from Diageo plc and Pernod Ricard SA won out. In the wake of this failed bid, Brown-Forman and Bacardi deepened their ties that already included the sharing of distributors in a number of U.S. states. Bacardi also distributed Brown-Forman's products overseas, particularly in Europe, and in 2002 Brown-Forman dropped Diageo as its U.K. distributor and instead began selling its products directly to the trade in the United Kingdom via a cost-sharing agreement with Bacardi. Brown-Forman and Bacardi, both family-controlled firms, were seen as natural partners, and possible candidates for a merger, because of their complementary brand portfolios, with Bacardi's strength in rum and Brown-Forman's in bourbon.

As it enjoyed increasing revenues mainly stemming from an upsurge in popularity of hard liquor, Brown-Forman pushed ahead with growth initiatives. In 2002 the company gained majority control of Finlandia by acquiring another 35 percent of the brand for $72 million. Brown-Forman then acquired the remaining 20 percent of Finlandia in December 2004 for $64 million. The company also acquired full control of Tuaca, an Italian liqueur flavored with vanilla and citrus, in early 2003.

Brown-Forman was thwarted, however, in its bid to acquire Glenmorangie, and the brand's new owner, the wine and spirits group of LVMH Moët Hennessy Louis Vuitton SA, in mid-2005 terminated Brown-Forman's contracts to distribute the brand. Around this same time, the company was part of a consortium vying to acquire U.K.-based Allied Domecq PLC, but Pernod Ricard ended up the winning bidder. Brown-Forman had thus missed out on a series of opportunities to quickly gain scale in a consolidating industry, but company executives believed that building strong individual brands was more important than accumulating an ever-larger number of brands.

FOCUSING FULLY ON SPIRITS AND WINE

In August 2005 Paul C. Varga was named president and CEO of Brown-Forman, becoming the third executive from outside the Brown family to lead the company. A veteran of nearly two decades, Varga had worked his way up from an entry-level position in sales and marketing to being named CEO of Brown-Forman Beverages in 2003. Right around the time of this management transition, Brown-Forman began the process of unloading its consumer durables business. In September 2005 the company sold its Lenox subsidiary to Department 56, Inc., for $196 million. Brown-Forman placed Hartmann on the auction block about a year later and finally sold the luggage maker to a private-equity firm in the spring of 2007. Divesting these noncore operations enabled the company to focus its full attention on its steadily expanding global alcoholic beverage business.

Although blockbuster deals had proven elusive, Brown-Forman did manage to add some important brands to its portfolio as it was shedding the consumer durables business. In May 2006 the company acquired Chambord, a superpremium black raspberry liqueur, for $251 million. The following January, Brown-Forman spent about $794 million for Grupo Industrial Herradura, S.A. de C.V., producer of two leading Mexican tequilas, Herradura and el Jimador. The company saw great potential for growth from this deal as these tequila brands had very little distribution in the United States or elsewhere overseas. In addition, at this time, tequila was one of the fastest-growing categories of liquor in the United States. On the wine side, Brown-Forman pruned its portfolio with the sale of the Bolla and Fontana Candida Italian wine brands in early 2009.

Brown-Forman remained on an upward trajectory through fiscal 2008, when two milestones were reached: sales of more than $3 billion and the generation of more than half of these revenues outside the United States. Net income reached a record $440 million. The global economic downturn, which began in late 2008, brought this growth trend to a halt as consumers cut back on their purchases of alcoholic beverages and/or traded down to less-expensive brands. Sales were down 3 percent in fiscal 2009, while profits dipped 1 percent, but the company extended its streak of paying regular quarterly dividends to 63 years. In April 2009 Brown-Forman implemented a cost-cutting program that among other measures reduced the firm's 4,100-employee workforce by about 250. Annual savings were projected at $15 million to $25 million. Brown-Forman also responded to the downturn by launching more pre-mixed products and ready-to-drink cocktails for sale at retail outlets for consumers cutting back on their visits to bars and restaurants.

April Dougal Gasbarre
Updated, David E. Salamie

PRINCIPAL SUBSIDIARIES

American Investments, C.V. (Netherlands); BFC Tequila Limited (Ireland); Brown-Forman Arrow Continental Europe, L.L.C.; Brown-Forman Australia Pty. Ltd.; Brown-Forman Beverages Europe, Ltd. (UK); Brown-Forman Beverages Japan, L.L.C.; Brown-Forman Beverages North Asia, L.L.C.; Brown-Forman Beverages Worldwide, Comercio de Bebidas Ltda. (Brazil); Brown-Forman Czech & Slovak Republics, s.r.o. (Czech Republic); Brown-Forman Dutch Holdings, B.V. (Netherlands); Brown-Forman Holdings Mexico S.A. de C.V.; Brown-Forman Italy, Inc.; Brown-Forman Korea Ltd.; Brown-Forman Netherlands, B.V.; Brown-Forman Polska Sp. z o.o. (Poland); Brown-Forman Spirits Trading, L.L.C. (Turkey); Brown-Forman Tequila Mexico, S. de R.L. de C.V.; Brown-Forman Thailand, L.L.C.; Brown-Forman Worldwide, L.L.C.; Brown-Forman Worldwide (Shanghai) Co., Ltd. (China); Canadian Mist Distillers, Limited (Canada); Chambord Liqueur Royale de France; Clintock Limited (Ireland); Cosesa-BF S.A., de C.V. (Mexico); Distillerie Tuoni e Canepa Srl (Italy); Early Times Distillers Company; Fetzer Vineyards; Finlandia Vodka Worldwide Ltd. (Finland); Jack Daniel's Properties, Inc.; Jack Daniel Distillery, Lem Motlow, Prop., Inc.; Limited Liability Company Brown-Forman Ukraine; Longnorth Limited (Ireland); Sonoma-Cutrer Vineyards, Inc.; Southern Comfort Properties, Inc.; Valle de Amatitan, S.A. de C.V. (Mexico); Woodford Reserve Stables, L.L.C.

PRINCIPAL COMPETITORS

Bacardi Limited; Beam Global Spirits & Wine, Inc.; Constellation Brands, Inc.; Diageo plc; E. & J. Gallo

Winery; Foster's Group Limited; Jackson Family Wines, Inc.; LVMH Moët Hennessy Louis Vuitton SA; Pernod Ricard SA.

FURTHER READING

Bary, Andrew, "Distilling Value from a Famous Name," *Barron's*, February 19, 2007, p. 34.

Benoit, Ellen, "Brown-Forman: Wall Street vs. the Family," *Financial World*, February 23, 1988, p. 14.

Branch, Shelly, "Brown-Forman Siphons Market Share from Its Rivals," *Wall Street Journal*, February 22, 2000, p. B4.

Dewson, Andrew, "Team Spirits," *Louisville*, January 2009, p. 30.

Fromson, Brett Duval, "Keeping It All in the Family," *Fortune*, September 25, 1989, pp. 86–87+.

Goetz, David, "Brown-Forman Cashes In on International Tastes," *Louisville Courier-Journal*, August 17, 1997, p. 1E.

———, "Brown-Forman Toasts Payoff of Global Push," *Louisville Courier-Journal*, July 23, 1999, p. 1E.

———, "Wine Venture Bears Fruit: When Brown-Forman Acquired Fetzer Vineyards, Both Cultures Profited," *Louisville Courier-Journal*, December 25, 1998, p. 22B.

Lucas, William F., *Nothing Better in the Market: Brown-Forman's Century of Quality, 1870–1970*, New York: Newcomen Society in North America, 1970, 32 p.

O'Connell, Vanessa, and Dennis K. Berman, "Brown-Forman to Buy Mexican Tequila Brands," *Wall Street Journal*, August 28, 2006, p. A8.

Pearce, John Ed, *Nothing Better in the Market*, Louisville: Brown-Forman Distillers Corporation, 1970, 96 p.

Song, Kyung M., "Brown-Forman Plans to Tap into Developing Spirits Markets," *Louisville Courier-Journal*, May 11, 1994, p. 8B.

———, "Lee Brown Hands Top Post at Brown-Forman to Brother," *Louisville Courier-Journal*, July 23, 1993, p. 1A.

Swibel, Matthew, "Drinking to the Dollar: How Distiller Brown-Forman Gets Rich by Exploiting the Greenback's Fall—and Pushing Its Brands Abroad," *Forbes*, April 18, 2005, p. 152.

BT Group plc

BT Centre
81 Newgate Street
London, EC1A 7AJ
United Kingdom
Telephone: (+44 121) 415 7178
Fax: (+44 1903) 833371
Web site: http://www.groupbt.com

Public Company
Founded: 1869
Incorporated: 2001
Employees: 111,858
Sales: £21.39 billion ($30.27 billion) (2009)
Stock Exchanges: London New York
Ticker Symbol: BT.A
NAICS: 517110 Wired Telecommunications Carriers; 517212 Cellular and Other Wireless Telecommunications; 517910 Other Telecommunications

■ ■ ■

BT Group plc is one of the world's leading telecommunications groups focused on the provision of fixed-line and Internet protocol (IP)-based communications services. BT Group includes the operations of British Telecommunications, the former U.K. telephone monopoly. As such, the company controls the United Kingdom's largest fixed-line network, with more than 125 million kilometers of copper wire and nearly 11 million kilometers of fiber-optic lines, as well as 5,600 exchanges, most of which have been converted to provide high-speed broadband access. Since the loss of its telephone monopoly, BT Group has expanded its operations internationally, and into 2010 counted more than 16 million customers in 170 countries around the world.

BT Group operates through four major divisions. BT Global Services accounts for 41 percent of group revenues, and provides a full range of managed network and information technology (IT) and other services, largely to a corporate and business clientele around the world. More than 60 percent of the *Fortune* Global 500 companies, and more than 65 percent of FTSE 100 companies are Global Services customers. In support of this division, BT Group has rolled out a high-speed, IP-based 21CN platform. BT Retail operates the company's fixed-line and broadband operations in the United Kingdom, and is the country's leading provider of high-speed Internet access. The company has also rolled out its own television service, BT Vision, a hybrid service using both broadband and digital terrestrial broadcasting platforms. BT Retail added 38 percent to the group's sales. BT Wholesale sells access to the group's fixed-line and broadband network to more than 700 communications providers in the United Kingdom, adding 16 percent to annual sales.

The fourth division, Openreach, fulfills BT Group's obligation to provide local loop unbundling (LLU) access (the direct connection to customers' homes and businesses) to competing communications groups. This division produces 5 percent of group revenues. BT Group is listed on the London and New York stock exchanges, and is led by CEO Ian Livingston and Chairman Michael Rake.

COMPANY PERSPECTIVES

■

Our vision is to be dedicated to helping customers thrive in a changing world. The world we live in and the way we communicate are changing, and we believe in progress, growth and possibility. We want to help all our customers make their lives and businesses better with products and services that are tailored to their needs and easy to use.

This means getting ever closer to customers, understanding their lifestyles and their businesses, and establishing long-term relationships with them.

We're passionate about customers and are working to meet the needs they have today and innovating to meet the needs they will have tomorrow.

TELEPHONE INDUSTRY IN ENGLAND: 1869–1969

British Telecommunications' administrative and technological roots are mingled with those of the U.K. Post Office and reach back into the second half of the 19th century, when inventors at home and abroad, such as Alexander Graham Bell, Thomas Edison, and Guglielmo Marconi, were applying electromagnetic principles to the development of practicable forms of telecommunications. Out of this the modern telegraph, followed by the telephone, was born. In 1850 the first submarine telegraph cable was laid across the English Channel.

In 1878 Bell demonstrated his newly patented telephone to Queen Victoria, and in 1879 England's first telephone exchange opened in London. It was in 1891 that the first international telephone call was made between England and France. The telegraph and telephone were at first exploited by private enterprises, but they were gradually taken over by a U.K. government department, the General Post Office. The reversal of that nationalization process was completed in the early 1990s.

In 1869 the Postmaster General was granted the exclusive right to transmit telegrams within the United Kingdom. At first the telephone was slow to catch on and was not regarded by the Post Office as a serious threat to its telegraphic network. The first independent U.K. telephone service provider, Telephone Company Ltd., was set up in 1879 and in 1880 merged with its competitor, Edison Telephone Company, to form United Telephone Company.

Seeing that the telephone was beginning to take customers away from its telegraph service, the Post Office embarked on a series of protective measures, and in 1880 the government brought an action against the recently formed United Telephone Company, claiming that it was operating in contravention of the Telegraph Act of 1869. The High Court subsequently decided that the telephone was a form of telegraph. The merger was revoked, and telephone companies were required to be licensed by the telegraph monopoly holder, the Post Office.

MONOPOLY IN 1912

The next stage in the process of squeezing out competition and establishing a state telephone monopoly was the building up of the Post Office's own system. In 1896 the Post Office completed its improved telephone network by taking over the trunk lines of National Telephone Company, the largest of its licensees, and started to set up its own local telephone exchanges. It was then decided that no more national licenses would be granted.

National Telephone Company continued to operate a local service until its license expired in 1911, but in 1912 the Post Office was granted a monopoly on the supply of telephone services throughout the United Kingdom. It took over all of National Telephone Company's exchanges and opened an automatic exchange in Epsom, south of London.

Since 1899 several of the larger towns and cities, including Glasgow, Brighton, Swansea, Portsmouth, and Kingston upon Hull (Hull), had each been operating an independent local telephone service, but their number gradually dwindled as they were bought out by National Telephone Company or the Post Office. In 1913 only Hull was left.

By cooperating with successive competitors (National Telephone Company and the Post Office) it survived, first as the Hull Corporation Telephone Department, a municipal enterprise run by the Hull City Council, and since 1987, as a limited company, Kingston Communications (Hull) PLC, wholly owned by Hull City Council and a licensed public telecommunications operator (PTO), with interconnection agreements with BT and BT's competitor, Mercury Telecommunications Limited.

POST OFFICE ACT OF 1969

A landmark in the prehistory of BT was the Post Office Act of 1969, which changed the status of the Post Office. This former government department became a

KEY DATES

1880: Telephone Company Ltd. merges with Edison Telephone Company to form United Telephone Company.
1969: Post Office Telecommunications is formed.
1981: British Telecommunications Act is passed.
1984: British Telecommunications plc becomes privatized.
1994: British Telecom enters strategic alliance with MCI Communications to form Concert Communications Company.
2001: BT Group plc is formed as a holding company.
2002: BT Group launches a new strategy focused on broadband and Internet protocol services.
2008: BT Group announces a $3 billion investment to build its fiber-optic network in the United Kingdom.
2010: Company reports a loss of £83 million on revenues of £21.4 billion.

state public corporation under the Secretary of State for Industry. The telecommunications services remained in the Post Office but were divided from the postal services into Post Office Telecommunications.

Three further events marked the telephone industry's move toward an environment of free competition. First came the passage of the 1981 British Telecommunications Act, which took Post Office Telecommunications out of the Post Office, turning it into an autonomous, though still state-owned, body known as British Telecommunications Corporation or, more familiarly, British Telecom. Second was the 1984 Telecommunications Act, which privatized BT and liberalized the telecommunications market, setting up a regulatory body. Third, the Duopoly Review in 1990 resulted in the government's 1991 decision to further increase telecommunications competition. The government also decided to sell off its remaining shares in BT, although this decision was not influenced by the Duopoly Review.

In July 1981 the British Telecommunications Act, which separated telecommunications from the Post Office and set up a new state public corporation to supply them, also gave the government powers to license competitors in the operation of the domestic telephone network. As well as modifying the state company's statutory monopoly of the telephone network, this act

took away its monopoly in the provision of telecommunications equipment, leaving it only with the right to supply and install a subscriber's first telephone. The act not only opened the market to competition in value-added services, such as data processing and storage, but also allowed other providers to use BT's lines.

NEW COMPETITION IN 1981

In October 1981 Mercury Telecommunications Limited was chosen to receive a 25-year renewable license to operate a national and international digital network (a system that encodes information as a series of on-off signals) to compete with BT's trunk traffic. Mercury had been set up early in 1981 by British Petroleum, Barclay's Merchant Bank, and Cable and Wireless plc (C&W) to enter the business of long-distance communications, offering a customized service to companies. The license allowed it to interconnect with the BT network and to enter the European and U.S. sectors.

In 1983 the government undertook for seven years not to license any company but BT and Mercury to carry telecommunications services over fixed links. Under this duopoly policy, Mercury, which began operating in 1986, was to be BT's single serious network competitor until the early 1990s. Less than a year after the 1981 act, the government announced its intention to privatize British Telecommunications Corporation.

At the end of 1982 the first telecommunications bill had reached the committee stage, when the general election of May 1983 was called. The bill immediately died, but was presented again in the new Parliament and finally became law in its second form, the Telecommunications Act of April 12, 1984. It had undergone 320 hours of debate and discussion, during which BT itself had briefed members of Parliament on its views and interests. By the act, BT lost its exclusive right to run telecommunications systems, and all PTOs had to be licensed.

The new company was to be sold as an integrated organization. Fragmentation, similar to the breakup of American Telephone and Telegraph Company (AT&T) in the United States, would have left the resulting entities too small to defend the home market from foreign competition, to stand up to multinationals in the world markets, and to command the technology and the financial strength for adequate research and development.

PRIVATIZED IN 1984

In November 1984, 3.01 billion ordinary shares of 25 pence were offered for sale at 130 pence per share, the first figure being the nominal or face value of the share, and the second its sale price, or market value, at the time of sale. The government retained a 48.6 percent stake in the new company, valued at the time of sale at £7.8 billion. All the offered shares were bought.

Under the terms of the 1984 act, BT's main activity was to supply telecommunications services in the U.K. market of 55 million people in accordance with a 25-year operating license from the Department of Trade and Industry. Starting in 1984, BT's performance and development were conditioned by an official regulatory body, the semi-independent Office of Telecommunications (Oftel), set up in August 1984 under the Secretary of State for Trade and Industry and headed by the director general of telecommunications (Bryan Carsberg being the first to hold the post).

A major role of this body was, by simulating the effects of real competition, to prevent BT from abusing its inherited dominance of the U.K. telecommunications market during the process of deregulation. Nevertheless, the fairness of the competition was often disputed by interested parties. In its severely regulated environment, BT had lost the security of being a state monopoly, without gaining the freedom of action of a wholly autonomous business.

Oftel monitored BT's pricing, accounting, investment policies, and quality of services; issued licenses to additional competitors; and continued to facilitate the interconnection of rival services to the BT network. Competitors, for their part, tended to feel that BT was favored by the regulator. The new British Telecommunications plc created by the 1984 act then shared its monopoly in telecommunications systems with Mercury as well as Kingston Communications, plus some general licensees.

When BT became a separate state corporation in 1981, before its rebirth in 1984 as a privatized company, it inherited from its Post Office days an evolved network. This network had to be brought up to date at the same time BT was taking on competition from operators starting from scratch. These competitors were using the latest technology, without public service obligations, and were able, for example, to go straight to digital systems and less expensive and more efficient fiber-optic cable, while BT still had copper wire circuits to be amortized.

FACING COMPETITION IN THE EIGHTIES

BT kept technology in the forefront, however, and spent 2 percent of its overall revenue on research and development to keep it there. The domestic telephone services sector was by far BT's largest operating division in terms of assets, revenue, and number of employees. In 1990 it accounted for nearly 75 percent of sales. Its core business was the public switched telephone network (PSTN). The 20 millionth U.K. telephone was installed in 1975, the system became fully automatic in 1976, and in the early 1990s BT, with more than 25 million lines, operated the world's sixth-largest telephone network, with nearly 100,000 public pay phones. In 1990 BTUK, the product of the 1987 merger of BT's local communications services and national networks divisions, was operating more than 7,000 local exchange units, of which nearly half were already digital.

Meanwhile, Mercury's market share in the early 1990s was variously estimated between 3.7 and 5 percent, but was increasing markedly. An efficiency and investment effort was BT management's response to this new competition and to growing demands and service expectations from its customers. Waiting times for connections and repairs were reduced, and new digital equipment was introduced into the network, including exchanges that used microchip technology to integrate the switching and transmission elements of the network, resulting in a higher quality of service and improved voice transmission. All trunk exchange units were digital since June 1990. BT aimed to have a fully digital network by the year 2000. In addition, new products, such as microwave radio transmission in the city of London, were offered.

Another area within which BT faced stiff competition was the capricious mobile communications market. BT's Mobile Telephone System 4, a noncellular service introduced in 1981, with 7,000 subscribers at the beginning of 1990, had capacity problems at peak periods and was being replaced by a cellular network, Cellnet, shared by BT and Securicor Communications. Its rival, using another network, was Racal-Vodafone. In February 1989 BT bought, for £907 million, a 20 percent interest in McCaw Cellular Communications, Inc., a U.S. mobile cellular telephone and broadcasting systems provider and operator.

In the late 1980s, BT offered a wide range of value-added network services (VANS, including such electronic mailbox services as Telecom Gold and Message Handling Service) in the United Kingdom. In November 1989, to further its strategies in the home and international VANS market, BT bought, for £231 million, the U.S. company Tymnet, one of the largest VANS companies in the world, and consolidated some of its own international services under a new company, BT Tymnet Inc.

BT started setting up an integrated services digital network (ISDN) that could eventually replace the other networks by offering all data, voice, text, and image network services at high speed, with circuit-switched digital connections from a single access point. Although ISDN was of primary importance in BT's plans for the future, like other telecommunications firms, BT had to move slowly in this area, needing to await definition of international standards and to raise the consciousness of potential customers. A pilot service was launched by BT in June 1985 that by the end of 1989 was available to 75 percent of business users.

ADAPTING TO A NEW COMPETITIVE MARKET FROM 1991

In the early 1990s BT faced major changes. The duopoly policy was reviewed in 1990, and a report issued in January 1991 was followed two months later by a government recommendation that both BT and Mercury should face greater competition in local, trunk, and international services. BT was still barred from offering entertainment services on cable television, but after some hard bargaining, Bryan Carsberg, director of telecommunications; Peter Lilley, secretary of state for trade and industry; and Iain Vallance, BT's chairman, agreed on amendments to BT's 25-year license. BT was then allowed to proceed with further rebalancing between telephone rentals and call charges and with customized tariffs. It was announced that the sale of a slice of the government's residual share in BT would take place in November 1991.

In the face of increasing competition, BT engaged in a rationalizing and restructuring operation. In the year ending March 31, 1990, a slimming-down and cost-control operation began, covered by an exceptional charge of £390 million. In the following year, 18,800 jobs were shed and overtime work was cut, while another 10,000 terminations were planned for 1991 and 1992.

In April 1991 the reshaped company announced that the three former operating divisions, BTUK, comprising Local Communications Services and National Networks; BTI, British Telecom International; and CSD, Communication Services Division, would be replaced. In their stead were placed two major divisions that dealt directly with customers: Personal Communications and Business Communications, both supported by a Products and Services Division. BT's international and U.K. networks were brought together into a new Worldwide Networks Division, and some business activities best managed separately, such as mobile communications and operator services, comprised a new Special Business Division.

Early in 1991 BT's intensified drive to consolidate its image as a smart, market-oriented world organization with a human face was signaled by its integration of the BT acronym into a new blue and red logo, representing a dancing piper apparently delivering a sound message. A new designer image was commissioned for the group and was widely publicized; public telephones were replaced by newly designed models; and the bright yellow of BT vehicles began to be replaced, in a notoriously expensive replace-or-respray operation, by a stylish gray.

FALLING MARKET SHARE IN THE NINETIES

As the 1990s continued, BT's challenges became more intense. While at least 98 percent of its revenues and profits continued to come from its home market, the additional competition allowed under the 1991 review of the duopoly policy combined with continued moves by Oftel to reduce BT's monopoly began to seriously erode BT's position in the U.K. market.

From 1991 to early 1996, some 150 firms started operations in the United Kingdom that were competitive with BT, several of the most important of which were cable firms owned by U.S. Baby Bell companies. As a result, BT's share of the U.K. telephone market tumbled, with its residential customer market share falling from 99 percent in 1991 to 93 percent in 1995 and its business customer market share falling from 94 percent to 83 percent during the same period. Some analysts were predicting that by 2000 BT's share of the U.K. residential market would fall to as low as 65 percent.

In response, BT continued the cost-cutting program it began in 1990. More than 100,000 jobs had been eliminated by 1995, reducing the BT workforce from 239,000 in 1990 to 137,500 in 1995. The program was to be continued into the late 1990s, moving toward a goal of a 100,000-employee workforce with productivity levels in line with the Baby Bells. BT's upstart competitors also forced the company to upgrade its service and lower its prices since they were luring away BT customers by offering low prices and better service. In 1995 BT reduced prices on both domestic and international long-distance calls, adding up to more than £800 million in savings for its customers for the year. That same year, BT increased capital expenditures 23 percent in order to improve customer service and upgrade its network.

Meanwhile, the often cantankerous relationship between BT and Oftel grew more confrontational in the mid-1990s. Perhaps not coincidentally, these BT-Oftel battles took place after 1993, the year in which the British government sold nearly all of its remaining stake in BT for $7.43 billion. In 1995, BT expressed support for the development of number portability (the ability of customers to keep the same phone number even if they changed telephone suppliers) but objected to a plan that the company felt would place a disproportionate share of the costs on BT.

In response to BT's rejection of the plan, Oftel referred the matter to the Monopolies and Mergers Commission, the first time BT had been subjected to such a referral. Later in 1995, the regulator announced that it wanted to reduce BT's return on capital from the 15.6 percent of 1995 to as low as 8 percent. If forced to accept this, the company's ability to invest for future growth might be seriously damaged. Such a possibility sent BT stock plunging throughout 1995.

The overall impact of the competition and regulation showed clearly in BT's revenues and profits. The company revenue growth had stagnated, with the £13.15 billion figure of 1991 only increasing to £13.89 billion in 1995. Profits fell in three of the four years from 1992 to 1995, and fell overall from £2.04 billion to £1.74 billion.

INTERNATIONAL ALLIANCES IN 1994

Embattled at home and certainly facing increasing pressure there for the foreseeable future, BT almost had no choice but to look overseas for its long-term survival. Early attempts at international expansion had failed, including the 1986 purchase of Mitel Corp., a Canadian phone equipment manufacturer that BT sold in 1992 at a loss of £120 million ($200 million), and the company's stake in McCaw Cellular, which it sold in 1992 to AT&T (which had just purchased a larger stake in McCaw) at a profit exceeding £200 million ($333 million).

According to Vallance, these investments no longer fit into the company's international plans, which now centered around building a global telecommunications network offering comprehensive services to multinational corporations. Vallance's first attempt at this failed, however. In 1991 the company set up a subsidiary, Syncordia Corp., in Atlanta, Georgia, to start such a network on its own, but had little success attracting either customers or the telecommunications partners it needed around the world to make the venture succeed.

Syncordia was shut down three years later, after BT realized it had erred attempting to go it alone. In mid-1993, BT's second attempt to go global began with the announcement of an alliance with the major U.S. telecommunications firm MCI Communications Corp. The alliance, which received final approval in mid-1994, involved BT purchasing a 20 percent stake in MCI for £2.86 billion ($4.2 billion). The two firms set up a joint venture called Concert Communications Company, based in England, which was 75 percent owned by BT and 25 percent by MCI. Syncordia was folded into the new venture, which would inherit Syncordia's charge of providing telecommunications services for multinational corporations.

To make Concert work, however, BT needed additional partners in other areas of the world. Over the next few years, BT set up alliances with several European companies including Norwegian Telecom, Tele Denmark, Telecom Finland, and Banco Santander of Spain. A foothold in the important German market also was secured in a 1995 alliance with the German conglomerate Viag AG, in which the partners planned to start a joint venture that would offer Concert services.

COURTING CABLE & WIRELESS IN 1995

BT now had a solid network of partners in Europe and North America, but remained weak in the critical Asian market, having allied only with International Telecom Japan Inc., a small international carrier. Meanwhile, AT&T was working furiously to set up its own system of global alliances through its WorldPartners program. By 1995, while AT&T had had more success than BT in Asia, having established partnerships with KDD of Japan and with Singapore Telecom, the U.S. giant was having difficulties making inroads in Europe.

In the midst of this, two top executives left the company, one retiring and one resigning. Vallance decided to step aside as CEO, while remaining chairman, and turned to an outsider, Peter L. Bonfield. Taking over as CEO in early 1996, Bonfield had been the chief executive of ICL PLC, a British computer company owned by Fujitsu Ltd. Observers noted that Bonfield's experience with Japanese business practices might help BT in its effort to enhance its alliances in Asia.

Heading into the new century, British Telecommunications was certainly being squeezed in its all-important home market. Its international activities were still very much in a start-up phase and needed time to turn the company's huge investments in them into profits. The question was whether cash would be drained faster at home than the payoff abroad. Perhaps needing to move faster than AT&T to secure a global network, it appeared in early 1996 that BT might try effecting a major merger to gain its missing Asian link.

The most significant possibility was that BT would merge with Cable and Wireless plc (C&W), which owned 80 percent of the main home market competitor of BT, Mercury. Merger talks between C&W and BT began in late 1995. If it happened, the merged firm would have to sell Mercury, but more important, BT would have gained C&W's 57.5 percent stake in Hong Kong Telecommunications Ltd. and its telecommunications businesses in Japan and Australia. BT might finally break free of its dependence on the U.K. market.

CHALLENGES OF GLOBALIZATION: 1997–2002

As the 21st century loomed, British Telecom found itself under increasing pressure to look abroad for new opportunities to expand its business. A number of factors contributed to the urgency of BT's position. By mid-1996 the Office of Telecommunications, wary of the near-stranglehold BT held on the domestic market (the company was still providing phone service to nearly 90 percent of all English households), was beginning to implement measures that would help reduce consumer telephone rates by up to 40 percent within a five-year span.

At the same time, the regulatory agency introduced procedures that greatly simplified the process by which customers were able to transfer phone numbers to new accounts. The new rules delivered a significant blow to BT; by the end of 1997, the company was losing close to 60,000 domestic customers a month. Finally, the imminent unification of Europe, along with the broader trend toward globalization, threatened to make the British phone industry too competitive for BT to retain its position as the United Kingdom's telephone powerhouse.

In the information age, it was becoming clear that corporations needed to be able to provide a full range of phone, Internet, and wireless services in order to remain competitive. Believing that the Internet would soon account for a higher volume of communications traffic than the telephone, BT began searching for a high-powered merger, with the aim of establishing itself as an international corporation with the capacity to meet the technological needs of the new century.

Although C&W seemed in many ways a perfect fit, the companies were ultimately unable to work out a deal, and BT was forced to look into other options. One possibility was to join forces with MCI, a company in which BT already owned a 20 percent stake. The two corporations entered negotiations in the summer of 1996, and by the following summer were on the verge of inking a $22 billion agreement. The deal stalled in August 1997, however, with MCI's announcement that it expected to suffer losses of up to $800 million for the previous year. The news struck trepidation in the hearts of BT's majority shareholders, and the two companies entered renegotiations. Unfortunately for BT, the merger was suddenly blindsided in October 1997, when Worldcom Inc., a fast-rising U.S. telecommunications firm, made an offer for MCI that exceeded BT's by nearly $13 billion. BT once again found itself without a partner.

PARTNERSHIP WITH AT&T IN 1998

The company immediately began searching for other possibilities. In July 1998 it entered into a promising new partnership with AT&T, wherein the companies merged their international operations into a single entity, called Concert. The combined businesses had the potential to generate more than $10 billion in revenue annually, and to place the two industry giants in a position to gain a foothold in newly deregulated telecommunications markets worldwide. One particularly attractive target was Japan. In March 1999, the companies acquired a combined 30 percent stake in Japan Telecom, the country's fourth-largest telephone company. Encouraged by the initial promise of the joint venture, the companies pooled their global wireless phone operations in September 1999. The new company, called Advance, boasted more than 41 million customers across the world, and promised to generate more than $12 billion a year.

In the end, however, BT's international expansion strategy proved to be hastily conceived. For one, Advance took longer than expected to generate a substantial product line. Worse, BT's efforts to achieve a wide global reach over a short period ultimately spread its resources far too thin, and by May 2001 the company had accumulated $43 billion in debt and was reporting its first fiscal year loss since becoming privatized. Under siege by investors, Chairman Sir Iain Vallance resigned, and BT was forced to dump many of its minority holdings in overseas telecommunications companies, including its shares in Japan Telecom, Rogers Wireless in Canada, Maxis Communications in Malaysia, and Airtel in Spain.

BROADBAND FOCUS FROM 2001

By October the joint venture with AT&T was defunct, and the company had undertaken a massive restructuring. The result was the formation of the BT Group, which became the holding company for British Telecom. In the meantime, the global telecommunications market, which had soared at the dawn of the new century, suddenly collapsed, sending stock prices plummeting.

BT Group's aggressive spending program, and especially the huge price it agreed to pay for a 3G mobile license, now pushed the group to the edge of financial collapse. As a result, BT Group was forced to sell off a number of its core operations. These included Yell Group, the telephone directory business, for £2 billion. Even more significant, however, was the de-merger of its mobile telecommunications operations, BT Wireless, which was renamed mmO2 and then re-branded as O2. As a result, BT Group became the only major telecommunications company in Europe without a mobile telephony subsidiary. This market, however, was set to achieve exponential growth in the new decade.

With debt levels still at $20 billion and losses of more than $4 billion, BT Group brought in a new CEO in 2002. Ben Verwaayen was a native of the Netherlands who had previously been vice-chairman of Lucent Technologies. Verwaayen charted a new course for BT Group's future, based on a two-pronged strategy of reinventing itself as a globally operating provider of IP-based network and IT services, while also becoming the United Kingdom's dominant broadband services provider. Verwaayen also launched a streamlining of the group's operations. By 2003, BT Group posted a profit of $4.2 billion.

In order to achieve these objectives, BT Group launched a massive $18 billion project to convert its telephone network to digital technology. The new network, called 21CN, for 21st Century Network, enabled BT to become one of the first in Europe to roll-out broadband services to its customers, starting in 2002. The 21CN effort also enabled the company to expand its range of IP services onto a worldwide level. These operations, targeted at the corporate and business markets, ultimately reached 170 countries, and included many of the world's largest corporations, as well as government and other public organizations.

FIBER OPTICS IN 2008

BT's broadband business expanded strongly through the decade, topping 10 million customers by 2007, and then nearly 13 million by 2009. In 2008, the company announced a new $3 billion spending program, extending its fiber-optic network to nearly 11 million kilometers by 2010. In this way, the company now oversaw one of Europe's most extensive and fastest broadband networks. The company had also begun to develop a broader multimedia and communications

services offering for its network, including the launch of its own IP and digital terrestrial broadcasting hybrid television service, BT Vision, in 2006.

Verwaayen retired in 2008, turning over the CEO job to Ian Livingston. Under Verwaayen, BT Group had successfully completed its transformation, remaining profitable through the decade while posting revenue gains from £18 billion in 2005 to more than £21 billion in 2009. The company's Global Services operation had become an important motor for its growth, accounting for 41 percent of its sales. At the same time, the group's domestic broadband operations, through the BT Retail division, provided the second major pole to its business, with 38 percent of revenues.

Into the beginning of 2010, however, BT Group faced new challenges amid the most severe global economic crisis since the late 1920s. The company's Global Services division was hit especially hard, and dragged the company into losses by the beginning of 2009. This led the company to announce plans to eliminate more than 15,000 jobs during that year. In 2010, as BT Group reported a net loss of £83 million, the company once again appeared set to sell off some of its operations, including a possible sale of its fixed-line business in Italy. Despite its difficulties, BT Group's core operations remained fundamentally solid as the company looked forward to a calmer climate in the new decade.

Olive Classe
Updated, David E. Salamie; Steve Meyer; M. L. Cohen

PRINCIPAL SUBSIDIARIES

British Telecommunications plc; Basilica Computing Limited; British Telecommunications plc; BT (Germany) GmbH & Co; BT Americas Inc. (USA); BT Australasia Pty Limited; BT Communications Ireland Limited; BT Conferencing Inc.; BT Conferencing Video Inc; BT Convergent Solutions Limited; BT ESPANA, Compania de Servicios Globales de Communication Telecommunicaciones, SA (Spain); BT Fleet Limited; BT France SA; BT Frontline Pte Ltd (Singapore); BT Global Communications India Private Limited; BT Global Services Limited (Hong Kong); BT Holdings Limited; BT Hong Kong Limited; BT Italia SpA (Italy); BT Limited; BT Nederland NV (Netherlands); BT Singapore Pte Ltd.

PRINCIPAL DIVISIONS

BT Global Services; BT Retail; BT Wholesale; Openreach; BT Design; BT Operate.

PRINCIPAL OPERATING UNITS

Digital Britain; BT Vision.

PRINCIPAL COMPETITORS

Nippon Telegraph and Telephone Corporation; AT&T Inc.; Verizon Communications Inc.; Siemens AG; Hutchison Whampoa Ltd.; China Mobile Communications Corporation; France Telecom S.A.; Telecom Italia S.p.A.; Vodafone Group PLC; Deutsche Telekom AG.

FURTHER READING

Armitage, Alex, "BT Profit Is Pushed Up by Rising Broadband Use," *International Herald Tribune*, May 18, 2007, p. 12.

Competition and Choice: Telecommunications Policy for the 1990s, London: HMSO, March 1991.

Cowell, Alan, "British Telecom Chairman Quits amid Stockholder Anger," *New York Times*, April 27, 2001, p. C2.

Dwyer, Paula, "The Sun Never Sets on British Telecom," *Business Week*, December 7, 1992, pp. 54–55.

Eglin, Roger, "BT Prepares to Beat the World," *Management Today*, July 1993, pp. 9–10.

Elder, Bryce, "BT Climbs amid Talk of Italian Wireline Unit Sale," *Financial Times*, February 20, 2010, p. 22.

———, "Solid Gains for BT as Tide of Confidence Starts to Turn," *Financial Times*, July 18, 2009, p. 22.

"Europe" and "The United Kingdom," *DATAPRO Reports on International Telecommunications 1990–91*, Delran, NJ: McGraw-Hill, 1990–91.

Flynn, Julia, Catherine Arnst, and Gail Edmondson, "Who'll Be the First Global Phone Company?" *Business Week*, March 27, 1995, pp. 176–80.

Flynn, Julia, and Mark Lewyn, "Why Telecom's Odd Couple Is Trying So Hard," *Business Week*, September 20, 1993, pp. 96, 98.

Flynn, Julia, Mark Lewyn, and Gail Edmondson, "What a Time to Take Over at British Telecom," *Business Week*, January 29, 1996.

Hass, Nancy, "The Whipping Boy: Meet British Telecom's Iain Vallance, the Rodney Dangerfield of Telecommunications," *Financial World*, September 15, 1992, pp. 48–49.

Hudson, Richard L., "BT Faces a Line of Potential International Competitors," *Wall Street Journal*, April 29, 1993, p. B4.

Lewis, Peter H., "MCI and British Telecom to Join Networks for Internet Market," *New York Times*, June 11, 1996, p. D5.

"Major Telecommunications Companies in Europe," *Profile of the Worldwide Telecommunications Industry*, Oxford: Elsevier Advanced Technology, 1990.

Newman, Karin, *The Selling of British Telecom*, London: Holt, Rinehart and Winston, 1986.

Palmer, Maija, "BT Plans Wi-Fi World-Beater," *Financial Times*, October 5, 2007, p. 6.

Purton, Peter, "Is BT Lost in the Fog of World Events?" *Telephony*, December 7, 1992, pp. 7–8.

Reinhardt, Andy, "Can a Grand Broadband Network Keep an Old-Line Telco Growing?" *Business Week*, July 26, 2004, p. 28.

———, "Strike up the Broadband," *Business Week*, May 30, 2005, p. 49.

Schenker, Jennifer L., "BT Rolls out a Massive Fiber Network," *Business Week Online*, July 16, 2008.

———, "BT's New CEO Has Work to Do," *Business Week Online*, May 30, 2008.

Schiesel, Seth, "AT&T and British Telecom Merge Overseas Operations," *New York Times*, July 27, 1998, p. A1.

"Shooting a Line," *Economist*, July 10, 1993, pp. 62–63.

Werdigier, Julia, "Beleaguered BT to Cut 15,000 Jobs and Its Dividend," *International Herald Tribune*, May 15, 2009, p. 16.

———, "BT Group to Cut 10,000 Jobs as Demand Tumbles," *International Herald Tribune*, November 14, 2008, p. 15.

C.O. Bigelow Chemists, Inc.

———————— ■ ————————

414 6th Avenue
New York, New York 10011
U.S.A.
Telephone: (212) 533-2700
Toll Free: (800) 793-5433
Fax: (212) 228-8107
Web site: http://www.bigelowchemists.com

Private Company
Incorporated: 1838
Employees: 40
NAICS: 424210 Drugs and Druggists' Sundries Merchant Wholesalers; 446110 Pharmacies and Drug Stores; 446120 Cosmetics, Beauty Supplies, and Perfume Stores

■ ■ ■

C.O. Bigelow Chemists, Inc., also known as C.O. Bigelow Apothecaries, has been a Greenwich Village institution since its early days as a one-man apothecary shop. Prescription medicines now form only a small portion of the store's revenues. It does the bulk of its business as a "destination for beautifully packaged health and beauty treatments." Bigelow sells "original formulary" products, which it makes using recipes from Clarence O. Bigelow's archives. These include high-end, hard-to-find European favorites, such as French hand-milled soaps and Italian toothpastes; homeopathic remedies; prescriptions; and surgical items, such as colostomy bags. The store is proud of its history and consciously maintains its old-time charm with most of its original fixtures in

place. Once frequented by Thomas Edison, Eleanor Roosevelt, and other American notables, today the store serves many show business celebrities.

FROM VILLAGE APOTHECARY SHOP TO NEW YORK INSTITUTION: 1838–1930

In 1838, Dr. Galen Hunter, a former Vermont physician, founded the Village Apothecary Shop in lower Manhattan's Greenwich Village. From the start, the Village Apothecary served both the prescription and beauty needs of its customers. The store on Sixth Avenue featured products from Dr. Hunter's tried and true formulary. One of its most well-known and sought-after products from 1838 was Dr. Hunter's Rose Wonder Cold Cream. In 1870, it introduced what became its best-selling Lemon Body Cream.

Clarence Otis Bigelow, one of Dr. Hunter's counter clerks, bought the apothecary shop from Hunter in 1880 with partners and changed its name to C.O. Bigelow Apothecary. With Bigelow at the helm, the shop expanded and became a neighborhood institution. In 1902, Bigelow built a new 2,700-square-foot building on Sixth Avenue to house his drugstore. This site became the store's permanent home. In 1920, he added a soda fountain with 40 stools. Bigelow, a tireless man, served for 40 years as treasurer of the Department of Pharmacy at Columbia University and for 17 years as president of the State Board of Pharmacy. He was also president of the West Side Savings Bank from 1911 until his death in 1922 at age 85.

COMPANY PERSPECTIVES

With our belief in the highest quality products, we travel the world, scouring for items that make a difference in the way you look and feel. For decades our landmark store has been a destination spot for discerning New Yorkers. Today, Bigelow continues to draw a cross section of dwellers, from celebrities (we won't go name dropping), to fashionistas, to neighborhood devotees who cherish the rarity of our old school approach. If you can't get it anywhere else, try Bigelow.

By this time, C.O. Bigelow was one of the busiest drugstores in New York City with the slogan: "If you can't get it anywhere else, try Bigelow's!" Six registered pharmacists worked on premises, filling 200 or more prescriptions a day, each of which was checked by three pharmacists before being dispensed. The store also had a fully stocked surgical department. It continued to offer a full line of cosmetics from the leading cosmetic manufacturers of the day (as well as its own line of original formulary creams and other items) and had a trained cosmetician on staff. Its reputation had grown worldwide, and it received regular orders for nonprescription items from customers in France, England, Poland, Hungary, and Palestine.

BLEND OF OLD & NEW: 1930S & 1940S

During the 1930s, the store remained a blend of the old and the new. It retained its original oak shelves and paneling, iron gas chandelier, and powder mixer, but also stocked up-to-date merchandise. Conscious of its place in U.S. history, Bigelow's maintained an archive of the prescriptions filled for its past rich and famous customers, including Thomas Edison (who came to see Dr. Hunter after burning his finger on a lightbulb), Samuel Clemens, Cornelius Vanderbilt, and Colonel William F. Cody.

However, by the 1930s the store had become rundown, and its profits were slipping. William B. Ginsberg, a pharmacist by training, sensed an opportunity and purchased C.O. Bigelow in 1939, becoming the first of three generations of Ginsbergs to own and run the store.

MIDTOWN STORE: 1962–65

Jerry Ginsberg, William Ginsberg's son, also a pharmacist, took over the store in 1952. He did so reluctantly at first, preferring to pursue a career as a jazz clarinetist and saxophone player. However, Ginsberg had a flair for the business, and C.O. Bigelow prospered during his tenure at the helm. In 1962, Bigelow opened a store called Bigelow Americana Chemists at the corner of Seventh Avenue and 53rd Street in New York in the new Americana hotel. Although the midtown branch was leased for 15 years, Bigelow sold its Americana business in 1965 when it received an offer that represented a tremendous profit.

Jerry Ginsberg's son, Ian Ginsberg, began working at Bigelow's soda fountain as a child in the 1970s. "I remember when E. L. Doctorow sat at one end of the counter and John Belushi sat on the other," he recalled in an October 31, 1999 *Daily News* article. (The food service at Bigelow's provided unlimited refills on 40 cent cups of coffee until it closed in 1984.) Like his father, Ian Ginsberg initially aimed for a career in music, but agreed, after discussion with Jerry Ginsberg, to complete a pharmacy degree as backup should his musical career fail. After becoming a licensed pharmacist in 1985, he joined the business.

NEW DIRECTIONS: THE EIGHTIES

However, Ian Ginsberg did not feel satisfied with his work at Bigelow, and so set out to transform the business. His vision was to make Bigelow into a destination for products that solved consumers' beauty dilemmas. He used the old counter for the soda fountain, which had closed in 1984, as a showcase for cosmetics. Preserving the store's old-fashioned charm, he stocked it with beautifully packaged health and beauty treatments and hard-to-find products from Europe and around the world.

This focus on making Bigelow a destination for specialty products served it well during the 1980s, a decade that witnessed the closing of many independent drugstores that were unable to compete with their new chain store competition. Bigelow also had a tough time succeeding against the chains. However, with its loyal customers, great windows, and well-renowned cosmetic lines, it was able to maintain its status quo.

NEW LINES & CATALOG SALES IN THE NINETIES

Bigelow embarked on several fortuitous new ventures in the 1990s. During the first half of the decade it

KEY DATES

—

1838: Dr. Galen Hunter founds the Village Apothecary Shop; he formulates Rose Wonder Cold Cream.

1870: Hunter's Lemon Body Cream becomes a best seller.

1880: Clarence Otis Bigelow, an employee, buys and renames the apothecary.

1902: Bigelow builds a new building to house his pharmacy.

1922: C. O. Bigelow dies.

1939: William B. Ginsberg purchases the store.

1995: Ian Ginsberg takes over the apothecary.

2005: Bigelow's introduces its personal care collection in partnership with Limited Brands.

of its business in beauty products, which included selling iconic brands such as Christian Dior, offbeat items from Europe, and its own product offerings.

PARTNERSHIP WITH LIMITED BRANDS

In 2005, Ginsberg created an original apothecary line of products based on C. O. Bigelow's original formulary. Drawing on artifacts and ledgers dating back to 1838 and re-creating the design of Bigelow's original packaging, the products targeted both genders by evoking the purity of ingredients such as rose water, lemon extract, peach nut oil, and witch hazel with artificial coloring or fragrances.

Bigelow partnered with Limited Brands, parent company of Bath & Body Works, in launching the line, which featured nostalgic packaging and debuted at its flagship store in New York, at a Limited Brands store located in the Easton Town Center in Columbus, Ohio, and in a Limited division store called Henri Bendel. A smaller product assortment was offered at Bath & Body Works' 70 flagship and 1,600 core stores.

"The whole line is [built] around problem solutions," explained Neil Fiske, chief executive officer of Limited Brands, in a December 2004 *WWD* article. In addition to reviving old formulas, the partnership also resurrected a product name that had fallen into disuse, cold cream, in its Rose Wonder Cold Cream. One of Dr. Hunter's first products, the cold cream had a rose petal base as a moisturizer and contained rose water as a tonic for itchy skin.

Limited Brands opened 10 C. O. Bigelow Stores in late 2004 and early 2005 to sell the full line of C.O. Bigelow products. Neiman Marcus and Nordstrom also carried some of the Bigelow line. By 2009, however, it had closed many of the stores, which, in retrospect, proved to be in less-than-choice locations.

dabbled in a few new products including soap and makeup, such as a line of nail polish named after herbs, which quickly took off. It started to produce an informal mail-order catalog in the mid-1990s, which was written and produced on low quality paper by Ian Ginsberg, "like something that The J. Peterman Company might have produced," he explained in an interview with Carrie Rothburd. The company also began to dabble in a few products (its own soap and makeup, branded as Alchemy) that proved a huge success. Within a few years the catalog had metamorphosed into a full-color, branded production on recycled paper.

In 1995, when Jerry Ginsberg retired, Ian Ginsberg took over the apothecary. Under the third-generation Ginsberg, Bigelow continued its emphasis on customer service. In making even a simple over-the-counter purchase, customers received one-on-one attention. "If you need Tylenol, you have to ask for it," explained Ginsberg in the 1999 *Daily News* article. "We have an incredible staff and we know a lot of stuff. So if you don't feel good, we can help you find the remedy that's best."

By 1999, Bigelow offered its products via catalog, messenger delivery, and personal telephone shopping. That year, the store also opened its third outpost at the Jeffrey New York, a department store located in Manhattan's meatpacking district. The store's brand, Alchemy, was sold at Sephora and Nordstrom's, and in countries around the world including Saudi Arabia, Japan, and the United Kingdom. During the early years of the new century, Bigelow was doing about 20 percent

As Bigelow closed out the first decade of the new century, Ginsberg continued his ongoing quest for new products, taking regular jaunts to Europe to find unusual and luxury items to bring back to the United States. The store continued to promote its online sales, sensing a great opportunity for an ever larger market. Moreover, Alec Ginsberg, Ian Ginsberg's son, was studying to become a pharmacist.

Carrie Rothburd

FURTHER READING

"Bigelow's Big Time," *Vogue*, March 2005, p. 450.

Colman, David, "The Racket Downstairs? Sounds Fine to Him," *New York Times*, November 26, 2006, p. 20.

Ginsberg, Ian, *Telephone interview with Carrie Rothburd,* April 9, 2010.

Hochwald, Lambeth, "RX for Success: The Friendly Pharmacists at Bigelow Are Just What the Doctor Ordered," *Daily News*, October 31, 1999.

"Limited Places a Big Bet on Bigelow," *WWD*, December 10, 2004, p. 18.

Canam Group Inc.

11505 1re Avenue, Bureau 500
Saint-Georges, Quebec G5Y 7X3
Canada
Telephone: (418) 228-8031
Toll Free: (800) 638-4293
Fax: (418) 228-1750
Web site: http://www.canamgroup.ws

Public Company
Incorporated: 1960 as Canam Steel Works
Employees: 2,923
Sales: CAD 625.8 million (2009)
Stock Exchanges: Toronto
Ticker Symbol: CAM
NAICS: 332312 Fabricated Structural Metal Manu-
   facturing

■ ■ ■

Canam Group Inc. is a Canada-based industrial
company operating 12 plants, its operations divided
among seven business units. Canam Canada produces
steel joists, girders, metal decks, and cladding, as well as
architectural and engineering services. Canam United
States offers similar products and the VertiSpace mezzanine system. Canam International partners with steel
fabricators in China, Romania, Russia, and Saudi
Arabia. Another business unit, Hambro, offers a
concrete floor system, mostly used in apartment and office buildings, while the Structural Heavy Steel
Construction unit fabricates heavy structural steel
components and aluminum risers. The focus of Structal-

Bridges is the manufacture of steel bridges, structural
bearings, and expansion joints. The final business unit,
Technix, offers three-dimensional modeling and
industrial detailing services. Canam Group is a public
company listed on the Toronto Stock Exchange and is
led by its longtime chairman and chief executive officer,
Marcel Dutil.

ORIGINS: 1960

The seeds of the Canam Group were planted in 1960
when Roger Dutil founded Canam Steel Works in St.
Gedeon de Beauce, Quebec, in 1960. In May 1961 the
company opened the doors to a 12,000-square-foot
plant and began fabricating steel joists from imported
steel. Two years later Dutil's 21-year-old son, Marcel,
who had worked at Canam as a student, joined the
company full-time. In 1966 he started his own company
in the barn behind his house, Manac Inc., to produce
semitrailers. In 1972 Marcel Dutil bought out his father
and U.S. partners to acquire Canam and merge it with
Manac, resulting in 1973 in the creation of Canam
Manac Group Inc. He also held an interest in Ottawa-
based Hambor and its patented composite floor system,
which Canam acquired in 1970.

Under the ambitious young chief executive, Canam
Manac Group enjoyed steady growth, spurred in large
measure by investments from the Desjardins Group of
Levis, Quebec, and the Caisse de Depot et Placement
du Quebec. While they acquired substantial stakes, Dutil retained majority control. The company opened a
plant in Boucherville, Quebec, in 1974 to fabricate steel
deck, and it also housed the first sales office and service

center for the Manac operation. In 1976 the company became involved in steel joist fabrication through the acquisition of a Boston company. Canam Manac then opened a steel joist fabrication plant in Mississauga, Ontario, in 1983.

COMPANY TAKEN PUBLIC: 1984

Dutil took Canam Manac public in 1984 and the company's stock was listed on the Montreal Stock Exchange. In that same year, the company expanded further through the acquisition of a pair of companies that specialized in steel joint fabrication: Toronto's Thames Steel Construction and Washington, Missouri-based Midwestern Joists. By this stage, Canam Manac was generating annual sales of CAD 203.8 million. In 1985 that amount increased to CAD 265.5 million. Along the way the company attempted, unsuccessfully, to become involved in prefabricated industrial buildings. Dutil also failed to acquire an ammunition manufacturer, Canadian Arsenals Ltd., when the government placed it up for sale, as well as making failed bids to add other assets. In 1985 office furniture manufacturer Nightingale Industries Ltd. was purchased and merged with company-owned Biltrite to create Biltrite Nightingale Inc., a venture that also did not perform as well as expected.

The second half of the 1980s brought further expansion. Maryland-based Standard Building Systems was acquired in 1986, helping Canam Manac to increase its share of the U.S. market in steel joists from 2 percent to about 10 percent. A year later, Murox Inc., a Quebec steel building system manufacturer, was added. Canam Manac also spent CAD 100 million to acquire Manitoba Rolling Mills and create vertical integration and prepare for a bid to enter the U.S. steel minimill industry. Canam Manac then added to its steel joist business in the United States by acquiring a fabrication plant in Indiana.

In that same year, the company bought a half-interest in another Quebec company, Tanguay Industries

Inc., a maker of logging machinery. Additionally during this period, Canam Manac acquired Quebec-based Comact Inc., maker of fiber-reinforced panels for vans and trailer bodies, and a steel product manufacturer in France, Société Coloco, providing a toehold in Europe. Canam Manac ended the 1980s by moving into the high-rise structures market when it won a contract to fabricate and erect the structural steel components for a 52-story building in Montreal.

RECESSION HURTS BUSINESS

The late 1980s also brought an effort at diversification that was far afield from the expertise of Canam Manac: the purchase of a half-interest in Noverco Inc., a gas distribution company mostly operating in Montreal. Because of difficult economic conditions, Dutil decided in 1991 to sell out to the other Noverco stakeholders. Not only did Canam Manac's steel business have to contend with a slump in the North American construction industry due to a recession, the company was adversely impacted by a strong Canadian dollar. The steel business remained profitable despite these drawbacks, but the time had come to focus on core areas. Noverco drained much needed resources, as did Biltrite Nightingale, and both were divested.

With a renewed emphasis on the steel fabrication business, Canam Manac resumed expansion after the recession abated. In 1993 a 32.3 percent interest in a Mexican structural steel fabrication business was acquired. In that same year, Canam Manac landed a major U.S. contract to fabricate and erect the structural steel components for a new arena in Boston, replacing the venerable Boston Gardens. Canam Manac expanded further into the United States in 1995 when it acquired a new plant in Columbus, Ohio, and purchased a Jacksonville, Florida, building that became a fabrication plant for structural steel components. The company also formed the Steel Plus Network, providing North American steel fabricators and steel construction industry suppliers with a number of services to help improve competitiveness and sales volume. It eventually limited its scope and became primarily a buying group.

Canam Manac's rate of growth accelerated in the second half of the 1990s as the North American economy soared. The company made several investments in 1996, including the acquisition of a Romsa, Monterrey, Mexico, operation; select assets of Lightsteel Industries Inc., a Quebec fabricator of steel sections used in the construction and manufacturing industries; a 45 percent interest in Quebec-based Structal Inc., fabricator of bridges and other complex steel structures; and the acquisition of a joist production plant in Calgary, Alberta.

KEY DATES

1960: Canam Steel Works is established.
1966: Manac Inc. is founded.
1972: Manac acquires Canam to create Canam Manac Group Inc.
1984: Company is taken public.
2005: Following reorganization, company is renamed Canam Group Inc.

INTERNAL & EXTERNAL GROWTH: 1997

The company pursued both internal and external growth in the late 1990s. In 1997 it acquired Marshall Steel Limited, a Quebec maker of cut-to-length beams used by structural steel fabricators, as well as Sun Steel of Sunnyside, Washington, a fabricator of joists and prefabricated steel buildings. In addition, Sun Buildings was launched, a new division that specialized in preengineered steel buildings, operating out of the Marshall Steel facility. A year later Canam Manac acquired the remaining shares in Structal, and in 1999 purchased an 80 percent stake in Expanpro, a Quebec load-bearing wall manufacturer. In 1998, as a result of its strong growth, Canam Manac topped the CAD 1 billion mark for the first time in its history.

Record revenues carried into the new century, exceeding CAD 1.11 billion in 2000, fueled in part by several major contracts for work on Pierre Elliott Trudeau International Airport in Montreal and a new football stadium for the New England Patriots in Foxboro, Massachusetts. A year later the company won a contract to fabricate and erect the structural steel components for the new stadium of the Philadelphia Eagles. The September 11, 2001, terrorist attacks on the United States had an adverse impact on U.S. commercial and industrial building, leading to overcapacity in steel joists and structural steel. A rise in the value of the Canadian dollar also hurt Canam Manac's profits, despite the company winning a number of major contracts.

Jobs secured in 2002 included the fabrication and erection of structural steel components for a new casino in Niagara Falls, Ontario, and Hartford, Connecticut's new convention center. In 2003 the Structural-Heavy Steel Construction unit won major contracts related to an Albany, New York-area generating station and the True North Spots and Entertainment Centre in Winnipeg, Canada. The Romania subsidiary also won a

contract for a new business complex in Bucharest. Moreover, Structal-Bridges secured the largest contract in its history in 2003, fabricating and erecting the beams used to construct a pair of 1,200-foot bridges across the North Saskatchewan River in Edmonton, Canada.

ADOPTION OF NEW NAME: 2005

Despite a strong performance on some fronts, Canam Manac was losing money. As a result, the company underwent a reorganization, laying off employees and selling some struggling units, including Tanguay, Manac, and a Mexican steel products plant, which fetched a combined CAD 75 million. With the loss of Manac, the company assumed a new name at the start of 2005, becoming Canam Group Inc. The company now focused on value-added products and the design and fabrication of construction products through its remaining business divisions, in particular joists, steel decks, heavy structural steel, bridges, concrete floor systems, high-rise residential buildings, and nonresidential construction projects. By the second quarter of 2005, Canam returned to profitability.

Canam tied up some loose ends in 2005 by selling the remaining Manac assets, including a building and some equipment. It also sold 55 percent of its interest in Steel Plus Network to fabricator members. Canam did not contract on every front, however. In October 2005 it introduced a new major project, the VertiSpace mezzanine system and components.

Positive developments continued in 2006. At the start of the year Canam International was formed to pursue the company's core businesses overseas through partnerships with established companies. Canam Canada expanded its headquarters, while Structal-Heavy Steel Construction enjoyed excellent success in both Canada and the United States. It won a contract in Toronto to fabricate and erect the structural steel components for the Metropolis retail and entertainment complex, and in New York City secured the contracts for work on both of the new baseball stadiums, worth CAD 110 million. A year later the unit also won the contract to fabricate the steel used in the new football stadium in East Rutherford, New Jersey, for the New York Giants and New York Jets, valued at CAD 100 million. In 2008 a contract for a new soccer stadium for the New York Red Bulls was added as well.

During this same period Canam acquired control of two Canadian companies, Goodco and Z-Tech, both of which manufactured structural bearings and expansion joints used in bridges and highways. Canam also acquired a 49 percent interest in a Chinese bridge and structural steel fabricator, United Steel Structures Limited, and Canam's U.S. subsidiary acquired Eastern Bridge, LLC, a New Hampshire fabricator of steel structures used in highway and railway bridges.

Canam recorded revenues of CAD 796.1 million and net income of CAD 48.4 million in 2008, and despite poor economic conditions the company looked to continue its strong growth. The company could not withstand a severe downturn in nonresidential construction in North America, however. Sales fell to CAD 625.8 million in 2009 while earnings were cut to CAD 20 million. Canam was hardly ready to retrench. In late 2009 it bought a stake in FabSouth LLC, a Fort Lauderdale structural steel fabricator, and in early 2010 increased its interest to 80 percent. Also in January 2010 Canam acquired InteliBuild Limited of Hong Kong. As a result, Canam was well positioned to take full advantage in an eventual turnaround in the construction industry.

Ed Dinger

PRINCIPAL OPERATING UNITS

Canam Canada; Canam International; Canam United States; Hambro; Structural Heavy Steel Construction; Structal-Bridges; Technix.

PRINCIPAL COMPETITORS

Commercial Metals Company; Gerdau Ameristeel Corporation; Steel of West Virginia, Inc.

FURTHER READING

Gibbens, Robert, "Expanding Canam Manac Feels Pressure of Success," *Globe & Mail,* June 10, 1986, p. B1.

Marotte, Bertrand, "Canam Manac on the Move but Stock Still Trades Ex-darling," *Globe & Mail,* March 7, 1988, p. B3.

———, "Canam to Focus on Long-Term Growth," *Globe & Mail,* April 30, 1988, p. B3.

Marshall, Samantha, "Quebec Steps Up NY Construction Jobs," *Crain's New York Business,* May 21, 2007, p. 33.

McKenna, Barrie, "Canam Sells Noverco Stake," *Globe & Mail,* March 15, 1991, p. B1.

"Reorganization by Canam Manac to Focus on Construction Products," *American Metal Market,* April 13, 2004, p. 4.

"Structural Fabricator Canam Upbeat as Net Income Falls," *American Metal Market,* February 25, 2010, p. 9.

Champagne Bollinger S.A.

BP 4
16 rue Jules Lobet
Ay, F-51160
France
Telephone: (+33 03) 26 53 33 66
Fax: (+33 03) 26 54 85 59
Web site: http://www.champagne-bollinger.fr

Subsidiary of Société Jacques Bollinger S.A.
Founded: 1829 as Renaudin Bollinger et Cie
Incorporated: 1986
Employees: 130
Sales: EUR 66 million ($90.2 million) (2008 est.)
NAICS: 424820 Wine and Distilled Alcoholic Beverage
  Merchant Wholesalers; 312130 Wineries

■ ■ ■

Champagne Bollinger S.A. is one of the oldest and most exclusive of the great French champagne houses, and is also one of very few to remain under the control of its founding family. Located in the village of Ay, Bollinger produces a limited selection of champagne styles. These include its classic Special Cuvée Brut, Bollinger Grande Année Brut, and the very rare Bollinger R.D. Extra Brut. Since 2008, Bollinger has also produced a Rosé champagne, blending Grande Année wines with red wines from Ay. In addition, the winery produces the highly exclusive Les Vieilles Vignes Français, a *blanc de noirs* based on extremely rare non-grafted vines; and Côte Aux Enfants Ay Rouge, a red wine produced only in good vintage years.

Bollinger supports its champagne production with 163 hectares of company-owned vineyards, producing the pinot noir, chardonnay, and meunier grape varieties. Bollinger's vineyards provide 60 percent of the grapes needed for its champagnes. The company is one of the last in the Champagne region to use traditional production techniques, including wooden cask aging. For this, the company employs its own cooper, the last champagne house to do so. Bollinger operates more than five kilometers of underground cellars, storing more than 14 million bottles. In 2009, the company shipped more than 2.5 million bottles, of which more than 85 percent went to the export market.

Bollinger is a subsidiary of Société Jacques Bollinger S.A. (SJB), established in order to ensure that the company remains under control of the founding family. That company also serves as the holding company for the family's other interests, which include Champagne Ayala, also based in Ay, which produces 400,000 bottles per year; the Burgundy wine house Chanson Père et Fils; exclusive Cognac brand Delamain; and the Loire Valley vintner Langlois-Château. SJB is also a partner in Tapanappa Winery in Australia, and holds a majority stake in U.K.-based Mentzendorff, which has handled the international distribution of the group's champagnes since 1858. Champagne Bollinger generated EUR 66 million ($90 million) in sales in 2008, while SJB's total revenues topped EUR 120 million. Family member Ghislain Montgolfier is the group's chairman. Since 2007, Champagne Bollinger has been led by CEO Jérôme Philipon, the first nonfamily member to head the company.

COMPANY PERSPECTIVES

A unique quality and style. Before becoming a great champagne, Bollinger is first of all a great wine. This idea is behind the passionate quest for excellence that the House has pursued for more than 180 years.

FOUNDING A CHAMPAGNE DYNASTY IN 1829

France's Champagne region had long been cultivated as vineyards. Like most of the region, it had come into the possession of France's aristocracy. In the village of Ay, the Villermont family became particularly prominent landholders, with properties dating back to the 15th century. The family's parcels remained scattered among different branches of the family until the middle of the 18th century. In 1750, the Comte de Villermont, Pierre-Gilles Hennequin, brought together the vineyards held by his family with those held by his wife's family in Ay. In that same year, King Louis XV gave Hennequin possession of the Château de Cuis there.

This house already produced wines, although not under the family name. This was according to the custom of the time that the country's aristocracy avoided becoming involved in commerce. Into the beginning of the 19th century, the family nevertheless began selling its wines, notably to the export market. By then, de Villermont's son, Athanase Louis-Emmanuel Hennequin de Villermont, had taken over his father's title. By then, the family's estates extended to Ay, Chouilly, Cramant, Cuis, and Grauves.

The growing renown for the Champagne region's sparkling wines introduced new financial opportunities during the first half of the century. The Villermont estates became particularly prized for the quality of their grapes, and the resulting champagne. In 1829, Villermont formed a partnership with Jacques Bollinger and Paul Renaudin to commercialize the estate's champagne. Bollinger, born in 1803 in Ellwangen, in the Kingdom of Würtemberg, Germany, had come to France to act as a sales agent for another champagne house, Muller Ruinart. Renaudin also worked for Muller Ruinart, helping Bollinger develop that company's sales to Germany, the Netherlands, and Belgium.

In keeping with family tradition, Villermont's name was left off the label of the new champagne house. Instead, the company became known as Renaudin Bollinger et Cie. Jacques Bollinger soon developed closer ties with Villermont, marrying his daughter Louise

Charlotte in 1837. Renaudin died in 1851, leaving no heir, so that the Bollinger-Villermont family became sole owners of the company.

ROYAL WARRANT IN 1884

From the start, Bollinger focused on producing a dry (Brut) champagne, developing its own blend of chardonnay and pinot noir grapes. The result was a distinctive and highly prized champagne that soon set the company apart from its rivals. The growing reputation of the company's champagne enabled Bollinger to develop a strong export business early. Bollinger initially targeted his native Germany, where Bollinger became a favorite of the various royal families and other dignitaries there.

England became another important market for Bollinger, starting in the 1850s. In 1858, the company developed a partnership with Ludwig Mentzendorff, a native of Riga who had come to London in 1850 in order to sell his own Mentzendorff Kummel. Mentzendorff became Bollinger's exclusive agent for the United Kingdom, before becoming the company's primary agent for nearly all of its exports. Mentzendorff succeeded in introducing Bollinger to the highest levels of British society. Bollinger's sons, Joseph and Georges, also played an important role in developing the international reputation of the company's champagne. This effort culminated with Queen Victoria awarding Bollinger the Royal Warrant as a supplier to the British court. This warrant was renewed at the beginning of the 20th century, and remained in place into the next century as well.

Georges and Joseph Bollinger took over as leaders of the company and began acquiring new vineyards to expand Bollinger's production. Under their leadership, the company added vineyards in Bouzy and Verzenay, as well as in Louvois. All three, like Ay itself, were later qualified as Grand Cru, denoting the high quality of the grapes they produced.

MADAME LILY FROM 1941

Bollinger's growing estate permitted the company to achieve a high degree of self-reliance. It also helped spare the company in 1911, when 6,000 grape growers revolted against the then-common practice among other champagne producers of importing grapes from other regions for wines labeled as champagne. That year was notable for the company for another reason, as the Mentzendorff company in England developed a new name, Special Cuvée, for part of Bollinger's champagne production. The Special Cuvée line referred to the company's nonvintage champagne.

KEY DATES

1829: Renaudin Bollinger et Cie is established by Jacques Bollinger, Athanase de Villermont, and Paul Renaudin to produce champagne in Ay, France.

1884: Bollinger receives a Royal Warrant from Queen Victoria of England.

1960s: Bollinger changes its name to Champagne Bollinger.

1986: Société Jacques Bollinger (SJB) is formed as a holding company for Champagne Bollinger and other family-owned businesses.

2005: SJB acquires the Ayala champagne house, also in Ay.

2009: Bollinger expands production to 2.5 million bottles per year as part of a EUR 25 million investment program.

Georges's son Jacques Bollinger took over the company after his father's death in 1918. Just 21 years old at the time, Jacques Bollinger continued to build the company, notably by expanding its winery as well as by extending and modernizing its cellars. The Bollinger cellars ultimately reached more than five kilometers in length, with a capacity to store and age more than 14 million bottles. Bollinger also purchased the company's future offices, a manor on the Boulevard du Maréchal de Lattre de Tassigny.

Bollinger's vineyard holdings had also been growing in the new century. Before World War I, Jacques and brother Edgar had acquired an important part of the group's estate, in Tauxières, which was also planted with pinot noir grapes, important to the company's champagne production. In 1930, Jacques Bollinger completed the purchase of the Louvois vineyard, while a cousin, Pierre Moret de Rocheprise, acquired a vineyard in Avenay for the family.

Jacques Bollinger died in 1941 soon after the start of World War II. His widow, Elizabeth Law de Lauriston Boubers, more familiarly known as Madame Lily, took over the direction of the company and oversaw its most impressive growth. By the early 1960s, Bollinger had more than doubled its production. The company had also added to its vineyards, purchasing part of its Grauves vineyard in 1955 (and acquiring the remainder in 1968) and a vineyard in Bisseuil in 1961. The company also expanded its vineyards in Ay, as well as in Mutigny.

Madame Lily also led Bollinger in its first diversification during the 1960s. The group's longtime distribution partner Mentzendorff had fallen into financial problems following World War II. This led Bollinger to acquire the company at the beginning of the 1960s. Bollinger also established its own champagne distribution company for the French market, BLD France. In 1964, Bollinger stepped outside the champagne market for the first time, buying Delamain Cognac in 1964.

BONDING IN 1973

Bollinger also debuted two new champagnes under Madame Lily. The first appeared in the 1950s, when the company created its new label, RD, for Recemment Dégorgé, starting with the 1952 vintage. The new champagne, based on the group's Grand Année vintage champagne, denoted bottles that were allowed to rest on their lees for an extended period, of not less than eight years, before being disgorged, or separated. In 1969, Bollinger debuted Les Vieilles Vignes Français, a champagne based on grapes grown on the rare ungrafted vines in two Ay vineyards. These vineyards had been among the rare vineyards to survive the great phylloxera outbreak that destroyed most of France's vineyards in the 1870s.

With no children of her own, Madame Lily turned over the direction of the company to her nephews, Claude d'Hautefeuille, who became the company's managing director in 1971, and Christian Bizot, who took over in 1978. By then, Bollinger had adopted the new name for its labels, becoming simply Champagne Bollinger during the 1960s.

Bizot and d'Hautefeuille continued the company's policy of expansion, modernizing its production while extending its vineyards to include Champvoisy and, in the 1980s, the extension of its Mutigny vineyard. In the meantime, the group had continued diversifying its holdings acquiring the noted Loire Valley vineyard Maison Langlois-Chateau in 1973.

Bollinger in the meantime had developed a novel means of raising its international profile. In 1973, a bottle of Bollinger became prominently featured in that year's James Bond release, *Live and Let Die*. This began a long-term relationship between the fictional secret agent and Bollinger, which, like Bond's Aston Martin, became an integral part of the development of the James Bond character.

NEW HOLDING IN 1986

In 1986, d'Hautefeuille and Bizot created a new holding company in order to regroup all of the family's holdings, including Champagne Bollinger. The new company, called Société Jacques Bollinger S.A. (SJB), effectively preserved Champagne Bollinger's independence as a family-owned company.

Bizot then set out to preserve the reputation of champagne itself. Into the 1980s, the reputation of the region's sparkling wines had begun to suffer as a result of overproduction and oversupply, particularly from a growing number of companies producing poor or mediocre wines labeled as Champagne. Bizot stepped in, establishing the Madame Bollinger Foundation in 1988 in order to promote professional and ethical standards in the Champagne region. Bizot then took his campaign a step further, publishing the Bollinger Charter of Ethics and Quality in 1992. This statement of principles committed Bollinger to maintaining the highest winemaking standards, and served as a gauntlet thrown down to its rivals. Bizot's charter later received credit for helping to restore the quality levels, and the reputation, of Champagne's wines.

Bizot became the company's chairman in 1994, turning over its direction to Ghislain de Montgolfier, the great-great-grandson of founder Jacques Bollinger. Through SJB, de Montgolfier continued the group's expansion, acquiring the well-respected Burgundy wine house Chanson Père et Fils in 1999, forming the Tapanappa Winery joint venture in Australia in 2004, and acquiring fellow Ay champagne house Ayala in 2005. In 2007, de Montgolfier became the company's chairman, appointing Jérôme Philipon, previously head of Coca-Cola Europe, as the first nonfamily member to lead Bollinger. Soon after, the company launched its new Rosé Champagne, in 2008.

RAISING PRODUCTION CAPACITY

Champagne Bollinger also invested in its growth in its own right. The company's vineyard holdings expanded again, with the purchase of the Vertus vineyard in the Champagne region, and the Venteuil and other vineyards in the Marne Valley region. In 2003, the company launched a major EUR 25 million investment program designed to modernize and expand its production capacity.

This effort, which continued through 2009, enabled the company to raise its total production from 2 million to 2.5 million bottles by 2010. The company's cellars held more than 14 million bottles, equivalent to six years of sales. At the same time, the company also expanded Champagne Ayala's production, from 400,000 to 700,000 bottles. This allowed Champagne Bollinger to claim the seventh place among the leading Champagne houses. By then, Bollinger was also one of the few remaining Champagne producers still owned by their founding families.

M. L. Cohen

PRINCIPAL COMPETITORS

Champagne Moët and Chandon SCS; Veuve Clicquot Ponsardin SCS; Boizel Chanoine Champagne S.A.; Vranken Pommery Monopole S.A.; Champagne Laurent Perrier S.A.; Champagnes P and C Heidsieck S.A.S.; Courvoisier S.A.S.; Champagne Louis Roederer S.A.; Taittinger Compagnie Commerciale et Viticole Champenoise S.A.S.; G H Mumm et Cie S.A.; Champagne Lanson S.A.S.; Kriter Brut de Brut S.A.

FURTHER READING

Ambrosi, Pascal, "Bollinger Arrose une Centaine de Pays," *Les Echos*, December 8, 2005, p. 18.

"Bollinger Confie les Rênes du Groupe Familial à Jérôme Philipon," *AFP*, September 15, 2007.

"Bollinger to Launch Rose Champagne," *Marketing*, May 7, 2008, p. 8.

"Cazes, Croser and Bollinger Form JV," *just-drinks.com*, March 4, 2004.

Duncan, Rob, "Bond and Bollinger," *Vietnam Investment Review*, November 24, 2008, p. S16.

Flallo, Laurent, "Bollinger Acquiert la Maison de Champagne Ayala," *Les Echos*, January 4, 2005, p. 15.

"Jacques Bollinger Reprend le Bourguignon Chanson Père et Fils," *Les Echos*, September 14, 1999, p. 12.

Laforce, Marguerite, "Au Fil des Ans, la Famille Bollinger A Construit un Véritable Groupe," *Les Echos*, May 25, 1998, p. 11.

Meignan, Géraldine, "La Maison Bollinger," *L'Expansion*, January 1, 2003.

Prial, Frank J., "Remembrances of a Champion of the Champagne World," *New York Times*, July 17, 2002.

Charles M. Schulz
Creative Associates

—■—

1 Snoopy Place
Santa Rosa, California 95403
U.S.A.
Telephone: (707) 546-7121
Web site: http://www.flyingace.net

Private Company
Incorporated: 1971 as Charles M. Schulz Creative
    Development
Employees: 10
Sales: $35 million (2009 est.)
NAICS: 533110 Lessors of Nonfinancial Intangible As-
    sets (Except Copyrighted Works)

■ ■ ■

Charles M. Schulz Creative Associates authorizes
licensed products and other derivative works based on
the comic strip *Peanuts*, which the firm's founder and
namesake drew from 1950 until his death in 2000. The
company has creative and editorial control over the strip
and its characters, and splits royalties with copyright
owner United Media. Schulz Creative Associates works
with approximately 900 licensees worldwide, which
market a wide range of toys, clothing, paper goods,
videos, and other items that feature beloved characters
including Snoopy, Charlie Brown, Lucy, and Linus. The
company is owned and managed by the heirs of Charles
Schulz.

BEGINNINGS

Charles Monroe Schulz was born on November 26,
1922, in Minneapolis, Minnesota. Nicknamed "Sparky"

after Sparkplug, a horse that appeared in the comic strip
Barney Google, Schulz wanted to be a cartoonist from a
very young age. When he was 15 a drawing of his dog
Spike was published in the popular *Ripley's Believe It or
Not!* strip, and after high school Schulz worked to hone
his skills by taking an art correspondence course.

Like millions of others, Schulz was drafted into the
U.S. Army during World War II, serving in Europe as a
staff sergeant in the 20th Armored Division. Following
the war he taught drawing for his former correspondence school, Art Instruction, Inc., while selling
occasional cartoons to the *Saturday Evening Post*. In
1947 he also started producing a weekly comic strip
about the foibles of a group of children for the *St. Paul
Pioneer Press,* called *Li'l Folks.*

In 1950 the *Pioneer Press* dropped Schulz's strip,
and he submitted a modified version of it to the United
Feature Syndicate, home to such hits as *Li'l Abner* and
Nancy. Although the odds against acceptance were about
a thousand to one, the distributor decided to take a
chance on it, but insisted on changing the name since
Li'l Folks was similar to that of another comic. The first
installment of *Peanut*s (a name Schulz would forever dis-
like) appeared on October 2, 1950, and during the first
year seven newspapers picked it up. As was standard
practice, United Feature Syndicate would own the strip's
copyright and split the income with the artist, who
received $90 for his first month of effort.

By 1953 the exploits of perpetual loser Charlie
Brown, his dog Snoopy, and friends Lucy, Linus,
Schroeder, and the rest had caught on with the public,
and Schulz was earning the then-handsome sum of

COMPANY PERSPECTIVES

Charles M. Schulz Creative Associates was established to work in partnership with United Media on the creative and business management of the Peanuts worldwide licensing program, providing creative oversight and art direction to the over 900 Peanuts licensees. Creative Associates is located in Santa Rosa, California, where the Peanuts creator maintained his studio for over thirty years.

$30,000 per year. Two years later he was honored by the National Cartoonists Society as outstanding cartoonist of the year, and by 1958 more than 350 U.S. and 40 foreign papers were carrying *Peanuts*. Schulz also started two other strips in the late 1950s, but abandoned each after several years.

The gently drawn children of *Peanuts* (adults were never seen), with oversized heads and simple but expressive features, lived lives that were largely bittersweet. When Charlie Brown tried to kick a football it was invariably pulled away at the last second; Lucy was always rejected by Beethoven-obsessed Schroeder; Linus never saw the Great Pumpkin; and even the daydreaming, carefree Snoopy, who several years into the strip had begun to have his thoughts revealed in balloons above his head, was always foiled in his attempts to shoot down World War I flying ace The Red Baron.

LICENSED PEANUTS PRODUCTS BEGIN APPEARING IN 1958

Compilations of *Peanuts* strips had been published starting in the early 1950s, and in 1958 the first licensed character toys were produced by Hungerford Plastics, with cards and party supplies appearing two years later from Hallmark. In 1958 Schulz, his wife, and their five children moved from Minnesota to Sebastopol, California (an hour north of San Francisco), and at the beginning of the 1960s the cartoonist formed a new licensing relationship with San Francisco-based Determined Productions.

Determined's first effort was a *Peanuts* date book that added striking graphic design to Schulz's drawings, and the firm subsequently convinced the skeptical artist to create a hardcover "microbook" on a single theme. Published in 1962, *Happiness Is a Warm Puppy* quickly became a phenomenon, spending months on the best-seller lists and leading to dozens of popular follow-ups.

Determined Productions soon began developing a range of plush toys, clothing, bedding, calendars, and more, and over the years would account for close to 90 percent of licensed *Peanuts* products. It also helped launch a chain of small *Peanuts* boutiques, which began appearing in department stores around the United States in 1967.

FIRST TV SPECIAL AIRS: CHRISTMAS 1965

In 1965 Schulz teamed up with producer Lee Mendelson and animator Bill Melendez (who had worked on Disney's *Bambi* as well as *Peanuts*-based Ford Falcon ads in 1960) to create "A Charlie Brown Christmas" for CBS television, after the Coca-Cola Company requested such a program. It was completed that December, but CBS executives were reportedly nervous about the show's lack of dramatic action and pianist Vince Guaraldi's jazz score, as well as the inclusion of a Gospel reading by Linus that former Sunday school teacher Schulz had insisted on including.

Their doubts were shown to be unfounded when the half-hour program was a critical and popular success, winning Emmy and Peabody awards and becoming a seasonal classic that was rerun each year. Several dozen other animated *Peanuts* specials would soon follow, with such titles as "It's The Great Pumpkin, Charlie Brown" and "A Charlie Brown Thanksgiving."

In 1967 a musical called *You're a Good Man, Charlie Brown* debuted off Broadway in New York. It, too, was a hit, enjoying a long initial run and later becoming a favorite of community and school theater groups. Two years later the first *Peanuts* feature film, *A Boy Named Charlie Brown*, was released. Schulz wrote the script for the movie, which like the TV shows was produced by the team of Mendelson and Melendez. It performed well at the box office and was followed by three other films.

If anyone now doubted that *Peanuts* had become a part of the cultural firmament, in 1969 NASA named the *Apollo 10* lunar excursion module "Snoopy" and the command capsule "Charlie Brown." During the year Schulz and his wife also opened the Redwood Empire Ice Arena near the cartoonist's studio in Santa Rosa, California, which would go on to play host to numerous concerts and skating events. In 1972 Charles and Joyce Schulz were divorced, however, and a year later the cartoonist married Jeannie Clyde, 16 years his junior, whom he had met at the skating rink.

EDITORIAL, CREATIVE CONTROL WON BY SCHULZ IN 1980

To coordinate his business interests, in 1971 Schulz founded Charles M. Schulz Creative Development (the

KEY DATES

1950: United Feature Syndicate begins distributing *Peanuts*.

1958: First toys based on *Peanuts* characters appear.

1965: "A Charlie Brown Christmas" airs on CBS-TV and other shows quickly follow.

1971: Charles M. Schulz Creative Development is founded.

1980: Schulz wins creative, editorial control of *Peanuts* from United Media, parent of United Feature.

2000: Schulz dies the night before last strip is published; control passes to his family.

2002: Schulz museum opens near cartoonist's studio in Santa Rosa, California.

last word later changing to Associates), shifting several key staffers from the ice arena to run it. In the mid-1970s, with *Peanuts* now appearing in more than 1,500 papers in the United States and abroad, he began seeking greater control over the strip, whose copyright was held by United Feature Syndicate. After a series of negotiations, in 1980 he won creative and editorial control over *Peanuts* and its licensed products, with United Media (the newly formed parent of United Feature Syndicate) continuing to own the copyrights, contract rights, and reprint rights.

In 1982 a new off-Broadway show, *Snoopy!!! The Musical,* opened. Like *You're a Good Man, Charlie Brown,* which now ranked as the most-produced musical in history, it would go on to become a staple of children's theater groups.

In 1984 *Peanuts* syndication reached 2,000 newspapers, and in 1985 insurance company Met Life began a long-running ad campaign that featured Snoopy. More than 20,000 separate licensed products were now being made, as well as many other unauthorized ones. *Peanuts* was especially popular in the Far East, where 40 percent of total licensing agreements were held by Japanese manufacturers.

By 1989 annual revenues from *Peanuts* products were worth an estimated $1 billion at retail. Schulz and United Feature Syndicate split a 5 to 10 percent royalty on the wholesale price of each item, with the cartoonist's annual earnings now reaching a peak of $62 million, up from $4 million 15 years earlier. Schulz was now one of the 10 highest-paid entertainers, according

to *Forbes*, and *Peanuts* was the most successful comic strip in history.

In anticipation of the 40th anniversary of *Peanuts*, in 1989 Determined Productions announced a slate of new products featuring Snoopy, including sportswear, bedding, baby bibs, and books. A Snoopy-themed shop was opened in the San Francisco FAO Schwarz store, and during the anniversary year there was a *Peanuts* Super Bowl halftime show and exhibits at the Smithsonian and Louvre museums. Some two-thirds of licensed products were now sold outside the United States, with clothing accounting for 20 to 30 percent of sales, toys and accessories 15 percent, books 10 to 15 percent, and the rest made up of greeting cards and other merchandise.

CHARLES SCHULZ DIES IN FEBRUARY 2000

In November 1999 Charles Schulz was diagnosed with colon cancer, and a month later he announced plans to publish the final *Peanuts* strip on Sunday, February 13, 2000. The cartoonist died in his sleep the night before it appeared.

While some popular comics such as *Blondie* continued to be drawn by others for years after their creators' retirement or death, Schulz had been adamant that *Peanuts* would end with him, and his contract with United Media guaranteed this. Nevertheless, the strip would continue to appear in more than 2,400 papers in 75 countries, rerun in sequence from 1974 to 2000 (when all the major characters had been clearly established), and new licensed products would continue to be authorized. Some 350 million people read *Peanuts* each day.

In 1998 Schulz had met a 34-year-old cartoonist and graphic designer named Paige Braddock at a cartoonist's convention, and the following August she began working for the six-person Charles M. Schulz Creative Associates as senior vice president and creative director, initially assigned the task of turning *Peanuts* TV specials into books. After Schulz's death she was assigned the task of selecting an existing drawing or creating a new one to meet the needs of licensees, as well as making sure that the products stayed true to the characters' established personalities.

Working in conjunction with United Media, a team of four proposal reviewers voted on each request, with split decisions resolved by an executive committee consisting of Schulz's widow Jeannie and son Craig, who was Schulz Creative Associates' president. Unusual requests required approval from the entire family.

LICENSING REQUESTS DOUBLE IN 2001

In the year after Schulz's death the number of licensing requests nearly doubled, from between 1,500 and 2,000 per month to more than 3,000. In November 2000 SnoopyStore.com was launched by Schulz Creative Associates and Colorado-based Concepts Direct, Inc., to offer *Peanuts* merchandise. The Web site drew on the latter firm's catalog, which had been introduced three years earlier. In the first year after its founder's death the company, which was still based at Schulz's studio in Santa Rosa, took in $19 million.

In March 2001 Universal Studios Japan opened a large amusement park called Snoopy Studios within its theme park, and in May the U.S. Postal Service issued a Snoopy stamp in tribute to Schulz, which was designed by Paige Braddock. In the fall a Hallmark-sponsored exhibit of original Schulz strips opened at the Norman Rockwell Museum in Stockbridge, Massachusetts, while a coffee-table book of his art was published. Other new products included Sony and Nintendo video games.

In February 2002 the newly produced "A Charlie Brown Valentine" ran on ABC television, previous shows having been seen on CBS. It was created by Schulz's original TV production team, Lee Mendelson and Bill Melendez. New books, overseen by Braddock, were also published during the year. *It's the Great Pumpkin, Charlie Brown*, *A Charlie Brown Christmas*, and *A Charlie Brown Valentine* were all strong sellers.

SCHULZ MUSEUM OPENS IN AUGUST 2002

In August the $8 million Charles M. Schulz Museum opened in Santa Rosa across from the Redwoods Empire Ice Arena. Developed by Jeannie Schulz, who had purchased much of the material after her husband's death (Schulz had given away many original drawings), it included a re-creation of his studio, *Peanuts*-inspired sculptures, and a Snoopy maze, along with an archive and research library.

In the fall of 2003 Schulz Creative Associates and United Media partnered with sports/media e-commerce provider FanBuzz to develop a new official *Peanuts* on-line store that would feature a mix of existing products and ones created specifically for the site, with hard-to-find foreign items a specialty. A new direct-mail catalog was created in conjunction with the relaunched SnoopyStore.com, with four mailings per year expected to reach one million *Peanuts* fans in 2004.

Schulz Creative Associates was now handling 24,000 product licensing requests per year, and in 2004 took in $35 million as estimated by *Forbes*, making Schulz second only to Elvis Presley on its list of top-earning "dead celebrities." Some 90 percent of United Media's $100 million in revenues for the year also came from *Peanuts*.

In December 2005 the 40th annual telecast of "A Charlie Brown Christmas" on ABC was rated first in its time slot with 15 million viewers, and advertisers paid up to $200,000 per 30-second ad. Originally produced for under $150,000, the show had become a Christmas viewing tradition and earned more than $50 million over the years.

WARNER HOME VIDEO LICENSES TV SHOWS IN 2007

In the fall of 2007 Warner Home Video was awarded rights to release DVDs of the 50 extant *Peanuts*-based television programs, including the perennial classic "A Charlie Brown Christmas." Each disc would include a remastered version of one of the original programs along with bonus features, some newly shot. Snoopy, Charlie Brown, and friends would join Warner's high-profile animation portfolio that included Bugs Bunny, The Flintstones, Dr. Seuss, and Popeye. "Be My Valentine, Charlie Brown" and "It's the Easter Beagle, Charlie Brown" were released in early 2008, and other titles followed.

Seeking to engage a new, younger generation of readers, in the fall of 2008, 20 new *Peanuts* "Webisodes" were made available online, intended for download to cellphones or iPods. The animated versions of strips from 1964 (which was felt to be a slightly edgier time in the strip's history), were originally offered at no charge, but would later be sold through the iTunes store.

In 2009 longtime U.S. amusement park licensee Cedar Fair introduced a new attraction called Planet Snoopy as an offshoot of its popular Camp Snoopy. Intended for small children, it featured *Peanuts*-themed rides, a *Peanuts* restaurant, and strolling costumed characters offering hugs and photo opportunities. It was added to the firm's chain of theme parks that included Cedar Point and Kings Island.

Ten years after Charles Schulz's death, and 60 years after *Peanuts* debuted in a small handful of newspapers, some 2,200 papers continued to publish reruns of the classic comic strip, and demand for licensed products remained strong around the world. Along with copyright holder United Media, Charles M. Schulz

Creative Associates appeared set for a long and prosperous run as steward of its founder's vision.

Frank Uhle

PRINCIPAL COMPETITORS

Dr. Seuss Enterprises, L.P.; The Jim Henson Company; MTV Networks; Paws, Inc.; Turner Broadcasting System; The Walt Disney Company; Warner Brothers Entertainment, Inc.

FURTHER READING

Arnold, Thomas K., "WHV Holds Ball for Charlie Brown," *Hollywood Reporter*, October 4, 2007.

Beckett, Jamie, "Snoopy Barrage on the Way," *San Francisco Chronicle*, August 3, 1989, p. C1.

Boxer, Sarah, "Charles M. Schulz, *Peanuts* Creator, Dies at 77," *New York Times*, February 14, 2000, p. 1A.

Gaudette, Karen, "New Museum for *Peanuts* Lovers Opens in Santa Rosa," *Associated Press Newswires*, August 15, 2002.

James, Meg, "Charlie Brown's Profitable Christmas," *Los Angeles Times*, December 11, 2005, p. E5.

Lauer, George, "*Peanuts* Empire Future Unclear," *Santa Rosa (Calif.) Press Democrat*, March 2, 2000, p. B1.

Michaelis, David, *Schulz and Peanuts*, New York: Harper, 2007.

Minton, Torri, "Good Grief, Charlie Schulz," *San Francisco Chronicle*, May 9, 1989, p. B3.

Smith, Chris, "*Peanuts* Power Licensing," *Santa Rosa (Calif.) Press Democrat*, February 18, 2001, p. A1.

Swartz, Susan, "Paige's World," *Santa Rosa (Calif.) Press Democrat*, September 16, 2007, p. D1.

City Lodge Hotels Limited

The Lodge, Bryanston Gate Park
Cramerview, Gauteng 2060
South Africa
Telephone: (+27 11) 557-2600
Fax: (+27 11) 557-2670
Web site: http://www.citylodge.co.za

Public Company
Incorporated: 1986
Employees: 800
Sales: ZAR 665.02 million (2009)
Stock Exchanges: Johannesburg
Ticker Symbol: CLH
NAICS: 721110 Hotels (Except Casino Hotels) and
Motels

■ ■ ■

City Lodge Hotels Limited operates four, moderately priced hotel chains in South Africa. The company owns 18 Road Lodge units with 1,695 rooms, its one-star hotel brand. Next on the company's price scale is its two-star brand, the nine-unit, 1,041-room Town Lodge chain. The company's flagship City Lodge brand comprises 11 three-star hotels with 1,802 rooms. Its most expensive brand is the Courtyard brand, a four-star chain consisting of six hotels and 451 rooms.

FOUNDER'S BACKGROUND

Hans Rudolf Enderle showed little promise as a teenager, never giving any indication that a pioneer of

the South African hotel industry was in the making. The Switzerland native took the exams required to advance to high school when he was 15 years old and he failed them. "I wasn't clever enough," he conceded in the January 13, 2010 edition of Johannesburg's *Sunday Times*. "It's as simple as that." His poor showing at exam time blocked off an academic path for Enderle, forcing him to choose another direction.

After leaving secondary school, Enderle got a job at a bakery in eastern Switzerland and began delivering bread. His first choice for a career was to become a chef, but after training as an apprentice, he again met with failure, describing himself as a "lousy chef" in his interview with the *Sunday Times*. Next, he set his sights on the hotel industry and enrolled in a hotel management program at the University of Lausanne. There, he found his calling, earning a certificate that provided entry into the industry that would become his life's passion.

Enderle's training in Lausanne was not a ticket to a position of influence in the hotel industry. In Switzerland, advancement to the top of the hotel industry began at the bottom, forcing Enderle to begin his rise by working as a waiter. He was working in such capacity during the mid-1960s when a conversation with a customer led to a momentous change in his life. The customer, the personnel manager for Amalgamated Hotels in Johannesburg, offered Enderle a job if he moved to South Africa. Enderle wanted to improve his English (he had been unable to secure a work permit for England or a green card for the United States) so he accepted the offer. He arrived in Johannesburg in 1966

COMPANY PERSPECTIVES

We will be recognised as the preferred Southern African hotel group. Through dedicated leadership and teamwork we will demonstrate our consistent commitment to delivering caring service with style and grace. We will constantly enhance our guest experience through our passionate people, ongoing innovation and leading edge technology. Our integrity, values and ongoing investment in our people and hotels will provide exceptional returns to stakeholders and ensure continued, sustainable growth.

and began working as a receptionist at the Langham Hotel, earning ZAR 100 per month.

Enderle did not remain in South Africa for long. What he had learned in Lausanne was not being practiced in Johannesburg. He found the hotel industry in Johannesburg to be in a sorrowful state, "terrible, really terrible," he said in his interview with the *Sunday Times*. He returned home to Switzerland after a stint at the Langham Hotel, but he soon gave South Africa a second chance, returning to the country where he would spend the rest of his life.

In 1970 Enderle was living in Switzerland when he received a telephone call and a job offer. A Holiday Inn chain was being started in South Africa and Enderle was asked to manage a hotel north of Johannesburg at what was then called Jan Smuts International Airport, the primary airport for domestic and international travel to and from South Africa. Enderle accepted the offer and quickly distinguished himself within the company. He was promoted to regional director in 1977 and rose to the top of the managerial ranks in 1983, when he was named chairman and managing director.

ENDERLE FORMS CITY LODGE HOTELS: 1985

Enderle's reign as the leader of the Holiday Inn chain was brief, but his accomplishments after his departure more than compensated for any bitterness he may have felt. In 1985 the Holiday Inn chain was sold to a company named Southern Sun. Enderle was told he would continue to lead the chain under Southern Sun's ownership, but after the deal was concluded Southern Sun installed a new managing director, relegating Enderle to second in command. Having been stripped of his title, Enderle no longer wanted to remain at

Holiday Inn, but before he left he made Southern Sun an offer. He offered to buy a half-built property north of Johannesburg in Randburg and Southern Sun agreed to the proposal. Enderle solicited the financial support of the Mine Employees Pension Fund, which agreed to put up ZAR 6.5 million to develop the hotel. "The deal was that they would get 65 percent for providing the capital and I, along with a couple of my colleagues, would eventually get 35 percent for doing the work," Enderle explained in the March 8, 2010 issue of *allAfrica*.

City Lodge Hotels began operating in 1985 when the 123-room City Lodge Randburg opened on August 1, National Day in Switzerland. By the time the City Lodge Randburg opened, Enderle was hatching bigger plans, never intending to operate a single hotel and shocked that Southern Sun had not required him to sign a restraint of trade agreement forbidding him from opening additional hotels. He approached the Mine Employees Pension Fund again with plans to open 1,000 rooms within the next five years. The managers of the fund agreed to back his efforts, giving Enderle ZAR 65 million to develop a chain of City Lodge Hotels. He had at his disposal the resources to build a sizable, regional hotel operator, one that would enjoy high occupancy rates because of the market strategy developed by its founder.

MID-MARKET COMPETITOR

When Enderle began building his City Lodge chain, he positioned the company as a mid-priced operator. The demand for hotel rooms in the region surrounding Johannesburg had reached a stage where rental rates had increased at a faster pace than inflation, creating a void in the middle segment of the market. Enderle jumped into the void, positioning City Lodge as a mid-market operator by offering rooms 25 percent to 50 percent less than any equivalent hotels in the area. He was able to offer the substantially lower prices and remain profitable by eliminating certain amenities and unprofitable appendages such as restaurants, convention rooms, and oversized lobbies. He emphasized service and cleanliness and offered only what his guests said they needed, creating a new lodging concept that would become known as "select service" hotels.

To fill his rooms, Enderle courted businesspeople during the week and families and groups attending weddings, sporting events, and other functions during the weekend. He created a range of special offers tailored to attract each particular type of guest and enjoyed immediate success. In 1987 his company opened two more City Lodge properties, then two more the following year. In 1989 the company's seventh hotel, the City

```
┌─────────────────────────────────────────────┐
│                                             │
│              KEY DATES                      │
│                  ━■━                         │
│  ─────────────────────────────────────────  │
│                                             │
│  1985:  First City Lodge Hotel opens near   │
│         Johannesburg.                       │
│  1990:  Second chain, Town Lodge, is created.│
│  1992:  City Lodge Hotels becomes a publicly traded│
│         company.                            │
│  1995:  Addition of Road Lodge and Courtyard gives│
│         the company four hotel chains.      │
│  2003:  One million room nights are sold during the│
│         year, a record total.               │
│  2009:  Hans Enderle announces his plans to retire as│
│         chairman.                           │
│                                             │
└─────────────────────────────────────────────┘
```

Lodge Bloemfontein, opened, marking the 1,000th room, completing Enderle's objective one year ahead of schedule.

TOWN LODGE IS BORN: 1990

Enderle continued to expand during the 1990s, using the success of the City Lodge chain to launch other hotel ventures, building a multi-brand lodging corporation. In 1990 he created Town Lodge, a more inexpensive version of City Lodge, starting the chain with a single property in Bellville, near Cape Town. Expansion during the next five years occurred in two directions, as Enderle used both vehicles to drive City Lodge Hotels' financial growth. In 1993 two new City Lodge properties were opened and the second Town Lodge debuted, with the grand opening of the units scheduled to coincide with Switzerland's National Day on August 1. In 1994 the date was used to unveil two new Town Lodge hotels, giving Enderle more than a dozen properties contributing to City Lodge Hotels' financial stature.

As Enderle's company diversified into a two-chain business, he took steps to secure the capital that would be required to open additional hotels. In 1992 City Lodge Hotels completed an initial public offering (IPO), listing its shares on the Johannesburg Stock Exchange. The year also marked Enderle's last days as City Lodge Hotels' CEO. After being attacked and held to the floor with a gun to his head by assailants at his home, Enderle moved to a golfing estate in the Western Cape where he presided as the company chairman, leaving day-to-day management of City Lodge Hotels to his management team.

ROAD LODGE & COURTYARD JOIN THE FOLD: 1995

Enderle's habit of launching major initiatives at five-year intervals was on display in 1995. He started another hotel chain, Road Lodge, moving further down the price spectrum. Road Lodge became the most inexpensively priced of the three City Lodge Hotels chains and the brand Enderle would expand most aggressively. The year also included another major addition to City Lodge Hotels' portfolio, Enderle's first move upmarket. He acquired a 50 percent interest in entities associated with the Courtyard Hotels chain, which featured rooms with dining tables, kitchenettes, and amenities such as personal shopping service.

City Lodge Hotels expanded in four directions during the second half of the 1990s, increasing the presence of its one-star Road Lodge brand, its two-star Town Lodge brand, its three-star City Lodge brand, and its four-star Courtyard brand. The period provided Enderle and his managers with their first great test, as occupancy rates steadily declined during the last years of the decade, slipping to 69 percent by 2000. At one point, Enderle considered expanding into neighboring countries as a way to mitigate the damage caused by rising room vacancies. Botswana, Zambia, and Namibia were named as likely candidates for the company's excursion beyond South Africa's borders, but Enderle never made the geographic leap.

Economic conditions improved at the start of the next decade and City Lodge Hotels' business flourished. In 2003 the company sold one million room nights during its fiscal year, the first time it had accomplished the feat in its history. Profits exceeded ZAR 100 million the following year when South Africa was chosen to host the 2010 F.I.F.A. World Cup, an event that promised to be a boon to the company's business.

PREPARATIONS FOR WORLD CUP & ECONOMIC DESPAIR: 2008–09

In preparation for the World Cup, City Lodge Hotels launched an ambitious expansion campaign. In 2008 the company began spending ZAR 397 million set aside for building seven new hotels. The scale of the capital investment program increased in early 2009, when the company said it intended to spend nearly ZAR 1 billion by 2011 to build 10 new hotels. City Lodge Hotels had achieved record-high occupancy rates of 82 percent during the previous two years, encouraging management to press forward, but deteriorating economic conditions soon delivered a swift and decisive blow to the company.

The recession at the end of the 1990s drained the company of vitality. During a three-year period, occupancy rates steadily fell, reaching a nadir of 69 percent. A decade later, the company's occupancy rate fell to the same low point, but the decline occurred with devastating speed, taking place during a six-month period in 2009.

City Lodge Hotels' management hoped the start of the World Cup in June 2010 would spark a return to the high occupancy rates historically enjoyed by the company. As executives waited for economic conditions to improve, they also braced themselves for the beginning of a new era, one without the leadership of Enderle. Enderle announced his retirement in late 2009, setting the date for his departure to coincide with City Lodge Hotels' 25th anniversary on August 1, 2010.

Jeffrey L. Covell

PRINCIPAL SUBSIDIARIES

Budget Hotels (Pty) Ltd.; City Lodge (Airport Property) Ltd.; City Lodge (Randburg) (Pty) Ltd.; City Lodge Holdings (Share Block) (Pty) Ltd.; Courtyard Management Company (Pty) Ltd.; Property Lodging Investment (Pty) Ltd.

PRINCIPAL COMPETITORS

InterContinental Hotels Group PLC; Marriott International, Inc.; Hilton Worldwide.

FURTHER READING

"Ambitious Expansion," *allAfrica*, March 8, 2010, p. 24.

Barron, Chris, "Hans Enderle: Chairman, City Lodge," *Sunday Times*, January 30, 2010.

Baumann, Julius, "South Africa: Hotelier Plans Retirement with Precision Timing," *allAfrica*, March 8, 2010.

"City Lodge Expands into Africa," *Africa News Service*, August 6, 2001.

"City Lodge Is Set for Major Expansion," *Africa News Service*, February 14, 2003.

D'Angelo, Audrey, "City Lodge Plans New World Cup Hotels," *Star* (South Africa), August 15, 2008, p. 3.

Columbia Manufacturing, Inc.

1 Cycle Street
Westfield, Massachusetts 01085
U.S.A.
Telephone: (413) 562-3664
Fax: (413) 568-5345
Web site: http://www.columbiamfginc.com

Private Company
Incorporated: 1877 as Pope Manufacturing Company
Employees: 125
Sales: $17.6 million (2009)
NAICS: 337127 Institutional Furniture Manufacturing;
   336991 Motorcycle, Bicycle, and Parts Manu-
   facturing

■ ■ ■

Columbia Manufacturing, Inc., is a Westfield, Massachusetts-based manufacturer of furniture and bicycles. Although the company's primary business is school furniture, Columbia is linked to the beginnings of the bicycle industry in the United States. Today, Columbia is a minor bike brand and the company offers a modest line of imported mountain bikes and classic-style bikes for men, women, and children. The company's furniture business, accounting for 95 percent of revenues, is focused on the school market and includes plastic molded chairs, desks, tables for grades K through 12, as well as chairs, tables, computer workstations, and combination chairs and desks for the college market. In addition, Columbia sells its school products to the religious market and serves the home and office

market with a variety of chairs, desks, workstations, and filing cabinets. The company also offers folding tables and chairs for event seating. Columbia furniture is sold through a network of authorized dealers covering all 50 states and Canada.

19TH-CENTURY ROOTS

The founder of Columbia Manufacturing was Albert Augustus Pope. He was born in 1843 into a well-known Boston family that had made its fortune in lumber, but his father elected to pursue real estate investments, which failed to pan out. Shunned by his disapproving family, Pope's father was a broken man, and Albert Pope was forced to begin working at the age of 10 to help support his family, ending his formal schooling five years later. He quickly proved to be an ambitious businessman. As a youth he bought fruits and vegetables from neighborhood farms and hired other boys to hawk his produce. Pope was still in his teens, working as a store clerk, when the Civil War broke out and he served with distinction, involved in a number of major battles. He advanced in rank until he became an honorary lieutenant colonel by war's end, and for the remainder of his life was known as Colonel Pope. Following the war Pope returned to his previous job, but soon used $900 in savings to start his own business, selling slipper decorations and shoe manufacturers supplies. He enjoyed immediate success and established himself as a prominent businessman.

Pope became interested in bicycles in 1876, when as a member of the city council of Newton, Massachusetts, he attended the Centennial Exposition in Philadelphia,

Pennsylvania. He was fascinated by a British-made high front-wheeler bicycle. A year later he formed Pope Manufacturing Company, imported a pair of the bicycles, and hired someone to make a copy using local materials. Pleased with the results and convinced that bicycles could be successfully manufactured in the United States, he secured the key patents and forged a partnership with Weed Sewing Machine Company in Hartford, Connecticut, contracting Weed in 1878 to produce 50 high-wheelers under the Columbia brand name. The Columbia sold so well that Weed began producing more bikes and fewer sewing machines, and in time Pope bought the Weed factory.

At the height of the bicycle craze in the mid-1890s, Pope was producing about 250,000 bicycles a year. The market was soon saturated, however. Pope diversified by applying some of the technology the bicycle industry had developed (pneumatic tires, differential axles, spring suspension, wire wheels, and ball and roller bearings) to the manufacture of automobiles. Pope championed the electric car and in the final years of the 1800s manufactured 500 electric as well as 50 gas-powered cars. To stabilize his bicycle business, he also joined forces with other manufacturers in 1900 to establish American Bicycle Company. One of the other firms was H.A. Lozier & Co. of Cleveland, Ohio, which opened a bicycle manufacturing plant in Westfield, Massachusetts, in 1897.

FOUNDER'S DEATH: 1909

American Bicycle Company did not fare well. It failed in 1901, was reorganized, and failed again in 1903. A year later Pope Manufacturing Company was reorganized, assuming control of many of the assets held by American Bicycle Company. Pope began consolidating the operations in the Westfield plant, but the company was unable to refinance its debt and was forced into receivership. Albert Pope's health began to deteriorate, and his son was appointed receiver. In August 1909 Pope died at the age of 66.

By 1913 all Columbia bicycle manufacturing was done in Westfield, and the following year the corporate

offices were also moved there from Hartford, Connecticut. Pope Manufacturing filed for bankruptcy in 1915, and a year later it emerged as Westfield Manufacturing Company and continued to produce Columbia brand bicycles. The company became a subsidiary of The Torrington Company of Connecticut in 1933.

It was in 1953 during Torrington's ownership that the company branched into school furniture. While on the surface bicycles and school furniture made an odd pairing, the combination made sense on a number of levels. Bicycles were a seasonal item and Westfield was eager to find a product to manufacture during the off-season. Because of its expertise in chrome-plated steel tubing, the factory was already set up, and its workers required little training to produce the standard framework of school chairs and desks. Thus, it was the ideal complement to the manufacture of bicycles, which continued but with less prestige than in years past. While older Columbia bicycles became collector's items, newer models were mostly inexpensive department store products.

ADOPTION OF COLUMBIA MANUFACTURING NAME: 1961

Westfield Manufacturing became an independent company once again in 1960. The following year it aligned itself with its brand to become Columbia Manufacturing Company. Its independence lasted only to 1967 when it merged with MTD Products Inc. Founded in Cleveland, Ohio, in 1932 as Modern Tool & Die Company, MTD started out supporting the automobile industry, but during the post-World War II era began producing gardening products for the emerging suburbs. In the late 1950s the company began producing lawnmowers, which led to the introduction of other outdoor power equipment in the 1960s. MTD then expanded through a series of acquisitions in the 1960s, including Columbia Manufacturing, whose bicycles fit MTD's growing outdoor profile.

While walk-behind and riding lawnmowers and garden tractors, along with snow throwers, remained core products for MTD, bicycles did not, especially in the 1980s when foreign competition crippled U.S. manufacturers. In 1987 Columbia filed for bankruptcy and a year later was bought by some members of its management, including President Kenneth Howard, Bruce Turcotte, and Emil Stang. The reorganized company held high hopes, as reflected by the title of its new catalog: "New Beginnings." Rather than toiling in the low-margin, value part of the market, Columbia planned to concentrate on the production of high-end bikes under the "Class by Columbia" name. The

```
┌─────────────────────────────────────────┐
│                                         │
│            KEY DATES                    │
│                 ■                       │
│  1877:  Pope Manufacturing Company is formed. │
│  1914:  Headquarters moves to Westfield, │
│         Massachusetts.                  │
│  1953:  Company begins producing school furniture. │
│  1961:  Columbia Manufacturing name is adopted. │
│  1993:  Company emerges from bankruptcy focusing │
│         on furniture.                   │
│                                         │
└─────────────────────────────────────────┘
```

company lacked the wherewithal to pursue this strategy, however. In order to pay off creditors, the company had been forced to sell equipment that made tubing, rims, and other parts, which now had to be jobbed out.

By the end of the 1980s, Columbia was generating $40 million in annual sales, 30 percent of which came from school furniture. Unable to turn a profit, the company was once again on the block, and in the spring of 1990 a deal was reached to sell it to Colorado-based Roadmaster Industries Inc. for $3.2 million. Roadmaster was the former bicycle division of AMF Corp., which had gone bankrupt in 1986 and was acquired by Henry Fong, the chief executive officer of Equitex Inc., which also acquired A.J. Enterprises, maker of golf bags, pool accessories, and fitness equipment. Columbia was deemed an excellent fit, but the acquisition fell through. Roadmaster claimed that Columbia was at fault because it failed to disclose it was facing serious environmental charges (the discharge of polluted wastewater into Westfield's sewer system), while Columbia officials maintained that Roadmaster was simply unable to obtain financing at a time when the country was suffering from the effects of a recession. The matter would become the subject of lawsuits and countersuits.

CHAPTER 11 BANKRUPTCY: 1991

After the deal with Roadmaster failed, Columbia attempted to sell the business to the employees' union, the International Association of Machinists and Aerospace Workers. A tentative agreement was reached to sell a controlling interest, but it never came to fruition. Faced with mounting losses, Columbia filed for Chapter 11 bankruptcy protection in March 1991, claiming total assets of $18.4 million, secured debt of $8.3 million, and unsecured debt of $4.7 million. A few days later Columbia laid off 59 workers and having run out of parts suspended bicycle production. A decade earlier Columbia had employed 600 people, but that number was now reduced to fewer than 100, of which

50 worked in the cavernous Westfield plant turning out school furniture.

One of Columbia's few remaining assets was its name. In early 1992 the company received permission from the bankruptcy court to license the production of Columbia bicycles to the Western Auto Supply retail chain. While 300 of the stores sold only auto parts, about 1,000 offered home items and bicycles. The three-year deal provided Western Auto with the Columbia name, trademark, logo, and other properties associated with the bicycles in exchange for a $2.50 royalty for every bicycle sold and a $50,000 minimum. Not only did the arrangement provide a source of revenue, however modest, it kept the trademark in the marketplace until Columbia could resume production. Columbia also considered selling its profitable school furniture business in 1992. An unidentified suitor from the institutional furniture business expressed interest in Columbia's remaining operating division, but nothing came of the matter.

Columbia emerged from bankruptcy in 1993, again led by Howard, Turcotte, and Stang, who acquired all of the remaining assets with the exception of the real estate. The company now leased space in its former factory where it continued to manufacture school furniture. While Columbia abandoned any hopes of returning to the mass market production of bicycles, it maintained ties to its original business by offering a limited number of bicycles for the specialty market, mostly through importing. While annual revenues were now less than $12 million, Columbia was at least a profitable concern.

GROWTH IN THE NEW MILLENNIUM

By focusing almost all of its attention on school furniture, Columbia grew at a double-digit rate in the late 1990s and beyond. A key to its success was better customer service and reliable delivery. The company also expanded its product offerings, introducing such items as activity tables, computer workstations, and upholstered furniture. It also expanded beyond the school market to sell to churches, companies, and homes. Business was strong enough that in the early 2000s, Columbia retired its waste treatment and plating line with a new automated system for nickel and chrome plating.

Columbia continued to sell bicycles. In addition to an imported line of mountain bikes, Columbia acquired parts to assemble commemorative bikes, such as its 125th anniversary special edition "Custom Deluxe" cruiser. Columbia also developed a new market for its classic-styled bikes, filled with nostalgia for people of a certain age, as a premium offering for corporation incentive programs. Although the Columbia brand was not likely to regain the luster it once possessed in the bicycle industry, it appeared that the company, with the revenues of its core school furniture business to rely on, would be able to maintain its proud tradition for many years to come.

Ed Dinger

PRINCIPAL DIVISIONS

Bicycles; Furniture.

PRINCIPAL COMPETITORS

Huffy Corporation; International Library Furniture, Inc.; Scholar Craft Products, Inc.

FURTHER READING

"Col. A.A. Pope Dies at Summer Home," *New York Times*, August 11, 1909.

Freebairn, William, "Columbia on Roll with Furniture," *Springfield (MA) Sunday Republican*, November 10, 2002, p. E01.

Geehern, Christopher, "Columbia Execs Sue Colo. Firm," *Springfield (MA) Union-News*, June 12, 1991, p. 26.

———, "Columbia Files under Chapter 11," *Springfield (MA) Union-News*, March 5, 1991, p. 1.

———, "Columbia Outlines Rebirth," *Springfield (MA) Union-News*, June 1, 1993, p. 17.

———, "Columbia Seeks Approval to Peddle Bicycles' Name," *Springfield (MA) Union-News*, December 10, 1991, p. 1.

———, "Potential Buyer Surfaces for Columbia Furniture Unit," *Springfield (MA) Union-News*, January 14, 1992, p. 17.

Goddard, Stephen B., *Colonel Albert Pope and His American Dream Machines*, Jefferson, NC: McFarland & Company, Inc., 2000.

Hachadourian, Kris, "Columbia Manufacturing Co. Lays Off 59 Factory Employees," *Springfield (MA) Union-News*, March 13, 1991, p. 24.

Dassault Aviation S.A.

78, quai Marcel Dassault
Saint Cloud, 92552 Cedex 300
France
Telephone: (+33 (0) 1) 47 11 40 00
Fax: (+33 (0) 1) 47 11 49 01
Web site: http://www.dassault-aviation.com

Public Company
Incorporated: 1936 as Société Anonyme des Avions Marcel Bloch
Employees: 12,000
Sales: EUR 3.42 billion ($4.9 billion) (2009)
Stock Exchanges: Euronext Paris
Ticker Symbol: AM
NAICS: 336411 Aircraft Manufacturing; 334511 Search, Detection, Navigation, Guidance, Aeronautical, and Nautical System and Instrument Manufacturing

■ ■ ■

One of Europe's last independent manufacturers of military aircraft, Dassault Aviation S.A. is also a leading producer of executive jets, focusing on the top end of the market. Dassault Aviation also makes electronic communications products through subsidiary Sogitec Industries S.A., while sister company Dassault Systèmes S.A. has been highly successful developing manufacturing software. Although listed on the Euronext Paris, only a small percentage of Dassault Aviation's shares are publicly traded. The founding family is the major shareholder through the holding company Groupe In-

dustriel Marcel Dassault S.A.S. (GIMD). The French government (via EADS) owns a 46 percent share in Dassault Aviation, which has long resisted attempts to combine it with other, nationalized aerospace firms. However, international cooperation has increasingly become the rule for military aircraft development in Europe. The Rafale, introduced in 1991, was expected to be Dassault's last independently developed fighter. The company was developing the nEUROn UCAV (unmanned combat air vehicle) in collaboration with the multinational European Aeronautics Defence & Space Co. (EADS).

Dassault with some justification has used the words "industrial revolution" to describe the development of its top-end business jet, the Falcon 7X. First delivered in 2007, it was designed entirely in virtual reality and bypassed the prototype stage altogether. More than two-dozen risk-sharing partners and 1,500 engineers worked on the project, enabled by software supplied by sister company Dassault Systèmes. Boeing Company adopted the same process for its massive 787 superjumbo airliner.

The last manufacturer of large executive jets left in Europe, Dassault produces major sections of Falcons at its factories at Saint Cloud near Paris for final assembly in Little Rock, Arkansas. The company has a total of 17 facilities and several sales offices globally.

AVIATION PIONEERS

Dassault was founded by Marcel-Ferdinand Bloch who was born in Alsace on January 22, 1892. As a schoolboy in Paris Bloch viewed his first airplane, built by the Wright brothers, making a low pass over the city and

COMPANY PERSPECTIVES

Technological excellence and innovation is the motto of Dassault Aviation on which its spirit, passion, and history are based. The Group ensures the quality, reliability, and safety of its aircraft through a strategy of constant innovation, its project management capability, and its mastery of complex systems.

then circling the Eiffel Tower. As a young man, still fascinated with aviation, Bloch attended the École Supérieure de l'Aéronautique, France's first school for aeronautical engineering. He established a factory in a converted garage, and persuaded his father-in-law to finance his small aeronautical business. During World War I Bloch developed a variable pitch propeller for the Spad fighter that gave French pilots the ability to outmaneuver their German adversaries. The Spad propeller made a great deal of money for Bloch who, after the war, went into housing construction.

Bloch began to manufacture airplanes again in the early 1930s when French military contracts were once more available. However, the complexion of French politics changed abruptly in 1936 when the Socialist-Communist "Popular Front" government of Léon Blum came to power. On January 1, 1937, Bloch's aircraft factories were nationalized by the Société Nationale de Constructions Aéronautiques du Sud-Ouest (S.N.C.A.S.O.), one of six state-controlled aeronautic factories. Bloch was retained as a civil servant and invested the compensation he received for his company in a variety of North American securities. After the Popular Front fell from power, Bloch founded a new aircraft company that later produced the highly successful Bloch 152 fighter.

After the Germans invaded France at the outset of World War II, Marcel Bloch, a Jew, was asked to build aircraft for the German war effort as an "honorary Aryan." Bloch refused to collaborate and was forced into hiding. He was later arrested in Lyon and jailed. Eight months before the war ended he was deported to the Buchenwald concentration camp where he remained until the area was liberated by U.S. forces in May 1945.

Bloch converted to Roman Catholicism after the war and changed his last name to Dassault, the *nom de guerre* of his brother who was a member of the French resistance. Although an "l" was added, the name literally means "on the attack." Marcel Dassault subsequently became an honored member of General de Gaulle's in-

ner circle, but since his company had been destroyed by the war it was once again nationalized.

POST-WORLD WAR II RENEWALS

Dassault recruited the most brilliant engineers from the best schools in France to work for a new company, Avions Marcel Dassault. Dassault's first project was the development of a small military liaison aircraft which was later manufactured for Air France under the name Languedoc. In 1951 the company began production of its Ouragan (Hurricane) jet fighter. When production of the Ouragan ended in 1953, the company had built 441 of the planes. In 1954 Dassault introduced its next jet, the Mystère. Designed as a subsonic fighter, the Mystère was the first European jet to break the sound barrier in level flight. The Mystère was followed by the Étendard attack jet. In 1953 Dassault acquired the manufacturing license for Armstrong Siddeley's Viper turbojet engine. The Viper was the intended power plant for Dassault's delta-wing Mirage fighter jet, which made its maiden flight in 1955.

Dassault had grown quickly in 10 years. Nonetheless, the company employed only a small workforce primarily composed of engineers and designers. Most of the actual production of aircraft was subcontracted to the state-owned company Sud-Aviation. Doing so was an intentional policy of Marcel Dassault. Unlike Dassault, state-owned companies were better able to keep workers employed while demand for their products was low. As a private company, however, Dassault was free to continue developing new aircraft designs without worrying about laying off production workers. The company's engineers were less specialized than others. Each was capable of designing an entire airplane. As a result, they could be moved easily from one project to the next, wherever they were needed most. In short, Dassault did not encounter the kinds of employment problems that plagued the state-operated companies.

FRANCE PULLS OUT OF NATO

In 1958 Marcel Dassault was elected a member of the French Parliament and represented the Beauvais region north of Paris. As a Gaullist deputy, Dassault continued to support the conservative political causes of his party. During this time France implemented a policy of independent military deterrence that culminated in the nation's 1966 decision to withdraw from the North Atlantic Treaty Organization (NATO). The defense of France was now solely the responsibility of the French military. Consequently, the demand for military equipment increased greatly, and the primary beneficiary was Avions Marcel Dassault.

```
┌─────────────────────────────────────────────┐
│                                               │
│              KEY DATES                        │
│                   ■                           │
│  ─────────────────────────────────────────    │
│                                               │
│  1936:  Marcel Dassault's aircraft factories are │
│         nationalized.                         │
│  1955:  Mirage jet fighter makes first flight. │
│  1967:  Avions Marcel Dassault acquires controlling │
│         interest in Breguet Aviation, four years before │
│         a full merger.                        │
│  1979:  New leftist government acquires minority │
│         stake in and veto power over Dassault- │
│         Breguet.                              │
│  1986:  Serge Dassault takes over company following │
│         death of his father.                  │
│  1991:  Rafale multi-role fighter is introduced. │
│  2000:  Longtime company veteran Charles Edel- │
│         stenne becomes first outside the family to │
│         serve as chairman and CEO of Dassault │
│         Aviation.                             │
│  2007:  Company completes first deliveries of the │
│         revolutionary Falcon 7X long-range business │
│         jet.                                  │
│                                               │
└─────────────────────────────────────────────┘
```

Dassault owned factories in nine locations across France. The design facilities and primary factories were located at Saint Cloud outside of Paris. The Bordeaux plant handled the final assembly of components manufactured by Sud-Aviation, while the other plants handled subassembly work and flight testing. The Martignas facility, however, later became primarily responsible for manufacturing missiles. Dassault also founded an electronics company in 1963 called l'Electronique Marcel Dassault. The electronics company, which was operated by Dassault's son Serge, provided his aircraft company with a variety of flight control and avionics devices.

RISE OF THE FALCON

Against the advice of several advisers, Marcel Dassault ordered the development of the Mystère into a small business jet. The civilian version of the Mystère was sold outside of France under the English name of Falcon (it was thought that this would increase its international marketability). The Mystère/Falcon later became one of the world's most popular private jets. In 1972 Dassault and Pan Am created a U.S. subsidiary called Falcon Jet Corporation for the sale and service of Falcon jets in the United States. (Dassault bought out Pan Am's interest in 1980.) In 1974 the company acquired a former Air-

motive facility in Little Rock, Arkansas, for final assembly of Falcons.

Besides assisting Sud-Aviation in the development of the French-British Concorde SST (supersonic transport) at this time, Dassault also developed improved versions of its Mirage fighter jet. Regarded as the most successful European jet since Britain's Canberra bomber, the Mirage was sold to over a dozen foreign air forces.

In June 1967 Avions Marcel Dassault purchased a 62 percent majority interest in Breguet Aviation, the French partner in the Franco-British Jaguar jet-fighter project. Breguet was founded in 1911 by French aviation pioneer Louis Breguet. The company was nationalized in 1936, but managed to regain a significant degree of independence three years later when it repurchased three of its former factories from the government.

MIRAGE'S ROLE IN THE SIX-DAY WAR

During June of the same year, Egypt, Syria, and Jordan launched a surprise attack on Israel in what later became known as the Six-Day War. Israel, however, was armed with Dassault's Mirage fighter jets that destroyed the Soviet-equipped Egyptian air force in three hours. The Mirages performed so well during the conflict that they were given much of the credit for the subsequent Israeli victory. President de Gaulle imposed an embargo on 50 additional Mirages bound for Israel. The embargo was lifted three years later by President Georges Pompidou, after it was learned that Israeli spies had acquired the plans for the Mirage and that modified versions were already being built in Israel. At approximately the same time, the French government also agreed to sell 110 Mirage fighters to Libya.

The French government, fully aware of the French aerospace industry's decreasing ability to compete internationally, campaigned for the rationalization (or merger) of several French aircraft manufacturers. The state-owned aircraft companies Sud-Aviation, Nord-Aviation, and Sereb (a missile manufacturer) were merged to form Aérospatiale in 1970. A year later, with the encouragement of the government, Breguet Aviation, a publicly traded company that was controlled by Marcel Dassault, merged with the larger, privately owned Avions Marcel Dassault. The new company, Avions Marcel Dassault-Breguet Aviation, operated 20 factories and accounted for 35 percent of all French aerospace production. Marcel Dassault's reason for merging his company with Breguet was that both companies could economize their operations by eliminating duplicated facilities and bureaus. Dassault also wanted to take advantage of Breguet's public stock listings in Paris and Brussels in order to raise capital. Dassault required a $280 million line of credit in order to develop a new 134-passenger commercial jetliner called the Mercure.

The Mercure was a twin-engine airliner very similar in appearance to the Boeing 737. In fact, the Mercure competed with the Boeing 737 for the same market. Only 10 Mercures had been sold by 1976, all of them to the French domestic airline Air Inter. The project was abandoned after the company failed to reach an agreement with McDonnell Douglas whereby the two companies would coproduce the subsequent Mercures.

FINANCIAL SCANDAL: 1976

Dassault-Breguet became involved in an unusual scandal during 1976 when the company's financial director, Hervé de Vathaire, disappeared with FRF 8 million from the company account. As the company accountant, de Vathaire was more familiar with the company's finances than anyone. He had become disillusioned a few months earlier after the death of his wife. He reportedly began assembling incriminating evidence against Dassault-Breguet, a photocopy of which fell into the hands of Jean Kay, a French right-wing "soldier of fortune" who became known for his flamboyant terrorist activities. Kay demanded FRF 8 million from de Vathaire for his copy of the dossier and threatened to turn the document over to news organizations if his demand was not met.

De Vathaire was introduced to Kay by his mistress Bernadette Roels, whose roommate was a friend of Kay's. Together with his mistress and Kay, de Vathaire went to Divone les Bains near the Swiss border. When French authorities began to search for de Vathaire, all three vanished. De Vathaire turned up a few weeks later in Corfu, and then returned to Paris where he surrendered to the police. In the meantime, an anonymous caller to a Paris television station announced that all FRF 8 million had been turned over to Lebanese Christians for arms purchases. Marcel Dassault also confirmed that Kay had returned the document.

Details of the document's contents were published in *Le Point* in October. Among other things, Dassault was accused of diverting funds for his personal use and attempting to avoid payment of taxes. According to the allegations, Marcel Dassault used company funds to build a replica of King Louis XIV's Petit Trianon palace at Versailles. The disclosures led to tax evasion investigations of Marcel Dassault and severely damaged his political position.

In 1978 French Socialist and Communist politicians pledged to nationalize Dassault-Breguet if they were elected. Marcel Dassault, who owned 90 percent of the company and was believed to have been the wealthiest man in France, stood for all that leftist politicians opposed. The leftists charged that the French government was allowing Mirage fighters to be sold to anyone who had the money to purchase them. Dassault-Breguet, they claimed, was interested only in making money by taking advantage of the ambitious military requirements of oil-rich and other third world nations. In answering these charges, Dassault maintained that these nations would purchase their arms from other manufacturers if they did not purchase them from Dassault and that its position as an arms supplier strengthened French political influence in the third world.

The following year leftists won enough seats in the national assembly to implement their nationalization policies. The government purchased a 21 percent share of Dassault-Breguet for $128.5 million. This included a special 33 percent voting interest which under French law enabled the government to exercise veto power over company decisions. When François Mitterrand was elected president of France in 1981, the government increased its share in Dassault-Breguet to 46 percent, with a special 63 percent voting majority. The move was regarded by many as an act of spite against the 89-year-old Marcel Dassault who continued to be regarded as a political opponent.

REMAINING COMPETITIVE

The French arms industry broke into the newspaper headlines again in 1982 during the brief South Atlantic war between Britain and Argentina over the Falkland Islands. During the hostilities Argentina destroyed a number of British ships with Matra Exocet missiles launched from a Dassault-Breguet Super Étendard. A French embargo on additional arms for Argentina had little effect on the losses suffered by British forces, who successfully completed their invasion of the Falklands and achieved an Argentine surrender.

Nonetheless, Dassault-Breguet remained in excellent financial condition due to its continued marketing success with improved versions of the Mystère/Falcon and Mirage fighter. Generally, the company remained competitive because it avoided the costs involved in developing new aircraft from scratch. Instead, Dassault-Breguet continually improved existing aircraft, the designs of which had been thoroughly proven. This was Marcel Dassault's rationale for campaigning against French participation in the four-nation Eurofighter program led by British Aerospace and MBB. Without a government commitment to purchase, Dassault-Breguet developed an entirely French-built fighter jet called the

Rafale, which was intended to serve as the basic instrument for the aerial defense of France.

Dassault-Breguet became involved in spacecraft engineering during 1985 when the French space agency Centre Nationale d'Études Spatiales assigned the company to lead the aeronautical development of the Hermes space plane as a subcontractor to Aérospatiale. The Hermes, similar in design to the U.S. space shuttle, was expected to fly into space atop an Ariane 5 rocket in 1995. Despite its position in the Hermes program, Dassault-Breguet had no plans to establish a space division.

SECOND GENERATION AFTER 1986

Marcel Dassault died on April 18, 1986, at the age of 94. His son Serge was placed in charge of the company. Dassault-Breguet remained through the 1990s France's most dynamic aeronautical manufacturer. In addition to the Super Étendard and Mirage and Falcon series, Dassault-Breguet was a partner with British Aerospace in the Jaguar fighter program, and with Dornier of West Germany in the Alpha jet program. The company also manufactured aircraft fuselages for Fokker of the Netherlands.

Serge Dassault would be roundly criticized as being a shadow of his powerful father. Nonetheless, Serge Dassault would fight tenaciously to maintain the long-cherished independence of the family-controlled company, renamed Dassault Aviation in 1990. After the failure of the Mitterrand government to nationalize the company in the early 1990s, the right-wing government led by family friend Jacques Chirac tried its hand at taming Dassault. In 1996, Chirac succeeded in winning an agreement to merge Dassault with Aérospatiale, but only after the larger state-owned aeronautics company would be privatized.

The defeat of the rightists in 1997 and the installation of a Socialist government under Lionel Jospin did not relax the pressure on Dassault, however. The Socialists, wary of job losses, refused to privatize Aérospatiale, suggesting a derailment of the merger agreement. Nonetheless, the merger of Dassault into Aérospatiale was expected to be forced through, one way or another. In 1997, the government stepped up the pressure on Serge Dassault by turning over documents to a Belgian court investigating bribery and other charges against him. The move effectively "imprisoned" Dassault within French borders.

In the face of global competition against such giants as Lockheed Martin, the restructuring of Dassault, Aérospatiale, and other important components (such as Matra, Snecma, and Thomson) of France's industrial military complex seemed inevitable in the late 1990s. Whether Serge Dassault and the Dassault family could be expected to maintain their grip on an important sector of France's aviation industry remained to be seen. Despite slowdowns in worldwide and French government aircraft purchases in the post-Cold War 1990s, and a corresponding drop in Dassault's revenues (from FRF 16.4 billion to FRF 13 billion in 1996) Dassault exhibited an impressive resiliency, maintaining its profitability and continuing the development of its aircraft. After the Rafale's debut in 1991, the company introduced new models of both this polyvalent aircraft and its Mirage predecessor. The company's civil aircraft, the Falcon, also saw its series expanded, as the company claimed 50 percent of the worldwide high-end executive jet market. In 1997, Dassault Aviation's revenues returned to a growth pattern, reaching FRF 16 billion of the group's FRF 20 billion total sales.

Total revenues were EUR 3.5 billion in 2000. Business-jet orders had reached new heights in the late 1990s and Dassault delivered a record 75 Falcons in 2001. In the spring of 2001 Dassault inked a $2.5 billion deal to supply 100 planes for United Airlines' short-lived business jet venture. The fractional-ownership company NetJets Inc. was another large customer.

2000 SUCCESSION

Charles Edelstenne, a 28-year company veteran, became chairman and CEO of Dassault Aviation in April 2000, the first outside the family to lead the aircraft manufacturer. Corporate policy had compelled Serge Dassault to step down upon reaching the age of 75, but he remained head of the family holding company, Groupe Industriel Marcel Dassault S.A.S. (GIMD). Edelstenne had been with Dassault Aviation for 28 years, becoming executive vice president of economic and financial affairs as well as chairman and CEO of sister company Dassault Systèmes.

Dassault escaped the industry consolidation that merged Aérospatiale into Matra and finally in 2000 into the transnational consortium EADS, which inherited the government's 46 percent holding in Dassault. Its role as an independent source of military hardware was highlighted by tensions between the United States and France leading up to the war in Iraq. The company won a large fighter order from the United Arab Emirates.

The United States had by far the largest military budget in the world, twice the size of all of Western Europe. Because of this, many countries preferred to buy its hardware to ensure the availability of future support. Dassault also had to contend with a relatively strong euro driving up its export prices.

The company blamed politics when South Korea chose the U.S.-designed F-15, despite the Rafale's superior performance evaluation. The company also faced competition from Lockheed Martin's state-of-the-art F-35 Joint Strike Fighter, which to Dassault's chagrin had been produced with help from European aerospace suppliers. There were also a handful of smaller, independent fighter-aircraft manufacturers in Western Europe and the former Soviet Union.

Production of the Mirage ended in 2007. About 2,800 had been built, making it one of the most ubiquitous fighter aircraft in history. Its replacement, the Rafale, entered service in 2001 and was expected to be the last developed specifically for the French military, as future European programs would be shared among the nations. This was the case with the nEUROn, an unmanned combat air vehicle (UCAV) Dassault was developing with participation from manufacturers in Greece, Italy, Spain, Sweden, and Switzerland.

COMMERCIAL SURGE IN 2005

Civil aviation had eclipsed military sales as Dassault's largest business segment, with the 63 Falcons delivered in 2004 accounting for sales of $2.7 billion, or 60 percent of total revenues. The industry was recovering after years of decline. Dassault sold 123 Falcons of all types in 2005. These included its latest offering, the Falcon 7X, which had an impressive 50 orders by the time it started flight testing during the year.

Deliveries of the Falcon 7X began in 2007. With a list price starting at $39 million, the 7X could span Paris-Los Angeles in a single hop and was intended to compete with the latest continent-crossing offerings from market leaders Gulfstream Aerospace Corporation and Bombardier Inc.

The 7X featured the fly-by-wire control systems perfected on previous fighter aircraft and Dassault's first entirely new business-jet wing in 30 years. Dassault spent $700 million on the development of the 7X, which was joined by 27 risk-sharing partners. It opened a new facility in Bordeaux specifically for the plane in 2003.

SURVIVING THE 2008 ECONOMIC CRISIS

Net sales peaked at EUR 4.09 billion in 2007, thanks to strong results for the Falcon and defense exports. More than three-quarters of sales came from abroad. Record business jet orders continued until the mortgage crisis

shook the global economy in the fall of 2008. Within a few months, demand had collapsed and the company was laying off workers in France and then Arkansas, where it had employed 2,400 people. The company employed another 400 at its marketing office in Teterboro, New Jersey, and 12,000 globally at 17 facilities and seven sales offices.

During the year Dassault was able to increase its holdings in French electronics firm Thales, which made the radar for the Rafale. It added a 20 percent holding once owned by Alcatel-Lucent, raising its stake to 25.9 percent.

Consolidated net sales slipped 9 percent in 2009, to EUR 3.42 billion. NetJets canceled orders of 65 Falcons it had scheduled for delivery after 2014. Dassault nevertheless delivered a record 77 Falcons and booked orders for another 98. Dassault also landed a EUR 5 billion ($7.5 billion) Rafale order from Brazil in 2009.

Perhaps suggesting pressure to make a sale, the Brazilian deal included substantial technology transfer. Having first invested 10 years earlier, Dassault owned roughly 1 percent of local manufacturer Embraer (Empresa Brasileira de Aeronáutica S.A.), which made business jets and regional airliners.

In a 2006 interview with *Aviation Week & Space Technology*, CEO Charles Edelstenne had questioned the wisdom of investing in potential future competitors through cooperative manufacturing arrangements, with Chinese companies in particular. He dismissed, however, the immediate threat from China's aviation industry, deeming its business-jet market too small and its technology not advanced enough.

Updated, M. L. Cohen; Frederick C. Ingram

PRINCIPAL SUBSIDIARIES

Dassault Falcon Jet Corp. (USA); Dassault Procurement Services, Inc. (USA); Dassault Falcon Service SARL; Sogitec Industries S.A.

PRINCIPAL OPERATING UNITS

Argenteuil; Saint Cloud; Seclin; Poitiers; Argonay; Martignas; Merignac; Cazaux; Biarritz; Istres; DFJ-Little Rock; DFJ-Wilmington; DFJ-Teterboro; SOGITEC-Suresnes; DFS-Le Bourget; Aero Precision; Dassault Procurement Services.

PRINCIPAL COMPETITORS

Gulfstream Aerospace Corporation; Bombardier Inc.; Cessna Aircraft Co.; Lockheed Martin Corporation; Eurofighter Jagdflugzeug GmbH; Saab AB; Russian Aircraft Corporation "MiG."

FURTHER READING

Birch, Stuart, "Dassault—Business Aviation Pioneer," *Aerospace Engineering*, January/February 2006, pp. 13+.

Bombeau, Bernard, "The Saga of the Mystère/Falcon," *Interavia*, Falcon Special Supplement, October 2000, pp. 27–35.

Carlier, Claude, *Serge Dassault: 50 ans de défis*, Paris: Perrin, 2002.

Christienne, Charles, and Pierre Lissarrague, *A History of French Military Aviation*, translated by Frances Kianka, Washington, DC: Smithsonian Institution Press, 1986.

"Family Values," *Flight International*, June 14, 2005.

Fitchett, Joseph, "Jospin's Cuts Take Aim at Dassault's Combat Plane," *International Herald Tribune*, August 13, 1997, p. 1.

"French Revolution," *Flight International*, June 7, 2005.

Jannic, Hervé, "Et si Dassault, loin de mourir, donnait plutôt l'exemple d'un ajustement à la crise?" *L'Expansion*, April 2, 1992, p. 57.

Matlack, Carol, "Dassault May Be Next in Line for Takeoff; Its Luxurious Falcon 7X Business Jet Could Catapult It to a Bigger Share of the Market," *Business Week*, March 7, 2005, p. 34.

Morrison, Murdo, "Dassault to Stand Down Workers as Business Jet Demand Collapses," *Flight International*, July 28, 2009.

Perry, Robert L., *A Dassault Dossier: Aircraft Acquisition in France*, Santa Monica, CA: Rand Memorandum No. R-1148-PR, September 1973.

Rocco, Anne-Marie, *Serge Dassault: Biographie*, Paris: Flammarion, 2006.

Romeges, Jean, "L'amorce d'un grand Meccano," *Le Point*, February 24, 1996, p. 56.

Saltmarsh, Matthew, "French Aviation Company Reaches beyond Borders," *New York Times*, October 20, 2009, p. B10.

Tillier, Alan, "Dassault: A Lesson in Survival," *Daily Deal*, August 9, 2001.

Vadepied, Guy, *Marcel Dassault; ou, Les ailes du pouvoir*, Paris: Fayard, 2003.

Wall, Robert, "Edelstenne in Depth," *Aviation Week & Space Technology*, Paris Air Show Sec., June 18, 2007, p. 120.

Deutsche Bank AG

Theodor-Heuss-Allee 70
Frankfurt am Main, 60486
Germany
Telephone: (+49 69) 910-00
Fax: (+49 69) 910-34225
Web site: http://www.db.com

Public Company
Incorporated: 1870
Employees: 80,456
Total Assets: EUR 2.2 trillion (2008)
Stock Exchanges: Frankfurt New York
Ticker Symbols: DBK (Frankfurt); DB (New York)
NAICS: 522110 Commercial Banking

■ ■ ■

Deutsche Bank AG, survivor of two world wars, three depressions, a divided Germany, and a 21st-century global financial crisis, ranks among the world's leading financial institutions. Its operations are divided into two divisions. The Corporate and Investment Bank Group serves corporate and institutional clients, offering investment banking and corporate financing services on a worldwide basis. The Private Clients and Asset Management Group focuses on retail banking and the worldwide provision of asset management services for both individuals and institutions. Deutsche Bank's global network spans 70 countries.

19TH-CENTURY ORIGINS

Deutsche Bank was founded in Berlin on March 10, 1870, with the approval of the king of Prussia. The company opened its doors for business a month later under the directorship of Georg von Siemens, with five million thalers in capital.

The company's creation coincided with the unification of Germany. After Germany's victory in the Franco-German War, France was required to pay an indemnity of FRF 5 billion, which greatly stimulated German industry, trade, and consumption. Deutsche Bank naturally assumed a position of leadership in the country's expanding economy. The founding of the Second German Reich in 1871 led to another important development: the thaler was replaced by the mark, a new currency based on gold.

Within two years, the bank had established domestic branches in Bremen and Hamburg and expanded into eastern Asia with offices in Shanghai and Yokohama. In 1873 it opened a London branch, and capital stood at 15 million thalers.

Many joint-stock banks, including Deutsche Bank, had been created in the wake of the liberalization of requirements for starting new companies, but many failed within a few years. During the financial crisis from 1873 to 1875 it appeared that the entire economic system was on the verge of collapse. Small shareholders as well as wealthy businesspeople were ruined, and in Berlin alone nearly 50 banks filed for bankruptcy. Deutsche Bank, because of its concentration on foreign operations, was largely unscathed by the financial panic.

Assets intact, the young bank began to make significant acquisitions, including Deutsche Union-Bank and the Berliner Bankverein, both completed in 1876. These purchases transformed Deutsche Bank into one of

COMPANY PERSPECTIVES

Our mission. We compete to be the leading global provider of financial solutions, creating lasting value for our clients, our shareholders, our people and the communities in which we operate. Our mission gives our business a clear purpose and direction. It is rooted in our brand. Our branch captures and projects a clear idea of who we are. It is something against which all our activities—products, services, behaviour and communications—can be judged. It is simple, succinct and unequivocal.

Germany's largest and most prestigious banks. In 1877 Deutsche Bank joined a syndicate of leading private banks popularly known as the "Prussian consortium." The bank was also employed by the government for the issue of state loans, and it grew rapidly in both influence and assets. By 1899 it was able to offer to float, without help from other financial institutions, a 125 million mark loan for Prussia and, at the same time, a 75 million mark loan for the German Reich.

Throughout the 1880s and 1890s Deutsche Bank was a leader in electrical development. It helped to form finance and holding companies and issued bonded loans and shares for the construction of dynamos, power plants, electric railways, tramways, and municipal lighting systems. By 1897, there were 750 power plants located across Germany. The bank also invested in the Edison General Electric Company in the United States and began to build a power plant in Argentina.

During the same period, the bank was a driving force behind railway development. In 1888, Deutsche Bank obtained a concession to build an east-west railway to open up Asiatic Turkey. A decade later, 642 miles of the Anatolian railway were in operation in Turkey. At the same time, in the United States the bank participated in the financial reorganization of Northern Pacific Railroad. All of this, of course, was done in addition to contributing significantly to the development of Germany's own extensive network of surface and underground railways.

CONSOLIDATION AND GROWTH: EARLY 20TH CENTURY

The continuity of bank operations was uninterrupted when von Siemens died in October 1901. At Deutsche Bank like most other German banks all decisions were

made by the board of directors, which customarily took credit for the company's successes. The firm had no official chairman, but selected one board member to act as "spokesman." Thus the absence of von Siemens had little effect on the bank, since management by consensus was the bank's guiding principle.

By the early years of the 20th century, the company had acquired interests in the Hannoversche Bank, the Oberrheinische Bank, and the Rheinische Creditbank, and in Italy, had participated in the 1894 founding of Banca Commerciale Italiana. In 1914 the acquisition of Elberfeld-based Bergische-Markische Bank and its branches in the Rhineland-Westphalia region increased Deutsche Bank's branch network from 8 outlets to 46. The bank's capital had increased more than six times since the founding.

The bank then entered a period of consolidation and growth. It built up its subbranches, improved and extended customer services, paid particular attention to the deposit business, and promoted checks for personal use. In association with numerous regional banks, Deutsche Bank also became involved in a wide range of business activities, including transportation, coal, steel, and oil, as well as railways and electrification. Shortly before World War I, with 200 million marks in capital backed by a 112.5 million mark reserve and deposits and borrowed funds of 1.58 billion marks, the *Frankfurter Zeitung* called it the world's leading bank. Growth continued during the war with the 1917 purchase of the Schlesischer Bankverein, which was based in Breslau (which became Wrocław, Poland, following World War II).

Deutsche Bank weathered the many economic problems during World War I. At the end of the conflict, the bank had offices at 182 locations throughout Germany, and a staff of nearly 14,000. However with the war lost, the German Empire gone, and the transition from monarchy to democracy threatened by revolution, Allied demands for reparations totaling 132 billion gold marks pushed the German banking system to the brink of ruin. By 1923, one gold mark was worth 1 trillion paper marks.

DEPRESSION & NAZI ERAS

In 1929 as financial chaos loomed, Deutsche Bank merged with its 20-year rival, the Disconto-Gesellschaft. The new entity was called Deutsche Bank und Disconto-Gesellschaft, a name that was used until 1937 when it was changed back to simply Deutsche Bank. At the time of their merger the banks were the two largest in Germany. Combined, their capital, reserves, and deposits were each at least twice as large as that of any

KEY DATES

1870: Deutsche Bank AG is founded in Berlin.

1873: London branch is opened.

1876: Deutsche Union-Bank and Berliner Bankverein are acquired.

1914: Acquisition of Bergische-Markische Bank increases the branch network from 8 outlets to 46.

1929: Deutsche Bank merges with Disconto-Gesellschaft to form Deutsche Bank und Disconto-Gesellschaft.

1933: Nazis come to power in Germany, beginning the period of collaboration between Deutsche Bank and the Hitler regime; Jewish board members are ousted.

1937: Bank's name reverts to Deutsche Bank.

1960s: Reestablishment of international operations begins.

1979: First U.S. branch office opens in New York.

1989: U.K. investment bank Morgan Grenfell is acquired.

1990: German reunification leads Deutsche Bank to quickly reestablish itself in Eastern Germany.

1993: Banco de Madrid is acquired.

1995: Global investment banking operations are consolidated under a new London-based unit, Deutsche Morgan Grenfell.

1999: U.S. investment bank Bankers Trust Corp. is acquired.

2002: First non-German is appointed to lead the company.

2008: Global financial crisis contributes to loss for the year.

2009: Deutsche Bank returns to profitability.

competitor. The merger, designed to cut administrative costs by closing competing operations, was very successful, and the resulting bank had enough capital and reserves to withstand the economic crisis. Before the collapse, Deutsche Bank and Disconto-Gesellschaft had handled about 50 percent of all business conducted by Berlin banks. By 1931 the bank was relying heavily on its undisclosed reserves and had twice reduced capital, but it remained solvent and required no government aid.

Under orders from the National Socialist government that came to power in 1933, unemployed workers were put to work under a "reemployment" plan. At first the government concentrated only on projects that were meant to counteract the high unemployment rate. The autobahns were the chief showpiece of this strategy. Although by 1936 a significant percentage of industrial production had been switched to the manufacture of weapons and munitions, and "reemployment" had become "rearmament." Deutsche Bank supported the program through the purchase of government securities. Also, in 1933 and 1934, three Jewish members of the board of managing directors (Oscar Wassermann, Theodor Frank, and Georg Solmssen) were forced to resign.

During World War II the government financed its budget deficit by printing new money, a misguided practice that quickly led to spiraling inflation. The problem was artificially suppressed by questionable banking measures. More treasury paper began to appear among the bank's assets. Deutsche Bank's enormous losses were made known only when Germany surrendered to the Allies in April 1945.

After the war Allied occupation authorities investigated possible war crimes committed by German banks. They found that Deutsche Bank and its rival Dresdner Bank bore substantial responsibility for the war through their lending to the Nazi government, their purchase of government securities, and the influence that they exerted over large industrial concerns through their shareholdings and corporate directorships. Both banks also had close ties to SS chief Heinrich Himmler and other Nazi officials, had exploited conquered nations by seizing the assets of their financial institutions, and had helped disenfranchise Jews in Germany. Four directors (including one Nazi Party member) and two executives of Deutsche Bank were arrested by the Allied authorities, but were never tried. Further investigations into Deutsche Bank's collaboration with the Nazis began to be conducted in the 1990s and shed additional light on this dark chapter in the bank's history.

POSTWAR REORGANIZATION, EXPANSION INTO RETAIL BANKING, AND INTERNATIONAL GROWTH

With the division of Germany into zones of occupation, and with Berlin in the Soviet zone, Deutsche Bank closed its head office there in 1945. The bank was run out of Hamburg. It lost all of its branches in what eventually became East Germany (in 1949 they became the basis for the newly formed Berliner Disconto Bank AG). From 1947 to 1948, the western operations of Deutsche Bank were divided into 10 separate regional institutions. After lengthy negotiations with the occupying forces, these institutions were formed into three banks. Norddeutsche Bank AG, Rheinisch-Westfalisene Bank AG, and Süddeutsche Bank AG served the northern, central, and southern areas of West Germany, respectively.

In 1957 these three banks were again reorganized to form a single Deutsche Bank AG with corporate headquarters in Frankfurt. At the time of its reunifica-tion, the bank employed more than 16,000 people and its assets totaled 8.4 billion marks. Hermann J. Abs, the strategist behind the reorganization of the bank and one of the key figures in West Germany's financial recovery, became its spokesman.

In the 1960s Deutsche Bank concentrated on improving services for its smaller depositors. The bank launched programs for personal loans of up to DEM 2,000 and medium-sized loans up to DEM 6,000 for specific purchases, as well as an overdraft facility of up to DEM 1,000 for consumers. Other services included personal mortgage loans, improvements in savings facili-ties, and the establishment of a eurocheque system. By the end of the decade, the bank had become the largest provider of consumer credit in West Germany.

Under the direction of Abs, Deutsche Bank began to reestablish its international operations (it had lost all of its worldwide holdings after the war). It first reopened offices in Buenos Aires and Rosario, Argentina, and São Paulo, Brazil, and then in Tokyo, Istanbul, Cairo, Beirut, and Tehran. In 1968 Deutsche Bank joined the Netherlands' Amsterdam-Rotterdam Bank, Britain's Midland Bank, and Belgium's Société Generale de Banque in founding the European-American Bank & Trust Company in New York. In 1972 Deutsche Bank founded Eurasbank (European Asian Bank) with members of the same consortium.

When Hermann Abs retired in 1967, Karl Klusen and Franz Heinrich Ulrich took his place, becoming cospokesmen. Abs had wielded such a great concentra-tion of economic and financial power that a special law limiting such influence was named after him. "Lex Abs" reduced the number of supervisory board seats a single person could hold simultaneously in West Germany.

During the 1970s Deutsche Bank became the dominant financial institution in West Germany. Under the guidelines of the "universal banking" system in place in Germany for more than a century, commercial banks were allowed to hold unlimited interests in industrial companies, underwrite and trade securities on their own, and play the foreign currency markets, in addition to providing credit and accepting deposits. Deutsche Bank took advantage of this rule during the 1960s and 1970s by investing in a wide range of industrial companies. In 1979, the bank held seats on the supervisory boards of about 140 companies, among

them Daimler-Benz, Volkswagen, Siemens, AEG, Thys-sen, Bayer, Nixdorf, Allianz, and Philipp Holzmann.

However, the bank's extraordinary influence in West Germany aroused concern about the extent of the bank's instruments in other companies. As a result of these concerns, Deutsche Bank began to reduce its industrial holdings in the 1970s. This trend was briefly interrupted in 1975 when Middle Eastern concerns flush with petrodollars supplanted the big banks as a source of capital investment. At the request of Chancel-lor Helmut Schmidt, Deutsche Bank purchased a 29 percent interest in Daimler-Benz from industrialist Friederich Flick to ensure that it would stay in German hands, with the understanding that the bank would resell the shares once the crisis had passed. Deutsche Bank already owned 25 percent of the famed automaker. In December of that year, it resold the shares to a consortium that included Commerzbank, Dresdner Bank, and Bayerische Landesbank.

GOING GLOBAL: EIGHTIES

During the 1980s Deutsche Bank made major expan-sions in its foreign operations, both in commercial banking and investment banking. It opened its first U.S. branch office in New York in 1979, and by 1987 had bought out all its partners in the Eurasbank consortium and renamed it Deutsche Bank (Asia), providing 14 more branches in 12 Asian countries. At nearly the same time, the company's capital-markets branch began operating and trading in Japanese, British, and U.S. securities. By the end of 1988, the bank had ap-proximately 7.2 million customers at 1,530 offices, more than 200 of them outside of West Germany.

In 1980 Deutsche Bank was the only one of the West German Big Three banks to turn a healthy profit. Unlike Commerzbank and Dresdner Bank, Deutsche Bank did not overexpand, but remained cautious in the face of high interest rates and continued recession. In 1984 it acquired a 4.9 percent stake in Morgan Grenfell, the British securities firm. In 1985 it bought scandal-plagued industrial giant Flick Industrieverwaltung from Friederich Flick, with the intention of taking it public. Then in 1988 it acquired a 2.5 percent interest in the automaker Fiat.

Another sign of Deutsche Bank's aggressive pursuit of foreign markets was the fact that in the wake of the stock market crash in October 1987, at a time when massive layoffs were taking place in the securities industry, its U.S. securities affiliate, Deutsche Bank Capital Corporation, expanded its workforce. In 1988 Deutsche Bank entered the treasury securities market at a time when many foreign firms were leaving. Two years later, the U.S. Federal Reserve recognized Deutsche Bank Government Securities Inc. as a primary dealer of government securities.

At home, Deutsche Bank took a large and controversial step toward becoming a one-stop financial service center in 1989 when it created its own insurance subsidiary to complement its commercial and investment banking businesses. Immediately, it was considered a strong rival for the Allianz Group, the West German-based company that was Europe's largest insurer. Wilhelm Christians and Alfred Herrhausen became Deutsche Bank's new cospokesmen in 1985. When Christians retired in early 1988, Herrhausen was appointed sole spokesman for the bank. Following Herrhausen's assassination by terrorists on November 30, 1989, Hilmar Kopper became spokesman.

INVESTMENT BANKING PUSH: LATE EIGHTIES TO EARLY NINETIES

In the late 1980s and early 1990s Deutsche Bank bolstered its investment banking arm through additional acquisitions, aiming to become a global investment bank. After acquiring the Toronto-based investment bank McLean McCarthy Ltd. in 1988, it purchased the remainder of Morgan Grenfell in 1989 for $1.5 billion. It also took a more aggressive approach to the North American market. In 1992 Deutsche Bank North America was formed. John A. Rolls as chief executive officer coordinated and managed all of Deutsche Bank's North American operations, including those in investment banking, McLean McCarthy and C.J. Lawrence Inc. among them. The latter was a U.S. investment bank acquired in 1986. The following year Deutsche Bank Securities Corporation was formed to specifically manage such areas as investment banking, securities transactions, and asset management services.

At the same time it aimed to become a global investment bank, Deutsche Bank also pursued a strategy of extending its position as a universal bank beyond Germany. Initially, it focused on Western Europe. However, with the fall of communism throughout Eastern Europe in 1989 and 1990, Deutsche Bank sought to become a Europe-wide institution. To that end, in 1986 it had acquired Banca d'America e d'Italia S.p.A. from the Bank of America for $603 million (in 1994 this bank was renamed Deutsche Bank S.p.A.).

In 1993 Deutsche Bank increased its presence in Italy when it purchased a majority interest in Banca Popolare di Lecco. That same year, the bank purchased Banco de Madrid in Spain, later integrated into Deutsche Bank, S.A.E. By 1994 Deutsche Bank operated 260 branches in Italy and 318 branches in Spain, and in both countries it was the largest foreign bank.

Following German reunification, Deutsche Bank quickly capitalized on the opportunity by entering into a joint venture with Deutsche Kreditbank to begin to restake its claim to Eastern German territory. By 1994 Deutsche Bank had more than 300 branches in Eastern Germany. It also opened offices elsewhere in Eastern Europe: Bulgaria, the Czech Republic, Hungary, Poland, and Russia.

The early 1990s were a time of rising fortunes for Deutsche Bank as net income more than doubled from 1990 to 1993. This trend was reversed in 1994 when a series of problems hit within a short period. First the bank suffered huge losses from loans of DEM 1.2 billion it had made to a property group run by Jurgen Schneider, which collapsed in early 1994. Then two firms in which Deutsche Bank had invested heavily ran into trouble. Balsam filed for bankruptcy and Metallgesellschaft (MG), an engineering conglomerate, nearly collapsed after losing $1.33 billion on speculative oil trades.

Kopper provoked additional controversy and public resentment when he called bills amounting to $33 million that the Schneider property group owed to construction workers "peanuts." Early in 1995 the former head of MG sued Deutsche Bank over who was responsible for MG's downfall. Also in early 1995, Deutsche Bank's ties to the Nazi government of Adolf Hitler were dredged up when East German files were made public for the first time.

The losses it suffered in 1994 forced Deutsche Bank to increase its loss reserves, which contributed to a reduction in net income to DEM 1.36 billion. In 1995 Deutsche Bank made significant moves to further establish itself as a global investment bank. Deutsche Bank North America acquired ITT Commercial Finance Corporation for $868 million to strengthen its presence in asset-based lending. The acquisition was immediately renamed Deutsche Financial Services Corporation.

Later in 1995 Deutsche Bank consolidated all of its investment banking operations into Morgan Grenfell under a new unit, Deutsche Morgan Grenfell (DMG), based in London and headed by Ronaldo Schmitz. The move shifted more than half of Deutsche Bank's business to London control rather than that of Frankfurt, a shift that the *European* called a "corporate revolution." The short-term consequence of this revolution was the creation of much bad blood between the bank's staffs in Frankfurt and London. To build up its investment banking operations, DMG poached some of the top names in investment banking from rival firms in New York and London, infuriating these companies.

CONFRONTING CHALLENGES: LATE NINETIES

In September 1995 Deutsche Bank unveiled Bank 24, the first full-service telephone bank in Germany. At the same time, the company was in the midst of a four-year effort, ending in 1996, to reduce the domestic staff by 20 percent, with much of these cuts coming from the traditional branch-based retail network. Further innovation came to the domestic operations in 1996 when Deutsche Bank opened its first supermarket banks. That same year, a scandal rocked DMG when a fund manager assigned bogus values to some securities in his portfolio. Reacting quickly, Deutsche Bank management fired four managers and spent $280 million to cover potential losses at two funds. In late 1996 Kopper announced his resignation from his position as spokesman (but remained chairman of the supervisory board), and Rolf-Ernst Breuer, who had headed the investment banking operations, became the new spokesman in early 1997.

During 1997 Deutsche Bank sold its 48-branch operation in Argentina to BankBoston Corporation for about $255 million. That year the bank set up an independent historical commission to research its role during the Nazi era. Such investigations were becoming increasingly common in the wake of the Cold War's end and the opening of archives in the former Communist states of Eastern Europe. In 1998 the bank admitted that it had profited from gold looted from Holocaust victims and that bank officials at the time likely knew the source of the gold. An $18 billion lawsuit was soon filed against Deutsche Bank and other German lenders in relation to such looted gold. Deutsche Bank revealed in 1999 that it had helped finance the construction of Auschwitz, the infamous Nazi death camp in Poland.

With problems continuing at DMG, Deutsche Bank in early 1998 transferred most of the management control of the investment banking operations back to Frankfurt. The Morgan Grenfell name itself began to be de-emphasized. Having failed to make much headway in the important U.S. investment banking market through DMG (primarily because of a clash of cultures between DMG's U.S. investment bankers and those hailing from Germany and England), Deutsche Bank turned to the acquisition route for another U.S. invasion. In November 1998 the company announced that it would acquire Bankers Trust Corp., a New York firm that specialized in underwriting securities for smaller companies and emerging markets.

Bankers Trust was the seventh-largest bank holding company in the United States. It had purchased Baltimore-based investment banking house Alex. Brown & Sons in 1997 and had subsequently renamed the unit BT Alex. Brown Inc. (under Deutsche Bank, it was rechristened Deutsche Banc Alex. Brown). Also in 1998 Deutsche Bank transferred several of its major industrial holdings, a total of DEM 40 billion ($24 billion) in stock, to a separate subsidiary in an effort to increase the transparency of its holdings. Among the transferred holdings were stakes in Allianz AG (7 percent), DaimlerChrysler AG (12 percent), and Metallgesellschaft AG (9.3 percent). This move was also seen as a prelude to the eventual unloading of some of these stakes.

The EUR 9.7 billion ($10 billion) takeover of Bankers Trust was completed in June 1999 but not before Deutsche Bank had received a great deal of negative publicity about its activities during the Nazi era. Under pressure from Holocaust survivors and others, Deutsche Bank finally agreed to contribute to a fund set up to settle Holocaust-era claims. The bank refused, however, to be held liable for its holdings in industrial companies that used forced laborers during that period. With the purchase of Bankers Trust, Deutsche Bank became the largest bank in the world with assets of about $750 billion. This position of preeminence proved short-lived, however, as the company was soon surpassed by Mizuho Holdings, which was formed in 2000 from the merger of three Japanese banks.

With the integration of Bankers Trust, investment banking was becoming an increasingly important part of the Deutsche Bank operations, accounting for 56 percent of pretax operating earnings for 1999, a huge jump from the 22 percent figure of 1998. On the other hand, the company was being bogged down by its inefficient retail banking operations, which accounted for only 5 percent of operating earnings in 1999. That year, the retail network was merged with the electronic banking unit Bank 24 to form Deutsche Bank 24 (DB24), which could then offer customers an array of online, telephone, and traditional branch services.

DISRUPTED PLANS: 2000-01

In March 2000 Deutsche Bank appeared to have a solution to its retail banking woes, namely offloading them, through a EUR 31 billion ($30 billion) merger with its longtime archrival Dresdner Bank. The deal would have included the combination of the retail networks of the two banks under the Deutsche Bank 24 unit, which would then have been spun off within three years, with Allianz, the number two insurer in Europe, taking a majority stake. The merger unraveled within weeks of its announcement, however, over the fate of Dresdner's investment banking unit, Dresdner Klein wort Benson (DKB).

Initially, Breuer agreed to merge DKB into Deutsche Bank's investment banking operations. The bank's investment bankers, however, felt that DKB's operations overlapped too much with their own, forcing Breuer to renege on his promise to absorb DKB and to insist that the unit be divested as a precondition to the merger. The Dresdner's board refused to go along with this and pulled out of the deal.

The failed merger was a huge blow to Deutsche Bank's aspirations to become an even bigger player in global investment banking. In the immediate aftermath, the company invested heavily in its e-commerce operations and announced that it would expand DB24 throughout Europe with a combined "clicks-and-bricks" retail structure. DB24 gained control of the bank's retail operations in Belgium, France, Italy, Poland, Portugal, and Spain, a network that included more than 2,000 branches and 21,000 employees.

Another significant development was a February 2001 reorganization that divided the bank's operations into two business units: the Corporate and Investment Bank Group and the Private Clients and Asset Management Group. The former encompassed the investment banking and corporate banking units, while the latter subsumed the retail banking (including DB24), private banking, and asset management units. Through the reorganization, Deutsche Bank hoped to facilitate cross-selling among the units, such as the selling of asset-management products through DB24.

Deutsche Bank's prospects in the early 21st century were clouded somewhat by the aftereffects of the collapse of the Dresdner deal. Deutsche Bank attempted to negotiate a cooperation agreement with Allianz whereby the latter would distribute insurance products through DB24. However, in March 2001, Allianz announced that it would acquire Dresdner. Deutsche Bank continued to seek partners, including negotiating with AXA, the French insurance firm, about a distribution deal. Despite the setbacks that Deutsche Bank had suffered in the late 20th century, the bank remained one of the most powerful financial institutions in the world.

The September 11, 2001, terrorist attacks on the United States, which left more than 2,700 dead and the twin towers of the World Trade Center a pile of rubble, stunned the world. Debris from the South Tower damaged Deutsche Bank's building, disrupting the bank's operations. Josef Ackermann, head of investment banking, flew to Canada, then to New York when U.S. air space reopened, *Institutional Investor* recounted. In the midst of the tragedy, he renewed efforts to take Deutsche Bank to the top ranks of Wall Street's investment banks. Deutsche Bank shares began trading on the New York Stock Exchange in October.

NEW LEADERSHIP: 2002–06

Deutsche Bank completed the purchase of the struggling U.S. asset manager Zurich Scudder Investments in 2002. Also during the year Deutsche Bank established a new corporate division, "Private & Business Clients," a combination of Deutsche Bank 24, Private Banking, parts of Corporate Banking, and an online broker. Another new operation, "Private Wealth Management," began serving high net worth and ultrahigh net worth individuals.

Ackermann, a Swiss, became the first non-German to lead the company when he succeeded Rolf Breuer as CEO in 2002. He wasted no time making changes, selling off equity interests in German companies and instating market rate loans, going forward. Management by consensus gave way to a strong chief executive model of management. Meanwhile back in the United States, Wall Street investment banks, Deutsche Bank among them, faced the ire of regulators over conflicts of interest in their securities research.

Deutsche Bank, under Ackermann, looked outside its borders for growth, acquiring private Swiss bank Rued Blass & Cie in 2003. The next year the bank opened a branch office in Beijing. A representative office had been operating there since 1981. On the home front, competitors including Barclays and JPMorgan Chase had been eroding Deutsche Bank's business. The third largest European bank announced domestic job cuts at the end of 2004. On a global basis, Deutsche Bank had cut nearly 14,500 jobs since 2000. Nevertheless, CEO Ackermann drew sharp criticism from both the political left and right over German job losses. The bank recorded a net profit of EUR 2.5 billion ($3.2 billion) for the year, an 87 percent increase in profit over 2003.

Ackermann directly linked the job cuts with his drive to attain a 25 percent return on equity by 2005. "That goal, he says, is necessary for Deutsche to achieve a capitalization that will help it compete in world markets with other financial heavyweights. Right now, Deutsche ranks sixth in the world by assets and tenth by net revenues, but it drops to 23rd by market cap: $50.5 billion," *Institutional Investor* reported in March 2005. Market value often was a key component of acquisition financing.

Ongoing cost-cutting contributed to a 53 percent climb in net income in 2005 to EUR 3.8 billion. Pretax return on equity reached the targeted 25 percent mark. The figure had been just 4 percent in 2002. Ackermann had executed the transformation of the German bank along with investment banking co-heads Anshu Jain and Michael Cohrs, an Indian and an American, respectively.

Investment banking produced two-thirds of revenues and three-quarters of profits.

Ultimately, Ackermann "abandoned a long-stated goal of achieving a 60-40 balance between investment and retail banking," the *Institutional Investor* reported. On a global basis Deutsche Bank had climbed to the upper reaches of the investment banking market. However, despite significant progress in the U.S. investment banking market by 2006, it had not yet breached the ranks of Goldman, Morgan Stanley, Merrill Lynch, Citigroup, and JPMorgan Chase.

Deutsche Bank, successes aside, had its share of trouble. During this period, the bank was hit with fines in the United Kingdom for trading infractions. In addition, regulatory problems sprang up in Italy over its participation in a bank takeover bid. Moreover, Deutsche Bank faced a number of lawsuits, one dating back to U.S. tax shelter activities in the late 1990s and early 2000s.

Continuing its foray into emerging markets, the bank completed the acquisition of United Financial Group in Russia, in December 2006. Its first stake, taken in 2004, gave Deutsche Bank a share of the country's growing initial public offering (IPO) and merger business. Other global action during 2006 included branch openings in Saudi Arabia and Dubai and the formation of a private wealth management unit in Shanghai. The next year Deutsche Bank announced the launch of private and business banking in China, but such news was eclipsed by a broader story.

FINANCIAL CRISIS: 2007–08

A credit crisis emerged in the second half of 2007, as the extent of the trouble in the U.S. home mortgage market was revealed. The collapse of a U.S. investment bank ushered in further turmoil, such as liquidity shortages and interbank lending constriction. Equity markets plummeted worldwide. By mid-2008, major banks had renewed their call for accounting rule changes, seeking to gain relief from write-downs linked to troubled assets. Opponents cited the need for transparency and consistency, contending risky investment practices by big banks had led to the economic crisis.

Allianz SE agreed to sell Dresdner Bank AG to Commerzbank AG in September 2008. The move propelled Commerzbank ahead of Deutsche Bank as Germany' largest bank by number of customers. Deutsche Bank nonetheless retained supremacy in terms of assets, holding approximately $2.93 trillion, according to the *America's Intelligence Wire*.

Accounting changes allowed Deutsche Bank to record a third-quarter profit instead of a loss.

"Germany's largest bank is the first big European institution to use the opportunity to avoid having to account for some of its assets at their severely impaired market value," the *Financial Times* reported in October. Ackermann was chairman and a spokesman for the Institute of International Finance, the alliance of banks that had lobbied U.S. and European central banks, regulators, and other agencies for change.

Areas of the bank hard hit by the financial crisis faced significant job cuts at year-end. While scaling back businesses such as credit origination, exotic structure products, and proprietary trading, the bank planned to grow foreign exchange, commodities trading, and cash equities, according to *Euroweek*. New York and London offices faced the largest hits in terms of employment. For the year Deutsche Bank reported a net loss of EUR 3.9 billion. Faced with continuing uncertainty in the global economy, Deutsche Bank extended Ackermann's tenure as CEO to 2013. The move ended troublesome succession speculation, according to an April 2009 *Financial Times* article.

RAPID REBOUND: 2009–10

A rebound in the equity markets, liquidity improvement, and increased activity in the capital markets during the later half of 2009 bode well for Deutsche Bank and other big financial institutions. Still, unemployment remained high and consumer credit was tight.

Ackermann pushed back against G20 summit regulatory changes proposed in October. He called for more input by bankers. "There is a trade-off between maximising stability of banks and optimising growth of the real economy. That balance [should] not be forgotten," he told the *Financial Times*. He warned of economic consequences if regulations were too stringent or localized.

Deutsche Bank meanwhile had developed a two-year strategic plan. Among the targets in the multi-pronged endeavor were Asian revenue growth and corporate and investment bank profitability improvement. Ackermann envisioned attaining pretax operating profits of EUR 10 billion ($14.6 billion) by 2011, according to a December 2009 *Financial Times* article.

The financial crisis was not bereft of opportunity for Deutsche Bank. To bolster its wealth-management business, Deutsche Bank had struck a deal to acquire Sal. Oppenheim's Luxembourg holding company and some of its subsidiaries. Its German operation was a leading private bank in terms of assets under management. Deutsche Bank also held a blocking stake in Postbank in Germany. Additionally, the bank planned to buy some corporate banking assets of ABN AMRO, in the Netherlands, according to the *Financial Times.*

Effects of the financial crisis lingered in 2009. Although the bank had dumped some riskier endeavors, impaired commercial property and leveraged finance assets remained on its books. Moreover, scrutiny and scorn were still being heaped on the industry. In December, Ackermann announced the bank would "globalize" the impact of Britain's 50 percent supertax on banks' bonus pools. Big banks' profits had been bolstered directly and indirectly by government bailouts, prompting the tax on executive compensation. Deutsche Bank had not taken direct state aid.

Deutsche Bank reported full year net profit of EUR 5 billion for 2009. "The profit comes a year after a low point of the financial crisis for Deutsche Bank. In the fourth quarter of 2008, proprietary trading, in which the bank bets its own money on securities markets, exposed Deutsche Bank to the fury of the meltdown, helping to cause the loss," the *International Herald Tribune* stated. Goldman Sachs, by comparison, earned $4.79 billion in the fourth quarter alone.

Big financial institutions had shown a remarkable recovery, but new problems loomed. Greece faced the possibility of bankruptcy and owed fellow European Union members billions of euros. Deutsche Bank's Ackermann said its share of the debt was "extremely small," *BBC Monitoring Europe* reported in February 2010. As the world had seen, however, the financial fate of one country was tied to another more closely than ever.

Updated, David E. Salamie; Kathleen Peippo

PRINCIPAL SUBSIDIARIES

Taunus Corporation (USA); Deutsche Bank Private- und Geschaftskunden Aktiengesellschaft; DB Capital Markets (Deutschland) GmbH.

PRINCIPAL DIVISIONS

The Corporate and Investment Bank Group; The Private Clients and Asset Management Group.

PRINCIPAL COMPETITORS

Commerzbank AG; UBS AG; Citigroup Inc.

FURTHER READING

"Ackermann under Fire," *Institutional Investor International Edition*, March 2005, p. 8.

"Allianz and Deutsche: And They Lived Unhappily Ever After," *Economist*, April 1989, p. 90.

Brierley, David, "Corporate Revolution in the Air as Deutsche Moves to London," *European*, July 21, 1995, p. 17.

Buerkle, Tom, "Three Outsiders: Three Foreigners—Indian, Swiss, and American—Have Taken Deutsche Bank Far beyond Its German Roots," *Institutional Investor*, May 2006, pp. 44+.

Carey, David, "Under Siege," *Financial World*, March 7, 1989, pp. 64+.

"Deutsche Makes Its Pan-European Move," *European Banker*, September 22, 2000.

"Deutsche Slashes Jobs to Match Its Rivals," *Australasian Business Intelligence*, December 2, 2004.

"Deutsche's Wayward Wunderkind," *Economist*, September 14, 1996, pp. 76–78.

"Deutsche to Slash 900 Jobs in Global Markets Business," *Euroweek*, November 21, 2008.

Duke, Simon, "Bankers Let the Good Times Roll," *Daily Mail*, February 12, 2010, p. 89.

"EU Members Agree to Help Greece Only in 'Complete Emergency,'" *BBC Monitoring European*, February 12, 2010.

Ewing, Jack, "Heavyweight of Finance Turns Page on the Crisis," *International Herald Review*, February 5, 2010, p. 15.

Fairlamb, David, and Stanley Reed, "Damage Control at Deutsche: The Failed Dresdner Deal Leaves German Banking in Turmoil," *Business Week*, April 17, 2000, pp. 150–51.

Fisher, Andrew, "Tough Guy at the Bank," *Financial Times*, November 21, 1994, p. FTS4.

Fuhrman, Peter, "A Faster Ship in a Richer Sea," *Forbes*, November 26, 1990, pp. 40–41.

Gall, Lothar, "Hermann Josef Abs and the Third Reich: 'A Man for All Seasons'?" *Financial History Review* 6, 1999, part 2, pp. 147–200.

Goff, Sharlene, et al., "Deutsche Bank to 'Globalise' Bonus Pain," *Financial Times*, December 18, 2009, p. 1.

Greenhouse, Steven, "Deutsche Bank's Bigger Reach," *New York Times*, July 30, 1989.

Grigsby, Jefferson, "Deutsche Bank uber Alies," *Financial World*, May 15, 1990, pp. 42–43.

Guerrera, Francesco, and Jennifer Hughes, "Banks Call for Easing of Rules," *Financial Times*, May 22, 2008, p. 17.

Guha, Krishna, "Top Bankers Launch Fightback against Feared Regulatory Overkill," *Financial Times*, October 3, 2009, p. 1.

"Herr Dobson's Fishing Trip," *Economist*, May 11, 1996, pp. 67–68.

"Herrhausen's Last Deal," *Economist*, December 2, 1989, pp. 87+.

Hughes, Jennifer, and James Wilson, "Deutsche Bank Profits from New Accounts Rules," *Financial Times*, October 31, 2008, p. 19.

James, Harold, *The Deutsche Bank and the Nazi Economic War against the Jews*, New York: Cambridge University Press, 2001, 254 p.

Jenkins, Patrick, and James Wilson, "Winner from Crisis Has Clear Aims," *Financial Times*, December 18, 2009, p. 21.

Kantrow, Yvette, "John Rolls' Grand Plan," *Investment Dealers' Digest*, August 29, 1994.

Kopper, Christopher, *Zwischen Marktwirtschaft und Dirigismus: Bankenpolitik im "Dritten Reich," 1933–1939*, Bonn: Bouvier, 1995, 400 p.

Kraus, James R., "Changing to Make Its Mark," *American Banker*, September 20, 1994.

Landler, Mark, "Big at Home, but Not Much Heft Globally," *New York Times*, August 26, 2005, p. C4.

Launder, William, "Deutsche Bank Buys Oppenheim," *Wall Street Journal*, October 29, 2009, p. C3.

"New Dreams at Deutsche Bank: Germany's Grandest Bank Has a New Vision of Its Future—A Rather More Modest One Than in the Past," *Economist*, June 22, 1991, pp. 79–81.

Paradis, Tim, "Insurer Allianz to Sell Dresdner Bank to Commerzbank AG for $14.38 Billion," *America's Intelligence Wire*, September 2, 2008.

Quint, Michael, "German Giant's Big U.S. Plans," *New York Times*, May 22, 1989, p. D1.

Seidenzahl, Fritz, *100 Jahre Deutsche Bank, 1870–1970*, Frankfurt: J. Weisbecker, 1970, 457 p.

Steinberg, Jonathan, *The Deutsche Bank and Its Gold Transactions during the Second World War*, Munich: Beck, 1999, 176 p.

"The 2002 Deals of the Year: The Slickest, the Shrewdest, the Sorriest Transactions of a Truly Miserable Time," *Institutional Investor*, January 2003, pp. 34+.

Walker, Marcus, "Deutsche Bank Shuffles Its Management," *Wall Street Journal*, January 26, 2001, p. A10.

———, "Deutsche Bank to Reorganize, Cutting Number of Divisions to Two," *Wall Street Journal*, December 5, 2000, p. A21.

Wilson, James, "Deutsche Bank Holds on to Chief in Effort to Silence Succession Talk," *Financial Times*, April 29, 2009, p. 15.

———, "Deutsche Bank Targets EUR10bn in Pre-Tax Profits by 2011," *Financial Times*, December 15, 2009, p. 17.

Disabled American Veterans

———■———

3725 Alexandria Pike
Cold Spring, Kentucky 41076
U.S.A.
Telephone: (859) 441-7300
Fax: (859) 441-1416
Web site: http://www.dav.org

Nonprofit Organization
Incorporated: 1920 as Disabled American Veterans of the
    World War
Employees: 615
Operating Revenues: $152 million (2008 est.)
NAICS: 813410 Civic and Social Organizations

■ ■ ■

Disabled American Veterans (DAV) is a nonprofit group chartered by the U.S. Congress that supports the needs of about 200,000 wounded military veterans and their families. With 1.2 million members, the Cold Spring, Kentucky, organization helps veterans, regardless of DAV membership, with claims for benefits from the Department of Veterans Affairs, the Department of Defense, and other government agencies, and conducts information seminars to inform them about their rights and benefits.

The organization also aids service men and women in making the transition to civilian life, supports homeless veterans outreach programs, provides veterans with free transportation to Veterans Administration (VA) hospitals, lobbies the government on behalf of veterans, and runs a voluntary services program that recruits

people to drive vans, work at VA hospitals, and help local veterans. Moreover, DAV is active in disaster relief efforts in the United States. The organization is divided into 21 districts and maintains 110 offices in the United States and Puerto Rico, including its National Services & Legislative Headquarters in Washington, D.C. It also boasts nearly 1,600 local chapters.

POST-WORLD WAR I ORIGINS

The man who provided the vision for DAV was Robert S. Marx, who had left his Cincinnati law practice to serve in the U.S. Army during World War I. Only hours before the armistice would go into effect on November 10, 1918, he was wounded by an artillery shell and spent the next several months recuperating in a French hospital. Upon his return to Cincinnati he was elected as a judge to the Superior Court of the city. It was at a Christmas party he hosted for a local veterans' service organization in 1919, attended by about 100 disabled veterans who were away from home while receiving health care or training, that he decided there was a need for a national organization to give voice to the concerns of the disabled veterans. Over 4.7 million Americans had served in the war, and more than 200,000 wounded soldiers had returned to a country ill-prepared to meet their needs. Disabled veterans not only had to come to terms with their injuries and physical losses, they were forced to navigate a bureaucratic maze to receive any government help.

A pair of Cincinnati area organizations had already prepared the soil before Judge Marx took up the cause of disabled veterans. The Ohio Mechanics Institute was

COMPANY PERSPECTIVES

Made up exclusively of men and women disabled in our nation's defense, the Disabled American Veterans is dedicated to one, single purpose—building better lives for all of our nation's disabled veterans and their families.

offering vocational training to hundreds of veterans, and a group of disabled veterans had been formed at the University of Cincinnati. The groups' leaders began meeting with Marx in the spring of 1920. He was also in contact with the War Department in Washington and learned that 741,000 veterans would be eligible to join a group of disabled veterans. The local initiative then began to assume greater scope as Judge Marx called for a national caucus to be held in Cincinnati on September 25, 1920, which DAV considers its birth date.

FIRST NATIONAL CONVENTION: 1921

At the September meeting 250 disabled veterans representing local groups gathered and created a national body that assumed the structure still used by DAV: a national organization comprising state-level departments, and local chapters. A national convention was then held in Detroit in June 1921 and Judge Marx was elected to be the first national commander. The delegates also laid the foundation for a permanent organization that would be known as the Disabled American Veterans of the World War (DAVWW). A constitution was written, dues were established, and a permanent headquarters was authorized in Cincinnati.

DAVWW quickly began lobbying Congress to create a single federal agency to coordinate veterans affairs. The organization also created its first fund-raising campaign in 1922, and at the convention held that year, the DAVWW Auxiliary was established. An effort was made to nominate Judge Marx as national commander for a second year, but he refused to accept it, adhering to the organization's constitution, which barred national commanders from succeeding themselves.

The early years for DAVWW were a struggle. After initial enthusiasm waned, membership tailed off and fund-raising efforts did not meet the organization's needs, forcing an increase in dues. A fund-raising arm, the Disabled American Veterans Service Foundation, was established in 1931. By that time the country was suf-

fering through the Great Depression, and budgetary constraints led to cutbacks in veterans benefits. In 1932 Congress recognized the importance of DAVWW and issued a federal charter to the organization. It now became the official voice of disabled veterans. Tough times and DAVWW's new status led to an increasing membership, which grew to 42,500 by the end of the decade.

INTRODUCTION OF IDENTOTAG PROGRAM: 1941

In 1941 DAVWW launched a fund-raising program that would provide the bulk of the organization's financial needs for the next 25 years. DAVWW worked with a Chicago company that manufactured IdentoTags, replica key-chain automobile license plates that were mailed to registered drivers. Should the keys be lost, the keys could be dropped in any mailbox to be sent to DAVWW headquarters where the tags were matched to a mailing list for return to the owners. The recipients of the IdentoTags were under no obligation, but resulted in donations, especially from drivers who had their lost keys returned to them. In its first year, the program generated $800,000 in income.

The money brought in by the IdentoTag program would be sorely needed. The United States entered another world war at the end of 1941 and soon there was a new generation of disabled veterans to serve. The equipment used to manufacture and mail the IdentoTag materials was purchased in 1945, providing employment for many disabled veterans, and after making the final payment in 1950, the organization assumed full ownership of the program. The operation was moved to a facility north of Cincinnati in 1952, where the majority of the 350 employees were disabled veterans.

NAME CHANGE: 1943

It was in 1943 during World War II that DAVWW shortened its name to Disabled American Veterans. The scale of World War II was enormous: 16.3 million Americans served in the military, resulting in 407,000 deaths, 671,000 personnel wounded, and 104,000 disabled veterans. As a result, DAVWW's membership ranks swelled, as did the need for the organization's services. In 1950, only five years after the end of World War II, the U.S. military was fighting in Korea. Although never a declared war, the conflict cost 36,000 lives and led to another 103,000 wounded Americans.

By 1960, DAV membership topped 200,000. Soon there would be another generation of disabled veterans, as the United States became mired in a war in Southeast

KEY DATES

1920: Disabled American Veterans of the World War is formed.
1932: Organization receives federal charter.
1943: Name is changed to Disabled American Veterans.
1986: DAV Charitable Service Trust is founded.

Asia, the Vietnam War that would escalate through the 1960s and linger into the following decade. DAV was quick to recognize the need to help disabled Vietnam veterans and used its influence to help pass the Veterans Readjustment Benefits Act of 1966. In that same year, the organization moved to its new headquarters in Cold Spring, Kentucky.

The 1960s was also notable because DAV began pursuing new fund-raising avenues. The IdentoTag program had slipped in effectiveness, in large part because states began issuing license stickers rather than new license plates each year. The mailings had been based on new license numbers and many states now allowed motorists to retain the same plate numbers. With a decrease in mailings came a decrease in donations, and in 1967 the program was discontinued (although DAV would continue to return lost keys well into the next century). In 1969 DAV hired a direct-mail veteran, Max Hart, to take charge of its fund-raising efforts. He built a sophisticated direct-mail fund-raising program that in 2001 led to his induction into the Direct Marketing Association Hall of Fame. By the time he retired in 2004, Hart helped raise more than $1.3 billion for DAV.

Membership surged to 427,000 because of the Vietnam War by the time DAV celebrated its 50th anniversary. To better serve veterans and their families, DAV created a mobile outreach program in 1974, using a fleet of six motor homes. The fleet grew to 18 vans, and during the 19 years the program operated it served more than 600,000 veterans and their families. The 1970s also saw the DAV use its influence in Congress to prevent cuts to the VA budget and defeat a measure that would eliminate veterans' preference in federal employment.

MEMBERSHIP REACHES ONE MILLION MARK: 1985

DAV began the 1980s with 600,000 members, or about one-quarter of the nation's 2.2 million eligible disabled veterans. Although the United States did not fight any major wars during the 1980s, the military saw action in Grenada, Panama, and other small countries, resulting in more wounded veterans. Compared to other conflicts their numbers were small, but these new disabled veterans helped to push DAV's membership ranks to the one million mark in 1985. During this decade DAV also recognized the importance of serving women veterans and urged the VA to form a Women's Advisory Committee. In 1987 the VA received cabinet-level status, something DAV had been advocating for years.

DAV continued to fight on behalf of Vietnam veterans, especially those who had suffered from the effects of the use of Agent Orange in Southeast Asia. An out-of-court settlement was reached with seven chemical companies in 1984. Neither were older veterans forgotten. DAV supported a federal case that resulted in a 1984 ruling that the government had been negligent in the way nuclear weapons were tested aboveground in the Nevada desert in the presence of troops from 1952 through 1962. In 1986 DAV founded the DAV Charitable Service Trust to help meet the needs of veterans and their families during a time of budget cuts. Also in 1987, after the government stopped assisting veterans with the cost of transportation to VA hospitals, DAV stepped in to create a national network of vans to provide medical center transportation.

The 1990s quickly brought a war in the Persian Gulf to expel Iraqi troops from Kuwait. Although brief, the war was not without its victims. Many returning veterans suffered from what was known as Gulf War syndrome, the symptoms of which were exhibited in about one-quarter of the nearly 700,000 veterans. DAV fought to have the malady recognized by the military and to provide help to the men and women who were affected by it. The 1990s also brought attention to another problem that DAV would champion: the plight of homeless veterans, the numbers of which began to grow in the late 1990s. At the end of the decade, DAV played a role in the enactment of The Veterans' Millennium Health Care Act of 1999.

FUND-RAISING SURGE

The 1990s were an especially fruitful period for DAV and its fund-raising efforts. While other organizations were pleased with a 2 percent return on its mailings, DAV enjoyed a success rate of 4 to 5 percent. The operation was also sophisticated enough to realize it could add a fifth renewal mailing to its 1997 schedule. Rather than cannibalize its own donations, the organization raised an additional $13 million. Moreover, DAV hired a new comptroller and made other changes to its fund-raising operations, so that between 1993 and 2003, the organization increased its net worth by 478 percent.

There was still a need for DAV as the new century dawned. While the nature of military threats may have changed with the rise of international terrorism, the need for soldiers remained the same. In fact, the development of high-tech personal armor saved many lives but resulted in a new generation of disabled veterans, who lost limbs that were not protected by the armor. New wars were fought in Afghanistan and Iraq that carried into the second decade of the 2000s. When wounded service men and women returned home, DAV was there to make sure they understood the benefits and services to which they were entitled. The use of military force was not likely to abate for many years to come,

nor would the need for DAV to serve those disabled in war.

Ed Dinger

PRINCIPAL SUBSIDIARIES

Disabled American Veterans Service Foundation.

FURTHER READING

Blum, Debra E., "A Veteran Direct-Marketing Fund Raiser's Bright View of the Future," *Chronicle of Philanthropy*, March 18, 2004.

Carpenter, Clint, "Change Is Good," *Non-Profit Times*, May 15, 2001, p. 32.

War & Scars, Cold Spring, KY: Disabled American Veterans, 2006.

Double Eagle Petroleum Co.

Double Eagle Petroleum Co.

777 Overland Trail, Suite 208
P.O. Box 766
Casper, Wyoming 82602
U.S.A.
Telephone: (307) 237-9330
Fax: (307) 266-1823
Web site: http://www.dble.us

Public Company
Incorporated: 1972 as Double Eagle Petroleum & Mining Co.
Employees: 26
Sales: $49.6 million (2008)
Stock Exchanges: NASDAQ
Ticker Symbol: DBLE
NAICS: 211111 Crude Petroleum and Natural Gas Extraction; 211112 Natural Gas Liquid Extraction

■ ■ ■

Double Eagle Petroleum Co. is an independent energy company that engages in exploration, development, and sales of domestic natural gas and crude oil principally in the Rocky Mountain basins of the western United States. The company's major development activities are in its coal-bed methane field in the Atlantic Rim of Eastern Washakie Basin and its natural gas play in the Pinedale Anticline, both in Wyoming. Double Eagle also transports gas through its natural gas pipeline. The company holds interests in 525,500 gross acres and in 1,125 producing wells.

COMPANY ORIGINS

The company traces its roots to geologist Dr. Richard B. Laudon. The son of a distinguished geologist, Richard Laudon developed a deep appreciation for nature as a boy by accompanying his father on research trips into the field. Not surprisingly, Laudon earned his first degree, a bachelor's from Tulsa (Oklahoma) University in 1952, in geology. After earning a Ph.D. in geology from the University of Wisconsin in 1959, Laudon went to work as a research geologist in the Tulsa area for what would become the Exxon Company. His specialty was sandstone reservoir geology, and during his 10 years with Exxon, he worked in 13 countries, including Australia where he was involved in early offshore research and discoveries. Laudon then accepted a job in 1969 as a senior geologist, exploring for uranium for an affiliate of United Nuclear Corporation in Casper, Wyoming.

Laudon was surrounded by numerous independent geologists in Casper, where he gained an appreciation for the freedom they seemed to enjoy. Moved to embrace such freedom in his own life, Laudon decided in 1972 to found his own firm, a public company he called Double Eagle Petroleum & Mining Co., based in Casper. Laudon launched his business with a $12,000 loan and some additional backing from friends and family. He started with a mercury mine in Nevada and some coal, gas, and zeolite leases.

Double Eagle's plan for an initial public offering appeared as if it might fail. However, just before the company's public debut, the firm made an oil discovery on a company lease in North Dakota. With the word of

COMPANY PERSPECTIVES

Our mission is to increase shareholder value; provide a positive and rewarding work environment for our employees; and profitably operate and expand our assets. In order to achieve this mission, we will economically expand our reserves; increase and enhance production of our existing properties; selectively pursue strategic acquisitions; expand our midstream business; and leverage the experience of our employees. These actions, together with our creative vision, will ensure the continued success of our company.

the discovery, the public offering succeeded. The rest of the company's first decade included a period of lean years when Laudon was nearly a one-man operation: He served as the company's treasurer, president, and chairman. John R. Kerns, a former Tenneco Oil Company geologist, served as company secretary and was also a director throughout the 1970s.

EIGHTIES: LEAN YEARS AND A YEAR OF PUBLICITY

For a very brief period during the 1980s, Double Eagle became a Wall Street darling of sorts. The small independent oil and gas firm was even featured in the *New York Times* business section for three consecutive quarters of earnings reports in 1985.

However, while Double Eagle's name rose like a gusher for a brief time, ink in its name fell off the pages of the *Times* quickly. In 1989, Laudon hired Stephen H. Hollis to serve as company vice president and director. Like Laudon, Hollis had worked as a geologist for an affiliate of United Nuclear Corporation in the 1970s. He was president of Hollis Oil & Gas Co. at the time he joined Double Eagle.

MID-90S: TRANSITION OF POWER & BUSINESS STRATEGY

During the mid-1990s, Double Eagle began to shift the executive power reins to Hollis and modify its business strategy. In 1994 Hollis was named president of Double Eagle while Laudon remained chairman, a post for which Hollis was preparing. In the early years of Hollis's presidency, Double Eagle struggled to earn a net profit, suffering net losses in 1994 and 1996 while earning

only $15,000 in 1995. During this period, Double Eagle's business strategy was to acquire large acreages and resell them, keeping a royalty stake.

However, in 1996, the company's business strategy shifted. Double Eagle began to focus not only on creating prospects in which it had a royalty interest but also on being involved in the developmental stage of wells, thereby using more capital for drilling as opposed to acquiring leases. This strategy was designed to bolster both reserves and cash flow. By 1996, Double Eagle held an interest in more than 180 producing wells, and oil represented about 55 percent of its production. Meanwhile, the company continued to sell its gas and oil production on the "spot market."

LATE 90S: GROWING AND GEARING UP FOR PROFITABILITY

In June 1996, Double Eagle's board of directors authorized an increase of common stock to 10 million shares. Laudon relinquished his role as chairman and retired from the firm he had created in 1997, just one year before his death, and Hollis assumed the additional post of chairman. In an effort to generate cash flow, a private placement of stock the following year was completed and netted the company nearly $506 million.

During the late 1990s, Double Eagle increased its lease holdings fourfold in order to expand its reserves and revenues through identified low-risk projects. In August 1999, Double Eagle purchased the assets of KCS Mountain Resources, a subsidiary of KCS Energy, Inc., which included wells in Cow Creek Field in southwestern Wyoming. That same year, the company used another private placement of stock, netting Double Eagle $1.1 million, which covered the firm's expenses for a year, including the development of wells in Green River and Wind River basins in Wyoming.

Double Eagle increased its revenues from 1998 to 2000, in part as a result of drilling and completing successful wells at Cow Creek, Mesa, and other plays. In 1999, revenues surpassed $1 million for the first time, and by 2000 net income was a record $125 million. The company was hitting its production stride at just the right time. As the company's online wells grew in number, the prices for gas and oil were likewise growing. Double Eagle's profit margins widened and its stock value had climbed from a low of 50 cents in 1995 to $4.65 a share in 2000.

Double Eagle entered the new century with a discernible focus on natural gas. In just four years, natural gas had grown from representing 45 percent of the firm's reserves to more than 80 percent in 2000. In directing its focus to natural gas, the company followed

KEY DATES

1972: Company is founded by Dr. Richard B. Laudon as Double Eagle Petroleum & Mining Co.
1989: Stephen Hollis becomes company vice president.
1994: Hollis is named president and chief executive.
1997: Laudon retires, and Hollis adds chairman to his roles.
1999: Double Eagle acquires acreage in the Cow Creek Field in southwestern Wyoming.
2001: Company changes its name to Double Eagle Petroleum Co.
2007: Hollis retires; Richard Dole becomes chairman.

the flow of domestic energy usage in the country.

The company's holdings by 2000 were predominantly in the Rocky Mountain basins, an area that a U.S. Geological Survey suggested held a significant percentage of known and possibly undeveloped natural gas reserves in the country. Double Eagle's leaseholds in these basins included significant acreage in the Washakie Basin, as well as plays in Green River Basin, Powder River Basin, and Wind River Basin. To develop these, Double Eagle planned to use its available capital on low-risk projects and locate partners to finance its more wildcat plays in which it held interests.

NEW NAME, INCREASING REVENUES

In February 2001, the company changed its name from Double Eagle Petroleum & Mining Co. to Double Eagle Petroleum Co. The following year, Double Eagle added 21 producing wells and almost doubled its 2001 natural gas production. The company concluded 2002 generating over five million cubic feet of natural gas per day, compared to 1.9 million cubic feet a year earlier. However, falling natural gas and oil prices kept earnings in check and the company recorded a net loss for the year.

Beginning in 2003, though, Double Eagle reeled off four consecutive profitable years, and it doubled its revenues between 2003 and 2004. Rising fuel prices in part drove the earnings surge and prompted the company to boost production wherever it could. In particular, the company focused on tapping its Mesa

and Cow Creek plays. In addition, the company acquired substantial acreage in 2003. Double Eagle purchased additional leases in the Eastern Washakie area of Wyoming, giving the company leaseholds representing more than 51,400 gross acres in the Washakie Basin, with Double Eagle having a 100 percent working interest in many of those leases.

Then in October 2003, Double Eagle turned to another private placement of 1.35 million shares of stock, primarily to generate funding for development drilling at the Pinedale Anticline and Cow Creek plays. In a November 2003 Bureau of Land Management lease sale, Double Eagle acquired leasehold interests of more than 8,000 acres in the Christmas Meadows play. This wildcat prospect brought Double Eagle's shared interest in Christmas Meadows to more than 30,000 acres, with Double Eagle having roughly a 28 percent working interest of that acreage.

EAGLE BEGINS TO SOAR

Double Eagle began increasingly focusing operations on its coal-bed methane play in Washakie Basin (Cow Creek) in the Atlantic Rim and its tight sands natural gas play in the Pinedale Anticline. For 2003, Double Eagle logged record production, revenue, and income. Nearly all of the company's sales growth arose from development drilling at the Mesa Unit in Pinedale and at Cow Creek. In 2004, Double Eagle anted more than $8 million in its annual investment of Mesa and Cow Creek plays which had driven revenues the year prior. The wager paid off, and Double Eagle earned $4 million on revenues of $13.3 million. Again, the major contributors to the company's growth were the same two plays. In total 111 successful wells contributed to Double Eagle's earnings, as the company sold about half its gas at a locked-in price, representing a shift in philosophy, as previously the company sold all of its product on the spot market.

By 2005, Double Eagle's strategy clearly was to continue tapping its two productive Wyoming plays. In 2005, higher oil and gas prices, and increased production at the coal-bed methane project in the Atlantic Rim and the Pinedale Anticline, drove earnings, which grew fourfold to $4 million on revenues of $20.5 million. In addition to further development and improvement of its coal-bed methane gas interests, the company's strategy also included engagement in high-potential exploration activities.

Seeking to expand its name among investors, in April 2006, Double Eagle hired Monarch Capital Consultants, Inc., to create an investor marketing strategy. Double Eagle's objective was to generate excitement among analysts, stock portfolio managers, and brokers and, as a result, generate a long-term shareholder base. That same year, Zacks Investment Research, a leading investment research firm, began coverage of Double Eagle with a "buy" recommendation.

During 2006, Double Eagle launched exploratory drilling at Christmas Meadows. The company also began transporting natural gas through its newly constructed pipeline that connected the Cow Creek Field with another pipeline system, owned by Southern Star Central Gas Pipeline Inc. The 13-mile Double Eagle pipeline constructed in late 2005 provided the company with the capacity to transport third-party gas and also provided the firm with a transportation system for its future Atlantic Rim projects.

The company began 2007 with a public offering of 450,000 shares of common stock, at $21.55 a share, with proceeds going toward repayment of loans from its revolving credit facility. The stock offering served as a good sign of the company's status and Hollis's tenure as chief executive. When Hollis became CEO in 1994, Double Eagle's stock was priced at just 37 cents a share. Thirteen years later, the company was preparing to make its largest wildcat play to date, the Christmas Meadows Field in Utah. The company started pumping money into the project, which had potentially big rewards, but the risks were just as big. As Hollis told the *Denver Post* in 2007, "Just this one project could catapult Double Eagle's value up to five or ten times. Or it could turn out to be a $20 million dry hole. ... It's a lottery ticket."

The Atlantic Rim Environmental Impact Statement released in May 2007 paved the way for Double Eagle to begin development drilling of more than 265 coal-bed methane wells in its Catalina Unit, a play the company had discovered in 1999 and begun to develop in the early 2000s with 14 successful wells. In addition, the impact statement set in motion approval for Double Eagle's partner Anadarko Petroleum Corp. to drill another 69 coal-bed methane wells in the Sun Dog Unit in the Pinedale Anticline, adjacent to Catalina. All told, the 2007 impact statement allowed Double Eagle to drill an additional total of 2,000 coal-bed methane and conventional gas and oil wells.

The timing of the impact study announcement also meant that the second leg of the Rocky Mountain (RME) Pipeline, a fairly new, large intrastate pipeline owned by major energy companies, would be completed when the first 34 Catalina wells were brought on line. This was a bounty for the company because Double Eagle's ability to transport gas via the RME Pipeline was expected to substantially increase the price it received for natural gas.

NEW LEADERSHIP, RECORD PRODUCTION & EARNINGS

Hollis resigned his post as chairman in December 2007 and was replaced by Richard Dole, a director since 2005 and chairman and chief executive of Petrosearch Energy Corporation, a Nevada-based oil and gas exploration firm. The following year, Dole assumed the roles of Double Eagle chief executive and president while keeping his chairman's post and the presidency of Petrosearch Energy. Double Eagle's proved reserves in 2008 hit a record 88 billion cubic feet of natural gas equivalent (Bcfe), fueled by production that doubled in a single year, mainly a result of the Catalina project in the Atlantic Rim and production from the Pinedale Anticline leases. For the year, the company's revenues gushed to a record $49.6 million while earnings rose to a record $10.4 million.

In 2009 Double Eagle signed a merger agreement with Petrosearch Energy, and, through a stock-for-stock swap, Petrosearch became a wholly owned Double Eagle subsidiary. Petrosearch, with no debt, brought the company $8.75 million in working capital and an early stage Texas Panhandle oil-water flood field.

As it neared the end of the decade, a number of barometers indicated how much Double Eagle had grown since the mid-1990s. By 2009 the company was the 33rd-largest producer of natural gas in Wyoming, a state where there were over 300 firms in the same industry. Its number of active wells had grown to about 800, and the company's interests in producing wells rose to 1,125. In addition, revenues, earnings, and stock price had all surged upward.

Double Eagle spent much of its first three decades as a company with a very lean balance sheet. As it neared the 2010s, the company's staff size of about 25 clearly was lean, another asset, and a company trait carried over from Laudon's reign. However, not until the 21st century, after Laudon's passing, did the company he established truly begin to hit pay dirt. That the company did, and that it still maintained a lean staff, was a credit to his astute leadership.

Roger W. Rouland

PRINCIPAL SUBSIDIARIES

Eastern Washakie Midstream Pipeline, LLC; Petrosearch Energy Corporation.

PRINCIPAL COMPETITORS

Abraxas Petroleum Corporation; Apollo Resources International, Inc.; Devon Energy Corporation; Stone

Energy Corporation; BP p.l.c.; Delta Petroleum Corporation; Exxon Mobil Corporation; Gasco Energy, Inc.; NGAS Resources, Inc; Noble Energy, Inc.; Platinum Resources Energy, Inc.; Samson Oil and Gas Limited; Stone Energy; Swift Energy Company.

FURTHER READING

"Double Eagle an Undervalued E&P," *Zacks*, November 22, 2008.

"Double Eagle Petroleum and Mining at Independent Petroleum Association of America Oil & Gas Investment Symposium New York Conference," *Fair Disclosure Wire*, April 22, 2009.

"Double Eagle Petroleum Co.: Interview," *Oil and Gas Investor*, September 2005, p. SS45.

Hall, Hubert H., and John R. Kearns, "Richard B. Laudon (1934–1998)," *AAPG Bulletin*, March 1999, pp. 526–27.

The Dow Chemical Company

———■———

2030 Dow Center
Midland, Michigan 48674
U.S.A.
Telephone: (989) 636-1000
Toll Free: (800) 422-8193
Fax: (989) 636-1830
Web site: http://www.dow.com

Public Company
Incorporated: 1947
Employees: 52,195
Sales: $44.87 billion (2009)
Stock Exchanges: New York
Ticker Symbol: DOW
NAICS: 325131 Inorganic Dye and Pigment Manufacturing; 325188 All Other Basic Inorganic Chemical Manufacturing; 325211 Plastics Material and Resin Manufacturing; 325611 Soap and Other Detergent Manufacturing; 325612 Polish and Other Sanitation Goods Manufacturing; 326122 Plastics Pipe and Pipe Fitting Manufacturing; 326130 Laminated Plastics Plate, Sheet, and Shape Manufacturing; 326150 Urethane and Other Foam Product (Except Polystyrene) Manufacturing

■ ■ ■

The Dow Chemical Company is the largest chemical company in the United States and the second-largest competitor in the world. Dow manufactures more than 5,000 products at 214 sites in 37 countries, organizing its business along eight business lines: electronic and specialty materials; coatings and infrastructure; health and agricultural sciences; performance systems; performance products; basic plastics; basic chemicals; and hydrocarbons and energy.

19TH-CENTURY BEGINNINGS

Herbert Dow began his career around 1890, when he convinced three Cleveland businessmen to back his latest project, which involved the extraction of bromide from brine. Dow's idea was to extract the huge underground reservoirs of brine, souvenirs of prehistoric times when Lake Michigan had been a sea. This brine was being used for salt, but Dow was determined to distill bromides and other chemicals from it. His first venture, called Canton Chemical, failed and was superseded by Dow Chemical.

Dow's use of an electric current to separate bromides from the brine was revolutionary. He was experimenting with electrolysis at a time when the electric lightbulb was still viewed with suspicion. (At the time, President Harrison refused to touch the newly installed light switches in the White House for fear of electrocution.) However, Dow constructed primitive cells from wood and tar paper, and began producing bromides, as well as bleaching agents, for another fledgling company by the name of Kodak.

In the first years of this century, Dow began to sell his bromides abroad, but the Deutsche Bromkonvention, a powerful group of German bromide producers, declared an all-out price war against Dow Chemical. German and British bleach makers (bromide is used in bleach) reduced the price of their product from $1.65 to

$0.88 a pound in the United States, which was less than cost. Dow's plants depended on a price of $1.65 in order to make a profit. While other U.S. bleach makers closed for the duration of the price war, Dow went deeper into debt and fought for his share of the domestic and foreign markets. One of his successful tactics was to purchase the imported bromide that the Germans were selling in New York at a price below cost, and then resell it in Europe where the price of bromide was still $1.65 per pound.

RESILIENCE THROUGH WAR AND DEPRESSION

After the bromide war came World War I, which, among other things, ended German domination of the world chemical industry. The German naval blockade forced U.S. industry to turn to U.S. chemical makers for essential supplies. Dow was pressed into the manufacture of phenol, used in explosives, and magnesium, used in incendiary devices. At the time these two substances had limited use outside of munitions, but they were later to play an important role in the development of Dow Chemical and the chemical industry in general. Phenol would become a key ingredient required for the manufacture of plastics, and magnesium would make aviation history.

After the war, Congress protected the fledgling U.S. chemical industry by imposing tariffs, so that the country would not become dependent on foreign chemical manufacturers again. By 1920 Dow Chemical was selling $4 million worth of such bulk chemicals as chlorine, calcium chloride, salt, and aspirin every year. By 1930 sales had climbed to $15 million and the company stock had split four times. Before the stock market crashed in 1929 the price per share had climbed to $500.

Dow's success drew the attention of du Pont, which wished to acquire the midwestern bromide manufacturer

until Herbert Dow threatened to leave the company and take his engineers with him. Without Herbert Dow's leadership and ingenuity the company was not regarded as worth the price of purchase and du Pont subsequently withdrew its offer.

Herbert Dow died just as the Depression began and was replaced by his son Willard. Willard Dow, like his father, considered research, as opposed to production or sales, the key to the company's future. Despite the state of the economy, Willard Dow approved expenditures for research into petrochemicals and plastics. The company's product line expanded to include iodine, ethylene, and materials to flush out oil from the ground. A new plant was constructed that would extract bromine from seawater, beginning in 1933. There was also a rumor on Wall Street that Dow's new method could extract gold from the seawater. The rumor turned out to be true. However, for every $300 worth of gold, $6,000 worth of bromine could be recovered.

WORLD WAR II: DEPRESSION-ERA STRATEGIES PAY OFF

During World War II, Dow Chemical's new research resulted in handsome rewards. Even before the United States' entrance into the war, Dow had started to expand in preparation for future hostilities. One of its first wartime contracts was with the British, who desperately needed magnesium. Dow produced some of this metal at its new plant in Freeport, Texas, which extracted magnesium from seawater. Dow later supplied the metal to the United States and even shared its patented process with other companies. In 1943, Dow and Corning Glass formed Dow Corning, a company that manufactured silicone products for the army. The company later expanded into civilian markets.

Before World War II the potential value of magnesium in the manufacture of airplanes had gone unnoticed, and during this time Dow Chemical was the only U.S. magnesium producer. Even with a monopoly on the metal, however, the company lost money on its production. This was typical of Dow Chemical at that time. It often invented a product and then patiently waited for a market. During the war, Dow produced over 80 percent of the magnesium used by the United States, which later led to federal investigations into whether or not Dow had conspired to monopolize magnesium production in the country. The U.S. press, however, sided with Dow and eventually the charges, which had included accusations of a conspiracy with German magnesium manufacturers, were dropped.

Besides manufacturing magnesium the company also made styrene and butadiene for synthetic rubber.

KEY DATES

1897: Herbert Dow founds The Dow Chemical Company.
1933: Dow begins extracting bromine from seawater.
1935: Dow enters the plastics business.
1943: Dow and Corning Glass merge to form Dow Corning Company, specializing in silicone products.
1953: Saran Wrap becomes a household product.
2001: Dow merges with Union Carbide.
2009: Dow acquires specialty chemicals maker Rohm and Haas for $16.3 billion.

During World War II the Japanese had conquered the rubber plantations of the Far East and soon this commodity was in short supply. Due to the fact that Dow had persisted in plastics research during the Depression, it was at the forefront of manufacturing synthetic products, including rubber. Besides making styrene and butadiene, it molded Saran plastic, now known as a food wrap, into pipes, or had it woven into insect screens to protect soldiers fighting in the tropics.

POSTWAR EXPANSION

After the war the company had to adapt to the postwar economy. One of management's concerns was that Dow Chemical had placed such a strong emphasis on research and development in the past that it sometimes ignored the fact that it was supposed to be making profits. The Marketing and Sales departments were reluctantly increased. Said one man employed at the time, "You got the feeling that Willard looked on sales as a necessary evil."

Despite having to share trade secrets with its competitors during the war, Dow ranked as the sixth-largest chemical company in the country and was well positioned to take advantage of the increasing peacetime demand for chemicals. Its product line was extensive and included chemicals used in almost every conceivable industry. Bulk chemicals accounted for 50 percent of sales and plastics accounted for 20 percent of sales, while magnesium, pharmaceuticals, and agricultural chemicals each accounted for 10 percent of sales.

Dow expanded significantly during the postwar period, going heavily into debt in order to finance its growth. The man who presided over this expansion was Willard Dow's brother-in-law, Lee Doan (Willard Dow

had been killed in a plane crash). One of Doan's first tasks was to reorganize the company and make it more customer-oriented. Willard's and Herbert Dow's tenures had been previously described by insiders as "capricious." The emphasis now was on long-range planning.

In the year of Willard's death, 1949, sales were $200 million, but 10 years later they had nearly quadrupled. Products such as Saran Wrap (introduced in 1953) began to make Dow a high-profile company. Dow's growth surpassed that of its competitors, and the company was soon ranked fourth in the industry. The company's plants had previously been located in Texas and Michigan, but during the 1950s important production centers were built elsewhere. Foreign partnerships like Ashai Dow in Japan were formed, and the company expanded its presence in the European market.

RESTRUCTURING, GROWTH, AND CONTROVERSY: 1960–69

Dow began the 1960s with a change of leadership. Ted Doan succeeded his father and, with Ben Branch and Carl Gerstacker, reorganized the company. Communication had become a problem because of Dow's vast size, so the company was broken into more manageable units that could be run like small businesses. Marketing, however, became more centralized. The management liked to think of their company as democratic, with overlapping lines of responsibility. The structure of the company was deliberately arranged so that employees would use their own initiative to invent new products and to manufacture existing products at a lower cost. The strategy worked.

In 1960, Dow purchased Allied Labs, thus entering the world of pharmaceuticals. Also in the early 1960s, Dow Corning began collaborating with two Texas plastic surgeons, Frank Gerow and Thomas Cronin, on silicone breast implants. This venture would spell trouble for Dow Corning and its parent companies, some 30 years later.

Throughout the 1960s, Dow's earnings increased approximately 10 percent each year. Among the company's hundreds of products, however, one began to receive an inordinate amount of publicity: napalm. Beginning in 1966 the company became the target of anti-Vietnam War protests. Company recruiters were overrun on college campuses by large numbers of placard-waving students. Dow defended its manufacture of the searing chemical by saying that it was not responsible for U.S. policy in Indochina and that it should not deprive U.S. troops of a weapon that the Pentagon thought was necessary. Critics charged that the gruesomeness of the weapon made it imperative for the company not to cooperate with the government. Right or wrong, the public outcry against Dow demoralized a company that wanted to be associated with Saran Wrap rather than with civilian Vietnamese casualties.

A TROUBLED DECADE: 1970–79

At the beginning of the 1970s, *Forbes* magazine predicted that Dow would have trouble growing because of its indebtedness. In 1974, however, the same *Forbes* reporter was subjected to criticism by CEO Carl Gerstacker because Dow had a record year. The oil embargo benefited Dow since it had its own petroleum feedstock with which to manufacture its various specialty chemicals; its competitors could not find the necessary petroleum. Noted Gerstacker: "Price wasn't the problem in '74; it was availability." Dow increased the price of many of its chemicals and its earnings increased, despite a strike in its hometown of Midland, Michigan. After the six-month strike, Dow gave the strikers a 10 percent bonus and gave each pensioner $2,000 worth of bonds. Company stockholders did not mind management's sudden display of generosity. That year they received a 30 percent return on equity.

The year 1975 was followed by an oversupply of petrochemicals and a business slowdown, and the company's earnings began to slide. Since the company was doing almost half of its business overseas, an unfavorable rate of exchange added to the above problems.

By 1978 a change of leadership was deemed necessary; Gerstacker's retirement from the board of directors was the end of an era. Carl Gerstacker's management strategy was, "you should have as much debt as you can carry." During recessions and slowdowns, borrowed money was used for research and development as well as plant expansion. He was an administrator in the tradition of Herbert Dow, but the moves that had catapulted Dow to a position of leadership in the chemical industry seemed unwise in the business climate of the late 1970s. P. F. Oreffice, who Gerstacker had referred to as "a little old lady in tennis shoes" because of his conservative fiscal policy, became president and CEO.

RECESSION AND RECOVERY: 1980–89

Soon after his promotion, Oreffice reorganized Dow as most of his predecessors had done after their appointment. These frequent reorganizations were less a testimony to the inadequacy of the previous organization than an admission that the company was outgrow-ing previously successful arrangements. This time management was reorganized on a geographical basis, since Dow had plants all over the world. In 1980, the year of the reorganization, sales exceeded $10 billion for the first time.

In the early 1980s a pattern of write-offs that depressed earnings began to emerge. In 1983 the write-off of two ethylene plants and a caustic soda plant caused earnings to drop 16 percent. Ethylene, a lead additive that prevents knocking in automobile engines, had been an important product for Dow at one time. In 1985 earnings fell 90 percent from the previous year as additional ethylene plants were closed.

Another factor that depressed 1985 products was the decrease in price and demand for basic chemicals. Dow derived 50 percent of its income from commodity chemicals that are sold by the ton. Foreign competitors, Arab chemical companies in particular, invaded the U.S. market in the same way that Dow once invaded the European bromide market. To make matters worse, the market for commodity chemicals is sensitive to world economic conditions. Dow's position as a U.S. company complicated matters further. When the dollar was strong, as it was in 1984 and part of 1985, the company's exports were harder to sell and its foreign earnings, when converted to dollars, were smaller.

In 1981, Dow purchased Merrell Drug, thus expanding its Pharmaceutical division. With the purchase Dow assumed liability for Bendectin, an anti-nausea drug that was blamed for birth defects. Despite the fact that Dow won practically all lawsuits (independent studies proved no connection between the drug and birth defects), the cost of continuing litigation forced the company to take Bendectin off the market.

ACQUISITIONS ADD DIVERSITY

In 1984, Dow purchased Texize, which boasted a strong line of detergent products, from Morton Thiokol. Research spending remained at almost 90 percent of cash flow. Extra-strong ceramics and plastics for the electronics industry were among the numerous specialty chemicals that Dow hoped would account for two-thirds of its sales in the 1990s. The company still placed a premium on innovation, however, and stated that it anticipated placing 15 to 25 new products on the market each year. However, some felt that the expansion into pharmaceuticals, specialty chemicals, and household products, required a new approach to management. According to an analyst with Kidder and Peabody, "If you're running a monolithic chemical business, management is the same across all products. Now they're going to have hundreds of small businesses to manage."

The company appointed a new chairman of the board, Robert Lundeen, and launched a new ad campaign, in which working for Dow was equated with "doing something for the world." Eager to rid itself of the adverse publicity surrounding topics such as Vietnam and alleged environmental abuse, Dow actually supported an increase in the Environmental Protection Agency's budget and a strengthening of rules regarding hazardous waste. This marked a significant philosophical turnaround for a company that had argued against a ban on dioxin in the 1970s.

Despite its changes in management, however, Dow was hurting in 1985, as it failed to recapture market share lost during the 1980 to 1982 recession. Profits tumbled from $805 million in 1980 to $58 million in 1985. Frank Popoff was promoted to president and CEO from his position as head of Dow Chemical/ Europe. Largely on the strength of Popoff's decisions, the firm improved marketing and sales of value-added products, which commanded higher prices. Dow began to win market share in this higher-margin area as it increasingly concentrated on finding new applications for existing products.

AUTOMOTIVE BUSINESS BRINGS RELIEF

The company's efforts found a ready-made market in the auto industry, which was in the midst of a campaign to increase efficiency and cut costs. Dow concentrated on other durable sectors as well, such as appliances, housewares, and electronics. It also looked into packaging and the recreation and health care industries. Since Dow already made so many plastics, chemicals, and hydrocarbons inexpensively, increased sales of these products at higher margins offered an immediate hike in profits. This strategy was immediately successful, and the company received a further boost when the U.S. dollar began to fall, making it easier for Dow to sell against German companies and other competitors.

Oil prices fell in 1986, further feeding Dow's recovery. With the dollar continuing to fall and the world economy humming, the spread between raw material costs and final prices expanded until the firm's plastics business was making a record 25 to 30 percent on sales during mid-1987.

Dow continued to diversify through acquisition, but tried to concentrate on firms with a base in chemicals, paying special heed to firms with technologies or distribution systems deemed not practical for Dow to develop internally. A joint venture in agricultural chemicals, called DowElanco, was begun with Eli Lilly. Dow acquired 39 percent of Marion

Laboratories, a pharmaceuticals firm, for $2.2 billion, then joined it with Dow Merrell, making it a public company with a 67 percent Dow stake.

By 1988 commodity chemicals accounted for just 53 percent of the firm's $13.3 billion in sales. Its move into pharmaceuticals was proving to be a success, with $1.1 billion in sales a year. Its star drug was Seldane, an antihistamine with sales that were reaching hundreds of millions of dollars. In 1989, Merrell Dow's Pharmaceutical division merged with Marion Labs to form Marion Merrell Dow, in which Dow had a 71 percent stake. Total Dow sales for 1989 reached $17.6 billion, an increase of $7 billion over five years earlier, with profits up to $2.5 billion.

PRICE WAR ERUPTS: 1990

In 1990 the world economy headed into recession. As in past recessions, the chemical industry, plagued by overcapacity, began a price war and began cutting output. Dow was the leading low-cost producer of commodity chemicals, hydrocarbons, and plastics. Rather than cut capacity, Dow continued to produce chemicals at a lower profit margin in the hopes of keeping its market share and driving out weaker competitors. Profits fell, but the company maintained its position in the marketplace. Even du Pont was forced to cut production of polymers.

The Persian Gulf War temporarily caused the price of oil to rise, further hurting Dow. When the war ended, the slowdown in the chemical industry continued. Many in the industry believed that it was just another cycle in a cyclical industry. Frank Popoff, however, maintained that the slowdown represented a more fundamental shift in the industry, one that was eroding the advantages of larger firms. The strategy, Popoff felt, was now to be as lean and fast as small firms while maintaining a research and development advantage.

Despite these beliefs, Dow was forced to build new plants for commodity chemicals when a Canadian supplier decided to become a competitor. Dow began building ethylene plants in Alberta, Canada, and Freeport, Texas. Even after 40 years in Asia, sales there still accounted for less than 10 percent, while European sales accounted for 31 percent of the total. However, with Europe mired in recession and European sales slowing, Dow began pushing into Asia again, building a petrochemicals plant in China, where it enjoyed an expanding polyurethane business. Although its growth had been slowed by the downturn in chemicals, Dow had nevertheless reduced its dependence on commodity chemicals from 80 percent of sales in 1980 to 45 percent in 1992, making it one of the world's most diversified chemical firms.

With success came growing controversy. Starting in the early 1980s, Dow Corning faced questions and lawsuits regarding the safety of its silicone breast implants. Many women claimed to have developed autoimmune diseases as a result of silicone leakage from the implants. Faced with many individual lawsuits, as well as class-action suits, Dow Corning filed for Chapter 11 bankruptcy protection in 1995 (emerging from Chapter 11 nine years later), and settled with breast implant recipients for $3.2 billion. Dow, however, as a 50 percent shareholder in Dow Corning, was named in many individual lawsuits. As of 2001, with over 20 independent studies done, no causal relationship between silicone breast implants and autoimmune diseases (or cancer) had been established.

UNION CARBIDE MERGER IN 2001

Another controversy erupted on August 4, 1999, when Dow announced plans to merge with Union Carbide, one of the world's leading manufacturers of polyethylene plastics, and a pioneer in the petrochemical industry. The announcement drew fire from various groups, including Dow shareholders. At issue was Union Carbide's reputation, and possible continuing liability, following the Bhopal gas leak disaster in India ("The world's worst industrial accident"). Plans for the $11.6 billion merger nevertheless moved on. To receive clearance from the Federal Trade Commission (FTC) and international regulators, Dow agreed to divest itself of a number of polyethylene plants worldwide. The FTC granted approval for the merger on February 5, 2001. Union Carbide became a wholly owned subsidiary of Dow.

Throughout the 1990s and into the new millennium, Dow continued to reinvent itself through sales and acquisitions of various assets. In 1995 Dow sold its stake in Marion Merrell Dow to Hoechst for $7.1 billion. In 1998 its consumer products subsidiary, known as DowBrands, was sold to S.C. Johnson & Son. DowBrands included the Home Food Management unit, responsible for familiar names such as Ziploc and Saran Wrap. The second DowBrands unit, Home Care Products, made products such as Spray 'N Wash and Fantastik. Dow purchased ANGUS Chemical from TransCanada Pipelines in 1999. In 2000 it acquired General Latex Chemical Corporation and Flexible Products Company, both manufacturers of foam products. Another foam business, Celotex Corporation (makers of foam insulation) was purchased in 2001. The same year Dow expanded its agricultural product line by acquiring the agricultural chemicals arm of Rohm and Haas.

LEADERSHIP PROBLEMS AT THE MILLENNIUM

Dow's interest in the assets owned by Rohm and Haas would deepen later in the decade, but before the company expressed its interest, it contended with pernicious difficulties. CEO William Stavropoulos handed his leadership duties to Michael Parker, a 34-year Dow veteran, in 2000, touching off a period of slumping profits and stock value. Potential Bhopal litigation as well as another liability inherited from the Union Carbide merger, potential asbestos litigation, cast a pall over Dow's fortunes. Compounding the company's difficulties was the escalating cost of oil and gas, which resulted in higher feedstock costs. Under Parker's command, Dow's profits plunged 80 percent and its stock value languished, prompting his departure and marking the return of Stavropoulos to the CEO post in December 2002.

Stavropoulos, who had handpicked Parker as his replacement, enjoyed far greater success with his second choice for a permanent replacement. In November 2004, he selected Andrew Liveris, an Australian, to become Dow's CEO. Liveris, who joined Dow in 1976 and rose to the post of chief operating officer before being tapped as CEO, initiated a major restructuring program when he took the helm, executing what he termed "an intervention" in a January 31, 2005 interview with *Business Week*. Liveris sold or shuttered dozens of manufacturing facilities and reduced Dow's global payroll by 14 percent, making the chemical giant a leaner organization. His changes coincided with a rising demand for Dow's chemicals and plastics, particularly from China, as the company's core industry shrugged off five years of anemic performance and began to record robust growth.

ROHM AND HAAS MERGER: 2009

Record high profits and revenues were reached during Liveris's first years in command. He began forming joint venture companies in fast-growing economies in the Middle East, Brazil, Russia, India, and China, injecting vitality in Dow and transforming it into "an aggressive, growth-oriented enterprise," as the April 28, 2008 issue of *Business Week* noted. Dow's restored luster enabled Liveris to move forward aggressively, leading to the announcement in mid-2008 that Dow intended to acquire specialty chemicals maker Rohm and Haas for $18.8 billion. The acquisition paved Dow's entry into the specialty chemicals business, which tended to have higher profit margins and greater stability than the basic chemicals business. "The addition of Rohm & Haas' portfolio is game-changing for Dow," Liveris said in the July 11, 2008 issue of *Investor's Business Daily*. "There aren't many jewels out there. This is one of them."

Liveris soon changed his appraisal. Not long after the deal was announced, deteriorating economic conditions prompted Dow to attempt to scuttle the merger. Rohm and Haas sued Dow in January 2009 for reneging on the agreement, but just before heading to trial Dow agreed to follow through on the merger. As part of the settlement, Rohm and Haas's two largest shareholders agreed to invest as much as $3 billion into the combined company, thereby reducing the valuation of the merger to $16.3 billion. The completion of the merger left Dow saddled with debt, but hopeful that a return to better economic times would justify the cost of the massive merger.

Updated, Scott M. Lewis; Adi R. Ferrara; Jeffrey L. Covell

PRINCIPAL SUBSIDIARIES

Buildscape, LLC; CanStates Holdings Inc.; CD Polymers Inc.; Centen Ag Inc.; Chemars Inc.; Chemars III LLC; DC Partnership Management Inc.; DCOMCO, Inc.; Denmerco Inc.; Diamond Capital Management Inc.; Dofinco, Inc.; Dow Capital International LLC; Dow Chemical (Australia) Limited; Dow Chemical (China) Investment Company Limited; Dow Chemical Delaware Corp.; Dow Chemical (Hong Kong) Limited; Dow Chemical International Ltd.; Dow Chemical (NZ) Limited (New Zealand); Dow Chemical Pacific Limited (Hong Kong); Dow Chemical (Singapore) Private Limited; Dow Credit Corporation; Dow Environmental Inc.; Dow Holdings LLC; Dow Internacional Mexicana S.A. de C. V. (Mexico); Dow International B.V. (Netherlands); Dow International

Technology Corporation; Dow South Africa Holdings (Pty) Ltd.; Rohm and Haas Company; Union Carbide Corporation; U.S. Laboratories, Inc.

PRINCIPAL OPERATING UNITS

Electronic and Specialty Materials; Coatings and Infrastructure; Health and Agricultural Sciences; Performance Systems; Performance Products; Basic Plastics; Basic Chemicals; Hydrocarbons and Energy.

PRINCIPAL COMPETITORS

BASF SE; E. I. du Pont de Nemours and Company; Exxon Mobil Corporation.

FURTHER READING

Carson, Ed, "Dow Chemical to Acquire Specialty Rival for $18.8 Bil," *Investor's Business Daily,* July 11, 2008, p. A1.

"Chronology of Silicone Breast Implants," *Frontline: Breast Implants on Trial,* program transcript, http://www.pbs.org, February 27, 1996.

Cimons, Marlene, "Long Shunned, Morning Sickness Drug May Be Staging a Comeback," *Los Angeles Times,* December 7, 2000.

Duerksen, Christopher J., *Dow vs. California: A Turning Point in the Envirobusiness Struggle,* Washington, DC: Conservation Foundation, 1982.

Harman, Adrienne, "Metamorphosis," *Financial World,* February 2, 1993.

"International Company News Richardson," *Globe and Mail,* March 19, 1981.

Marcial, Gene, "Dow Chemical: Not So Dowdy," *Business Week,* April 28, 2008, p. 132.

Meyer, Richard, "Avoiding the Fifth," *Financial World,* November 15, 1988.

Poland, Alan Blair, *A History of the Dow Chemical Company,* Ann Arbor, MI: University Microfilms, 1980.

Quickel, Stephen, "Uncle!" *Financial World,* May 15, 1990.

Electricité de France S.A.

22-30, Avenue de Wagram
Paris, 75382 Cedex 08
France
Telephone: (+33 1) 40 42 40 43
Fax: (+33 1) 40 42 32 17
Web site: http://www.edf.fr

Public Company
Incorporated: 1946
Employees: 160,000
Sales: EUR 66.33 billion ($92.8 billion) (2009)
Stock Exchanges: Euronext Paris
Ticker Symbol: EDF
NAICS: 221122 Electric Power Distribution

■ ■ ■

Electricité de France S.A. (EDF) is Europe's largest electrical power generator, and the world's leading operator of nuclear power stations. EDF is also the dominant supplier of electrical power to the French market, which accounts for nearly 26.5 million of EDF's total client base of 38 million. EDF's international operations account for 47 percent of the group's revenues, which totaled EUR 66.33 billion ($93 billion) in 2009. EDF operates across the full spectrum of the electrical power sector. The group's government-regulated operations in France include Transmission and Distribution, through subsidiaries RTE, operator of the French power grid, and ERDF, its power distribution subsidiary.

EDF also competes in the deregulated European energy market. The group's Generation division is the largest in Europe, with a total capacity of nearly 610 terrawatts per hour (TWh). This includes more than 478 TWh generated in France, 65 percent of which is produced through the group's 58 nuclear pressurized water reactors (PWRs) located in 19 plants across the country. EDF also operates hydropower generation and other renewable energy facilities in France, while thermal plants account for 14 percent of its French production. Outside of France, the company controls British Energy PLC, the leading nuclear power group in the United Kingdom, which operates eight plants that account for 20 percent of the country's total electrical power supply. In Germany, EDF owns 45 percent of EnBW, that country's third-largest power supplier. EDF also controls the majority of Italy's Edison, the country's number two electricity group and number three natural gas supplier. Other shareholdings include ESTAG in Austria; EDF Belgium; Hispaelec Energia and Elcogas in Spain; BERt and Demasz in Hungary; ECW, Elektrowia Rybnik, and others in Poland; SSE in Slovakia; and Alpiq in Switzerland. EDF also competes in two other deregulated energy markets, Energy Selling and Trading, on a European-wide basis.

Beyond Europe, EDF owns 49.99 percent of Constellation Energy in the United States, and has launched plans to operate four evolutionary power reactors (EPRs) there before 2020. The company has also begun constructing two EPRs in China, through a 30 percent share of Taishan Nuclear Power Joint Venture Company. Both reactors are expected to be operational by 2015. In France, the company expects to commission a new EPR in 2012, while launching construction of a second that same year.

EDF is listed on the Euronext Paris. The French government nonetheless retains more than 80 percent of the company. EDF announced in October 2009 that it would replace CEO Pierre Gadonneix, architect of much of the company's international growth, with Henri Proglio, chairman of Veolia Environnement and a personal friend of French President Nicolas Sarkozy.

1946 ORIGINS

EDF was formed in 1946 when the French government decided to nationalize the production and distribution of electricity. This was part of a general wave of nationalizations of key industries in France and elsewhere in Europe following the end of World War II.

Before 1946, the French electrical industry was in the hands of a large number of private companies, providing production, distribution, and other services connected with the industry under a variety of agreements with local authorities and regional administrations. The system had developed with no centralized planning following the appearance of the first distribution networks in 1884.

By the outbreak of World War II, electricity was provided by about 200 companies engaged in production, another 100 in transport, and about 1,150 involved in distribution. An estimated 20,000 concession-holders provided equipment and other services to these companies. The system was irrational and inefficient, going as far as having two companies providing electricity to the same place, such as in the Lyon region, where two companies competed directly, one selling alternating current from its hydroelectric plant, the other offering direct current produced at a coal-fired thermal station.

The main reason for the government's decision to consolidate the electrical industry into a single national-ized utility was its determination to speed up industrialization and urbanization after World War II. Defeat by the German forces had revealed the weaknesses of the French economy, and there was a widespread agreement on the need to modernize what was still a largely rural, agricultural society. The electric industry was central to these plans for industrialization, and the government regarded a single utility as the best way of providing the resources for the swift increase in productive capacity that would be needed, as well as overcoming the inefficiencies of the old system.

The decision to establish a nationalized utility, rather than a private one, was largely due to the influence of Marcel Paul, a Communist who in November 1945, seven months after being freed from the Nazi concentration camp at Buchenwald, was appointed minister for industrial production by the head of the government, Charles de Gaulle. Besides strong technical arguments for nationalization as the most efficient means of rationalizing the industry, Paul brought a firm ideological commitment to nationalization, as well as the bitter enmity of the French political left toward the private electricity owners, who had often funded right-wing political organizations and were widely suspected of collaborating with the Nazi occupiers during the war. Paul's work toward nationalization paid off on April 8, 1946, when the National Assembly voted almost unanimously in favor of the law nationalizing electricity and gas.

EXPANDING GENERATION CAPACITY IN THE FIFTIES

Given the task of dramatically increasing France's output of electricity, the new organization immediately began work on a massive program of hydroelectric plant construction, which was the method favored by Marcel Paul and by Pierre Simon, whom Paul appointed as first president and director general of EDF. Simon was the former director of hydroelectric energy at the Ministry of Public Works. The dam-building program dominated EDF's activities throughout the late 1940s and 1950s. Although generally well received by the public, the program gave the utility its first encounter with public opposition, when its first dam, which required the flooding of the village of Tignes in the Alps, met strong local resistance, including the bombing of a crane at the building site in 1946. Nevertheless, EDF pressed on with the program.

Seven new hydroelectric installations were delivered in 1949. Another 26 were delivered over the next three years. By 1957, a further 15 hydroelectric facilities were brought into service, turning the French Alps into the heart of the French electrical industry. The dam-

KEY DATES

1946: French government nationalizes its electrical industry, bringing about the creation of Electricité de France (EDF).
1962: Company's first nuclear power plant goes into service.
1990: Nuclear power supplies 75 percent of France's electricity.
1996: European Union decides to open all markets to competition for electricity.
2004: EDF completes its privatization with a listing on the Euronext Paris.
2009: EDF acquires 49.99 percent of Constellation Energy in the United States.
2010: EDF plans partnership with Russia's Rosatom.

building program culminated in the largest project, the redirection of the Durance River inland from Marseille, a project that created one of the largest lakes in France when it began operating in 1960.

This vast hydroelectric expansion increased EDF's production by 250 percent, and made water power the most important part of the French electrical system. Until 1961, hydroelectric installations provided at least half of EDF's total production every year except in two years of drought. In 1960, the dams and their associated plants produced over 37.1 billion kilowatt hours of electricity, representing 71.5 percent of EDF's total production, compared with 18 percent provided by coal-fired thermal stations and only 3 percent by oil-burning stations.

The hydroelectric program had succeeded in providing France with a solid electrical supply. In the 1960s, however, as demand for electricity continued to increase in response to the rapid growth of the French economy, EDF turned away from its hydroelectric policy in the search for more highly productive capacity. Urbanization and general prosperity had caused a sharp increase in the use of domestic electrical appliances, creating much greater variation in the seasonal and daily demand for electricity. To cater to these changes, EDF turned to oil-fired thermal power stations, which burned a cheap fuel and were capable of providing a flexible output of current in accordance with the demand for energy. By 1973, EDF's oil-fired power stations were producing 59.7 billion kilowatt hours of power, provid-

ing 43 percent of EDF's total output compared with only 3 percent 13 years before. Over the same period, hydroelectricity had dropped to only 32 percent of EDF's output compared with 71.5 percent in 1960.

FIRST NUCLEAR PLANT IN 1962

Although oil had come to dominate EDF's activities, the company had also begun relatively small-scale developments in producing electricity from nuclear fission. Closely connected with the French military's development of its own arsenal of nuclear weapons, a civil nuclear project was begun in the late 1940s. In 1957 EDF decided to build its first nuclear power station at Chinon in the Loire Valley, using technology developed by the French Atomic Energy Commissariat (CEA).

Compared with later projects, the Chinon plant was fairly small, using natural uranium as fuel, graphite as a moderator, and carbon gas as a refrigerant. The first phase of the project, with a capacity of just 68 megawatts (MW), came into service in 1962; the second 200 MW stage in 1965; and the third in 1967, with capacity of 500 MW. Research and development programs were launched on heavy water reactors and PWRs. It was determined that PWR was the more efficient technology, and the government began work on a 1,300 MW system. As nuclear power gradually increased in importance within EDF during the 1960s, the utility commissioned more plants, turning from gas-graphite technology to the more efficient PWR. By 1973, nuclear stations were producing 14 million kilowatt hours of electricity a year, representing 8 percent of EDF's output.

Despite this development, nuclear power remained the poor relation of the French electrical family, dominated by oil and hydroelectricity, until oil was delivered a devastating blow in 1973. When the Organization of Petroleum Exporting Countries (OPEC) decided to increase oil prices sharply in that year, the importance of oil to the industrialized West was crudely illustrated. In France, the prospect of a huge increase in the oil bill for the electrical industry prompted the government to swing strongly in favor of rapid nuclear development, which had previously been considered too expensive compared to oil. Now, as oil prices shot up, the slogan of French independence, which had prompted the postwar hydroelectric projects, reemerged as the rationale for a massive nuclear power project to ensure that France would never again depend on other countries' whims for its energy.

FOCUSING ON NUCLEAR POWER
IN THE SEVENTIES

The French prime minister, Pierre Messmer, outlined the pro-nuclear case in a speech on national television on March 6, 1974: "France has not been favored by nature in energy resources. There is almost no petrol on our territory, we have less coal than England and Germany and much less gas than Holland. ... [O]ur great chance is electrical energy of nuclear origin because we have had good experience with it since the end of World War II. ... In this effort that we will make to acquire a certain independence, or at least reduced dependence in energy, we will give priority to electricity and in electricity to nuclear electricity." The Messmer Plan, as it became known, involved a huge and sudden swing toward nuclear dependence, foreseeing the launch of 13 nuclear power plants, each with a capacity of 1,000 MW, within two years.

In 1974 alone, three new plants (Tricastin, Gravelines, and Dampierre, with a combined capacity of nearly 11,000 MW) were begun. By 1977 work had begun on another five stations, all using PWR, with a total capacity of 13,000 MW. As part of a consortium of European utilities, EDF also began building the most ambitious of all its nuclear installations: the FRF 27 billion Superphénix fast-breeder reactor. Situated at Creys-Malville on the banks of the Rhone, the Superphénix was the world's only commercial fast-breeder reactor and used enriched uranium and plutonium and capable of generating 12,000 MW.

The Messmer plan succeeded in turning France into a nuclear-powered country. In the six years to 1979, nuclear energy's share of EDF's total output rose from 8 percent to 20 percent. By 1983 it had jumped to 49 percent, and by 1990 nuclear plants were providing 75 percent of EDF's electricity. By contrast, the share produced by stations burning oil or coal fell from 53 percent in 1973 to 24 percent in 1983, and down to just 11 percent in 1990. The importance of hydroelectricity also continued to decline, although less sharply, dropping from 32 percent in 1973 to 14 percent in 1990. EDF's total nuclear capacity had reached 54,000 MW by the end of 1990, with another 6,800 MW under construction, giving France a nuclear capacity greater than that of West Germany, the United Kingdom, Spain, and Sweden combined.

OVERCAPACITY IN THE EIGHTIES

EDF's nuclear buildup faced opposition from antinuclear groups, but the utility and the government refused to yield to any pressure to moderate their ambitious nuclear plans, or even to accept a public debate on the issue. When huge demonstrations took place at the building site for the Superphénix plant in 1977, the authorities relied on firm police action to disperse the protesters. One demonstrator was killed in the violent clashes that followed. The unimpeded nuclear program finally slowed in 1981, when the newly elected Socialist government of François Mitterrand froze reactor construction. However, the government soon changed its position and allowed construction to continue, but at a greatly reduced rate.

In the mid-1980s it gradually became clear that the frenzied rush toward nuclear dependence had been overambitious. The construction program had compelled EDF to borrow heavily and, although building a standardized reactor had allowed the company to streamline the construction process and thus cut costs, this saving would be realized only if the plants were operating at full capacity. The sheer size of the nuclear buildup, caused by incorrect energy demand forecasts made in the late 1970s and by the obsession with energy independence, had, however, left EDF with an immense overcapacity. By 1988, EDF's nuclear units were operating at an average load factor of 61 percent, compared with West Germany's 74 percent, and the much more efficient systems of smaller nuclear operators such as Switzerland, at 84 percent, and Finland, at 92 percent.

During this period EDF began to sell its expertise and its product in foreign markets. The utility became closely involved in power projects in French-speaking countries in Africa and in 1985 began a series of projects in China, working on thermal, hydroelectric, and nuclear generation, distribution networks, maintenance, and training. By 1990, EDF had signed 20 contracts in China, had become project consultant for a controversial 1,800 MW seawater-cooled nuclear plant at Daya Bay and on the construction of a 1,200 MW pumped storage power station.

INTERNATIONAL SALES FROM
1986

EDF also began a concerted campaign to export its electricity to neighboring countries. In 1986, after six years of building, an undersea electrical cable was completed between France and Britain. Although this was theoretically to allow each country to draw on the other's power grid in times of shortage, it effectively became a one-way cable for the export of electricity from France to Britain. By 1990, France was exporting 11.9 billion kilowatt hours of power a year to Britain, close behind its two largest customers: Italy, with 12.9 billion kilowatt hours, and Switzerland, with 13.6 billion kilowatt hours. EDF also exported large bands of power to Germany, the Netherlands, Belgium, and

Luxembourg and in 1990 signed an agreement worth $4 million to supply the Spanish electrical grid with 1,000 MW of capacity beginning in the mid-1990s.

The utility was also quick to take advantage of the dramatic changes in Eastern Europe following the collapse of Communism in 1989 and 1990. In 1991, EDF was on the verge of joining a German-led consortium to modernize East Germany's power network, and was leading an international team providing technical and management advice to Bulgaria's troubled nuclear industry. EDF was also broadening its activities in more developed markets. In July 1991, the utility became a key part of a consortium with Britain's East Midlands Electricity and several other companies to build a £400 million, 800 MW gas-fired power station in Lincolnshire, in a direct challenge to the two main British power companies, National Power and Power-Gen, on their own territory. The consortium, Independent Power Generators, planned to invest in private power projects around the world.

While these foreign moves went ahead, EDF was also trying to stimulate demand for electricity within France to soak up its spare capacity. EDF also set out to encourage industrial companies to build power-consuming plants in France. However, large companies would do this only if EDF offered them power at a heavily subsidized rate, which the utility agreed to do when the aluminum producer Pechiney threatened to move its production to Venezuela because French power was too expensive. Instead, Pechiney, in partnership with EDF, built a new plant at Dunkirk in 1988, to which EDF agreed to provide electricity at half the production cost per kilowatt hour for the first six years, with the price rising gradually over subsequent years. The European Commission (EC) regarded the deal as nothing less than anticompetitive electricity dumping and forced EDF to renegotiate it on more competitive grounds, but EDF received EC approval in 1990 for similar cheap power deals with Exxon Chemicals and Allied Signal, two U.S. companies.

TURNING POINT IN THE NINETIES

The problems confronting EDF crystallized in 1989, when the utility reported an annual loss of FRF 4 billion, a result that EDF's president, Pierre Delaporte, described in the *Financial Times* of January 31,1990, as "catastrophic, though mainly due to unforeseen problems, such as the mild winter, drought, and reduced availability of the PWR 1300 MW series." In 1990, it received a further blow when the overseer of nuclear technology in France, EDF's former partner, the CEA, released a report sharply criticizing EDF's overinvest-

ment in nuclear capacity and calling for urgent solutions to unresolved problems of nuclear waste disposal. By 1990, EDF had begun looking for ways to diversify its power sources.

Although EDF returned a small profit in 1990, a nuclear program costing FRF 800 billion had left the utility with long-term debt of FRF 226 billion. The long-term problems of waste disposal needed to be dealt with, while many of EDF's older reactors would soon be due for decommissioning, an operation whose cost, although unknown, was expected to be very high and would provide no financial return. However, the problem of overcapacity had been reduced, owing to the development of exports and increasing demand from French heavy industries.

EDF ordered a new nuclear plant in 1991 and anticipated further investment in peak facilities and nuclear plants. From 1990 onward, debt was also decreasing. By 1990 repayment exceeded borrowing by FRF 3 billion, with a provisional figure of FRF 13 billion for 1991. EDF's rates, meanwhile, although already among the lowest in Europe, continued to decrease at 1.5 percent per year in real terms.

A new vision took shape for EDF in the early 1990s. With limited potential for growth on the domestic front, the company expanded its international efforts. Spending abroad increased from FRF 300 million to FRF 3 billion in 1994. The company purchased stakes in Sweden's Sydkaft and Italy's Ilva SE. In 1996 EDF joined a consortium of companies to buy a major Brazilian electric company.

A year later it purchased 55 percent of a Polish power station. On the distribution side, EDF invested in Massachusetts-based American Superconductor Corporation to develop new technology that would permit 5 to 10 times more electric power to be conveyed over the same size cable or conduit. EDF also joined forces with Texaco, Inc., to build an integrated gasification/combine-cycle plant in Normandy, France, despite the company's general reluctance to add to its already high electric power capacity. The new plant would allow EDF to offer process steam and industrial gases to industrial clients, thus providing a competitive edge when the European Union (EU) allowed open competition in the electricity market.

EU DEREGULATION IN 1996

In 1996, the EU energy ministers met to discuss the opening of its markets to allow consumers to choose among competing suppliers of electricity. France was reluctant to agree to the proposal, afraid of the effects on its state-run monopoly, in particular the loss of jobs.

It was estimated that as much as 30 percent of the workforce would have to be trimmed if EDF lost its privileged status in France. EDF workers were members of a strong union, and it was certain that they would rally in the streets of Paris, much to the discomfort of the politicians. Jobs were also the payoff to local communities for accepting reactors in their backyards.

As the *Economist* noted in a 1996 article: "If EDF loses its reputation as a creator of jobs, public support for its nuclear programme may begin to ebb. Meanwhile, competition would certainly encourage suppliers in other countries to question whether EDF had incorporated all the costs of decommissioning reactors in its tariffs; they would also demand that EDF be financed at market rates. EDF is a mighty edifice which has so far been supported by powerful union, political and industrial interests. Take one leg away, however, and the whole structure could collapse."

Only after a meeting between the French president, Jacques Chirac, and German chancellor, Helmut Kohl, did France finally agree to European deregulation of electricity. The plan was to be phased in over several years beginning on February 19, 1999, when high-volume customers would be allowed to choose suppliers, with a minimum market opening of 25 percent. When that date arrived, however, legislation had still not been completed to provide for France's participation. In the meantime, EDF completed its most ambitious acquisition when, for $2.3 billion, it purchased London Electricity. France's subsequent failure to comply with EU deregulation sparked outrage from many governments, whose own companies were barred from competing in the French market.

PRIVATIZED IN 2004

Ironically, it was the lobbying of EDF itself that would finally lead to France opening its markets to a minimum level of compliance. François Roussely, who had become chairman and chief executive of EDF in July 1998, was convinced that the utility could prosper under the new conditions. He set a goal of EDF realizing half its revenues from business other than electricity in France by 2005. That portion in 1999 stood at just 18 percent of revenues. Roussely also set an ambitious target for a return on capital, growing it from 7.4 percent to 10 percent.

Despite Roussely's belief that EDF was destined to play a major role in Europe and the world in general, he still had to contend with the nature of the utility's ownership. To prosper, EDF had to act like a private-sector company. Roussely inaugurated a new customer-focused corporate culture. (According to the *Economist*,

EDF had never referred to its clientele as "customers" before Roussely came onboard.) As part of this effort, Roussely restructured EDF's management into two separate divisions, one focused on customer service, the other on operations.

In 2000, EDF redoubled its efforts to reduce its reliance on the French electricity sector, announcing plans to generate as much as half of its revenues outside of France by the middle of the decade. The company established a new Energy Trading division, which quickly achieved profitability. EDF also began expanding its range of foreign shareholdings, most notably through adding a 45 percent stake in Germany's third-largest electricity player, EnBW. In the United Kingdom, EDF acquired several parts of the future British Energy, including London Electricity, Eastern Electricity, and Seeboard. The company also added to its holdings in Italy and Spain. In this way, the company had gained a presence in all of Europe's largest energy markets.

RUSSIAN PARTNERSHIP IN 2010?

By 2003, EDF's international holdings generated more than 25 percent of its total revenues. EDF continued to develop its international presence, and by the end of the decade had established a presence in nearly 20 countries. Amid this expansion, EDF had finally overcome the political and social resistance at home in order to complete its privatization. In 2004, the company reincorporated as a limited company, Electricité de France SA. Then, in November 2005, EDF went public, listing its shares on the Euronext Paris. The French government nonetheless maintained control of more than 80 percent of the company, considered as vital to France's economic and political interests. By then, EDF had come under new leadership, as Pierre Gadonneix took over as CEO.

This government ownership exposed EDF to criticism as it continued to expand into other, fully liberalized energy markets. The French government had taken some steps to open the country's electricity market to competition, including allowing major corporations to seek alternative energy providers from 2000. In 2007, the government carried out a liberalization of the rest of the energy sector, exposing EDF to competition in the consumer and business sectors for the first time. Nonetheless, EDF retained control of both the country's power grid, operated by subsidiary RTE, and its distribution network, operated by ERDF. The latter continued to dominate the distribution sector in 2010, claiming some 95 percent of the total market.

EDF's long-term commitment to nuclear power technology had given the company a distinct edge in the second half of the decade as prices for oil and other energy sources skyrocketed. With oil reserves fast becoming depleted, coal representing a major environmental hazard, and other renewable energy sources still years away from true commercial viability, nuclear power appeared to be the best near-term investment for the future of electrical power generation.

By then, EDF had completed a new series of acquisitions that firmly established it as Europe's nuclear power leader and one of the world's major nuclear power players. These included the takeover of British Energy, finally completed in September 2008, making EDF the largest energy producer in the United Kingdom. The company also gained majority control over Italy's Edison through a number of direct and indirect shareholdings.

In 2009, EDF moved into the United States, paying $4.5 billion for a 49.99 percent stake in Constellation Energy. That company then announced its intention to build four new EPRs in the United States by 2020. In the meantime, EDF had also entered the Chinese market, acquiring a 30 percent stake in a joint venture to build two EPRs in Tianjin by 2015. EDF also neared completion of its newest French EPR, in Flamanville, expected to be commissioned by 2012. The company prepared to launch construction of a second EPR that year, in Penly, in partnership with Italy's ENEL.

With revenues of nearly EUR 66.4 billion ($93 billion) in 2009 and a total power generation capacity of nearly 610 TWh, EDF stood out as Europe's power generation heavyweight. The company continued to seek new horizons, and in March 2010 was reported to have begun planning a partnership with its Russian counterpart, Rosatom, to build and operate nuclear power facilities outside of their home markets. By then, EDF had gained new management, after Gadonneix reportedly fell out of favor with the French government. In his place was named Henri Proglio, head of Veolia Environnement and personal friend to President Nicolas Sarkozy. Under Proglio, EDF could be expected to carry out more closely the French government's strategic aims for the company, which had become one of the country's largest employers, and one of the leaders of the global electricity sector.

Richard Brass
Updated, Ed Dinger; M. L. Cohen

PRINCIPAL SUBSIDIARIES

RTE EDF; Électricité Réseau Distribution France; PEI Group; EDF Energy; EnBW; Edison; Transalpina di Energia; EDF Trading (UK); EDF International; ECK Cracovie (Poland); Société d'Investissement en Autriche France (80%); SSE Slovakia; Groupe ATEL (Switzerland; 24.83%); EDF Development UK Ltd; EDF Production UK Ltd; EDF Belgium; Hispaelec (Spain); EDF Développement Environnement SA; EDF Holding SAS; EDF Développement USA; Unistar Nuclear Energy USA (50%); Ute Paracambi (Brazil); Figlec (China).

PRINCIPAL DIVISIONS

Generation; Transmission; Distribution; Energy Selling; Trading.

PRINCIPAL OPERATING UNITS

RTE Reseau de Transport Electricité; ERDF Electricité Reseau Distribution France.

PRINCIPAL COMPETITORS

ENI S.p.A.; E.ON AG; SUEZ; Essel Mining and Industries Ltd.; Iberdrola S.A.; Hutchison Whampoa Ltd.; ENEL S.p.A.; National Grid PLC; RWE AG.

FURTHER READING

Davies, Graeme, "EDF Finally Seals British Energy Takeover," *Investors Chronicle*, September 24, 2008.

"EDF Plans to Collaborate with Rosatom," *International Resource News*, March 9, 2010.

"EDF to Study Options for Selling Power Distribution Networks Business," *International Resource News*, October 2, 2009.

"EDF to Swap Power for Gas with Gazprom," *International Resource News*, December 23, 2009.

"Electricité de France: A Giant Awakes," *Economist*, November 4, 2000, p. 71.

"Energetic Manoeuvres," *Economist*, October 3, 2009, p. 77EU.

George, Gerry, "The Global Giants," *Transmission & Distribution World*, 2000, pp. 30–50.

Holmes, A., *Electricity in Europe: Power and Profit*, London: Financial Times Business Information Ltd., 1990.

"How the French Get Power," *Economist*, May 11, 1996, p. 62.

Matlack, Carol, "Time to Tame This Electrical Storm," *Business Week*, June 21, 2004, p. 22.

Picard, J.-F., A. Beltran, and M. Bungener, *Histoires de l'EDF*, Paris: Dunod, 1985.

Pugsley, Justin, "EDF Takes Nuclear Dream beyond France," *Acquisitions Monthly*, June 2009, p. 16.

"A Very Big French Turn-off: Electricité de France," *Economist*, July 3, 2004, p. 55US.

Empire Industries Ltd.

717 Jarvis Avenue
Winnipeg, Manitoba R2W 3B4
Canada
Telephone: (204) 589-9300
Fax: (204) 582-8057
Web site: http://www.empireindustriesltd.com

Public Company
Incorporated: 2005 as Ryjencap Inc.
Employees: 800
Sales: CAD 180.01 million (2008)
Stock Exchanges: Toronto
Ticker Symbol: EIL
NAICS: 332312 Fabricated Structural Metal Manufacturing

■ ■ ■

Empire Industries Ltd. is a Winnipeg, Canada-based manufacturer of structural steel and specialty engineered products. The structural steel business is conducted by four wholly owned subsidiaries: Empire Iron Works Ltd., George Third & Son Ltd., Empire Dynamic Structures Ltd., and Tornado Technologies Inc. Additionally, Empire holds a 49 percent stake in Sorge's Welding Ltd. Mostly serving western Canada, these units provide structural steel fabrication, module fabrication, plate steel fabrication, pipe fabrication and spooling, infrastructure fabrications and installations, steel erection services, and emergency welding repair services. Products include industrial tanks, pipes, staircases, and bridges for use in refineries, office buildings, highway projects, and airports.

Empire's specialty engineered products are manufactured by Tornado Technologies and Empire Iron Works and its two wholly owned subsidiaries: Parr Metal Fabricators Ltd. and Ward Industrial Equipment Ltd. They manufacture oil and gas production and combustion equipment, stationary industrial vacuums, industrial air cleaning equipment, bulk material handling equipment, amusement rides, and observatory telescopes. In addition to nine Canadian offices, Empire maintains operations in the United States in Buffalo, New York; Bellingham, Washington; and Alleyton, Texas. Empire is a public company listed on the Toronto Stock Exchange.

ORIGIN AS EMPIRE IRON WORKS: 1958

The foundation for Empire Industries was established in Winnipeg in 1958 with the launch of the Empire Iron Works, which was incorporated in Manitoba in 1964. The company started out as an ornamental metal fabricator, but diversified its operations over the years. In 1968 it began supplying and erecting structural steel in the Winnipeg area, and three years later hired a full-time engineering staff. It then added wheelabrating and paint facilities in 1974, and two years later launched a separate company to produce stainless steel, aluminum, and light gauge carbon steel products. Empire Iron ended the 1970s by expanding to the Alberta area where in 1979 it purchased a facility in Edmonton to provide steel fabrication and installation services.

Empire Iron continued to grow in the 1980s and 1990s. It expanded to the Vancouver market in 1983, opening offices and a steel fabrication and installation operation in Delta, British Columbia. The company added a construction services division in Winnipeg in 1988. The multi-discipline operation included ironworkers, millwrights, carpenters, boilermakers, pipefitters, electricians, cement masons, and engineers. They constructed new plants, renovated or shut down old plants, and provided maintenance services. Sectors served included pulp and paper mills, water and sewage treatment plants, mine process plants, oil refineries, boiler and power plants, gas process plants, compressor stations, oil sands and heavy oil recovery plants, and materials handling facilities. Another construction services division was then opened in Edmonton in 1991.

GUY NELSON TAKING THE HELM: 1996

There was a change in the top ranks at Empire Iron in 1996 when K. Guy Nelson assumed the chairmanship. He was also the head of Nelson Advisors, which provided consulting services and invested in steel fabrication, manufacturing, and other companies. Empire Iron now began to pursue external as well as internal growth. In 1999 it acquired Welland, Ontario-based Hopkins Steel Works Ltd. The industrial, structural steel fabrication company was established in 1966. Empire Iron added a detailing division in Edmonton in 2000 to provide full-service drafting including software modeling to determine the impact that certain materials and equipment might have on a steel structure.

Empire Iron experienced declining revenues in the early 2000s, falling from CAD 43.8 million in 2002 to CAD 36.3 million in 2004. The company also posted net losses in both 2003 and 2004. A year later the company enjoyed a rebound, as revenues more than doubled to CAD 78.2 million, resulting in net income

of CAD 260,000. In the spring of 2006 the board of directors at Empire Iron decided that in addition to organic growth it would make a concerted effort to use the company as an acquisition vehicle to build up its western Canada business in the industrial, commercial, and institutional market segments. In May 2006, Empire Iron acquired Ward Industrial Equipment Ltd., a maker of bulk material handling equipment and environmental equipment since 1966. The deal also set the stage for the creation of Empire Industries.

REVERSE MERGER TAKES COMPANY PUBLIC: 2006

After raising CAD 6 million in a private placement of stock in May 2006, Empire Iron went public through a reverse merger with a public capital pool corporation, Ryjencap Inc., formed in 2005. After the transaction was completed in July 2006, Ryjencap changed its name to Empire Industries Ltd. and its stock began trading on the Toronto Stock Exchange. The company's largest shareholder was Guy Nelson, who in June 2006 became chairman and chief executive officer of Empire Industries.

Empire lost little time in using its public status to further its acquisition strategy. In August 2006 it paid CAD 9.4 million, which included CAD 2.1 million in working capital, to acquire George Third & Son Partnership, a well-established British Columbia steel fabricator. The family-owned business was founded as a blacksmith shop, Third & Dundas, by 25-year-old Scottish immigrant George Third in 1910. The company assumed the George Third & Son name in 1946 and became involved in steel fabrication, in particular steel tanks used by gas stations. George Third died in 1972 and the business was continued by his sons, grandsons, and great-grandsons Rob and Brett Third who stayed with the company after it was acquired by Empire and received an equity stake in the new corporate parent. The business also added about CAD 18 million in annual sales to Empire's balance sheet.

Empire was now the second-largest steel fabricating company in western Canada and had its sights set on the market leader, Edmonton-based Supreme Steel Ltd., which was twice as large. Before 2006 came to a close, Empire completed a pair of deals at a combined cost of CAD 2.1 million. It bought Ft. McMurray, Alberta-based Sorge's Pro Welding Ltd., a fabrication business, as well as a 49 percent interest in Sorge's Welding Ltd., an Aboriginal majority-owned welding business. The addition of these operations strengthened Empire's position in northern Alberta.

```
┌─────────────────────────────────────────────┐
│                                               │
│              KEY DATES                        │
│          ────────────●────────────            │
│                                               │
│   1958:  Empire Iron Works is established.    │
│   1996:  Guy Nelson is named chairman.        │
│   2006:  Company goes public in reverse merger as │
│          Empire Industries.                   │
│   2007:  AMEC Dynamic Structures Ltd. is acquired. │
│   2010:  Empire refinances.                   │
│                                               │
└─────────────────────────────────────────────┘
```

ACQUISITION OF DYNAMIC STRUCTURES: 2007

More acquisitions followed in 2007. In April Empire paid CAD 11 million for AMEC Dynamic Structures Ltd., a division of AMEC PLC, a United Kingdom company that was in the process of divesting noncore assets. British Columbia-based Dynamic Structures produced a variety of complex structures, including telescopes and enclosures, bridges, ski jumps, automatically guided vehicles, roller coasters, and motion theater attractions. It was founded in 1926 as Vancouver Art Metal and assumed the name Coast Steel Fabricators Limited in 1952. The company built its first telescope, the Canada-France-Hawaii telescope, in the 1970s.

It became known as AMEC Dynamic Structures Ltd. after AMEC acquired the company in 2001. Under Empire's ownership, Dynamic Structures turned over its 61,000-square-foot fabrication shop to George Third & Son, and focused on telescopes and amusement rides, two business segments in which it had developed into a world leader. Also in April 2007 Empire, at the cost of CAD 8 million, acquired KWH Constructors Ltd. and its Somerset Engineering division, a well-respected North American bridge builder. KWH had been incorporated in 1989, while Somerset was founded in 1981.

Empire completed two more acquisitions in 2007. In November it bought Tornado Technologies Inc. for CAD 18 million. Tornado mostly served Alberta's oil and gas industry, offering steel fabrication services as well as selling proprietary combustion and production equipment. In addition, Tornado sold Hydrovac and Vacuum trucks to oil and gas customers. The company had been launched in 1984 as Tornado Combustion Technologies with the introduction of a flare pit igniter. Tornado brought with it three fabrication plants in Alberta and one in Houston, Texas. At the close of 2007 Empire acquired Parr Metal Fabricators for $1.1 million. The Winnipeg company was founded in 1976 and was a major custom fabricator of stainless steel, carbon steel, and aluminum pressure vessels, pressure piping, tanks, and silos. As a result of its acquisition spree, Empire increased revenues to CAD 117 million in fiscal 2007, and grew operating incomes from CAD 1.2 million to CAD 8.9 million.

Business conditions in western Canada appeared promising for Empire. Not only did demand for construction services exceed the region's supply, nonresidential capital spending, especially in the mining and oil and gas industries, was expected to continue to grow to record heights. Having more than tripled its fabrication and installation capacity, Empire appeared well positioned to take advantage of a multitude of opportunities.

POOR ECONOMY TAKES TOLL: 2008

A confluence of events, however, combined in 2008 to create extremely arduous business conditions. A credit crunch led to a financial market downturn, making it exceedingly difficult to borrow funds for capital expenditures, adversely impacting Empire's sales. Moreover, the company's primary customers in the energy industry had to contend with declining oil and gas prices. Although the nonresidential construction market in western Canada was stronger than the rest of the country, it was not strong enough to withstand the softening conditions that only worsened as the year went on. Empire was able to increase revenues to CAD 180 million in 2008, but margins did not hold up, and the company posted a net loss of CAD 1.76 million, due entirely to the performance of the steel fabrication group, the sales of which remained relatively flat while margins eroded. The engineered products group, on the other hand, enjoyed the benefits of the acquisitions completed in 2007. Sales more than tripled from CAD 23.9 million in 2007 to CAD 83.34 million in 2008.

The financial market slump also hurt the price of Empire's stock, so that its market capitalization fell below the book value of its assets. As a result, Empire retained the services of The Equicom Group, an investor relations consulting firm, as it considered possible ways to maximize shareholder value, including the sale of undervalued or redundant assets. There were some other positive developments for Empire in 2008, however. In October Sorge's Welding acquired Lemax Machine and Welding for CAD 1.1 million plus CAD 300,000 in working capital. Lemax maintained a machine shop in Ft. McMurray, where it provided welding services as well as field machining and welding services in the Wood Buffalo region.

The continuing recession led to increasing difficulties for Empire in 2009. The company responded by initiating a restructuring plan that, in short, called for a narrowing focus on "adding value to steel." Thus, some redundant assets were divested, such as the sales and leaseback of a facility and the sale of a combustion business. Empire also took steps to cut costs and limit capital expenditures, including reduced work weeks, salary cuts, layoffs, and a hiring freeze.

Empire worked with its banks to improve its financial position. In August 2009 the company was able to negotiate extensions on debts owed by Empire Iron, George Third, and Dynamic Structures. In March 2010, Empire completed a CAD 17.5 million refinancing with Canadian Western Bank that included a CAD 10 million revolving credit line and CAD 7.5 million in term debt. Together the facilities allowed Empire to fully repay the money Empire owed Royal Bank of Canada and HSBC Bank of Canada. As the economy began to show improvement, Empire appeared to have restored health to its balance sheet and was positioned to resume a growth strategy.

Ed Dinger

PRINCIPAL SUBSIDIARIES

Empire Iron Works Ltd.; George Third & Son Ltd.; Empire Dynamic Structures Ltd.; Tornado Technologies Inc.

PRINCIPAL COMPETITORS

ADF Group Inc,; Butler Manufacturing; Canam Group Inc.

FURTHER READING

"Empire Falls Deeper in the Red," *Toronto Star*, August 29, 2009, p. B5.

"Empire Industries Ltd. Closes Acquisition of George Third Partnership," *Canadian Corporate News*, September 1, 2006.

"Empire Industries Ltd. Successfully Closes $17.5 Million Refinancing," *TendersInfo*, March 9, 2010.

McNeill, Murray, "Hoping to Grow an Empire," *Winnipeg Free Press*, September 7, 2006, p. B5.

"Ryjencap Acquires Empire Iron," *Canada Stockwatch*, July 6, 2006.

"Sales Fall at Steel Maker but Contract Profit Soars," *Toronto Star*, May 1, 2007, p. C6.

"Steel Fabricator Buying Ski Firm for $9.8 Million," *Toronto Star*, April 18, 2007, p. F8.

TECHNOLOGIES

EMS Technologies, Inc.

660 Engineering Drive
Norcross, Georgia 30092
U.S.A.
Telephone: (770) 263-9200
Fax: (770) 263-9207
Web site: http://www.ems-t.com

Public Company
Incorporated: 1968 as Electromagnetic Sciences, Inc.
Employees: 1,300
Sales: $359.97 million (2009)
Stock Exchanges: NASDAQ
Ticker Symbol: ELMG
NAICS: 334290 Other Communications Equipment
Manufacturing; 334220 Radio and Television
Broadcasting and Wireless Communications Equip-
ment Manufacturing; 541710 Research and
Development in the Physical, Engineering, and Life
Sciences

■ ■ ■

EMS Technologies, Inc., is a supplier of communications equipment used in military and commercial
applications. The company began as a developer of
microwave systems for satellite communications. It has
expanded on this expertise by making systems for tracking inventory at warehouses and providing satellite and
terrestrial data links for moving vehicles. It is the
dominant player in the market for Cospas-Sarsat
satellite-based tracking systems used in search and
rescue.

Subsidiary LXE Inc. was formed in 1983 to commercialize such technology and pioneered its use in
logistics handling. By 2009 it had been installed in more
than 7,500 locations, with more than half of LXE's annual sales coming outside the United States. The success
of LXE has helped EMS reduce the proportion of total
sales to the U.S. government to less than 30 percent.
EMS's customers include defense contractors, militaries
and government agencies, and global corporations. The
company has principal facilities in Atlanta; Moorestown,
New Jersey; and Ottawa.

ATLANTA ORIGINS

EMS Technologies, Inc., was founded in Atlanta by Dr.
John E. Pippin. A graduate of the Georgia Institute of
Technology and a Harvard Ph.D., Pippin had led
research at Scientific-Atlanta (later part of Cisco
Systems) for four years. He acquired a line of microwave
devices from Scientific-Atlanta, which was also generous
with providing test equipment to get the company
started. Pippin was joined by several colleagues from
Scientific-Atlanta, best known as a maker of cable boxes.
EMS was incorporated in Georgia as Electromagnetic
Sciences, Inc., and counts November 1, 1968, as its
founding date.

EMS's products were used in the first weather satellites and communications satellites. From the beginning
the company operated on the cutting edge of microwave
communications technology. Early work included antennas and other components for the Defense Satellite
Communications System in 1976. Annual revenues
grew steadily through most of the decade, reaching $6.3
million in 1980.

Annual revenues were $9.6 million in 1981. The company had been consistently profitable for five years. The business grew rapidly during the Reagan era defense buildup. EMS branched out from satellite hardware into communications tools, electronic countermeasures, and other types of defense electronics. In 1983 EMS acquired California's Gamma F Corp., which expanded its capacities into millimeter-wave technology.

EMS reached sales of $33 million in 1985. At the time, the U.S. government was the end customer for more than three-quarters of its business. However, in spite of the defense boom, the company had already moved to adapt its existing technologies for use in the commercial sector.

COMMERCIAL OFFSHOOT IN 1983

EMS experimented with supplying wireless communications devices for the Washington, D.C., police in the mid-1970s, but the technology of the day proved ungainly and impractical. The company then began applying its wireless communications expertise to commercial tracking solutions for logistics. It later formed a subsidiary, LXE Inc., to market such products.

LXE had developed its inventory-control system with the help of Milliken Inc., the Spartanburg, South Carolina, textile giant. It soon attracted other corporate customers with very large warehouses, such as Ford Motor Company and AT&T.

The end of the Cold War depressed the value of EMS's shares, as it did those of other companies predominantly geared toward defense. Revenues slipped 17 percent to $55.6 million in 1989 and net income fell from a record $7.5 million to $2 million. There were about 800 employees. EMS had remained profitable largely due to its fast-growing LXE logistics equipment business, but it posted a loss in 1990 as the Navy's A-12

naval attack aircraft program was suddenly canceled. The company responded by laying off 100 workers and consolidating some of its plants.

The company's fortunes soon experienced a resurgence with U.S. military operations in the Persian Gulf. It made a $6.4 million profit as revenues exceeded $75 million in 1991. By this time, military sales accounted for only half of EMS's total revenues. Although the economy in general was slow, EMS's logistics management products remained in demand as a tool for controlling costs, noted *Business Atlanta*. EMS posted total revenues of $150 million in 1996. Profits were $5 million.

ESTABLISHING A SATELLITE UNIT IN 1993

In 1993 EMS acquired a controlling 70 percent interest in CAL Corporation, an Ottawa manufacturer of satellite antennas for aviation. CAL was one of the few companies to field products able to gather the fainter signals from new high-altitude satellites, whose coverage extended across larger swaths of Earth's surface than that of low-orbit satellites.

Formerly Canadian Astronautics Ltd., CAL had about 260 employees when it was acquired. It had been formed in 1974 by three engineers working out of a garage making satellite antennas for the military. In the 1980s it developed a specialty in search-and-rescue technology. It became the basis of EMS SATCOM after the acquisition.

In January 1999 EMS added Spar Aerospace Ltd.'s satellite plant near Montreal for CAD 20 million. Spar, known for supplying the Canadarm robot arm to the space shuttle, was exiting the high profile but notoriously unprofitable satellite business after years of overbuilding in the industry.

The unit being sold had produced Canada's famous Anik telecommunications satellites, as well as antennae for Radarsat satellites and the International Space Station, sometimes working alongside EMS engineers. It had been established in the 1940s as a division of RCA Canada, which in 1967 built a new plant in Ste. Anne de Bellevue, a town near Montreal. Spar Aerospace Ltd. bought the unit in 1977.

After being acquired by EMS in 1999, the Montreal business was merged with previously acquired CAL into EMS Technologies Canada Ltd. EMS was unable to turn the Montreal unit around, although it had reached annual sales of about CAD 70 million. After rounds of layoffs reduced it to 525 employees, less than half its early 1990s peak, EMS put it up for sale in July 2003.

KEY DATES

1968: Electromagnetic Sciences, Inc., (EMS) is formed by former Scientific Atlanta engineers.
1983: EMS subsidiary LXE Inc. pioneers use of wireless technology in logistics handling.
1999: Company is renamed EMS Technologies, Inc.; Spar Aerospace's satellite business is acquired.
2007: EMS posts record results; Australia's DSpace Pty. Ltd. Is acquired.
2010: New Aviation business unit combines EMS SATCOM with recent acquisitions Sky Connect LLC and Formation, Inc.

It took more than two years for a buyer to emerge, giant Vancouver-based engineering firm MacDonald Dettwiler & Associates Ltd., which had been one of its customers.

NEW NAME IN 1999

In March 1999 Electromagnetic Sciences was renamed EMS Technologies, Inc. Company founder Pippin had retired the previous year. He was succeeded by Thomas E. Sharon, who had joined EMS in 1971, just three years after it was founded. Sharon resigned as CEO in January 2001 to start his own company. He was succeeded by Alfred Hansen, a retired four-star Air Force general who had been corporate vice president of Lockheed Martin.

EMS opened an addition to its Norcross, Georgia, headquarters in early 2000 in order to support growth at its booming wireless business. Ottawa's Digital Space Systems Inc., which had worked with EMS on the multinational Cospas-Sarsat satellite system used for search and rescue, was added to the SATCOM division at the end of the year. In May 2001 the company acquired Dallas's CI Wireless Inc., which made repeaters and other components for RF wireless networks. EMS bought Ottercom Ltd., a Tewkesbury, England-based supplier of portable terminals for Inmarsat satellite networks, in April 2002.

Drawing on its experience with aviation, by 2003 EMS SATCOM had launched a maritime venture to bring satellite data communications to ocean vessels. It originally focused sales efforts on the leisure market, where it was more likely to get quick approvals from yacht owners than would be the case with corporate shipowners.

In July 2004 EMS bought small Clearwater, Florida, defense electronics firm Multitech Corp. By this time EMS employed 1,700 people. The company lost $10.8 million in 2005 on revenues of $310 million. EMS finally sold off its Montreal space business toward the end of 2005. The company posted a loss of $10.8 million on revenues of $310 million for the year.

RENEWED FOCUS AFTER 2006

In early 2006 a small satellite networking unit, the last remnant of the Montreal operation, was also divested, to Advantech Advanced Microwave Technologies Inc. for a reported $8.9 million. The company later sold EMS Wireless, which made antennas for cellphone towers, to wireless equipment manufacturer Andrew Corp. for $50.5 million. By this time the division had 200 employees.

Revenues were $260 million in 2006. After the divestments the company had 1,000 employees. Paul B. Domorski became president and CEO of EMS in June 2006. He had previously held a number of executive positions in the tech industry, including CEO of RSL Communications Ltd. and most recently vice president of Avaya Corporation's services operations business.

A recovering commercial aviation industry renewed interest in broadband Internet access for airliners and other aircraft. Boeing closed its much-hyped Connexion in-flight data connectivity offering in 2006 after just two years in business, however. While Boeing had been oriented toward large international airlines, EMS's new Enfusion system was at first marketed more toward business jet operators in North America. It seemed an enduring concept, and a few airlines continued to bring out new in-flight broadband offerings aimed at meeting this demand from productivity-minded business travelers.

MILESTONE YEAR: 2007

In 2007 EMS announced a deal to develop hybrid mobile/satellite phones for London-based satellite operator Inmarsat PLC. In July of the same year Australia's DSpace Pty. Ltd. was acquired for a reported AUD 6.6 million. DSpace, established in 1995, had developed BGAN satellite radio protocols for Inmarsat. EMS also began offering anti-jam technology to the commercial satellite market during the year.

EMS posted the best results of its history in 2007. U.S. government end use accounted for only one-quarter of the total. As it grew, the company hired dozens of workers and made plans to build a 34,000-square-foot addition to its headquarters. More acquisitions were soon underway. *Forbes* magazine pronounced EMS one of the country's 200 best small companies. The year was also marked by the passing of company founder John Pippin at the age of 79.

EMS was a contractor for the latest generation of military communications satellites from Lockheed Martin. In 2007 it made some of the same anti-jam technology used in these available to commercial users. EMS was also providing antennas for Northrop Grumman to connect B-2 stealth bombers with data connections to satellites.

Stockholm's Akerstroms Trux AB became part of LXE in February 2008. EMS paid $15.5 million for the 20-employee unit, which enhanced its presence in the faster growing European logistics-tracking market and added a Windows-based product line. Six months later EMS paid about $15.5 million for Sky Connect LLC, based in Maryland, which made products for general aviation and tracking and phone systems based on the Iridium satellite network.

Formation Inc., a Moorestown, New Jersey, manufacturer of in-flight wireless networking products used in military and commercial aviation, was acquired in January 2009 in a deal potentially worth $55 million. The company specialized in shielding components so they would not interfere with an aircraft's other electronic systems in flight. It had nearly collapsed when airlines retrenched following the September 11, 2001, terrorist attacks on the United States. It also made communications systems for commuter trains.

Renamed EMS Formation, it was combined with EMS Sky Connect and EMS SATCOM in the new Aviation business unit in January 2010. EMS's other business units were Global Tracking, LXE, and Defense and Space. In February 2009 EMS also bought Britain's Satamatics Global Ltd., a supplier of Inmarsat-based tracking systems.

Paul Domorski stepped down as EMS president and CEO in November 2009 and was replaced by Neilson A. Mackay, a company veteran of 17 years who had been made chief operating officer in the previous year. An $18.5 million goodwill impairment charge relating to the LXE division contributed to a $20.1 million loss for 2009, although revenues rose 7.5 percent to $360 million. The company then had about 1,300 employees.

PRINCIPAL SUBSIDIARIES

Sky Connect LLC; Formation, Inc.; LXE Inc.; EMS Technologies–LXE S.e.n.c. (Luxembourg); EMS Holding S.a.r.l. (Luxembourg); LXE Belgium NV; LXE France SARL; LXE GmbH (Germany); LXE Italia SRL (Italy); LXE Netherlands BV; LXE Scandinavia AB (Sweden); Akerstroms Trux AB (Sweden); LXE Singapore; LXE UK, LTD; Akerstroms Trux Inc.; EMS Technologies Canada, Ltd.; EMS Pacific Pty. LTD (Australia); DSpace Pty. Ltd. (Australia); EMS SATCOM UK, LTD; EMS Acquisition Company Limited (UK); Satamatics Global Limited (UK); Satamatics Brasil Comercialização de Segmento Espacial Ltda. (Brazil).

Frederick C. Ingram

PRINCIPAL DIVISIONS

EMS Defense and Space; EMS Aviation; EMS Global Tracking; LXE.

PRINCIPAL OPERATING UNITS

EMS Defense & Space; EMS SATCOM; LXE; EMS Sky Connect; EMS Formation; EMS Satamatics.

PRINCIPAL COMPETITORS

Intermec Inc.; Motorola, Inc.; Psion Group; L-3 Communications Corporation; DRS Technologies, Inc.; TECOM Industries, Inc.; Chelton, Inc.; Thrane & Thrane A/S; Lockheed Martin Corporation.

FURTHER READING

Allison, David, "EMS Is Building Arsenal of Major Defense Contracts," *Atlanta Business Chronicle*, May 5, 1986, p. 3A.

———, "Gulf War Gives Norcross Defense Firm a Shot in the Arm," *Atlanta Business Chronicle*, February 4, 1991, pp. 1A+.

Brady, Margret, "Masters of Communicating with the Far Side of the World; Solo Sailor Derek Hatfield Will Have a New Canadian Satellite System," *National Post's Financial Post & FP Investing*, June 21, 2004, p. FP7.

Cassoff, Derek, "The Web from Space: EMS Adds a Return Channel to Satellite TV That Provides High-Speed Wireless Net Access," *Gazette* (Montreal), September 9, 2000, p. S5.

Davidson, Charles, "EMS Turns from Defense to Wireless Age," *Atlanta Business Chronicle*, August 19, 1994, p. 7A.

Frandzel, Steve, "High-Tech Defense Shores Up EMS," *Business Atlanta*, March 1991, pp. 56–59.

Hill, Bert, "Heavenly Helper; Ottawa Company's Satellite Technology Aids Rescue of Nova Scotia Fishermen," *Ottawa Citizen*, February 3, 1993, p. C7.

Key, Peter, "EMS Formation's Flight Communications Line Is Taking Off," *Philadelphia Business Journal*, March 27, 2009.

Layman, Tonya, "Domorski Leads EMS Team through Record Results," *Atlanta Business Chronicle*, June 23, 2008.

Mehlman, William, "Revived Market Could Give Second Look to ELMG," *Insiders' Chronicle*, May 28, 1984, pp. 1, 9–11.

Pasztor, Andy, "EMS Technologies to Make Mobile Phones for Satellite Operator," *Globe & Mail*, August 22, 2007, p. B9.

Pearson, Michael, "EMS Technologies: With Business Booming, Firm Plans to Expand," *Atlanta Journal-Constitution*, May 1, 2008, p. B5.

Ravensbergen, Jan, "EMS Set to Dump Satellite Division," *Gazette* (Montreal), July 12, 2003, p. B1.

Shalom, François, "325 Secretly Laid Off at EMS, More Cuts Possible; Company Denies Rumours of Sale," *Gazette* (Montreal), November 2, 2002, p. B1.

Smith, William, "How a Prescient Pentagon Contractor Entered Civilian Life; The Key Was Using Its Own Battlefield Technology to Develop Commercial Products," *New York Times*, April 12, 1992, p. F9.

Sumner, Gary O., "Missions to Mars Give Norcross Firm a Boost," *Atlanta Business Chronicle*, November 6, 1998, p. 3A.

Young, Mary Lynn, "MDA Takes One for Canada's Space Future," *Globe & Mail*, November 11, 2005, p. B2.

Eutelsat S.A.

70 rue Balard
Paris, F-75502 cedex 15
France
Telephone: (+33 01) 53 98 47 47
Fax: (+33 01) 53 98 37 00
Web site: http://www.eutelsat.org

Subsidiary of Eutelsat Communications
Founded: 1977 as European Telecommunication Satellite
    Organization
Incorporated: 2001
Employees: 550
Sales: EUR 940.54 million ($1.34 billion) (2009)
NAICS: 517212 Cellular and Other Wireless Telecom-
    munications; 517910 Other Telecommunications

∎ ∎ ∎

Eutelsat S.A. is the world's third-largest operator of
communications satellites. The Paris-based company
owns and operates a fleet of 26 satellites reaching over
150 countries, and more than 180 million homes. Video
Applications, especially television broadcasting, remains
the largest part of the company's operations, accounting
for 72 percent of the group's revenues in 2009. At the
beginning of 2010, Eutelsat's fleet broadcast nearly
3,450 television channels, including more than 100
high-definition (HD) channels. In addition, the
company has begun testing next-generation 3D television broadcast services.

Eutelsat is also a leading provider of satellite-based
Internet and broadband services, under its Tooway

brand, serving corporate and remote residential and
other customers. Data and Value-added Services/
Broadband generates more than 19 percent of the
group's sales. The company also provides professional
data network and broadband services, which contributed
nearly 9 percent to its sales in 2009. Europe, the Middle
East, and Africa remain the company's major markets,
although Eutelsat has also built up a strong presence in
the Latin and North American markets, as well as in
Asia. Eutelsat is listed on the Euronext Stock Exchange
and is led by CEO Michel de Rosen. The company
posted revenues of EUR 940.54 million ($1.34 billion)
in 2009.

IGO IN 1977

Prior to the 1960s, all long-distance communications
required the existence of land-based or subsea cable
networks, providing physical links among locations. The
developments of the first rockets capable of reaching
beyond Earth's atmosphere opened up the potential for
developing new satellite telecommunications
technologies. The use of satellites circling Earth at fixed
orbits made it possible to relay telecommunications and
other transmissions from one continent to another. The
development of fiber-optic technologies toward the end
of the century later made subsea cabling systems more
competitive against satellite transmissions. By then, the
satellite market had largely shifted toward providing
television broadcasting services.

The first true telecommunications satellite, Telstar,
was launched in 1962 by a consortium including
AT&T, Bell Laboratories, and NASA in the United

COMPANY PERSPECTIVES

In today's digital environment satellites are a privileged source of bandwidth, able to offer universal coverage of all territories for content delivery direct to users or to terrestrial networks, and for enabling complete communications networks to be rapidly set up, even in the most remote areas.

States, and in Europe, the British Post and France PTT, the telecommunications monopolies in the United Kingdom and France. The international tone of this early launch provided the basis for a broader cooperative effort to develop and launch new satellites. In 1964, the government-owned telephone monopolies from 14 countries joined together to form an intergovernmental organization (IGO) called Intelsat, which launched its first satellite in 1965. By the early 1970s, more than 80 countries had joined Intelsat, which was to remain the largest satellite services provider into the next century.

The development of the first telecommunications-based data transmissions placed new demands on the satellite system. At the same time, the launch of satellite-based television broadcasting services further increased demand for bandwidth. Into the late 1970s, the Western European countries recognized the need for a new IGO focused on developing satellite transmission services specifically for Europe. This led to the creation of the European Telecommunication Satellite Organization, or Eutelsat, in 1977. Like Intelsat, Eutelsat, owned by state telecommunications monopolies, functioned as a provider of technical services, with little or no concern for commercial operations. Intelsat, Eutelsat, and a third company, Inmarsat, established in 1979, also functioned as monopolies in their own right. Private companies seeking to launch their own satellite services were required to obtain approval from the IGOs.

FIRST SATELLITE IN 1983

Eutelsat succeeded in putting its first satellite into orbit in 1983. The company launched several more of the Eutelsat I series through the end of the decade. By then, the satellite market had begun its shift from a telecommunications focus to one based largely on television transmissions. By 1990, television broadcasting, including the first direct-to-home systems, accounted for 75 percent of Eutelsat's annual revenues. Other technologies, such as VSAT (Very Small Aperture Terminal), introduced new data transmission possibilities, placing

additional demands on the capacity of Eutelsat's fleet of satellites.

By then, too, Eutelsat had begun to expand its membership base. With the collapse of the Soviet Union, Eutelsat brought the Eastern and Central European markets into its consortium, starting in 1989. By 1991, the company included 27 member-nations. This rose to 46 by 1998. Nearly all of these countries were also part of the Intelsat consortium, which had itself grown to 121 member nations at the beginning of the 1990s. Into that decade, Eutelsat also began opening its ranks to the African and Middle Eastern markets.

The expansion of its base of operations, as well as the need to adapt to newly emerging technologies, led Eutelsat to develop a new generation of satellites, Eutelsat II. The new satellite design, developed by a consortium including Aeritalia, Aerospatiale, Alcatel Espace, and CASA, provided a 60 percent increase in capacity over the previous generation. By the end of 1991, Eutelsat had launched three Eutelsat II satellites, bringing its total fleet to seven.

The satellite sector remained limited by the inherent risks involved with space technology. As a result, Eutelsat faced a series of setbacks in 1975, with four of its satellite launches ending in failure. The company's dominant position had also come under increasing pressure as a number of new satellite players arose in the private sector. Chief among Eutelsat's rivals was SES, which had deployed its Astra satellites based on the "hot bird" concept. The concept involved positioning several satellites to serve the same video "neighborhood" (that is, the direction satellite dishes needed to face in order to receive broadcast signals). In this way, Astra was able to broadcast hundreds of television stations at a time. This flexibility enabled Astra to leapfrog ahead of Eutelsat to become the world's number three satellite player.

HOT BIRDS FROM 1996

Part of Eutelsat's difficulties lay in its status as an IGO, which left it exposed to the demands of its many nation-owners, all of which had the right to sit on its board of directors. As a result the company lacked the full flexibility for responding to the changing market. At the same time, Eutelsat lacked the same incentive toward profitability as its private sector counterparts. This situation too began to change as Europe's telecommunications sector opened to competition.

Eutelsat began taking its own steps toward raising its own commercial viability. Leading this effort was Giuliano Berretta, a native Italian who previously worked at the European Space Agency before joining Eutelsat in 1990. Berretta became Eutelsat's sales director charged with boosting the company's commercial

1977: European Telecommunication Satellite Organization (Eutelsat) is founded as an intergovernmental organization to provide satellite services for the European Union.
1983: Eutelsat launches its first satellite.
1995: Eutelsat launches its first Hot Bird satellite for the television broadcasting market.
2001: Eutelsat is privatized as Eutelsat S.A.
2009: Eutelsat launches the Tooway satellite Internet and broadband service.

operations. Among Berretta's first initiatives was to steer the company away from its reliance on telephone communications to develop itself as a major player in the faster-growing satellite television broadcasting sector. Through the decade, Eutelsat scored a number of major contracts, notably with Canal Plus, the largest pay-TV operator in Europe, in 1998. By then, the company claimed to reach more than 70 million homes.

Backing this growth, Eutelsat began launching a new generation of satellites as part of its own Hot Bird strategy in the mid-1990s. The first of the new fleet, Hot Bird 1, went into orbit in 1995. This was followed with the Eurobird 9 (later called W48 after its position was redirected toward 48° east), in 1996. In 1997, the company added the Eurobird 4 (later W75), as well as its Hot Bird 5, which became a major part of the company's direct-to-home broadcasting strategy. By the end of the decade, the company had positioned five Hot Bird satellites, providing the company with the capacity for broadcasting hundreds of television channels.

PUBLIC OFFERING IN 2001

Eutelsat began moving toward its privatization at the end of the 1990s, as Europe's telecom majors not only faced the loss of their domestic monopolies and the prospect of growing international competition, but also turned their interest toward the booming mobile telephone market. In 1999, Giuliano Berretta was named CEO of Eutelsat and began preparing the company for its coming privatization. The company completed several new satellite launches into the next decade, including the W3 (later W6), launched in 1999, and the W4, Eurobird 4, and Sesat 1, all deployed in 2000.

In July 2001, Eutelsat completed its privatization, becoming Eutelsat S.A. Under terms of the privatization

agreement, Eutelsat promised to go public within two years in order to allow its existing shareholders to sell their stakes in the company. The newly private company quickly moved to expand its commercial business. At the same time, the company exited the telephone services sector entirely.

By October 2001, Eutelsat had completed its first expansion effort, buying more than 21 percent of Hispasat, the national satellite operator in Spain. The two companies then announced plans to form a joint venture, Amazonas, in order to launch a satellite serving the Latin American markets in 2003. Eutelsat's stake in Hispasat later rose to nearly 28 percent.

Eutelsat boasted strong revenue growth in its first year as a private company, topping $600 million in sales for the year, and posting profits of $285 million. Much of this growth came from the company's television broadcasting wing, as it continued to expand its satellite fleet. Between 2001 and 2003, the company launched a total of seven new satellites. These were also growing increasingly sophisticated, allowing the company to achieve significant growth in its capacity. The company also beefed up its commercial operations, launching a subsidiary in Italy, called Skylogic Italia, in order to develop the group's satellite-based multimedia operations in that market.

Eutelsat targeted Internet and broadband services as a major growth area into the new century. In 2003, the company launched a new satellite, called the e-Bird, which had been designed especially for providing broadband communications services, including Internet. This new capacity enabled the company to target the business and institutional markets. At the same time, the company also began developing its first consumer-oriented Internet access services. These were targeted primarily to homes in rural and remote areas not served by fixed-line broadband services.

Other satellite launches through the decade, such as the Hot Bird 7A added in 2006, enabled the company to boost the range of its television broadcasting operations. By then, the Hot Bird "neighborhood" alone reached 113 million homes, and boasted 850 television channels and 550 radio stations. The company's total broadcasting capacity became even more impressive, as its total number of television channels topped 3,400 by the end of the decade.

TOOWAY LAUNCH IN 2009

Eutelsat was less successful in pursuing its public offering. Originally slated for 2003, the company put the offering on hold due to poor trading conditions. Instead, the company's largest shareholders regrouped their holdings into a new company, Eutelsat Communications, which then controlled more than 95 percent of the company's shares. The new structure permitted a number of the company's existing owners to exit its shareholding, while bringing in new investors, including Eurazeo, Texas Pacific Group, Goldman Sachs, Spectrum, Cinven, and others. In 2007, Spanish construction giant Abertis paid more than EUR 1 billion ($1.4 billion) to buy out a number of Eutelsat's shareholders, to become the company's largest shareholder with a 32 percent stake.

In the meantime, Eutelsat's Internet business grew only slowly during the decade. This effort had been hampered in large part because of technological limitations, as the company's original service provided only for satellite-based reception of data. Users were still required to maintain a fixed-line connection in order to transmit data. The early equipment was also extremely expensive, while subscription rates remained high.

By 2009, Eutelsat had largely solved these limitations, leading to the launch of Tooway, a two-way broadband service that year. The company quickly reached an agreement with two French companies, Numeo and Sat2Way, to introduce the service in France. By June 2009, the company had also reached an agreement with the state of Brandenburg, in Germany, to begin introducing Tooway as part of that government's "Broadband supply for rural areas" program. By the end of that year, the group's broadband operations accounted for nearly 20 percent of the group's total sales, which now topped EUR 940 million ($1.34 billion).

Television broadcasting nonetheless remained Eutelsat's bread and butter. Eutelsat's fleet expansion program had brought its total to 26 satellites by 2010, with plans to launch at least four more by the end of 2011. This enabled the company to boost its total number of television channels, adding more than 500 new channels in 2009 alone. The company had also been expanding its HD television carrying capacity during the decade, and by the beginning of 2010 offered more than 100 HD channels. The company also pledged to remain at the cutting-edge of the broadcast market, and in that year began testing its first 3D television broadcasts.

M. L. Cohen

PRINCIPAL SUBSIDIARIES

Eutelsat America Corp. (USA); Eutelsat Broadband Corp. (USA); Eutelsat do Brasil S.A. (Brazil); Eutelsat Inc. (USA); Eutelsat Italia (Italy); Eutelsat Polska s.p.z. o.o. (Poland); Eutelsat Services und Beteiligungen GmbH (Germany); Eutelsat UK Limited; Eutelsat VAS S.A.S.; Fransat S.A.S.; Hispasat (Spain); Skylogic Italia s.p.a. (Italy); Solaris Mobile Limited (Ireland; 50%); Tooway Management S.A.S.; VisAvision GmbH (Germany).

PRINCIPAL DIVISIONS

Video Applications; Data and Value-added Services/Broadband; Multi-usage.

PRINCIPAL COMPETITORS

Intelsat Ltd.; SES Global SA; Telesat/Loral; Loral Space and Communications Inc.

FURTHER READING

"Abertis Buys into Eutelsat for US$1.42bn," *Acquisitions Monthly*, January 2007, p. 35.

"Brandenburg and Eutelsat Partner to Deliver Broadband to Rural Homes," *Space Daily*, June 30, 2009.

"Eutelsat Breaks the Barrier of 100 HDTV Channels," *Space Daily*, October 13, 2009.

"Eutelsat Launches Broadband Satellite," *BEN (Broadcast Engineering News)*, September 30, 2003.

Forrester, Chris, "Eutelsat Ready for Battle," *Television Europe*, April 2001, p. 18.

Koeleman, Donald, "Eutelsat's Brave New Orbit," *Multichannel News International*, January 2002, p. 8.

"Privatizing the Skies," *Multichannel News International*, October 2001, p. IV.

Reinhardt, Andy, "Eutelsat Sets Its Sights on the Internet," *Business Week*, April 14, 2003, p. 26.

"Russia Set to Launch Eutelsat Satellite from Baikonur," *UzReport*, November 23, 2009.

"View from the Top," *Via Satellite*, March 1, 2010.

Forest Laboratories, Inc.

—■—

909 Third Avenue
New York, New York 10022-4731
U.S.A.
Telephone: (212) 421-7850
Toll Free: (800) 947-5227
Fax: (212) 750-9152
Web site: http://www.frx.com

Public Company
Founded: 1954
Incorporated: 1956
Employees: 5,225
Sales: $3.92 billion (2009)
Stock Exchanges: New York
Ticker Symbol: FRX
NAICS: 325412 Pharmaceutical Preparation Manufacturing

■ ■ ■

Forest Laboratories, Inc., develops, manufactures, and sells both brand-name and generic prescription drugs in the United States and Europe. The main therapeutic areas that the company concentrates on include depression, Alzheimer's disease/neuropathic pain, hypertension, infectious diseases, and respiratory ailments. Since 1998, Forest has derived the bulk of its revenues first from the antidepressant drug Celexa and subsequently from a second-generation version of Celexa called Lexapro. In fiscal 2009, Lexapro accounted for around 60 percent of the company's sales. More than a quarter of sales are generated by Namenda, a treatment for moderate to severe Alzheimer's disease. Other key products include Bystolic, a beta-blocker used to treat hypertension; Campral, an alcohol dependence medication used to treat alcoholism; and Savella, a treatment for the chronic pain disorder fibromyalgia. Most of the pharmaceutical products marketed by Forest Laboratories were developed by other companies and then licensed by Forest.

EARLY YEARS: TRANSITIONING FROM LAB SERVICE TO GENERIC DRUG MARKETER

Forest Laboratories was founded in 1954, and incorporated two years later, as a small laboratory service company. It helped larger pharmaceutical companies, which had hefty research and development funds, to create new drugs. After Forest developed a drug, it would hand the new product off to its client, who would then market, sell, and distribute the offering. Forest achieved a degree of success in its niche and found a steady demand for its services during the late 1950s and early 1960s. In addition, the company swerved slightly from its pharmaceuticals focus by diversifying into other markets. It invested particularly heavily in food businesses, principally candy and ice cream, and also sold branded vitamins. Its foray into other ventures was an attempt to bolster the company's bottom line and to protect it from risks associated with the drug industry.

Forest, which went public in 1967, continued to enjoy the greatest amount of success in its core drug development business. One of its most successful achievements was its creation of Synchron, a controlled-release technology that allowed an ingested drug to be slowly released inside the body. It was this penchant for exploiting profitable niches that would later become the base of the company's meteoric rise.

By the mid-1970s accusations had been raised against the company's chairman, Hans Lowey, that he had inflated profits. Howard Solomon, who at the time was serving as outside counsel for Forest, was asked to investigate the charges. He found evidence to support the allegations, Lowey resigned, and Solomon took over as CEO of the company in 1977. Solomon sold off Forest's lagging food businesses and dropped out of the vitamin business to focus on the pharmaceutical market. He then led the company through an important transition from a service firm to a company that actually manufactured and sold its own pharmaceuticals.

Recognizing that the big profits in the drug industry were garnered from the marketing and sale of new drugs, Solomon began looking for a way to break into that side of the business. The company lacked the vast resources, however, that were necessary to fund the development, testing, marketing, and distribution of an entirely new drug. It was entirely feasible that, even if Forest could gather enough capital to fund a new drug, the venture could go bust for any number of reasons and force the company into bankruptcy. For example, a newly developed drug could fail to pass federal approval, rendering it commercially useless, or the drug could simply fail to achieve commercial appeal.

Rather than trying to develop and market new drugs, Solomon decided to steer the company toward the drug marketing business through a sort of back door: generics. Generic drugs (drugs that perform the same essential function as the brand-name drugs they mimic, but cost less) were becoming increasingly popular during the late 1970s as an alternative to expensive brand-name pharmaceuticals. Because generics lacked patent protection, however, profits were typically elusive. The first company to introduce the drug could make big profits for a short time, until lower-priced generics from competing companies entered the market.

Solomon was able to successfully exploit the limited opportunities offered in the generics business by focusing on Forest's controlled-release Synchron technology. Forest had already succeeded in applying the technology to drugs for several major pharmaceutical companies. Solomon correctly suspected that a viable market existed for controlled-release versions of several popular drugs. As a result, the company shifted its corporate focus to generics, realizing sound revenue and profit growth during the late 1970s and early 1980s.

Despite its success with generics, Forest Labs' management in the early 1980s was still eager to participate in the potentially lucrative business of marketing brand-name, patented drugs. It had most of the tools necessary to compete in the industry, having maintained a talented research and development arm, which had long been one of its core competencies, and having accrued a degree of manufacturing, sales, and distribution knowledge through its generics business. However, Forest still lacked the resources it needed to go toe-to-toe with the industry giants.

SHIFTING FOCUS FROM GENERICS TO LICENSED BRAND-NAME DRUGS

Forest embarked on a new corporate strategy in the mid-1980s that it hoped would allow it to market and sell proprietary drugs without having to face pharmaceutical industry leaders. It would look for branded drugs that had already been developed and marketed by larger companies, but that served very small customer niches. If it found a drug that it felt was undervalued, it would purchase or receive a license to the product and increase its value through aggressive marketing. The reasoning behind the strategy was that the big companies tended to ignore their smaller drugs, focusing their resources instead on popular, high-profile, high-profit offerings.

The only weapon needed to carry out the new strategy that was still missing from Forest Labs' armory was a sales force. Thus, in 1984 Forest purchased the assets of O'Neal, Jones & Feldman Inc., a St. Louis, Missouri-based pharmaceuticals company. O'Neal, Jones & Feldman was put on the block after its president and another executive were convicted and jailed for selling a drug that had not been approved by the Food and Drug Administration (FDA). Tragically, 27 infant deaths were linked to the misbranded drug before the company pleaded guilty to 17 violations.

KEY DATES

1954: Forest Laboratories is founded as a small laboratory service company.

1956: Company is incorporated.

1967: Company goes public.

1977: Howard Solomon takes over as company CEO and subsequently shifts the company's focus to drug marketing, initially of generic drugs.

1980s: Company shifts focus from generics to licensed brand-name drugs.

1984: Forest significantly boosts its sales force with the purchase of O'Neal, Jones & Feldman Inc.

1986: Company purchases Aerobid, an antiasthma drug.

1998: Marketing of the antidepressant Celexa begins.

2002: Sales of Celexa surpass the $1 billion mark; Forest begins selling Lexapro, a next-generation version of Celexa.

2007: Forest acquires Cerexa, Inc., a firm specializing in injectable antibiotics.

Forest paid $8.3 million for its new acquisition and assumed an additional $1.5 million in debt. In what turned out to be a savvy purchase, Forest immediately gained an established 71-member sales force. In a carefully plotted stratagem, the company began tagging new drugs on to its existing line of generics and branded drugs, some of which had belonged to O'Neal, Jones & Feldman. For example, the company bought a drug called Esgic, a stress headache remedy, and was able to significantly boost its sales. Forest also purchased other small pharmaceutical companies, continually increasing the size and scope of its sales force and gaining access to new proprietary drugs. In 1989, for instance, Forest acquired UAD Laboratories for $33 million in stock. This deal increased the sales force to 300 and added to the company portfolio a narcotic analgesic product, Lorcet, which within a few years had annual sales of $60 million. All the while, the company's generics business remained strong.

Forest's growth strategy during the late 1980s and early 1990s was relatively simple and straightforward, yet few other firms were successfully implementing the same tactics. Before it purchased an undervalued drug, it would make sure that the product was a good match with the company's existing product line. By emphasizing a small number of therapeutic categories, such as asthma and headache relief, Forest was able to increase the potency of its sales force and achieve a higher number of prescriptions written per sales call. Whereas many pharmaceutical firms would send salespeople to general practitioners, offering them a range of drug lines, most Forest salespeople focused on a few groups of specialists, particularly allergists, internists, and pulmonary physicians.

Forest's knack for turning an undervalued drug into an industry overachiever was evidenced by its 1986 purchase of Aerobid, an asthma drug, from industry giant Schering-Plough Corporation, for $6 million. Although Aerobid sales totaled only $2.3 million annually at the time of purchase, Forest was able to generate huge returns from the drug. By 1991, in fact, Aerobid revenues had exploded to $30 million annually. Furthermore, bolstered by independent research that recommended increased use of the drug in certain applications, sales of Aerobid eventually rocketed past the $100 million mark by the mid-1990s. Aerobid, along with Forest's other two major drugs (Tessalon, a cough medication, and Propranolol, a generic used to treat high blood pressure), accounted for more than 40 percent of the company's sales by 1993.

RAPID REVENUE GROWTH IN EARLY NINETIES

By the early 1990s it was clear that Forest Labs' new strategy was a shrewd one. The company's annual revenues had ballooned since the mid-1980s to about $133 million by 1990, of which $30 million was profit. Sales increased to $176 million in 1991 as income leapt to approximately $40 million. Importantly, Forest's sales force had swelled to more than 500, including more than 50 salespeople employed by subsidiaries acquired in Europe. "The large sales force is really helping the company pick up drugs that fall through the cracks," observed industry analyst Martin Bukoll in a November 1991 issue of *Crain's New York Business.*

The strength of Forest's overall operations was exhibited by a setback that it encountered in 1991. Forest had spent $20 million for a license to market a new drug called Micturin, which had been developed through a joint venture between E.I. du Pont and Merck & Co., Inc. Forest hoped the drug would become one of its primary offerings with over $100 million in annual sales. Unfortunately, the FDA, citing negative side effects, chose not to approve the drug. Although the company's stock price plummeted 30 percent, within a few months it had regained most of its value on expectations of growth from other segments of Forest's operations. Furthermore, growth of Forest's sales, earnings, and equity value continued unabated through 1991 and 1992.

As Forest Labs continued to acquire low-profile underachievers that were being ignored by the major manufacturers, which generally showed little interest in products that did not have the potential to generate revenues in excess of $100 million per year, sales mushroomed. Solomon watched his company's sales jump to $239 million in 1992, $285 million in 1993, and to an amazing $348 million in 1994 (fiscal year ending March 31, 1994). Likewise, net income tracked revenue growth, soaring more than 30 percent in 1992 to $50 million, to $64 million during 1993, and then to $80 million in 1994. The company's workforce had multiplied to about 1,300 worldwide.

To accommodate the company's 100 percent sales growth in less than three years, Forest hurriedly expanded its U.S. and overseas facilities. Its major St. Louis subsidiary, Forest Pharmaceuticals, Inc., which accounted for roughly two-thirds of company sales in 1993, was consolidated into a newly renovated 87,000-square-foot facility replete with high-tech manufacturing and distribution systems. The company added 65,000 square feet to a manufacturing operation in Cincinnati and boosted its New York production facility, which manufactured generics, to 150,000 square feet. Forest in 1994 also completed a major new production facility in Ireland, which began supplying its clients in Eastern and Western Europe.

Although Forest's established brand-name drugs and generics had provided consistent growth for the company since the mid-1980s, it was forced to continue its search for new acquisitions that would supplant its fading superstars. Many of the brand-name drugs that it had licensed had only a few years of patent protection remaining before generics would diminish their profit margins. As a result, Forest was reliant on new additions to its pharmaceutical arsenal to sustain its rampant growth. Reflecting the company's intent to introduce new products was its growing emphasis on research and development (R&D). Annual R&D expenditures by Forest increased from $10 million in 1990 to nearly $30 million during 1993.

Forest reached a peak in fiscal 1996 when record revenues of $461.8 million were recorded. Leading the way was Aerobid, with sales of $147 million. The very next year, however, the company was hit by several setbacks, leading to a 37 percent decline in revenues and the first loss ($25 million) in company history. During the year, Aerobid began facing stiff competition from a new asthma drug from Glaxo Inc. called Flovent. Sales of Forest's number two drug, the painkiller Lorcet, plunged after its patent expired and generic competitors were quickly introduced into the market. Forest's own generic product business suffered from severe competition from both industry giants and hundreds of smaller players. In addition, while the company's product pipeline remained promising, delays in getting government approvals for several new drugs cost the company additional potential sales.

CELEXA-FUELED BOOM

Forest Labs' downturn proved temporary, and the company soon began a new period of even more explosive growth. In fact, the foundation had already been laid for the turnaround. Late in 1995 Forest licensed the U.S. rights for Tiazac from Biovail Corporation, a Toronto firm. The 1996 introduction of Tiazac, a once-daily calcium channel blocker used to treat hypertension and angina, marked Forest's entrance into the huge cardiovascular market. After achieving $30 million in sales during its year of introduction, Tiazac generated $158 million in revenues by 2000.

While Tiazac was certainly a success, it and all of Forest Labs' other products were soon far overshadowed by a drug called Celexa. This latest turn in the company's fortunes began in 1994 when CEO Solomon's son Andrew fell into a deep depression. Solomon began researching treatments for his son and discovered a European antidepressant named Cipramil, which had been developed by the Danish company H. Lundbeck A/S. Cipramil had achieved market share in Europe of more than 40 percent mainly because it was considered to have fewer side effects than the U.S. blockbusters Prozac (Eli Lilly and Company) and Zoloft (Pfizer Inc.) The head of Lundbeck had tried to license the drug to several large U.S. drug companies, but each deal fell through, the companies apparently having concluded that Cipramil's sales potential was not large enough for them. For Forest, however, Cipramil was a perfect fit, and so Solomon signed a deal with Lundbeck in early 1996 to license the drug for sale in the United States under the name Celexa.

The FDA approved Celexa in July 1998. To help market the drug, Solomon reached a copromotion deal with Warner-Lambert Company. This alliance ended after only a year, however, because Warner-Lambert agreed in 1999 to be acquired by Pfizer. Rather than pursue another copromotion alliance, Forest elected to go it alone. The company's sales force was substantially beefed up, growing from 850 representatives to 1,425, an increase of 70 percent. The reps touted Celexa's minimal side effects, and to give the product a further edge Forest offered the drug for 20 percent less than the cost of its formidable rivals. The strategy proved brilliant. Celexa quickly grabbed a 9 percent share of the $6 billion antidepressant market. Sales in fiscal 1999, specifically, from launch in September 1998 through March 1999, amounted to $91 million. Celexa sales then mushroomed to $427 million the following year, with the drug reaching blockbuster status as a $1 billion product by 2002. By that year, Celexa's market share had reached 17 percent.

Overall sales and profits for Forest Labs ballooned thanks to the great success of Celexa. The company posted net income of $77.2 million on sales of $624 million for fiscal 1999, but by 2002 these figures were $338 million and $1.6 billion, respectively. During this same period, the company's stock surged as well, nearly quadrupling in value. In 1999 the stock began trading on the prestigious New York Stock Exchange, having been listed for three decades on the American Stock Exchange. On the down side, Forest was slated to lose patent protection on Celexa in mid-2003, with generic competition expected to be introduced in early 2005, so there was a pressing need to find other winning products, particularly because Celexa was generating more than 60 percent of revenues by fiscal 2001.

A minor success for Forest came in October 1999 when Infasurf was launched. Infasurf was used to treat and prevent respiratory distress syndrome, an affliction that occurred in tens of thousands of infants annually and could cause death or physical abnormalities. Forest had licensed the drug from ONY, Inc., in 1991. Sales during fiscal 2000 totaled less than $5 million. A much more significant product introduced by Forest was Benicar, an agent used to treat hypertension and therefore a follow-up to the successful Tiazac. Benicar had been developed by Sankyo Pharma Inc., and through an agreement signed in December 2001, it was copromoted by Forest and Sankyo following the receipt of FDA approval in April 2002.

LEXAPRO FOLLOW-ON

Forest hoped its next blockbuster would be Lexapro. This drug was a new version of Celexa that the company touted as being more pure and powerful than the original. Lexapro was approved by the FDA in August 2002, and Forest launched it the following month. At the same time it stopped promoting Celexa and added an additional 175 sales representatives to further strengthen the sales force. Lexapro got off to a strong start, achieving sales of $244.7 million during its first six months on the market. Sales surpassed the $1

billion mark in fiscal 2004. To further expand the market potential of the drug, Forest worked to gain FDA approval for the use of Lexapro in treating other disorders. In December 2003 Forest secured the regulatory agency's approval to begin marketing Lexapro for the treatment of generalized anxiety disorder, but the FDA nixed later attempts to extend the drug into the treatment of social anxiety disorder and panic disorder.

As expected, by early 2005, a number of generic versions of Celexa had been introduced into the market, prompting the drug's sales to plunge. By fiscal 2006, Celexa's sales amounted to only $19 million, but Forest's follow-on strategy was a clear success. Lexapro generated $1.87 billion in sales that year, representing about two-thirds of Forest's total revenues of $2.79 billion. The drug had also captured more than 20 percent of the market for its category of antidepressants.

During this period, Forest suffered a number of setbacks on the drug development front, but its pipeline yielded a major new product in October 2003 when the FDA approved memantine hydrochloride for the treatment of moderate to severe Alzheimer's disease. This drug, which Forest had jointly developed with Merz + Co. of Frankfurt, Germany, while not representing a cure for the disease, had shown the ability to slow down the cognitive deterioration and functional loss experienced by Alzheimer's patients. Marketed by Forest in the United States as Namenda, the drug by fiscal 2009 had become the company's number two product, with its $949.3 million in sales that year accounting for 26 percent of the overall total.

In 2005 Forest Laboratories began marketing two drugs that had been approved by the FDA the previous year. Campral was an alcohol dependence medication that helped recovering alcoholics continue abstaining from alcohol, while Combunox was a pain reliever combining the opioid oxycodone and the anti-inflammatory drug ibuprofen. With these drugs, Forest continued its strategy of securing licenses for the U.S. market for drugs that had been developed by European companies: Germany's Merck KGaA in the case of Campral and BTG Group of the United Kingdom for Combunox. Forest also maintained its presence in the hypertension field by gaining FDA approval for Bystolic in December 2007. The company the following month began marketing this beta-blocker under a license agreement with Mylan Inc. In February 2008, however, Forest paid Mylan $370 million to terminate the latter's commercial rights to the drug in the United States and Canada and to reduce Forest's future royalty payments to Mylan.

COUNTERING A KEY PATENT EXPIRATION

Bystolic was one of a number of drugs with the potential to generate large, if not blockbuster, sales that Forest Labs was counting on to make up for the revenue shortfall that was sure to follow the expiration of Lexapro's patent protection in 2012. Countering the imminent introduction of generic versions of Lexapro was a major challenge given that the antidepressant's sales by fiscal 2009 had ballooned to $2.3 billion, or about 60 percent of Forest's $3.92 billion in total revenue. Among the other products in which Forest saw the most potential was Savella, a treatment for fibromyalgia, a chronic pain disorder affecting more than six million Americans a year. After the FDA granted its approval of Savella in January 2009, Forest began marketing the drug under a license from Cypress Bioscience, Inc., a biotechnology firm based in San Diego.

In January 2007 Forest Laboratories gained another promising new drug and entered a new treatment area through the $494 million acquisition of Cerexa, Inc., a privately held biopharmaceutical concern based in Alameda, California, specializing in injectable antibiotics. Among other R&D activities, Cerexa was in late-stage testing of the compound ceftaroline acetate as an antibiotic for two hospital-based infectious diseases: so-called complicated skin infections and community-acquired pneumonia. In 2008 and 2009 Forest reported positive results from Phase III studies of ceftaroline acetate as an antibiotic for both of these infections, setting the stage for a formal application of approval with the FDA.

As it steadily moved products through its pipeline to counter the impending loss of patent protection for not only Lexapro but also Namenda, Forest encountered another challenge in early 2009 on the legal front. The U.S. Department of Justice charged that the company had between 1998 through at least 2005 illegally marketed Celexa and Lexapro for unapproved uses in children and teenagers. The government's civil complaint also accused Forest of offering kickbacks, in the form of cash, expensive meals, and other valuables, to doctors to induce them to prescribe the antidepressants.

Forest in fiscal 2009 set $170 million aside as a reserve to cover a possible settlement of this case and the costs of litigation. In May 2009 Forest and the government reached an agreement in principle on a settlement, with the company reporting that the amount of the settlement was likely to fall within the parameters of the reserve. This proposed settlement covered the civil case but not possible criminal charges that Forest might face in connection with this matter.

Dave Mote
Updated, David E. Salamie

PRINCIPAL SUBSIDIARIES

Cerexa, Inc.; Forest Laboratories Ireland Ltd.; Forest Laboratories UK Ltd.; Forest Pharmaceuticals, Inc.; Forest Research Institute, Inc.; Forest Tosara Ltd. (Ireland); Inwood Laboratories, Inc.; Pharmax Healthcare Ltd. (UK).

PRINCIPAL COMPETITORS

Pfizer Inc.; GlaxoSmithKline plc; Eli Lilly and Company; Merck & Co., Inc.; Abbott Laboratories; Novartis AG; Bristol-Myers Squibb Company.

FURTHER READING

Alson, Amy, "Expansion Sustains Health at Forest," *Crain's New York Business*, February 9, 1987, p. 10.

Bennett, Johanna, "Forest: Out of the Woods, Still Unloved," *Barron's*, February 11, 2008, p. 43.

Benson, Barbara, "Drugmaker Forest Branches Out," *Crain's New York Business*, October 16, 1995, p. 31.

Berfield, Susan, "A CEO and His Son," *Business Week*, May 27, 2002, pp. 72–76+.

Boggs, Jennifer, "Forest Gets Late-Stage Antibiotic through $480M Cerexa Buyout," *BioWorld Today*, December 15, 2006.

Davison, Robin, "Forest Development Gambit Pays Off," *European Chemical News*, September 20, 1993, pp. 16+.

"Forest Gets Some High Marks for Its Slate of New Products," *Chemical Marketing Reporter*, January 4, 1993, p. 7.

France, Mike, "From a Raw Deal to a Winning Hand," *Business Week*, June 7, 1999, p. 75.

Hovey, Hollister H., "Surging Sales of Antidepressants Have Forest Labs Rolling in Green," *Wall Street Journal*, October 30, 2002, p. B5A.

Kamen, Robin, "Unwanted Drugs a Powerful Elixir," *Crain's New York Business*, November 4, 1991, sec. 1, p. 3.

Marshall, Samantha, "European Drug Strategy Makes Forest Stand Out," *Crain's New York Business*, December 8, 2003, p. 29.

Meier, Barry, and Benedict Carey, "Drug Maker Is Accused of Fraud," *New York Times*, February 26, 2009, p. B1.

Reingold, Jennifer, "Forest Laboratories: Beyond the Trees," *Financial World*, April 11, 1995, p. 16.

Rudinsky, Howard, "Sardines, Not Whales," *Forbes*, December 5, 1994, pp. 47+.

Sonenclar, Robert, "The Credibility of Mr. Solomon," *Financial World*, June 26, 1985, pp. 82+.

Temes, Judy, "Local Drug Company Swallows Bitter Pill: First Year of Losses," *Crain's New York Business*, May 26, 1997, p. 3.

The Gorman-Rupp Company

600 South Airport Road
Mansfield, Ohio 44903
U.S.A.
Telephone: (419) 755-1011
Fax: (419) 755-1263
Web site: http://www.gormanrupp.com

Public Company
Incorporated: 1934
Employees: 1,008
Sales: $266.2 million (2009)
Stock Exchanges: American
Ticker Symbol: GRC
NAICS: 333911 Pump and Pumping Equipment Manufacturing

■ ■ ■

The Gorman-Rupp Company is one of the largest pump manufacturers in the United States, producing more than 4,000 models of pumps. The company's product line ranges from small pumps for soft-drink dispensers and household appliances to massive machines capable of moving more than 750,000 gallons of fluid per minute. The larger pumps are used in such applications as boosting water pressure in municipal water systems and pumping petroleum products, as well as in the ground refueling of aircraft. Over the company's several decades of operation, and through both organic and acquisitive growth, the product line has expanded to include an increasingly diverse array of pumps and related equipment, including products for municipal water and sewerage systems, the construction industry, fire protection systems, a variety of industrial applications, original equipment manufacturers, government agencies such as the U.S. military, and petroleum applications.

Gorman-Rupp maintains about 1.5 million square feet of manufacturing and warehousing facilities, the bulk of which is located in the company's headquarters city of Mansfield, Ohio. Other facilities are situated in Bellville, Ohio; Toccoa, Georgia; Royersford, Pennsylvania; Sand Springs, Oklahoma; Sparks, Nevada; St. Thomas, Ontario; County Westmeath, Ireland; Leeuwarden and Culemborg, Netherlands; and Bangkok, Thailand. The facilities outside the United States support the company's efforts to penetrate international markets, and by the end of the first decade of the 21st century, 36 percent of sales were generated overseas from customers located in more than 100 countries.

FOUNDING DURING THE GREAT DEPRESSION

Gorman-Rupp's roots stretch more than three-quarters of a century to 1933 when two engineers, J. C. Gorman and Herbert E. Rupp, pooled $1,500 and started a pump manufacturing business in a barn outside the small town of Mansfield, Ohio. By that time, pumps had long been integral to many businesses. In fact, pumps remained the second most common machine used in industry into the 1990s. Perceiving an opportunity to carve out a profitable niche in this highly fragmented industry, Gorman and Rupp worked diligently to design pumps with particular features for specific tasks.

COMPANY PERSPECTIVES

Over seventy five years ago, The Gorman-Rupp Company was established upon a philosophy of, and a commitment to, product quality and technological leadership in the pump industry. Gorman-Rupp's philosophy of growth and service is reflected in the mission statement made by co-founders J. C. Gorman and H. E. Rupp, which reads: "To provide a quality product, competitively priced, delivered on time, backed by reliable service, at a profit that provides an equitable return to our shareholders, as well as providing our employees with competitive wages and benefits."

The fulfillment of this commitment has provided the foundation for The Gorman-Rupp Company to become a world pump leader.

They established a long-standing corporate reputation for product development early on, launching "the first simplified self-priming centrifugal pump with no valves or orifices" in 1933. These relatively quiet, rugged, and inexpensive devices were most often used to remove water (known in industry parlance as "dewatering") at intermittently wet construction sites, sewers, and quarries. Self-priming centrifugal pumps formed the core of Gorman-Rupp's product line.

WORLD WAR II & THE POSTWAR ERA

Within six years of its creation, the company was generating about $345,000 in annual sales. In the 1940s, Gorman-Rupp developed a solids-handling trash pump that featured a removable endplate for easy maintenance. The company later called it a "bellwether" product, one often imitated by competitors. Fueled in part by wartime contracts with the U.S. Army and Navy, for which the company was awarded an "E" for excellence, Gorman-Rupp sales multiplied to more than $2 million by 1949. Manufacturing capacity grew correspondingly, and the company moved from its rural barn to a factory in town during this decade.

Sales continued to mount rapidly in the postwar era, when Gorman-Rupp's close attention to the dewatering needs of the construction industry paid off. In 1952, the company reengineered a diaphragm pump for this market. Diaphragm pumps incorporate a flexible, but impenetrable membrane that prevents the material

being pumped from coming in contact with the inner workings of the pump and vice versa. They are designed to pump abrasive or uncontaminated substances and can also tolerate extended dry runs. Gorman-Rupp improved on the basic diaphragm pump design by decreasing the pump's weight and increasing its capacity. The pump manufacturer benefited indirectly from the residential housing boom of the 1950s. Its revenues tripled over the course of the decade, from $2.3 million in 1949 to $7.1 million by 1959.

PROGRESSIVE DIVERSIFICATION

Company executives realized, however, that they could not rely on a single market, especially one as cyclical as the construction industry, for consistent sales and earnings growth. The seeds of the diversification process were sown in 1953, when the firm established its Gorman-Rupp Industries Division in nearby Bellville, Ohio. Created to meet the needs of original equipment manufacturers (OEMs), Gorman-Rupp Industries made small, specialized pumps used in larger machines such as photocopiers, coffee machines, kidney dialysis machines, and photo-processing equipment. This division's emphasis on research and development helped make it the parent company's highest-margin segment by the mid-1990s.

In 1960 the company went international with the construction of a 12,000-square-foot plant in St. Thomas, Ontario, Canada. Gorman-Rupp of Canada Limited mirrored the parent company's main plant in Ohio, and its product line grew accordingly.

Gorman-Rupp also began to diversify within the pump category in earnest in the 1960s. It launched new lines of submersible pumps for mining, centrifugal pumps and fiberglass pumping stations for municipal sewage systems, specialty pumps for moving home heating oil and aircraft fuel quickly and safely, as well as pumps for the consumer market (i.e., the "handy pump") and a backpack pump for firefighters. These technological developments and the new markets they opened helped triple Gorman-Rupp's sales for the second consecutive decade, from $7.1 million in 1959 to $21.4 million by 1969. The workforce grew to encompass more than 500 employees by decade's end.

PENETRATING NEW MARKET NICHES

The company continued to penetrate new niches of the pump industry in the 1970s, launching a magnetic drive pump that could be used to move liquid metals. A key development of this decade was the creation of the

KEY DATES

■

1933: J. C. Gorman and Herbert E. Rupp start a pump manufacturing business in a barn outside Mansfield, Ohio.

1934: Business is incorporated as The Gorman-Rupp Company.

1940s: Company develops a solids-handling trash pump with a removable endplate.

1953: Gorman-Rupp Industries Division is formed to meet the needs of original equipment manufacturers.

1960: International expansion begins with the construction of a plant in Ontario, Canada, and the formation of the subsidiary Gorman-Rupp of Canada Limited.

1968: Company goes public.

1977: Ramparts, Inc., maker of diaphragm pumps for the chemical industry, is acquired.

1988: Gorman-Rupp acquires Patterson Pump Company, producer of large-volume centrifugal pumps used for flood control and irrigation as well as fire pumps.

2002: Company completes two acquisitions: American Machine and Tool Co., Inc., and Flo-Pak, Inc.

2009: Construction is completed on a major new manufacturing facility and headquarters in Mansfield.

Gorman-Rupp International Division, which marketed the entire line of pumps via overseas distributors. This segment's contribution to sales rose from 7 percent in 1980 to about 11 percent by 1995. Gorman-Rupp hoped to further increase its share of global pump sales by emphasizing the petrochemical, municipal, and industrial markets. Driven by these developments, total corporate sales doubled over the course of the 1970s, exceeding $50 million in 1978 and reaching $58.3 million by 1979. Having gone public in 1968, Gorman-Rupp common stock was listed on the American Stock Exchange in the 1970s.

A fairly modest industry contraction saw manufacturers of pumps and pumping equipment shrink from 613 in 1977 to 528 in 1987. Gorman-Rupp played a role in this trend, executing three acquisitions during this period. In 1977 the company acquired Ramparts, Inc. (becoming Gorman-Rupp's Ramparts Division), which manufactured air-driven diaphragm pumps and replacement parts for the chemical industry. These specialized machines were most often used to move highly corrosive and/or viscous liquids like sulfuric acid and hydrochloric acid. Although the Ramparts Division was still only generating 1 percent of Gorman-Rupp's annual sales 20 years after its acquisition, the parent company considered its high profit margins an important contributor to long-term growth.

Like many manufacturers, U.S. pump makers faced heavy competition from foreign producers in the 1980s. To combat this problem, Gorman-Rupp acquired the IPT Pumps Division, a manufacturer of economically priced, portable, and durable pumps for the construction market, in 1986. Although this division also contributed only 1 percent of annual revenues and scant profits, it helped Gorman-Rupp maintain a presence in this competitive industry segment.

1988 ACQUISITION OF PATTERSON PUMP

Gorman-Rupp made its largest acquisition to date in 1988, when it paid Banner Industries $14.8 million for control of the Patterson Pump Company. Based in Toccoa, Georgia, Patterson manufactured a comprehensive line of large-volume centrifugal pumps used for flood control and irrigation as well as fire pumps for automatic sprinkler systems and fire hydrants. Patterson complemented Gorman-Rupp's existing water, sewer, and fire-fighting lines, enabling the company to offer custom-designed, large-scale fluid transport systems to these key markets.

Although Patterson added $24 million to Gorman-Rupp's sales tally, its returns were less than stellar. Treating its newest affiliate as a turnaround situation, Gorman-Rupp pumped an additional $20 million into plant and office renovations over the ensuing eight years. In the meantime, sales reached $114.3 million by 1989.

Several key factors contributed to Gorman-Rupp's record of growth through the early 1990s. The company had long emphasized innovation and product quality. So confident were Gorman and Rupp in the capabilities of their products that they empowered their distributors "to put a Gorman-Rupp contractor's pump on any pumping job, anytime, anywhere, beside any competitor's pump of comparable size." The company guaranteed that its products would move more volume more efficiently and for a longer time. In addition, "if it wasn't the best all-around pump, our distributors would accept the return and pay the user any installation expense incurred."

Gorman-Rupp's reputation for excellent customer service was predicated on its network of knowledgeable distributors and its thorough inventory of new and replacement products. Gorman-Rupp supported its nearly 1,000 distributors in North America with in-depth product and process training. Sales representatives, distributors, engineers, and customers alike were able to attend corporate educational programs at one of two permanent training centers. The company also outfitted three recreational vehicles as mobile exhibitions for on-the-spot training and demonstrations. Although many industries and companies made the transition to just-in-time inventory in order to cut costs, Gorman-Rupp perceived its reserve as a key element of customer service. As James C. Gorman, CEO and son of the founder, told *Barron's* magazine in 1982, "Some 20 percent to 30 percent of our business is crisis business. They don't buy anything from us until they are up to their noses in water."

A prime example of the wisdom of this strategy came in 1989, when Gorman-Rupp was able to provide an estimated 90 percent of the pumps used to clean up after the *Exxon Valdez* oil spill. In a brief article for *Fortune* magazine in 1990, CEO Gorman crowed, "Our Alaskan distributor called us on Saturday, and at six Sunday evening we had the first DC-8 load of pumps in Anchorage." In addition to its ready supply of new pumps, Gorman-Rupp estimated its trade in replacement parts was at 20 percent to 25 percent of total revenues. This segment was doubtless another vital factor in the company's customer service equation.

Although Gorman-Rupp operated as a nonunion manufacturer, it cultivated such a good working environment that one industry observer characterized the company as "paternalistic." It had launched hospitalization and profit-sharing programs in the mid-1930s and had carefully avoided layoffs in the recessions of the 1970s and 1980s, a policy that possibly reflected its Depression-era origins. In return for its fair treatment of employees, Gorman-Rupp enjoyed low turnover and a strike-free history. Healthy labor-management relations also helped give Gorman-Rupp one of the industry's highest productivity rates. In 1996 the company's volume of sales per employee stood at $153,800, having risen from $120,000 in 1991.

Also in 1996, 72-year-old James C. Gorman drew the lines of corporate succession, ceding the chief executive office to President John A. Walter. It was expected that Gorman's son, Jeffrey S., who was named executive vice president at that time, would eventually follow in his father's (and grandfather's) footsteps. Two years later he did just that, being named president and CEO in April 1998. Gorman remained chairman, and Walter retired but remained on the board of directors.

ACQUISITIONS ABROAD & AT HOME

The period of the late 1990s and early 21st century was particularly noteworthy for the firm's aggressive pursuit of overseas revenues. In 1996 the company set up an office in Greece as a way to improve its distribution to the Middle East and Europe. Through a majority-owned subsidiary called Patterson Pump Ireland Limited, Patterson Pump Company began manufacturing pumps in Ireland in 1998 for sale in Europe. (In March 2002 Patterson purchased the minority holding in the subsidiary, making it wholly owned.) In 1999 the Mansfield Division opened a warehouse in Grindstead, Denmark, and another distribution center was opened in Singapore in 2001 to serve markets in Asia. The warehouse in Denmark was closed in 2001, however, and was replaced by one near Amsterdam. That year, about 16 percent of overall revenues were generated outside the United States.

In 2002 Gorman-Rupp completed two significant acquisitions, the first in 14 years. In February, American Machine and Tool Co., Inc., (AMT) was purchased for $12.6 million. Based in Royersford, Pennsylvania, AMT was a producer of small centrifugal and diaphragm pumps for industrial, construction, agricultural, marine, and household use. The firm provided pumps under its own name as well as private-brand products for national distributors. In March 2002 Patterson Pump acquired Atlanta-based Flo-Pak, Inc., for about $6.5 million. Flo-Pak specialized in prepackaged pumping systems for the municipal, fire protection, industrial, plumbing, and heating, ventilating, and air conditioning (HVAC) markets.

The stellar history of Gorman-Rupp was reflected in the company's achievement of 15 consecutive years of increased revenue and earnings through the year 2001. That year, revenues surpassed the $200 million mark for the first time, hitting $202.9 million. The difficult economic climate finally brought an end to this streak in 2002, however, as revenues fell 4.4 percent and earnings were down 38.7 percent. Gorman-Rupp remained in recovery mode over the next two years, before growth returned in earnest in 2005 when the company posted record profits of $10.9 on record sales of $231.2 million.

NEW PRODUCTS & RECORD REVENUES

In advance of the recovery, the company invested heavily in new product development efforts, and this investment paid off with a number of 2005 introductions, including the Pro-Max HVAC pump and the

Ultra V Series trash pumps. The Pro-Max featured a high-efficiency design to cut energy consumption, while Ultra V models were high-performance, self-priming centrifugal pumps offering up to a 300 percent increase in pressure and a 40 percent increase in flow over traditional self-priming pumps of a similar size. Also of note during 2005 was Gorman-Rupp's role in the devastating aftermath of Hurricane Katrina, including the company's donation of a number of pumps to help dewater New Orleans and surrounding parishes. Later, in 2007, the Patterson Pump unit delivered eight large flood-control pumps to the U.S. Army Corps of Engineers for installation in New Orleans.

Gorman-Rupp maintained its forward momentum through 2008, another record-breaking year with profits of $27.2 million on sales of $330.6 million. The company's international operations became increasingly important during this period and were the subject of additional investments. In 2006, for instance, Gorman-Rupp more vigorously pursued sales in various Asian markets when it began operating a warehouse and distribution center in Bangkok, Thailand. In April 2007 Gorman-Rupp acquired a controlling 90 percent stake in Wavo Pompen B.V., a Dutch manufacturer of pumps with facilities in Leeuwarden and Culemborg. The name of this company was subsequently changed to Gorman-Rupp Europe B.V. By 2008 Gorman-Rupp was selling its pumps in more than 100 countries around the world, and that year it generated more than $100 million in sales outside the United States, representing 31 percent of total sales.

The global economic downturn that began in late 2008 affected a number of the company's key markets, including the construction, industrial, municipal, fire protection, and OEM sectors. As a result, profits for 2009 were down 32.8 percent to $18.3 million, and sales fell as well, dropping 19.5 percent to $266.2 million. Gorman-Rupp launched a number of cost-cutting initiatives to deal with the downturn, and it also completed construction on a $53 million, 460,000-square-foot facility in Mansfield designed to increase the efficiency and capacity of the operations in the home base. The Mansfield Division's manufacturing operations and offices, along with Gorman-Rupp's headquarters, were shifted into the new facility during the fourth quarter of 2009.

Although the economic downturn brought a halt to another period of pronounced growth, Gorman-Rupp and its products nevertheless continued to prove good at pumping profits for shareholders. The firm in 2009 increased its dividend for the 37th consecutive year. Its

financial performance was also recognized by *Forbes* magazine, which that year, for the fourth consecutive year, named Gorman-Rupp to its list of the 200 best small companies in the United States.

April Dougal Gasbarre
Updated, David E. Salamie

PRINCIPAL SUBSIDIARIES

American Machine and Tool Co., Inc. of Pennsylvania; The Gorman-Rupp International Company; Gorman-Rupp of Canada Limited; Gorman-Rupp Europe B.V. (Netherlands; 90%); Patterson Pump Company; Patterson Pump Ireland Limited.

PRINCIPAL DIVISIONS

Gorman-Rupp Industries Division; Gorman-Rupp Mansfield Division.

PRINCIPAL COMPETITORS

Ampco-Pittsburgh Corporation; Colfax Corporation; Flowserve Corporation; Graco Inc.; Haskel International, Inc.; IDEX Corporation; ITT Corporation; KSB AG; Roper Industries, Inc.; The Weir Group PLC.

FURTHER READING

Autry, Ret, "Gorman-Rupp," *Fortune*, June 18, 1990, p. 93.

Brammer, Rhonda, "Gorman-Rupp Gets No Respect," *Barron's*, November 22, 1999, p. 26.

Gleisser, Marcus, "Pumping Up Profits in Mansfield," *Cleveland Plain Dealer*, June 28, 1998, p. 2H.

Pramik, Mike, "Mansfield Company Ready to Bail Out New Orleans," *Columbus (Ohio) Dispatch*, September 1, 2005, p. 1E.

Rosenbaum, Michael, "Pumping Profits: Gorman-Rupp Builds Revenues in a Harsh Climate," *Barron's*, January 4, 1982, pp. 44–45.

Sabath, Donald, "Gorman-Rupp Succession in Place," *Cleveland Plain Dealer*, May 29, 1996, p. C1.

Winter, Ralph E., "Gorman-Rupp CEO: All Sectors of Business Doing Very Well," *Dow Jones News Service*, August 21, 2007.

———, "Gorman-Rupp Hopes Expansion Helps It Capitalize on Upturn," *Dow Jones News Service*, August 20, 2009.

———, "Gorman-Rupp Hopes to Maintain Growth Streak," *Wall Street Journal*, August 28, 2001.

The Great Atlantic & Pacific Tea Company, Inc.

---

2 Paragon Drive
Montvale, New Jersey 07645-1718
U.S.A.
Telephone: (201) 573-9700
Fax: (201) 571-8719
Web site: http://www.aptea.com

Public Company
Founded: 1859
Incorporated: 1900
Employees: 48,000
Sales: $9.52 billion (2008)
Stock Exchanges: New York
Ticker Symbol: GAP
NAICS: 445110 Supermarkets and Other Grocery (Except Convenience) Stores

■ ■ ■

The Great Atlantic & Pacific Tea Company, Inc., (A&P) is one of the dozen largest grocery store operators in North America. At its peak in the 1930s, A&P was the largest grocery chain in the United States, with 15,737 stores from coast to coast. By the beginning of the second decade of the 21st century, however, it operated around 435 stores in eight states (Connecticut, Massachusetts, New York, New Jersey, Pennsylvania, Delaware, Maryland, and Virginia) and the District of Columbia. Store banners include A&P, Food Basics, The Food Emporium, Super Fresh, Pathmark, and Waldbaum's. Tengelmann Group, a German retailer, acquired a majority interest in A&P in 1979, but this

stake has since been reduced to less than 39 percent. The Yucaipa Companies LLC, a private-equity firm, owns a 27.6 percent stake in A&P.

EARLY HISTORY: FROM TEA MERCHANT TO GROCERY CHAIN

In 1859 George Huntington Hartford and George Francis Gilman formed a partnership. Using Gilman's connections as an established grocer and the son of a wealthy shipowner, Hartford purchased coffee and tea from clipper ships on the waterfront docks of New York City. By eliminating brokers, Hartford and Gilman were able to sell their wares at "cargo prices." Initially, the operation was strictly a mail-order affair. However, the enterprise proved so successful that Hartford and Gilman opened a series of stores under the name Great American Tea Company. The first of these, which opened in 1861, soon became a landmark on Vesey Street in New York City. By 1869 there were 11 such stores.

The company's appeal to the 19th-century consumer was enhanced by the lavish storefronts and Chinese-inspired interiors that Gilman designed. Inside the Chinese paneled walls, cockatoos greeted customers, who brought their purchases to a pagoda-shaped cash desk. Outside, the red-and-gold storefronts were illuminated by dozens of gas lights that formed a giant "T," and on Saturdays customers were treated to the music of a live brass band.

Despite the company's extravagant trappings, its success was largely due to its innovative strategy of offering savings and incentives to the consumer. A&P's "club plan" (introduced in 1866), which encouraged the formation of clubs to make bulk mail-order sales for an additional one-third discount, was so successful that by 1886 hundreds of such clubs had been formed. Pioneering the concept of private labels and house brands, The Great American Tea Company introduced its own inexpensive tea and coffee blends, continuing to direct its efforts at the price-conscious consumer. In 1882 Eight O'Clock Breakfast Coffee was introduced. The Eight O'Clock blend remained a hallmark house brand until A&P sold it in 2003.

In 1869 the company became The Great Atlantic & Pacific Tea Company, to commemorate the joining of the first transcontinental railroad and to separate its retail stores from its mail-order operations. A&P's gradual national expansion began shortly thereafter. The company established a foothold in the Midwest in the aftermath of the Chicago Fire of 1871, when A&P sent staff and food to help the devastated city, and stayed to open stores in the region. By 1876 the company had become the first significant grocery chain, having reached the 100-store mark.

EXPANSION & PROMOTION

Careful thought and planning were given to A&P's expansion. New store openings were complemented by promotions and premiums. In the Midwest and the South, new stores gave away items such as crockery and lithographs in order to attract customers, and in other areas, showy "Teams of Eight" became legendary symbols of A&P. The brainchild of the flamboyant John Augustine Hartford, parades of teams of eight horses decorated with spangled harnesses and gold-plated bells drew red and gold vehicles through the towns; the

person who best guessed the weight of the team was awarded $500 in gold.

In 1878, after Gilman's retirement, Hartford gained full control of the business. His two sons, George Ludlum and John Augustine, were each apprenticed at the age of 16. Years later, a writer in the *Saturday Evening Post* observed that "in discussing the two brothers, tea company employees seldom get beyond the differences between the two." The older brother, who became known as Mr. George, earned a reputation as the "inside man" because of his concern for the books, and was considered to be the "conservative, bearish influence in the business."

The younger, flamboyant Mr. John was described as an "old-school actor-manager." He was well-suited for his responsibility for promotions and premiums and generally ensured a "personal touch" in each of A&P's stores, which by 1900 numbered nearly 200 and generated $5.6 million in annual sales. Mr. John was also responsible for A&P peddlers, who by 1910 were carrying A&P products along 5,000 separate routes into rural areas in easily recognized red-and-black A&P wagons.

INTRODUCING THE CASH-&-CARRY CONCEPT

Responding to a dramatic rise in the cost of living in the first decade of the 20th century, when food prices increased by 35 percent, Mr. John devised the first cash-and-carry A&P Economy Store, which opened its doors in Jersey City, New Jersey, in 1912. Initially dismissed by both younger and elder George Hartford, economy stores obviated the problem of capital depletion posed by premiums, credit, and delivery.

The cash-and-carry stores followed a simple formula, whereby $3,000 was allotted for equipment, groceries, and working capital. Only one man was needed to run an economy store, and he was expected to adhere strictly to Mr. John's "Manual for Managers of Economy Stores," which outlined, in meticulous detail, how to run the stores. Among other things, Mr. John insisted that all the stores have the same goods at the same location. A&P legend has it that Mr. John could find the beans in any of his stores, blindfolded.

CHAIN'S PEAK ERA

When George Huntington Hartford died in 1917, the younger George Hartford became chairman of A&P, while John Hartford became president. By 1925 A&P had 14,000 economy stores, with sales of $440 million, marking one of the greatest retail expansions ever. At this point, the company's national expansion was so far-

KEY DATES

1859: George Huntington Hartford and George Francis Gilman form The Great American Tea Company to sell discount tea via mail order.

1861: First store opens in New York City.

1869: Company is renamed The Great Atlantic & Pacific Tea Company (A&P).

1930: Chain reaches its all-time store count peak of 15,737.

1937: With the opening of the first A&P supermarket, the chain begins transitioning to the innovative new grocery format.

1958: Family control of the company ends, and A&P is taken public.

1979: Tengelmann Group, a West German retailer, purchases majority control of a financially troubled A&P.

1980: James Wood is appointed chairman and CEO and initiates a major restructuring.

1998: Christian Haub is named CEO of A&P; revitalization program is launched.

2007: A&P acquires Pathmark Stores, Inc.

reaching that A&P had to be divided into five geographical divisions to decentralize management.

During the 1920s, A&P continued to diversify, opening bakeries and pastry and candy shops. It also expanded its manufacturing facilities to produce its own Ann Page brand products and set up a corporation to buy coffee directly from Colombia and Brazil. "Combination stores" added hitherto unheard-of meat counters to the grocery chain and, when lines at these counters became a problem, A&P devised a system to make prepackaged meats available to customers, who had never before been offered such a convenience. At the same time, A&P introduced food-testing laboratories to maintain quality standards in its manufactured products. In 1929 when the stock market crashed, causing other retail companies to fold, merge, or sell out in the subsequent Great Depression, A&P was so firmly established and soundly managed that it was virtually unaffected. Sales reached the $1 billion mark in 1929, and the following year the chain's store count peaked at 15,737 outlets. Responding to consumers' needs, A&P began publishing literature with money-saving tips and recipes. The public's reception of these publications prompted the company to begin

publishing *Woman's Day* magazine in 1937, at two cents per issue.

The 1930s marked the advent of supermarkets in the United States. The Hartfords found the supermarket idea distasteful and were slow to respond to the trend, but as A&P began to lose market share, they were swayed and opened their first such outlet in Braddock, Pennsylvania, in 1937. The following year, supermarkets represented 5 percent of A&P's stores but 23 percent of its business. By 1939 the total number of A&P stores had dropped to 9,100, of which 1,100 were supermarkets, and A&P's sales had regained the level they first achieved in 1930. The company's size, however, although smaller than the 15,737 stores it had at its height, was a distinct liability.

In 1936 the Robinson-Patman Act was passed, marking the beginning of the antitrust woes that shook A&P's hegemony. Anti-chainstore legislation, passed at the instigation of small independent grocers who claimed chains practiced unfair competition, imposed severe taxes and regulations on A&P and other chains, limiting pricing and other competitive advantages afforded to them by virtue of their size and purchasing power. Restrictions were based simply on store numbers, hitting A&P particularly hard. The company sought to redeem its damaged public image by publicizing its sense of corporate responsibility to consumers, producers, and employees. The loss of a suit in 1949, however, imposed limitations on A&P's purchasing practices that were more severe than any others in the industry. With this final blow, the company's position as an esteemed industry leader disintegrated.

DECLINING FORTUNES AT MID-CENTURY

In 1950 Ralph Burger, who had started at A&P in 1911 as an $11-a-week clerk, became president of the company. Much of A&P's early success had stemmed from Mr. George and Mr. John's scrupulous attention to the business, or, in Mr. John's term, to "the art of basketwatching." As the *Saturday Evening Post* article on the Hartfords had concluded in 1931, "who will watch the baskets after the Hartfords are gone? Neither has any children and although the 10 grandchildren get their due shares of income from the family trust, the direct line of shrewd vigilance will be broken." Burger remained loyal to the Hartford brothers even after their deaths, John in 1951 and George in 1957.

With George's death, family control of A&P ended and the company was taken public the following year, but Burger, as president not only of A&P, but also of the Hartford Foundation, the charity to which the Hartfords had willed their A&P shares and which owned more than one-third of the company's shares, retained control of A&P. He ran the company, if not imaginatively, then at least reasonably successfully, until his death in 1969. At that point, despite its dusty image, A&P was still the grocery-industry leader, with sales of well over $5 billion a year, more than twice its closest competitor.

With the end of Burger's tenure, and the Hartford heirs' disinclination to enter business, A&P had no clear line of management succession. The "direct line of shrewd vigilance" was broken, and management continued to change throughout the 1970s. The company's direction foundered so much that A&P, once an innovative industry leader, was no longer able even to follow the lead of its competitors. Failing to capitalize on suburban development and to adapt to changing consumer tastes, A&P's sales dropped and its reputation suffered serious injury. A&P's once "resplendent emporiums" were now perceived as antiquated, inefficient, and run-down.

NEW MANAGEMENT, CLOSURES, RENOVATIONS, & ACQUISITIONS

In 1973, as A&P reported $51 million in losses and Safeway took its place as the largest food retailer in the country, Jonathan L. Scott was hired from Albertson's, marking the first time in history that A&P had looked outside its ranks for management. Scott's attempt to revive A&P by closing stores and cutting labor costs resulted only in more dissatisfied customers, and more losses. Finally, in 1979, the Tengelmann Group, a major West German retailer, bought 52.5 percent of A&P's stock. By this point, the A&P chain, which had consisted of more than 4,000 stores in the 1960s, was down to about 1,500 locations.

The Tengelmann Group appointed James Wood, the former CEO of the Grand Union Company, as chairman and CEO of A&P, in 1980. Wood's reputation as a turnaround manager underwent a trial by fire, but his radical restructuring of the company was later lauded by analysts as "an outstanding success." By 1982 close to 40 percent of the company's stores had been shut down. In addition, virtually all manufacturing facilities had been eliminated (the coffee-roasting plants were the exception). Management had won labor concessions in key markets, and the company returned to profitability. Between 1986 and 1990, A&P's earnings grew an average of 27 percent annually. With a formidable cash flow, Wood initiated an aggressive capital-spending program to rejuvenate the store base, develop new store formats, and make prudent acquisitions.

While some markets were abandoned, others were the focus of store recycling and expansion. High-growth areas (such as Phoenix, Arizona, and Southern California) were avoided in favor of markets in which A&P's presence was firmly established amid a stable and slow-growing population (such as Philadelphia, New York, and Detroit). Concentrating efforts in the most promising areas of its six major operating regions (the Northeast, the New York metropolitan area, the mid-Atlantic states, the South, the Midwest, and Ontario, Canada), the company had the flexibility to tailor store formats, product mixes, service, and pricing to local customer bases.

Initially, tens of millions of dollars were spent to remodel and expand 85 percent of A&P's extant stores to give them a more up-to-date presentation, rid the company of its tarnished reputation, and add service departments to accommodate consumers' changed tastes. Improved sales allowed the company to begin to undertake new-store construction by 1985. The "new" A&P aimed for an upscale, service-oriented image and catered to one-stop shoppers. In addition, two new store formats addressed different market niches. Futurestores stressed A&P's broad variety of quality products, and Sav-A-Centers took a strong promotional approach by offering warehouse prices.

Wood also focused on growth through the purchase of regional chains, permitting A&P to establish itself as the top food retailer in certain regional markets without the risk and expense of building new facilities and establishing a market niche. Initial purchases included 17 Stop & Shop stores in New Jersey, purchased in 1981 and converted to the A&P name; the Kohl's grocery chain in Wisconsin, bought in 1983; 20 Pantry Price Stores in Virginia, acquired in 1984; and 92 Dominion stores in Ontario, Canada, brought onboard in 1985. The Waldbaum and Shopwell/Food Emporium acquisitions in 1986 combined to make A&P the market leader in the New York metropolitan area, where the company had its strongest presence, and its 1989 acquisition of the 79-store, Detroit-area Farmer Jack chain from Borman's Inc. resulted in a majority share of the Detroit market.

SHIFTING FOCUS IN THE LATE EIGHTIES

After the company's restructuring under Wood, operating income per store more than doubled. Emphasizing high-profit-margin departments, including full-service delis, cheese shops, fresh seafood, and floral departments, the company departed radically from low-price generic product offerings. In 1988 Master Choice, a private-brand label of specialty chocolates, pastas, sauces, and herbal teas was introduced in order to compete with what industry experts considered the real competition: restaurants and fast-food chains.

In 1989 A&P made a bid for Gateway Corporation, the third-largest grocery chain in Britain. Gateway would have offered A&P a whole new arena for growth, one that was of considerable interest to Erivan Haub, Tengelmann's owner, who wished to shore up his European retailing empire in preparation for the unification of the common market in 1992. The Gateway bid ultimately failed. A&P also had trouble with another international venture, its $250 million acquisition of 70 Miracle Food Mart stores in Ontario in 1990. Ontario was soon hit by recession, as were A&P's other major markets in the United States, and sales fell in the Canadian stores by 5 percent the next year.

CONTINUING STRUGGLES IN THE NINETIES

A&P's acquisitions had given the company top market share in many cities. Its 1989 acquisition of Farmer Jack in Detroit, along with its earlier purchases of Kohl's in Milwaukee and Waldbaum's in New York, put it in the top spot in these major markets. The company had trouble, however, hanging on to its market share. Its stores averaged half the size of newly built supermarkets, and many were old and run-down. Waldbaum's in New York was cited in 1991 as the worst of all area grocery chains for numerous problems with rodents and cockroaches. The company was slow to respond, and Waldbaum's sanitation record improved only slightly the next year. Earnings for the company dropped from $151 million in 1990 to $71 million in 1991. Then sales for 1992 fell a shocking $1.1 billion, and the company was in the red, losing $189.5 million. By 1993 stores run by A&P had lost market share in six major markets. Faced with a poor economy and declining profits, the company cut back the amount it was spending on renovations.

A&P decided to focus its marketing efforts on a new store-brand product line in 1993. Wood had sold or closed most of the company's store-brand manufacturing plants in the 1980s, but A&P thought it was time to emphasize cost-cutting store brands again. The company consolidated nine different private labels into one such line, America's Choice, which was soon found at all its different chains. Some 3,500 private-label items were consolidated into 1,600 America's Choice items, which were promoted on television in major market areas.

A&P also remodeled more than 100 stores in 1993 and built 20 new ones. Analysts frequently noted that

A&P could spend much more on remodeling and on opening larger stores. In 1994 A&P upped its capital spending 40 percent, to $340 million, and announced that it would concentrate on opening 50,000- to 60,000-square-foot stores, on par with those of its competitors. The company was still plagued with problems, though. Its Ontario chains, Miracle Food Mart and Ultra Mart, were closed by a 14-week strike during 1993–94. A&P had attempted to lower its labor costs by cutting wages and relying on more part-time workers, setting off the strike. A&P finally settled with the unions, but the long strike had given Ontario customers plenty of time to build loyalty to competitive stores. A&P's Atlanta stores also faltered. The company bought 40 stores in the Atlanta area in 1993 in order to fight back competitors who were opening new stores in the area. The Atlanta stores, however, lost money and began to show a profit only in the fourth quarter of fiscal 1994.

REVITALIZING UNDER HAUB

The company gained a new president in 1994, Christian Haub, the 29-year-old son of Erivan Haub, the principal owner of A&P's majority owner Tengelmann Group. This was the first time a member of the Haub family had direct involvement with managing A&P. Haub planned to improve the image of A&P stores by emphasizing cleanliness, checkout service, and other highly visible areas of customer service. More than this, the company opened 16 new stores in 1994–95, remodeled or expanded 55 more, and closed 87 stores. According to Haub, A&P planned to open 50 stores a year after 1996. The company put aside $1.5 billion for store development over the next five years. Problems with the Canadian stores seemed to be improving by 1996. That, coupled with excellent results from the company's Michigan stores, helped A&P post a 28 percent increase in profits for the fiscal year ending in February 1997.

During 1997 Haub was promoted to president and co-CEO and then became sole CEO in May 1998, with Wood remaining chairman. Haub soon launched a new revitalization effort. In December 1998 A&P announced that it would shut 127 smaller, underperforming stores. The closures were designed to enable the company to concentrate on its better-performing outlets in its strongest markets, those in which it had the potential to be the number one or number two player. A&P subsequently exited from the Atlanta; Richmond, Virginia; and Tidewater, Virginia, markets. The company also said that it would, over the next three years, open as many as 200 larger-format superstores and modernize 225 existing stores. The closed stores were expected to generate one-time cost savings of $90 million and lead to improved overall profitability. In turn, rising profits would place A&P in a better position to pursue acquisitions at a time when the supermarket industry was undergoing a significant consolidation wave. Restructuring charges of about $120 million led A&P to post a net loss of $67.2 million for the fiscal year ending in February 1999.

The store closures left A&P with three core markets: the Northeast, the Midwest (principally Michigan and Wisconsin), and Ontario. The company identified New Orleans as a fourth core area and in 1999 acquired six Schwegmann stores there that were later rebranded under the Sav-A-Center name. In addition to budgeting $400 million for capital improvements, A&P also set aside another $250 million for a second phase of the restructuring program involving the installation of a state-of-the-art computer system. This effort, launched in 2000, was designed to improve efficiencies throughout the company's entire supply chain and operations, from manufacturing through checkout. Between 90 and 95 percent of the firm's computer systems were to be replaced.

EARLY 21ST CENTURY: A STALLED TURNAROUND

Following several executive defections in 2000, including that of the COO, Elizabeth Culligan was brought onboard as executive vice president and COO in early 2001 (she was promoted to president and COO about a year later). Culligan was a former executive at Nabisco Holdings Corp., and her background in food manufacturing made her an unconventional choice to head a major food retailer. In the middle of that year, Christian Haub was named chairman and CEO, bringing an end to Wood's long A&P tenure. In November the company announced the closure of another 39 underperforming supermarkets, most of which had been opened during the previous five years in what A&P now said was a "flawed" program of expansion. Investors reacted positively both to the closure plan and to the frank admission of past failure, and the company's stock began to rise.

In a hopeful sign for the company, A&P posted a profit for the fourth quarter of fiscal 2002, its first quarter in the black since the first quarter of 2000. The turnaround soon began stalling out, however, hampered by the stagnating U.S. economy and stepped-up competition in the company's main markets. A&P encountered a further setback in the middle of 2002 when it was forced to restate its financial results for the previous three fiscal years because of problems with the way it was accounting for inventory in certain regions and with vendor allowances, or payments made by manufacturers to retailers for promoting their products in stores. The company's stock began declining, reaching an all-time low in October 2002, the same month that Culligan tendered her resignation.

At that same time, A&P announced that it was dividing its retail operations into two operating units: A&P U.S. and A&P Canada. A&P officials felt that its chains within the two countries were in markedly different operational situations. The Canadian chains, under the direction of Brian Piwek, had been successfully turned around and had entered a growth phase. By contrast, there was still much work to be done to turn the U.S. chains into competitive and consistently profitable properties. In fact, many of the programs that had been instrumental in the Canadian turnaround were to be transferred to the U.S. operations. For example, the Canadian A&P and Dominion chains had placed large emphasis on high-quality fresh foods and customer service.

A&P had also developed a successful low-price/limited-assortment format in Canada under the Food Basics banner. After testing the format in the United States, the company in December 2002 announced that it would convert 120 of its 700 stores to the Food Basics format. Management too was shifted to the south, Piwek having been named president and CEO of A&P U.S. Eric Claus took a similar position with A&P Canada. Claus came to A&P from Co-op Atlantic, a New Brunswick-based retail and wholesale food company, where he was president and CEO. Both Piwek and Claus began reporting directly to Haub, who added the title of president to his other duties.

These moves came as A&P was in increasingly dire straits. For the fiscal year ending in February 2003, the company suffered a net loss of $147 million. Burdened with more than $900 million in total debt, the company needed to raise cash and cut costs. It subsequently completed a series of asset sales during the fiscal year ending in February 2004. The company sold its 17 stores in northern New England, thus exiting from Massachusetts and New Hampshire and reducing its New England operations to just its stores in Connecticut. A&P sold its seven Kohl's stores in Madison, Wisconsin, and then closed its 23 remaining Kohl's stores, located in the Milwaukee area. A&P also sold its Eight O'Clock coffee business to Gryphon Investors, a San Francisco-based private-equity firm, for $107.5 million. In the Detroit market, in an effort to be more competitive, A&P lowered prices permanently at its Farmer Jack stores, replacing the need for customers to use a savings club card for weekly sales specials. In addition, several Farmer Jack stores were shut down and 13 were converted to the Food Basics format. This round of store divestments reduced the number of company stores to around 630, while total debt was slashed to just under $700 million.

RETRENCHING TO THE NORTHEAST

Shortly after reporting a net loss of $188.1 million for the fiscal year ending in February 2005, A&P announced its intention to downsize again, pulling back to its core market in the Northeast. In August 2005 the company sold its Canadian division to Montreal-based Metro, Inc., in a $1.47 billion deal that included $982 million in cash and $409 million in stock. The stock portion left A&P with a stake in Metro of nearly 16 percent. Around this same time, Haub stepped aside as CEO and became the firm's executive chairman, while Eric Claus, who had headed the Canadian division, was named A&P's CEO.

The sale of the Canadian division greatly improved A&P's financial position as total debt was cut to less than $300 million. The greater financial strength, coupled with the sale of the company's stake in Metro, enabled A&P to acquire Pathmark Stores, Inc., for about $1.4 billion in cash, stock, and assumed liabilities in December 2007. Pathmark, based in Carteret, New Jersey, operated about 140 supermarkets in the New York, New Jersey, and Philadelphia metropolitan areas. Adding Pathmark made A&P the grocery market-share leader in the Northeast. In the meantime, A&P completed its retrenchment to the Northeast in 2007 by selling or closing its Sav-A-Center stores in New Orleans and its Farmer Jack stores in Michigan.

A little more than a year after the Pathmark deal closed, A&P completed an integration that yielded about $150 million in annual cost savings. During the period of integration, A&P began repositioning Pathmark as its "price impact" banner, aiming to make the chain a "destination price leader" offering prices strikingly less expensive than competitive conventional supermarkets. This new format became part of A&P's multiformat strategy designed to meet the needs of an increasingly diverse base of consumers. Food Basics was the firm's limited-choice, discount chain, while A&P, Waldbaum's, and Super Fresh used a format dubbed "fresh" that included the full offerings of a traditional grocery store but also featured a wide array of fresh, prepared, specialty, natural, and organic food products. The Food Emporium, finally, was A&P's high-end gourmet chain, operating mostly in Manhattan.

One other consequence of A&P's purchase of Pathmark was to push Tengelmann's stake in A&P to under the 50 percent mark. In mid-2009 this stake was reduced still further, to less than 39 percent, when Yucaipa Companies LLC, a private-equity firm, made a major investment in A&P as part of new agreements that provided the company with $400 million in financing. Yucaipa emerged with a 27.6 percent interest in A&P and two seats on the company board.

The Pathmark stores performed poorly after their acquisition by A&P, with both sales and earnings on a downward trajectory. After A&P suffered a net loss of $80.3 million for the second quarter of 2009, with Pathmark's struggles the prime culprit, Claus was pushed out and Haub began serving as interim CEO. In January 2010 A&P announced a net loss of $559.6 million for the third quarter. This was the firm's seventh consecutive quarterly loss and the largest in more than a decade. The loss included a $412.6 million impairment charge to write down the value of the Pathmark acquisition. In early 2010 Ron Marshall resigned from his position as CEO of book retailer Borders Group, Inc., to become A&P's new CEO. Marshall, whose résumé included a stint as CFO of Pathmark, faced the daunting task of turning around a beleaguered company.

Marie J. MacNee
Updated, A. Woodward; David E. Salamie

PRINCIPAL SUBSIDIARIES

APW Supermarket Corporation; APW Supermarkets, Inc.; Best Cellars, Inc.; Compass Foods, Inc.; Food Basics, Inc.; The Food Emporium, Inc.; Kwik Save Inc.; Montvale Holdings, Inc.; Pathmark Stores, Inc.; Shopwell, Inc.; Super Fresh Food Markets, Inc.; Super Fresh Food Markets of Maryland, Inc.; Super Fresh/Sav-A-Center, Inc.; Supermarket Distribution Services, Inc.; Super Plus Food Warehouse, Inc.; Waldbaum, Inc.

PRINCIPAL COMPETITORS

Acme Markets, Inc.; Costco Wholesale Corporation; Foodarama Supermarkets, Inc.; Genuardi's Family Markets, Inc.; Giant Food Stores, LLC; King Kullen Grocery Company, Inc.; Kings Super Markets, Inc.; Shaw's Supermarkets, Inc.; The Stop & Shop Supermarket Company; Wakefern Food Corp.; Wal-Mart Stores, Inc.; Weis Markets, Inc.; Whole Foods Market, Inc.

FURTHER READING

DeMarrais, Kevin G., "A&P Looks for a Fresh Start," *Hackensack (N.J.) Record*, November 5, 2000, p. B1.
———, "Can New CEO Deliver the Goods for Troubled A&P?" *Hackensack (N.J.) Record*, January 28, 2010, p. L7.

————, "Strategic Retreat: A&P Shrinking to Focus on Northeast," *Hackensack (N.J.) Record*, May 11, 2005, p. B1.

Dowdell, Stephen, "A&P Is on Fresh Path to Growth in Future," *Supermarket News*, July 31, 1995, pp. 13+.

Hoyt, Edwin P., *That Wonderful A&P!* New York: Hawthorne Books, 1969, 279 p.

Marcial, Gene G., "Spicing Things Up at the A&P," *Business Week*, February 1, 1999, p. 112.

"Portrait of a Survivor: America's First Grocery Chain Has Proved an Enduring Fixture—through Good Times and Bad," *Supermarket News*, December 19, 1994, pp. 10+.

Ruth, João-Pierre S., "A&P Tries to Reinvent Itself—Again," *NJBIZ*, June 18, 2007, pp. 3, 8.

Springer, Jon, "A&P Posts Loss, Ousts CEO Claus," *Supermarket News*, October 26, 2009, p. 1.

————, "A History of Reinvention," *Supermarket News*, December 8, 2008, p. 14.

————, "Marshall Returns to Northeast, and to Company in Crisis," *Supermarket News*, February 15, 2010, p. 20.

————, "Metro to Buy A&P Canada," *Supermarket News*, July 25, 2005, p. 4.

————, "Pathmark Acquisition Ends Three Years of Anticipation," *Supermarket News*, December 10, 2007, p. 1.

Walsh, William I., *The Rise and Decline of The Great Atlantic & Pacific Tea Company*, Secaucus, NJ: L. Stuart, 1986, 254 p.

Wilson, Marianne, "A&P's Great Expectations," *Chain Store Age*, April 1999, pp. 36–39.

Great Canadian Gaming Corporation

13775 Commerce Parkway, Suite 200
Richmond, British Columbia V6V 2V4
Canada
Telephone: (604) 303-1000
Fax: (604) 279-8605
Web site: http://www.greatcanadiancasinos.com

Public Company
Incorporated: 1990 as Jetta Resources Ltd.
Employees: 5,300
Sales: CAD 403.7 million (2008)
Stock Exchanges: Toronto
Ticker Symbol: GC
NAICS: 713990 All Other Amusement and Recreation Industries; 711212 Race Tracks; 713120 Amusement Arcades; 722110 Full-Service Restaurants

∎ ∎ ∎

Great Canadian Gaming Corporation is a gaming company that owns casinos and horse-racing properties in British Columbia, Ontario, Nova Scotia, and in the United States in Washington State. The company operates four casinos, one bingo hall, and two horse-racing facilities in British Columbia. Great Canadian operates two racing complexes in Ontario. The company operates two casinos in Nova Scotia. In Washington, operating through a subsidiary, Great American Gaming Corporation, the company owns four casinos, all within an hour's drive from Seattle. Great Canadian's signature casino is the River Rock Casino Resort in Vancouver, British Columbia, which accounts for 30 percent of the

company's annual revenue. The company is led by founder, Chairman, and CEO Ross J. McLeod.

BEGINNINGS IN 1982

The company that expanded at a furious pace during the first decade of the 21st century began its business life in 1982 as a firm named Jetta Resources Ltd. The venture's founder and the individual who would preside over its development for the next three decades was Russ J. McLeod, who would become a major contributor to the regulatory mandates governing gambling in British Columbia.

When McLeod formed Great Canadian's predecessor, there were no permanent casinos in Canada. Winnipeg, Manitoba, would become home to the nation's first permanent, "year-round" casino in 1989. Gambling restrictions did not apply to temporary casinos or charitable casinos, however, the type of business McLeod began running in 1982. The first year-round charitable casino, dubbed "Cash Casino," opened in Calgary, Alberta, two years before McLeod launched Jetta Resources.

McLeod lived an itinerant existence during his first years shepherding Jetta Resources. He moved from city to city, operating temporary casinos set up for charitable causes. Frequently, given the fledgling state of his business, McLeod hired his employees on a part-time basis when he arrived at a new location, training his staff on site just prior to opening his casino. It was a modest beginning, but McLeod began displaying greater ambition when federal and provincial gambling restrictions began to loosen. Canada had declared a complete ban

COMPANY PERSPECTIVES

The company considers the knowledge of its people to be one of its most important assets. Success in the gaming industry requires a very high level of technological sophistication and solid gaming experience to meet the new challenges of the industry. The officers and directors of the company are professionals who have extensive expertise and highly-technical experience particular to the gaming and horse racing industry. Several members of our management team are considered to be pioneers within the Canadian gaming industry, and have specialized knowledge that is essential for our gaming and horse racing operations.

on all gambling activities nearly a century earlier, but gradually attitudes changed, providing McLeod with opportunities he would exploit.

FIRST PERMANENT CASINO OPENS: 1987

McLeod's caravan came to a stop in 1987. His company opened its first permanent location, the Casino on Broadway, in Vancouver, British Columbia. The Vancouver suburb of Richmond became the hub of his operations, the site of his headquarters where he would begin establishing what would become the largest gaming company in British Columbia. By 1997, gambling restrictions had eased, allowing gaming proprietors to operate for longer hours, to offer a wider selection of table games, and, for the first time, introduce slot machines into their properties. McLeod changed the name of his company during the watershed year, choosing Great Canadian Gaming Corporation as the name for the vehicle that he would use to secure a dominant position in the gaming industry. At roughly the same time, he formed a subsidiary, Great Canadian Casino Inc., the entity that would spearhead the charge forward.

In 1998, a year after McLeod changed the name of his business, regulatory changes gave him further ability to turn Great Canadian into an industry leader. In British Columbia the charity casino system was replaced by government management, giving the British Columbia Lottery Corporation control over all casinos in the province. McLeod, comparatively anonymous in the industry for the previous 16 years, moved aggressively

ahead. By the following year, Great Canadian ranked as the largest gaming company in the province, controlling one-third of British Columbia's casinos. The company owned six casinos and possessed a license from the British Columbia Lottery Corporation for an additional casino in southwest British Columbia. McLeod bolted into the lead, but his impressive start to an expansion campaign did not satisfy his vision for Great Canadian.

GREAT CANADIAN CROSSES THE BORDER: 1999

As McLeod quickly rose to the top of the British Columbia gaming industry, he armed himself with another corporate vehicle to fuel his company's growth. In March 1999, he formed a subsidiary, Great American Gaming Corporation, which he would use to begin his expansion into the United States. Several months earlier, he and his management team had decided to expand into markets adjacent to British Columbia, a plan that included crossing the border south. "How much of the market do you really want before you start looking around?" Great Canadian's general manager asked in the October 15, 1999 issue of *Puget Sound Business Journal.* "We need to diversify a bit."

Great Canadian began looking for opportunities to diversify by examining markets in Alberta and Washington State. By the fall of 1999, the company had made its first move, brokering a deal to acquire a 50 percent interest in Washington's second-largest casino, the Riverside Casino in Tukwila, 20 miles south of Seattle. Great Canadian gave Riverside's owner, SBD Inc., $600,000 for a stake in the casino, which offered live music, dancing, dining, card games, and pull tabs. Washington became the focal point of Great Canadian's expansion outside British Columbia, where provincial authorities had imposed a cap on new casino development. The company ended the decade with CAD 54 million in revenues, a total that would increase substantially in the decade ahead as McLeod aggressively expanded his business.

Great Canadian entered the new century shoring up its presence in British Columbia and expanding in Washington. At the start of the decade, the company closed two casinos, the Mayfair gaming facility near Victoria and the Surrey gaming facility in Vancouver, and replaced them with two new, 35,000-square-foot properties in Coquitlam and Victoria. The replacements gave the company a total of six casinos in British Columbia with 900 slot machines and 172 table games. Meanwhile, in Washington, Great Canadian strengthened its presence, constructing new casinos in Tukwila (the Riverside had since closed) and Algona that opened in 2002. The year also saw the company

KEY DATES

1982: Great Canadian is founded.
1987: Company opens its first permanent casino in Vancouver, British Columbia.
1999: Company enters the United States for the first time.
2004: First horse-racing facility is acquired.
2005: Expansion into eastern Canada begins.

purchase Big Al's Casino in Everett, 30 miles north of Seattle, for $5.8 million. Big Al's featured 15 table games, a nightclub with live entertainment, and a restaurant.

EXPANSION ACCELERATES: 2004

A turning point occurred in Great Canadian's history in 2004, a year that marked the beginning of an energetic acquisition campaign and the company's entry into a new line of business. In scope and scale, the company expansion efforts were unprecedented, creating a gaming concern with far-flung properties. At the heart of the company's operations was its most important casino, a property that underpinned its financial performance during the decade. Great Canadian secured the land for the casino in 2002, when it purchased 18 acres of land known as the Bridgepoint Market site on River Road in Richmond, British Columbia. The land was occupied by buildings, a marina, and a pub that Great Canadian transformed into its signature property, the River Rock Casino Resort. The company signed a 10-year operational service agreement with the British Columbia Lottery Corp., received its liquor license from the British Columbia Liquor Control and Licensing Branch, and opened the casino in June 2004. The facility began operating 24 hours per day, featuring 1,000 slot machines, 75 gaming tables, a food court, and a 100-seat lounge. At the time of the opening, construction was underway for a 222-room hotel adjacent to the casino, a property that was scheduled to open in early 2005.

The grand opening of the River Rock Casino Resort was not the only event for Great Canadian officials to celebrate in 2004. The year saw the company jump into the "racino" business. Great Canadian acquired Hastings Entertainment Inc., a company that owned Hastings Racecourse, a thoroughbred racetrack in Vancouver. Before the end of the year, Great Canadian tripled its interests in horse-racing properties, signing a

purchase agreement to acquire Orangeville Raceway Limited. Orangeville owned two standardbred racing facilities in British Columbia, Fraser Downs Racetrack & Casino in Surrey and Sandown Park on Vancouver Island. The acquisition of Orangeville was completed in the first half of 2005 for CAD 40 million, making Great Canadian the largest standardbred and thoroughbred racing operator in British Columbia.

By the end of 2004, Great Canadian's revenues reached a record high of CAD 178.5 million, a 56 percent increase from the previous year's total and more than three times the total registered at the end of the 1990s. The company's net income shot upward as well, increasing by 86 percent to CAD 26.7 million. McLeod, energized by the glowing financial performance of his company, charged ahead, completing a flurry of acquisitions during the next several years.

COMPANY MARCHES EASTWARD: 2005

One month before Great Canadian completed its acquisition of Orangeville, it signed an agreement to acquire another racing property that extended its geographic presence substantially. The company signed an agreement in April 2005 to acquire Georgian Downs Limited and Georgian Downs Holdings Inc., two companies that operated a slots and standardbred racing facility in Innisfil, Ontario, 45 minutes north of Toronto. Great Canadian paid CAD 25 million and assumed CAD 23 million of debt to purchase the racetrack, which became its fourth racetrack and casino, racino, operation.

The geographic leap eastward was extended with Great Canadian's entry into Nova Scotia. In mid-2005 the company purchased two casinos from Caesars Entertainment Inc., paying $70 million for Casino Nova Scotia Halifax and Casino Nova Scotia Sydney. The Halifax property operated as a full-service gaming facility with 750 slot machines, 41 table games, and three licensed restaurants. The Sydney facility featured 387 slot machines, 11 table games, and two licensed restaurants. Several months later, McLeod added another property to Great Canadian's portfolio of racetrack properties, paying CAD 50 million plus debt for Flamboro Downs, a standardbred racing facility in Flamborough, Ontario.

The dizzying pace of expansion slowed after the purchases completed in 2005, ending a two-year spree that saw Great Canadian become a nationally oriented company with sizable holdings in casinos and racinos. Sales swelled to CAD 385.2 million by 2006 and the company's stock, which had traded for CAD 2 per share in 1998, rose impressively in value, reaching a high of CAD 22.36 per share in April 2005. The aggressive expansion paid dividends, but it also engendered problems, pocking Great Canadian's otherwise stellar record.

GROWING PAINS SLOW EXPANSION: 2006–09

The company stumbled in its eastward expansion, experiencing difficulties that contributed to a CAD 18.6 million loss in 2006. The casinos in Nova Scotia, for instance, attracted fewer U.S. visitors than expected, primarily because of the strong Canadian dollar. "Every jurisdiction is a little different and a little more competitive and a little bit harder to crack into," an analyst said in the October 20, 2005 issue of the *America's Intelligence Wire*. "It's kind of going from Nirvana to the regular world—it just doesn't go that well. Great Canadian is growing, but as they're growing they're changing their stripes and they're getting into different businesses and different jurisdictions that aren't as profitable and not as easy and not as protected."

Revenue remained essentially flat during the second half of the decade, holding at roughly the same level reached in 2006 as Great Canadian eased back on expansion efforts. The last years of the decade were not without activity, however. In 2006 the company thoroughly revamped its casino in Coquitlam, nearly tripling its size and rebranding it as the Boulevard Casino. By the end of the decade, the Boulevard Casino was generating 17 percent of the company's total revenue, second only to the 30 percent generated by the River Rock Casino Resort. The company also redeveloped its Hastings Racecourse facility, finishing the work in 2008. The new 42,000-square-foot facility featured 600 slot machines, a licensed lounge, and a restaurant. Other capital improvement projects were suspended in 2009, but the company ended the decade as a profitable concern poised to reap the benefits of McLeod's bold expansion.

Jeffrey L. Covell

PRINCIPAL SUBSIDIARIES

Flamboro Downs Limited; Georgian Downs Limited; Great American Gaming Corporation; Great Canadian Casinos Inc.; Great Canadian Entertainment Centres Ltd.; Hastings Entertainment Inc.; Metropolitan Entertainment Group; Orangeville Raceway Limited; TBC Teletheatre B.C. (50%).

PRINCIPAL COMPETITORS

Churchill Downs Incorporated; Magna Entertainment Corp.; Harrah's Entertainment, Inc.

FURTHER READING

Erb, George, "BC Firm Rolls Dice on Riverside," *Puget Sound Business Journal*, October 15, 1999, p. 3.

"Great Canadian Gaming Corporation/Media Advisory: Vancouver Saddles Up for the Grand Opening of Its Multi-Million Dollar Entertainment Facility at Hastings Racecourse," *Canadian Corporate News*, August 7, 2008.

"Great Canadian Gaming Corporation Reports Results for 2004: A Profitable Year Full of Growth, Acquisitions and Opportunities," *Canadian Corporate News*, March 8, 2005.

"Great Canadian Gaming Corporation: River Rock Casino Resort," *Canadian Corporate News*, June 22, 2004.

Milicia, Joe, "A Winning Streak Ends: Great Canadian Gaming's Plans Hit a Snag," *America's Intelligence Wire*, October 20, 2005.

The Heritage Foundation

214 Massachusetts Ave NE
Washington, D.C. 20002-4999
U.S.A.
Telephone: (202) 546-4400
Fax: (202) 546-8328
Web site: http://www.heritage.org

Nonprofit Organization
Incorporated: 1971 as Analysis and Research Association
Employees: 244
Operating Revenues: $63.57 million (2008)
NAICS: 813920 Professional Organizations

■ ■ ■

The Heritage Foundation is widely recognized as one of the most influential public policy centers, both in the United States and around the world. A not-for-profit think tank, Heritage (as it is more commonly known) uses funds from private and corporate donors to promote conservative values. Intent on expanding its work beyond Capitol Hill, Heritage has made an admirable foray into a variety of social media outlets. William E. Simon, quoting historian James A. Smith, wrote, "Heritage is the salesman and promoter of ideas par excellence."

EARLY BEGINNINGS

Heritage was the brainchild of two young congressional staffers in the early 1970s, Paul Weyrich and Edwin (Ed) J. Feulner. Weyrich and Feulner both noticed the need for a conservative public policy center to rival the powerful, liberal Brookings Institution. There were already two well-known conservative think tanks in the nation (the American Enterprise Institute, or AEI, and the Center for Strategic Initiatives at Georgetown University) but due to their distance from Capitol Hill and their insistent coverage of long-range policy over immediate current events, they were unable to influence legislation. Furthermore, the two centers were divided by their respective concentrations of domestic and international policy studies.

Convinced of the need for a comprehensive conservative think tank, Weyrich, along with fellow conservatives Victor Fediay, an analyst at the Library of Congress; James Lucier, an assistant to Senator Strom Thurmond; and Fritz Rench, a Wisconsin businessman, drafted a business proposal and attempted to find corporate support. They met with little success, however, until beer magnate Joseph Coors began to express interest in becoming more politically engaged. Weyrich's group persuaded Coors to invest in their vision of a new public policy institution. With Coors's investment, the Analysis and Research Association (ARA) was formed, with Lucier serving as president.

ARA did not last long, however. Although its members were passionate and dedicated, they were not unified, as Joseph Coors recalled to Lee Edwards in *The Power of Ideas: The Heritage at 25 Years.* Frustrated with the dissonance within the organization, as well as alarmed by the prospect of being the sole corporate sponsor, Coors told Weyrich to reconfigure the organization or risk losing it.

COMPANY PERSPECTIVES

Founded in 1973, The Heritage Foundation is a research and educational institution, a think tank, whose mission is to formulate and promote conservative public policies based on the principles of free enterprise, limited government, individual freedom, traditional American values, and a strong national defense.

It did not take Weyrich long to find a new answer. The dormant Robert M. Schuchman Memorial Foundation needed new funding and a new direction, which, with the assistance of Coors, Weyrich could provide. Shortly after his discussion with Coors, the reconstituted Schuchman Foundation opened its offices on Massachusetts Avenue. Weyrich served as its first president, with Coors, Jack Wilson, and Ed Feulner joining him on the board.

As it turned out, older members of the board were less eager to affect legislative processes as directly as Weyrich and Feulner desired, and often opted instead for more traditional approaches to policy, such as conferences and paper publication. With the increasing divide over direction on the board, it appeared at first as though a simple split would be possible: Schuchman would be reconstituted again as a public-interest law center, while a separate public policy center would be created. By February 16, 1973, the Heritage Foundation was formally incorporated, with Weyrich serving as its first president.

Nevertheless, soon afterward, Heritage became formally divorced from the Schuchman Foundation. In November 1973, Coors announced that he, Weyrich, Feulner, and Wilson were resigning from the board. Almost immediately afterward, Heritage began operating under its new tax-exempt status, working in the old Schuchman Foundation offices, while they moved to offices near the Supreme Court. Within 18 months, the Schuchman Foundation was nearly nonexistent.

SEARCH FOR A PRESIDENT

Heritage could have easily been left to the same fate. When the Watergate scandal shook the Republican Party in 1974, Weyrich, the ever-ready activist, left Heritage to start the Committee for the Survival of a Free Congress. Jerry P. James was picked to succeed him, but as Edwards wrote, it was soon evident that he was not the ideal candidate for the job, and moreover, he was eager to return to his home state of Oklahoma. Once again, the search for a president resumed, and by June 1975, Frank J. Walton was found. Walton, former secretary of business and transportation under the gubernatorial Reagan cabinet, brought to Heritage a dose of credibility, as well as its first real sense of security. Under Walton's guidance, Heritage's income first passed the $1 million mark in 1976. Additionally, Walton launched the first direct-mail fund-raising for Heritage, which, in its first run, produced several thousand donors. During this time, Heritage also moved to a larger location, a renovated movie theater just off C Street.

Despite these triumphs, Walton was not planning on staying long. Upon first coming to Heritage, he had told the board that he would stay for two years, and not longer. Too soon, Heritage was once again looking for a leader. This time, conversely, the choice was clear.

A member of the board since 1973 and acting corporate secretary since 1975, Feulner was selected as the new president. In addition to his direct involvement in the foundation, Feulner also had a decade of Capitol Hill work, election into the prestigious Mont Pelerin Society, and his M.B.A. from the Wharton School of Commerce and Finance (Feulner would go on to earn his Ph.D. in political science from the University of Edinburgh while serving as Heritage's president).

Under Feulner, Heritage flourished. Feulner came in with ambitious goals for the Foundation, and with every intention of accomplishing them. Above all, Feulner wanted to establish Heritage as a significant force on Capitol Hill, and the site of the new conservative coalition. In order to accomplish this, almost immediately after his June 1, 1977 succession to president, Feulner hired several new key players. Among these was Hugh C. Newton, whom Feulner charged with the establishment of a public relations department, and Willa Johnson, responsible for creating the Heritage Resource Bank and the subsequent core of all things conservative.

One of Feulner's most decisive hires was Phillip N. (Phil) Truluck, a longtime associate of Feulner at the Republican Study Committee, and newly named director of research for Heritage. Under Truluck's command, Feulner hoped to reinvent research departments, to create a department that could quickly and consistently condense the most complicated issues of the day into easily read articles and papers. This was the fruition of the early dream held by Feulner and Weyrich and quickly became the format of policy analysis that all think tanks would use. Truluck would later go on to serve as Heritage's chief operating officer.

KEY DATES

1971: Analysis and Research Association (ARA) opens with funding from Joseph Coors.
1972: ARA reconstitutes under the Robert M. Schuchman Memorial Foundation.
1973: The Heritage Foundation is formally incorporated.
1980: *Mandate for Leadership* is completed and handed to newly elected President Ronald Reagan.
1989: The Ronald Reagan Chair in Public Policy is established.
1991: Heritage joins the culture war with the release of its study, "The Index of Leading Cultural Indicators."
2008: Heritage launches "Leadership for America" campaign.

Within the first 18 months under Feulner's leadership, Heritage increased its budget to $2.8 million and expanded its financial grassroots supporters to more than 120,000. Corporate support was on the rise as well, and Heritage could now boast an array of well-known supporters, including General Motors, Pfizer, and Sears Roebuck. By 1979, Heritage was receiving donations from 87 corporations, and its budget topped $4 million. Heritage's rapid rise to prominence, and its increasing monetary security, readied the foundation for what would be its largest challenge at that time.

MANDATE FOR LEADERSHIP

With the 1970s coming to a close, Heritage grew increasingly confident that a conservative revolution would dawn with the election of a new president. Well aware of the challenges that the nation's new leader would face, Heritage set out to produce a manual to aid the incoming president in his duties. The final product, *Mandate for Leadership: Policy Management in a Conservative Administration*, was roughly the size of Tolstoy's *War and Peace*, and was finished in just under a year.

Heritage's success with the project did not go unnoticed. Early on, Charles Heatherly, a key force behind the manual, wrote to both the Carter-Mondale and Reagan-Bush campaigns, offering to meet with them about the project. Carter's team refused, but Ronald Reagan was enthusiastic from the beginning. Thus, less than two days after Reagan's election in

November 1980, Heritage personally delivered copies of *Mandate* to top Reagan officials, and soon after, Reagan was handing out copies at his first board meeting. Later, as Reagan began to staff his administration, he often turned to the writers of *Mandate*, reasoning that if one was able to write a book on how to run a government agency, that person was certainly capable of running it. Nearly 20 Heritage staffers joined the Reagan administration, a partnership that was to last long into the future.

Mandate set the tone of Heritage for many years to come and established the foundation as one of the premier intellectual resources on Capitol Hill. When in 1985 Heritage published its second edition of *Mandate* (*Mandate for Leadership II: Continuing the Conservative Revolution*), the book was lauded by the press. According to Edwards's records, the *New York Times* called it "the hottest ticket in town." With Reagan's reelection certain, *Mandate II* addressed the conservative action that could be taken under a conservative administration. Even after Reagan's two terms in office, Heritage continued the message of *Mandate* with two more editions, *Mandate for Leadership III: Policy Strategies for the 1990s* (1988) and *Mandate for Leadership IV: Turning Ideas into Action* (1997). However, rather than focusing on the executive branch, the latter two *Mandates* turned their attention to "retraining" the federal government's spending habits and emphasizing the importance of legislative initiative within the House and Senate.

After the success of *Mandate*, it was decided that Heritage needed to be as physically present in Washington as it was intellectually. In 1981, with the purchase of the eight-story, former Annex of the Library of Congress, Heritage's place inside the beltway was set in stone. The new building, located on Massachusetts Avenue, provided more than enough room for the staff of 100 plus. By the summer of 1983 the building was bought, renovated, and ready to open, all for a little over $9 million.

MAJOR PUBLICATIONS

Mandate, and its successive editions, was just the beginning of Heritage's broad success with media outlets, and surprisingly, its next major achievement was actually in a realm that had been purposely avoided from the start: domestic, particularly cultural, policy.

Since the foundation of Heritage, cultural policy, and all the controversy encompassed within it, had been purposely avoided. However, at the urging of its corporate and grassroots sponsors (who, at the time, numbered above 140,000), Heritage reconsidered its position and soon hired former Secretary of Education

William J. Bennett as Distinguished Fellow in Cultural Policy Studies in 1991. That hire soon proved advantageous to Heritage in 1993, when Bennett along with Empower America and the Free Congress Foundation published a 22-page report titled "The Index of Leading Cultural Indicators."

Less than one year later, in 1995, Heritage released its third major best seller, *The Index of Economic Freedom*. Originally suggested by renowned economist Milton Friedman, the *Index* measured the correlation between a country's economic freedom and its growth or reduction. The first *Index*, coauthored by Brian T. Johnson and Thomas P. Sheehy, examined the economies of over 100 countries, based on over a dozen factors, including trade and taxation policies, capital flow and foreign investments, and property rights. Tied for first were Hong Kong and Singapore. The United States came in at number four, falling in later years to number eight.

Perhaps one of the most prescient publications of Heritage, though, was an article that appeared in October 1979. The article, written by James Phillips and titled "Afghanistan: The Soviet Quagmire," predicted that before long, the Soviet Union would have no choice but to invade the increasingly rebellious Afghanistan. Within 32 days after the article's publication, the Soviet Union did invade, and the Phillips article was lauded as prophetic.

Under Feulner's directions, Heritage began to produce a new magazine titled *Policy Review*, which quickly moved to the top ranks of policy journals. The journal officially became a publication of the Hoover Institution of Stanford University in 2001.

The intellectual vigor of Heritage became further apparent with the hire of Burton Yale Pines as vice president of research in 1981. Pines, who had once been *Time* magazine's youngest foreign correspondent, multiplied the research output of Heritage from a mere 52 papers a year in 1980 to over 250 five years later. Under Pines's watchful eye, Heritage became one of the most sought-after research organizations, especially by the Reagan administration.

REAGAN & THE HERITAGE FOUNDATION

President Reagan's association with the Heritage Foundation did not end with his acceptance of the *Mandate*. Throughout his presidency, he frequently sought the advice of top Heritage researchers, and although Heritage did not always agree with the choices that the Reagan administration made, the two groups remained close associates.

In the spring of 1989, with funds raised by Ambassador Holland (Holly) Coors, and a grant from the Grover M. Herrmann Foundation of Chicago, Heritage established the Ronald Reagan Chair in Public Policy. This was the only chair that was ever officially approved by the former president. Since inception, Reagan's own attorney general, Edwin (Ed) Meese III, held the post.

LOOKING TO THE FUTURE

Entering the 2000s, Heritage continued to market itself through a variety of mediums. Heritage experts frequently appeared on television shows and radio shows internationally. In fact, Heritage hosted two of the most popular conservative radio programs in the nation directly from its own radio station, *The Laura Ingraham Show* and *Sean Hannity*. Heritage's first foray into the blogosphere began with Townhall.com (later passed on to Salem Communications Corporation), a creation that gradually evolved into Heritage's own private blog, The Foundry. Finally, Heritage aggrandized its presence on the social media scene, at sites including Facebook, YouTube, and Twitter. Such aggressive and modern marketing was not just aimed at broadening Heritage's media base. It also served to establish Heritage as more influential than other large think tanks in Washington, including Cato, AEI, and Brookings.

Within the walls of its primary Massachusetts Avenue office (which received a facelift in 2008), Heritage also looked broadly into the future. In 2008, Heritage began implementing 10 initiatives titled "Leadership for America." These initiatives were: First Principles, American Leadership, Education, Energy & Environment, Entitlements, Entrepreneurship, Family & Religion, Health Care, Protect America, and Rule of Law. Heritage hoped that pursuit of its 10 goals would continue to draw new and old conservatives together, both in Washington and around the globe.

Laura Rydberg

PRINCIPAL DIVISIONS

Domestic Policy; Government Relations; The Kathryn and Shelby Cullom Davis Institute for International Studies; Information Technology; Strategic Initiatives.

PRINCIPAL COMPETITORS

Brookings Institution; Cato Institute; The Manhattan Institute; The Hoover Institution; The Economic Policy Institute.

FURTHER READING

"The Charge of the Think-Tanks," *Economist*, February 15, 2003, p. 33.
Edwards, Lee, "Ash Heap or Mountain Top?" *National Review*,

January 25, 2010, pp. 48–49.

———, *The Power of Ideas: The Heritage Foundation at 25 Years*, Ottawa, IL: Jameson Books, Inc., 1997.

Posen, Adam S., "Think Tanks: Who's Hot and Who's Not,"

International Economy, Fall 2002, pp. 8+.

Simon, William E., "An American Institution," Foreword in *The Power of Ideas: The Heritage Foundation at 25 Years*, by Lee Edwards, Ottawa, IL: Jameson Books, Inc., 1997.

Hillyard, Inc.

—■—

302 North 4th Street
St. Joseph, Missouri 64501
U.S.A.
Telephone: (816) 233-1321
Toll Free: (800) 861-0256
Fax: (800) 861-0256
Web site: http://www.hillyard.com

Private Company
Incorporated: 1907 as Hillyard Disinfectant Co.
Employees: 700
Sales: $55 million (2009 est.)
NAICS: 325612 Polish and Other Sanitation Good
      Manufacturing

■ ■ ■

Hillyard, Inc., is a family-owned company based in St. Joseph, Missouri, that manufactures and distributes a wide variety of institutional and household cleaning and related supplies. The company is best known for its wooden gym floor treatments and its contributions to popularizing the game of basketball. Other Hillyard products include aerosol air fresheners and sanitizers; carpet and floor cleaners; disinfectants and deodorizers; sanitizing products for foodservice use as well as drain maintenance products; and products to care for stone and concrete floors.

Additionally, Hillyard offers housekeeping equipment, including carpet and wet-dry vacuums, automatic scrubbers, extractors, floor buffers, pressure washers, and air movers. Hillyard products are sold in all 50 states and much of Canada through a network of corporate and independent distributors. The company owns about 35 warehouses and its products are kept in 125 strategically located independent warehouses. Also affiliated with the company is Hillyard University, School of Facility Management. Its program is geared toward facility managers, covering not only cleaning products and equipment, but also budgeting, time management, safety and compliance, human resources, communication skills, and team building. Hillyard is owned and led by fourth-generation family members with participation from a fifth.

FOUNDER MOVES TO ST. JOSEPH: 1891

Hillyard Inc. was founded by Newton Scott Hillyard. Born in 1867 or 1868, he was raised on an Iowa farm. In 1891 he struck out on his own with little more than $5 in his pockets but blessed with an inventive mind. He settled in St. Joseph, Missouri, a transportation nexus and bustling town of the 1800s. Working during the day to support his growing family, Hillyard spent his evenings developing maintenance products as well as miscellaneous inventions.

During his lifetime he would receive dozens of patents for such items as a portable standing liquid-soap dispenser, a nursery soap dispenser, a dust mop with a head that was completely covered by the swab to prevent the accidental marring of a floor, a combined mop and wringer, a cleaning wiper, toilet paper and paper towel dispensers, a trash receptacle, a mechanical desk calendar, an ink blotter holder, an electric fan "air spreader" attachment, a key carrying container, a revolver to fire gas-producing shells, an automatic rifle with a banana clip, a police patrol car stop signal, and a pair of manacles for police use. He would make his mark, however, with his work as a chemist, developing disinfectants and cleaning products.

In 1907, despite the country lapsing into a depression, Hillyard quit his job and started a chemical manufacturing business in his home under the name Hillyard Disinfectant Co., which would later become known as Hillyard Chemical Company. It was little more than a one-man band, with Hillyard playing multiple parts, including chemist and researcher, salesman, accountant, and president. He also bought a used milk wagon and a pair of ponies to act as delivery boy. The company enjoyed immediate success, due in large measure to his commitment to customer service, allowing Hillyard to move the business to a small building located on Messanie Street in St. Joseph.

"SHINE-ALL" DEBUTS: 1915

It was with wooden gym floor treatments that Hillyard made his mark. One of his sons, Marvin R. Hillyard, demonstrated a talent for basketball and persuaded his father to sponsor a team. He did, but ever the inventor, N. S. Hillyard grew displeased with the condition of the gym floors that relied on oil dressings and caused the players to slip and incur unnecessary injuries. He went to work on the problem and developed a coating that not only provided sure footing, but was long-lasting and easy to maintain. Around 1915 he began selling the treatment under the name "Shine-All." The trademark depicted the name against a background of a radiating sun.

Hillyard products became better known for the trademarked checkerboard design that continues to adorn its products. According to company lore, the origins of the Hillyard Checkerboard dated to a trip N. S. Hillyard made to New York City, where in the 1920s the first Checker taxicabs were introduced. Taken by the checkerboard design that adorned the side of the cabs,

he appropriated it for Hillyard products and it became the symbol for the company and found its way onto all labels, packaging, and promotional materials. The company also made use of a cartoon figure named Newt, an allusion to the founder's first name, who wore a tall hat reminiscent of the company's signature 55-gallon container. The hat was also adorned with two bands of the checkerboard pattern. While Newt did not stand the test of time, the Hillyard Checkerboard did, and over the years the company assiduously defended and protected the trademark.

The commitment to basketball grew deeper for N. S. Hillyard. His son Marvin was inducted into military service during World War I and died overseas. Like many in the military and in civilian ranks, he succumbed at the age of 20 to the influenza pandemic that swept the world in 1918. Marvin Hillyard had wanted to develop a basketball team that was a national powerhouse, and in honor of his son, N. S. Hillyard committed the money to make that dream a reality. Another son, Robert B. Hillyard, took over as manager of the team, known as the Hillyard Shine Alls.

In 1920 the company began building a new plant and office building that would have one unusual feature. On the top floor N. S. Hillyard installed a 90-foot by 140-foot wood floor gymnasium flanked on either side by tiers of bleachers. The $30,000 gym opened in 1922. It was at the time the largest gym floor west of the Mississippi River. Aside from serving as the home of the basketball team, the gym was a proving ground for new wood gym floor finishes and seals Hillyard developed.

HILLYARD SPONSORS CHAMPIONSHIP TEAMS: 1926–27

In the 1920s the Hillyard Shine Alls grew to become the championship team that Marvin Hillyard had envisioned. Although college basketball was popular, professional basketball, aside from touring clubs such as the legendary Harlem Globetrotters, was still in its infancy. The American Basketball League was launched in 1925 by the owners of the Chicago Bears and Washington Redskins of the National Football League, which was itself far from established, and folded a few years later. Company teams, including the Shine Alls, provided ex-college players with an opportunity to continue playing while providing a steady income. In 1923 University of Kansas star player Forrest DeBernardi was hired by Hillyard, and part of his job was to manage the Shine Alls. He led the club to a pair of Amateur Athletic Union (AAU) national championships in 1926 and 1927. He then took a job with Cook Paint

KEY DATES

1907: N. S. Hillyard forms Hillyard Disinfectant Co.
1926: Hillyard Shine Alls win AAU basketball championship.
1936: N. S. Hillyard dies.
1973: George W. Roth, who had joined the company following World War II, retires.
2007: Hillyard celebrates centennial.

Company in Kansas City, directing that team to AAU championships the next two seasons.

The success of the Shine Alls was good for Hillyard's business. The brand exposure helped to drive the sale of Shine-All, which became the wood floor treatment of choice for gymnasiums of all types from high schools and colleges to grade schools, community centers, and civic arenas. The Hillyard family's dedication to basketball was far from fleeting, however. Not only was N. S. Hillyard well respected by players, coaches, and sports writers, his descendants continued to support basketball organizations including the Basketball Hall of Fame, where in the main lobby a permanent exhibit depicts the Hillyard family's contributions to the rise of basketball.

FOUNDER DIES: 1936

N. S. Hillyard died of a heart attack in March 1936 at the age of 69. He left behind a company that he had built into a national concern. Not only did he pioneer a number of maintenance products, he led the way on education as the products became more advanced. To help train the custodians who were the main users of Hillyard products, to maximize the potential of his products, he teamed up with the Colorado State Teachers College in Greeley, Colorado, to create the first professional maintenance school. This effort laid the foundation for the future Hillyard University. In addition, Hillyard developed training programs for his own salespeople and service staff to ensure they kept up with new products and procedures to help train customer custodial staffs.

N. S. Hillyard was succeeded as president by his son Robert. He was in turn succeeded by George W. Roth, who had married into the family. After returning from service in the infantry in the Pacific during World War II, he married Jacklyn Hillyard in 1946. A year later he went to work for the Hillyard companies and ultimately became president. He retired in 1973 and eventually his son, Robert W. Roth, would become president, representing the fourth generation of family ownership.

The generations that followed N. S Hillyard continued to develop new formulas and introduce new products. They also expanded the company's distribution system. To deliver the Hillyard products, horses and wagons gave way to Plymouth business coupes in the 1930s and trucks in the 1950s. Hillyard turned to rail transport in the early 1960s for five years before returning to trucks as a primary means of transport. By the time Hillyard celebrated its centennial in 2007, the company was operating a private fleet that included 18 tractor-trailers that operated out of its main facility in Saint Joseph. Another 85 to 90 straight trucks served the three-dozen company warehouses and 125 independent warehouses that delivered Hillyard products to customers across the United States and much of Canada. The company also took advantage of its hauling capacity to bring return loads to other St. Joseph companies.

CENTENNIAL: STILL FAMILY OWNED

After 100 years in business, Hillyard controlled 150 formulas and offered 300 products, but it also kept up with changes in the marketplace. In the early 2000s Hillyard introduced a number of environmentally friendly "green" products. Ironically, one of its oldest products, Shine-All, now known as Super Shine-All, which had not been reformulated in half a century, met the Green Seal Certified standards without requiring any changes. As a result, Hillyard was well positioned to take advantage of new laws that were enacted across the country requiring the use of green cleaning products in schools. One such law went into effect in Missouri with the 2009–10 year. Many of Hillyard's customers, such as the local St. Joseph school district, were essentially in compliance already because of the reformulation of Hillyard products.

By 2010 Hillyard was generating an estimated $55 million in annual revenues. The company's truck fleet was capable of handling almost all of its business, with only 15 percent of its transportation needs handled by outside carriers. There was a chance that Hillyard would launch a separate trucking operation. While most family-owned companies were fortunate to make it past the second generation, Hillyard was ready to pass the torch to a fifth generation. There was every reason to believe that the company would continue to prosper well into its second century.

Ed Dinger

PRINCIPAL SUBSIDIARIES

Hillyard Enterprises, Inc.; Hillyard Industries, Inc.

PRINCIPAL COMPETITORS

Ecolab, Inc.; The Procter & Gamble Company; S.C. Johnson & Son, Inc.

FURTHER READING

Hall, Jennifer, "Hillyard Begins Century Celebration," *St. Joseph News-Press*, September 9, 2006.

———, "There's Green in Going Green," *St. Joseph News-Press*, February 14, 2010.

Hull, Nancy, "Striving for a Green Clean," *St. Joseph News-Press*, July 21, 2008.

Mires, Susan, "A Century of Clean," *St. Joseph News-Press*, September 16, 2007.

Petty, Gary, "Centennial Celebration," *Fleet Owner*, February 1, 2007.

Scherer, Ray, "Former Hillyard Executive Dies at 91," *St. Joseph News-Press*, February 3, 2010.

"Sponsor of Champ Basketball Teams Dies in St. Joseph," *Jefferson City Post-Tribune*, March 26, 1936, p. 7.

Hormel Foods
Corporation

---

1 Hormel Place
Austin, Minnesota 55912-3680
U.S.A.
Telephone: (507) 437-5611
Toll Free: (800) 523-4635
Fax: (507) 437-5489
Web site: http://www.hormelfoods.com

Public Company
Founded: 1891 as George A. Hormel & Company
Incorporated: 1901
Employees: 18,600
Sales: $6.53 billion (2009)
Stock Exchanges: New York
Ticker Symbol: HRL
NAICS: 311412 Frozen Specialty Food Manufacturing; 311421 Fruit and Vegetable Canning; 311422 Specialty Canning; 311423 Dried and Dehydrated Food Manufacturing; 311611 Animal (Except Poultry) Slaughtering; 311612 Meat Processed from Carcasses; 311615 Poultry Processing; 311830 Tortilla Manufacturing; 311919 Other Snack Food Manufacturing; 311999 All Other Miscellaneous Food Manufacturing

■ ■ ■

Hormel Foods Corporation is a diversified producer of branded, packaged-food products, including hams, bacon, franks, luncheon meats, turkey products, stews, chilies, hash, meat spreads, microwavable entrees, bouillons, and a variety of ethnic food items. Hormel has successfully evolved from meatpacker to value-added food manufacturer over its more than 115 years in business. In addition to its flagship SPAM brand, Hormel also produces and sells products under such brands as Black Label, Chi-Chi's, Cure 81, Di Lusso, Dinty Moore, Doña María, Farmer John, Herb-Ox, Herdez, House of Tsang, Jennie-O Turkey Store, Kid's Kitchen, Marrakesh Express, Mary Kitchen, Peloponnese, Stagg, Valley Fresh, and, of course, Hormel. Nearly three dozen of the company's brands rank either number one or two in their respective categories. Hormel's Specialty Foods division caters to foodservice customers, including restaurants, healthcare facilities, and retailers, offering such products as sugar and sugar substitutes, creamers, salt and pepper, sauces and salad dressings, dessert and drink mixes, and nutritional food products and supplements.

Although Hormel focuses mainly on the U.S. market, with 95 percent of its sales generated at home, it also actively markets its products overseas, through either subsidiaries or joint ventures, with the larger markets including Australia, Canada, China, England, Japan, Mexico, and Micronesia. The Hormel Foundation, which was formed in 1941 by the founder of the company and his son, maintains an ownership stake of about 48 percent, an arrangement that has kept Hormel Foods an independent company.

FOUNDING A MEATPACKING BUSINESS IN LATE 19TH CENTURY

Hormel's history began when the company's founder, George A. Hormel, borrowed $500 in 1887 to form a retail meat market and pork packing business with his partner, Albrect Friedrich. Hormel established a powerful precedent when he refused to be complacent about their early success and pushed ahead with his plans to set up and operate a packinghouse. He and Friedrich agreed to disband their partnership in September 1891, and in November of that same year Hormel and employee George Petersen had transformed a small, abandoned creamery in Austin, Minnesota, into a meat-packing plant complete with smokehouse and slaughterhouse, operating under the name George A. Hormel & Company. In addition, he opened the Hormel Provision Market to sell his products. It quickly became the town's largest and most successful retail meat business.

Faced with low profit margins and competition from large meatpackers who could afford state-of-the-art refrigeration facilities, Hormel made expansion his first priority. Within the first few years his two brothers and other members of his family had joined the business, allowing George Hormel to put down his cleaver and devote himself exclusively to management. In 1899 Hormel spent $40,000 to upgrade his facilities, building a new refrigeration facility, new pumps and engines, an electric elevator, smokehouses, and a slaughterhouse. In 1901 the company was incorporated and also acquired several acres of adjacent land, and two years later it

constructed additional facilities such as a casing processing room and a machine shop. In 1908 it also opened a new office facility, which the company used for more than 60 years.

During this period of expansion Hormel also worked to refine and improve its products. In 1903 it registered its first patent, "Dairy Brand," with the U.S. Patent Office. In 1915 Hormel began to produce several lines of dry sausage, a product that proved particularly popular with ethnic consumers.

In an effort to increase sales volume, Hormel sent salesmen outside of Austin to set up branches and distribution centers. By 1920 the company operated branches in Minneapolis, Duluth, St. Paul, San Antonio, Dallas, Atlanta, Birmingham, and Chicago. In 1905 George Hormel traveled to England to establish the foundation for an export business. Between 1905 and the end of World War I, exports grew to constitute about a third of the company's yearly volume.

Hormel & Company participated fully in the country's World War I effort. To control the price and supply of meats, the government regulated the meat-packing industry. Hormel expanded its labor force and the hours worked to help satisfy the increased demand for meat both at home and abroad. With so many American men, including George Hormel's son Jay, away at war, the company employed women for the first time in its history. In addition to producing meat for the war effort, Hormel employees bought Liberty bonds and donated an hour's wages per day to the Red Cross.

SURVIVING SCANDAL FOLLOWING WORLD WAR I

When Jay Hormel returned from the war, he rejoined the company and uncovered a scandal that very nearly put Hormel out of business. The company's assistant controller, "Cy" Thomson, had embezzled more than $1 million from the company and had channeled it into several poultry farms. The company had borrowed $3 million that year for operating expenses and hoped to repay the sum at the end of the year. At year-end, however, they were unable to do so, and George Hormel had to confront his bankers and persuade them to extend the loan.

The embezzlement scandal provided George Hormel with additional incentive to fortify his company. He did so by arranging for more reliable capital management, by dismissing unproductive employees, and by continuing to develop new products. In 1926, after years of research, Hormel introduced "Hormel Flavor-Sealed Ham," the world's first canned ham. Two years later, Hormel & Company went public.

KEY DATES

1891: George A. Hormel begins operating a meat-packing plant in Austin, Minnesota, forming George A. Hormel & Company.

1901: Company is incorporated.

1926: Company introduces the world's first canned ham.

1928: Hormel goes public.

1935: Dinty Moore beef stew is introduced.

1937: Hormel launches SPAM luncheon meat.

1941: Company founder and his son form the Hormel Foundation, which now controls the company through holdings of its capital stock.

1985–86: A bitter, nationally publicized strike takes place at the company's Austin plant.

1986: Hormel acquires Jennie-O Foods, a turkey-processing company.

1993: Company changes its name to Hormel Foods Corporation.

2001: Turkey Store Company is acquired in the largest purchase in company history.

In 1929 Jay C. Hormel became the company's second president, and his father, George, became chairman of the board. Under the new president the company continued to expand its product line. Some of the company's best-known products, Dinty Moore beef stew (1935), Hormel chili (1936), and SPAM luncheon meat (1937), entered the market and became extremely popular.

The company survived a bitter labor strike in 1933, during which disgruntled union employees, armed with clubs, physically removed Jay Hormel from the company's general offices and shut off the plant's refrigeration system. The two parties reached a compromise within three days. Soon, the company gained recognition for its innovative labor relations policies. Jay Hormel developed the "Annual Wage Plan," under which employees were paid weekly, their working hours fluctuated according to need, employment was considered permanent, and workers were guaranteed a year's notice before they could be terminated. In addition, the company introduced profit sharing, merit pay, a pension plan, and a joint earnings plan. Under this plan, in 1983 Hormel employees received more than $4 million.

In 1941, during his tenure as president, Jay Hormel cofounded (with his father) the Hormel Foundation, which controlled the company through holdings of its capital stock, and thus served as a bulwark against unwanted takeover attempts, and which also served "religious, charitable, scientific, literary, or educational purposes." Since 1945, a prime activity of this foundation has been funding the Hormel Institute, an Austin-based research unit of the University of Minnesota that has conducted highly respected research on fats and other lipids and how they affect human life as well as on cancer prevention and control.

SPAM BECOMING STAPLE DURING WORLD WAR II

During World War II, Hormel & Company became a "war facility" and once again increased its meat production. By 1945 Hormel was selling 65 percent of its total production to the U.S. government. SPAM, Hormel's canned spiced ham and ground pork product, became the staple of U.S. forces throughout the world. In 1941 Hormel was producing 15 million cans a week, and the government was distributing it under the lend-lease program. Overfamiliarity bred substantial contempt and ridicule during and after the war, but the product demonstrated uncanny resilience. By 1959, Hormel had sold more than one billion cans of SPAM.

When George Hormel died in 1946, Jay Hormel took his place as chairman of the board of directors and H. H. Corey became Hormel's third president. During the eight years under Corey, the company continued to renovate and upgrade its existing plants and acquire new facilities. It purchased several new packing operations, located in Mitchell, South Dakota; Fort Dodge, Iowa; and Fremont, Nebraska. With the wartime restrictions on tin now lifted and with a tremendous demand for Hormel's canned meat products, the company improved its canning facilities in its Dallas and Houston plants and arranged for independent canning companies to manufacture Hormel products. In addition, Hormel made a concerted effort to make better use of its raw material, and in 1947 the company began to produce gelatin from pork skins.

Hormel's product line expanded along with the company's facilities. Mary Kitchen Roast Beef Hash, Corned Beef Hash, and Spaghetti and Beef in Sauce appeared in 1949, along with a new line of meat spreads.

With its constant expansion, the company had to consider how to dispose of its increased waste material. Hormel researchers developed an anaerobic digestive system that removed waste cleanly and efficiently. In 1946 the company financed a $2.25 million sewage system that it shared with the Austin community.

In 1954 Jay Hormel died, and Corey assumed his chair on the board of directors, while R. F. Gray succeeded Corey as president. He held this position for 10 years, during which the company continued to pursue quality and efficiency. Hormel added several more slaughtering, processing, and packing facilities throughout the country, and in 1965 it added a new 75,000-square-foot automated sausage manufacturing building to its Austin plant.

Several new products appeared in this decade as well. In 1960 the company introduced its "Famous Foods of the World" line. The following year Little Sizzlers' sausage entered the market, followed two years later by a fully cooked sausage product, Brown'n Serve. The largest success of the decade, however, was the Hormel Cure 81 Ham, a skinless, boneless, cured ham with the shank removed. It debuted in 1963.

After another decade of progressive growth under two different presidents, M. B. Thompson and I. J. Holton, the directors realized that to remain competitive in the industry, Hormel needed to undertake a wholesale renovation of its Austin plant. In 1975 the company began planning a $100 million state-of-the-art facility, which opened in 1982. At more than a million square feet, it was among the largest and most productive in the industry and featured robotic technology and automatic ham deboners. Hormel continued to diversify its product lines as well, introducing precooked bacon and three new varieties of Perma Fresh luncheon meats. By 1980 Hormel was producing more than 700 different products.

BITTER STRIKE & MOVING AWAY FROM MEATPACKING

Although this new facility was capable of processing more than two million hogs a year and producing more than 200 million pounds of products annually, the industry began to shrink in the 1980s and Hormel began to feel the effects. In the 1980s consumers began to eat less meat, and meat producers for the first time had to struggle to make their products appealing. With a 40 percent increase in the price of hogs, Hormel was pinched. It asked employees to accept wage cuts in Austin of more than $2 an hour. In August 1985 the union decided to strike. A total of 1,500 workers left their jobs. Under the glare of national publicity, striking workers harassed the 700 replacements whom Hormel hired five months later. Five hundred union workers eventually returned to work, under lower pay scales, but the others were either dismissed or forced into early retirement.

The wounds from this bitter strike (which had lasted into early 1986) were slow to heal, but Hormel moved ahead, and under the company's then president, chairman, and CEO, Richard L. Knowlton (who had accepted a $236,000 raise in the midst of the strike), it adjusted to a rapidly changing market by moving away from the traditional meatpacking business and its many problems and concentrating on satisfying consumers' appetites for processed foods.

In an 18-month period in the late 1980s, Hormel introduced 134 new products, including Top Shelf vacuum-packed unrefrigerated meals with a shelf life of 18 months. Knowlton considered this "one of the most important products ever introduced by Hormel. It represents a revolutionary breakthrough in packaging technology and offers consumers a new level of convenience." After acquiring Willmar, Minnesota-based Jennie-O Foods, a turkey-processing company, in late 1986, Hormel went on to acquire a small producer of fresh marinated chicken breast entrees in 1988 and targeted its fish operations for expansion in an effort to exploit the more health-conscious market. With these new and acquired products, Hormel overcame a period of sluggish sales and earnings between 1979 and 1984 to record net earnings of $60.1 million in 1988, up from $29.4 million in 1984.

FOCUSING ON HEALTHFUL, CONVENIENT, ETHNIC FOODS

In the 1990s, Hormel worked hard to react quickly to consumers' increasing appetite for more healthful and more convenient foods as well as ethnic foods. It did so by seeking out targeted acquisitions and through new products and line extensions. The company also sought additional opportunities for international expansion.

Hormel's continuing move away from meatpacking and toward value-added food production was highlighted by the 1992 appointment of Joel W. Johnson as president. Johnson became the first president not to have risen through the Hormel ranks, having been hired away from rival Kraft General Foods. Johnson added the CEO title in 1993, then became chairman of the Hormel board as well upon Knowlton's retirement in 1995.

In 1991 Hormel celebrated 100 years in business. The following year, the three grandsons of George Hormel (George Hormel II, James Hormel, and Thomas Hormel) who held control of the company through the Hormel Foundation, filed suit to attempt to force the foundation to diversify its holdings, which consisted almost entirely of Hormel stock. After an initially favorable ruling, the Hormel heirs eventually lost the suit in 1994. By 1996, the company's decision to repurchase as many as five million shares of Hormel stock was destined to further increase the foundation's Hormel holdings.

Meanwhile, in 1993 the company's own diversification efforts precipitated the first name change in company history: George A. Hormel & Company became Hormel Foods Corporation, a name more reflective of Hormel's food products orientation of the 1980s and 1990s. At the same time, however, the company did not abandon longtime mainstays such as SPAM. Johnson was credited with reviving SPAM sales by repositioning the canned pork mix as a quick and easy base for a "SPAMburger." He called it the "only hamburger made out of ham." The SPAM line was also successfully expanded with low-sodium and light extensions. In 1993 SPAM maintained a stunning 80 percent market share of its sales category.

Hormel aggressively went after the leaner food products category in the early 1990s. In 1992 the company introduced Light & Lean 97 hot dogs, which were 97 percent fat-free and were praised for their taste by *Eaters Digest*, a consumer magazine. Additional Light & Lean 97 products were soon introduced, including all-beef hot dogs, boneless ham, turkey breasts, smoked sausages, and packaged luncheon meats.

The ethnic foods category was an area targeted for expansion in the 1990s primarily through acquisitions. In 1992 the House of Tsang and Oriental Deli brands were acquired, with Dubuque meats and Herb-Ox instant broths and seasonings added the following year. In mid-1995, Hormel purchased from Rockridge Trading Company the Péloponnèse brand, a line of Mediterranean-based specialty foods including olives, olive oil, peppers, stuffed grape leaves, and salad dressings. Later that same year, the assets of Melting Pot Foods were acquired, which featured Po River Valley risotto rice, Marrakesh Express couscous, and Terrazza pasta and beans.

The acquisition of American Institutional Products, Inc., (AIP) in 1994 brought Hormel a presence in the distribution of food products to hospitals, nursing homes, and other healthcare facilities. AIP made instant food thickeners and pureed food products. AIP was later renamed Hormel HealthLabs, Inc.

Hormel also spent heavily to add to and upgrade its facilities in the early to mid-1990s. In 1993 it bought from Rochelle Foods a 1.8-million-head hog processing plant located in Rochelle, Illinois, then spent $4 million in renovating the site. Hormel also spent $15 million to upgrade its Davenport, Iowa, gelatin/proteins plant, and $20 million to expand and renovate its Fremont, Nebraska, hog processing plant. In 1995 alone, the company spent $97.2 million in capital additions and improvements, the most ever in company history.

Meanwhile, in fiscal 1994, Hormel Foods exceeded the $3 billion revenue level for the first time.

LATE-CENTURY INTERNATIONAL EXPANSION

Several of lawsuits involving Hormel made headlines in 1995. Hormel sued Jim Henson Productions over a wild boar named Spa'am that appeared in the movie *Muppet Treasure Island*. Although Hormel contended the character tarnished its SPAM trademark, a circuit judge rejected the argument and said it was legitimate satire. Hormel settled a more serious case out of court when it agreed to pay $7.5 million to settle a class-action suit brought by fish distributors and processors who claimed that Hormel's Farm Fresh Catfish Company and six other catfish wholesalers conspired to fix prices for nearly a decade. While some of the smaller defendants had admitted guilt, neither Hormel nor the other major defendants, ConAgra Inc. and Delta Pride Catfish Inc., admitted responsibility. Late in 1996, Hormel sold Farm Fresh Catfish for an undisclosed sum, taking a $5.4 million charge related to the divestment.

In the mid-1990s, Hormel increasingly looked overseas for growth opportunities, and often turned to joint ventures to pursue foreign revenue as well as domestic sales. After opening sales offices in Hong Kong and Mexico earlier in 1994, Hormel in December of that year joined with Beijing Agriculture Industry and Commerce to form Beijing Hormel Foods Co. In 1996 this venture began constructing a hog processing plant, which was completed in early 1998. The plant could process 300,000 hogs each year and began producing a variety of pork products under the Hormel brand for sale in China. In Mexico, Hormel Alimentos S.A., a joint venture with Grupo Herdez S.A. of Mexico, was formed in 1995 to market U.S.-manufactured Hormel products in Mexico. Another 1995 joint venture was with Darling Downs Bacon Cooperative Association Limited of Australia.

The following year saw additional joint ventures. In January 1996 Hormel and the U.K.-based Patak Spices Ltd. formed Patak's Foods USA to import and market Indian sauces, pastes, pickles, and chutneys in the United States. In July Hormel and Grupo Herdez formed a second joint venture, Herdez Corp., to distribute Mexican foods products in the United States under the Herdez, Búfalo, and Doña María brands. Then in December Hormel spent $64.3 million to purchase a 21.4 percent interest in Campofrio Alimentación, S.A., a food company based in Madrid that sold ham, sausage, and turkey products in Spain, Russia, and Latin America. All of these 1996 activities expanded

Hormel's already extensive presence in the ethnic foods category.

During this same period, the company was not inactive on the domestic front. In October 1996 Hormel acquired Stagg Foods, Inc., maker of the Stagg brand of chili products, for $50 million in cash and stock. In the fall of 1997, Hormel acquired Heartland Foods Co., which operated a 117,000-square-foot plant in Marshall, Minnesota. Under Hormel, the plant began processing whole turkeys and bone-in turkey breasts for sale under the Jennie-O and Heartland brands as well as under private labels. The Heartland acquisition helped boost Jennie-O into position as the top turkey processor in the United States, with production of 855 million pounds of turkey in 1998. Early in 1998, Hormel sold its Davenport, Iowa, gelatin/proteins plant to Goodman Fielder Limited of Sydney, Australia, for $71.4 million. Hormel completed the sale to further its focus on consumer-branded meat and food products.

By fiscal 2000, Hormel Foods had achieved record net sales of $3.68 billion. The 9.5 percent increase over the previous year was fueled in part by a significant upsurge in purchases of nonperishable products, including SPAM, during the final months of 1999 as nervous consumers stocked up in advance of impending Y2K problems that never materialized. The company also recorded a strong profit margin of 4.63 percent, well above the 2.5 to 4 percent margins that prevailed during the early 1990s and more than double the levels of the mid-1980s.

INCREASING ACQUISITION ACTIVITY IN EARLY 21ST CENTURY

Hormel stepped up its acquisition activity during the first years of the 21st century. Two deals bolstered the firm's expanding Hormel HealthLabs unit, which supplied foods to the rapidly growing healthcare portion of the foodservice industry, specializing in modified foods for people with dietary restrictions, such as swallowing difficulties, bowel problems, and diabetes. In December 2000 Hormel acquired Quakerstown, Pennsylvania-based Cliffdale Farms, a supplier of texture-modified foods with annual sales of $3.4 million. Then in April of the following year, Hormel paid about $65 million to Imperial Sugar Company for the nutritional products division of Diamond Crystal Brands. The acquired unit, which had annual sales of about $50 million, produced more than 170 nutritional products, including thickened ready-to-serve juices, frozen pureed meats, fortified shakes and breakfast mixes, and ready-to-serve instant breakfasts. These acquisitions helped propel Hormel HealthLabs past $100 million in annual revenues.

Hormel's largest deal, however, and in fact the largest in company history, was the purchase of Jerome Foods, Inc., which did business as the Turkey Store Company, in February 2001 for $334.4 million. Based in Barron, Wisconsin, the Turkey Store processed about 375 million pounds of turkey annually and had revenues of $309 million for the year ending in February 2000. The Turkey Store was merged into Jennie-O to form Jennie-O Turkey Store (JOTS), which ranked as the largest processor of turkey in the world, processing more than 1.2 billion pounds per year. Heading JOTS was Jerry Jerome, the son of the founder of the Turkey Store and that firm's CEO and chairman. During fiscal 2001, JOTS accounted for 20 percent of overall Hormel Foods revenues and 22 percent of operating profits.

By this time, Hormel also had ended, for the most part, its efforts to curtail alternate uses of the term *spam*, most notably its increasingly common usage as a term meaning junk e-mail. This latter meaning apparently had been inspired by a sketch by the British comedy troupe Monty Python in which several Vikings repeatedly chant "Spam," in the process drowning out normal conversation. Hormel eventually gave up fighting the use of the term *spam* for junk e-mail but emphasized that the brand should be rendered in all capital letters, SPAM, while the junk e-mail term should appear in lowercase, spam. The company continued to object to and to discourage the use of the luncheon meat's image in connection with junk e-mail.

An important initiative of the early 21st century was the continuing drive to convert the company's fresh meat products from commodity to branded, value-added products. This program began in the mid-1990s with the introduction of the Hormel Always Tender line of marinated, flavored, and precut pork loins and tenderloins. In April 2002 Hormel and the Excel Corporation subsidiary of Cargill, Incorporated created Precept Foods, LLC, a joint venture that began marketing fresh, prepackaged beef and pork under the Hormel Always Tender brand. The venture, by leveraging Excel's position as the second-largest beef processor in the United States, enabled Hormel to get into the value-added beef market without having to invest a great deal of resources. Excel later changed its name to Cargill Meat Solutions.

In December 2002 Hormel acquired Diamond Crystal Brands from Imperial Sugar for $115 million in stock. Diamond Crystal was a maker of soups, beverages, sauces, seasonings, and gravy and dessert mixes primarily for foodservice customers and had annual sales of about $160 million. Hormel delved further into the foodservice sector via the July 2003 purchase of Century Foods International of Sparta, Wisconsin, for $116.5 million. These two operations were subsumed within a newly created Specialty Foods division, which also included Hormel HealthLabs.

Hormel benefited in the 2003 and 2004 fiscal years from the low-carb diet craze among U.S. consumers, which boosted demand for protein-rich meats such as pork, beef, and turkey. At the same time, higher raw material costs from such commodities as meat and grain put pressure on the firm's bottom line. In response, Hormel in the spring of 2004 announced plans to raise the prices of hundreds of its packaged foods from 4.5 percent to 6.5 percent, its first such general price increase since 2000. That same year, the company divested its minority stake in Campofrio Alimentación, and its JOTS unit introduced Oven Ready frozen turkeys, which could go straight from freezer to oven and be ready to serve in three and a half hours.

PURSUING EASY-TO-DIGEST ACQUISITIONS

In addition to such innovations on the new product front, Hormel continued to pursue smaller, easy-to-digest acquisitions of companies specializing in complementary product lines. In December 2004 Hormel acquired Clougherty Packing Company, a pork processor based in Vernon, California, with annual sales of around $420 million. Clougherty enjoyed a strong position in the southwestern United States through its Farmer John brand of bacon, breakfast sausage, and sliced hams. The Farmer John brand was popular among Hispanic Americans in that region, making it a complementary addition to Hormel's existing Hispanic brands. Among these brands was the Chi-Chi's line of salsas and other Mexican foods. The brand was originally licensed from the Chi-Chi's restaurant chain, but Hormel acquired full ownership of the trademark for retail products in 2004.

Hormel pushed further into the ethnic food market in January 2005 when it spent $48 million for New Berlin, Wisconsin-based Arriba Foods, Inc., a producer of premium Mexican flour and corn tortillas, salsas, seasonings, and tortilla chips. Two months later, Hormel bolstered the foodservice-based Specialty Foods division via the $43.2 million acquisition of Mark-Lynn Foods Inc., a firm based in Bremen, Georgia, that supplied restaurants with salt and pepper packets, ketchup and mustard, sauces and salad dressings, creamers, sugar packets, jellies, desserts, and drink mixes. Hormel next purchased Lloyd's Barbeque Company from General Mills, Inc., for $50.5 million. Lloyd's, based in St. Paul, Minnesota, produced a full range of pork, beef, and

chicken barbecue products that complemented Hormel's existing line of refrigerated entrees.

Upon Johnson's retirement at the beginning of 2006, Jeffrey M. Ettinger became only the ninth president/CEO in Hormel's century-plus history. Ettinger, who had joined the company as a corporate attorney in 1989 and was named president and COO in May 2004, was charged with the chairmanship as well later in 2006. Hormel remained largely on the same course following the transition with modest acquisitions continuing as one strategic centerpiece. In March 2006, for example, the company spent $80.4 million for Valley Fresh, Inc., a firm based in Turlock, California, that ranked number one in the United States in the canned, ready-to-eat chicken category. The company also scored on the new product front in 2006 with its introduction of the Hormel Natural Choice line of lunchmeat and deli items. Natural Choice products contained no preservatives and no artificial colors or flavors, and they thus meshed well with the growing consumer demand for natural products.

REMAINING ON COURSE THROUGH DOWNTURN

The following year, the company relaunched its line of Hormel shelf-stable microwavable meals as Hormel Compleats, prompting a 40 percent increase in sales. Hormel in August 2007 purchased Iowa-based Burke Corporation for $111.5 million, gaining a producer of pizza toppings and other fully-cooked meat products. Acquisition activity slowed down over the next two years during the economic downturn. Although sales declined slightly in fiscal 2009, falling 3.3 percent to $6.53 billion, Hormel reaped some benefits from the tough economy as budget-conscious consumers turned to inexpensive canned staples, including not only SPAM but also Dinty Moore stew, Hormel chili, and Mary Kitchen hash. Net earnings for fiscal 2009 jumped 20.1 percent to $342.8 million.

Deal-making returned late in 2009 when Hormel and Grupo Herdez expanded their partnership into the creation of a 50-50 joint venture called MegaMex Foods LLC, which was given responsibility for marketing a wider range of Mexican food brands in the United States, including Búfalo, Chi-Chi's, Del Fuerte, Doña María, El Torito, Embasa, Herdez, and La Victoria. This array of brands brought in revenues initially amounting to about $200 million a year. In a move intended to bolster the firm's offerings in the refrigerated convenient meals category, Hormel in January 2010 agreed to acquire from Unilever the Country Crock line of chilled side dishes, which generated annual sales of about $50 million. The deal did not include the line of spreads sold by Unilever under the Country Crock trademark.

Hormel Foods had sustained its remarkably consistent history through the first decade of the 21st century. The company maintained its continuous level of profitability, having operated in the black every year since its founding. Hormel had not missed a dividend payment since becoming a public company in 1928, and in fiscal 2009 the company increased its cash dividend for the 43rd straight year. With a strong balance sheet and low debt load, it was well positioned to grow through targeted acquisitions. Another of the company's strengths was the large ownership stake held by the Hormel Foundation. This ownership structure lessened the chances of Hormel becoming a takeover target and also shielded the firm from the heavy pressure to achieve quarterly financial goals that most public companies face.

Updated, David E. Salamie

PRINCIPAL SUBSIDIARIES

Clougherty Packing, LLC; Dan's Prize, Inc.; Hormel Foods International Corporation; Jennie-O Turkey Store, Inc.

PRINCIPAL DIVISIONS

Grocery Products; Refrigerated Foods; Foodservice; International; Specialty Foods.

PRINCIPAL COMPETITORS

Tyson Foods, Inc.; Smithfield Foods, Inc.; Sara Lee Corporation; ConAgra Foods, Inc.; General Mills, Inc.; Campbell Soup Company; Cargill, Incorporated; Butterball, LLC.

FURTHER READING

Dougherty, Richard, *In Quest of Quality: Hormel's First 75 Years*, Austin, MN: George A. Hormel & Company, 1966, 357 p.

Egerstrom, Lee, "Hormel's Acquired Tastes: Company Expands beyond Meats to Become Player in Ethnic Foods," *St. Paul Pioneer Press*, May 20, 2005, p. C1.

Fusaro, Dave, "Comfort Food in a Time of Anxiety," *Food Processing*, December 2008, pp. 18+.

Garrison-Sprenger, Nicole, "Hormel CEO Focusing on R&D, Acquisitions," *Minneapolis/St. Paul Business Journal*, June 2, 2006, pp. 1+.

Gray, Steven, "Hormel Struggles to Add Upscale Foods without Alienating Lovers of Its Spam," *Wall Street Journal*, November 29, 2006, p. B1.

Knowlton, Richard L., with Ron Beyma, *Points of Difference: Transforming Hormel*, Garden City, NY: Morgan James Publishing, 2010, 328 p.

Lee, Thomas, "The Head of the Table at Hormel: Ettinger Plans a Long Stay as Company's CEO," *Minneapolis Star Tribune*, June 30, 2004, p. 1D.

———, "Hormel Acquires Big Pork Producer: $186 Million Deal Is for Clougherty Packing, Maker of Farmer John Meat," *Minneapolis Star Tribune*, December 31, 2004, p. 1D.

———, "Small, Tasty, and Easy to Digest: While the Giants of the Food Industry Are Gorging Themselves on Huge, Difficult Acquisitions, Hormel Is Nibbling on Smaller Companies That Add Quickly to Profits," *Minneapolis Star Tribune*, April 14, 2005, p. 1D.

Lund, Doniver Adolph, *The Hormel Legacy: 100 Years of Quality*, Austin, MN: George A. Hormel & Company, 1991, 231 p.

McClenahen, John S., "Hungry for Growth: As It Carves Out New Markets, Hormel Is Proving to Be Much More Than SPAM," *Industry Week*, November 2001, pp. 46–47.

Merrill, Ann, "Hormel Stays Hungry: Hormel Foods Aggressively Pursues New Products and New Markets," *Minneapolis Star Tribune*, August 3, 2001, p. 1D.

———, "Hormel to Buy Turkey Store and Merge It with Jennie-O," *Minneapolis Star Tribune*, January 24, 2001, p. 1D.

Stynes, Tess, "Hormel Posts 53% Profit Rise," *Wall Street Journal*, November 25, 2009, p. B4.

Webb, Tom, "Hormel Wants Bigger Slice of Pizza: Buys Toppings Company to Expand in Hot Market," *St. Paul Pioneer Press*, August 24, 2007, p. C1.

Hussey Seating Company

38 Dyer Street Extension
North Berwick, Maine 03906
U.S.A.
Telephone: (207) 676-2271
Toll Free: (800) 341-0401
Fax: (207) 676-2222
Web site: http://www.husseyseating.com

Private Company
Incorporated: 1835 as Hussey Plow Company
Employees: 200
Sales: $50 million (2008 est.)
NAICS: 337900 Other Furniture Related Product
   Manufacturing

■ ■ ■

A private company under sixth-generation family leadership, Hussey Seating Company is a major provider of bleachers, chairs, and seats for a wide variety of markets, with about three-quarters of its revenues coming from K-12 schools. The North Berwick, Maine-based company serves this market with telescopic gym seating, sold under the MAXAM Wall and Courtside names. More than bare planks of wood, these contemporary rollout bleacher systems are ergonomically designed, offering contoured seats, back rests, and seat spacers as well as built-in safety rails. The company's Concertina Stage also elevates gymnasium floors to create auditoriums. Hussey provides the same bleacher solutions to colleges and universities as well as outdoor stadium seating and lecture hall and auditorium seating.

Hussey also sells auditorium seating to the religious, corporate, and government markets.

In addition, the company serves sports and entertainment customers, providing seating to cinemas, performing arts venues, and arenas and stadiums used by such sports franchises as the Arizona Diamondbacks, Colorado Rockies, Denver Broncos, Kansas City Chiefs, Kansas City Royals, Minnesota Timberwolves, New England Patriots, Philadelphia Phillies, Seattle Mariners, and Washington Redskins. Hussey is a recognized leader in its field, doing business in more than 75 countries around the world. Products are sold through a network of more than 60 dealers. Hussey offers parts and service through its Hussey Advantage Division. While some parts are produced in China and Taiwan, core manufacturing is done in Maine.

19TH-CENTURY AGRICULTURAL ROOTS

The Hussey family became involved in seating almost a century after William Hussey started the business in North Berwick in 1835. A farmer well familiar with the rocky New England soil, Hussey developed a new design for a forged iron plow blade that could more effectively turn hard ground than anything else available at the time. He organized the Hussey Plow Company, also known as the Hussey Plow Works, to produce his invention, and the business was passed down through the generations.

Hussey Plow was almost put out of business in 1895 when a fire struck the works, causing extensive damage, a situation made worse because only a few days earlier the company's fire insurance had lapsed. The facility was rebuilt, but the company's capital was all but exhausted. Now in the hands of Augustine J. Hussey, the founder's grandson, the company began to shift its focus away from plow blades, the demand for which was beginning to fall. In 1908 Augustine Hussey was asked by a bank president if his company could use its expertise to fashion a pair of steel ladders so he could make repairs to a cattle barn. Hussey took the job. Later in that year a company salesman exaggerated the company's newfound abilities by telling a school superintendent that Hussey could build and install fire escapes. Having never tackled such a project before, Augustine Hussey quickly traveled to Portland, Maine, where he inspected a number of steel fire escapes, made sketches, and produced a blueprint that secured the contract.

COMPANY REORGANIZATION: 1913

With the company's change in focus came a change in name. In 1913 Augustine Hussey and his son, Philip Hussey, organized Hussey Manufacturing Company. They used their steel shaping capabilities to produce hand rails, bridge supports, ski lifts, ski jumps, and such waterfront equipment as docks and diving boards. Diversity became increasingly imperative by the 1930s due to the prevalence of tractors that supplanted the need for the kind of animal-drawn plow Hussey produced.

Hussey's transformation into a seating company began in 1931 when it was contracted to do work for the new Portland Boys Club. Portland, Maine, native Cyrus Curtis, a wealthy Philadelphia publisher, donated the money for the new club, which included a gymnasium with wooden bleachers. Hussey provided the iron parts for the bleachers. The work was so admired that Hussey was soon asked to produce a complete set of bleachers for a local school. Despite lacking the necessary woodworking equipment, the company took the job, opening the door for a much needed new line of work.

Recognizing a business opportunity, Augustine and Philip Hussey paid a visit to Washington, D.C., and the

U.S. Commerce Department to study the bleacher market. They discovered that the closest competitor was located almost 400 miles away from Maine and that most of the bleacher companies were even more distant. Believing there was a large market potential in New England, Hussey Manufacturing invested in the necessary equipment to become a full-fledged bleacher provider. Moreover, Philip Hussey had in mind a design for an outdoor portable bleacher. It proved popular and was installed throughout the Northeast and opened the door for Hussey to provide permanent grandstand seating.

POSTWAR GROWTH

Like many companies, Hussey devoted itself to the production of war materials during World War II. Following the conflict, returning servicemen and servicewomen married and raised families in the new suburbs, resulting in the baby boom generation and the opening of large numbers of schools in the 1950s to educate them. For Hussey, this meant a surge in demand for its bleacher products for the gymnasiums and playing fields of the new schools. Indoor retractable bleachers was the product that drove the company's growth during this period. Hussey also made a mark in the industry in 1952 when it introduced the "closed deck" bleacher, which closed the gap between seating slats. Not only did this innovation prevent personal items from falling beneath the riser but also prevented injury due to missteps.

By the end of the 1950s, Hussey's annual sales were in the $1 million range. The next major development in the company's growth came in 1960 when it installed its first telescopic platform, accommodating fold-down chairs, at the Pittsburgh Civic Center. The system, which allowed venues to gain floor space as needed, became very popular with arenas and civic centers that needed flexibility in order to host a wide variety of events, including sports, concerts, and trade shows. Hussey followed up in 1964 with an electrically powered system, Pow-R-Trac, to open and close telescopic bleachers and platforms. Because the bleachers did not have to be operated manually, weight was less of a factor and bleachers could be built longer and higher, up to 30 rows, thus maximizing the seating potential of a space.

Necessity drove the next stage of Hussey's development. Despite the popularity of its telescopic platforms, no adequate chairs were being made for the system. The company corrected that absence by developing its own fold-down chair, the Sentinel, in 1971. The Augusta Civic Center in Augusta, Maine, ordered 3,500 of the new product, the first of more than a million Sentinels that would be installed around the world over

KEY DATES

1835: Hussey Plow Company is formed.
1913: Business is reorganized as Hussey Manufacturing Company.
1931: Company becomes involved in the manufacture of bleachers.
1980: Ideal Seating Company is acquired.
1996: Timothy B. Hussey becomes chief executive, representing the sixth generation of family leadership.

the next four decades. To become more vertically integrated, Hussey acquired a local plastic molding company in 1977 to produce plastic seating parts used in the Sentinel and other seating products to follow.

PURCHASE OF IDEAL SEATING COMPANY: 1980

Hussey expanded its offerings during the following decade. In 1980, it became involved in the upholstered auditorium chair market with the acquisition of Grand Rapids, Michigan-based Ideal Seating Company. Three years later the operation was moved to Maine. Hussey used its new expertise in plastic in 1981 to begin development of an all-plastic gymnasium seat. The resulting Comfort Curve design was not only more comfortable than traditional wooden bleacher systems, it was available in a variety of colors that could match school colors in a gymnasium. In 1985 Hussey applied its efforts in plastic seating to outdoor stadium seating, introducing the Olympiad chair. It found a ready market, first installed in the 65,000-seat National Stadium in Riyadh, Saudi Arabia. Other venues that followed suit included Toronto's Sky Dome, Miami's Joe Robbie Stadium, Jacksonville's Jaguar Stadium, and the new Comiskey Park in Chicago. To support its plastic seating business, Hussey acquired a molding company in Tyngsboro, Massachusetts.

The 1980s brought the involvement of the sixth generation of the Hussey family. In 1982, Timothy B. Hussey joined the company after receiving a bachelor's degree from Colby College and a master's of business administration from Cornell University. Over the next dozen years he became well familiar with all aspects of the company, serving in a variety of posts in manufacturing, sales, and operations. In 1995, at 38 years of age, he was named company president, and a year later became chief executive officer.

Timothy Hussey took the reins during a boom time for the company. Across the United States and Canada, communities were building new arenas and stadiums at an unprecedented rate, facilities that required tens of thousands of quality seats. In major league baseball cities, following decades of playing in nondescript multipurpose stadiums, there was a renewed interest in the ballparks of a bygone era. To serve the needs of these "retro" stadiums, Hussey in 1995 introduced the Legend stadium seat reminiscent of the slatted seats of the 1940s. Coors Field in Denver, home of the Colorado Rockies, became the first of several new stadiums to adopt the Legend seats. Also in the late 1990s Hussey introduced the Medallion stadium chair, offering ergonomic support and the Ensemble theater chair with added lumbar support.

NEW STADIUMS AND ARENAS DRIVE SALES

In the final years of the 1990s and into the new century, Hussey experienced a 10 percent increase in annual sales. During the stadium and arena boom, Hussey installed seats in the new facilities used by the Arizona Diamondbacks, Chicago Blackhawks, Colorado Avalanche, Florida Panthers, Philadelphia Phillies, and Washington Redskins. During this period, in 1998 Hussey received the largest contract in its history, supplying the seats for a pair of adjoining stadiums in Kansas City, home to baseball's Royals and football's Chiefs.

By the time the building spree petered out, Hussey increased annual sales to about $110 million in 2001 and employment swelled to more than 600, spread across the New Berwick facility, the Tyngsboro molding plant, a paint shop in Sanford, Maine, and sales offices in five countries. As new construction came to an end, Hussey had to rely on its core school business. To better serve that market and differentiate itself from the competition, Hussey redesigned its indoor folding bleachers. In the summer of 2000 the company unveiled the MAXAM bleacher line, offering a number of new advantages. The system included half as many parts as the old bleachers, speeding up installation, and there were no sharp edges so that people with disabilities could more easily negotiate the bleachers.

Through most of the first decade of the new century, Hussey contracted in the aftermath of the stadium building surge. Sales fell to $50 million and the workforce decreased to 200. Nevertheless, the company remained healthy and innovative. In 2009 Hussey introduced a new stadium seat, the Quattro Extreme Series, which combined the durability and weather resistance of an outdoor seat with the comfort provided by an upholstered seat. The first 3,500 of the new chairs were installed in the twin Kansas City stadiums. The Quattro seats were then installed in a new 45,000-seat soccer stadium in Mexico. Although contracts for stadiums used by professional sports teams were glamorous, school sales would remain the heart of Hussey's business in the years to come.

Ed Dinger

PRINCIPAL OPERATING UNITS

College & University; Corporate; Education K-12; Government; Sports & Entertainment; Worship.

PRINCIPAL COMPETITORS

Irwin Seating Company; Sauder Manufacturing Company; Virco Mfg. Corporation.

FURTHER READING

Bluestein, Adam, "The Success Gene," *Inc.*, April 2008, p. 82.

"Heartfelt Tribute Traces Hussey Family History," *Maine Sunday Telegram*, June 2, 1996, p. 9G.

Leech, Barbara, "Hussey Seating Remains an Industry Leader," *Weekly Sentinel*, October 16, 2009.

"Maine's Oldest Business Ready for New Millennium," *Lewiston (ME) Sun Journal*, June 7, 1999, p. A2.

Verespej, Michael A., "Sitting Pretty," *Industry Week*, March 5, 2001, p. 49.

Isetan Mitsukoshi Holdings Ltd.

———■———

5-6-10 Shinjuku
Shinjuku-ku
Tokyo, 160-0022
Japan
Telephone: (+81 03) 5843 5115
Fax: (+81 03) 5273-5321
Web site: http://www.imhds.co.jp

Public Company
Founded: 1886 as Iseya Tanji Drapery; 1904 as Mitsuko-
shi Dry-Goods Store Company Ltd.
Incorporated: 2008
Employees: 17,350
Sales: ¥1.27 trillion ($13.72 billion) (2009)
Stock Exchanges: Tokyo
Ticker Symbol: 3099
NAICS: 452111 Department Stores (Except Discount
Department Stores)

■ ■ ■

Isetan Mitsukoshi Holdings Ltd. is Japan's largest department store group. The company was formed through the 2008 merger between Mitsukoshi, which opened Japan's first modern department store in 1904, and Isetan, its smaller rival. In Japan, Isetan Mitsukoshi operates more than 25 stores, including six Isetan department stores and 10 Mitsukoshi stores, as well as a small number of specialty shops. The company has been building its overseas operations, focusing especially on the Asian markets. In 2010, the company counted more than 30 foreign stores, in China, Thailand, Singapore,

Taiwan, and Malaysia. The group also operates several smaller stores catering to the Japanese tourist market in Orlando, Florida; Paris; London; Rome; and Madrid. The company announced plans to shut the Paris store in autumn 2010. Isetan Mitsukoshi is listed on the Tokyo stock exchange and is led by Chairman and CEO Nobukazu Muto and President and COO Kunio Ishizuka. The company posted total revenues of ¥1.27 trillion ($13.72 billion) in 2009.

ISETAN'S KIMONO SHOP ORIGINS

In common with other top Japanese department stores, Isetan traces its origins back to a kimono shop. Whereas Mitsukoshi, Daimaru, and Takashimaya have histories going back hundreds of years, Isetan's story begins in 1886, with the opening of the Iseya Tanji Drapery in Tokyo's Kanda district, then a bustling center of commerce located near the Kanda River. Its founder, Tanji Kosuge, was born Tanji Nowatari in 1859. At the age of 12 he was apprenticed to the Isesho Drapery in Kanda. By the age of 20 Tanji had risen to the position of *banto*, or head clerk. In 1881 he married Hanako Kosuge, the daughter of one of Isesho's best customers, a local rice merchant, and took the surname Kosuge. Five years later, with the blessing of his employer, Tanji Kosuge went into business for himself.

Kanda was one of the most densely populated areas of the city, and the new shop's location near a busy intersection guaranteed it a steady stream of business. Because of the shop's proximity to several well-known geisha districts, Kosuge's customers included many geisha who needed to maintain a well-stocked wardrobe of fine kimonos. He created his own range of original products, and the Iseya Tanji Drapery came to be associated with exquisite obi, the belt used to tie the kimono, and quality design.

Tanji Kosuge began expanding the business in various ways. He experimented with staying open at night, sent out salesmen with samples of the stores' original designs, introduced seasonal bargain sales, and began buying out other kimono stores. In 1899, as business prospered, he enlarged the Kanda store. So successful had he been that by 1900, the Iseya Tanji Drapery had entered the ranks of Tokyo's top five dry goods stores.

Nevertheless, there was still a big gap between Kosuge's store and those of its long-established rivals. While the older stores were thinking of moving to a department store format, complete with display cabinets for their products and a wider variety of merchandise, Kosuge was still concentrating on building up the kimono business.

NEW NAME IN 1907

In an effort to bring the store's image more in line with those of its rivals, in 1907 he simplified the store's name to Isetan Drapery, combining the first two syllables of Iseya with the first syllable of Tanji. Three years later he considered building a department store in Tokyo's Hibiya district but shelved the idea as premature. At his death in 1916, Isetan was well established as a kimono store, but had yet to make the switch to a department store.

Kosuge was succeeded by his son-in-law, Gihei Takahashi. Takahashi had married Tanji Kosuge's eldest daughter in 1908, taking the family name of Kosuge. Upon his father-in-law's death, he took the name Tanji as well.

Takahashi had been working for another kimono store when he first came to the attention of Isetan in 1908. One day he bought 20 obi for his store at a 10 percent discount from an Isetan salesman, who assured him that the obi were not being sold at the Isetan store. Walking past Isetan some days later, he discovered that the same obi were being sold, and for a 20 percent discount. Going in to complain, he handled himself so well that he got a further discount. He impressed the man he dealt with (Tanji Kosuge's younger brother) as both a good businessman and a potential husband for Tanji's eldest daughter. Takahashi joined Isetan shortly afterward and was married within six months.

A man who read widely, Takahashi had many ideas about retailing. As Tanji Kosuge II, he began to lay the groundwork for Isetan's transformation from a kimono shop to a department store. His first move was to place Isetan on a more businesslike footing by creating the Isetan Partnership to run the store in 1917. It was, however, a catastrophic event six years later that would really move Isetan's plans forward.

REBUILDING AFTER THE GREAT QUAKE OF 1923

The Great Kanto Earthquake of September 1, 1923, killed some 130,000 people. The Kanda store burned to the ground, along with much of the rest of Kanda. The necessity of rebuilding the Kanda store provided Kosuge with the opportunity to introduce a department store format. When Isetan reopened in 1924 it was selling not only kimonos but also children's clothes, toys, umbrellas, cosmetics, stationery, household goods, and food. If the store had changed, so had Kanda, and it gradually became apparent that Kanda was no longer the prime site it once had been.

There were three reasons for this. First, within Kanda, the devastation caused by the earthquake and subsequent conflagration resulted in a changed street configuration, and Isetan no longer was situated near the corner of a busy intersection. Second, transportation was improving steadily, making the public more mobile. As the subway system was extended, Ginza and Nihonbashi, where Tokyo's leading department stores were located, became more accessible. With the completion of the Yamanote Line, a surface railway that circled Tokyo, new shopping and recreational areas grew up around stations such as Shibuya, Shinjuku, and Ikebukuro. Third, and in many ways most far-reaching, as a result of the Great Kanto Earthquake the center of the population moved away from the devastated areas in central and eastern Tokyo to the suburbs in the west.

By 1928 it was clear that there was no future for Isetan in Kanda. It abandoned a project to build a new eight-story department store there, although four stories

KEY DATES

1886: Isetan is founded by Tanji Kosuge, who opens a kimono shop called Iseya Tanji Drapery in Tokyo's Kanda district.

1904: Mitsukoshi Dry-Goods Store Company Ltd. is established as Japan's first modern department store.

1924: Isetan reopens as a department store.

1928: Mitsukoshi shortens its name to Mitsukoshi Ltd.

1961: Isetan goes public on the Tokyo stock exchange.

1971: Mitsukoshi begins to open overseas stores.

1993: Isetan opens its first store in China, in Shanghai.

2007: Mitsukoshi agrees to merge with Isetan, forming Isetan Mitsukoshi Holdings Ltd.

2010: Isetan Mitsukoshi opens sixth store in China amid streamlining of its Japanese stores.

of the building had been completed, and began looking for an alternative site. Hibiya, in downtown Tokyo, was considered once more, but after Tanji Kosuge had spent three days looking at the proposed site, he decided that there would not be enough customers and continued the search elsewhere. His eventual choice was Shinjuku, in the west of Tokyo, an area that had begun to develop after the opening of Shinjuku Station in 1875, but which had really taken off after the Great Kanto Earthquake. It was a decision that was to be as important for Shinjuku as it was for Isetan, and the two have grown in tandem ever since.

DEPARTMENT STORE FORMAT IN THE THIRTIES

In 1930, in preparation for its move into the department store business proper, Isetan formed itself into a limited company, Isetan Company Limited, capitalized at ¥500,000. In 1931 it purchased the land on which its new flagship store would stand, adjacent to an existing department store called Hoteiya. Work began on the Isetan building in 1932, and the main building was completed in 1933. It consisted of two floors below ground and seven above, including an auditorium. On its first day of business, it attracted 130,000 customers. Three months later, the old store in Kanda closed.

In 1935 Isetan bought the ailing Hoteiya department store for ¥2 million. This included the building,

the land it stood on, and the entire contents of the store. It borrowed ¥3.3 million from the Bank of Japan to pay for the purchase and redevelopment of the store as part of Isetan. A year later, this new addition to Isetan was open for business.

Shinjuku was by then established as one of Tokyo's new city subcenters. It was frequented by middle-class salaried workers and their families, attracted to its shops, cafes, and cinemas. As a new, up-and-coming department store, Isetan blended in perfectly. A play on a popular catch phrase of the day captures the mood of those times. "Today the Imperial Theatre, tomorrow Mitsukoshi" went the original, linking together these bastions of tradition in the heart of downtown Tokyo. "Today the Moulin Rouge [a new Shinjuku theater that opened in 1931], tomorrow Isetan," went the other, clearly identifying Isetan as something of a trendsetter, appealing to those who preferred black comedy to traditional Kabuki.

SURVIVING WORLD WAR II AND THE ALLIED OCCUPATION

During World War II, Isetan remained open for business almost until the end of the war, although its displays grew barer and its sales area gradually shrank to 50 percent of prewar levels. Escalators and elevators were removed and melted down for the war effort in 1943. That year, Isetan was asked by the Imperial Japanese Army to manage a hotel and store taken over by the Japanese in Sumatra, which it did until the end of the war. The Allied fire bomb raids on the night of March 10, 1945, devastated large areas of Tokyo, reducing the old Kanda store to ashes, but Isetan's flagship store remained standing. Quick action that night on the part of employees put out a fire that threatened to rage out of control. Neighboring buildings, however, were not so lucky.

According to one of his sons, Tanji Kosuge shrugged off the despondent comments of his employees on August 15, 1945, the day the Japanese emperor announced Japan's surrender. "What are you saying? The store's still standing, isn't it? You've got nothing to worry about. I'm going back to work tomorrow." Kosuge's wish for a quick return to business as usual was not fulfilled for several years, however. Apart from the problem of the lack of merchandise, the Allied occupation authorities had taken a liking to the building, and in 1945 requisitioned it for Allied use from the third floor up. Not until the end of the occupation, in 1952, would Isetan have the building to itself again.

The department store business after World War II saw a much greater emphasis on Western-style clothing.

In the years immediately following the war, women made do with what they had, blouses and Japanese-style pantaloons called *monpei*. From the late 1940s, however, there was a growing fashion-consciousness, initially inspired by the "military look" sported by women in the Allied occupation forces. In 1951 Isetan sponsored Tokyo's first postwar fashion show, Tokyo Fashion 51, which presaged a boom in fashion shows, modeling, and modeling schools.

LAUNCHING A POSTWAR EXPANSION

In 1956 Isetan underwent its first major postwar extension. Three new buildings were added, increasing the sales area by 25 percent. The purpose was not simply to increase Isetan's size. It was to reaffirm Isetan's image as a fashion leader. From this period Isetan introduced modern merchandising techniques, dividing up customers very specifically on the basis of age, sex, taste, and spending power. The new-look Isetan (it also changed its logo) celebrated the completion of its refurbishment with a grand opening in October 1957.

In 1960 Tanji Kosuge II stepped down as president and was succeeded by his eldest son, Toshio, who took the name Tanji upon his father's death two years later. The new president was a graduate of Keio University who had joined Mitsui Trading Company in 1941, before being drafted into the Imperial Japanese Army in 1942. After the war he had spent three years at Showa Textile Company before joining Isetan as a director in 1948.

Under Tanji Kosuge III, Isetan maintained its reputation for innovation during the 1960s. Anticipating the growth in private car ownership, it opened a parking garage adjacent to the store in 1960, becoming the first Japanese department store to have its own car park. In 1963 it introduced designer brands to the store with a Pierre Balmain haute couture salon, and in 1964 took the initiative in rationalizing women's clothing sizes, developing a system that has since been used by all Japanese department stores.

In 1968 it opened a new annex devoted entirely to menswear. Many were opposed to the move, but Kosuge believed that by removing all men's clothes from the main building he could both create space for more women's and children's clothing and target the different categories of male shoppers more effectively in a building designed for that purpose. "Bring him along, too," said the publicity as Isetan sought to reach out to male shoppers through wives, girlfriends, sisters, and daughters who already shopped regularly at Isetan. Meanwhile, Isetan had become a publicly traded company in 1961.

By the late 1960s Isetan had established itself as the number one fashion merchandiser in Japan and recorded Japan's highest sales per month for a single store. In a move to strengthen its fashion merchandising capability further, in 1967 it established the Isetan Research Institute Company, Ltd., a think tank for collecting and analyzing information about the latest fashion, industrial, and consumer trends. The institute was an important source of ideas for Isetan's new product development. A year later, it opened its first overseas representative office, in Paris, which, along with other offices opened subsequently, also acted as a source of information on fashion trends.

EXPANDING OVERSEAS & DIVERSIFYING

From the 1970s Isetan began a period of expansion, opening new stores both at home and overseas. Isetan's first overseas store opened in Singapore in 1972, followed by a store in Hong Kong a year later. The increase in stores continued in the 1980s, accompanied by the growing diversification of Isetan's business activities in the areas of fashion, food, leisure, and finance.

Subsidiaries set up in these areas in the 1980s included J.F. Corporation, which supplied Isetan with originally developed brands and also created brands for specialty stores around the country; Prio Company, Ltd., an importer-wholesaler of quality women's wear; Queen's Isetan Co., Ltd., a gourmet foods store; Isetan Travel Service Company, Ltd., which arranged package tours to domestic and overseas destinations; and Isetan Finance Company, Ltd., which was responsible for a wide range of nonbanking financial operations including the credit management of Isetan's charge card, the I-Card, the use of which was extended in 1988 to all shoppers at Isetan, as well as cashing, leasing, and loan services.

Isetan also ran a chain of supermarkets through Queen's Isetan Co., Ltd.; operated a nationwide restaurant chain of approximately 100 outlets through Isetan Petit Monde Company, Ltd., started in 1957; and imported and sold cars through Isetan Motors Company, Ltd., started in 1970.

Under Kuniyasu Kosuge, who succeeded his father, Tanji Kosuge III, in 1984, the company continued to grow. A graduate of Keio University who subsequently studied in the United States, Kosuge worked for Mitsubishi Bank for seven years, including a stint in London, before joining Isetan as a director in 1979. His overseas experience was useful as he presided over a growing international network of companies.

In Europe, Isetan operated stores in London, established in 1988, and Vienna, opened in 1990, which together with the company's representative offices in Paris, Milan, and Barcelona strengthened their business capabilities, including the procurement of merchandise through licensing agreements, product development projects, and information gathering. In 1988 Isetan established an international finance company in Amsterdam to support its overseas business activities. It opened a store in Barcelona in October 1991.

Active in the United States since the opening of a representative office in New York in 1979, Isetan moved into the U.S. market with more purpose when it entered into a joint venture with New York-based Barneys, Inc., an upscale retailer of clothing and sundry goods, in 1989. Isetan looked to strengthen its merchandising and increase its expertise in specialty-store management through the joint venture, while helping Barneys to open new stores across the United States. The tie-up also resulted in the opening of a branch of Barneys in Tokyo in November 1990. The Shinjuku store became the largest joint venture between a Japanese and a U.S. retailer, and Isetan had plans to open Barneys outlets in other Japanese cities.

STRUGGLING THROUGH THE EARLY NINETIES

In the mid-1990s Isetan suffered from the aftermath of the rapid decline of the Japanese economy and the souring of the Barneys joint venture. When the Japanese economic bubble burst in 1991, the economy was thrown into a lengthy downturn featuring a precipitous drop in consumer spending. In 1992 overall department store sales fell 3.3 percent, the first such decline in 27 years. Isetan's sales began to decline as well (they fell for the first time in company history in 1992) and at a particularly inopportune time, given the company's far-ranging expansion in the heady days of the late 1980s that left it with a mountain of debt.

In the depressed climate of the mid-1990s, Isetan also faced increased competition from the burgeoning ranks of discount stores such as Ito-Yokado Co., Ltd. In fact, Isetan in 1993 was threatened with a takeover by Ito-Yokado after Isetan's largest shareholder, Shuwa Corporation, a financially troubled real estate firm, sought to unload its 29 percent stake. Mitsubishi Bank, Isetan's main bank, intervened, forcing Kuniyasu Kosuge to step down as president in favor of 30-plus-year company veteran Kazumasa Koshiba, and arranging the sale of the Shuwa shares to 41 of Isetan's major existing shareholders and business partners.

The pushing of Kosuge into the honorary chairman's seat marked the end of the Kosuge family's reign over Isetan. Meanwhile, the culminating moves of

Kuniyasu Kosuge's overseas expansion also came in 1993 when new stores opened in Bangkok, Thailand (Isetan's largest unit in Southeast Asia), and in Shanghai, China.

The company's new president put a halt to any more store building and concentrated on improving profits. He closed underperforming affiliates, including the company's stores in Hong Kong, a fitness club in Tokyo, and Isetan Motors. In the short term, however, Isetan was haunted by the overexpansion of the 1980s. The Amsterdam-based finance company formed in 1988 suffered large losses from secret derivatives trading during the 1994 fiscal year, leading Isetan to post an extraordinary loss of ¥9.7 billion ($89 million).

EXITING BARNEYS IN 1999

The relationship with Barneys soured in 1994 when the U.S. retailer requested more money from Isetan to fund its newly expanded operations. However, Koshiba refused to do so as his company had already poured more than $600 million into the joint venture. This led Barneys, unable to make the rent payments on its stores, to file for Chapter 11 bankruptcy protection in early 1996. For the fiscal year ending in March 1996 Isetan posted its first net loss since 1961 as a result of writing off billions of yen in loans to Barneys.

Legal action ensued as well, with both sides suing each other over the original terms of their joint venture agreement. Kuniyasu Kosuge, the architect of the Barneys venture, voluntarily resigned from the Isetan board in mid-1996, leaving a 0.43 percent stake as the only connection between the founding family and the company. In the meantime, Isetan had continued to expand its Asian operations, opening its Tampines store in Singapore in 1996, a second store in Shanghai in 1997, and a store in Kuala Lumpur in 1998.

The dispute with Barneys was not resolved until early 1999 when the company emerged from bankruptcy under a reorganization plan in which the company's creditors received more than 90 percent of the equity. Isetan came away with a stake of about 7 percent as well as various concessions that settled the lawsuits. Isetan gained ownership of Barneys stores in New York, Chicago, and Beverly Hills, California, the exclusive right to license the Barneys name in Japan, and a 30 percent stake in a joint venture with Barneys to license the name elsewhere in Asia. Isetan also continued to operate two Barneys units in Japan, located in Tokyo and Yokohama, before selling them in 2006.

NEW PARTNER IN 2008

Its dispute with Barneys settled, Isetan turned toward shoring up its ailing operations in Japan. Like all of Japan's department store groups, Isetan remained confronted both with the country's fragile economy and a number of new factors affecting the retail sector. The rise of Internet shopping became an increasingly attractive draw for shoppers. At the same time, consumers had begun shifting their interests to the growing number of specialist and branded retail shops. These included many of the luxury and high-end designer names traditionally found only in department stores. Into the new decade, these companies increasingly began opening their own retail boutiques.

In response, Isetan began remodeling a number of its existing stores, developing a more up-to-date look and format. The company relocated its store in Tachikawi in 2001, and completed several new store openings. These included a store in Kokura in 2004, and in Jinan in 2005. By then, the group had also introduced a new flagship store format, in Iwataya, in 2004. By 2006, Isetan had also carried out the remodeling of its Urawa store.

Isetan nonetheless recognized that Japan's declining birthrates, rapidly aging population, and continued economic difficulties promised few expansion prospects for the near future. Instead, the company began targeting a wider expansion into the Asian region. In 2006, the company announced its intention to add as many as 20 new Asian-region stores before 2015. The company targeted China especially for this expansion, with plans to open as many as two stores per year in that market. At the same time, the company earmarked $1.7 billion toward the remodeling of the group's existing stores abroad and in Japan. In 2007, Isetan unveiled a new store concept, Isetan NOVO, in Chengdu, China, designed to capture the growing "trendy youth" market there.

Japan's economic woes and the ongoing evolution of its retail markets continued to plague Isetan and the other major department store groups. A number of these companies had begun to move toward a consolidation of the sector, initially through a number of alliances and partnerships. Isetan itself had formed an earlier partnership with Hankyu Department Store in 1996. By the early years of the new century, however, mergers became a common feature among department store groups. Isetan, then the country's fifth-largest department store company, began to seek its own merger partner. This led it to its fourth-place rival, Mitsukoshi, one of the country's oldest and most prestigious department store names.

MITSUKOSHI'S 17TH-CENTURY ROOTS

Mitsukoshi's origins dated back past its establishment in 1904 as Japan's first modern department store to the nation's feudal days in the 17th century. The Lord of Echigo, head of the noble House of Mitsui, fled from the forces of a samurai who eventually unified Japan by subduing the protectors of the hereditary estates. Because Matsusaka, the place of refuge, was a busy market center near a popular port in a fertile province, the Lord of Echigo, no longer in a position to collect income from his estates, renounced his title in order to become a merchant. After an inauspicious effort operating a brewery of sake and soy sauce, a merchandising dynasty was launched through the work of the former lord's eldest son, Mitsui Sokubei Takatoshi, and his wife, Shuho, daughter of a successful merchant.

The drapery business they opened in 1673 was called Echigo-ya in recognition of the family's noble heritage, differentiating it from other businesses and attaching some prestige to its wares. A luxurious ambiance, in which transactions were discussed secondarily to elaborate social amenities, quickly attracted a loyal clientele, but the couple soon introduced some business practices that greatly broadened their customer base.

First, they maneuvered to become purveyors of textiles to the new government, which by that time had settled down under the thumb of the Tokugawa shogun to a lengthy period of peace and isolation from the outside world. Second, the couple opened a store where customers could view the merchandise and make cash transactions. This was a drastic departure from the practices of the late 17th century, when merchants made house calls on wealthy families, the only persons who could afford to buy, and would have to wait for payment until the lord of the manor collected the annual or semiannual rentals from tenants, who paid in rice rather than currency. That, in turn, would have to be converted into negotiable instruments by professional moneychangers or bartered for other goods.

Centralizing the purchase process in a store eliminated the transportation costs of making house calls, a savings that Echigo-ya could pass on to customers in the form of reduced prices. The couple also introduced fixed prices. This eliminated the uncertainty on both sides that had accompanied the traditional haggling and speeded the purchase process, making it possible to handle more transactions.

HOUSE CODE IN 1722

The success of the first store led to the opening of a second, in Edo, which became modern Tokyo. It also led to the establishment of a second business, a financial arm. Customers found it convenient to have a moneychanger on the premises, and the financial service eventually grew to gigantic proportions. It became known as the powerful Mitsui Bank, another independent member of the Mitsui group.

In pioneering consumer-oriented business practices, the change that had the greatest effect on attracting new customers was to make merchandise available in quantities small enough to be affordable for the common people. Previously, fabric had to be purchased by the bolt. Echigo-ya was the first store to allow the customer to limit the purchase to the amount needed. This resulted in an unprecedented volume of sales, and the couple was able to open additional stores in other urban centers during the following decades. It was not until the Bon Marche store was opened in Paris in 1852 that such practices became known throughout the occidental world.

Another legacy of the founders was the Mitsui House Code, derived from Takatoshi Mitsui's will in 1722. This was a guide for the Mitsui heirs for management of the family's companies, which were proliferating through the country. It was also a code of ethics intended to ensure that the founders' principles and traditions of service would be followed by future generations. For example, Echigo-ya was so accommodating that an early patron wrote, "When ceremonial costumes are required in a hurry, the shop lets the servants wait and has the regalia made up immediately by several dozens of their own tailors. ... This is an example of a really big merchant."

In the ensuing 150 years, trust in the Mitsui name grew to be so entrenched that when the Tokugawa shogunate was succeeded in 1868 by the restoration of the imperial government, Mitsui's financial arm became, for all practical purposes, its banker. The management system that the Mitsui House Code had established was no longer adequate, however, to handle the rambling empire of businesses and industrial enterprises that the Mitsui heirs were struggling to keep in order in the late 19th century. Japan's business climate had changed drastically with the opening of the nation to foreign trade and the new Meiji emperor actively encouraging openness to Western concepts. Moreover, the various Mitsui enterprises often did not work in harmony with one another, and each was bound by its own traditional ways of doing business.

MITSUI DRY GOODS IN 1896

Rizaemon Minomura, a talented manager, was recruited by the Mitsuis and given power of attorney to make any changes needed to solve the internal problems of the businesses, which by then represented almost all types of commercial, financial, and industrial enterprises. He was eminently successful. One of his methods was to release

certain companies from direct control of Mitsui, but to retain a small share in businesses that were foundering as a result of mismanagement. One of these was the Tokyo Echigo-ya store.

The Tokyo Echigo-ya gained its independence in 1872, under the management of a related family named Mitsukoshi. The store prospered under its new management. Known first as the Mitsui Clothing Store, it became the Mitsui Dry-Goods Store in 1896 to reflect its expansion into additional lines of merchandise. Capitalizing on the Mitsui reputation for high quality and the growing popular fancy for Western-style fashions, the store brought in a designer from France to develop a new apparel department. The designs caught on, along with other innovations, including a display of merchandise in the open, life-size poster displays at railway stations as well as a catalog sales department. Home delivery by auto was instituted in 1903. Stocking foreign-made goods also attracted customers.

JAPAN'S FIRST MODERN DEPARTMENT STORE IN 1904

The following year, under new Director Osuke Hibi, the store was reorganized as Mitsukoshi Dry-Goods Store Company and announced its metamorphosis into Japan's first modern department store, with newspaper advertisements emphasizing the convenience of one-stop shopping for an ever-increasing variety of merchandise, simulating "in part, the department stores of the United States." As well as adding items such as jewelry, luggage, food, and photography to its wares, Mitsukoshi also held events such as expositions and exhibitions to contribute to the cultural life of the area. This had the effect of elevating the status of the store and attracted so many new customers that additional Mitsukoshi stores were opened.

By 1914, the Mitsukoshi stores were firmly established as sources of high-quality merchandise that were accessible and affordable for most shoppers, and other stores had begun to copy their innovations. The new Renaissance-style building constructed to house the flagship store that year sported Japan's first escalator. Mitsukoshi was also firmly associated with cultural activities, having participated in the refurbishing of the Imperial Theater, among many community projects.

Japan's eventual entry into World War I did not slow Mitsukoshi's growth. If anything, wartime industries furnished employment that enabled many more persons to become customers. Reduced-price special sale days and the introduction of gift coupons also stimulated sales.

The Great Kanto Earthquake of September 1, 1923, marked a turning point for all Japanese department stores. Along with many other buildings in Tokyo, they were all burned to the ground. Small mobile units were quickly set up throughout the city to supply essentials to the people, many of whom had never before been customers. A large number of customers acquired in this way continued to shop at Mitsukoshi throughout the rebuilding process and remained loyal patrons. The new stores, built as high-rises with many architectural innovations, offered further convenience. They ended the practice of having customers remove their shoes at the entrance and pad through the stores in cotton slippers. Fashion shows were held and beauty salons added. Business burgeoned. In 1928, to reflect the great variety of goods and services offered, Mitsukoshi dropped the Dry-Goods part of its name and became Mitsukoshi Ltd.

In the 1930s, mobilization for war again created industrial activity that increased the number of workers who could become part of Mitsukoshi's customer base. The Mitsukoshi name had begun to be recognized overseas as a result of participation in world's fairs and other expositions in Europe and the United States, increasing the number of foreign customers. As part of the Mitsui group, Mitsukoshi profited from its association with Japan's top business-industrial conglomerate, or *zaibatsu*. However, government constraints on the business, instituted in 1938 and continuing throughout World War II, along with the wartime damage resulting from direct bombing, left Mitsukoshi in a greatly weakened state.

POSTWAR GROWTH

The trust in the company's integrity that had been built up over many generations enabled Mitsukoshi to begin the recovery period by successfully combating the black market with fixed prices. Working with the new government established during the Allied occupation of Japan, Mitsukoshi was able to make rapid progress in rebuilding its business. Reaching out to customers through its continuing involvement in cultural events, as well as adopting Western-style products and retail techniques, Mitsukoshi had recovered enough by 1954 to celebrate its 50th anniversary with exhibitions of fine art and the introduction of new fashions that quickly became popular.

The phenomenal recovery and growth of Japanese business and industry in general brought Mitsukoshi a host of new customers. As Mitsukoshi added new products made possible by Japanese technological advancement, a consumer boom resulted that carried through the 1960s and made it possible for Mitsukoshi to open overseas stores in such locations as Paris and Hong Kong, beginning in 1971. By 1974, Mitsukoshi's

flagship store was importing Rolls-Royces for purchase. During the 1970s, Mitsukoshi stores opened in London, New York, and Rome.

Mitsukoshi's profits dropped in the early 1980s. In September 1982, Mitsukoshi's directors dismissed Shigeru Okada from the presidency, and Akira Ichihara became president. In 1986 he became chairman of the board.

By 1985, the company's catalog sales, as well as its stores' travel, construction, and decorating departments, had become so large that they were reorganized as independent business divisions. Mitsukoshi continued opening new department stores, expanding existing ones, and establishing numerous specialty shops. In 1989, Mitsukoshi purchased 1.5 million shares of stock in Tiffany and Co. Mitsukoshi's president, Yoshiaki Sakakura, was appointed a director of Tiffany later that year.

During this period, Mitsukoshi was still tied to the Mitsui group through the shares Mitsui held and through its own participation in the Mitsui group's leadership conferences. Like the rest of the Mitsui group, Mitsukoshi expanded through takeovers and joint ventures as well as through self-developed businesses. Mitsubishi recovered from World War II somewhat faster than the Mitsui group because all of its businesses were self-developed and therefore closer-knit and easier to control. That was why the Mitsui group had not regained its prewar *zaibatsu* number one position. However, its number two position, under the postwar *keiretsu* system, was not seriously threatened. Along with the Mitsui group, Mitsukoshi, too, appeared to be securely established as a frontrunner, both internally in Japan and worldwide. A sign of the ever-widening circle of Mitsukoshi activities was its joint venture with Marubeni Corporation in 1990 to set up cable television services in Europe.

OVERCOMING PROBLEMS IN THE NINETIES

Problems arose in the 1990s, however, that threatened to usurp Mitsukoshi from its top spot. In 1992, the company was forced to forgo a costly expansion plan it had started in 1990 due in part to sluggish sales in its luxury goods segment. That year, the company also started to reorganize its executive and management structure, believing that mismanagement was the cause for much of the company's financial woes. By September 1992, the company was reporting major declines in pretax profits.

Mitsukoshi was dealt another blow in April 1997 when Japan raised its consumption tax from 3 to 5 percent. This tax increase, along with a crisis in Asia's financial sector, weakened consumer confidence. The company and its competitors began to feel the crunch as sales began to dwindle. Many of these companies had expanded significantly during the 1980s and early 1990s and were now left with too much floor space. According to a 1999 *Nikkei Weekly* report, sales per square meter of floor space declined by more than 30 percent from 1990 to 1999. Nevertheless, Mitsukoshi opened its new Fukuoka location in October 1997. Over 180,000 visited the store on its grand opening day.

Despite the challenging economic climate, Mitsukoshi was determined to enter the new century on solid ground. The firm launched a new management strategy in the late 1990s with five major goals: to secure strong sales and profitability, to bolster the performance of company businesses, to restructure financial operations in order to promote future growth, to adopt a new corporate culture, and to remain a good corporate citizen. As part of this plan, the firm sold its interest in Tiffany and Co., set plans in motion to overhaul operations at three of its stores in the Kansai region, and stopped a golf course development project in the Chiba Prefecture. For the first time since it was listed in 1949, Mitsukoshi was forced to cancel its dividend payment in fiscal 1999.

SEEKING PARTNERS FROM 2000

Consumer spending continued its downward trend in the early years of the new century. Company sales declined for the third year in a row in fiscal 2000, prompting Mitsukoshi to look for new growth avenues. In 2000, the company launched its "Only You" e-commerce Web site and joined the Yahoo! Japan Shopping online shopping mall the following year, hoping that increased Internet sales would make up for lackluster traditional retail sales. During 2001, plans were set in motion to refurbish the Mitsukoshi Nihombashi store in preparation for its 100th anniversary celebration in 2004. Management hoped the revamped store would become a landmark in the Nihombashi area. A relocation strategy for the Osaka location was also in the works.

Taneo Nakamura took over the helm of Mitsukoshi in February 2002. Under his leadership, the company continued to divest unprofitable businesses and focused on entering high profit areas. In early 2003, the firm announced that it would merge four of its subsidiaries: Nagoya Mitsukoshi, Chiba Mitsukoshi, Kagoshima Mitsukoshi, and Fukuoka Mitsukoshi. Nakamura commented on the strategy in a 2003 *Japan Economic Newswire*, stating, "We will enhance our competitiveness and earning power by focusing management resources on our mainline department store operation."

Like Isetan and other department store groups, Mitsukoshi began seeking partners to help solidify its operations. In 2000, the company announced an early partnership with rival Takashimaya, which called for the companies to integrate their purchasing, e-commerce, and back-office operations. The two companies remained independent of each other, and later separated again.

Mitsukoshi continued to struggle through the first half of the new decade, and by 2004 had posted losses for four out of the previous eight years. The company launched a five-year plan in 2003, which led to a major restructuring of its business the following year. In October 2004, the company announced plans to close 10 of its stores, including seven smaller stores as well as three of its large-scale department stores in Osaka, Yokohama, and Kurashiki. Mitsukoshi also made moves to develop its own specialty store business during this period. In 2004, the company converted its Shinjuku to a new luxury-brand specialty format. At the same time, the company completed a $150 million expansion of its Nihonbashi flagship store in Tokyo.

MERGING WITH ISETAN IN 2008

Mitsukoshi completed several new store openings in the second half of the decade. In 2006, the company debuted a new "suburban" store concept, as it opened a store at the new Diamond City mall in Musashi Murayama. The company added a second suburban store, in the Diamond City mall in Nahori, in 2007.

By 2007, however, Mitsukoshi had posted losses for six years in a row. The value of the company's properties was said to be worth more than the company itself. In the meantime, the company found itself surrounded as a number of its rivals joined forced in a series of mergers. This situation drove Mitsukoshi into the arms of smaller but profitable Isetan in August 2007.

The merged company took the name Isetan Mitsukoshi Holdings Ltd., and became Japan's largest department store group with annual sales of ¥1.58 trillion ($13.9 billion). Mitsukoshi's president, Kunio Ishizuka, became president of the new company, while Isetan's president, Nobukazu Muto, assumed the role of chairman. Isetan Mitsukoshi Holdings was formally incorporated in April 2008. In November of that year the company launched a new three-year plan starting in 2009. This plan included the integration and streamlining of most of the two department store chain's support and back-office functions, including their store card operations.

Another part of the plan called for the full-scale remodeling of the group's three Tokyo flagship stores, and the expansion of the Mitsukoshi Ginza store, expected to be completed by the autumn of 2010. At the same time, Isetan Mitsukoshi's strategy recognized that the group's future growth lay outside of Japan, especially in the fast-growing Chinese market. At the beginning of 2010, the company opened its sixth store in China, in Tianjin, boasting 17,000 square meters of floor space. This opening came ahead of the group's plans to open five more stores in that country before 2014.

In the meantime, Isetan Mitsukoshi had been hard hit by the global economic recession of the end of the decade. With losses mounting through 2009, the company was forced to announce a new series of store closings, starting with two Mitsukoshi stores in May 2009. In November of that year, the group announced its intention to close 11 more Mitsukoshi stores, as well as an Isetan store by March 2010. Also included in this new restructuring was the group's small, money-losing shop in Paris, to be closed in September 2010. With this new streamlining, Isetan Mitsukoshi hoped to revitalize its operations for the decade ahead.

Updated, M. L. Cohen

PRINCIPAL SUBSIDIARIES

Centresta Co., Ltd.; Century Trading Co., Ltd.; Fortnum & Mason Japan Co., Ltd.; Garden Hotel Shanghai Mitsukoshi; Isetan Co., Ltd.; JTB Isetan Travel Service, Inc.; Leo d'Or Trading Co., Ltd.; Leo Mart Co., Ltd.; Leotex Co., Ltd.; London Mitsukoshi; Mammina Co., Ltd.; Mitsukoshi Insurance Service Co., Ltd.; Mitsukoshi, Ltd.; Niko, Ltd.; Orlando Mitsukoshi; Paris Mitsukoshi; Queen's Isetan Co., Ltd.; Rome Mitsukoshi; Shin Kong Mitsukoshi Department Store Co., Ltd. (Taiwan); West Japan Railway Isetan Ltd.

PRINCIPAL DIVISIONS

Department Store Business; Overseas Stores; Credit & Finance Business; Women's Wear Specialty Store Business; Supermarket Business; Real Estate Business; Other Businesses.

PRINCIPAL OPERATING UNITS

Isetan Department Stores; Mitsukoshi Department Stores.

PRINCIPAL COMPETITORS

Seven and I Holdings Company Ltd.; AEON Company Ltd.; Jardine Strategic Holdings Ltd.; Ito-Yokado Company Ltd.; Uny Company Ltd.; J Front Retailing Company Ltd.; Daiei Inc.; Takashimaya Company Ltd.

FURTHER READING

Furukawa, Tsukasa, "Isetan, Mitsukoshi Join Forces," *WWD*, August 24, 2007, p. 2.

———, "Japanese Chain Plans to Shutter 10 Stores, Cut 800 Jobs," *WWD*, October 8, 2004, p. 22.

Hirano, Koji, and David Moin, "Isetan to Sell Barneys Japan Operation," *Daily News Record*, June 26, 2006, p. 18.

Isetan hyakunenshi, Tokyo: Isetan, 1990.

"Isetan Mitsukoshi to Open 6th Store in China, Shut Paris Site," *AsiaPulse News*, February 5, 2010.

"Isetan to Open Outlet in Shanghai," *Yomiuri Shimbun*, August 15, 2009.

"Japan's Isetan Mitsukoshi to Open Renovated Chinese Store on Wed.," *AsiaPulse*, March 3, 2010.

"Japan's Isetan to Open 20 Overseas Stores by 2015," *AsiaPulse News*, February 28, 2006.

"Japan's Mitsukoshi to Trim Staff, Revamp Operations," *AsiaPulse News*, December 6, 1999.

Li, Sandy, "Retailers Fighting Pessimism," *South China Morning Post*, April 16, 2003, p. 3.

"Mitsukoshi Sets Offering for Its Tiffany Holdings," *WWD*, January 8, 1999, p. 11.

"Mitsukoshi to Merge 4 Subsidiaries in Reorganization," *Japan Economic Newswire*, January 30, 2003.

"More Pain for Major Department Stores," *Nikkei Weekly*, February 22, 1999, p. 7.

"Reorganization Plan for Barney's Is Cleared by Bankruptcy Judge," *Wall Street Journal*, December 22, 1998, p. B7.

Roberts, John G., *Mitsui: Three Centuries of Japanese Business*, New York: Weatherhill, 1989.

Rowley, Ian, "Upscale Shopping's Downbeat Outlook," *Business Week*, November 1, 2004, p. 20.

Shirouzu, Norihiko, "Cooperation Sparks Interest in Two Retailers," *Asian Wall Street Journal*, February 7, 1996, p. 15.

———, "Isetan Doesn't Want to Divorce Barney's," *Wall Street Journal*, January 22, 1996, p. A9.

"Stores Already Feeling That Wintry Chill," *Nikkei Weekly*, December 1, 1997, p. 6.

"Takashimaya Net Falls 41 Percent, Mitsukoshi Back in Black for Half," *WWD*, October 20, 2000, p. 22.

Terazono, Emiko, "Isetan Hangs On to Heritage by Thread," *Financial Times*, June 20, 1996, p. 27.

KESKO

Kesko Corporation

—■—

Satamakatu 3
Helsinki, FI-00016 Kesko
Finland
Telephone: (+358 10) 5311
Fax: (+358 9) 174 398
Web site: http://www.kesko.fi

Public Company
Incorporated: 1940
Employees: 19,184
Sales: EUR 8.45 billion ($11.78 billion) (2009)
Stock Exchanges: NASDAQ OMX Helsinki
Ticker Symbols: KESAV KESBV
NAICS: 424410 General Line Grocery Merchant
  Wholesalers; 441110 New Car Dealers; 442110
  Furniture Stores; 443112 Radio, Television, and
  Other Electronics Stores; 444110 Home Centers;
  444220 Nursery, Garden Center, and Farm Supply
  Stores; 445110 Supermarkets and Other Grocery
  (Except Convenience) Stores; 445120 Convenience
  Stores; 448210 Shoe Stores; 451110 Sporting
  Goods Stores; 452111 Department Stores (Except
  Discount Department Stores); 452910 Warehouse
  Clubs and Supercenters; 454111 Electronic Shop-
  ping; 454113 Mail-Order Houses; 551112 Offices
  of Other Holding Companies

■ ■ ■

Kesko Corporation is the largest trading company in
Finland. Its largest business, generating about 45 percent
of overall revenues, is its grocery trade operations. The
company manages a network of more than 1,000 food
stores in Finland operating under the names
K-citymarket, K-supermarket, K-market, and K-extra.
These stores are run by independent chain entrepreneurs
known as K-retailers, with Kesko responsible for such
functions as centralized product purchasing, logistics,
and chain development. Kesko's food operations also
include Kespro, the leading Finnish wholesaler to hotels,
restaurants, and other catering companies.

About 18 percent of sales are derived from Kesko's
home and specialty goods trade operations, which
consists of about 450 stores in Finland, about 200 of
which are owned by the company. These stores include
hypermarkets, department stores, sporting goods stores,
furniture stores, home electronics stores, and shoe stores.
The firm's building and home improvement trade unit,
which contributes about 27 percent of sales, includes
around 330 home improvement stores in Finland,
Sweden, Norway, Russia, and the Baltic countries, plus
about 90 agricultural supply stores in Finland. Kesko
also imports into Finland and markets Volkswagen,
Audi, and Seat passenger cars and imports and sells a
variety of brands of construction, environmental, and
agricultural machinery, trucks and buses, and
recreational vehicles.

EARLY 20TH-CENTURY ORIGINS

Kesko was formed following mergers and dissolutions of
nearly a dozen retailer-owned wholesale companies active in Finland prior to World War I. By the beginning
of World War II, only four such companies, called the
group of rural retailer companies, were left to vie for

market share against other competitors in the rural foodstuffs industry. These four were Maakauppiaitten Oy, founded in 1906 and headquartered in Helsinki; Kauppiaitten Oy, founded in 1907 and located in Vaasa; Oy Savo-Karjalan Tukkuliike, founded in 1915 and centered in Vyborg; and Keski-Suomen Tukkukauppa Oy, founded in 1917 and located in Jyväkylä. The early association of these four main companies represented a transition in Finland's goods distribution system from traditional wholesale trade to owner-operated wholesale companies, a transition upon which Finland's entire cooperative movement was ultimately modeled. Two large central companies already in existence, the Finnish Co-operative Wholesale Society SOK and the Central Cooperative Society OTK, would eventually be surpassed by this group that joined to form Kesko. Even during their infancy, three of the core four (Maakauppiaitten, Kauppiaitten, and Savo-Kaijalan Tukkuliike) represented sizable businesses with extensive office networks and net sales second only to the two central co-ops.

According to the corporate publication *50 Years of Kesko*: "Attempts were made to merge the retailer-owned wholesale companies almost from the very beginning, as the first negotiations on the matter took place as early as in 1908." Although prior to the formation of both Savo-Karjalan Tukkuliike and Keski-Suomen Tukkukauppa, these original negotiations led to a series of meetings throughout the 1910s and 1920s, during which time several small mergers took place. A large merger of the core four almost succeeded in 1928, prevented only by "the 'strong men' of the two biggest companies," who had "firm opinions about the principles of the new company, and the other companies could not accept them." The firm opinions, of course, pertained to how the new company would be managed and what degree of administrative clout each of the original managers would retain following the merger.

One positive outcome of the 1928 negotiations was the foundation of two organizational bodies, Vähittäiskauppiaiden Tukkuliikkeiden Yhdistys (VTY) and Kauppiaitten Keskuskunta. The purpose of the former was to serve as a consortium for more uniform purchasing by the four. The latter was to serve as a joint-service cooperative for the importation of wholesale goods as well as domestic industrial production, as the Kauppiaitten company already operated a Lahti shirt factory and a Helsinki coffee roastery. According to *50 Years of Kesko*, "Kauppiaitten Keskuskunta did not become a very significant company during the 1930s but, in the end, it became the seed of Kesko" because of its registration of the K-emblem and the Kesko logo.

In late March 1940, following another decade of ongoing but disappointing negotiations as well as the conclusion of the Winter War with Russia, new talks among the four companies resumed. Despite one potentially considerable stumbling block, Savo-Karjalan Tukkuliike's loss of most of its eastern Finland operations to Russian control during peace negotiations, Kesko Oy became a reality by October. Combined sales at the time totaled FIM 1.25 billion. Retailer-shareholders for the group numbered some 5,800.

Fittingly, the chair of the largest merged company, Maakauppiatten's Oskari Heikkilá, was elected Kesko's first chairperson. The company's original supervisory board consisted of 21 other members, with seats apportioned according to the net sales of the predecessor companies. The name Kesko, which had no historical ties to any of the founding companies, was adopted. Interestingly, the formation of Kesko did not legally constitute a merger because all four companies dissolved themselves and distributed their net assets to shareholders, who in turn subscribed to new shares of capital in Kesko, a wholly new limited liability company.

POSTWAR GROWTH

From the end of World War II to 1950, Kesko's district network grew from 19 to 22 regional offices while K-emblems spread to the stores of some 3,700 shareholders. Through the formation of consultative committees, introduction of purchase discounts, and implementation of support services, Kesko began to transform itself from a strictly wholesale concern to a central company devoted to its members. Beginning in 1950, the emphasis on district expansion and internal restructuring was exchanged for diversification beyond foodstuffs, into the related areas of animal feed, fertilizer, and agricultural machinery, as well as the construction industry.

During the late 1950s, as Finland altered from a primarily agrarian and rural to a primarily industrial and urban economy, Kesko adapted itself as well. Large numbers of K-stores located in outlying regions had to be closed, while nearly as many new K-stores had to be erected closer to urban centers. Coincident with this dramatic upheaval for Kesko retailers, the central

KEY DATES

1940: Kesko is formed from the merger of four regional wholesaling companies.

1960: Company goes public with a listing on the Helsinki Stock Exchange.

1971: First Citymarket hypermarket opens in Lahti, Finland.

1997: Plussa customer loyalty marketing system is introduced.

2005: Acquisitions of Norway-based Byggmakker and the Russian chain Stroymaster help make Kesko one of the five largest building and home improvement retailers in Europe.

company faced shortages in capital, spiraling growth in personnel, and mounting transportation and distribution expenses.

The most significant action taken by the company during this period of growth and transformation was the decision to take Kesko public, through a division of the company's stock into exclusive and ordinary shares. Thus, in 1960, Kesko was listed on the Helsinki Stock Exchange, and new capital was available to solve its problems while governance of the company remained in the hands of the exclusive shareholders, the retailers themselves. Enormous advancements during the 1960s, including the completion of a central warehouse in 1965 and the implementation of long-term retail development programs, paved the way for significant growth during the 1970s.

During this decade, Kesko came into its own and saw its combined market share rise from 23 percent to almost 30 percent. Among the growth initiatives of the period was the 1971 opening in Lahti, Finland, of the first Citymarket hypermarket. Confident, after weathering the rationing policies and manufacturing shortages of the 1950s and 1960s, that foodstuffs could steadily generate at least half of corporate sales, Kesko poised itself for more rapid growth in its agricultural and builders' supplies division.

CHANGES IN THE LATE 20TH CENTURY

During the 1980s, Kesko fulfilled its longtime plan of divesting itself of most of its manufacturing operations, which over the years had come to include a margarine factory, flour mill and bakery, match factory, rye-crisp company, meat-processing company, bicycle factory, clothing factory, and coffee-roasting plant. The process had been a slow one, for at the beginning of the decade the last three still remained within the company's holdings. Management decided to retain only the roastery, the strongest performer in net sales of all Kesko's manufacturing units. "The necessity of having a coffee roastery of our own has been generally approved," according to *50 Years of Kesko*, "because coffee has been the most important campaign product ever since the Second World War." Kesko's establishment in 1991 of Viking Coffee Ltd., a roastery jointly owned with a Swedish central company, affirmed the company's continuing commitment to this important "micro-market." In the meantime, the 1980s also saw Kesko introduce into the K-stores its own Pirkka line of private-label products.

Having become the largest central trading company in Finland, Kesko entered the 1990s streamlined (its district offices progressively pared down to just nine) and prepared for strong continuing growth. Because of a depressed national and global economy, however, the company saw net sales decline by 6.5 percent from 1991 to 1992. Eero Utter, the chairman and chief executive, nonetheless found cause for optimism in the increased market share for most of Kesko's product groups: "Although the Kesko Corporation's profit for 1991 decreased from the previous year, the Corporation and the whole K-Group has coped and will continue to cope with the recession very well in comparison with other companies."

The company was back on track soon, with profits for 1994 of FIM 462 million, up from FIM 285 million the year before, on a sales increase of 4.8 percent. The following year was even better, with a total profit of FIM 689 million on sales of FIM 26.4 billion. Expanding outside Finland, Kesko had begun opening several different types of stores in Sweden, and later in Russia. The K-stores chain had restructured in 1994, with stores now classed into four different size categories, ranging from "One-K," the smallest, to "Four-K," with a store's sign now showing from one to four letter "K"s on it as appropriate. Each size had a different emphasis, with the smallest ones, for example, posting a list of "10 principles" on the wall near the entrance that stated such ideals as, "You can always have a few words with the shopkeeper," or "You'll always feel cozier in our store than in big supermarkets." Despite the variations in size, the stores were organized identically, enabling shoppers to find things easily in any store in the chain.

The year 1996 saw Kesko acquire a large commercial trading house, Kaukomarkkinat Oy, while it sold Keskometalli Oy, a steel and metal service center and distributor. An attempted acquisition of the Tuko chain of supermarkets, however, was thwarted by the Commission of the European Union after the Finnish government requested that it examine the case. The country could not intercede itself, as it had no laws governing large corporate mergers. Control of Tuko, the second-largest supermarket chain in Finland after K-stores, would have given Kesko nearly 60 percent of this market, and the European Union ruled against Kesko because it believed that this would significantly impede competition. Having already begun the acquisition process, Kesko was forced to sell most of the portions of Tuko that had already been purchased.

This setback was not a total debacle, however, as Kesko reported that it was selling off its Tuko stake at cost, and by 1998 the company was posting another record year for profits and sales. The company installed a new CEO, Matti Honkala, and announced plans to add wine sales to its food retail outlets and expand further into the Baltic states. Another acquisition of this period was Anttila Oy, a department store retailer and mail-order business that ranked as the largest retailer of home specialty goods in Finland. In 1997 Kesko launched its Plussa customer loyalty marketing system, which encompassed several of its retailing concepts. By the end of the 1990s, more than half of the households in Finland had joined the Plussa program.

INTERNATIONAL EXPANSION

Around the turn of the millennium, Kesko accelerated its international expansion. The K-rauta hardware and builders' supplies store concept was extended into Sweden and later into Estonia and Latvia. Acquisitions also played an important role in Kesko's expansion of its building and home improvement business. The 2004 purchase of the Senukai chain made Kesko the market leader in the Baltic countries. In 2005 the company acquired both Byggmakker, the leading hardware and building materials chain in Norway, and Stroymaster, a do-it-yourself store chain based in St. Petersburg. The Stroymaster stores were later rebranded under the K-rauta name. This expansionary drive turned Kesko into one of Europe's five largest players in the building and home improvement retail sector.

In 2003 Kesko sold Viking Coffee, its last remaining manufacturing unit. By this time, the company had also expanded its food retailing operations into the Baltic countries, both organically and via acquisition,

with a concentration on two types of stores: hypermarkets and hard discounters. At the beginning of 2005, however, Kesko and Sweden's ICA AB combined their respective food retailing operations in the Baltics into a 50-50 joint venture called Rimi Baltic AB. Kesko then sold its share in Rimi Baltic to ICA in December 2006 for EUR 190 million.

Matti Halmesmäki, who had headed Kesko's hardware and builders' supplies business, began serving as the company's president and CEO in March 2005, succeeding the retiring Honkala. Also in 2005 Kesko expanded its home and specialty goods unit and became the market leader in the Finnish furniture trade by acquiring Indoor Group Ltd. and its Asko and Sotka furniture store chains. Indoor Group, which also operated furniture stores in Sweden, Estonia, and Latvia, generated annual sales of about EUR 170 million.

Acquisitions activity slowed over the next few years, although growth remained on the agenda in the form of new store openings. In 2008, for instance, 37 new food stores and two new building and home improvement stores were opened in Finland, while 12 stores debuted in other countries. Kesko was also actively working to refurbish a large portion of its existing food stores. After having earlier delved into the e-commerce sector through, for example, its NetAnttila online department store, Kesko in the fall of 2008 launched Konebox, an online home electronics store. Konebox leveraged the experience in home electronics retailing the company had gained through its Musta Pörssi chain. Similarly, Kesko had built a significant position in sporting goods retailing with its Intersport, Budget Sport, and Kesport chains, and in the spring of 2009 the company launched an online Budget Sport store.

In 2008 Kesko managed a 3.4 percent increase in sales to EUR 9.59 billion ($14.11 billion), although the beginning of the global economic downturn helped push pretax profits down 19.4 percent to EUR 288.5 million ($424.5 million). The deteriorating economic environment in 2009 particularly affected Kesko's car and machinery trading operations and its building and home improvement retailing business. Sales dropped nearly 12 percent to EUR 8.45 billion ($11.78 billion), while pretax profits fell a further 24.9 percent to EUR 217 million ($302 million). Kesko nevertheless remained a singularly important Finnish company, controlling some 34 percent of the country's overall food retailing market and looming large in a number of other retailing and wholesaling sectors. The company had also built a significant array of businesses in neighboring countries and was actively seeking opportunities to expand its overseas presence, particularly in Russia and the Baltic countries.

Jay P. Pederson
Updated, Frank Uhle; David E. Salamie

PRINCIPAL SUBSIDIARIES

Anttila Oy; Indoor Group Ltd.; Intersport Finland Ltd.; Kenkäkesko Ltd.; Keslog Ltd.; Kesko Agro Ltd.; Musta Pörssi Ltd.; Kesko Food Ltd.; Rautakesko Ltd.; VV-Auto Group Oy.

PRINCIPAL COMPETITORS

Bauhaus; Heinon Tukku Oy; Lidl Dienstleistung GmbH & Co. KG; Meiranova Oy; Metro-tukku; S Group; Starkki; Suomen Lähikauppa Oy.

FURTHER READING

Fifty Years of Kesko, Helsinki: Kesko Oy, 1990.

"Kesko Sees FY Profits Drop 44%," *just-food.com*, February 5, 2010.

McCabe, Jane, "Commanding Respect (Finland's Coffee Industry)," *Tea and Coffee Trade Journal*, February 2, 1995, p. 16.

McIvor, Greg, and Emma Tucker, "Brussels Blocks Big Finnish Merger," *Financial Times*, November 21, 1996, p. 2.

Raphael, Murray, and Neil Raphael, "The One-Idea Trip," *Progressive Grocer*, March 1, 1996, p. 23.

Vinha, Laura, "Kesko Profit Tops Forecasts, Dividend Pleases," *Reuters News*, February 4, 2004.

Royal Wessanen nv

Koninklijke Wessanen nv

Beneluxlaan 9
P.O. Box 2635
Utrecht, 3500 GP
Netherlands
Telephone: (+31 30) 298 8888
Fax: (+31 30) 298 8816
Web site: http://www.wessanen.com

Public Company
Founded: 1765 as Wessanen and Laan
Incorporated: 1913 as N.V. Verenigde Fabrieken Wessanen and Laan
Employees: 2,139
Sales: EUR 702.5 million ($980.5 million) (2009)
Stock Exchanges: Euronext Amsterdam
Ticker Symbol: WES
NAICS: 311212 Rice Milling; 311230 Breakfast Cereal Manufacturing; 311412 Frozen Specialty Food Manufacturing; 311421 Fruit and Vegetable Canning; 311422 Specialty Canning; 311423 Dried and Dehydrated Food Manufacturing; 311812 Commercial Bakeries; 311821 Cookie and Cracker Manufacturing; 311911 Roasted Nuts and Peanut Butter Manufacturing; 311920 Coffee and Tea Manufacturing; 311941 Mayonnaise, Dressing, and Other Prepared Sauce Manufacturing; 311999 All Other Miscellaneous Food Manufacturing; 312111 Soft Drink Manufacturing; 424410 General Line Grocery Merchant Wholesalers; 551112 Offices of Other Holding Companies

■ ■ ■

Based in the Netherlands, Koninklijke Wessanen nv is a multinational producer, marketer, and distributor of natural and specialty foods, with an emphasis on organic products. Wessanen's core business is the manufacturing of a wide variety of organic food products for the grocery and health food store channels, principally in the Benelux countries, France, Germany, and the United Kingdom. Key brands include Allos, Bjorg, Bonneterre, Ekoland, Gayelord Hauser, Kallo, Tartex, Whole Earth, and Zonnatura. In addition, the company's Beckers and Favory businesses offer frozen snack food brands and private-label products in the Netherlands, Belgium, and elsewhere in Europe.

Wessanen also owns the U.S.-based American Beverage Corporation, producer of noncarbonated fruit drinks and nonalcoholic cocktails, but has earmarked this business for divestment as part of its withdrawal from the North American market to concentrate on its core European operations. Founded in the mid-18th century, Wessanen has evolved from a local seed trader into a multinational food company focusing on the organic sector.

SEED TRADING ORIGINS

On March 22, 1765, cheese merchant Adriaan Wessanen and his 31-year-old nephew Dirk Laan established Wessanen and Laan, with a capital of NLG 12,000. The company originally traded in a variety of seeds and grains. In 1789, nearly 25 years after the company began, Wessanen retired and Laan took control of the company. The company continued to prosper, eventually becoming active in the milling of various grains.

When Laan himself died in 1791, his son Remmert became head of the company. Remmert Laan faced new challenges. The French under Napoleon dominated the European continent by the early 1800s, and Holland was part of the French Empire, which was at war with the British, among others. Britain's navy was a serious barrier to Dutch ships carrying raw materials to the Netherlands from its colonies and transporting finished goods back to them. As a result, many of Wessanen's trading activities were restricted.

Political changes in Europe after 1814 enabled Wessanen to establish new trading affiliations throughout the continent in such cities as Hamburg, Antwerp, and Ghent. Although seed trading remained one of the company's largest businesses, Wessanen became increasingly active in the trade of wheat, oats, and barley. Before long, encouraged by the Netherlands Trading Company (a company set up in 1824 by King William I to facilitate colonial trade and also a forerunner of the modern-day Algemene Bank Nederland N.V., which itself later merged into ABN AMRO Bank N.V.), Wessanen also began trading in milled rice, a staple in the Dutch East Indies. During these years Remmert Laan's sons Jan and Adriaan took an increasing role in the operation of the family business.

In 1839 the company undertook factory-like processing on a major scale when it purchased a facility for the refining of vegetable oils. The purchase of the factory signaled a significant change in the character of the company and in the primary products in which the company dealt, from unprocessed grains and seeds to milled grains and processed oils. Wind was the primary source of power for Wessanen's new plants for some time. By 1865, the year of the company's centennial, Wessanen and Laan was an active cheese broker and producer of flour, vegetable oil, milled rice, barley, and related products, and employed about 100 people.

In 1868 Jan Laan died, leaving his five sons to run the business. That same year the company opened a new steam-powered flour-milling plant, built with the most up-to-date technology to replace a facility that had burned down. Only the plants for milling rice and barley continued to use windmills.

FOCUSING ON PROCESSED PRODUCTS IN THE EARLY 20TH CENTURY

Wessanen and Laan left the cheese, seed, and grain trades around 1900 and focused on processed products. The company's largest commodity was milled rice, now produced in steam-powered factories. The company had been under the direction of the Laans for five generations. Taking into consideration the risks of modern enterprise, in 1913 the family changed the structure of the company to a corporation, with a paid-in-capital of NLG 7 million. The name N.V. Verenigde Fabrieken Wessanen and Laan was adopted, but was changed in 1916 to Wessanen's Koninklijke Fabrieken N.V. ("Koninklijke" [meaning "royal"] is an honorary title bestowed upon distinguished corporations by the Dutch monarchy.)

During World War I Wessanen continued to trade much as usual, but the company lost a major export market for its finished products and a significant supplier of raw material when the Russian Revolution terminated trade between Russia and the West. Wessanen compensated for this loss by entering rolled-oat production and by starting to produce cocoa and cocoa butter.

During the 1920s, as a favorable trade climate prevailed throughout Europe and in the Americas, Wessanen regularly upgraded its production facilities. The company also sought to build factories abroad to increase productivity but repeatedly faced stiff opposition from local governments. In 1927, however, the company did open a factory near Kraków, Poland, as a joint venture with rival Dutch rice miller Van Schaardenburg. When the Polish rice market collapsed several years later, the venture was abandoned.

Wessanen survived the Great Depression relatively well. Food producers were protected from drastic shrinkage of their markets because people needed to eat even in hard times, and the company had good product diversification. In 1938 Wessanen organized its animal-feed unit as a separate division. Although these products made up a minor proportion of the company's total sales, their volume was significant.

During World War II Wessanen operated at lower levels of production. Holland was invaded by the Nazis, while the Dutch East Indies were occupied by the Japanese. Raw materials could no longer be imported from, nor finished goods exported to, the colonies. The loss of this trade was a severe blow to Wessanen, and it was compounded by the growing inclination of rice-producing nations to mill their own rice rather than export it for processing. In 1951 Wessanen was forced

KEY DATES

1765: Adriaan Wessanen and his nephew Dirk Laan establish Wessanen and Laan to trade in a variety of seeds and grains.

Early 20th Century: Company begins focusing on processed products.

1913: Company is incorporated as N.V. Verenigde Fabrieken Wessanen and Laan.

1916: Company's name is changed to Wessanen's Koninklijke Fabrieken N.V.

1959: Company goes public.

1992: Sale of grain division completes shift from bulk manufacturer to marketer of consumer food products.

1993: Wessanen merges with Koninklijke Distilleer-derijen Erven Lucas Bols N.V., a Dutch distiller, to form Koninklijke Bols Wessanen N.V.

1994: BolsWessanen substantially beefs up its breakfast cereal portfolio with several purchases.

1998: Company divests its French wine division and its Bols spirits operation to focus fully on food.

1999: Company is renamed Koninklijke Wessanen nv.

2000: Distriborg Group, the leading marketer of natural and specialty foods in Europe, is acquired; company announces shift in focus to "wellness" food products.

2003: Wessanen gains majority control of Natudis BV.

2009: Company begins concentrating on branded organic food products, principally in western Europe.

to shut down its largest rice-milling factory in Holland, but it remained a large miller in the United States.

POSTWAR TRANSITION TO PUBLIC COMPANY

Throughout the 1950s, economic recovery encouraged Wessanen to enter new product areas. Research in the area of milk replacers (products used to feed calves that are raised away from their mothers) proved extremely profitable for Wessanen. At the end of 1958, the company's paid-in-capital was NLG 68 million, up from

NLG 7 million in 1913, and in 1959 the Laan family decided to take the firm public. Wessanen's initial public offering (IPO) was completed on September 7 of that year on the Amsterdam Stock Exchange.

The transition from private to public corporation was overseen by Wessanen President T. Verspyck and Raymond Laan. In 1962 the last Laan left the company's board of directors, marking the end of nearly 200 years of direct family control of Wessanen. The Laan family remained its main stockholder for several years, however.

By Wessanen's bicentennial in 1965, the company had about 2,100 employees. The late 1960s brought some unfavorable developments in the company's markets. Cocoa-producing countries began refining their products at home, Europe experienced a flour glut, and competition in edible oils put pressure on Wessanen's market share.

LAUNCH OF GLOBAL DIVERSIFICATION

In 1971 Gerrit Hendrik van Driel became the managing director of Wessanen and began to formulate a plan to bring the company into new markets. Under van Driel's leadership, the company acquired a number of meat and animal-fat-processing facilities and in 1973 laid out a plan for global diversification. Van Driel emphasized decentralized management and conservative handling of the financial risks that accompany broad expansion plans. His strategy included a transition from bulk products to higher-margin consumer products. This led to the acquisition of a cheese factory, a cheese trading company, and a milk-powder factory. Also acquired were Delicia, a Dutch maker of chocolate products, in 1972; Gelderland Frischwaren GmbH, a German maker of meat specialty products, in 1973; and Baars, maker of Leerdammer cheese, in 1976. The company also looked to the United States as the prime area for geographic diversification and, in the Dutch tradition, planned to grow by relying on its own assets rather than through borrowing. When necessary the company raised capital through new equity issues.

In 1978 Wessanen began to execute its program when it purchased Marigold Foods Inc. of Minneapolis, Minnesota, for $20 million. Marigold produced consumer dairy products such as milk, yogurt, ice cream, and cottage cheese, as well as fruit juices and drinks. A year later, Wessanen augmented its Marigold acquisition with the purchase of the Clover Leaf Creamery in Minneapolis. The acquisition made Marigold the market leader in many products and increased its coverage throughout Minnesota.

In 1979 Wessanen withdrew from almost all of its milk-replacer activities and sold a 51 percent interest in Wessanen Cacao to British commodity trader S. & W. Berisford in 1980. A year later it got out of the raw cocoa trade entirely, focusing instead on lower cost cocoa oil substitutes. Wessanen's Friwessa unit distributed these products and other vegetable oils, including palm oil, which was experiencing an increase in demand worldwide.

Profits began to improve for Wessanen after two unsatisfactory years in the late 1970s. By 1982 more than 60 percent of Wessanen's sales were generated from markets other than the Netherlands. In 1983 Wessanen acquired Crowley Foods, Inc., of Binghamton, New York, for about $16 million. Crowley, like Marigold, was primarily a dairy concern. The acquisition helped Wessanen post record earnings. Profits tripled between the 1979 and 1983 fiscal years, from NLG 13 million to NLG 39 million.

COMPLETING SHIFT FROM BULK MANUFACTURER TO CONSUMER PRODUCT MARKETER

The mid-1980s brought Wessanen continued success. Profits increased markedly, as 30 percent of the company's total revenue came from the higher-margin consumer goods division in the United States. At the end of 1986 Wessanen bought the health food distributor Tree of Life Inc. in St. Augustine, Florida, which soon became a major part of Wessanen's U.S. operations, and announced a joint venture with a cheese factory in Ireland. In 1987 the company purchased Cheshire Wholefoods, a granola producer in the United Kingdom for about £14 million. The following year Wessanen acquired Gourmet Foods of St. Paul, Minnesota, and Award Foods of Dallas, Texas, for an undisclosed amount. Those two companies, which were active in the distribution of specialty food products and which were combined to form Gourmet Award Foods, added about $60 million in sales to Wessanen's sales. Later that year Wessanen also bought Week's Dairy of Concord, New Hampshire, and the Ohio Pure Foods group (later renamed American Beverage Corporation) of Verona, Pennsylvania.

Wessanen's acquisitions in the United States were organized under a holding company called Wessanen USA and benefited from each other's research and product development. For example, the Marigold unit in Minnesota brought a hard-pack frozen yogurt to market in 1987 and its success helped Crowley Foods and Axelrod Foods (another East Coast acquisition of this period) to sell a similar product in their own markets.

By the end of the 1980s Wessanen was a significantly different company than it had been just 15 years before. In 1989 van Driel, the architect of the restructuring and chairman of the managing board, divided Wessanen's operations into three main areas: consumer products, semi-manufactured products, and bulk specialties. Consumer products included the U.S. dairy-related and fruit-juice operations as well as health foods, processed meats, cheeses, mueslis, and chocolate products in Europe. Altogether they accounted for more than 64 percent of group sales by the end of the 1980s. Bulk specialties such as wheat, rye, cereal by-products, and animal feeds, once the mainstay of the company, amounted to only about 20 percent of sales, and semi-manufactures such as refined oils and fats, milk powders, and starches (sold primarily to industrial bakers and chocolate manufacturers) made up 16 percent of revenues at the end of the decade.

In late 1989 Wessanen suddenly withdrew completely from the animal-feeds sector by selling its three remaining compound feeds factories in the Netherlands and its last milk-replacers unit in the United States. The withdrawal from the animal-feeds sector was followed in mid-1990 by the divestment of the Dutch oils and fat company Friwessa. These sell-offs were two of the final moves in the company's shift from bulk manufacturer to marketer of consumer food products.

Van Driel retired at the end of 1990, when this transformation was nearly complete. Succeeding him as chairman was Peter Bakker Schut, who had joined the company in 1979 and had served on the board of managing directors since 1986. Bakker Schut completed the company's transformation in 1992 when he sold the grain division to Goodman Fielder Wattie of Australia for AUD 200 million ($149 million). Meanwhile, Wessanen continued to expand its stable of consumer food products through three 1991 acquisitions: Levaillant S.A., a French cheese packaging and distribution company that became part of Baars Kaas BV; Den Hartog Holding BV, a Dutch maker of ice cream and frozen desserts; and Duif Holding BV, a maker of high-quality snack foods, mainly Asian snacks and related products.

1993–98: THE BOLSWESSANEN INTERREGNUM

Partly to fulfill the firm's desire to pursue larger acquisitions, Wessanen in April 1993 merged with a major Dutch distiller, Koninklijke Distilleerderijen Erven Lucas Bols N.V. Founded in 1575, Bols was best known for its Bols and Bokma brands of gin, Dry Sack sherry, and Pisang Ambon and Zwarte Kip liqueurs. More than 40 percent of Bols's revenues were derived from the sale of spirits, with the remainder coming from wines and nonalcoholic beverages. Nearly 90 percent of the firm's revenues were generated in Europe.

Bols was much smaller than Wessanen in terms of revenues, with 1992 sales of about NLG 1.29 billion, compared to Wessanen's NLG 3.7 billion. Bols's profits were nonetheless about the same as that of Wessanen, so the merger, in the form of a full stock swap, was structured nearly as a merger of equals. Bols shareholders secured about 45.5 percent of the new company, while Wessanen holders controlled the other 54.5 percent. It was hoped that the profits generated from the drinks side of the combined company, which adopted the name Koninklijke BolsWessanen N.V., would fund further, and larger, acquisitions of food companies.

Bakker Schut, Wessanen's chairman, continued in the same role at BolsWessanen, but he then retired in April 1994. Rob Schipper, who had been deputy chairman, was named the new chairman. Under Schipper, BolsWessanen began implementing the acquisition plan, with a particular emphasis on purchasing breakfast cereal makers. After acquiring the Netherlands-based Dailycer in 1994, BolsWessanen later that year acquired U.K.-based Telford Foods and the French firm H&C Céréales from Harrisons & Crosfield plc, a U.K. conglomerate, for about £75 million ($113 million).

Following the deals, BolsWessanen commanded about 50 percent of the European market for private-label breakfast cereals and about 10 percent of the overall European breakfast cereals market. Telford Foods also brought to the company its lines of instant dry soups, desserts, chocolate drinks, and other dry grocery products. Early in 1995, BolsWessanen transferred its Italian drinks business to Davide Campari-Milano in return for a 35 percent stake in the Italian drinks firm.

Poor financial results in 1994, which were blamed largely on problems with the company's Italian beverage operations, led to a sharp decline in the company's stock price in early 1995 and also to the resignation of Schipper. Mac Zondervan, a member of the three-person management board, was appointed to succeed him. Within a month, Zondervan had announced that BolsWessanen would shift its growth strategy toward food and away from drinks and that the company would gradually be transformed into predominantly a food company. The shift in strategy mirrored the shift in executives as Schipper had come to BolsWessanen from the Bols side, whereas his successor had been a Wessanen executive.

Zondervan also began tinkering with the portfolio of food businesses, aiming to concentrate on several core areas: cheese, cereals, and convenience foods in Europe

and dairy products and fruit drinks in the United States. Divestments of units outside of these areas began, including the mid-1995 sale of Den Hartog to Unilever. Soon thereafter, the first drinks divestment was completed: the sale of BolsWessanen's 60 percent stake in Williams & Humbert, a producer of sherry based in Spain. In October 1995 the company sold Cain Foods, a U.S. maker of mayonnaise, salad dressing, and pickles. During the first half of 1996, the divestment of Bols Strothmann, a German maker of schnapps with annual sales of DEM 200 million ($139.5 million), was finalized.

While struggling to turn its fortunes around, BolsWessanen completed several acquisitions to strengthen its core operations. During 1996, Gourmet Award Foods was expanded into the western United States through the purchase of McLane America, a specialty foods distributor with a distribution center in Salt Lake City, Utah, and annual sales of $60 million. Similarly, a specialty food distributor in the Pacific Northwest was gained in early 1998 when Ray's Food Service, Inc., was acquired. Based in Clackamas, Oregon, Ray's had sales of $80 million. Late in 1996, BolsWessanen reached an agreement to acquire Barber Chestergate, a U.K. producer of private-label breakfast cereals, from Hillsdown Holdings plc. In March 1998 Marigold Foods was bolstered through the purchase of Becker's Dairy, a Chicago-based foodservice dairy distributor with approximate annual sales of $45 million.

POST-BOLS FOCUSING ON "WELLNESS"

Results for 1997, including a 19 percent increase in revenues and a 10.1 percent jump in profits, showed that BolsWessanen's fortunes were finally beginning to turn. It was in the wake of this positive news, however, that the gradual unbundling of the Wessanen-Bols merger reached its culmination. In March 1998 BolsWessanen announced that it would sell its alcoholic beverage operations in order to focus fully on food. One month later the French wine division was sold to management, and then in July the company reached an agreement to sell the Bols spirits unit to CVC Capital Partners, a European venture capital firm. The only remaining drinks interest was the 35 percent stake in Campari. In early 1999 BolsWessanen renamed itself Koninklijke Wessanen nv.

The new Wessanen immediately began making acquisitions to strengthen its food businesses. The U.S. food distribution operation was enlarged with the early 1999 purchase of the North American specialty food unit of Hagemeyer N.V. (Hagemeyer Foods USA), which included New Jersey-based Liberty Richter, the Canadian firm Ashley Koffman, MBC Foods of Milwaukee, and Fine Distributing, which operated out of Atlanta and Fort Lauderdale, Florida. Annual revenues of the acquired operations exceeded $300 million.

Later in the year, Tree of Life grew even larger still with the purchase of the $225-million-in-sales A-1 International Foods, Inc., a specialty food distributor based in Los Angeles with a subsidiary in San Antonio. Wessanen's U.S. dairy operations grew as well, through the July 1999 purchases of two dairies in the Midwest (Rapid City, South Dakota-based Gillette Dairy of the Black Hills, Inc., and Nebraska Dairies, Inc.) and the early 2000 acquisition of Oak Grove Dairy, which operated in Minnesota and Wisconsin.

ACQUIRING DISTRIBORG GROUP

The company turned its acquisitive eye on Europe during 2000, starting with the buyouts of two German convenience food makers: Karl Kemper GmbH, producer of frozen meal components, mainly chicken and meat specialties; and Vegeta GmbH, which specialized in vegetarian products. Having established a national distribution network in the United States for natural and specialty foods, Wessanen sought to form a similar position in Europe. The company took a major step toward that goal in mid-2000 by acquiring the France-based Distriborg Group, the leading marketer of natural and specialty foods in Europe, with operations in France, the United Kingdom, Italy, Belgium, the Netherlands, and Spain. Wessanen paid about EUR 150 million for Distriborg, which had annual sales of EUR 250 million. Next came the purchase of Boas BV, a distributor of specialty products in the Netherlands bought in late 2000.

In October 2000 Wessanen announced another change of direction. The company said that it would focus on the "health and wellness market," by producing, marketing, and distributing natural and specialty food products aimed at health- and quality-conscious consumers. The U.S. dairy businesses, Crowley Foods and Marigold Foods, were put up for sale as was Leerdammer, its only European dairy operation. Although the divestment of the latter was put on hold during 2001 because of the European outbreak of foot-and-mouth disease, the U.S. dairy unit was sold for $400 million in September 2001 to a partnership that included the farmer-owned cooperative Dairy Farmers of America Inc. Also divested during 2001 were Golden Foods International, a producer of chicken products in Thailand, and the bulk of the 35 percent stake in Campari (the remainder was sold in February 2002).

Meanwhile, several strategic acquisitions were completed during 2001 in line with the new company mission, including Zonnatura, a leading Dutch brand of healthful and natural foods; Food for Health Co., Inc., a natural food distributor with operations in Phoenix, Arizona, and Melbourne, Florida; a 41 percent interest in Natudis BV, the Netherlands' leading distributor of branded natural and health food products; and two Canadian food distributors, Preisco Foods Ltd. and Jentash Specialty Foods L.P.

During 2002 Wessanen enhanced its focus on natural and specialty foods by completing two more divestments. In July the U.K. dry soup business, Telford Foods, was sold to Leeds-based Brand Partnership, and in December Leerdammer was sold to Paris-based Fromageries Bel S.A. for EUR 190 million, completing the company's exit from dairy. The preceding year, the European distribution operations had been placed under a new unit called Tree of Life Europe, and this unit bulked up in 2002 via the purchases of Nature's Store, a U.K. distributor of health food products; and Kallo Foods Ltd., a U.K. producer of organic food products, such as rice cakes and breadsticks. In June 2002, meanwhile, Tree of Life North America signed a three-year contract making it the main national distribution company for Wild Oats Markets, Inc., for natural, organic, and specialty food products. Wild Oats was the operator of one of the largest chains of natural foods stores in the United States, operating more than 100 outlets across the country.

TRANSITION TO CONCENTRATION ON BRANDED ORGANIC PRODUCTS

Wessanen posted disappointing results during 2002, largely as a result of the poor performance of Tree of Life North America, which was hit hard by the continuing economic stagnation and intense pricing pressure in the United States. In January 2003 the company cut its profit forecasts for both 2002 and 2003, leading Zondervan to announce his resignation, although he stayed onboard until Ad Veenhof arrived as the new president and CEO in June. Veehhof was a former executive at Royal Philips Electronics N.V. During the executive transition, Wessanen increased its stake in Natudis to 70.65 percent.

Veenhof quickly launched a company-wide cost-reduction program that eventually yielded annual savings in excess of EUR 100 million. Much attention was also paid to returning Tree of Life North America to profitability by making its distribution system leaner and more efficient. European streamlining included the combining of the Dutch operations of Boas and Beckers into a subsidiary called Wessanen Nederland BV.

A strategic review of the company's wide-ranging businesses concluded that Wessanen's troubles stemmed in large measure from its focus on low-margin operations, particularly its private-label and distribution units. The company thus began to place increased emphasis on its branded food lines, with a concentration on two areas: natural and organic foods and "premium taste" foods. The latter included various ethnic specialty food products sold under such brands as Beckers and KA-ME.

FURTHER DIVESTMENTS AND ACQUISITIONS

In 2005 Wessanen began divesting some of its noncore businesses, selling Gelderland Frischwaren, part of its private-label operations, to Balvers Group. Then in February 2007 the company sold its remaining private-label operations, including the Dailycer and Delicia units, to the financial investment firm One Equity Partners for EUR 104 million. On the acquisition front, Wessanen in 2006 purchased full control of Natudis and also acquired Bio Slym S.r.l., an Italian producer of soy milk. The following year Wessanen and a unit of Rabobank Group combined their frozen snack businesses into a joint venture called Favory Convenience Food Group, with Wessanen holding an initial 60.6 percent stake. In July 2008, in a follow-up to its purchase of Bio Slym, Wessanen acquired the soy-based beverage brand So Good, which ranked as the second-largest dairy-alternatives brand in the United Kingdom.

In early 2009 Veenhof resigned abruptly after clashing with the company board over the firm's direction. Wessanen, under the interim leadership of Frans Koffrie, soon altered its strategy to focus principally on branded organic food products with a narrower geographic footprint consisting mainly of the Benelux countries, France, Germany, and the United Kingdom. By January 2010 the German frozen food business Karl Kemper, the U.S. branded business Liberty Richter, and the North American distribution unit Tree of Life had all been divested. A planned sale of Wessanen's sole remaining major North American business, American Beverage Corporation, was delayed after accounting irregularities were uncovered at the unit, but Wessanen aimed to sell the company in 2011.

Impairment charges and a dampening of sales of organic products because of the global economic downturn added up to a net loss of EUR 221.6 million ($309.3 million) during Wessanen's tumultuous 2009. Sales, after accounting for the various divested and discontinued businesses, amounted to only EUR 702.5 million ($980.5 million). Having nearly completed its slimming down to a new core, and having staked its future on the organic sector, Wessanen in March 2010 raised EUR 18.4 million ($25 million) through an equity offering to fund possible acquisitions. The company also hired Piet Hein Merckens, a former executive at both the Procter & Gamble Company and Sara Lee Corporation, to become CEO starting in June 2010.

Updated, David E. Salamie

PRINCIPAL SUBSIDIARIES

Beckers Benelux BV; Favory Convenience Food Group (64.1%); Natudis Nederland BV; Wessanen Europe BV; Wessanen Finance BV; Wessanen Nederland BV; Beckers Belgium BV; Distriborg Groupe SA (France); Wessanen France Holding S.A.S.U.; Allos Walter Lang GmbH (Germany); CoSa Naturprodukte GmbH (Germany); Tartex + Dr. Ritter GmbH (Germany); Wessanen Deutschland GmbH (Germany); Bio Slym S.r.l. (Italy); Wessanen Italy S.r.l.; Kallo Foods Ltd. (UK); Tree of Life UK Ltd.; Wessanen Great Britain Holdings Ltd. (UK); American Beverage Corporation (USA); Wessanen USA Inc.

PRINCIPAL COMPETITORS

Groupe Danone; The Hain Celestial Group, Inc.; Koninklijke FrieslandCampina N.V.; Nestlé S.A.

FURTHER READING

Best, Dean, "Dutch Courage Needed at Wobbly Wessanen," *Just-Food*, January 15, 2010.

——, "Wessanen Talks Up Potential of Organic Food," *Just-Food*, February 27, 2010.

Bickerton, Ian, "Wessanen to Focus on Core Markets," *Financial Times*, September 1, 2004, p. 24.

"BolsWessanen: Hard Cheese," *Economist*, June 20, 1998, p. 75.

Cramb, Gordon, "Sell-Off Ends BolsWessanen Merger," *Financial Times*, July 22, 1998, p. 29.

Du Bois, Martin, "Bols and Wessanen in the Netherlands Agree on Merger," *Wall Street Journal*, January 21, 1993, p. A10.

Fusaro, Dave, "Lowfat Cats, Not Bureaucrats," *Prepared Foods*, April 15, 1996, pp. 8+.

Hollinger, Peggy, "Dutch Group Buys H&C Food Units for £81.6m," *Financial Times*, August 18, 1994, p. 18.

Van de Krol, Ronald, "Dutch Group to Refocus on Foods Side," *Financial Times*, August 15, 1995, p. 18.

"Wessanen Acquires Kallo Foods," *Eurofood*, August 15, 2002, p. 8.

Korea Gas Corporation

215 Jeongja-dong
Bundang-gu
Seongnam
Gyeonggi-do
Seongnam-si, 463 754
South Korea
Telephone: (+82 82) 317100114
Fax: (+82 82) 317100117
Web site: http://www.kogas.or.kr

Public Company
Founded: 1983
Incorporated: 1999
Employees: 2,848
Sales: KRW 19.39 trillion ($15.4 billion) (2009)
Stock Exchanges: Seoul
Ticker Symbol: 036460
NAICS: 221210 Natural Gas Distribution

■ ■ ■

Korea Gas Corporation was founded by the South Korean government in 1983 in order to ensure the country's supply of liquefied natural gas (LNG). As such, Korea Gas, or KOGAS, holds the monopoly over South Korea's wholesale LNG market. KOGAS is also the world's largest LNG importer, bringing in nearly 25 million tons per year in order to supply the commercial, industrial, and residential markets. Each year South Korea consumes more than 1.2 trillion cubic feet of natural gas. In South Korea, KOGAS operates three LNG regasification terminals, as well as nearly 2,740

kilometers of pipeline supplying distributors throughout the country. KOGAS has made an effort to diversify its LNG sources, long centered on the Persian Gulf region. Qatar and Oman together account for nearly 50 percent of the company's total LNG supply. Other major sources include Indonesia, with provides 25 percent, and Malaysia, which supplies 21 percent.

KOGAS has also been diversifying into natural gas and petroleum exploration and development as part of a strategy to raise its self-generated capacity to 25 percent of its total imports by 2017. This effort has led the company to launch development projects in more than nine countries, including Nigeria, Uzbekistan, Oman, and Qatar. In 2010, KOGAS entered the Canadian market in partnership with EnCana Corporation with a CAD 565 million investment. In March of that year, the company also announced plans to launch operations in crude oil exploration and development.

KOGAS has been listed on the Seoul Stock Exchange since 1999. The South Korean government owns nearly 27 percent of the company directly and a total of 61 percent indirectly through its control of KO-GAS's other major shareholder, Korea Electric Power Corp. The company is led by CEO Choo Kangsoo.

DEVELOPING SOUTH KOREA'S
LNG MARKET IN 1983

South Korea's industrialization and modernization effort, launched in the 1960s, had impressive results by the early 1980s. By then, the country had emerged as one of the world's fastest-growing industrial centers. The modernization of the once impoverished country also brought about radical changes in its housing sector. Large-scale construction projects in Seoul and elsewhere had begun to transform the country's skylines with a growing number of multistory residential complexes.

With no natural resources of its own, South Korea adopted a multifaceted approach to ensuring its utility supplies. The government-owned electric utility launched a nuclear power program in the 1970s. Into the 1980s, the country also began adopting natural gas for its residential and commercial heating needs. A number of gas distribution companies were formed in the late 1970s and early 1980s to serve the different local and regional markets. Because South Korea had no natural gas reserves of its own, these companies at first relied on manufactured gas based on naphtha, a petroleum derivative.

The dependence on petroleum supplies, however, left the country vulnerable to the volatility of that market during the period. This led the South Korean government to form a new company, Korea Gas Corporation (KOGAS), which would serve as an importer and wholesale supplier of liquefied natural gas (LNG) to the country's gas distribution companies. Natural gas held a number of advantages over other fuel resources. One major advantage was that it was possible to liquefy the gas at low temperatures, making it easier to transport around the world. Natural gas also burned more cleanly than other fossil fuels, and in this way played a central role in addressing growing concerns over pollution levels accompanying the rapid growth of South Korea's urban and industrial areas. The discovery of increasingly vast natural gas reserves around the world also meant that natural gas had become the least expensive of the fossil fuels.

KOGAS was charged with building an LNG terminal, including regasification unit, in the port of Pyeongtaek, and then with constructing and operating a national pipeline transmission system. The company also entered into negotiations with LNG producer nations in order to secure its natural gas supply. The company's first supply contracts came from Indonesia, and in October 1986 KOGAS took delivery of its first LNG shipments. By November of that year, the company had launched its distribution arm, supplying the power plant at Pyeongtaek.

NATIONAL GAS GRID FROM 1990

During this time, KOGAS had also been laying its first pipeline system, including a 98-kilometer high-pressure transmission linking its LNG terminal to the gas-based power plant in Incheon, the industrial city near Seoul, as well as to the capital city itself. KOGAS also built a 112-kilometer distribution pipeline encircling Seoul in order to supply the seven gas distributors serving the Seoul market. The completion of these projects enabled KOGAS to launch distribution to Seoul and Incheon in February 1987. By April of that year the company had also completed the Pyeongtaek LNG terminal, which reached its full capacity of 400,000 kiloliters.

KOGAS's LNG imports grew strongly through the end of the decade, topping two million metric tons in 1989. Most of the company's capacity went to supply the power stations at Pyeongtaek and Incheon, operated by the government-owned electrical power utility, Korea Electric Power Corporation (Kepco). Demand from the residential and commercial sectors rose steadily as well, topping 354,000 metric tons in 1989, and rising past 550,000 metric tons in 1990. At the same time, Kepco had launched plans to construct five new medium-sized gas-burning power plants to serve the Seoul-Incheon basin, home to approximately 25 percent of South Korea's 40 million population.

The Korean government had begun developing plans to construct, through KOGAS, a national gas transmission grid. This project, expected to cost $2.3 billion, was to be carried out in two phases. KOGAS launched the first, and smaller phase, in 1990. This phase included the expansion of its distribution capacity to the Seoul and Incheon markets, and the extension of the transmission grid with a 130-kilometer high-pressure pipeline to Taejon in 1993.

KOGAS then launched construction of the second and far larger phase of the transmission grid project, which involved the extension of the pipeline system to the south, including a western leg to Kwangju, and an eastern leg to Pusan. Kwangju was the first to be connected, in 1995. The company also began supplying the Honam and Yeongnam markets that year. Construction of the 298-kilometer link to Pusan began in 1996, and was completed in 1998. KOGAS also constructed a second LNG terminal, in Incheon, which began receiving its first LNG shipments in 1996.

KEY DATES

1983: Korea Gas Corporation (KOGAS) is founded by the South Korean government.
1990: KOGAS launches construction of a national natural gas transmission grid.
1999: KOGAS is privatized with a listing on the Seoul Stock Exchange.
2010: KOGAS enters Canada through a partnership with EnCana Corporation.

PRIVATIZATION IN 1999

By then, Korea's natural gas consumption had soared, making the company the fastest-growing natural gas market in Asia. By 1997, the country's annual consumption had topped 12 million metric tons per year. This level was expected to more than double over the next decade. In order to secure its supply, the company negotiated a number of new long-term contracts, notably from Ras Laffan LNG (Rasgas) in Qatar and Oman LNG. These two markets then came to account for nearly 50 percent of the company's total supply.

KOGAS's reliance on long-term supply contracts became a liability, however, amid South Korea's economic collapse in the late 1990s. The recession caused a sudden drop in demand, catching KOGAS off-guard. As a result, the company was forced to carry out a drastic cost-cutting exercise, including laying off nearly half of its employees in June 1998. Meanwhile, the International Monetary Fund had stepped in to arrange a bailout and drastic restructuring of South Korea's economy. As part of this process, the South Korea government announced plans for KOGAS's privatization. This was completed at the end of 1999, when KOGAS listed on the Seoul Stock Exchange. The Korean government ultimately reduced its direct stake in the company to just under 27 percent. At the same time, however, Kepco, which remained majority-owned by the government, stepped in as KOGAS's second-largest shareholder, with nearly 25 percent.

DIVERSIFYING SUPPLY IN 2004

KOGAS's difficulties proved temporary as the South Korean economy, and the country's gas consumption, once again grew strongly into the new century. By the end of 2000, the company's annual imports neared 15 million metric tons, then surged to more than 20 million metric tons by 2003. The company had also continued to extend its infrastructure, completing a third LNG terminal in Tongyeong in 2002.

By then, natural gas distribution had been extended to some 30 percent of the country's total households. Natural gas also represented a significant share of the country's electrical power generation as well. While the company's long-term contracts in Oman and Qatar ran through 2025, South Korea's consumption continued to grow strongly and by 2004 had begun to outstrip KOGAS's existing supplier base.

By mid-decade, KOGAS had launched a new effort seeking to diversify its supplier base. This led the company to secure a new supply contract with Yemen in 2004, as well as a minority stake in Hyundai Yemen LNG Company. The company's diversification drive also led it to pursue active operations in natural gas exploration and development. In 2006, for example, the company reached an agreement with Uzekneftegaz to launch an exploration and development joint venture in Uzbekistan's Surgil gas field, located near the Aral Sea.

WORLD'S LARGEST LNG IMPORTER IN 2010

KOGAS sought other areas for diversification from the middle of the decade. This effort came in part because of the South Korean government's decision to deregulate the country's natural gas market, including the wholesale distribution sector, starting in 2004. KOGAS's dominant position in the market at first allowed it to maintain its de facto monopoly over the sector. Into the second half of the decade, however, the government began developing plans to spin off the group's distribution activities into a separate company.

In the meantime, KOGAS's diversification drive led it into Vietnam, where it began providing consultation services for the construction of that country's natural gas pipeline system. The group's consultation operations soon expanded to Qatar and Nigeria as well. In Russia, the company teamed up with China's CNPC on a national gas development project in Irkutz. The company also joined in on the exploration of the A-1 gas field in Myanmar.

By 2009, KOGAS's natural gas exploration and LNG production had reached nine countries, including Oman and Qatar. The company also targeted further expansion of these operations, with an interest in joining projects in Australia, Nigeria, and Papua New Guinea, as well as further gas field projects in Oman. The company also expected to take part in plans to exploit the natural gas reserves in the Arctic Sea. These efforts came as part of KOGAS's newly announced strategy that year of boosting its rate of self-development to 25 percent of its total LNG imports by 2017.

By 2008, KOGAS's total LNG imports had topped 25 million metric tons, making it the world's largest LNG importer. The company's sales had also grown strongly, rising from KRW 7.3 trillion ($6.1 billion) in 2001 to KRW 23.4 trillion ($18.6 billion) in 2008. The company faced a new setback the following year, however, as the global economic crisis caught up to South Korea as well. As a result, the company's LNG deliveries dropped by 6.4 percent, to 24.64 million tons, while its sales dropped below KRW 19.5 trillion ($15.4 billion).

KOGAS's expansion program nonetheless remained intact. At the beginning of 2010, the company's Uzbekistan project appeared to be nearing a launch point, as the company reached an agreement calling for a total investment of $4 billion there. In March 2010, the company added Canada to its list of active markets, when it announced plans to invest CAD 565 million in a gas field development partnership with that country's EnCana Corporation. At the same time, KOGAS announced a new plan to expand its operations into crude oil development and production. From its base as South Korea's natural gas giant, KOGAS hoped to claim a place among the world's energy leaders.

M. L. Cohen

PRINCIPAL SUBSIDIARIES

Gyeonggi CES Co. Ltd. (54.64%); Hyundai Yemen LNG Company (49%); Korea Gas Technology Corp.; Korea LNG Ltd. (24%); Korea Ras Laffan LNG Ltd. (60%).

PRINCIPAL DIVISIONS

LNG Import and Distribution; Resources Development Division; Resources Business Division; LNG Terminal Division; Trunk Line Division.

PRINCIPAL COMPETITORS

E.ON AG; SUEZ; Gaz de France; PetroChina Company Ltd.; Gazprom Russia Joint Stock Co.; Petroliam Nasional Bhd.; Petronas Nasional Bhd.; Osaka Gas Company Ltd.; SembCorp Industries Ltd.

FURTHER READING

Hayes, David, "Moves to a National Grid," *Gas World International*, December 1990, p. 26.

"Kogas Eyes Global Gas Fields," *Pipeline & Gas Journal*, February 2009, p. 16.

"Kogas Ups Stake in YLNG," *MEED Middle East Economic Digest*, August 11, 2006, p. 16.

"Kogas' Uzbek Project Gaining Steam," *UzReport*, February 10, 2010.

"Korea Gas Announces Fiscal 2009 Results," *International Resource News*, February 5, 2010.

"Korea Gas Plans to Expand into Crude Oil Development, Production and Sales Business," *International Resource News*, March 5, 2010.

"Meteoric Rise Gives Way to a Sudden Slump," *MEED Middle East Economic Digest*, August 21, 1998, p. 12.

"25% Self-Development in 2017," *Business Korea*, March 2009, p. 24.

Korean Air Lines Co., Ltd.

———————— ■ ————————

Korean Air Operations Center 1370, Gonghang-dong, Gangseo-gu
Seoul, 157-712
South Korea
Telephone: (82 822) 26567857
Toll Free: (800) 438-5000
Fax: (82 822) 26565709
Web site: http://www.koreanair.com

Public Company
Incorporated: 1969 as Korean Air Lines
Employees: 19,178
Sales: KRW 9.39 trillion (2009)
Stock Exchanges: Korea
Ticker Symbol: 003490
NAICS: 481111 Scheduled Passenger Air Transportation; 481112 Scheduled Freight Air Transportation; 488190 Other Support Activities for Air Transportation; 721110 Hotels (Except Casino Hotels) and Motels

■ ■ ■

Korean Air Lines Co., Ltd., (KAL) is South Korea's leading airline and part of the giant Hanjin Group, which deals in land, sea, and air transport, construction, heavy industry, finance, and information services. After a slew of accidents in the late 1990s, KAL revamped its training and safety culture while maintaining aspirations for the highest standards of customer service. It became a founding member of the SkyTeam global alliance in 2000.

More than 20 million passengers fly KAL every year, which boasts the largest cargo operations of any passenger airline. The company operates a fleet of 127 planes, 22 of them dedicated freighters. Its route network includes 105 destinations in 35 countries. The company is involved in extensive ancillary activities such as hotels and in-flight catering, but 96 percent of total revenues in 2009 came from air transportation.

ORIGINS

Korean Air Lines Co., Ltd., has throughout its history been controlled by the Hanjin Group, which has its origins in Hanjin Transportation Co. Cho Choong-hoon started the company in 1945, at a time when the Korean economy was in a state of chaos following World War II. Cho saw a market for trucking services, and his first major customer was the United States Armed Forces, who were busy establishing bases in Seoul, Pusan, and other Korean cities.

The hostilities between North and South Korea from 1951 to 1954, which involved combined United Nations forces against North Korean and Chinese forces, proved beneficial to business in South Korea. The huge U.S. military investment in South Korea required various local services, transport being one of the most important. Hanjin expanded rapidly and in 1956 was the prime transporter of U.S. military cargo in Korea. In 1960 the company was granted an air transportation license, which proved important in its later expansion in this sector. The company founded Air Korea, which initially dealt with cargo. In 1961 and 1964, respectively, Hanjin Sightseeing Bus Company and

Korea Vehicle Transportation were established, with Daejin Shipping Company joining the group in 1967. Cho's company had become a leading private transportation firm in South Korea. In 1969 the South Korean government recognized Hanjin for its performance as an earner of foreign exchange and presented it with the Presidential Flag Citation. This same year the Korean government would transfer operations and ownership of the bankrupt state-owned carrier Korean National Airlines (KNA) to the Hanjin Group. The new name for the carrier was Korean Air Lines (KAL).

KNA had folded in 1962 because of a combination of low demand, inability to compete with foreign carriers, and inexperienced management dealing with poor technology. The enterprise had been started by the government shortly after World War II and consisted of nine small aircraft. The Korean government could not afford to keep the airline afloat, however, and began the search for suitable private-sector investors. The task of rehabilitating the airline was at first taken on by Cho's Hanjin Group, in part out of a sense of patriotic duty and in part as a business challenge.

At the time the prospect of a mismanaged, ill-equipped airline competing with the world's largest carriers seemed daunting. Cho realized that the domestic market for air travel within South Korea was limited by the country's small size, and international travel originating out of country was severely restricted by a government ban on its citizens traveling abroad. Despite these limitations Cho put his acute business sense to work on the airline, which he acquired in March 1969.

BUILDING THE NATIONAL CARRIER AFTER 1969

The first step Cho took was to build up an Asian network based on cargo rather than passenger business. The freight business remained a mainstay of KAL, accounting for 40 percent of revenues. Although a freight network could be built up to serve the explosion of manufacturing that was taking place at the time, finding a passenger market proved to be a different matter. The growing volume of business travel and visits to South

Korea by tourists was not enough to maintain a civil carrier, and Cho's strategy, therefore, was to use Seoul as a transit route in the busy Asian region. Japan proved to be the strongest market in this category, with cost-conscious tour groups prepared to travel an indirect route to the United States or Europe via Seoul.

The first activities of the new airline consisted of the opening of branches in Taipei, Hong Kong, Saigon, and Bangkok, plus the commencement of service to Osaka in Japan from Pusan, followed by flights to Taipei, Hong Kong, and Bangkok from Seoul. In 1970 KAL moved into a new 26-story building built by the Hanil Development Company, a member of the Hanjin Group. New hangars also were constructed in 1970 to accommodate KAL's new fleet of planes. The operation of a Seoul-to-Los Angeles cargo route was followed closely by the 1973 acquisition of KAL's first Boeing 747, which was put into immediate service on the route. Although KAL began its first regular flight to Europe with a cargo service to Paris in 1973, the airline remained at a severe disadvantage in flying to Europe. Whereas other Asian airlines took advantage of the direct route to Europe over the U.S.S.R., South Korean aircraft were not granted such privileges by a Soviet government that still refused to recognize South Korea as an independent state.

KAL, therefore, concentrated on transpacific service to the United States and became the first airline to offer an all-cargo 747 service across the Pacific. Cho saw the need to keep pace with his international competitors' technological advances. KAL opened a modern engine shop at Seoul's Kimpo International Airport and introduced an IBM mainframe computer in its push toward full computerization. In 1975 KAL became one of Airbus's first customers with the purchase of three A300s, which were put into immediate service in the Asian routes.

In 1976 KAL established an aerospace division to contribute to South Korea's aviation and defense industry. Borrowing engineers from its maintenance department and using the resources of the Hanjin Group, KAL formed the Korean Institute of Aeronautical Technology as a subsidiary in 1978. The company was involved initially in the assembly of helicopters for McDonnell Douglas of the United States. In 1981, with the help of Northrop, it built South Korea's first domestically produced fighter aircraft, the F-5EF. The aerospace division planned to develop a short-range commuter aircraft eventually.

On the civil passenger side of operations KAL continued its expansion with services to Paris, Manila, Bahrain, Zurich, Nagoya, Kuwait, Colombo, and Abu Dhabi by 1979. To accommodate these routes KAL

KEY DATES

∎

1945: Cho Choong-hoon establishes Hanjin Group.
1969: Government privatizes its airline holdings as Korean Air Lines (KAL), controlled by Hanjin Group.
1976: KAL establishes its aerospace division.
1983: KAL Flight 007 is shot down after it strays into Soviet airspace.
1988: Seoul Olympics offers KAL a chance to showcase its services to international travelers.
1989: Government lifts restrictions on overseas travel by South Korean citizens.
2000: KAL becomes founding member of SkyTeam global alliance.
2006: KAL's fleet renewal program includes massive $5.5 billion Boeing order.

placed an order with Boeing that represented the second-largest single order in commercial aviation history: 18 Boeing 747 jets. Nonstop KAL service to New York and Los Angeles began shortly thereafter. The lack of access to trans-Siberia passage to Europe continued to be problematic for KAL. The airline was forced to fly to destinations in Europe via Anchorage.

FLIGHT 007 DISASTER IN 1983

In 1983 disaster struck KAL Flight 007, which strayed off course into Soviet airspace. The Boeing 747 was intercepted and destroyed by a squadron of Soviet fighter aircraft; 269 passengers and crew members were killed. The incident resulted in international condemnation of the U.S.S.R. and counteraccusations by the Soviet government that the KAL flight was being used to gather intelligence, a claim hotly contested by KAL and the South Korean government. The incident was a severe setback for the airline and strained relations between South Korea and the U.S.S.R. for several years afterward. KAL's strategy for the next three years was to increase its freight network, and the airline invested heavily in freight terminals in Tokyo, Los Angeles, and New York.

KAL acquired a state-of-the-art control system for its freight network and in 1983 computerized its passenger reservation system with the introduction of a ticketing system called TOPAS. KAL scored a coup in 1986 when it became one of the first airlines to supply Boeing with parts for its aircraft, in the form of a contract to deliver wingtip extensions for the Boeing

747-400. KAL continued to be one of Boeing's prized customers with an order for 10 of the aircraft in 1988.

1988 OLYMPICS & LIFTING OF TRAVEL RESTRICTIONS

In that year KAL began services to London, Vancouver, Toronto, Jakarta, and Frankfurt. The Olympic Games held in Seoul in 1988, although marred by a boycott from the U.S.S.R. and other Communist nations, was a financial success for the country. KAL was named official carrier for the games and took advantage of the influx of visitors to the country to display the full range of comforts it offered passengers. Cho had long stressed the need to offer quality service on par with the world's best airlines. As a result, KAL's first-class service was noted worldwide for its comfort and convenience.

Governmental restrictions on overseas travel by South Korean citizens were lifted in 1989, resulting in a 100 percent annual increase in passenger volume out of the country in each of the last two years, with more growth predicted in the near future. KAL's first scheduled flight to Moscow from Seoul occurred in 1991, and the breakup of the U.S.S.R. eased relations between South Korea and the former Soviet states. The airline aimed at continued aggressive expansion and sought strategic partners to achieve this. Leading contenders in this included the Philippines' national airline, PAL.

NEW ROUTES

The company also began serving Chinese destinations. Negotiation for "beyond" rights, however, the right to carry passengers from Beijing to another international destination, remained a point of contention. Still, KAL's long-term ambitions included establishing Seoul as a gateway to China (contingent upon development of Korea's new airport at Inchon). In addition, scheduled cargo flights were not included in the Sino-Korean agreement.

In the 1990s, buoyed by generally excellent financial results, KAL maintained its ambition of being the world's best airline with a route network extending around the globe, as *Air Transport World* reported. New routes were continually added. KAL became the first Asian airline to fly directly to Africa. A vigorous acquisition policy kept the company supplied with new planes. Operating revenues passed $3 billion in 1993 as Korean travelers took to the skies in unprecedented numbers, thanks to the relaxation of travel restrictions in 1989 and a booming domestic economy. The cargo market was even more robust. Then the world's third-largest freight carrier, the company grew 20 percent a year in the mid-1990s. Operating revenue reached $4.4 billion in 1995. At the same time, increasing competition from international carriers and potential industry overcapacity gave KAL managers cause for concern.

OVERCOMING TRAGEDY & OTHER CHALLENGES

In 1996, thanks to these worries and rising jet fuel prices, KAL lost KRW 210 billion ($235.5 million) on revenues that remained steady from 1995. Its losses were compounded by unfavorable exchange rates. The 1997 deficit was KRW 280 billion ($281.9 million).

A second catastrophic accident befell the company in August 1997 when Flight 801 crashed in Guam, killing 226 people. U.S. investigators implicated pilot error as the precipitating factor. KAL officials, however, blamed inadequate airport landing instruments.

In the late 1990s the devalued won had made Korea an attractive destination for Korean expatriates living in the United States, although domestic travelers flew less. While its smaller rival Asiana lost a deposit on a large Airbus order it canceled, KAL coped with lessened demand by selling aircraft as new shipments of Boeings continued. The company also laid off a 10th of its upper level managers.

Aircraft production projects in the 1990s included the UH-60 Black Hawk helicopter for the South Korean air force, as well as military fighter and trainer programs. The aerospace division had grown to 2,400 employees. The company also operated an extensive maintenance division, providing support for more than 30 airlines. Its catering operation served an equivalent number of carriers and garnered the International Flight Catering Association's top in-flight meal award in 1998.

Such advantages allowed KAL to again announce a profit, of KRW 250 billion, for 1998. The results seemed to justify the company's aircraft purchases, which let it boast one of the youngest fleets in the world, as well as sales of about 18 older aircraft in 1997. Asian and Pacific traffic was expected to account for half of all air travel by 2010, according to the International Air Transport Association. Nonetheless, a $5 billion debt guaranteed navigating the company would remain a challenge for Cho Yang-ho, who succeeded his father as president in 1992.

REBUILDING AFTER 1999

KAL recovered relatively quickly from the effects of the Asian financial crisis as the South Korean economy surged on the strength of technology-related exports. It

would not be as easy to slough off safety concerns.

The company had begun a cargo service to China in 1998 and the fatal crash of a freighter in China in April 1999 was its fourth major loss in two years. Delta Air Lines, Air Canada, and Air France subsequently suspended their code-share arrangements with KAL.

In the aftermath company founder Cho Choong-hoon relinquished his chairman's post to his son, Cho Yang-ho. The younger Cho had earned an M.B.A. at the University of Southern California and was reportedly an admirer of U.S. business culture. He set out to change the rigidly hierarchical culture on the flight deck, which was a legacy of Oriental societies in general as well as the military, from which many of its pilots had been drawn. It became a safety consideration when subordinate officers were afraid to alert captains of errors.

REBRANDING CAMPAIGN IN 2005

An extensive revamp of the operations ensued, with the company contracting FlightSafety Boeing. Over the next several years the airline also invested billions in new aircraft interiors, new planes, and other features to lure lucrative business travelers. The company's turnaround efforts were crowned with a rebranding campaign in 2005 with the theme "Excellence in Flight." KAL endured a pilots' strike in December of that year, a few months after one at rival Asiana.

KAL continued to play a prominent role on the world stage. In 2000 the company was a founding partner in the new SkyTeam global alliance along with Delta Air Lines, Air France, and Aeromexico. A new airport, Incheon International Airport, opened in 2001, becoming the base for most of KAL's long-haul routes, while domestic and regional flights were served from Gimpo International. Even so, KAL lost $352 million in 2000 and another $450 million in 2001.

KAL remained aloof from the industry consolidation that joined South Korea's Samsung Aerospace, Hyundai Space and Aircraft, and parts of Daewoo Heavy Industries & Machinery in 1999 to form Korean Aerospace Industries (KAI). KAL Aerospace contributed 6.8 percent of revenues and 17.5 percent of profits in 1998. More than half of its business was with U.S. and South Korean military customers, although in the 1990s it had built up a significant business manufacturing subassemblies for Boeing and Airbus airliners. In 2003 KAL expressed interest in buying a stake in KAI, but dropped the bid three years later. KAL's own aerospace division had revenues of $470 million by 2008.

KAL posted a KRW 241 billion loss in 2003, a year known for the SARS crisis and high fuel prices. The airline responded by cutting routes and deferring aircraft purchases. However, in 2004 the cargo unit placed ambitious orders that would add freighters to the fleet at the rate of two per year. The South Korean government was aiming to position the country as a trade gateway, upgrading the facilities at Incheon into a major cargo hub to support the still growing South Korean economy.

KAL found a ready market among the hundreds of Korean-run companies in China. The government began to ease restrictions on head-to-head international competition between Korean carriers beginning with a few Chinese routes in April 2004. KAL also looked to India, Japan, and Eastern Europe for growth potential.

OPTIMISTIC AMID COMPETITION, ECONOMIC SLOWDOWN

Meanwhile, a crop of new budget airlines was providing price competition on domestic routes. In July 2008, KAL fielded its own budget airline, Jin Air Co., Ltd., beginning with just one plane (a Boeing 737) flying between Seoul and Jeju Island. The country then had about 20 small airlines operating domestic or regional routes. KAL's domestic routes were generally unprofitable.

In November 2006 KAL placed a huge $5.5 billion order for 25 Boeing aircraft as it waited for delivery of Airbus's much-delayed A380 superjumbo. KAL had earlier ordered 10 of Boeing's competing 787, which would not be delivered for a few years. The airline was spending about $1 billion a year on capital expenses such as new planes and various service upgrades.

The company also had to contend with very high fuel costs and unfavorable exchange rates, and posted a net loss of KRW 1.95 trillion ($1.6 billion) on revenues of KRW 10.19 trillion ($8.16 billion) in 2008. With the global economic slowdown, revenues slipped about 13 percent to KRW 9.39 trillion in 2009. The airline then served 105 destinations in 35 countries with a fleet of 127 aircraft, including 22 dedicated freighters. The group's spending on fleet upgrades and a new hotel in Los Angeles was conspicuous in such a depressed economy, noted the *Los Angeles Times*, but KAL had big plans for the future, aiming for KRW 25 trillion in operating revenues by 2019.

Dylan Tanner
Updated, Frederick C. Ingram

PRINCIPAL SUBSIDIARIES

Jin Air Co., Ltd.; Korean Air Lines Cargo Co., Ltd.; Korea Airport Service Co., Ltd. (58.9%).

PRINCIPAL DIVISIONS

Passenger; Cargo; Catering & In-Flight Sales Business; Hotel Business; Aerospace Business.

PRINCIPAL COMPETITORS

Asiana Airlines Inc.; Singapore Airlines Limited; Cathay Pacific Airways Limited; Jeju Air Co.; Air Busan Co.

FURTHER READING

"Aircraft Deals Lift Korean Air Profit," *South China Morning Post*, February 23, 1999.

Dunn, Graham, "Interview: Korean Air Chief Executive Cho Yang-ho," *Airline Business*, June 18, 2009.

Mackey, Michael, "Pall over Asia," *Air Transport World*, September 1998, pp. 30–38.

———, "The 'Reluctant Dragon,'" *Air Transport World*, April 1996, pp. 43–47.

———, "Unification Watch," *Air Transport World*, August 1994, pp. 87–88.

Nelms, Douglas W., "Make, Manage and Maintain," *Air Transport World*, August 1997, pp. 97–98.

"On a Won and a Prayer," *Economist*, November 15, 1997, p. 69.

Pae, Peter, "Korean Air Bucks Trends amid Industry Turbulence," *Los Angeles Times*, June 24, 2009.

Putzger, Ian, "Korean's View; After Becoming the World's Largest International Air Cargo Carrier, Korean Air Finds Turbulence at the Top," *Air Cargo World*, September 2005, pp. 18–19.

Taehan Hanggong, and Chusik Hoesa, *Wings of Korea: The First 15 Years of Korean Air Lines, 1969–1984*, Seoul: Korean Air Lines Public Relations Dept., 1984.

Thomas, Geoffrey, "The Flight to Quality," *Air Transport World*, September 2005, pp. 40–46.

Vandyk, Anthony, "Korean: Still Riding the Tiger," *Air Transport World*, June 1993, p. 204.

The World of Korean Air, Seoul: Korean Air Lines, 1990.

Yu, Roger, "Korean Air Upgrades Service, Image; CEO's Safety-First Philosophy Helps Airline Grow," *USA Today*, August 24, 2009, p. B1.

Legacy Health System

———————————■———————————

1919 Northwest Lovejoy Street
Portland, Oregon 97209
U.S.A.
Telephone: (503) 415-5600
Fax: (503) 415-5777
Web site: http://www.legacyhealth.org

Nonprofit Organization
Incorporated: 1989
Employees: 9,168
Sales: $1.18 billion (2009)
NAICS: 622110 General Medical and Surgical Hospitals; 622210 Psychiatric and Substance Abuse Hospitals; 622310 Specialty (Except Psychiatric and Substance Abuse) Hospitals; 624230 Emergency and Other Relief Services

■ ■ ■

Legacy Health System is the second-largest hospital system in the Portland, Oregon, area, trailing Providence Health & Services, which operates 27 hospitals. Legacy operates six hospitals as well as a number of primary care and specialty clinics and outpatient laboratories. The company's hospitals are Legacy Emanuel Medical Center, The Children's Hospital at Legacy Emanuel, and Legacy Good Samaritan Medical Center, each of which is located in the central Portland area. Legacy Mount Hood Medical Center is located east of Portland in Gresham, a suburb. Legacy Meridian Park Medical Center is located southwest of Portland in the suburb of Tualatin. Legacy also operates Legacy Salmon Creek

Medical Center, a hospital located near Vancouver, Washington.

MERGER CREATES LEGACY: 1989

Legacy, created through a merger, was one of the three largest health care systems in Portland, Oregon, at its birth. In April 1989 two health care providers joined forces, seeking to gain an advantage by marrying their assets. Good Samaritan Hospital & Medical Center, a hospital founded in 1875, united with Healthlink, owner of four hospitals, Holladay Park Medical Center, Meridian Park Hospital, Mount Hood Medical Center, and its signature property, the Emanuel Hospital & Health Center, founded in 1912. The two hospital operators also owned a home health care agency and several nursing homes and intermediate care centers, which, combined with the five hospitals, gave the newly created Legacy $446 million in annual revenues and control over 28 percent of the hospital business in the Portland area.

Although Healthlink brought four hospitals to the merger, the newly created company took its leader from Good Samaritan. Chester Stocks, who had spent the previous 27 years serving as CEO of Good Samaritan, became Legacy's president and CEO upon its formation. Stocks, 61 years old, had a formidable challenge before him. Legacy was impressive in stature, but it was riddled with problems.

Stocks presided over five former competitors who now found themselves thrust into a position of working together for the better good of Legacy. The transition did not go smoothly, exacerbated by redundancies within the organization that made the five-hospital system one of the most costly systems in Oregon. Additional problems plagued Legacy from the start, namely the debt carried by each of the hospitals and money-losing nursing home operations. During its first full year of business in 1990, Legacy reported a loss of $3.4 million. The company's problems became more profound when it lost its leader. Stocks died in December 1990 of a heart attack, leaving the ailing Legacy to search for a new CEO capable of stanching its losses.

Legacy turned to its chief financial officer to lead the company on an interim basis while it searched for a permanent replacement for Stocks. While Legacy's board of directors conducted its search, measures were taken to ease the company's financial burdens. In early 1991 Legacy organized a $200 million bond offering, one of the largest hospital bond issues in the country, to refinance its existing debt and to reimburse its five hospitals for recent capital spending. The bond offering reduced the company's annual interest costs by $1.5 million and buoyed hopes for profitability in the near future. Company morale brightened considerably when a replacement for Stocks arrived midway through the year. Legacy, as the coming years would demonstrate, had found the individual to put the company on a firm financial footing.

CEO KING LEADS RESTRUCTURING EFFORTS

John King became president and CEO of Legacy in July 1991. He joined the company after serving as the president and CEO of Chicago-based Evangelical Health Systems, where he had spent the previous 11 years. Although King traveled nearly 2,000 miles to accept his new job, he occupied familiar ground when he took the helm at Legacy. Evangelical Health Systems, like Legacy,

operated five hospitals. In 1989, Evangelical Health Systems generated $479 million in revenues, a total only slightly more than the $446 million recorded by Legacy.

When King joined Legacy the company was in the midst of trimming its payroll in an effort to reduce overhead. King embraced the initiative and took it to a higher level, focusing his efforts on developing a restructuring plan that not only would eliminate positions within the organization but also consolidate health care programs, centralize administrative services, and end Legacy's involvement in certain practice areas. He sought to make Legacy a leaner, smaller health system that was more efficient and financially stable.

By early 1992 Legacy was nearly three years into an effort to cut costs and reduce its payroll. King announced another three-year-long campaign to reduce expenses, revealing that Legacy planned to eliminate another 200 positions and bring the company's payroll down to approximately 4,800 staff. "This isn't going to be accomplished, necessarily, in one short burst of activity," he said in the March 30, 1992 issue of *Business Journal-Portland.*

TRIMMING PAYROLL, CONSOLIDATING SERVICES: 1992–95

By the fall of 1992 Legacy had eliminated 100 positions, including 40 management positions. King's efforts to reorganize the company went deeper, as he faced a glut of medical service providers in his market, each competitor vying for contracts with insurers. He consolidated the services offered by the five hospitals he governed, getting rid of overlapping programs and assigning each hospital specific areas of focus.

Heart and cancer services became Good Samaritan Hospital's specialty. Orthopedics and neurology were based at Emanuel Hospital. Holladay Park, which was stripped of its emergency room, acute surgical care functions, and its nuclear medicine department, assumed responsibility for non-urgent laboratory work. King centralized clerical and administrative services, empowered a single management team led by one president to control the company's three central city hospitals (Good Samaritan Hospital, Emanuel Hospital, and Holladay Park), and went as far as legally merging Emanuel Hospital and Holladay Park. "We are moving from a system that I would call a hospital-based system to a managed care system," King said in the November 23, 1992 issue of *Business Journal-Portland.* "And that means that we're becoming more customer-directed, more focused on relationships with health clients, and providing health plan alternatives to the community."

King's actions injected financial vitality into a struggling organization. In 1993 he formed an alliance with Blue Cross and Blue Shield of Oregon, seeking to make Legacy more competitive in managed care by collaborating on business planning, data networks, product development, and marketing with the health care giant. Within 18 months, he sold Tigard Immediate Care Clinic, closed Milwaukie Care Clinic, and sold Gresham Intermediate Care Center, ridding Legacy of its immediate care centers, each founded as for-profit clinics by Good Samaritan during the 1980s. By the end of 1996, King could point to strong evidence of his success. Legacy ended the year with revenues of $485 million and nearly $40 million in net income.

LEADERSHIP TRANSITION: 1997–99

King had achieved his objective as Legacy entered the second half of the 1990s. When he joined the company in 1991, he said his tenure would be limited, and in 1997 he followed through on his promise. He accepted an offer to become president of the American Hospital Association during the year and began developing a plan to hire his replacement. Robert J. Pollari was appointed chief financial officer and effectively took over day-to-day management of Legacy while King, focused on national health issues, spent as much as 30 percent of his time away from Legacy. Pollari's performance as chief financial officer was scrutinized by Legacy's board of directors for nearly two years, his actions and demeanor assessed in what amounted to a crucible of his leadership skills. Pollari passed the test, earning the endorsement of King and the company's board of directors, becoming Legacy's president and CEO in February 1999.

The financial stability established under King's guidance enabled Pollari to pursue an agenda of expansion. For the first time in its history, Legacy began to add to its holdings. Reports of the company's new, growth-minded stance emerged in early 2001, when plans were made public for the construction of a new 130-bed hospital that was expected to cost $130 million. Pollari intended to build the new hospital north of Vancouver, Washington, 20 miles from Portland. The project promised to give Washington its first new hospital since 1979 and it raised the ire of Southwest Washington Medical Center, the only hospital in the region. Legacy pressed ahead, nonetheless, amplifying the scope of the project. By mid-2001, the company was proposing to build a 200-bed, $170 million hospital along with a $10 million, 15-bed newborn intensive care unit.

NEW WASHINGTON HOSPITAL OPENS: 2005

As construction commenced at the Washington site, Legacy invested in improvements of its Portland properties. In 2003 the company completed a $3 million expansion of its family birth center at Mount Hood Medical Center in Gresham. The highlight of the period, however, was the new facility near Vancouver, which had been named Legacy Salmon Creek Medical Center. The project ultimately cost $278 million to complete, resulting in a 475,000-square-foot, 220-bed, six-story hospital that opened in mid-2005.

Reorganization had been King's crowning achievement and the construction of Salmon Creek Medical Center proved to be Pollari's lasting contribution to Legacy. Pollari left Legacy several months after Salmon Creek Medical Center opened. In January 2006 he was replaced by Lee Domanico, whose stay at Legacy was relatively short. Domanico resigned in October 2007 to pursue other opportunities in the health care field. The search for a replacement lasted nearly a year, concluding with the selection of George J. Brown in August 2008. A former brigadier general in the U.S. Army, Brown previously had served as chief operating officer of Multi-Care Health System, a Tacoma, Washington-based health care provider.

LEGACY TURNS 20

Brown assumed control over Legacy during a difficult period for the company. Deteriorating economic conditions at the end of the decade weakened the company's financial footing. It reported a loss on its investments during its 20th anniversary in 2009 and faced surging demand for charity care, which taxed the company's financial resources. Despite the turbulent economic times, the company was pressing ahead with capital expenditure efforts.

In 2009 the company launched a major project, announcing plans to build a new home for the children's hospital at Emanuel Medical Center. The facility was designed to accommodate more than 160 acute and intensive care rooms. Legacy was a 20-year-old company when it began moving forward with the project, having triumphed during its first great test in the years immediately following its creation. As the company celebrated its anniversary, the specter of another trying period loomed, one that would test the skills of Legacy's executive team.

Jeffrey L. Covell

PRINCIPAL OPERATING UNITS

The Children's Hospital Legacy Emanuel; Legacy Good Samaritan Medical Center; Legacy Meridian Park Medical Center; Legacy Mount Hood Medical Center; Legacy Salmon Creek Medical Center; Legacy System Office; Legacy Clinical Research & Technology Center; Legacy Hospice; CareMark Behavioral Services; Managed HealthCare Northwest; Legacy Medical Group.

PRINCIPAL COMPETITORS

Providence Health & Services; Kaiser Permanente; Adventist Health.

FURTHER READING

Brock, Kathy, "King Abdicates Legacy's Throne," *Business Journal-Portland*, February 12, 1999, p. 3.

———, "Legacy Head Sees Restructuring as Crowning Achievement," *Business Journal-Portland*, November 23, 1992, p. 12.

———, "Legacy to Cut 200 Positions in Year Ahead: Large Employer Puts Programs under the Knife to Stay Competitive in Managed Care Arena," *Business Journal-Portland*, March 30, 1992, p. 1.

"King Will Rule Five-Hospital Legacy Chain," *Business Journal-Portland*, May 13, 1991, p. 2.

"Legacy Health System," *Hospitals & Health Networks*, August 2008, p. 57.

Stout, Heidi, "Duel for New Hospital Goes to the Next Round," *Business Journal-Portland*, March 30, 2001, p. 13.

Linamar Corporation

———————■———————

287 Speedvale Avenue West
Guelph, Ontario N1H 1C5
Canada
Telephone: (519) 836-7550
Fax: (519) 824-8479
Web site: http://www.linamar.com

Public Company
Incorporated: 1966 as Linamar Machine Limited
Employees: 9,000
Sales: CAD 2.26 billion ($1.84 billion) (2008)
Stock Exchanges: Toronto
Ticker Symbol: LNR
NAICS: 333112 Lawn and Garden Tractor and Home
   Lawn and Garden Equipment Manufacturing;
   333923 Overhead Traveling Crane, Hoist, and
   Monorail System Manufacturing; 333924 Industrial
   Truck, Tractor, Trailer, and Stacker Machinery
   Manufacturing; 336311 Carburetor, Piston, Piston
   Ring, and Valve Manufacturing; 336312 Gasoline
   Engine and Engine Parts Manufacturing; 336350
   Motor Vehicle Transmission and Power Train Parts
   Manufacturing

■ ■ ■

The principal business of Canada-based Linamar
Corporation, one that generates about 80 percent of the
firm's revenues, is the manufacturing of precision metallic
components for automobiles and other motor
vehicles. Ranking as Canada's second-largest auto parts
supplier, trailing only Magna International Inc.,

Linamar specializes in components, modules, and
systems for light-vehicle and heavy-duty engines,
transmissions, and drivetrains. Its largest customers for
these vehicle parts include Caterpillar Inc., Chrysler
Group LLC, Ford Motor Company, and General Motors
Corporation. Linamar also owns Skyjack, Inc., a
producer of aerial work platforms and rough-terrain
forklifts, and Linamar Consumer Products Ltd., maker
of cordless rechargeable lawnmowers and utility trailers.
In addition, Linamar has majority control of Linamar
Hungary Nyrt., a publicly traded Hungarian company
that produces agricultural implements. The global
operations of Linamar include about three-dozen
manufacturing plants, five research and development
centers, and 10 sales offices in Canada, the United
States, Mexico, the United Kingdom, Germany,
Hungary, Sweden, China, Japan, and South Korea.

EARLY HISTORY

The driving force behind the development of Linamar
Corporation was its founder, Frank Hasenfratz, who
remained the firm's chairman and largest shareholder
through the first decade of the 21st century. A native of
Hungary, Hasenfratz emigrated from the land of his
birth in 1956 during the chaotic and violent Soviet
invasion and occupation. Arriving in Austria as a
refugee, he served as a translator for his fellow Hungarians
who also fled after the Soviet invasion. Working his
way to France, he met some Italian crewmen who allowed
him to travel free to Canada on their freighter.
Met by immigration officials when the ship docked in
Quebec City, Hasenfratz was interviewed, given immigration
status, and provided with a total amount of

CAD 5.00 to start a new life. Not knowing where to go, the young man of 22 years remained a few days in the railway station in Quebec City and then traveled to Guelph, Ontario, when he heard of an employment opportunity. He was hired by W.C. Woods Company as a machinist but was laid off after a short stint of six months.

Undismayed, and full of confidence in himself, Hasenfratz soon found another job as a machinist. From 1958 to 1964, he worked diligently in order to save his money for the right entrepreneurial opportunity. In 1964 the time was ripe. With CAD 600 he had saved from his six years of work, he opened a one-man machine shop in his own garage. His first contract was for the manufacture of automotive oil pumps. In 1966 Hasenfratz incorporated his firm as Linamar Machine Limited, naming it after his daughters Linda and Nancy and his wife Margaret. By that year, Linamar had grown large enough to employ five people at the Linamar Ariss Plant in Guelph. During the same year, the ambitious businessman received his big break, a contract to manufacture automotive oil pumps for Ford Motor Company of Canada.

Throughout the late 1960s and the decade of the 1970s, Hasenfratz worked hard to expand the customer base of Linamar. Gradually, the company garnered larger and larger contracts for component parts not only from Ford Motor Company of Canada but also from defense industry firms located in both the United States and Canada. As his customer base grew, so did revenues and the number of employees. By the end of the 1970s, Linamar's revenues totaled CAD 7 million and more than 80 people were employed at the company's Ariss Plant in Guelph.

GROWTH & EXPANSION DURING THE EIGHTIES

By 1980, sales at Linamar had increased to CAD 10 million, and Hasenfratz was ready to implement an aggressive acquisitions strategy to quicken the pace of his company's growth. One of the first purchases made during the 1980s was White Farm Equipment of Canada, Ltd. Having previously engaged in subcontract work for the company, Hasenfratz jumped at the opportunity to acquire White Farm which, in spite of its annual sales base of approximately CAD 280 million, had filed for bankruptcy. The first year after White Farm's acquisition, Linamar made a handsome profit, but shortly thereafter a minority partner in the transaction activated a provision in a shareholder agreement and Hasenfratz was forced to sell his interest in the company. Nonetheless, Linamar had greatly benefited from the acquisition, because the company had gained expertise in the design and manufacture of farm equipment.

Like many other companies during the 1980s, Linamar's growth stemmed from its acquisition policy. The difference between Linamar and other larger corporations at the time was that Linamar integrated acquisitions quickly into its manufacturing operations, rather than breaking up its acquisition into divisions or component parts and then selling them to the highest bidder. Major acquisitions during this period included Bata Engineering (renamed Invar Manufacturing Ltd.), located in Batawa, Ontario. The rationale behind the acquisition was to take advantage of the company's expertise in the production of sophisticated components for defense and commercial applications. Perhaps the most important acquisition during the 1980s, however, was Western Combine Corporation. Western manufactured the Rotary Combine model 8570 for Massey Ferguson in North America, and was soon selling it globally under the auspices of Linamar.

The strategic acquisitions of Bata Engineering and Western Combine were augmented by Linamar's policy of developing its own semiautonomous subsidiaries. Located mostly in Guelph, the first of these subsidiaries was Linex, created to provide more high-precision metal component parts for the automotive and defense industries, as well as office equipment manufacturers. Hastech was initially formed to manufacture aerospace and defense components, while Spinic manufactured high-volume brackets, spindles, and water pumps for the automotive industry. Emtol was established to provide Linamar with a new facility able to produce large component parts for the defense, agricultural, and automotive industries, including such items as engine blocks, injector bodies, and antilock-braking-system valve housings. Similarly, both Roctel and Transgear

KEY DATES

1966: Frank Hasenfratz incorporates his Guelph, Ontario, machine shop as Linamar Machine Limited.

1989: Following push for auto contracts, Linamar is generating 80 percent of its sales as an automotive parts supplier.

1992: Company is renamed Linamar Corporation; Linamar acquires a Hungarian producer of agricultural equipment components called Mezogep (later Linamar Hungary).

2002: Linda Hasenfratz, daughter of the founder, succeeds her father as CEO of Linamar.

2009: Expanding into green energy, Linamar wins a large contract to produce nacelles for wind turbines.

were created to provide highly specialized machined components for the automotive industry.

The impetus behind Linamar's formation of its own network of subsidiaries was the changing scene of the North American automotive industry during the early and mid-1980s. As foreign car companies captured more of the automobile market during the entire decade of the 1970s, U.S. car manufacturers began to fight back. The 1980s saw a renewed commitment to higher quality and more durable automobiles by the Big Three manufacturers: Ford, Chrysler, and General Motors. In order to achieve the goal of consumer satisfaction and, consequently, a larger share of the car market, the Big Three companies began a comprehensive policy to reduce the number of suppliers, and increase the outsourcing of components rather than individual automotive parts. As a result, Ford, Chrysler, and General Motors took extreme measures to evaluate all their suppliers, and awarded long-term contracts to those who had a passing grade. If supplier firms did not receive a passing grade, their contracts were not renewed or they were asked to upgrade their manufacturing facilities.

Linamar management recognized that the Big Three intended to reduce the number of their suppliers, and immediately established a pilot program at the Transgear subsidiary to meet the newly formulated expectations. Linamar reduced costs, began taking time studies of value-added activities, converted its production lines to the new Japanese Kaisen system (which reduced inventories up to 40 percent), clustered its machinery in team groupings that manufactured an entire component,

and retrained its employees to work as a team rather than as individuals on an assembly line. With all of its effort to satisfy the demands of the Big Three, Linamar was justly rewarded. By the end of the 1980s, the company had won major contracts from Ford, Chrysler, and General Motors. Most importantly, however, in a complete turnaround from just 10 years earlier, nearly 80 percent of all the company's business came from the automotive industry.

With an established reputation for reliability, meticulous accuracy, and low manufacturing costs, Linamar began to reap the benefits of its hard work. In 1992 alone, the same year that Linamar Machine Limited was renamed Linamar Corporation, the company's Spinic subsidiary won the Ford Quality 1 Preferred Customer Award, its Linex subsidiary won the Saco Defense Supplier of the Year Award, and parent Linamar received the extremely prestigious Canada Award for Business Excellence in the Quality Category. When any customer visited one of the company plants located in Guelph, one saw streaming flags indicating Ford's Quality 1, Chrysler's Pentastar, and General Motors' Mark of Excellence Awards.

OVERSEAS VENTURES

Hasenfratz, of course, was not the kind of entrepreneur to rest on his laurels. During the 1980s, a state-owned firm located in Hungary, Mezogep, had improved upon a component made for combines by a German corporation. Linamar had been importing the component, called a "cornhead," since 1989. Recognizing the potential market for the component, Hasenfratz returned to his native land and purchased Mezogep in 1992. Industry analysts initially criticized the purchase as misguided, because Hungary had developed a notorious reputation as an unproductive labor market. Hasenfratz thought this criticism itself was mistaken, especially because the industry held the traditional attitude of most foreign firms working in Eastern Europe, namely, that a U.S. or Canadian manufacturing firm should take advantage of the inexpensive labor force to lower its own manufacturing costs.

Defying traditional attitudes, Hasenfratz decided to take the opposite approach toward the labor market. He strongly believed that, if the management was good, then the assembly line workforce would be equally good. Hasenfratz proceeded to hire hardworking, corruption-free managers who, in turn, hired people like themselves. He also reached a unique agreement with his Hungarian management team, including ownership and profit incentives if certain manufacturing goals were met. By 1995, results from the Mezogep operation had even outstripped Hasenfratz's own expectations. Growing into one of Linamar's most successful businesses, Mezogep recorded profits of more than $3 million, reported efficiency levels between 80 and 90 percent, and had added two divisions while employing 560 people. Mezogep widened its manufacturing base to include an automotive division producing component parts for the international automotive market.

Hasenfratz did not stop with the purchase of Mezogep, which merely seemed to whet his appetite for overseas expansion. In 1992, in conjunction with its Western Combine Corporation subsidiary, Linamar airlifted over 100 tons of farm equipment to Russia by employing the world's second-largest airplane. Although there had been a long history of failed dealings between Russian farmers and other North American and German combine manufacturers, Hasenfratz was confident that his company would not make the same mistakes. Consequently, Hasenfratz sent along three Russian-speaking farmers from Canada, along with a comprehensive system that included not only combines but also large drying machines and huge storage bins for grain. Again, Hasenfratz had anticipated what was needed to create a successful project. Working closely with their Russian counterparts in the city of Chelybinsk, the Canadian farmers helped collect one of the largest harvests ever in the area.

Insisting on supervising the harvest of grain for a period of three years, and implementing both a training program and a repair program for the equipment, the experience soon became a showcase for international cooperation. Proving that grain-handling equipment and methods used in North America could be adapted to regions in Russia with the same production of high-quality grain at lower costs, additional pilot programs were quickly established. Equipment and technical assistance from Canada were used in Kazakhstan and Ukraine, and Linamar also set up a joint venture plant in Russia to manufacture combine equipment. Interestingly, the plant chosen for the operation was a former military plant used by the Russian army but closed because of a lack of funds.

In addition to expanding the company's activities in Eastern Europe and Russia, Hasenfratz positioned Linamar to take advantage of the burgeoning North American market. Hasenfratz saw the North American Free Trade Agreement (NAFTA), an accord between the United States, Canada, and Mexico that went into effect at the beginning of 1994, as the counterpart and answer to the European Common Market. A strong advocate of a thoroughgoing, unregulated free trade among the United States, Canada, and Mexico, Hasenfratz in 1993 negotiated a five-year contract with Volkswagen of Mexico to manufacture automobile components for the Golf and Jetta models.

During the second half of the 1990s, Linamar refocused most of its attention back on the auto industry. With the exception of Mezogep, the company divested its ventures in Eastern Europe, as well as its North American agricultural equipment business, and it also in early 1997 completed an initial public offering of Mezogep stock on the Budapest Stock Exchange, emerging with a stake in the Hungarian company of about 60 percent.

BILLION-DOLLAR MILESTONE

A boom period for North American automakers in the late 1990s propelled Linamar's sales well past the CAD 1 billion mark by decade's end. Concentrating mainly on engine, transmission, and steering system components, the company benefited from the continued outsourcing push among the major carmakers. During the late 1990s, Linamar gained its first manufacturing assets in the United States, and it also established a subsidiary in Mexico that oversaw the construction of a new plant near Saltillo in order to manufacture transmission parts for General Motors. In addition, in the first step toward a shift at the top, Frank Hasenfratz in 1997 named his daughter Linda to the COO post. Two years later she was named company president. Linda Hasenfratz had joined Linamar in 1990, working her way up from her initial job as a machine operator and earning an M.B.A. along the way.

Growth stalled at the beginning of the 21st century as the North American auto industry was hit hard by a downturn in the larger economy. The 2001 sales of CAD 1.21 billion were down 9 percent from the previous year. Linamar nevertheless managed in 2001 to book a record CAD 460.6 million in new automotive supply business. The company also ventured that year to diversify its interests to a small degree by gaining majority control of another Guelph-based business, Skyjack, Inc., a producer of scissors-type aerial work platforms. The following year Linamar acquired Skyjack's remaining shares, making it a wholly owned subsidiary.

In August 2002 Linda Hasenfratz was named CEO of Linamar, succeeding her father, who remained company chairman. Shortly after this change in leadership, Linamar restructured its business into five groups, three of which focused on specific vehicle areas, namely chassis, engines, and transmissions. Another group concentrated on European operations, while the fifth centered on industrial markets and included the Skyjack subsidiary. This overhaul was designed to foster the development of more efficient production methods by grouping similar products together.

Linamar strengthened its engine components business in 2002 by acquiring another manufacturing plant in Saltillo, Mexico, to supply camshafts to both General Motors and Chrysler. The following year the company acquired a plant in Crimmitschau, Germany, that had a contract to manufacture camshafts for Bayerische Motoren Werke AG (BMW). Also in 2003, Mezogep's name was changed to Linamar Hungary.

STAYING AFLOAT IN ROUGH TIMES

The company kept on a growth track through the year 2007, when sales reached a record CAD 2.31 billion ($2.34 billion). During this period, while remaining vulnerable to production cuts from the major Detroit-based automakers, Linamar for a number of reasons avoided the financial troubles that beset numerous other North American auto suppliers. One advantage was the company's operations outside the auto industry, including not only Skyjack but its business supplying parts to makers of heavy-duty vehicles, such as Caterpillar Inc. The latter business was expanded in 2003 with the construction of a new 200,000-square-foot plant in Guelph for the production of cylinder heads for Caterpillar.

Skyjack grew as well, purchasing CareLift Equipment Limited, a manufacturer of rough-terrain forklifts, also known as telehandlers, marketed under the name Zoom Boom. CareLift was based in Breslau, Ontario. Skyjack's telehandler operations were augmented via the 2008 purchase of AB Volvo's material handling division, which was based in Shippensburg, Pennsylvania. Also in 2008, Linamar introduced into the North American market a line of cordless rechargeable lawnmowers that featured a company-designed advanced engine.

Also benefiting Linamar was its effort to create a more geographically diverse auto supply business. In Asia the company set up plants in both South Korea and China and began supplying parts not only to Asian automakers but also to U.S. and European companies producing cars in China. Linamar expanded in Europe as well, purchasing a former Visteon Corporation plant in Swansea, Wales, that produced transfer units, transfer cases, and axles. This 2008 deal was preceded by the earlier acquisition of another former Visteon plant with a similar product profile located in Nuevo Laredo, Mexico.

The growth trend halted abruptly when the global economic downturn that began in 2008 had an outsized impact on the North American auto industry and eventually pushed both General Motors and Chrysler to reorganize under Chapter 11 bankruptcy protection.

Sales fell 2.4 percent that year, and the net income figure of CAD 70.4 million ($57.5 million) represented a drop of more than 35 percent over the previous year's total. The company saw its stock fall almost 90 percent before recovering as Linamar was lumped in with other auto suppliers with weaker balance sheets and less diversified operations. Linamar was nevertheless forced to retrench, slashing its global workforce from more than 12,000 to around 8,000. It also postponed an ambitious CAD 1.84 billion expansion plan that had been announced in 2006 and been touted as creating 3,000 new jobs by the year 2010.

Linamar posted net losses for the first two quarters of 2009 before returning to the black in the third quarter. By early 2010 the company appeared to be firmly on the rebound. Its workforce figure was back up to around 9,000, and during 2009 the company had won CAD 300 million in new business, much of which involved work taken over from other companies exiting the automotive sector. Further brightening Linamar's prospects was its promising new green-energy business. Late in 2009 the company announced it had entered into a 10-year agreement to provide two other Ontario firms with nacelles (engine housings) for wind turbines. The diversification into nacelles leveraged Linamar's experience in automotive drivetrains, as these systems housed all the mechanical gear used to generate electricity in wind turbines. The company expected its energy business to generate CAD 1 billion in annual sales by 2020, by which time Linamar aimed to be pulling in overall revenues of CAD 10 billion.

Thomas Derdak
Updated, David E. Salamie

PRINCIPAL SUBSIDIARIES

Linamar Holdings Inc.; Skyjack, Inc.; Linamar Hungary Nyrt. (70.1%).

PRINCIPAL DIVISIONS

Linamar Consumer Products Ltd.

PRINCIPAL COMPETITORS

Magna International Inc.; Dana Holding Corporation; ArvinMeritor, Inc.; Federal-Mogul Corporation; Denso Corporation.

FURTHER READING

Bagnall, James, "Linamar's Profit Prescription," *Financial Times of Canada*, March 18, 1991, pp. 10+.

Dias, David, "GM Is Cutting Contracts. Ford Is Ditching Staff. Times Must Be Hard in the Parts Biz. Linda Hasenfratz Says: Bring It On," *National Post*, Financial Post Business Magazine, January 1, 2007, p. 28.

"Economy Stalls $1.8B Plan for Expansion," *Waterloo Region (Ont.) Record*, August 29, 2008, p. A1.

Enchin, Harvey, "Linamar Marches to Different Tune," *Globe and Mail*, October 12, 1992, p. B1.

Erwin, Steve, "Daughter Takes the Reins from Father at Linamar," *Toronto Star*, August 13, 2002, p. C6.

Hamilton, Tyler, "Green Machining: Linamar Joins Pack of Auto Parts Makers Retooling to Build the Gear That Drives Wind and Solar Energy," *Toronto Star*, November 21, 2009, p. B1.

O'Flanagan, Rob, "Hasenfratz Sees Many Opportunities for Growth for Linamar in Days Ahead," *Guelph (Ont.) Mercury*, October 20, 2009, p. A1.

———, "Linamar Poised for Growth While Other Auto Suppliers Fail," *Guelph (Ont.) Mercury*, May 13, 2009, p. A1.

———, "Linamar Rebounds from Recession," *Guelph (Ont.) Mercury*, January 8, 2010, p. A1.

Pitts, Gordon, "Linamar Faces Roadblocks beyond Succession," *Globe and Mail*, November 1, 1999, p. M1.

Thompson, Laura, "Going Up: Product Diversification and Geographic Expansion Seem to Be Delivering Value to Linamar's Stock," *Guelph (Ont.) Mercury*, June 6, 2008, p. A1.

Magnotta Winery Corporation

---

271 Chrislea Road
Vaughan, Ontario L4L 8N6
Canada
Telephone: (905) 738-9463
Fax: (905) 738-5551
Web site: http://www.magnotta.com

Public Company
Incorporated: 1990
Employees: 112
Sales: CAD 24.04 million (2009)
Stock Exchanges: Toronto
Ticker Symbol: MGN
NAICS: 312130 Wineries

∎ ∎ ∎

Listed on the Toronto Stock Exchange, Magnotta Winery Corporation is a Canadian company based a few miles north of Toronto that is licensed to produce and sell wine, beer, and spirits. The company has won numerous awards for its wines, mostly blends of wine produced from Ontario Niagara grapes and vintages from other parts of the world. In addition to 180 acres of vineyards in Ontario, the company owns a 351-acre vineyard in the Maipo Valley in Chile that supplies wine for its blends and sells its excess juice to other Chilean wineries. In addition, Magnotta brews a line of natural premium beers, distills icewine brandy, icewine Eau de Vie, ice grappa, vodka, and gin, and sells beer-making kits and juices for producing homemade wine.

Magnotta is also known for its longtime feud with the Liquor Control Board of Ontario (LCBO), and for many years its products were not carried in LCBO stores. As a result, Magnotta developed its own retail operation, selling its products at its Ontario winery in Beamsville, Ontario; the winery, brewery, and distillery at its main facility in Vaughan, Ontario, that also houses its corporate offices; as well as five retail stores in the Greater Toronto area, the Niagara Peninsula, and southwestern Ontario.

GABRIEL MAGNOTTA, ITALIAN BORN: 1949

Magnotta Winery was founded in 1990 by Gabriel Magnotta and his wife, Rossana. He was born in 1949 in Andretta, Italy, where he claimed to get his start in the wine business by filling carafes at his family tavern when he was eight years old. At age 11 he immigrated to Canada. After graduating from York University in 1974 he became a teacher but soon turned his attention to business. In 1980 he began exporting live bait to the United States. He then turned his attention to the wine trade. In 1986 he launched Festa Juice to provide juice for homemade winemakers. More importantly he was able to make full use of his cold storage facility, using it for nightcrawlers during fishing season and juices during the off-season.

A change in Ontario law led to Magnotta deepening his commitment to the wine industry. The law required that for a wine to be marketed as an Ontario product it could contain no more than 30 percent foreign vintage. The impact of free trade forced a change in the Wine Content Act in 1989 as a way to help On-that the price for quality grapes was rising as supply was falling short of demand. To guarantee supply, Magnotta sought to grow its own Niagara grapes and began acquiring land in the Niagara Peninsula. Later in the 1990s the company also acquired a vineyard in Chile's renowned Maipo Valley. Not only did Magnotta secure its supply, it produced enough surplus juice to create another revenue stream.

GOING PUBLIC: 1995

After two years in business Magnotta was selling more than 100,000 cases of wine a year and grossing about CAD 5 million. The company also continued to irk the LCBO. It introduced a premium imported blend under the International Vintages label, but the board complained that the name infringed on their Vintages stores, forcing Magnotta to resort to the International Series label. By 1995 Magnotta was ready to expand its operation. In the fall of that year the company went public, making an initial offering of stock to raise money to fund the construction of a new manufacturing plant, headquarters, and retail store. The 75,000-square-foot facility, including a winery, microbrewery, and distillery, opened in Vaughan in May 1997 and quickly became a tourist attraction. Also in 1997 Magnotta struck a deal with Springfield, Ohio-based Francis A. Bonnano Inc. to distribute its wines in the United States.

Magnotta began entering its wines in international competitions and enjoyed excellent results, winning more awards than any other Ontario winery. By the end of the 1990s, Magnotta was operating five retail stores and generating annual sales of about CAD 22 million from the sale of wines as well as beer and such spirits as vodka and grappa. In addition to Canada and the United States, Magnotta products were now available in the United Kingdom, Asia, and northern American Duty Free Shops.

The company was also generating some income from LCBO stores, which now carried Magnotta icewine (produced from grapes picked during the winter) but only through special order. The relationship between Magnotta and the LCBO had not improved, however. LCBO Chairman Andrew Brandt in a 1993 radio interview claimed that the board's price thresholds were in place to protect the public health. A year later Brandt held a press conference to warn about the dangers of drinking "contraband" wine, and one of the bottles presented for filming carried a Magnotta label. The implication that Magnotta wines were threats to the public health and that the company was involved in illicit conduct, did not sit well with Gabriel and Rossana Magnotta.

tario wineries remain competitive. Now blends could contain as much as 70 percent foreign vintage. Sensing an opportunity, in 1989 Gabriel and Rossana Magnotta paid CAD 250,000 for a small Charal winery in Vaughan, Ontario, primarily for the license to produce and sell wine. In 1990 they moved the stock, vats, and equipment to Concord, Ontario, to establish Magnotta Winery. The couple also began to look for foreign vintages from around the world to blend with the wine they produced from fermented Ontario grapes.

MAGNOTTA WINERY OPENS: 1990

In December 1990, shortly after the changes in the Wine Content Act went into effect, the Magnotta Winery opened for business. It had also begun fighting with the LCBO. Magnotta had applied for the 15 to 17 listings controlled by Charal, and initially the LCBO indicated the company could receive seven listings. That number was cut to just four, and only days before the winery was to open and wine was to ship to LCBO stores, the company was informed there was no room in the warehouse for any of the Magnotta products. As a result, the company was forced to rework its marketing plan and begin selling directly to the public. The LCBO, on the other hand, insisted that Magnotta voluntarily chose not to be carried by LCBO stores.

In any event, Magnotta gained a pricing edge in the market by selling direct, avoiding a steep LCBO markup, 44 percent, plus a handling and distribution charge of CAD 1.25 a liter. Magnotta was able to attract attention by offering a bottle of quality blended wine at CAD 3.95 a bottle, a move that not only drew attention from the public but the ire of the LCBO, which forced the company to raise the price. Gabriel Magnotta also upset Ontario vintners because he was open about his use of foreign juices, a practice they also followed but preferred to keep from the public.

An important factor in Magnotta's favor was the Festa Juice business, which provided steady income. In addition, its operation was able to work with both fresh wine juice and imported vintages. Magnotta searched the globe for wine to blend, mostly using vintages from California, Chile, and Argentina. It became apparent

---

KEY DATES

1989: Gabriel and Rossana Magnotta acquire Ontario winery.
1990: Magnotta Winery is formed.
1995: Company is taken public.
1999: Company sues Liquor Control Board.
2009: Gabriel Magnotta dies.

Magnotta hired a private investigator who tape-recorded conversations with LCBO liquor store clerks who made disparaging remarks about Magnotta products, calling the icewine "shabby" and not "the real thing," and one clerk told the investigator if he served Magnotta icewine to his boss "it'll end your career." One LCBO manager suggested that the investigator wrap the bottle in a napkin or liner so that his guests would not know they were being served a "lesser icewine."

Magnotta filed a lawsuit in 1999, accusing the LCBO of conspiring against it because Magnotta would not participate in the system. Moreover, Gabriel Magnotta insisted that it was a point of honor, claiming that he pursued a lawsuit only because his children were being taunted by schoolmates for running a nefarious business. "It's our name on the bottles," he told the press. "Pride is important, honour is important. They're denigrating us, not only our company."

LAWSUIT SETTLEMENT: 2001

The lawsuit against the LCBO was settled out of court in 2001, and some of Magnotta's icewines began to be carried on the shelves of select stores. In the meantime, the company continued to grow on a number of fronts. It expanded its sales into the United States and also completed the planting of its acreage in Ontario as well as in Chile. In 2002 Magnotta opened two more retail locations, bringing the total number of stores to seven. It made its first sales of icewine in Europe. Magnotta began to shift its marketing focus, positioning itself as a lifestyle brand. In addition, it began to sell some of its products via the Internet. A year later it entered the home beer brewing market with the introduction of "Festa Brew," a wort, or unfermented beer product. Sales topped the CAD 20 million mark in 2003.

Magnotta enjoyed steady growth but was soon adversely impacted by the health concerns of Gabriel Magnotta. An avid outdoorsman who enjoyed taking his dogs to bird trials, he was bitten by a tick in 2006 and

contracted Lyme disease. A heavy treatment of antibiotics deprived him of energy, leading his wife to take over as chief executive. The family and winery now became actively involved in raising money for the Canadian Lyme Disease Foundation.

BUYOUT BID FAILS: 2007

Rossana Magnotta took charge of a company that while successful was not appreciated by investors and the stock was seldom traded. In 2007 the Magnottas, who owned more than 60 percent of the company, made an offer to buy the shares they did not own and take the company private in a deal valued at CAD 19.9 million. Because more than 5 percent of shareholders voted against the plan, the offer was eventually canceled. Rossana Magnotta also had to contend with more problems with the LCBO, which began opening stores close to Magnotta's outlets. Moreover, a new bottle deposit return system that went into effect in February 2007 added to her workload.

Magnotta continued to win awards and grow sales in 2008. To attract new customers the company increased its marketing budget, adding a mainstream radio campaign in southern Ontario. The radio campaign continued in 2009 as sales inched above CAD 24 million and net earnings totaled CAD 2.64 million.

In fiscal 2009 Gabriel Magnotta was forced to retire due to his deteriorating health. On December 30, 2009, he died suddenly at home from the complications of Lyme disease. Not only was the loss felt by his family and employees, Gabriel Magnotta, despite his earlier differences with other Ontario vintners, had become an involved business leader, a man respected for his originality of thinking and someone who, according to *Wines & Vines,* "brought about positive changes in the wine industry." He left behind a company that was well established and likely to continue to grow under the experienced hand of Rossana Magnotta.

Ed Dinger

PRINCIPAL SUBSIDIARIES

Magnotta Brewery (Vaughan) Ltd.: Magnotta Distillery Ltd.; Festa Juice Co. Ltd.

PRINCIPAL COMPETITORS

Cristaelerias de Chile S.A.; E. & J. Gallo Winery; Vincor International Inc.

FURTHER READING

Aspler, Tony, "Winery Goes Its Own Way," *Toronto Star,* January 16, 1993, p. G1.

Brehl, Robert, "Winery Finds Way to Beat LCBO Prices," *Toronto Star,* March 25, 1991, p. B1.

Cattell, Hudson, "Remember Feisty Vintner Magnotta," *Wines & Vines,* February 2010, p. 53.

Grech, Caroline, "Maverick Vaughan Winemaker a 'Down to Earth' Guy Who Made Difference to Many," *Vaughan Citizen,* January 7, 2010.

McArthur, Keith, "Magnotta Winery Plans to Go Private," *Globe & Mail,* February 8, 2007, p. B6.

Spears, John, "'White Knight' Led Unorthodox Winery," *Toronto Star,* January 11, 2010, p. GT04.

"Wine's Scrappy Duo," *Toronto Star,* January 24, 2007, p. 4.

Manhattan Beer
Distributors LLC

———————— ■ ————————

400 Walnut Avenue
Bronx, New York 10454
U.S.A.
Telephone: (718) 292-9300
Toll Free: (800) 233-7462
Fax: (718) 292-6348
Web site: http://manhattanbeer.com

Private Company
Founded: 1978
Employees: 1,324
Sales: $592.9 million (2008)
NAICS: 424810 Beer and Ale Merchant Wholesalers

■ ■ ■

Manhattan Beer Distributors LLC is one of the largest beer distributors in the United States and the largest operating in a single market, in this case the New York City metropolitan area. It directly services more than 25,000 accounts and represents over 50 suppliers from all over the world. No longer based in Manhattan, it operates out of three warehouses in the city and two in the suburbs. All of the company's customers are offered service every day, with no minimum order required.

STARTING OUT ON MANHATTAN'S LOWER EAST SIDE

Simon Bergson, founder, president, and chief executive officer of Manhattan Beer Distributors, was born in

Austria after World War II to survivors of the Auschwitz concentration camp. They settled in New York, where his father went into the garment trade. Simon was living in Arizona when his father lured him back to the city by purchasing a discount beer and soft-drink home-distribution center on Manhattan's Lower East Side in 1975.

The home distribution business was created by the state of New York to give returning World War II veterans an opportunity to work for themselves. They were allowed to sell all brands of beer and soft drinks in all package sizes and were free to negotiate the best price from producers. Combining elements of retail and wholesale, the home distributor sold to individuals coming in off the street but also to the many thousands of small retailers, such as convenience and grocery stores, in the metropolitan area.

This business was no bonanza. Bergson worked long hours seven days a week in quarters on Houston Street that had neither heat nor air conditioning. Urban crime was rampant, and so he carried two guns in addition to the shotgun he kept under the counter. He liked the beer business but yearned to go strictly wholesale, so that he could at least have his Sundays off.

Bergson's opportunity came when he learned that the Rheingold brewery, one of the city's largest, was closing. This made available the local distribution rights to two brands, Carling Black Label and Tuborg Gold, and Bergson obtained them because, he later told Andrea Foote of *Beverage World*, "nobody else wanted them." He added, "I figured that if I could get a busi-

COMPANY PERSPECTIVES

As a diversified distributor of high quality beverages, we are focused on providing complete customer satisfaction, serviced by well-trained company personnel in an environment that recognizes and rewards teamwork and commitment toward our shared goals.

We are truly dedicated and committed to the growth and development of each associate. Our mission is to profitably grow our business through attainment of clearly communicated goals.

ness up to four or six trucks that I would do well for myself and be able to make a living."

Manhattan Beer opened on July 4, 1978, with three used trucks purchased from the Carling brewery in Baltimore for $500 each and driven separately to New York by Bergson himself. He and his employees loaded beer in and out of a 4,000-square-foot warehouse in Alphabet City, a part of the Lower East Side even rougher than Houston Street. Bergson soon added two brands popular elsewhere but little known in New York: Brahma, the best seller in Brazil, picked up from a Philadelphia importer, and Rolling Rock, a low-priced Pennsylvania beer.

SCUFFLING FOR BUSINESS: 1979–88

Despite its name, Bergson's company was not based in Manhattan for long. Interviewed by *Modern Brewery Age* in 2005 at its Bronx headquarters (and still toting a pistol in a holster at his hip), Bergson explained, "The reason we moved to the [South] Bronx in 1979, is that they had just burned it, and everyone had moved out. It was cheap as can be. We had to have a pack of German Shepherd guard dogs in the warehouse."

Operating in the big city presented other challenges not familiar to beer distributors based elsewhere. Manhattan Beer's trucks had to double-park to make deliveries, which was legal, but more often than not they were ticketed anyway for obstructing traffic. The city imposed a significant tax on commercial rentals and a similar tax on mortgage payments or on fair market value if a company chose to buy rather than rent. Competitors located elsewhere in the region sometimes bootlegged the product in the city in violation of the company's exclusive territorial distribution rights.

Such transshipment was a vexing problem. Although breweries and wholesalers signed agreements providing exclusive sales within a given territory, the state did not recognize wholesaler franchises or exclusive territories, so these agreements were not legally enforceable. Manhattan Beer Distributors and other wholesalers needed to monitor their customers closely to make sure that the orders being filled were for consumption only. The ensuing years severely tested the ability of Manhattan Beer and other small beverage distributors to survive. The largest breweries and the largest retailers had one common goal: reduce dependence on independent middlemen.

As a result, the number of independent beer wholesalers in the United States fell from 3,800 in 1985 to 2,000 in 1995, when just six breweries were producing 97 percent of the beer in the United States. In New York City the number of beer distributors dropped, Bergson estimated, from about 30 in 1978 to probably only four in 2005. One advantage for Manhattan Beer and the other survivors was that the elimination of competitors greatly reduced the transshipment problem.

Manhattan Beer seems to have turned the corner in 1988 when it won a distribution contract from the importer of Corona, a run-of-the-mill Mexican beer that, perhaps because of its long-neck bottle, was becoming hip in the United States. In that year the company opened a second warehouse, in Plainview, Long Island. This operation later moved to Wyandanch.

MORE BRANDS, MORE SALES, MORE WAREHOUSES: 1995–2005

By 1995 Manhattan Beer was selling four million cases a year. Corona and Rolling Rock each accounted for more than one million, with some 35 other brands constituting the remainder. Annual sales volume had reached $63 million. On-premise accounts, primarily bars taking draft beer, represented about 40 percent and supermarkets about 25 percent. The company was serving all five boroughs in New York City, Long Island, and Westchester and Putnam counties north of the city. By now it was in its fourth South Bronx home, a 250,000-square-foot warehouse in the Port Morris neighborhood.

Manhattan Beer's second wind came in 1998, when it doubled its distribution to more than 20 million cases by merging with Coors Distributing of New York and thus becoming the exclusive distributor of Coors brands there and hence the largest Coors distributor. Other brands carried included Beck's and Samuel Adams. The company also carried a number of beverages, including wine coolers and bottled water. A third facility, in

```
┌─────────────────────────────────────────────┐
│                                               │
│             KEY DATES                         │
│                   ■                           │
├───────────────────────────────────────────────┤
│  1978:  Manhattan Beer Distributors opens on the │
│         borough's Lower East Side.            │
│  1988:  Company lands its first big client, Corona. │
│  1998:  Manhattan Beer doubles output by becoming │
│         a Coors distributor.                  │
│  2007:  Company loses its right to distribute some │
│         popular European beers.               │
│  2009:  Manhattan Beer purchases a warehouse in the │
│         Hunts Point section of the Bronx.     │
│                                               │
└─────────────────────────────────────────────┘
```

Monroe, New York, was headquarters for distribution in counties north of the city. Manhattan Beer bought a fourth warehouse in Brooklyn in 2001.

Manhattan Beer had become a major enterprise and now fielded a fleet of mostly new trucks, all with diesel engines, automatic transmission, and air conditioned cabs. Besides the more than 200 trucks with beverage bodies, there were several tractors and trailers, 50 vans, and 130 or so company cars. A recently installed software model downloaded inventory and sales data to the managers. This data was integrated with separate loading and routing software programs.

By 2005 half of the company's beer was arriving at Port Morris by means of three rail spurs built by Manhattan Beer at a cost of $3 million. Corona, arriving there on a daily train from Mexico City, was accounting for more than a third of company sales. Another daily train, from Colorado, accounted for nearly half of the company's Coors supply. Besides Corona and Coors the company was carrying almost 50 brands, with an emphasis on specialty and imported beers. Manhattan Beer was credited with making Belgium's Stella Artois an important draft beer in New York bars.

Manhattan Beer opened its fifth warehouse in the borough of Queens in 2005. It had moved its facility for serving six counties north of the city from Monroe to Harriman. Its fleet included 40 trucks powered by compressed natural gas. "They run quieter and cleaner with the same amount of power," Bergson told *Modern Brewery Age*. "When these trucks are lined up in the morning outside the warehouse, you don't have to walk through a choking blue haze of diesel emissions." In back of its Bronx warehouse, now occupying one million square feet, was a recycling plant for all glass, cardboard, wood, and aluminum.

PUSHING SPECIALTY AND CRAFT BEERS: 2007–08

Manhattan Beer lost Stella Artois, Beck's, Bass, and several other beers in 2007, when their owner, InBev S.A., made the local distributor of Anheuser-Busch Cos., Inc., the exclusive importer for its European brands. These brands had represented about 2.5 million of Manhattan Beer's 28.6 million cases sold in 2006. To soften the blow from lost commissions and avoid losing experienced route salespeople, senior management raised pay and incentives substantially for these staffers.

Manhattan Beer focused on increasing sales volume for its specialty beers, such as Blue Moon, Newcastle Brown Ale, and Kronenbourg 1664. In creating a specialty product division for its smallest-volume beverages, it concentrated on selling craft beers such as Black Dog and Sierra Nevada and little-known imports such as Germany's Spaten. As a result, the company made up the difference in lost sales in only 10 months.

Manhattan Beer moved its north-of-the-city warehouse to Suffern in 2008. There was a general sales manager for each warehouse, plus one for the home distribution market and one, Rob Mitchell, for the specialty beer division. Mitchell, an 18-year company veteran, hired a team of knowledgeable beer professionals to go door to door, visiting restaurants and bars looking for out-of-the-ordinary beers. "Our strength is that we'll deliver five or six days a week with no minimums, in all of our counties," Mitchell told *Beverage Industry*.

The new division, named World Class Beverages, focused on promoting and selling the products of local and regional craft brewers. These included Captain Lawrence, Kelso, Lake Placid, Southampton, and Sly Fox, plus Arcadia and Keegan ales. Its mission also was to communicate with the rest of the sales organizations so that the average route salesperson or on-premise supervisor could speak confidently about these brands.

MANHATTAN BEER IN 2009–10

Hunts Point, the southeast Bronx site for the city's central produce, meat, and fish market, became the locale for a new $20 million Manhattan Beer warehouse in 2009. The advantage for moving into the Leggett Avenue facility was its proximity to such links as the Bruckner Expressway, a rail yard, and two major bridges. The purchase was partially financed by more than $9 million in municipal tax exemptions.

In addition to its many domestic and imported mainstream beers, craft beers, and microbeers, Manhattan Beer was selling and distributing a large variety of other beverages. The company Web site listed numerous exotic soft drinks, including 27 Boylan sodas. There were 18 wines, 17 bottled waters, five ciders, four nonalcoholic beers, and many premixed cocktails. The company had grown substantially since its humble beginnings and anticipated continued growth in the years ahead.

Robert Halasz

PRINCIPAL COMPETITORS

Anheuser-Busch Sales and Service of New York; Boening Brothers Inc.; Clare Rose, Inc.; The Gambrinus Company; Oak Beverages Inc.; Phoenix Beverages, Inc.; Union Beer Distributors LLC.

FURTHER READING

"Beer Distributors: Big City Wholesaler Keeps Its Focus Small," *Beverage Industry*, February 2008, pp. 33–34, 36.

Davis, Tim, "Mean Streets," *Beverage World*, March 1995, pp. 44, 46.

Deierlein, Bob, "Coping with Growth in Gotham," *Beverage World*, October 15, 1999, p. 81.

Fickenscher, Lisa, "Beer Wars at a Head," *Crain's New York Business*, August 22, 2005, pp. 2, 26.

Foote, Andrea, "New York State of Mind," *Beverage World*, August 15, 2006, pp. 24–30.

Landi, Heather, "First in Class," *Beverage World*, October 15, 2009, pp. 61–62.

McDonnell, Sharon, "New Lines Fermenting Beer Agent's Growth," *Crain's New York Business*, February 28, 1995, p. 35.

Potkewitz, Hilary, "One-Stop Shopping in Hunts Point Gets Heady Meaning," *Crain's New York Business*, July 27, 2009, p. 14.

"Prince of the City," *Modern Brewery Age*, Fall 2005, pp. 12–16, 39–40.

"Storming the City," *Beverage World*, August 2007, pp. 48, 50, 52–53.

Mars, Incorporated

———■———

6885 Elm Street
McLean, Virginia 22101
U.S.A.
Telephone: (703) 821-4900
Fax: (703) 448-9678
Web site: http://www.mars.com

Private Company
Incorporated: 1911 as Mar-O-Bar Co.
Employees: 65,000
Sales: $28 billion (2010 est.)
NAICS: 311320 Chocolate and Confectionery Manufacturing from Cacao Beans; 311340 Nonchocolate Confectionery Manufacturing; 311520 Ice Cream and Frozen Dessert Manufacturing; 311111 Dog and Cat Food Manufacturing; 311212 Rice Milling; 311919 Other Snack Food Manufacturing; 311991 Perishable Prepared Food Manufacturing; 311999 All Other Miscellaneous Food Manufacturing; 333311 Automatic Vending Machine Manufacturing

■ ■ ■

From its origins in candy and confectionery products, Mars, Incorporated has diversified to become a world leader in multiple markets, including snack foods and chocolates, pet care and pet food products, main meal foods, electronic automated payment systems, and vending machines systems. In spite of its large size and geographic reach, the company remains privately owned. It has fostered an ostensibly egalitarian corporate culture since the 1960s. The company has a reputation for being notoriously secretive despite the millions it spends to promote its products.

ORIGINS IN 1911

Mars began in 1911 as Mar-O-Bar Co., a snack food business founded by Frank C. Mars of Tacoma, Washington, who made a variety of buttercream candies in his home. Quality and value were the foundations of his first candy factory, which employed 125 people. In 1920 Frank Mars relocated to larger quarters in Minneapolis, where Snickers (without the chocolate coating) and Milky Way bars were created. The company posted a loss of $6,000 in 1922. By 1924, however, sales exceeded $700,000. Mars changed his company's name to Mars Candies in 1926. With the rapid growth of the company, Mars sought larger quarters and built a new plant in suburban Chicago in 1928. Sales actually quadrupled during the lean years of the Great Depression and new products were introduced, including the Mars Almond Bar, Snickers Bar (now sporting a chocolate covering), and 3 Musketeers.

Frank Mars hired his son Forrest E. Mars to work in the candy operation after his graduation from Yale University, but the two reportedly had a stormy relationship. In the early 1930s, Frank, giving Forrest some money and the foreign rights to manufacture Milky Way, ordered his son to start his own business abroad. Moving to England, Forrest established a confectionery and a canned pet food company, which met with great success.

In 1940 Forrest Mars returned to the United States and founded M&M Limited in Newark, New Jersey, to manufacture chocolate candies in a sugar shell. At that time, stores reduced their stock of chocolate in the summer because of the lack of air conditioning, and Forrest hoped to capitalize on the unique construction of M&M's to sell the candy year round. The name of the candy was derived from the initials of Mars and an associate, Bruce Murrie. M&M's Peanut Chocolate Candies were introduced in 1954, the same year the famous slogan "the milk chocolate melts in your mouth—not in your hand" was first used.

Frank Mars's business was also experiencing great success. In 1943 Mars ventured into the main meal business, which included a wide selection of rice products, including whole grain, savory, boil-in-bag, fast cook, instant, and frozen rice as well as other products. Uncle Ben's rice used a rice-processing technology called parboiling, which was developed in England and was first used in the United States by a Texas food broker with whom Forrest E. Mars Sr. formed a partnership. Several months after their first production facility was completed, they began selling rice to the U.S. Army, which they continued to supply throughout World War II.

After the war, the company introduced converted rice to the U.S. public, and by 1952 it sold the country's number one brand of rice. Around this time, the company adopted the name "Uncle Ben" for a locally famous rice grower known for producing high-quality rice crops. Uncle Ben's eventually became the leading brand of rice worldwide, sold in more than 100 countries, with manufacturing facilities in the United States, Australia, Belgium, Germany, the Netherlands, and the United Kingdom. Other popular brands included Country Inn rice, Dolmio spaghetti sauces, pasta, and oriental dishes named Suzi Wan, primarily sold in Europe and Australia.

UNITED IN 1967

Because of increased production, Mars constructed a new plant in Hackettstown, New Jersey, in 1958. In the early 1960s, facilities were extended to Europe with a factory at Veghel in the Netherlands. In 1967 Forrest merged his business with the Mars Company owned by his father and took over operation of the new company. He established a radically egalitarian system at the company in which workers were called associates and everyone, from the president down, punched a time clock. Offices were eliminated and desks were arranged in a wagon-wheel fashion, with the higher-ranking executives in the center, to facilitate communication between individuals and functional areas. Notoriously demanding, Forrest rewarded his associates with salaries that were substantially higher than those in other comparably sized companies.

In 1968 Mars (the largest dog food packer in the world, with subsidiaries in Europe, South America, and Australia) acquired Kal Kan Foods, Inc., a dog food company founded in 1937 that later supplied food for dogs in the U.S. military during World War II. With assistance from Mars, Kal Kan expanded by adding a second canned pet food plant in Columbus, Ohio, and a dry pet food plant in Mattoon, Illinois, while expanding into midwestern and eastern markets. New product development of Mars pet care products was aided by the creation of the Waltham Centre for Pet Nutrition in the United Kingdom, which was formed to study the nutritional preferences and needs of pet animals. Nutritional studies were published regularly in scientific and veterinary journals, and Waltham became a world authority on pet care and nutrition.

Mars Electronics International (MEI) began operating in Britain in 1969 and expanded to the United States in 1972. MEI was responsible for the introduction of electronics to the vending machine industry. In 1985 MEI expanded its product line to include advanced bill technology and cashless payment systems. In addition to serving the vending industry, MEI also provided products for use in pay phones and amusement parks. MEI's electronics technology had also been applied to data acquisition and laser scanning devices. In 1987 the company's British and U.S. operations were merged to form the largest international manufacturer of electronic coin machines. In addition to its two manufacturing facilities, MEI had marketing and sales offices throughout the United States, Europe, Australia, and the Far East.

Forrest Sr. retired from Mars in 1973. His elder sons, Forrest E. Mars Jr. and John Mars, took over Mars as co-presidents, joined in 1983 in the office of the president by their sister, Jackie, who took a lesser role in running the company. In his retirement, Forrest Sr. started a candy business named Ethel M. Chocolates (after his late mother) to produce premium boxed

KEY DATES

1911: Frank C. Mars starts a candy factory in Tacoma, Washington.
1920: Mars relocates to Minneapolis; company begins selling Snickers and Milky Way bars.
1926: Business is renamed Mars Candies.
1940: After starting operations in Europe, son Forrest brings M&M's to United States.
1943: Mars begins making parboiled (instant) rice for the U.S. Army.
1967: Frank and Forrest Mars merge their respective businesses.
1968: Mars, a leading dog food maker, buys and expands Kal Kan.
1973: Forrest Mars retires; elder Mars children become co-presidents.
1986: Mars enters frozen snack business with purchase of Dove International.
1999: Founder Frank Mars dies.
2002: Company merges Mars Confectionery and Pedigree Masterfoods and changes its corporate name to Master Foods USA.
2006: Company reverts to the name Mars, Incorporated.
2008: Mars purchases Wm. Wrigley Jr. Co. in a cash transaction.

chocolates. Around 1988 Ethel M. Chocolates was purchased by Mars.

SWEET BATTLE IN THE SEVENTIES AND EIGHTIES

Despite its unorthodox corporate culture, the Mars company thrived. Hershey Foods and Mars historically fought a battle to hold the number one spot in the U.S. candy market, an honor that passed between them. Mars took over the top spot in the early 1970s and by late in the decade had pushed its market share 14 percentage points ahead of Hershey. According to an industry executive quoted in *Fortune*, "it took the Hershey people seven or eight years to realize that Mars was not going to go away. … Then it took them another five years to get their act together."

Hershey responded with a flurry of new product introductions, heavy advertising, and innovative marketing efforts. In the mid-1980s Mars tried to combat this by creating a new image for candy as a sweet snack, not just junk food. Mars paid $5 million to have M&M's and Snickers named "the official snack foods of the 1984 Olympic Games." Commercials featured athletes getting quick energy from sugary snacks. By 1985 industry analysts noted that the two companies were neck and neck, with Mars's recent brand introductions including Bounty Bars, Combos, Holidays M&M's, Kudos, Starburst, Skittles, and Twix Cookie Bar.

Mars added frozen snacks to its repertoire when it acquired Dove International in 1986. The Dove Bar, a hand-dipped ice cream bar with a thick chocolate coating, was created in 1956 by Leo Stefanos, the proprietor of a Chicago candy shop. For many years, the bar was available only in the Chicago area. It appeared in selected U.S. markets during the early 1980s. Doveurope was established in 1988. Other Mars frozen treats included Dove miniatures and ice cream versions of 3 Musketeers, Milky Way, and Snickers bars.

In 1988 Hershey Foods Corporation surpassed Mars as the largest U.S. candy maker when it acquired Cadbury Schweppes's U.S. division, boasting the Mounds and Almond Joy brands. In 1989 Mars suffered another setback when it tried to launch Sussande chocolate bars, a high-priced European-style bar, which, according to a report in *Forbes*, was a costly failure.

MORE BRANDS FOR THE NINETIES

The company rivalry between Mars and Hershey reversed itself in 1991, when Mars increased its percentage of the total candy market from 16.7 percent to 17.9 percent while Hershey's market share remained flat at 17 percent, according to the *Wall Street Journal*. Mars was very successful with its 1990 introduction of peanut butter M&M's, which took a toll on Hershey's number two-ranked Reese's peanut butter cups. Mars launched 12 new products in 1991, including a dark chocolate candy bar under the Dove name, mint and almond M&M's, Milky Way Dark, and Peanut Butter Snickers.

Also in 1991 Mars introduced Expert, a superpremium dog and cat food line meant as an alternative to Hill's Science Diet and Iams, which was sold only in pet stores and feed shops. An industry analyst noted in the *New York Times* that "people are feeding their pets like they feed their children. The nutrition kick has moved over to our pets." To meet customer demand, Mars quickly moved into the specialty pet food area, but made the product accessible by selling it in supermarkets. Mars's other pet care lines continued to do well. According to company literature, Kal Kan was the fifth-largest pet food manufacturer in the United States. Other top sellers in Australia, Europe, and the

United States included Pedigree and Partners dog foods; Whiskas, Sheeba, and Brekkies cat food; and Winergy Horsesnacks.

Mars also explored more healthful alternatives for its traditional snack products when, in 1992, the company became the first customer of Procter & Gamble Co.'s caprenin, a low-calorie cocoa butter substitute. Mars used caprenin in Milky Way II bars, launched on the West Coast in April 1992. Made of fatty acids naturally found in other fats such as peanut oil, cheese, and milk, caprenin was not subject to Food and Drug Administration approval as were fat substitutes. Some of the sugar in Milky Way II was replaced with polydextrose, a low-calorie carbohydrate. The resulting candy bar was 25 percent lower in total calories and had 50 percent fewer calories from fat than the original Milky Way. By introducing Milky Way II, Mars became the first candy manufacturer to try to gain or retain calorie- and fat-conscious customers.

The company did not ignore its strengths, however. In the early 1990s, the company rested near the top of the confectionery products, dog and cat food, and rice milling industries. In late 1992, Mars began testing Mahogany, a line of premium chocolates, in Germany. These candies included truffles, bars, and boxed chocolates in reddish-brown and gold packaging with such South American motifs as palm trees and colonial style houses. The candy was relatively expensive, with a small box of eight truffles costing almost $4 and a 50-gram chocolate bar selling for more than $1.

Analysts questioned Mars's future stability, particularly in light of the Mars brothers' reputed inability to share power with top managers who did not carry the family name, and it remained unclear who would assume control of the company when they retired. John and Forrest Mars Jr. had trouble through three presidents in the first four years in the early 1990s. Demanding taskmasters, they often paid double the going rate for management talent. In the middle of 1993, as its competitors downsized, the company offered voluntary separation agreements to its U.S. employees.

"WAKING UP" IN THE MID-NINETIES

Market share in several categories slipped in the early 1990s. The overall European market was shrinking. Mars suffered a conspicuous lack of successful new products, an area in which archrival Hershey excelled. However, reported *Fortune*, the Mars brothers seemed unfazed, likely more focused on long-term concerns than momentary fluctuations in sales. *Fortune* questioned the effectiveness of the company's "one

world, one brand" policy, maintaining regional differences were still an important factor in marketing. Mars, however, still beat Hershey's overseas; it was estimated to have shipped 100,000 tons of chocolate to Russia alone in 1993.

Mars dumped its ad agency, Bates Worldwide, in favor of BBDO in 1995. Mars wanted a more image-building approach such as had been successful for Visa and Pepsi. The company did hire former Bates executives to head its European marketing.

Mars tried several new tricks in the late 1990s. It acquired a small organic foods marketer, Seeds of Change, in late 1997. The reportedly foul-tasting VO2 Max Energy Bar, Mars's shot at a $300 million-a-year market, was launched but quickly pulled due to poor sales. A version of M&M's with crisped rice added to the chocolate center was much more successful. It began shipping in late 1998.

Forrest Mars Sr. died in Miami in July 1999 at the age of 95. His children had been legally barred from selling the company without his consent until his death, leading to speculation that the company would go public or change hands within a few years. After its founder's death, the company began to consolidate several divisions and agencies. It planned to merge its candy, pet care, and food businesses in continental Europe into a single unit.

Forbes believed Mars, Incorporated had become sluggish and, being private, inattentive to the quarterly profit demands of Wall Street. Its chocolates trailed 10 points behind those of its rival from Pennsylvania. The Uncle Ben's division, once the leading rice producer in the United States, let market share fall to Quaker Oats' Rice-A-Roni and Carolina and Mahatma rice from Riviana Foods until it actually lost money in 1998. In 1999, after terminating 100 of its 540 "associates," the division found a hit in frozen dinners, microwaveable bowls of rice topped with meat, vegetables, and sauce.

In early 2000, Mars launched a Web site, Cocoapro.com, dedicated to celebrating recent research claiming health benefits for certain of chocolate's plant-derived components. The company's extensive process for manufacturing chocolate was also presented.

CHANGING ITS NAME TO MASTERFOODS: 2002

In spite of its market share setbacks, Mars, Incorporated was still a serious marketing force around the world at the beginning of the millennium. The company had facilities in more than 60 countries and sold products in more than 150. It was spending $850 million a year advertising brands such as M&M's candies, Snickers candy bars, Uncle Ben's rice, and Pedigree dog food.

In 2002 the company merged Mars Confectionery and Pedigree Masterfoods to centralize its three top divisions and changed its corporate name to Master Foods USA in an attempt to reflect its role as a major player in the food business, rather than a simple candy manufacturer. Master Foods, which was already in use in Canada, Asia, Australia, South Africa, and Europe, came to represent M&M/Mars, Uncle Ben's, Mars Pet Food, and Seeds of Change worldwide.

The switch followed a reorganization of Mars' sales force in which sales representatives assumed the responsibility of pitching several brands across multiple categories. A small number of direct sales reps retained responsibility for the company's core brands, such as M&M's and Snickers. Overall, Masterfoods employed 30,000 people in manufacturing facilities and offices in more than 60 countries; its products were consumed in more than 100 countries.

Nonetheless, the company retained its intensely private way of doing business. "We are a private company and we run our business like a private company," explained Michelle Weese, Masterfoods' marketing director in a 2002 *NJBIZ* article. Weese also proclaimed that Masterfoods was "a company with a rich heritage. It's quite exciting to have the entrepreneurial freedom to focus on long-term success. Our activities are not bound by short-term goals and reporting. It gives us the latitude to experiment more and really invest for the success of our brand."

One of the ways in which the company experimented was to set up a factory in Hyderabad, India, in 2003 for its international pet foods businesses of snacks and whole meals for cats, dogs, caged birds, aquarium fish, and horses. Masterfoods' pet food included the Pedigree, Cesar, Whiskas, Sheba, Kitekat, Trill, Winergy, and Aquarian brands.

CHOCOLATE HISTORY AND HEALTH BENEFITS: 2006

In 2006 it also set up its Historic Division with the vision of becoming the undisputed leader in chocolate history. Working with researchers from the University of California at Davis, Colonial Williamsburg, Fort Ticonderoga, and other institutions focused on preserving and teaching American history, the division explored the place of chocolate in the lives of Americans during the Revolutionary era. American Heritage chocolate snacks, manufactured by Masterfoods, with a slightly gritty texture, and a spicy and slightly sweet taste, sold at historic sites around the United States, such as Mt. Ver-

non, Monticello, and The Smithsonian, in addition to Colonial Williamsburg and Fort Ticonderoga.

The company also invested heavily in research in partnership with the University of California at Davis and Harvard University to understand the potential health benefits of cocoa. It funded at least 20 health-related studies between 1997 and 2007, establishing its Mars Botanical division to develop "leading edge science and technologies in the field of phytonutrients" while promoting sustainability in cacao growing regions around the world.

Also in 2006, in a reversal of the philosophy that led the company to centralize in 2003, Masterfoods decentralized its three top divisions and reverted to the name of Mars, Incorporated. There had been confusion over the firm's identity. Following this decision, Mars purchased 100 percent of Wm. Wrigley Jr. Co. in a cash transaction in mid-2008. The combined company, which had 64,000 employees and $27 billion in sales, hoped for enhanced growth opportunities. According to Mars President Paul S. Michaels, the merger brought together "[t]he strong cultural heritage of two legendary American companies." The company expected to see continued growth based on its combined commitment to "innovation, quality, and best-in-class global brands."

Janet Reinhart Hall
Updated, Frederick C. Ingram; Carrie Rothburd

PRINCIPAL SUBSIDIARIES

Mars Electronics Incorporated; Uncle Ben's; American Heritage Chocolates; Ceipa France; Dolma Italy; Kal Kan Foods.

PRINCIPAL DIVISIONS

Snack Foods; Pet Care; Main Meals; Electronics; Drinks.

PRINCIPAL COMPETITORS

Cadbury Schweppes; Hershey Foods Corporation; Nestlé S.A.; Ralston Purina Company.

FURTHER READING

Benady, David, "Mars Acts to Halt European Decline," *Marketing Week*, September 6, 1996, pp. 24+.

Brabbs, Cordelia, "Unwrapping the Changing Future of Mars," *Marketing*, January 13, 2000, p. 13.

Branch, Shelly, "Chocolate Lovers, Relax! Mars Points to Web Site Touting Cocoa's Benefits," *Wall Street Journal*, January 28, 2000, p. B2.

Brenner, J. G., *The Emperors of Chocolate*, New York: Random House, 1999.

Cantoni, Craig J., "Quality Control from Mars," *Wall Street Journal*, January 27, 1992.

Dahlberg, Carrie Peyton, "Candy Maker's a Sugar Daddy for UCD Cocoa Health Studies," *Knight-Ridder/Tribune Business News*, February 19, 2007, p. 1.

Fairclough, Gordon, "Mars Inc.'s Future Is Unclear after Death of Patriarch," *Wall Street Journal*, July 6, 1999, p. A22.

Hwang, Suein L., "Peanuts and Caramel Combine to Create Sticky Competition," *Wall Street Journal*, April 14, 1992.

Katayama, Frederick H., "Snickers Ice Cream Bar," *Fortune*, August 13, 1990.

Koselka, Rita, "Candy Wars," *Forbes*, August 17, 1992.

Lawrence, Steve, "Bar Wars: Hershey Bites Mars," *Fortune*, July 8, 1985.

Leonhardt, David, "It's Not All Kisses in Candyland" (review of *The Emperors of Chocolate*), *Business Week*, February 22, 1999, p. 18.

"A Little Illustrated Encyclopedia of M&M/Mars," Hackettstown, NJ: M&M/Mars, 1992.

"Mars Acquires the Dove Bar," *New York Times*, August 12, 1986.

"Mars Buys Wrigley in Cash Deal Worth Billions," *Candy & Snack Business*, May 2008, p. 6.

"Mars Merger Talks Denied by Nestlé," *New York Times*, September 20, 1991.

McKnight, Marshall, "A Clandestine Company Creeps Out of Its Shell," *NJBIZ*, September 30, 2002, p. 10.

McNatt, Robert, and Roy Furchgott, "It's the Taste, Stupid," *Business Week*, June 1, 1998, p. 6.

Mistry, Bhavna, "On a Global Mission," *Marketing*, October 9, 1997, pp. 39–42.

Noble, Barbara Presley, "Will the American Pet Go for Haute Cuisine?" *New York Times*, December 16, 1990.

"On the Wings of a Dove," *Washington Post*, May 13, 1991.

"Our Most Important Ingredient Is Quality," McLean, VA: Mars, Incorporated, 1980.

"P&G Sells Caprenin to Mars, Achieving Product's First Sale," *Wall Street Journal*, January 20, 1992.

Palmen, Christopher, "Wake Up, Mars!" *Forbes*, December 13,1999.

Rutherford, Andrea C., "Candy Firms Roll Out 'Healthy' Sweets, but Snackers May Sour on the Products," *Wall Street Journal*, August 10, 1992.

Saporito, Bill, "The Eclipse of Mars," *Fortune*, November 28, 1994, pp. 82+.

———, "Uncovering Mars' Unknown Empire," *Fortune*, September 26, 1988.

Sprout, Alison L., "Milky Way Light," *Fortune*, February 24, 1992.

Steinhauer, Jennifer, "America's Chocoholics: A Built-in Market for Confectioners," *New York Times*, July 14, 1991.

MDU Resources Group, Inc.

1200 West Century Avenue
Bismarck, North Dakota 58506-5650
U.S.A.
Toll Free: (866) 760-4852
Fax: (701) 530-1698
Web site: http://www.mdu.com

Public Company
Incorporated: 1924 as Minnesota Northern Power
    Company
Employees: 8,081
Sales: $4.18 billion (2009)
Stock Exchanges: New York
Ticker Symbol: MDU
NAICS: 213115 Support Activities for Nonmetallic
    Minerals (Except Fuels); 213113 Support Activities
    for Coal Mining; 221210 Natural Gas Distribution;
    325120 Industrial Gas Manufacturing; 486210
    Pipeline Transportation of Natural Gas; 551112 Of-
    fices of Other Holding Companies

∎ ∎ ∎

Headquartered in Bismarck, North Dakota, MDU
Resources Group, Inc., is a leading player in several
regulated and nonregulated businesses including energy,
utility resources, and construction materials. The
company's operations, which span 44 states, involve
everything from electric and natural gas utilities and
natural gas and oil production to natural gas pipelines,
energy and construction services, and construction
materials/contracting.

FORMATIVE YEARS

R. M. Heskett founded Minnesota Northern Power
Company, the progenitor of MDU, in 1924. Heskett
was an engineer who began his career building electric
streetcar systems in Wisconsin. After the automobile
caused the decline of the streetcar industry, he entered
the electric utility business with the financial backing of
Wausau, Wisconsin, investors Cyrus C. Yawkey, Aytch
Woodson, and the Alexander brothers. Heskett
undertook his first venture during the 1910s and early
1920s, when he built and then sold Minnesota Utilities
Company. He then retired briefly, but at the age of 53
he began the company that would become MDU
Resources Group, Inc.

On March 14, 1924, he and his Wausau backers
incorporated Minnesota Northern Power Company.
Heskett ran the company from Minneapolis and served
as vice president and general manager. Cyrus C. Yawkey
and Walter Alexander served as president and secretary,
respectively, but had no operational responsibilities.
Minnesota Northern began its operational life by
purchasing three utilities: Minnesota Electric Light and
Power Company in Bemidji, Minnesota; Glendive Heat,
Light and Power Company in Glendive, Montana; and
the municipal electric utility at Sidney, Montana.

In 1926 Heskett bought 80 acres of land near
Cabin Creek, in eastern Montana, and drilled for
natural gas. Drillers found enough gas for Heskett to
commission a site report from Hope Engineering. Hope
claimed the acreage held enormous reserves, so Heskett
quickly bought up the surrounding property. In 1927
Heskett hired Montana gas wildcatter Harry V. Mathews

COMPANY PERSPECTIVES

■

Provide value-added natural resource products and related services that exceed customer expectations.

to run Gas Development Company, a subsidiary that would explore for and develop gas, and build pipelines. Gas Development set up four wells in 1927 and 18 wells in 1928. It acquired development interests in the Bowdoin Dome in northeastern Montana and the Pondera Field outside of Conrad, Montana.

Minnesota Northern sold this gas to an increasing territory of homeowners and businesses in the upper Midwest. It built pipelines to Marmarth, North Dakota, and Miles City, Montana, and it laid pipe southeast into the Black Hills of South Dakota. In 1929 the company committed $8 million for a 90-mile line to connect Glendive, Montana, with Williston, North Dakota, and a 220-mile line from the Baker Field site to Bismarck, North Dakota. In addition to this geographic expansion, the company pursued acquisitions as another method of increasing business. In January 1929 Heskett acquired Havre Natural Gas Company, and in 1930 he bought Montana Cities Gas Company, Northern Natural Gas Development Company, and the manufactured gas properties at Sheridan, Wyoming.

ELECTRIC BUSINESS GROWS

Through the late 1920s Heskett's electric business followed a similar path of acquisition and extension. In 1925 alone Minnesota Northern acquired electric plants in seven North Dakota towns and seven Montana communities. In most cases Heskett built long transmission lines, closed inefficient isolated plants, and dropped rates. Growth continued in 1926. That year Heskett acquired the Terry, Montana, power plant. In addition, he installed a 600-kilowatt generator at Fairview, Montana, and hung several transmission lines between Montana and North Dakota, including a line from Bainville, Montana, to Williston, North Dakota.

Such acquisitions and line extensions continued, but the most significant activity of the late 1920s was a successful battle with Montana Power Company for the Miles City, Montana, electric franchise. Both companies organized publicity campaigns that urged Miles City residents to vote for their interests. Minnesota Northern also worked to expand per-customer electrical usage by selling refrigeration equipment to businesses and appliances to homeowners. Consumers could buy an automatic washer through their electric bill for one dollar down and a dollar a month. According to the official company history, *The Mondakonians: Energizers of the Prairies*, Minnesota Northern promoted the offer as "a copper washer for a silver dollar."

DIFFICULTIES DURING THE GREAT DEPRESSION

The Depression struck Minnesota Northern's territory in the late 1920s, when drought and depressed farm prices affected the Dakotas and eastern Montana. Following the stock market crash in 1929, conditions became even worse. Heskett committed $5 million to capital projects at the urging of President Herbert Hoover. U.S. utility executives had been encouraged to continue major construction projects in an attempt to aid the ailing U.S. economy. It soon became apparent, however, that business could not spend its way out of the Depression. Credit tightened and Minnesota Northern's income fell from $4 million in 1930 to $3.2 million in 1934.

Longtime employee H. N. Elvig noted in *The Mondakonians* that the company's financial structure "was held together by such slender financial threads as to require the founders of the company to guarantee its debts with their own assets." Heskett refinanced troublesome short-term debt, cut wages across the board, and inaugurated a sales campaign led by merchandise manager W. L. "Bill" Hayes. Perhaps most importantly, he relied on the essential financial soundness of Minnesota Northern's Wausau-based backers.

In 1935 Minnesota Northern was faced with another type of threat when Congress passed the Public Utility Holding Company Act (PUHC), which limited utility holding companies to one operating subsidiary. The law was a reaction to the abuses of several giant electric utility holding companies who then dominated the industry, but it applied to all utility companies. Heskett opposed the bill. Nevertheless, he consolidated all Minnesota Northern's subsidiaries into one operating utility called the Montana-Dakota Utilities Co. Montana-Dakota conformed to the PUHC and was able to continue operations without interruption.

Growth returned in the later half of the 1930s. The needs of natural gas and electric customers expanded, especially around Fort Peck, where the U.S. Army Corps of Engineers was damming the Missouri River. Between 1935 and 1939 revenues fluctuated between $4.4 million and $4.6 million, finally breaking the $5 million mark in 1940. Economic conditions improved further as Europe went to war. In the spring of 1941, Heskett told shareholders that "the year 1940 was one of the most

KEY DATES

1924: R. M. Heskett founds Minnesota Northern Power Company.

1925: Minnesota Northern acquires electric plants in seven North Dakota towns and seven Montana communities.

1930: Company buys Montana Cities Gas Company, Northern Natural Gas Development Company, and the Sheridan, Wyoming, manufactured gas properties.

1935: Minnesota Northern consolidates its subsidiaries into one operating utility and changes its name to Montana-Dakota Utilities Co.

1966: Company headquarters moves from Minneapolis, Minnesota, to Bismarck, North Dakota.

1985: Individual lines of business are grouped under the new MDU Resources Group, Inc., which is structured as a holding company.

1999: MDU consolidates all its oil and natural gas production and reserve assets under WBI Holdings, Inc.

2007: Cascade Natural Gas is acquired for $475 million.

2008: Boise, Idaho-based Intermountain Gas Company is acquired for $328 million.

satisfactory in the history of the company. ... For the first time in its history, total operating revenues of the company exceeded $5 million and net income after all deductions exceeded $1 million," according to *The Mondakonians*.

Also in 1940, the company acquired the gas franchise of Crookston, Minnesota, and completed a 117-mile pipeline from Fort Peck to Glendive, which added six communities to its customer base and connected the Bowdoin Field reserves to its growing pipeline system. By year's end sales of equipment and appliances were up 25 percent and MDU had 23,757 gas customers and 18,052 electric customers.

As the nation geared up for war, many Mondakonians, as Montana-Dakota employees called themselves, joined up, were drafted, or left the region. By June 1942 close to 10 percent of the company's prewar workforce was in the service. During the war itself, labor and materials shortages made repairs difficult and expansion

nearly impossible. After the war, Montana-Dakota expanded and took its modern-day shape.

POSTWAR BOOM BEGINS

On the electric side, MDU made two key acquisitions. In October 1945 it paid $7 million for the Dakota Public Service Company, an electric and mining firm whose subsidiaries provided electricity to 91 communities, including Bismarck, North Dakota, and had yearly revenues close to $2 million. Two years later, Montana-Dakota paid $1.8 million for the Sheridan County Electric Company, its first electric utility in Wyoming.

The company took a variety of steps to secure electricity for its new customers. It bought power from the federal government's Fort Peck dam and agreed to transport power to area electric cooperatives in exchange for 5,000 kilowatts of firm power from the Bureau of Reclamation's Fort Peck dam along the Missouri River. In terms of generating capacity, Montana-Dakota constructed several small diesel and coal-fired generators in the 3,400 to 8,500 kilowatt range and completed its first large steam generator, the 25,000-kilowatt, coal-fired R. M. Heskett Station.

Overall generating capacity increased from 14,837 kilowatts to 68,270 kilowatts between 1945 and 1951. Transmission mileage was up from 973 to 2,616. Kilowatt-hour sales grew from 40.5 million to 221.6 million, and electric revenues skyrocketed from $1.5 million to $6.88 million.

In the gas business, Montana-Dakota's primary postwar aim was to firm up supplies, which had begun to run short in 1944 and 1945. In the summer of 1947 Montana-Dakota began storing gas for winter usage in Carter Oil Company's Billy Creek Field south of Buffalo, Wyoming. In 1948 it started buying gas from Pure Oil Company's Worland, Wyoming, field, and in 1950 it built a 334-mile, 12-inch gas transmission pipeline from the Worland field to the gas storage field at Cabin Creek.

BOOM CONTINUES

With established supplies, the gas business again began expanding. In May 1951 Montana-Dakota acquired Billings Gas and the Rocky Mountain Gas Company. Billings Gas owned natural gas properties in Billings, Montana, and eight other Montana towns, and Rocky Mountain owned the Big Horn Pipeline and held the gas franchises in four Wyoming communities. Billings and Rocky Mountain increased Montana-Dakota's natural gas customers by 16,000 and helped push its 1951 gas revenues to $9.1 million. Montana-Dakota's total revenues for 1951 were $16.8 million.

Montana-Dakota also explored new business areas after the war. It acquired the Knife River Coal Mining Company, which switched from underground to surface mining, in the 1945 deal for Dakota Public Service. Then in the 1950s, oil reserves in eastern Montana were tapped. Rather than exploit the oil themselves, Montana-Dakota executives signed a net proceeds agreement with Shell Western E & P. Shell Western operated the company's 90,000-acre leased properties, which by 1958 were producing more than 860,000 barrels and paying $300,000 to Montana-Dakota.

By the mid-1950s growth in electrical usage demanded further generating capacity. On June 6, 1956, the company broke ground for the Lewis & Clark Station, a 44,000-kilowatt, lignite-fired unit on the Yellowstone River outside Sidney, Montana. Completed in 1959 for $12 million, Lewis & Clark was succeeded a scant two years later by groundbreaking on a $10.5 million, 66,000-kilowatt addition to Heskett Station.

EXPANSION CONTINUES

As electrical demand continued to increase (kilowatt-hour sales would more than double in the 1960s), Montana-Dakota looked for innovative ways to increase capacity. In 1962 it proposed a seasonal swap of electricity with the Bureau of Reclamation's Pick-Sloan dams but was turned down. In January 1963 it joined the 20-member Mid-Continent Area Power Planners, an organization that worked to strengthen transmission ties in the upper Midwest. In 1965 Mid-Continent members agreed to build a 5,400-mile grid of high-voltage transmission lines across a state region, enabling members and others to buy and sell excess capacity.

In 1964 R. M. Heskett, then in his nineties, stepped down after 30 years at the head of the company. Cecil Smith was named chairman of the board, and his nephew and Heskett's son, David Heskett, was named Montana-Dakota president and CEO. David Heskett reorganized the company according to modern management practices. He delegated authority to department heads, installed a conventional chain of command, and brought in new outside directors. Two years after R. M. Heskett's death in 1966, David Heskett moved the company headquarters from Minneapolis, Minnesota, to Bismarck, North Dakota.

In the late 1960s Montana-Dakota experienced continued customer and usage growth. To satisfy electric demand, in 1969 David Heskett and officials of Minnesota's Otter Tail Power Company and South Dakota's Northwestern Public Service Company announced a joint venture to construct a 400,000-kilowatt, lignite-powered generating station near Big Stone Lake in eastern South Dakota. Montana-Dakota would contribute $20 million to the $100 million project, which would break ground in 1971 and be completed in 1975. The plant, the construction of which marked the end of a long rivalry between Montana-Dakota and Northwestern Public Service, would be fueled by coal mined at Knife River Coal Mining Company's Gascoyne Mine in Bowman County in southwestern North Dakota.

CHALLENGING TIMES

In the early 1970s the company expanded its natural gas distribution system in two "Progress" projects. "Progress '70" extended gas pipelines 227 miles eastward across North Dakota, bringing service to 12 new communities at a cost of $18.5 million. "Progress '72" extended the gas system north to the U.S. Army's Perimeter Acquisition Radar site near Cavalier, North Dakota, and led the way to gas service for five North Dakota communities. To supply these new customers, Montana-Dakota explored for gas in the five sedimentary basins of the Rocky Mountain High Plains Region, and in 1974 acquired gas from the Rapelje Lake Basin northwest of Billings.

The major event of 1972 was the Rapid City, South Dakota, flood. On June 9, Rapid Creek overflowed, killing 238 people and damaging or destroying more than 2,000 dwellings. Montana-Dakota crews worked through the night for the next two weeks restoring service to the Black Hills and rebuilding much of the devastated gas transmission system.

The Big Stone Plant was finished on time in 1975, but at a higher cost than anticipated. A major component in its $160 million price tag was $30 million for pollution abatement. Pollution control was becoming a major cost throughout the Montana-Dakota system. Between 1973 and 1975, the company spent $8.7 million on electrostatic precipitators, scrubbers, and new smokestacks at existing generators.

At Knife River, surface mining was subject to increasingly stringent North Dakota reclamation laws. Pollution control was not the only area where costs rose in the middle and late 1970s. Inflation, high interest rates, and increasingly expensive natural gas squeezed finances and forced the company to repeatedly seek rate relief.

CAPACITY ISSUES

Despite these pressures, Montana-Dakota again needed new generating capacity by the mid-1970s. In 1977 Montana-Dakota and four regional partners announced that they would build a 410,000-kilowatt, lignite-powered generating station at Beulah, North Dakota. Situated adjacent to the Beulah Mine of the Knife River Coal Mining Company, Coyote Station would be a mine-mouth plant, cooled by piped-in Missouri River water.

Montana-Dakota also needed new gas. In the late 1970s a nationwide natural gas shortage exacerbated the problems the company faced in the cold winter of 1977–78. Because it stored gas in underground formations, Montana-Dakota survived the winter without any major mishaps. It did, however, interrupt service to industrial customers.

A major leadership change occurred during the late 1970s. On January 1, 1978, David Heskett retired, and Montana-Dakota's chief financial officer, John A. Schuchart, became president. Schuchart aimed to reorganize Montana-Dakota in ways that would exploit its technical know-how.

In the early 1980s, however, the company faced natural gas supply problems brought about by changing policies. To meet a growing demand for gas, Montana-Dakota contracted for supplies of deregulated gas. Deregulated gas proved too pricey for customers, however. Consumers conserved and industrial customers switched to less expensive alternate fuels, leaving Montana-Dakota with multimillion-dollar contracts for gas it could not use.

REORGANIZATION

On the electric side, Schuchart spent the 1980s rearranging Montana-Dakota's supply structure. He retired several older plants and in 1985 acquired further shares of the Big Stone and Coyote generating stations. In June 1986 he bought capacity at Basin Electric Power Cooperative's Antelope Valley II plant.

By the mid-1980s Schuchart was able to institute his reorganization plan. In 1985 he created MDU Resources Group, Inc., structured as a holding company under which he grouped the individual lines of business, although still operating within the bounds of the PUHC. Schuchart explained in *The Mondakonians* that the reason for the restructuring, begun in 1985, "was to better enable us to develop the individual assets which prior to that time had really been embedded and lost in the Montana-Dakota Utilities Co. structure."

Among the new subsidiaries, Williston Basin Interstate Pipeline Company faced a difficult time in the gas supply, production, and transmission business. Under deregulation, the role of the pipeline company changed from merchant to transporter. Rates fell, which

was good news for the consumer but bad news for MDU, whose overall gas business suffered as deregulation and warmer than normal winters caused a downward spiral in prices.

The Fidelity Oil Group took proceeds from the Shell-run Cedar Creek Anticline property and invested them in oil and gas operations in the western half of the United States and Canada. At the beginning of the program in 1986, reserves totaled 12 million barrels. Fidelity increased reserves to 17 million barrels by the end of 1991.

SHIFTING FOCUS

At Knife River Coal Mining Company, the late 1980s saw business suffer for two reasons: coal was in oversupply, and sales volume dropped sharply in 1987 after a crack in the rotor shaft caused a shutdown of the Big Stone Plant. After the reorganization, Knife River executives began looking at mineral and aggregate mining and clean coal technology as new ways to exploit their expertise. This effort intensified during the early 1990s, when clean air legislation put the future of the lignite coal business in doubt. In June 1992 it acquired KRC Aggregate, Inc., a sand and gravel mining company based in Lodi, California.

The last element in Schuchart's reorganization was Prairielands Energy Marketing, which expanded markets for the corporation's energy products. In 1991 Prairielands signed a 17-year capacity agreement with the Northern Border Pipeline system. The agreement provided a link between regional natural gas reserves and major national markets. In 1992 Prairielands began using the natural gas futures market.

Through a series of acquisitions in the 1990s, the Knife River Coal Mining Company changed its focus from lignite coal mining to aggregate mining and sales of construction materials. In 1993 the company acquired three aggregate operations in California and Oregon and the assets of an aggregate and construction materials company in Alaska. In 1995 it gained a 50 percent ownership in Hawaiian Cement, one of the largest construction suppliers in Hawaii, then acquired the remaining 50 percent two years later. To better express its broadened business concerns, the subsidiary dropped the reference to coal mining in its name in 1997, becoming Knife River Corporation.

Knife River continued its expansion in aggregate mining and construction materials sales, a lucrative area given the boom in road building in the Pacific Northwest. The Transportation Equity Act of 1998 dedicated some $150 billion to road building, mainly in the West, between 1998 and 2004, and Knife River had more business than it could keep up with. Its backlog in early 2001 hit $126 million. The company stepped up its acquisitions. By the end of 1999, it had acquired four more construction materials businesses, including Oregon-based Morse Bros, and JTL Group, which expanded Knife River's operations into Montana and Wyoming. In 2000, it purchased nine additional companies in California, Oregon, Montana, and Alaska. By mid-2000, the company's aggregate reserves had grown to 880 million tons, giving the company supplies for the next 40 years at current consumption levels.

More important, the growth of Knife River's aggregate business offset the decline of its coal mining operations. In May 2001 the company made the transformation complete by selling its coal mining operations to Westmoreland Coal Company. "Knife River's coal mining operations have been a part of MDU Resources since 1945, so making the decision to exit the coal mining business was not easy," said Terry D. Hildestad, president and CEO of Knife River, in a company press release. "However, with Knife River's growing construction materials operations providing over 90 percent of Knife River's revenues, it is prudent to concentrate on that business and take advantage of Westmoreland's interest in our coal operations."

GROWTH AND EXPANSION

MDU created Utility Services, Inc., in 1997, contributing to its increasing diversity. As a full-service engineering, design, and build company, the new subsidiary specialized in the construction and maintenance of electric lines and natural gas distribution and transmission systems. By 2000 the company had $169 million in annual sales and was expected to bring in almost $300 million in 2001. Its rate of growth looked promising as utility companies struggled to replace aging lines.

MDU continued its program of expansion for Fidelity Oil with great success in the 1990s. Reserves reached 22 million barrels in 1994, and production passed three million barrels. In 1996 the subsidiary acquired two new companies, with properties in Texas, New Mexico, and Alabama. The next year, its operating revenues exceeded $68 million. A significant purchase, the Willow Springs gas field in east Texas, was completed in 1998.

Williston Basin Interstate Pipeline Company changed its name to WBI Holdings, Inc., in 1998 to acknowledge its growing lines of business in energy marketing and to prepare for the consolidation of all the corporation's oil and natural gas production and reserve assets. The following year Fidelity Oil Group was renamed Fidelity Exploration & Production Company

and became a subsidiary of WBI Holdings. WBI made further acquisitions in the next few years, including a Wyoming pipeline, a gas storage field in western Kentucky, a large coalbed natural gas producer, and an energy technology firm specializing in pipeline and cable location and tracking.

Early in the new millennium, MDU had reduced its emphasis on its utility business. Utility services accounted for less than 10 percent of sales in 2000. Its growth in other areas, fueled in large part by acquisitions (70 between 1993 and 2001), was disciplined rather than haphazard: It purchased only in areas of expertise or closely related enterprises, and the strategy seemed very effective. The company's revenues, which were $464 million in 1995, reached $1.9 billion in 2000.

LEADERSHIP CHANGE, SHIFTING FOCUS

A major leadership change took place in October 2000 when Chairman John A. Schuchart announced that he would retire in January 2001. At that time he was succeeded by Martin A. White, who continued serving in the capacity of president and CEO. That same year the company sold its coal interests and began concentrating on aggregate-based construction materials.

In 2001 MDU Resources' Knife River business acquired Oregon-based Metro Rock & Construction. In addition, the company acquired the Portland, Oregon-based electrical contractor Oregon Electric Construction, as well as Bell Electrical Contractors Inc. Acquisitions continued in 2002 when MDU Resources acquired a total of six companies: Thornton Inc., Gesell Concrete Products Inc., Granite City Ready-Mix Inc., ESI Inc., Buffalo Bituminous Inc., and Bemidji Blacktop Inc. The year ended on a high note when *Fortune* magazine included the company on its 100 Fastest Growing Companies list, with a ranking of 83rd.

Acquisitions continued in 2003. That year the company added Young Brothers Inc., Young Contractors Inc., Young Materials Corp., and Brazos Motor Transport Inc. to its corporate family. In addition, it entered the wind power market by purchasing a 67 megawatt (MW) wind power farm in Southern California from the National Energy Group of PG&E Corp. for $102.5 million. Other highlights in 2003 included the completion of one of the largest natural gas transmission pipeline projects in MDU Resources' history.

In early 2004 MDU Resources acquired Spring Grove, Minnesota-based Roverud Construction Inc. and Decorah, Iowa-based Fred Carlson Company Inc., which became part of Knife River Corp. It was around this time that the company sold $46.6 million worth of stock to cover capital expenditures from 2003. Midway through the year CEO Martin White was named Best Executive at the American Business Awards. One final highlight from 2004 was the acquisition of Stratford, Iowa-based Becker Gravel Company Inc. in August.

ACQUISITIONS INTENSIFY

In 2005 MDU Resources parted with $145 million to acquire natural gas and oil properties in South Texas. In addition, the company purchased Las Vegas, Nevada-based Bombard Mechanical LLC, an HVAC equipment installation and maintenance company, which became part of its Utility Services Inc. operation. Growth of the company's Knife River business continued via the acquisition of several companies during the second half of the year. In addition to Post Falls, Idaho-based Norm's Utility Contractor Inc., the company acquired Sioux City, Iowa-based Jebro Inc., along with the assets of Irving F. Jensen Co. Inc. and Brower Construction Co.

Knife River expanded further in 2006 when MDU Resources acquired Jefferson State Redi-Mix Inc., Concrete Products Industries Inc., Jefferson State Asphalt Inc., Cherry Creek Aggregate Inc., Allied Concrete Pumping Inc., Keith Hamilton Trucking Inc., and HDP Leasing Inc. Other acquisitions made by MDU Resources in 2006 included the Reno, Nevada-based sprinkler company Desert Fire Holdings Inc. and the Stockton, California-based liquid asphalt producer Kent's Oil Service. Finally, the company's international business, MDU Brasil Ltda., parted with $50 million for a stake in an electric energy transmission partnership in Brazil.

Several important developments took place at the corporate level in 2006. In January the company named Dan Moylan chief accounting officer. Midway through the year the company announced a three-for-two stock split following several years of strong performance. The retirement of Martin White in August prompted several changes at the leadership level. Harry J. Pearce was appointed chairman, and Terry D. Hildestad was named president and CEO.

In 2007 MDU Resources acquired Cascade Natural Gas Corporation for $475 million. To help fund the acquisition, the company made the largest asset sale in its history, agreeing to sell its independent power production portfolio, along with its Colorado Energy Management LLC business, to Bicent Power LLC for $636 million. Other deals that year included the acquisition of Fargo, North Dakota-based Ames Sand &

Gravel Inc.; the Las Vegas, Nevada-based specialty excavation and utilities contractor Lone Mountain Excavation and Utilities LLC; Cheyenne, Wyoming-based Star Aggregates Inc.; and Beaumont, Texas-based Quality Concrete & Materials Co. Ltd.

UTILITY BUSINESS PROSPERS

Acquisitions continued during the closing years of the decade. In November 2008 MDU Resources purchased Boise, Idaho-based Intermountain Gas Company for $328 million. The deal meant the addition of approximately 300,000 new customers. The following month, the company's Montana-Dakota Utilities Co. division revealed plans to expand its 10.5 MW Diamond Willow wind facility near Baker, Montana, and construct a new 19.5 MW wind generation facility in southwestern North Dakota. Billings, Montana-based Total Corrosion Solutions Inc. was acquired in 2009, becoming part of the company's Bitter Creek Pipelines subsidiary.

In 2009 lower natural gas and oil prices pushed MDU Resources' consolidated earnings down to $260.4 million, compared to $377.2 million in 2008. However, the company's utility business achieved record earnings, thanks to the acquisition of Intermountain Gas Company in 2008. By this time the utility group served 950,000 customers in eight states. Moving forward, the organization appeared to be positioned for continued success during the 21st century's second decade.

Jordan Wankoff
Updated, Susan Windisch Brown; Paul R. Greenland

PRINCIPAL SUBSIDIARIES

MDU Resources Group, Inc.; MDU Energy Capital, LLC; Cascade Natural Gas Corporation; Intermountain Gas Company; Centennial Energy Holdings, Inc.; Williston Basin Interstate Pipeline Company.

PRINCIPAL COMPETITORS

Black Hills Corporation; NorthWestern Corporation; Vulcan Materials Company.

FURTHER READING

Beck, Bill, *The Mondakonians: Energizers of the Prairie*, Duluth, MN: MDU Resources Group, Inc., 1992.

"Bicent Power LLC Completed Its Previously Announced Acquisition of the Domestic Independent Power Production Business Unit of MDU Resources Group Inc. in a Transaction Valued at $636 Million," *Power Engineering*, August 2007, p. 16.

"MDU Resources Completes Intermountain Gas Acquisition," *Pipeline & Gas Journal*, November 2008, p. 10.

"MDU Resources Group, Inc.," *On Wall Street*, October 2000, p. 6.

"MDU Resources Will Mark Its Entry into the Wind-Power Business with the Expected Closing This Week of a $102.5 Million Purchase of a Southern California Wind Farm, an MDU Spokesman Said," *Power, Finance and Risk*, February 3, 2003, p. 6.

Shinkle, Kirk, "Erstwhile Utility Player Eyes Growth Elsewhere," *Investor's Business Daily*, April 17, 2001.

Merit Energy Company

13727 Noel Road, Suite 500, Tower 2
Dallas, Texas 75240
U.S.A.
Telephone: (972) 701-8377
Fax: (972) 960-1252
Web site: http://www.meritenergy.com

Private Company
Incorporated: 1989
Employees: 780
Sales: $1.83 billion (2009)
NAICS: 211111 Crude Petroleum and Natural Gas
Extraction

■ ■ ■

Merit Energy Company is an energy company that
forms equity-based limited partnerships catering to
institutional investors and high-wealth individuals.
Merit is an acquisition-driven, privately held company
that invests in mature producing oil and gas properties
that retain a high percentage of reserves and uses
advanced exploitation techniques to tap into those
reserves and increase the value of the properties. Merit's
tight control over its operations also helps to generate
profits. All told, Merit has more than $4 billion in com-
mitted equity capital under management and nearly an
equal amount in total assets.

The company owns interests in more than 12,500
wells located in Alberta, Canada, and 13 U.S. states,
mostly in the mid-continent, the Rockies, the South,
and Southwest, but also in the Gulf of Mexico and

Michigan. Production capacity approaches 95,000 barrels of oil equivalent (BOE) per day. Merit's proved
reserves, as reported in 2008, are in excess of 470 million BOE. The company was founded by its chairman,
William Gayden, and other former executives with
Petrus Oil and Gas L.P.

GAYDEN, LONGTIME ROSS PEROT ASSOCIATE

After graduating from the University of Texas in 1964,
William Gayden went to work for H. Ross Perot at
Electronic Data Systems (EDS), where for the next 20
years he held a number of top level positions, including
senior vice president of corporate development and
president of EDS World Corporation. He was also a
member of the board of directors until 1972. In that
year he negotiated the sale of EDS to General Motors.
In 1985 he was hired as the president of Petrus Oil
Company and charged with reorganizing and expanding
the business. Petrus Oil and Gas was founded in Dallas
in 1976 by the Perot family and quickly developed a
large amount of reserves. Under Gayden's watch, Petrus
built its proven reserves to 13.7 million barrels of oil
and 81.47 billion cubic feet of natural gas, and
controlled 61,267 acres of leased land. The business
dressed up, Gayden sold it in the fall of 1988 on behalf
of Perot to an Australian company, Bridge Oil Ltd., for
$112 million in cash.

After the sale to Bridge Oil, Gayden and other
Petrus managers formed Merit Energy Company in
September 1989, and launched its first partnership with

Perot acting as the initial investor in the $14 million pool. Rather than pursue exploration and assume the attenuating risks, the company planned to acquire, develop, and operate mature oil and gas assets, operating them on behalf of equity-based, reinvestment-oriented limited partnerships and reinvesting the cash flow over a 10-year time frame.

FIRST PROPERTY: 1989

The first property acquisition was completed on the final day of 1989. Over the next three years Merit cobbled together an asset base through the acquisition of small, individual properties, paying on average $6 million. Merit focused most of its early attention on onshore properties in Texas and New Mexico. Merit then became involved in the Hamilton Dome play in northwest Wyoming, which by the mid-1990s contained the company's largest concentration of assets. Merit also held properties in the Coleman Ranch in west Texas and the La Reforma area in Hildalgo County, Texas.

Merit's philosophy and expertise quickly paid off for Perot and other investors. In 1990 the company posted investor return of 14 percent (after the allocation of the general partner's profits). In that year Merit raised additional capital of $45 million while investing $46 million in acquisitions. Much of that new money came from tax-exempt institutions, such as university endowments, pension plans, and private foundations. Thus, taxable partnerships were established to own the working interests while tax-exempt partnerships owned the net profit interests. In 1992 three new institutional investors made $45 million in equity commitments.

ADDING VALUE: 1993

A key to Merit's success was its skill in identifying the properties it acquired and then adding value to them. An example of how Merit approached the exploitation of its properties was demonstrated by the handling of a property in the south Texas gas field of La Forma. After conducting preliminary field studies in 1993, Merit brought in Schlumberger Oilfield Services. Schlumberger was hired to discover if the field was operating to its potential, and if not, to determine the most economical way to stimulate production. This review, as part of the agreement, would be paid for by the enhancement services Schlumberger provided. In another example of its value-oriented approach, Merit would only consider enhancement services that would pay out in less than six months.

Schlumberger compared the five wells in the La Reforma field and determined that one was underperforming. Further analysis of that well revealed formation damage, a "skin" that hampered performance. Fracture stimulation was then identified as the best way to economically reduce the skin to spur production. Stimulation was recommended for two areas in the well and Schlumberger also identified five new gas zones that could be released through the treatment. Taking an incremental approach, Merit agreed to stimulate one of the zones. It proved successful as gas production increased more than one million cubic feet per day. The second zone was then stimulated, providing an equal improvement in production. The well, in fact, was approaching the production levels of 1981 when it originated. Merit's investment was recovered in less than a month. Only then did the company fund a 3D seismic survey of the area, which led to eight new well locations for future drilling.

In 1995 Merit entered the Rocky Mountains by acquiring $52 million of assets. Raising funds was not a problem. Merit's sophisticated, systematic approach of maximizing production and minimizing operating expenses in the exploitation of mature oil and gas properties earned the confidence of investors. In 1996 Merit raised $150 million, the largest fund-raising program in its brief history. Investors included three pension plans, nine university endowments, four private foundations, and several family trusts. With those funds, Merit formed a new partnership and increased the capital commitment to two other partnerships. Merit also benefited from higher oil and gas prices during the year, and posted record revenues of $83 million, resulting in net income of $27 million and an investor return of 15.1 percent. The company spent $14 million on development projects. Moreover, in 1996 Merit partnerships acquired the onshore properties of Murphy Oil

KEY DATES

1989: Company is formed, aided by initial financial investment of H. Ross Perot.
1990: Merit begins to attract institutional investors.
1995: Merit enters Rocky Mountain area.
2003: Merit acquires $420 million in Shell Exploration assets.

Company that it did not already own, and added four states to its area of operation, altogether spending $47 million on oil and gas properties, mostly located in Alabama, Arkansas, Mississippi, and Texas. Not only did they contain 13 million BOE of proved reserves, they held manifold exploitation opportunities.

ACQUISITIONS TOP $100 MILLION: 1997

Another first followed for Merit in 1997. The $122 million it spent on acquisitions was the first time in company history that it purchased more than $100 million in properties in a year. They were primarily located in Texas and the Rocky Mountains and added reserves of 35 million BOE. The company continued to benefit from high oil and gas prices in 1997. Revenues increased to $107.7 million and net income to more than $36 million. By this stage Merit managed over $335 million in committed capital.

Strong growth continued in the second half of the decade. Merit raised $300 million in equity capital in 1998 and spent $100 million in acquisitions, including the first oil and gas assets in Michigan. A year later the company spent a further $205 million in properties, including the $105 million purchase of a property in the Rocky Mountains, Merit's single largest acquisition to date.

By the end of the 1990s, after 10 years in operation, Merit increased the amount of committed capital it managed to $635 million, about 55 percent of which came from university endowments, 19 percent from pension plans, 17 percent from private foundations, and the rest from family trusts and individuals. Altogether it managed 16 limited partnerships with aggregate capital commitments of more than $1 billion. By every measure the company had exceeded the goals of its founders. Merit had hoped that after 10 years it would generate annual revenues of $30 million. Instead, the company posted revenues of $186 million in 1999 and net income of $61 million instead of the $10.5 million

envisioned. Moreover, cash flow totaled $110 million as opposed to the projected $18 million, and daily production of 2,500 BOE paled in comparison to the 44,000 BOE Merit's wells produced at the close of 1999.

NEW CENTURY BRINGS ACCELERATED GROWTH

The new century brought accelerated growth for Merit. Oil and gas prices surged to 10-year highs leading to a spike in revenues to $402 million and net income of $206 million in 2000. The company also completed its 2000 Fundraising Program, adding $500 million in new equity commitments, bring the total to more than $1.1 billion. The property acquisition market grew tight, on the other hand, and Merit completed only $75 million in acquisitions for the year. Opportunities increased a year later when Merit spent $165 million on new producing properties, primarily located in the Rocky Mountain region. A year later Merit spent $405 million on new producing properties, all but $10 million of which were included in a single acquisition, properties owned by Oklahoma City-based Devon Energy Corp. Merit attracted further investments as well. In 2002 it added $250 million in new equity commitments from its Canadian Fundraising Program as Merit entered the Canadian acquisition market.

After recording revenues of $436 million and net income of $139 million in 2002, Merit increased those totals in 2003 to $646 million in revenues and $281 million in net income. The company also closed on $778 million of property acquisitions, most of which were concentrated in a pair of deals. In July Merit paid $288 million for an asset package spread across five states. Another $420 million was spent on properties owned by Shell Exploration & Production Co. in Michigan, expanding Merit's presence in that area by adding 491 wells as well as gas-processing and transportation facilities. Merit also completed its first acquisition in Canada for its Canadian-specific partnership, spending $34 million on the Leduc Field located south of Edmonton.

As the first decade of the new century progressed, Merit became an ever-larger player. In 2004 it bought the U.S. onshore assets of Anadarko Petroleum for $850 million in cash plus interests in a pair of Wyoming oil and gas fields. Revenues kept apace, reaching $1.4 billion in 2005. As energy prices climbed so too did Merit's performance. In 2008 revenues increased 20.2 percent to $2.2 billion. *Forbes* magazine listed Merit number 267 on its list of the nation's largest private companies. A year later, the company moved up to 223rd. After 20 years in business, Merit had made money for its investors during good times and bad. Given the company's track record, this strong performance was likely to continue well into the future.

Ed Dinger

PRINCIPAL SUBSIDIARIES

Merit Energy Partner Llp.

PRINCIPAL COMPETITORS

Forest Oil Corporation; Newfield Exploration Company; Stone Energy Corporation.

FURTHER READING

"Apache, Morgan Stanley Take Anadarko GOM Assets," *Oil and Gas Investor*, October 2004, p. 101.

Haines, Leslie, "Merit Energy Co. Poised to Buy More Producing Properties," *Oil and Gas Investor*, July 2003, p. 17.

"Merit Energy Co., Dallas Plans to Buy the Michigan Exploration and Production Co., Houston, for $445 Million," *Oil and Gas Investor*, November 2003, p. 86.

"Merit Energy to Acquire Shell's Michigan Properties," *Oil & Gas Journal*, September 29, 2003, p. 41.

Sullivan, John A., "Dallas Firm Harnessing Digital Age to Rein in Far-Flung Assets," *Natural Gas Week*, June 9, 2008, p. 6.

Tremble, T. Porter, and Jay Haskell, "Production Reviews Payout Quickly for Two Texas Operators," *Oil & Gas Journal*, February 13, 1995, p. 60.

Merkle Inc.

7001 Columbia Gateway Drive
Columbia, Maryland 21046
U.S.A.
Telephone: (443) 542-4000
Web site: http://www.merkleinc.com

Private Company
Incorporated: 1971 as Columbia Computer Corporation
Employees: 1,000
Sales: $223 million (2009 est.)
NAICS: 541613 Marketing Consulting Services

■ ■ ■

Privately held Merkle Inc. is a Columbia, Maryland-based company that bills itself as a customer relationship marketing agency. In short, Merkle helps its commercial and nonprofit clients to take full advantage of their direct-marketing databases. By providing clients with a better understanding of their customers or contributors, Merkle helps clients to refine their marketing strategies, leading to better campaigns, stronger long-term customer/contributor relationships, and greater profits or fund-raising. In addition to strategic consulting, Merkle offers analytics, database services, creative services for direct marketing, full-range direct-mail-execution services, e-mail and other interactive marketing services, and fund-raising strategy and execution services.

Commercial clients include Bank of America, Dell, DirecTV, GlaxoSmithKline, New York Life, Nike, Procter & Gamble, and Wachovia. Nonprofits include AARO, the American Heart Association, Easter Seals, and The Salvation Army. Branch offices are located in Hagerstown, Maryland, as well as Boston, Denver, Little Rock, Philadelphia, and Seattle. Merkle is owned by its chairman and chief executive officer, David Williams.

COMPANY ORIGINS: 1971

Merkle Inc. was founded in Columbia, Maryland, in 1971 as Columbia Computer Corporation, a data-processing company that became a mailing list, subscription, and accounting service provider. In 1977 the business was acquired by Pubco Corporation of Glenn Dale, Maryland, and renamed Merkle Computer Systems Inc. The man who provided the company with its new name was Edgar A. Merkle, Pubco's chairman.

Born in Woodstock, Maryland, in 1900, Merkle became a reporter for the *Ellicott City Times* and *Baltimore Sun.* In 1932 he bought Ransdell Incorporated, a Washington, D.C., printing firm. He grew the business and in 1944 renamed it Merkle Press. By the early 1960s the company was printing 21 million magazines each month, including copies of *Sports Illustrated* and *Time.*

In 1962 he retired from active management and sold the business to Pubco Corporation and became Pubco's chairman. Pubco had been established just four years earlier in Washington, D.C., as Publishers Company Inc., a company that published and sold Bibles, devotional books, and encyclopedias door to door. In the early 1960s it expanded through acquisitions, and after Merkle assumed the chairmanship the acquisition spree continued. Nevertheless, Merkle Press

COMPANY PERSPECTIVES

■

In today's competitive environment, it's not enough to provide great products and services. What matters is how these capabilities create and support marketing strategies that influence consumer behavior over time. This is Merkle's mission.

remained Pubco's largest business, providing more than half of the company's revenues by the time Columbia Computer Corporation was purchased and renamed.

DIVESTING MERKLE COMPUTER SYSTEMS: 1981

Because Pubco did not keep its printing facilities up to date, the quality of its work began to suffer and its customer base eroded, eventually leading to the company declaring bankruptcy in the early 1980s. In 1981 Merkle Computer Systems was divested, acquired by a former Air Force pilot and flight instructor who lived in Boston, Harvey Blanton. He ran the business for several years, growing annual sales to $2.6 million, but by 1988 was ready to retire and sell the company. One of his Boston neighbors was 25-year-old David Williams, who became interested in Merkle.

Williams was an aspiring entrepreneur. While earning a degree in business administration at Shippensburg University in Pennsylvania, he launched a landscaping business. It was by way of advice from one of his clients that Williams became a stockbroker for a Philadelphia, Pennsylvania, investment bank, Butcher & Singer. In hopes of brokering the sale of Merkle Computer Systems through his employer, Williams paid a visit to Merkle, where Blanton showed him the operation. After two days of learning about the business, Williams found it fascinating and decided he wanted to buy the company for himself.

Blanton, who had mentored many young fighter pilots during his Air Force days, was eager to sell Merkle to a young person, albeit at a price he considered fair: $5.3 million. Blanton also agreed to sign a two-year consulting agreement to teach Williams the business. Although the terms were settled, the financing was not. Williams sought bank loans but was turned down 12 times, due in large measure to his age and inexperience. His family became concerned and at a family gathering dispatched older brother Lance Williams to an outdoor deck to talk some sense into him over beers.

While the elder brother agreed that Merkle was an interesting opportunity, he pointed out that David, who had a young family, had been neglecting his job, which was commission-based. He simply could not pursue both opportunities. The younger brother agreed and declared he would quit his job. "It kind of backfired," Lance Williams later told *Smart CEO*. "It was hard for me to go back into the house and explain it to the rest of the family."

DAVID WILLIAMS BUYS COMPANY: 1988

Williams's perseverance, and full-time devotion to the project, paid off. Perpetual Savings Bank of Washington, D.C., agreed to provide financing, and along with the money he raised from selling some assets, Williams was able to complete the acquisition. Thus, 25-year-old David Williams bought Merkle in 1988 and became the company's 24th employee. His problems were just beginning, however. Williams soon lost his hard-earned lines of credit when Perpetual Savings became ensnared in the savings and loan scandal of the 1980s and was taken over by the Resolution Trust Corporation, established to sell assets of failed trust companies. Merkle also lost its second-largest client, which accounted for almost one-quarter of annual revenues. To make matters worse, in the first six months under Williams's leadership Blanton suffered a heart attack and was unable to provide the guidance on which the young CEO had counted.

To help him guide Merkle through these difficult conditions, Williams brought in his older brother, who was a chemical engineer by training but was now selling insurance to oil refineries and power plant customers and eager for a change. Lance Williams joined the executive team and helped Merkle develop a five-year plan in 1990. Blanton was also healthy enough by that point to at least provide some input. At the time, Merkle focused mostly on unions and associations, but it had one *Fortune* 500 client, Bell Atlantic, one of the seven "Baby Bells" that resulted from the government-enforced breakup of AT&T. Bell Atlantic became the focal point of Merkle. "We put all of our energy behind trying to build around that brand," David Williams recalled in an interview with *Smart CEO*.

The attention paid to Bell Atlantic paved the way to additional clients. A Bell Atlantic contact also provided a link to another telecom, long-distance service provider MCI. In 1991 Merkle became involved in MCI's acclaimed "Friends & Family" direct-mail marketing campaign. As a result, Merkle made a national name for itself. Not only did it win MCI as a

```
┌─────────────────────────────────────────────┐
│                                               │
│              KEY DATES                        │
│              ───────■───────                  │
│                                               │
│  1971:  Company is founded as Columbia Computer│
│         Corporation.                          │
│  1977:  Pubco Corporation acquires business and│
│         renames it Merkle Computer Systems.   │
│  1988:  David Williams acquires company.      │
│  1997:  Merkle Direct Marketing, Inc., name is │
│         adopted.                              │
│  2005:  Reorganizing leads to new name, Merkle Inc.│
│                                               │
└─────────────────────────────────────────────┘
```

client, it added other telecom contracts, allowing it to gain entry into new sectors.

Merkle adopted a second five-year plan and increased sales through the mid-1990s. By 1997 the company was in a position to acquire its competitors. A major deal came in 1997 when Merkle bought Electronic Banking Systems. In that same year, Merkle changed its name to Merkle Direct Marketing, Inc. A year later Merkle acquired Worldwide Direct and moved its headquarters to Lanham, Maryland. Merkle closed the decade with the addition of several major new clients, starting with British Telecom in 1999 and quickly followed by Dell Computers, Capital One Bank, and Procter & Gamble.

EXPANSION IN THE NEW MILLENNIUM

Now well established in its field, Merkle enjoyed steady growth into the new century. Annual revenues reached $58 million in 2002 while employment increased to 700 spread across five Maryland offices. A year later, as sales improved to the $75 million range, Merkle opened an office in Philadelphia and added a professional services group to develop database marketing solutions for both its commercial and nonprofit clients, including the tracking of customer activity across multiple channels, and improving customer response rates or donor acquisitions.

Merkle completed another acquisition in 2004, adding an Atlanta consulting firm, Sigma Analytics and Consulting, a specialist in the development of statistical marketing solutions. Because of its expanded offerings, Merkle reorganized its operation in 2005, forming three new divisions: Consumer Marketing, Financial Services, and Fundraising. It also changed its name to Merkle Inc., opened satellite offices in Denver and Boston, and completed a pair of acquisitions in 2005. Seattle-based direct-response fund-raising agency the Domain Group

was purchased, as was Quris, Inc., a full-service e-mail marketing agency based in Denver.

Annual revenues were about $100 million in 2005, prompting the company to hire a chief financial officer for the first time in its history a year later. More acquisitions followed in 2007, including the response division of AB&C Group, a McLean, Virginia-based provider of direct-response processing services. Another direct-marketing agency was added in CFM Direct of Chicago, bringing with it $17 million in annual sales and a number of major clients: Bank of America, Capital One, HSBC, RBS, and TIAA-CREF. For the year, revenues increased to $181 million, making Merkle the 13th-largest marketing services agency in the United States, according to *Advertising Age*.

Also of note in 2007, Merkle opened a new 20,000-square-foot office in Denver to consolidate the company's operations in the area. Construction was underway in Columbia, Maryland, where Merkle opened a new $65 million campus in 2008 that included a five-story, 120,000-square-foot headquarters, a $10 million data center, and room for 575 employees. Additionally, the company acquired four acres of adjacent property on which it planned to add a 70,000-square-foot building to house another 350 employees. Merkle also relocated its Hagerstown response management division to a new 125,000-square-foot building, and later in the year a new office opened in Little Rock.

ADDING A MARKET RESEARCH PRACTICE: 2009

Despite an economy that was beginning to struggle, Merkle continued to grow, primarily because its services proved to be more valuable during lean times as companies were eager to make the most out of their marketing budgets by better targeting their customer and contributor lists. Sales increased 17 percent to $211 million in 2008 and continued to climb in 2009 as Merkle bolstered its capabilities.

To better serve its pharmaceutical clients, the company added a health care marketing practice. A mobile market practice was launched to help clients across a variety of markets to more effectively deliver product news and information through mobile devices. In addition, a market research practice was formed in 2009 to provide clients with insights on how beliefs and attitudes helped to determine a customer's purchasing and other decisions.

Merkle supplemented its offerings through acquisitions as well in 2009. Marketing technology company CognitiveDATA, with offices in New York and Chicago, was acquired in May. Two months operations were expanded through the acquisition of Minneapolis-based CMS Direct, a catalog marketing services provider. In September Merkle acquired Analytici, a New Jersey database marketing service firm. Moreover, Merkle launched a new business in 2009. Based in New York, LogicLab used data and analytic practices to strengthen the media buying process.

Having long portrayed itself as a database marketing agency, Merkle changed its positioning in 2009 by adopting the Customer Relationship Marketing Agency label, which described the company's aspirations as much as the current reality. The company posted revenues of $223 million in 2009. Williams expressed a desire to build Merkle into a $1 billion company. Whether he would succeed or not remained to be seen, but there was no doubt that the company's growth was continuing an upward trend.

Ed Dinger

PRINCIPAL SUBSIDIARIES

Merkle Response Services, Inc.

PRINCIPAL COMPETITORS

Epsilon Data Management, LLC; Acxiom Corporation; Harte-Hanks, Inc.

FURTHER READING

Cho, Hanah, "Merkle on Move as Agency Grows," *Baltimore Sun*, May 15, 2008, p. 1D.

"A 'Diamond' That's Rough No More," *Washington Post*, April 24, 2003.

"Edgar A. Merkle, 84, the Founder of the Merkle Press," *Washington Post*, August 17, 1984, p. C10.

Knight, Jerry, "Pubco Corp., Penn Co. Post Improved Results," *Washington Post*, April 4, 1978, p. D11.

Levy, Claudia, "Merkle Press Inc. to Close, Victim of Sales Siphoning," *Washington Post*, March 28, 1981, p. D8.

Tegler, Eric, "Have You Been to the Mailbox Today?" *Smart CEO*, October 2008, p. 28.

NAVISTAR®

Navistar International Corporation

4201 Winfield Road
Warrenville, Illinois 60555
U.S.A.
Telephone: (630) 753-5000
Toll Free: (800) 448-7825
Fax: (630) 753-2303
Web site: http://www.navistar.com

Public Company
Incorporated: 1902 as International Harvester Company
Employees: 17,900
Sales: $11.57 billion (2009)
Stock Exchanges: New York
Ticker Symbol: NAV
NAICS: 336211 Motor Vehicle Body Manufacturing; 336120 Heavy Duty Truck Manufacturing; 336212 Truck Trailer Manufacturing; 333924 Industrial Truck, Tractor, Trailer, and Stacker Machinery Manufacturing; 336213 Motor Home Manufacturing; 336312 Gasoline Engine and Engine Parts Manufacturing; 336992 Military Armored Vehicle, Tank, and Tank Component Manufacturing; 522220 Sales Financing; 522291 Consumer Lending; 532120 Truck, Utility Trailer, and RV (Recreational Vehicle) Rental and Leasing

∎ ∎ ∎

Navistar International Corporation is a holding company involved primarily in heavy-duty truck manufacturing and related enterprises. Navistar's subsidiaries and affiliate companies develop and manufacture products that include commercial and military trucks with the International brand; diesel engines with the MaxxForce brand; school and commercial buses with the IC brand; RVs with the Monaco, Holiday Rambler, Beaver, McKenzie, R-Vision, and Safari brands; and motor home and step-van chassis with the Workhorse brand. The company also designs and produces private-label diesel engines for pickup trucks, step vans, and SUVs. Navistar has production facilities in North, Central, and South America and partnerships and distribution operations on five continents, although the company garners most of its sales in North America. A subsidiary provides financing services for customers and dealers.

ORIGINS

Navistar traces its roots to 1831, when Cyrus Hall McCormick invented a machine for reaping grain. McCormick's reaper did not gain immediate acceptance among the nation's farmers. In fact, 10 years passed before he sold his first reaper, and, by then, his patent had expired. To stay ahead of the competition, McCormick developed such sales techniques as the warranty and the extended guarantee. Early reapers were bulky and noisy, and, as the *Times* of London disparagingly referred to McCormick's entry at the Great Exhibition in 1851, looked like a "cross between ... a chariot, a wheelbarrow, and a flying machine." Soon thereafter, however, the reaper became increasingly popular. The reaper and The McCormick Harvesting Company would eventually prove to have a dramatic impact on the farming industry.

COMPANY PERSPECTIVES

By the turn of the last century, our company's influence as International Harvester stretched around the world. While the past few decades found us focused on North America, locations around the globe once again power Navistar's business. Today, our products, parts, and services are sold throughout a network of nearly 1,000 dealer outlets in the United States, Canada, Brazil, and Mexico and more than 60 dealers in 90 countries throughout the world. With facilities on five continents—including North America, South America, Europe, Africa, Asia and Australia—we have the power to provide the most strategic and innovative technology solutions to our customers, no matter where they are.

While McCormick died in 1884, his company continued to experience rapid growth. In 1902, McCormick Harvesting was merged with four other struggling agriculture machinery manufacturers to form International Harvester Company. This merger was contested by critics who charged that the new firm represented a monopoly on the industry and, for more than 20 years, the company would be involved in several antitrust suits. However, Cyrus H. McCormick, descendant of the inventor and the company's first president, defended the merger by arguing that it gave the new company opportunities and resources that were beyond the reach of smaller companies. "Presently," he wrote, "there was afforded to the business world the unique spectacle of five competitors in one line coming together for the preservation of their concerns and of the industry, and for the fulfillment of their hopes of a future that was to count for much in the swelling total of American enterprise."

The courts eventually agreed that Harvester neither raised prices nor stifled competition and that the conglomerate actually helped farmers by developing and marketing new equipment. Harvester's product line expanded to include a wide range of tools used to speed the production of food, including disk harrows, harvester combines, feed grinders, and manure spreaders. In 1907, Harvester introduced a new piece of farm equipment called the auto wagon, a high-wheeled, rough vehicle designed to carry a farmer, his family, and his produce over rutted mud roads to the marketplace. Prompted by the success of the auto wagon, the company eventually designed new models with water

and air-cooled engines as well as lower, rubber tires rather than wooden wheels.

INTERNATIONAL EXPANSION

The company also began marketing its machinery abroad. Between 1903 and 1912, sales climbed from $53 million to $125 million, capitalization more than doubled, and foreign sales rose 388 percent to $51 million. By 1912, more than 36,000 dealers in 38 countries were selling McCormick products. During this time, the company's workforce grew to 75,000, and management invested in iron mines, coal mines, and acres of forest property, all of which provided the raw materials for producing farm machinery. Although the company suffered a huge loss during the 1917 Russian Revolution, when its Russian interests were taken over by the new government, Harvester's growth continued into the 1920s, as the U.S. economy expanded, new roads were built for trucks, and the international demand for agricultural equipment increased.

While Harvester continued to enhance its offerings, introducing a line of walk-in freezers in the 1930s, for example, the company sought to promote competition in the agricultural machinery industry by refusing to invoke tariffs and by protecting its patents for no more than five years. The company also experienced vigorous competition in both the construction and the truck industries while building up a vast dealer and supplier network. Eschewing any corporate restructuring during this period of rapid growth, Harvester simply added new divisions, over which managers had relatively little control and had to clear even minor decisions with the central offices. As a result, Harvester became a rather large and unwieldy collection of businesses, gaining a reputation for conservatism, antiquated management techniques, and strictly in-house promotions. Nevertheless, this form of organization saw Harvester through the Great Depression and into World War II.

FIRST DEFENSE CONTRACTS AND CHANGING POSTWAR MARKET

In 1940, Harvester accepted $80 million in defense contracts from the government. Even before the Japanese attack on Pearl Harbor, which prompted the United States' entrance into the war, 20 percent of the company's total output was defense related. Harvester employed its dealer network to haul in millions of tons of ferrous scrap from the fields of farmers and also sent its mechanics into the army in order to service and maintain military vehicles. Moreover, Harvester subsidiaries in Great Britain during the war were able to raise agricultural production there by one-third.

KEY DATES

1831: Cyrus Hall McCormick invents a machine for reaping grain.

1902: Five companies merge to form International Harvester Company.

1985: Company sells its agricultural holdings and the International Harvester name.

1986: Firm is renamed Navistar International Corporation and focuses its product lines on trucks and engines.

2009: Navistar reaches settlement with the Securities and Exchange Commission regarding investigation of the company's financials between 2002 and 2005.

Wartime production accounted for $1 billion in sales, and the company's contributions to the war effort garnered a *Business Week* cover story and several awards.

However, the war left Harvester financially weakened, and the company was unprepared for the postwar years. High taxes and a concentrated research effort cut profits. In 1945, the company reported $24.4 million in profits on $622 million in sales, a significant decrease from 1941's earnings of $30.6 million on $346.6 million in sales. Moreover, one Harvester official noted in *Forbes* that "the company's leadership in many articles of farm equipment [was] almost too well-established to bear expansion without charges of monopoly."

Nonetheless, the company continued to expand whenever possible. Harvester entered the consumer market for air conditioners and refrigerators, introduced a mini tractor, the Farmall Cub for small farmers, and manufactured an 18-ton crawler tractor for the construction market. A mechanical cotton-picker, introduced in 1942, sold well, as did a self-propelled combine and pickup baler. Furthermore, the company's overall market changed, and, by 1948, farm equipment accounted for less than half of the company's total sales. Trucks were the company's single largest item. Construction equipment and refrigeration equipment comprised the remainder of its product line.

LACKLUSTER POSTWAR YEARS

These new units and a capital improvement program improved profits, which peaked at $66.7 million in 1950, representing a performance that Harvester would not match for nine years due to an overextended budget, conservative management, and intransigent unions. Harvester's efforts to reduce labor costs were opposed by some of its 80,000 workers and 28 unions. An innovative pension fund program and in-house promotions placated workers, but even more difficulties arose when Harvester tried to reduce wages during the McCarthy era. During this time, the company accused the leaders of the Farm Equipment Workers union of communist sympathies, while the workers accused Harvester of using such "red smoke screens" to cover up wage cuts. Nevertheless, Harvester won an "Industrial Statesmanship Award" from the National Urban League during this time for establishing racially integrated plants in Memphis and Louisville. "Fair employment," remarked one Harvester manager, "is good business."

The company's profit margin remained dangerously low, however, due to high labor costs, poor management, an inadequate organizational structure, and its failure to introduce innovative products, many of which, competitors claimed, were merely redesigns of existing machines. Moreover, Harvester's much touted policy of in-house promotions was actually stifling research and technological advances. Most Harvester officers stayed with the company for as long as 30 years.

In 1955, Harvester sold its line of refrigeration equipment but kept its other losing ventures and failed to modernize antiquated plants. Intent on conserving its resources, the company failed to emphasize growth and began a slow and steady decline. "For too many years, as long as there was cash to cover the dividends, few executives really cared about how much the company made," one Harvester director later observed. Moreover, tradition was valued to a fault at Harvester. Although sales for one of its truck models remained poor, for example, the truck was kept in production. While Harvester continued to retain its market share, competitors alleged that it did so only by making government and fleet deals at cost.

NEW MANAGEMENT, NEW PRODUCTS, SCALED-DOWN OVERHEAD

Beginning in the late 1950s, a series of company presidents attempted to reverse the economic fortunes of the company. Frank W. Jenks, president from 1957 to 1962, standardized production, reduced district offices by half, reduced the number of dealers from 5,000 to 3,600, and increased expenditure for research and development. In 1961, Harvester reentered the consumer market with a jeep called the Scout and a small lawn and garden tractor named the Cub Cadet. The company also expanded its promotional campaign for a station wagon, the Travelall, which resembled a scaled-down truck.

All three of these new products could be produced inexpensively, as the company did not have to retool its plants to manufacture them, and they could be sold through the company's already existing distributor network. While new products increased sales, profits only rose temporarily before Harvester found itself ranked the second in the farm machinery industry, having been surpassed by John Deere & Company. In response, management tried to improve upon Harvester's 10 to 15 percent share of the construction industry but failed to gain any ground on Caterpillar and other competitors. By 1964, Harvester's truck line was its only viable product, comprising close to half the company's total sales. Harvester had the largest market share of the heavy-truck market: 31 percent.

GROWING COMPANY DEBT IN THE SIXTIES AND SEVENTIES

Throughout the 1960s, Harvester's profits declined, as the company expended more capital and went deeper into debt. Its labor costs were higher than General Motors; its management had poor communication channels; and low-selling products, such as the in-city truck, named the Merco, continued to be produced at high volume. Moreover, Harvester's decentralization policy failed to allow plants in different countries to share research or manufacture interchangeable parts. Although these plants would eventually work more closely during the 1970s, Harvester's construction products were still sold under several brand names, in direct competition with one another. In 1974, such products were combined under the Pay Line name to present "a united front to the industry."

Even though Harvester was larger than most of its competitors, it ranked second or lower in each of its three industries. In 1968, Cyrus H. McCormick's grandnephew, Brooks McCormick, took charge of the company, closing several inefficient plants, including the famed McCormick Works in Chicago. Under McCormick, younger executives were hired, dealerships were reduced, and a Chrysler executive named Keith Mazurek was appointed head of advertising. Mazurek promptly doubled the advertising budget, put the best-selling models on the main assembly lines, and reorganized the district dealer network along regional lines. However, profits continued to decline. While sales in 1971 passed $3 billion, profits reached a mere $45 million. *Forbes* described the company as virtually all sales and no profits and warned that Harvester's profits were far behind all its main competitors.

In 1977, Harvester brought in Xerox executive Archie R. McCardell, who quickly reduced costs and engineered a profit increase from $203.7 million to $370 million in his first year. However, McCardell's cutbacks led to a crippling strike in 1979. Over the next year, the company suffered more than $1 billion in losses, falling $4.2 billion into debt. When McCardell resigned in 1982, industry experts predicted that the company would soon file for bankruptcy. New managers tried to restructure the company, but, as one observer noted, "The new management is doing some very good things, but it is like putting a band-aid over a massive stomach wound."

Moreover, Harvester's share in the construction and farm markets continued to decline, and it fell to a number two ranking in heavy trucks, after Ford Motor Co. Although the company had cut its employment from 98,000 to 15,000 and shuttered all but seven of its 42 plants, it still lost $3.3 billion between 1979 and 1985. Troubled by soft markets and persistent creditors, Harvester entered a period of continuous restructuring. The corporation sold its construction line in 1982 and then its agricultural holdings, and, in the process, its International Harvester name, in 1985. The sale of its agricultural line to Tenneco for $488 million in 1985 helped the company reduce its long-term debt to less than $1 billion.

A NEW START

In 1986, Harvester was renamed Navistar International Corporation, a name that management hoped would reflect its new focus on high technology (and, a name which phonetically was similar to the former one). The company left the gasoline-powered truck market, relying primarily on its line of diesel-powered medium- and heavy-duty trucks. Navistar manufactured diesel engines for the medium trucks and used engines from other companies for the heavier trucks. The emphasis on fuel-efficiency, along with the solid construction and reliability of the trucks, prompted Navistar to redesign a majority of its truck line and advertise them as "LCO," or lowest cost ownership. In 1986, after recording its first annual profit since 1979, Chief Financial Officer James Cotting petitioned investors for a $471 million stock offering. The cash infusion helped Navistar retire a significant amount of its high-interest debt and thereby avoid bankruptcy. The following year Cotting was named Navistar chief executive officer and chairman.

Beginning with its 1989 introduction of an industry first, the smokeless diesel engine, the company began rebuilding its reputation as a company known for its environmentally friendly technology. Navistar also began expanding its Latin American interests and, in 1991, increased its stake in Dina Camiones, a Mexican truck maker, to 17 percent. That same year, Navistar signed original equipment manufacturer (OEM) agreements to provide engines to Perkins Group in the United Kingdom and Detroit Diesel in North America.

In the late 1980s and early 1990s, Navistar held one-fourth of the heavy- and medium-duty truck market (the leading share) but continued to face several challenges. Fallout from reorganizational divestments included a $14.8 million settlement with 2,700 employees of former subsidiary Wisconsin Steel, who had charged that their parent company had deliberately spun them off to a purchaser who had no experience in the steel business. Moreover, intense competition from better-funded domestic and international rivals in a declining truck market, which sank to a five-year low in 1990, also hindered Navistar's efforts to realize consistent earnings gains.

One of the most costly problems faced by the corporation evolved in part from its drastic labor cuts of the 1980s. The pension plan that was regarded as innovative in the 1950s became unacceptable in the 1990s, as Navistar found itself with 3.3 benefit-consuming retirees for every active employee. Health benefits consumed 7 percent of the company's annual sales. In 1992, Navistar made an innovative move to revamp its benefits structure by filing a declaratory judgment action in federal court. The legal maneuver, which was immediately countersued by the United Auto Workers, asked the court to sanction the company's plan to reduce benefits to 40,000 pensioners and their 23,000 dependents. Navistar held out what amounted to half-ownership of the company in exchange for the benefits concessions. In August 1993, under the supervision of the federal court, labor and management agreed on a two-tier plan, which actually reduced overall costs and improved benefits. The settlement slashed Navistar's liability from $2.6 billion to $1 billion but compelled the company to engineer a 1-for-10 reverse stock split.

NEW PRODUCTS, NEW MANAGEMENT, PROFITABILITY IN THE NINETIES

Navistar restructured its production line around utilities of specific trucks during the early 1990s, launching its Navtruck Program in 1992. This first new product line in six years targeted North American niche markets with particular trucks: the Dairy Diamond, for the milk-transport field in the Midwest; the Michigan Diamond with specialized "centipede" trucks exclusively used in that state; the Sun Diamond for construction and agricultural industries in Florida; and the Western Logger for the timber industry in the Pacific Northwest.

During this time, Cotting oversaw investments in not only product development but also modest overseas expansion, automation, and plant renovation. While these investments brought product and production improvements, initially they did not result in profits. In 1993, Navistar had still not recorded an annual net income and reported losses of $501 million. Nevertheless, Cotting expressed his unflagging confidence in the company's ability "to translate Navistar's traditional strengths—a broad product line and a strong and capable distribution network—into bottom-line results." That product line was enhanced in 1994 when Navistar introduced an industry-leading clean-burning truck and van engine, fueling an expansion of the company's sales of diesel engines. Navistar in 1994 finally reported a very modest profit, of $82 million, but it was a harbinger of consistent profitability in years to come. In 1995, the company rolled out its 9300 Conventional Truck, dubbed the Golden Eagle, with the truck's customers including several NASCAR racing teams. That same year, John Horne became chief executive officer and in 1996 was named chairman.

Navistar's sales flattened during the mid-1990s as competition in the heavy-truck market increased. The company sold its Columbus Plastics subsidiary, renamed Core Materials, to RYMAC Mortgage, although Navistar held onto a 45 percent interest in the firm. By the late 1990s, the economy had stabilized, Navistar had simplified its product lines, and the company had nudged further into Latin America. In 1998, Navistar opened a manufacturing plant in Mexico and launched sales of trucks and truck parts in Brazil. The cumulative result was that Navistar's earnings almost doubled, to $299 million, in 1998. The following year, the company completed its entry into the South American market and acquired a 50 percent stake in Brazil's leading manufacturer of diesel engines, Maxion Motores. The new joint venture was named Maxion International Motores and sold diesel engines to South American factories for Ford and General Motors. In 1999, Daniel Ustian, who would play an important role in the company's future, was named president of Navistar's engine group, a new position expected to guide the group's development of new diesel engines, especially those in the development stages of what it called "Green Diesel Technology."

NEW LEADERSHIP & BUSINESS LINES

Navistar opened the new century reorganizing operations under a new name. In 2000, the company adopted as its operating name International Truck and Engine Corporation. It also adopted the "International" name for all of its business groups in order to unite truck, engine, and finance operations under a single brand. The name change sent a signal that Navistar was going to change both its product line and its image. To alter the latter, the company launched a new logo featuring the traditional International orange triple diamond, replicated in such a way as to reflect the company's century-old history but using a new chrome border and deeper orange hue to highlight the triple diamond. In conjunction with the unveiling of the new logo, the company embarked on a new advertising campaign, building on its television ad campaign begun a year prior. The purpose of the campaign and name changes were to connect Navistar to its pre-Navistar history as an innovator in general and the International brand's roots, dating to the company's first truck, in particular. Along with the name-related restructuring, Navistar formed a new subsidiary, International Engine Corporation, for its engine business.

During the initial years of the new century, Navistar made significant investments in mostly non-truck operations, sales volumes of which fell as a result of an economic downturn. Meanwhile, the company took strides to build its diesel, engine, and bus operations. In 2001, Navistar consolidated its American Transportation school bus-body operations and its International Truck and Engine chassis operations into the new subsidiary IC Corporation (later, IC Bus, LLC). Navistar also acquired complete control of Maxion International Motores which it renamed International Engines South America. That same year, Navistar and Ford formed a 50-50 commercial-truck production joint venture, Blue Diamond Truck, in Mexico, to produce Ford brand trucks.

The year 2002 marked a turning point in Navistar's growth strategy. Ustian was named president and chief operating officer, designated to oversee truck and engine businesses and guide future expansion strategy for the company. Ustian became chief executive the following year. Planning to capitalize on its expertise in medium trucks, diesel engines, and parts operations, Navistar in 2003 launched a fledgling business unit specifically designed to compete for U.S. military contracts, International Military and Government, LLC. In 2003, Ustian assumed the additional title of chief executive, and the following year he succeeded the retiring John Horne as chairman and took full control of running the company.

Initially, under Ustian, Navistar focused heavily on diesel and diesel emission-control activities. Navistar was named an Environmental Protection Agency (EPA) partner in the evaluation of vehicle diesel emissions control in 2004, and that same year, the company joined with MAN Nutzfahrzeuge, a leading diesel engine producer in Europe, to collaborate on the design and manufacture of commercial truck and diesel engine systems. Navistar also became a leading supplier of trucks for the U.S. Postal Service, signing a contract to provide 1,700 low-emissions medium-duty trucks. Additionally, Navistar also manufactured 24 prototype diesel-electric hybrid medium-utility trucks in 2004.

Navistar in 2004 also unveiled its first two concept military vehicles, the SmarTruck III and MarTruck III. MarTruck III included a weapons station with sniper control abilities and remote controlled .50-caliber machine gun. SmarTruck III featured a defense system for rocket-propelled grenades and antitank missiles. It could likewise deploy antimissile missiles. In 2005, Navistar landed a three-year $62 million contract for provision of more than 2,750 Afghanistan National Army vehicles, including transport trucks and specialty vehicles.

SEC ISSUES, ACQUISITIONS, AND JOINT VENTURES

Mid-decade for Navistar marked a period of Securities and Exchange Commission (SEC) problems as well as a flurry of acquisitions and joint venture start-ups. Beginning what would become a nearly five-year ordeal, in January 2005, Navistar announced it would not meet the normal 10-K filing deadline nor would it meet an extended deadline for filing its 2004 10-K and that it would be restating fiscal 2002 and 2003 figures. Two months later, the SEC announced it was formally investigating Navistar.

The same year the company acquired MWM Motores Diesel Ltda (MWM), a leading diesel engine maker in Brazil that manufactured medium- and high-speed diesel engines for vans, pickups, and light and semi-heavy trucks and vehicles for commercial applications. The acquisition, renamed MWM International Industria da Motores da America do Sul Ltda., brought with it a significant list of OEM customers that included General Motors, Nissan, and Volkswagen and annual revenues of $370 million.

Navistar also formed a joint venture with Mahindra & Mahindra Limited of India to manufacture light commercial vehicles and medium- and heavy-duty diesel engines to be marketed under the Mahindra brand and sold in India. In another joint venture, Navistar teamed up in 2005 with Germany's MAN Nutzfahrzeuge to develop and produce 11- to 13-liter engines for class 8 vehicles.

Navistar also expanded its chassis and bus manufacturing operations, developing cleaner-emissions vehicles for the latter. The company moved into the motor home, RV, and step-van chassis market in 2005 by acquiring Workhouse Custom Chassis. Navistar that year became the first school bus manufacturer to offer factory-installed GPS tracking in its school buses and, in 2006, in conjunction with partner Enova Systems, Inc., became the first North American firm to produce a hybrid school bus. In 2006, Navistar also entered the commercial bus market, drawing upon its experience and reputation in the school bus manufacturing business. The company introduced five models: a small bus; a low-floor bus; a medium-duty bus; a front-engine bus; and a rear-engine transit bus. In 2006, the EPA revealed its first hydraulic-hybrid diesel urban vehicle, a result of a joint effort between Navistar, the EPA, the U.S. Army, and the United Parcel Service (UPS).

Between 2006 and 2007, Navistar was actively engaged in engine and pickup truck development and production. In 2006, Navistar and Caterpillar agreed to jointly produce truck engines and other products, and Navistar became an OEM provider of a 6.4.-liter diesel engine for Ford's 2008 F-Series Super Duty truck. Navistar also rolled out its new global brand of on-highway engines, MaxxForce, in 2006. That same year, the company unveiled, after five years of development and consumer testing, its International ProStar with the MaxxForce which Navistar boasted as being more aerodynamic and fuel efficient than any other North American class 8 truck. The company also launched its International MXT 4x4 pickup, targeting the "image" truck market, for owners who wanted a truck reflecting their personality. On the heels of the MXT release, Navistar debuted in 2007 its International MXT Limited, a 4x4 pickup with a 300 horsepower V-8 engine.

EXPANSION: HYBRID, MILITARY, RV, & BUS PRODUCTS

Navistar also expanded its product line and hybrid technology in 2007, in part through joint ventures both in the United States and abroad. In 2007, Navistar began a joint venture with Monaco Coach Corporation to produce rear-end diesel engines. Navistar claimed a 51 percent interest in the venture, named Custom Chassis Products LLC. Navistar officially entered the $14 billion RV and motor home market by launching a partnership with Conquest Motorhomes, a division of one of the industry's leading manufacturers, Gulf Stream Coach. That same year, Navistar and Mahindra & Mahindra teamed up in a second joint venture to make diesel truck and bus engines for the Indian market. Navistar took a 49 percent stake in the venture, Mahindra International Engines Ltd. Navistar in 2007 also became the first firm to begin line production of

hybrid trucks for commercial applications. The company's first such vehicle, International DuraStar Hybrid, was a diesel hybrid-electric medium-duty truck.

Navistar's subsidiary International Military and Government in 2007 won its first major contract, a $623 million deal to provide the U.S. Marine Corps with 1,200 Category I Mine-Resistant Ambush Protected (MRAP) vehicles. Several other military contracts followed and, by the end of the year, more than 4,470 MRAP vehicles had been ordered by the U.S. military in just eight months in contracts totaling $1.18 billion. International Military and Government also teamed with BAE Systems in 2007 to produce a Joint Light Tactical Vehicle (JLTV) for the U.S. military and to explore markets for other military customers.

In February 2007, Navistar stock began trading over the counter under the symbol NAVZ after being delisted from the New York Stock Exchange for failure to complete its restatement of 2005 financial statements. At the end of 2007, Navistar submitted to the SEC its 2005 10-K, which included restated figures for fiscal 2003, 2004, and 2005. The company reported net losses of $333 million and $44 million for 2003 and 2004, respectively. For 2005, though, Navistar reported earnings of $139 million. As it climbed into the black, Navistar's sales rose from $7.7 billion in 2003 to $12.1 billion in 2005. Subsequent late fiscal 2006 financial results revealed sales for 2006 were $14.2 billion while net income rose to $301 million, more than doubling earnings over the previous year. In May 2008, Navistar submitted to the SEC its fiscal 2007 10-K, bringing the company up to date in its filing. For fiscal 2007, the company recorded $12.3 billion in sales but lost $120 million, in part due to expenses related to late filing. In June 2008, Navistar was reinstated on the New York Stock Exchange and again began trading under the ticker symbol NAV.

In 2008, the company's military-products subsidiary changed its name to Navistar Defense, LLC. By 2008, Navistar Defense was producing 500 vehicles a month, and military orders in the previous 10 months totaled more than $3 billion. As sales for medium and heavy trucks and school buses shrank due to downturns in those market segments, the company weathered the storm with ongoing military orders that propelled the company's strategy for sustained profitability. One such contract from the U.S. Army in 2008 was worth $1.3 billion for MaxxPro vehicles to be used in Iraq and Afghanistan. In 2008, Navistar Defense added a heavy equipment transporter and trailer to its line of products and earned an $11 million contract from the Iraqi Ministry of Defense. The company also began production on its new International MaxxPro Dash, a smaller

MRAP armored vehicle created specifically for Afghanistan conditions. Navistar Defense further expanded its product line through conversion of commercial vehicles for military use after winning a $60.4 million U.S. military contract for refrigerator trucks and passenger buses for use in Afghanistan and Iraq.

Navistar made several moves to expand its Latin American operations and bus business in 2008. General Motors Brazil and Navistar subsidiary MWM International Motores signed an agreement to produce a new diesel engine for GM's 2011 line of vehicles in Brazil and other export markets. Navistar's Mexican subsidiary Camiones y Motores International de Mexico, S.A. de C.V., formed a joint venture with Brazilian bus builder San Marino Ônibus e Implementos LTDA in 2008 to produce bus bodies for commercial and public buses. That same year, 10 bus models made by Navistar's IC Bus became the first commercial and school buses added to the Internal Revenue Service's list of vehicles qualifying for the Alternative Fuel Motor Vehicle Credit. In addition, the company joined with San Marino Ônibus e Implementos Ltda., a Brazilian maker of bus bodies selling the Neobus brand, to produce commercial and public buses. Navistar's Global Bus Operations unit took control of managing the product line, which was initially marketed to Latin American customers. Navistar's bus subsidiary also announced its intention to enter the motor coach business in 2010.

In 2008, the company debuted its first big-bore MaxxForce diesel engines, MaxxForce 11 and MaxxForce 13, which established new fuel-efficiency standards for heavy-duty diesels and provided competition to Caterpillar Inc. and Cummins Inc., the only alternative providers of big-bore engines for International trucks. In another sign of Navistar's growing reputation for fuel-efficient technology, in 2008, the U.S. Department of Energy selected Navistar to participate in a program to develop aerodynamic trailers that would substantially reduce fuel consumption.

REORGANIZATION OF TRUCK OPERATIONS, NEW JOINT VENTURES, AND ACQUISITIONS

Reorganizing its truck operations to better facilitate company growth and customer service, Navistar in 2008 established four business units: Global Bus Operations, Global Truck Operations, Navistar Defense, and North American Truck Operations. That same year, Navistar rolled out its International LoneStar truck, featuring a classic-retro design with long-nose aerodynamic qualities and fuel economy 20 percent better than its competitors in the long-haul market. Using the LoneStar and Pro-

Star to drive expansion efforts, Navistar began adapting its MaxxForce engine, designed for U.S. emission standards, for Mexico and Brazil and later India, China, and Russia.

Ultimately, Navistar's strategy was to push the wheels of its truck business into emerging markets in the Middle East and South Africa. Where the truck business went, the parts business followed. The company also planned to use the ProStar to help it garner sales from a recovering class 8 truck market. For 2008, Navistar's revenues rose to $14.7 billion, a 20 percent increase, largely powered by increased military contracts, increased class 8 truck sales driven by ProStar, increased engine sales in South America, and global expansion. Net income was $134 million, compared to a loss of $120 million a year prior.

In 2009, Navistar became a partner in several joint ventures. Navistar and Caterpillar Inc. formed the 50/50 joint venture NC2 Global LLC to produce and distribute commercial trucks with both International and CAT brand names in markets that included Russia, South Africa, Australia, Turkey, and Brazil. NC2 Global then reached an agreement to establish a joint venture in China with Anhui Jianghuai Automobile Co., Ltd., to produce and market trucks and truck parts. In addition, Navistar Defense and Czech Republic heavy-truck producer Tatra, a.s., reached an agreement to jointly manufacture and sell military tactical off-road trucks. The initial vehicle produced was expected to use a Navistar engine and Tatra's backbone-tube chassis design and suspension system. Navistar also formed a joint venture with U.K.-based Modec Limited to manufacture all-electric class 2c-3 commercial trucks to be marketed in North, South, and Central America.

Navistar also made some significant acquisitions in 2009. The company acquired North America's largest private mixer manufacturer, Continental Mfg. Company, Inc. The acquisition of the Houston-based manufacturer of CBNW brand products was designed to bolster Navistar's slate of purpose-driven vehicles. Navistar planned to have Continental operate independently but distribute its mixers through International truck dealerships. Navistar also acquired for $47 million the RV manufacturing business of bankrupt Monaco Coach (renamed Monaco RV), which increased Navistar's RV chassis and diesel operations, supplemented its Workhorse Custom Chassis operations, and gave the company more U.S. manufacturing plants. Additionally, Navistar acquired Continental Diesel Systems US, LLC (renamed Pure Power Technologies, LLC), a manufacturer of fuel injection parts for Navistar's MaxxForce engines. In conjunction with the acquisition, Navistar created a research and development operation for diesel parts, and Pure Power operations were integrated into the research center, aimed at developing advanced emission control systems. In December 2009, Navistar also acquired Amminex, a Danish firm specializing in providing technology for clean-burning engines.

Navistar Defense in 2009 added the Canadian Department of National Defence and the U.K. Ministry of Defence to its clientele. For the Canadian military, Navistar Defense produced Military Commercial off the Shelf (MILCOTS) vehicles. Navistar Defense also added to its product line in 2009, unveiling the International Husky Tactical Support Vehicle, a lighter and more mobile MRAP than earlier versions designed for the U.K. Ministry of Defence to protect against ballistics, bombs, and roadside mines in rough Afghanistan terrain. In 2009, Navistar Defense also debuted a new MRAP vehicle, the International MaxxPro Wrecker, which provided small crews with the ability to recover disabled or damaged vehicles.

COMPETITIVE ADVANTAGES & CHALLENGES

In October 2009, Navistar reached a settlement with the SEC that the company expected would sufficiently resolve the investigation of the company's financials between 2002 and 2005. At the end of 2009, Navistar's revenues were being fueled by a rise in sales to large commercial fleets and ongoing defense contracts. Additionally, the International ProStar was increasing in popularity given its status as the most fuel-efficient class 8 truck. U.S. military sales, though, were decreasing, and material costs were rising, cutting into the company's profit margin. However, even though the U.S. and Canadian truck market continued to weaken due to lack of customer demand driven by the downturn in the economy, the company earned a record $320 million, although sales fell to a five-year low of $11.57 billion.

Navistar also unveiled its International WorkStar Hybrid 4x4, the first hybrid four-wheel-drive commercial truck, in 2009. In early 2010, Navistar released the next generation of its engines, the MaxxForce Advanced EGR (exhaust gas recirculation) engine. That year, the Navistar and CAT joint venture began to develop a vocational heavy-duty CAT truck for North American markets with CAT's dealer network to sell and service the truck, expected to be in production by 2011. The alliance also was expected to develop commercial trucks for other global markets.

As it entered the next decade, Navistar had competitive advantages but faced the most challenging

market for truck sales since the early 1960s. In particular, the worldwide economy had spawned a significant downturn in sales of diesel engines. In the short term, Navistar looked to its leadership in the class 8 truck market that was improving. In the long term, Navistar was clearly focused on four product areas: truck, bus, defense, and engine operations. Additionally, the company was picking up speed in its drive to create an expanded presence in burgeoning markets. The company had actively developed its commercial truck business in Central and South America and was beginning to expand that to other markets including India, Korea, and South Africa. Moreover, Navistar's parts business was growing with the expansion of its worldwide truck and engine operations. Ultimately, the company expected its globalization and its competitive advantages to pay off.

Those advantages included being at the forefront of hybrid truck and other environmentally friendly truck technology. Navistar was accelerating its development of hybrid technology through government grants and corporate partnerships. In addition, the company was working with the EPA, UPS, and Eaton Corporation to create a diesel series hydraulic urban delivery vehicle, relying on hydraulic pumps and storage tanks to store and use energy.

MAJOR MILITARY SUPPLIER

Additionally, Navistar had the advantage of being a rapidly growing defense business to which the U.S. government turned. During the second half of the decade, Navistar established itself as a major supplier of military vehicles and garnered more than $3 billion in U.S. government contracts for military vehicles, including those for more MRAP vehicles than any other government contractor. By the end of the decade, government sales represented better than one-quarter of all company sales. Navistar also had become a supplier for other national militaries, including those of Afghanistan, Canada, Israel, and the United Kingdom. Heading into the 2010s, Navistar Chairman Ustian projected that the company would net annual defense sales of $1.5 billion to $2 billion.

Overall, Navistar's major competitive advantage was that to which the company regularly pointed: leveraging its existing operations to start new businesses or enter new businesses through supplemental acquisitions. Since taking control of the company in the early 2000s, Ustian had guided the firm into several new profitable product lines, including defense contracts and the RV and motor homes business. Moreover, Navistar had achieved significant milestones. Navistar was North America's largest school bus manufacturing business, the leading class 8 truck producer, a growing military contractor, and at the forefront of hybrid technology. How much profit the company could gain from leveraging its own expertise remained uncertain in 2010, but Navistar seemed well positioned to expand the presence of the International name.

Updated, April Dougal Gasbarre; Roger Rouland

PRINCIPAL SUBSIDIARIES

Navistar Inc.; International of Mexico Holding Corporation; Navistar Canada, Inc.; Navistar Financial Corporation; IC Bus, LLC; SST Truck Company, LLC; Navistar Defense, LLC.

PRINCIPAL DIVISIONS

Trucks; Engines; Parts; Financial Services.

PRINCIPAL OPERATING UNITS

North American Truck; Global Truck; Global Bus; Navistar Defense.

PRINCIPAL COMPETITORS

Daimler AG; Daimler Trucks North America; PACCAR Inc.; AB Volvo; Blue Bird Corporation.

FURTHER READING

Durr, Kenneth, and Lee Sullivan, *International Harvester, McCormick, Navistar: Milestones in the Company That Helped Build America*, Portland, OR: Graphic Arts Center Publishing Company, 2007.

Loomis, Carol J., "The Strike That Rained on Archie McCardell's Parade," *Fortune*, May 19, 1980.

"M&M to Launch Truck in JV with Navistar," *Economic Times*, December 9, 2009.

Marsh, Barbara, *A Corporate Tragedy: The Agony of International Harvester Company*, Garden City, NY: Doubleday, 1985.

Miller, James P., "Navistar Misses Annual Report Deadline," *Chicago Tribune*, January 18, 2006.

"Navistar Buys Privately Held Continental Mfg.," *Boston Globe Online*, December 7, 2009.

Ozanne, Robert W., *A Century of Labor-Management Relations at McCormick and International Harvester*, Madison: University of Wisconsin Press, 1967.

Wendel, C. H., *150 Years of International Harvester*, Sarasota, FL: Crestline Publishing, 1981.

Williams, Winston, "Long Strike Is Called Key McCardell Error," *New York Times*, May 4, 1982.

Winninghoff, Ellie, "US: When Giving Employees Half Saves the Whole," *Global Finance*, July 1993, pp. 13–14.

Pacific Continental Corporation

---

111 West Seventh Avenue
Eugene, Oregon 97440
U.S.A.
Telephone: (541) 686-8685
Toll Free: (877) 231-2265
Fax: (541) 344-2807
Web site: http://www.therightbank.com

Public Company
Incorporated: 1972 as Pacific Continental Bank
Employees: 270
Total Assets: $1.19 billion (2009)
Stock Exchanges: NASDAQ
Ticker Symbol: PCBK
NAICS: 551111 Offices of Bank Holding Companies;
522110 Commercial Banking

■ ■ ■

Pacific Continental Corporation is a bank holding company for its primary operating subsidiary, Pacific Continental Bank. Pacific Continental Bank provides comprehensive banking services to consumers, community-based businesses, nonprofits, and professional service providers. The bank operates in three primary markets: Portland, Oregon, and southwest Washington; Seattle, Washington; and Eugene, Oregon. The bank oversees 14 banking offices in its three markets. In Eugene the bank operates five branches, as well as individual branches in nearby Springfield and Junction City. There are two branches in central Portland and individual offices in the outlying com-

munities of Tualatin and Beaverton. Pacific Continental maintains a branch office in Vancouver, Washington, 13 miles north of Portland. There are two branches in operation in the Seattle area. The holding company is the only publicly traded bank company based in Eugene.

FOCUSED ON ONE COMMUNITY FROM THE START

Pacific Continental, a bank that prided itself on functioning as a local, community-oriented institution throughout its history, remained close to home for decades. The bank was founded in 1972 as Pacific Continental Bank. Pacific Continental offered banking services to residents and small businesses in Eugene at its inception, operating as a hometown bank in a small city in central Oregon. As the years progressed, the bank began to develop into a notable, regionally oriented financial institution. Pacific Continental's evolution occurred in measured steps.

The first significant development in the bank's history had nothing to do with its physical expansion. The decision to hire J. Bruce Riddle six years after its formation figured prominently in its maturation into a respected banking institution. Riddle joined the company in 1978 and wasted little time in distinguishing himself to Pacific Continental's board of directors. A mere two years passed before Riddle, 35 years old, was named president and CEO of the Eugene bank. For the next two decades, Pacific Continental had its top executive, gaining the leader who would orchestrate the bank's geographic expansion and guide the enterprise through its evolution into a bank holding company.

Pacific Continental never pined for national fame. The bank never plotted to erect a vast network of branch offices capable of serving myriad communities. Instead the bank stuck close to home, satisfied to remain within the confines of central Oregon. Riddle embraced the bank's expansion philosophy, only stretching the territory of Pacific Continental's influence after careful consideration.

The addition of Pacific Continental branch offices represented significant steps in the bank's development. Pacific Continental tested the waters at first, directing its initial efforts to familiar areas. The bank opened a branch in Springfield, just east of Eugene. It opened a branch in Junction City, 13 miles to the north of Eugene. Its first great geographic leap occurred as its 25th anniversary neared.

EXPANSION INTO PORTLAND: 1996

From Eugene to Seattle to the north, Interstate 5 (I-5), stretched as a cord connecting two cities separated by 250 miles. Pacific Continental began to move up the I-5 corridor in 1996, 16 years after Riddle had taken control of the bank. Pacific Continental opened a branch office in Beaverton, a Portland suburb. From there, the company pressed ahead into Portland, establishing a presence in the state's largest city.

After shepherding Pacific Continental 100 miles north, he made the boldest move of his leadership tenure. In June 1999 Pacific Continental reorganized as a bank holding company. Pacific Continental Corporation was formed as the holding company and given control over its primary operating subsidiary, Pacific Continental Bank. The reorganization, made popular by much larger financial institutions during the late 1960s, enabled Riddle's company to enjoy greater flexibility in raising capital, it eased its ability to acquire other banks and non-financial institutions, and it gave the company greater legal authority to purchase its own stock.

At the time of the reorganization into a bank holding company, Pacific Continental existed as a six-branch bank with 121 employees. The company registered $213 million in deposits and recognized three counties (Lane, Washington, and Linn) as its primary operating territory. Although the formation of a holding company gave the company greater regulatory freedom to pursue expansion, it adhered to the philosophy created at its formation. Pacific Continental Corporation presided over a community-based bank, a financial institution that had gradually widened its scope beyond Eugene, but a financial institution that remained committed to supplying banking services its much larger rivals either ignored or were unable to provide.

As Pacific Continental entered the 21st century, the company focused its efforts on serving residents in its communities and it allied itself with local business owners. Between 1997 and 2000, Pacific Continental originated more Small Business Administration loans in Oregon than any other lender. "Our real niche is to be a resource to business," a company executive said in the July 2000 issue of *Oregon Business*. At the time, Pacific Continental served approximately 15,000 business customers.

CHANGE IN LEADERSHIP: 2002

The steady development of Pacific Continental was disrupted with an announcement in mid-2002. After 22 years leading the company, Riddle suddenly resigned, surprising everyone within the organization. Publicly, no reason was offered for his departure. Riddle remained silent. "This was Bruce's decision," the company's chairman, Robert Ballin, offered in the July 16, 2002 edition of Eugene's *Register-Guard*. "Bruce has done a marvelous job for our bank. There were no improprieties."

Riddle's replacement was waiting a few doors down from the CEO's vacant office. Hal Brown, 48 years old, was serving as Pacific Continental's chief operations officer when Riddle's departure created a leadership void. Brown began his banking career while he was attending college. He worked as a part-time teller for United California Bank in Downey, California, and joined the bank on a full-time basis after completing his studies. In 1981 he moved to Oregon to accept a position at Greater Pacific Bank in Albany. In 1985 he was offered employment at Pacific Continental, joining the bank when it operated only in the greater Eugene area. "Pacific Continental, in 1985, was quite a small institution," Brown said in the April 1, 2008, edition of the *Register-Guard*. "So I joined the bank with several hats."

During the next 17 years, Brown distinguished himself, earning several promotions. He began as a

```
┌─────────────────────────────────────────┐
│                                         │
│            KEY DATES                    │
│              ■                          │
│  ─────────────────────────────────────  │
│  1972:  Pacific Continental Bank is     │
│         founded.                        │
│  1996:  Bank opens its first branch in  │
│         Portland.                       │
│  1999:  Pacific Continental Corporation │
│         is formed as a bank holding     │
│         company for Pacific             │
│         Continental Bank.               │
│  2005:  Acquisition of NWB Financial    │
│         Corp. extends the company's     │
│         presence to the Seattle market. │
│  2008:  Assets exceed $1 billion for    │
│         the first time.                 │
│                                         │
└─────────────────────────────────────────┘
```

cashier, earned a promotion to operations officer, gained greater authority when he was named senior operations officer, and joined the top tier of management when he was appointed chief financial officer. In 2000 he was named chief operations officer, the position he held when Riddle left.

A new era of leadership began during the bank's 30th anniversary. Expansion into Portland sparked speculation that Pacific Continental might relocate its headquarters, but Brown quashed the rumors, saying that the company would always regard Eugene as its home. Brown's declaration of the bank's commitment to the community in Eugene did not mean he was reluctant to expand geographically, however. Midway through the decade, he orchestrated arguably the boldest move in Pacific Continental's history, extending the bank's presence 250 miles to the north.

ENTRY INTO SEATTLE: 2005

By 2005 Pacific Continental possessed more than $550 million in assets. The total would swell once the company completed one of the rare acquisitions in its history. In August 2005 Brown announced his intention to acquire NWB Financial Corp., the bank holding company for Northwest Business Bank. The proposed acquisition represented a momentous event in Pacific Continental's history, a "strategic inflection point of Pacific Continental," according to Brown in the August 18, 2005 release of *Fair Disclosure Wire*.

NWB Financial Corp., led by President and CEO Basant Singh, was based in Seattle where it operated one branch and another east of the city in Bellevue. The two-branch bank's assimilation into Pacific Continental marked the Eugene-based company's first step into Washington, into the biggest market in the state. The acquisition also paved the way for further expansion in the state. "Importantly," Brown said in the August 18, 2005 release of *Fair Disclosure Wire*, "this transaction

also provides a future opportunity to branch into any Washington city, including Vancouver, Washington, a natural expansion of our metropolitan Portland footprint."

The acquisition was completed before the end of 2005. Pacific Continental paid $14.5 million in cash plus stock to acquire NWB Financial Corp. for a total consideration of $39 million. NWB Financial Corp.'s assets, $143 million at the time of the merger, gave Pacific Continental approximately $700 million in assets. Bolstered by the addition of NWB Financial Corp., Pacific Continental ended the year with a presence in three of the Pacific Northwest's largest commercial markets, including the largest commercial markets in Oregon and Washington. As predicted, the acquisition set the stage for Pacific Continental's expansion into Vancouver. In March 2006 the company opened a branch in a building formerly occupied by the retailer J.C. Penney, giving Pacific Continental a total of 14 branches.

STORM CLOUDS GATHER: 2007–09

After the bold move into Washington, Pacific Continental braced itself for tumultuous times. The subprime mortgage crisis near the end of the decade delivered a stinging blow to banks across the country, as mortgage delinquencies and foreclosures mushroomed. The housing market lost its luster, peaking at the end of 2006, and severe recessive economic conditions soon followed. U.S. consumers and businesses reeled from the reverberative effects of a profoundly stricken economy. Some banks closed, others teetered on the brink of insolvency, prompting the U.S. government in 2008 to create the Troubled Asset Relief Program, TARP, to purchase assets and equity from financial institutions in an effort to stabilize the financial sector.

Pacific Continental occupied a vulnerable position. Exposed to the anemic real estate market and its health tied to the health of small businesses in the region, the company prepared for turbulence ahead. Pacific Continental posted a profit of $3.3 million in the final quarter of 2007, but warning signs were beginning to emerge, signaling trouble. The company listed 17 residential construction loans as nonperforming assets at the beginning of 2008.

Brown, wary of public perception that Pacific Continental would be swept aside by the pernicious forces causing severe damage to other banks, reassured onlookers in a public statement. "We employ the best practices in the industry when it comes to our loan portfolio management and identification of the inherent risks associated with bank lending," he said in the January 24, 2008, edition of the *Register-Guard*. "Pacific Continental's overriding philosophy to lending is quality first, profitability second, and growth third."

Pacific Continental avoided damage in 2008 because of its prudence and because its three primary markets fared far better than other parts of the country. The company posted $12.9 million in net income during the year and, for the first time in its history, its assets eclipsed $1 billion. Instead of buckling under the force of the economic pressures, Pacific Continental came to the aid of its hometown community, hosting a private panel discussion in Eugene on budget cuts and the effect of the cuts on nonprofits. In early 2009 Brown opted not to participate in the U.S. Treasury Department's bank bailout program after gaining preliminary approval to receive as much as $30 million in TARP funding. "It became apparent we didn't need the money ... for our capital position," Brown said in the January 15, 2009 edition of the *Register-Guard*. Brown believed Pacific Continental was sturdy enough to stand on its own during the global economic crisis that extended into the next decade, convinced Eugene's largest bank would persevere and go on to thrive in the years ahead.

Jeffrey L. Covell

PRINCIPAL SUBSIDIARIES

Pacific Continental Bank; PCB Service Corporation; PCB Loan Services.

PRINCIPAL COMPETITORS

Umpqua Holdings Corporation; Wells Fargo & Company; West Coast Bancorp.

FURTHER READING

McCarthy, Nancy, "A Community Service to Bank On," *Oregon Business*, July 2000, p. 59.

Mosley, Joe, "Local Bank Passes on Bailout," *Register-Guard*, January 15, 2009, p. D19.

———, "Pacific Continental Banks on Eugene," *Register-Guard*, April 1, 2008, p. L3.

———, "Pacific Continental Results Up," *Register-Guard*, January 24, 2008, p. B11.

"Pacific Continental Corporation Conference Call and Webcast Relating to Acquisition of NWB Financial Corporation—Final," *Fair Disclosure Wire*, August 18, 2005.

Russo, Ed, "Pacific Continental Bank Loses Longtime Executive," *Register-Guard*, July 16, 2002.

Palmer and Harvey Group PLC

P and H House
106-112 Davigdor Road
Hove, BN3 1RE
United Kingdom
Telephone: (+44 01273) 222100
Fax: (+44 01273) 222101
Web site: http://www.palmerharvey.co.uk

Private Company
Founded: 1925
Incorporated: 1984
Employees: 3,518
Sales: £4.03 billion ($7.72 billion) (2008)
NAICS: 424940 Tobacco and Tobacco Product Merchant Wholesalers; 424450 Confectionery Merchant Wholesalers; 424810 Beer and Ale Merchant Wholesalers; 424820 Wine and Distilled Alcoholic Beverage Merchant Wholesalers

■ ■ ■

Palmer and Harvey Group PLC is the largest wholesale distributor in the United Kingdom. Palmer and Harvey is also the third-largest privately held company in the United Kingdom, with annual revenues of more than £4 billion ($7.7 billion). Palmer and Harvey focuses on supplying delivery wholesale services (as opposed to the cash-and-carry wholesale), boasting an array of 69,000 product lines. The company also provides turnkey retail services, with four main fascia, Mace, Mace Express, Your Shop, and Supershop. These services include signage, store layout, lighting and fittings, electronic point-of-sale systems, and product offerings tailored to the retailers' specific location and market segment.

Palmer and Harvey has further developed distinct product lines for its three largest retail channels, CTN (Convenience, Tobacco, News) Retailers; Convenience Retailers; and Forecourt Retailers. The company serves both independent and multiple group customers, including Esso, Shell, Total, Welcome Break, One-Stop, Blockbuster, Star News, and Moto. Palmer and Harvey supplies a number of major grocery retailers, including Tesco, Sainsburys, and Makro. The company also provides distribution services for a number of manufacturers, including Coca-Cola Company, Nestlé, McVitie's, and GSK. Through subsidiary P&H Snacksdirect, the company provides van delivery services. The company supports its operations with a network of distribution depots located throughout England, Wales, and Scotland. Palmer and Harvey is led by CEO Chris Etherington and Chairman Christopher Adams, who spearheaded a management buyout of the company in 2008.

FOUNDING A WHOLESALE EMPIRE IN 1925

Palmer and Harvey Group originated as a small tobacconist shop opened in London in the early years of the 20th century. The company's founder was Archibald William Stone, born in 1882. Around 1900 Stone left England for Canada, where he worked on farms and in the logging industry. On his return to England, Stone came to north London, where he opened his tobacconist store in 1906. By 1925, Stone had moved into the wholesale sector, founding what was to become the United Kingdom's leading wholesaler, Palmer and Harvey.

In the 1960s, Palmer and Harvey gained a new chairman after Donald Gosling, cofounder of National Car Parks, married into the founding family. Under Gosling's leadership, Palmer and Harvey grew significantly. By the end of the decade the company was posting sales of more than £40 million.

Acquisitions played a significant part of Palmer and Harvey's growth through the next decade. The company helped set the pace of a consolidation movement among the wholesale sector, in part to counter the effects of the ending of the Retail Price Maintenance scheme. Under this system, manufacturers had been allowed to set minimum prices for their goods. Its repeal promised to place the wholesale sector under new pressure, squeezing their profit margins. In order to counter this effect, Palmer and Harvey sought to expand its own trading volumes.

ACQUIRING SCALE IN THE SEVENTIES

The company's acquisition drive started with the purchase of Singleton & Cole, the wholesaling operation of Cavenham Foods, for £2 million in 1968. The purchase added an additional 25 new cash-and-carry stores to Palmer and Harvey's own network, which topped 60 locations by the end of the 1970s. The purchase of Singleton & Cole also boosted the company's annual revenues by another £27 million, giving the company control of more than 1 percent of the total U.K. market.

Palmer and Harvey completed several more acquisitions through the 1970s. The company bought C. Baker & Co. (Wholesalers) in 1972. This was followed by the takeover of the CTN operations of Barker & Dobson in 1974. This £1.1 million purchase gave the company control of three new businesses, Allsop & Wagner, H.

Jenkins of Skewen, and Waller & Hartley (Wholesale). Palmer and Harvey thus strengthened its presence in England's southeast and northwest, as well as in south Wales.

By then, Palmer and Harvey was ranked as the leading wholesale supplier to the CTN trade. Other acquisitions during the decade included Rugby-based Lennon Brothers, for £1.5 million in 1977. The company also completed a smaller purchase that year, paying £174,500 for confectionery wholesaler Edward McGregor. The following year, the company completed a still more ambitious acquisition, paying £5.3 million for the wholesale and retail operations of Drakes Sweets and Marketing, manufacturers of the world famous Licorice Allsorts.

NEW DIRECTIONS IN THE NINETIES

Palmer and Harvey completed two more notable acquisitions in the 1980s. In 1984, the company engineered the £1.28 million takeover of P. Panto, a wholesale CTN and grocery supplier that had slipped into losses. The company also added Sinclair & Collis, purchased from Imperial Tobacco in 1987. Two years later, the group added the Moffat wholesale group as well.

Palmer and Harvey also prepared for its own change in ownership, following A. W. Stone's death at the age of 100 in 1982. The company remained controlled by the Stone family through that decade. In 1988, Gosling divorced from his wife and resigned from his director's position with the company. Soon after, the Stone family sold Palmer and Harvey through a management buyout. This proved to be the first of several, as Palmer and Harvey clung to its status as a private company through the close of the century.

The company prepared for an even stronger expansion in the 1990s. In 1992, the company built a new 72,000-square-foot central warehouse in Coventry. A few years later, the company refitted that facility, which became fully automated in 2005. In this way, the facility's output soared, from just 130 "outers" per hour to up to 6,000 per hour.

This expanded capacity provided the foundation for the company's transformation in the 1990s. Through most of its history, Palmer and Harvey had focused on the traditional CTN market, supplying tobacco products, confectionery, soft drinks, and snacks. However, the company began courting the wider grocery market as well. Toward this end, the company developed a range of canned and fresh products.

In 1994, Palmer and Harvey launched a new service delivering chilled and frozen foods to complement its offerings. This launch was quickly followed with the acquisition of another major wholesaler, McLane UK Ltd., which focused especially on the grocery market. McLane also operated a delivered wholesale business from its Rushden, Northhamptonshire, site. Delivered wholesale, as opposed to cash-and-carry store operations, now became Palmer and Harvey's own primary business.

NEW SYMBOL IN 1996

Palmer and Harvey expanded its frozen foods and grocery lines again in 1995, acquiring the two wholesale operations of the Safeway supermarket chain that year. This deal gave the company control over the 10-depot Snowking Frozen Foods business, as well as 13 Mojo Cash & Carry stores. The company sold off the Mojo depots during the year, consolidating its operations into its own wholesale grocery business.

In 1996, the company plugged a gap in its operations, when it struck a deal with Winerite, a distributor of wines and other alcoholic beverages. The deal added 650 alcohol lines to the group's offering, targeted especially at the convenience store sector. This retail market had been growing strongly, in part because of the development of a number of large-scale chains.

The growth of the larger chains, however, opened new opportunities for wholesalers to consolidate their relationship with the large number of independent retailers. For this, Palmer and Harvey began developing its own operations, developing turnkey store formats and product lines. In this way, retailers could sign on

with Palmer and Harvey, which then supplied nearly everything the retailer required, from store signs to flooring, lighting, and store fittings. Palmer and Harvey's first symbol (or package) became its Supershop format. In 1996, the company added a second symbol, called Your Store.

These efforts helped stimulate Palmer and Harvey's sales growth through the decade, as the company's revenues topped £2 billion, and then reached £2.3 billion by 1999. During this period, the company launched a £15 million expansion of the Coventry site, which grew to 190,000 square feet. The company also began investing in its information technology infrastructure, dedicating a special budget of £10 million.

ADDING MACE IN 1999

The company also celebrated a major expansion of its Supershop symbol in 1998, when the 24,000-member National Federation of Retail Newsagents chose that symbol as its main retailing partner. By the end of that year, the company had signed up nearly 200 Supershop members. At the same time, the Your Shop symbol had expanded to 128 shops.

Palmer and Harvey also completed several new acquisitions. The largest and most significant of these was the purchase of the Mace business for the England and Wales markets from Booker Wholesale Foods, completed in 1999. The Mace brand was one of the oldest and most well-known convenience store brands in the United Kingdom, with branches in Scotland, Northern Ireland, and the Republic of Ireland as well. As part of the Booker purchase, the company also acquired the Select & Save name. The retailers in this chain rebelled, however, against the change in ownership, leading the company to sell the brand that year. The company also bought the Winerite business that year.

These acquisitions were followed the next year by the purchase of YP Electronics Ltd., a major U.K. developer and supplier of IT services and systems to the retail sector. In this way, Palmer and Harvey were able to offer electronic point-of-sale services and related support services to its growing customer base. Also in 2000, Palmer and Harvey bought KP Van Sales, formerly part of United Business. The company converted that van fleet to providing quick delivery of chips and other snacks. This service later became known as P&H Snacksdirect.

MANAGEMENT BUYOUT IN 2002

Palmer and Harvey rounded out 2001 with the purchase of a 200,000-square-foot depot in Scotland. At the same time, the group beefed up its operations in the south of England, acquiring a warehouse facility in Crawley. The company had also been taking steps to shore up the aging Mace brand, which had gone through a series of ownership changes before arriving at Booker Wholesale Foods. As a result, the Mace chain had received little in the way of investment.

Under Palmer and Harvey, the chain began preparing a relaunch of its signage. The company also introduced a new format, Mace Express, signing its first customers in 2002. Mace Express targeted smaller retailers, including small grocers, post offices, and especially service station forecourts. The new format became a strong success for the company, with more than 200 stores signed by 2005. In that year, also, Palmer and Harvey acquired the rights to the Mace brand in Scotland, giving it full control of the brand in Great Britain.

Palmer and Harvey's own ownership structure changed during that decade. In 2002, Chairman Chris Adams led a new management buyout (MBO) of the company, backed by 1,100 of its employees and managers. The total purchase price of the MBO topped £160 million. By then, Palmer and Harvey's revenues had grown to £3.4 billion, making it the third-largest privately held company in the United Kingdom.

Despite its size, Palmer and Harvey remained saddled by its low margins, which dipped to just 0.6 percent, compared to around 1 percent for the delivered wholesale market as a whole. In order to shore up its profits, the company brought in a new chief executive officer, Chris Etherington, in 2007.

SURVIVING THE CRISIS

Etherington then instituted a review of the company's operations. Among the changes implemented by the company was an exit from alcohol distribution, with the sale of Winerite in 2008. The company also targeted expansion in the fresh and chilled foods categories, which had become the main drivers of the retail convenience sector. Palmer and Harvey also completed a new management buyout led by Etherington, which now valued the company at £298 million. The MBO followed on the acquisition of WH & HM Young, based in Leeds, boosting the group's total revenues past £4 billion.

Palmer and Harvey soon felt the effects of the growing economic crisis, which struck the United Kingdom particularly hard at the end of the decade. Through 2009, more and more of the group's customers, including the First Quench, Wine Cellars, and Borders UK chains, as well as a growing number of

independent retailers, had been forced out of business. The company also lost a number of important contracts, including those for WH Smith and Somerfield, as well as the One Stop chain. By March 2010, Palmer and Harvey was forced to cut 85 jobs, and implement a pay freeze for its remaining employees.

Palmer and Harvey nevertheless maintained its commitment to its remaining customers. In December 2009, for example, the company rolled out a new transactional Web site, providing its customers with 24-hour ordering capabilities. The company also extended its successful Snacksdirect van service to the confectionery market, unveiling Sweetsdirect that year. As the United Kingdom's wholesale leader, and the country's third-largest privately held company, Palmer and Harvey remained a major force behind the country's retail industry.

M. L. Cohen

PRINCIPAL SUBSIDIARIES

P&H Snacksdirect; YP Electronics; BB Printing.

PRINCIPAL DIVISIONS

CTN Retailers; Convenience Store Retailers; Forecourt Retailers.

PRINCIPAL OPERATING UNITS

Mace; Mace Express; Your Store; Supershop.

PRINCIPAL COMPETITORS

Booker Plc; Bestway Plc; Costco Wholesale Inc.; Makro Plc; Brakes Foodservice Solutions Plc; 3663 First for Foodservice Plc.

FURTHER READING

Hegarty, Ronan, "P&H Overhauls Pricing to Enable Comparisons," *Grocer*, April 25, 2009, p. 12.

"Is P&H Up for Sale, 'Possible' MBO May Flush Out Bidders," *Grocer*, February 2, 2008.

"Mace Makes Its Debut," *Grocer*, March 29, 2008, p. 60.

"P&H Closes Down Its Winerite Depot," *Grocer*, August 30, 2008, p. 9.

"P&H Launches Long Shelf Life Fresh Range," *Grocer*, July 25, 2009, p. 11.

Phillips, Beth, "Acquisitive P&H Swoops," *Grocer*, August 18, 2007, p. 4.

———, "The Great Rebranding Drive," *Grocer*, May 16, 2009, p. 42.

———, "One Stop Deal as P&H Boosts Chilled Ranges," *Grocer*, May 3, 2008, p. 11.

———, "P&H Loses One Stop but the Gains Make Up for It," *Grocer*, September 5, 2009, p. 12.

———, "P&H Takes a Fresh Approach," *Grocer*, January 26, 2008, p. 36.

———, "P&H to Give Mace Its Second Relaunch in Two-Year Period," *Grocer*, March 21, 2009, p. 11.

Plug Power Inc.

—■—

968 Albany-Shaker Road
Latham, New York 12110
U.S.A.
Telephone: (518) 782-7700
Fax: (518) 782-9060
Web site: http://www.plugpower.com

Public Company
Incorporated: 1997 as Plug Power LLC
Employees: 208
Sales: $17.9 million (2008)
Stock Exchanges: NASDAQ
Ticker Symbol: PLUG
NAICS: 335999 All Other Miscellaneous Electrical
   Equipment and Component Manufacturing

■ ■ ■

Plug Power Inc. is a NASDAQ-listed company based in Latham, New York, that develops and manufactures proton exchange membrane (PEM) fuel cells. The company focuses on a pair of commercial product lines. The GenDrive systems are an alternative to traditional lead-acid batteries used by electric lift trucks. Not only do the power systems last longer than batteries, they require less time to refuel than recharging a battery. Plug Power's other product, and its original line, the GenSys system is an off-grid, power generating system aimed at the residential home market that also provides heat to customers.

Compared to traditional internal combustion engine-powered generators, the GenSys fuel cell requires less maintenance, costs less in fuel, creates fewer emissions, and has a longer life. Adoption has been hampered by the high cost of the unit, but the price has been steadily falling. Hence, GenSys remains at the heart of Plug Power's future potential. In addition to its corporate headquarters, the Latham operation includes a 50,000-square-foot manufacturing facility as well as a research laboratory. Other branch offices providing research, engineering, sales, and customer support are found in Sidney, Ohio, and Apeldoom, Netherlands. The company also has offices in Gallatin, Tennessee, and Richmond, British Columbia.

BEGINNINGS AS JOINT VENTURE: 1997

Plug Power was formed in June 1997 as a joint venture between Latham-based Mechanical Technology Inc. (MTI) and Detroit-based Edison Development Corporation, a subsidiary of DTE Energy, to pursue clean fuel-cell technology. The principle behind fuel cells was hardly new. In 1802 Sir Humphry Davy discovered that water decomposed through electrolysis could be reunited with hydrogen and oxygen atoms to produce electricity and water. A seemingly simple concept, fuel-cell technology proved difficult to harness. It was not until the 1950s that viable fuel cells began to take shape. In the 1960s the technology turned the corner when NASA chose fuel cells over nuclear power to provide electricity and drinking water for the Gemini and Apollo spacecrafts.

In essence, fuel cells are like a continuous fuel battery, converting the chemical energy of a fuel directly into electricity without the need for generators or turbines. As long as the cells are supplied with fuel and air they generate a steady stream of electricity. Like batteries, they can also be "stacked" to create more powerful units. Continuous energy fuel cells are not, however, to be confused with automobile fuel cells, which must be able to start and stop generating power instantaneously without emitting excess heat.

MTI was one of the companies that pursued the development of automobile fuel cells. Founded in 1961 by a pair of engineers, MTI had been reliant on defense contracts, but with the end of the Cold War the company struggled to make the transition, leading to significant losses as it searched for new commercial pursuits. A group of investors led by the firm of First Albany acquired MTI and looked to take advantage of the company's research and development efforts that had been hampered by a lack of funding. The company's initial fuel cell work for automobiles was funded by the Ford Motor Company. A key MTI advance in fuel-cell technology was its method to make a proton exchange membrane with a small amount of platinum, one of the most expensive materials used in the cells. Moreover, MTI developed a method to manufacture fuel cells using stainless steel plates rather than machined graphite, which required a time-consuming process. As a result, MTI was able to find a much larger company, Edison Development Corp., as a joint venture partner, leading to the creation of Plug Power.

Plug Power's initial goal was to develop and manufacture fuel cells to generate electricity for home use. The company was soon able to attract public funding. Later in 1997 it received a $15 million grant from the U.S. Department of Energy to bring its prototype fuel cell into mass production, using natural gas as a fuel source to convert into hydrogen. The first product was expected to generate 7,000 watts of power,

more than the energy demands of a 2,000-square-foot home. Another $25 million in federal and state government grants soon followed.

DEMONSTRATION HOME OPENS: 1998

To demonstrate the potential of the product, Plug Power in June 1998 outfitted a model home with a prototype hydrogen fuel cell system. Late in 1998 Plug Power demonstrated methanol-fueled and gas-fueled residential systems. Plug Power's potential attracted commercial attention as well. GE Power Systems bought a 12 percent interest worth $37.5 million. Moreover, in February 1999 Plug Power formed a joint venture with GE On-Site power called GE Fuel Cell Systems, LLC, to market, sell, install, and service Plug Power fuel cells. Southern California Gas Co., a Los Angeles-based natural gas utility, was also interested in the technology and acquired a stake in Plug Power for $7.5 million.

Plug Power was now ready to begin fuel cell production, and in June 1999 broke ground on a state-of-the-art 51,000-square-foot manufacturing plant in Latham, which would be completed in February of the following year. To fund further growth, Plug Power went public, completing an initial offering of stock in November 1999, netting $93 million. Plug Power used $15 million of its cash in February 2000 to acquire a Dutch company, Gastec, which was a leading developer of fuel process technology. A month later Plug Power used $1.5 million in cash and 7,000 shares of stock to acquire a 28 percent stake in Advanced Energy Systems, Inc., a maker of power electronic inverters for fuel cell systems. Also in March 2000 Plug Power agreed to a joint development project with GE MicroGen and Joh. Vaillant Gmbh to develop a fuel cell system that took advantage of the heat it produced to also power a furnace and hot water heater.

CEO RESIGNS: 2000

Plug Power hoped to bring its first product, about the size of a refrigerator, to market in 2001 and within two years have different sizes to offer to different market segments. The company's prospects appeared bright and investors bid up the price of Plug Power's stock from its initial $15 a share to $79 a share by early 2000. The stock eventually peaked at $150. Investors soon grew concerned, however, when General Electric, which was to put its logo on the fuel cells, rejected Plug Power's prototypes because they failed to meet its specifications. Not only did Plug Power postpone the release date of its initial product to 2002, it reported higher than expected losses. In August 2000 the company's president and

KEY DATES

1997: Plug Power is formed as a joint venture.
1999: Company goes public.
2001: First product is delivered.
2007: Canadian forklift companies are acquired.
2008: Andy Marsh is named chief executive officer.

chief executive officer, Gary Mittleman, abruptly resigned after three years in charge. He maintained that his strengths of launching new ventures was not suited to the manufacturing and marketing stage that Plug Power was now entering. Taking his place on an interim basis was COO Greg Silvestri, who had been recruited by Mittleman a year earlier.

At the end of 2000, following a four-month search, Plug Power hired a new chief executive, 57-year-old Roger B. Saillant, a man with a background in chemistry who was also well familiar with manufacturing. He was an executive at auto parts maker Visteon Corp., a Ford Motor Company spin-off, serving as vice president and general manager of the Energy Transformation Systems department. By the time he took the helm at Plug Power, the price of the company's stock had fallen below $11. He would also have to contend with some disgruntled investors who filed lawsuits charging that the company had not been forthcoming about its problems as a way to maintain the price of its stock.

SALE OF FIRST SYSTEMS: 2001

Early on, Plug Power had established the lofty goal of becoming the first company to sell one million fuel cell systems. To become competitive with traditional power suppliers, however, the company would have to drop its price significantly, but until sales volumes grew to high enough levels it would be difficult to achieve that goal. In the summer of 2001 Plug Power sold its first 75 fuel cell systems for $7 million to the Long Island Power Authority, but the price per kilowatt was about $12,000. Before fuel cells attracted a mass market that amount would have to fall to the $500 range. Nevertheless, the company's prospects remained promising enough that it was able to raise $54 million in 2001 through a secondary stock sale, including $10 million from two of its largest investors, GE and DTE.

To conserve its cash and weather difficult economic conditions, Plug Power implemented cost-cutting measures in 2001, including a 20 percent reduction in

staff. It was a slow climb to build the business as the company's engineers reduced the number of parts to cut expenses while at the same time improving reliability. Although revenues doubled to $11.8 million in 2002, the company still lost $47.2 million for the year.

Plug Power also diversified its business to improve its chances. It worked with Honda to develop a home hydrogen refueling system to generate hydrogen from natural gas for use in a fuel cell vehicle while also providing power and heat to a house. In 2005 Plug Power received funding from the U.S. Defense Department, a longtime backer, to begin field testing of its next-generation continuous-run fuel cell systems. Providing a foundation for the new design would be the 425 systems the company had installed since 2001 around the world. A year later Plug Power and a partner, Ballard Power Systems, received a $2 million grant from the military to develop a PEM fuel cell for backup power applications. On the commercial side, Plug Power began testing a backup power system for cellular phone towers.

MOVE INTO FORKLIFT BUSINESS: 2007

Further changes took place in 2007. Not only did Plug Power reorganize its structure, it completed a pair of acquisitions to gain entry to a new market for fuel cells, power forklift trucks. Because of their use indoors, forklifts had to rely on exhaust-free batteries. Because fuel cells did not emit any pollutants, they were a natural substitute for acid-lead batteries and held a number of advantages, including usage time and costs. In April 2007 Plug Power acquired a Canadian company that specialized in forklifts using fuel cells, Cellex Power Products Inc., for $45 million. A month later Plug Power paid another $10 million to acquire General Hydrogen Corporation, located a short distance away from Cellex in Richmond, British Columbia. While Cellex produced smaller forklifts that operated in warehouse and distribution centers, General Hydrogen focused on larger, industrial lift trucks. Together they participated in a market worth $1.5 billion each year.

In October 2007 Saillant announced that he planned to retire in April 2008 when he turned 65. Replacing him as president and CEO at that time was Andy Marsh, the former CEO of Valere Power, which sold direct-current power products to the telecommunications sector. Upon taking the reins at Plug Power, he moved quickly to cut costs further, immediately trimming headcount by 80, followed by the elimination of another 90 jobs by the end of 2009. Plug Power had never recorded a profitable year, but with its new forklift business it was moving ever closer to realizing that achievement. He also cut research and development expenditures, electing instead to focus on marketing the company's existing products.

The telecommunications business continued to offer promise. Plug Power sold 200 of its GenSys prime power systems to the tower unit of India's Tata Teleservices. India, with its vast rural areas lacking reliable grid power, offered a great deal of potential sales. By 2012 Plug Power hoped to be selling 5,000 systems each year in India. The home power system market, too, offered a great deal promise for Plug Power, particularly as the cost of production fell.

Ed Dinger

PRINCIPAL SUBSIDIARIES

Plug Power Energy India Pvt. Ltd.

PRINCIPAL COMPETITORS

Arotech Corporation; Avista Corporation; FuelCell Energy, Inc.

FURTHER READING

Aaron, Kenneth, "Building Plug Power," *Albany (NY) Times Union*, February 3, 2002, p. E1.

———, "Plug's CEO Resigns," *Albany (NY) Times Union*, August 24, 2000, p. E1.

Anderson, Eric, "Plug Power Expands Reach," *Albany (NY) Times Union*, May 8, 2007, p. E2.

———, "Plug Power Names New Chief," *Albany (NY) Times Union*, April 8, 2008, p. C1.

Denn, James, "Plug Power's $8M Contract to Produce 15 Jobs," *Albany (NY) Times Union*, October 23, 1997, p. E1.

Hughes, Claire, "Plug Power Fuels Interest," *Albany (NY) Times Union*, January 16, 2000, p. C1.

Johnston, Jo-Ann, "Latham Firm Adds Fire to Fuel Cell," *Albany (NY) Times Union*, June 18, 1998, p. A1.

Kane, Tim, "Latham Firm Developing Home Fuel Cell," *Schenectady (NY) Daily Gazette*, October 22, 1997, p. A1.

"Plugging Away at Profitability," *Albany (NY) Times Union*, April 29, 2009, p. D1.

Smyth, Julie Carr, "MTI Plans Deal to Develop Fuel Cells for Home Use," *Albany (NY) Times Union*, May 30, 1997, p. E4.

Premium Brands Holdings Corporation

———————■———————

7720 Alderbridge Way
Richmond, British Columbia V6X 2A2
Canada
Telephone: (604) 656-3100
Fax: (604) 656-3170
Web site: http://www.premiumbrandsholdings.com

Public Company
Incorporated: 1984 as Fletcher's Fine Foods Ltd.
Employees: 1,667
Sales: CAD 449.36 million (2008)
Stock Exchanges: Toronto
Ticker Symbol: PBH-T
NAICS: 424470 Meat and Meat Product Merchant
   Wholesalers; 424420 Packaged Frozen Food
   Merchant Wholesalers; 424490 Other Grocery and
   Related Products Merchant Wholesalers; 311812
   Commercial Bakeries; 311612 Meat Processed from
   Carcasses

■ ■ ■

Premium Brands Holdings Corporation owns a broad
range of branded specialty food businesses that
distribute food to foodservice, retail, and concessionary
customers. Premium Brands distributes sandwiches,
meat snacks, deli products, pastries, muffins, hamburgers, and related items under a variety of brand names,
including Creekside, Bread Garden, Gloria's, Hempler's,
Hygaard, McSweeney's, Grimm's, and Quality Fast
Foods. The company serves approximately 25,000
customers, utilizing manufacturing and distribution

facilities in British Columbia, Alberta, Saskatchewan,
Manitoba, and Washington State.

FOUNDED UNDER THE FLETCHER'S NAME

Throughout much of the 20th century, Premium Brands
operated under a different name and led a quiet
existence. A new century brought sweeping changes,
witnessing the Premium Brands corporate banner unfurl
for the first time. More profound were the reorganization efforts undertaken during the first decade of the
21st century, as Premium Brands altered its business
model, seeking to find the ideal corporate strategy to
pursue.

The company began as Fletcher's Limited in 1917,
a Vancouver, British Columbia-based concern involved
in processing meat, primarily pork. In 1984 the
company changed its name to Fletcher's Fine Foods
Ltd., but it continued to pursue its original business,
operating as a processor and distributor of commodity
meat products, mainly pork. In 1996 the company
began to display greater ambition, converting to public
ownership by completing an initial public offering
(IPO) of stock on the Toronto Stock Exchange.

EMPHASIS ON PORK PRODUCTION

An ambitious objective was revealed to the public at the
end of the decade. Fletcher's Fine Foods ranked as a
leading processor of fresh and prepared pork products in
Canada, but it desired a greater stature. The company

wanted to become, as the November 22, 1999 issue of *Feedstuffs* noted, "the leading manufacturer and marketer of branded, processed, and value-added pork products in Canada and the western United States." Possessing meat-processing operations in Alberta, British Columbia, Saskatchewan, and south of the border in Washington and Oregon, the CAD 255 million company wanted to become much more powerful, but to do so it needed to promote the growth of its industry. Fletcher's Fine Foods began building a western Canada pork production system.

Fletcher's Fine Foods resolved to invest in hog farming and pork production operations to ensure it had the supplies and market stability necessary to reach its objectives. A series of partnerships, joint ventures, and investments within the industry followed Fletcher's Fine Foods' announcement that it sought to be the industry leader. In late 1999 the company reached an agreement to take a 40 percent stake in Peace Pork, Inc., an entity that produced approximately 110,000 hogs per year. With Fletcher's Fine Foods' investment, Peace Pork estimated it would be able to double its annual production total, an output to which Fletcher Fine Foods was guaranteed access.

Additional alliances within the industry followed the agreement with Peace Pork. In early 2000 the company brokered an arrangement with Quadra Group, a hog production system based in Outlook, Saskatchewan. One month later Fletcher's Fine Foods announced a partnership with Rocky Mountain Pork, a Red Deer, Alberta-based company that provided management and financing services to pork producers.

FLETCHER'S BECOMES PREMIUM BRANDS: 2000

As Fletcher's Fine Foods set out bolstering pork production in its marketing territory, it recast its identity. In mid-2000 the company changed its name to Premium Brands, Inc., a new corporate title meant to reflect its evolution from a single-brand pork processor to a food processor marketing its products under several brand names.

The implementation of the company's new strategy continued after the name change. In August 2000 the company sold its Stone Mill salad business to Reser's Fine Foods Inc., deeming the asset too outside the scope of its core business. At the end of 2000, another investment was made in western Canada's pork production system. Premium Brands acquired a 33 percent stake in Community Pork Ventures Inc., a holding company created to acquire hog production operations in Saskatchewan. The investment was expected to enable hog operations to double their production within two years and it gave Premium Brands full rights to the production.

Just as Premium Brands' efforts to strengthen its pork production system were reaching full steam, the campaign shuddered to a stop. A transforming event caused the company to change its strategic course, and disentangle itself from the alliances, partnerships, and joint ventures it had formed during the previous two years. As a result, Premium Brands shelved its commodities-based business and turned into a branded specialty food and distribution company, beginning the new century with a new business model.

MAJOR CHANGE IN STRATEGY: 2001

The event that triggered the wholesale change occurred in May 2001. Saskatchewan Wheat Pool, a publicly traded agricultural cooperative, decided to focus on its core business of grain handling and marketing agricultural products. The decision led the company to divest its non-core assets, which included a 41 percent controlling stake in Premium Brands. Premium Brands acquired Saskatchewan Wheat Pool's stake for CAD 46.3 million and used the event to reassess its future.

Premium Brands' management, led by President George Paleologou, perceived Saskatchewan Wheat Pool's departure as an opportunity to pursue a new strategic mission. Compared to commodity foods, branded specialty foods delivered more stable and higher profit margins, convincing Paleologou and his management team to build a new business platform and divest assets they considered to be non-core businesses.

Assets were steadily shed in the wake of Saskatchewan Wheat Pool's decision, notably Premium Brands' equity stake in Peace Pork Inc. in March 2002. "We are continuing to focus on the reallocation of capital from commodity to specialty niche food businesses," Paleologou commented in the March 21, 2002 issue of *Canadian Corporate News*. "Over the next 12 to 24 months we expect to raise an additional CAD 22 million in proceeds from the sale of assets and investments

KEY DATES

1917: Premium Brands is founded as Fletcher's Limited.

1984: Fletcher's Limited changes its name to Fletcher's Fine Foods Ltd.

1996: Fletcher's Fine Foods converts to public ownership.

2000: Fletcher's Fine Foods changes its name to Premium Brands, Inc.

2001: Premium Brands begins transformation into a specialty food and distribution company.

2009: After operating as an income trust for the previous four years, Premium Brands converts to a corporation.

that are not contributing to the company's cash flow and CAD 5 million from non-core businesses."

Less than a year later, Premium Brands made another sizable divestiture. In May 2003 the company announced the sale of its label printing businesses, Adam's Label & Tag Ltd. and Apex Label & Systems Inc. Premium Brands sold the companies to Tapp Technologies Inc., stripping itself of nearly CAD 6 million in annual sales. In October 2004 the company sold its processed meats operation in Vancouver and Algona, Washington, to Quality Meat Group Ltd., gaining CAD 25 million from the sale. "The sale of these operations is consistent with our strategic focus on selling our commodity based assets and investing in specialty food businesses," Paleologou said in the October 18, 2004 issue of *Canadian Corporate News*.

NEW CORPORATE STRUCTURE: 2005

After shedding approximately CAD 170 million of non-core assets, Premium Brands announced it was at the end of its three-year restructuring plan in 2005. At this point, Paleologou decided to convert the company into an income trust to enable shareholders to realize the full value of the sweeping restructuring efforts undertaken. The conversion was expected to increase the consistency of the dividends paid to the fund's unit holders. The conversion to a publicly traded income trust required a new name, marking the emergence of Premium Brands Income Fund as the company's official corporate title. At the time of the conversion, the company's annual revenues stood at CAD 182 million.

After completing its restructuring efforts, Premium Brands focused on making strategic acquisitions to strengthen its position as a specialty food distributor. In 2005 the company acquired Harlan Fairbanks, western Canada's largest distributor of concessionary products and equipment. Harlan Fairbanks served more than 8,000 customers, including hotels, restaurants, recreation facilities, and carnivals, selling popcorn, nachos, frozen beverage supplies, hot beverage supplies, waffle mixes, and concession equipment. The company generated CAD 24 million in sales in 2004. The year also saw Premium Brands complete the acquisition of Quality Fast Foods, the largest manufacturer of prepackaged sandwiches and hamburgers in western Canada, which complemented the company's purchase of a similar type of company, Hygaard Fine Foods, in 2004.

ACQUISITIONS FUEL GROWTH: 2006–09

Premium Brands' financial stature, diminished by the restructuring efforts that included major divestitures, began to increase as the company added to its portfolio of specialty food businesses. In 2006 the company merged its U.S. meat snack business with Bellingham, Washington-based Hempler Enterprises, Inc., a company founded in 1934 that ranked as one of the Pacific Northwest's leading specialty sausage and premium meat brands. The transaction created Hempler Foods Group LLC, a company 60 percent owned by Premium Brands that moved into a new 28,000-square-foot facility in Ferndale, Washington. Several other acquisitions were completed during the year, including Gloria's Catering, Pop's E-Z Popcorn & Supply, and Creekside Custom Foods. Sales by the end of 2006 reached CAD 216 million.

The acquisition campaign pressed ahead during the last years of the decade. The largest purchase completed during the period occurred in 2007, when Premium Brands acquired Centennial Foodservices for CAD 84.7 million. Centennial ranked as western Canada's largest specialty distributor of protein products to the foodservice industry. In 2008 the company bolstered its infrastructure and increased its roster of branded food businesses. A new 20,000-square-foot meat snack production facility opened in Langley, British Columbia, and a fleet of seven trucks was added through the purchase of Noble House Distributors, which operated in northern Alberta. Mrs. Willman's Baking Limited was acquired for CAD 1.4 million as was B&C Food Distributors Ltd., a CAD 8 million purchase that gave the company a distributor serving customers on Vancouver Island.

By the end of 2008, Premium Brands' revenues had climbed to CAD 449 million, a substantial increase from the CAD 182 million recorded when the company converted to an income trust. In 2009, the company shed its status as an income trust and returned to the designation of a corporation, which prompted a name change from Premium Brands Income Fund to Premium Brands Holdings Corporation. The year also included two acquisitions: S.J. Irvine Fine Foods Ltd. for CAD 2.5 million and Multi-National Foods for CAD 1.6 million. S.J. Irvine processed meat for the foodservice and retail industries, operating out of a 40,000-square-foot facility in Saskatoon, Saskatchewan. Multi-National, based in Calgary, Alberta, functioned as a food brokerage business, generating CAD 9 million in annual sales.

By the end of the decade, Premium Brands was a 93-year-old company, but in many respects it was far younger. Its role as a producer, marketer, and distributor of specialty branded food products was less than a decade old. With Paleologou at the helm, the company continued to march forward on the acquisition front in an effort to strengthen its holdings. In 2010 the company acquired South Seas Meats Ltd., a leading distributor of specialty meats to restaurants, hotels, and specialty butcher shops in the greater Vancouver area. Such additions to the company's profile were expected in the future, as Premium Brands sought to secure its position as the leading distributor of specialty foods in Canada.

Jeffrey L. Covell

PRINCIPAL SUBSIDIARIES

Centennial Foodservice; Direct Plus Food Group; Grimm's; Bread Garden; McSweeneys; Grimm's Fine Foods; Harlan Fairbanks; Hempler Foods Group LLC (60%); Creekside Custom Foods; Quality Fast Foods; Hygaard Fine Foods Ltd.

PRINCIPAL COMPETITORS

George Weston Limited; Kraft Foods Inc.; Sepp's Gourmet Foods Ltd.

FURTHER READING

"Premium Brands Inc. Announces Sale of Non-Core Assets," *Canadian Corporate News*, March 21, 2002.

"Premium Brands Inc. Announces the Sale of Two Mainstream Processed Meat Operations for $25 Million and a New Strategic Alliance with Quality Meat Group," *Canadian Corporate News*, October 18, 2004.

Smith, Rod, "Fletcher's Changes Name to Reflect Brands," *Feedstuffs*, July 10, 2000, p. 19.

———, "Fletcher's Plans to Invest, Expand in Hog Operations," *Feedstuffs*, November 22, 1999, p. 6.

QUALCOMM
Incorporated

5775 Morehouse Drive
San Diego, California 92121-1714
U.S.A.
Telephone: (858) 587-1121
Fax: (858) 658-2100
Web site: http://www.qualcomm.com

Public Company
Incorporated: 1985
Employees: 16,100
Sales: $10.41 billion (2009)
Stock Exchanges: NASDAQ
Ticker Symbol: QCOM
NAICS: 334220 Radio and Television Broadcasting and Wireless Communications Equipment Manufacturing; 533110 Owners and Lessors of Other Non-Financial Assets

∎ ∎ ∎

QUALCOMM Incorporated (Qualcomm) is the largest manufacturer of chips for cellphones in the world. Its patented code division multiple access (CDMA) technology is used throughout the world and has played an integral role in the development of a single international standard for wireless communications. Royalties from the company's CDMA technology account for approximately two-thirds of its annual profit total. Qualcomm maintains administrative, research and development, and marketing offices in the United States, Mexico, India, Taiwan, China, Korea, England, Israel, and Singapore.

BIRTH OF MOBILE COMMUNICATIONS

In 1959, two former engineering classmates at the Massachusetts Institute of Technology (MIT), Irwin Jacobs and Andrew Viterbi, reunited at an academic conference. They resowed the seeds of a friendship that during the 1960s evolved into a consulting business and then, in 1968, into Linkabit, a San Diego-based manufacturer of digital communications equipment. After graduating from MIT in 1959, Jacobs had become a professor of electrical engineering and in 1965 authored *Principles of Communication Engineering*, later described as "the first comprehensive textbook on digital communications." Viterbi had gone into research, helping to design the telemetry equipment of the first successful U.S. satellite, *Explorer I*, and playing a pioneering role in developing the potential of digital transmission technology for the telecommunications systems of space and satellite equipment.

At Linkabit, Jacobs and Viterbi applied their considerable talents to developing satellite communications applications for the television industry and by 1980 had transformed tiny Linkabit into a thriving communications enterprise with more than 1,000 employees and more than $100 million in sales. In August 1980, Linkabit merged with M/A-COM, forming M/A-COM Linkabit, a developer of cable television, data transmission, and other electronics technologies. Although Jacobs had risen to M/A-COM's executive vice presidency by 1983, mobile satellite communications technology had developed to the point where both he and Viterbi saw a golden opportunity to create a new business with the potential to dominate its industry. If

COMPANY PERSPECTIVES

Life. Connected with technology. From the written word, to image and photos, to music, to videos, games, streaming content, and more, Qualcomm is on a never-ending quest to feed the mind. Whether by developing our technologies or partnering with companies who share our vision, we're leading the charge in the digital revolution.

they could work out the as-yet unsolved technical obstacles, Jacobs and Viterbi reasoned that the wireless mobile communications (WMC) market was so young, and so complex, that they could grab an insurmountable three- to five-year head start over any future competition.

REVOLUTIONIZING THE TRUCKING INDUSTRY: 1985–88

In 1985 they left M/A-COM (which was later sold and broken up) to form Qualcomm Inc., a provider of contract research and development services and which *Business Week* later described as a "tiny military house." Their real goal, however, was a full-fledged integrated research-to-manufacturing business, and they began to cast about for an application of digital satellite communications with commercial potential. Military uses were considered first but Jacobs soon decided that the transportation industry offered the best opportunity for building a WMC-based company.

If there was any segment of the U.S. transportation industry that needed the help of wireless, long-distance communications it was the trucking industry. Valuable shipping time was routinely lost as truckers pulled off the road to call into their dispatchers with updates on their location and expected arrival, and dispatchers' inability to precisely monitor and coordinate their fleets' schedules meant many "deadhead" miles as truckers wasted return trips with empty trucks that could have been used to haul more freight. Moreover, shippers themselves often had to act as ersatz dispatchers, continually checking in with trucking companies to see if their shipments would arrive on time. To solve these problems, between 1985 and 1988 Jacobs and Viterbi began developing a wireless, two-way messaging and positioning system that would enable trucking firms to closely track their drivers' progress while enabling drivers and dispatchers to send messages to each other.

Christened OmniTRACS, the system would lease the capability of existing communications satellites to create continent-wide coverage. Qualcomm's proprietary signal processing technology meant that OmniTRACS could operate without interfering with other satellite transmissions, and the position-reporting component would use either the federal government's Global Positioning System (GPS) satellites or a signal generated on a leased satellite using Qualcomm's own automatic satellite position-reporting system. Down on Earth, a keyboard-and-terminal hardware and software package would be located next to the driver in the cab and a huge integrated network management facility in San Diego would route messages between truckers and dispatchers.

By 1988 Qualcomm was ready to unveil OmniTRACS to the public. Jacobs invited 300 trucking industry leaders to San Diego for a demonstration of the 30-pound device. It worked, and within months Qualcomm had signed up its first customer, Schneider National Inc. of Wisconsin, one of the largest long-haul truckers in the country. The Schneider contract alone was worth $20 million and involved 5,000 trucks, and by the end of 1989 Qualcomm's revenues had soared to $32 million. Qualcomm established OmniTRACS systems for Canada and Europe, and in August 1991 OmniTRACS enjoyed its first profitable month. On the eve of Qualcomm's initial public stock offering (IPO) as a public corporation in the fall of 1991, it landed a deal to launch OmniTRACS for Brazil's and Japan's trucking industries, and by early 1992 more than 23,000 OmniTRACS terminals had been installed worldwide by some 150 transportation companies and 50,000 trucks and their dispatchers were generating 400,000 messages and position reports each day. By 1993 Jacobs was being anointed by *Fleet Owner* magazine as "The Man Who Changed Trucking."

REVOLUTIONIZING THE CELLPHONE INDUSTRY: 1989–91

In the late 1940s, AT&T's Bell Laboratories conducted the first test to determine the commercial feasibility of cellular communications technology. In 1970 the Federal Communications Commission (FCC) set aside radio frequencies for land mobile communications and by 1977 had announced the construction of two cellular development systems in Baltimore/Washington and Chicago. A U.S. cellular phone industry began to emerge in the 1980s, and by 1985 some 300,000 Americans were making cellphone calls from their car phones. It was clear to Jacobs and Viterbi that the analog transmission technology with which the cellular industry had started would eventually be replaced by

KEY DATES

1968: Irwin Jacobs and Andrew Viterbi found Linkabit.
1980: Linkabit merges with M/A-COM to form M/A-COM Linkabit.
1985: Qualcomm Inc. is formed.
1993: U.S. Telecommunications Industry Association adopts Qualcomm's CDMA technology as a cellular standard.
2002: China Unicom agrees to implement Qualcomm's CDMA technology.
2005: Irwin Jacobs's son, Paul Jacobs, is named CEO.
2009: Revenues eclipse $10 billion for the first time.

digital signals (which transformed the electrical signals of the traditional phone into the zeros and ones of computer technology), and they began to develop a new standard that they hoped would become the sole medium by which all cellphone calls would eventually be made.

In 1989, however, the Cellular Telecommunications Industries Association adopted a cellphone standard developed by Sweden's Ericsson called time division multiple access (TDMA), which divided phone conversations into blocks of digital data that were streamed one after the other over specific radio frequencies, allowing cellphone channels to carry three to six times as many callers as traditional analog systems.

Jacobs and Viterbi's own standard, called code division multiple access (CDMA), took a different approach. Instead of assigning an entire frequency channel to each cellphone call, CDMA tagged each conversation with a code that could be identified and retrieved only by the phone of the intended recipient. Once coded, the call was divided into 10 different digital pieces that were then transmitted across all available cellphone channels. By thus using the cellular frequencies more efficiently, voice quality could be sustained over greater distances, reducing the number of antennas needed to cover a given territory and cramming twice as many conversations onto the airwaves as TDMA phones, and 10 times as many as analog phones.

CDMA TRUMPS TDMA

The catch was twofold: The cellphone industry had already adopted TDMA, and Qualcomm's CDMA was untested and, as far as the industry was concerned, thus only a theory. In 1989 Jacobs nevertheless pitched CDMA's advantages before the Cellular Telecommunications Industries Association. He was given a cool reception but resolved to rally the financial support of key industry firms to conduct a series of tests that would conclusively establish the superiority of CDMA over TDMA. The wireless division of Pacific Telesis agreed to commit $2 million toward a CDMA trial, and throughout 1989 Qualcomm lined up some $30 million to construct limited CDMA test networks in San Diego and New York City. While Qualcomm closed licensing or development agreements with such companies as Nokia, Motorola, Northern Telecom, and Sony; established international CDMA partnerships in Europe, Japan, and Canada; and convinced AT&T and Nynex to adopt the CDMA standard for their cellular service, it continued to test CDMA's call quality, coverage area, and call capacity.

In November 1991, 14 international and domestic cellular carriers and manufacturers conducted a large-scale field validation test of Qualcomm's CDMA technology. The tests were conclusive enough to persuade the Cellular Telecommunications Industries Association to reopen the cellular standard debate. Buoyed by the news that its technology might indeed become the new cellular standard, Qualcomm nevertheless faced a daunting challenge. A national CDMA infrastructure simply did not exist, and to make CDMA cellphones a commercial reality a huge base station and network system had to be created, at Qualcomm's expense. To help raise the funds, Qualcomm went public in December 1991, generating $53 million.

While Jacobs and Viterbi were recasting Qualcomm into a cellular industry giant, they also were pursuing other cutting-edge technologies. In 1991, Qualcomm continued research on high-definition television (HDTV) signal processing components, data link systems, specialized modems, and custom VLSI (very large-scale integrated) circuits, as well as a number of classified communications-related research projects for the U.S. government. It also formed a joint venture with satellite-maker Loral Corporation to develop a network of low Earth orbit satellites called Globalstar that would use CDMA technology to provide, beginning in 1998, mobile communications service to regions of the world that could not be economically served by ground-based cellular systems. It also unveiled Eudora, a cross-platform e-mail software program originally licensed from the University of Illinois that by 1997 claimed some 18 million Internet users.

CDMA APPROACHING CRITICAL MASS: 1992–94

Although 1992 represented the third straight year in which Qualcomm suffered a net loss, its sales continued to climb and its future continued to brighten. It prepared for the rollout of CDMA in 1993 by signing a technology agreement with Nokia and a licensing agreement with Northern Telecom; by promoting CDMA in Korea, Australia, Switzerland, and Germany; and by opening regional offices in Pittsburgh, Dallas, Atlanta, Salt Lake City, and Washington, D.C. It secured a license from the FCC to tailor CDMA technology for the new personal communications service (PCS) niche of the cellular industry and created a PCS corporate group to create applications for this market. By bundling traditional cellular phone service with paging, messaging, fax, and e-mail service all from a single all-purpose "pocket communicator," PCS appeared to have become the future of CDMA and of the cellphone industry as a whole. Sales of OmniTRACS meanwhile leaped 68 percent over 1991 to 36,000 installed units and 200 trucking customers in North America. In 1992, OmniTRACS' first and largest customer, Schneider National Inc., renewed its OmniTRACS contract; Qualcomm added Werner Enterprises, one of the five largest truckload carriers in the United States, to its stable; and Mexico, Japan, and Brazil committed to adopting the OmniTRACS system in 1993.

The tidal shift toward the CDMA cellular standard began to snowball in 1993. The U.S. Telecommunications Industry Association adopted CDMA as a cellular standard; three Bell regional operating companies and Alltel Mobile Communications placed orders with Qualcomm and its partners for CDMA handsets and infrastructure equipment; and major telecommunications firms conducted tests of CDMA service.

Internationally, companies in Korea and the Philippines placed orders with Qualcomm for CDMA systems. Chile, China, India, Malaysia, Pakistan, and Russia signed memoranda edging them closer to the adoption of Qualcomm's CDMA technology for the wireless local loops (WLL). WLL would take the place of traditional copper wire for connecting telephone switching centers to homes in the developing world. OmniTRACS, however, remained, at least for the time being, Qualcomm's money machine, and the company sold 62 percent more units in 1993 than it had the year before. Moreover, 50 new trucking firms adopted the system, including J.B. Hunt, the largest truckload carrier in the United States.

The CDMA rollout anticipated for 1993 was delayed until 1995 while the FCC began auctioning off PCS licenses to potential service providers and Qual-

comm battled off patent suits brought by competitors who claimed it had lifted its CDMA technology from their own research. A growing number of U.S. cellular carriers (including AirTouch, GTE, Sprint, and Ameritech) prepared to deploy or test CDMA-based PCS service in major U.S. markets, and the International Telecommunications Union adopted CDMA as one of four global wireless communications standards.

Moreover, China and Argentina began testing CDMA cellular systems, and Qualcomm opened offices in Beijing, New Delhi, and Buenos Aires. With more and more companies signing onto the CDMA/PCS standard, Qualcomm moved to fill the void of manufacturers offering CDMA/PCS equipment by partnering with Sony Electronics to create Qualcomm Personal Electronics, a joint venture to manufacture and market up to a million PCS cellphones a year.

OmniTRACS, meanwhile, had increased its customer base to 425 and by the end of 1994 was processing 2.5 million trucking messages and position reports every day on 13,000 OmniTRACS units in 25 countries. Qualcomm augmented its OmniTRACS software offerings by acquiring Integrated Transportation Software Inc. in 1994 and continued to integrate the 10,000 customers of Motorola's CoveragePLUS ground-based radio operation that it had acquired in late 1993 into its OmniTRACS network. Qualcomm's long-planned Globalstar satellite communications system also got a welcome boost when Qualcomm signed the largest development contract in its history, valued at $266 million, to develop Globalstar's ground communications equipment and telephones.

QUALCOMM'S "ARRIVAL": 1995–97

For all the billions spent on development, testing, equipment, and marketing, by mid-1995 CDMA still remained, in large part, an unknown quantity. In a feature article on Qualcomm's battle to establish CDMA as the cellular standard, Britain's *Economist* magazine described CDMA as a "clever—but fiendishly complicated and unproven—technology" that was still "a good year away from the market" and one that might never be made to work as well as the thoroughly operational TDMA standard. Moreover, despite 1995 earnings estimated at only about $30 million, Wall Street investors had driven Qualcomm's stock valuation to an atmospheric $2.4 billion. What is more, Qualcomm was entering a telephone equipment market in which it was dwarfed by such giants as AT&T, NEC, and Motorola.

Nevertheless, by July 1995 Qualcomm could claim that 11 of the 14 largest telephone carriers in the United

States had committed to CDMA. In addition, 12 cell-phone suppliers, including Motorola, NEC, Mitsubishi, Matsushita, and Sony, had each paid Qualcomm $1 million for its CDMA technology, and six manufacturers, including AT&T, Northern Telecom, and Motorola, had each surrendered $5 million for the right to make CDMA network equipment. From its CDMA royalty fees and microchip sales alone Qualcomm stood to profit handsomely in the years to come. In August 1995, it raised $500 million in a public stock offering to fund its transformation from a cellular standard licensor to a cellular phone maker.

COMMERCIAL CDMA DEBUTS IN 1995

By partnering with virtually every major telecommunications carrier and manufacturer in as many markets as it could, Qualcomm sought to translate the CDMA PCS market from an idea into a foregone conclusion almost overnight. In late 1995 the first telephone calls on a commercially installed system using CDMA were made by Primeco customers, and Air-Touch announced plans to launch the first commercial CDMA system in Los Angeles.

Qualcomm's equipment joint venture with Sony received an $850 million order for handheld phones in 1996, and by midyear a Qualcomm/Sony truck departed from San Diego for the East Coast with thousands of PCS phones ready for delivery to Primeco customers. When it was discovered that a software bug rendered the phones' menu screens inoperable, however, a Qualcomm team was dispatched to the Primeco warehouse with the software fix. Four days later, the 40,000 handsets had been reprogrammed and over-nighted to Primeco's anxious retail outlets. In March 1997 Qualcomm introduced its newest PCS handset, the Q phone. Motorola sued Qualcomm for stealing the Q phone design from Motorola's own StarTAC phone, but a San Diego court ruled in Qualcomm's favor a month later.

By mid-1997, 57 percent of all digital wireless systems under construction used Qualcomm's CDMA standard, which now boasted some four million users, and Primeco and Sprint had agreed to spend $850 million over the next two years to buy Qualcomm/Sony handsets. Handsets and equipment orders from China, Korea, Russia, and Chile were expected to add another $500 million to Qualcomm's coffers, and Qualcomm made plans for new equipment factories in Asia and Latin America. In June 1997, it opened a Moscow sales office and could claim that it had licensed CDMA to more than 45 leading telecommunications manufacturers worldwide.

Because it was wedded to the CDMA standard, however, Qualcomm's fortunes as a cellular phone maker were threatened by its larger phone-making rivals, who had long offered handsets for every cellular standard. Nevertheless, by the end of its 1997 first quarter, Qualcomm's sales were a full 165 percent greater than a year earlier and, with the penetration of the U.S. wireless communications market expected to increase from 16 percent to 48 percent by 2006, Qualcomm appeared to have plenty of room to grow. Its onetime cash cow, OmniTRACS, had in the meantime grown to encompass 200,000 terminals at 800 transportation companies in 32 countries worldwide. When Qualcomm announced in May 1997 that San Diego's Jack Murphy sports facility had been officially renamed Qualcomm Stadium, Jacobs and Viterbi's dream of building a communications business that could dominate its industry appeared to have been fulfilled beyond anyone's rosiest expectations.

CELLULAR TECHNOLOGY AT THE MILLENNIUM

As the millennium approached, Qualcomm continued to work tirelessly to establish CDMA as the global standard for cellular communications. As the sole producer of CDMA, however, the company encountered a great deal of opposition from the nation's phone industry, which was wary of relying on a single supplier for its cellular technology. Qualcomm responded to this resistance by loosening its licensing restrictions, making CDMA technology available to a range of manufacturers, many of them in Asia. The reasoning was simple: By broadening the production capacity for CDMA, Qualcomm hoped to make prices more competitive, thereby providing the major telecommunications corporations with a wider range of choices. At the same time, Qualcomm saw this strategy as a means of establishing a more powerful presence for CDMA technology in the global marketplace.

In the late 1990s the company undertook a series of initiatives designed to expand its reach into emerging cellphone markets in Asia. The biggest prize was China, where the number of cellphone users was projected to exceed 70 million by the year 2000. Despite a number of promising tests of CDMA technology in the Chinese marketplace, however, China continued to favor GSM, which was still the industry standard in Europe. After failing in its initial bid to forge a strategic alliance with China Unicom, one of the country's largest cellphone companies, Qualcomm signed research-and-development deals with seven Chinese cellphone manufacturers in June 2000, in the hope that the increased presence of CDMA on the production level might stir up greater interest among the larger Chinese telecom companies.

The competitive advantage held by GSM technology in the late 1990s, however, still posed a serious threat to the future of CDMA. Companies such as Ericsson, reluctant to give Qualcomm the opportunity to promote CDMA as an alternative to GSM in Europe, successfully lobbied regulators to maintain a single European standard, effectively closing the door on foreign competition. The conflict came to a head in 1998, when Ericsson introduced a new technology that was based on CDMA, but not compatible with it. A patent infringement lawsuit ensued, with the two companies reaching a settlement in March 1999. The agreement created a new standard in Europe, that would allow for compatibility among the various competing technologies.

The agreement with Ericsson turned out to be a watershed moment for Qualcomm. No longer distracted by concerns of being shut out of international cellphone markets, the company was able to devote more attention to the development of its third-generation, or 3G, wireless technologies. The company had set the stage for the creation of its 3G products in November 1998, when it joined with Microsoft to create Wireless Knowledge, a joint venture dedicated to the integration of data transfer capability with mobile communications. The new technology, known as high data rate (HDR), would allow subscribers to access the Internet and e-mail accounts from their cellphones. In April 2000 Qualcomm purchased a 10 percent share of Net Zero, with the intention of making the Internet provider the first to use HDR in the United States.

3G TECHNOLOGY DEBUTS IN 2002

The company achieved another breakthrough in January 2002, when Verizon Wireless launched the nation's first 3G mobile phone service, called Express Network, using Qualcomm's patented CDMA2000 technology. That same month Qualcomm finally reached an agreement with China Unicom to implement CDMA as the Chinese telecom's standard. Having established a foothold in China, Qualcomm then turned its attention to other emerging markets. It invested $200 million in the Indian company Reliance Communications Ltd., with the aim of laying the foundation for the introduction of CDMA to the subcontinent. The long-awaited acceptance of CDMA on the international stage, combined with the meteoric development of 3G technology in the United States, put Qualcomm on firm ground heading into the new century.

Qualcomm's near-monopoly on the CDMA market did not mean the company was free from worry, however. Rivals and customers, tired of paying royalties

for Qualcomm's technology, were intent on making their own CDMA chips. In 2003 Samsung, one of Qualcomm's largest customers, announced it would begin making its own CDMA chips. Nokia, the world's largest manufacturer of cellphones, formed a partnership with chipmakers Texas Instruments and ST-Microelectronics to produce CDMA chips for its handsets.

FROM FATHER TO SON: 2005

The incursion of competitors and making the next evolutionary step in technology became the challenges inherited by Jacobs's successor, the first transfer of power in Qualcomm's history. Jacobs relinquished his duties as CEO in 2005 during Qualcomm's 20th anniversary, ending his two-decade campaign to usher wireless voice service into the mainstream. He passed the reins of command to his son, 42-year-old Paul Jacobs, who earned a doctorate degree in robotics from the University of California at Berkeley. Before being named CEO, the younger Jacobs spent the previous four years as president of the Qualcomm Wireless & Internet Group, spearheading projects that utilized the array of data services that could be delivered on 3G networks. The training was pertinent to his new role as CEO: His father had devoted his career to bringing wireless voice into the mainstream, and his challenge would be bringing wireless data into the mainstream.

Jacobs, like his father, preached the wonders Qualcomm's technology could deliver. Mobile e-mail, Web surfing, gaming, television, and a host of other sophisticated services became available to cellphone subscribers during the first years of Jacob's leadership tenure. He tirelessly promoted the adoption of data services and foresaw the use of Qualcomm's thumbnail-size microprocessing units in a range of other devices, such as thermostats that regulated energy use and in medical devices. As the use of data services increased, developing into a $33 billion business by 2008 (a 46 percent increase from the previous year), Qualcomm's financial stature grew substantially. Revenues nearly doubled during Jacob's first five years in charge, jumping from $5.6 billion in 2005 to $10.4 billion in 2009. Industry observers praised Jacobs's efforts, perceiving the Qualcomm scion as a leader well equipped to seize the opportunities that lay ahead. "Jacobs has far greater ambitions for Qualcomm than simply to sell chips and collect royalties on his dad's pioneering patents," the July 6, 2009 issue of *Fortune* observed. "He seems to be seeking to build a wireless technology company, churning out new products and platforms capable of generating billions of dollars in revenue for Qualcomm."

Paul S. Bodine
Updated, Steve Meyer; Jeffrey L. Covell

PRINCIPAL SUBSIDIARIES

FLO TV Incorporated; QUALCOMM Global Trading, Inc. (British Virgin Islands); QUALCOMM CDMA Technologies Asia-Pacific Pte. Ltd. (Singapore); QUALCOMM GT Holdings, Inc. (British Virgin Islands); QUALCOMM Mauritius Holdings Limited; QUALCOMM CDMA Technologies Malaysia SDN.BHD; QUALCOMM Canada Inc.; QUALCOMM (UK) Limited; Spike Technologies LLC; QUALCOMM India Private Limited; QUALCOMM Communication Technologies Ltd. (Taiwan); QUALCOMM CDMA Technologies GmbH (Germany); QUALCOMM Finland Oy; QUALCOMM CDMA Technologies, T.Y.K. (Japan); QUALCOMM CDMA (Korea) Y.H. (South Korea); QUALCOMM Wireless Semi Conductor Technologies Limited (China); QUALCOMM Netherlands B.V.; QUALCOMM Italia S.r.l. (Italy).

PRINCIPAL DIVISIONS

Integrated Circuits; Licensing; Wireless Device Software and Related Services; Asset Tracking and Services; Mobil Banking; FLO TV; Display.

PRINCIPAL COMPETITORS

Broadcom Corporation; Nokia Corporation; Texas Instruments Incorporated.

FURTHER READING

Aguilera, Mario, "CDMA Gets the Press While OmniTRACS Pulls the Qualcomm Wagon," *San Diego Transcript*, January 6, 1995.

Angell, Mike, "Son Seeks to Repeat Father's Success in the Changing of Guard at Qualcomm," *Investor's Business Daily*, July 1, 2005, p. A4.

Armstrong, Larry, "Qualcomm: Unproven, but Dazzling," *Business Week*, September 4, 1995.

Bauder, Don, "Analysts See Growth in Asian Markets as Key for Qualcomm," *San Diego Union-Tribune*, January 20, 2002.

Davies, Jennifer, "Chinese Tap CDMA Technology; Network Launch Aids Qualcomm," *Los Angeles Times*, January 9, 2002.

Douglass, Elizabeth, "Tracking Trucks Is Big Business for Qualcomm," *San Diego Union-Tribune*, April 14, 1989.

Flanigan, James, "Torpedo That Hit Qualcomm Carried a Message," *Los Angeles Times*, July 12, 1998.

Hempel, Jessi, "What's Next for Qualcomm?" *Fortune*, July 6, 2009, p. 17.

Krause, Reinhardt, "Qualcomm vs. Ericsson Reaches a Critical Stage," *Investor's Business Daily*, February 18, 1999.

Mele, Jim, "The Man Who Changed Trucking," *Fleet Owner*, October 1993.

Schine, Eric, "Qualcomm: Not Exactly an Overnight Success," *Business Week*, June 2, 1997.

Quality King Distributors, Inc.

———————— ■ ————————

35 Sawgrass Drive
Bellport, New York 11713-1548
U.S.A.
Telephone: (631) 737-5555
Fax: (631) 439-2202
Web site: http://www.qkd.com

Private Company
Founded: c. 1960
Employees: 900
Sales: $2.68 billion (2008)
NAICS: 424210 Drugs and Druggists' Sundries
Merchant Wholesalers

■ ■ ■

Quality King Distributors, Inc., is, in terms of annual revenue, the largest privately owned company on Long Island. The company purchases health and beauty care aids, pharmaceutical products, fragrances, and groceries at a discount and then sells this merchandise to other wholesalers, wholesale clubs, and retailers such as supermarket chains, pharmacies, and discount stores. In all, it distributes more than 10,000 products.

Quality King Distributors has often been in the news because of its practice of selling so-called gray-market goods: products manufactured in the United States and exported to other countries but then transported back to the United States for sale at a discount from recommended retail price. Buying, transporting, and selling gray-market goods outrages original manufacturers and has resulted in many lawsuits, but the courts have consistently declined to sanction Quality King's methods of doing business. The family-owned company keeps as low a profile as possible but defends its interests vigorously.

GRAY-GOODS MARKET

Brooklyn-born Bernard Nussdorf was attending college when his father was killed in an auto accident. He took charge of the family business, a Jewish catering hall. By the early 1960s, however, he was apparently operating on a considerably smaller scale. According to an obituary, he founded Quality King Distributors out of the back seat of his station wagon in 1964. Other accounts maintain that he, with his wife Ruth, started Quality King Distributors as a small beauty-supply shop in Queens or New Hyde Park (just east of the city and county line), in 1960 or 1961. In any case, Nussdorf's way of doing business proved consistent: A 2007 *Long Island Business News* article quoted him in these words: "I buy for 5 cents, sell for 6 cents and count the pennies."

In the early 1970s distributors began to invest heavily in computer technology so that they could better satisfy their customers: manufacturers and retailers. In the pharmaceutical industry, for example, companies found that an alliance with a technologically savvy wholesaler might well provide an improved indication of demand, enabling better management of production and inventory. These wholesalers locked up business from druggists, for example, by offering a computerized order system.

KEY DATES

c. 1960: Bernard and Ruth Nussdorf found Quality King Distributors.
1985: Quality King has been sued by at least three manufacturers for selling gray goods.
1996: Quality King has become the largest private company on Long Island.
1999: Upon Bernard Nussdorf's death, his sons Glenn and Stephen assume management.
2007: Quality King moves its corporate headquarters to Brookhaven.

During the following decade there developed increasing awareness of a gray market in merchandise selling below the manufacturer's suggested retail price. This traffic took many forms. Hong Kong, Singapore, Dubai, and Panama, for example, were centers of gray-market operations that brought consumer electronics items deriving from Japanese manufacturers into the United States. Little was done to combat this traffic, even when the complainant was a U.S. corporation. The Reagan administration, for example, overruled an International Trade Commission in favor of Duracell International Inc., which demanded that batteries made in its Belgian plant and intended for sale in Europe be barred from entering the United States.

Sometimes gray-market goods never left the United States. For example, one former owner of a wholesale drug company said that at least 20 major pharmaceutical companies sold drugs, at discount prices, to hospitals in quantities vastly greater than needed. The surplus was then diverted to the gray market by the hospitals for sale at higher prices. In other cases a manufacturer's authorized distributor simply unloaded merchandise it could not sell.

QUALITY KING DISTRIBUTORS IN AND OUT OF COURT: 1984–88

The cases disputed in court, however, usually involved goods made in the United States and exported but then resold in the United States at a price that undercut the manufacturer's authorized distributors or marketers. By 1985 Quality King Distributors had been sued by at least three U.S. manufacturers, including Johnson & Johnson (which lost its case).

The manufacturer of Old Spice toiletries, for example, was pursuing racketeering charges against three companies, one of them Quality King. The plaintiff,

Shulton Inc., argued in federal court that the three had wired money to an exporter who said he would send the merchandise to Latin America but instead sold it in the United States. Quality King and the other defendants denied knowing how the exporter obtained the goods.

Interviewed by Pete Engardio of *Business Week* in 1988, Nussdorf declined to name his suppliers and claimed he never asked where their goods originated. Sometimes, he said, manufacturers sold directly to Quality King, even allowing his company to load its trucks with their products at their own loading docks. He shrugged off manufacturers' complaints with the words: "They'll use us, abuse us, and call us names—when they don't need us."

Counterfeit goods were another matter, however, particularly when they involved prescription drugs. Quality King Distributors had been cited for buying counterfeit birth-control pills and antibiotics in 1984 in a case that a U.S. Food and Drug Administration official characterized as probably the most serious counterfeit prescription-drug violation the agency had ever experienced. Federal agents seized 20 cartons containing a total of about 5,000 oral contraceptive tablets as part of a shipment from Panama. Nussdorf denied knowing that the pills were counterfeit and testified against a man convicted of criminal charges, including the sale of counterfeit drugs. With regard to the counterfeit antibiotic, Quality King was fined $4,000 and placed on probation for two years as a wholesale distributor of prescription drugs.

This event, however embarrassing to Quality King, failed to stem its growth. Engardio was impressed by the company's offices, which he described as "a sleek Long Island headquarters that dispels any impression of a fly-by-night business." He noted a profusion of leather furniture and artworks and a 186,000-square-foot warehouse filled with standby items such as Pampers, Tylenol, and Phillips' Milk of Magnesia. Quality King was said to be selling such products at a discount of as much as 30 percent below listed wholesale prices. The company's annual sales had reached $350 million, and it was enjoying sales growth of 20 percent a year. It became Long Island's largest private company in 1996, when its sales passed the $1 billion mark.

MORE LITIGATION: 1995–2001

Quality King returned to public scrutiny in 1995. Federal marshals, armed with a court order, raided the company's two warehouses and seized thousands of bottles of counterfeit Head & Shoulders shampoo. Its owner, giant Procter & Gamble Company (P&G), then sued Quality King for selling the goods as well as trademark and package-design infringement. The lawsuit charged that "Quality King has a long history of dealing in consumer products that are counterfeit or otherwise violate trademarks or have been fraudulently diverted." A spokesman for Kroger Company, a supermarket chain that had ordered a small supply of the shampoo, said it did not intend to use Quality King as a supplier in the future.

Quality King replied that it had not bought the counterfeit product knowingly but had obtained it from another supplier, who contended that it was not the original source either. The trail became even murkier despite the efforts of investigators hired by P&G. After Quality King was found guilty of violating P&G trademarks in 2001, a settlement was reached.

The next aggrieved manufacturer to sue Quality King Distributors was L'anza Research International Inc., a manufacturer of hair-care products that sold its merchandise to distributors forbidden to resell it outside their own exclusive but limited territories. Quality King obtained the products from L'anza's U.K. distributor at a deep discount and brought them back to the United States, where it sold them to a California drugstore chain for a bargain price that undercut L'anza's authorized U.S. distributors. The U.S. Supreme Court, in 1998, ruled unanimously in favor of the defendant. Writing for the court, Justice John Paul Stevens maintained, "Once the copyright owner places a copyrighted item in the stream of commerce by selling it, he has exhausted his exclusive statutory right to control its distribution."

This decision did not apply to John Paul Mitchell Systems, which had a more basic grievance with Quality King Distributors: product counterfeiting. In a 1999 lawsuit, the plaintiff contended that Quality King had purchased 10 tractor-trailer loads of fake Paul Mitchell shampoo from a man who was later convicted of counterfeiting. The manufacturer also sued a retailer, Filene's Basement Corp.

Bernard Nussdorf had died earlier in the year, leaving management of the business to his sons Glenn and Stephen. Glenn, who had been president of the company's health and beauty aids division, succeeded his father as chief executive officer. He denied that Quality King was deliberately engaged in counterfeiting and maintained that it had found no evidence of counterfeit products in its warehouses or on Filene's shelves. He declared that the plaintiff had been trying for 15 years to keep Quality King from selling Paul Mitchell shampoo in the marketplace. A settlement was reached in which Quality King agreed to destroy $1 million worth of the counterfeit merchandise.

QK HEALTHCARE: 2000–03

Quality King, in 2000, made preliminary steps to spin off its medical-supply division into a public company, QK Healthcare, Inc. Quality King believed it could collect as much as $210 million from an initial public offering (IPO) of stock while still maintaining majority control. However, the national economy soured that year as a result of the collapse on Wall Street of overpriced high-technology stocks, and in 2001 the company canceled its plans.

There was speculation at the time that the Nussdorf heirs were in need of cash to pay taxes on their inheritance. In 2006 the U.S. Internal Revenue Service charged that family members had abused a tax shelter in 1999 to avoid taxes on $80 million of income. They were resisting a demand for $45 million in taxes and penalties.

The QK Healthcare prospectus reported that Quality King's medical-supply division had quadrupled in sales between 1996 and 2000, when it reached $1.24 billion. The unit had concentrated its efforts on marketing a limited range of products in bulk in order to take advantage of discounts offered by manufacturers. Significantly, one-quarter of its revenues came from sales to the giant distributor McKesson Corporation, indicating that no company was too big to disdain gray-market goods. (Retailers who bought products through Quality King included Wal-Mart Stores, Inc., and Target Corporation.)

QK Healthcare experienced bad publicity in 2003, when it reported that it had recalled 20 bottles each containing 5,000 counterfeit tablets purporting to be Lipitor, a popular anti-cholesterol drug. It sued the company that had allegedly supplied the recalled product, which had been sold by QK to a mail-order entity within WellPoint Health Networks Inc.

EMPHASIS ON FRAGRANCES: 2007–08

By 2002 pharmaceuticals constituted 60 percent of Quality King's business, according to the company's executive vice president. He said that gray-market goods now came to only about 5 percent of Quality King's nonpharmaceutical business. At least one gray-market dispute, however, continued to hang over the company: a lawsuit by The L'Oréal Group, one of the world's largest cosmetics companies.

L'Oréal had, in 1990, obtained a court injunction barring Quality King from buying and reselling a line of shampoos and conditioners made by L'Oréal for exclusive use, it said, by company-trained professionals working in salons. In a 2004 lawsuit, however, the company charged that Quality King had violated the injunction by using a spin-off company, New Jersey-based Pro's Choice Beauty Care Inc., to continue buying L'Oréal products and selling them to discount stores and chain pharmacies. A federal judge, in a 2007 decision, ruled against the plaintiff, suggesting that the problem lay in diversion of merchandise by L'Oréal's own distributors.

In that year Costco Wholesale Corp. sued Yves Saint Laurent Perfums S.A., YSL Beauté Inc., and Quality King Distributors in federal court, claiming that it had purchased 2,500 units of counterfeit Opium perfume from the latter. The YSL entities had previously filed suit against Costco for purportedly repackaging and selling cosmetic and beauty products. YSL Beauté reached a settlement with Costco and Quality King in 2008.

Fragrances were very much on Quality King's mind in the new decade. The company had established Five Star Fragrance Company, Inc., in 2000 and had acquired a company called Smell This in 2002. In 2003 Quality King and another party considered purchasing Parlux Fragrances, Inc., a producer and distributor, but could not find a lender. Quality King continued to eye Parlux, however. In 2007 Parlux sued Glenn Nussdorf and Quality King for soliciting shareholders to unseat members of the board. Parlux alleged several antitrust and securities-law violations and also what it called misconduct by the Nussdorf family, which held a minority stake in the company.

By 2008 the Nussdorfs' fragrance holdings had been placed into the manufacturer and distributor Model Reorg Inc., whose subsidiaries included Quality Fragrance Group, a distributor; Five Star Fragrance, a manufacturer; and Scents of Worth, a retailer with kiosks in big discount stores. Model merged that year with Perfumania Holdings Inc., in which the Nussdorf family also had a significant stake. Perfumania had secured a $250 million credit facility that was expected to fund the opening of new Perfumania stores.

NEW QUARTERS IN 2007

Quality King opened a warehouse in North Carolina in the late 1990s but shut it down about five years later, after receiving economic incentives to stay on Long Island by the state of New York and the town of Brookhaven. The company, which had run out of room to expand at its main location in Ronkonkoma, purchased 37 acres in Brookhaven Industrial Park and began construction of a 580,000-square-foot corporate headquarters and distribution facility that occupied a space larger than 10 football fields. The company was thereby remaining true to its Long Island roots, even though to some outsiders it seemed counterintuitive to locate a national distribution company on a long, narrow island with only a few main roads for its trucks to negotiate.

In erecting this structure, however, Quality King added a third floor without receiving a permit from the board of the town of Brookhaven. An agreement reached in 2007 provided that the company would pay three times the cost of its building permit in fines, hold a job fair for local applicants, hire some 100 workers from the area, and contribute $75,000 for infrastructure improvements in the area.

Robert Halasz

PRINCIPAL SUBSIDIARIES

QK Healthcare, Inc.

PRINCIPAL DIVISIONS

Fragrances; Hair Care; Health and Beauty; Pharmaceuticals.

PRINCIPAL COMPETITORS

AmerisourceBergen Corporation; Bindley Western Drug Company; Cardinal Health, Inc.; McKesson Corporation.

FURTHER READING

Anastasi, Rick, "Quality King Lays Claim in Yaphank," *Long Island Business News*, March 21–27, 2004, pp. 1A, 56A.

Gilgoff, Harry, "Counterfeit!" *Newsday*, August 27, 1995, Money and Careers section, p. 5.

Kessler, Robert E., "In a Lather over Shampoo," *Newsday*, February 14, 2006, pp. A35, A38.

———, "Legal Wrangle a Washout for L'Oréal," *Newsday*, November 27, 2007, pp. A36–A37.

Narisetti, Raju, "Investigators follow a Trail of Shampoo to Some Dry Ends," *Wall Street Journal*, pp. A1, A6.

Scholl, Tammy, "B. Nussdorf, 72, Quality King Distributors Founder," *Newsday*, March 20, 1999, p. A28.

Strugatch, Warren, "Quality King in Court over Shampoo Ado," *Long Island Business News*, April 23, 1999, pp. A1+.

"There's Nothing Black-and-White about the Gray Market," *Business Week*, November 7, 1988, pp. 172–73, 176.

Wagner, Daniel, "Town Accepts Quality King's Payback," *Newsday*, March 20, 2007, p. A44.

Willoughby, Jack, "Gray-Market IPO," *Barron's*, January 10, 2000, p. 30.

RehabCare Group, Inc.

7733 Forsyth Boulevard, Suite 2300
St. Louis, Missouri 63105-1817
U.S.A.
Telephone: (314) 863-7422
Toll Free: (800) 677-1238
Fax: (314) 863-0769
Web site: http://www.rehabcare.com

Public Company
Incorporated: 1982
Employees: 13,500
Operating Revenues: $743.1 million (2008)
Stock Exchanges: New York
Ticker Symbol: RHB
NAICS: 622310 Specialty (Except Psychiatric and Substance Abuse) Hospitals; 621498 All Other Outpatient Care Facilities

■ ■ ■

RehabCare Group, Inc., is one of the leading providers of physical rehabilitation facility and program management. The company provides acute care rehabilitation program management to more than 110 hospitals, operating within hospital facilities and receiving a percentage of Medicare and insurance reimbursement fees for service. Inpatient, acute care services include physical, occupational, and speech therapy for patients recovering from stroke, head injuries, and orthopedic conditions. Subacute care rehabilitation involves patients requiring less than three hours of therapy per day, such as in the case of recovery from heart failure and cancer. Outpatient services are offered at 35 in-hospital or in freestanding clinics, and usually involve sports and work-related injuries. Contract therapy operations include neurological, orthopedic, and other physical rehabilitation at more than 1,068 skilled nursing, assisted living, and long-term care facilities.

RehabCare owns and operates several freestanding hospitals, including physical rehabilitation hospitals and long-term, acute care hospitals for conditions requiring more than 25 days. Long-term acute care services involve patients with complex health issues requiring continual monitoring and ongoing medical care. These cases include respiratory failure, neuromuscular disorders, brain and spinal cord injuries, cardiac disorders, and renal disorders requiring dialysis.

PHYSICAL REHABILITATION PROGRAM MANAGEMENT: 1983

RehabCare Group began operations in 1983, when the original company established its first inpatient rehabilitation unit at a Portsmouth, Virginia, hospital. Operating on a contract basis, the company's responsibilities involved complete operational management of the rehabilitation unit. RehabCare utilized existing hospital space to provide physical therapy, occupational therapy, and speech therapy for patients recovering from acute conditions, such as stroke, head injuries, and orthopedic problems. By providing a therapy program at a lower cost than a hospital could

COMPANY PERSPECTIVES

The vision of RehabCare is to provide a clinically integrated continuum of post-acute care that helps people regain their lives.

manage itself, the company directed its expertise toward market leadership in a new area of hospital services.

RehabCare did not become a substantial presence in hospital-based physical rehabilitation until it became a subsidiary of Comprehensive Care Corporation (Comp-Care) in 1986. While CompCare provided financial support for expansion of the RehabCare concept, federal legislation created demand for independent rehabilitative services. The 1987 Omnibus Budget Reconciliation Act required hospitals to shift acute care physical therapy to separate, long-term care facilities. Such facilities could still be located within hospitals, as long as they were independently managed.

Under the then-new name of RehabCare Corporation, the company grew rapidly. RehabCare obtained contracts to operate 22 new physical rehabilitation units in the fiscal year ending May 31, 1988. However, financial problems at CompCare hampered further expansion, with only 10 units opening in fiscal 1989, and only five units in 1990. Fiscal 1991 brought profits of $2.6 million on revenues of $38.4 million, but RehabCare paid special dividends to CompCare which exceeded profits. These funds offset losses from Comp-Care's primary operations in drug and alcohol abuse treatment.

RehabCare became an independent company in May 1991, following a forced change in leadership at CompCare the previous summer. RehabCare CEO James Usdan and CFO Alan Henderson led a management buyout that occurred in conjunction with an initial public offering of stock. The 1991 stock offering of 800,000 shares for RehabCare, priced at $13 per share, garnered RehabCare $8.8 million in proceeds to expand operations. CompCare retained a substantial interest in RehabCare, but RehabCare purchased the remaining stock in October 1992 through a private placement of $3.8 million in preferred stock.

At this time RehabCare employed 735 people and held contracts to manage physical medicine and rehabilitation units at 50 acute care hospitals and one extended care facility, an aggregate of 1,022 hospital beds.

BUSINESS STRATEGY FOR EXPANSION DURING NINETIES

Once RehabCare became an independent company, management initiated an expansion strategy that diversified the company's business outlets. RehabCare expected rapid growth in subacute cure, which required less than three hours of physical therapy daily, leading to occasional outpatient visits. The company looked to growth in outpatient care generally associated with sports and work injuries. Two acquisitions stemmed from this diversification. In 1993 RehabCare purchased Advanced Rehabilitation Resources, increasing its managed acute care units by 50 percent and subacute and outpatient programs by 10 percent. The October 1994 acquisition of Physical Therapy Resources added 17 subacute, outpatient clinics in Florida and Texas.

Internal growth at RehabCare followed from opportunities for new inpatient rehabilitation unit development. Heightened cost oversight by health insurance companies led to shorter hospital stays, thus reducing hospital revenues. By converting the excess of unused beds for physical rehabilitation patients, hospitals created a new stream of income from services that might otherwise be provided by a nursing care center or other long-term care facility. Benefiting from these changes, RehabCare obtained several new contracts at hospitals in San Jose, Ventura, and Santa Ana, California, bringing total operations in that state to 13 units. A new unit in Laredo increased activity in Texas to 18 contracts and a new contract in Michigan brought operations there to seven units.

Establishment of a new rehabilitation center involved substantial investment, as qualification for Medicare reimbursement required an inpatient rehabilitation program be in operation for a full year. With 85 percent of its revenue stemming from Medicare, RehabCare lost money the first year of each new contract. However, RehabCare structured its contracts so that the company lost $175,000 the first year, earned a modest profit of $125,000 the second year, and garnered an overall profit of $550,000 for the duration of a five-year contract. RehabCare renewed 80 percent of its contracts, and the renewal period reaped profits that offset losses associated with new contracts. By 1995, RehabCare reported $83.2 million in sales that resulted in $8.5 million in net earnings.

RehabCare had the competitive advantage as new opportunities in rehabilitation program services abounded. RehabCare held a substantial lead over its competitors in experience and command of the market. Of 900 hospitals in the country, 150 used contracted outside management for inpatient physical rehabilitation by the late 1990s. Of those 150 programs, RehabCare

KEY DATES

1986: Original company is purchased by Comp-Care, begins rapid expansion.

1991: RehabCare becomes an independent, public company.

1996: Temporary staffing operations are initiated and expanded through several acquisitions.

2005: Newly established hospital division purchases RehabCare's first freestanding rehabilitation hospitals.

2009: Triumph Healthcare acquisition contributes to hospital development capabilities.

managed approximately 100 units, and the remaining units were managed by numerous smaller companies. Changes in Medicare reimbursement, as established by the Balanced Budget Act of 1997, promised additional business development for RehabCare. As Medicare's new flat fee payment replaced the cost-of-treatment basis for reimbursement, more hospitals would choose to outsource rehabilitation operations.

In addition to building internal growth, RehabCare continued its diversification through acquisition strategy. The July 1998 acquisition of Rehabilitative Care Systems of America added outpatient therapy contracts. RehabCare established a presence in contract therapy for freestanding skilled nursing and long-term care facilities through the acquisition of Therapeutic Systems in September 1998.

BUSINESS EXPANSION IN TEMPORARY STAFFING

As company expansion met with increasing demand for health care services, RehabCare faced a shortage of physical therapists and clinicians. Hospitals frequently requested temporary staff from RehabCare, prompting the company to enter the physical therapy staffing field. In 1996 RehabCare acquired Healthcare Solutions, Inc., and HCH, Inc., doing business as Health Tour, the largest provider of temporary therapists in the country. That year, the company changed its name from RehabCare Corporation to RehabCare Group, to reflect its growing range of services.

The acquisition trend continued in 1997 with Team Rehab, in the St. Louis area, and Moore Rehab. These companies extended RehabCare's temporary staffing business into nursing homes, providing long-term and short-term rehabilitation therapy. RehabCare made its

largest acquisition in the temporary staffing field in August 1998, with the combined purchase of StarMed Staffing and Wesley Medical Resources. These companies specialized in nurses and nurse assistants. Expansion in 1999 included the $6.6 million acquisition of Salt Lake Physical Therapy and the $17.3 million acquisition of All Staff, Inc., in Iowa. These companies added medical records and billing clerks and laboratory and pharmacy technicians to RehabCare's staffing business. All staffing operations were consolidated under StarMed as the StarMedStaffing Group.

Temporary staffing became a dominant force for growth at RehabCare as delays in implementation of the new Medicare reimbursement structure for rehabilitative care hindered demand. While rehabilitation services remained stable, staffing services accounted for more than 50 percent of total revenue. In 2001 health care staffing garnered $304.57 million in revenue while hospital rehabilitation services yielded $173.03 million and contract therapy, $63.66 million. The company's substantial growth as an independent company prompted a shift from the NASDAQ to the New York Stock Exchange in 2000.

RENEWED FOCUS ON REHABILITATIVE CARE

Operating losses and pending changes in the health care industry led RehabCare to reevaluate its position. Interim President and CEO John Short, who replaced Alan Henderson after his retirement in 2003, led the company toward a renewed focus on rehabilitation programs and services. Short restructured the company's operating structure in alignment with revenues. For instance, a decline in temporary staffing prompted the company to sell the MedStar Group to InteliStaf Holding, Inc., in December 2003. The stock transaction gave RehabCare a 25 percent interest in InteliStaf, then the largest privately held integrated staffing company with aggregate revenue of $450 million in 2003.

With less attention given to staffing, Short directed RehabCare toward addressing the complete continuum of care. This involved adding more post-acute rehabilitative services, establishing operations in long-term acute-care, and offering home health therapy services. In January 2004, the company acquired the Neurological Rehabilitation and Research Unit of UCLA, which provides long-term acute care rehabilitation related to neurological conditions from spinal cord injuries and to degenerative diseases, including multiple sclerosis and amyotrophic lateral sclerosis. These acute care situations involved hospital stays that averaged 120 days. Through a partnership with Signature Healthcare Foundation,

RehabCare developed outpatient clinics and began offering home therapy health in the St. Louis area.

Geographic location also played a role in RehabCare's growth strategy. Through the acquisition of CPR Therapies, Inc., RehabCare gained market share in contract therapy in Colorado and in skilled nursing services in California. In March 2004 RehabCare acquired American VitalCare, Inc., and Managed Alternative Care, Inc., subsidiaries of Health Net, Inc., for $14 million. The two VitalCare entities managed more than 800 hospital beds in California, approximately half of the available beds for such acute care rehabilitation in the state. One of the leading managed contract specialists in California, VitalCare was expected to contribute $14 million in annual revenue to RehabCare.

Short became permanent in June 2004. In conjunction with the election of Short, RehabCare acquired Phase 2 Consulting, a health care management consulting firm, for $5 million. John Short was a managing partner and majority shareholder in Phase 2. However, as the company developed along other lines, the company sold its consulting operations in 2009.

ESTABLISHMENT OF HOSPITAL DIVISION AND EXPANSION OF CONTRACT THERAPY

With the baby-boomer generation on the verge of retirement and life expectancy increasing, RehabCare saw its future in the development of acute-care specialty hospitals. Toward that end, RehabCare sought partnerships in which risk and revenues are shared. In November 2004 RehabCare formed a joint venture with Howard Regional Health System to operate a rehabilitation facility at the West Campus Specialty Hospital in Kokomo, Indiana. In addition to 40 percent ownership in the 60-bed hospital, RehabCare signed a management agreement with the joint venture to operate a 30-bed physical rehabilitation center. Plans for the remaining 30 beds involved development of a long-term acute care hospital, with the service provider to be determined at a later time.

RehabCare established its hospital division in 2005 with the acquisition of Meadowbrook Healthcare. The acquisition of freestanding hospitals involved two acute rehabilitation facilities and two long-term care facilities located in Oklahoma, Florida, Louisiana, and Texas. RehabCare opened its first company-developed freestanding specialty hospital in Arlington, Texas. In 2006 RehabCare purchased Solara Hospital in New Orleans for $19.7 million. The acquisition added a 44-bed long-term acute-care facility and a 12-bed specialty

hospital nearby. The two Solara facilities were renamed West Jefferson Specialty Hospital.

RehabCare sought to develop its contract therapy business through small and large acquisitions. In December 2005 the company purchased Cornerstone Rehabilitation, a contract therapy management company based in Shreveport, Louisiana. The business included contracts for 40 rehabilitation units in northern Louisiana, 10 in Texas, and 1 outpatient facility in southeast Shreveport. The acquisition added approximately $12 million to RehabCare revenues.

RehabCare became one of the largest rehabilitation management service providers in the United States with the May 2006 acquisition of Symphony Health Services, of Hunt Valley, Maryland. The $101.5 million deal included Rehab Works, a contract therapy company operating at 470 locations, and VTA Management Services, which provided contract therapy staffing throughout the state of New York. The Polaris Group subsidiary offered consulting services to post-acute health care providers.

In addition to gaining more than $230 million in annual revenue, RehabCare expected to save up to $12 million through integration of administrative functions. The acquisition expanded RehabCare's activities to management of 1,400 facilities in 42 states, the District of Columbia, and Puerto Rico. The company employed 15,000 people handling 24,000 patient visits per day.

RehabCare continued to develop its hospital and contract therapy businesses. The company entered the Rhode Island market through the acquisition of Landmark Health System in the fall of 2007. RehabCare became a majority owner and manager of the 41-bed rehabilitation hospital in Woonsocket. RehabCare gained its first multi-hospital system contract with the West Penn Allegheny Health System in 2008.

A FUTURE IN HOSPITAL DEVELOPMENT

The company pursued new business development through joint ventures with other hospitals. A $7.5 million joint venture with St. Luke's Hospital, in west St. Louis, culminated in the opening of a 35-bed inpatient rehabilitation facility in November 2008. A joint venture with Methodist Medical Center in Peoria, Illinois, involved development and management of a 56,000-square-foot, 50-bed long-term acute care hospital. The facility, which opened in 2009 near downtown Peoria, served patients who completed initial treatment at an acute care hospital and required long-term, specialized care on a 24-hour basis due to chronic or medically complex conditions stemming from brain injury, neuropathy, ventilator dependency, cardiopulmonary disease, or chronic pain.

At the end of 2009, RehabCare finalized a merger with Triumph HealthCare of Houston. As a developer and operator of long-term acute care hospitals (LTACH), Triumph contributed significant expertise in this area to RehabCare. Triumph brought 23 independent hospitals to RehabCare, and the subsidiary became the manager of RehabCare's seven hospitals. To partially fund the transaction, RehabCare offered 4.5 million shares of common stock for $24 per share. The offering raised $127.4 million toward the $570 million acquisition of Triumph HealthCare.

Triumph expanded further when RehabCare completed its acquisition of St. Agnes Long-Term Care Hospital, a 58-bed facility in Philadelphia. A joint-venture agreement with Gulf States Health Services, a physicians group, involved a freestanding 60-bed LTACH in Dallas. The venture purchased the facility from Gulf States Health, with RehabCare holding an 80 percent interest. The newly renamed Dallas LTAC Hospital would be operated by Triumph.

RehabCare and Seton Family Hospitals began development of a physical rehabilitation and long-term care facility in Austin, Texas, in 2009. Construction of the $45 million facility followed from an existing relationship between the two organizations, as RehabCare operated a rehabilitation unit at Seton Medical Center. Moving rehabilitation to a new location provided Seton with additional space for surgery patients while adding rehabilitation and long-term care for hip or joint replacements, neurological disorders, and amputations. The new rehabilitation facility complemented Seton's strength in handling strokes and brain and spinal cord injuries. Hence, the development contributed to a continuum of care at Seton, allowing patients to remain within one hospital system over the course of care.

The 80,000-square-foot Central Texas Rehabilitation Hospital was expected to house 38 rehabilitation beds and 40 long-term care beds. RehabCare and Seton divided ownership of the facility at 80 percent and 20 percent, respectively. Construction was scheduled for completion in late 2010.

RehabCare expected to focus on hospital development as it looked ahead. With progressive growth in sales and profits and significant reduction of debt since 2006, RehabCare was well positioned to endure whatever changes might occur in the nation's health care system, particularly after the passage of the Patient Protection and Affordable Care Act in 2010.

Mary Tradii

PRINCIPAL SUBSIDIARIES

Polaris Group, Inc.; Triumph Healthcare Holdings, Inc.; VTA Management, Inc.; VitalCare America, Inc.

PRINCIPAL DIVISIONS

Program Management Services; Hospitals.

PRINCIPAL COMPETITORS

HealthSouth Corporation; Kindred Healthcare, Inc.; Select Medical Corporation.

FURTHER READING

Lau, Gloria, "Rehab without the Real Estate," *Forbes,* February 24, 1997, p. 92.

Manning, Margie, "New Contracts Pump Up Sales at Rehab-Care," *St. Louis Business Journal,* May 15, 2000, p. 1.

———, "RehabCare Group Expects 8–12% Growth in Rehab Units," *St. Louis Business Journal,* October 19, 1998, p. 38.

Miller, Patricia, "RehabCare Corp. Leaving Parent, Comprehensive Care," *St. Louis Business Journal,* May 20, 1991, p. 7A.

Mueller, Angela, "RehabCare Group Grows with Addition of Triumph," *St. Louis Business Journal,* December 21, 2009.

———, "Short's RehabCare Flush with Cash," *St. Louis Business Journal,* May 25, 2009.

"RehabCare Group, Inc. Elects President and Chief Executive Officer," *Managed Care Weekly,* May 31, 2004, p. 119.

Zaragoza, Sandra, "Seton, RehabCare to Build $45M Hospital," *Austin Business Journal,* January 19, 2009.

The Renco Group, Inc.

1 Rockefeller Plaza
New York, New York 10112
U.S.A.
Telephone: (212) 541-6000
Fax: (212) 541-6197
Web site: http://www.rencogroup.net

Private Company
Incorporated: 1986
Employees: 13,000
Sales: $5.5 billion (2008 est.)
NAICS: 212231 Lead Ore and Zinc Mining; 212299 Other Metal Ore Mining; 336211 Motor Vehicle Body Manufacturing; 336360 Motor Vehicle Fabric Accessories and Seat Manufacturing; 551112 Offices of Other Holding Companies

■ ■ ■

The Renco Group, Inc., is a private holding company whose affiliated operating companies are engaged in a number of industries, including mining and minerals recovery, metals production and fabrication, and automotive assembly and furnishings. These operating companies include The Doe Run Company and US Magnesium, LLC, which mine lead and magnesium, respectively, and AM General LLC, which manufactures and assembles the Humvee military vehicle and its civilian counterpart, Hummer. Renco is owned almost entirely by Ira Rennert, an entrepreneur whose net worth has been estimated at several billion dollars.

Renco Group assembled its empire by purchasing distressed companies at discount prices, with borrowed money. The companies, usually in the mining and metals field, then issued so-called junk bonds: securities that carried poor credit ratings but that paid high rates of interest. Renco immediately took a large cash dividend for arranging the financing. The acquired companies typically depended for their profits on high prices for their commodities. Since commodity prices fluctuate greatly, in many cases these companies fell deeply into debt. Several of them declared bankruptcy and forced the bondholders to sustain heavy losses, but Renco, having taken its money off the top, continued to prosper.

FORMING THE RENCO GROUP

Born in Brooklyn, Rennert received degrees from Brooklyn College and New York University's Stern School of Business before working as a credit analyst, salesman, and securities dealer. In 1960 he opened his own securities firm, I.L. Rennert & Co., but had to shut it down four years later when the National Association of Securities Dealers revoked his registration for operating with insufficient capital. Nevertheless, he had done well enough as a consultant by 1975 to acquire a company, Consolidated Sewing Machine Corporation, that made industrial sewing machines, plus their motors and parts. He was also financing leveraged buyouts of other small firms, generally family-owned, by selling unregulated private-equity bonds to investors.

Although Renco's Web site claims the company was formed in 1986, Michael Shnayerson maintained in a 1998 *Vanity Fair* article that it was established in 1980.

By 1988, according to Shnayerson, the holding company consisted of 15 diversified operating companies that he characterized as "a grab bag of dreary profit-makers" with combined annual sales of perhaps $200 million.

MOSTLY MINERALS AND METALS COMPANIES: 1988–99

Renco raised its profile in 1988, when it purchased a steel mill in Warren, Ohio, from LTV Steel Co., part of bankrupt conglomerate LTV Corp. The mill and another steel operation were acquired through a leveraged buyout for $112 million in cash and a $30 million loan from LTV itself. The mill became part of Warren Consolidated Industries Inc., which later became WCI Steel Inc. In the next few years Renco Group collected $208 million in dividends from junk bonds issued by WCI Steel or its holding company, Renco Steel Holdings Inc.

Cash flow from WCI enabled Renco in 1989 to purchase a plant from Amax Corporation that extracted magnesium from brine in Utah's Great Salt Lake. This plant was the only primary magnesium producer in the United States. The purchase price was undisclosed, but Amax had been seeking $65 million.

These Renco acquisitions had in common a record of spewing toxic emissions into the atmosphere and nearby water. In 1998 the U.S. Department of Justice sued WCI on charges that included illegal dumping of copper, lead, hydrochloric acid, and other industrial waste into the Mahoning River. The magnesium plant, renamed Magnesium Corporation of America, was described by Shnayerson as "the single worst polluting facility in the entire United States of America," emitting clouds of chlorine gas, a by-product of the extraction process, and toxic chemicals into channels deemed likely to leach into the Great Salt Lake.

In 1992 Renco had purchased another bankrupt company, AM General Corporation, from LTV

Corporation. Renco paid about $133 million for the company, which had produced the Humvee armored vehicle to acclaim in the recent Persian Gulf War. However, the Humvee was not in demand by the Pentagon once hostilities ended. AM General found new life in 1992 by introducing the seven-foot-wide Hummer civilian version, widely touted by no less than film star Arnold Schwarzenegger. This vehicle later was renamed the H1 Hummer as the company added the smaller but still tank-like H2 Hummer sport-utility vehicle in 2002 in collaboration with General Motors Corporation, which had assumed the distribution and marketing of the Hummer models in 2000.

Renco enhanced its portfolio in the mining and metals business in 1994, when it acquired Ohio-based Baron Drawn Steel Corporation from Cooper Industries and purchased Doe Run Resources Corporation (also known as The Doe Run Company) from Fluor Corporation for an estimated $175 million. The latter enterprise was the world's largest primary lead producer, with five mines and four mills in Missouri supplying concentrates to two smelters. Because of low lead prices it had been losing large amounts of money for at least two years. Its smelters had been cited as one of Missouri's two biggest polluters. In 1998 Renco purchased the other one from Asarco Inc. for about $55 million in cash. This purchase included two lead-zinc mines.

This acquisition made Renco Group, according to Shnayerson, the largest private polluter in the country. The smelter in Herculaneum, Missouri, for example, which was the nation's largest, had been found responsible for high levels of lead, a highly toxic substance, in the vicinity. A 2002 state report concluded that one-fourth of all children under six years tested near the smelter were suffering from lead poisoning.

Doe Run and Renco Resources Inc. of Canada, in 1997, also purchased a metallurgical smelter/refinery complex from Empresa Minera del Centro del Perú S.A. (Centromín), a state-owned company. The price was $126.5 million for 51 percent of the complex and an agreement to invest another $121 million to acquire the remainder. According to Shnayerson's 2003 account, the initial sum was returned to Renco as an interest-free loan.

The Peruvian operation, almost a century old, centered on a company town called La Oroya where studies had concluded that almost all the children had elevated levels of lead in their blood as a result of sediment falling from the smelter smokestack towering over the town and effluents flowing into the river below. The Blacksmith Institute, a nonprofit group that studies such sites, described La Oroya as one of the world's 10 most polluted places.

```
┌─────────────────────────────────────────────┐
│                                               │
│             KEY DATES                         │
│                  ■                            │
│  ───────────────────────────────────────      │
│                                               │
│  1988:  The Renco Group consists of 15 small-scale, │
│         diversified operating companies.      │
│  1989:  Renco purchases the only U.S. primary │
│         producer of magnesium.                │
│  2002:  Renco subsidiaries and affiliated companies │
│         have issued 10 junk-bond offerings.   │
│  2004:  Renco shores up its finances by selling 70 │
│         percent of AM General for $930 million. │
│  2008:  Renco buys a unit of bankrupt Delphi  │
│         Corporation.                          │
│                                               │
└─────────────────────────────────────────────┘
```

Renco entered coal mining in 1998, when it purchased Costain Coal Inc., a firm based in Lexington, Kentucky, from U.K.-based Costain plc for $32.5 million. This company was renamed Lodestar Holdings Inc. A Renco subsidiary quickly issued a $150 million bond offering, and the parent company's share of the take came to $27.8 million.

Little was heard about Unarco Materials Handling, Inc., a Tennessee-based company that Renco purchased in 1999. Unarco was a manufacturer of racks and material-handling systems used by warehouses and retail stores, among other customers. It acquired Kingway Material Handling Co. in 2007.

TAKING JUNK-BOND PROCEEDS OFF THE TOP

What these acquisitions had in common was that the purchase price was seldom higher than the value of the assets. The purchase money came almost entirely from financial institutions that issued loans to Renco on the basis of the value of the assets of the acquired companies. Congress Financial Corporation (which later became part of Wachovia Capital Finance Corporation) was usually the lender. Once in control of these companies, subsidiaries of Renco Group issued the junk bonds: speculative securities that, however, paid generous interest. Sometimes as much as half the proceeds went to Renco as a dividend.

According to Shnayerson, in a 2003 follow-up *Vanity Fair* article, what distinguished Rennert from others who played the junk-bond game, was "a twist that made even his own bankers call him rapacious. Instead of putting all the money raised into his new company, Rennert took a huge chunk for himself as a onetime 'dividend.' … The dividend gambit was entirely legal,

because Rennert declared right on his bond offering how much he would shovel upstairs."

By 2002 Renco's practices had attracted outrage not only from environmentalists but from the holders of the 10 bond issues floated by the firm's subsidiaries and affiliated companies as their holdings lost value in the wake of falling world prices for minerals and metals. In a *Forbes* article, Nathan Vardi contended that Rennert had "gotten rich off junk bonds issued by metals companies he acquired, paid fines to clean up what he's had to, stopped interest payments on bonds and bought back assets at pennies on the dollar."

SHOWER OF BANKRUPTCIES: 2001–03

Lodestar was the first Renco Group company to fall, failing to make the semiannual interest payment on its bonds in November 2000. The largest bondholder forced Lodestar into involuntary bankruptcy in 2001, and it was liquidated in 2003. The assets, six coal mines, were purchased by a private-equity and hedge-fund firm for about $26 million. Among unhappy investors were the ones who bought $150 million worth of junk bonds from Renco Metals Inc., the parent of Magnesium Corporation of America (MagCorp). Debt-ridden Mag-Corp filed for Chapter 11 bankruptcy in 2001 and was reorganized as US Magnesium, LLC, the following year. Federal authorities claimed that MagCorp's financial problems stemmed from Renco Metals paying $75 million from the bond offering to Renco Group. This maneuver, according to a U.S. Justice Department brief rejected in court, enabled an affiliate of the latter to sidestep the bondholders and buy back MagCorp's assets the following year for only $23 million.

WCI Steel suffered a severe operating loss in 2001. As a result, its parent, Renco Steel, began to miss interest payments on the $120 million in bonds it had sold (of which $100 million went to Renco Group). The parent company bought back half the outstanding debt of its subsidiary for 10 to 20 cents on the dollar. WCI itself went bankrupt in 2003 after missing payments due on its own $300 million junk bond.

WCI emerged from bankruptcy in 2006. Renco retained no stake in the company and agreed to assume responsibility for the company's pension fund, which provided benefits to about 2,000 workers and retirees. According to the federal government's pension agency, the pension fund had $138 million in assets and $255 million in obligations.

Doe Run bondholders were informed in March 2002 that the company would not be making its semiannual interest payment on $305 million in bond debt. Renco bought out some of the bondholders for 15 to 25 cents on the dollar. In an out-of-court settlement the others later agreed to accept between 58 and 68 cents on the dollar and 40 percent of the company's equity in the form of warrants.

In this case there was no bankruptcy filing, according to one observer interviewed by Shnayerson, because then creditors could have claimed the Peruvian operation. While Doe Run Peru had invested significant sums to improve environmental conditions in La Oroya, it was, in 2009, reluctant to commit more in view of financial problems that had caused most of its mining and smelting operations in the area to close.

In a 2002 article in *American Metal Market*, Renate F. Mas presented much the same scenario as Vardi in *Forbes*. She wrote that Rennert, "a one-time associate of junk-bond king and one-time jailed financier Michael Milken, has bought metal companies cheaply, issued bonds on the assets, paid the proceeds to himself and when times got tough, let the companies go to the wall. And when his companies go bust he buys back the assets for fire-sale prices."

SALES AND PURCHASES: 2004–09

AM General, not dependent on falling metals prices for income, was in better shape but nevertheless received support in 1999 from General Motors in return for an option on 40 percent of the company's equity. To shore up Renco's finances, Rennert sold 70 percent of AM General to fellow entrepreneur Ron Perelman's MacAndrews & Forbes Holdings Inc. in 2004 for $930 million.

Renco resumed its modus operandi in 2008, when it purchased the interiors and closures unit of bankrupt automotive supplier Delphi Corporation. The holding company thereby acquired 17 facilities on three continents and renamed the unit Inteva Products, LLC. Renco sold struggling Baron Drawn Steel in 2009 to Hercules Drawn Steel Corporation for an undisclosed sum.

LAVISH ESTATE

Renco's holdings also included Fair Field, a 100,000-square-foot U-shaped complex consisting of an Italian-style mansion and outbuildings on a 63-acre seaside site in Sagaponack, Long Island. Fair Field was said to be the largest private residence in the United States and included 29 bedrooms, 39 bathrooms, 3 dining rooms, 3 side-by-side swimming pools, a 164-seat theater, a

recreation pavilion with a gym, bowling alley, and squash and basketball courts, and a huge parking garage. Federal authorities had threatened to seize the property unless Renco agreed to assume responsibility for meeting its pension obligations to WCI workers and retirees.

Forbes estimated Rennert's worth at $6 billion in 2008. Renco's revenues that year were estimated at $5.5 billion by *Crain's New York Business*. Following the financial crisis and economic recession that ensued, Rennert's worth was estimated to have fallen to $4 billion by *Forbes*, but the magazine estimated that it had rebounded to $5.3 billion by early 2010.

Robert Halasz

PRINCIPAL SUBSIDIARIES

AM General LLC; The Doe Run Company; Doe Run Peru S.R.L.; Inteva Products, LLC; Unarco Material Handling, Inc.; US Magnesium, LLC.

FURTHER READING

Barkholz, David, and Robert Sherefkin, "Industrialist Poised to Buy Delphi Interiors," *Automotive News*, February 12, 2007, pp. 1, 73.

Berman, Dennis K., and Lee Hawkins Jr., "Perelman Is Near to a Deal for Control of AM General," *Wall Street Journal*, August 10, 2004, p. D2.

Mas, Renate F., "The Fine Art of Asset Juggling," *American Metal Market*, September 9, 2002, p. 4.

Miller, Joe, "GM Moves Ahead on Strategy for Hummer Plan," *Automotive News*, November 29, 1999, p. 4.

Romero, Simon, "In the Andes, a Toxic Site Also Provides a Livelihood," *New York Times*, June 24, 2009, p. A6.

"St. Louis-Area Lead-Mining Company Makes Deal to Restructure Its Debt," *St. Louis Post-Dispatch*, April 16, 2002, p. C1.

Sandler, Linda, "Hamptons Mansion Turns Focus on Multimillionaire," *Wall Street Journal*, June 18, 1998, p. C1.

Shnayerson, Michael, "Devastating Luxury," *Vanity Fair*, July 2003, pp. 130–33, 160–64.

———, "Sand Simeon," *Vanity Fair*, August 1998, pp. 80+.

Thornton, Emily, "Ira Rennert's House of Debt," *Business Week*, February 17, 2008, pp. 78–80.

Vardi, Nathan, "Man with Many Enemies," *Forbes*, July 22, 2002, pp. 44, 46.

Walsh, Mary Williams, "U.S. Moves to Seize Bankrupt Steel Maker's Pension Plan," *New York Times*, February 4, 2006, p. C4.

Rotana Hotel Management Corporation LTD.

———■———

Abu Dhabi Mall
7th Floor, East Tower
Tourist Club Area
P.O. Box 43500
Abu Dhabi,
United Arab Emirates
Telephone: (+971 2) 644-4412
Fax: (+971 2) 644-1412
Web site: http://www.rotana.com

Private Company
Founded: 1992
Employees: 10,000
NAICS: 721110 Hotels (Except Casino Hotels) and
    Motels

■ ■ ■

Rotana Hotel Management Corporation LTD. is one of the fastest-growing hotel management groups in the Middle East and North African region. Founded in Abu Dhabi in 1992, Rotana has been expanding aggressively throughout the region, and expects its portfolio to grow to at least 70 hotels, and as many as 100 hotels by 2012. Hotels managed by the company include its first hotel, the Beach Rotana resort in Abu Dhabi, and the Rose Rayhaan in Dubai, which, at 72 floors, claims to be the world's tallest hotel. The company operates 10 more hotel properties in Dubai, including the Al Bustan Rotana, included in the list of The Leading Hotels of the World. Other current and upcoming markets include Oman, Lebanon, Syria, Egypt, Saudi Arabia,

Iraq, Kurdistan, Algeria, Kuwait, and Sudan.

Rotana's hotels operate under four distinct brands. Rotana Hotels and Resorts is the company's flagship brand, grouping its four- and five-star properties. The company launched a mid-market brand, Centro Hotels by Rotana, in 2006. Under the Rayhaan Hotels by Rotana brand, the company provides alcohol-free accommodations. The company also operates a number of all-suite apartment hotels under the Arjaan by Rotana brand.

Rotana is led by cofounder and CEO Selim El Zyr, ranked number one in the Hotelier Middle East Power 50 in 2009. The company remains a private company and does not release its financial details. In 2010, however, Rotana indicated its intention to pursue a public offering as early as 2012.

FOUNDING A UAE HOTEL GROUP IN 1992

Rotana Hotel Management Corporation was founded in 1992 by two hospitality industry veterans, Nasser Al Nowais and Selim El Zyr. Economist and New York University graduate Al Nowais had been the driving force behind Abu Dhabi National Hotels Company, which was created by taking over a number of government-owned hotels in the 1970s. Over a 14-year period, Al Nowais expanded that company into the region's leading hotel and industrial catering group.

By the early 1990s, the United Arab Emirates (UAE), and especially Dubai, had begun to emerge as the leading business center for the Persian Gulf region,

COMPANY PERSPECTIVES

Our Vision: To be the Leading Hospitality Management Company within the Middle East and North Africa operating a comprehensive range of products and brands that aim to meet all the requirements of our guests.

Mission: Treasured Time. In today's busy, pressured world, time is our most precious commodity. How and with whom we choose to spend it is perhaps one of the most important decisions we make in our lives. At Rotana, we have chosen to acknowledge this fact by embracing the challenge of making all time spent with us, Treasured Time. This means that we pledge to understand and meet the individual needs of all who we deal with. In so doing, we strive to continually build long-term relationships with our owners and partners, our colleagues and, of course, our guests. Treasured Time is Rotana today.

and the Middle East in general. The UAE states had long been important trade centers for the region, a position reinforced through a series of major investments in order to develop port facilities capable of handling the world's largest vessels. The UAE offered a relatively moderate religious climate, compared to most of its neighbors, as well as greater political stability and an openness to the international market.

While a number of international hotel groups had begun to build a presence in the region, Al Nowais recognized the potential for building a new company, focused on developing luxury hotel accommodations and based in the UAE. Al Nowais turned to El Zyr to help him build the new company. El Zyr's own hospitality industry dated back to the 1960s. As he recalled in a corporate press release, "Since 1964, which was the first time I was in a hotel, I knew that's where I wanted to be. I was simply bewitched: the colors, the cars stopping at the front porch, the uniformed bell boys. ... I stayed for ten minutes by the door, plenty of time for me to watch the people coming and going on the escalators. Then I moved to the lobby, which was even grander. The sights I saw in the hotel that day triggered my lifelong interest in hotels."

Soon after, El Zyr enrolled in the prestigious Swiss hotel school, L'École Hôtelière de Lausanne, graduating in 1970. From there, El Zyr continued his studies at Cornell and Columbia University, then launched his

career as the chief steward at New York's Waldorf Hotel. El Zyr's career next took him to Hilton International, where he eventually returned to the UAE as the company's regional director. In the early 1980s, however, El Zyr developed an entrepreneurial bent and moved to Beirut, Lebanon, where he launched the Juicy Burger fast-food chain in 1982. From there, El Zyr once again returned to the UAE, taking up the position of vice president at Abu Dhabi National Hotel under Al Nowais.

Al Nowais, who later joined the UAE government as under secretary of the Ministry of Finance and Industry, became chairman of Rotana, while as chief executive El Zyr took over the day-to-day task of building Rotana into the leading UAE hotel management group. The company then set out developing its first property, the Beach Rotana Hotel, a 254-room five-star hotel in Abu Dhabi. That hotel, opened in 1996, was later accepted as a member of the exclusive The Leading Hotels of the World list.

ENTERING DUBAI IN 1996

Rotana next targeted the fast-growing Dubai market, which had become one of the most vibrant business markets in the entire Middle Eastern region. Rotana opened its first hotel in Dubai in 1996, with the opening of the Rimal Rotana Suites. This hotel also introduced a relatively novel concept to the region, featuring an all-suite, apartment-style rooms policy. The company later rebranded its Rotana Suites properties as Arjaan by Rotana.

By then, Rotana had strengthened its management, bringing in Nael Hashweh to develop the group's financial foundation. Hashweh, another Abu Dhabi National Hotels veteran, had also spent 11 years with the Intercontinental Hotel Company, developing expertise in hotel finance and management. At the same time, the group hired Imad Elias, another industry veteran, in order to lead the group's international marketing effort. Elias's own career included 22 years with Hilton International. Elias, who became Rotana's vice president and chief operating officer, was credited with developing the company's successful strategic marketing arm.

Rotana added a second Dubai property, the Al Bustan Rotana, in 1997. This five-star hotel also gained membership among The Leading Hotels of the World, and paved the way for the group's further expansion in that UAE state. Rotana continued to progress strongly into the end of the decade, and by 1998 had signed management contracts for 10 hotels in Abu Dhabi and Dubai, as well as its first hotel in Al-Ain. By the end of

KEY DATES

1992: Rotana Hotel Management Corporation is founded by Nasser Al Nowais and Selim El Zyr in Abu Dhabi.

1996: Company opens its first hotel under management, the Beach Rotana.

1999: Company signs its first international management contract in Beirut.

2006: Rotana launches its mid-market brand, Centro Hotels; company sells 40 percent of its shares in a private placement.

2010: Rotana announces plans to go public as early as 2012.

the decade, the company had added the 135-suite Rihab Rotana in Dubai, which opened in 1999; and the Trade Centre Rotana, providing 400 rooms near Dubai's World Trade Centre. These were followed by two new UAE properties, the 100-room Rotana Suites in Muscat, and the 250-room Fujairah Rotana Hotel, both opened in 2000.

MIDDLE EAST EXPANSION IN 2000

The company's vision, however, soon extended beyond the UAE. Rotana targeted growth throughout the Middle East and North African markets, with plans to expand its portfolio to include properties in all of the region's major cities. The company took a first step in this direction with the opening of the Gefinor Rotana Hotel in Beirut, Lebanon, in 1999. Next, the company targeted Egypt, which remained one of the most popular tourism destinations in the region. In 2000, the company added two sites in that country, the Coral Beach Tiran, in Sharm El Sheikh, and the Coral Beach Al Arish.

By then, Rotana's total portfolio had grown to 15 properties. The company had also been developing its amenities, including its own health club and spa brand, Zen, and a range of restaurants. By 2001, Rotana's restaurant operations included 50 outlets. The company's payroll had also increased significantly, growing to 3,000 employees by then.

Rotana remained on the lookout for new hotel management properties. This led the group into Syria in 2002, when the group took over the management contract for the Queen Center Rotana Suites, slated to

open in Damascus in 2005. In that year, also, the company completed a $68 million expansion of its original Beach Rotana hotel. As a result, that property became the single-largest hotel in Abu Dhabi, with nearly 560 rooms.

MID-MARKET BRAND IN 2006

Rotana's portfolio continued to grow through the first half of the decade. Part of the group's success could be attributed to the growing recognition it enjoyed among the international hotel and tourism industries, as the company began building up an impressive series of awards. In 2003, the company added two new Beirut properties, the Hazmieh Rotana Hotel and the Raouche Rotana Suites, which opened in 2003 and 2005, respectively. In 2004, the company added five new management contracts, including its first in Doha and Kuwait, and three in Dubai, all scheduled to open by the end of 2006. The group's new Dubai sites included the 400-room Jumeirah Beach resort, and the construction of a $180-million, 72-story hotel.

The company moved into Sudan at mid-decade, taking on the management of the five-star Al Salam Rotana Hotel in Khartoum, which opened at the beginning of 2007. The company also teamed up with Egypt's Orascom for the first time, signing the management contract for that company's The Cove Rotana Resort & Spa, in Ras Al Khaimah in 2006. In that year, also, Rotana's founding shareholders brought in a new round of investors, in a private placement of 40 percent of the company led by SHUAA Capital. In 2007, the company announced plans to go public, targeting 2010 for its initial public offering (IPO).

Rotana's portfolio by then had grown to more than 50 properties expected to be opened by 2010. While the group continued to expand its luxury four- and five-star hotel holdings, it had also begun developing a new mid-market concept. The company first unveiled the Centro Hotels by Rotana brand in 2006, focused on building up a portfolio of three-star hotels in the UAE and Middle East. The first Centro opened in Abu Dhabi at the beginning of 2009. The company also formed a joint venture with Orascom and SHUAA to open five Centro hotels in Egypt. Rotana hoped to operate as many as 25 Centro hotels by 2014.

WORLD'S TALLEST HOTEL IN 2010

Maintaining its successful expansion, Rotana added a number of important markets at the end of the decade. These included the contract to manage its first property in Iraq, a 250-room hotel in Erbil, in the Kurdistan region, expected to open in 2010. In 2008, the company also signed a contract to manage a luxury hotel in Bagdad, the Shams Rotana, under construction in the International Green Zone in that city and expected to be completed in 2012. Also in 2008, Rotana reached an agreement with SHUAA Capital Saudi Arabia to develop 17 hotel properties across that country, for a total of more than 5,000 rooms.

For this, Rotana rolled out a new brand in 2008, Rayhaan Hotels by Rotana, an alcohol-free hotel concept in accordance with the Islamic ban on alcohol consumption. The first Rayhaan hotel opened in Mecca in 2009. The company applied the brand to its high-profile 72-story hotel project in Dubai, which at last opened at the beginning of 2010 under the Rose Rayhaan name. That property then claimed to be the world's tallest hotel.

Amid the global recession, the hotel and tourism market contracted sharply at the end of the decade. For 2009, Rotana reported a 30 percent drop in revenues (but did not reveal its actual sales figures). Nonetheless, the company remained committed to its expansion across the Middle East and North Africa region. The company already managed, or held contracts to manage, 70 properties by 2012. At the same time, the group targeted as many as 10 to 15 new hotel openings per year, suggesting that the group's portfolio could easily top 100 properties by then. While the company had been forced to postpone its IPO, it reaffirmed its interest in going public, possibly by as early as 2012. In the meantime, Rotana had grown into one of the largest hotel management companies in one of the world's most dynamic markets.

M. L. Cohen

PRINCIPAL SUBSIDIARIES

Beach Rotana Hotel and Towers.

PRINCIPAL DIVISIONS

Hotels; Restaurants; Spas.

PRINCIPAL OPERATING UNITS

Arjaan Hotel Apartments by Rotana; Centro Hotels by Rotana; Rayhaan Hotels & Resorts by Rotana; Rotana Hotels & Resorts.

PRINCIPAL COMPETITORS

Hilton Hotels Corp.; Dubai World; Orascom Group; DUTCO Transport Company L.L.C.; Al Hamed Enterprises; Caisse de Depot et de Gestion; The Emirates Group; Ahmad Hamad Algosaibi and Brothers; Tamimi Group.

FURTHER READING

Parsons, Matt, "Jordan's Revival Reflected by Rotana's Hotel Plan," *Travel Trade Gazette UK & Ireland*, April 6, 2007, p. 21.

Rai, Bindu, "Rotana Records 30% Drop in 2009 Hotel Revenues," *Emirates Business 24-7*, January 7, 2010.

"Room for Expansion," *Middle East MICE & Events*, September 26, 2009.

"Rotana Hotel to Be 'World's Tallest,'" *Travel Trade Gazette UK & Ireland*, November 20, 2009, p. 16.

"Rotana: New Names, New Products," *Arabian Business*, March 31, 2008.

"Rotana Storms Ahead with Expansion Plans," *Travel & Tourism*, March 1, 2010.

"Rotana to Launch Mid-Market Centro Brand," *Hotels*, January 2006, p. 12.

"Rotana to Manage Hotels in Iraq," *CPI Financial*, May 5, 2009.

Sambidge, Andy, "Rotana Commits to MENA Expansion Despite Downturn," *Arabian Business*, September 24, 2009.

———, "Rotana Eyes 100% Occupancy for Dubai Shopping Fest," *Arabian Business*, January 25, 2010.

Scoviak, Mary, "Dubai's New Oases," *Hotels*, June 2006, p. 36.

RTI International Metals
Inc.

Westpointe Corporate Center One
1550 Coraopolis Heights Road, 5th Floor
Pittsburgh, Pennsylvania 15108-2973
U.S.A.
Telephone: (412) 893-0026
Fax: (412) 893-0027
Web site: http://www.rti-intl.com

Public Company
Incorporated: 1951 as Mallory-Sharon Titanium
    Corporation
Employees: 1,643
Sales: $609.9 million (2008)
Stock Exchanges: New York
Ticker Symbol: RTI
NAICS: 331491 Nonferrous Metal (Except Copper and
    Aluminum) Rolling, Drawing, and Extruding

∎ ∎ ∎

RTI International Metals, Inc., is one of the world's
major producers of titanium products, dividing its business
among three divisions: Titanium, Fabrication, and
Distribution. The company produces a variety of milled
titanium parts, including bars, billets, bloom, ingot,
pipe, extrusions, plate, sheet, slab, strip, tubing, and
wire. RTI also makes custom designed and manufactured
assemblies and machine parts from titanium, and
offers value-added services such as heat treating, shearing,
and water jet cutting as well as stocking and inventory
management programs.

Markets served by RTI include aerospace (structural
air frames, engine components, and other uses), defense
(airplanes, tanks, howitzers, and other uses), energy
(drill pipe, down hole tubing, and drilling risers and
other parts used in offshore drilling platforms), medical
(wheelchairs, spectacle frames, surgical devices, dental
implants, bone screws and plates, and joint replacements),
and sporting equipment (including golf clubs
and tees, bicycle frames, baseball bats, lacrosse sticks,
tennis rackets, skis, camping equipment, and
horseshoes). In addition to its corporate headquarters in
Pittsburgh, Pennsylvania, RTI maintains operations in
12 other U.S. cities, as well as Canada, England, France,
and China. RTI is a public company listed on the New
York Stock Exchange.

POST-WORLD WAR II ORIGINS

According to *Business Week,* "Titanium earned its reputation
as a wonder metal at the dawn of the Space Age,
when NASA engineers used the light, superstrong material
for jet turbines and rocket parts." RTI's origin
predates the 1958 creation of NASA (National
Aeronautics and Space Administration). Because it is
lighter than steel and stronger than aluminum, enjoys
excellent heat tolerance, and has few peers in its
resistance to corrosion, titanium became an ideal material
for the jet and atomic age that emerged after World
War II and a new industry took shape. DuPont and
Titanium Metals Corporation produced the basic metal,
called sponge. This was a tricky process because while
titanium was the fourth most common element on
Earth, it readily combined with nearly every solid as
well as such common gases as oxygen and nitrogen.

COMPANY PERSPECTIVES

The mission statement of RTI International Metals, Inc., is to deliver superior quality products, services, and solutions to our global customers on time, and in a manner that maximizes long-term shareholder value, while providing an environment that promotes safety, employee satisfaction, ethical conduct, continuous improvement, and corporate responsibility in the communities in which RTI operates.

Converting sponge into ingots was also a difficult task, requiring high temperatures and working in a vacuum or under cover of helium, argon, or another inert gas to grind up and melt the sponge into ingots. One of three companies established to turn the sponge into ingots and then fabricate it into sheets, strips, bars, wire, and other usable forms, was RTI's predecessor: Mallory-Sharon Titanium Corporation. It was founded in Niles, Ohio, in 1951, a joint venture between Sharon Steel, a now defunct Pittsburgh steel maker, and P.R. Mallory & Co., a battery company that eventually adopted the Duracell name.

The titanium industry enjoyed robust growth into the mid-1950s. For its part, Mallory-Sharon was shipping 5,000 pounds of the metal by 1952. A year later shipments increased to 120,000 pounds, and the company opened its first titanium research lab. Three new furnaces were opened in 1954, and the following year the company acquired Sharon Steel's rolling mill division, also located in Niles. With the addition of a new melt shop boosting production, titanium shipments reached 2.5 million pounds in 1956. The titanium industry experienced a slump in 1957, caused by the cancellation of some military projects and aircraft orders that were stretched. Mallory-Sharon's earnings fell from $3 million to $1.2 million. It was the start of a boom-or-bust syndrome that would characterize the titanium business for the next half-century.

RENAMED REACTIVE METALS: 1960

Mallory-Sharon experienced a number of changes in 1957 that continued into the 1960s. It changed ownership in 1957 and was renamed Mallory-Sharon Metals Corporation, and also joined with National Distillers and Chemical Corporation that year to establish a joint venture in Ashtabula, Ohio, called Reactive Metals. In 1958 Reactive Metals was folded into Mallory-Sharon,

which also acquired Stauffer Chemical of Ashtabula; Mallory-Schwartzkopf of Huntsville, Alabama; and a National Distillers' subsidiary, Johnson & Funk Metallurgical Corporation of Wooster, Ohio. National Distillers, as a result, became a one-third owner of Mallory-Sharon, which was then renamed Reactive Metals Inc. (RMI) in 1960. National Distillers then bought out P.R. Mallory and Sharon Steel to gain full control of the business. In 1964 U.S. Steel became a half partner.

The titanium industry enjoyed an up-cycle in the early 1960s spurred by the increase in passenger jet travel and production of the Boeing 747 and Lockheed C5A, the former requiring 20 to 30 tons of titanium in each craft and the latter 15 tons. In addition, there was a demand for titanium alloys for other commercial and military jet planes as well as jet engines and other aircraft components. Moreover, NASA was in the midst of its push for a moon landing and required titanium for its projects. To meet increased demand for titanium for the Apollo program, RMI launched a $70 million, four-year expansion program in 1966 that included new processing equipment in Niles and Ashtabula. By the end of the 1960s the titanium industry increased shipments to 32 million pounds.

BECOMING RMI COMPANY IN 1971

Reactive Metals was renamed RMI Company in 1971 (and incorporated in Ohio four years later as RMI Titanium Company), the same time as another downturn in demand for titanium, the result of cutbacks in commercial and military aircraft programs as well as competition from Japan and Russia. The situation grew so dire that RMI and the United States' other major titanium producer, Titanium Metals Corporation of America, told the government that they would be forced to close down unless they could sell titanium to the defense stockpile, created to protect the United States from dependence on foreign supplies of titanium and other scarce metals in time of war. Thus, the companies were allowed to sell sponge to the stockpile, but were required to buy back the stockpile at 1972 prices if the sponge was ever declared excess and authorized for disposal.

In 1973 the stockpile was so declared but a year later a titanium shortage developed and RMI and Titanium Metals Corporation found themselves in a position to enjoy windfall profits by acquiring the sponge at 1972 prices. The Defense Department, which now needed the titanium in the stockpile for defense contractors, was upset over the two companies essentially controlling all excess titanium in the stockpile, leading to congressional investigations that revealed poor management of the nation's defense stockpiles.

In the 1970s RMI was also involved in a price-fixing investigation conducted by the U.S. Justice Department, which in 1978 filed an antitrust suit against RMI and other titanium producers, accusing them of sharing price information to rig bids. RMI pleaded no contest to the charges in 1979 for fixing prices of titanium mill products from 1970 to 1976, and in March 1980 the matter was settled, with the company agreeing to pay a fine and cease sharing pricing information.

By the start of the 1980s, the titanium industry was shipping 46 million pounds, 45 percent of which was devoted to commercial aerospace, 38 percent to defense aerospace, and 17 percent to non-aerospace purposes. With the election of Ronald Reagan as president of the United States in 1980 came a defense buildup that led to another surge in demand for titanium. In 1981 RMI invested $8 million to increase its manufacturing capacity, and at the end of the year the company launched a $50 million modernization program, including a $20 million melt shop that opened in Niles in 1983 and a welded tub mill located in Hermitage, Pennsylvania, that opened two years later. The new capabilities allowed RMI to enter the tube and pipe market in 1982. A year later RMI entered the powder business by acquiring Salt Lake City-based Micron Metals, Inc. The company also established itself in the offshore oil and gas exploration market through the 1985 introduction of a new titanium alloy, Beta-C, which also had applications in other harsh environments.

GOING PUBLIC: 1990

RMI became a public company in 1990 when Quantum Chemical Corporation, the successor to National Distillers, liquidated its 50 percent stake through a public offering on the New York Stock Exchange. Once again, however, the industry was about to enter another difficult stretch, as the demand for titanium plummeted, due in large part to the end of the Cold War and cuts in military spending that led to the production of fewer jet fighters and cargo transport planes. Defense demand for titanium that totaled 15 million to 18 million pounds in the 1960s now tumbled to seven million pounds in 1991. As a result, RMI struggled through the first half of the decade, complicated by labor strife. When workers refused to grant wage concessions, the company elected to close two Ashtabula plants as well as implement other cost-cutting measures. To maintain the price of its stock, the company resorted to a 1-for-10 stock split. All told, RMI lost $117.4 million from 1991 to 1995.

The lean years of the first half of the 1990s prompted RMI to pursue commercial markets for titanium to offset the aviation slump, including medical devices and offshore oil and gas structures, as well as oversized titanium golf clubheads that became extremely popular during this period (sales peaked in 1997). The company also opened an office and warehouse in Birmingham, England, to drum up further business in Europe. As the economy began to pick up, RMI enjoyed a major comeback in 1996. A year later revenues improved 27 percent to $318.5 million and earnings nearly doubled to more than $60 million.

FORMATION OF HOLDING COMPANY: 1998

Mindful of the cyclical nature of the titanium business, RMI did not neglect the further development of commercial markets. In 1996 the company produced the first titanium geothermal casing, and the following year began to produce titanium golf tees. RMI was also in the market for acquisitions. In 1997 it bought a 90 percent interest in Canton, Ohio-based Galt Alloys, and a year later acquired Solon, Ohio-based New Century Metals, Inc., to enter the extrusion and specialty metals distribution sectors, and Houston-based Weld Tech Engineering to add both engineering and fabrication assets and bolster the company's services to the oil and gas industry. RMI was also reorganized during this period through the 1998 formation of an Ohio holding company that assumed the name RTI International Metals Inc.

Expansion continued on several fronts at the dawn of the new century. The company was selected by the U.S. Army in 2000 to provide the titanium components used in a new lightweight howitzer. In that year RTI also expanded its European footprint by adding German and Italian operations and acquiring a French company, Reamet, S.A., and in 2002 secured contracts to provide titanium for the Eurofighter Typhoon fighter jet and Airbus passenger liners. While these were positive developments, the company also had to contend with the adverse impact on air travel of the September 11, 2001, terrorist attacks on the United States, which led to an aircraft industry slump. By the summer of 2002, RTI was forced to close the Niles plant for a month and take other cost-cutting measures as titanium reached extremely low prices. One benefit of inexpensive titanium was that the metal could now be used in a variety of new products that bode well for the future, including bicycle frames, eyeglass frames, electronic products, watches, laptops, and cameras.

The titanium market began to recover in 2004 as aerospace and defense orders picked up, leading to the October acquisition of a Canadian company, Claro Precision Inc., a manufacturer of precision-machined components and assemblies used in the aerospace industry. A yearlong employee lockout came to an end at the close of 2004. The resulting labor deal lowered RTI's costs, better positioning the company to take advantage of improving conditions.

MOVING TO PITTSBURGH AREA

In 2006 RTI won contracts to supply titanium products for the Boeing 787 and Airbus commercial aircraft. To support this business, the company announced a $35 million expansion program to upgrade its melting and forging capabilities. A year later RTI realized record sales of $626.8 million and net income of $75.7 million and signed supplemental long-term contracts with Boeing and Airbus. The company's prospects appeared bright as it relocated its corporate headquarters from Niles to a Pittsburgh suburb in 2008 and made plans to build a new forging and rolling plant in Virginia and a sponge plant in Mississippi.

As the economy began to stall in 2008, demand for titanium softened. The Boeing 787 "Dreamliner" project was postponed and RTI was forced to delay its $400 million expansion plan, which was pushed back to 2009. Conditions grew only worse, leading to some layoffs in the spring of 2009. It became apparent to many observers that the $300 million Mississippi project would be scrapped, leading Wall Street to begin bidding up the price of RTI stock, which continued to grow as Boeing announced a new delivery and production

schedule and rumors circulated that RTI might be an acquisition target. However, demand for titanium remained deflated and the company did not anticipate an upturn in the market until the end of 2010. Despite efforts over the years to diversify and find new commercial uses for titanium, RTI remained very much dependent on commercial and military aircraft sales, and was still subject to the cyclical nature of the titanium industry.

Ed Dinger

PRINCIPAL SUBSIDIARIES

RMI Metals, Inc.; RMI Titanium Company; RTI Europe Ltd.

PRINCIPAL COMPETITORS

Allegheny Technologies Incorporated; Titanium Metals Corporation; VSMPO-AVISMA Corporation.

FURTHER READING

Aston, Adam, "A 'Magical Metal' for the Masses," *Business Week*, December 2, 2002, p. 104B.

"Company on the Rise after a Bad 5 Years," *Akron Beacon Journal*, October 21, 1996, p. D2.

Corwin, Phillip, "Proving Its Mettle," *Barron's*, July 25, 1966, p. 11.

Elliott, J. Richard, Jr., "More Titanium," *Barron's*, June 25, 1956, p. 3.

Gerdel, Thomas W., "RMI Titanium Back Up to Par," *Cleveland Plain Dealer*, July 23, 1996, p. 1C.

———, "RMI Titanium Still Losing Money as It Copes with Changing World," *Cleveland Plain Dealer*, April 14, 1992, p. 6F.

Haflich, Frank, "RTI Reverses Gear, Delays Expansion," *American Metal Market*, November 5, 2008, p. 8.

Melvin, Chuck, "RMI Titanium, Inc. Demand Is Soaring for Company's Lightweight Metal," *Cleveland Plain Dealer*, June 18, 1998, p. 7S.

Perham, John C., "Miracle Metal?" *Barron's*, March 1, 1954, p. 11.

"Reactive Metals Sold to Distiller," *New York Times*, March 1, 1962.

"RMI Titanium Inc. Hit Hard by the End of the Cold War," *Cleveland Plain Dealer*, November 15, 1992, p. 6E.

Russell, John, "RMI Titanium Turns Alloys into Gold Mine," *Akron Beacon Journal*, June 28, 1998, p. H5.

"Shifts in Steel," *Barron's National Business and Financial Weekly*, April 21, 1958, p. 11.

Stundza, Tom, "RTI Delays Expansion as 2009 Demand Outlook Has Softened," *Purchasing*, December 11, 2008.

Thomas, Jo, "Millions Held Lost on Sale of Minerals," *New York Times*, July 16, 1979.

Vinarsky, Cynthia, "Niles, Ohio-Based Metal Firm Sees Stock Tumble with Aerospace-Industry Fall," *Vindicator*, September 21, 2001.

St. Jude Children's Research Hospital, Inc.

---

262 Danny Thomas Place
Memphis, Tennessee 38105
U.S.A.
Telephone: (901) 595-3300
Toll Free: (866) 278-5833
Fax: (901) 595-3103
Web site: http://www.stjude.org

Nonprofit Organization
Incorporated: 1959
Employees: 3,500
Operating Revenues: $1.05 billion (2009 est.)
NAICS: 622310 Specialty (Except Psychiatric and Substance Abuse) Hospitals

■ ■ ■

St. Jude Children's Research Hospital, Inc., is one of the leading medical institutions involved in research and patient care for catastrophic diseases in children, specifically cancers, sickle-cell disease, genetic disorders, infectious diseases, and some immune deficiencies. Research specialties include the molecular, genetic, and chemical origins of disease. The hospital's operations are based on a "bench to bed" patient care philosophy, in which research from the laboratory is implemented as patient care as quickly as possible. As such, St. Jude's facilities are designed to integrate research and clinical facilities in order to foster interaction between doctors and scientists.

Patient care is based on the requirements of research protocols. Children are never turned away from St. Jude

because of their parents' inability to pay. The hospital provides care to about 5,700 patients per year, treating more than 260 patients daily, primarily on an outpatient basis. Children admitted to the hospital tend to remain in the hospital for several months, so St. Jude offers classroom education and generates fun through sibling involvement, holiday parties, and recreational activities. St. Jude employs some of the top doctors and scientists in the world, and is especially renowned for developing groundbreaking treatments for pediatric cancers.

DANNY THOMAS'S PRAYERFUL PROMISE

St. Jude Children's Research Hospital was the inspiration of entertainer Danny Thomas (1914–1991). In distraught moments Thomas found himself praying to St. Jude Thaddeus, the patron saint of hopeless causes. He asked St. Jude for guidance and promised to build a shrine to the saint. Thomas prospered as a Detroit radio comedian, a Chicago nightclub entertainer, and as a film and television actor. During the 1950s and 1960s, he won Emmy awards for his long-running comedy television shows *Make Room for Daddy* and *The Danny Thomas Show.* He produced many popular shows, including the *Dick Van Dyke Show.*

Having found his road to success, Thomas began the process of determining how to fulfill his vow to St. Jude. As he discussed this with his wife and friends, the idea emerged of establishing a unique hospital devoted to curing catastrophic diseases in children. In 1951 colleagues in the entertainment industry helped him form the St. Jude Foundation of California, and they began fund-raising through benefit shows. Thomas's friends in the entertainment industry, including Frank Sinatra, Bob Hope, and Sammy Davis, performed at benefit concerts. Cardinal Stritch, whom Thomas had known as an altar boy in Toledo, suggested Memphis as a populated area where more children could be helped, and he referred Thomas to influential businessmen in the city.

Thomas traveled to Memphis and began developing relationships with local supporters. Plans for the hospital quickened in 1955, when Thomas promised to raise $1.5 million. Although they were not convinced that Memphis needed another children's hospital, the Memphis Steering Committee formed with an agreement to raise $500,000 locally. Dr. Lemuel Diggs, a member of the medical advisory committee, recommended that Thomas consider a research hospital for children with catastrophic illnesses. At this time, no institution in the world was dedicated to such a purpose.

By 1953 Thomas had gained national recognition with the launch of *Make Room for Daddy*, and his new celebrity status contributed to successful fund-raising. In an appearance on "Break the Bank," a national television show, Thomas asked children to break their piggy banks and donate one dollar to help other children. Thousands of children and adults responded. The incident established average donors as the primary base of support for St. Jude Hospital.

Thomas contributed personal funds to the hospital. Thomas kicked off the first benefit concert in Memphis with a song he wrote for the occasion, "Bring Back My Beale Street," in honor of Memphis's famous blues district. Proceeds from the recording were donated to St. Jude Hospital. Also, he donated all of the income he received from making television commercials.

FROM PROMISE TO REALITY

With funds for construction in hand, Thomas faced the question of how to fund daily operations. Committed to the idea of providing medical care regardless of ability to pay, Thomas approached Arab-American clubs around the country. He asked them to contribute to the hospital as a sign of gratitude for the freedoms their immigrant forefathers enjoyed in the United States. In 1957 the American Lebanese Syrian Associated Charities (ALSAC) fund-raising arm of St. Jude was established with a commitment to raise $300,000 annually.

St. Jude Foundation purchased land in downtown Memphis and held a groundbreaking ceremony in 1958. However, construction was delayed until 1960. In the meantime, St. Jude Hospital established bylaws and incorporated in 1959. The Memphis Steering Committee evolved into the Board of Governors.

St. Jude hired Dr. Donald Pinkel as medical director. At age 34 Pinkel had already distinguished himself in the application of chemotherapy for pediatric cancer. Under Pinkel's guidance St. Jude established an unusual, for its time, collaborative relationship between the doctors and biomedical scientists. They worked closely in the development and evaluation of cancer treatments with the goal of finding both the cause and a cure for leukemia and other diseases.

St. Jude Hospital opened in downtown Memphis in 1962. The five wings of the building housed only 38 patient beds, as the bulk of the 85,000-square-foot space was dedicated to clinical laboratories and basic research. Dr. Pinkel wanted to accommodate more research space than planned, so St. Jude formed an agreement with neighboring St. Joseph Hospital to use surgery facilities there. With a staff of 100 doctors, scientists, nurses, and administrators, St. Jude cared for 126 patients its first year, and another 300 patients in 1963 and 1964.

RESEARCH AND SUCCESSES DURING THE SIXTIES

Although St. Jude offered general pediatric care to poor children, the hospital focused on leukemia, a blood cancer that affects bone marrow and the body's overall immunity. Acute lymphoblastic leukemia (ALL), the most common form of childhood cancer, had a 4 percent survival rate. Children with ALL suffered from low production of white blood cells, allowing cancer and other infections to spread throughout the body.

Within three years of opening, doctors at St. Jude Hospital began what would become a prestigious record of research on how to diagnose and treat leukemia in children. In 1965 Dr. Warren Thomas developed the first method for diagnosing solid tumors from an immunological point of view. In 1966 Dr. Pinkel decided that St. Jude would stop treatment for patients with leukemia in remission who were cancer free. He viewed

KEY DATES

1951: Danny Thomas establishes the St. Jude Foundation and begins fund-raising.
1957: ALSAC, the fund-raising organization for St. Jude, is established.
1962: St. Jude Hospital opens in downtown Memphis.
1990s: Series of expansion projects attracts top doctors and scientists to St. Jude.
2010: St. Jude becomes involved in the Pediatric Cancer Genome Project.

long-term treatment as harmful to children, so he designed a program of regular checkups to ensure appropriate care was given and clinical evaluations concluded. The high-risk decision improved the quality of life for patients, and it allowed St. Jude to provide care for more children. By 1968 the hospital attended to 1,000 patients annually.

Research at St. Jude revolutionized the way doctors perceived and treated childhood cancer. Dr. Omor Hustu discovered that treatment with both chemotherapy and radiation improved the survival rate of children with Ewing sarcoma, bone tumors that are frequently malignant. In 1971 Pinkel found that treatment with both chemotherapy and radiation of the brain and spinal cord cured more than half of children with ALL. Pinkel also developed a Total Therapies protocol for ALL that applied a combination of drugs for optimal effectiveness. Unthinkable at the time, these forms of treatment showed pediatric cancer to be 50 percent curable.

EXPANSION OF FACILITIES, REPUTATION

After 10 years in operation, St. Jude required more space to accommodate its growing research and the accompanying clinical care. In 1971 St. Jude began construction on a seven-story, 118,000-square-foot building. Completed in 1975, the facility housed two floors for patient care and three for research. In 1981, St. Jude constructed a research facility with state-of-the-art technology for handling biological matter and research laboratories.

Despite its larger size, under the leadership of Dr. Alvin Mauer, who took over as medical director in 1973, St. Jude sustained its intimate style of personal care. Mauer stressed not simply easing the pain of sick

and dying children but boosting survival rates and the possibility of a healthy quality of life for its patients.

Research at this time included clinical study of a new drug combination for the treatment of recurrent leukemia. Another study found numerous variations of ALL in children, which led to further developments in understanding and treating ALL. In 1977 doctors at St. Jude discovered a new treatment for neuroblastoma. The second most common form of solid tumor in children, neuroblastoma affected the peripheral nervous system and carried a high death rate. The treatment proved effective for 55 percent of patients.

Dr. Joseph Simone became head of St. Jude Hospital in 1983. Under his leadership, St. Jude narrowed its field of care to childhood cancer and related diseases exclusively in 1984. The change underlined the hospital's growing reputation for effective specialized research. That year St. Jude doctors made several discoveries which contributed to an understanding of how well patients responded to various drugs and other forms of treatment.

Simone oversaw the beginnings of a 10-year, $125 million expansion and renovation of St. Jude's facilities. The project doubled the hospital's size, adding more than 350,000 square feet, including the five-story Danny Thomas Research Tower, which opened in 1991. Hospital operations were temporarily located to the building while the original hospital was demolished. The new Patient Care Center opened in 1994, and the tower became available for basic scientific research. The state-of-the-art laboratories and equipment helped Simone to attract some of the country's leading doctors and scientists. They, in turn, improved St. Jude's status as a research institution through publication of numerous articles and papers.

Throughout its growth, the ongoing fund-raising efforts of ALSAC continued to sustain St. Jude's research and operations. Celebrities continued to play a role in fund-raising, such as in the Country Cares for Kids radiothon, featuring live performances by country music stars. Richard Shadyac, the CEO of ALSAC at the time, improved the organization's fund-raising strategy, as he restructured direct-mail solicitations and developed a donor services department to encourage gift planning from wealthy philanthropists.

NEW AREAS OF RESEARCH & OFF-SITE EXPANSION

New research activities at this time included tumor cell biology, and St. Jude established itself as a leader in brain tumor research. Innovations in immunological research led St. Jude to become involved in AIDS/HIV research. In 1992 St. Jude and two Memphis-area hospitals opened a pediatric AIDS Clinical Trial Unit, for research on the effects of new AIDS drugs on children. Other areas of research included sickle-cell anemia, a blood disease, and infections as side effects of illness or treatment, such as pneumonia and strep throat.

Dr. Arthur Nienhuis came to St. Jude from the National Institutes of Health in 1993, bringing further prestige to St. Jude. Applying his expertise in gene therapy, genetic testing, hematology, and bone marrow transplant, Nienhuis organized 12 new research laboratories focused on the genetic basis for cancer development. Also, he established the Department of Developmental Neurobiology in 1995, marking St. Jude's entry into brain tumor research. The $20 million investment attracted leading neuroscientists to St. Jude.

Expansion at St. Jude took the form of affiliations with several hospitals. These hospitals participated in St. Jude protocols and extended St. Jude's knowledge and available care without requiring patients to travel to St. Jude as often. They also expanded St. Jude's base of clinical research.

St. Jude initiated the International Outreach Program to developing countries. Doctors traveled to Brazil, Chile, El Salvador, China, Russia, and other countries, providing training in treatment protocols, adapted to available local resources. ALSAC established a new position to concentrate on funding for international outreach efforts.

1999 PLANS FOR GROWTH AND IMPROVEMENT

St. Jude continuously labored to resolve its ever-growing need for new facilities. St. Jude redesigned and expanded the outpatient center in 1999 to accommodate its 47,000 outpatient visits per year. In 1999 St. Jude initiated a five-year plan to further expand and renovate hospital facilities. With construction of five new buildings, the project more than doubled existing space, to 2.5 million square feet, and space for inpatient care increased from 60 to 78 beds. St. Jude also acquired and renovated the neighboring facility formerly housed by St. Joseph Hospital.

The expansion project accommodated new and existing research departments, the latter involving the Department of Immunology. In 2005, St. Jude established the Department of Epidemiology and Cancer Control, for research into causes of childhood cancer and preventive medicine, and the Department of Chemical Biology and Therapeutics, intended for drug development. The new Good Manufacturing Practices,

established in 2003, provided St. Jude scientists with a "clean room" to produce small batches of vaccines and specialized treatments to be used in clinical research and patient care. It was the first on-site pediatric research center in the nation dedicated to drug and treatment production.

Hospital improvements included acquisition of state-of-the-art technology. In 2003 St. Jude purchased a high-powered nuclear magnetic resonance (NMR) imaging machine capable of providing clearer, more detailed pictures of DNA cells than smaller NMR or MRI equipment. The new machine allowed doctors to see the structural damage caused by cancer as well as the effects of treatment. St. Jude was one of two hospitals in the United States to own one of the $2.3 million magnets.

Marlo Thomas, actress and daughter of Danny Thomas, contributed to the fund-raising efforts of AL-SAC at this time. With help from a new celebrity fund-raising office in Hollywood, Ms Thomas initiated the Thanks and Giving annual program in 2004.

OTHER FACILITIES

In 2007 St. Jude opened the Chili's Care Center. The seven-story, 340,000-square-foot facility housed major research initiatives in both diagnostic and therapeutic radiology. The main motivation for constructing the Chili's Care Center was driven by the need to expand and modernize facilities for the Radiological Sciences department, including Diagnostic Imaging and Radiation Oncology. The patient care areas were some of the last to be renovated from the initial 1962 and 1975 building. Chili's Bar & Grill funded the $134 million project.

A year after opening the Chili's Care Center, St. Jude began a $16 million construction project to renovate 90,000 square feet and to add 8,000 square feet on the first floor of the Patient Care Center. Rapid growth in treatment of sickle-cell anemia and solid tumors required St. Jude to address a shortage in space for examinations. The project involved adding 16 new patient rooms to the outpatient clinic and combining the clinic with the central pharmacy on the first floor. Other facility reorganization allowed for St. Jude to double its space for physical rehabilitation, to renovate the school's classrooms, and to add administrative offices.

St. Jude formed associations with other hospitals to share resources and information, thus expanding without new facilities. In July 2007 St. Jude formed an affiliation with Rady Children's Hospital in San Diego and University of California at San Diego. The collaboration on scientific and clinical research contributed to St. Jude's base of information while spreading St. Jude's treatment protocols to patients in San Diego. Also, St. Jude contributed $7 million toward the upgrade of neurosurgery facilities at Le Bonheur Children's Medical Center in Memphis, where all St. Jude patients with brain tumors receive neurosurgery.

INTO THE 21ST CENTURY WITH GENETIC RESEARCH

Its earlier entry into genetic research placed St. Jude among the premier research institutions concentrating on pediatric cancer research. New research at St. Jude confirmed the long-held opinion that the e-Myc gene contributed to tumor malignancy in mice. The 2002 discovery implied that confirmation of the gene's role in human tumor growth would lead to improvement of anticancer treatment. In 2005 St. Jude researchers discovered a mechanism that stimulates the p53 protein, known to assist the body's resistance to stress that damaged cells by mutating DNA. The discovery was expected to lead to treatments that increased p53 activity in order to reduce cancer causing cell mutations.

Research in cell immunology and genetics came to fruition. In 2006 research on blood stem cells showed potential of transplanting cells from family members to treat leukemia resistant to chemotherapy. In June 2007 St. Jude released results from a study on the role of certain genetic proteins and enzymes in supporting or preventing apoptosis, the self-destruction of cells into cancerous tumors. Another genetic study found three proteins that hindered the growth of certain kinds of brain tumors, showing potential for preventive medicine. Scientists identified genetic mutations involved in the development of chronic myelogenous leukemia, a discovery that could lead to new treatments for this frequently fatal type of ALL.

Three years of research by Dr. Charles Mullighan in the Department of Pathology, culminated in knowledge of how DNA mutated a normal, healthy cell into a leukemic cell. After studying 20,000 genes for each of 242 patients, Mullighan discovered a common mutation in 30 percent of ALL patients, a missing sequence of proteins in the PAX5 gene. The PAX5, EBP, and Ikaros genes were mutated in 40 percent of patients. Potential applications for this new knowledge involved diagnostic testing, and further research involved experimental modeling of genetic mutations and monitoring ongoing genetic mutations.

St. Jude began collaboration in genetic research with the Washington University School of Medicine's Genome Center in January 2010. Washington University was the first institution to decode the entire genetic sequence of a patient with cancer, a woman with leukemia. The collaborative project involved complete sequencing of genomes of children with leukemia. For this project (called the St. Jude Children's Research Hospital—Washington University School of Medicine Pediatric Cancer Genome Project), St. Jude brought more than 50,000 DNA samples from the cancerous tumors of 600 children, comprising one of the largest repositories of genetic information on pediatric cancer. As the primary sponsor, Kay Jewelers pledged a $20 million donation to the $65 million project, expected to take three years to complete.

Mary Tradii

PRINCIPAL SUBSIDIARIES

Children's GMP, LLC.

PRINCIPAL DIVISIONS

St. Jude Children's Research Hospital has more than 100 departments ranging from Human Resources to Structural Biology, Pathology, Oncology, and Epidemiology.

PRINCIPAL COMPETITORS

Children's National Medical Center; City of Hope; Nationwide Children's Hospital Inc.

FURTHER READING

"Cells Re-Energize to Come Back from the Brink of Death," *Space Daily*, June 7, 2007.

"Children's Hospital Launches Thanks & Giving Campaign to Fight Childhood Disease," *Managed Care Weekly*, December 13, 2004, p. 130.

Cotton, Richard C., "Mullighan's Childhood Leukemia Research Leads to Big Discovery," *Memphis Business Journal*, November 28, 2008.

"Danny Thomas," *Broadcasting & Cable*, November 10, 1997, p. HF38.

Fischman, Josh, "For the Sickest Kids," *U.S. News & World Report*, July 12, 2004, p. 68.

Jones, Palmer Thomason, *From His Promise: A History of AL-SAC and St. Jude Children's Research Hospital*, Memphis: Guild Bindery Press, 1996.

"Mechanism Controlling Response to DNA Damage Discovered," *Biopharm International*, November 2005, p. 16.

"St. Jude Researcher Discovers Tumor Gene," *Memphis Business Journal*, October 3, 2002.

Sells, Toby, "Cyclotron Can Produce Radioactive Atoms, Helping St. Jude Researchers Fight Cancer," *Memphis Business Journal*, December 14, 2007.

———, "St. Jude's Patient Care Center Undergoing $16M Renovation, Adding New Space," *Memphis Business Journal,* November 28, 2008.

Shepard, Scott, "St. Jude Buys Super Magnet," *Memphis Business Journal,* May 16, 2003.

"That Girl's Crusade: Cake, Confetti, Unheard-of Cure Rates; Marlo Thomas Talks about the Miraculous Hospital Her Father Founded," *O: The Oprah Magazine,* December 2004, p. 80.

"Washington University, St. Jude Team on $65M Pediatric Cancer Genome Project," *Memphis Business Journal,* January 25, 2010.

Saks Incorporated

12 East 49th Street
New York, New York 10017
U.S.A.
Telephone: (205) 940-5305
Fax: (205) 940-4987
Web site: http://www.saksincorporated.com

Public Company
Incorporated: 1919
Employees: 13,000
Sales: $3.03 billion (2009)
Stock Exchanges: New York
Ticker Symbol: SKS
NAICS: 452110 Department Stores; 454111 Electronic Shopping; 454113 Mail-Order Houses

■ ■ ■

Saks Incorporated, once one of the top domestic department store operators, focuses solely on its luxury Saks Fifth Avenue business, which consists of about 53 Saks Fifth Avenue department stores and 55 Off 5th outlet stores. Founded in 1919 as Proffitt's, the firm bought several department store chains during the 1980s and 1990s, which it later sold. The company also does e-business by catalog and at www.saks.com.

UNDER THE PROFFITT FAMILY: 1919–84

Proffitt's was founded in 1919 by David W. Proffitt. It was a department store in Maryville, Tennessee (near Knoxville), selling everything from clothing and bedding to furniture and farm implements. Evidently no place for sophisticates, it attracted customers to anniversary sales during the 1920s and 1930s by hurling live poultry from its second floor windows. Another Proffitt's was opened later in Athens, Tennessee. D. W.'s son Harwell took charge of Proffitt's in 1958. He closed the Maryville store in 1962, moving to a strip shopping center his family had developed a mile away in suburban Alcoa. "My father thought that was awful," he told a *Norfolk Virginian-Pilot* reporter in 1993. "Then, after we doubled our sales, he thought it was just great."

Proffitt's opened a store in Knoxville's first mall in 1972 and a store in Oak Ridge two years later. In 1984, when a fifth store opened in another Knoxville mall, D. W.'s heirs, including another son and daughter, began looking for a buyer who would keep the family on as managers. They found their man in Brad Martin, who, at the age of 21, became in 1972 the youngest state legislator in Tennessee history. While serving in the state assembly for 10 years he earned two degrees, pieced together deals to build shopping centers in three states, and became a venture capitalist. Martin and his partners bought Proffitt's in October 1984 for $14 million. At this time the company had annual sales of about $40 million.

FIRST EXPANSION MOVES: 1987–93

After Martin pulled out of a planned race for governor in 1986, he began to take a more active role in his investment. He succeeded Harwell Proffitt as chairman

The company is primarily a fashion retail organization, offering a wide assortment of distinctive fashion apparel, shoes, accessories, jewelry, cosmetics, and gifts. SFA stores are primarily free-standing stores in exclusive shopping destinations or anchor stores in upscale regional malls.

of the company in 1987 and Harwell's son, Fred, as chief executive officer in 1989. Proffitt's went public in 1987, offering 28 percent of its common stock at $8 a share. The company had record net sales of $43.5 million and net income of $1.4 million in fiscal 1987 (the year ended January 31, 1987) but also had a long-term debt of $18.4 million.

The $8 million or so raised by public subscription enabled Proffitt's to buy the Loveman's, Inc., five-unit chain, based in nearby Chattanooga, in 1988 for $9.3 million in cash and notes. Proffitt's thereby doubled in size overnight but also assumed Loveman's considerable debt, weakening earnings in 1989 and 1990. During 1990 Proffitt's also opened stores in Chattanooga and Asheville, North Carolina, but closed one that was unprofitable.

By selling more stock at $12 a share in 1992, Martin raised an added $29 million. He then bought eight stores from Hess Department Stores Inc., seven in eastern Tennessee and the eighth in Bristol, Virginia. In April 1993 Proffitt's bought eight more stores from Hess (five in the Hampton Roads area of Virginia, two in Kentucky, and one in Georgia) for $7.4 million, selling more stock to finance the purchase and to pay for store renovations. Two months later Proffitt's bought two more Hess stores in Richmond, Virginia, for about $1.6 million.

This acquisition proved to be one of Martin's few mistakes because Hess's unprofitable stores cut into company income. Revenues rose from $128 million in fiscal 1993 to $201 million in fiscal 1994, but net income dropped from $6.7 million to $5.7 million. In December 1996 Dillard Department Stores agreed to buy the Hampton Roads and Richmond stores for an undisclosed sum, and Proffitt's took a $2 million after-tax charge on the sale.

MCRAE'S ACQUISITION: 1994

Martin's next move was bolder. In March 1994 he purchased McRae's, Inc., a retailer about twice Proffitt's

size, for $176 million in cash and $32 million in notes. Founded in 1902 by Samuel P. McRae in Jackson, Mississippi, as a dry goods store, McRae's was a privately held chain with 28 stores (compared with Proffitt's 25) in Mississippi, Alabama, Louisiana, and Florida, with $419 million in sales in 1993. It was strong in home furnishings, men's apparel, and cosmetics. Thirteen of its 14 Alabama stores had been purchased from Pizitz, Inc., in 1987. In acquiring McRae's, Proffitt's assumed about $109 million in long-term debt and other financing and also paid $18 million to purchase four regional mall stores owned by McRae family partnerships. The McRae's stores retained their name and operated as a subsidiary.

Despite the high price Proffitt's paid, investor reaction was favorable. McRae's was regarded as one of the most successful family-owned businesses in the United States, its sales having grown from only $1 million in 1955 to $10 million in 1970. Just months before the sale, Richard McRae Jr., president and chief executive officer, told the *Daily News Record*, "Our debt-to-equity ratio is the lowest it's been since the early 1970s, yet all of our growth has been from internal financing. We are sound. No one has ever lost a dollar by selling McRae's. … In fact, we have a higher Dun & Bradstreet rating than any of our competitors."

YOUNKERS ACQUISITION: 1996

With the acquisition of McRae's, Proffitt's revenues swelled to $617 million in fiscal 1995, and its net income grew to $16.1 million. In April 1995 Proffitt's acquired a majority interest in Parks-Belk Co., owner and operator of four Tennessee department stores. This transaction paled in relation to Proffitt's purchase, in February 1996, of Younkers, Inc., a midwestern 53-store chain with annual sales slightly larger than Proffitt's own.

Based in Des Moines, Iowa, Younkers had a history even longer than Proffitt's or McRae's, dating back to 1856. Acquired by Equitable of Iowa in 1979, it became an independent company again in 1992 but soon found itself the object of a takeover bid by Carson, Pirie Scott & Co. Younkers's management turned down Carson's offer of about $163 million for the company, but succumbed to Proffitt's bid of $216 million. Like McRae's, Younkers continued to operate under its own name as both a division and a subsidiary of Proffitt's. Counting Younkers, Proffitt's revenues for fiscal 1996 surpassed $1.3 billion. Younkers was described by Martin as a "fashion-driven" business. Proffitt's converted its shoe departments from leased to in-house, and Martin said there were opportunities for the chain to grow in cosmetics and accessories.

<table>
</table>

KEY DATES

1919: David Proffitt founds first store in Maryville, Tennessee.
1984: Brad Martin buys the Proffitt's chain.
1988: Firm makes its first major acquisition, buying Loveman's, Inc.
1996: Proffitt's buys Younkers chain, moving the company into the Midwest for first time.
1998: In its largest acquisition to date, the firm acquires Saks Holdings, and changes its name to Saks Inc.
2006: Stephen Sadove replaces Brad Martin as chief executive; company sells its Northern Department Store Group and Parisian.
2007: Saks opens the first Saks Fifth Avenue in Mexico City.

PARISIAN ACQUISITION: 1996

Hardly had Martin completed the Younkers acquisition when he purchased Parisian, Inc., a 38-store chain in the Southeast and Midwest with annual sales of $675 million, for $110 million in cash, $100 million in stock, and assumption of $243 million in debt. Well regarded for quality and customer service, Parisian began as a Birmingham, Alabama, fabric store in 1887. It was acquired by the Hess and Hollner families in 1920. Until 1963 Parisian was a single store, but over the next 14 years it built a network of a half-dozen stores, all in Alabama.

Parisian sold stock to the public for the first time in 1983. It was acquired in a leveraged buyout by Australia-based Hooker Corp. in 1988, but after Hooker filed for bankruptcy the following year, Birmingham's Hess and Abroms families bought it back, with investment from Lehman Merchant Bank Partners. The new owners opened stores in Atlanta, Indianapolis, Cincinnati, suburban Detroit, Nashville, and Orlando. Because of the large debts inherited from Hooker and disappointing 1994 results, Standard & Poor's placed $125 million in notes issued by the company on its CreditWatch. The company lost $5.5 million in 1994 but returned to profitability the next year, earning $8.8 million.

Like Younkers and McRae's, Parisian became a division and subsidiary of Proffitt's, but its corporate offices were moved to Jackson. Martin indicated that Parisian would be the company's upscale division and that home furnishings might be added to what had been almost

purely an apparel chain. Interviewed by *WWD* in 1997, he said, "We see it as the premier specialty store, with many resources that aren't in traditional department stores." Parisian President and Chief Executive Officer Donald Hess remained president and joined Proffitt's board of directors.

HERBERGER'S AND CARSON PIRIE SCOTT: 1996–97

Proffitt's topped off 1996 by agreeing, in November, to acquire G.R. Herberger's for $153 million. Based in St. Cloud, Minnesota, Herberger's was a chain of 40 department stores in 10 midwestern and western states that became Proffitt's fifth division. Strong in women's, children's, and moderately priced men's apparel, Herberger's was scheduled to develop lines in shoes and cosmetics. Martin indicated that it would focus on branded businesses, adding name brands such as Nautica, Ralph Lauren, and Tommy Hilfiger.

Founded in 1927, the chain was sold by the Herberger family in 1972, a year in which it consisted of 11 department stores and six fabric stores with $17 million in sales. In subsequent years it made a transition from downtown locations to anchor tenant in regional malls. In 1993, when the company had sales of $265 million and income of $5.5 million, it was about 55 percent owned by an employee stock option plan. About 450 employees, including officers and directors, owned the rest of the stock. Herberger's had revenues of $327 million in 1995. The acquisition was ratified as Proffitt's ended its 1997 fiscal year in early February 1997. Because of its acquisitions, Proffitt's in fiscal 1996 more than doubled its revenues. The company lost $6.4 million after special charges of $31.4 million, including merger, restructuring, and integration costs of $20.8 million. During fiscal 1997 Proffitt's had net income of $37.4 million on sales of $1.89 billion. Its long-term debt was $510.8 million in November 1996.

As fiscal 1997 ended on February 3 of the calendar year, Proffitt's had 19 stores in its Proffitt's division (12 in Tennessee), 29 in the McRae's division (14 in Alabama and 12 in Mississippi), 48 in the Younkers division (18 in Iowa and 17 in Wisconsin), 40 in the Parisian division (15 in Alabama), and 39 in the Herberger's division (14 in Minnesota). A Proffitt's Merchandising Group had recently been formed to coordinate merchandising planning and execution, as well as visual, marketing, and advertising activities between the merchandising divisions. Certain departments in Proffitt's stores were being leased to independent companies and included fine jewelry, beauty salon, and maternity departments.

During fiscal 1997 women's apparel was the leading sales category in all five Proffitt's divisions. Men's apparel ranked second in all but the Proffitt's division, where it trailed cosmetics. The other categories, in order of overall sales, were home furnishings, cosmetics, children's apparel, accessories, shoes, and lingerie.

Next the company went for another midwestern retailer, the Chicago-based Carson Pirie Scott chain. In November 1997 Proffitt's offered $790 million in stock for Carson's, which had 52 stores in Illinois, Wisconsin, Indiana, and Minnesota. Carson's was a regional chain, much like the other southern and midwestern department store chains Proffitt's had picked up earlier. Carson's was a big retailer, with 1997 sales of $1.1 billion, and its acquisition vaulted Proffitt's into the number four spot in department store retailing, behind Federated, May Department Stores, and Dillard's Inc.

SAKS INC. IN THE LATE NINETIES

Proffitt's growth had been tremendous after Brad Martin took over the company. Starting with the acquisition of Loveman's in 1988, Proffitt's had been growing nonstop. Barely a year separated the Herberger's deal from the buyout of Carson's, and about a month after the Carson's transaction was finalized in February 1998, Proffitt's bought the small North Carolina retail chain Brody's and Bullock & Jones, a posh San Francisco men's clothier. The biggest deal of all came later in 1998, with the acquisition of the preeminent New York retailer Saks Fifth Avenue. Saks Fifth Avenue was a storied New York store, with a high-fashion pedigree that Proffitt's previous acquisitions lacked. Saks had been owned since 1990 by an investment group based in Bahrain, Investcorp.

Investcorp had previously owned the luxury retailers Gucci and Tiffany, and it expected to handle Saks as it had these others: run it for a few years, then cash out. Saks, however, apparently lacked retail focus and was not consistently profitable. It went public in 1996, but its stock did not do well. It had grown to close to 100 stores, including more than 40 outlet stores called Off 5th, when its owners decided to put it up for sale.

Proffitt's was quick to offer a stock swap estimated at about $2.1 billion for the chain. The deal was consummated in a matter of months, and in late 1998 Proffitt's changed its corporate name to Saks Incorporated. Industry analysts were divided about the wisdom of the merger. On the one hand, Saks was wildly different from Proffitt's previous acquisitions, which had filled the moderate-to-better niche. Saks offered cutting-edge couture, with almost no merchandise

overlap with any other Proffitt's chains. On the other hand, Saks had been run by bankers since 1990, and perhaps it would prosper even more under the guidance of an experienced retailer such as Proffitt's. Proffitt's Brad Martin promised he could save Saks around $65 million by combining some financial and management functions with his other chains.

However, the Saks Fifth Avenue acquisition did not go as smoothly as most of the company's others. A year after the merger, Saks Inc.'s stock had fallen 55 percent. Problems with Saks Fifth Avenue merchandise led the company to post lower than expected earnings. The company admitted that it was having trouble integrating the luxury retailer with its other operations. Although same-store growth increased overall by 4 percent in 1999, the rate was lower than Saks Inc.'s management expected or desired.

CONSOLIDATION & SELLING BUSINESSES IN HARD TIMES

In August 2000 Saks Inc. announced that it would spin off Saks Fifth Avenue into a separate, publicly owned company with New York City headquarters. The new entity would include the Saks Fifth Avenue stores, the Off 5th outlet stores, and the chain's e-business and catalog division. This plan was short-lived, however. While in early 2000 Saks Fifth Avenue sales were growing (when other chains such as Younkers and Carson's were declining), the fourth quarter of 2000 told a different story, with 1.3 percent same-store sales growth at the regional chains and a drop of 3.4 percent for the upscale Saks. With the luxury goods sector as a whole declining, and with the Saks.com Web site pulling in losses of around $7 million, the spin-off no longer seemed a safe bet. Saks Inc. canceled the split-up in early 2001. At the same time, it sold nine of its southern regional stores, including five Proffitt's, three Parisians, and one McRae's, to May Department Stores Co. for $310 million.

Losses continued throughout the high-end department store market through 2001 as well-heeled consumers began to stay away or shop in less-expensive stores. Saks' share price also declined overall, leading Mexican billionaire Carlos Slim Helu to increase his total holdings in the company to slightly more than 15 percent late in the year. The company shuttered its catalog operations and sold Bullock & Jones, the men's clothing company it had acquired in 1998. However, the following year, the company opened four new stores and acquired Club Libby Lu, a specialty retailer for preteen girls.

It was not until 2004 that the beleaguered department store segment began to recover, and Saks Inc., driven by gains at its Saks Fifth Avenue stores, took the lead with a same-store sales increase of 25.3 percent in the first quarter. Focusing on its Saks brand in 2005, it sold Proffitt's and McRae's to Belk Inc. and began to look for buyers for its Northern Department Store Group, which included Younker's, Herberger's, Carson Pirie Scott, Bergner's, and Boston Store. The stores were sold to Bon-Ton Stores in first quarter of 2006, leaving Saks with only its Saks Fifth Avenue enterprises, Parisian, and Club Libby Lu.

PLOTTING A COMEBACK UNDER A NEW CHIEF EXECUTIVE IN 2006

Following the company's consolidation, Stephen Sadove, who had been with Saks since 2002, succeeded Brad Martin as chief executive in 2006. Sadove exited the slower growth department store business with the sale of Parisian's 38 stores to Belk in 2006. Characterizing Saks as an "old-new" company, he aimed at reviving its 53 Saks Fifth Avenue stores, 50 Off 5th outlets, Saks.com, and Club Libby Lu. Sadove believed that the key to his company's comeback lay in its sharper identity, leaner management structure, and a cultural transformation that included tailoring merchandise to local demand. His plans included pruning nonproductive assets and growing Saks.com, as well as moving headquarters close to its flagship store in New York City. After a year of repositioning, Saks began to show progress. Total sales for 2006 rose almost 6 percent to $2.94 billion.

In 2007 Sadove replaced Martin as chairman of the board in time to settle with the Securities and Exchange Commission on a charge first brought in 2005 that it had improperly collected more than $34 million from vendors in markdown allowances. The scandal, which had resulted in the ouster of three senior executives in 2005, culminated in the reimbursement to vendors of $48 million. The same year, Saks announced that it was in default on $230 million worth of convertible notes. On a more positive note, the company opened its first Saks Fifth Avenue in an upscale part of Mexico City in late 2007.

Once again, in 2008 the nation saw a precipitous decline in department store shopping. Saks went from double-digit growth in 2007 to double-digit decline by year's end. "It's the toughest environment I've seen in my career," announced Sadove in a November 19, 2008 *WWD* article. The company discontinued its Club Libby Lu brand, shuttering all its stores, after trying and failing to sell it.

As losses began to trail off in early 2010, Saks added more exclusive lines to its Saks stores in a bid to grab a large share of the high-end department store market. By the end of the first quarter, same-store sales were slightly on the rise, and Saks had experienced a surge in stock price. What the future would hold for Saks in an unstable economy was still unclear, but the company saw itself poised for growth in hard economic times.

Robert Halasz
Updated, A. Woodward; Carrie Rothburd

PRINCIPAL SUBSIDIARIES

Saks Fifth Avenue; Off 5th.

PRINCIPAL COMPETITORS

Barneys New York, Inc.; Bloomingdale's Inc.; The Neiman Marcus Group Inc.; Bluefly, Inc.; Brooks Brothers Inc.; Dillard's, Inc.; Loehmann's Holdings Inc.; Macy's Inc.; Nordstrom, Inc.; Ann Taylor Stores Corporation; J. Crew Group, Inc.; The Talbots, Inc.; Tiffany & Co.

FURTHER READING

"Accord Is Signed to Acquire Herberger's for $153 Million," *Wall Street Journal*, November 11, 1996, p. B4.

Barr, Elizabeth, "Proffitt's Signs Agreement to Buy Loveman's," *Daily News Record*, March 10, 1988, p. 11.

Carey, Susan, "Saks Backs Away from Spinning Off Fifth Avenue Stores," *Wall Street Journal*, February 9, 2001, p. B7.

Clark, Ken, "Dept. Stores Unite: Carson's Said to Fit Well with Proffitt's," *HFN*, November 3, 1997, p. 1.

Dinsmore, Christopher, "Brad Martin: Pushing Proffitt's to the Max," *Norfolk Virginian-Pilot*, Bus. Sec., June 13, 1993.

Hazel, Debra, "Man with a Mission," *Chain Store Age*, August 1996, pp. 41–43.

Hierlmaier, Christine, "Herberger's Legacy Lives, Thanks to CEO," *St. Cloud Times*, January 30, 1997, pp. C6+.

Lawson, Skippy, "Keeping It Friendly," *Women's Wear Daily* (*WWD*), March 26, 1991, pp. 6–7.

Lee, Georgia, "Dillard's to Acquire 7 Proffitt's," *WWD*, December 16, 1996, pp. 2–3.

———, "Proffitt's Power Play," *WWD*, February 3, 1997, pp. 8–9.

Lloyd, Brenda, "McRae's Plans to Acquire Pizitz," *Daily News Record*, December 11, 1986, p. 2.

Moin, David, "Difficult Spring Ahead: Saks Plans Cutbacks after Loss of $42.8M," *WWD*, November 19, 2008, p. 1.

———, "Heading the Right Way: Saks Inc. Profits Soar, but Lots of Work Ahead," *WWD*, March 8, 2007, p. 1.

———, "A New Chapter for Saks," *WWD*, November, 15, 2006, p. 4B.

———, "Proffitt's Offers $2.1B in Stock to Acquire Saks," *WWD*, July 6, 1998, p. 1.

———, "Shake-up at Saks Fifth Avenue," *WWD*, December 12, 2006, p. 7B.

"Proffitt's to Acquire 8 Units in Tenn., Va. from Hess's," *WWD*, October 27, 1992, p. 12.

"Saks Inc. Appoints Christina Johnson CEO and President," *Wall Street Journal*, November 10, 1999, p. B19.

"Saks Inc. Says Daniel Resigned from Post as Top Merchandiser," *Wall Street Journal*, September 23, 1998, p. B18.

"Saks Inc. Spinning Off Saks Fifth Avenue," *Marketing News*, August 14, 2000, p. 21.

"Saks Profit Falls 54%, Hurt by Weak Sales at Its Flagship Stores," *Wall Street Journal*, March 14, 2001, p. B7.

Wieffering, Eric J., "The Wealthiest Minnesotans," *Corporate Report Minnesota*, August 1994, pp. 34+.

Zissu, Alexandra, "Proffitt's Sees Payoff on Money Spent," *WWD*, February 19, 1997, p. 30.

SHARP

Sharp Corporation

——————◼——————

22-22 Nagaike-cho
Abeno-ku
Osaka, 545-8522
Japan
Telephone: (+81 6) 6621-1221
Fax: (+81 6) 6627-1759
Web site: http://www.sharp-world.com

Public Company
Incorporated: 1935 as Hayakawa Metal Industrial
Laboratory
Employees: 54,144
Sales: ¥2.84 trillion ($29.35 billion) (2008)
Stock Exchanges: Tokyo
Ticker Symbol: 6753
NAICS: 334310 Audio and Video Equipment
Manufacturing; 334220 Radio and Television
Broadcasting and Wireless Communications Equip-
ment Manufacturing; 334419 Other Electronic
Component Manufacturing; 335228 Other House-
hold Appliance Manufacturing

◼ ◼ ◼

Sharp Corporation develops, produces, and markets
advanced consumer electronics, business products, and
electronic components. The company makes liquid
crystal display (LCD) panels for a variety of electronic
devices, most notably large LCD televisions. Sharp also
manufactures consumer audio and video products, cell
phones, personal computers, printers, and household
appliances. The company ranks as one of the world's
largest producers of photovoltaic solar cells. Sharp generates roughly half of its revenue from sales in Japan.

HAYAKAWA METAL INDUSTRIAL LABORATORY: 1912–42

The company was founded as a small metal works in
Osaka in 1912 by an inventor and tinkerer named
Tokuji Hayakawa. After three years in business, earning
a modest income from gadgets and repair jobs, Hayakawa engineered a mechanical pencil he called the
Ever-Sharp. Consisting of a retractable graphite lead in a
metal rod, the Ever-Sharp pencil won patents in Japan
and the United States. Demand for this simple and
durable instrument was immense. To facilitate greater
production, Hayakawa first adopted an assembly line
and later moved to a larger factory.

Hayakawa's business, as well as his personal life,
were dealt a devastating blow on September 1, 1923.
On that day, the Great Kanto Earthquake caused a fire
that destroyed his factory and took the lives of his wife
and children. Hayakawa endured severe depression, and
it was a year before he reestablished his factory. The
Hayakawa Metal Industrial Laboratory, as the company
was called, resumed production of the Ever-Sharp
pencil, but Hayakawa became interested in manufacturing a new product: radios.

The first crystal radio sets were imported into Japan
from the United States in the early 1920s. Hearing one
for the first time, Hayakawa immediately became
convinced of its potential. With little understanding of

COMPANY PERSPECTIVES

We do not seek merely to expand our business volume. Rather, we are dedicated to the use of our unique, innovative technology to contribute to the culture, benefits, and welfare of people throughout the world. It is the intention of our corporation to grow hand-in-hand with our employees, encouraging and aiding them to reach their full potential and improve their standard of living. Our future prosperity is directly linked to the prosperity of our customers, dealers, and shareholders—indeed, the entire Sharp family.

radios, or even electricity, he set out to develop Japan's first domestically produced crystal radio. After only three months of study and experimentation, Hayakawa succeeded in receiving a signal from the broadcasting service that had begun programming to a very small audience only a few months before, in 1925.

The radio entered mass production shortly afterward, and sold so well that facilities had to be expanded. Crystal radios, however, are passive receivers whose range is limited. Hayakawa felt that powered radios, capable of amplifying signals, should be the subject of further development. While competitors continued to develop better crystal sets, Hayakawa began work on an AC vacuum tube model. When the company introduced a commercial model, the Sharp Dyne, in 1929, Sharp was firmly established as Japan's leading radio manufacturer. The company expanded greatly in the following years, necessitating its reorganization into a corporation in 1935.

The laboratory, for all its success, was not a leader in a wide range of technologies. It led only in a narrow section of the market. In addition, the company did not have the benefit of financial backing from the *zaibatsu* conglomerates or the government. In the realm of the national modernization effort, it was an outsider. This may have been its saving grace, however, as the government had become dominated by a group of right-wing imperialists within the military. Whatever their political opinions, the leaders of Japan's largest corporations were compelled to cooperate with the militarists in their quest to establish Japanese supremacy in Asia. Hayakawa, on the other hand, was for the most part left alone.

WORLD WAR II & POSTWAR CHALLENGES

During World War II, Hayakawa and his company were forced to produce devices for the military, and even to restructure, as new industrial laws intended to concentrate industrial capacity were passed. Renamed Hayakawa Electric Industries in 1942, the company emerged from the war damaged but not destroyed. While other industrialists were purged from public life for their support of the militarists, Hayakawa was permitted to remain in business. His biggest concerns were rebuilding his company and surviving Japan's postwar recession.

By 1950 more than 80 of Hayakawa's competitors were bankrupt. Hayakawa's officials, however, personally guaranteed the company's liabilities when the company suffered a critical drop in sales, and Hayakawa Electric was able to obtain the cooperation of underwriters until the first major expansion in the Japanese economy occurred in 1952.

Hayakawa considered television, a field that had not yet proved commercially successful, a highly promising new area. The company began development of an experimental TV set in 1951, even before plans had been made to begin broadcasting in Japan. Two years later, when television broadcasting started, Hayakawa Electric introduced its first commercial television set under the brand-name Sharp, in honor of the pencil. Hayakawa's good timing was essential in allowing the company to establish and maintain a significant and profitable market share.

INNOVATION: 1950–70

The company started development of a color television in the mid-1950s. In 1960, with the advent of color broadcasting in Japan, Hayakawa introduced a line of color sets. This was followed in 1962 by a commercial microwave oven, and in 1964 by a desktop calculator. The Compet calculator was the first in the world to use transistors. In 1966 the microwave oven received a rotating plate and calculators shrank with the use of integrated circuits.

Hayakawa recognized the great sales potential of the United States. A sales subsidiary was established there in 1962. It served the dual purpose of facilitating sales and observing the market. By the late 1960s, the Sharp brand name had become well-established in North America. Sales in the United States provided the company with a large and increasing portion of its income. In addition, subsidiaries were established in West Germany in 1968 and Britain in 1969. Hayakawa Electric made two major breakthroughs in 1969. That

```
┌─────────────────────────────────────────────────┐
│                                                   │
│                  KEY DATES                        │
│                      ■                            │
│  ─────────────────────────────────────────────    │
│                                                   │
│  1912: Tokuji Hayakawa founds company as Hay-     │
│        akawa Metal Industrial Laboratory.         │
│  1929: Company introduces the Sharp Dyne radio.   │
│  1942: Company is renamed Hayakawa Electric       │
│        Industries.                                │
│  1953: Hayakawa Electric introduces its first com-│
│        mercial television set under the brand-name │
│        Sharp.                                     │
│  1970: Akira Saeki replaces Hayakawa as president; │
│        company changes name to Sharp              │
│        Corporation.                               │
│  1973: Sharp introduces handheld calculator with  │
│        liquid crystal display (LCD).              │
│  1986: Haruo Tsuji becomes Sharp's new president. │
│  1998: Katsuhiko Machida replaces Tsuji as president │
│        and focuses the company's efforts on produc- │
│        ing LCD televisions.                       │
│  2003: Sharp controls 50 percent of the market for │
│        LCD televisions.                           │
│  2008: Sharp begins selling 108-inch LCD monitors, │
│        the world's largest commercial-use LCD.    │
│                                                   │
└─────────────────────────────────────────────────┘
```

year the company introduced the Extra Large Scale Integration Calculator, a device now reduced to the size of a paperback book. The other new product was the gallium arsenide light-emitting diode (LED), in effect, a tiny computer light. Like the radio and television before them, improved versions of both the calculator and LED were subsequently introduced in future years.

NEW LEADERSHIP: 1970

Tokuji Hayakawa retired from the day-to-day operations of his company in 1970, assuming the title of chairman. He was replaced as president by Akira Saeki, a former executive director. Saeki oversaw an important reorganization of the company intended to establish a new corporate identity and unify product development efforts. That year, Hayakawa Electric Industries also adopted its new name: Sharp Corporation.

Saeki, who witnessed the Apollo moon landing while in the United States, decided that the company's future efforts should center on the development of semiconductors, the electronic components that had made the lunar mission possible. He initiated construction of a massive research complex called the Advanced Development and Planning Center. The project was a

significant investment for Sharp, since its budget was already seriously strained by the construction of an exhibit for Expo '70. Nevertheless construction was begun on a 55-acre research complex in Tenri, Nara Prefecture. When completed, the research complex cost ¥7.5 billion, representing about 70 percent of Sharp's capitalization.

Perhaps the most important product to come out of the Tenri research facility was the very large-scale integration (VLSI) factory automation system. Building upon existing integration technologies, VLSI production lines enabled manufacturers to reduce defects and raise productivity through the use of industrial robots and other mechanical apparatus.

During the 1970s, Sharp consolidated its position in consumer goods by broadening its product line to include refrigerators, washers, portable stereos, copiers, desktop computers, video equipment, and Walkman-type headsets. Perhaps Sharp's most significant development during this period occurred in 1973, when the company introduced the first handheld calculator using an LCD screen. LCD screens had been discovered in 1963 at RCA Labs, but the U.S. company had been largely uninterested in the discovery. Having just pioneered cathode-ray tubes in color, RCA did not see any use for LCD screens. Sharp, on the other hand, incorporated LCD screens into its calculator, making it smaller and lighter. Although Sharp's LCD screen did not seem like a tremendous breakthrough at the time, the technology would later prove central to Sharp's development.

In an effort to head off impending protectionist trade legislation, Sharp built new factories in its largest overseas markets, principally the United States. The company's decision to build a plant in Memphis, Tennessee, was criticized at first. RCA had closed a plant in Memphis in 1966, favoring production in Taiwan. Sharp maintained that RCA had merely suffered from inept management and went ahead with the plant. By pushing its U.S. suppliers for parts with zero defects and incorporating the Japanese concept of full worker involvement, the Memphis plant proved highly successful.

EMBRACING LCD: 1986–89

President Saeki retired in 1986, continuing to serve the company as an adviser. He was succeeded by Haruo Tsuji, a "numbers man" with an exemplary record in middle and upper management. During Saeki's tenure, Sharp had diversified into a wide range of consumer products. By 1986 Sharp operated 12 research laboratories and 34 plants in 27 countries and its employees were equally divided between Japan and foreign countries. The logistics of running a truly international corporation took a toll on Sharp's earnings, however, particularly as the value of the Japanese yen strengthened against other currencies in the mid-1980s. In 1986, for example, Sharp's earnings plunged 42 percent to ¥20.78 billion ($137.5 million). Nevertheless, Saeki had left his company, with its 18 divisions, poised for a future of vigorous growth.

Eschewing the more glamorous development paths of rivals such as Sony and Matsushita, who expanded by acquiring a number of Hollywood-based entertainment companies during the 1980s, Sharp instead focused on research and development. In consumer electronics and appliances, the company engaged in a measured effort to move upmarket, introducing more expensive, but higher quality, products. By the late 1980s Sharp had developed a number of innovations in its product line such as a video disc player capable of reproducing three-dimensional images, a cordless telephone with a 100-meter range, and Zarus, a highly successful computerized personal organizer, capable of reading handwritten Japanese text.

The most significant changes took place in another area of business. President Tsuji quickly recognized the potential of LCD devices, and unflinchingly focused the company's resources on developing the technology. Tsuji committed 10 percent of Sharp's total sales revenues to research and development. With this push, Sharp soon began to add LCD screens to all its products. By the late 1980s, Sharp succeeded in producing a thin film transistor LCD, a display with impressively sharp definition that opened the door to color laptop computers and portable televisions.

LCD TECHNOLOGY UNDERPINS GROWTH: 1989–94

In 1989, Tsuji appointed Kiyoshi Sakashita, a company board member and an expert in industrial design, to lead a team of 50 engineers focused on further exploiting Sharp's LCD technology. Three years and countless brainstorming sessions later, the company unveiled ViewCam, an ingeniously redesigned video camcorder that presented the image on a four-inch LCD screen as it was being recorded. First shown at Japan's prestigious consumer electronics show in Osaka, Sharp's ViewCam "set the industry abuzz," according to the *Far Eastern Economic Review*. The ViewCam represented a direct challenge to Sony's best-selling Handycam. Within two years, over 1.6 million ViewCam units were sold, at an average price of ¥223,000 ($2,275).

Sharp's LCD advances propelled the company forward. Between 1991 and 1994, Sharp's LCD business grew by more than 35 percent each year, and by the close of fiscal 1994, LCD screens accounted for over 30 percent of Sharp's total revenue. While rivals Sony and Matsushita watched their profits drop in 1994, Sharp's earnings rose by 25 percent over the same period.

INVESTMENTS IN RESEARCH AND DEVELOPMENT

The company did not rest on its laurels, however, as it remained committed to development. In the early 1990s Sharp completed two new research and development centers: the Makuhari Building in Tokyo, which focused on multimedia, networking, and software for advanced information systems; and Sharp Laboratories of Europe Ltd. in Oxford, United Kingdom, which focused on areas such as pan-European translation technology and optoelectronics. In 1992 alone, the company spent over ¥100 billion ($660 million) on research and development.

Sharp also fortified its television manufacturing operations in the United States, Spain, Thailand, and Malaysia, and shifted some of its other production facilities abroad as well. Late in 1994, for example, the company transferred LCD front-end manufacturing facilities to its plant in Camas, Washington. A few months later, Sharp established an LCD production facility in Wuxi, China. During this period, the company also entered into key relationships with Intel Corporation and Apple Computer, Inc., to jointly develop flash memory chips and personal information equipment. In 1994 Tsuji announced that the company would invest $1 billion over three years to build the world's largest LCD plant. By mid-1994, *Far Eastern Economic Review* announced that Sharp was "poised to usurp Sony as the electronics maker to watch in the 1990s—provided it can keep churning out good products."

As its chief competitors struggled to catch up with its advances, Sharp continued to pin its future on LCD technology. In 1995 Sharp announced that it would again increase capital investments in its electronic devices division. In particular, the company planned to pour funds into its LCD and semiconductor manufacturing operations. Sharp's goal was not merely to produce LCD screens. Rather, the company sought to place cutting-edge LCD technology at the core of the emerging multimedia field. Sharp launched a bevy of products to further this agenda, including the Mebius notebook computer, the Super High-Resolution LCD Projector, and the pen-operated infrared transmission LCD Office Station. At the same time, Sharp entered into an alliance with AT&T to jointly develop the next generation of videophone technology. "In the 21st century, I envision the future will be involved with three important things—multimedia, semi-conductors, and LCDs," Tsuji told the *New Jersey Business News* on January 1, 1996.

OVERCOMING DIFFICULTIES: 1996–2001

The economic climate of the late 1990s confronted Sharp with new challenges, however. Starting in 1996, Sharp, like other Japanese electronic companies, saw its sales eroded by the high value of the yen (which made Japanese products more expensive). "The production cost in Japan has become the highest in the world," Tsuji complained to the *Wall Street Journal*. In response, Sharp shifted more of its manufacturing overseas.

As LCD technology continued to go mainstream, the prices the displays commanded began to decline sharply, falling more than 50 percent in 1996 alone. Nevertheless, Sharp continued to boost production. The company also announced that it would produce and sell notebook personal computers in the United States to complement the company's burgeoning sales of copiers to U.S. customers. Thanks to decisions such as these, Sharp appeared to be unscathed by the strong yen and the slumping LCD prices, even as many of its competitors went through painful restructurings. Early in 1997, Tsuji announced that Sharp would increase its production of LCDs by 43.8 percent for the year and would continue to invest heavily in LCD research and development.

However, 1997 inaugurated a more difficult period. Sharp's LCD products faced tremendous competition from Matsushita Electric Industrial Co., as well as from manufacturers in Korea and the United States. The competition drove down prices and raised the supply of LCDs. To top it off, Sharp had failed "to develop new high margin products that could guarantee it a steady stream of profits," according to the *Asian Wall Street Journal*. As a result, the company's profits and sales declined for the first time in five years.

Sharp's troubles only grew more intense with the onset of a severe Japanese recession in 1998 (the country's worst since World War II). Sales of Sharp's usually steady "white goods" sector (appliances such as refrigerators, washing machines, and air conditioners) plummeted as Japanese consumers shied away from major purchases. Caught in this crunch, Sharp's profits fell another 43 percent in 1998.

MACHIDA BETS FUTURE ON LCD TECHNOLOGY: 1998

In response to the crisis, Tsuji stepped aside and was replaced by Katsuhiko Machida as president. Describing the situation as "the worst in the history of Sharp," Machida instituted a number of changes to right the foundering company. In August 1998 he announced that Sharp would entirely replace its production of cathode-ray-tube televisions by 2005. In their place, the company would introduce sets using LCD screens, thereby driving demand for the displays in which Sharp specialized. In 1999, Machida also brought sweeping changes to Sharp's production and management systems. According to *Industry Week*, Machida sped up Sharp's decision-making process and allocated more responsibilities to his three deputies. More importantly, he freed the company's numerous subsidiaries, appointing local executives to key positions. In 1999, for instance, he named the first American head of Sharp's U.S. subsidiary. Machida also cut costs, especially in the company's flailing semiconductor segment, and reduced Sharp's product lines.

Sharp recognized that it would have to wait out Japan's economic turmoil for its fortunes to recover completely. The company also continued to develop new products in the hopes of finding its next "hit." In 2000 Sharp once again boosted capital investments, the bulk of which went to increased production of LCD panels. Sharp also planned to design a device that combined the functions of television with personal computers. In 2001 Sharp began plans to manufacture next-generation LCDs, low-temperature, liquid continuous-grain silicon display systems that incorporated semiconductor chips. Sharp also looked to strengthen its position in other areas. In 2000, for example, Sharp teamed up with Xerox Corporation to develop next-generation ink-jet printers and copiers.

As the decade progressed, the astuteness of Machida's commitment to manufacture LCD televisions was on display. The company seized control of 50 percent of the global market for LCD televisions by 2003, enjoying a commanding lead over all rivals that was fueled by substantial investments in new production facilities. In 2002 the company began constructing a $1.5 billion plant in Kameyama devoted to producing next-generation LCD televisions. The plant, capable of handling the entire production process from fabricating LCD panels to final assembly of television sets began operating in 2004, by which time Sharp ranked as the most profitable electronics maker during the previous five years. In 2005 the company posted record profits of $708 million, a 26.6 percent increase over the previous year's total.

SHARP'S DOMINANCE EBBS: 2005

Sharp's impressive lead in the global LCD market gradually began to disappear as competition in the market reached fever pitch. By 2004 Sharp's share of the global market had slipped to 35 percent and by the fourth quarter of 2005 the company had lost its worldwide lead, the first quarter Sharp did not rank as the market leader since the inception of the LCD television market. Sony, its rise fueled by the introduction of the popular BRAVIA series, became the market's new front-runner. As Sharp fell behind, Machida passed his duties as president to Mikio Katayama. Katayama joined Sharp in 1981 and distinguished himself quickly, earning seven promotions during the eight years leading up to his appointment as president in April 2007.

Under Katayama's command, Sharp continued to concentrate on the LCD market. Construction of a new LCD panel manufacturing plant in Sakai began in 2007, the same year Sharp unveiled the world's first 108-inch LCD television. The size of the massive television signaled Katayama's approach to the LCD market. He intended to let rivals such as Sony and Samsung battle it out in the 30-inch market while he focused on televisions 40 inches and larger, a segment of the LCD market that was growing faster than that for smaller televisions.

MARKET RECOVERS: 2009

By the time the Sakai plant began operating in 2009, Samsung held the lead in the global LCD market. Perhaps more worrisome to Sharp was the onset of a global economic crisis that delivered a stinging blow to all makers of LCD televisions. Between 2008 and 2009, the worldwide industry suffered a 5.2 percent decline in revenue. Conditions soon improved, however, as the industry returned to profitability in the second half of 2009, which led analysts to predict revenue growth in the months that followed. Global revenue from the shipment of large-sized LCD panels was expected to increase 40 percent in 2010, providing a fertile climate for the pioneer of LCD technology to regain its leadership position.

Updated, Maura Troester; Rebecca Stanfel; Jeffrey L. Covell

PRINCIPAL SUBSIDIARIES

Sharp Electronics Marketing Corporation; Sharp System Products Co. Ltd.; Sharp Manufacturing Systems Corporation; Sharp Engineering Corporation; Sharp Document Systems Corporation; Sharp Amenity Systems Corporation; Sharp Niigata Electronics Corporation; Sharp Trading Corporation; Sharp Business Computer Software Inc.; Sharp Yonago Corporation; SD Future Technology Co. Ltd.; Sharp Electronics Corporation (USA); Sharp Manufacturing Company of America (USA); Sharp Electronics of Canada Ltd.; Sharp Electronics (Europe) GmbH (Germany); Sharp Electronics (Svenska) AB (Sweden); Sharp Electronics (UK) Ltd.; Sharp Precision Manufacturing (UK) Ltd.; Sharp Electronics GmbH (Austria); Sharp Electronics (Schweiz) AG (Switzerland); Sharp Electronica Espana S.A. (Spain); Sharp Corporation of Australia Pty. Ltd.; Sharp Manufacturing France S.A.; Sharp-Roxy Sales (Singapore) Pte. Ltd.; Sharp Electronics (Singapore) Pte. Ltd.; Sharp Electronics (Taiwan) Company Ltd.; Sharp Appliances (Thailand) Ltd.; Sharp-Roxy (Hong Kong), Ltd.; Sharp Thebnakorn (Thailand) Co. Ltd. (STLC); Sharp-Roxy Electronics Corporation (M) Sdn. Bhd. (Malaysia); Sharp Laboratories of Europe (England) Ltd.

PRINCIPAL COMPETITORS

Samsung Electronics Co., Ltd.; Sony Corporation; Panasonic Corporation.

FURTHER READING

Eisenstodt, Gale, "Unidentical Twins," *Forbes*, July 5, 1993, p. 42.

Friedland, Jonathan, "Sharp's Edge: Prowess in LCD Screens Puts It Ahead of Sony," *Far Eastern Economic Review*, July 28, 1994, p. 74.

Gross, Neil, "Sharp's Long-Range Gamble on Its Innovation Machine," *Business Week*, April 29, 1991, pp. 84–85.

Hamilton, David, "Sharp's Edge Dull, Leaving Shares Adrift," *Asian Wall Street Journal*, September 17, 1997.

Kelly, Tim, "Go Big or Go Home," *Forbes*, June 4, 2007, p. 70.

Morris, Kathleen, "The Town Watcher," *Financial World*, July 19, 1994, pp. 42–45.

Prior, James, "Sharp Pioneers Society's 21st Century Products," *New Jersey Business News*, January 1, 1996.

Teresko, John, "Japan: Reengineering vs. Tradition," *Industry Week*, September 5, 1994, pp. 62–70.

Smithfield Foods, Inc.

———————■———————

200 Commerce Street
Smithfield, Virginia 23430-1204
U.S.A.
Telephone: (757) 365-3000
Fax: (757) 365-3017
Web site: http://www.smithfieldfoods.com

Public Company
Incorporated: 1936 as Smithfield Packing Company
Employees: 52,400
Sales: $12.49 billion (2009)
Stock Exchanges: New York
Ticker Symbol: SFD
NAICS: 112210 Hog and Pig Farming; 311611 Animal (Except Poultry) Slaughtering; 311612 Meat Processed from Carcasses; 311615 Poultry Processing

■ ■ ■

Smithfield Foods, Inc., is the world's largest pork processor, with annual production of about 7.6 billion pounds of fresh pork and processed meats. It is also the world's largest hog producer (approximately 20 million hogs annually). In addition to North Carolina, where it operates the world's largest hog-processing operation, the company owns industrial pig farms in Illinois, Iowa, Nebraska, South Dakota, Virginia, Poland, and Romania. It is also involved in hog processing in Mexico through joint ventures. Known as a leader in vertically integrated pork processing since 1987, Smithfield raises, slaughters, and processes meat. Its line of hams, hot dogs, bacon, sausage, deli and luncheon meats, and specialty products is marketed wholesale, under private labels, and under such brand-name labels as Smithfield, Farmland, John Morrell, Gwaltney, Armour, Eckrich, Lean Generation, Cook's, Esskay, and Jamestown. Smithfield Foods also holds a 49 percent stake in Butterball, LLC, the largest turkey producer in the United States. In addition to its hog processing operations overseas, Smithfield owns controlling interests in meat processing and distribution operations in Poland, Romania, and the United Kingdom. Smithfield also holds a 37 percent interest in Madrid-based Campofrío Food Group, S.A., the largest pan-European packaged meat company.

Many industry observers argue that Smithfield's competitive edge is synonymous with the firm's longtime leader, Joseph W. Luter III. After reclaiming in 1975 the company founded by his father and grandfather, Luter ushered Smithfield into the high-tech age by acquiring companies, forging partnerships, reducing overhead, and instituting capital improvements to boost efficiency. More importantly, he elevated Smithfield to the elite ranks of those *Fortune* 500 companies offering the highest total returns to investors.

ALL IN THE FAMILY: 1936–69

Since colonial times the small town of Smithfield, Virginia, had been known for its quality hams. Even today, under Virginia law, a ham may be marketed as a "genuine Smithfield" only if it has been cured for six months within the confines of the town. One such marketer, family-owned Gwaltney Packing, was the employer of Luter's father and grandfather during the 1930s. In 1936 these two decided to establish their own ham business and succeeded in raising $10,000 from local investors. They opened across the street from Gwaltney and built their small private company into a multimillion-dollar entity.

When Luter's father died suddenly of a heart attack in 1962, Luter, near graduation from college, shelved his plans to attend law school and returned to oversee the business. Seven years later the company, with annual revenues of $35 million, had attracted the interest of Washington, D.C.-based Liberty Equities Corporation, a small conglomerate. Luter sold the family company for $20 million but was retained as manager. After being summarily dismissed by the new owners six months later, Luter promptly launched a second career in real estate development.

FROM NEAR BANKRUPTCY TO FIRST BILLION

The packing plant, operating as Smithfield Foods, Inc., fattened itself through non-pork acquisitions and unnecessary staff expansion. By the mid-1970s Smithfield was floundering along with Liberty Equities, and Luter saw an opportunity to repurchase the company at a fraction of its worth. Because of actions taken by the Securities and Exchange Commission, Liberty had essentially reduced itself to Smithfield Foods, a failing $100 million pork-processing and fish wholesale business, further hampered by a nonproductive chain of 27 seafood restaurants.

Price inflation throughout the food industry, as well as poor management, had severely affected the company. Its debt had risen to $17 million, while net worth had plummeted to $1 million. Creditors were demanding a management change, and Luter agreed to a salary and stock options package that encouraged turnaround. As one analyst in a 1988 *Financial World* article claimed, "Essentially, Joe Luter got the company back for ten cents on the dollar."

Luter quickly reduced Smithfield's debt by selling the non-pork operations. He achieved profitability within seven months by slashing nearly $2 million in overhead through the elimination of middle managers and via sharp reductions in data-processing costs. Thus streamlined and firmly back in the meat business, Smithfield began to expand through acquisition. In 1978 it purchased a plant in Kinston, North Carolina. In 1981 Smithfield snatched up Gwaltney (at 35 cents on the dollar) for $34 million. Luter derived special satisfaction from this acquisition because not only had Gwaltney been a longtime competitor, it had also succumbed to the trappings of conglomerate spending under ITT Corp. Luter continued to seek out and buy at bargain rates other underperforming pork companies throughout the 1980s. These included Hancock's Country Hams, Patrick Cudahy Incorporated, and Schluderberg-Kurdle Co. (renamed Esskay, Inc.). By 1988 annual revenues had skyrocketed to $864 million, well within striking range of the billion-dollar mark.

CONSISTENT AND PREDICTABLE GROWTH

In 1987, in a particularly prescient move, Luter launched a 50-50 partnership with Carroll's Foods, Inc., the country's fifth-largest pork producer. Strategically located in North Carolina, within single-day transportation of half the U.S. population, Smithfield-Carroll's helped the company lessen its dependence on Midwest hog farmers, the traditional source for the pork-packing industry. Coupled with hogs supplied by East Coast giant Murphy Farms, Inc., the partnership-generated pigs helped to account for 50 percent of Smithfield's annual requirements. In addition to saving on high transportation costs, Luter also benefited from lower weight loss during shipment, thereby enhancing his product line's quality and marketability.

According to Sharon Reier, writing in *Financial World* in 1988, "What is remarkable about Luter's resurrection of Smithfield is that he did it in an industry plagued by plant overcapacity and a flat consumption pattern in pork product over the past ten years, and dominated by large, well-heeled conglomerates that could subsidize poor margins in meatpacking operations with profits from other divisions." Of course, even Luter's Midas touch had little control over four-year cycles in hog prices, which directly affected the company's profitability. When prices are high, more pigs are raised and the eventual oversupply results in falling prices and undersupply, a true indicator of a high-risk commodity business. As a consequence of this predictable cycle, net income for Smithfield totaled $7 million in 1990 but rose sharply to nearly $29 million in 1991. Net income

KEY DATES

1936: Smithfield Packing Company is founded by Joseph W. Luter Sr. and Joseph W. Luter Jr.

1975: After a brief period of nonfamily ownership, Joseph W. Luter III regains control of what is now known as Smithfield Foods, Inc.

1981: Smithfield buys its competitor Gwaltney.

1987: Smithfield begins joint hog production with Carroll's Foods, Inc.

1999: Carroll's Foods is acquired.

2000: Smithfield purchases Murphy Farms, Inc.

2006: Company acquires several brands from Con-Agra Foods, Inc., including Cook's, Armour, and Eckrich, as well as a 49 percent stake in turkey producer Butterball.

2009: Major restructuring is launched as company suffers its first yearly net loss since 1975.

for 1992 began cycling downward again to $21 million.

Out of necessity, Smithfield was forced to take a long-term view of earnings performance through compound growth rates. In the 1991 letter to shareholders it explained, "an analysis of the Company's performance over the last 16 years provides some enlightening results. When the 16 years are divided into four, four-year segments, the Company's earnings fall into a consistent and predictable growth pattern. ... The Company's sales, net income and net income per share have shown compound growth rates of 14 percent, 31 percent, and 33 percent, respectively, over the last 16 years."

One distinct advantage of these cycles, both for the company and for investors, was that Smithfield stock prices also followed a dip-and-rise pattern. With his extra profits, Luter had capitalized on downswings to buy back some 50 percent of the company's shares during the same 16-year period and had increased his individual stake to approximately 20 percent, according to a 1992 *Forbes* article.

To keep Smithfield on the cutting edge, Luter concentrated on his niche markets, avoided high advertising budgets, and relegated more than half of his production to nonbranded commodity pork sales for the supermarket and foodservice industries. Most promising for the future was Luter's quest for the genetically perfect pig: lean, hardy, and easy-to-process. An exclusive contract between Smithfield-Carroll's and National Pig Development Co. (NPD), a family-owned

British firm, proved to supply the answer. The first generations of NPD's transplanted stock were raised at the North Carolina facility. In July 1992, according to David Ress, "Mr. Luter ran some tests on a 265-pound hog ... comparing it with an especially lean American hog culled from the best of Smithfield's current stock. The American pig had an inch of fat on its back. The British pig had less than half that, Mr. Luter said. The raw, or 'green' ham from the American pig yielded 52 percent lean meat after boning and after the fat was trimmed. The British pig's yield was 62 percent."

Development and marketing of the pigs was expected to continue, particularly through Smithfield's formation of Brown's of Carolina and its centerpiece, a state-of-the-art slaughtering plant located in Bladen County, North Carolina, which opened for production in September 1992. Around this time, the company phased out a dated Baltimore facility, acquired a John Morrell plant in Wilson, North Carolina, and searched for a plant situated to serve the West Coast.

BECOMING A PORK-INDUSTRY GLOBAL FORCE

The Bladen County plant played a pivotal role in Smithfield Foods' transition from a small, regional packer to the largest pork-packer in the world. By April 1998 operations expanded, changing the primary nature of the facility from a pork-processing plant to the central warehousing/distribution center for Smithfield Packing Co. In 1999 Smithfield received approval to increase processing from 24,000 to more than 30,000 hogs a day. By 2001 the plant was slaughtering 32,000 hogs per day, twice the capacity of a typical plant.

By the mid-1990s, pork processing was an industry in flux. Production was becoming more horizontally concentrated and vertically integrated. At this time, the meat-processing industry faced mounting federal regulations, a seesaw marketplace, and food-safety challenges. At Smithfield, though, the company saw a smoother road. The trade publication *National Provisioner* described Smithfield Foods as the market leader in vertically integrated fresh pork production, with the implementation system necessary to support future growth: long-term production agreements for hogs, and its high-tech North Carolina facility designed to ensure product consistency and quality.

Even in 1998, a year that saw a struggling pork industry, Smithfield was thriving. Planning and strategic initiatives contributed to sales of almost $4 billion in pork products, with profitable product sales and marketing achievements that allowed the company to turn its attention to global expansion. Product development strides included a new line of low-fat Italian sausage and a new precooked sausage line by Smithfield's Wisconsin-based Patrick Cudahy division.

Luter knew that turning the nation's chicken eaters into pork lovers would not be easy. The company's meat would have to go outside the country. Smithfield Foods entered long-term production agreements with customers in Japan. In addition, the company acquired majority control of Canada's Schneider Corporation (Kitchener, Ontario), a pork producer, in November 1998. In August 1999 Smithfield further pursued its international expansion through a 50 percent owned integrated pork joint venture in Mexico. In September 1998 Smithfield acquired the largest private-label manufacturer of ham, pork shoulder, and bacon products in France. The following year, Smithfield acquired a French meat processor, which doubled the company's processed meats business in that country. Later Smithfield acquired majority control of Poland's largest meatpacking firm, Animex SA.

Around this time, Smithfield Foods faced a minefield of opposition to corporate pig farming in the United States. In 1997 Smithfield Foods drew a record civil penalty of $12.6 million, assessed for violations of the Clean Water Act. It was also ordered to pay $3.8 million for about 22,000 pollution violations in Virginia. In September 2000 Smithfield Foods and its North Carolina swine-production firms signed an agreement with the state of North Carolina that included a $15 million research and development commitment to conduct research on environmentally superior swine waste technology to protect the state's water quality.

Environmentalists, animal-rights activists, and independent farmers continued to rail against the company in 2001, with lawsuits charging that Smithfield Foods for years intentionally and systematically violated environmental laws, including the Clean Water Act. In March 2001 a North Carolina judge dismissed two lawsuits brought against the company and its hog-production subsidiaries in the state.

In this hostile climate, Smithfield needed to diversify its offerings to supermarkets and find new arenas for growth. Between 1998 and 2000, Smithfield purchased or invested in 12 companies, many outside the United States. The acquisitions provided production operations to offset declining meat-processing margins. Because there was more money in raising pigs than slaughtering them, Smithfield bought out its hog-farm partners Carroll's Foods and Murphy Farms in 1999 and 2000, respectively, as the price of hogs fell to a historic low.

Meanwhile, NPD genetics played a role in Smithfield's Lean Generation pork products, which Luter

believed could emulate Purdue and Tyson's heart-healthy branding of chicken products. By late 2000 Smithfield was one of the few stocks that resisted the market's downswing, thanks to a contract to supply Wal-Mart Stores, Inc., with prepackaged meats, an agreement Luter predicted would triple Smithfield's sales of fresh-wrapped pork.

EARLY 21ST-CENTURY ACQUISITIONS

In early 2001 Smithfield and Tyson, the nation's largest poultry company, fought for control of IBP, Inc., the country's largest beef company. Tyson prevailed and thus became the nation's largest meat producer. Shortly thereafter, in June 2001, Smithfield bought Moyer Packing Company, a smaller beef processor based in Souderton, Pennsylvania, for about $90.5 million in cash and assumed debt. In October of the same year, Smithfield acquired Packerland Holdings, Inc.. for around $250 million in stock and assumed debt. Based in Green Bay, Wisconsin, Packerland was the fifth-largest beef processor in the United States. Moyer and Packerland were subsequently combined within a new beef division, which by 2003 was generating nearly a quarter of the company's total revenues of $8.82 billion. In addition to its foray into beef, Smithfield acquired full control of Schneider in September 2001.

In a streamlining move announced in the spring of 2003, Smithfield merged its Gwaltney and Smithfield Packing pork-processing units under the Smithfield Packing umbrella. In October 2003 Smithfield Foods acquired Farmland Foods, Inc., for $377.4 million in cash. Farmland, based in Kansas City, Missouri, was the sixth-largest pork processor in the United States, with annual production of 1 billion pounds of fresh pork and 500 million pounds of processed meat. It sold its products under the Farmland, Carando, Ohse, and Roegelein brands. To help pay for the Farmland purchase, Smithfield sold Schneider to Toronto-based Maple Leaf Foods Inc. in April 2004 for about $380 million in cash and assumed debt.

In its most significant acquisition of 2004, Smithfield spent $136.9 million for a 22.4 percent stake in Campofrío Alimentación S.A. Spanish pork-processor Campofrío had additional operations in Portugal, Russia, Romania, and France and exported its pork products to more than 40 countries. Its annual sales were approximately EUR 1 billion ($1.25 billion).

Back in the United States, Smithfield Foods was seeking to increase the portion of its sales that were derived from higher-margin, value-added pork products as opposed to fresh pork. Thus, in April 2006 the company acquired the Cook's ham business from ConAgra Foods, Inc., for $260 million. Cook's, based in Lincoln, Nebraska, was a major producer of traditional and spiral-sliced smoked bone-in hams, corned beef, and other smoked meat products. Later in 2006, Smithfield opened a 240,000-square-foot, state-of-the-art cooked ham manufacturing facility in Kinston, North Carolina. In September 2006 C. Larry Pope took over the day-to-day operations as company president and CEO, while Luter continued to oversee acquisitions and long-term strategy as nonexecutive chairman. Pope had joined Smithfield in 1980 as controller, was named CFO in 2001, and was then elected president and COO a year later.

Over the next few years, a series of transactions significantly altered the operations and holdings of Smithfield Foods. In a follow-up to the purchase of Cook's, Smithfield in October 2006 acquired most of ConAgra's refrigerated meats business for $571 million in cash. In addition to gaining the Armour, Eckrich, Margherita, and LunchMakers packaged meat brands, Smithfield secured a 49 percent stake in Butterball, LLC, the largest turkey processor in the United States. In May 2007 Smithfield's hog-production division grew even larger with the purchase of the number two U.S. hog-farm operator, Premium Standard Farms, Inc., for about $800 million in stock, cash, and assumed debt. Premium Standard's operations were located in Missouri, North Carolina, and Texas.

In August 2006 Smithfield and Oaktree Capital Management, LLC, formed a 50-50 joint venture called Groupe Smithfield Holdings S.L., which then acquired the European meats business of Sara Lee Corporation for $575 million in cash and $39 million in assumed liabilities. Smithfield Foods contributed its French operations to the venture. In December 2008 Campofrío Alimentación and Groupe Smithfield merged to form Campofrío Food Group, S.A., the largest pan-European packaged meat company and one of the five largest in the world. Smithfield Foods emerged from these deals with a 37 percent stake in Madrid-based Campofrío Food Group. Also in 2008, Smithfield exited from the beef industry by selling its beef processing and cattle feeding operations to the Brazilian firm JBS S.A. for $575.5 million. Smithfield's beef operations had performed well but were a relatively minor player compared to the giants of the industry, and company executives elected to concentrate their efforts on the firm's much stronger pork business.

MAJOR 2009 RESTRUCTURING

High grain prices, an oversupply of market hogs, and a drop in pork sales because of the perceived risks stem-

ming from the outbreak of H1N1 influenza (widely called "swine flu") made for a very problematic fiscal 2009 at Smithfield. In February 2009 the company launched a major restructuring aimed at cutting annual operating costs by $125 million by fiscal 2011. Six U.S. plants were shut down, including one of the two plants in the firm's hometown of Smithfield, Virginia. Plants in Florida, North Carolina, Kansas, Ohio, and Nebraska were also shuttered, and Smithfield streamlined the number of operating companies in its pork division from seven to three.

A hog-production loss of $171 million during the fourth quarter, coupled with restructuring and impairment charges of $88.2 million, sent Smithfield into a net loss of $190.3 million for 2009. This was the company's first yearly loss since 1975. After two more quarters operating in the red, Smithfield in March 2010 reported a profit of $37.3 million for the third quarter of fiscal 2010. While its hog-production business showed some improvement thanks to cuts to its hog herd to counter the industry-wide oversupply, it was Smithfield's packaged meat business that continued to lead the way, with an 18 percent increase in earnings.

Jay P. Pederson
Updated, Michelle Feder; David E. Salamie

PRINCIPAL SUBSIDIARIES

The Smithfield Packing Company, Inc.; Cumberland Gap Provision Co.; Smithfield Specialty Foods Group; John Morrell & Co.; Armour-Eckrich Meats, LLC; Curly's Foods, Inc.; Patrick Cudahy, Inc.; Farmland Foods, Inc.; Cook's Ham, Inc.; North Side Foods Corp.; Stefano Foods, Inc.; Smithfield Foods International Group; Carroll's Foods LLC; Animex Sp. z.o.o. (Poland); Smithfield Prod S.R.L. (Romania); Smithfield Foods, Ltd. (UK); Murphy-Brown, LLC; Premium Standard Farms, LLC; AgriPlus Sp. z.o.o. (Poland); Smithfield Ferme S.R.L. (Romania).

PRINCIPAL COMPETITORS

Cargill, Incorporated; ConAgra Foods, Inc.; Hormel Foods Corporation; JBS S.A.; Johnsonville Sausage LLC; Kraft Foods Inc.; National Beef Packing Company LLC; OSI Industries, LLC; Perdue Incorporated; Pilgrim's Pride Corporation; Sanderson Farms, Inc.; Sara Lee Corporation; Seaboard Corporation; Tyson Foods, Inc.

FURTHER READING

Davis, Michael, "Staying Fat in Lean Times: Low Pork Prices Hurt Smithfield Despite Efforts to Diversify Assets," *Norfolk*

Virginian-Pilot, August 10, 2003, p. D1.

Forster, Julie, "Who's Afraid of a Little Mud?" *Business Week*, May 21, 2001, p. 112.

Kilman, Scott, "Smithfield Foods CEO Welcomes Backlash over Its Hog Farms," *Wall Street Journal*, August 31, 2001, p. B4.

Koselka, Rita, "$ Oink, $ Oink," *Forbes*, February 3, 1992, pp. 54+.

McWilliams, Jeremiah, "Move over Bacon, Here Comes Turkey," *Norfolk Virginian-Pilot*, August 1, 2006, p. D1.

Reier, Sharon, "High on the Hog," *Financial World*, June 28, 1988.

Ress, David, "Britain's Low-Fat Pigs Expected to Beef Up U.S. Pork Market," *Journal of Commerce and Commercial*, July 1, 1992.

Smith, Rod, "Smithfield Plans to Restructure Pork Operations," *Feedstuffs*, February 23, 2009, p. 6.

Walzer, Philip, "Smithfield Sees First Annual Loss since '75," *Norfolk Virginian-Pilot*, June 17, 2009, p. A13.

———, "Smithfield to Lay Off Fewer Than 30 Instead of 340," *Norfolk Virginian-Pilot*, January 8, 2010, p. A1.

———, "With Sale, Smithfield Trims Beef from Lineup," *Norfolk Virginian-Pilot*, March 6, 2008, p. D1.

Young, Barbara, "Corporate Rotation," *National Provisioner*, June 2006, pp. 40, 42, 46.

Strand Book Store Inc.

828 Broadway
New York, New York 10003
U.S.A.
Telephone: (212) 473-1452
Fax: (212) 473-2591
Web site: http://www.strandbooks.com

Private Company
Incorporated: 1927
Employees: 200
NAICS: 451211 Book Stores

■ ■ ■

Strand Book Store Inc. owns one of New York's largest collections of used, new, and rare books, which it sells at discount prices from its building at Broadway and 12th Street. The iconic store, run by the Bass family, also sells first and signed editions of many modern books and hard-to-find art and photography books. In addition to selling to individual book lovers, Strand rents books by the linear foot for use on film and television sets and prepares book collections for decorators and homeowners.

FAMILY BUSINESS STARTS OUT
NEW YORK'S BOOK ROW: 1927

In 1927 Benjamin Bass opened a small used bookstore called Strand Book Store on Eighth Street in New York City. Shortly thereafter, he moved his store to Fourth Avenue, home to New York's legendary Book Row,

which started in the 1890s and ran from Union Square to Astor Place. During the 1930s and 1940s, Book Row was the location of close to 50 used and antiquarian booksellers. According to Marvin Mondlin, a former Strand employee, Strand himself was a lover of books and an avid book collector, who ran his business more as a collector than a businessman. He would occasionally toss valuable first editions into the store's remainder bin to provide the thrill of the hunt to other book aficionados.

Named after the famous street in London's publishing and book district and after the *Strand* magazine that published some of Arthur Conan Doyle's Sherlock Holmes stories, the Strand was situated in a building built in 1901. Originally a publishing house, the interior featured tall neoclassical revival columns. From the start, the Strand was a "fiercely independent family business," as its Web site still proclaims. Bass's son, Fred Bass, began working in the store at 10 years of age. After serving in the military, he returned home and to the Strand full time, assuming its leadership in 1956. Soon after, he moved the store to Broadway at 12th Street, where he rented 4,000 square feet of space, a large space at that time, and continued gradually to expand the store.

When Fred Bass's own daughter, Nancy Bass, was growing up in the 1960s, she, too, worked in the store. As a child, she used to sharpen pencils for employees and begged to help out in other ways. She remembers "thinking I was the luckiest girl on the whole planet," according to a February 2005 article in *Reading Today*, because she "could pick any book [she] wanted."

MAINTAINING ITS QUIRKY IDENTITY

By the 1970s, the Strand was a New York City institution, "the eight miles worth saving in this city are at the corner of Broadway and 12th Street," according to Pulitzer Prize-winning journalist George F. Will, as quoted on the Strand's Web site. During the late 1970s, the Strand found itself in hot water over its practice of offering cash to book reviewers on the resale of books sent to them for review. The objection to this practice was that the author received no royalty, nor the publisher any publicity on resold advance copies of books. The *Denver Post*'s book editor resigned after his sale of books became public, and Gannett News Service conducted a two-month investigation that revealed that an employee at the *Cincinnati Enquirer* was also involved in the practice.

The quirky Strand relished its rebel status, however, and so did the public. In 1975 the Strand opened two distinctive red kiosks outside Central Park at 60th Street and Fifth Avenue. These were followed by two other kiosks at the former site of Strand stalls at the Roosevelt Island Tramway Plaza on Second Avenue as, throughout the 1980s and 1990s, the Strand continued to grow.

In 1990 it started the Strand Annex, the only used bookstore in lower Manhattan, which bounced from one downtown location to another before settling at 95 Fulton Street in 1998. There the Strand Annex eventually grew to fill the 15,000 square feet. In 1995 it was outbid on the rent on its uptown stalls and had to relinquish the site, much to the dismay of Fred Bass.

NEXT GENERATION & CHANGE

Nancy Bass joined the Strand in 1996 at age 25 after graduating from college with a dual major in business and literature and after completing a two-year stint with Exxon. She assumed leadership of the review books department. According to *Victoria*, Bass was a woman of expansionist vision and business acumen. "I just want to run the greatest bookstore ever and I want to run it like a perfect machine." Bass built upon the Strand's service of amassing collections for private customers, such as a library of modern American literature, all first editions, or a collection of art books.

However, the Strand remained unchanged in many ways, still known for its laid back and even dingy atmosphere. The original bright red, crudely painted signs that pointed shoppers in the right direction stayed in place. Staff members' attire was informal. Books were stacked unsorted on tables that had been built in the 1950s.

Fred Bass explained his reluctance to institute changes in a 1998 *Wall Street Europe* article: "If I clean up the place and make it neat, sales will go down. I know it because I've tried it." Bass occupied the same office without walls that he had since moving to the Strand's Fourth Avenue location and occasionally jumped in when lines to buy used books got too long. The Strand still sold reviewers' copies up to eight weeks before their actual release date at 50 percent off list price and publishers' overstocks of successful books at up to 90 percent off. New best sellers sold at a 31 percent discount, 6 percent more than competitor Barnes and Noble. Books were offered to the public in the basement and on the first and third floors.

DEVELOPING A PRESENCE ONLINE

By the close of the century, the Strand was being described in the press as the world's largest bookstore with annual sales of about $20 million. In 1998 it purchased the building it had occupied since 1956 and planned to expand from 47,500 to 57,500 square feet by turning the second floor into retail space and connecting it with an escalator. A new elevator would also link all four retail floors.

In 2001 the Strand's collection became available online at strandbooks.com. Computerizing the store's collection of 2.4 million books took several years with the help of Savant Solutions. "We're already set up to do a lot of this," explained Nancy Bass, referring to the store's mail-order business. In order to accommodate the additional business from online sales, the Strand expanded into another 5,000 square feet, using its third floor to house the staff required for its online operations.

The Strand also took another major step to facilitate its online presence in 2001: It alphabetized its books by category instead of arranging them simply by

```
┌─────────────────────────────────────────┐
│                                           │
│              KEY DATES                    │
│                   ■                       │
│  ├─────────────────────────────────────┤ │
│  1927:  Benjamin Bass opens Strand Book   │
│         Store.                            │
│  1956:  Bass's son, Fred Bass, assumes    │
│         leadership of the business.       │
│  1975:  Strand opens two outdoor book     │
│         kiosks.                           │
│  1995:  Strand closes its Central Park    │
│         kiosks after being outbid for     │
│         the site.                         │
│  1998:  Company opens a second retail     │
│         location on Fulton Street in the  │
│         seaport district.                 │
│  2001:  Strand launches its Web site.     │
│                                           │
└─────────────────────────────────────────┘
```

subject on tables and shelves. To preserve some of the old feel of the hunt, however, it posted new acquisitions on its site each week. Also in 2001, the Strand signed a deal to sell merchandise on eBay's online marketplace Half.com. By 2002 online sales accounted for 15 percent of business. The store's site, according to Nancy Bass, helped more people learn about the Strand.

MORE THAN 16 MILES OF BOOKS

The Basses estimated that they probably had about 10 miles of books by 2002 and were expanding onto another floor. By 2005 the estimated shelf space in miles was up to 16, and the store correspondingly changed its longtime motto to reflect the increased inventory. Nancy Bass had plans for becoming "the best source for art books old and new. They're really hot and they don't go out of date," she was quoted on Gothamist.com, a local news Web site.

In 2007, 27 percent of revenues were coming from online purchases, and the Strand was celebrating its 80th birthday with a party cohosted by *Publishers Weekly*. Former Mayor Ed Koch was the master of ceremonies and a number of notable New York writers and artists toasted the Strand, including Gay Talese, Frank McCourt, Nora Ephron, Adam Gopnik, and Art Spiegelman.

Used bookstores with their bargain prices tended to be more recession proof than some other businesses, but in 2007 the Strand fell victim to increasing rents. When the owner of its Fulton Street annex tripled the rent at the same time that construction work on a water main directly outside the store was forecast to continue for six months or more, the Basses decided to close their second bookstore. The construction on Fulton Street meant that the Strand had been unable to place its racks of used books on the sidewalk. "Sales just fell tremendously after the construction began," owner Fred

Bass said in a phone interview quoted in Gothamist.com.

In other upsetting news, the union accused the Strand of violating its labor contract with workers. After the union's last contract expired in August 2007, management and the union went back and forth on negotiations until March 2008 while the threat of a walkout loomed. Workers argued that, despite the Strand's financial success, the new contract offered fewer benefits and cited a working atmosphere that was tense.

Nonetheless, customers continued to shop happily at the Strand and the Bass family committed themselves to keeping the Strand a "fiercely independent" business. The last years of the decade passed without incident. There were plans for more book-related events and perhaps a juice or coffee bar for patrons. Books were written, bought, sold, and resold. Collections were amassed and dismantled, and the Strand Book Store continued to play a starring role among the literati of New York.

Carrie Rothburd

PRINCIPAL COMPETITORS

Barnes and Noble, Inc.; Border's Books; Powell's Books, Inc.; The Tattered Cover Book Store; Third Place Books LLC; Amazon.com, Inc.

FURTHER READING

Archer, Michael, "Sixteen Miles of Books: New York's 77-Year-Old Strand Book Store Adds a New Floor of Inventory and Increases Online Sales," *Publishers Weekly*, September 13, 2004, p. 24.

Canfield, Kevin, "The Legendary Strand: The Strange, Wonderful Store That Offers '8 Miles of Books' Continues to Thrive in New York's 'Book Row,'" *Hartford Courant*, February 2, 2003, p. F1.

Curan, Catherine, "Storied Retailer to Increase Volume," *Crain's New York Business*, September 1, 2003, p. 3.

Deahl, Rachel, "At 80, the Strand Feels as Young as Ever," *Publishers Weekly*, May 28, 2007, p. 25.

Finn, Robin, "Those Books Look Good? Imagine Reading Them," *New York Times*, November 4, 2003, p. B2.

Freeman, Matt, "Maintaining the Mystique," *Reading Today*, February/March 2005, p. 3.

Hirschhorn, Michael Weis, "It May Be Bookish, but This Store Has a Tough Streak—Strand of New York Prospers by Driving Hard Bargain," *Wall Street Journal*, August 21, 1986, p. 1.

Mondlin, Marvin, and Roy Meador, *Book Row: An Anecdotal and Pictorial History of the Antiquarian Book Trade*, New York: Carroll & Graf Publishers, 2003.

Timberlake, Colten, "New York's Strand Is a Bit of Book
    Heaven—It's Musty and the Paint Is Peeling but Literati

Love It," *Wall Street Europe*, April 24, 1998, p. 16.
Waller, Kim, "Born to Books," *Victoria*, June 2002, p. 38.

Suffolk Construction Company, Inc.

---

65 Allerton Street
Boston, Massachusetts 02119
U.S.A.
Telephone: (617) 445-3500
Fax: (617) 541-2128
Web site: http://www.suffolkconstruction.com

Private Company
Incorporated: 1982
Employees: 800
Sales: $1.7 billion (2009 est.)
NAICS: 236220 Commercial and Institutional Building Construction; 236116 New Multi-Family Housing Construction (Except Operative Builders); 236210 Industrial Building Construction; 541310 Architectural Services: 561110 Office Administrative Services

■ ■ ■

Suffolk Construction Company, Inc., is a diversified construction company with offices in Massachusetts, Virginia, Florida, and California. The company provides a range of services, including preconstruction, construction management, design/build, and general contracting. Suffolk Construction serves a variety of markets as well. The company builds commercial, science and technology, and health care facilities. It builds educational buildings, government buildings, and residential developments. Suffolk Construction builds retail buildings, entertainment complexes such as movie theaters, and buildings used by nonprofit organizations.

CEO JOHN FISH

John Fish first practiced the tireless, unflagging work ethic that created a multibillion-dollar construction company while he was attending college. Fish suffered from severe dyslexia, requiring him to spend an extraordinary amount of time completing his course work. At Bowdoin College in Maine, Fish spent most of his waking hours in the library, where his hard work paid off. He graduated with honors, earning a bachelor's degree in political science.

Fish returned home to Massachusetts after completing his studies. He immediately gravitated toward the construction industry and began working as a project manager at a firm his brother managed, Peabody Construction Co. Inc. After several months, his father, Ed Fish, intervened, suggesting his son either stay at Peabody or take over another construction company, Suffolk Construction, that he had founded several months earlier. John Fish chose the entrepreneurial option and took charge of Suffolk Construction in 1982 at the age of 22.

Although Suffolk Construction was founded by Ed Fish, it was a company entirely created by John Fish. His penchant for hard work and long hours was fully expressed at the fledgling construction company, where he instilled a workplace culture that some industry observers likened to a military operation. Fish awoke each workday at 3:30 a.m. to arrive at Suffolk Construction's office in Suffolk County by 5:00 a.m., where he remained until the evening, a schedule he adhered to rigorously. Suffolk Construction employees either followed suit, or their time with the company was electric growth during the late 1980s. In 1987 the company completed its first project for a national client, Marriott Corporation, the first of a host of projects that the company would complete in the hospitality sector for Marriott. At around this point in its development, Suffolk Construction grew "with reckless abandon," as Fish described the period in the February 16, 2001 issue of *Boston Business Journal*. The first great test of his leadership was imminent, however, showing how quickly feast could turn to famine in the construction industry.

WITHSTANDING RECESSION AND EXPANDING INTO FLORIDA: 1991–94

Rampant growth in the late 1980s transmogrified to recessive economic conditions in the early 1990s. The construction industry reeled in the face of deteriorating economic conditions. Large commercial construction projects were suspended or aborted, but Suffolk Construction withstood the downturn, relying on its Special Projects division to provide a steady source of income. The company spent the period working on smaller projects for the health care sector. "When times get tough in our business, people who have the discipline and tenacity to compete—and have humility—will survive," Fish said in his February 16, 2001 interview with *Boston Business Journal*. "In the late 1980s, Mickey Mouse could have made a buck."

Suffolk Construction shouldered past the early 1990s recession and occupied a position of strength when the economic climate improved. One of the boldest moves in the company's history followed next, when Fish opened an office in West Palm Beach, Florida, in 1994 and laid the foundation for Suffolk Construction's Southeast division. Construction projects in Florida became a vital contributor to the company's business, equaling its achievements in Massachusetts and serving as the springboard for Fish's vision of making Suffolk Construction a general contractor with a national presence.

Suffolk Construction asserted itself as one of the premier general contractors in Massachusetts during the 1990s. The company fattened its portfolio on a diet of large, high-profile projects. Suffolk Construction completed the exterior renovation of the Massachusetts State House, a $42 million project; a thorough rehabilitation of a former Sears building that created the Landmark Center in Boston's Fenway neighborhood, a $55 million project; and the $43 million contract to construct the Rollins Square affordable housing project. The company also completed a host of commercial projects, renovating large sections of major streets in Boston, giving a new look to swaths of Cambridge

brief, creating an energetic, driven firm that quickly established itself as a prominent general contractor in the state.

Suffolk Construction began compiling its long list of notable achievements not long after its formation. In 1983, after generating $300,000 in revenue during its first year, Suffolk Construction completed its first $1 million project, an office complex in Chelmsford, 25 miles north of Boston. The following year, the company completed its first project in the education sector, building a residence hall at Brandeis University, nine miles west of Boston. Not long afterward, just as his company was beginning to distinguish itself and attract numerous clients, Fish demonstrated prudence, exhibiting a cautious business stance even as business was booming.

FAST GROWTH: 1986–89

In 1986 Fish opened a Special Projects office, establishing a business arm that would help the company withstand the notoriously cyclical construction industry. The Special Projects office was set up to govern the company's smaller projects, contracts typically worth less than $5 million. Through the division, the company took on tenant improvements, educational and institutional jobs, hotel renovations, and multifamily housing remodeling. Suffolk Construction would build its reputation and fill its coffers by completing major construction projects, but Fish felt he needed to pay attention to smaller projects in sectors less subject to the caprices of the commercial market. The Special Projects office insulated Suffolk Construction from market fluctuations and it diversified the company's client base. "There is no job too small for us," Fish remarked in the February 16, 2001 issue of *Boston Business Journal*. "We'll build a doghouse if we can make a buck at it."

Before Fish had to worry about a downturn in the construction industry, he enjoyed Suffolk Construction's

```
┌─────────────────────────────────────────────┐
│                                             │
│              KEY DATES                      │
│                                             │
│  ─────────────────■─────────────────        │
│                                             │
│  1982:  Suffolk Construction is founded.    │
│  1986:  Special Projects office is opened   │
│         to court educational, residential,  │
│         and institutional clients.          │
│  1994:  Southeast division is formed with   │
│         the opening of an office in West    │
│         Palm Beach, Florida.                │
│  2002:  Office is opened in Irvine,         │
│         California, establishing the        │
│         company's West Coast division.      │
│  2009:  William A. Berry & Son is acquired. │
│                                             │
└─────────────────────────────────────────────┘
```

Street, Summer Street, Congress Street, and Dartmouth Street. The steady flow of major projects lifted Suffolk Construction's annual revenue total to $750 million by the millennium, making it the second-largest construction company in Massachusetts.

PROJECTS IN FLORIDA: 2000–01

A meaningful percentage of the company's work by the start of the 21st century came from its West Palm Beach office. The Southeast division employed 50 people by 2000, generating $90 million in annual revenue. Suffolk Construction, in the six years since it had entered the region, had developed lasting ties with clients, completing numerous projects for Marriott, for instance. The company also completed a series of projects for Muvico Theaters, constructing multiplex entertainment properties designed around a particular theme. Suffolk Construction built the Muvico Theaters Parisian 20, a $22.4 million, multistory movie theater in West Palm Beach; the Muvico Baywalk 20, a $13.5 million, 20-screen complex in St. Petersburg; and the Muvico Starlight 20, a $10.8 million, 20-screen theater in Tampa, among other projects for Muvico Theaters. Its largest Muvico Theaters project, completed in 2000, was the $25.7 million Muvico Boca Raton, a 20-screen movie theater with a seating capacity of more than 4,000 and a two-level parking garage.

During its first 20 years in business, Suffolk Construction recorded phenomenal revenue growth. Financially, the company was more than 2,000 times larger than it was when Fish took command, but he continued to look after every aspect of the company's operations. "I'm focused on real minutiae in the company," he said in his February 16, 2001 interview with *Boston Business Journal*. "If you pay attention to the

pennies and the nickels and the dimes, you'll always be able to account for the bigger picture."

ESTABLISHING A WEST COAST PRESENCE: 2002

Fish's focus heading into the new century centered on expansion, as he sought to make Suffolk Construction a national construction corporation. He expanded his headquarters in Roxbury in 2001, building a 40,000-square-foot, five-story addition to the existing structure occupied by the company. The following year, he made the greatest geographical leap of his career, establishing a West Coast division by opening an office in Irvine, California. The Southeast division expanded in 2003 by opening its second Florida office, a branch located in Miami. The opening coincided with the division securing a contract shared with Kraft Construction to build Ave Maria University, the first new Catholic university constructed in the United States in 50 years. The project was massive, valued at $163 million, which required Suffolk Construction to open its third Florida office in Naples in 2004 to support the project.

Suffolk Construction ended 2004 with more than $1 billion in revenue, the first time the company had reached that financial milestone. The total was expected to grow in the years ahead as Fish concentrated on giving the company a national footprint. In 2005 he took a step toward realizing his objective when he hired Thomas N. O'Brien as executive vice president. O'Brien, a former director of the Boston Redevelopment Authority, had spent the previous five years serving as managing director of Tishman Speyer Properties LP, a New York-based real estate development firm. Although O'Brien was experienced in development, Fish did not intend to diversify into development. He had another reason for hiring O'Brien: "The story line of this relationship," Fish said in the August 11, 2005 edition of the *Boston Globe*, "is to assist Suffolk to realize its potential on a national level as a general contractor."

Suffolk Construction moved steadily toward the $2 billion-in-sales mark during the second half of the decade. Sales generated by the Southeast division, $90 million at the start of the decade, increased to $325 million by 2006, benefiting from the contributions of three major projects in Florida: Ave Maria University in Collier County, Latitude on the River in Miami, and the Diplomat Oceanfront Residences in Hollywood. Fish formed Suffolk Ventures in 2006 to meet the demand for development and preconstruction services, but his boldest move occurred at the end of the decade when he completed an acquisition, a rare event in Suffolk Construction's history.

ACQUISITION OF WILLIAM A. BERRY & SON: 2009

In 2009 Fish acquired William A. Berry & Son, Inc., using the purchase to form Suffolk Construction's Berry division. William A. Berry & Son was formed more than a century before Fish's father established Suffolk Construction, beginning as a builder founded outside of Boston in 1857. Ownership of the company remained within the Berry family until 1984, when it was purchased by John E. Kavanagh III and Peter Campot. Under their leadership, the company, which had subsisted on moving historical buildings, realized substantial financial growth and underwent a transformation. Its core business became building projects for institutional clients, particularly health care clients. In the decade before it was acquired by Suffolk Construction, the company expanded into Maine, Vermont, and Connecticut, increasing its annual revenue to $500 million by the end of the decade.

Fish dedicated the Berry division to specializing in the health care and science and technology sectors. The acquisition accelerated Suffolk Construction's expansion into the northeastern United States, occurring at roughly the same time Fish formed another division, the Mid-Atlantic division, by opening an office in Falls Church, Virginia. With his two new divisions, Fish shored up his presence throughout the Eastern

Seaboard. To fulfill his objective of turning Suffolk Construction into a national company, Fish needed to head west, the likely direction of his company's expansion in the years ahead.

Jeffrey L. Covell

PRINCIPAL DIVISIONS

Berry; Northeast; Mid-Atlantic; Southeast; West Coast.

PRINCIPAL COMPETITORS

Kraus-Anderson Companies, Inc.; McCarthy Building Companies, Inc.; Tutor Perini Corporation.

FURTHER READING

Archambeault, Bill, "John Fish," *Boston Business Journal*, February 16, 2001, p. 3.

Burrows, Kate, "Suffolk Builds Partnerships," *Construction Today*, October 2008, p. 186.

"From the Ground Up," *South Florida Business Journal*, July 21, 2000, p. 1.

Miller, Joanna, "Suffolk: Driven to Succeed," *Construction Today*, July 2006, p. 24.

Palmer, Thomas, Jr., "Construction Firm Hires an Executive Vice President," *Boston Globe*, August 11, 2005.

Reliable People ::: Reliable Products ::: Reliable Power!

SunWize Technologies, Inc.

1155 Flatbush Road
Kingston, New York 12401
U.S.A.
Telephone: (845) 336-0146
Fax: (845) 336-0457
Web site: http://www.sunwize.com

Wholly Owned Subsidiary of Mitsui & Co., Ltd.
Incorporated: 1997
Employees: 140
Sales: $105 million (2009 est.)
NAICS: 334413 Semiconductor and Related Device Manufacturing; 541690 Other Scientific and Technical Consulting Services

■ ■ ■

SunWize Technologies, Inc., is a leader in solar power systems design and installation for commercial, residential, governmental, and industrial locations. The company offers more than 400, pre-designed solar system kits, and each complete kit can be ordered from a single stock-keeping number through any of the company's 11 North American distribution centers. The company supplies photovoltaic panels and related products to other solar installers as well. SunWize's government and industrial solar systems include remote, off-grid equipment for military, oil and gas, security, traffic, telecommunications, and other special situations.

Off-grid systems utilize SunWize's proprietary, protective polymer encapsulation technology suitable for lightweight portability and harsh weather conditions.

SunWize develops custom systems at the company's research and development laboratories, located at its Kingston, New York, headquarters. The company operates 19 sales offices in nine states and Canada. An international sales office in Washington serves customers in Africa, Latin America, Europe, and the Middle East.

EARLY INVENTIONS & PRODUCTS

SunWize Technologies, Inc., originated as a subsidiary of Bestcorp Group. Both were founded by Michael Zinn, regarded as a visionary entrepreneur in the alternative energy field. Bestcorp operated power cogeneration projects, primarily in New York, and its Bio-Energy Systems subsidiary developed solar thermal and heat transfer technology. Between 1979 and 1983 engineers at the company received seven patents for solar water heating technology and related tools and components. The company's principal product, the SolaRoll, employed an elastomeric tubing that withstood adverse conditions and provided better heat retention and transfer than copper pipe. Bio-Energy products provided heat for commercial buildings and greenhouses and hot water for domestic uses and swimming pools.

The formation of SunWize in 1992 marked the beginning of Bestcorp's development of photovoltaic-based power generation technology. Zinn planned to develop SunWize in three areas: consumer products, solar electricity infrastructure development, and marketing and distribution. The Power and Infrastructure Projects division handled all aspects of large-scale, solar power generation projects, from system design to installation and maintenance. The PV Product Fabrication and Distribution division marketed and distributed Sun-Wize solar products and systems.

PV Module Manufacturing and Integration involved development of solar power systems for wireless electronics and cellular telephones. This division oversaw the company's proprietary polymer encapsulation technology, applied to solar products for consumer, commercial, and industrial situations. The use of polymer instead of glass decreased the price of solar photovoltaic systems and made the modules lighter and portable.

FINANCIAL CHALLENGES

Some of the company's product development occurred with the financial support of the New York State Energy Research and Development Authority (NYSERDA). Cost-sharing agreements allowed SunWize to repay NYSERDA loans from profits on consumer products that emerged from various projects. The loans covered up to three-fourths of research and development.

Another cost-sharing agreement, signed in March 1996, involved production and installation of 10 skid-mounted photovoltaic hybrid power systems. Nine were distributed to remote New York locations at government and nonprofit facilities. The last was tested by an independent laboratory. Additional funding supported development of proprietary system controllers that improved energy efficiency.

During its first four years in operation, SunWize reported a steady increase in revenues. In 1992 the company garnered $2.21 million in revenue, which doubled to $4.3 million in 1996. Although SunWize operated at a loss, profits at other Bestcorp businesses sustained the subsidiary.

In 1996 SunWize began production of small solar modules that used the company's polymer encapsulation

technology. The technology provided a foundation for SunWize's off-grid solar systems. Applications included oil and gas field automation, surveillance cameras and other security devices, telecommunications equipment, and various kinds of outdoor monitoring equipment. SunWize Power Ready Systems and Power Stations provided from 10 to 2,400 watts of power.

In February 1998 SunWize introduced the Portable Energy System (PES) for laptop computers. Weighing less than five pounds, the kit included a solar panel, 11 inches by 16 inches and one-half inch thick, a stainless-steel stand, and cables. Uses of the systems included scientific field research, military situations, disaster relief, and field rescue efforts.

Changes at Bestcorp in 1997, prompted by Zinn's conviction in a federal campaign finance case, led the company to divest its power cogeneration interests. In November 1998 Lion Gate LLC, an investment company owned by Thamer bin Said al-Shanfari, of Oman, acquired the remaining operations of Bestcorp.

2000 ENTRY INTO GRID-TIED SOLAR SYSTEMS

SunWize began a new phase in its history in 2000, when the company relocated to new headquarters in Kingston, New York. The facility housed corporate offices, a laboratory, and manufacturing and distribution operations. The move supported business development in grid-tied solar systems, just as technological innovations and government initiatives contributed to industry growth.

Advances in solar technology at this time involved the capability of connecting an individual solar power system with the electricity transmission lines of a major power company. By connecting to the power grid, a solar user was assured access to electricity 24 hours a day without the use of a storage battery. Moreover, at peak daylight hours, when solar modules produced an excess of required energy, a connection to the power grid allowed the solar system owner to divert excess electricity to the power grid. The sale of solar generated electricity through a grid-tied solar system offset the cost of installing an individual power source.

The development of solar technologies dovetailed with growing social concern for the effects of carbon dioxide emissions produced by fossil fuels-based power generation. Government incentives, particularly in California, lowered the up-front costs of purchasing and installing solar systems, and contributed to demand for grid-tied, single meter solar systems.

SunWize developed a business strategy for promoting grid-tied systems in residential areas, called the Sales

```
┌─────────────────────────────────────────────┐
│                                               │
│              KEY DATES                        │
│          ─────────■─────────                  │
│                                               │
│   1992:  SunWize is formed.                   │
│   1996:  SunWize begins production of small   │
│          solar modules for off-grid systems.  │
│   1998:  SunWize launches Portable Energy     │
│          System for laptop recharging.        │
│   2001:  Grid-tied residential solar          │
│          installations push revenues past     │
│          $10 million, garner first profit.    │
│   2006:  Solar supplier Mitsui & Co. acquires │
│          SunWize.                             │
│   2009:  SunWize launches neighborhood        │
│          promotional programs and initiates   │
│          franchise development.               │
│                                               │
└─────────────────────────────────────────────┘
```

Connect program. In preparation for commencing its program SunWize built models of residential solar systems in New York and Illinois. The introduction of SunWize Grid-Tie Systems contributed to the company's first profitable year in 2001, derived from revenues of more than $10 million.

To support residential expansion SunWize opened several sales offices in Southern California, including a sales, warehouse, and distribution facility in Oxnard in March 2002. In Willits, in northern California, the sales office was combined with a warehouse. Also, to ensure an adequate base of qualified solar installers, SunWize provided sponsorship to the North American Board of Certified Energy Practitioners, the organization responsible for the solar industry's voluntary certification examination.

In addition to installing many individual grid-tied solar power systems, SunWize handled larger residential projects. In 2004 SunWize completed installation of eight grid-tied solar systems at newly constructed homes in the Grand View Estates development in Clear Lake, California. The community was expected to include a total of 90 homes.

2001–05: OFF-GRID PRODUCTS & GOVERNMENT CONTRACTS

Off-grid solar projects remained the primary market for SunWize products. To complement its existing products, SunWize began distributing other off-grid solar products. These included solar powered Solus Refrigeration products, by Electrolux of Sweden. The highly insulated refrigerators and freezers required as little as 100 watt hours of energy per day. SunWize obtained an agreement to distribute SunDanze products that incorporated Electrolux's insulated chests into direct current refrigerators and freezers. SunWize offered the products through its North American dealer network, and its worldwide distributors would make the products available to communities in remote locations where utility power was absent or minimal.

An agreement with Global Solar Energy gave SunWize exclusive marketing and distribution of several products in the United States and nonexclusive rights for other worldwide markets. Global Solar Energy products were used by the U.S. military and humanitarian aid groups. These included Power Flex Modules, which used materials that allowed the modules to mold to irregular surfaces. Also, they folded for easy transport and storage. Transportable AC Systems and Portable Power Packs fit into a backpack. As the largest supplier of photovoltaic systems to the federal government, Global Solar Energy thus formed a strong, mutually beneficial alliance with SunWize.

Off-grid systems were suitable to meet the needs of remote national parks. For Joshua Tree National Park, in Southern California, SunWize designed a photovoltaic water pumping system at the Cottonwood Campground. One of the largest such systems of its kind in the United States, it replaced a noisy diesel generator. SunWize installed a solar system at the park's maintenance facilities and visitors' center in Twentynine Palms as well.

SunWize designed, equipped, and installed a comprehensive renewable energy project at the Navajo reservation near Fort Defiance, Arizona. The project included wind turbines and 63 photovoltaic power stations. All components of the energy system were chosen to withstand the extreme weather of the high desert. SunWize and Sandia Laboratories provided training to the Navajo Tribal Utility Authority's electricians to maintain the system. Completed in the summer of 2004, the project provided electricity to about 18,000 homes on the reservation, many of them in remote locations.

2006 ACQUISITION BY NEW PARENT COMPANY

A long-standing relationship between SunWize and Mitsui & Co. USA culminated in Mitsui acquiring the company in October 2006. SunWize projects frequently implemented Mitsui solar modules. The acquisition by Mitsui provided SunWize with additional industry expertise, international distribution opportunities, and financial support for expansion. Mitsui's ambitious plans involved increasing revenues to $400 million over the next three to five years.

Expansion activities in 2007 included the opening of a 70,000-square-foot manufacturing and distribution facility, located in Rancho Cucamonga, west of Los Angeles. SunWize merged local solar system installers, including GenSelf Corporation, a residential and commercial solar system design and installation firm based in Irvine, California.

Organizational restructuring prepared SunWize for growth. The Distributed Power Group covered residential off-grid solar systems, and on-grid residential and commercial systems. The Industrial Power Group handled industrial, international, and mobile systems, including custom solar panels, and SunWize brand Power Ready Systems and Power Stations. The Operations Group oversaw business support functions, such as information technology, supply chain management, and human resources management.

By mid-2008 growth in commercial and residential solar systems led SunWize to divide the Distributed Power Group into two divisions, the Residential Power Systems Division and Commercial Power Systems. The group moved to a new office location in downtown San Jose, a center for green technology businesses. Also, Sun-Wize acquired Mitsui Comtek's solar assets, thus completing operational integration with Mitsui. In 2008 SunWize supplied more than 10 percent of the photovoltaic panels purchased in the United States.

SunWize's position as one of the primary solar power systems contractors for the federal government contributed to the company obtaining contracts with the Department of Veterans Affairs (VA). SunWize designed and installed a 309 kilowatt DC solar energy system at the Jerry L. Pettis Memorial Medical Center in Loma Linda, California. The project was completed in September 2008. SunWize installed a similar system at the VA' Dallas Medical Center in Texas in July 2009. The VA awarded SunWize a $7.8 million contract for another 10 solar projects for hospitals across the country, as well as in Pago Pago and American Samoa.

2009: FOCUS ON RESIDENTIAL SOLAR PROGRAMS

New state and federal incentives contributed to Sun-Wize's expansion, especially into the green-friendly markets in Oregon and California. In Los Angeles, Sun-Wize became involved in a community reward program with One Block off the Grid (1BOG). The largest solar buying collective in the country, 1BOG negotiated volume discount purchases for members. Residents of Los Angeles received a group discount rate of $5.56 per watt by joining a 1BOG community. SunWize supported the development of solar systems at 1BOG com-

munities by paying each member $100 for going solar, plus $10 for each of the other members that purchased a solar system.

In January 2010 SunWize launched a Solar Challenge in Salem, Oregon, home to a recently established solar cell manufacturing facility operated by Sanyo. Meeting the 75,000-watts-in-75-days goal meant supporting the local business, as well as a $7,500 donation to a local food bank, Marion-Polk Food Share. Every customer to purchase a system during the challenge received a company rebate of $100 plus another $10 for each additional participant.

As ideas about a new "green" economy became more widespread, SunWize prepared to capitalize on the solar industry's growth. In the fall of 2009 the company became the North American distributor of solar modules for Solon Corporation, which produced high-quality 225-watt and 230-watt polycrystalline solar modules in Tucson, Arizona. An agreement with Fronius USA involved utilization of the Fronius IG Plus and DATCOM inverter and monitoring products as Sun-Wize's standard choice for small scale solar energy projects, such as residential and small commercial systems. Standardized components simplified the ordering process and installation of the company's pre-designed solar system kits.

Pre-designed solar system kits provided the basis for expansion through SunWize's new franchise program. The kits included permits and allowed flexibility for individual home solar projects. Franchise support included proprietary marketing materials and promotional and lead generation programs. SunWize hoped to obtain its first franchise contracts in early 2010.

Mary Tradii

PRINCIPAL OPERATING UNITS

Residential Power Systems; Commercial Power Systems; Industrial Power Group; Operations Power Group.

PRINCIPAL COMPETITORS

Akeena Solar, Inc.; Borrego Solar Systems, Inc.; groSolar, Inc.

FURTHER READING

Byrne, James, "Solar Panels Can Juice Up Your Notebook Battery Life," *Government Computer News,* February 23, 1998, p. 36.

Duan, Mary, "SunWize Sees Jobs in Franchise Plan," *San Jose Business Journal,* November 24, 2009.

"Solar M & A: Mitsui to Acquire SunWize Technologies," *Energy Resource,* October 30, 2006.

"SunWize Commercial Power Systems Awarded $7.8 Million in Federal Contracts," *Health & Medicine Week,* January 18, 2010, p. 31.

"SunWize Customers Recognized for Renewable Efforts," *Renewable Energy Today,* November 25, 2003.

"SunWize Unveils New Residential Solar Financing Program," *Manufacturing Close-Up,* July 7, 2009.

SUPERVALU

SUPERVALU INC.

———— ■ ————

11840 Valley View Road
Eden Prairie, Minnesota 55344-3691
U.S.A.
Telephone: (952) 828-4000
Fax: (952) 828-8998
Web site: http://www.supervalu.com

Public Company
Incorporated: 1926 as Winston & Newell Company
Employees: 178,000
Sales: $40.59 billion (2010)
Stock Exchanges: New York
Ticker Symbol: SVU
NAICS: 445110 Supermarkets and Other Grocery (Except Convenience) Stores; 446110 Pharmacies and Drug Stores

■ ■ ■

Minnesota-based SUPERVALU INC. (Supervalu) is the third-largest retail grocer and one of the leading grocery wholesalers in the United States. Supervalu owns and operates more than 1,550 stores in 40 states, including 850 combination food and drug stores, more than 350 food stores, and more than 300 limited-assortment food stores. Supervalu stores operate under several brand names, most of them located in regional markets. Save-A-Lot is the largest store brand, with more than 1,175 corporate-owned and licensed stores across the United

States, followed by Albertsons with more than 460 Albertsons stores in the western states. Jewel operates more than 180 combination stores in Chicago and the Midwest, while Acme Markets counts 125 stores in Pennsylvania. Shaw's and Star Markets brands have more than 175 stores in Boston and five New England states. Cub Foods' 78 stores in the Minneapolis area include 30 franchised locations. Farm Fresh's 44 stores are located around Richmond, Virginia, and Shop 'n Save's 41 stores are in the St. Louis area. Shoppers Food & Pharmacy brand includes more than 60 stores in the Baltimore and Washington, D.C., area. Four brands have fewer than 20 stores each: Bristol Farms and Lucky in Southern California, bigg's in the Cincinnati area, and Hornbacher's in Fargo, North Dakota. In-store pharmacies operate in 850 stores under the Sav-on and Osco brands, and 130 stores offer automotive fuel.

Supervalu's wholesale grocery business operates from 33 warehouse and distribution centers supplying products to 2,000 independent stores in 48 states and abroad. These include regional and national chain supermarkets, mass merchandisers, and e-tailers. The W. Newell & Company subsidiary distributes fresh produce. Total Logistics, Inc., offers supply chain management and consulting services to retail grocery stores, automotive parts distributors, and manufacturing companies. Business support service offerings include consumer and market research; private labeling; personnel training; accounting; insurance brokerage and services; store site selection, construction and design; category management; and business planning.

COMPANY PERSPECTIVES

Our mission at SUPERVALU always will be to serve our customers better than anyone else could serve them. We will provide our customers with value through our products and services, committing ourselves to providing the quality, variety and convenience they expect.

We shall pursue our mission with a passion for what we do and a focus on priorities that will truly make a difference in our future.

LATE 19TH TO EARLY 20TH CENTURY: MINNEAPOLIS WHOLESALER ROOTS

Supervalu's origins lie in the 1871 merger of the Minneapolis wholesale grocery firms B.S. Bull and Company and Newell and Harrison Company. The new Newell and Harrison existed for only three years. In 1874 George R. Newell bought out his partners and renamed the company George R. Newell Company.

Meanwhile, one of Newell's former partners, Hugh G. Harrison, formed a wholesaling venture called H.G. Harrison Company in 1879. After a series of reorganizations (including Harrison's sale of his interest), this company became Winston, Harper, Fisher Company in 1903, headed by F. G. Winston, a Minneapolis railroad contractor; J. L. Harper, a merchandiser; and E. J. Fisher, a financier. In 1916 Harrison's grandson, Perry Harrison, joined Winston, Harper, Fisher as vice-president and co-owner.

In 1926 George R. Newell Company and Winston, Harper, Fisher Company merged to form Winston & Newell Company, with Perry Harrison and L. B. Newell, Winston's son-in-law, as principal shareholders. Winston & Newell was incorporated in 1926 in response to the threat that independent retailers faced from the emerging grocery store chains that began developing in the 1920s. Winston & Newell hoped to improve services to these independent retailers so they could withstand the competitive impact of the chain stores. At the time of its creation, Winston & Newell was serving some 5,000 small grocery stores and had sales of $6 million, making it the largest grocery wholesaler in the Midwest.

With Minnesotan Thomas G. Harrison at its helm, Winston & Newell became one of the first wholesale distributors in the nation to join the new Independent Grocers Alliance (IGA). Harrison, the son of Perry Harrison, had joined Winston, Harper, Fisher Company in 1919 as an assistant sales manager. He successively became assistant treasurer and executive vice-president, directing the operations of Winston & Newell and later Super Valu in a variety of executive positions from 1926 until his retirement as CEO in 1958.

Harrison, in guiding the company through the Great Depression, was primarily responsible for introducing many practices that changed the way in which grocery stores conducted business. Cash-and-carry and self-service shopping, almost unheard of at the time, were two of his innovations at Winston & Newell. He broke with tradition again when he stopped using a pricing structure with an arbitrary markup and began charging instead the manufacturer's price plus a percentage fee that declined with volume. This practice gave the company impressive cumulative profits. During the 20-year period from 1942 to 1962, *Fortune* reported that the company's sales volume increased from about $10 million to more than $300 million.

EARLY FORTIES TO SIXTIES: FORMATION OF VOLUNTARY ASSOCIATIONS

It was during World War II that Winston & Newell began the march to becoming Supervalu and attaining its position as the world's largest food wholesaler and distributor. Although no acquisitions were made during the 1940s, in 1942 the company ended its affiliation with IGA and formed its own association, known in the industry as a "voluntary." Winston & Newell offered independent retailers services such as food processing and packaging, preparation of advertising for individual store use in local newspaper advertising, and store-planning assistance, in addition to supplying most of the merchandise sold. This voluntary association introduced the Super Valu name and operated independently from the wholesale business. Super Valu and another voluntary association called U-Save (which was also formed under the auspices of Winston & Newell) were familiar to grocers in Iowa, Minnesota, and North Dakota. By 1942 the company had wholesale sales of $10 million and some 400 stores belonged to its wholesale-retail team.

In 1954 Winston & Newell Company changed its name to Super Valu Stores Inc. in order to clarify the connection between itself and the voluntary association. During the 1950s Super Valu began to grow by acquiring other voluntary associations. In 1955 it purchased Joannes Brothers of Green Bay, Wisconsin, a firm that had begun serving stores in northern Michigan and northeastern Wisconsin in the 1870s. Joannes Brothers

KEY DATES

1871: Minneapolis wholesale grocery firms (B.S. Bull and Company, and Newell and Harrison Company) merge to form the early forerunner to Supervalu.

1926: Company incorporates as Winston & Newell Company.

1954: Company changes its name to Super Valu Stores Inc.

1955: Company begins acquiring regional wholesalers.

1971: With acquisition of ShopKo, company begins major investments in the nonfood, general merchandise business.

1989: Company opens its first hypermarket in Cleveland, Ohio.

1992: Company changes its name to Supervalu Inc.

1999: Supervalu acquires Richfood Holdings, Inc., a leading mid-Atlantic food distributor and retailer.

2000: Sales surpass $20 billion.

2002: Supervalu opens its 1,000th Save-A-Lot store.

2006: Supervalu becomes third-largest grocery retailer with acquisition of New Albertsons.

became Super Valu's Green Bay Division. In 1958 Russell W. Byerly became president of Super Valu. Byerly, a North Dakota native who joined Winston & Newell in 1932 as a bookkeeper, served as president until 1964 and later was chairman of the board and chief executive officer.

SERIES OF ACQUISITIONS IN THE SIXTIES

Acquisition followed acquisition during the 1960s as Super Valu expanded throughout the Midwest. In 1961 Super Valu moved into the Ohio Valley with the purchase of the Eavey Company, one of the nation's oldest food wholesale distributors. In 1963 the company acquired the J.M. Jones Company of Champaign-Urbana, Illinois, and the Food Marketing Corporation of Fort Wayne, Indiana. Each of these companies could trace its beginnings to the early days of the grocery business. Jones began as a general store and developed into a large wholesale business. Food Marketing dated back to the early 1800s, as Bursley & Company and the Bluffton Grocery Company. The Food Marketing

acquisition also brought Super Valu into the institutional market. After the acquisition, these two companies were operated as autonomous divisions in a company that historically gave its divisions and stores as much free rein as possible.

In 1964 Super Valu expanded its area of operation outside the Midwest by acquiring Chastain-Roberts Company, which had begun in 1933 as a wholesale flour and feed company, and the McDonald Glass Grocery Company, Inc., of Anniston, Alabama. These acquisitions formed the basis for Super Valu's Anniston Division.

In 1965 Super Valu acquired the Lewis Grocer Company of Indianola, Mississippi. The Lewis Grocer Company was founded by Morris Lewis Sr. in 1895 and eventually became a multimillion-dollar wholesale grocer, branching out later into the retail grocery business. The 1960s were a growth period for Super Valu in ways other than acquisition. The company expanded its retail support services to include accounting, efficiency studies, budget counseling, and store format and design advice. In 1962 Super Valu established Planmark, a department that offered engineering, architectural, and design services to independent retailers, subsidiaries, and corporate stores. Planmark became a division in 1975. With Studio 70, its commercial design arm, Planmark used computer-assisted design to analyze and develop plans for construction, expansion, or remodeling. This innovation, implemented in the recessionary years of the late 1970s, allowed Super Valu retailers to take a project from planning to opening faster than their competition. Super Valu also began providing financial assistance for retailers building new stores, bankrolling some 500 stores in a three-year period in the 1960s. Super Valu also signed leases on its retailers' behalf, allowing them to locate in prime space in shopping centers and other locations.

In 1968 Preferred Products, Inc., (PPI) was incorporated as a subsidiary of Super Valu to develop its private-label program. A food packaging and processing division, it was started in the 1920s as a department of Winston & Newell.

Super Valu also formed an insurance agency, Risk Planners, Inc., in 1969. This wholly owned subsidiary began by providing insurance on retail property for the company and its retail affiliates. Tailored specifically to the needs of retailers, its products have expanded to include all types of insurance for Super Valu and its stores and franchises, as well as independent retailers' employees and families.

DIVERSIFIED OPERATIONS IN THE SEVENTIES

Diversification was the moving force at Super Valu in the 1970s, in part because the U.S. government in the late 1960s made it clear that it was not going to allow further consolidation of the food industry. Beginning with the 1971 acquisition of ShopKo, a general merchandise discount chain, Super Valu began what proved to be a highly profitable program of nonfood marketing operations. ShopKo, founded by James Ruben in Chicago in 1961, opened its first store in Green Bay, Wisconsin, in 1962. In 1971 Super Valu acquired Daytex, Inc., a textile goods company, but the venture proved unsuccessful and its assets were liquidated in 1976. Meanwhile, Super Valu sales surpassed $1 billion for the first time in 1972.

When Jack J. Crocker became chairman and CEO of Super Valu in 1973, he initiated another diversification venture, County Seat. A success story in its own right, County Seat opened its first store in 1973 selling casual apparel, including the complete Levi's jeans line. By 1977 there were 183 County Seat stores, and the chain's earnings were $8 million in that fiscal year. When it was sold for $71 million to Carson Pirie Scott and Company of Chicago in 1983, there were 269 stores in 33 states.

Crocker, a CPA who came to Super Valu from the presidency of the Oregon-based grocery and pharmacy chain Fred Meyer, Inc., also directed the company's continuing acquisition and expansion program. Very much a part of the trend toward consolidation in the food wholesale industry, Super Valu continued to purchase smaller food wholesalers, acquiring Pennsylvania-based Charley Brothers Company in 1977. Charley Brothers, which began as a retail grocery store in 1902 and moved into wholesaling in 1918, served Shop 'n Save stores and other independent retailers in Pennsylvania.

The advent of universal price codes and scanning equipment in the grocery business led to the introduction, in the mid-1970s, of Testmark, an independent research center providing store measurement data. These data had been available from Super Valu stores since 1965 and, during the period before Testmark was established, had been handled by Super Valu merchandising research, an internal department for clients who preferred not to use commercial research companies. In direct competition with these commercial research companies, Testmark, with Super Valu's backing, offered its customers the advantage of cooperation within the Super Valu network and with major chains and independents nationwide. Testmark's autonomy was enhanced by its Hopkins, Minnesota, location, separate from Super Valu's corporate headquarters.

Crocker's tenure at Super Valu was characterized by his success in running what was one of the better-capitalized and stronger wholesalers in the country and by the casual no-frills operation he ran. Company headquarters were in a warehouse, not a plush office. Crocker personally founded a professional soccer team, the Minnesota Kicks, in 1976. They, too, were a Crocker success story, becoming popular in their home territory.

Crocker's successes were apparent on the bottom line as well. By 1978 earnings per share had increased approximately 50 percent since Crocker's first year with Super Valu. Crocker commented to *Financial World* in 1977, "I don't think about profits very much. If you're doing things right, profits always follow." By the end of the 1970s Super Valu's sales were $2.9 billion.

MOVE INTO RETAIL GROCERIES WITH CUB FOODS IN 1980

Super Valu ushered in the 1980s with the acquisition of Cub Foods, a discount grocery store operation. Warehouse stores, with bare bones facilities and prices, were a phenomenon of the 1970s. Cub Foods was founded by the Hooley family, grocers since 1876 in Stillwater, Minnesota. The Hooleys opened their first warehouse store with the Cub name in a Minneapolis suburb in 1968. When Super Valu purchased the chain in 1980, there were five Cub stores and a Hooley supermarket in Stillwater. Culver M. Davis was appointed president and chief executive officer of Cub Foods in 1985. Davis had joined the Hooley organization in 1960 and was a founder, with the Hooley family, of the discount stores.

Super Valu originally acquired the Cub chain to boost its wholesale sales. *Business Week* reported in 1984, the company soon realized it had a "tiger by the tail," and that Cub had "taken on a (retailing) life of its own." Super Valu improved the atmosphere of Cub Foods stores by using attractive decor, keeping the stores clean, and increasing product offerings, including perishables, which the early warehouse stores did not offer. As a result, Cub Foods evolved into a combination of the conventional grocery store and the warehouse store, known in the industry by the late 1980s as a "super warehouse."

Although Cub Foods competed directly with a number of Super Valu's customers' stores and its own corporate stores, the company saw a benefit in the opportunity Cub offered its retailers to learn about warehouse-store operations from the inside. Several of its retailers did not totally agree, citing a 10 to 15 percent reduction in business when a Cub Foods store opened in their market area. To address this complaint, Super Valu started franchising its Cub stores and also developed County Market, a downsized version of Cub with the same low prices, but aimed at smaller communities and at independent retailers who could not meet the financial commitment that buying a Cub franchise required. By 1989, 74 Cub Foods stores (of which Super Valu owned 34) were in nine states and had sales of approximately $3 billion.

By 1986 Super Valu had introduced another variation on the Cub theme. Developed for retailers who needed to improve their stores' look and style to meet competition, the Newmarket format combined warehouse pricing with an upscale product line and services such as video rental, check cashing counters, and baggers. The first Newmarket store opened in the St. Paul-Minneapolis area, and was so successful that the company opened more stores in other locations.

In June 1981 Jack Crocker, at age 57, stepped down from his position as CEO. Crocker, who headed Super Valu for nine years, brought the company to just over $4 billion in sales. He is reported to have handpicked Michael W. Wright, who had joined Super Valu as an executive vice president in 1977 and became president in 1978, to be the next CEO. Wright had first come to Crocker's attention when he handled some legal matters for the company in Minneapolis. Wright, a former captain of the University of Minnesota football team, had put himself through law school by playing professional football with the Canadian Football League.

1980S: EXPANSIONS IN THE WEST & SOUTH

Super Valu took its expansion west in 1982 when it acquired Western Grocers, Inc. Western had distribution centers in Denver, Colorado, and Albuquerque, New Mexico. In 1984 these two centers became separate divisions. Super Valu also moved into Nebraska in 1982 by acquiring the Hinky Dinky distribution center near Omaha from American Community Grocers, a subsidiary of Texas-based Cullum Companies. In 1984 Super Valu sold the center back to Cullum.

With intentions of gaining a strong market presence in Florida, in 1983 and 1984, respectively, Super Valu purchased Pantry Pride's Miami and Jacksonville distribution centers. In what Super Valu considered a breach of their agreement, Pantry Pride began selling off its stores. With this and the fact that the Florida market had historically been dominated by the chains, Super Valu, claiming that the Florida market would take a large amount of capital to develop, sold the Miami

center to Malone & Hyde in 1985, and the Jacksonville center to Winn-Dixie in 1986.

In 1985 Super Valu created its Atlanta Division when it acquired the warehouse and distribution facilities of Food Giant. Through this division the company supplied Food Giant, Big Apple, Cub Foods, and independent stores. Food Giant, according to a 1988 *Financial World* report, "refused to implement Super Valu's turnaround plan for store upgrading," and the retail stores that Super Valu owned through the original transaction and a later acquisition of stock lost money for the company. By 1988 the company had divested itself of these stores, but operated or franchised seven Cub stores in the Atlanta area.

Also in 1985, Super Valu acquired West Coast Grocery Company (Wesco) of Tacoma, Washington. Wesco, founded by the Charles H. Hyde family in 1891, was Super Valu's largest acquisition to that time. Wesco had distribution centers in two Washington cities and Salem, Oregon, and a freezer facility in another Washington city. Super Valu's West Coast operations were hurt when the Albertsons chain opened a distribution center to supply its own stores in Washington.

In 1986 and 1987 Super Valu acquired two more distribution centers in Albuquerque and Denver, respectively. These centers were owned by Associated Grocers of Colorado, which, at the time of the Denver purchase, was in Chapter 11 bankruptcy proceedings. In December 1988, Super Valu acquired the Minneapolis; Fargo, North Dakota; and Green Bay, Wisconsin, distribution centers of Red Owl Stores, Inc. The former Denver and Albuquerque divisions of Western Grocers were moved into these new facilities.

By the mid-1980s Super Valu had developed a substantial presence in the military commissary marketplace. The company had been supplying both product and retail support to military commissaries in the United States and abroad and, in 1986, demonstrated its commitment to international operations by appointing a military and export product director. Super Valu International had its beginnings with the Caribbean and Far East markets and eventually supplied fresh goods and private-label canned goods, general merchandise, and health and beauty aids to most countries of the world.

During the 1980s ShopKo continued to expand and to turn in substantial profits for the company. At the end of fiscal 1989 ShopKo operated 87 stores in 11 states from the Midwest to the Pacific Northwest and had sales of $1.28 billion. Super Valu's only nonfood retail operation at the time, ShopKo had its headquarters and distribution center in Green Bay,

Wisconsin, and distribution centers in Omaha, Nebraska, and Boise, Idaho.

It was perhaps the successes of ShopKo and of Cub Foods that led Super Valu to its largest venture in retailing in the 1980s: the "hypermarket," a retailing concept that originated in Europe after World War II. The first hypermarkets introduced in the United States in the early 1970s were not successful, but in the mid-1980s Hyper Shoppes, Inc., a predominantly French consortium, reintroduced the hypermarket in the United States. Super Valu was a 10 percent investor in the venture, which opened bigg's, a 200,000-square-foot food and general merchandise store in the Cincinnati, Ohio, area.

With the experience of this venture under its belt, Super Valu created its own version of the hypermarket, Twin Valu. A combination of a Cub Foods and a ShopKo, this 180,000-square-foot store opened in early 1989 in Cleveland. A second Twin Valu opened in Cleveland in 1990. The hypermarket concept as executed by Super Valu emphasized low prices, good selection, and brand-name merchandise.

In 1988 Super Valu lost its position as the world's largest wholesaler when Oklahoma City-based Fleming Companies bought Malone & Hyde, a purchase Super Valu declined to make. At the end of the 1980s, Super Valu served some 3,000 independent retailers in 33 states. The company still owned and operated 70 conventional grocery stores and some Cub Foods stores and served its corporate stores and customers from 18 retail support and distribution centers.

WETTERAU & OTHER PURCHASES HIGHLIGHT EARLY NINETIES

Super Valu entered the 1990s having to contend with the loss of $220 million in business from the sale or closing of three major customers in 1989: Red Owl stores in Minneapolis, Skaggs Alpha Beta stores in Albuquerque, and two Cub Foods stores in Nashville. The loss of business through acquisition of its independent retail customers by major chains, nearly all of whom were self-distributing, would continue to pose a threat to Super Valu and other wholesalers throughout the 1990s. Part of Super Valu's response to this threat was to further bolster its own retail operations.

Meanwhile, Super Valu's ShopKo subsidiary had grown so rapidly it was beginning to be too large for Super Valu to manage. The company decided to divest itself of part of ShopKo through an initial public offering (IPO). In October 1991 the IPO resulted in the sale of 54 percent of ShopKo to the public, netting Super

Valu $420 million. Wright told *Grocery Marketing* that if Super Valu had not taken this step, "it was a case where we would have ended up with the tail wagging the dog."

The very next month Wright began to reinvest the cash, and to boost the company's retail sector through the purchase of Scott's Food Stores, a 13-store chain based in Fort Wayne, Indiana. With the addition of Scott's, Super Valu became the 25th-largest retailer in the United States.

In early 1992, Super Valu Stores Inc. changed its name to Supervalu Inc. Later that year, the company made its largest acquisition to date when it acquired Wetterau Inc., the fourth-largest wholesaler in the country, in a $1.1 billion deal. The addition of Wetterau's $5.7 billion in sales volume to Supervalu's $10.6 billion leapfrogged Supervalu over rival Fleming and back into the top spot in U.S. grocery wholesaling. Wetterau, founded in 1869 and based in Hazelwood, Missouri, was led at the time of the merger by Ted C. Wetterau, a member of the fourth generation of Wetteraus to run the company. With Wright, Wetterau became vice chairman of Supervalu and a company director. Wetterau retired late in 1993, leaving Wright in sole control of Supervalu once again.

In addition to bolstering Supervalu's wholesaling operation, Wetterau brought Supervalu a significant retail operation: 180 stores in 12 states (added to Supervalu's stable of 105 stores in 11 states). Most significantly, Wetterau's stores included the Save-A-Lot chain of limited-assortment stores, a format new to the Supervalu fold and one that would expand under Supervalu's supervision. The newly combined retail operations moved Supervalu into 14th place among U.S. food retailers. The company set a long-term goal of being one of the top 10 retailers by the end of the 1990s.

The Wetterau acquisition was soon followed by additional acquisitions, several in retail. Late in 1993 Supervalu acquired Sweet Life Foods Inc., a wholesaler based in Suffield, Connecticut, with $650 million in revenues and a few retail operations in New England, one of Supervalu's weaker regions. In March 1994, the 30-store Texas T Discount Grocery Stores chain was acquired. Then in July, Supervalu bought Cincinnati-based Hyper Shoppes, Inc., which ran seven bigg's stores in Cincinnati, Denver, and Louisville, Kentucky, and had more than $500 million in annual revenues. Meanwhile, in June 1994, Fleming leapfrogged back over Supervalu into the number one wholesaling position when it acquired Scrivner Inc., then number three. At that time, Fleming claimed $19 billion in revenue to Supervalu's $16 billion.

MID-NINETIES TO 2002: SUPERVALU RESTRUCTURES WHILE STILL GROWING

Supervalu announced in late 1994 that it would begin to implement a restructuring program called Advantage in early 1995. Over a two-year period, the company eliminated about 4,300 jobs (10 percent of the total workforce) and divested about 30 underperforming retail stores. The Advantage program also centered around three chief aims: revamping the distribution system into a two-tiered system in order to lower the costs to retailers; creating a new approach to pricing called Activity Based Sell; and developing "market-driving capabilities" that would increase sales for Supervalu's retail customers, chiefly through category management.

The last of these goals also involved the realignment of the company's wholesale food divisions into seven marketing regions: Central Region, based in Xenia, Ohio; Midwest Region, Pleasant Prairie, Wisconsin; New England Region, Andover, Massachusetts; Northeast Region, Belle Vernon, Pennsylvania; Northern Region, Hopkins, Minnesota; Northwest Region, Tacoma, Washington; and Southeast Region, Atlanta, Georgia. Supervalu took a $244 million charge in 1995 to implement the Advantage program, which was the company's response to increasing market pressures (low inflation, industry consolidation, a slowdown in growth, and changes in the promotional practices of manufacturers) that had yet to hurt the company's earnings but were certain to begin to do so if the company took no action.

In late 1996 Supervalu bought the 21-store Sav-U Foods chain of limited assortment stores from its rival, Fleming Companies. The purchase provided Supervalu its first Southern California retail presence. The stores were to be converted to Save-A-Lot stores, small, warehouse-style retail markets offering a limited assortment of 1,200 to 1,300 food items. The company made plans to eventually open 200 to 300 Save-A-Lot stores in the area.

Also in late 1996, ShopKo and Phar-Mor Inc., a chain of more than 100 deep-discount drug stores, merged under the umbrella of a new holding company called Cabot Noble Inc. Although initially Supervalu was to have no stake in the new company, the final agreement gave Supervalu 6 percent of Cabot Noble in order to reduce the amount of financing needed for the merger. Supervalu also gained about $200 million as a result of the purchase of most of its shares in ShopKo. In 1997 the company exited its 46 percent investment in ShopKo, making about $305 million in net proceeds. Supervalu had also started to take some tentative steps toward expanding its presence overseas, through a 20 percent stake it held in an Australian wholesaler and its agreement to supply products to a new supermarket in Moscow.

By mid-1998, the company had a strong first quarter to boast about, a two-for-one stock split, and opened or completed acquisitions of 73 stores. The company focused its expansion efforts that year on growing the Save-A-Lot unit. That same year, Supervalu began its investment in the pharmacy business: Scott's Foods stores acquired Keltsch Pharmacy of northeast Indiana, which included 11 freestanding pharmacies and three in-store ones. Supervalu also lost one of its larger customers, Bellevue, Washington-based QFC, which was acquired by Portland's Fred Meyer.

In 1999 Supervalu reported record sales of $17.4 billion for 1998, and shortly thereafter, still riding the crest of the previous year's revenue wave, acquired Richfood Holdings, Inc., the leading mid-Atlantic food distributor and retailer. As a result, Supervalu took over the Shoppers Food Warehouse, Metro, and Farm Fresh retail food chains and gained about 800 new customers. Supervalu then divested Hazelwood Farms Bakeries to focus its investments on core food distribution and retail businesses, but maintained its link with the bakeries (and new owner Pillsbury Bakeries & Foodservice) as a supplier.

Along with various cost-reduction initiatives, Supervalu's continued focus on core businesses and the boost from the Richfood acquisition helped Supervalu see another record year for sales. By mid-2000, Supervalu's sales surpassed the $20-billion mark. An ever-growing, increasingly more efficient company, Supervalu was operating more than 194 price superstores (including Cub Foods, Shop 'n Save, Shoppers Food Warehouse, Metro, and bigg's), 839 limited assortment stores (including 662 licensed locations under the Save-A-Lot banner), and 85 other supermarkets. It was also the primary supplier to about 3,500 supermarkets and franchises of its own retail chains, and a secondary supplier to approximately 2,600 stores, including 1,350 Kmart stores. The company also joined the Worldwide Retail Exchange, a premier retail-focused, business-to-business exchange, and signed a multiyear national supply agreement with Webvan Group, Inc., of Foster City in California.

As was the trend among wholesalers at this time, Supervalu planned to continue its expansion of retail stores in order to gain more control of its core businesses. By 2001 Supervalu's retail food business represented about 60 percent of total company operating earnings, and was growing even more. One of the company's goals was to increase retail square footage by about 5 percent for the 2001 fiscal year. The pharmacy side of Supervalu's retail business, however, was apparently not considered a core one, as the company closed 30 stores in three states, 18 of which contained pharmacies.

The distribution side of Supervalu's business took a blow when Kmart ended its contract with the company, resulting in $2.3 billion in reduced revenue for the year. Supervalu also lost a $400 million annual supply contract with the Genuardi's chain, once the East Coast chain was bought by Safeway in mid-2001. Supervalu continued to consolidate its distribution centers and announced that it would cut 4,500 jobs, or 7.3 percent of its workforce.

JEFF NODDLE AT THE HELM AS CEO

When he replaced the retiring Mike Wright as chief executive officer in 2001, Jeff Noddle pursued an aggressive expansion strategy to offset the loss of distribution business. During 2002, Supervalu opened 115 new stores, including 103 Save-A-Lot stores, 11 price superstores, and one conventional supermarket, and closed 49 stores. In mid-2002, the company announced its plans for 2003: It would open 10 to 15 superstores and at least 150 extreme-value food stores. In another move to gain control over its core business, Supervalu announced that it would purchase St. Louis-based Deal$-Nothing Over a Dollar LLC, adding 53 stores to its general merchandise business. Supervalu's Save-A-Lot chain also opened its 1,000th store in 2002.

In 2003 Noddle negotiated a swap with C&S Wholesale Grocers, offering its New England distribution business for operations in Wisconsin and Ohio. Also, Supervalu obtained the retail distribution business of Flemings, which discontinued those operations in 2003.

Supervalu parlayed its expertise in supply chain management into a subsidiary offering retail distribution logistics management. In October 2003 the company launched Advantage Logistics, expanding on the Advantage brand used for existing Kroger accounts. As a third-party logistics coordinator, Advantage offered its proprietary logistics technology for warehouse, distribution, and transportation management. Flexibility in the technology allowed for easy interface with a client's existing information technology. Success with the concept led Supervalu to expand with the acquisition of Total Logistics, Inc., for $234 million. The 2005 acquisition expanded Supervalu's business into nonfood areas, including automotive parts and office supplies.

Supervalu continued to expand its distribution network. The company added 49 SuperTarget stores in Texas, Oklahoma, Louisiana, Colorado, and Utah. Supervalu started a new distribution business in 2005, W. Newell & Company, which distributed fresh produce to grocery retailers.

In the extreme-value segment, Supervalu continued to expand its highly profitable Save-A-Lot brand through corporate expansion and licensed stores. By the end of fiscal year 2005, more than 1,270 Save-A-Lot stores were in operation.

2006 ALBERTSONS ACQUISITION

Previously the 11th-largest retail grocer in the country, Supervalu ranked third after its 2006 merger with New Albertsons. Recorded as a $17.4 billion acquisition, the deal involved store locations in the western states and along the West Coast operating under Albertsons and Bristol Farms names. Operations in the Midwest and East added Acme Market, Jewel, Shaw's Supermarkets, and Star Markets brands. Supervalu nearly doubled in size with the addition of 1,125 stores to approximately 1,400 existing stores. The Osco and Sav-on in-store pharmacy brands contributed 900 units. Other operations included corporate headquarters in Boise, Idaho; regional offices; and 10 distribution centers.

Supervalu began an extensive overhaul of operations systemwide. Integration with Albertsons maximized the efficiency of its supply chain network and administrative functions. Supervalu closed poorly performing stores or stores in close proximity to better stores. Most of the company's $1.2 billion annual renovation budget for 2007 and 2008 was applied to 100 to 150 newly acquired stores. Supervalu maintained identities of its many brands to preserve regional customer loyalty.

The multiyear project involved updating the company's merchandising strategy. Its new Premium, Fresh & Healthy atmosphere included the Wild Harvest store-within-a-store concept offering organic foods and improvements to the perishable foods areas. In 2006 Supervalu introduced in-store health clinics, Now Care Clinics. Shop the World offered international foods. Shoppers Food Warehouse became Shoppers Food & Pharmacy. The store retained its low cost pricing, without the warehouse atmosphere. At the 202-store Shaw's chain Supervalu shifted from sale prices designed to increase traffic to an everyday low-price strategy.

To simplify merchandising across Supervalu chains, the company initiated the Own Brands program. The company offered a smaller range of brands across three pricing and quality categories, entry-level, national-brand-equivalent, and premium selections. Supervalu introduced several private-label brands, developed at the company's new East View Innovation Center. Test kitchens, sensory laboratories, and related facilities supported new product development. Private-label brands included Homelife Value, Shoppers Value, Wild Harvest, Baby Basics, and Java Delight. Culinary Circle offered fresh-prepared, casual foods.

Supervalu opened several stores under many of the acquired brands, as well the company's existing brands. These involved approximately 25 new supermarkets and 75 limited-assortment stores.

After its first full year operating as one of the top three retail grocers, Supervalu reported $44.05 billion in sales for the fiscal year ending February 23, 2008. Retail accounted for 90 percent of sales, compared to approximately 50 percent before the Albertsons acquisition. Integration of operations resulted in $40 million in savings and operating income rose 31.5 percent to $1.55 billion, resulting in net income of $593 million.

ECONOMIC CONTRACTIONS OF THE GREAT RECESSION

Supervalu continued to expand. However, the economic crisis of late 2008 led to another round of operational and management restructuring, especially after Noddle's retirement in 2009. As consumer spending declined, same-store sales suffered, leading Supervalu to close 22 marginal stores across several brands and throughout the country in late 2008.

Taking the helm as CEO of Supervalu in May 2009, Craig Herkert closed 50 stores and sold the company's 36 Albertsons stores in Utah. He reduced the budget for store remodeling and streamlined the management structure, which had become bloated during the initial integration phase of the Albertsons acquisition. In early 2010 Supervalu sold 16 Shaw's Markets in Connecticut. Herkert pursued a plan of slow development, with an emphasis on the expansion of the Save-A-Lot chain of extreme-value stores.

Nina Wendt
Updated, David E. Salamie; Heidi Wrightsman; Mary Tradii

PRINCIPAL SUBSIDIARIES

Total Logistics, Inc.; W. Wendell & Company.

PRINCIPAL OPERATING DIVISIONS

East; Midwest; West.

PRINCIPAL COMPETITORS

Ahold USA, Inc.; ALDI Group; Alex Lee, Inc.; Allou Enterprise; Associated Wholesalers, Inc.; Bozzuto's, Inc.; D&W Food Centers, Inc.; Delhaize America, Inc.; Di Giorgio Corporation; Dierbergs Markets, Inc.; Dominick's Finer Foods, LLC; Fresh Brands Distributing, Inc.; Giant Eagle, Inc.; The Great Atlantic & Pacific Tea Company, Inc.; Jetro Cash & Carry Enterprises, LLC; Krasdale Foods, Inc.; The Kroger Co.; Marsh Supermarkets, Inc.; McLane Company, Inc.; Meijer, Inc.; Nash-Finch Company; Roundy's Supermarkets, Inc.; Safeway, Inc.; Schnuck Markets, Inc.; Sherwood Food Distributors; Shurfine International; Spartan Stores, Inc.; Topco Associates, LLC; Wakefern Food Corporation; Wal-Mart Stores, Inc.; Winn-Dixie Stores, Inc.

FURTHER READING

Canning, Kathie, "Looking to Lead," *Private Label Buyer*, September 2008, p. 20.

Desjardins, Doug, "Supervalu Kicks Off Major Remodeling Project," *Drug Store News*, April 23, 2007, p. 101.

Levy, Melissa, "Supervalu's Third-Quarter Earnings Slip 19 Percent," *Minneapolis Star Tribune*, December 19, 2000, p. 2D.

Lewis, Len, "Plan-A-Lot: Supervalu's Noddle Charts a Course That Combines Aggressive Expansion with Fiscal Prudence," *Progressive Grocer*, November–December 2001, p. 71.

Merrill, Ann, "Dented but Undaunted; A New Supervalu Executive Team Aims to Freshen Earnings, in Part by Rejuvenating Some Cub Foods Stores," *Minneapolis Star Tribune*, December 11, 2000, p. 1D.

Morris, Kathleen, "Beyond Jurassic Park: Meet the First Big Company Likely to Make It Out of 'Dinosaur-Hood,'" *Financial World*, June 22, 1993, p. 28.

"New CEO Herkert Begins to Put His Stamp on Supervalu," *MMR*, January 11, 2010, p. 56.

"No National Link for Kmart," *Food Logistics*, September 15, 1999, p. 13.

Smith, Rod, "Supervalu to Create Extreme-Value Centers," *Feedstuffs*, June 3, 2002, p. 9.

"Supervalu Announces Store Closings, Restructures," *MMR*, June 25, 2001, p. 138.

"Supervalu Closes Stores," *Drug Store News*, July 23, 2001, p. 4.

"Supervalu Falls 22% after Revealing False Accounting," *New York Times*, June 27, 2002, p. C10.

"Supervalu: 50 Years on the Road to Excellence," special section of *Grocery Marketing*, 1992.

"Supervalu Inc. (The Bottom Line)," *Des Moines Business Record*, February 4, 2002, p. 24.

"Supervalu Inks Richfood Deal," *Food Logistics*, July–August 1999, p. 12.

"Supervalu Is Stung by Accounting Fraud," *Drug Store News*, July 22, 2002, p. 6.

Tosh, Mark, "Wholesale Changes," *Progressive Grocer*, January 1999, p. 29.

Weinstein, Steve, "The Reinvention of Supervalu," *Progressive Grocer*, January 1996, p. 26.

———, "Tomorrow the World," *Progressive Grocer*, October 1992, p. 58.

Susser Holdings Corporation

4433 Baldwin Boulevard
Corpus Christi, Texas 78408
U.S.A.
Telephone: (361) 884-2463
Toll Free: (800) 569-3585
Fax: (361) 884-2494
Web site: http://www.susser.com

Public Company
Incorporated: 1938
Employees: 6,567
Sales: $4.24 billion (2008)
Stock Exchanges: NASDAQ
Ticker Symbol: SUSS
NAICS: 447110 Gasoline Stations with Convenience Stores

■ ■ ■

Susser Holdings Corporation is a Corpus Christi operator of a convenience store chain and serves as a motor fuel distributor through Susser Petroleum Company. The company operates more than 525 convenience stores in Texas, Oklahoma, New Mexico, and Louisiana under the company's proprietary Stripes brand as well as the Town and Country, and Village Market banners. In addition to fuel, foods, beverages, snacks, and general merchandise, many of the stores include ATMs and the Susser-developed restaurants Laredo Taco Company and Country Cookin'. Susser also offers a variety of proprietary items, including Royal brand cigarettes, Café de la Casa coffee, Slush Monkey frozen carbonated drinks, Quake energy drink, Thunderstick meat snacks, Smokin' Barrel beef jerky, and Monkey Loco candies.

Based in Houston, Susser Petroleum works through a network of more than 350 dealers to supply the Susser-owned stores as well as hundreds of independent convenience stores and other customers with motor fuels from Chevron, CITGO, Conoco, Exxon, Shell, Texaco, and Valero. In number of gallons, Susser Petroleum considers itself the largest non-refining motor fuel distributor in Texas. Moreover, Susser is the largest non-refining operator of convenience stores in Texas based on store count. Susser is a public company listed on the NASDAQ. Wellspring Capital Management owns 38.3 percent of the shares and Wellspring partner (and Susser Director) William F. Dawson Jr. owns another 38.4 percent. Samuel L. Susser, grandson of the founder, holds a 13.9 percent stake and serves as the company's president and chief executive officer.

BEGINNINGS IN 1938

Susser Holdings dates its origins to 1938 when Sam Susser took over the management of two Victoria, Texas, gas stations his wife, Minna, inherited. She had been 12 years old when her parents died and left her the businesses. She was raised by her aunt and uncle, the gas stations operated under a trust by the Corpus Christi National Bank until her husband took charge. Susser took a more active role in growing the business than the bank. To obtain a better price on gasoline, he bought a tanker truck and purchased fuel directly from the refinery. He also took advantage of the truck to begin supplying other local gas stations, laying the foundation for a distributorship, Susser Petroleum. Under his direction it grew into the largest non-refiner fuel distributorship in Texas.

Susser's sons, Jerry and Sam J. Susser, joined the family company in the 1960s and soon made their own mark, playing a key role in the 1970s in the development of the first pay-at-the-pump system. Their gas stations had been using a meter system at the pumps to calculate how much customers needed to pay. The brothers were making the rounds to take meter readings when they discovered one pump was malfunctioning so that drivers were filling up for free. According to Jerry Susser, he was the one who suggested that a computerized system could do a better job of keeping tabs on sales. He recalled the incident with the *Corpus Christi Caller-Times*: "I said, 'I'll call IBM, you call Dad and let him known we just lost $10,000 worth of gas.'" The timing for the call to IBM was fortuitous, because the company had just developed a pump-measuring system.

A pair of former NASA engineers, their services no longer needed by the space agency following the end of the Apollo lunar missions, were dispatched from Houston to work with the Susser brothers. Together they developed a system that allowed customers to use their credit cards at an unattended pump, which was linked to a computer by telephone line to complete the transaction. The system took the name $ave-A-$ Club and was manufactured and sold across the country by the Susser family. The Sussers also received membership fees from customers, who paid $5 to enjoy the convenience of paying at the pump. Because of the Arab oil embargo that led to sharp spikes in the cost of motor fuels, control of fuel became critical, creating even greater demand for the Sussers' metering technology.

FORMATION OF SOUTHGUARD CORPORATION: 1988

Samuel J. Susser's son, Samuel L. Susser, joined his father and uncle in 1988. With a degree in finance from the University of Texas, he had spent the previous three years in New York City working in the merger and acquisitions department at Salomon Brothers Inc. At the time, Susser Petroleum was operating Save-A-Dollar gas

stations and generating annual revenues of $8.4 million. The family's retail holdings grew significantly in 1988 when the Sussers and 12 outside investors formed Southguard Corporation to acquire 26 7-Eleven stores. The five Save-A-Dollar gas stations were also converted to the 7-Eleven format.

In the 1990s Southguard added to its slate of 7-Eleven stores, including the acquisition of 27 units in 1992. Two years later Southguard acquired Susser Petroleum along with another business, Susser Environment Services, which installed and removed the underground storage tanks used by gas stations and convenience stores and also provided environmental consulting services. In June 1994 Applied Petroleum Technologies, Ltd., was formed to take over this business as well to sell and install motor fuel pumps, cash registers, credit card readers, and other convenience store-related equipment.

CIRCLE K ALLIANCE: 1995

By 1995 Southguard was operating 59 7-Eleven stores and now forged a joint venture with Phoenix, Arizona-based Circle K Corporation, a major convenience store operator that focused on the Sun Belt states. The joint venture, called SSP Partners (standing for "Sales Service Partners"), called for Southguard's 7-Eleven stores to be rebranded as Circle K units, which would also be operated with 105 existing Circle K stores. All told, 137 units were located in south Texas, making SSP the largest convenience store operator in the area, and another 27 stores were found in the Texas-Oklahoma border area. They were operated on a franchise basis, with Samuel L. Susser serving as president and chief executive officer of SSP Partners as well as Southguard.

SSP expanded in early 1996 when it acquired the 22-year-old 10-unit Ice Box convenience store chain with locations in Port Aransas, Aransas Pass, Rockport, Ingleside, and Portland, Texas. Total annual sales for SSP increased to $300 million. Later in 1996, less than two years after forming SSP with Circle K, Southguard bought out its partner to gain 100 percent ownership of the convenience store chain. In 1998 Samuel L. Susser formed Susser Holdings L.L.C., which became the holding company for Southguard, SSP Partners, and Applied Petroleum Technologies.

ACQUISITION OF A.N. RUSCHE: 1999

The next major step in the growth of Southguard took place on the fuel distribution side in 1999 with the acquisition of A.N. Rusche Distributing Company, Inc.,

KEY DATES

1938: Sam Susser takes over the management of two inherited gas stations.

1988: Susser family forms Southguard Corporation to own 7-Eleven stores.

1995: Southguard creates joint venture to operate Circle K stores.

2001: Susser acquires 121 Coastal Maverick and CoastalMart convenience stores.

2006: Company is taken public.

2007: Town & Country Food Stores is acquired for $361 million.

2009: Susser acquires 25 Quick Stuff stores.

a Houston-based distributor of motor fuel to 200 outlets for the Chevron, CITGO, Exxon, and Texaco brands. Rusche was founded by Albert Nelson Rusche, a World War II veteran who used the G.I. Bill to earn a degree in business administration from Stephen F. Austin State University in 1949. After growing dissatisfied selling dairy equipment, Rusche became an inventory clerk for Gulf Oil, and while he liked the industry, he did not care for the paperwork. Instead, he became a gas station owner, acquiring a Gulf Oil station in 1951.

He next became a commissioned agent for Gulf Oil, and moonlighted by delivering diesel fuel to construction sites and readied the heavy equipment for the next day by filling up their fuel tanks. When another commissioned agent decided to retire, Rusche bought him out in 1956, laying the foundation for A.N. Rusche Distributing Company. Rusche would also add a string of car washes and gas stations as well as Handy Plus convenience stores that operated alongside many of the gas stations. By the end of the 1990s Rusche was ready to sell his businesses and retire, much to the benefit of Susser Petroleum, which now moved the headquarters of the operation to Houston.

In the second half of the 1990s SSP added to its convenience store holdings through new openings and a series of acquisitions, including the addition of other brands. By the start of the new century SSP was operating 440 units, of which 179 were Circle K stores and 261 were divided among the Chevron, Citgo, Exxon, and Texaco brands. About 35 more Circle K stores were soon added, many of them in a new large format that was becoming popular in the convenience store industry, and in 2001 SSP completed a pair of significant acquisitions. In March of that year 30 Tex-Mart

convenience stores were acquired, followed in October by the addition of 121 Coastal Maverick and Coastal-Mart convenience stores. The latter deal also brought 23 unattended fuel sites and 15 motor fuel dealer locations. As a result of this expansion, Susser Holdings increased annual revenues from $766 million in 2001 to more than $1 billion in 2002.

Providing the funds for Susser's growth were three private-equity firms: Banc Boston Ventures Inc., Arena Capital Investment Fund of New York, and Houston's The Cap Street Group. In order to fuel further growth, in late 2005 Susser engineered a new investment agreement with another New York investment firm, Wellspring Capital Investments LLC. Wellspring Capital formed Stripes Acquisitions LLC and merged it with Susser Holdings, which became the surviving entity, a large stake of which was owned by Wellspring. The Stripes name was no idle choice. Several months later in May 2006, Susser announced that it was going to make a public offering of stock and with the expiration of its licensing agreement for the Circle K name, its Circle K stores were going to be rebranded Stripes. A change in fuel brands was also made later in the year, as Stripes dropped Citgo, signing an 11-year agreement with Valero Energy Corporation. In addition, some of Susser Petroleum's wholesale dealers would operate under the Valero brand.

GOING PUBLIC: 2006

On the strength of posting annual revenues of $1.9 billion for 2005, Susser completed its initial public offering in October 2006, raising $113 million, the money earmarked to trim debt. The company was now in a position to pursue further growth in 2007, while also completing the task of rebranding Circle K stores to Stripes and making the transition from CITGO gas to Valero. Susser opened 18 new convenience stores while adding 30 new locations to its wholesale business. It also expanded into west Texas and eastern New Mexico by acquiring privately held Town & Country Food Stores for $361 million in cash in October 2007. The deal included seven Village Market small-format grocery stores and 161 Town & Country convenience stores, of which 140 were located in central and west Texas and the Texas Panhandle and 28 units were located in eastern New Mexico. Altogether, these stores generated annual sales of more than $840 million and helped Susser to increase revenues to $2.72 billion in 2007.

The Town & Country acquisition had a greater impact in 2008 after contributing to the balance sheet for an entire year. Revenues grew to $4.4 billion, aided by the opening of 12 new retail stores and another 27 dealers to the wholesale operation, but more so by the spike in gasoline prices. Moreover, Town & Country provided about $10 million in what the company called "cost synergies."

Susser continued to expand through external means in 2009. In August of that year, Susser acquired 25 Quick Stuff convenience stores in Texas and Louisiana from Jack in the Box Inc., which was exiting the convenience store sector. Susser was already familiar with many of the operations, its wholesale unit supplying fuel to 11 of the stores. Through three-quarters of 2009, Susser's revenues lagged behind the results of the previous year, but that was the result of fluctuating fuel prices. Merchandise sales, on the other hand, had increased. There was every reason to expect Susser and its Stripe convenience store chain to find more room for growth in the years to come.

Ed Dinger

PRINCIPAL SUBSIDIARIES

Stripes Holdings LLC.

PRINCIPAL COMPETITORS

7-Eleven, Inc.; Exxon Mobil Corporation; Valero Energy Corporation.

FURTHER READING

Chirinos, Fanny S., and Tom Whitehurst Jr., "Changing Its Stripes," *Corpus Christi Caller-Times*, May 13, 2006, p. A1.

Copp, Tara, "Sussers Pumped about Expansion," *Corpus Christi Caller-Times*, November 21, 1999, p. D1.

Nelson, Amanda, "The Susser Strategy," *Corpus Christi Caller-Times*, March 21, 2005, p. D4.

Nelson, Nick, "Susser Holdings Announces Agreement," *Corpus Christi Caller-Times*, November 16, 2005, p. D1.

Phelps, Grady, "7-Eleven Stores Here to Become Circle K's," *Corpus Christi Caller-Times*, May 3, 1995, p. D7.

———, "Southguard Purchases All of Partnership in Stores," *Corpus Christi Caller-Times*, November 28, 1996, p. B10.

Van Wagenen, Chris, "Susser Tells Tech Roundtable How Firm Built Success by Listening to Customer," *Lubbock Avalanche-Journal*, February 23, 2007.

T&D Life Group

T&D Holdings Inc.

Shiodome Shika-Rikyu Bldg.
1-2-3 Kaigan
Minato-ku
Tokyo, 105-0022
Japan
Telephone: (+81 3) 3434 9111
Fax: (+81 3) 3434 9055
Web site: http://www.td-holdings.co.jp/e

Public Company
Founded: 1893 as Nagoya Life Insurance Company
Incorporated: 2004
Employees: 108
Total Assets: ¥12.49 trillion ($128.47 billion) (2009)
Stock Exchanges: Tokyo
Ticker Symbol: 8795
NAICS: 551112 Offices of Other Holding Companies

∎ ∎ ∎

T&D Holdings Inc. is the holding company for three Japanese insurance companies, Taiyo Life Insurance, Daido Life Insurance, and T&D Financial Life. Each company focuses on a specific market segment. The largest is Daido Life, which targets the small and mid-sized enterprise market with individual term life insurance and related products. This company represents 66.5 percent of the group's total policies in force at the beginning of 2010. Daido Life conducts its sales both through its own staff of sales representatives as well as through a network of independent sales agents. Taiyo Life provides death protection and medical and nursing care insurance products to the retail household sector, and represents nearly 30 percent of the company's total policy value in force. Taiyo Life's sales are generated through its in-house sales staff. The smallest of the three is T&D Financial Life, which provides individual annuities and other financial products through an agency-based network of banks, securities firms, and other financial institutions.

T&D also operates through T&D Asset Management, including a small U.S. subsidiary, and provides pet insurance through Pet & Family Small-amount and Short-term Insurance Company. T&D Holdings' combined operations generated revenues of ¥2.54 trillion ($25.86 billion) in 2009, making it Japan's fifth-largest life insurance company. T&D Holdings is listed on the Tokyo Stock Exchange, and is led by its president, Naoteru Miyato.

ROOTS IN THE MEIJI ERA

Although created only in 2004, T&D Holdings Inc. traced its roots to the early years of Japan's life insurance industry, during the Meiji era (1867–1912). The country's earliest life insurance company was founded in Tokyo in 1881, and that city remained the major center of Japan's insurance industry. Near the end of the century, new insurance companies appeared in other Japanese cities, such as Nagoya Life Insurance Company, created in 1893. That company later became known as Taiyo Life Insurance Company, and became one of the founding partners of T&D Holdings.

In 1902, three other life insurance companies, namely Asahi Life, Hokkai Life, and Gokoku Life,

COMPANY PERSPECTIVES

T&D Life Group's Corporate Philosophy: With our "Try & Discover" motto for creating value, we aim to be a group that contributes to all people and societies. T&D Life Group's Management Vision: Aim to provide the best products and services to increase customer satisfaction. Aim to increase the value of the group by expanding and creating value in areas where the group can take full advantage of its strengths. Broadly fulfill our social responsibilities with high ethical standards and strict compliance practices. Aim to be an energetic group whose employees are encouraged to be creative and to take action.

merged together to form Daido Seimei Hoken Kabushiki Kaisha (The Daido Life Insurance Company). The new company took Osaka as its home, and came under control of the Hirooka family. This family had long been one of Osaka's most prominent and influential merchant families during the Tokugawa Shogunate earlier in the 19th century. The Hirooka family was also among the few of the city's powerful merchant families to survive into the Meiji Restoration period, and later expanded their operations into the banking sector as well as the insurance industry.

Unlike most of its contemporaries, Daido was structured from the start as a hybrid joint-stock company and mutual insurance concern. The company's founding principles reflected its mutualist leanings, and included stipulations that premiums be kept as low as possible, and that the largest portion of its profits should benefit its policyholders, rather than its shareholders. Daido initially focused on merging and restructuring the operations of its three life insurance businesses. The end of Japan's war with Russia soon after brought a major boom in Japan's life insurance industry. As a result, Daido signed on a growing number of new policyholders, and secured more than ¥50 million in the immediate postwar period.

This growth allowed the company to expand rapidly into new markets in Japan. By 1915, the company operated branches in Osaka, Kobe, Hiroshima, Kyoto, Tokyo, Fukuoka-keu, Sendai, Kanazawa, Nagoya, Sappora, as well as in Seoul, then under Japanese control. In addition to its branch offices, Daido had also established a national network of agencies, with more than 1,150 agents generating policies for the company.

MUTUAL STATUS AFTER WORLD WAR II

Daido grew into one of Japan's larger insurance companies in the years leading up to World War II, although lagging behind the industry's big four companies. These, however, were closely linked to Japan's four largest *zaibatsu*, the family-controlled conglomerates that dominated Japan's economic and industrial landscape in the first half of the 20th century. Nevertheless, Daido profited too from the rising growth of interest in life insurance in Japan. In 1919, life insurance penetration rates remained at less than 3 percent of the total population. By 1929, this figure approached 20 percent. This contrasted strongly with the beginning of the 21st century, when life insurance penetration rates reached 95 percent.

By the outbreak of World War II, more than 40 life insurance companies competed for the Japanese market, with Daido Life and Taiyo Life among them. Many of these companies were extremely profitable, in large part because the life insurance industry had received an exemption from Japan's anti-profiteering laws. The companies also benefited from their close association with the country's *zaibatsu*, which had become essential to the Japanese military and industrial buildup. As a result, the life insurance companies played a major role in helping to finance the war effort.

Japan's surrender, and the large-scale destruction of much of the country's industrial and economic infrastructure, brought the life insurance sector to near collapse following the war. The U.S. occupation forces pushed through the economic restructuring of the country, including the breakup of the *zaibatsu*. Among the economic reforms were new laws governing the insurance industry, including the elimination of the hybrid mutual status put in place by Daido and other insurance companies. Instead, privately held life insurance companies were allowed to operate either as pure joint-stock companies or as mutual life insurance companies.

The majority of Japan's life insurance companies chose the latter form. As a result, Daido reincorporated as Daido Mutual Life Insurance Company in 1947. Nagoya Life Insurance became Taiyo Mutual Life Insurance Company in February of the following year. The end of the 1940s and the beginning of the 1950s remained difficult for both companies, reflecting the financial struggles of Japan as a whole.

GROWTH IN THE SIXTIES

Japan's rapid recovery helped the life insurance sector regain its footing, and by the mid-1950s, the industry

KEY DATES

1893: Taiyo Life Insurance Company is founded as Nagoya Life Insurance Company.

1902: Daido Life Insurance Company is founded through the merger of three life insurance companies.

1947: Daido Life becomes Daido Mutual Life Insurance Company.

1948: Nagoya Life becomes Taiyo Mutual Life Insurance Company.

1999: Daido Mutual and Taiyo Mutual agree to form a business alliance, T&D Life Group.

2001: Daido and Taiyo jointly acquire Tokyo Mutual Life (renamed T&D Financial Life).

2004: Daido, Taiyo, and T&D Financial merge under T&D Holdings.

had returned to its prewar levels. Japan now entered a period of sustained economic growth, as the country emerged as one of the world's major industrial and economic powerhouses. The shortage of men during the period also led insurance companies to turn to the country's women to act as insurance agents, particularly for the door-to-door market. Women continued, even in the next century, to make up the majority of Japan's insurance agents.

By the mid-1960s, life insurance penetration had made strong gains, reaching 70 percent of the country's households. With more than 50 million policies in circulation, with a total worth of more than ¥24 trillion, Japan had become the fourth-largest life insurance market in the world, trailing the United States, the United Kingdom, and Canada.

Both Taiyo Mutual Life and Daido Mutual Life posted their own gains during this period. Taiyo in particular made a mark as a developer of innovative insurance products targeting the household insurance sector. By 1951 the company had introduced an insurance savings product, based on monthly payments and a five-year maturity period. At the same time, Taiyo shifted its marketing strategy to focus on Japan's major urban centers, including its larger regional cities.

Other products developed by Taiyo Mutual Life over the next decades included its Himawari endowment insurance policies, starting with a five-year maturity policy launched in 1968. In 1974, the company launched a new product, the 10-year Kenko Himawari, which provided medical protection benefits over a 10-year span. This was followed by Kenko Himawari Lady, introduced in 1986 and providing medical protection benefits specifically for women-related illness. Taiyo Mutual Life also developed a small business serving the community of Japanese nationals living in the United States.

Daido Mutual Life's development followed a different path, as the company emerged as a major provider of insurance products to the small and midsized enterprise sector. Toward this end, Daido established a number of partnerships, including an initial alliance with Sanwa Bank, later known as the Bank of Tokyo-Mitsubishi, in 1954. In 1971, the company teamed up with AIU Insurance Company, part of American International Group, Inc. Like Taiyo, Daido also entered the United States, serving the Japanese corporate market there. Into the middle of the 1970s, the company formed a partnership with TKC National Federation, developing a new product, called the TKC Corporate Defense Plan.

BUSINESS ALLIANCE IN 1999

Japan's life insurance market had maintained its steady growth through the 1980s. Into the 1990s, however, the industry faced new difficulties as Japan entered a new and extended period of economic decline and stagnation that lasted through the first decade of the next century. Adding to its woes, the life insurance industry faced heightened competition as the Japanese government launched the deregulation of the country's financial sector. This allowed banks, securities firms, and other financial businesses to begin developing insurance products for the first time.

At the same time, the life insurance market faced added pressure from the rapid aging of the Japanese population. By 1990, the Japanese population included nearly 14 million people aged 65 or older. The country also boasted longevity rates among the world's highest. This number was set to grow significantly, a concern further exacerbated by the country's low birth rate. The inevitable decline in new policies meant that too many life insurance companies competed for the shrinking market.

Into the late 1990s, the deregulation of Japan's financial and insurance industries had exposed the weakness underlying many of the country's life insurance players. By the end of the decade, a number of companies were already on the verge of collapse. The Japanese government began putting pressure on the life insurance industry to consolidate in order to create a smaller pool of financially healthy companies.

Daido Mutual Life and Taiyo Mutual Life became among the first to comply with the government's wishes.

In January 1999, the two companies announced that they had forged a business alliance, including the creation of a mutually held insurance company, called T&D Life Group.

T&D HOLDINGS IN 2004

Daido and Taiyo set to work cementing their alliance through that year. The partners established a new joint venture, T&D Asset Management, in order to extend their operations into the asset management sector. The joint venture was strengthened by Daido's acquisition of the investment trust operations of bankrupt Long-Term Credit Bank of Japan in February 1999. Daido and Taiyo also created a joint sales force, as well as their U.S. operations, then founded a second joint venture, T&D Confirm Ltd., which took over both companies' policy confirmation business.

A new step toward the future T&D Holdings came in 2001, when the two companies jointly acquired another bankrupted company, Tokyo Mutual Life Insurance Company. Following its takeover, that company was renamed T&D Financial Life Insurance Company. The company was also "demutualized," and reorganized as a stock company held jointly by Taiyo and Daido. T&D Financial then refocused its operations on developing annuities and other financial insurance products, launching its first variable annuities in 2003. For this, the company focused on sales through banks and other financial institutions. The success of this venture led T&D to shut down T&D Financial's 46-strong sales office network in 2005.

In the meantime, its parent companies had completed their merger, forming T&D Holdings in 2004. Daido took the first step in this process in April 2002, when it became the first of Japan's mutual life insurance companies to restructure as a joint-stock company and go public, listing its shares on the Tokyo Stock Exchange. Taiyo followed suit one year later, and in April 2004 Taiyo Life, Daido Life, and T&D Financial became subsidiaries of a newly created holding company, T&D Holdings. That company was then listed on the Tokyo and Osaka stock exchanges.

NEW CAPITAL IN 2009

T&D Holdings now emerged as Japan's fifth-largest life insurance company, and the country's largest publicly held life insurance group. In 2006, the company consolidated the head offices of its three main subsidiaries, as well as T&D Asset Management, into a single headquarters in Tokyo, further cementing their status as parts of a group. T&D Asset Management, which had been held as a joint venture between Taiyo and Daido, was restructured as a direct subsidiary under T&D Holdings in 2007.

Each of T&D Holdings' life insurance subsidiaries targeted specific and complementary markets. The company moved to expand its range of markets in 2007, with the acquisition of Japan Family Insurance Planning Inc. This purchase allowed the group to enter the small but growing market for pet insurance. The new subsidiary was then renamed Pet & Family Small-amount Short-term Insurance Company.

Amid the global economic crisis at the end of the decade, the company's premium revenues slipped from ¥1.9 trillion in 2006 to ¥1.6 trillion ($16.8 billion) in 2009, despite an increase in overall revenues, to ¥2.54 trillion ($25 billion). However, T&D Holdings also faced its first loss that year, of ¥89 billion ($907 million). Despite these difficulties, T&D successfully completed a series of capital increases, including raising ¥40 billion for T&D Financial and then nearly ¥70 billion ($731 million) to shore up the capital base of Daido Life and Taiyo Life. In this way, the company sought to weather the financial turmoil while seeking new investments for its future growth.

M. L. Cohen

PRINCIPAL SUBSIDIARIES

Alternative Investment Capital, Ltd.; Daido Life Insurance Company; Daido Management Service Co., Ltd.; Nihon System Shuno, Inc.; Pet & Family Small-amount Short-term Insurance Company; T&D Asset Management (USA) Inc.; T&D Asset Management Cayman Inc.; T&D Asset Management Co., Ltd.; T&D Confirm Ltd.; T&D Customer Services Co., Ltd.; T&D Financial Life Insurance Company; T&D Lease Co., Ltd.; Taiyo Credit Guarantee Co., Ltd.; Taiyo Insurance Agency Co., Ltd.; Taiyo Life Career Staff Co., Ltd.; Taiyo Life Insurance Company; Zenkoku Business Center Co., Ltd.

PRINCIPAL DIVISIONS

Household Market; Small and medium-sized Enterprise Market; Individual Variable Annuities Market.

PRINCIPAL OPERATING UNITS

Daido Life; Taiyo Life; T&D Financial Life; T&D Asset Management.

PRINCIPAL COMPETITORS

Dai-Ichi Mutual Life Insurance Co.; Meiji Yasuda Life Insurance Co.; Mitsui Life Insurance Company Ltd.;

Nippon Life Insurance Co.; Sony Financial Holdings Inc.; Rga Reinsurance Co.; Transatlantic Reinsurance Co.; Aioi Insurance Company Ltd.; Dai-ichi Mutual Life Insurance Company; Nipponkoa Insurance Company Ltd.; Sompo Japan Insurance.

FURTHER READING

"Daido Life, Taiyo Life, T&D Financial to Form Holding Firm," *Japan Weekly Monitor*, October 14, 2003.

"First Life Insurer Lists in Japan," *Reactions*, May 2002, p. 8.

"Japan's T&D Had US$389 Mln. Net Profit on Securities at June-end," *AsiaPulse News*, July 15, 2009.

"Japan's T&D Holdings Reports Fiscal 2008 Loss on Investments, Lower Premiums," *A.M. Best Newswire*, May 20, 2009.

"Japan's T&D Holdings Says Value of Life Insurers at Record High," *AsiaPulse News*, May 18, 2007.

"Kida Picked as New Daido Life Pres.," *Jiji*, January 26, 2010.

Lai, Iris, "Japan's T&D Holdings Issues New Shares to Raise Capital for Subsidiaries," *A.M. Best Newswire*, February 24, 2009.

———, "Japan's T&D Holdings to Raise Capital through Public Offering," *A.M. Best Newswire*, December 2, 2009.

"Nomura and T&D among Bidders for Citi Japanese Unit," *Global Banking News*, June 16, 2009.

"T&D Holdings Group to Add Pet-Insurance Firm," *Kyodo News International*, November 29, 2006.

Talecris Biotherapeutics Holdings Corp.

4101 Research Commons
79 T.W. Alexander Drive
Research Triangle Park, North Carolina 27709
U.S.A.
Telephone: (919) 316-6300
Fax: (919) 316-6316
Web site: http://www.talecris.com

Public Company
Incorporated: 2005
Employees: 5,000
Sales: $1.53 billion (2009)
Stock Exchanges: NASDAQ
Ticker Symbol: TLCR
NAICS: 325414 Biological Product (Except Diagnostic)
Manufacturing

■ ■ ■

Talecris Biotherapeutics Holdings Corp. is a North Carolina-based maker of plasma- derived protein therapies for primary immune deficiencies (PI), chronic inflammatory demyelinating polyneuropathy (CIDP), alpha-1 antitrypsin deficiency, bleeding disorders, infectious diseases, and severe trauma. The company's flagship product is Gamunex IGIV, which accounted for more than $825 million in worldwide sales in 2009. Gamunex is used to treat immune deficiency conditions and leukemia as well as to help patients recover from bone marrow transplants. Another major product is Prolastin A1P1, generating about $320 million in worldwide sales in 2009.

To ensure a supply of plasma, the liquid component of blood that is the building block of Talecris products, the company maintains about 70 plasma collection centers and also purchases plasma from third parties. The company operates a pair of manufacturing facilities and sales and marketing operations in the United States, Canada, Germany, and other international regional locations. Talecris is a public company listed on the NASDAQ.

WORLD WAR II-ERA HERITAGE

Talecris traces its lineage to Cutter Laboratories, Inc., named for founder Edward A. Cutter, who established a small manufacturing pharmacy in Fresno, California, in 1897. His sons were brought up in the company and eventually assumed control. As they expanded the company, it became best known to the public in the 1950s for its insect repellent, generically called "Cutters." Like the product Off!, it made use of the compound commonly known as deet, and combined with a lotion it became a mainstay for backpackers and sportsmen. Cutter Laboratories also pioneered plasma fractionation and in 1942 developed its first blood product, albumin, laying the foundation for Talecris.

Talecris's ties to North Carolina were established in 1974 when Cutter Laboratories opened a production facility in Clayton to produce blood products. In that same year, Cutter was acquired by Miles Laboratories, Inc., and in 1978 Miles was in turn acquired by Germany's pharmaceutical giant Bayer AG. Miles operated independently for the next 15 years. During that time, in 1981, it received approval for the first intravenous immune globulin, which was marketed under the Gamimune name. In 1988 Miles introduced the first proteinase inhibitor product, sold as Prolastin. In 1992 Bayer combined all of its U.S. operations under Miles, Inc., which in 1995 was renamed Bayer Corporation. The former Cutter operation was now the Bayer HealthCare Biological Products Division (Bayer BP).

ADVANCES: 2001–04

The North Carolina operation continued to grow in the meantime. By the end of the 1990s its fractionation capacity approached two million liters per year. Bayer BP expanded its products and capabilities as well. It achieved an industry first in 2001 with the introduction of the Western Blot Assay method of testing plasma purification during plasma protein manufacture. A year later it became the first biological products company to use tamper-evident packaging. In 2003 the company became the first to employ viral inactivation technology to produce Intravenous Immune Globin (IVIG), part of an effort to replace Gamimune. The company's researchers essentially re-imagined the company's highly successful product. The successor, Gamunex, received U.S. Food and Drug Administration (FDA) approval in August 2003 and was introduced to the market in 2004. Also in that year, Bayer BP became the first plasma fractionator to receive FDA approval for the in-house nucleic acid testing of human immunodeficiency virus (HIV).

A key concern for Bayer BP was maintaining a reliable supply of plasma. The parent company attempted to acquire a competitor that owned a blood plasma collection network, but when that bid failed Bayer AG elected to sell Bayer BP. In the spring of 2005 the business was sold for $303.5 million to a management team led by Lawrence D. Stern with the financial backing of a pair of investment firms, New York buyout firm Cerberus Capital Management and Ampersand Ventures, a venture capital firm based in Wellesley, Massachusetts. Included in the sale was the Clayton plant, and the laboratory and former Bayer BP headquarters in Raleigh, North Carolina. The assets were transferred to

a newly formed company, Talecris Biotherapeutics Holdings Corp. Bayer, in the meantime, moved the headquarters of its Biological Products Division to Berkeley, California.

At the same time the Bayer BP business was being acquired, the owners of Talecris supplemented production capacity by adding Ampersand Ventures-owned Precision Plasma Services, a Melville, New York-based contract manufacturer of blood plasma products. Precision Plasma got its start as Melville Biologics Inc. in 1980 when its New York Blood Center facility was licensed by the FDA. It adopted the Precision Plasma name upon Ampersand Ventures acquiring the company in 2001. After becoming part of Talecris it retained the Precision name until 2008 when its operations and name were merged completely into Talecris.

Lawrence Stern served as the CEO for Talecris until October 2005, when he turned over day-to-day control to his successor, although he remained chairman of the board. (About two years later, Martinex would leave the company, and Stern once again became CEO as well as chairman.) The new CEO was Dr. Alberto Martinez, who was well familiar with the plasma products field, having served as former vice president of commercial operations of a plasma products subsidiary of the Australia pharmaceutical firm CSL Ltd. In addition, a chief financial officer was installed as was a senior vice president of human resources.

CANADIAN AND EUROPEAN EXPANSION

Talecris made progress on multiple fronts in 2006. It expanded into Canada in April and on December 1 expanded into Europe as well with the opening of a regional headquarters in Frankfurt, Germany, to serve 15 European countries. The company established Talecris Talents, a grant program to fund basic and clinical research related to the use of Intravenous immunoglobulin. Perhaps of most importance to Talecris was an acquisition that laid the foundation for Talecris Plasma Resources, a plasma collection operation that ensured a reliable, safe supply of plasma needed to manufacture the company's products. In November 2006 Talecris purchased Lafayette, Louisiana-based International BioResources LLC, which operated 58 plasma collection centers spread across 21 U.S. states. Securing plasma supplies was especially important because a supply agreement with CSL Limited was set to expire at the end of 2008.

The corporate parents of Talecris were not in the habit of holding on to properties and quickly sought an exit strategy that provided them with a healthy return

KEY DATES

1942: Cutter Laboratories develops first blood product.
1974: Cutter opens production facility in Clayton, North Carolina.
1995: Former Cutter operation becomes Bayer BP.
2005: Bayer BP is sold to a management team; Talecris Biotherapeutics is created.
2009: Talecris goes public.

on their investment. An initial public offering (IPO) was planned for the spring of 2007. It was hoped the company could raise $1 billion to pay down debt as well as pay a dividend to its investors and a termination fee for a management agreement with Cerberus and Ampersand. Poor market conditions caused by a credit crisis forced the offering to be shelved, however.

A year later a buyer was being sought after Talecris encountered several problems that adversely impacted its prospects for a successful stock offering. The company was $1.3 billion in debt, and debt ratings agency Moody's questioned the ability of Talecris to repay its debt. Another concern, in light of the lapsing agreement with CSL, was plasma supply. Moreover, Talecris was sued in May 2008 by a U.S. rival, Baxter International, which claimed that Talecris infringed on patents Baxter held on a way to test donated blood for infectious agents. Talecris faced some clear challenges that required the infusion of cash that only a sale or stock offer could provide. Not only did Talecris need to pay down its debt, it required funds to invest in drug development, build new facilities and upgrade old ones, and expand its blood plasma sources.

AGREEMENT TO SELL COMPANY: 2008

Talecris appeared to have an answer for its concerns in August 2008 when an agreement was reached to sell the business to CSL for $3.1 billion. It was a deal that made sense for both parties. CSL was the second-largest blood-plasma products company, trailing only Baxter, while Talecris was the third largest. Together they were larger than Baxter, and the addition of Talecris provided the Australian company entry into both the North American and European markets. Cerberus and Ampersand were also in a position to net $2 billion, representing a hefty profit on their $303.5 million initial investment.

The CSL deal was subject, however, to regulatory approval, and in the spring of 2009 the U.S. Federal Trade Commission (FTC) filed a complaint in U.S. District Court to oppose it on antitrust grounds, worried that because of CSL's greater size the price of medicines made from blood plasma would increase. CSL had offered to sell as many as 25 of its plasma collection centers in the United States as well as divest some of its blood products, but had failed to secure FTC support. Rather than fight the FTC in court, CSL elected to withdraw its bid and pay Talecris a $75 million breakup fee.

TAKEN PUBLIC: 2009

Once again Talecris turned its attention to the capital markets, reviving its plans for an IPO. Since the last time the company had pursued such a course, interest in technology and biotechnology stocks had improved. Nevertheless, only a handful of companies had conducted successful IPOs in 2009. In its new filings, Talecris indicated a desire to sell 44.7 million shares at $18 to $20 a share, potentially grossing $894 million. When the offering was held in October 2009, Talecris was able to fetch $19 a share and sell more stock than anticipated, resulting in $950 million being raised, making it the second-largest stock offering of 2009. Moreover, the company raised another $550 million through the sale of its debt as part of a debt restructuring. Combined, Cerberus and Ampersand continued to hold about 70 percent of their initial investment.

Talecris indicated that it planned to spend about $750 million of the money it raised to improve manufacturing facilities. A month later the company announced a $269 million expansion on its Clayton manufacturing facility. Because of the 259 new jobs that would result, the company received local and state grants.

After Talecris stock began trading on the NASDAQ it increased in value 17 percent by the end of the year. The price dipped somewhat in February 2010 when the company reported disappointing fourth-quarter results. Although revenues exceeded expectations, earnings per share fell short of analyst predictions, totaling $1.4 million compared to $26.2 million for the same period in 2008. For the year, revenues increased 11.6 percent to $1.53 billion and net income grew 133.9 percent to $153.9 million. A strong performance of Gamunex IGIV was a primary reason for the company's success. Boding well for 2010 and beyond was the October 2009 FDA approval for Talecris's next generation A1P1 product, Prolastin-C, which was also approved for use in Canada in February 2010. Talecris was ramping up production of the plasma product for a North American launch in 2010. With other drugs in the pipeline and expanding production capacity in the offing, Talecris appeared to be well positioned for ongoing growth.

Ed Dinger

PRINCIPAL SUBSIDIARIES

Talecris Biotherapeutics Limited; Talecris Plasma Resources; Talecris Biotherapeutics GmbH.

PRINCIPAL COMPETITORS

Baxter International Inc.; CSL Behring, LLC; Grifols, S.A.

FURTHER READING

Cox, Jonathan B., "Talecris Plans IPO to Raise $1 Billion," *Raleigh (NC) News & Observer*, July 28, 2007.

Demetrakakes, Pan, "Talecris Has Medical Distribution Down Cold," *Food & Drug Packaging*, May 2005, p. 47.

"Talecris Launches European Operation," Triangle Business Journal, December 1, 2006.

"Talecris to Create 259 Clayton Jobs with $269 Million Clayton Expansion," *Triangle Business Journal*, November 13, 2009.

Vollmer, Sabine, "Talecris Pumps Itself Up," Raleigh (NC) News & Observer, June 25, 2008.

———, "Talecris Sale Has Nerves Tingling," *Raleigh (NC) News & Observer*, August 15, 2008.

———, "Talecris to Buy Plasma Centers," *Raleigh (NC) News & Observer*, November 7, 2006.

Wolf, Alan M., "CSL Drops $3.1 Billion Bid for Talecris," *Raleigh (NC) News & Observer*, June 8, 2009.

———, "Talecris Giving Wall Street Another Try," *Raleigh (NC) News & Observer*, July 28, 2009.

———, "Talecris Toasts Successful IPO," *Raleigh (NC) News & Observer*, October 2, 2009.

TDK Corporation

1-13-1 Nihonbashi
Chuo-ku
Tokyo, 103-8272
Japan
Telephone: (+81 3) 5201-7102
Fax: (+81 3) 5201-7114
Web site: http://www.tdk.co.jp

Public Company
Incorporated: 1935 as Tokyo Denki Kagaku Kogyo K.K.
  (TDK Electronics Company, Ltd.)
Employees: 66,429
Sales: ¥727.4 billion ($7.42 billion) (2009)
Stock Exchanges: Tokyo London
Ticker Symbols: 6762; TDK
NAICS: 327113 Porcelain Electrical Supply Manufacturing; 334112 Computer Storage Device Manufacturing; 334414 Electronic Capacitor Manufacturing; 334415 Electronic Resistor Manufacturing; 334416 Electronic Coil, Transformer, and Other Inductor Manufacturing; 334419 Other Electronic Component Manufacturing; 334613 Magnetic and Optical Recording Media Manufacturing; 335311 Power, Distribution, and Specialty Transformer Manufacturing; 335911 Storage Battery Manufacturing

∎ ∎ ∎

TDK Corporation is a major global manufacturer of a variety of electronic materials and devices. The company's largest product area, generating about one-third of overall sales, is recording devices. TDK ranks as the world's top producer of magnetic recording heads used in hard disk drives, and it also manufactures suspension assemblies for such drives. About 23 percent of sales comes from electronic devices, such as inductive devices, high-frequency components, and power supplies. Electronic materials generate another 20 percent of sales; these included multilayer ceramic chip capacitors, rare-earth and ferrite magnets, and ferrite cores for coils and transformers. For much of its history TDK was best known as one of the world's leading makers of recording media, including audio and videotapes and rewritable CD and DVD discs, but this business was divested in 2007. TDK subsequently bolstered its core electronic materials and devices operations via the 2008 acquisition of the German firm Epcos AG.

ORIGINS AS MARKETER OF FERRITE TECHNOLOGY

The initial success of TDK paralleled the commercial development of a remarkably versatile material known as ferrite, a magnetic material with ceramic properties. Ferrite is composed of ferric oxide and any of a number of other metallic oxides, but usually zinc. Ferrite can be produced in several variations, each with somewhat different properties, and it can be categorized in two groups: hard and soft. Hard ferrite can be easily and permanently magnetized. Soft ferrite, on the other hand, does not stay magnetized for any great length of time but has other properties that make it suitable for many electronics applications.

COMPANY PERSPECTIVES

The spirit of craftsmanship, of creating products that have true value—this is what our manufacturing power is all about. As a company that has the needs of its customers at heart, we believe that we must be ready to swiftly adapt to market changes. Using our resources and potential of manufacturing to turn dreams into reality—this will continue to be our aim in the future.

Ferrite was invented in 1933 by two Japanese scientists, Dr. Yogoro Kato and Dr. Takeshi Takei, at the Tokyo Institute of Technology. Two years later, Kenzo Saito founded TDK Corporation (originally known as Tokyo Denki Kagaku Kogyo K.K., or TDK Electronics Company, Ltd.) to market the scientists' discovery. Saito had been searching for a manufacturing business that he could establish in his hometown of Nikaho, a town in the prefecture of Akita that was wholly dependent on agriculture. When Kato and Saito met by chance, each was impressed by the other, and soon Kato granted Saito the use of the ferrite technology he and Takei had developed.

TDK's first application was a soft ferrite product, marketed as an "oxide core" and employed in transformers and coils. The demand for ferrite was very limited at this time, however, and TDK's first years were hard. As the number of electrical appliances in the world increased, however, demand for TDK's ferrite cores increased dramatically. Early in its history, TDK made research and development (R&D) a priority by exploring the properties of ferrite and finding new ways to employ it. Soon, the use of ferrite cores became widespread in consumer electronics products such as radios and televisions, markets that grew considerably during the 1940s and 1950s. Saito left TDK in 1946 and later became a member of the Diet (Japan's parliament).

DIVERSIFYING MANUFACTURING AND EXPANDING OVERSEAS

Eventually TDK branched into the manufacture of materials other than ferrite. In 1951 the company began to produce ceramic capacitors. These components are used to store electrical energy, inhibit the flow of direct current, or facilitate the flow of alternating current, and are widely used in the production of electronic devices. Establishing itself as a key components manufacturer,

TDK would benefit as the Japanese electronics industry grew.

In 1952 TDK introduced its first magnetic recording tape. TDK's line of recording tape eventually became the industry standard, and at one point it accounted for half of the company's sales. In Japan TDK led the development of recording tape, becoming the first domestic manufacturer of audiocassettes in 1966. Two years later the company defied skeptics when it produced the world's first high-fidelity cassettes, marketed by TDK as Super Dynamic tape.

Meanwhile, a TDK researcher named Yasuo Imaoka was looking for a material that could be used to replace chromium dioxide in video and audiotapes. Chromium dioxide, while offering excellent sound quality, is rare and expensive. Imaoka and his team came up with a process that combined ferric oxide with metal cobalt. The resulting material was named Avilyn, and it had a greater coercivity, a measure of magnetic substances, than chromium dioxide. Avilyn videotapes hit the market in 1973. The formula was soon improved by using cobalt hydroxide instead of metal cobalt, and the resulting Super Avilyn (SA) audiotapes revolutionized the industry when TDK unveiled its SA line, the first nonchrome high-bias tape, in 1975. In 1985 the Japanese Council of Industrial Patents named Avilyn as one of the country's top 53 inventions of the century.

As TDK developed technological innovations, its marketing strength also improved. The company entered foreign markets as early as 1959, opening a representative office in New York City. TDK opened a second U.S. office in Los Angeles four years later, and TDK Electronics Corporation, the first overseas subsidiary, was established in New York in 1965. TDK's international operations grew extensively during the late 1960s and the 1970s. In 1968 TDK set up a subsidiary in Taiwan to manufacture ferrite cores, ceramic capacitors, and coil components. Over the course of the next 10 years, TDK established subsidiaries in West Germany, Hong Kong, Great Britain, Brazil, Korea, Mexico, the United States, Singapore, and Australia. To ease trade imbalances and to insulate the company from currency fluctuations, TDK set up manufacturing facilities in many of these countries. TDK or its subsidiaries began producing magnetic heads in the United States in 1972 and audiotape a year later, ferrite cores in Korea in 1973, ferrite magnets in Mexico in 1974, ferrite cores in Brazil in 1979, and videotape in the United States in 1980. By the mid-1980s nearly half of TDK's business was generated outside of Japan. In the meantime, TDK went public in 1961 with a listing on the Tokyo Stock Exchange.

KEY DATES

1935: Kenzo Saito founds Tokyo Denki Kagaku Kogyo K.K. (TDK Electronics Company, Ltd.) to market ferrite cores.

1951: Company diversifies, launching production of ceramic capacitors.

1952: TDK begins production of magnetic recording tape.

1961: Company goes public with a listing on the Tokyo Stock Exchange.

1965: TDK Electronics Corporation, the first overseas subsidiary, is established in New York.

1966: Production of audiocassettes begins.

1973: Avilyn videotapes are introduced.

1983: Company's name is changed to TDK Corporation.

2000: TDK acquires Headway Technologies, Inc., producer of recording heads.

2002: Company posts first net loss since it began reporting consolidated earnings results in 1975.

2007: The global TDK-brand recording media unit is sold to Imation Corporation.

2008: TDK acquires EPCOS AG, a major producer of electronic components based in Germany.

VCR-FUELED BOOM TIMES

In the mid-1970s TDK's already impressive growth rate took off for a number of reasons. Technological developments in consumer electronics created new demand for the company's expertise in ferrite and other materials. More sensitive audio equipment created strong demand for TDK's SA tapes, and the introduction of videocassette recorders (VCRs) to the consumer market created new demand for both the software (videotapes) and hardware (magnetic tape heads and other components) that TDK was capable of producing. The company's sales went through the roof as the videocassette market expanded 60 percent each year in the late 1970s.

Videocassettes and audiocassettes made up half of TDK's sales in the early 1980s. In 1983, however, an oversupply of videotapes sent prices into a downward spiral. While TDK's audiotapes sales continued to improve, revenue from videotape declined even though total volume increased. Just as the videotape crunch was at its worst, Yutaka Otoshi, the former chief of the tapes division, took over as TDK president and CEO. Otoshi

increased TDK's R&D budget from 3.4 percent to 5 percent of sales to ensure the company's technological edge. New products such as the compact 8mm camcorders and players and recordable optical videodiscs were expected to give a boost to the market. Nonetheless, Otoshi focused on expanding TDK's nontape business. As he told *Business Week* in 1983, "we have never thought it was a good idea to concentrate too much on one product." Also in 1983, the company changed its name to TDK Corporation.

R&D SUCCESSES IN THE EIGHTIES

In 1984 TDK launched its Components Engineering Laboratory in Los Angeles. At this lab TDK's researchers worked with marketing personnel to develop custom prototypes of transformers, microwave products, and other components for use by U.S. customers. In addition to customization, the new lab reduced the time required to go from product development to full-scale production. TDK's research efforts also resulted in the development of a number of new products in the 1980s. The company made breakthroughs in the development of thin-film heads for increased recording sensitivity, in multilayer hybrid circuits that allowed equalization in headphone cassette players to be performed in one-third the usual space, and in sensor technology.

Another area in which TDK excelled in the 1980s was the field of anechoic chambers, rooms lined with a material that absorbs radiowaves. Anechoic chambers are used to measure the electromagnetic emission of electronic products and also a product's vulnerability to interference from such emissions. TDK's success with anechoic chambers grew out of its experience with microwave absorption. The company first began research in that field in 1964 and by 1968 had marketed its first ferrite-based microwave absorbers. The popularity of microwave ovens, which use a ferrite and rubber compound to keep the cooking process inside the oven, bolstered TDK's bottom line. In 1975 the company applied its expertise in microwave absorption to anechoic chambers, and in the 1980s, as demand for these facilities grew on the back of a booming electronics industry, TDK became a major force in the field.

In 1987 the company embarked on a joint venture with the Allen-Bradley Company, of the United States, to produce motor magnets for the automobile industry. Allen-Bradley/TDK Magnetics began production at a plant in Oklahoma in April of that year. TDK benefited from its partner's long-standing relationship with U.S. automakers, and Allen-Bradley benefited from TDK's magnetics expertise.

The late 1980s also saw the miniaturization of and increased demand for higher-density circuits and components. Manufacturers of these products required extremely precise equipment for their production facilities. TDK's Avimount and Avisert automated assembly equipment was in greater demand as a result. Sales in 1988 were up 25 percent over the previous year and were expected to continue to rise.

TDK's focus on broadening its nontape products was successful. By 1988 the nontape sector accounted for 64 percent of the company's total sales. TDK did not, however, neglect its recording-media development. TDK's floppy disks, first produced in 1982, garnered a respectable market share partly based on the company's excellent reputation in audio and video recording media. In 1987 the company introduced digital audio tape into the Japanese market and prepared to enter foreign markets as soon as copyright problems were settled. Such tapes were able to play and record music digitally, like compact discs. In 1988 it introduced a top-of-the-line videotape called Super Strong, a new product that allowed TDK to raise prices and still maintain market share.

TDK continued to grow on its own and make acquisitions when appropriate. In 1988 the company acquired Display Components Inc. (Discom), of Westford, Massachusetts. The purchase allowed Discom access to TDK's advanced production techniques while TDK received Discom's state-of-the-art magnetic field technology.

OVERSEAS PRODUCTION AND INCREASING R&D

In 1989 TDK purchased a large U.S. manufacturer of mixed-signal integrated circuits, Silicon Systems Inc. (SSI), for $200 million, further diversifying its range of products. SSI proved to be a problematic acquisition for TDK, however. SSI struggled during its first few years under TDK, even after a $100-million-plus infusion from the parent to help SSI beef up its U.S. production. By the mid-1990s, even this had not provided SSI with the capacity it needed to compete with the giants of the semiconductor industry. Rather than sinking more money into the troubled firm, TDK decided to sell SSI in 1996 and found a willing buyer among these same giants, namely Texas Instruments Incorporated. Terms were $575 million in cash plus further contingent payments.

This sale did not mark TDK's complete withdrawal from semiconductor-related areas, however. Not included in the deal were SSI's Communications Products Division and TDK Systems Division, leaving TDK with such products as PC cards and integrated circuits for telecommunications. These were not insignificant, as evidenced particularly by TDK's success in the area of fax/modem PC cards, a product that experienced explosive sales growth in the mid-1990s as the Internet and online services became everyday business and personal tools.

In the early to mid-1990s, TDK had to contend with a glut in the videotape market and the consequences of an extremely strong yen, both of which depressed company sales, and consequently earnings. TDK moved aggressively to cut costs, consolidating Japanese production of blank audio and videotapes in one factory in 1993. To mitigate the effects of the strong yen, TDK shifted much of its production overseas. Ferrite products began to be manufactured in Dalian, China, in 1993. By 1995, more than half of TDK's audio and videotapes were produced outside Japan, namely in Luxembourg, the United States, and Thailand. In May 1996 TDK announced a plan to shift all its floppy disk manufacturing overseas, some to a California subsidiary, some to several Southeast Asian companies. In the fall of 1996, a new plant in Hungary began manufacturing transformers, ferrite cores, and other components.

Under the guidance of President Hiroshi Sato, TDK further bolstered R&D by spending 6 percent of overall sales on new product development. One product area targeted was that of ceramic filters for mobile telecommunications, another high-growth sector. Overall, R&D was directed to make TDK even less dependent on the mature areas of magnetic products and tapes. An example of the company's search for non-tape revenue was the joint venture with Duracell International Inc. announced in early 1996, whereby the two companies would jointly develop and manufacture ion electrode sets, a key component in the increasingly popular lithium-ion rechargeable battery.

The production shifts and emphasis on new products began to pay off in 1996, with TDK posting healthy increases of 11.6 percent in net sales and 41.1 percent in operating profit over 1995, which represented the best consolidated results in five years. The company cited electronic components for computers, home electronics, and telecommunications products as the main contributors to these gains. Continued strong sales in overseas markets and the yen's weakness against the dollar sent sales and profits soaring still higher in fiscal 1997. Revenues increased another 15 percent, and operating profits surged by nearly 43 percent.

ACQUISITIONS, HEADS FOR HARD DISK DRIVES

Continuing its policy of making strategic acquisitions, TDK acquired Grey Cell Systems Limited in September 1997. Based in the United Kingdom, Grey Cell specialized in PC card and software-based data communications products. Grey Cell was later renamed TDK Systems Europe Ltd. Having produced CD-Rs (rewritable compact discs) for the first time in 1993, TDK maintained its position on the cutting edge of recording media by launching production of DVD-R discs in April 1998, well in advance of any sizable market for the product. In June 1998 Sato retired from his position as president of TDK and was succeeded by Hajime Sawabe.

By the late 1990s one of TDK's major product areas was that of magnetoresistive recording heads, a key component of computer disk drives. TDK was one of the leading makers of an advanced version of these heads that were known as giant magnetoresistive (GMR) heads, and much of the company's profits were derived from the sale of GMR heads. In March 2000 TDK bolstered its position in this sector with the purchase of Headway Technologies, Inc., for about $122 million. Based in Milpitas, California, and founded in 1994, Headway produced a variety of recording heads but was particularly strong in the area of GMR heads. The company reported net income of $1 million on sales of $160 million for 1999.

Despite TDK's commitment to remaining on the cutting edge of technological development and its selected use of acquisitions and strategic alliances as growth generators, profits came under increasing pressure around the turn of the millennium as the Japanese economy continued to struggle. One response to this profit squeeze was a restructuring of the product lines. Products were now arranged into five sectors: electronic materials, electronic devices, recording devices, semiconductors, and recording media.

Another strategy was diversification, and TDK in 2000 moved beyond its traditional position as provider of recording media by branching out into the manufacture of related hardware devices for sale to consumers. Early in 2000 the company began selling TDK brand CD-R/RW drives for personal computers. In November of that year the company introduced its first audio CD recorder, and in January 2001 TDK began selling computer speakers. Meanwhile, in December 2000, TDK paid $26 million for U.S. semiconductor maker Sierra Research and Technology Inc. Established in 1993, Sierra specialized in the design of CMOS (complementary metal-oxide semiconductor)

products for networking and data communications applications.

RESTRUCTURING AMID TECH DOWNTURN

By late 2001 TDK was forced to launch a major restructuring effort as the technology market entered a severe slump precipitated by a slowdown in the U.S. economy and by a global downturn in information technology investment. Inventories for a broad range of electronic components soared as the predictions for worldwide demand for mobile phones and personal computers proved to be far too optimistic. The huge inventories placed downward pressure on prices, cutting into revenues.

In October 2001 TDK responded by announcing plans to cut 8,800 jobs, or 20 percent of its workforce by March 2004, with 2,300 of the job cuts earmarked for the company's domestic operations. Two manufacturing plants in Japan and one in Germany were closed, and several subsidiaries were consolidated to improve efficiencies. The number of jobs to be eliminated was increased by 400 in February 2002. Restructuring charges for the fiscal year ending in March 2002 totaled ¥25.87 billion ($194.5 million). This led to TDK's first net loss since it began reporting consolidated earnings results in 1975. For fiscal 2002, the company lost ¥25.77 billion ($193.8 million) on net sales of ¥575.03 billion ($4.32 billion). The sales figure represented a 16.7 percent decline from the previous year, despite a further weakening in the yen.

As TDK returned to the black in fiscal 2003 and demand for electronic components began picking up, the company pursued growth in three main areas: consumer home electronics, broadband networks, and car electronics. TDK benefited from growing demand for its magnetic heads for hard disk drives in part because such drives were increasingly moving beyond computers into such consumer electronics products as DVD recorders. In the broadband networks field, TDK in March 2003 acquired the U.S. firm Innoveta Technologies, Inc. Innoveta specialized in DC-DC converters, a key electronic component used in a variety of communications and data network applications to convert a source of direct current (DC) from one voltage level to another. TDK was also a pioneer in the market for DC-DC converters for the burgeoning field of hybrid electric vehicles. These converters represented only part of TDK's presence in the field of power supply components, an area that meshed with the company's historic development given that ferrite was a core component of power supplies.

China was a key growth market for TDK at this time, and by 2004 the company's Chinese operations, which included several manufacturing facilities, were generating nearly 20 percent of the firm's overall sales. In a streamlining move, TDK in 2005 placed four of its Chinese manufacturing units under a new holding company called TDK China Co., Ltd. In May 2005 TDK ventured deeper into China, while also entering the market for rechargeable batteries, by acquiring Hong Kong-based Amperex Technology Limited for about $100 million. At its factory in China, Amperex produced polymer lithium rechargeable batteries for use in mobile phones and other portable devices. Also in 2005, TDK divested its semiconductor subsidiary and thus exited from that sector, and it bolstered its power supply operations by acquiring majority control of Lambda Power Group, the power supply business of the U.K.-based Invensys plc, for ¥24.2 billion ($207 million).

DEAL-ALTERED TDK

In June 2006 Sawabe was named chairman and CEO, while Takehiro Kamigama, who had headed the firm's magnetic heads business, took over day-to-day operations as president and COO. This leadership team accelerated the pace of deal-making and in the process significantly reconfigured the company's product portfolio. In August 2007 TDK sold the business for which it was still best known, its global TDK-brand recording media unit, which had generated about 12 percent of the company's fiscal 2007 sales of ¥862.03 billion ($7.31 billion). The business was sold to the U.S. firm Imation Corporation for about $250 million in cash and stock, and TDK thus emerged with a stake in Imation of about 20 percent. The deal included TDK's audiotape, videotape, CD-R, and DVD operations, as well as a license to use the TDK name, but not its business in tape-based data storage media for computers. This divestment enabled TDK to concentrate on its operations with greater growth potential.

One of TDK's key areas was magnetic heads for hard disk drives, and the firm strengthened itself in this sector via the September 2007 purchase of the magnetic heads business of Alps Electric Co., Ltd., for ¥34.43 billion ($344 million). TDK and Alps had been the world's last two remaining independent producers of magnetic heads, and with TDK's takeover of Alps, TDK's only competitors in this field were manufacturers of hard drives that produced component parts in-house. In November 2007 TDK ventured into a closely related field by acquiring majority control of Thailand-based Magnecomp Precision Technology Public Company

Limited, a producer of suspension assemblies for hard-disk-drive magnetic heads. Around this same time, TDK began producing magnetic heads for third-generation high-capacity hard drives featuring perpendicular magnetic recording (PMR) technology. TDK supplied the heads for PMR hard drives produced by South Korea-based Samsung Electronics Co., Ltd. This relationship made Samsung TDK's largest customer, accounting for nearly 12 percent of net sales during fiscal 2008.

TDK maintained its positive momentum through fiscal 2008, when the company garnered net income of ¥71.46 billion ($714.6 million) on ¥866.29 billion ($8.67 billion) in revenue. For the first time in eight years, TDK's operating income ratio topped the 10 percent mark, reflecting the firm's cost-containment efforts. From this position of strength, TDK completed its boldest acquisition to that point in October 2008. For a total price of ¥163.73 billion ($1.67 billion), TDK significantly expanded its global passive electronic components operations by acquiring EPCOS AG. Based in Munich, Germany, and originally a division of Siemens AG, EPCOS had generated net sales of EUR 1.48 billion ($2.08 billion) for the fiscal year ending in September 2008.

TDK subsequently merged its existing electronic materials and devices operations with EPCOS to form TDK-EPC Corporation. This subsidiary combined TDK's strength in general-purpose ceramic capacitors and inductive devices for consumer electronics and personal computers with EPCOS's strength in customized products such as piezo actuators for automobile fuel-injection systems, surface acoustic wave (SAW) filters for mobile phones, and aluminum electrolytic and film capacitors for industrial electronics. Acquiring EPCOS also geographically diversified TDK's revenue streams as EPCOS generated 65 percent of its sales in Europe whereas most of TDK's sales originated in Japan or elsewhere in Asia. A further benefit was to lessen TDK's dependence on its core magnetic heads business, which was vulnerable to changes in the volatile personal computer market.

Around the same time that TDK was wrapping up its takeover of EPCOS, the world economy fell sharply into recession, cutting demand for electronic devices and thus causing electronic component orders to plunge. TDK quickly launched restructuring efforts that included a 10,000-person workforce reduction and the closure of four plants located outside Japan. Restructuring costs of ¥15.88 billion ($162 million) contributed to a net loss for the fiscal year ending in March 2009 of ¥63.16 billion ($644.5 million). Despite six months of contributions from EPCOS, net sales fell 16 percent to

¥727.4 billion ($7.42 billion). As demand for electronic devices began recovering, TDK reported a net profit for the first nine months of fiscal 2010, although full-year results were projected to be well below the record level set in 2008.

Updated, David E. Salamie

PRINCIPAL SUBSIDIARIES

TDK-EPC Corporation; TDK-Lambda Corporation; TDK Design Inc.; TDK-MCC Corporation; TDK Ujo Corporation; TDK Yurihonjo Corporation; TDK Ugo Corporation; TDK Iwaki Corporation; TDK Shonai Corporation; TDK Micro Device Corporation; TDK-Lambda Facilities Corporation; TDK Iida Corporation; Media Technology Corporation; TDK Sagara Corporation; TDK China Co., Ltd.; TDK Korea Corporation; TDK Taiwan Corporation; TDK U.S.A. Corporation; TDK Electronics Europe GmbH (Germany); EPCOS AG (Germany).

PRINCIPAL DIVISIONS

Ceramic Capacitors Business Group; Magnetics Business Group; Systems Acoustics Waves Business Group; Piezo & Protection Devices Business Group; Sensors Business Group; Aluminum-Electrolytic Capacitors Business Group; Film Capacitors Business Group; Power Systems Business Group; Ferrite & Magnet Products Business Group; Data Storage & Thin Film Technology Components Business Group; Storage Media Business Group; Energy Devices Business Group.

PRINCIPAL COMPETITORS

AVX Corporation; Fuji Electric Holdings Co., Ltd.; FUJIFILM Holdings Corporation; Fujitsu Limited; Hitachi, Ltd.; Kyocera Corporation; Murata Manufacturing Co., Ltd.; Panasonic Corporation; Pioneer Corporation; Samsung Electronics Co., Ltd.; Seagate Technology; Showa Denko K.K.; Sony Corporation; Taiyo Yuden Co., Ltd.; Toshiba Corporation; Vishay Intertechnology, Inc.; Western Digital Corporation.

FURTHER READING

Kawa, Toshinari, "TDK Embarks on Push to Beef Up Parts Ops," *Nikkei Weekly*, August 17, 2009.

Matsuda, Takuya, "Changing of Guard at TDK Not End to Progress," *Nikkei Report*, April 19, 2006.

Palenchar, Joseph, "TDK Drives for Diversification," *Twice*, October 9, 2000, p. 10.

Sender, Henny, "TDK, Nimble and Innovative, Typifies the Companies Driving Japan's Growth," *Wall Street Journal*, June 19, 2006, p. A2.

"TDK in Megadeal to Buy Germany's Epcos," *Nikkei Weekly*, August 4, 2008.

"TDK Launches New Round of Product Development," *Tokyo Business Today*, July 1995, p. 18.

"TDK Moving to 'Head' of Its Class," *Nikkei Weekly*, September 3, 2007.

"TDK to Cut 8,000 Jobs, Post Loss," *Wall Street Journal Asia*, January 9, 2009, p. 5.

"A Volatile Tape Market Has TDK on a Roller Coaster," *Business Week*, July 25, 1983, pp. 36+.

Zaczkiewicz, Arthur, "TDK Cautiously Adds Capacity," *Electronic Buyers' News*, May 15, 2000, p. 52.

Teknion Corporation

—■—

1150 Flint Road
Toronto, Ontario M3J 2J5
Canada
Telephone: (416) 661-3370
Fax: (416) 661-4586
Web site: http://www.teknion.com

Private Company
Incorporated: 1981
Employees: 8,930
Sales: CAD 631.3 million (2006)
NAICS: 337210 Office Furniture (Including Fixtures)
 Manufacturing

■ ■ ■

Based in Toronto, Canada, Teknion Corporation is a privately held major international designer, manufacturer, and marketer of office systems, including panel-based, freestanding, and desking systems. The company also offers a variety of seating products, including executive, general use, lounge, and stacking chairs; storage and filing cabinets; case goods; tables; and workplace accessories, such as lighting products and clocks. The company operates 22 manufacturing plants in Canada, three in Malaysia, and one in the United States. Products are sold in more than 50 countries through a network of about 400 authorized dealers. In addition to Canada, Teknion maintains offices and showrooms in the United States, the United Kingdom, Malaysia, Russia, India, and Dubai. Teknion mostly

caters to large and mid-sized national and multinational companies and government entities.

FOUNDER SURVIVES HOLOCAUST

Teknion's founder, Saul Feldberg, was born in Poland, a Jew who survived the Holocaust of World War II. In 1953, at the age of 17, he immigrated to Canada with his parents and younger brother. Although he wanted to attend college, he postponed his education in order to help support his penniless family. Barely able to speak English and essentially without skills he was fortunate to find work at a furniture factory where he earned $30 a week and learned the craft of upholstery. The factory was far from an ideal workplace and Feldberg also had to contend the company's demeaning owners. It was an experience that would one day shape the way Feldberg conducted his business and how he treated his employees. Despite the cyclical nature of the furniture business, Feldberg would refuse to lay off workers during lean times, instead putting them to work cleaning and painting.

Feldberg eventually received his college education, graduating from York University. In 1966 he decided to start his own business, Global Company, using his knowledge as an upholsterer to design an inexpensive version of a popular tilting office chair, which was retailing for $300 or more. Feldberg's chair cost $78 and established Global in the value-priced segment of the office furniture market. The company added other value-priced products including desks, filing cabinets, case goods, and storage products, and later added mid-priced items.

FORMATION OF TEKNION: 1981

In 1981 Feldberg founded Teknion as a separate company to focus on the contract segment of the office furniture market. The company made its mark two years later with the introduction of its flexible T/O/S ("Teknion Office System") office system. It was designed by Ford & Earl Associates, the premise of which was that office partitioning had to be able to accommodate next-generation technological needs, some that might not be predictable. T/O/S was the company's only product until 1990, when the company added complementary items. In the meantime, Feldberg had to contend with a sea change in the Canadian furniture industry.

In the late 1980s the free trade movement began to take shape. For many years Canadian furniture manufacturers had enjoyed the benefits of a 15 percent protective tariff that crippled foreign competition. Not only was that tariff removed, Canadian manufacturers had to contend with the impact of a recession that struck the North American economy in the early 1990s. While hundreds of furniture manufacturers went out of business during this period, Feldberg not only kept his people employed at Teknion and Global, he hired more staff, expanded his offices in the United States, and developed international sales channels. A Teknion subsidiary was formed in Israel in the late 1980s to manufacture the company's full line of products and market them in Europe. In a matter of three years, the Israeli company was generating exports of $5 million.

Teknion was also making significant headway in the United States. In 1992 the company's U.S. subsidiary won a $30 million contract to supply the Boeing company with more than 7,000 office workstations. The world's largest office furniture company, Steelcase Inc., now took notice of the upstart. Steelcase began offering cash prizes to salespeople for taking away business from Teknion. Steelcase even printed a wanted poster as part of the promotion, featuring a headline that read "Wanted: Terrible Teknion." Making Teknion a more serious competitor was the 1990 expansion beyond office systems to include seats, cabinets and shelving, tables, and ergonomically designed furniture.

DAVID FELDBERG BECOMES CHIEF EXECUTIVE: 1994

In 1994 Teknion established a manufacturing subsidiary in Malaysia with its Pacific Rim distributor, Vanguard Interiors Pte. Ltd. Teknion owned 80 percent of the new business. A change at the top ranks of Teknion also took place in 1994 when Saul Feldberg's son, David Feldberg, succeeded him as president and chief executive officer. The younger Feldberg was well seasoned in the business, having launched his career in 1984 by going to work for Global. His father remained Teknion's chairman, while David Feldberg soon added the vice chairman title.

Teknion's growth continued under the leadership of its new chief executive. Sales increased from CAD 124 million in fiscal 1994 (the year ending November 30) to CAD 330.2 million in fiscal 1997. Of that amount, 78 percent resulted from the sale of office systems. The product lines added in 1990 accounted for the other 22 percent. Net income improved from CAD 7.9 million to CAD 32.1 million. Also of importance in 1997 was the introduction of the Ability line of mobile case goods and a rebranding effort.

In July 1998 Teknion went public, completing an initial offering of stock that netted CAD 112.8 million. Nearly CAD 85 million of that went to the principal shareholders, Saul Feldberg-controlled A-Tean Holdings Ltd., and Deaj Properties Ltd., a David Feldberg-owned entity. The remaining CAD 28 million was earmarked for the construction of a new headquarters of the U.S. subsidiary as well as expanded showrooms and upgrades to the manufacturing operations.

Teknion quickly became a favored stock. In the first week that Teknion stock traded on the Toronto Stock Exchange, it increased in value 31 percent. The company's performance continued to inspire confidence. Sales surged to CAD 443.4 million and earnings to CAD 53.25 million when the results for fiscal 1998 were posted. Teknion then maintained its momentum through external growth. In early 1999 it acquired Halcon Corporation, a Minnesota designer, manufacturer, and distributor of high-end hardwood office desks, tables, and other office furniture products. In May of that year Teknion acquired Quebec-based Roy & Breton, Inc., a company founded in 1954 that targeted the educational and institutional markets and was best known for its desk products. The two companies had been working together for the past decade and operated a plant together.

KEY DATES

1981: Saul Feldberg founds the company.
1990: Teknion expands beyond office systems.
1994: David Feldberg succeeds father as CEO.
1998: Company goes public.
2008: Teknion returns to private company status.

Also in 1999 Teknion's Malaysian subsidiary acquired Lion Seatings Sdn, Bhd., a major Malaysian manufacturer of seating, filing, and storage products. The deal brought a 160,000-square-foot manufacturing facility that Teknion planned to use to expand its production capacity in Southeast Asia, an important consideration as the region prepared for free trade in 2003.

MAINTAINING STRONG GROWTH

As the new century began, Teknion continued to maintain strong sales growth in the 40 percent range, spurred in part by the distribution of the Japanese-made Contessa chair by Giugiaro Design and other stylish products. Sales increased from CAD 629.3 million in fiscal 1999 to CAD 917 million in fiscal 2000, while net income improved from CAD 61.2 million to nearly CAD 94 million. It was an especially impressive performance because only a small percentage of the sales increase, 3.7 percent, was contributed by Halcon and Roy & Breton. The lion's share of sales, CAD 636.9 million, was produced in the United States, where Teknion grew its operation in fiscal 2000 by expanding an Atlanta showroom and opening a new showroom in Los Angeles. Teknion also benefited from the opening of a San Francisco showroom the prior year and a 50 percent expansion of the U.S. sales force.

The year 2001 presented more of a challenge, however. The economy was already softening when the terrorist attacks on New York City and Washington, D.C., on September 11, 2001, greatly exacerbated the situation. Business furniture sales fell as a result, and Teknion was not immune to the downturn. Sales for fiscal 2001 fell to CAD 770.9 million and net income dipped to CAD 35.83 million. Nevertheless, Teknion recorded some notable achievements. It introduced more new products in 2001 than in any other year in its history, added over 700,000 square feet in manufacturing space, and opened a new facility in New Jersey for its U.S. subsidiary, including new corporate offices, showroom, and a marketing and design center.

The full impact of the recession was more apparent in fiscal 2002 when sales continued to fall to CAD 516.6 million as customers delayed or canceled orders. Teknion recorded a net loss of CAD 32 million, by far the most difficult year in the company's history. The company continued to invest in upgrading its manufacturing facilities, and even made an acquisition, adding its first operation in the United Kingdom through the purchase of Squirewood Furniture Solutions, a small contract furniture maker in North London.

Demand continued to fall in 2003. Teknion's revenues slipped to CAD 502.8 million and the company lost a further CAD 30.1 million. Teknion did manage to introduce new products and increase its market share in the key U.S. market. Moreover, the company made progress in reducing its cost structure. Further cuts in overhead were achieved in 2004. Teknion had to contend with the impact of a weak U.S. dollar as well as a significant increase in the price of raw materials, and net sales continued to fall in 2004 to CAD 497.3 million, but overall unit sales revenues increased and the cost-cutting moves began to pay off. While the company recorded a net loss of CAD 417.8 million, it achieved positive earnings of about CAD 7 million before depreciation.

The upturn continued in 2005 as revenues grew 22 percent to $606 million, albeit the company lost another CAD 20.7 million. Before depreciation, however, Teknion posted positive earnings of more than CAD 24 million. An especially positive development was that revenues increased in Canada and the United States as well as the international market. Furthermore, sales increased sharply in the fourth quarter of the year, and that momentum carried into 2006. Sales again improved across all markets in fiscal 2006 to CAD 631.3 million and Teknion reported net earnings of CAD 3.5 million. The company's performance was even stronger but hidden somewhat by the depreciation in the U.S. dollar. Teknion also opened a new showroom in New York during the year and redesigned the showrooms in Toronto and London, England.

COMPANY TAKEN PRIVATE: 2008

In late 2007 the Feldberg family elected to again take Teknion private. In a friendly deal worth CAD 76.8 million, and approved by outside directors, the controlling shareholder of the company, A-Tean Holdings, bought all of the stock it did not already own. The transaction was completed in January 2008. While the company was no longer required to make its financial statements public, there was every reason to believe that Teknion was continuing to do well.

Teknion introduced a number of award-winning products, including its District furniture system, Marketplace worktable, Optos full-height glass wall, and Fitz task seating. To better present these products, Teknion redesigned its showroom at its U.S. headquarters in Mount Laurel, New Jersey, in late 2008. The following year the New York City showroom was also redesigned, followed by a renovation in the Vancouver showroom in 2010. The company also opened a second showroom in California in 2009 in Santa Monica, and in March 2010 opened a new logistics and customer service center in Levis, Quebec. Everything considered, Teknion was well positioned to enjoy further prosperity.

Ed Dinger

PRINCIPAL SUBSIDIARIES

Teknion LLC; Teknion Furniture Systems; Teknion Europe; Teknion Furniture Systems SDN BHD; Teknion Furniture Systems (India) Pvt. Ltd.; Teknion Furniture Systems (UAE).

PRINCIPAL COMPETITORS

Haworth, Inc.; Herman Miller, Inc.; Steelcase Inc.

FURTHER READING

Bell, Kevin, "Teknion Soars on Shareholder Purchase," *Globe & Mail*, December 26, 2007, p. B6.

Hirschmann, Thomas, "Teknion Seeks Interior Growth," *Financial Post*, July 22, 1998, p. 17.

Olive, David, and David Akin, "The Richest Canadians," *National Post*, April 22, 2000, p. E06.

"On a Roll," *Business Week*, November 29, 1999, p. 101.

"Teknion Turns 25," *Interior Design*, August 2008, p. 138.

"You're (Still) Hired (Alternatives to Downsizing)," *Report on Business*, December 1996, p. 54.

TELUS Corporation

555 Robson Street
Vancouver, British Columbia V6B 3K9
Canada
Telephone: (604) 697-8044
Toll Free: (877) 310-6110
Fax: (604) 432-9681
Web site: http://www.telus.com

Public Company
Incorporated: 1990
Employees: 36,600
Sales: CAD 9.65 billion (2008)
Stock Exchanges: Toronto New York
Ticker Symbols: T; TU
NAICS: 517110 Wired Telecommunications Carriers;
517212 Cellular and Other Wireless Telecom-
munications; 517910 Other Telecommunications

■ ■ ■

TELUS Corporation (Telus) is a leading telecommunications company in Canada, providing wireline,
wireless, and Internet access services to approximately 12
million customers. Telus provides four million wireline
network access lines, enjoying a dominant market position in British Columbia, Alberta, and eastern Quebec.
The company provides service to 6.5 million wireless
subscribers and 1.2 million Internet subscribers. Telus
also offers all-digital television service and satellite television service in British Columbia, Alberta, and eastern
Quebec, serving approximately 170,000 customers.

PRIVATIZATION OF TELECOMMUNICATIONS SPAWNS TELUS: 1990

Telus Corporation was created on October 4, 1990, following several years of effort by both public and government entities to privatize the public telephone system in
Alberta, Canada. In the largest share offering in
Canadian history, more than 130,000 Albertans
purchased 74.7 million common shares of Telus. A sale
of remaining government shares on the Alberta, Montreal, and Toronto stock exchanges about one year later
made Telus a 100 percent publicly traded company. The
overall privatization scheme garnered $1.8 billion and
spread ownership of the company to 55,000 Albertans.

Several subsidiaries were organized under the Telus
holding company umbrella. The largest of those
underlings was Alberta Government Telephones Ltd.
(AGT), which was formerly Alberta's telephone utility.
AGT's history reaches back to the early 1900s when
Canada was installing its nationwide telephone network.
Because of the advanced technology and massive
infrastructure required to develop regional telephone
systems, government-backed companies were usually
established to generate funding, build, and then manage
the equipment and services. The first of those utilities in
Canada was the Bell Telephone Company of Canada
(Bell Canada), which was established in 1880 to bring
telephone service into Montreal, Ottawa, Quebec, other
eastern Canadian cities.

BELL CANADA IN THE LATE 19TH CENTURY

Within a year of its inception, Bell Canada was supplying telephone service to 14 major cities, employing about 150 workers, and servicing more than 2,000 telephones. Furthermore, the company had set up agencies in a number of other towns to secure subscribers and develop new exchanges. In fact, Bell Canada's long-term goal was to extend service throughout Canada. The company obtained rights to provide service throughout much of the country and began investing in the construction of equipment and facilities in several provinces. Soon, telephone infrastructure was being built as far west as Alberta and was even being extended to very small towns.

It eventually became apparent that Canada's vast geography would preclude a single company from efficiently developing and managing a system for the entire country. Among other operations, therefore, Canada Bell sold its telephone operations in Prince Edward Island, Nova Scotia, and New Brunswick in the late 1880s. Many citizens in the Prairie Provinces, including Alberta, were dissatisfied with Bell Canada by the early 1900s. That was partly because Bell Canada had been successful mostly in bringing service only to urban areas (voice clarity was possible only over distances of less than 20 miles). To get phone service from the city to rural residents, public telephones were commonly installed at the ends of the Bell Canada lines. Thus, many Alberta customers wanted to transfer ownership of the telephone system to the province government, which they felt would be able to provide a more cohesive system that focused on their needs.

In 1906 Alberta's first Legislative Assembly approved the province's entry into the field of telephone service. Two years later the province purchased all of Bell Canada's plants and equipment along with the privileges and rights to provide service throughout Alberta. The entire telephone system was placed under the control of the Alberta government, although several small farmer-owned services remained intact. To help balance the will of bureaucrats with the needs of the citizens, the province placed the telephone system under the regulation of the Alberta Public Utilities Board in 1915. Then, in 1927, the system was placed under the control of an autonomous Ministry, with the general manager elevated to the rank of deputy minister. The service remained in that form until 1958, when Alberta Government Telephones Commission was established to end direct government control of the phone system. Thus, AGT became what is known as an agency of the crown.

TECHNOLOGICAL ADVANCEMENTS: 1915–74

Under various forms of government control, AGT picked up where Bell Canada left off and expanded service throughout Alberta during the early and mid-1900s. The exception was Edmonton, Alberta, which continued to be handled by the independent Edmonton Telephone into the 1990s. Telephone technology advanced rapidly during the period. Importantly, the vacuum tube repeater was introduced in 1915. That mechanism, which could theoretically transmit a voice an infinite distance, allowed AGT to become part of a transcontinental telephone network that gave an entirely new meaning to "long distance" telephone communication.

Of similar import was an improvement over early telephone systems that required batteries to be installed at the subscriber's premises. "Central energy switchboards" eliminated that inconvenience. Another major breakthrough was the phantom circuit, whereby two pairs of wires with special equipment at each end could transmit a third conversation. The third "phantom" line even offered higher quality transmission than the other two lines.

By the 1950s telephone technology had improved to the point where the service was viewed as a necessity by many people. To expand and improve service, AGT initiated a $93 million, 10-year effort in 1964 to bury rural telephone cables and bring four-party, divided-ringing service to virtually every farm in Alberta. Meanwhile, AGT continued to buy up the old farmer-owned phone systems to secure its monopoly on the Alberta phone system (still with the exception of Edmonton Telephone). In 1976, AGT purchased the last of the farmer-owned systems. Two years later the number of telephones serviced by AGT reached one million. In 1983 AGT was incorporated to act as the owner of AGT and to separate nonregulated operations. During the 1980s AGT also branched out into communications services other than basic, traditional, regulated telephone service.

PUSH FOR PRIVATIZATION BEGINS: 1980

The government-supported, monopolistic environment that characterized Alberta's telephone system served the country well for roughly a century. Governments often mandated that all customers requesting service receive a phone line, regardless of their location, and multimillion-dollar projects were forced into action through political mandate. The result was that everybody got quality telephone service and equipment, and usually at reasonable rates. By the 1980s, however, many people were beginning to question the validity of the system. Much of the costly infrastructure was already in place, so the role of the bureaucracy had diminished. Many people felt that the system was antiquated and was hindering innovation and growth. A number of new technologies, such as wireless telecommunications, were poised to take off, and many insiders believed that add-on telephone services were not being developed quickly enough.

In fact, AGT was widely believed to have become a cumbersome, inefficient bureaucracy. The utility had long been as much a political tool as it was a member of the business community. For example, politicians often appointed people to executive posts in the company as a political reward rather than because they were the best people to handle the job. AGT did introduce new services. In 1982, for example, AGT commenced operation of Canada's first cellular telephone system using 400 megahertz bandwidth. Three years later AGT began offering conventional 800 megahertz cellular service, and also launched Individual Line Service for all Albertans. Despite those initiatives, however, many

customers and government insiders believed that change was due. Throughout the 1980s public pressure to privatize AGT's long-distance services mounted.

AGT BECOMES TELUS: 1990

In 1990 the Alberta legislature passed the Alberta Government Telephones Reorganization Act. That act was designed to reorganize the Alberta Government Telephones Commission and to place all of the shares of AGT under a holding company to be named Telus Corporation. The idea was to privatize the phone system and allow the free market to exert greater influence on the long-distance telecommunications sector. The effort had a big impact on AGT, which began a turbulent transformation from a government-regulated monopoly to a relatively unprotected combatant in the increasingly competitive world of telecommunications. During the next few years the company was forced to slash its long-distance rates by 40 percent and to eliminate fully 25 percent of its staff. The huge workforce cutbacks, which seemed to confirm critics' claims that the organization was bloated and inefficient, did little for employee morale.

Besides reducing long-distance rates and cutting payrolls, AGT attempted to diversify its service offerings to compensate for profit stagnation in its traditional businesses. The company had started AGT Directory in 1988, which was a Talking Yellow Pages service offered to customers in Calgary. AGT Directory also offered *Yellow Pages* books. Telus started another subsidiary after privatization called AGT Mobility, which became the first North American company to offer digital cellular service. Within two years the division was serving 15,200 paging subscribers and about 100,000 cellular telephone customers. Also in 1992, Telus launched ISM Alberta, a joint venture, to provide state-of-the-art computer systems and technical expertise on a contract basis to business and government customers.

At about the same time that it joined ISM, Telus became involved in Stentor, an alliance owned by nine Canadian telecommunications companies. The consortium company offered better long-distance services, as well as commercial satellite service between Canada and 240 countries and territories around the globe. In 1993 Telus entered the cable television/telephony business in the United Kingdom through a partnership with CUC Broadcasting. Dubbed Telecential, the pioneer venture combined telephone and cable television services and managed to accrue about 150,000 customers by the end of 1993. AGT Mobility became profitable for the first time that year, adding to Telus' overall net income for the year of about $180 million. Despite turbulence in its core AGT subsidiary, Telus managed to keep sales and net income steady around $1.2 billion and $180 million, respectively, during the early 1990s.

Regardless of its rapid diversification and stable earnings, Telus' board of directors decided that the company was due for a management shakeup in 1993. Shortly before Telus was formed, the last political appointee to head AGT was named. Neil Webber took the helm as chairman in 1989. Webber had worked in government for several decades before being tapped as chairman by political ally and premier Don Getty. He was considered a member of the old guard, so his retirement was greeted with enthusiasm by many investors. Still, under Webber's command Telus managed to post major gains. The number of AGT employees per 1,000 telephone access lines, for example, plummeted from about 9.3 in 1991 to just 5.8 by late 1993. At the same time, the number of access lines increased by more than 100,000.

LEADERSHIP CHANGE AND MERGER WITH ED TEL: 1994–95

George K. Petty took over as chairman and chief executive of Telus late in 1994. A telecommunications veteran, Petty had worked for telecom giant AT&T from 1969 to 1994 and had most recently served as vice president of global business services. Before AT&T he had been a U.S. Navy communications officer after graduating from New Mexico State University with a degree in electrical engineering. At Telus, he quickly announced his intent to slash costs, diversify services, and focus on customer satisfaction. He also welcomed increased efforts by the CRTC to increase competition within the industry. "From my experience, deregulation immediately increases the ability to communicate," Petty said in the January 13, 1995, *Calgary Herald.*

Importantly, in 1995 Telus finalized the acquisition of the operations of Edmonton Telephones Corporation (Ed Tel) for CAD 467 million. Ed Tel was incorporated in 1893 as Edmonton District Telephone Company and owned by the city of Edmonton from 1904 to 1995. Throughout the century it survived as the only telephone company in Alberta outside of AGT's control. By 1994 Ed Tel was supporting about 400,000 access lines in the Edmonton area, or about one-third the number of lines operated by AGT. Ed Tel also had about 36,000 cellular subscribers. The merger brought 2,000 new employees to Telus, which had managed to cut its AGT payroll from 10,200 workers to just 6,300 by 1994. Telus management believed that it could integrate Ed Tel into its operations to achieve economies of scale. Telus also hoped to cut costs and improve efficiency at the new subsidiary.

By 1994 Telus was operating, or partnering in, six subsidiaries. Most of its sales and profits were derived from AGT. Telus' subsidiaries, though, were expected to contribute much more to the holding company's bottom line in the future. Most of Telus' companies were achieving steady sales and earnings gains going into the mid-1990s and were building market share in growing niches of the fast-paced communications industry. The holding company's sales increased to $1.36 billion in 1994 while net income jumped a healthy 18 percent to $212 million. Ed Tel was expected to add about $325 million to Telus' revenue base in 1995.

BCTEL AND CLEARNET COMMUNICATIONS ACQUISITIONS: 1999–2000

The second half of the 1990s witnessed significant growth at Telus. The purchase of Ed Tel had turned the company into the premier telecommunications company in Alberta, but dominance in one province was not sufficient in the rapidly changing telecommunications industry. The company began using the Telus name as a consumer brand in 1996, terminating the use of AGT and Ed Tel for promotional purposes, and gained a much larger audience to market its name after completing the largest merger in its history in 1999. Telus merged with its British Columbian counterpart, BCTel, a transaction that immediately made Telus a national force. The company moved its headquarters to Vancouver, British Columbia, after the merger, where it ended the decade as the second-largest telecommunications company in Canada. Telus controlled 22 percent of the market, trailing only Bell Canada, which held a 42 percent market share.

Telus wasted little time before making another bold move on the acquisition front. Leading the charge forward was Darren Entwistle, who was appointed president and CEO in 2000 after spending the previous seven years working for a telecommunications company, Cable & Wireless PLC, in the United Kingdom. During Entwistle's first year at the helm, Telus jumped headlong into the fast-growing wireless market, spending CAD 4.6 billion to acquire Clearnet Communications, a cellular company based near Toronto, Ontario. The acquisition created a new subsidiary, Telus Mobility, that became arguably the most important aspect of the company's business in the early 21st century. Within four years, Telus Mobility was serving 3.75 million customers throughout Canada with a full range of wireless voice, Internet, and data services through its wireless networks.

Midway through the decade, Entwistle united Telus' two business segments. Telus Mobility was merged with

Telus Communications, the company's wireline business, to create a single operating structure. The restructuring was part of his plan to offer integrated services on a national basis. At the time of the reorganization, Telus had 4.7 million network access lines, representing its wireline business, and 4.3 million wireless customers.

INVESTMENT IN
INFRASTRUCTURE: 2005–09

Telus' wireless business grew in importance during the second half of the decade, aping the global trend that saw wireless businesses usurp the dominant position held by wireline businesses. Beginning in 2005 Entwistle began investing heavily in completing Telus' wireless broadband rollout, spending CAD 100 million by 2008 to install hardware at more than 1,100 cell sites in British Columbia and Alberta. The capital investment program was completed with an installation on Mount Bing on Vancouver Island, giving Telus' customers wireless data speeds of up to 3.1 megabits per second throughout 95 percent of British Columbia and Alberta. The number of Telus' wireless subscribers by the time the network was completed had reached 5.6 million.

Entwistle remained committed to improving Telus' capabilities as he finished his first decade as CEO. In 2009 he earmarked large sums for upgrading Telus' broadband infrastructure, directing the funds to be spent across Canada in anticipation of launching High Speed Packet Access technology nationally by 2010. The technology was expected to facilitate Telus' transition to the emerging worldwide standard for fourth-generation, or 4G, networks.

In British Columbia, where Telus had spent more than CAD 19 billion in capital and operating expenditures during Entwistle's tenure, the company planned to invest CAD 500 million on improving wireless and wireline broadband infrastructure. In Alberta, the company intended to invest more than CAD 700 million on improving its broadband infrastructure, adding to the CAD 18 billion the company had spent in the province since 2000. In Quebec, Telus was spending CAD 250 million to improve its infrastructure. Under Entwistle's guidance, Telus was striving to remain on the technological vanguard, a necessity in the rapidly evolving realm of telecommunications in the 21st century.

Dave Mote
Updated, Jeffrey L. Covell

PRINCIPAL SUBSIDIARIES

TELUS Communications Inc.; TELUS Communications Company.

PRINCIPAL COMPETITORS

BCE Inc.; Bell Mobility Inc.; MTS Allstream Inc.

FURTHER READING

Crawford, Anne, "Quantum Change; AGT, for Years Operated as a Government-Run Monopoly, Is Trying to Adapt to Face Stiff Corporate Competition," *Calgary Herald*, June 26, 1993, p. F1.

————, "Taking Care of No. 1: New Telus Boss Puts Customers First as the Company Faces Stiff Competition," *Calgary Herald*, January 13, 1995, p. E6.

Geddes, Ashley, "Edmonton Tel Takeover Approved," *Financial Post*, March 1, 1995, Sec. 1, p. 6.

"Telus Merges Wireline and Wireless Segments," *Wireless News*, November 27, 2005.

"Telus Speeds Things Up in Western Canada," *CNW Group*, February 28, 2008.

"Telus to Invest More Than $700 Million in Alberta," *CNW Group*, April 14, 2009.

Thomas&Betts

Thomas & Betts
Corporation

———•———

8155 T&B Boulevard
Memphis, Tennessee 38125-8888
U.S.A.
Telephone: (901) 252-8000
Fax: (901) 252-1354
Web site: http://www.tnb.com

Public Company
Incorporated: 1917 as Thomas & Betts Co.
Employees: 8,500
Sales: $1.9 billion (2009)
Stock Exchanges: New York
Ticker Symbol: TNB
NAICS: 334220 Radio and Television Broadcasting and Wireless Communications Equipment Manufacturing; 334290 Other Communications Equipment Manufacturing; 334417 Electronic Connector Manufacturing; 335129 Other Lighting Equipment Manufacturing; 335931 Current-Carrying Wiring Device Manufacturing; 335932 Noncurrent-Carrying Wiring Device Manufacturing; 332312 Fabricated Structural Metal Manufacturing; 333415 Air-Conditioning and Warm Air Heating Equipment and Commercial and Industrial Refrigeration Equipment Manufacturing

■ ■ ■

Thomas & Betts Corporation (T&B) is a leading global manufacturer of electrical components. The company's electrical segment, responsible for about 82 percent of net sales, produces and markets thousands of different products, including fittings and accessories for electrical raceways; wire fastening products; compression and mechanical connectors for wiring and cables; indoor and outdoor switch and outlet boxes, covers, and accessories; emergency and hazardous lighting products; and radio frequency connectors. Generating around 12 percent of revenues is the steel structures segment, which manufactures tubular steel poles and lattice steel structures used in power transmission and distribution. The remaining 6 percent of sales belong to the HVAC segment, which specializes in heating and ventilation products for commercial and industrial buildings. T&B has more than 50 manufacturing, distribution, and office facilities located in about 20 countries. Two-thirds of T&B's revenues originate in the United States, 17 percent in Canada, and 11 percent in Europe.

EARLY 20TH-CENTURY BEGINNINGS

From its earliest years in business, Thomas & Betts demonstrated an ability to transform electrically charged business ideas into readily marketable products. In 1898 Robert McKean Thomas and Hobart D. Betts, both engineering graduates from Princeton University, established an agency in New York City for selling electrical conduit. Within a year, they were joined by Adnah McMurtrie, another engineer whose in-house designs added to the fledgling agency's list of salable products. The partners formed a New York corporation, Thomas and Betts Company, in 1905. As early as 1906, T&B's innovative products changed the electric industry. The Erickson coupling, for example, enabled electricians to join two conduits without having to

COMPANY PERSPECTIVES

For over 100 years, Thomas & Betts has been a leader in the electrical industry. No other company can match our record of product "firsts" or our influence in shaping safe and consistent electrical standards and practices. Our brands are asked for by name, known for their quality and trusted by electricians, installers, engineers and consumers to be best.

Our corporate goals are simple: We want to be the brand of choice for the end user of our products; the supplier of choice for our distributor and utility customers; the employer of choice for our employees; and the investment of choice for our shareholders.

rotate either, or to separate conduits without disassembling the whole conduit run. These early patents set industry standards and were still widely used more than a century later. Such products made for healthy sales around the beginning of the 20th century.

To accelerate their young firm's growth, however, the three colleagues realized that they had to begin manufacturing the goods they designed and sold. To that end, in 1912 they purchased Standard Electric Fittings Company of Stamford, Connecticut. The following year, they solicited the expertise of Robert Thomas's nephew, George C. Thomas Jr., who pushed the company's manufacturing capabilities to unprecedented levels. With design, manufacturing, and sales efforts all advancing at a healthy rate by 1917, the time came to centralize resources and consolidate operations. That year, the Thomas & Betts sales agency and the Standard Electric Fittings Company were merged to form one, new corporation, Thomas & Betts Co. Central headquarters were established on Butler Street in Elizabeth, New Jersey, a site that remained T&B's largest manufacturing facility into the early 1990s.

Following its incorporation, T&B entered a period of diversification and geographic expansion that would last uninterrupted until the outbreak of World War II. In 1928 G. C. Thomas Jr. rose to the position of CEO, a tribute to the importance of the manufacturing initiatives he had managed over the previous decade and would continue to expand into the 1970s. Under Thomas Jr.'s leadership, T&B also pushed into broader markets, founding Thomas & Betts Limited in order to sell products in Canada.

The onset of World War II forced T&B into product development that it otherwise might have neglected. The military's drive to reduce weight in aircraft, for example, spurred the firm's development of the first successful compression lugs for connecting aluminum conductors. This breakthrough led to the development of a complete line of color-coded compression connectors, as well as hand and hydraulic tools and dies. After the war, these and other innovations served numerous civilian applications, adding significantly to the company's product line.

POSTWAR ERA: GOING PUBLIC & EXPANDING

Product changes were accompanied by organizational changes as the company entered the 1960s. T&B became a public company in 1959 and was first listed on the New York Stock Exchange in 1962. The company changed its name to Thomas & Betts Corporation in 1968. Meanwhile, in 1960, Thomas Jr. retired as CEO and was replaced by Nestor J. MacDonald, the former vice president of marketing.

Early in MacDonald's tenure, T&B continued to stride assiduously into new, international markets. Building on its Canadian presence, the company established a new international division in 1962. By 1963 the company was emphasizing closer field contact with licensees in Great Britain, Europe, and Mexico. In order to speed up the development of European markets, the company also established a new European subsidiary, Thomas & Betts of Belgium, S.A., in June of that year. By 1983 a Luxembourg facility had been established to produce electronic connectors for even broader European markets. Moreover, Ouest Electronic Connecteurs, a French maker of electronic connectors and custom components of which T&B had acquired 80 percent in 1982, provided additional research and development and manufacturing capabilities in Europe. Other international points of contact included an Australian location to supply the South Pacific.

While delving into foreign markets in the 1960s and 1970s, T&B also began to push aggressively beyond its traditional expertise in electric supplies and into electronic components. Its initial forays in that direction were bolstered by the purchase of Arthur Ansley Manufacturing Company in 1966 and Digital Sensors, Inc., (DSI) in 1968. After J. David Parkinson, former head of the company's electrical business, succeeded MacDonald as CEO in 1974, electronic product development was stepped up again. In 1975 T&B merged its Ansley and DSI divisions to form the Ansley

KEY DATES

1898: Robert McKean Thomas and Hobart D. Betts form a New York City agency for selling electrical conduit that is later called Thomas and Betts Company.

1912: The partners become manufacturers through the acquisition of Standard Electric Fittings Company of Stamford, Connecticut.

1917: Thomas and Betts Company and Standard Electric Fittings merge to form Thomas & Betts Co. (T&B), which is headquartered and incorporated in New Jersey.

1959: T&B goes public.

1968: Company name is changed to Thomas & Betts Corporation.

1992: American Electric is acquired.

1993: T&B relocates its headquarters to Memphis, Tennessee, where American Electric had been based.

2000: T&B's global electronics connectors business is divested; the company falls into the red.

2007: Company acquires Lamson & Sessions Co., the largest producer of plastic electrical boxes and other fixtures in North America.

Electronics Division (subsequently renamed the Thomas & Betts electronics division in 1981).

Progress in electronics built on a solid foundation of innovation that had already distinguished T&B as a market leader in the electrical market. Through the 1980s, many of the company's past developments were still considered milestones in the industry at large: conduit fittings with integrally insulated throats in 1954; new cable ties and straps in 1959; use of steel in rigid conduit fittings line in 1968; new designs in floor boxes in 1970; heat-shrinkable insulating covers and caps in 1974; and a line of flat conductor cables for under-carpet wiring systems in 1980. That list was supplemented by a growing line of electronic interconnection products for professionals in electronic engineering, telecommunications, and automotive electronics. Among T&B's best performers were the FLEXPAC Termination system, consisting of flexible conductor cables, jumpers, and circuits; connectors for leadless chip carriers, designed for multilayer printed circuit boards in advanced computer systems; and dual in-line package sockets for interconnecting integrated circuits.

STRATEGIC ACQUISITIONS: EIGHTIES AND EARLY NINETIES

Through the late 1980s, T&B continued to aggressively seek new markets. The firm began a series of strategic acquisitions under the guidance of T. Kevin Dunnigan, a seasoned veteran who had progressed from Canadian sales in the 1960s to president and COO in 1980, and finally to president and CEO in 1985. In 1987 the company acquired Vitramon, Inc., a manufacturer of surface-mount ceramic chip capacitors (an integral part of the power management process in all electronic systems). Vitramon's surface-mount technology permitted direct soldering of the chips onto printed circuit boards, thereby simplifying the manufacturing process and saving space. This acquisition was quickly followed by the 1988 acquisition of Nevada Western Supply Co., specializing in voice and data wiring products that could be easily and cost-effectively installed using ordinary telephone wiring. Both these acquisitions were a step away from T&B's core line of electrical and electronic connectors, and both were intended to capitalize on new demands related to computer and communications networking.

The 1989 acquisition of Holmberg Electronics Corporation, a manufacturer of electronic connectors, was more in line with T&B's historical field of specialty. The effect of that deal on core business was soon far eclipsed, however, by what at the time ranked as the largest acquisition in the company's history. On January 2, 1992, T&B spent $436.8 million to purchase FL Industries Holdings, Inc., known in the electrical industry as American Electric, a firm with annual revenues of nearly $500 million. The corporation's electrical business and American Electric were merged into a new Thomas & Betts electrical division, which, along with the existing corporate headquarters, was relocated to Memphis, Tennessee, on the site of the former American Electric, in 1993. By the first quarter of 1994, T&B's electronics division headquarters also moved to Memphis, thereby joining the newly energized core. (T&B itself reincorporated in Tennessee in 1996.)

Critical to that core was the competitive edge that American Electric brought to T&B. Founded in 1958, American Electric had undergone a series of transformations and buyouts. In 1968, when American Electric still focused on its original business of manufacturing lighting and related products to the utility market, it was acquired by ITT Corporation. After becoming the nation's largest streetlight manufacturer, American Electric was sold to Forstmann Little & Co., a leveraged buyout firm, in June 1985. Under that management, the company began a rapid chain of acquisitions, including the Electrical Products Division of Midland-

Ross Corporation, the Lighting Division of North American Phillips, Anchor Metals, and American Pole. With such a dynamic range of constitutive parts, American Electric was better suited to give T&B "a broader market presence, and [to] function more effectively as a single global unit," as Chairperson and CEO Dunnigan remarked in the 1993 letter to shareholders.

CONSOLIDATING AND OPTIMIZING THE ENLARGED OPERATIONS

T&B's acquisition of American Electric triggered a series of other strategic moves and organizational changes designed to consolidate operations and optimize efficiency of the larger company. On January 1, 1994, Clyde R. Moore became president and COO. He brought to the post experience as previous president of Thomas & Betts' electrical division and president of American Electric before the acquisition. Six months later, T&B sold Vitramon, the manufacturer of ceramic chip capacitors it had acquired in 1987, to Vishay Intertechnology, Inc., for $184 million. The move represented an effort to focus on T&B's core businesses of electrical and electronic connectors, components, and systems.

In continuation of that process, on September 16, 1994, the company announced pretax charges of approximately $90 million to cover the costs for various initiatives to "optimize operations," according to a T&B press release on that date. According to Dunnigan, "the actions covered by these charges are expected to result in savings of approximately $8 million in 1995 and over $20 million annually in subsequent years."

In the effort to optimize operations, one of the first areas of concentration was quality control. Starting in 1987, the firm launched its "total quality excellence" program, involving all employees in an ongoing effort to improve product quality and reduce costs. T&B began implementing statistical quality control and just-in-time manufacturing techniques in all its plants, as well as computer-aided design and manufacturing. The program's goals included improving on-time delivery, reducing defects, and setting competitive prices.

Declaring in its promotional literature that "the era of electronic commerce has arrived," T&B also dedicated significant resources to marketing strategies employing electronic data interchange with its customers. In an effort to optimize customer service for its electrical distributors, T&B's largest single market, the company designed Signature Services, a marketing package that sped up the order entry process and reduced paperwork for shipping billing. Taking that system a step further in 1993, T&B implemented Distributor/Manufacturer Integration, an interactive system that made inventory management a responsibility (and ideally a simple one) shared by both the distributor and the company. A similar service, Easy Access, was designed for electronics customers. Distributors and buying manufacturers in that market could check T&B's inventory and pricing, as well as the status of their orders, while corresponding instantaneously via e-mail. These state-of-the-art systems represented important steps toward reducing costs while increasing direct contact with market trends via the company's customers.

Revenues during 1994 topped the $1 billion mark for the first time, while profits increased 20 percent, hitting $67.8 million. In August of that year, T&B acquired a minority stake of about 29 percent in Leviton Manufacturing Co., Inc., the leading manufacturer of wiring devices in the United States. The purchase was seen as a possible prelude to a full acquisition, but the CEO of the privately held, family-run Leviton, who with his wife held more than half of the common stock, opposed T&B's investment in the company, and the two companies were soon involved in litigation. Through relationships between T&B and certain Leviton managers, T&B was able to have some influence over the company, but this influence essentially ended in January 2002 when T&B's main liaison with Leviton retired from that company.

LATE-CENTURY ACQUISITIONS OF AMERACE AND AUGAT

For T&B, the mid-1990s were dominated by acquisitions. During 1995 the company acquired E.K. Campbell Company, a maker of custom industrial heating and cooling equipment based in Osawatomie, Kansas, and Catamount Manufacturing, Inc., located in Orange, Massachusetts, which specialized in cable ties, wire connectors, and various nylon hardware products. The former purchase bolstered T&B's heating, mechanical, and refrigeration division, which sold commercial and industrial heating and ventilation equipment under the Reznor brand (a business gained via the American Electric acquisition).

Two more acquisitions negotiated in 1995 were consummated in January 1996: Bowers Manufacturing Corporation, a Southgate, California-based supplier of metallic and nonmetallic electrical boxes for the construction industry, and Amerace Corporation, based in Chicago. Bowers was purchased from Masco Corporation for $8.5 million, while Amerace was purchased from Eagle Industries Inc. for $220.6 million.

The latter firm, which had 1995 sales of $215 million, produced electrical products for utility and industrial markets, with its most important product line being underground power and distribution connectors and components sold under the Elastimold brand name.

Six more acquisitions were completed in 1996, with the most significant being a December deal for Augat Inc. The stock swap, which cost T&B $560 million in stock, eclipsed the deal for American Electric as the largest in T&B history. Based in Mansfield, Massachusetts, Augat produced electronics connectors for the communications, computer, automotive, and industrial markets. The firm had 1995 revenues of $535 million. The addition of Augat made T&B one of the five largest connector makers in the United States. Merger, restructuring, and other charges totaling $97.1 million were taken in the fourth quarter of 1996, resulting in a net earnings total for the year of just $59.9 million. As a result of the heavy acquisition activity, revenues for the year increased 15 percent, finishing just a shade below $2 billion.

In May 1997 Moore took over as CEO of Thomas & Betts, with Dunnigan remaining chairman. That year T&B spent another $62 million on six smaller acquisitions, and the company also formed a joint venture with Exemplar Manufacturing Company, a private company based in Ypsilanti, Michigan, to manufacture and market power distribution, battery cable, and wiring systems to the U.S. automotive industry.

Acquisition activity increased again in 1998 as nine purchases were completed. The largest was the acquisition in November of Kaufel Group Ltd. for $100 million in cash and the assumption of $60 million in debt. Based in Montreal, Kaufel was a maker of emergency lighting products and systems with 1997 sales of CAD 230 million ($152 million). T&B also gained entrance into a new market sector with the purchase of Telecommunication Devices, Inc., (TDI) in July 1998 for about $74 million in stock.

The privately held TDI, which had three plants in the Chicago area and a fourth in Scotland, was a major manufacturer of battery packs for cellular telephones and laptop computers. TDI recorded revenues of $145 million for 1997. Soon after completion of this deal, T&B announced a major restructuring involving several plant closures and the loss of more than 750 jobs. The cost-cutting came in response to a downturn in the electronic connector industry as well as fallout from the Asian economic crisis that erupted the previous year. Special charges of $108.5 million once again led earnings to fall dramatically, from $154.9 million in 1997 to $87.5 million in 1998.

In January 1999 T&B reached an agreement to acquire AFC Cable Systems Inc. for $504 million. AFC produced armored cable, modular wiring systems, and other devices used in transmitting power, voice, and data. The deal began unraveling, however, after the Securities and Exchange Commission (SEC) began an inquiry into the compensation that the chairman of AFC was slated to receive as part of the deal. The delay in completing the deal enabled other suitors to move in, and Tyco International Ltd. trumped T&B's bid with an offer of $578 million. T&B ended up completing three acquisitions during 1999 for $70.7 million: Ocal, maker of PVC-coated conduit and components for corrosive industrial environments; L.E. Mason Co., a Boston-based manufacturer of weatherproof electrical boxes; and Shamrock Conduit Products Inc., a small Ohio-based maker of steel and aluminum conduit elbows, couplings, and nipples.

Acquisition activity slowed down considerably in the final months of 1999 as T&B began contending with a whole host of problems, including difficulties arising from relocating a number of plants to low-cost locations, such as Mexico and Eastern Europe, and the botched launch of a new Internet-based order management system. In November 1999 the company restated earnings for two quarters of 1999 after finding accounting errors that were related to the system conversion.

MAJOR RESTRUCTURING IN THE EARLY 21ST CENTURY

The beginning of the 21st century proved turbulent for Thomas & Betts. Executive turnover, divestment of significant operations, accounting problems, and net losses replaced the management continuity, acquisitions, and profits of the previous decade. In May 2000 Moore replaced Dunnigan as company chairman, but only three months later Moore resigned, and Dunnigan was called back to become chairman and CEO once again. In July, meantime, John R. Mayo was hired away from competitor Framatome Connectors International as president and COO of T&B, but Mayo also resigned after only a brief stint, leaving in October 2000. Dunnigan assumed the additional title of president. In July 2000, during this period of turmoil, T&B completed the sale of its global electronics connectors business to Tyco International for $750 million. The divestment, which represented 27 percent of the firm's 1999 revenues and included virtually all of the product lines acquired through the acquisition of Augat, was intended to return the company to a focus on electrical connectors and components. Proceeds were earmarked for debt reduction and a stock repurchase program.

In late August 2000, soon after Moore's resignation, T&B replaced a complex matrix organizational structure that had been adopted in 1997, and that was now blamed for some of the operational difficulties that were plaguing the company, with a much simpler market-focused divisional structure. Also in August, T&B announced an unexpected loss for the year's second quarter thanks to a revenue decline of 40 percent and $223.9 million in special charges stemming from restated sales, disputed customer invoices, excess and obsolete inventory, and other items. The company also announced that it would revise its 1999 financial statements.

In response, T&B's stock plunged to a 52-week low of $18.94, down from the high of $53.44 that had occurred in September 1999. Investors soon began suing the company, alleging that securities laws had been broken and that the company had issued false financial statements. In early 2001 the SEC initiated a formal investigation into the firm's accounting practices. For 2000, T&B reported a net loss of $25.8 million on revenues of $1.76 billion. Additional pretax charges of $60 million were recorded for the final quarter, and the company also restated its results for 1996 through 1999.

Restructuring efforts continued in 2001 and 2002. During the two years, the workforce was reduced from 14,000 employees to 10,000. Late in 2001 a plan to reduce costs and improve profitability was launched whereby about one-third of the 30 plants in the electrical products division were shuttered. Restructuring charges of $110.2 million contributed to a net loss for the year of $146.4 million, while 2001 revenues of $1.5 billion represented a 15 percent drop from the preceding year. Continuing to focus more tightly on core operations, T&B in late 2001 sold its American Electric and Dark-to-Light commercial lighting product lines to National Service Industries, Inc., for $80 million.

As the turnaround efforts continued in 2002, and appeared to be making progress in spite of the difficult economic conditions, T&B announced in October that it had reached an agreement to settle five class-action lawsuits that had been filed against the company alleging violations of securities laws. The company agreed to pay the plaintiffs $46.5 million, without admitting liability or wrongdoing, in exchange for dismissal of the suits. The judge overseeing the case approved this settlement in December 2002. The cost of the settlement, coupled with a variety of other charges and the effect of an accounting charge, resulted in another net loss, totaling $53 million, while the weak economy sent sales down a further 10 percent.

RETURN TO PROFITABLE GROWTH

In 2003 T&B reached a settlement with the SEC over the alleged improper accounting practices. The company neither admitted nor denied the allegations, but the agency fined three former executives for their actions. With its restructuring complete and the economy on the mend, T&B returned to the black that year, posting profits of $42.8 million on flat sales of $1.32 billion. Having returned to the company and shepherded it through this turnaround, Dunnigan stepped aside from the CEO position, while remaining chairman, to make way for the elevation of Dominic J. Pileggi to the top executive post. Pileggi had played a key role in the turnaround, first as head of the electrical business starting in October 2000 and then as president and COO starting in January 2003. At the end of 2005, Dunnigan retired from the chairmanship, a position also assumed by Pileggi.

Both profits and sales grew steadily through 2006, reaching $175.1 million and $1.87 billion, respectively, by that year. The improved results and a strong balance sheet enabled Thomas & Betts to begin once again seeking out major strategic acquisitions to broaden the offerings in its core electrical products business and create a wider platform for future growth. In July 2007 the company spent $282 million in cash to acquire the Joslyn Hi-Voltage and Power Solutions businesses from Danaher Corporation. These units manufactured high-voltage overhead power distribution products for electric utilities as well as products and services that ensured a reliable flow of power for companies' mission-critical applications, such as data centers.

In an even larger deal, T&B in November 2007 acquired Lamson & Sessions Co., based in Cleveland, Ohio, for about $450 million in cash. Already the largest producer of metallic electrical boxes in North America, T&B through this takeover gained the continent's largest manufacturer of plastic electrical boxes and other fixtures with annual sales in 2006 of $561.3 million. About 40 percent of this revenue, however, stemmed from Lamson & Sessions' PVC pipe and conduit operations, which T&B immediately decided to divest. The operations were sold to the Japanese firm Mitsubishi Corporation during the third quarter of 2008. Also that year, T&B sold its 29 percent stake in Leviton Manufacturing back to that company after further takeover overtures fell on deaf ears. T&B received $300 million for the stake, which it had acquired 14 years earlier for $50.6 million. In January 2008 T&B acquired the Homac Manufacturing Company, a producer of secondary underground distribution connectors used by utility and telecommunications companies. Homac operated plants in Florida and California.

Sales fell sharply in 2009 as a result of the deep economic recession, plunging 23 percent to $1.9 billion. T&B nevertheless managed to stay profitable, posting net earnings of $107.9 million thanks to a number of cost-cutting initiatives, including reductions in the overall workforce from around 10,000 employees to 8,500. The company continued to seek opportunities for future growth, particularly overseas.

After opening a new manufacturing plant in Saudi Arabia in 2009 to serve industrial markets throughout the Middle East, Thomas & Betts in February 2010 agreed to acquire PMA AG for approximately EUR 85 million ($120 million). Based in Zurich, Switzerland, the privately held PMA was a leading manufacturer of cable protection systems and sold its products in more than 45 countries in Europe, Asia, the Middle East, and North America. In addition to having the financial strength to pursue this type of strategic acquisition, T&B's future prospects were further brightened by predicted growth in the global electricity market, which promised to increase demand for the company's key product lines.

Kerstan Cohen
Updated, David E. Salamie

PRINCIPAL SUBSIDIARIES

Jennings Technology Company, LLC; T&B Power Solutions, LLC; Thomas & Betts International, Inc.; Lamson & Sessions, Ltd. (Canada); T&B Limited (Canada); T&B Investments Ltd. (Canada); T&B Manufacturing, Inc. (Canada); T&B Division Mexico S. de R.L. de C.V.; T&B de Mexico S. de R.L. de C.V.; T&B Monterrey S. de R.L. de C.V. (Mexico); T&B Communicaciones S. de R.L. de C.V. (Mexico); T&B Corporacion Mexicana S.A. de C.V. (Mexico); T&B Procesos de Mexico S. de R.L. de C.V.; T&B Australasia Pty. Ltd. (Australia); LMS Asia Limited (Hong Kong); T&B Sales Limited (Hong Kong); T&B Japan Ltd. KK; T&B Sales Co., Ltd. (Japan); T&B Asia BHD (Malaysia); T&B Asia Pte. Ltd. (Singapore); T&B LLC (Saudi Arabia); T&B European Centre S.A. (Belgium); T&B Benelux BVBA (Belgium); Reznor N.V. (Belgium); Kaufel France S.A.; Gaz Industrie S.A.S. (France); Kaufel S.A. (France); Drilling Technical Supply (France); Gaz Industrie SCP (France); SCI ICL (France); T&B Vertriebs GmbH (Germany); Kaufel Van Lien Barendrecht GmbH (Germany); KVBL Beteiligungsverwaltungs GmbH (Germany); Kaufel GmbH & Co. (Germany);

T&B Gyarto Kft. (Hungary); T&B Italy Sales Srl.; Thomas & Betts Netherlands B.V.; T&B Europe C.V. (Netherlands); T&B Holdings Limited (UK); T&B Limited (UK); W.J. Furse & Co. Ltd. (UK); Royce Thompson Limited (UK).

PRINCIPAL COMPETITORS

3M Company; Amphenol Corporation; Cooper Industries plc; Eaton Corporation; Hubbell Incorporated; ITT Corporation; Methode Electronics, Inc.; Molex Incorporated; Siemens AG; Tyco International Ltd.; Valmont Industries, Inc.

FURTHER READING

Barton, Christopher, "Thomas & Betts Says It's Settled Slew of Lawsuits," *Memphis (Tenn.) Commercial Appeal*, October 4, 2002, p. C1.

———, "Thomas & Betts to Close Plants, Cut 1,000 More Jobs," *Memphis (Tenn.) Commercial Appeal*, December 19, 2001, p. C1.

———, "Thomas & Betts to Sell Big Chunk," *Memphis (Tenn.) Commercial Appeal*, May 9, 2000, p. B5.

Flaum, David, "Thomas & Betts Sells Stake Back to Leviton," *Memphis (Tenn.) Commercial Appeal*, June 26, 2008, p. C2.

Funk, Dale, "T&B Buys Homac, to Sell PVC Pipe Business," *Electrical Wholesaling*, February 2008, p. 10.

———, "Thomas & Betts Sells PVC Conduit and Pipe Business to Mitsubishi," *Electrical Wholesaling*, September 2008, p. 8.

Hicks, Ed, "Thomas & Betts Corp. Trying to Pull Out of a Deep Hole," *Memphis Business Journal*, September 28, 2001, p. 38.

Lasseter, Diana, and Mukul Pandya, "Thomas & Betts Strikes a Deal That Will Double Its Size," *Business for Central New Jersey*, November 27, 1991, p. 5.

Paulk, Michael, "Thomas & Betts Seeks Turnaround," *Memphis Business Journal*, July 14, 2000, p. 1.

Roberts, Jane, "Chair Retiring Again After Saving T&B," *Memphis (Tenn.) Commercial Appeal*, December 28, 2005, p. C1.

———, "T&B Buys Ohio Competitor: Purchase Gives Memphis Company Presence in Plastic Electrical Boxes," *Memphis (Tenn.) Commercial Appeal*, August 17, 2007, p. A9.

Sharpe, Anita, and Steve Stecklow, "Thomas & Betts to Acquire Augat for $515 Million," *Wall Street Journal*, October 8, 1996, p. A4.

Thompson, Richard, "Retooled and Ready: T&B Poised to Plug In When Market Turns On," *Memphis (Tenn.) Commercial Appeal*, May 1, 2003, p. C1.

Watson, Mark, "Thomas & Betts Restructuring Efforts Increase Efficiency," *Memphis (Tenn.) Commercial Appeal*, March 14, 2004, p. G1.

TimberWest Forest Corp.

———— ■ ————

1055 West Georgia Street, Suite 2300
Vancouver, British Columbia V6E 3P3
Canada
Telephone: (604) 654-4600
Fax: (604) 654-4662
Web site: http://www.timberwest.com

Public Company
Incorporated: 1997
Employees: 88
Sales: CAD 163.7 million (2008)
Stock Exchanges: Toronto
Ticker Symbol: TWF.UN-T
NAICS: 423310 Lumber, Plywood, Millwork, and
    Wood Panel Merchant Wholesalers; 423990 Other
    Miscellaneous   Durable   Goods   Merchant
    Wholesalers

■ ■ ■

TimberWest Forest Corp. is western Canada's largest
private timber and land management company. Timber-
West owns 322,000 hectares or 796,000 acres of private
forest lands located on Vancouver Island in the province
of British Columbia. Most of the company's land supports the growth of Douglas fir, a tree species well suited
for structural purposes. The company also holds renewable long-term public tenures, giving the right to harvest
logs on federally owned land. TimberWest contracts out
all logging activities to small- and medium-sized logging
operations. Through Couverdon Real Estate, Timber-
West is using approximately 134,000 acres of its land

for real estate development projects. To help maintain
sustainable management of its timberland, the company
operates the Mount Newton Seed Orchard on the Saanich Peninsula, north of Victoria, British Columbia.

FLETCHER CHALLENGE CANADA SPINS OFF TIMBERWEST: 1993

When Fletcher Challenge Canada Ltd. decided to
sharpen its strategic focus in the early 1990s, the stage
was set for the emergence of what would become the
largest private landowner in western Canada. Fletcher
Challenge Canada, controlled by New Zealand-based
Fletcher Challenge Ltd., owned timberland, licenses to
harvest federally owned timber, sawmill and logging
operations, and pulp and papermaking operations. The
company decided to focus its efforts on one area, papermaking, which led it to spin off most of its wood
products assets in December 1993.

The separation of Fletcher Challenge Canada's
wood products assets occurred through an initial public
offering (IPO) of stock. A newly formed subsidiary,
TimberWest Forest Ltd., sold 15.2 million shares of
stock at CAD 13 per share, completing a CAD 197.6
million IPO that netted Fletcher Challenge Canada
CAD 187.7 million and left it owning 51 percent of
TimberWest's stock. TimberWest debuted in the business world with licenses to harvest Crown timber,
210,000 hectares of timberland in British Columbia,
and logging and lumber mill operations in Campbell
River on Vancouver Island and in the province's interior
at Williams Lake. TimberWest began as a CAD 330
million company that sold all its chips and pulpwood to

Fletcher Challenge Canada, supplying its former parent company's papermaking operations.

The assets included in the IPO marked Fletcher Challenge Canada's first step in paring away its non-papermaking assets. Other divestments followed and TimberWest became the new owner of the assets. After completing a profitable first full year of operation in 1994, TimberWest repaid all of its CAD 66 million in long-term debt, giving it one of the strongest balance sheets in the industry.

The company's firm financial footing allowed it to expand through acquisitions. This occurred after Fletcher Challenge Canada revealed its intention in early 1996 to sell two sawmills in Mackenzie, British Columbia. TimberWest acquired the two mills, which had a combined annual capacity of 350 million board feet per year, for CAD 167.4 million, giving it a total of five sawmills with an annual capacity of 675 million board feet per year. The deal rid Fletcher Challenge Canada of its last remaining wood products assets, all of which had been consolidated within TimberWest. Later in the year, Fletcher Challenge Canada relinquished its stake in TimberWest, selling 31 million shares for approximately CAD 530 million.

FIRST SAWMILLS ARE SOLD: 1997

After acquiring Fletcher Challenge Canada's assets, TimberWest decided to shed some of its assets, beginning the company's gradual exit from the processing side of the business. In mid-1997, the company sold its sawmill operations in Williams Lake to Riverside Forest Products Ltd. At roughly the same time, the company sold its Mackenzie sawmill operations to Slocan Forest Products Ltd. TimberWest, which had owned five mills at the peak of its processing activities, was left with sawmills in Campbell River, the company's Elk Falls property, and Cowichan Lumbermill in Youbou, British Columbia, after the divestitures.

One month after selling its sawmills, TimberWest added to its holdings. The company joined forces with Doman Industries Ltd., a coastal British Columbia-based company that later became Western Forest Products Inc. The companies reached an agreement with Avenor Inc. to acquire Pacific Forest Products Ltd. in a CAD 573 million transaction. Doman took possession of Pacific Forest Products' three sawmills, a business TimberWest no longer had interest in, and TimberWest acquired Pacific Forest Products' private timberland, consisting of 124,000 hectares primarily on Vancouver Island. The acquisition was completed in December 1997.

Organizational changes followed the Pacific Forest Products acquisition. TimberWest incorporated in 1997, the year TimberWest Timber Trust was formed as an income trust to acquire the company's operations. The following year, the company reorganized its structure for investing purposes, becoming TimberWest Forest Corp.

FROM LOGGER TO LAND MANAGER: 2004

One of the most important events in TimberWest's history occurred shortly after the company celebrated its 10th anniversary. During its first decade, the company logged its timberland and the federally owned land it had a license to log, typically performing 50 percent of the harvesting work in-house. Beginning in 2004, as part of its decision to become a company focused on land management, TimberWest turned to third-party contractors to perform the work. The company solicited bids from logging operations to build the roads and harvest its timberland and ceased functioning as a logging company.

TimberWest spent its second decade of business recasting its identity, disentangling the assets it inherited from Fletcher Challenge Canada. The company bowed out of harvesting. After closing its Cowichan mill in 2001 and putting its last remaining sawmill, Elk Falls, up for sale in 2005, it turned away from processing logs. The company focused its efforts on land management, holding sway as the largest private landowner in western Canada. Financially, its stature declined as it embraced

```
┌─────────────────────────────────────────────┐
│                                             │
│           KEY DATES                         │
│              ─────■─────                     │
│                                             │
│  1993:  TimberWest is spun off from Fletcher Chal-  │
│         lenge Canada.                        │
│  1997:  TimberWest begins divesting its sawmill  │
│         properties.                          │
│  2004:  Log harvesting is contracted out to third-  │
│         party operators.                     │
│  2009:  With the assistance of Rennie Marketing  │
│         Systems, TimberWest enters the real estate  │
│         business.                            │
│                                             │
└─────────────────────────────────────────────┘
```

its single focus, as annual revenues declined from CAD 371.8 million in 2004 to CAD 318 million by 2007 before plunging to CAD 163.7 million in 2008.

SEARCH FOR NEW OPPORTUNITIES: 2005–08

The second half of the decade proved to be a difficult period for TimberWest, as its anemic financial performance reflected. Sagging lumber sales plagued the company, prompting it to look for alternative ways to exploit its timberland asset base. Industry conditions, far from ideal midway through the decade, became decidedly worse at the end of the decade, when a global economic crisis struck the construction market with a telling blow, causing timber companies to suffer severe losses and lumber mills to suspend operation. In the first half of 2008 alone, Canada's forest industry lost more than CAD 1 billion.

One way TimberWest was looking to make more profitable use of its dominant landownership position emerged before the economic debacle at the end of the decade. As early as 2005, the company began looking at 166 hectares of land it owned in Vancouver Island's Comox Valley and considered using it for purposes other than logging. By 2008, which the company described as the most difficult year it experienced since its inception, it had decided to stop harvesting the land for timber and, instead, begin using the land to grow food. "When you look at how [Vancouver Island] has changed over the last five or 10 years, you realize you can make way more money off this land than just growing trees on it," a TimberWest spokesperson explained in the October 14, 2008 edition of *Globe & Mail*. "If you look at Comox and the kind of boutique agriculture that's going on, we really think that's going to drive up the value of land."

The 11 parcels of land in Comox Valley sat within an Agricultural Land Reserve, which essentially made the area off limits to residential development, but not all of TimberWest's vast land holdings were subjected to such a stipulation. The company identified 134,000 acres to use for purposes other than forestry, setting aside three large tracts that had the greatest potential value as real estate holdings.

LAUNCH OF COUVERDON REAL ESTATE: 2009

To facilitate its entry into the real estate business, TimberWest collaborated with Rennie Marketing Systems, led by Bob Rennie, who had made his fortune in Vancouver converting property into condominiums years earlier. In 2009 the two companies formed a partnership called Couverdon, a name derived from the city in the Netherlands where the ancestors of Captain George Vancouver were born. "It's about creating real land and real land uses for homeowners, whether that's manufactured home parks or homesteading on one-acre or five-acre developments, farming, we're going to look at real needs," Rennie said in the February 8, 2009 edition of *Maple Ridge News*, explaining the mission of Couverdon.

TimberWest organized its activities into six operations, evenly divided within its forestry and real estate segments. The company's logging activities were conducted in the South Island Operation, Oyster River Operation, and Johnstone Strait Operation. The South Island Operation stretched from Parksville and Port Alberni on Vancouver Island south to Sooke on the southern tip of the island. The Oyster River Operation comprised timberland west of Courtney and Campbell River on the east coast of Vancouver Island. The Johnstone Strait Operation, based north of Campbell River in Middleton, consisted of timberland along the east of Vancouver Island from Quadra Island in the south to Hanson Island in the north. TimberWest's real estate projects operated under the names Campbell River Airport Land, Jubilee Heights, and Headquarters, each located on Vancouver Island.

The end of the decade proved to be the harshest period TimberWest had experienced in its history. Log sales were plummeting, thrusting the company into a precarious position. TimberWest refined its contractor model during the period, distancing itself from large logging operations. The company began to favor small- and medium-sized contractors instead, choosing the smaller operators because of their focus on safety and their habit of offering competitive prices. Until the construction market recovered, however, the state of TimberWest's logging operations was not expected to improve, no matter how efficiently its harvesting activities were conducted. Moving forward, the company intended to make real estate an increasingly important aspect of its business.

Jeffrey L. Covell

PRINCIPAL OPERATING UNITS

Couverdon Real Estate.

PRINCIPAL COMPETITORS

Tembec Inc.; International Paper Company; Canfor Corporation.

FURTHER READING

Clarke, Brennan, "From Timberland to Boutique Agriculture," *Globe & Mail*, October 14, 2008, p. S3.

Fletcher, Tom, "Realtor Moves to Homesteads," *Maple Ridge News*, February 12, 2009, p. 30.

———, "TimberWest Lands a Unique Opportunity in North America, Developer Says," *Saanich News*, February 8, 2009, p. 22.

Lush, Patricia, "TimberWest Debt-Free after Profitable Year," *Globe & Mail*, October 17, 1995, p. B4.

"TimberWest Places Sizeable Asset on the Block," *Mergers & Acquisitions Report*, October 17, 2005.

Tolko Industries Ltd.

3000 - 28th Street
PO Box 39
Vernon, British Columbia V1T 6M1
Canada
Telephone: (250) 545-4411
Fax: (250) 550-2550
Web site: http://www.tolko.com

Private Company
Founded: 1956 as Lavington Planer Mill
Incorporated: 1961 as Lavington Planer Mill Ltd.
Employees: 3,700
Sales: CAD 1.5 billion ($1.52 billion) (2007)
NAICS: 321113 Sawmills; 321212 Softwood Veneer and
     Plywood Manufacturing; 321219 Reconstituted
     Wood Product Manufacturing; 322121 Paper
     (Except Newsprint) Mills

∎ ∎ ∎

Tolko Industries Ltd. is a major Canadian forest
products company with facilities across the western
provinces of British Columbia, Alberta, Saskatchewan,
and Manitoba. From its beginnings running a single
sawmill in Lavington, British Columbia, Tolko has
grown to encompass 18 operations producing lumber,
specialty kraft papers, plywood and veneer products,
engineered wood, and other forest products. Tolko's
mills have the capacity to produce more than two billion board feet of lumber per year, with lumber accounting for more than 60 percent of the company's total
revenues. Plywood and veneer products bring in about

16 percent of sales, with kraft papers, which are used to
make paper bags and packaging, accounting for around
14 percent. Several of the company's mills use wood
waste to generate biomass energy. Tolko generates nearly
half of its total sales in the United States and about one-
third in Canada. The company remains privately owned
by the founding Thorlakson family.

FOUNDING AS LAVINGTON PLANER MILL

Harold Thorlakson, the founder of Tolko Industries, was
the fourth of six sons of Thorlakur and Ingibjorg Thorlakson, who in the 1890s had separately immigrated to
Canada from Iceland, met in Winnipeg, and married.
The Thorlaksons raised their family on a ranch in the
Okanagan Valley, located in southern British Columbia
near the town of Vernon. Surrounded by the rich British
Columbian forests, it was not surprising that some of
the children eventually pursued careers in the logging
industry.

In the early 1950s Harold Thorlakson began logging in the local area, while his younger brother Joe
traveled around the area with a portable sawmill cutting
railroad ties and clearing timber from government-
owned lands to make way for hydroelectric power lines.
Joe eventually set up shop on leased land in Lavington,
located about 10 miles southeast of Vernon, and in
1954 Harold joined Joe and a son of Joe's in this business, having concluded that marketing finished lumber
products offered him better prospects than logging. The
partners soon found, however, that the nascent operation was too small to support two families, and so

Harold in 1956 purchased full control of the enterprise and Joe and his son returned to the portable sawmill business.

At what he called the Lavington Planer Mill, Harold Thorlakson bought rough lumber from operators of portable sawmills working in the surrounding forests and then planed it with the help of a machinist who had brought his self-built, portable planer to the mill. Thorlakson sold the finished lumber to a variety of customers in the Okanagan Valley. He soon secured his first big break, a contract to supply the timbers and lumber for the building of the Okanagan Lake Floating Bridge in Kelowna, located about 30 miles south of Vernon. This bridge, spanning nearly a mile in length, opened in 1958. In the wake of this successful job, Thorlakson in 1959 purchased a planer and thus was able to move beyond marketing and start manufacturing forest products. He incorporated the business as Lavington Planer Mill Ltd. in 1961.

One of the key early suppliers of rough timber to Lavington Planer was the Schunter family, who were engaged in logging operations and also ran a portable sawmill. During the 1960s this family decided to concentrate their efforts on logging and began supplying raw logs to Lavington, a practice they continued into the 21st century. At the same time, Thorlakson brought people into his company with sawmill experience, and by 1968 the company had established a permanent sawmill at the Lavington facility.

FIRST WAVE OF GROWTH AS TOLKO

Also during the 1960s, the second generation of Thorlaksons came into the business. Most notable among these was Harold's son Al, who after gaining an engineering degree from the University of British Columbia and practical experience at another forest products concern, Weldwood of Canada Limited, returned to Lavington Planer with a focus on the manufacturing side of the business. He was named president of the company in 1972. Al's brother John around this time was placed in charge of the firm's

marketing and sales operations. In 1973 Lavington Planer Mill was renamed Tolko Industries Ltd., the name created from every other letter of the Thorlakson family name.

The first major growth initiative at Tolko occurred in 1973 when Hoover Sawmills Limited was acquired in what amounted to a doubling of the business. When a fire destroyed the Hoover facilities two years later, Tolko elected to maintain its enlarged capacity by adding a second sawmill line and a graveyard shift to the Lavington mill and shifting the Hoover employees to Lavington. In the late 1970s Harold Thorlakson handed control of the company over to his sons, although he retained the CEO title. When the founder died in 1981, Al Thorlakson was officially named CEO.

Also in 1981, Tolko ventured further afield with the purchase of Ernst Forest Products, operator of a sawmill in Quesnel, a town in central British Columbia about 60 miles south of the city of Prince George. Tolko subsequently modernized this mill, and it became a division known as Quest Wood Products. The company's growth spurt continued in 1987 when Balco Industries was acquired. Through Balco, Tolko gained several facilities to the north and south of the British Columbia city of Kamloops, including sawmills in Merritt and Louis Creek and a plywood plant in Heffley Creek. The company's entrance into the plywood business marked the first diversification of its product line. By the end of the 1980s, aided by the addition of an export department to facilitate sales outside Canada, Tolko's annual sales had reached approximately CAD 250 million ($215 million).

DIVERSIFYING GEOGRAPHICALLY AND IN PRODUCT VARIETY

Tolko diversified further in the 1990s, in terms of both product and geographic area of operation. In 1995 the company completed construction of its first "greenfield" (built-from-scratch) manufacturing facility, an oriented strand board (OSB) plant located in the northern Alberta town of High Prairie. An alternative to plywood, OSB was a multilayered board made from wood strands "oriented" in various directions. The strands were held together by a mixture of wax and resin and compressed under intense heat. Tolko was simultaneously planning to build another OSB plant in northwestern Ontario in the Kenora area, but in 1998 the provincial government pulled the plug on the project apparently because of the company's delays in submitting a firm proposal for the project's completion.

In the meantime, Tolko acquired the Manitoba subsidiary of Repap Enterprises Inc. in 1997. Tolko thus gained two operations in the northern Manitoba town of The Pas, a sawmill and a kraft paper mill. The kraft paper produced was used mainly for multiwall bags and shipping sacks. After acquiring the sawmill, Tolko embarked on an expansion to increase its existing capacity of 100 million board feet of lumber per year. The company rounded out the decade with the 1999 purchase from Daishowa-Marubeni International Ltd. of another sawmill located in the northern Alberta town of High Level. One of the largest lumber producers in Alberta, the High Level mill ranked as Tolko's most productive lumber operation in the first years of the 21st century, with an output of more than 250 million board feet per year. Its latest growth initiatives helped push Tolko's sales up to CAD 922 million ($640 million) by 1999.

In the first years of the 21st century, sales stagnated in part because of a trade dispute between Canada and the United States. Following the expiration of a trade agreement between the two nations in March 2001, the United States began imposing duties on softwood lumber imports from its northern neighbor, charging Canadian producers with dumping their products below cost. These duties had a large effect on Tolko because it exported to the United States about two-thirds of the lumber it produced. The trade dispute coupled with the rocky state of the North American economy led Tolko to intermittently shut down its sawmill in The Pas in 2001.

During this same period, the company was in the midst of a multiyear effort to build a new, state-of-the-art OSB mill near Meadow Lake, a town in northwestern Saskatchewan. This plant, which was constructed in partnership with a number of local Aboriginal communities, began production in mid-2003. Back in British Columbia, wildfires raged across the province in what were called the driest conditions in 50 years. In July 2003 a wildfire destroyed Tolko's Louis Creek sawmill, and the company concluded that rebuilding the plant did not make sense from an economic standpoint. That same year, the company consolidated its marketing, sales, and transportation operations into a new wholly owned subsidiary called Tolko Marketing and Sales Ltd. Among other duties, this unit was responsible for marketing Tolko products in about 20 countries around the world.

BOOM & BUST

With housing starts surging in the United States, sales began moving sharply higher in 2004 and Tolko pursued additional growth initiatives. Early in the year, the company purchased from Weyerhaeuser Company an OSB mill located in Slave Lake, Alberta, that had an annual production capacity of 240 million square feet. Then, much later that same year, Tolko completed the largest acquisition in its history, winning a takeover battle with International Forest Products Limited over control of Riverside Forest Products Limited. Tolko prevailed with an offer that amounted to about CAD 377 million ($307 million). With eight production facilities, Riverside ranked as the fourth-largest lumber producer in British Columbia, with an annual production capacity of more than one billion board feet, and the second-largest producer of plywood and veneer in Canada. It was based in Kelowna, not far from Tolko's headquarters in Vernon. The takeover of Riverside vaulted Tolko into the number seven position among North America's lumber producers. It also helped propel revenues to a record CAD 2.3 billion ($2 billion) in 2005.

In October 2006 the Canadian and U.S. governments finally reached a settlement on the lengthy softwood lumber dispute. The U.S.-imposed duties were replaced by a Canadian-imposed export tax, or a combination of a lower tax and a quota, and the deal also required the U.S. government to refund with interest all duties that had been collected. Thus in 2006, Tolko enjoyed a boost in its profits from softwood duty refunds.

Ironically, around the same time that this lumber dispute was settled, the North American lumber market went into a sharp and prolonged decline as the credit/subprime mortgage crisis devastated the U.S. housing market. According to Tolko officials, this downturn featured the worst market conditions for softwood lumber in the company's entire 50-plus-year history.

The company was forced to shut down a number of mills on either a permanent or temporary basis, and sales by 2007 had plunged to just CAD 1.5 billion ($1.52 billion). In what turned out to be an ill-timed investment, Tolko in mid-2005 had begun building a CAD 200 million OSB and laminated-strand lumber plant in Slave Lake with a capacity of 800 million square feet per year. The plant opened in November 2007, but Tolko had to shut it down in early 2009 as the global economic crisis led to lower prices and weak demand for the plant's products. The company planned to reopen the plant when market conditions improved. Later in 2009, Tolko indefinitely shut down its sawmill in High Level, Alberta. Company officials anticipated enduring a long wait before market conditions improved enough to justify the resumption of production at the shuttered plants.

David E. Salamie

PRINCIPAL SUBSIDIARIES

Tolko Marketing and Sales Ltd.

PRINCIPAL DIVISIONS

BRITISH COLUMBIA: Armstrong Division; Ashcroft Treating Division; Creekside Division; Heffley Creek Division; Kelowna Division; Lake Country Division; Lakeview Lumber Division; Lavington Planer Division; Nicola Valley Division; Quest Wood Division; Soda Creek Division; White Valley Division. ALBERTA: Athabasca Division; High Level Lumber Division; High Prairie Division. SASKATCHEWAN: Meadow Lake OSB. MANITOBA: Tolko Manitoba Kraft Papers; Tolko Manitoba Solid Wood.

PRINCIPAL COMPETITORS

Weyerhaeuser Company; West Fraser Timber Co. Ltd.; Canfor Corporation; AbitibiBowater Inc.; Georgia-Pacific LLC; Sierra Pacific Industries; Hampton Affiliates.

FURTHER READING

Cash, Martin, "Tolko Mill Threatened by Crippling U.S. Tariffs," *Winnipeg Free Press*, March 27, 2002, p. B5.

Greenwood, John, "Tolko Locks Up Takeover of Riverside," *National Post*, October 27, 2004, p. FP4.

Hamilton, Gordon, "Tolko Reacts to Low Prices by Taking Down-Time, Cutting Shift," *Vancouver (B.C.) Sun*, May 15, 2007, p. D3.

Mah, Bill, "Slave Lake Sawmill Shuts Down," *Edmonton Journal*, February 14, 2009, p. E1.

McKie, Paul, "Terms Reached for Repap Sale," *Winnipeg Free Press*, July 22, 1997, p. B5.

"Tolko Industries: 50th Anniversary, 1956–2006," Vernon, BC: Tolko Industries Ltd., 2006, 12 p.

TruFoods LLC

14 Penn Plaza, Suite 1305
New York, New York 10122
U.S.A.
Telephone: (212) 359-3600
Fax: (212) 359-3601
Web site: http://www.trufoods.com

Private Company
Incorporated: 2002 as TruFoods Corporation
Employees: 30
Sales: $40 million (2008 est.)
NAICS: 722211 Limited-Service Restaurants

■ ■ ■

Privately held TruFoods LLC is a New York City-based multi-concept, quick-serve restaurant franchiser that owns about 100 eateries, mostly located in the eastern half of the United States. Concepts include Pudgie's Famous Chicken, Arthur Treacher's Fish & Chips, Ritter's Frozen Custard, and Wall Street Deli. Known as a company that specializes in turning around tired brands, TruFoods has itself been the object of a turnaround since its acquisition by CEO Andy Unanue, a member of the family that owns Hispanic foods manufacturer Goya Foods and a former executive of the concern.

FOUNDER, BROOKLYN BORN

TruFoods was founded by Jeffrey Bernstein. Born in the Far Rockaway section of Brooklyn, New York, he was the son of a grocery products manufacturer's rep. After graduating from Brooklyn University in 1970, Bernstein went to work as a salesman for his father's Long Island-

based company, Harrison Food Brokerage Co., playing a role in the successful introduction of "Juicy Juice" to supermarkets. After his father died he ran the business for awhile, and then took an executive position at a New York City restaurant chain, Cooky's Steak Pubs. After three years, when the company was sold, he became CFO and COO in 1989 for a real estate firm, Intercapital Organization, helping to shepherd it through Chapter 11 bankruptcy protection. That experience led Bernstein to start Consolidated Services Inc. in 1990, a consulting business that specialized in insolvency-crisis management and corporate turnarounds. Over the next several years he became involved in more than 100 corporate restructurings.

It was Bernstein's sojourns in bankruptcy court that led to his return to the restaurant business. In June 1998 he was in court in White Plains, New York, when he overheard two lawyers mention that the 39-unit Pudgie's restaurant chain had filed for Chapter 11 bankruptcy protection and that its assets were for sale. Founded in Bethpage, New York, in 1981, Pudgie's was a takeout and delivery concept that offered skinless, bone-in fried chicken. It grew in popularity on Long Island and was also one of Bernstein's favorite eateries. "I saw an opportunity," Bernstein told *Long Island Business News*. "I decided to do a turnaround for myself instead of working for others."

BERNSTEIN ACQUIRES PUDGIE'S: 1998

Bernstein acquired Pudgie's out of bankruptcy court in June 1998 for $425,000 and the assumption of

$700,000 in debt. He quickly stabilized the operation by closing 20 locations. As part of his turnaround effort, one of the Pudgie's stores, located in West Babylon, New York, also began offering selected items from Arthur Treacher's Fish & Chips. Bernstein then merged Pudgie's with Arthur Treacher's Inc. in October 2000. Arthur Treacher's was an older but equally troubled concept. Now mostly forgotten, Arthur Treacher was a British-born actor who became the announcer and sidekick for television talk show host Merv Griffin in the 1960s. Treacher's popularity in the United States was used to launch a fish and chips chains under the Arthur Treacher's Fish & Chips, Inc., banner in 1969, although the extent of his personal involvement was uncertain. Treacher died in 1975 but the chain carried on, numbering 900 units at its peak.

Mrs. Paul's, Inc., acquired Arthur Treacher's in 1979 and in 1982 sold it to Lumara Foods of America, Inc. Just one year later Lumara filed Chapter 11 bankruptcy and in December 1983 its assets were acquired by a newly formed Ohio corporation, Arthur Treacher's, Inc. Three months later this company merged with El Charro, Inc. By the 1990s the chain was reduced to less than 200 units. It was acquired in 1996 by an investment group headed by investment banker Bruce R. Galloway, who served as chairman and in 1998 took over as chief executive officer. It was at his behest that co-branding with Pudgie's was begun. He was also interested in Internet ventures and formed Digital Creative Development Corporation in February 2000, and through some legal maneuvering Arthur Treacher's Inc. assumed the Digital Creative name two months before Bernstein merged Pudgie's with the company and became the new CEO.

BERNSTEIN BUYS OUT PARTNER: 2002

Bernstein furthered the co-branding of Pudgie's and Arthur Treacher's, and by the end of 2000 was operating 27 company-owned stores and another 138 franchised operations that also included 15 units co-branded between Treacher's and the Nathan's hot dog chain, 43 units co-branded with Miami Subs, and one unit co-branded with the Kenny Rogers Roasters chicken chain.

Because of the collapse of the Internet market, publicly traded Digital Creative was unable to fund expansion, and in February 2002 Bernstein bought out Galloway and took the company private.

Given a free hand, Bernstein increased the company's co-branding efforts and enjoyed some success in building sales at a number of locations. He revamped the menus, dropping some of the less popular items in favor of new selections. Bernstein was also eager to bring new concepts into the fold. In March 2002 he brought the 60-unit Wall Street Deli restaurant chain out of bankruptcy paying about $4.3 million for the assets.

Wall Street Deli was founded in Birmingham, Alabama, in 1966 as Stand N Snack by Alan Kaufman and did not assume the Wall Street Deli name until 1987, when the entire concept was reimagined as an upscale New York-style deli. The chain grew to more than 100 restaurants but by the early 2000s it was reduced to 80 units in a handful of cities, including Birmingham, Chicago, Dallas, Denver, Houston, Los Angeles, and Washington. It was also losing more than $8 million a year, because while half of the company-owned and franchised restaurants were profitable, the other half were not. Moreover, corporate overhead was onerous.

Bernstein became aware of Wall Street Deli when he ate at one of the Birmingham restaurants when in town on a visit in March 2001. He liked the operation, inquired, and discovered that the Kaufman family was interested in selling the business. Bernstein offered his consulting services to help turn around the chain, primarily by making Wall Street Deli a pure franchise operation. The Kaufmans declined his advice as well as his bid to buy the chain, and they tried to revive the business by closing a large number of units.

The changes in Wall Street Deli did not have much of a chance to work. In the wake of the economic turmoil that followed the terrorist attacks on the United States of September 11, 2001, a key lender cut the company's credit line and in October 2001 Wall Street Deli was forced into Chapter 11 bankruptcy. Wise in the ways of such proceedings, Bernstein bought $1.5 million in company debt from Birmingham bank Am-South, which was at the top of the creditor list. He was now able to come into bankruptcy court as the largest creditor, foreclose on the debt, and force a sale to an investment group he put together under the name FWSD (Funding Wall Street Deli) Inc.

FORMATION OF TRUFOODS: 2002

To house the three restaurant concepts, Bernstein formed TruFoods Corporation in March 2002. All told

KEY DATES

1998: Jeffrey Bernstein acquires Pudgie's Famous
Chicken restaurant chain.
2000: Pudgie's merges with Arthur Treacher's Inc.
2002: Trufoods Corporation is formed.
2007: Company is sold, renamed TruFoods LLC.
2008: Ritter's Frozen Custard is acquired.

the company operated 300 units generating systemwide sales of about $56 million in fiscal 2003, the year ending on June 30. TruFoods looked to drive growth through further co-branding efforts, but Bernstein also remained interested in acquiring additional brands. His next opportunity came in May 2003 when TruFoods acquired Burritoville, Inc., a chain of 11 company-owned "fresh Mex" restaurants located in Manhattan, New York.

Founded in 1992, Burritoville carved out a niche in Manhattan with its healthful Mexican fare, and expanded to New Jersey, Connecticut, and Pennsylvania. The impact of the September 11, 2001, terrorist attacks on the United States also crippled the company, which closed its out-of-state stores and focused on its Manhattan operations. Matters grew worse, however, when employees complained to New York State Attorney General Eliot Spitzer that the company failed to pay them overtime. Burritoville insisted that the workers were all in fact managers or in supervisory positions and therefore not entitled to overtime. Regardless, investigating the matter cost the company money it could ill afford to spend. Bernstein was aware of Burritoville's situation and was interested in buying the chain. Rather than face bankruptcy or liquidation, the owners elected to sell to TruFoods, the purchase price including $500,000 to settle the back wages claim.

The addition of Burritoville, and a sister concept, California Burrito, helped to boost TruFoods' systemwide sales to about $75 million in fiscal 2004. By this time another distressed restaurant chain, Piccadilly Cafeterias Inc., had caught Bernstein's attention. The 145-unit operation had been in business since 1944 when T. H. Hamilton acquired the Piccadilly Cafeteria & Coffee Shop in Baton Rouge, Louisiana. Two years later he opened a second restaurant and in 1965 incorporated Piccadilly Cafeterias Inc., which he took public in 1979 two years before his death.

The chain continued to grow but began to falter by 2000. In October 2003 it filed for Chapter 11 protection. One day after the filing, Piccadilly agreed to a $53 million joint offer from TruFoods and Miami venture capital firm H.I.G. Capital. The deal did not close, however. Instead the bankruptcy court held an auction in February 2004 and Trufoods was outbid by Los Angeles-based Yucapia Companies, which paid $80 million for the restaurant chain.

SALE OF COMPANY: 2007

In the wake of the failed Piccadilly purchase, TruFoods experienced its own share of difficulties. By the fall of 2004 the California Burrito chain was closed. Systemwide sales fell to $40 million and in November 2007 Trufoods was acquired by Andrew Unanue, whose grandfather founded Goya Foods, a major manufacturer of Hispanic foods. Unanue was a former vice president and chief operating officer of Goya and also made headlines by considering a run to be a U.S. senator from New Jersey despite living in New York City. Now operating as TruFoods LLC, the company soon added another restaurant concept, the 40-unit, eight-state Ritter's Frozen Custard, which was acquired in April 2008.

Ritter's was founded in 1989 when John Ritter, a retired animator, opened his first store in Franklin, Indiana, in 1989. He began franchising the operation and by 2005 there were 60 locations. Stiff competition from Cold Stone Creamery and Maggie Moo's took its toll, however, and the company under the leadership of John Ritter's son, Bob, ceased franchising and focused on its healthy stores as the number of units began to dwindle.

With four restaurant concepts in hand, Unanue's priorities were to improve Wall Street Deli's northeast presence, and then grow the other three brands in markets where they were already established. The long-term goal was to expand all of the chains nationwide. Because of the credit crunch that would come, it was fortunate that TruFoods had the deep pockets of its CEO to draw upon. In 2009 Unanue hired veteran franchiser Gary Occhiogrosso as TruFoods chief development officer, and late in the year Occhiogrosso spearheaded the relaunch of the Pudgie's brand. While the company planned to focus its attention on its four portfolio brands, Unanue did not rule out the possibility of further acquisitions.

Ed Dinger

PRINCIPAL COMPETITORS

Captain D's, LLC; Dunkin' Brands, Inc.; YUM! Brands, Inc.

FURTHER READING

Crecca, Donna Hood, "Turnaround Artist: TruFoods Looking for Trouble," *Chain Leader,* November 1, 2003.

Curan, Catherine, "Franchisor's Dig Deep to Fund Own Growth," *Nation's Restaurant News,* November 24, 2008, p. 1.

Fickenscher, Lisa, "Reheated Burritoville Set to Feed East Coast," *Crain's New York Business,* May 26–June 1, 2003.

Frumkin, Paul, "Operator Seeks Brands 'Tru' Form," *Nation's Restaurant News,* March 18, 2001, p. 4.

Gautreau, Chris, "Bankruptcy Buyouts TruFoods Focus," *Baton Rouge (LA) Advocate,* November 4, 2003.

Solnik, Claude, "Local Man Has Knack for Bankruptcy Turn-Arounds," *Long Island Business News,* April 12, 2002.

———, "TruFoods Acquires 11 Burritovilles," *Long Island Business News,* May 16, 2003.

Stall, Sam, "Ritter's Buyer Retools Chain," *Indianapolis Business Journal,* May 4, 2009, p. 3.

Strugatch, Warren, "Resuscitating Two Familiar Restaurant Chains," *New York Times,* December 2, 2001.

Williams, Roy L., "Bread Winners," *Birmingham News,* February 3, 2002, p. 1D.

Truman Arnold
Companies, Inc.

---

702 South Robison Road
Texarkana, Texas 75501
U.S.A.
Telephone: (903) 794-3835
Toll Free: (800) 235-5343
Fax: (903) 831-4056
Web site: http://www.trumanarnoldcompanies.com

Private Company
Incorporated: 1969 as Truman Arnold Distributing, Inc.
Employees: 450
Sales: $2.5 billion (2009 est.)
NAICS: 424710 Petroleum Bulk Stations and Terminals;
488190 Other Airport Operations; 447110
Gasoline Stations with Convenience Stores; 531120
Lessors of Nonresidential Buildings (Except
Miniwarehouses)

■ ■ ■

Truman Arnold Companies, Inc., distributes petroleum
products, operates pipeline terminals, and operates
general aviation facilities. The company has smaller
interests in operating convenience stores, managing real
estate, and operating a cattle ranch. Through TAC
Energy, one of its three main divisions, the company
distributes more than two billion gallons of diesel,
gasoline, and aviation fuels throughout the country.
TAC Terminals operates petroleum storage operations in
Caddo Mills, Texas, and North Little Rock, Arkansas,
capable of storing more than 1.3 million barrels of
refined petroleum products. TAC Air provides fueling,

hangar facilities, and other services at 13 airports in the
United States. Truman Arnold Companies operates two
Road Runner convenience stores equipped with fuel
pumps.

ORIGINS AS A CONOCO JOBBER

Otis Truman Arnold launched his multibillion-dollar
business empire with $2,500, the amount it cost to
become a commissioned agent for Conoco Inc. and
begin his career as a branded petroleum jobber. Arnold
was 27 years old in 1964 when he began purchasing
refined fuel from Conoco and selling the fuel to gasoline
stations. He wasted little time before expanding his
business, displaying the ambition that eventually made
him the largest independent petroleum distributor in
the United States.

Arnold built his own Conoco dealership outlet a
year after he started his business, establishing it in Texarkana, Texas, a location that would play a significant role
in the development of Truman Arnold Companies. He
incorporated his business as Truman Arnold Distributing in 1969, the same year he formed Truman Arnold
Transportation as a business unit assigned to transport
fuel to retail customers. The year's most notable event
was a modest effort that gradually developed into the
driving force propelling Arnold's business forward. He
opened his first gas station in 1969, a location in Texas
that operated under the name Road Runner. The outlet,
which sold gas, candy, cigarettes, and motor oil, became
the first in its industry to offer self-service gasoline of a
major oil company brand.

COMPANY PERSPECTIVES

Regardless of the industry, TAC has a passion for service like no one else. We've made a reputation for ourselves to take what others are already doing, then do it like no one else does. It's what sets us apart from the competition, and what has made us a major force in the following industries: aviation services; wholesale petroleum marketing; petroleum terminal services; branded petroleum marketing. Each of our divisions is staffed by the finest associates and managed by leaders who are, themselves, experienced leaders in their respective industries. The divisions benefit from both the combined experience of Truman Arnold Companies, but also the flexibility they're given to use his or her expertise to respond instantly to industry demands.

FIRST CONVENIENCE STORE: 1973

The scope of Arnold's business expanded considerably during the 1970s. He used his relationship with Conoco to his advantage, buying the company's assets in Little Rock, Arkansas, in 1972 and the oil giant's assets in Arkansas and eastern Texas in 1975. The first half of the decade also included the opening of the first Road Runner convenience store, a $25,000 unit located in Texarkana. The Road Runner location opened in 1973 boasted a far more comprehensive selection of merchandise than the gas station that debuted in 1969. It became the prototype of a chain of Road Runner units, each featuring six fueling pumps and a range of food and sundry items for sale.

A decade after starting his locally oriented business, Arnold had become a regional petroleum marketer with a budding retail operation. The expansion created logistical difficulties, growing pains that were peculiar to operating out of a headquarters location as small as Texarkana. To manage his burgeoning empire, Arnold needed to fly to various sites, a weekly chore that proved difficult because of limited airline service to and from Texarkana. In 1976, after completing the second Conoco acquisition that scattered his assets throughout two states, Arnold purchased a twin-engine Cessna 402, Truman Arnold Companies' first aircraft.

Arnold's need to use the company's Cessna would increase as Truman Arnold Companies' retail business developed into its mainstay business. A chain of Road

Runners emerged, expanding into Colorado and a handful of other states by the beginning of the 1980s. In 1982 the company broadened its offerings in the retail locations, becoming one of the first competitors in the convenience store industry to offer fast-food products.

TAC ENERGY TAKES SHAPE: 1980–84

Meanwhile, as the Road Runner chain blossomed into a major component of Truman Arnold Companies' business, another facet of the company developed. In 1980 Truman Arnold Companies collaborated with Coulson Oil Company to open a petroleum storage terminal, Arkansas Terminaling and Trading. The facility was built under the aegis of a joint venture agreement between Truman Arnold Companies and Coulson Oil, serving as a springboard for Arnold's further involvement in the storage and terminal side of the petroleum industry. In 1984, on its own, Truman Arnold Companies constructed a second storage facility, establishing it in Caddo Mills, Texas.

Arnold branched out into other businesses during the 1980s. In 1988 he launched a wholesale marketing and products trading operation, assembling a team to purchase and sell petroleum products. His most important diversifying move during the period occurred in 1986, a decade after he had acquired his first aircraft. By the mid-1980s there were approximately 100 Road Runner stores operating in a territory stretching from Arkansas to the Rocky Mountains. The company's wholesale business encompassed a much larger operating territory, distributing more than one billion gallons of fuel annually throughout 24 states. The sprawling size of each operation meant that Arnold and his team of managers were making weekly flights aboard company-owned aircraft, creating a need for a cost-cutting initiative to reduce the expenses incurred from the flurry of flights emanating from Texarkana.

ENTRY INTO THE AVIATION BUSINESS: 1986

Arnold needed to reduce the cost of fueling his aircraft at the Texarkana airport. In 1986 he purchased the airport's fueling operation, acquiring his first fixed base operation (FBO), businesses that served the general aviation sector by providing services such as fueling, hangar leasing, pilot lounges, and other amenities. The operation, initially named Road Runner Aviation, formed the foundation of TAC Air, Truman Arnold Companies' aviation services division. TAC Air began as a way to save money, but once Arnold realized how profitable the business was, he began to acquire other FBOs, creating

KEY DATES

1964: Otis Truman Arnold begins working as a Conoco distributor.

1969: First Road Runner gas station opens.

1986: Truman Arnold Companies acquires its first fixed base operation (FBO).

1989: Road Runner chain is sold to Total Petroleum Inc.

2002: Sales eclipse $1 billion for the first time as the company's wholesale operation expands.

2009: Truman Arnold Companies acquires its 13th FBO.

a vibrant business that became the company's profit-making jewel.

Before Arnold began purchasing FBOs, he surprised industry observers with a decision he made in 1989. Arnold was regarded as innovative, tenacious, and ambitious, having gained prominence primarily because of the success of the Road Runner retail chain. Pundits were shocked when he sold the business, along with other substantial assets in 1989. "He was, to put it mildly, probably the last independent in the world that might be expected to sell any of the stations and stores that he had spent so many years in collecting or building from the ground up into first-class operations," the September 1989 issue of *National Petroleum News* noted of Arnold.

DEPARTURE OF ROAD RUNNER: 1989

In a two-part transaction, Total Petroleum Inc. acquired 125 Road Runner stores in seven states and rights to the Road Runner name, which it never used, re-branding the units under a different banner. Total Petroleum also acquired Truman Arnold Companies' transport system, consisting of 18 trucks, terminals, real estate holdings, and the company's headquarters in Texarkana. The deal stripped Truman Arnold Companies of between $300 million and $400 million in annual revenues from the Road Runner operation alone and left Arnold in possession of several terminals, gas stations, and little else. The company went from having 1,200 employees to 50 employees within a matter of weeks.

Financial details of the transaction were never disclosed, but they underpinned Arnold's decision to sell. "When we sold our retail operation, the business was not for sale," Arnold's son, Greg Arnold, explained

in the March 24, 1997 issue of *Arkansas Business*. "However, Total Petroleum made us an offer that we couldn't refuse."

Truman Arnold Companies entered the 1990s ready to rebuild, its retail business gone but its strategy still determined by a leader with an unflagging drive to succeed. Arnold turned to his wholesale operations, acquiring the largest inland petroleum storage terminal in the United States in 1990, a facility located in West Memphis, Arkansas. The company's wholesale business grew rapidly, increasing revenues to $500 million by the end of the year, as Truman Arnold Companies' marketing and distribution activities spread throughout a 30-state territory.

TAC AIR EXPANDS: 1989–96

Arnold also renewed his efforts in another direction. Operating FBOs had proven to be Truman Arnold Companies' most profitable activity, encouraging the company to add to TAC Air's holdings. In 1989, Arnold acquired FBOs from Shreveport Air Center in Shreveport, Louisiana, and Grady Stone Aviation in Fort Smith, Arkansas. In 1993 his company acquired an FBO based in Amarillo, Texas, and three years later acquired two more FBOs, one in Lexington, Kentucky, and another in Greensville, South Carolina. The FBOs, although accounting for only 10 percent of Truman Arnold Companies' annual revenues, were generating 40 percent of its annual earnings, recording profits at a rate four times higher than the company as a whole. "We would like to double it in size from a revenue standpoint in the next three to five years," Greg Arnold said in the March 24, 1997 issue of *Arkansas Business*, when TAC Air was producing $60 million in annual sales. "That would probably involve adding one or two key locations per year."

With Greg Arnold serving as president and his father serving as CEO, Truman Arnold Companies delved deeper into the FBO business. In 1998, the company acquired an aviation services business in Omaha, Nebraska. The following year it purchased two FBOs, one located in Denver, Colorado, and the other located in Hartford, Connecticut.

As Truman Arnold Companies entered the 21st century, the loss of Road Runner a decade earlier was a distant memory. The sale of the retail chain had stripped the company of its main source of revenue, but during the 1990s it developed powerful replacements for Road Runner. The company's wholesale business, run through TAC Energy, recorded phenomenal growth at the millennium, contributing to a 130 percent increase in revenues between 1999 and 2000 due largely to a dramatic increase in the price of petroleum fuels. By 2002, TAC Energy had extended its operating territory to include all 48 contiguous states, enabling Truman Arnold Companies to record more than $1 billion in revenue for the first time in its history.

SECOND GENERATION TAKES THE HELM: 2003

In 2003 leadership of Truman Arnold Companies passed from one generation to the next. Greg Arnold was named president and CEO of the company, taking on the duties held by his father for the previous four decades. "This company has been my life's passionate vocation and nothing could please me more than to pass the baton to Greg on his 40th birthday," Truman Arnold said in the September 15, 2003 issue of *Arkansas Business*. "As chief operating officer, Greg has already assumed most of the responsibilities of this position and I'm extremely happy to recognize him with the earned and deserved title."

At roughly the same time Greg Arnold took command of the company, he and his father made an important discovery, one that brought them back to familiar territory. In the fall of 2003 they learned Total Petroleum's ownership of the Road Runner trademark had expired and they decided to resurrect the retail brand. They opened a test site and added a second store before the end of the year, spending $1.5 million to open each unit, both of which were located in Texarkana. "Our plans right now are not to grow the retail business right away," Greg Arnold said in the January 19, 2004 issue of *Oil Express*. "We have been out of retail for a while and need to acclimate ourselves to the business and how it has changed over the past 15 years."

TAC AIR AND TAC ENERGY EXPAND: 2005–09

The Arnolds took a cautious approach to expanding the Road Runner concept. They did not open another store before the end of the decade, but they did move aggressively on other fronts. In 2005, the company attempted to build its first FBO from the ground up, a $17 million project slated for the Little Rock National Airport. The company was unable to work out an acceptable lease, however, prompting it to return to its standard way of expanding TAC Air. The company acquired Cherokee Aviation at McGhee Tyson Airport in Knoxville, Tennessee, and purchased the airport's other FBO, Knox-Air, making it the sole supplier of aviation services at the airport. By the time of the acquisitions, the company had reached its goal of doubling TAC Air's annual revenue volume, collecting $120 million in 2005 from its 12 FBOs.

Truman Arnold Companies ended the decade by adding to the operations of its two main businesses. In January 2009 TAC Air gained its 13th FBO when the assets of Jet Direct were acquired, giving the division a presence at Spirit of St. Louis Airport in Missouri. Later in the year, TAC Energy strengthened its already extensive distribution network with the November acquisition of Fuel Managers Incorporated's wholesale fuels business. The Tulsa, Oklahoma-based company possessed distribution operations in 18 states. Further acquisitions by the company's main divisions were expected in the years ahead, as industry observers waited to see if the Road Runner retail chain would once again spread across the landscape.

Jeffrey L. Covell

PRINCIPAL DIVISIONS

TAC Air; TAC Energy; TAC Terminals.

PRINCIPAL COMPETITORS

Atlantic Aviation FBO Inc.; Million Air Interlink, Inc.; Sun Coast Resources Inc.

FURTHER READING

Haman, John, "TAC Air Venture Takes Flight," *Arkansas Business*, March 24, 1997, p. 1.

Shaner, J. Richard, "Why Arnold Buyout Gives Total a Bigger Image," *National Petroleum News*, September 1989, p. 68.

"SW Marketer Resurrects Long-Time C-Store Brand," *Oil Express*, January 19, 2004, p. 1.

"TAC Air, a Division of Truman Arnold Cos. of Texarkana, Has Officially Begun Services at Spirit of St. Louis, Chesterfield, Mo.," *Arkansas Business*, January 26, 2009, p. 13.

Turner, Lance, "Greg Arnold to Head Truman Arnold Cos.," *Arkansas Business*, September 15, 2003, p. 11.

Tulikivi Corporation

Juuka, FIN-83900
Finland
Telephone: (+358 0207) 636 000
Fax: (+358 0207) 636 130
Web site: http://www.tulikivi.com

Public Company
Incorporated: 1980
Employees: 500
Sales: EUR 53.1 million ($74.2 million) (2009)
Stock Exchanges: Helsinki
Ticker Symbol: Tulav
NAICS: 327991 Cut Stone and Stone Product
 Manufacturing; 212319 Other Crushed and Broken
 Stone Mining and Quarrying

■ ■ ■

Tulikivi Corporation is the world's leading producer of soapstone fireplaces. Tulikivi, which means "fire stone" in Finnish, operates through two primary divisions: Fireplaces and Natural Stone Products. The Fireplaces division is the company's largest, generating more than 90 percent of its revenues. This division produces soapstone-based fireplaces, including custom-designed fireplaces, as well as combined fireplace-bakeovens and self-standing stoves. The company also produces lining stones for other fireplace manufacturers. Tulikivi's Natural Stone Products division supplies kitchen countertops, floor and wall tiles, and other architectural stone products, as well as paving stones and other construction stone products. Tulikivi also operates a small utility

ceramics division, focused largely on kitchen utensils and cooking tools aids. Tulikivi operates five factories in Finland, including at its Juuka headquarters. The company operates its own soapstone quarry in Karelia, assuring its supply.

Finland remains the company's largest market, with nearly 49 percent of sales. Europe accounts for most of the rest, with 2 percent of sales generated in the United States. Tulikivi is listed on the Helsinki Stock Exchange but remains controlled by the founding Vauhkonen family. Heikki Vauhkonen, son of the founder, is the company's managing director. Hard hit by the global recession, Tulikivi's sales slipped to EUR 53 million ($72 million) in 2009, down from EUR 82 million in 2006.

WOOD-BURNING STOVES FROM THE 16TH CENTURY

Fire served as the principal source of heat for much of European and human history, and the fireplace was a prominent feature in most homes. Fireplaces did not, however, serve as the most efficient heat source, as much of the heat produced by the fire disappeared up the chimney. The search for more efficient heating systems developed especially during the mid-16th century, a time that later became known as the Little Ice Age. This led to the appearance of the first wood-burning stoves, with the first design receiving a patent as early as 1567.

The wood-burning stove offered a major advantage over the fireplace in that the fire could be used to heat a firebox, which in turn radiated the heat outward, rather than up the chimney. The abundance of stone made this a natural material for the early primitive stove designs. Stones provided the added advantage of retaining and then releasing heat over a sustained period. Not all types of stone were suited to the high temperatures produced by the wood-burning stove, nor did all stone retain heat equally. In general, the denser the stone, the greater its heat retention properties. Stone that contained a high talc content was more likely to offer greater heat resistance.

Soapstone, found in abundance in the Karelian mountains of Finland, was a particularly dense type of stone that was also especially heat resistant. Soapstone provided another significant advantage in that, despite its higher weight relative to its size, it was easily carved. As a result, Soapstone had long been widely used to carve ornaments and religious icons.

MODERN WOOD-BURNING STOVE DESIGN IN THE 18TH CENTURY

The Scandinavian region's emergence as a center of masonry stove technology dated from the second half of the 18th century. The region's colder climate meant that it was much more reliant on wood for its heating needs. The growth of the population, however, had already begun to put its forests under pressure. At the same time, the earlier masonry stoves remained highly inefficient in their design.

To address these problems, the king of Sweden turned to noted architect and engineer Count Carl Johan Cronstedt in 1767, giving him a commission to develop a new stove design. Working with Field Marshal Fabian Wrede, Cronstedt set out to redesign the masonry stove entirely, and in the process raised its efficiency by a factor of eight. Cronstedt and Wrede's design incorporated a system of long flues, which guided the heated gases and smoke from the firebox through a stone housing, which retained the heat before finally allowing the smoke to escape through the chimney.

The new design proved highly efficient, using far less wood to produce heat over longer periods. The Cronstedt stove, which became known as the masonry or tiled stove in English, required wood to be burned only once or twice a day. The heat produced by the stone was radiant heat, which, like heat from the sun, more easily penetrated the barrier of the skin, thus generating a better sensation of heat at lower temperatures. Radiant heat also spread more evenly throughout a room, as opposed to convection heat which gathered near the ceiling.

Cronstedt and Wrede published the results of their work in 1775, and sparked something of a revolution in residential design. The layouts of homes were adapted to take greater advantage of the radiant heat produced by the masonry stove, so that more rooms could now be heated from a single heat source.

INCORPORATING SOAPSTONE IN THE 19TH CENTURY

Improvements on the original masonry stove design continued to be made through the 19th century. In Finland, craftsmen began building soapstone stoves, further increasing the design's efficiency. The use of the easily carved soapstone also enabled craftsmen to develop a wider variety of design shapes and sizes. By the late 19th century, soapstone became a highly popular construction material in its own right, finding use in a large number of applications, including columns, staircases, floor and wall tiles, building facades, and other building structures.

Demand for soapstone soon spread to the rest of Europe, becoming especially fashionable among the continent's royalty and the wealthy classes. The development of new machinery and power sources during the Industrial Revolution had also led to the industrial production of soapstone elements. This in turn made it possible to introduce newer, more compact, and less-expensive fireplace and stove designs as well.

In order to meet the rising demand for soapstone products including construction elements and masonry stoves, a group of investors from a number of leading Swedish industrial families joined together to form a new company, Finska Täljstens AB, in 1893. The company later adopted its Finnish name, Suomen

KEY DATES

1893: Finska Täljstens AB (later Suomen Vuolikivi Oy) is founded to quarry soapstone in Juuka, Finland.

1960s: Suomen Vuolikivi Oy shuts down its quarrying operations.

1979: Reijo Vauhkonen acquires Suomen Vuolikivi and launches production of soapstone fireplaces.

1994: Renamed Tulikivi, the company goes public on the Helsinki Stock Exchange.

2006: Tulikivi completes its largest-ever acquisition, of Kermansavi Oy.

2010: Tulikivi introduces its new Whirlbox Combustion Technology in its fireplaces.

Vuolukivi Oy. Vuolukivi grew strongly, developing a strong business exporting to Russia and other European markets. A major part of the company's growth came through the rise of the Art Nouveau movement, which had a major impact on architecture of the period and in turn stimulated demand for soapstone throughout the continent.

REVIVING FINLAND'S SOAPSTONE LEGACY IN 1980

Finland gained its independence from Russia in 1917, leading to the loss of the company's largest export market. Vuolukivi instead refocused its operations on supplying the Finnish market. Into the middle of the century, the company became confronted with a major change in the home heating market. The increasing availability of electricity had led to a major shift toward central heating systems and the use of electric cookers to replace wood-burning stoves. At the same time, the architectural market turned to other materials, such as iron and steel, to replace soapstone. As a result, Vuolukivi slipped into a slow decline, ending its soapstone quarrying operations in the 1960s.

The late 1970s, however, were marked by a revival in interest in traditional and natural building materials. In 1979, a young entrepreneur, Reijo Vauhkonen, decided to purchase the Vuolukivi quarry and revive its fireplace production. Vauhkonen turned to Makron Oy, a producer of stone-working tools and equipment in Finland, to help him develop a new set of machinery for cutting and machining soapstone.

By 1980, Vauhkonen was ready to launch production. Starting with fewer than 20 employees, Vauhkonen also began developing the company's own fireplace designs, with wife Eliisa leading the company's design team. As part of the design effort, the company developed a modular system, which enabled the company to disassemble its fireplaces for shipping, to be reassembled by skilled craftsmen on location.

Vuolukivi's designs rapidly gained attention in Finland. The company created its own brand name for its fireplaces, Tulikivi, which means "fire stone" in Finnish. At the same time, Vuolukivi grew into a major original equipment manufacturer (OEM) supplier of soapstone elements that could be incorporated in other fireplace and stove manufacturers' designs. In the meantime, the company revived its production of natural stone architectural and construction elements, ultimately setting up dedicated factories for these operations. In 1987, the company launched a subsidiary, Mittakivi Oy, which focused on developing custom-tailored fireplaces, which fetched prices as high as $100,000.

PUBLIC COMPANY IN 1994

Vuolukivi took a step toward a public listing in 1988, when it placed its shares on the Helsinki Stock Exchange's over-the-counter market. The public offering came to a head of the company's decision to begin developing an international sales network. As part of this effort, the company targeted an entry into the United States, and established a production facility in Virginia in the late 1980s. Through that decade, the company slowly established the reputation of the Tulikivi brand in that market. Its sales in the United States remained small, however. Instead, the company's true export focus remained on Europe, which grew to account for more than 40 percent of the company's total revenues into the early 1990s. By 1994, the company's sales neared FIM 163 million ($20 million).

By then, the growing international success of the Tulikivi name led the company to adopt it as its own name in 1993. The following year the company also launched a full-fledged public offering, listing its shares on the Helsinki Stock Exchange proper.

Tulikivi hit a bump in the middle of the decade, as its sales slipped amid organizational difficulties. The company's U.S. manufacturing subsidiary, in particular, had become a drain on the company's resources, and in 1998 Tulikivi decided to sell that facility. Instead, the company launched construction of a new plant in Suomussalmi, in 1999. The company also launched a reorganization of its structure, separating its operations into four business centers. At the same time, Vauhkonen's son Heikki Vauhkonen was sent to the United States to oversee its sales operations there.

HITTING A PEAK IN 2006

The Suomussalmi plant was completed in 2000, and became the home of a new subsidiary, Kiantastone Oy, which focused on the production of stove stones both for the company and the OEM market. By then, the company's sales had once again begun to rise, reaching EUR 20.6 million ($18 million) in 2000.

This growth encouraged Tulikivi to make a series of acquisitions through the middle of the decade, starting with the purchase of granite processor SKT-Granit Oy in 2000. This purchase enabled the company to extend its range of architectural and building products. At the same time, the company expanded into construction services, buying Marmorimestarit Oy, which specialized in stone delivery and installations, at the end of 2000, and A.W. Liljeberg, a full-service stone company, at the beginning of 2001.

Tulikivi launched a new restructuring in 2002, creating Tulikivi Corporation as a holding company. The company then merged most of its subsidiaries into that company by 2003. By then, Tulikivi had acquired rival fireplace maker Kivia Oy, based in Kuhmo. Tulikivi at first maintained the Kivia range alongside its own. In 2006, however, the company decided to phase out that brand, and instead focus all of its fireplace sales on the Tulikivi brand.

Tulikivi's sales continued to grow strongly through the first half of the decade, boosted in particular by its growth in Russia. In 2005, the company decided to establish a dedicated presence for that market, forming subsidiary OOO Tulikivi. By then, Tulikivi's sales neared EUR 59 million. The following year, Tulikivi completed its largest-ever acquisition, buying rival Finnish fireplace group Kermansavi. That purchase, which also gave the company a small household ceramics business, helped the company hit a new sales peak, of more than EUR 82 million in 2006. Heikki Vauhkonen took over as the company's managing director the following year.

STRUGGLING INTO 2010

Vauhkonen soon faced a series of challenges into the second half of the decade, however. For one, the home heating market had begun to expand with the introduction of a number of renewable energy technologies, such air-source heat pumps, geothermal heating, and wood-pellet stove systems, draining sales away from the company's more expensive masonry fireplaces. The European market also saw an upsurge in the number of fireplace and wood-burning stove manufacturers, particularly with the introduction of tax incentives encouraging households to abandon electrical and fossil-fuel based heating systems. A drop-off in new home building in Finland, and a slowdown in Germany, which had previously been the company's largest export market, also contributed to the steady drop in the company's sales. By the end of 2007, Tulikivi's revenues had dropped back to EUR 70 million.

Tulikivi responded to the difficult conditions by restructuring its Finnish sales operation into a smaller network of company-owned showrooms. Tulikivi also merged Kermansavi into its main business, then once again refocused itself around its core Tulikivi brand. These efforts enabled the company to maintain its profitability for 2007. Into 2008, as Europe succumbed to the global economic crisis of the end of the decade, Tulikivi's sales continued to decline. The group responded with a series of job cuts, shedding more than 200 jobs by the beginning of 2010. By then, the company's sales had dropped to EUR 53 million, as it slipped into net losses for the first time.

Despite the gloom of the market, Tulikivi remained committed to developing its fireplace business, and claimed the title as the world's largest producer of soapstone fireplaces. The company continued to seek to improve the efficiency of its fireplaces, while also reducing its carbon footprint, both in terms of fireplace emissions and the impact of its production and logistics operations. Among the innovations introduced by the company was its new Whirlbox Combustion Technology, introduced across its entire fireplace range in March 2010. The new technology permitted the fireplaces to burn an even higher proportion of gases, further reducing emissions. Tulikivi remained one of the world's leading names in fireplace design.

M. L. Cohen

PRINCIPAL SUBSIDIARIES

AWL Marmori Oy; Kivia Oy; OOO Tulikivi (Russia); Tulikivi Oyj Niederlassung Deutschland; Tulikivi U.S., Inc.

PRINCIPAL DIVISIONS

Fireplaces; Natural Stone Products; Ceramics.

PRINCIPAL OPERATING UNITS

Tulikivi Heating & Environment; Tulikivi Interior Design; Tulikivi Cooking.

PRINCIPAL COMPETITORS

Nibe AB; Hark GmbH; Heat Wärmesysteme GmbH; NunnaUuni Oy.

FURTHER READING

"Finland's Tulikivi Corporation to Cut 67 Jobs," *Nordic Business Report*, January 8, 2008.

"Finland's Tulikivi Corporation to Merge Subsidiary with Parent Company," *Nordic Business Report*, June 29, 2007.

"It's on the Table, Tulikivi Has to Cut 120 Jobs," *Neweurope*, February 9, 2009.

Reis, Michael, "Spreading the Warmth of Finnish Soapstone," *Stone World*, September 2001, p. 114.

Robbins, Jim, "Rolls-Royce of Hearths, a Hit in the Rockets, Heads East," *New York Times*, January 21, 1999.

"Tulikivi Corporation Focuses Its Marketing Strategy under One Brand Name," *Nordic Business Report*, January 18, 2005.

"Tulikivi Corporation Receives Prospecting and Industrial Rights for Soapstone in Karelia," *Nordic Business Report*, January 19, 2006.

"Tulikivi Corporation Reorganises Finnish Distribution Operations," *Nordic Business Report*, October 30, 2006.

"Tulikivi Corporation to Acquire Kermansavi Oy," *Nordic Business Report*, April 3, 2006.

"Tulikivi Corporation to Build New Production Plant," *Nordic Business Report*, January 4, 2006.

"Tulikivi Fireplaces Have a Lifecycle of Several Decades," *Euroinvestor*, January 21, 2010.

Tully Construction Co. Inc.

———————■———————

127-50 Northern Boulevard
Flushing, New York 11368
U.S.A.
Telephone: (718) 446-7000
Fax: (718) 446-6072
Web site: http://www.tullyconstruction.com

Private Company
Incorporated: 1924 as Tully & Di Napoli, Inc.
Employees: 97
Sales: $579.2 million (2008)
NAICS: 221320 Sewage Treatment Facilities; 237310
Highway, Street, and Bridge Construction; 485112
Urban Commuter Rail Systems; 562111 Solid
Waste Collection; 562211 Hazardous Waste Treat-
ment and Disposal; 562910 Remediation Services

■ ■ ■

Tully Construction Co. Inc. is one of the leading public
works contractors in the New York City metropolitan
area. Its roots lie in heavy highway, bridge, and airport
construction, but it has expanded to construction of a
wide range of infrastructure projects, including building
construction projects, landfill, sewage treatment, dewatering facilities, and project management. Tully
Environmental, Inc., an associated company, is engaged
in the development of composting facilities, solid-waste
transfer stations, and construction-material recycling
facilities.

Tully Construction became known nationally for its
role as one of the four contractors cleaning up the debris

from the World Trade Center twin-tower collapse following the September 11, 2001, terrorist attacks on the
United States. The company followed this effort in
lower Manhattan by reconstructing damaged below-site
rail lines.

PAVING NEW YORK FOR THREE DECADES

Vincent Peter Di Napoli began working for himself at
the age of 17, hauling coal in a truck. In 1924 he
teamed with Edward Tully to form Tully & Di Napoli,
Inc. (T&D), based in New York City's borough of
Queens. They started with only a few trucks and men.
Whatever gains they made in the 1920s seemed to have
ended with the Great Depression. When Di Napoli
came to the office of Thomas Shanahan, a banker,
legend has it that he had to borrow a nickel for the fare
back to Queens.

Shanahan was, at this time, one of the few bankers
who, on face value, would lend money to a small
contractor who needed funds just to meet his payroll.
He liked what he saw in Di Napoli and helped steer
business to his firm. In 1932 T&D submitted the low
bid for snow removal the next winter in four of the five
city boroughs. The contractor was required to post a
$300,000 bond and hire 270 teams of four men each,
with five trucks assigned to each team. When a weekend
snowstorm struck New York in February 1933, T&D
had to hire crews and trucks from New Jersey to meet
its obligations.

A potent fund-raiser for the city's Democratic Party,
Shanahan was campaign manager for William

O'Dwyer's successful mayoral bid in 1945. By then contractors "were making money by the carload," according to *The Power Broker*, Robert A. Caro's Pulitzer Prize-winning biography of Robert Moses, the master builder of public works who over a 34-year period presided over the construction of hundreds of miles of highways, as well as housing, bridges, parks, and beaches, in the metropolitan area.

Shanahan's influence at City Hall continued through the 1950s, but he also had close ties to Moses, who commanded an array of autonomous public bodies from his quarters at the Triborough Bridge and Tunnel Authority. Tully & Di Napoli, in 1936, won the contract for paving the Bronx approach to the newly constructed bridge and building an end ramp. Over the next 20 or so years the firm built parts of the Long Island Expressway and Grand Central Parkway in Queens and the Bruckner and Major Deegan expressways in the Bronx. It constructed roads leading to the grounds of the 1939–40 and 1964–65 world's fairs in Flushing, Queens.

In 1944 Tully & Di Napoli purchased a 180,000-square-foot vacant tract in Flushing to be developed as storage yards for materials and other purposes. The company moved its headquarters from Astoria to a brick building erected in 1950 on this site.

Tully & Di Napoli remained one of the major contractors for regional infrastructure through the 1950s and 1960s. It was involved in work on such facilities as the Cross Bronx Expressway, Southern State and Garden State parkways, New Jersey Turnpike, Whitestone Bridge, LaGuardia and Idlewild (later Kennedy) airports, and also the foundation for the World Trade Center.

TWO DECADES IN THE WILDERNESS: 1968–88

The old political order had passed away by 1968, when 14 major contractors and 13 individuals were indicted for collusion over a decade in obtaining contracts. One of the indictments alleged that Di Napoli had designated which firm would be the low bidder in secur-

ing more than $24 million in contracts from Consolidated Edison Company of New York, Inc., the city's main supplier of electricity. Di Napoli pleaded guilty and was fined $12,000 the following year. T&D was fined $35,000 and blacklisted by the city.

Blowback came swiftly and ironically when a 15-inch snowfall struck New York City in February 1969. Three days later, streets and roads in large sections of Queens were still clogged, to the fury of the many who felt that Manhattan-resident Mayor John V. Lindsay had no regard for the outer boroughs. The city hurriedly authorized T&D and another indicted construction firm to clear major portions of three Queens parkways on an emergency, day-to-day basis.

Edward Tully had died in 1964, and, with no Di Napoli heirs, ownership passed to the four Tully sons involved in the firm, which reorganized as Willets Point Contracting Corp. in 1971. Work was completed for agencies such as the city's transportation and sanitation departments, the state's transportation department, and Port Authority of New York and New Jersey. However, amid the deteriorating economy of the early 1970s, both the city and state were falling deeply in debt, and few new public works projects were underway. Kenneth Tully, who assumed leadership, traveled as far as Ecuador and Nigeria to seek construction contracts. Tully Construction Co. was established in 1978. It was not able to resume highway construction in earnest until 1988.

Even when city work was available, Tully Construction's brush with the law had proven costly to its reputation. In the early 1990s the firm was investigated by the controller with regard to financial issues associated with its investment in concrete businesses.

TURNING TO ENVIRONMENTAL MATTERS: 1992–99

With little work available from the city, the firm, through Willets Point Contracting, moved into new areas, securing its first project for solid-waste disposal in 1985. Tully Environmental, Inc., was founded in 1992 to concentrate efforts in this field and became one of the largest privately held waste-hauling companies in the United States. It built the first waste-transfer station on Long Island for the town of Oyster Bay and was awarded the subsequent contract to haul and dispose of the town's waste. A joint venture of Willets Point and Tully was contracted to haul and dispose of waste in Bergen County, New Jersey, and to operate a temporary waste-transfer station in Lyndhurst, New Jersey.

KEY DATES

1936: Tully & Di Napoli is on its way as a major road builder in the metropolitan area.

1968–69: Di Napoli pleads guilty to bid rigging; he and the firm are fined.

1978: Tully Construction Co. is established.

1992: Tully Environmental, Inc., is formed.

2001–02: Tully takes part in the World Trade Center site cleanup.

Tully Construction won a big contract in 1994, when the board of Westchester County (the county just north of The Bronx), approved an agreement to pay the firm and another company $226 million over 23 years to truck sludge from a sewage-treatment plant in Yonkers serving 26 communities to a facility in Harmony, New Jersey, where it would be converted to fertilizer. For decades before the federal government forbade the practice, the county had been dumping sewage sludge into the Atlantic Ocean.

Tully Environmental entered the field of biosolids management and disposal in 1991, when it signed a contract to haul and dispose of dewatered sludge cake from a facility in Wantagh, New York. A facility in Tremont, Pennsylvania, was subsequently established to receive biosolids and process this waste into compost. Customers, besides New York City, came to include several counties and cities in Connecticut and Pennsylvania as well as New York.

Tully Environmental was assigned the job of removing hazardous and contaminated soil when Tully Construction was rebuilding Manhattan's West Side Highway in 1996. It delved further into remediation work by removing 300,000 cubic yards of oil-contaminated soil along Newtown Creek, a waterway separating parts of Brooklyn from Queens.

Willets Point, a 75-acre peninsula west of Queens' Flushing River, became the site of a Tully Environmental solid-waste transfer station in 1999. Under a $150 million contract from the city's Department of Sanitation, this facility became operational the next year, shipping curbside garbage and trash to a variety of landfills and incinerators in the metropolitan region. Also that year, the company established the largest fill-material recycling facility in the city at Willets Point. It became an important disposal site not only for material that Tully Construction generated from its many projects but also for other construction projects.

GROUND ZERO CLEANUP AND AFTER: 2001–10

Following the collapse of the World Trade Center towers, Tully Construction was chosen in October 2001 as one of the four contractors to clear the 16-acre Ground Zero site of debris and restore utility links. Each of the four was assigned a quadrant of the site and an emergency contract of $250 million for the work. Three of the four were giant multinational companies who generally relied on subcontractors. Although the publicity-shy Tully clan avoided exploiting the company's role in the undertaking, as the only local firm of the four, Tully emerged as "everyone's favorite, the hardworking red-meat guys," according to William Langewiesche's book *American Ground: Unbuilding the World Trade Center*.

Tully Construction was awarded the job because it had a large inventory of trucks and heavy equipment, as well as experienced workers, and also because it had teamed with the city's managing Department of Design and Construction in the past. Tully assigned about three-quarters of its 900 workers to the task. The company had only recently emerged from five years' prohibition from doing business with the city. After receiving a negative evaluation arising from unpaid taxes, alleged organized-crime ties and other issues, Tully had, in 1996, signed an independent monitoring agreement that ended in early 2001. Even before the end of this period, however, Tully had helped complete the closing of the city's Fresh Kills landfill on Staten Island.

By this time Peter Tully had succeeded his father as chief executive of the firm. He took a leading role in urging federal lawmakers to indemnify the site contractors against lawsuits. Thousands of construction workers, as well as firefighters, police officers, and emergency responders subsequently sued the city and the four contractors with regard to illnesses that they claimed they had developed, chiefly due to exposure to contaminants on the site.

In March 2010 a settlement of up to $657.5 million was reached to compensate about 10,000 plaintiffs, with the funds to come from a federally financed insurance company. A week later, however, the federal judge who was overseeing the litigation rejected the settlement, contending it did not offer enough compensation to the plaintiffs.

A joint venture of Tully and two other construction companies was awarded in early 2002, a $300 million contract to build a temporary Port Authority PATH underground rail station to replace the destroyed one beneath the Ground Zero site. The contact also called for the repair of tunnels between the New Jersey side of the Hudson River and Manhattan and the expansion of a PATH station in Jersey City. This job was completed in 2003. A few weeks later, Tully and a partner submitted the low bid of about $92 million to rebuild two city subway stations under the damaged site. The work was completed in only nine months, much less time than expected, and earned the partners a $3 million early-completion bonus, the largest one ever paid by the contracting Metropolitan Transit Authority.

Tully Construction did not see eye to eye, however, with Mayor Michael Bloomberg concerning the city's planned redevelopment of Willets Point. The plan called for this grimy site of junkyards and hundreds of small auto-repair shops to be transformed into a retailing and entertainment district, including a hotel and convention center. However, the Tully waste-transfer station and recycling plant would be dismantled. A lawsuit by business owners challenging the city's eminent-domain powers was turned aside in court, and the redevelopment of the point was proceeding in 2010.

Robert Halasz

PRINCIPAL SUBSIDIARIES

Tully Environmental, Inc.

PRINCIPAL COMPETITORS

Macquarie Infrastructure Company; Slattery Skanska Inc.

FURTHER READING

Caro, Robert A., *The Power Broker*, New York: Random House, 1974, ch. 33.

"Edward A. Tully Sr., 69, Dies; Contractor Headed Queens Firm," *New York Times*, March 8, 1964, p. 87.

Hetter, Katia, "Monitors for WTC Cleanup," *Newsday*, October 10, 2001, p. A37.

Langewiesche, William, *American Ground: Unbuilding the World Trade Center*, New York: North Point Press, 2002, p. 68.

Navarro, Mireya, "Deal Is Reached on Health Costs of 9/11 Workers," *New York Times*, March 12, 2010, pp. A1+.

Pristin, Terry, "A Redevelopment Scuffle in Queens," *New York Times*, May 17, 2006.

Rubin, Debra K., "Tully Construction Bursts on Scene after 80 Years of Building Hometown," *ENR/Engineering News-Record*, February 17, 2003, pp. 26+.

Tolchin, Martin, "13 Indicted Here in Rigging of Bids on Utility Work," *New York Times*, August 21, 1968, pp. 1, 35.

"Westchester Accord on Sludge Disposal," *New York Times*, August 31, 1994, p. B6.

"WTC Contractor on Winning Teams for Jobs beneath Site," *ENR/Engineering News-Record*, February 18, 2002.

 Tyson Foods, Inc.

Tyson Foods, Inc.

2220 Don Tyson Parkway
Springdale, Arkansas 72762-6999
U.S.A.
Telephone: (479) 290-4000
Toll Free: (800) 643-3410
Fax: (479) 290-4061
Web site: http://www.tyson.com

Public Company
Incorporated: 1947 as Tyson Feed & Hatchery, In-
corpora-ted
Employees: 117,000
Sales: $26.7 billion (2009)
Stock Exchanges: New York
Ticker Symbol: TSN
NAICS: 311615 Poultry Processing; 311999 All Other
Miscellaneous Food Manufacturing; 311412 Frozen
Specialty Food Manufacturing; 311611 Animal
(Except Poultry) Slaughtering; 311612 Meat
Processed from Carcasses

■ ■ ■

Founded in 1935, Tyson Foods, Inc., is the world's largest processor and marketer of beef and pork and second-
largest processor and marketer of chicken. The company
produces a wide variety of brand-name, processed food
products, including fresh meats, processed and
precooked meats, refrigerated and frozen prepared foods,
and animal feed and pet food. It is the recognized
market leader in almost every retail and foodservice
market it serves. Tyson supplies more than 25 billion
pounds of chicken, beef, and pork per year to Mc-
Donald's, Wal-Mart, and most major supermarket and
restaurant chains in the United States. The company
operates over 300 facilities in 26 states and 20 countries,
and it contracts with more than 6,000 family farmers to
care for company-owned chickens. Its products are sold
in more than 90 countries through offices in 18
countries. International production operations are
located in Mexico, Brazil, China, India, and Argentina.
The Tyson family controls 80 percent of the company's
voting power.

EARLY YEARS

During the Great Depression, John Tyson moved to
Springdale, Arkansas, with his wife and one-year-old son
Don. In 1935, he bought 50 "springer" chickens and
hauled them to Chicago to sell at a profit. Two years
later, he named his business Tyson Feed & Hatchery.
Over the next 13 years the company prospered by buying and selling chickens, aided by the postwar boom,
which brought improved kitchen appliances and the first
supermarkets. Gradually, however, Tyson became
involved in raising chickens, which allowed him better
control over the quality of what he sold. In 1947, the
company was incorporated.

Five years later, Don Tyson graduated from college
and joined the company as head of operations. Father
and son were said to have made a dynamic team, the
older Tyson more cautious and the younger one pushing
forward. For example, Don persuaded his father to raise
Rock Cornish game hens, a market that Tyson would
one day dominate.

For the next six years, Tyson focused on expanding production facilities, and, in 1957, the company opened a processing plant in Springdale, Arkansas, the site of the company headquarters. Tyson also introduced its first ice-pack processing line, which brought the company into a more competitive industry bracket. By achieving more complete vertical integration, its dependence on other suppliers lessened.

During the early 1960s, many amateur chicken producers were lured into the market by the drop in feed-grain prices and the easy availability of credit. As a result, broiler production rose about 13 percent between 1965 and 1967. The glut that followed caused big price cuts and accounted for about $50 million in losses in the industry. Several small companies were forced out of business, but the demand for low-priced chicken soared. People were eating four times as much chicken as they did in 1950.

GROWING COMPANY IN A NEW INDUSTRY

In 1963 Tyson went public and changed its name to Tyson's Foods, Incorporated. It also made its first acquisition, the Garrett Poultry Company, based in Rogers, Arkansas. In 1966 John Tyson and his wife died in an automobile accident, and Don Tyson took over the business as president.

Technological improvements in the 1960s fundamentally changed the poultry industry. Broiler production had become one of the most industrialized, automated parts of U.S. agriculture. Through the development of better feeds and better disease control methods, chickens were maturing more quickly. These improvements, combined with increased competition, meant lower prices for consumers, but, for processors, it meant lower earnings. In 1967, despite a 37 percent gain in sales, Tyson lost more than a dollar per share in earnings. The company took advantage of this situation, in which several smaller companies were floundering. With its acquisition of Franz Foods, Inc., Tyson continued its pattern of buying out smaller poultry concerns. It also began to give its corporate name more

visibility, printing "Tyson Country Fresh Chicken" on its wrappers instead of the name of the supermarket to which the chickens were sold.

In 1968 Tyson went to court with two other processors when an Agriculture Department officer alleged that the processors had discriminated against Arkansas chicken farmers who were members of an association of poultry farmers. At that time, processors customarily hired farmers to raise their chickens; Tyson and the others had been accused of "boycotting and blacklisting" association members in 1962. In 1969 a federal appeals court ruled that the Department of Agriculture had "erred" in treating the chicken processors like meatpackers. Therefore agriculture officials did not have the authority under existing laws to take any action against chicken processors.

Also in 1969, Tyson acquired Prospect Farms, Inc., the company that became its precooked chicken division. That year Tyson produced more than 2 percent of the nation's chickens, 70 percent for retail sale and 30 percent for institutions. The company had grown from 15 to 3,000 employees and operated five chicken-processing plants and four protein-processing plants in northwest Arkansas and southwest Missouri.

Tyson continued to grow and diversify. In 1970 a new egg facility was built, and in 1971 a computerized feed mill and a plant in Nashville, Arkansas, were completed. Also in 1971 the company's name was changed from Tyson's Foods to Tyson Foods. In 1972 Tyson acquired the Ocoma Foods Division of Consolidated Foods Corporation, including three new plants, as well as Krispy Kitchens, Inc., and the poultry division of Wilson Foods. That year Tyson began selling the Ozark Fry, the first breaded chicken breast patty. The company also bought a hog operation in Creswell, North Carolina, from First Colony Farms.

The year 1972 was a shakeout year in the poultry business, and several large processors sold out to those with better prospects of survival, easing competition. Because of the rising prices of beef and pork, chicken consumption was increasing at a rapid rate. Also, new products and technological developments seemed to promise improved profits for the industry. Tyson was already a leader in introducing new products such as its chicken patty, chicken hot dog, and chicken bologna. By 1979 it offered 24 specialty products. Tyson also operated three plants that used the new deep chill (rather than ice-pack) process. The moisture of the bird was frozen at 28 degrees, one degree warmer than the temperature at which chicken meat freezes, leaving the meat still tender and doubling shelf life to about 25 days.

KEY DATES

1935: Company founder, John Tyson, begins selling chickens in Springdale, Arkansas.
1947: Tyson Feed & Hatchery is incorporated.
1963: Company goes public and changes its name to Tyson's Foods, Incorporated.
1966: Founder's son, Don, becomes president of the company.
1971: Company name changes to Tyson Foods.
1989: Tyson acquires Holly Farms and nearly doubles its national market share.
1992: Tyson goes into the seafood business with the purchase of Arctic Alaska Fisheries, Inc., and Louis Kemp Seafood.
1997: Tyson announces plans to acquire longtime competitor Hudson Foods.
2001: Tyson acquires IBP and becomes the world's largest processor and marketer of chicken, beef, and pork.
2007: Tyson seeks to offset decline in sales volume through international expansion.

In the early 1970s Tyson closed its unprofitable plant in Shelbyville, Tennessee, but reopened it in 1974 to produce more popular processed and precooked chicken products. In 1973 Tyson bought Cassady Broiler Company, another small poultry concern, and in the next year acquired Vantress Pedigree, Inc. A civil antitrust lawsuit brought against Tyson and other broiler processors in 1974 for conspiring to fix, maintain, and stabilize broiler prices was settled in 1977. Tyson agreed to pay a $975,663 fine to about 30 chicken purchasers. In 1978 Tyson acquired the rest of Wilson Foods Corporation. A year later the company sold its two North Carolina chicken processing plants.

BIG GAINS

By the early 1980s, consumers' nutritional concerns and the continuously high prices of beef and pork caused the nation's poultry consumption to increase by 30 percent since 1970. This increase was also partly due to innovative, easy-to-prepare products from companies including Tyson and the industry's ability to improve breeding and feed techniques. Some of Tyson's experiments had produced six-pound chickens in just six weeks.

In 1980 Tyson introduced its Chick 'n Quick line of products, which included a variety of chicken portions that were easy to prepare. By then Tyson was the largest grower of Rock Cornish game hens and one of the nation's largest hog producers. As it perfected its precooked chicken patty for restaurants, its institutional sales grew. In 1983 Tyson implemented its new advertising slogan, "Doing our best ... just for you" with television commercials on all three major networks in the United States. The company also acquired Mexican Original Products, Inc., a manufacturer of tortillas, taco shells, tostados, and tortilla chips.

In 1984 Cobb, Inc., and Tyson began a joint venture called Arkansas Breeders to breed and develop the Cobb 500, a female with fast growth, low fat, and high meat content. Later that same year, Tyson acquired 90 percent of another poultry firm, Valmac Industries. By then Tyson had expanded its operations into six states (Georgia, North Carolina, Missouri, Tennessee, Louisiana, and Arkansas) and many of its products were being distributed internationally. In 1986, the *Wall Street Transcript* named Don Tyson the gold award winner in the meat and poultry industry. The company acquired Lane Processing Inc., a closely held poultry-processing firm that had been bankrupt since 1984.

In October 1988 Tyson made a takeover bid for Memphis-based Holly Farms Corporation, the national leader in brand name chicken sales. Holly Farms began more than a century before as a cotton compressor. Over the years it had evolved into a chicken and food-service firm with vast holdings and a 19 percent share of the brand-name chicken market. It was the first processor to use its own name rather than the retail seller's on its packaging, which gave the company a long-standing credibility with consumers.

Brand recognition made it a very attractive acquisition. Holly Farms rejected the bid, nodding to Tennessee takeover laws, and agreed to merge with ConAgra, Inc., one of the nation's largest food companies and a leading poultry producer. Holly Farms also agreed to sell its poultry assets to ConAgra should the merger not come to fruition. In mid-November Tyson sued Holly Farms and ConAgra to stop the merger. A federal judge ruled that Tennessee's antitakeover laws were unconstitutional and could not be used to halt Tyson's bid. This act opened an eight-month fight between Tyson and ConAgra for control of Holly Farms.

GROWING PAINS

Tyson's rapid growth in the fast-food chicken business had put a strain on its production facilities, and Tyson needed Holly Farms' chicken supply. More than half of Tyson's business now was with institutions and restaurants, and Tyson's name was not as popular as Holly Farms' in grocery stores. Finally in June 1989, Don Tyson agreed to pay $1.29 billion for Holly Farms, and the company was fully merged into Tyson later that year. In 1990, its first full year with Holly Farms under its wing, Tyson's sales increased 50.7 percent. The purchase of Holly Farms made Tyson the undisputed king of the chicken industry. It also gained a stronger position in beef and pork through Holly Farms' further-processing operations. Tyson's Beef and Pork Division grew substantially over the next several years and claimed 11 percent of the company's revenue by 1995.

In 1991 Leland E. Tollett, a college classmate of Don Tyson whom Tyson had brought into the firm in the late 1950s, was named president and chief executive officer. Tyson remained chairman of the board, but was slowly reducing his responsibilities.

Tyson next turned its attention to seafood in an effort to further diversify its operations. In 1992 Tyson acquired Arctic Alaska Fisheries Corporation, a vertically integrated seafood products company, and Louis Kemp Seafood Company, which was purchased from Oscar Mayer Foods Corporation. Tyson's resulting Seafood Division experienced some rocky initial years, and the firm was forced to take a write-down of $205 million on its seafood assets in 1994, the first major write-down in Tyson's history. The Seafood Division was subsequently revamped and then bolstered by the 1995 acquisition of the seafood division of International Multifoods Corporation. That company had $65 million in sales in 1994 and produced simulated crabmeat, lobster, shrimp, and scallops.

EMBROILED IN CONTROVERSY

Arkansas Governor Bill Clinton's presidential election campaign and his subsequent term in office brought unwanted attention to the condition of Tyson's chicken processing plants and eventually embroiled the company in controversies. As governor of Arkansas, Clinton had strongly supported the chicken industry, and Don Tyson was a major contributor to Clinton's presidential bid. During the campaign several journalistic investigations of the chicken industry in Arkansas, such as one published in *Time*, revealed that many of the plants were unsanitary and dangerous and staffed by low-paid workers often subject to such difficult conditions as line speed-ups. Environmentalists had also charged that Clinton, while he was governor, had allowed the Arkansas poultry industry to dump tons of chicken waste in Arkansas streams.

After Clinton took office, the close ties between Tyson and the president aroused controversy first when reports stated that James Blair, Tyson's general counsel and a close friend of Bill Clinton and Hillary Rodham Clinton, had helped Hillary Rodham Clinton make a

killing in the commodity markets. Then came reports in 1994 that Mike Espy, agriculture secretary under Clinton, had accepted a trip on a Tyson jet and football tickets from Tyson in exchange for favorable treatment from poultry inspectors. Espy subsequently resigned over this matter. Tyson denied any wrongdoing.

Tyson had traditionally expanded its chicken processing capacity through the purchase of existing facilities, but when it decided it needed to expand in 1994, no suitable plants could be found that were for sale. The company then decided to build, at a cost of about $400 million, four new poultry plants over a four-year period, each of which would be able to process 1.3 million chickens a week. That year Tyson also bought a controlling interest in Trasgo, S.A. de C.V., a Mexican joint venture started in 1988. Trasgo held the number three position in the growing chicken market in Mexico.

Also in 1994, Tyson acquired Culinary Foods, Inc., a maker of specialty frozen foods mostly for the foodservice market, and Gorges Foodservice, Inc., a further processor of beef for the foodservice market. Tyson failed, however, to acquire a much larger prize, WLR Foods Inc., a $700 million Virginia-based producer of high-quality turkey and chicken products sold primarily under the Wampler-Longacre brand. Similar to Tyson's experience with Holly Farms, WLR management fought Tyson's $330 million attempt to take over the company in early 1994, an attempt that then turned hostile. WLR instituted a takeover defense, which Tyson fought in federal district court as unconstitutional. This time, unlike the Holly Farms case, the judge ruled against Tyson in a decision that summer.

The Seafood Division write-down had soured Tyson's 1994 results and it posted a $2 million loss, its first in years. Not to be deterred, the company continued its aggressive expansion in 1995. Tyson purchased the chicken plants of Cargill, which had decided it could no longer compete with Tyson's chicken empire. This purchase added more than 2.5 million chickens per week to Tyson's processing capacity. Another 2.4 million chickens per week were added later in the year with the acquisition of McCarty Farms Inc., a Mississippi-based closely held firm.

An important era for Tyson ended in April 1995 when Don Tyson retired as chairman, denying that the firm's recent controversies had prompted the move. Tyson remained involved in the firm as senior chairman, but day-to-day operations were handed over to Tollett, who became chairman in addition to his previous position as CEO. Donald "Buddy" Wray became president in addition to his previous position as chief operating officer. Like Tollett, Wray was another college classmate of Tyson's and had joined the firm in 1961. John Tyson, Don's then-41-year-old son, was reportedly being groomed to eventually run the company and held the position of president of the Beef and Pork Division.

TYSON'S PLATE GETS CROWDED

By 1995, Tyson Foods enjoyed a strong position as the leading chicken firm in the United States and looked forward to continuing tremendous growth. Sales had more than doubled from the pre-Holly Farms level of $2.54 billion in 1989 to $5.11 billion in 1994. Tyson was diversifying its operations to become more than just a poultry company, aiming to be a leader in all "center-of-the-plate" proteins. In 1994, poultry accounted for only 75 percent of Tyson's revenues.

From this strong position, Tyson pursued overseas opportunities. These included the formation of a joint venture in the People's Republic of China in 1994, and the opening of an office in Moscow in 1995. The formation in 1995 of a subsidiary, World Resource, Inc., was designed to help Tyson's customers throughout the world source products. About 10 percent of the firm's revenues (about $500 million) derived from international sales.

Tyson's past investment in seafood continued to be problematic. In February 1996, the company agreed to pay Alaska up to $5.85 million over 10 years to settle allegations of illegal fishing off the Alaska Peninsula in the early 1990s. Tyson assumed this legal problem when it purchased Arctic Alaska Fisheries Corp. in 1992. Later in 1996, the Securities and Exchange Commission accused Donald Tyson of tipping off a friend who then made a quick profit in the stock of Arctic Alaska Fisheries while the sale of the seafood company to Tyson was pending. Tyson quickly agreed to pay a civil penalty of $46,125.

In the fall of 1997, Tyson announced that it planned to acquire the fourth-largest U.S. poultry processor, Hudson Foods Inc., for $642.4 million. The move meant that Tyson would gain control of 30 percent of the U.S. poultry market. However impressive the move, the year ended on an embarrassing note for Tyson, with the company pleading guilty to giving former Agriculture Secretary Mike Espy $12,000 in illegal gratuities. According to Susan Schmidt writing for the *Washington Post*, "Tyson Foods admitted to lavishing gifts on Espy—including football tickets, airline trips, meals and scholarship money for his girlfriend—at a time when his department was considering action on several matters affecting the company's business, including safe handling instructions on poultry packaging." Tyson consented to pay $6 million in fines and costs.

As the poultry industry was faced with an oversupply and low prices, Tyson took a number of measures designed to reduce production, improve its product mix, and focus on higher added-value products. Consequently, 1998 and 1999 for Tyson were years marked by restructuring and streamlining, including some divesting of non-chicken businesses. In 1998, Tyson closed a laying-hen-processing plant in Bloomer, Arkansas, and sold off a turkey processing plant in Minnesota. That same year, the company created a new division, the Tyson Prepared Foods Group, under which many of Tyson's businesses realigned. In 1999, Tyson sold its seafood and pork groups.

RENEWING GOAL TO BECOME A DIVERSIFIED MEAT COMPANY

After about 20 years of double-digit profit growth, Tyson shares peaked in late 1998, and then dropped sharply over the next two years. Despite its efforts to address a chicken oversupply and low prices, Tyson saw a dramatic 45 percent drop in its second-quarter profits for 2000. Nonetheless, Tyson had its 65th anniversary to celebrate. As part of the celebration, the company launched a major campaign to fight hunger. Partnering with Share Our Strength (SOS), Tyson committed to providing $10 million in product and support to local communities over three years. The company also announced that it would donate 650,000 pounds of chicken to local hunger organizations.

Total sales for 2000 fell just short of the previous year's, at $7.15 billion, compared to 1999's $7.36 billion. Year 2000 net income fell to $151 million, from the previous year's $230 million. In 2001, Tyson began test marketing an organically grown chicken product, Nature's Farm Organic Chicken, in an effort to find a way to compete in the growing organic and natural foods markets.

Even though Tyson's past was checkered with failed attempts to diversify into beef, pork, and seafood, the company still sought a way to go beyond chicken. In mid-2001, Tyson made its boldest move to diversify, and this time, the company seemed to get it right. New CEO John Tyson, grandson of the founder, engineered the acquisition of IBP, the world's largest beef processor, for $4.4 billion, transforming the company from a giant chicken-only operation into the largest diversified meat company in the world. The acquisition made Tyson a $23 billion enterprise, responsible for processing nearly one-quarter of all meat sold in the United States. The company gained a third-place U.S. ranking as a packaged food company, behind Philip Morris's Kraft Foods division and ConAgra.

GROWING WITH ACQUISITION OF IBP

Profits and sales surged after the acquisition: Profits tripled in the most recent quarter after the sale. Chicken prices rose during the summer as glut-busting production cuts took effect and demand for wings and legs improved. Pork sales grew by more than 10-fold to $508.7 million.

The year for Tyson ended on a negative note, however, as the company faced serious allegations of illegal hiring practices, brought on by a two-and-a-half-year investigation by the Department of Justice. Tyson and several employees were indicted for conspiring to smuggle illegal immigrants across the U.S.-Mexico border and put them to work with false documentation. Tyson was investigated for financial gains derived from the alleged offense, which was estimated to be in excess of $100 million.

IBP's businesses continued to benefit Tyson's bottom line into 2002. Tyson's midyear profits jumped to a sixfold increase, raising net income to $107 million, compared to 2001. Also, in that same time frame, revenue tripled to $5.9 billion from $1.92 billion. International sales, however, were less successful. Russia, the world's leading poultry importer, halted purchases from the United States, citing concerns over sanitation and handling practices. China also imposed import restrictions, further hurting Tyson's foreign sales.

2002 PRODUCT DEVELOPMENT FOR CUSTOMER CONVENIENCE

Tyson strove to maximize the opportunities that stemmed from its leading position in the animal protein market, especially given the potential of economies of scale and market trends. In 2002 IBP Chief Executive Richard Bond chose a select group of executives to develop products within the new Refrigerated Processed Meats Division. First, the team reorganized operations, closing some plants and upgrading some facilities. New operations included a dinner meat processing facility in Council Bluffs, Iowa, and a bacon processing plant in Omaha.

Tyson extended its success in creating convenient chicken products to beef and pork. As such, product development followed the dining trend toward fresh preparation of meals at home with seasoned or precut fresh meats. These included more than 18 flavors of ready-to-cook premium dinner meats. Dinner ham was available in six varieties, and bacon was available precooked or fully-cooked as well as in smokehouse options. A new line of sliced deli-style lunch meats included chicken, turkey, beef, and pork. In addition to

providing added value to animal protein, the products sold at a higher potential profit margin than plain, basic cuts.

Tyson promoted its new products through a $100 million marketing campaign that included more than $40 million in new advertising on television and radio and in print. The company continued to use the advertising tagline "Tyson, It's What Your Family Deserves," established in 2000. Other initiatives involved in-store and online promotions, and multicultural marketing.

Tyson sought to improve chicken production efficiency with the acquisition of Choctaw Maid Farms in Carthage, Mississippi. Installation of new automated processing equipment allowed the company to relocate processing of 850,000 chickens from its Jackson facility, bringing production at Carthage to 2.3 million chickens weekly.

FOCUS ON VALUE-ADDED PRODUCTS

In January 2005 the company purchased a 537,000-square-foot meat processing and packaging facility in Sherman, Texas, and began a $100 million renovation. Tyson continued to expand its line of value-added meat products. As an adjunct to rotisserie chicken offered hot at grocery deli counters, Tyson offered such items as meatballs, barbeque pork ribs, Mexican style beef, and Cajun pork chops. During 2005 the company introduced 420 new products, primarily ready-to-cook meals. "Ingredient meats" were popular among consumers, as they made fresh food preparation easier.

Committed to providing consumers with new value-added products, Tyson broke ground on a $52 million research and development facility in 2005. Located at the corporate campus in Springdale, the Discovery Center housed 18 test kitchens, a pilot plant to test production, and a packaging laboratory. The center opened in May 2007 with a staff of 65 food technologists.

STRUGGLE FOR PROFITABILITY

Although the integration of IBP went smoothly, Tyson struggled to post a return for investors. Grocers were hesitant to bring Tyson's prepared dinner meats into their stores as competitors to similar store brand products. Sales representatives were slow to offer pork and beef products to restaurants. Mad cow disease led most countries to block beef imports from the United States in 2003 and 2006. Moreover, Hurricane Katrina closed ports used for export, and avian flu reduced poultry consumption in Asia. As the company faced a rapid increase in the price of grain and lower demand for beef and chicken, factory production declined and economies of scale suffered. When Bond replaced John Tyson as CEO in May 2006, he faced the company's first financial losses in several years.

Bond started a cost-reduction program aimed at cutting $110 million in expenses, later increased to $200 million. Tyson eliminated more than 4,000 jobs, including 420 management positions. The company postponed annual merit raises to senior management and suspended matching stock options. Management restructuring in late 2007 further reduced staffing. Also, a glut of chicken on the commodities market prompted Tyson to reduce production by 5 percent, closing plants in Idaho, Iowa, and Nebraska and selling five poultry plants in Alabama.

GAINING PRESENCE IN DEVELOPING COUNTRIES

Tyson's strategic plans involved establishing a presence in developing countries, where population growth and rising incomes would encourage demand for animal protein. In China the company formed two joint ventures. Jiangsu Tyson Foods, in which Tyson owned a 70 percent interest, produced and distributed Tyson brand meat products in eastern China. In Shandong Tyson Xindung Foods Company, Tyson owned a 60 percent interest. Tyson acquired a 51 percent interest in Godrej Foods, one of the largest poultry processors in India.

Expansion in South America involved the acquisition of two companies in Argentina in 2007 and three companies in southern Brazil in 2008. Tyson preferred vertically integrated organization, with the joint ventures handling all aspects of meat production, from animal husbandry to processing, packaging, and distribution.

Tyson sought environmentally sustainable ways to create new business. The Renewable Products Group used meat scraps to create fresh, refrigerated pet foods, a venture that involved restarting an idle plant. Given increased public interest in alternative fuels, Tyson saw an opportunity to capitalize on its enormous supply of animal fats to produce biofuel. The company formed a joint venture with Syntroleum Corporation, Dynamic Fuels, and was expected to open a biofuel production plant in Louisiana in the summer of 2010.

Although meat production declined worldwide, Tyson's international operations offset lower sales volume in the United States. Also, Tyson raised prices on its products. The company lost money on its chicken operations, and beef and pork products carried the

company to profitability. As excess inventory of frozen chicken sold during late 2009, Tyson began to rebuild chicken production. Higher production was expected to improve cost efficiency, if not strengthen the company's bottom line.

Updated, David E. Salamie; Heidi Wrightsman; Mary Tradii

PRINCIPAL OPERATING UNITS

Foodservice and International Unit; Fresh Meats; Refrigerated Processed Meats Division; Retail and Consumer Products Unit; Renewable Products Group.

PRINCIPAL COMPETITORS

Cagle's, Inc.; Cargill, Inc.; ConAgra Foods, Inc.; Continental Grain Company Corporation; Farmland Industries; Foster Poultry Farms; Hormel Foods Corporation; Keystone Foods, LLC; Perdue, Inc.; Pilgrim's Pride Corporation; Sanderson Farms, Inc.; Sara Lee North American Retail; Smithfield Foods, Inc.

FURTHER READING

"After Acquiring Beef Producer, Tyson Foods Says Profit Is Up," *New York Times*, November 13, 2001, p. C4.

Barboza, David, "Why Is He on Top? He's a Tyson, for One," *New York Times*, March 4, 2001, p. 1.

Behar, Richard, "Arkansas Pecking Order," *Time*, October 26, 1992, pp. 52–54.

Capshaw, Mike, "CEO Turns Tyson Back from Brink," *Arkansas Business*, March 26, 2007, p. 1.

Edmundson, Sheila, "Real Home of the McNugget Is Tyson," *Memphis Business Journal*, July 9, 1999, p. 21.

Fusaro, Dave, "'It's Good to Be Tyson,' Despite the Pitfalls of the Animal Protein Market, North America's Biggest Food Processor for Years Has Been Adding Value to Meats, Tightly Running Its Plants and Staying Close to Its Arkansas Values," *Food Processing*, December 2005, pp. 22+.

Garrison, Bob, "Seize the Moment: Tyson Foods' New Refrigerated Processed Meats Division Literally Makes a Name for Itself as a New, $500 Million Player in the Category," *Refrigerated & Frozen Foods*, August 2003, p. 14.

Heath, Thomas, "A Booming Business Runs Afowl of Politics: Tyson Foods' Troubles Escalated Following Clinton's Election," *Washington Post*, July 23, 1995, p. H1.

McGraw, Dan, "The Birdman of Arkansas," *U.S. News & World Report*, July 18, 1994, pp. 42–46.

Miller, Bill, "Tyson Foods Executive Sentenced in Espy Case," *Washington Post*, September 26, 2000, p. A6.

"Profit Increases Sixfold at Tyson Foods," *New York Times*, July 30, 2002, p. C8.

Ruggless, Ron, "Don Tyson: Chairman, Tyson Foods Inc., Springdale, Arkansas," *Nation's Restaurant News*, January 1995, pp. 213–14.

Schmidt, Susan, "Tyson Foods Admits Illegal Gifts to Espy; Firm to Pay U.S. $6 Million; Executives to Testify at Trial of Former Cabinet Member," *Washington Post*, December 30, 1997, p. A1.

Schwartz, Marvin, *Tyson: From Farm to Market*, Fayetteville: University of Arkansas Press, 1991, 158 p.

Stein, Nicholas, "Son of a Chicken Man," *Fortune*, May 13, 2002, pp. 136–46.

Stewart, D. R., "Tyson Forecasts Its Future in Faster Foods," *Arkansas Democrat-Gazette*, January 14, 1995, pp. D1–D2.

"Tyson Foods Expands International Interests," *Nation's Restaurant News*, June 25, 2001, p. 154.

"Tyson Launches Major Campaign to Fight Hunger," *Food Management*, July 2000, p. 24.

"Tyson Struggles as Low Prices Take Their Toll," *Eurofood*, May 11, 2000.

"Tyson to Sell Pork Group," *ID: The Voice of Foodservice Distribution*, December 1999, p. 20.

"Tyson Will Realign Several Food Businesses," *News & Record* (Piedmont Triad, NC), September 11, 1998, p. B6.

Walsh, Sharon, "Tyson Foods to Buy Competitor Hudson; Rival Had Been Hit by Massive Beef Recall," *Washington Post*, September 5, 1997, p. G1.

Young, Barbara, "Tyson Foods' Karma," *National Provisioner*, June 2002, p. 10.

Zeller, Wendy, "The Wal-Mart of Meat; Tyson Foods Produces One of Every Four Pounds of U.S. Beef, Chicken, and Pork. Is That a Problem?" *Business Week*, September 20, 2004, p. 90.

Umeco plc

Concord House
24 Warwick New Road
Leamington Spa, Warwickshire CV32 5JG
United Kingdom
Telephone: (+44 1926) 331800
Fax: (+44 1926) 312680
Web site: http://www.umeco.com

Public Company
Incorporated: 1917 as University Motoring and Engineering Company Limited
Employees: 1,723
Sales: £415.3 million (2009)
Stock Exchanges: London
Ticker Symbol: UMC.L
NAICS: 423840 Industrial Supplies Merchant Wholesalers; 423860 Transportation Equipment and Supplies (Except Motor Vehicles) Merchant Wholesalers; 541330 Engineering Services; 541614 Process, Physical Distribution, and Logistics Consulting Services; 332996 Fabricated Pipe and Pipe Fitting Manufacturing; 332999 All Other Miscellaneous Fabricated Metal Product Manufacturing; 336413 Other Aircraft Parts and Auxiliary Equipment Manufacturing; 811310 Commercial and Industrial Machinery and Equipment (Except Automotive and Electronic) Repair and Maintenance

∎ ∎ ∎

Umeco plc is a U.K. company with two main lines of business: distributing aerospace components and supply-

ing materials used in manufacturing composites. Although its main focus is the aerospace industry, Umeco's composite materials are also used in the wind energy, automotive, and motorsports industries.

Originally a London-area auto distributor, in 1983 the company became involved in aviation through the acquisition of Fluid Transfer Limited, which made aircraft refueling trucks. New management took over in 1997, eventually selling this and other businesses while focusing subsequent acquisitions on distributing low-cost aerospace components such as seals and fasteners while developing a composite materials business.

In 2007 the company initiated a sell-off of its repair and overhaul and chemicals distribution units in order to concentrate on its two main divisions. Most of Umeco's revenues come from Europe, although the company supplies Boeing Company and has moved to increase its participation in the U.S. defense industry through strategic acquisitions.

ORIGINS

Umeco plc's name comes from University Motoring and Engineering Company Limited, a motor vehicle distributorship established in southern England in 1917. George R. A. Metcalfe, former joint managing director of the Bath and Portland Group, became Umeco's group managing director in 1983 and chief executive the next year. He soon shifted the business toward aerospace with the acquisition of Fluid Transfer Limited, supplier of aircraft refueling equipment for airports and Britain's Ministry of Defence. Umeco then acquired B&K Resin,

COMPANY PERSPECTIVES

Umeco is a leading innovator in distribution and supply chain management to the aerospace and defence industries, harnessing new methods for enhancing its customers' performance and profitability. Umeco also has significant manufacturing interests in advanced composite materials for a growing range of applications in its core aerospace and defence markets and in other high performance technology industries such as motor sport, automotive and wind energy.

a maker of adhesives and its first exposure to composite materials, which would become a major business unit.

Umeco lost £32,000 in the fiscal year ended March 1985, but was soon profitable again after divesting the last of its automobile distributorships. Revenues were then about £5 million a year. The loss-making subsidiary Loheat, a manufacturer of transformers, was sold off to management for £385,000 in 1991.

INTO SUPPLY CHAIN SUPPORT IN 1987

In 1987 Umeco acquired Pattonair, a distributor of low-cost aerospace components such as nuts, bolts, seals, bearings, and connectors that it kept for original equipment manufacturers for delivery on a just-in-time basis. This allowed manufacturers to free up capital otherwise tied up in inventory and greatly simplified billing. This was at the time a much more accepted model in the United States than in Europe.

Umeco's revenues approached £10 million for the year ended March 1989 and the company was consistently profitable. In July 1989 its shares appeared on the Unlisted Securities Market in an offering that valued the company at £5.4 million. A full listing on the London Stock Exchange followed five years later.

In January 1994 Umeco acquired Tortube, which supplied piping for gas cookers and boilers. The pace and scope of acquisitions stepped up with the arrival of a new management team in 1997.

NEW MANAGEMENT IN 1997

Brian McGowan and Clive Snowdon had been chairman and CEO, respectively, of Solihull engineering firm Burnfield for five years when it was acquired by rival

Fairey Group for £60 million. McGowan had previously cofounded Derby's Williams Holdings, a conglomerate built up through aggressive corporate takeovers in the 1980s, and had also chaired House of Fraser.

In 1997 McGowan and Snowdon together acquired an approximately 5 percent stake in Umeco, taking over its management. They relocated the company from Hungerford to Leamington Spa and launched an acquisition drive focused on the supply-chain and composite materials businesses. They paid £1 million for Med-Lab Limited, which had a materials distributor as a subsidiary. Fluid Transfer, the refueling equipment business, was sold off in the fall of 1998.

Umeco grew rapidly over the next two years. At the same time, the company gained a sterling reputation for asset utilization. Snowdon told *Aviation Week* he aimed for return on invested capital of 25 percent.

In 1998 the Pattonair unit signed an 11-year contract to supply basic parts at Rolls-Royce plc's U.K. aerospace operations. By the end of the next year this was expanded to Rolls-Royce's plants throughout Europe.

Outsourcing was becoming more accepted in the aviation industry in Europe. Umeco was able to secure long-term deals with British Aerospace and GKN-Westland Helicopters. Rather than trying to compete in the U.S. market, Umeco focused on expanding in Europe, particularly France and Germany.

EMPHASIZING COMPOSITES AFTER 1999

In March 1999 Umeco acquired Aerovac Systems, a leader in supplies for the European vacuum-bagging industry. A year and a half later it added Richmond Aircraft Products, Inc., its first large venture into the United States, for £23.5 million. Richmond supplied composite materials used on aircraft structures and power-generating wind turbines.

Once the province of makers of kit-planes and experimental craft, composite construction was fast becoming accepted in the aerospace mainstream. Both Airbus and Boeing were using it in their latest and largest airliners. The materials allowed manufacturers to save weight, always a consideration in aircraft, and opened new design possibilities.

Umeco focused on providing supplies such as resin and fabric used to make composite parts, rather than the components themselves. It did manufacture tooling of composite construction, which offered huge cost savings over traditional metal tools.

In June 1999 Umeco announced the purchase of five businesses from TI Group for £11.8 million. Two of them, Compstock and Flightspares' electronics division, brought electronics into its product mix. The deal included chemicals businesses Aerocontracts Chemicals and R.D. Taylor as well as AEM, which repaired aircraft components for airlines.

After the Richmond acquisition, Umeco had 650 employees serving 14 operating subsidiaries. Revenues rose 72 percent to £165 million in the year ended March 2001.

INDUSTRY SLOWDOWN AFTER 2001

In June 2001 Umeco acquired U.S. aerospace fasteners distributor Abscoa Industries, later called Pattonair USA, in a deal worth $22 million (£15.4 million). Abscoa was profitable on annual revenues of $34 million. Its clients included Lockheed Martin Corporation.

The industry-wide slowdown following the September 11, 2001, terrorist attacks on the United States grounded Umeco's soaring share price. Exposure to the declining civilian aerospace market was tempered by increased military sales.

Increased U.S. defense spending in the years following the attacks led to more involvement in the North American market. In January 2004 Umeco landed a long-term parts-supply contract with Canadian business jet manufacturer Bombardier worth potentially £44 million a year.

In February 2004 Umeco acquired a majority stake in Tailored Logistics Corporation, Inc. (TLC), which

supplied aircraft overhaul kits primarily to the U.S. military. It had annual revenues of about $15 million. Umeco agreed to pay up to $15 million (£8.4 million) for the business.

In May 2004, after five years of pursuit, Umeco bought Advanced Composites Group (ACG) for £44 million. Based in Heanor, Derbyshire, ACG had been founded by Roger Sloman in 1975 to supply plastics for Formula One race cars. Umeco soon expanded this facility.

SIGNS OF RECOVERY BY 2005

Acquisitions helped lift revenues for the fiscal year ended March 2005 to £242.4 million from £184.5 million the year before. The commercial aviation sector was showing signs of recovery as passengers returned to the skies.

In 2005 the company added Avionics Mobile Services to its maintenance, repair, and overhaul (MRO) business. Provest, a distributor of aerospace fasteners based in Milan, Italy, was acquired in November 2005 for EUR 20 million. It became a part of Pattonair. During the year Umeco also acquired Aeromedic Innovations and Aviation Windings. At the same time it was also investing more in China, where it had long seen much potential for growth.

In June 2006 Umeco acquired Capetown, South Africa's Aerodyne Advanced Composites for £1.5 million. It had 130 employees and primarily supplied sports car manufacturer McLauren Automotive. It was renamed ACG South Africa.

Pattonair landed a long-term supply deal with France's Thales in December 2006, followed several months later by a contract with France's Turbomeca. Miami-based distributor US Airmotive International Inc. was acquired in 2006. By the end of the year Umeco had 1,450 employees.

In October 2006 Umeco acquired Antavia, a small French repair and overhaul company. Antavia had been established in 1989 and counted Air France as its largest client. This was Umeco's first foray into the MRO business in continental Europe.

REFINED FOCUS IN 2007

Los Angeles, California-based composite materials supplier J.D. Lincoln, Inc., was acquired in September 2007 for £60 million. Lincoln was a leader in phenolic resin fabrics used in aircraft interiors. Umeco followed up this purchase two months later with the £3 million acquisition of George Cole Technologies (doing business as Primco), a Manchester-based supplier of phenolic resin materials with annual sales of more than £5 million.

In November 2007 the repair and overhaul business was sold to AMETEK, Inc., for £36 million ($74 million), leaving the company to focus on its faster-growing supply-chain and composite materials businesses. At the same time Umeco's supply contract with Rolls-Royce was extended through 2015, increasing the scope to include much more expensive items and potentially doubling the value of the contract to £140 million a year. Within a few months Umeco opened a £7 million facility near Rolls-Royce's Derby plant.

In March 2008 Umeco divested a pair of chemicals distribution businesses, Aeropia and R.D. Taylor & Co., which had combined sales of £28 million. The buyer, Germany's Haas TCM Group, paid £13 million.

Snowdon told *Flight International* that in spite of its recent acquisitions, most of the company's recent growth had been organic. He was bullish on aviation industry's long-term prospects in Asia and the Middle East.

In November 2008 Pattonair landed a long-term contract with ATK in North America. Italy's Industria Plastica Monregalese SpA (IPM), manufacturer of vacuum bagging films used in composites manufacture, was acquired in December.

Although revenues rose nearly 12 percent to £415.3 million in the year ended March 2009, and pretax profits were up more than 30 percent to £29 million, investors were becoming increasingly wary of the company's increasing debt load, which had more than doubled to £120 million in one year. Moreover, the share price had fallen to just a quarter of its two-year high. Subsequently, Chairman Brian McGowan stepped down to be replaced in October 2009 by Neil Johnson, formerly chief executive of motorists' group RAC plc.

Although the composites business was proving more vulnerable to the economic downturn, it remained central to the aviation industry. Umeco was the materials supplier for Airbus's £100 million Next Generation Composite Wing project, a group of 16 British businesses and agencies aiming to make future airliners more efficient.

While Boeing's massive 787 superjumbo continued to experience delays, there remained a large backlog for Umeco's supply-chain business for civil aircraft. By 2010 the wind turbine industry was showing signs of an early recovery, and excellent long-term prospects, as governments from the United Kingdom to China devoted more attention to alternative energy sources.

Frederick C. Ingram

PRINCIPAL SUBSIDIARIES

Advanced Composites Group Limited; Advanced Composites Group Manchester Limited; Advanced Composites Group, Inc. (USA); Advanced Composites Group SA (Pty) Limited (South Africa); J. D. Lincoln, Inc.; GRPMS Limited; GRPMS Sweden AB; GRPMS Estonia OU; Aerovac Systems Limited; Aerovac Systemes France Sarl; Aerovac Systems Italia S.r.l. (Italy); Richmond Aircraft Products, Inc. (USA); Industria Plastica Monregalese SpA (Italy); Med-Lab Limited; Pattonair Limited; Pattonair SAS (France); Pattonair S.r.l. (Italy); Pattonair (Derby) Limited; Pattonair (Wolverhampton) Limited; Pattonair (Berlin) GmbH (Germany); Ulogistics Canada, Inc.; Pattonair USA, Inc.; Tailored Logistics Corporation, Inc. (USA); Pattonair do Brasil Serviços e Logística Ltda. (Brazil); Umeco Asia Pte. Limited (Singapore); Pattonair (Xi'an) Trading Limited (China).

PRINCIPAL DIVISIONS

Umeco Supply Chain; Umeco Composites.

PRINCIPAL COMPETITORS

Airtech International, Inc.; First Aviation Services, Inc.; Lawson Products, Inc.; Saywell International Ltd.; Alcoa Inc.

FURTHER READING

Bennett, Neil, "Umeco Engineers £5.4m Valuation with Placing," *Times* (London), Bus. Sec., July 3, 1989.

"Efficiency Key to Umeco Rise," *Aviation Week & Space Technology,* May 31, 1999, p. 62.

Felsted, Andrea, "Umeco Launches £26m Rights for Abscoa Buy," *Financial Times,* June 2, 2001.

Guthrie, Jonathan, "Winner: Clive Snowdon of Umeco," *Financial Times,* FT Report: Mid Market Companies 2008, Surveys MMC1, March 7, 2008, p. 3.

Harrison, Michael, "McGowan Back on Track as He Snaps Up Formula 1 Supplier," *Independent* (London), March 20, 2004, p. 56.

Leach, Andrew, "Ready for Takeoff; £15m Deal Boosts US Expansion," *Mail on Sunday,* July 1, 2001, p. C1.

Marcaillou, Laurent, "Antavia passe sous le pavillon du britannique Umeco," *Les Echos,* October 17, 2006, p. 22.

Thisdell, Dan, "Umeco Has Composites Mix," *Flight International,* June 10, 2008.

"Umeco Profits from Fluid Situations," *Investors Chronicle,* July 13, 1990, p. 56.

"Umeco Retains Top Ranking," *Aviation Week & Space Technology,* July 10, 2000, p. 80.

Urquhart, Lisa, "Umeco Is Flying Well on Civil Aviation Recovery," *Financial Times,* June 2, 2005, p. 24.

United Business Media

United Business Media Limited

Whiteley Chambers
Don Street
St. Helier, Jersey JE4 9WG
United Kingdom
Telephone: (+44 20) 7921 5000
Fax: (+44 20) 7928 2717
Web site: http://www.unitedbusinessmedia.com

Public Company
Incorporated: 1918 as United Newspapers Limited
Employees: 5,800
Sales: £847.6 million ($1.33 billion) (2009)
Stock Exchanges: London
Ticker Symbol: UBM
NAICS: 511120 Periodical Publishers; 519110 News Syndicates; 519130 Internet Publishing and Broadcasting and Web Search Portals; 561920 Convention and Trade Show Organizers

■ ■ ■

United Business Media Limited (UBM) is a leading U.K.-based international business media firm specializing in business-to-business (B2B) products and services. UBM's largest unit, B2B Communities, focuses on about 70 specific B2B markets, such as game developers, chief information officers, and primary care physicians. For such markets, this unit, which generates more than 80 percent of overall revenues, organizes trade shows, conferences, and other events; provides data, services, and online products; and publishes specialty print magazines (including *Information Week* and the *Journal of Commerce*).

UBM's remaining revenues are generated by its B2B Distribution, Monitoring and Targeting unit, which is the largest distributor of commercial news and information in the world. This unit's flagship business is PR Newswire, a distributor of corporate press releases via the Web, e-mail, fax, wire, and other channels. Nearly half of UBM's revenues originate in the Americas, about 20 percent in the United Kingdom, 17 percent in continental Europe and the Middle East, and 15 percent in the Asia-Pacific region.

UBM's earliest roots are in the newspaper field, and it was known for most of its history as United Newspapers. The company changed its name to United News & Media plc in 1995 to reflect widening interests, and one year later gained a number of broadcasting and entertainment properties through a merger with MAI PLC. In 2000, after the sale of its newspaper unit and most of its consumer-related media properties, the company adopted the name United Business Media plc. UBM later divested its remaining consumer media assets as well as its broadcasting and market research interests. In 2008 the company restructured under a newly created Jersey-based holding company, United Business Media Limited, and, for tax purposes, set up headquarters in Ireland. Its main office nevertheless remained in London.

EARLY HISTORY OF UNITED NEWSPAPERS

From the middle of the 19th century the newspaper industry had grown faster in the United Kingdom than in any other country in the world. Educational reform

COMPANY PERSPECTIVES

Our strategy is to build businesses which target the needs of specialist communities in B2B and business information distribution, monitoring and targeting. We provide information, data, marketing services and distribution products. We aim for each of our businesses to be at the heart of commercial and professional communities, providing a complete range of information, data, services and media products. We provide the "industry leading" event, the "must read" online or print content, the "business critical" market analysis or information resource and the "most comprehensive" distribution network and database. Our core expertise lies in providing continuous valued services and transferring the know-how and expertise from one community to another, from one geography to another and from one medium to another.

provided a literate readership interested in foreign affairs and domestic politics, and rapidly improving road and rail links facilitated distribution throughout the country. The industrial revolution had created towns and cities that were able to provide a local newspaper with readers and advertisers. Advances in technology, such as Linotype and rotary presses, typewriters, telephones, and telegraphs, enabled local and national newspapers to operate profitably.

Politicians were quick to realize the great influence that newspaper editors had over the electorate, and from the 1850s onward there was a considerable interchange between the Parliament and Fleet Street, the traditional home of U.K. journalism. David Lloyd George, prime minister in the United Kingdom during World War I, was an adept user of the press and was not afraid to exercise his influence to negate the effects of a political crisis. When the *Daily Chronicle* employed as a military correspondent a stern critic of his policies, Lloyd George responded by calling together a group of Liberals to buy out the owners of the paper.

United Newspapers Limited was formed in 1918 by these supporters of the prime minister. The company bought two papers in the deal, of which the *Daily Chronicle* was the most important. The other paper, *Lloyd's Weekly News*, had been founded in 1842 and held the distinction of being the first newspaper with a circulation of one million readers. The board of United Newspapers soon began to publish a northern edition of the *Daily Chronicle* as a rival to the Conservative Lord Northcliffe's *Daily Mail* and also acquired the *Edinburgh Evening News* and the *Doncaster Gazette*, papers that carried on the strong Liberal tradition of Lloyd George and his politically minded associates. In 1925 the company went public as United Newspapers plc.

In 1927 the company was sold for £2.9 million to the Daily Chronicle Investment Group, a joint venture of Liberal interests led by the Marquis of Reading, Sir David Yule, and Sir Thomas Catto. A covenant in the sales document restricted the owners to running the paper "in accordance with the policy of Progressive Liberalism" to further social and industrial reform, free trade, and "other programmes of Liberal and Radical measures adopted by the Liberal party." Within a year United Newspapers was again in the hands of a new owner, William Harrison, a Yorkshireman who had trained as a solicitor in London. Although Harrison was a Conservative, he proclaimed that the group would continue to support Lloyd George and the Liberal cause. As chairman of the Inveresk Paper Company, Harrison bought a controlling interest in United Newspapers. The latter was then amalgamated in 1929 with Provincial Newspapers Ltd., an umbrella organization taking in some 17 local newspapers that Harrison had acquired in the early and mid-1920s.

Harrison's belief in the regional market molded United's acquisition strategy for the next 50 years, but this strategy was also responsible for his downfall. In the autumn of 1929, 80 percent of the value of the shares in the Inveresk Paper Company was written off because of the Great Depression. In December Harrison resigned as chairman when it was revealed that Inveresk had debts of £2.5 million and that United Newspapers had no immediate means to pay for a £500,000 modernization program for the *Daily Chronicle*. Both companies were highly leveraged at a time when investment capital in all sectors of the economy was nearly impossible to secure.

FIRST MAJOR CRISIS

The board of United Newspapers (led by Sir Bernhard Binder, founder of the chartered accountants Binder Hamlyn, and managing director Jack Akerman) was now facing a major crisis. Its solution was to merge the *Daily Chronicle* with the *Daily News* to produce a new title, the *Daily News and Chronicle*. In a move to provide finance for United's provincial press, 50 percent of the ownership of the new paper was sold to News and Westminster Ltd.

The mid-1930s were difficult for United Newspapers. It was a time of depression and mass

KEY DATES

1918: Supporters of David Lloyd George, the U.K. prime minister, buy two newspapers, the *Daily Chronicle* and *Lloyd's Weekly News*, forming United Newspapers Limited.

1925: Company goes public as United Newspapers plc.

1982: PR Newswire, a corporate and financial news agency, is acquired.

1995: United Newspapers changes its name to United News & Media plc (UNM).

1998: Firm's regional newspaper business is divested.

1999: UNM acquires CMP Media Inc.

2000: Divestments totaling £3.2 billion are completed; company is renamed United Business Media plc (UBM) to highlight new focus on business publishing and business services.

2004: UBM acquires MediMedia's European and Asian operations.

2006: Commonwealth Business Media, Inc., is acquired.

2008: Company is restructured under a newly created Jersey-based holding company, United Business Media Limited.

unemployment, especially in United's marketplace, the north of England. Fears for the company's survival increased when Lord Rothermere announced his venture, Northcliffe Newspapers, with a stated aim of producing an evening paper in every city and metropolitan area served by United Newspapers. However, in a move executed by Jack Akerman and Sir Herbert Grotrian, who had replaced Binder as chairman, United Newspapers sold its 50 percent share in what (in June 1930) had become the *News Chronicle* for £500,000 and was instantly freed from its debt. The reaction from the City was ecstatic, and United's preference shares rose from one shilling sixpence to 25 shillings, as final proof that the crisis had been averted.

The war years were less difficult for United than they were for those newspaper groups that were based in heavily bombed Fleet Street. An increase in news was cruelly matched by newsprint rationing, distribution and communication problems, and government censorship. Although Sheffield and Hull suffered damage from Luftwaffe bombing comparable to that inflicted on London, presses in Scotland, Leeds, and the West Country fared better, and United Newspapers was able to consolidate its success in these areas.

THE DRAYTON ERA

The next event of importance for the directors of United Newspapers occurred in the winter of 1946 with an invitation to dinner at the Hyde Park Hotel from Harold Charles Drayton. Drayton, always known as "Harley," was the epitome of the self-made man. Born in rural Lincolnshire, he started his working life as a £1-a-week office boy and rose through the ranks of the City, eventually controlling the 117 Old Broad Street Group, a large and diverse empire of companies with worldwide interests.

Although Drayton described himself as almost uneducated, he was in truth an erudite and imaginative businessman. He realized that United Newspapers was holding assets of immense value, in the shape of offices and printing houses in the center of major towns and cities throughout the United Kingdom. Within a few weeks of the Hyde Park dinner, Drayton began negotiating with United Newspapers and eventually bought 500,000 shares, representing approximately one-third of the equity of the company. After several months as an ordinary board member, Drayton became chairman on New Year's Day 1948.

Years of steady but unspectacular profits for United followed, enlivened by a number of small and cautious acquisitions. Drayton realized that the directors of the company, three of whom were in their 70s, would soon have to be replaced. Two important additions were made to the board. Significantly, they were both men who had risen through the ranks of Provincial Newspapers, a company associated with United that had been formed in 1930.

Ken Whitworth had been advertising manager of a group of local newspapers based in south London before joining the Royal Air Force in 1939. He returned from four years as a prisoner of war in Japan to prove his business worth as a member of several of Provincial's boards. William Barnetson had started as an editorial writer on the *Edinburgh Evening News* and swiftly rose to become editor. He demonstrated his management skills on the board of the Edinburgh paper and later on the board of Provincial. After the quiet years of the 1950s, when the United Kingdom struggled to recover from the ravages of World War II, United Newspapers entered the 1960s with the commercially minded Whitworth and the editorially gifted Barnetson as joint managing directors. With Harley Drayton as chairman it was to be the first golden age of United Newspapers.

United Newspapers entered the 1960s as a wealthy company with an established stable of widely read regional newspapers. It was to Barnetson's credit that he did not rush headlong into reckless expansion but instead formulated a cautious acquisition strategy that relied as much on the goodwill of competitors as on his own undoubted capacity for striking deals. United's move in 1963 to larger premises in Tudor Street was indicative of United's imminent emergence as a major player in the U.K. newspaper industry.

In 1963 the *Nelson Leader* and the *Colne Times*, both struggling Lancashire papers, were bought by United, which rationalized operations by transferring printing to its own underused plant at Burnley. Later in the same year United sold the 49 percent stake in the *Hull Daily News*, held by Provincial, for £1.7 million to Associated Newspapers. In November, United gave the *Edinburgh Evening News* to the Thomson group in exchange for two Sheffield papers, the *Telegraph* and the *Star*. For Thomson it meant the end of competition for its *Evening Dispatch* in Edinburgh and for United the loss of a fine paper was offset by the strengthening of its position in Yorkshire.

This deal was followed by an agreement to sell United's *Yorkshire Evening News* for 20 percent of the equity of the far stronger Yorkshire Post Newspapers. Drayton adroitly realized that it was necessary to lose a battle, or at least to appear to lose a battle, to win the war. The purchase of the group of newspapers centered on the Blackpool office of the *West Lancashire Evening Gazette* and further consolidated United's position in the north of England.

ENTERING THE PERIODICALS MARKET

Harley Drayton was succeeded as chairman by William Barnetson in April 1966. Barnetson followed Drayton's strategy and tactics when he sold the *Doncaster Gazette* to Yorkshire Post Newspapers in exchange for 49 percent of a new joint venture company, Doncaster Newspapers Ltd., which was set up to publish the *Doncaster Evening Post*. With Ken Whitworth's help as managing director, United introduced new economies in preparation for the company's greatest years of expansion.

The year 1969 started quietly with the acquisition of a group of weekly papers in north London. United then took the brave step of entering the periodicals market when Bradbury Agnew and Co., fearing hostile predators, offered its flagship *Punch*, the *Countryman*, and a number of printing houses to the company. During the tail end of the 1960s *Punch* had been suffering from a problem that was to recur with some regularity over the next 20 years. Seen as a magazine for dentists' waiting rooms, it found itself out of step with

contemporary humor, but United worked closely with then editor William Davis to counter this problem.

While the deal with Bradbury Agnew was being finalized, United had begun to increase its shareholding in Yorkshire Post Newspapers. In October 1969 United acquired the total equity of the group in a transaction that was more of a mutually beneficial merger than a hostile takeover. In just one year United Newspapers had more than doubled in size.

EXPANDING GEOGRAPHICALLY UNDER STEVENS

The 1970s saw a further period of deliberate consolidation for United Newspapers. Under Lord Barnetson the company had become firmly established as one of the Big Four of the U.K. regional press, and acquisitions were designed to increase further its share of the local market. When Barnetson died in 1981 his successor David Stevens, later Lord Stevens of Ludgate, knew that if the group was to survive it would have to venture beyond traditional areas of interest and concluded that expansion abroad was vital. He instigated a process of rationalization that saw the closure of unprofitable papers in Sheffield, Doncaster, and Wigan and the sell-off of the group's printing interests.

Stevens's leadership of United coincided with the rise of the 1980s media magnates. Rupert Murdoch and Robert Maxwell did more than simply buy out the interests of the Astors, the Beaverbrooks, and the Rothermeres. They replaced the old-fashioned newspaper proprietor with an aggressive, profit-driven businessman who was prepared almost continually to buy and sell media interests. Stevens, with a public profile deceptively lower than that of his major competitors, ensured that United Newspapers did not lag behind.

In January 1985 United Newspapers bought a 15 percent stake in Fleet Holdings, owner of the *Daily Express*, the *Sunday Express*, the *Star*, and the Morgan Grampian Group, from Maxwell's Pergamon Press. When Lord Matthews, chairman of Fleet, refused to elect him to the board, Stevens initially launched a £223 million takeover offer in August 1985. This was well below the price of the company's shares at the time and was accepted by less than 1 percent of Fleet shareholders. The bid was subsequently raised to £317 million, significantly larger than the market value of United Newspapers itself. The skills Stevens had learned as a fund manager in the City enabled him to gain complete control of Fleet Holdings by October.

Express Newspapers gave United Newspapers its first national newspaper in 50 years, but the return to

Fleet Street was to be far from easy. The *Daily Express* had been losing readers in the middle market and was further hit by the launch of *Today* in 1986. Numerous changes in editorial staff led to a confused editorial style, and the paper's image problem was not helped by a steady turnover of advertising agencies.

INVESTMENTS IN TECHNOLOGY, ACQUISITIONS, DIVERSIFICATION

Stevens initially reduced the number of regular employees from 6,800 to 4,700 and forced through new agreements with the national printing unions and the paper's own chapels. In the ensuing years to 1990, the number was further reduced to 1,700. Electronic production and direct input of copy to computers meant that the labor-intensive process of hot metal composition could be bypassed. A ban on secondary picketing, enforced by the Employment Acts of 1980 and 1982, further weakened the hold of the traditional printing unions, which had already been shaken by protracted strikes and violent demonstrations in Warrington and Wapping. These measures returned the newly acquired national papers to profitability, enabling Express Newspapers to embark on a program of investment to ensure the future viability of its newspapers. This strategy involved the utilization of the new print technology, investment in color presses, increased paginations, and reduced advertising proportions, with the clear aim of improving the papers' appeal to their target audiences.

By 1990 there were strong indications of the success of this strategy, with all Express titles showing stable circulation and strong shares of their respective advertising markets. By the end of the 1980s the *Daily Express* and the *Daily Star* were, respectively, the fourth and sixth most popular daily titles in the United Kingdom. The *Sunday Express* was by far the largest-selling Sunday broadsheet paper and the fifth most popular of all national Sunday newspapers.

Stevens's first major overseas acquisitions took place in the United States. PR Newswire, a corporate and financial news agency, was acquired in 1982. Gralla, a family-run publisher of trade magazines and promoter of trade shows, was the next U.S. acquisition, purchased in 1983, followed by Miller Freeman, publisher of a number of medical and computer trade magazines.

Stevens also was determined to diversify into different markets. In 1987 Extel, a provider of financial and sporting information, was bought for £250 million. Benn Brothers plc, producer of directories and tax guides, was bought in 1987. In 1989 the *Daily Express* was the last national newspaper to leave Fleet Street, moving to the other side of the Thames River to new offices at Blackfriars Bridge.

THE UNM ERA: 1995–2000

By the beginning of the 1990s Lord Stevens had transformed United Newspapers from a publisher of regional U.K. newspapers to a diversified media group whose additional interests included the national U.K. papers *Express* and *Daily Star*, trade magazines, advertising publications, news services, and trade show activities. Geographically, the company had gained a considerable presence in the United States and was expanding certain businesses, most notably Miller Freeman and PR Newswire, into Asia. In 1995 this diversification was highlighted through the company changing its name to United News & Media plc.

Even more dramatic changes were in the cards for UNM during the remainder of the decade, under the continued direction of Stevens. In February 1996 a £2.9 billion ($4.5 billion) merger joined the operations of UNM with those of MAI PLC, with the combined entity retaining the United News & Media name. MAI's interests included two television licenses in the United Kingdom for the Independent Television Network (ITV); a 29 percent stake in Channel 5, a national commercial broadcasting service in the United Kingdom that made its on-air debut in 1997; NOP Research Group, a market research company; and various financial services firms. In addition, MAI had an agreement, also concluded in February 1996, with Time Warner to partner on a £225 million ($344 million) Movie World theme park and film studio complex to be built just west of London. However, it was the extension into television broadcasting, production, and distribution that made the MAI merger most attractive to UNM. Following the merger, the head of MAI, Clive Hollick, became chief executive of UNM, while Stevens remained chairman.

Within just a few years of this blockbuster deal, United News & Media made a series of acquisitions and divestments that further transformed the company. In late 1996 UNM bolstered its trade show operations through the £592.5 million ($905 million) purchase of U.K.-based Blenheim Exhibitions and Conferences Ltd., which was soon integrated into Miller Freeman. This acquisition made UNM into the largest exhibitions group in the world. During 1997 United News acquired HTV, a Welsh independent television broadcaster; Telecom Library, a magazine publisher and trade show organizer in the United States; and Lemos Britto, a Brazilian trade show organizer.

In early 1998 UNM made a dramatic break from its past with the divestment of its regional newspaper business through three separate sales, totaling £450 million ($700 million). In November of that same year, the company demerged the financial services businesses inherited from MAI into a separate public company called Garban plc. These moves left a more focused UNM, with three main business segments: business services, which included Miller Freeman, PR Newswire, and market research operations NOP and Mediamark Research; broadcasting and entertainment, which included the independent television licenses, the Channel 5 stake, and television show production and distribution activities; and consumer publishing, which included the *Express* and the *Daily Star* national U.K. newspapers and advertising periodicals in the United States and the United Kingdom. In the late 1990s more than half of the company's revenues were generated by business services, which was also UNM's most profitable sector.

During 1999 Ronald Hampel, former CEO and chairman of Imperial Chemical Industries plc, succeeded Stevens as chairman. That year, UNM made several more acquisitions, with the deals bolstering core operations and highlighting an ongoing interest in U.S. growth and an increasing interest in Internet-based opportunities. In January, United News & Media, through its PR Newswire unit, acquired NEWSdesk International, a leading European Internet distributor of corporate news for the high-tech industry. Two months later UNM spent $42.5 million for Audits & Surveys Worldwide Inc., a leading U.S. market research firm, and $111 million for Continuing Medical Education, Inc., a provider of continuing medical education resources for U.S. physicians, including conferences and seminars, trade magazines, home study products, and Web sites.

Then in June, United News purchased CMP Media Inc. for $920 million. The Manhassat, New York-based CMP's operations included the publication of such high-tech trade magazines as *Information Week, Computer Reseller News,* and *Electronic Engineering Times,* and the maintenance of 40 online Web sites, including Tech Web and Channel Web. CMP became a part of Miller Freeman but maintained a separate identity.

The company's transformation into a focused business publisher and provider of business services reached its culmination in 2000, with the process being launched in the final months of the preceding year. In November 1999 UNM announced its intention to divest a number of businesses in order to create a more focused group. In March 2000 Visual Communications

Group, a stock photo library acquired in 1994, was sold to Getty Images, Inc., for $220 million. UNM's U.S. advertising periodicals business, UAP, Inc., was sold in May to Trader Publishing Company for $520 million; United Advertising Publications plc, the U.K. advertising periodicals unit, was retained. Two months later the U.S. side of Miller Freeman, minus CMP Media, was sold to the Dutch publisher VNU N.V. for $650 million, and Miller Freeman Europe was sold to Reed Elsevier for £360 million.

PLANNED MERGERS, THEN DIVESTMENTS

As these disposals were being made, there were also significant developments with the company's television assets. In November 1999 UNM reached an agreement with Carlton Communications plc, another ITV licensee, on an £8 billion ($12.6 billion) merger. U.K. regulators gave conditional approval to the merger, requiring that the combined company divest one of its ITV licenses. This led to the collapse of the merger. UNM also discussed a merger with Granada Media plc, a third ITV licensee.

In the end, however, United News & Media elected to sell its three ITV licenses and related assets to Granada for £1.75 billion, in a deal completed in December 2000. UNM retained stakes in several television and related businesses, including its stake in Channel 5, which had been increased to 35 percent in January 2000; a 20 percent stake in Independent Television News Limited, a news provider; and a 33 percent interest in SDN Limited, a digital multiplex operator.

Soon after deciding to sell the ITV licenses, UNM made another important decision to sell off its remaining newspaper interests in order to focus fully on business publishing and services. In November 2000 the Express Newspapers unit was sold to the Northern & Shell Group for £125 million. This brought the total for the year's disposals to £3.2 billion. To emphasize the shift in focus the company changed its name to United Business Media plc. Of the proceeds, portions were earmarked for debt reduction and future acquisitions, with £1.25 billion returned to shareholders in April 2001.

EMERGENCE OF UNITED BUSINESS MEDIA

UBM emerged from the whirlwind of activities in 2000 as a major player in professional media, news distribution, and market research. The balance of operations had shifted significantly toward the United States, with

75 percent of operating profit now originating in North America. The U.S. focus was enhanced with the completion of two major acquisitions in 2001: the June purchase of Allison-Fisher International, Inc., for $45 million and the August buyout of Roper Starch Worldwide LLC for $88 million. Based in Detroit, Michigan, Allison-Fisher was the leading supplier of syndicated market research for the automotive industry. Roper Starch, based in New York City, was a leading U.S. consumer market research firm. It was merged with Audit & Surveys Worldwide to form RoperASW. UBM also offered to acquire MediaLink Worldwide Inc., a New York company specializing in video news releases, but was rebuffed.

Unfortunately, the UBM era got off to a rough start thanks to the economic downturn that began in 2001. Magazine publishers were hit hard as companies sharply cut back on their advertising, and the high-tech oriented CMP Media suffered a stiffer blow than most (because of the tech stock implosion) and had to endure a 26 percent drop in ad pages during 2001. To stem losses and cut operating costs, the workforce was slashed, with 1,400 jobs shed during the year. Operating profits from continuing businesses fell 50 percent over the previous year and stood at £81.1 million. Including restructuring and other charges that totaled £448.9 million, UBM reported a pretax loss of £541.2 million. The operating environment continued to be a rough one in 2002, leading the company to announce the elimination of a further 500 positions, with large reductions at CMP Media and PR Newswire. The latter was suffering from a serious downturn in the volume of press releases because of the economic sluggishness; the severe drop in mergers, acquisitions, and initial public offers; and the fallout from the wave of corporate scandals, which led companies to be more publicity-averse than usual. As UBM awaited a turnaround in the advertising market, Hampel retired as chairman in October 2002, with longtime board member Geoff Unwin assuming his position.

IMPROVING ECONOMIC CLIMATE

In the later months of 2003, UBM began to reap the benefits of improvements in the economic climate for its major markets. As a result, the firm's operating profits for the year jumped more than 53 percent over the previous year's figure. Cost-cutting efforts over the previous few years had also paid off in improved cash flow. A healthy amount of cash on hand, coupled with access to credit lines, enabled UBM to build up its core B2B media operations, particularly in its key sectors, which included technology, health care, and construction.

In July 2003, for instance, the company acquired Aprovia UK for £86.6 million, gaining the Builder Group, a publisher and event organizer specializing in the U.K. construction industry, and Barbour Index, an information services provider serving professionals in the U.K. construction and health and safety sectors. This new growth spurt also led to the creation of a unit called CMPMedica, which encompassed drug information, patient education, and pharmaceutical marketing solutions businesses in Europe and Asia. The core of this unit was built from the 2004 acquisition of MediMedia's European and Asian operations for EUR 299.9 million.

In September 2004 Hollick announced his intention to retire the following spring. Later in the year, David Levin was named Hollick's successor as CEO. Levin had previously headed Symbian Limited, a mobile phone software licensing company, and had an earlier stint at the international business publisher Euromoney Institutional Investor. In the early months of 2005, before the handover occurred, Hollick placed NOP World, UBM's market research arm, on the auction block. Soon after Levin came onboard, UBM completed the sale of NOP to the German firm GfK AG for £383 million.

Also in 2005, UBM sold its stakes in both Channel 5 and SDN, leaving it with only one remaining television holding: its 20 percent stake in Independent Television News. Part of the proceeds from the divestments was returned to shareholders via a special dividend totaling £298 million. The company spent an additional £250 million buying back its own shares and bonds.

FOCUSING ON B2B COMMUNITIES

Levin thus essentially began his leadership tenure in charge of a company focused on B2B print and online publishing and events, headed by the CMP businesses, and news distribution, headed by PR Newswire. He then centered the company on the creation of B2B communities of shared interests, such as health care and construction, bringing together buyers and sellers in print, online, at events, and through information products and services. Acquisitions were a central avenue for growth, and in 2006 more than a dozen modest, bolt-on acquisitions were completed, with a particular emphasis on gaining online products and services to lessen UBM's dependence on print publications.

The company pursued larger deals as well, such as the July 2006 purchase of U.S.-based Commonwealth Business Media, Inc., for $152 million. UBM thus gained the leading provider of information to the global trade and transportation industry. Commonwealth, which later evolved into a unit called UBM Global Trade, was involved in print publishing, including the *Journal of Commerce*, and organizing exhibitions and other events but generated more than 60 percent of its revenues from online products and proprietary databases.

Because of the acquisition of Commonwealth and other overseas entities, along with the divestments of numerous U.K. assets, UBM by 2008 was generating 85 percent of its revenues outside the United Kingdom. To avoid certain complexities and burdens of the U.K. tax code, particularly in relation to bringing earnings back to the United Kingdom from overseas operations, UBM that year restructured under a newly created Jersey-based holding company, United Business Media Limited, while also setting up its tax residence in Ireland. UBM retained its listing on the London Stock Exchange, and its main office stayed in London.

Between 2007 and 2009, UBM completed about three dozen acquisitions, all of a modest variety. These deals further lessened the company's dependence on print publications, placing it on a path toward generating less than 15 percent of its revenues from an ever-shrinking number of magazine titles by the end of 2010. At the same time, UBM targeted emerging markets as a key growth area, both organically derived and acquisition-based. By 2009 China, India, and Brazil contributed nearly 14 percent of overall revenues and more than 20 percent of operating profits. That year, profits took a hit both from the global economic downturn and from a £153 million impairment charge to write down the value of several units with a heavy concentration of print titles, including CMPMedica and UBM Global Trade. The group thus reported an operating loss of £25.8 million ($40.5 million) for 2009, while revenues fell 4 percent to £847.6 million ($1.33 billion).

Andreas Loizou
Updated, David E. Salamie

PRINCIPAL SUBSIDIARIES

CMP Asia Limited (Hong Kong); CMPMedica Asia Pte Limited (Singapore); CNW Group Limited (Canada; 50%); Commonwealth Business Media, Inc. (USA); Maypond Holdings Limited (Ireland); Medizinische Medien Informations GmbH (Germany); PR Newswire Association, LLC (USA); PR Newswire Europe Limited; Société d'Editions Scientifiques et Culturelles SA (France); UBMi B.V. (Netherlands); UBM Information Limited; United Business Media; United Business Media Finance, Inc. (USA); United Business Media Finance Sarl (Luxembourg); United Business Media Group

Limited; United Business Media, LLC (USA); United Finance Limited; Vidal S.A. (France); Wenport Limited (Ireland).

PRINCIPAL DIVISIONS

B2B Communities; B2B Distribution, Monitoring and Targeting.

PRINCIPAL COMPETITORS

Emap International Limited; International Data Group, Inc.; The Nielsen Company B.V.; OneSource Information Services, Inc.; Pearson plc; Reed Elsevier Group plc.

FURTHER READING

Burt, Tim, "UBM to Hand Shareholders £300m from NOP Sale," *Financial Times*, April 16, 2005, p. 4.

Burt, Tim, and Maija Pesola, "David Levin Named UBM Chief," *Financial Times*, December 17, 2004, p. 22.

Davidson, Andrew, "Lord Stevens," *Management Today*, March 1995, pp. 53–54, 56.

Edgecliffe-Johnson, Andrew, "UBM Plans Tax Move to Ireland," *Financial Times*, April 29, 2008, p. 21.

Grande, Carlos, "Hollick the Time Lord Awaits Finest Hour," *Financial Times*, December 27, 2002, p. 18.

Harding, James, and Ashling O'Connor, "Failed Merger Leads to a Scattering of the Assets," *Financial Times*, July 22, 2000, p. 14.

Harverson, Patrick, and Raymond Snoddy, "Express in £3Bn Merger Deal with TV Group MAI," *Financial Times*, February 9, 1996, p. 1.

Isaac, Debra, "The News at United," *Management Today*, July 1985, pp. 42+.

Kirchgaessner, Stephanie, and Friederike Tiesenhausen Cave, "UBM in EUR 283m Medical Publishing Expansion," *Financial Times*, June 2, 2004, p. 22.

McCall, Margo, "UBM Remains Hot on Acquisition Trail," *Tradeshow Week*, March 13, 2006, pp. 1, 6.

Newman, Cathy, "United Sells Regional Titles for £450m," *Financial Times*, February 28, 1998, p. 18.

Rich, Motoko, "United's Swift Move Wins Battle of Blenheim," *Financial Times*, October 16, 1996, p. 30.

Schofield, Guy, *The Men That Carry the News: A History of United Newspapers Limited*, London: Cranford Press, 1975, 201 p.

Snoddy, Raymond, "Lord Stevens Looks to a Richer Future," *Financial Times*, April 10, 1995, p. 10.

Taylor, A. J. P., "Lloyd George: Rise and Fall," in *Essays in English History*, London: Hamish Hamilton, 1976.

Tricks, Henry, and Clay Harris, "Record Breaker Bows Out of Public Eye," *Financial Times*, September 4, 2004, p. 2.

Wray, Richard, and Mark Sweney, "Favourable Tax Deal Helps UBM in 'Brutal' Year for Media Firms," *Guardian* (London), March 6, 2010, p. 34.

United States Steel Corporation

600 Grant Street
Pittsburgh, Pennsylvania 15219
U.S.A.
Telephone: (412) 433-1121
Toll Free: (866) 433-4801
Fax: (412) 433-5733
Web site: http://www.ussteel.com

Public Company
Incorporated: 1901
Employees: 49,000
Sales: $23.75 billion (2008)
Stock Exchanges: New York
Ticker Symbol: X
NAICS: 331513 Steel Foundries (Except Investment);
331111 Iron and Steel Mills; 331210 Iron and Steel
Pipe and Tube Manufacturing from Purchased Steel;
213114 Support Activities for Metal Mining;
212112 Bituminous Coal Underground Mining;
237210 Land Subdivision; 541330 Engineering
Services; 324199 All Other Petroleum and Coal
Products; 541611 Administrative Management and
General Management Consulting Services

■ ■ ■

United States Steel Corporation (U.S. Steel) is the largest integrated steel company in the United States. U.S.
Steel, with major production operations in North
America and Europe, supplies its own iron ore and coke
to make steel, boasting an annual production capacity of
31.7 million net tons of raw steel. The company operates through three segments: flat-rolled products, U.S.
Steel Europe, and tubular products, serving the automotive, container, construction, and appliance markets.

STEEL INTERESTS COME
TOGETHER: 1873–1900

The origin of United States Steel Corporation (U.S.
Steel) is virtually an early history of the steel industry in
the United States, which in turn is closely linked to the
name of Andrew Carnegie. The quintessential 19th-
century self-made man, Carnegie began as a bobbin boy
in a cotton mill, made a stake in the railroad business,
and, in 1864, started to invest in the iron industry. In
1873 he began to establish steel plants using the Bessemer steelmaking process. A ruthless competitor, he led
his Carnegie Steel Company to be the largest domestic
steelmaker by the end of the century. In 1897 Carnegie
appointed Charles M. Schwab, a brilliant, diplomatic
veteran of the steel industry who had worked his way up
through the Carnegie organization, as president of Carnegie Steel.

At about the same time, prominent financier John
Pierpont Morgan became a major participant in the
steel industry as a result of his organization of the
Federal Steel Company in 1898. Morgan's personal
representative in the steel business was Elbert Henry
Gary, a lawyer, former judge, and director of Illinois
Steel Company, one of the several steel companies co-
opted into Federal Steel, of which Gary was made
president. Carnegie, Schwab, Morgan, and Gary were
the key participants in the organization of U.S. Steel.

By 1900 the demand for steel was at peak levels, and Morgan's ambition was to dominate this market by creating a centralized combine, or trust. He was encouraged in this by rumors of Carnegie's intention to retire from business. U.S. President William McKinley was known to approve of business consolidations, and his support limited the risk of government antitrust claims in the face of a steel industry combination. In December 1900 Morgan attended a now-legendary dinner at New York's University Club. During the course of the evening Schwab gave a speech that set forth the outlines of a steel trust, the nucleus of which would be the Carnegie and Morgan steel enterprises, together with a number of other smaller steel, mining, and shipping concerns.

With Schwab and Gary as intermediaries between Carnegie and Morgan, negotiations were concluded by early February 1901 for Carnegie to sell his steel interests for about $492 million in bonds and stock of the new company. The organization plan was largely executed by Gary, with Morgan arranging the financing. On February 25, 1901, United States Steel Corporation was incorporated with an authorized capitalization of $1.4 billion, the first billion-dollar corporation in history. The 10 companies that were merged to form U.S. Steel were American Bridge Company, American Sheet Steel Company, American Steel Hoop Company, American Steel & Wire Company, American Tin Plate Company, Carnegie Steel Company, Federal Steel Company, Lake Superior Consolidated Iron Mines, National Steel Company, and National Tube Company.

EARLY YEARS OF U.S. STEEL

At Morgan's urging Schwab became president of U.S. Steel, with Gary as chairman of the board of directors and of the executive committee. Two such strong personalities, however, could not easily share power. In

1903 Schwab resigned and soon took control of Bethlehem Steel Corporation, which he eventually built into the second-largest steel producer in the country. Gary stayed on as, in effect, chief executive officer to lead U.S. Steel and to dominate its policies until his death in August 1927.

His stated goal for U.S. Steel was not to create a monopoly but to sustain trade and foster competition by competing on a basis of efficiency and price. Steel prices did drop significantly in the years after the company began. Because of competition, U.S. Steel's market share of U.S. steel production dropped steadily over the years from about 66 percent in 1901 to about 33 percent from the 1930s to the 1950s.

U.S. Steel's history is notable for continual acquisitions, divestitures, consolidations, reorganizations, and labor disputes. In 1901 U.S. Steel acquired the Bessemer Steamship company, a shipping concern engaged in iron-ore traffic on the Great Lakes. Shelby Steel Tube Company was purchased in 1901, Union Steel Company in 1903, and Clairton Steel Company in 1904. A number of other, smaller acquisitions were made in those early years. In 1906 U.S. Steel began construction on a large, new steel plant on Lake Michigan together with a model city designed primarily for its employees. The new town was named Gary, Indiana, and was substantially completed by 1911. A major acquisition in 1907 was that of Tennessee Coal, Iron and Railroad Company, the largest steel producer in the South. A presence in the West was established with the purchase of Columbia Steel Company in 1910. In addition to steel manufacture, U.S. Steel also maintained large coal-mining operations in western Pennsylvania. These operations were based on former properties of H.C. Frick Coke Company, which included some of Carnegie's coal properties and which became a part of U.S. Steel when it was formed in 1901. The coal produced by these mines was used to fuel U.S. Steel's operations.

U.S. STEEL'S FIRST BRUSH WITH ORGANIZED LABOR: 1919

The 12-hour workday, standard in industry during U.S. Steel's early years, was a major labor issue. U.S. Steel's workers originally were unorganized, and Gary was a staunch enemy of unionization, the closed shop, and collective bargaining. He took a leading role among businessmen, however, by calling in 1911 for the abolition of the 12-hour workday. Little was actually done, however, and a general strike was called against the steel industry in 1919. The strike failed and was abandoned

KEY DATES

1873: Andrew Carnegie founds Carnegie Steel Company.

1898: J. P. Morgan founds Federal Steel Company.

1901: Ten steel companies, including Carnegie and Federal, merge to form United States Steel Corporation.

1911: Antitrust charges are brought against U.S. Steel.

1915: U.S. Steel is cleared of antitrust charges.

1937: U.S. Steel signs a contract with the Steel Workers Organizing Committee, the predecessor of the United Steel Workers of America.

1982: U.S. Steel acquires Marathon Oil Company.

1991: A restructuring renames U.S. Steel USX and creates two tracking stocks: USX-U.S. Steel Group and USX-Marathon Group.

2002: USX is broken into independent companies: United States Steel Corporation and Marathon Oil.

2003: U.S. Steel acquires National Steel Corp. for $1.05 billion.

2007: U.S. Steel spends $3.1 billion to purchase Lone Star Steel and Stelco.

in 1920. The 12-hour workday eventually was abolished, and in 1937 U.S. Steel signed a contract with the Steel Workers Organizing Committee, which in 1942 became the United Steelworkers of America. U.S. Steel's labor relations were historically adversarial, characterized by divisive negotiations, often bitter strikes, and settlements that were sometimes economically disastrous for the company and, in the long run, for its employees.

The U.S. government's tolerant view of big corporations ended with the administration of President Theodore Roosevelt. On Roosevelt's instructions, an antitrust investigation of U.S. Steel was begun in 1905. Gary cooperated with the investigation, but the final report to President William Howard Taft in 1911 led to a monopoly charge against U.S. Steel in the U.S. Circuit Court of Appeals. This court's 1915 decision unanimously absolved U.S. Steel from the monopoly charge and largely vindicated Gary's claim that U.S. Steel was designed to be competitive rather than a monopolistic trust.

ROBUST EXPANSION THROUGH TWO WORLD WARS

U.S. Steel's business boomed during World War I with sales more than doubling between 1915 and 1918 and remaining strong at about $2 billion annually through the 1920s. Gary's personal domination of U.S. Steel ended with his death in 1927. J. P. Morgan Jr. became chairman of the board of directors from 1927 to 1932, but during this period U.S. Steel essentially was under the leadership of Myron C. Taylor, chairman of the finance committee from 1927 to 1934 and chairman of the board from 1932 until his resignation in 1938. Taylor brought about extensive changes in U.S. Steel's makeup. Numerous obsolete plants were closed, others were modernized, and a new plant was added with total capital expenditures of more than $500 million. By the end of Taylor's tenure, about three-quarters of U.S. Steel's products were different or were made differently and more efficiently than they had been in 1927, with the principal realignment being the change from heavy steel for capital goods to lighter steel for consumer goods.

After Taylor's resignation in 1938, Edward R. Stettinius Jr. served as chairman of the board until he left in 1940 to undertake government service and eventually to become secretary of state. Benjamin F. Fairless, an important figure in U.S. Steel history, became president in 1938, and Irving S. Olds succeeded Stettinius as chairman of the board in 1940. Olds served as chairman until 1952, when he was succeeded in that office by Fairless.

During this period U.S. Steel's business recovered from its Depression slump, buoyed by the enormous demand for steel products generated by World War II and the postwar economic boom. Revenues more than quintupled from $611 million in 1938 to more than $3.5 billion in 1951. U.S. Steel was present in every geographical market in the United States except the East, so in 1949 it announced plans to build a large integrated steel plant in Pennsylvania on the Delaware River to be known as the Fairless Works. This plant, operational in 1952, was intended to compete with Bethlehem Steel for the eastern market and to take advantage of ocean shipment of iron ore from U.S. Steel's large ore reserves in Venezuela.

POST-WORLD WAR II REORGANIZATION

In 1951 a change intended to simplify the structure of United States Steel Corporation took place when a single company was formed from its four major operational subsidiaries. This reorganization, completed in 1953, created a tightly knit, more efficient organizational structure in place of the former aggregate of semi-independent units. In 1953 Clifford F. Hood was appointed president and chief operating officer, sharing overall responsibility for the company with Board Chairman Fairless and Enders W. Voorhees, who continued as chairman of the finance committee.

Fairless's tenure as chairman of the board included one of the longest strikes in U.S. Steel's history, resulting from the company's refusal to allow substantial wage increases and tighter closed-shop rules. Just before the strike was to begin in April 1952, President Harry S. Truman seized the company's properties in order to ensure steel production for the Korean War. This unusual action was declared unconstitutional by the U.S. Supreme Court in June 1952. An industry-wide strike ensued that was settled in August, ending a unique episode in U.S. Steel's labor history. A more productive occurrence was the groundbreaking in 1953 for the building of a new research center near Pittsburgh. Fairless retired in May 1955 and was succeeded by Roger M. Blough as chairman of the board and chief executive officer.

Due to improved administrative, operating, and plant efficiencies, U.S. Steel set a postwar record for profitability in 1955, although market share continued to decline to around 30 percent. In 1958 a further corporate simplification took place when wholly owned subsidiary Universal Atlas Cement Company was merged into U.S. Steel as an operating division, as were the Union Supply Company and Homewood Stores Company subsidiaries. Profits were being squeezed between rising operating costs and relatively stable prices, and in April 1962 U.S. Steel unexpectedly announced an across-the-board price increase that triggered a storm of criticism, including an angry protest to Blough from U.S. President John F. Kennedy.

Within a week U.S. Steel was forced to rescind the price increase, using the face-saving excuse that other steel companies had not agreed to support the new price level. This situation resulted from U.S. Steel's continued decline in market share to about 25 percent in 1961, together with deteriorating profitability, in part caused by excessive capital spending in relation to market volume.

DECLINE AND CONSOLIDATION: 1960–70

In response to its difficulties, U.S. Steel announced in 1963 a further reorganization and centralization of its steel divisions and sales operations in order to concentrate management resources to a greater extent on

sales and consumer services. In 1964 U.S. Steel created a new chemicals division called Pittsburgh Chemical Company. Effective in 1966 United States Steel Corporation was reincorporated in Delaware to take advantage of that state's more flexible corporation laws.

In 1967 Edwin H. Gott became president and chief operating officer, and in 1969 he succeeded Blough as chairman of the board and CEO. Edgar B. Speer, a veteran steel man, moved up to the presidency. In 1973 Gott retired and Speer assumed his duties as chairman and CEO. Significantly, Speer immediately announced plans to expand U.S. Steel's diversification into nonsteel businesses. Prospects for long-term growth in steel were fading rapidly because of rising costs, competitive pricing, and foreign competition.

During Speer's tenure, U.S. Steel closed or sold a variety of facilities and businesses in steel, cement, fabricating, home building, plastics, and mining. Capital expenditure, much of it for environmental purposes, remained high. There was little significant diversification, however. In 1979 U.S. Steel lost $293 million. Also that year, former President David M. Roderick became chairman and CEO. He announced a major liquidation of unprofitable steel operations and increased efforts to diversify. In 1979, 13 steel facilities were closed with an $809 million write-off. Universal Atlas Cement, once the United States' largest cement company, was sold, and various real estate, timber, and mineral properties were leased or sold.

The long-promised diversification move came in 1982 with United States Steel Corporation's $6.2 billion acquisition of Marathon Oil Company, a major integrated energy company with vast reserves of oil and gas. Marathon's revenues were about the same as those of U.S. Steel. Thus, the company's size was doubled, with steel's contribution to sales dropping to about 40 percent.

MARATHON OIL'S LEGACY

Marathon had been incorporated on August 1, 1887, as Ohio Oil Company by Ohio oil driller Henry Ernst and four of his fellow oil men, primarily in order to compete with Standard Oil Company. Ohio Oil quickly became the largest producer of crude oil in Ohio and was bought out by Standard Oil in 1889. When Standard was broken up on antitrust grounds by the U.S. government in 1911, Ohio Oil again became an independent company with veteran oilman James Donnell as president. Under Donnell and his successors, Ohio Oil grew into an international integrated oil and gas company with large energy resources and extensive exploratory and retail sales operations. Its name was changed to Marathon Oil Company in 1962.

U.S. Steel continued to improve the efficiency and profitability of its steel operations with the 1983 closing of part or all of 20 obsolete plants. By 1985 Roderick had shut down more than 150 facilities and reduced steelmaking capacity by more than 30 percent. He cut 54 percent of white-collar jobs, laid off about 100,000 production workers, and sold $3 billion in assets. U.S. Steel continued its diversification program in February 1986 with the $3.6 billion acquisition of Texas Oil & Gas Corporation. Founded in 1955 as Tex-Star Oil & Gas Corporation, the company is engaged primarily in the domestic production, gathering, and transportation of natural gas. In July 1986 United States Steel Corporation changed its name to USX Corporation to reflect the company's diversification.

In October 1986 corporate raider Carl Icahn threatened to make a $7.1 billion offer for USX after purchasing about 29 million USX shares. Roderick fought off the takeover attempt by borrowing $3.4 billion to pay off company debts with the provision that the loan would be called in the event of a takeover. Icahn gave up his attempt in January 1987 but kept his USX shares and began a long program of urging USX management to spin off or sell its underperforming steel business. In 1987 Roderick shut down about one-quarter of USX's raw steelmaking capacity, but by 1988 U.S. Steel, the steel division of USX, had become the most efficient producer of steel in the world.

RESTRUCTURING: 1991

In May 1989 Roderick retired and was succeeded as chairman and CEO by Charles A. Corry, a veteran of the USX restructuring. In October 1989 Corry announced a plan to sell some of Texas Oil & Gas's energy reserves in order to pay off debt and implement a large stock buyback. In June 1990 the company stated that it would consolidate Texas Oil's operations with Marathon Oil in order to cut costs. On January 31, 1991, Icahn won his long battle to have USX restructured when the company announced that it would recapitalize by issuing a separate class of stock for its U.S. Steel subsidiary although both businesses, energy and steel, would remain part of USX. In May 1991 USX shareholders approved the plan. Common shares of USX Corporation began trading as USX-Marathon Group, and new common shares of USX-U.S. Steel Group were issued. In May 1992 USX shareholders approved the creation of a third common share, USX-Delhi Group, which reflected the performance of the Delhi Gas Pipeline Corporation and related companies engaged in the gathering, processing, and transporting of natural gas.

In 1991 the two stocks rose 28 percent and the steel shares actually outperformed the oil. Several factors influenced the positive performance of the company and its stock. Marathon, unlike many of its competitors, had prepared for growth in the 1990s. The 1991 discovery of a potentially large oilfield in Tunisia and two new Gulf of Mexico strikes had the early 1990s looking promising for USX-Marathon. The addition of its East Brae field in the North Sea in 1995 held promise of boosting crude output by 25,000 barrels per day from about 200,000 barrels per day. In addition, while other oil companies reduced their exploration budgets, USX-Marathon increased its capital and exploration budget by almost one-third.

In the early 1990s, USX-U.S. Steel reduced its fixed costs and boosted productivity by cutting its raw steel capacity in half, closing four of its seven plants and reducing its total number of employees by 56 percent between 1983 and 1990. From 1991 to 1992 alone U.S. Steel reduced its operating capability by three million tons to 13.5 tons. The drastic cuts paid off for U.S. Steel. By 1993 the company was the lowest-cost fully integrated steel producer in the United States.

U.S. Steel had also worked to bring its quality up to par with foreign competitors, especially the Japanese, by forging joint ventures with such companies as Japan's Kobe Steel and Korea's Pohang Iron and Steel Co. The company also spent $1.5 billion in the early 1990s to upgrade its facilities to industry benchmark standards.

As the decade proceeded, however, these measures proved insufficient to remedy USX's many problems. Internationally, the industry suffered from production that exceeded demand. Domestically, the traditional integrated steel companies, including USX, bore the crushing burden of "legacy costs," the pension and health benefits that union contracts obligated them to pay to the thousands of retired and laid-off employees that had resulted from the restructurings of the previous decades.

THREAT FROM FOREIGN PRODUCERS: 1992–98

Facing this difficult environment, USX cooperated with the rest of the industry in bringing "antidumping" trade suits against foreign producers. In 1992 and 1998, the industry accused foreign companies of selling steel in the United States at prices below those they sold it for at home. If successful, these actions would cause the U.S. government to impose prohibitive tariffs on foreign steel, thus eliminating foreign competition. These efforts were not, however, initially successful. Only in 2001 did the industry succeed in invoking such antidumping penalties.

Internally, the company continued to suffer the extreme cyclical nature of the industry, moving into and out of profitability during the decade. By 1998 USX cut production at its Fairless Works and planned to spend $10 million to encourage 540 management and salaried employees to retire early.

In 1997 USX, the largest U.S. steel producer but only the 11th largest globally, began a search for a company or companies that would allow it to become a strong international competitor. The search extended over several continents and three years. In October 2000, USX announced the acquisition of a nearly bankrupt former communist steelmaker in the Slovak Republic. U.S. Steel-Kosice, as the unit was renamed, was expected to sell steel to automobile makers in much of Eastern Europe.

SPLIT FROM MARATHON OIL: 2002

The tracking stock structure, in which USX-Marathon and USX-U.S. Steel Group remained units of a single parent but traded separately on the stock exchange, came under criticism in 1999. The oil industry had been suffering a down cycle, and several large companies had merged. The tracking stock arrangement made Marathon an unattractive acquisition target because payment for its acquisition would be taxable to USX unless a purchaser bought the entire company, an unlikely happening. The existence of the Marathon unit also made it more difficult for the U.S. Steel unit to seek acquisitions or acquirers. Marathon Oil and the United States Steel Corporation became independent companies on January 1, 2002.

As it entered the new century, United States Steel reclaimed its original name and identity as an integrated steel manufacturer. The environment in which it operated, however, was still an exceedingly difficult one. At the end of 2001 it took a $35 million to $45 million charge to close most operations at its Fairless Works.

By the beginning of 2002, U.S. Steel proposed a major reorganization of the entire U.S. integrated industry. It began discussing a merger with bankrupt Bethlehem Steel. The company quickly followed this move with a more comprehensive proposal that all integrated companies consolidate in order to improve their efficiency and compete better with foreign producers and the domestic minimills that made steel by less costly methods.

The prospects for such a consolidation were not good. As prerequisites, the industry, represented by U.S. Steel, demanded that the government establish very high barriers to protect it from foreign competition. They also asked that the government take over responsibility for paying the industry's legacy costs. Even if these conditions were met, the consolidation would undoubtedly meet strong protests by foreign governments for violations of international trade agreements, including World Trade Organization rules. At the beginning of the 21st century, the future of U.S. Steel and of the rest of the U.S. integrated steel industry appeared cloudy.

MERGERS RESHAPE THE STEEL INDUSTRY: 2003–07

U.S. Steel's prospects brightened as the decade progressed, however, precisely because a period of consolidation swept through the industry, leaving the steel giant in a more powerful position than it occupied previously. The company's rise began under the leadership of John P. Surma, a former Price Waterhouse partner and Marathon Oil executive who was named president of U.S. Steel in 2003 and CEO the following year. In 2003, as Surma rose to power, U.S. Steel acquired bankrupt National Steel Corp., beating out rival AK Steel to purchase the struggling firm for $1.05 billion. The acquisition added seven million tons of steelmaking capacity and strengthened U.S. Steel's position in the higher profit margin markets for automotive, container, and construction markets. It also enabled the company to overtake International Steel Group, which had purchased Bethlehem Steel earlier in the year, as the nation's largest steel producer.

Back at the top of its industry, the company slimmed down even as it added National Steel's integrated facilities to its operations. Surma signed new labor contracts that reduced the company's domestic payroll by 27 percent, part of $320 million in annual operating costs that the company eliminated between 2002 and 2004.

Mergers continued to represent the dominant theme of the steel industry as the years passed. The largest of the decade occurred in 2006, when Mittal Steel Co., which had acquired International Steel Group in 2005, merged with Arcelor S.A. to form ArcelorMittal, the world's largest steel company. Surma remained active on the acquisition front during the period, spending $2.1 billion to acquire Lone Star Steel and $1 billion to acquire Canada-based Stelco in 2007. The wave of mergers concentrated power, leaving the three largest steel companies responsible for nearly 70 percent of the output in most product lines. "There has been a tremendous amount of consolidation after years of underinvestment in this industry," an analyst observed in the May 9, 2008 issue of *Investor's Business Daily*. "This makes it easier to pass along costs to customers even in difficult economic times."

Difficult economic times loomed ahead as U.S. Steel absorbed the assets acquired in the Lone Star and

Stelco transactions. A global economic crisis threatened to end the stellar financial record posted by Surma, who had increased U.S. Steel's revenues from $13.9 billion in 2004 to $23.7 billion by 2008. Uncertainty and business cycles were nothing new to U.S. Steel, however, putting the company in its accustomed position of weathering a storm and preparing itself for a return to more salubrious economic conditions.

Bernard A. Block
Updated, Anne L. Potter; Jeffrey L. Covell

PRINCIPAL SUBSIDIARIES

Chrome Deposit Corporation; Double Eagle Steel Coating Company; Essex Minerals Company; Stelco Holding Company; Texas & Northern Railway Company; Birmingham Southern Railroad Company; U.S. Steel Canada Inc.; HLE Mining GP Inc.; U.S. Steel China, LLC; U.S. Steel Europe B.V.; Lone Star Brazil Holdings 1 Ltda.; United States Steel Credit Corporation; United States Steel Export Company de Mexico, S.R.L. de C.V.; United States Steel International, Inc.; Chicago Lakeside Development, LLC; USX International Sales Company, Inc.; USS Tubular Processing, Inc.

PRINCIPAL OPERATING UNITS

Flat-rolled Products; U.S. Steel Europe; Tubular Products.

PRINCIPAL COMPETITORS

AK Steel Holding Corporation; ArcelorMittal; Nucor Corporation.

FURTHER READING

Adams, Chris, "Ailing Steel Industry Launches a Battle Against Imports," *Wall Street Journal*, October 1, 1998, p. B4.

Cooper, Helene, "Move to Impose Steel Duties May Fail," *Wall Street Journal*, February 16, 1999, p. A24.

Cotter, Arundel, *The Authentic History of the United States Steel Corporation*, New York: Moody Magazine and Book Co., 1916.

Crandall, Robert W., "Whistling Past Big Steel's Graveyard," *Wall Street Journal*, March 19, 1999, p. A18.

"Feds Are Asked to Support a Big Steel Combination," *Mergers and Acquisitions*, January 2002, pp. 14–15.

Fisher, Douglas A., *Steel Serves the Nation, 1901–1951*, Pittsburgh: United States Steel Corporation, 1951.

Jackson, Stanley, *J. P. Morgan*, New York: Stein and Day, 1983.

Kelly, Brad, "United States Steel Corp.; Pittsburgh, Pennsylvania; Big Steel Producer Benefits from High Prices and Strong Demand," *Investor's Business Daily*, May 9, 2008, p. A9.

Matthews, Robert Guy, "A Big Stick: The U.S. Won't Take 'No' for an Answer at Paris Steel Summit," *Wall Street Journal*, December 14, 2001, p. A1.

Vranken Pommery Monopole S.A.

———————————— ■ ————————————

BP 1049
5 Pl. du General Gouraud
Reims, F-51689 Cedex 2
France
Telephone: (+33 03) 26 61 62 63
Fax: (+33 03) 26 61 63 88
Web site: http://www.vranken.net

Public Company
Founded: 1976
Incorporated: 1988 as Financière Vranken
Employees: 628
Sales: EUR 267.3 million ($373 million) (2009)
Stock Exchanges: Euronext Paris Euronext Brussels
Ticker Symbol: 0062796 (VRAP)
NAICS: 312130 Wineries

■ ■ ■

Vranken Pommery Monopole S.A. is the second-largest producer of champagne, behind the LVMH luxury products group, with sales of nearly 20 million bottles per year. The company owns 265 hectares of vineyards in the Champagne region of France. Vranken Pommery Monopole controls a number of major champagne brands and their cellars and production facilities. The group's brands include Pommery, which accounts for one-third of its sales; Heidsieck & Cie, which adds nearly 25 percent; and Charles Lafitte, for more than 10 percent. Vranken, named after the company's founder, adds nearly 18 percent to sales. These brands are marketed and distributed both in France and for the

export market, which accounts for nearly half of the group's annual revenues. In addition, Vranken Pommery Monopole produces and distributes a range of smaller brands for the French market.

Champagne sales remain the most important part of Vranken Pommery Monopole's operations, at more than 94 percent of its sales of EUR 267 million ($373 million) in 2009. The company also owns the high-end Porto brands, Rozès and São Pedro, in Portugal. Vranken Pommery Monopole also oversees Domains Listel, a major producer of rosé wines, including more than 2,000 hectares of vineyards in France's Provence region. Vranken Pommery Monopole is listed on the Euronext exchanges in Paris and Brussels. Nearly 71 percent of the company is controlled by founder, CEO and Chairman Paul-François Vranken through his holding company, Compagnie Vranken pour le Haut Commerce.

FOUNDING A MODERN CHAMPAGNE DYNASTY IN 1976

Born in Belgium, Paul-François Vranken's father died when he was still young. Vranken was instead raised by his uncle, who owned a Porsche dealership. Vranken studied law at the University of Liège, while working nights at a service station to support himself. At the same time, through his uncle, Vranken was initiated into the world of high society. These contacts led Vranken to start his career with Belgian drinks group Bass and Charrington. Vranken, just 23 years old, offered to develop that company's small and flagging champagne brand, De Castellane, in exchange for a percentage of the profits. Within two years, Vranken succeeded in boosting De Castellane's sales from next to nothing to 160,000 bottles. Vranken's share of the profits came in the form of a check for FRF 130,000.

This success had also given Vranken a taste for champagne. In 1974, Vranken moved to France, setting up his own business in the Champagne region. Vranken's timing was auspicious. The early 1970s marked a difficult period for the champagne industry, burdened by overproduction during the economic downturn brought on by the oil crisis. For Vranken, however, the period provided opportunity. In 1974, Vranken purchased 10,000 bottles *sur lattes* for FRF 9.5. *Sur lattes* referred to the practice of wine and champagne producers of selling their excess production to third parties, which then took over the finishing of the product, and affixed their own labels to the bottles. The system permitted producers to sell off their excess stock. On the other hand, it also exposed the champagne market to speculation.

In Vranken's case, this speculation paid off. A year after the purchase, champagne prices once again began to rise, and Vranken resold his stock for more than double the purchase price. This new success provided Vranken with the foundation for the creation of his own company, and his own champagne brand, Vranken, in 1976.

Vranken's ambitions went beyond the *sur lattes* market. The entrepreneur became determined to develop and produce his own champagne. To this end, Vranken rented a facility from a winegrower in the

region, and negotiated his first grapes purchase, of two marcs, or enough to produce 7,000 bottles, with an agreement to pay for the grapes only after a year. Using borrowed equipment, Vranken produced his first vintage that year, which he quickly sold. This sale in turn enabled him to negotiate a loan to buy more wine the following year, just as champagne prices had once again begun to soar. In this way, Vranken's young business had generated a profit of more than FRF 1.3 million.

ADDING BRANDS IN THE EIGHTIES

Vranken's true success, however, came through his willingness to break with tradition. In the mid-1970s, champagne growers largely avoided selling their wines through the fast-growing large-scale supermarket groups, preferring the traditional specialized retail channel. Vranken approached two of the largest supermarket groups, Casino and Prisunic, proposing to place his champagnes on their shelves. If other champagne producers treated Vranken as a heretic to tradition, he nonetheless gained first advantage. During the 1980s, Vranken succeeded in placing his champagnes with nearly all of the country's large supermarket groups, as well as the growing number of central purchasing groups.

In order to supply this ever-expanding customer base, Vranken began developing his range of champagne brands, largely targeting the mid-level and lower-end champagne segments. In 1978, Vranken completed his first acquisition, buying Veuve Monnier, a champagne house founded in 1880.

In 1983, Vranken acquired another well-known name, Charles Lafitte & Cie, founded in 1848 by Jean-Baptiste Lafitte. Although based in Cognac, Lafitte had long supplied champagne bottlers with its distilled "esprits de Cognac," used in the production of commercial champagne. Following the acquisition, Vranken used the Lafitte name to introduce a new champagne brand. Lafitte grew into one of Vranken's top-selling champagnes, both in France and internationally.

Vranken received a new sales boost in 1985, when Socadep, one of the largest supermarket buying groups, chose the company to produce its own private-label champagne, starting with an initial order for 300,000 bottles. In that year, Vranken acquired Chateau de Castaignes, located in Les Demoiselles, a hamlet near Reims. The company followed this purchase with the launch of a new champagne brand, Cuvée Demoisselle, that year.

INTERNATIONAL EXTENSION IN
THE NINETIES

Vranken also acquired its first vineyards in 1985, through its purchase of the Charles Collin champagne brand, founded in 1952 by a group of winegrowers in Fontette. This acquisition gave the company control of 18 hectares of highly prized Champagne vineyards.

While champagne remained the heart of Vranken's business, the company began developing a more diversified, and international, business in the 1990s. This process started in 1986 with the purchase of the Quinta monastery in Portugal's Douro valley, along with 184 hectares of vineyards. This allowed the company to launch its own porto brand, São Pedro, that year.

Vranken's international expansion continued in 1988, with a move into Spain's Penedès region where it launched the Senora sparkling wine brand. Vranken then returned home to Belgium in 1989, acquiring the wine and spirits distributor Histoires de Vin, in Liège. In order to provide a structure for the company's growing collection of brands and subsidiaries, Vranken created a new holding company, Financière Vranken, in 1988.

Champagne and the Champagne region nonetheless remained at the core of Vranken's business. In 1987 the company acquired a new house, Champagne Sacotte based in Epernay, adding to its range of brands for the French national distribution market. In the meantime, the champagne sector had begun to feel the effects of a new and deeper crisis, brought on in part by the recession at the beginning of the 1990s. Part of the sector's difficulty, however, stemmed from its overproduction and a rising number of inferior quality champagnes, often produced with grapes from outside the Champagne region. At the same time, wine producers in other regions, including California, Chile, South Africa, and Australia, had made enormous progress in improving the quality of their still and sparkling wines, further exacerbating the difficulties in Champagne.

Their difficulties, however, provided new opportunities for Vranken's own expansion. Vranken completed three major acquisitions, buying Champagne Lallement in 1992, Champagne Barancourt in 1993, and Champagne A. Charbaut & Fils in 1995. These purchases not only added to the group's list of prominent champagne brands, each added to Vranken's vineyard holdings. While Lallement added 10 hectares of all-important pinot noir vineyards, Charbaut gave the group the long-term contract for another 45 hectares. Meanwhile, Barancourt helped boost Vranken among the larger Champagne landowners, with its 93 hectares of vineyards. Vranken also added Barancourt's distribution subsidiary in Germany, and Charbaut's sales operations in the United States. By then, Vranken's production had topped 8.5 million bottles per year, generating revenues of more than FRF 600 million ($100 million).

GOING PUBLIC IN 1998

Through these purchases, Vranken gained the scale to pursue an even larger and more prestigious target. In 1996, the company reached an agreement with Mumm, the champagne subsidiary of Seagram, to acquire Champagne Heidsieck & Cie. Monopole. That company traced its origins back to 1785, when German-born Florens-Louis Heidsieck founded his champagne house. When he died in 1828, this house was taken over by his oldest nephew, Henri-Louis Walbaum Heidsieck and his cousin and brother-in-law Auguste Heidsieck. This business added the Monopole to its name in 1860, in order to distinguish itself from two competing champagne houses, Piper-Heidsieck and Charles Heidsieck, each founded by another one of Florens-Louis Heidsieck's nephews.

The purchase of Heidsieck gave Vranken its first true *grande marque*, as the Champagne region's most prestigious wine labels were known, while adding another 130 hectares of vineyards, and boosting its production by another 1.2 million bottles per year. Heidsieck also gave the group its first significant international sales operations, with a particularly strong position in the U.K. market.

By 1998, Vranken's total production had topped 10 million bottles. In that year, Vranken went public, listing its shares on the Paris Stock Exchange. This listing was followed one year later by a second listing on the Brussels Stock Exchange. Paul-François Vranken nonetheless retained control of the company, and maintained more than 70 percent of the company's shares.

Vranken remained on the lookout for new acquisition candidates. In 1999, the company bought the Germain champagne brand, as well as its stock of 2.5 million bottles. This purchase helped elevate Vranken to an elite group of the top five Champagne producers, alongside Laurent-Perrier. Also in 2009, the company acquired prestigious Maison Rozès and its porto brand in Portugal. In France, the company bought Pressoirs Meneclier, adding another 30 hectares to its vineyard holdings.

VRANKEN POMMERY MONOPOLE
IN 2002

Vranken boosted its international sales and distribution operations, adding a subsidiary in the United Kingdom in 2000, and in Switzerland in 2001. In that year, Vranken, like the rest of the champagne industry, suffered from the aftereffects of the Year 2000 celebrations, which failed to generate the sales companies had anticipated. As a result, the champagne market once again faced an oversupply problem, if only temporarily.

The weakened market was enough, however, to provide a new expansion opportunity for Vranken. In 2002, the company announced that it had agreed with the LVMH luxury products group to acquire Maison de Champagne Pommery & Greno, producers of the world-renowned Pommery champagne brand.

The original company was founded in 1836, but it was not until 1856 that Alexandre Pommery joined as a partner. Pommery died just two years later, leaving his wife, Louise, in charge of the company. The Veuve (widow) Pommery, as she became known, not only took over the business, she was credited with revolutionizing the champagne industry itself. Among her innovations, Pommery was credited with developing and popularizing the less sugary "brut" or dry champagne style, that became highly popular in the United Kingdom, the United States, and ultimately throughout the world. As a result, Pommery became one of the most well-known and highly prized of the Champagne region's *grande marques*. Following its acquisition, Vranken changed its name to Vranken Pommery Monopole S.A.

Vranken Pommery Monopole continued to seek new expansion possibilities as it moved steadily toward the Champagne market's number two position, behind LVMH. The company acquired Champagne Guy Jacopin and its 20 hectares of vineyards in Vertus in 2003. In that year, the company also acquired, through Charles Lafitte, Maison George Goulet, a champagne house founded in 1834. In another acquisition, in partnership with Moët et Chandon, the company added the Bricout and Delbeck champagne brands as well.

NUMBER TWO IN 2010

Vranken Pommery Monopole targeted a move into still wines in the middle of the decade. For this, the group launched a distribution agreement with Vins Listel, a major producer of rosé wines in the south of France. This agreement soon led to the acquisition of Listel by Paul-François Vranken, who instituted a new strategy of raising the quality of Listel's wines into the higher-end categories. By the end of 2009, this process was well underway, leading Vranken to transfer his holding to Vranken Pommery Monopole.

By then, Vranken Pommery Monopole had claimed the number two position among leading Champagne producers, selling more than 20 million bottles in 2006.

The company also developed a number of new brands, including the high-end Diamant par Vranken, launched in 2006, and the small-sized champagne bottle brand POP!, launched in 2005 and marketed toward the young drinkers segment in the United States, the United Kingdom, and elsewhere.

Vranken took steps to expand its international distribution wing around the end of the decade. The company took control of its U.S. distribution in 2007, renaming its subsidiary there Vranken-Pommery America. Also that year, the company created new sales subsidiaries in Japan and Italy. These helped boost the group's champagne exports, which represented half of the company's total champagne sales. Champagne in turn represented nearly 95 percent of the company's total revenues, which neared EUR 286 million in 2008.

Like the rest of the champagne sector, Vranken suffered from the brutal economic downturn, which provoked the most severe global depression since the 1930s at the end of that decade. Nevertheless, Vranken's strong portfolio of both internationally recognized *grandes marques* and well-segmented national brands in France enabled the group to escape the full force of the downturn. By the beginning of 2010, the group outperformed the rest of the industry, which saw sales drop by as much as 45 percent in 2009. Vranken, however, posted a drop in champagne sales of just 6.5 percent, bringing its total sales for the year back to EUR 267.3 million ($373 million). Under the direction of Paul-François Vranken, Vranken Pommery Monopole had become one of the leaders of the modern Champagne industry.

M. L. Cohen

PRINCIPAL SUBSIDIARIES

Champagne Charles Lafitte; Charles Vranken; Pommery S.A.; Domains Listel S.A.; Quinta do Grifo (Portugal); Rozès S.A. (Portugal); Vranken Japan; Vranken Pommery Belgium; Vranken America (USA); Vranken Pommery GmbH (Germany); Vranken Pommery Italia; Vranken Pommery Suisse; Vranken-Pommery Monopole U.K. Ltd.

PRINCIPAL DIVISIONS

Champagne; Porto; Rosé.

PRINCIPAL OPERATING UNITS

Veuve Pommery; Vranken; Hiedsieck & Cie.; Charles Lafitte; Rozès; Listel.

PRINCIPAL COMPETITORS

Pernod Ricard S.A.; Belvedere S.A.; Champagne Moët and Chandon SCS; Moët Hennessy S.N.C.; Rémy Cointreau S.A.; Veuve Clicquot Ponsardin SCS; Boizel Chanoine Champagne S.A.; Laurent-Perrier S.A.; Champagnes P and C Heidsieck S.A.S.

FURTHER READING

"Champagne Sales Hold Up at Vranken-Pommery Monopole," *just-drinks.com*, January 27, 2010.

Franco, Victor, "Paul Vranken, un Belge Qui Fait Trembler Epernay," *L'Expansion*, May 19, 1994.

Héron, Susie Manning, "The Birth of POP!" *Wine Report*, November–December 2005.

Rekik, Catherine, "Le 'Gentleman' Begle a Conquis la Champagne," *Journal Des Finances Hebdo*, September 20, 2008.

Todd, Stuart, "Vranken Pommery to Raise Capital for Acquisition," *just-drinks.com*, December 2, 2009.

"Vranken in EUR20m Vineyard Acquisition," *just-drinks.com*, April 26, 2006.

"Vranken Pommery Envisage des Accords avec des Groupe Etrangers dans le Vin," *Les Echos*, October 19, 2006, p. 23.

"Vranken-Pommery Monopole Sales Drop, Losses Deepen," *just-drinks.com*, September 1, 2009.

"Vranken s'Attend à une Poussée de Ses Ventes à l'Export en 1999," *Les Echos*, May 3, 1999, p. 16.

WE: Women's Entertainment LLC

———————— ■ ————————

11 Penn Plaza, 19th Floor
New York, New York 10001
U.S.A.
Telephone: (212) 324-1300
Web site: http://www.we.tv

*Wholly Owned Subsidiary of Rainbow Media
      Holdings LLC*
Founded: 1997
Employees: 35
NAICS: 515210 Cable and Other Subscription Pro-
      gramming

■ ■ ■

WE: Women's Entertainment LLC operates WE tv, a
cable network that delivers entertaining women's-
focused original programming, syndicated reruns, movies, and specials. Popular original shows have included
The Locator, Bridezillas, Women behind Bars, and the
Single in the City franchise. The network relies heavily
on reality-based programming and unscripted series to
fill its lineup. Launched as Romance Classics by
American Movie Classics in 1997, the network is viewed
by more than 75 million U.S. households.

NICHE NETWORK WITH GOOD
DISTRIBUTION: 1997–2000

In 1992 American Movie Classics (AMC) announced
that it would spin off a new niche programming service
dedicated to classic love stories by early 1994. The new
network would be called Romance Classics. AMC's

move was a strategic response to an anticipated explosion of growth in the cable industry. Thanks to new
digital compression technology, hundreds of channels
would soon be available. Executives at AMC got the
idea to launch Romance Classics from the huge success
of the Sunday afternoon programming block airing on
AMC in the early 1990s. Research showed that the
block, which featured old-fashioned films celebrating the
boy-meets-girl love story, outperformed everything else
on the network.

Romance Classics' launch was postponed at least
three times, including in the fall of 1994 and the
winters of 1995 and 1996. By the summer of 1996,
when AMC announced winter 1997 as the official
launch date, industry pundits were skeptical AMC
would deliver. However, this time AMC was true to its
word. Romance Classics debuted as a 24-hour
commercial-free cable network on January 1, 1997, to
1.8 million homes.

At almost two million households, Romance's
distribution rate was high for a brand-new niche cable
network. Romance was able to achieve this exposure due
to its ownership. Its parent company, Rainbow Media
Holdings, was 75 percent owned by the sixth-largest
cable operator in the United States, Cablevision
Systems. The remaining 25 percent was owned by NBC.
Additionally, Romance was aggressively competitive with
the glut of new networks, extending free subscriptions
to cable operators in a bid for them to sign up. A few
months after launch, Romance struck a deal with satellite companies DirecTV and PrimeStar, extending its
reach to another 4.1 million homes.

In its first several years on the air, Romance's programming subtly shifted focus from the original theme of boy-meets-girl to shows with a more widespread appeal. At launch, movies came directly from the vaults of AMC and were almost exclusively made in the 1940s and 1950s. The schedule featured such classics as *Rebecca, Notorious, An Affair to Remember,* and *The Long Hot Summer,* and a prime-time soap opera from the mid-1960s, *Peyton Place.* As a result, Romance mostly appealed to women whose median age was mid-50. By 1999, 70 percent of the schedule was dated post-1980 in a bid to win over a younger audience. That year, original programming also debuted, including a travel show, *Romance in America,* and a lifestyle show to rival Martha Stewart's, *Colin Cowie's Everyday Elegance.*

Romance gained popularity fairly quickly thanks to lucrative distribution deals and its association with AMC, which had 68 million subscribers. By the fall of 1999 its subscriber count had jumped to 19 million. At the time, Romance was number two in the women's cable market. Its biggest competition was Lifetime, which launched in 1982, and Oxygen, which trailed in third place after launching in 1998. To differentiate itself from the competition and create a distinctive brand, Romance's president, Katie McEnroe, positioned the network as an oasis for women. "Men have timeout in sports. Women want timeout programming for themselves. Women are looking to distress and decompress," McEnroe said in a 1999 *New York Times* article.

By 2000, the network was almost in the black with revenues of $38 million. Nearly all its revenue came from the nine cents per month that cable operators paid per subscriber. That year, Romance reached 23 million homes. Its competitors, Lifetime and Oxygen, had 78 million and 13 million, respectively.

REBRANDING THE NETWORK: 2001–02

One year later, in 2001, Romance reached 37 million households and underwent a complete transformation. The network's programming schedule was completely revamped and Romance was renamed. The new name, WE: Women's Entertainment, was meant to reflect the network's new focus. "Romance sounded more like their mother's channel," McEnroe said in a 2001 *USA Today* article. The network's extreme about-face was prompted by a two-year market research study, which included findings that their target audience was looking for different programming besides the classic romance.

To further differentiate itself from its competition, McEnroe said in a 2001 *USA Today* article: "Oxygen is more news- and service-oriented, Lifetime often programs emotionally dramatic stories, and Romance is about relaxing narrative programming." WE's branding and market position in relation to Lifetime and Oxygen was important to future profits. In the past, the network had hinted it would eventually evolve into an advertising-based revenue model. Its programming needed to appeal to advertisers; its ranking would determine how much it could demand for advertising spots.

In WE's new lineup, vintage tearjerkers were replaced with original series, specials, and films. While still concerned with stress relief and entertainment, shows provided ideas and inspiration for a variety of lifestyle topics, such as entertaining, fashion, and design. The network's film library expanded to include *Peggy Sue Got Married, Soapdish, An Officer and a Gentleman,* and *Desperately Seeking Susan.* Four high-profile spokeswomen—supermodels Cindy Crawford and Rachel Hunter, Academy Award-winning actress Faye Dunaway, and actress/producer Debbie Allen—were recruited to be WE spokeswomen. They also had projects airing on the network.

New series that year included *Style World,* a lifestyle show focused on design around the world, and *Cool Women,* a Debbie Allen show that featured ordinary women doing extraordinary things. In addition, Cindy Crawford hosted a four-part series, *Fashion Flashback,* and Faye Dunaway made her directorial debut with Tennessee Williams's *The Yellow Bird.* In February, the network debuted its first reality show, *Journey Women off the Map,* a show that followed women traveling to exotic places. At the time, industry pundits agreed WE's focus on specialized programming was sound. However, some opined that the brand's new direction was indistinguishable from competitors. John Rash, a senior executive at Interpublic Group, said in a 2001 *Advertis-*

```
╔══════════════════════════════════════════╗
║                                            ║
║            KEY DATES                       ║
║              ──■──                         ║
║                                            ║
║   1997:  American Movie Classics launches  ║
║          Romance Classics to 1.8 million   ║
║          households.                       ║
║   2001:  Romance Classics is re-branded    ║
║          as WE: Women's Entertainment.     ║
║   2002:  Network switches to a traditional ║
║          commercial advertising format.    ║
║   2006:  WE: Women's Entertainment         ║
║          becomes WE tv.                    ║
║   2010:  Network reaches 75 million U.S.   ║
║          households.                       ║
║                                            ║
╚══════════════════════════════════════════╝
```

ing Age article: "[WE] faces significant challenges getting noticed because it's an imitator."

In March 2001 WE had 40 million subscribers and was still commercial-free. However, that month it signed an agreement with Johnson & Johnson (J&J), making it WE's exclusive sponsor. According to the terms of the agreement, J&J would run advertisements before and after shows, and J&J product packaging would carry WE messaging. The agreement extended through the third quarter of 2002, which is when WE planned to switch to a traditional commercial advertising format.

SWITCH TO COMMERCIAL PROGRAMMING: 2002–03

In a bid to appeal to advertisers and attract a young audience, in 2002 WE debuted a reality dating show, *Single in the City*, which was a real-life counterpoint to HBO's *Sex in the City*. It ended up being a sleeper hit and boosted WE's exposure among women in the 18 to 34 demographic. (At the time, WE's median age was 42.) By the time WE started airing commercials in the fourth quarter of 2002, its programming budget for 2003 had grown to $59 million, up from $55 million in 2002.

The new programming schedule in 2003 was full of lighter content and a slew of reality-based programs. In its first scripted sitcom series, *The Tinsley Bumble Show*, a young woman tried to make it on her own after her wealthy father is busted for white-collar crime. New reality shows included *Bridezillas* (a behind-the-scenes show about brides on the brink), *Diva Detectives* (a program about an all-female Las Vegas detective agency), and a lifestyle makeover series, *Mix It Up*. More versions of the *Single in the City* franchise based in Las Vegas and Miami's South Beach were also scheduled.

By March 2003, WE's new shows were enjoying popularity and garnering the attention of younger audiences. In addition, an extensive distribution deal with Time Warner that month helped boost total subscriber count to 50 million, surpassing the network's growth expectations (in 1999 the stated goal for 2003 was 35 million). The network was experiencing unprecedented success. WE was still the biggest of Lifetime's challengers. However, Oxygen was gaining ground in the competition with 48 million subscribers.

A few months later in May 2003 WE began a marketing campaign around its new branding position with the tagline, "Live. Love. Laugh." It also hired pop artists including the B-52s to write original songs to accompany the network's new look. To reach viewers and agency media buyers, WE leased billboards across New York City, including Penn Station, Times Square, Herald Square, and Madison Avenue locations. Other outdoor media were scheduled for Chicago and Los Angeles. In addition, a massive TV advertising campaign was launched across various Rainbow Media Holdings. At the time, the network reached 52 million homes. Its advertisers had grown from a single sponsor to 85 within approximately six months.

SCANDAL & SETBACK: 2003

However, the network faced a setback in June 2003 when it was rocked with an accounting scandal. News broke when it was announced that 14 of WE's top executives were fired, including Katie McEnroe, who had spent nearly 23 years in various positions at Rainbow Holdings. Waves of surprise and disbelief passed through the cable industry. "That was the most shocking news I've ever heard," an industry veteran said at the time in a 2003 *Multichannel News* article. "Katie McEnroe getting fired … is like a presidential assassination." One person dubbed the scandal "Katie-gate."

The scandal revolved around an internal probe that uncovered allegedly improper expense accruals of $6.2 million relating to marketing, "and in some cases, fabricated invoices," according to a 2003 *Multichannel News* article. The accruals should have been charged in earlier years. Many industry executives were perplexed by the situation. The accounting irregularities were small in comparison with Cablevision's overall revenue of $6 billion. Additionally, they were an understatement of earnings for strictly internal budgeting purposes. The goal of the creative bookkeeping had been to take advantage of strong years to make it easier to hit big-budget targets set the next year by Rainbow Media.

Despite the disclosures, Cablevision stock was relatively unscathed. Most analysts said the accounting irregularities were minor. In a November 2003 *Multichannel News* article, Janco Partners cable analyst Matt Harrigan said, "I think it's fair to say you could go through quite a number of large companies and find similar irregularities." Analysts were more concerned with third-quarter results, which showed sluggish subscriber growth. By the end of the year, for the first time in WE's history, the network lost its second place standing in women's network ratings, falling behind Oxygen as Lifetime's closest competitor.

NEW LEADERSHIP & A NEW NAME: 2004–05

More than a year later, at the end of 2004, WE appointed Kim Martin as the network's new general manager. The post had been vacant since the accounting probe. At the time, Martin voiced an intention to de-emphasize films in favor of original programming. Many shows from the schedule would be renewed, including *Bridezillas*, *Full Frontal Fashion*, and *Single in the City*. However, they would be tweaked to fit the network's evolving personality. By the spring of 2005, the past two years of scandal and lack of leadership had taken a toll on the network's growth. WE's subscriber count totaled 56 million homes, an increase of only four million in two years.

To increase the network's profile, in May 2005 Martin announced WE's first service initiative, WE Empowers Women. The initiative focused on supporting organizations and charitable groups with the goal of creating confident women. A series of editorials by well-known female politicians and celebrities speaking about women's issues and documentaries were aired. The move was seen by some industry pundits as an attempt by WE to follow in Lifetime's footsteps. Lifetime had a long history of public service efforts. According to Martin, WE's effort was based instead on the cable industry's overall history of public service.

In May 2005 WE was focused on developing more original programming to differentiate itself from the competition. More reality shows were on the roster, with *Kiss & Tell*, a series about the dating adventures of 12 singles, and *Daddy's Little (Spoiled) Girl*, a show about the outrageous behavior of wealthy parents. To define how these new shows fit in with WE's brand, in a 2005 *TelevisionWeek* article Martin said, "WE is a network that is about three things. It's about relationships, pop culture, and style." That year, several shows were renewed, including *Bridezillas*, *McLeod's Daughters*, and the *Single in the City* franchise.

In an effort to embrace younger audiences, in May 2006 WE announced a new name and new tagline. The network would be called WE tv with the tagline, "WE Have More Fun." Of the changes, Martin said in a 2006 *TelevisionWeek* article, "It really brings to life the personality of the brand. When you're coming to this network, you're going to have a good time." The move was identical to Lifetime's strategy at the time.

To accompany the new look, Martin banked on several new lighthearted reality shows to push WE's ranking higher. Topping the lineup were *Doggie Daycare*, a series about high-end day care for pampered pups, and *Ghost Moms*, a show about ghost-hunting homemakers. There was also docu-soap about cheerleaders on the schedule, *Cheerleader U*. (Lifetime had also recently unveiled plans for its own cheerleading docu-soap, but Martin said the network was not trying to emulate the brand: "If you have a good idea, there's room for more than one," she said in a 2006 *TelevisionWeek* article.) Pop culture, relationships, and personal style were WE's programming focus because they cast a wide net.

WE's new look worked. The network's direct competition with Lifetime seemed to help boost ratings, putting it close to overtaking Oxygen for the first time since 2003. Lifetime's executive vice president of research, Tim Brooks, said in a 2006 *TelevisionWeek* article: "They're breathing down Oxygen's neck this year."

FOCUS ON REALITY-BASED PROGRAMMING: 2007–10

A year later, in 2007, Martin shifted programming to more wedding-related originals with Sunday nights dedicated to the wedding theme. Research on behalf of the network concluded that 49 percent of WE viewers responded positively to matrimonial-related shows. They were also avid consumers. By 2008 WE had expanded its bridal lineup with a fifth season of *Bridezillas*, a third season of *Platinum Wedding*, and added new wedding-themed shows including *Amazing Wedding Cakes*, *My Fair Wedding*, and *Wedding Central*. (Taking advantage of the genre's popularity, in 2009 Rainbow Media launched a new network, the Wedding Channel.)

In 2008 WE saw record prime-time viewership growth among its core 18 to 49 demographic, as well as women aged 25 to 54. Much of the network's growth was attributed to *Bridezillas* and *The Locator*, a documentary-style series that featured the psychic John Edward traveling across the country helping families connect with deceased loved ones.

In 2009 WE defined its three brand genres as: "WE Go Bridal," showcasing wedding content, "WE Reveal," featuring life stories of noteworthy women, and "WE Transform," highlighting life stories of women undergoing personal change. That year, WE also announced a new tagline: "Simply Fascinating." Popular shows in 2009 and 2010 included reality-based programming, including *Sex Change Hospital*, *Raising Sextuplets*, *Platinum Babies*, and *Downsized*. While WE had successfully managed to stay at the top of women's focused networks, with 75 million subscribers in 2009, it still lagged behind Lifetime and Oxygen.

Carrie Rothburd

PRINCIPAL COMPETITORS

Oxygen Media, LLC; SOAPnet, LLC; The Oprah Winfrey Network, LLC; iVillage Inc.; Lifetime Entertainment Services, LLC; Discovery Communications, Inc.; E! Entertainment Television, Inc.

FURTHER READING

Ault, Susanne, "Romance Classic Taking New Tack," *Daily Variety*, May 8, 2000, p. A5.

Fischler, Marcelle, "Long Island Journal: Creating a Refuge for Women with Television and the Internet," *New York Times*, August 22, 1999, p. 4.

Hazan, Jenny, "Love Is off the Air," *Realscreen*, February 1, 2001, p. 34.

Hibberd, James, "Ain't WE Got Fun?" *TelevisionWeek*, May 1, 2006, p. 3.

Keveney, Bill, "WE Offers Women Another Cable Option," *USA Today*, January 17, 2001, p. 4D.

Lafayette, Jon, "WE Committed to an Originals Path," *TelevisionWeek*, May 16, 2005, p. 3.

Liebeskind, Ken, "Fight to Reach Women Viewers Shows No End; Fare Improves as Lifetime, WE, Oxygen Extend Partnerships, Reach," *Advertising Age*, April 16, 2001, p. S6.

Moss, Linda, "Kim Martin," *Multichannel News*, January 31, 2005, p. 38A.

——, "McEnroe Colleagues Stunned," *Multichannel News*, June 23, 2003, p. 1.

Umstead, R. Thomas, "WE Scripts a Shift to Younger Viewers," *Multichannel News*, April 21, 2003, p. 26.

Wilbur-Ellis Company

———■———

345 California Street, 27th Floor
San Francisco, California 94104
U.S.A.
Telephone: (415) 772-4000
Fax: (415) 772-4011
Web site: http://www.wilbur-ellis.com

Private Company
Incorporated: 1921
Employees: 3,000
Sales: $2.57 billion (2009)
NAICS: 424910 Farm Supplies Merchant Wholesalers;
423840 Industrial Supplies Merchant Wholesalers;
115112 Soil Preparation, Planting, and Cultivating;
424690 Chemical and Allied Products Merchant
Wholesalers

■ ■ ■

Wilbur-Ellis Company is a marketer and distributor of
agricultural products, animal feed, and specialty
chemicals and ingredients. Through its agribusiness division, the company supplies crop protection, plant nutrition, and seed technology products. Its feed division
supplies feed ingredients, supplements, and forage to the
livestock, pet food, and aquaculture industries. The
Connell Brothers division ranks as one of the largest
distributors of specialty chemicals and ingredients in the
world, serving a host of industries, including paper,
construction, plastics, coatings, and personal care.

FOUNDING OF CONNELL BROTHERS: 1895

Wilbur-Ellis was founded in 1921, the date recognized
by the company, but an acquisition completed during its
first decade of business stretched its roots deeper into
the annals of U.S. business history. The company
could claim rights to a legacy beginning in the late
19th century, to the founding of Connell Brothers in
1895.

Connell Brothers' formation was predicated on a
gamble. In 1895 financial failure put ownership of a
cargo of flour in Hong Kong into the hands of a bank,
leaving the bank to search for a way to liquidate the
distressed merchandise. J. J. Connell, with his brother
M. J., purchased the single load of flour from the bank
and used it to build a bustling distribution business that
operated under the name Connell Brothers.

The location of their company's first load of
nondurable goods gave the brothers their geographic focal point. Connell Brothers developed into a business
built around trade in Asia, becoming a familiar name in
a host of countries. The company opened its first
overseas office three years after its formation, establishing a presence in Yokohama, Japan. From there, the
brothers focused on trading flour, which led them to
open additional offices in rapid succession in Shanghai,
China; Hong Kong; and the Philippines.

During the first decade of the 20th century, Connell Brothers developed into a recognized brand in the
Orient. The brothers expanded beyond flour and began
trading in condensed milk as well as fresh fruit from

COMPANY PERSPECTIVES

We are Wilbur-Ellis. And we know the lay of this land like no other. You'll find us in fields and fairways, forests and byways across the country bringing you local expertise in the solutions we offer. And we bring a better understanding of what it takes to make everything that grows here thrive.

California. The company broadened its operating territory during the period, particularly after World I, opening offices in China and Singapore.

The death of M. J. Connell in 1925 triggered a period of transition for Connell Brothers. After the loss of his brother, J. J. Connell lost interest in managing the company's affairs and began looking to sell his company. The founders of a young import-export business based in San Francisco learned of J. J. Connell's desire to sell his company and purchased Connell Brothers in 1931, uniting a 36-year-old trading business with a burgeoning company named Wilbur-Ellis Company.

FORMATION OF WILBUR-ELLIS: 1921

A decade before completing the acquisition, three friends who met while studying at the University of Washington founded Wilbur-Ellis. The three friends (Wilbur, Ellis, and Franck) launched the company by pooling $5,000, the start-up capital used to start a fishmeal and fish oil trading company in San Francisco. Their brokerage business prospered, enabling the founders to diversify into trading fertilizer before the end of the 1920s and to complete their seminal acquisition of Connell Brothers.

The combination of Wilbur-Ellis and Connell Brothers had a transforming effect on both companies. For Connell Brothers, the corporate marriage fueled its growth, leading to rapid expansion that soon saw the business trading industrial chemicals and semi-manufactured goods in its area of influence in the Orient. For Wilbur-Ellis, the acquisition of Connell Brothers gave it an immediate and extensive presence in Asia and a range of additional goods to import and export. The company, quickly developing beyond its original business scope, began trading everything from flour and canned fish to gunpowder.

EMPHASIS ON AGRICULTURE EMERGES: 1940–49

During the 1940s, the modern version of Wilbur-Ellis began to take shape. Agriculture started to become the company's main industry, beginning with the establishment of crop protection and treatment facilities in California and Arizona. The decade's most impressive achievement was related to its original business, however. Wilbur-Ellis, which first demonstrated its willingness to enter overseas markets with the purchase of Connell Brothers, showed its mettle again after World War II. The company became a global company, turning a potentially damaging development into a reason to continue its march into foreign countries.

Wilbur-Ellis's headquarters location and its original business of trading fishmeal and fish oil was tied to Monterey, 80 miles south from San Francisco, where the fishing industry was based. The bond existed for a quarter-century, but after the war the fishing industry left the piers of Monterey and led Wilbur-Ellis's management to make a bold move. Although the company remained in San Francisco, it moved its canning machinery to other epicenters of the fishing industry, establishing its operations thousands of miles away in Peru and South Africa. The move overseas represented the first major instance of Wilbur-Ellis's ability to be adaptive to change, a skill that would serve the company well as it evolved during the second half of the 20th century.

Agriculture, not fishing, became Wilbur-Ellis's mainstay in the years after expanding into South America and Africa. During the 1950s the company began to distribute agricultural chemicals. Because of its acquisition of Connell Brothers, the company became one of the first foreign-based companies to reestablish commercial activity in Japan after World War II. In the 1960s the company began exporting industrial chemicals, minerals, fibers, and machinery goods, using Connell Brothers' relationships in Asia to bring the new products eastward. Domestically, advancements in the formulation of fertilizer and crop protection products made the market more attractive, prompting Wilbur-Ellis to begin an acquisition campaign that would continue at a measured pace for the next half-century.

During the 1960s Wilbur-Ellis began to acquire fertilizer and crop protection businesses in California, Washington, Oregon, and Texas. Ownership of the company by this time was held closely by the Wilbur family, from whose ranks came the son of one of the company's founders, Brayton Wilbur Jr. He earned a history degree from Yale University and a graduate degree in business from Stanford University before joining the family business in 1964 as a trainee. A quarter-

<table>
<tr><td colspan="2">

KEY DATES

1921: Wilbur-Ellis is founded with a $5,000 investment.

1931: Connell Brothers is acquired.

1940s: Company begins to open crop protection and treatment locations for the first time.

1970s: Company's business is organized into three divisions: agribusiness, Connell Brothers, and feed.

1990: Annual sales near $1 billion.

2009: Acquisitions during the decade push annual sales above $2.5 billion.

</td></tr>
</table>

century would pass before he rose to the top of the company's managerial ranks, time that gave Wilbur an opportunity to observe the company's two modes of growth: internal and external expansion. Wilbur arrived when growth through acquisitions, external means, was in fashion, but once he took the helm he demonstrated an equal propensity to acquire other businesses and to bolster Wilbur-Ellis's operations through internal means.

BUSINESS DEVELOPS IN THREE DIRECTIONS: 1970–79

The corporate structure supporting Wilbur-Ellis during the 21st century began to take shape in the 1970s. Connell Brothers, organized as a division, began to narrow its focus on distributing specialty chemicals during the decade, complementing the product lines of fertilizer and crop protection products distributed by the company's agribusiness division. The acquisition of nutritional businesses in California and the Pacific Northwest during the 1970s formed the foundation of a third division, Wilbur-Ellis's feed division, which focused on supplying feed ingredients, supplements, and forage to the livestock, pet food, and aquaculture industries.

By the beginning of the 1980s, Wilbur-Ellis was generating $450 million in annual sales, making it one of the largest privately owned companies in the country. The company's revenue volume swelled during the 1980s, expanded by a series of acquisitions that made it an industry leader in the agricultural chemicals market. Wilbur-Ellis purchased Arizona Agro-Phosphate Co., a distributor of phosphoric acid, L. H. Butcher Co., an agricultural chemical formulator, and Western Chemical Co., a specialist in pelletized fertilizers. The company purchased Brayton Chemicals, Inc., which distributed

farm chemicals in 17 states, and it purchased Tide Products Co., a regional competitor in the agricultural chemicals business. By the end of the decade, the company's sales had nearly doubled, soaring to $840 million.

BRAYTON WILBUR JR., CEO: 1989

Brayton Wilbur Jr. took command of the company after its energetic growth during the 1980s. He was appointed president and CEO in 1989 and expressed his intention to continue expanding by using both external and internal methods of realizing growth. "If a market is saturated with good competitors," Wilbur said in the December 13, 1991 issue of the *San Francisco Business Times*, "you're probably better off buying someone than killing yourself with less good accounts. You can get a lot more quickly [by completing an acquisition], but then you have to train them your way. It takes a while to meld a different organization into your own; growing from within is often slower but surer."

Wilbur-Ellis marched toward the $1 billion sales mark during the 1990s. The company's agribusiness was expanded through several acquisitions of California-based companies, solidifying its position as a leading supplier of crop protection products. The largest purchase of the decade occurred in 1999, when Wilbur-Ellis acquired Sacramento, California-based John Taylor Fertilizers. John Taylor was one of the 11 largest retailers of pesticides, fertilizers, and seed and application services in the United States, generating more than $100 million in sales in 1998. The addition of John Taylor's operations helped Wilbur-Ellis eclipse $1.5 billion in sales by the start of the 21st century.

ACQUISITIONS: 2003–09

The decade to follow saw Wilbur-Ellis continue to record robust financial growth, perpetuating an expansion campaign that began in 1980. The period began with a change in leadership, as Brayton Wilbur Jr. assumed the role of chairman. He handed his duties as president and CEO to the company's vice president and treasurer, Herbert B. Tully, who had spent the previous 18 years working for Wilbur-Ellis. Under Tully's watch, further acquisitions were completed. Notable purchases included the acquisition of Western Feed Supplements Inc., a mineral and vitamin pre-mixer, in 2003, and a fertilizer and crop protection business named Hughson Chemical Co. in 2004, and another agricultural fertilizer and crop protection business named Woodburn Fertilizers Inc. in 2005.

Another managerial change occurred midway through the decade, engendered by the loss of an individual instrumental to the company's development during the previous four decades. In 2006 Brayton Wilbur Jr. died while visiting India, leaving the company without a chairman. Tully was elected chairman in the weeks following Wilbur's death and John P. Thacher, Wilbur-Ellis's executive vice president, was appointed president and CEO.

Under Thacher's command, acquisitions continued to play a significant role in the company's development. Wilbur-Ellis's agribusiness division received a boost several months after Thacher took charge when the company acquired an agricultural products formulation business located in San Joaquin, California. The company's feed division benefited from the acquisition campaign in 2008, receiving a 20 percent increase in its revenues by absorbing the marketing and distribution business of ProFood USA Inc. ProFood served the dairy industry in Idaho as well as the export market to Asia. The year also saw the company acquire Ripon Farm Services, LLC, a fertilizer and crop protection distribu-

tor in Ripon, California. Wilbur-Ellis completed the decade with two more acquisitions, pushing its sales above $2.5 billion as it prepared for the future. The acquisitions, both finalized in December 2009, added two retailers and aerial applicators of plant protection products, Ag Flight, Inc., based in York, Nebraska, and Muckel's Aerial, Inc., based in Prosser, Nebraska.

Jeffrey L. Covell

FURTHER READING

Blitzer, Carol, "Wilbur-Ellis Co. Building Its Agribusiness through Both Acquisitions and Expansions," *San Francisco Business Times*, December 13, 1991, p. S2.

Fatka, Jacqui, "Wilbur-Ellis Acquires ProFood," *Feedstuffs*, June 2, 2008, p. 52.

Fujii, Reed, "Ripon Farm Absorbed by S.F. Company," *Stockton (Calif.) Record*, November 11, 2008.

"Wilbur-Ellis Buys Hughson Chemical," *Feedstuffs*, April 12, 2004, p. 7.

The Wine Group, Inc.

315 Montgomery Street
San Francisco, California 94104
U.S.A.
Telephone: (415) 986-8700
Fax: (415) 986-4304
Web site: http://www.franzia.com

Private Company
Incorporated: 1981
Employees: 250
Sales: $500 million (2009 est.)
NAICS: 312130 Wineries

■ ■ ■

The Wine Group, Inc., (TWG) is the third-largest wine producer in the world and the second-largest wine producer in California. At its vineyards in California and New York, TWG produces a variety of wines sold under numerous brand names, including Franzia, Corbett Canyon, Concannon, Mogen David, Inglenook, and Almaden. Through the company's Underdog Wine Merchants unit, TWG caters to young adults with a selection of premium wines that include Cardinal Zin, Tempra Tantrum, and Pinot Evil.

FORMATION OF LIMITED PARTNERSHIP: 1981

In the early 1980s several large conglomerates began divesting wine companies that they had acquired just a few years earlier. Among the sellers were The Coca-Cola Company, R.J. Reynolds, Schlitz Brewing Company, and Coca-Cola Bottling Company of New York. For various reasons, the wineries no longer fit into the conglomerates' plans for growth and diversification. The Coca-Cola Company had in fact caused a stir in 1977, when it created the Wine Spectrum, a subsidiary consisting of the Monterey Vineyard and Sterling Winery in California and Taylor Wine Company and Great Western Winery in New York. Some critics questioned the advisability or propriety of the soft-drink giant's entry into the alcoholic beverage market. Whether it took such concerns seriously or not, it sold its winery holdings to The Seagram Company in 1983.

By that time, Coca-Cola Bottling Company of New York, which had owned three wineries, had already divested its holdings. These consisted of Franzia, Mogen David, and Tribuno, which were bought in 1981 by The Wine Group, a limited partnership formed for the purpose of buying the wineries. The partnership was headed by Arthur A. Ciocca, who was the president and CEO of Franzia and formerly a marketing executive with Gallo. He was joined in the venture by some other members of his team, men who had been charting Franzia's way under the ownership of Coca-Cola Bottling Company of New York and were opposed to a buyout involving a third party.

LEGACY OF FRANZIA: 1915–71

Franzia was a well-established California winery offering a range of varietal wines. It also shipped wine, grape concentrates, and brandy in bulk to the Mogen David winery in Westfield, New York, to be used in such

KEY DATES

1915: Giuseppe Franzia founds family winery in California.
1981: The Wine Group (TWG) partnership is formed to buy Franzia Bros., Mogen David, and Tribuno brands.
1988: TWG acquires Corbett Canyon, formerly known as the Lawrence Winery.
1997: Franzia is the top-selling brand of wine in the United States.
2004: TWG acquires Golden State Vintners, Inc., gaining control of nearly 10,000 acres of vineyards in California.
2008: Inglenook and Almaden wine brands are acquired from Constellation Brands, Inc.

Mogen David products as MD 20-20 and Golden Chablis. Mogen David also had a long history and was noted for its regional kosher wines, notably its sweet concord grape and blackberry table wines. Tribuno vermouths, both sweet and dry, bottled in New Jersey, were also established products. The brand was the number one premium vermouth produced in the United States. It and Lejon, a leading popular-priced vermouth, were two high-volume brands of TWG. Both produced sweet (red) and dry (white) vermouth. The wines, often used in standard cocktails including martinis and Manhattans, were also used as both aperitif and dessert wines.

At the time of its acquisition by The Wine Group, Franzia had been in existence for 66 years. In 1893, Giuseppe Franzia, its founder, immigrated to California from his native Italian city of Genoa. He worked in small truck farms around San Francisco, earning a meager salary that kept him at the poverty level for several years. He was very frugal, however, and by 1906 he had saved enough to plant and cultivate a small vineyard of his own. He founded the first Franzia family winery in 1915. It was not a particularly auspicious moment, however. The country was two years away from entering World War I and just five from passing the infamous 18th Amendment, which cleared the path for the Volstead Act, barring the manufacture, sale, or transportation of intoxicating liquors.

Franzia had no choice but to close his winery during Prohibition, which lasted from 1920 to 1933. During that period, Franzia's five sons continued cultivating the vineyard, and when the repeal came in the form of

the 21st Amendment, they reopened their father's business under the name Franzia Brothers. Initially, the sons sold their wine in bulk to eastern bottlers. Then, late in World War II, they began bottling their own branded wine, using the mass-production methods that had been introduced by their in-laws, Ernest and Julio Gallo, who had opened bottling plants in Los Angeles and New Orleans. In addition to an assembly-line method of bottling, the Gallos used screw-caps rather than corks to seal the bottles, something considered almost a criminal act by some wine connoisseurs but defended as a sanitary improvement by health-conscious customers.

In 1971, a family squabble over the future of the winery resulted in its sale to a group of investors in the East who subsequently sold it to Coca-Cola Bottling Company of New York (itself acquired by Coca-Cola Enterprises Inc. of Atlanta in 1997). However, some members of the Franzia family continued in the business, creating the JFJ Bronco Winery near Modesto, California.

The Mogen David Winery, located in Westfield, New York, also had been around a long time when TWG acquired it. Originally, the company was located in Chicago, but it relocated to upstate New York in 1967, a practical move to put it closer to its supply of grapes for its Concord wines. At the time it was purchased by TWG, it was producing about six million gallons of wine annually and was the world's largest producer of Concord wines. Not all of its wines were the kosher wines for which it was best known. Popular among a younger audience, specifically college students, was its MD 20/20 affectionately know as "Mad Dog" 20/20, a line marketed in several flavors that recalled nonalcoholic drinks, including pink grapefruit, wild berry, and Hawaiian blue.

BECOMING A MAJOR MARKET PLAYER: 1982–89

TWG faced some troubling prospects in the early years. By 1983, the California wine boom of the 1970s had ended, leaving an industry in a slump and with a major marketing problem. In the decade prior to TWG's formation, California had at last won the long battle to establish itself as a world-class producer of wines. State vintners, buoyed by a new optimism, added considerable acreage with new grape plantings, developed new technologies, and created new wineries. One of these was the Lawrence Winery, the forerunner of Corbett Canyon. In 1982, after a decade of annual average growth of 10 percent, wine shipments flattened out. About half of California's leading wineries shipped fewer cases than in the previous year, and between the 1981 and 1982 harvests, wine inventories climbed by 16 percent to 685 million gallons. The 3.1 million ton grape crush of 1982 broke all previous records. It also caused wine prices to plummet, aided by a general recession that was reining in growth in the sales of all alcoholic beverages.

The wine glut compelled wineries to use new marketing strategies, and it soon became clear that the 1980s would be ruled by the low-cost producers and marketers. TWG responded with some innovative measures for producing and marketing its array of bargain-priced wines. Notably, with Franzia, TWG pioneered the "wine tap" container, a box containing a pouch with a tap. It would become the fastest-growing wine package of the 1990s. Because a loophole in federal wine standards allowed boxed wine producers to dilute the wine with water and still market it under classic varietal names such as Merlot and Cabernet Sauvignon, the new packaging caused some industry flack. Also with Franzia, TWG helped initiate the wine cooler craze in the 1980s.

In 1988, the company took an important expansion step, buying Corbett Canyon from Glenmore Distilleries Co. The vintner was originally established in 1979 as the Lawrence Winery but was reestablished as Corbett Canyon in 1983. From grapes grown on its 350-acre Los Alamos Vineyards in the Edna Valley, outside of San Luis Obispo, California, the winery was producing a line of award-winning Coastal Classic varietals and Reserve designated wines. Its line would eventually grow to include Cabernet Sauvignon, Chardonnay, Merlot, Muscat, Muscat Canelli, Sauvignon Blanc, White Zinfandel, and Zinfandel. Growing sales would also compel it to buy some of its grapes from other producers.

TWG'S BRANDS FLOURISH: 1995–97

In most ways, TWG fared very well in the 1990s. It enhanced its reputation as an innovator, introducing, for example, freshness assurance dating to the wine industry and garnering some awards for the distinct design of some of its bottles. Both its Franzia and Corbett Canyon brands were highly successful. According to A.C. Nielsen ratings, in the mid-1990s, Corbett Canyon was the fastest-growing domestic wine. From 1995 to 1996, Corbett Canyon produced one million cases, a 67 percent leap in production.

The winemaker, one of 19 wineries and vineyard members in the Edna Valley Arroyo Grande Valley Vintner's Association, was so successful that it had to close its doors to the public. It needed its tasting-room space for additional barrel storage to accommodate its growing product line and sales. In 1995, after cultivat-

ing additional acreage, it added Merlot and Zinfandel to its range of Californian varietals. However, the closing move made it the only winery in the association to turn away visitors and prompted some criticism because the vintner, immensely popular, had previously drawn many visitors to the area, a benefit to all the other area wineries.

It was also in 1996 that Corbett Canyon received a *Wine Business Monthly* Clear Choice Award for package design for its 1.5-liter bottles that tapered from rounded shoulders to square bases, a distinct, innovative shape. Still, it was not just TWG's break from the traditionally shaped bottle that made Corbett Canyon a great seller. It won plenty of accolades for its caliber, and even "wine snobs" were buying some of Corbett Canyon's line, its Sauvignon Blanc, for example, that in 1997 still cost under $5 for a 750-milliliter bottle.

As for Franzia, in 1997 it was the top-selling brand of wine in the country. In that year it recorded depletions of 18 million nine-liter cases, 6.6 million cases ahead of its closest competitor, Carlo Rossi. Even Mogen David continued to lead in its particular market sector. In 1998, 1.5 million adults were drinking Mogen David, beating out its chief competitor, Canandaigua's Manischewitz, by 100,000. Demographics indicated that the drinkers of the kosher wines produced by Mogen David and rival Manischewitz were not typically part of a kosher community or even Jewish. The nonvintage kosher wines, with their relatively high sugar content, had an appeal to a broader customer base, principally to consumers who preferred sweet dessert wines in such traditional flavors as blackberry and concord. Mogen David was also tapping into a more youthful market, a mainstay of TWG.

INNOVATION & ACQUISITIONS AT THE MILLENNIUM

In 1999, TWG started shipping its new, clear-bottled Lyrica brand in a variety of flavors: Raspberry Merlot, Passion Berry White Zinfandel, Peach Chardonnay. The bottles, created at the San Francisco design shop Primo Angeli, were again unique, reinforcing the impression that TWG always did things a little differently than other wineries. However, in 2000, it appeared that TWG was also going to invest more in standard varietals and pricier wines. Sebastiani Vineyards Inc. agreed to sell its Turner Road Vintners division, the largest in the Lodi, California, area, to TWG. The facilities included a crushing and winemaking complex with a 275,000-square-foot bottling plant and distribution warehouse located nearby. Turner Road Vintners produced about 7.8 million cases of wine per year (about 90 percent of Sebastiani's wine) bottled under a variety of brand names: Talus, Vendange, Farallon, Nathanson Creek, Heritage, and La Terre.

In addition to being an industry leader in the development and marketing of new varietals and blends, TWG played an exploratory part in the development of new markets, including Mexico. The North American Free Trade Agreement (NAFTA) that went into effect at the start of 1994 encouraged wineries in the United States to make a serious attempt to export wines to Mexico and other south-of-the-border countries. Mexico's tariff was reduced by 20 percent and would continue to decline by 2 percent per year until it would finally be eliminated. Arthur Ciocca, TWG's CEO, noted that once the tariff barrier was sufficiently lowered NAFTA would give U.S. winemakers an opening in a market with enormous potential.

ACQUISITIONS INCREASE STATURE: 2002–08

The first decade of the 21st century was a period of consolidation in the wine industry. The largest acquisition of the decade created the largest wine producer in the world, a stature achieved by Constellation Brands when it purchased Australia's BRL Hardy for $1.1 billion in 2003. TWG, ranking as the third-largest wine company in the United States, was on the march as well, making significant additions to its portfolio of brands. The company's creation occurred at a time when major wine producers were shedding assets, but survival 20 years later hinged on keeping pace with the acquisitive activities of competitors on the prowl for assets.

Under the direction of CEO David Kent, TWG strengthened its market presence through acquisitions. In 2002 the company paid $83 million to Diageo PLC for the Glen Ellen and MG Vallejo brands, adding nearly three million cases to its annual production total. The addition of Glen Ellen gave the company the second-best-selling wine brand in the 1.5-liter segment for wines retailing for more than $10, a new market niche for TWG. Later in the year, TWG purchased Concannon Vineyards, gaining 190 acres of vineyards in California's Livermore Valley.

Kent's next moves on the acquisition front strengthened TWG's market position at two different points of the price spectrum. In 2004 he won a bidding war to acquire Golden State Vintners, Inc., a publicly traded company that primarily made premium bulk wines for other wine producers, counting Gallo, Sutter Home, and Sebastiani as its largest customers. TWG paid approximately $106 million for Golden State, gain-

ing control of the company's nearly 10,000 acres of vineyards in central and northern California. In 2006 Kent formed Underdog Wine Merchants as an operating unit of TWG, using the entity to sell premium wines to young adults. He acquired the Big House and Cardinal Zin brands from California-based Bonny Doon Vineyard at roughly the same time, and put the two brands under the stewardship of Underdog Wine Merchants, which also marketed a stable of irreverently named wine brands that included Pinot Evil, Tempra Tantrum, and Herding Cats.

The end of the decade saw Kent continue to add heft to TWG's brand portfolio. In 2008 he brokered a deal with Spanish wine producer Grupo Osborne to make TWG the exclusive U.S. distributor of brandies, spirits, and a collection of wines that included Montecillo, Solaz, and Osborne. The largest acquisition of the period gave TWG two of the most well known wine brands in the United States. In a deal with Constellation Brands, TWG acquired the Madera Winery and the Almaden and Inglenook brands, paying $134 million in 2008 to complete the deal. The acquisition made TWG the second-largest wine producer in California and the third-largest wine producer in the world.

John W. Fiero
Updated, Jeffrey L. Covell

PRINCIPAL OPERATING UNITS

Underdog Wine Merchants.

PRINCIPAL COMPETITORS

Constellation Brands, Inc.; E. & J. Gallo Winery; Kendall-Jackson Wine Estates, Ltd.

FURTHER READING

"California Wineries Seek to Develop Mexican Consumer Market for Wines," *Knight-Ridder/Tribune Business News*, September 19, 1994.

Fujii, Reed, "San Francisco-Based Wine Group Inc. to Buy Brands from Diageo for $83 Million," *Record*, March 20, 2002.

Moran, Tim, "San Francisco-Based Wine Firm to Buy Vintners Division," *Knight-Ridder/Tribune Business News*, September 1, 2000.

Sewall, Gilbert T., "Trouble for California Wine Makers," *Fortune*, April 18, 1983, p. 54.

"The Wine Group Buys Almaden and Inglenook Brands," *Western Farm Press*, March 3, 2008.

Worthington Industries, Inc.

200 Old Wilson Bridge Road
Columbus, Ohio 43085-2247
U.S.A.
Telephone: (614) 438-3210
Fax: (614) 438-3136
Web site: http://www.worthingtonindustries.com

Public Company
Incorporated: 1955 as The Worthington Steel Company
Employees: 6,400
Sales: $2.63 billion (2009)
Stock Exchanges: New York
Ticker Symbol: WOR
NAICS: 331221 Rolled Steel Shape Manufacturing;
    332323 Ornamental and Architectural Metal Work
    Manufacturing; 332420 Metal Tank (Heavy Gauge)
    Manufacturing

∎ ∎ ∎

Worthington Industries, Inc., is a diversified metal processing company, with operations in both value-added steel processing and the manufacture of metal products. Its Worthington Steel Company subsidiary, which generates about 43 percent of overall sales, is one of North America's largest intermediate processors of flat rolled steel, purchasing steel coils from integrated steel mills and minimills and processing them to the precise specifications of about 1,100 customers in the automotive, appliance, construction, furniture, office equipment, and other industries. This subsidiary operates 11 manufacturing facilities in the United States.

Around 24 percent of revenues is generated by the firm's Worthington Cylinder Corporation subsidiary, which ranks as the world's largest manufacturer of pressure cylinders for industrial, commercial, and consumer markets, including liquefied petroleum gas cylinders, propane tanks, refrigerant cylinders, helium balloon kits, and small high-pressure cylinders for medical applications. Worthington Cylinder operates eight plants in Austria, Canada, the Czech Republic, Portugal, and the United States.

Worthington Industries' Dietrich Industries, Inc., subsidiary is the largest U.S. producer of metal framing products for the commercial and residential construction industries, manufacturing such products as steel studs, floor and wall system components, and roof trusses at 14 facilities in the United States and two in Canada. Dietrich accounts for about 23 percent of Worthington Industries' sales. Worthington is also involved in a number of joint ventures, including the Worthington Armstrong Venture (WAVE), a producer of metal grids for suspended ceiling systems that is jointly owned and operated with Armstrong World Industries, Inc. In addition, the company owns the Gerstenslager Company, a leading supplier of aftermarket body panels for the automotive and commercial truck industries.

STEEL FOUNDATION

Worthington's development largely reflects the determination, entrepreneurial skills, and exceptional management philosophy of founder John H. McConnell. Maintaining the company's golden rule ("we treat our customers, employees, investors, and sup-

COMPANY PERSPECTIVES

Worthington Industries has established a tradition of leadership in value-added steel processing and metals related industries. We believe that leadership is about action—not simply position. Operating under a long-standing Philosophy based on the Golden Rule, with earning money for our shareholders the first corporate goal, we are building on our strengths and redefining industry leadership in the markets we serve.

pliers as we would like to be treated"), McConnell built up a highly motivated, well-rewarded, and highly productive workforce.

Born in 1923 in New Manchester, West Virginia, the son of a steel worker, McConnell went to work in the Weirton Steel Company mills when he graduated from high school in 1941. After three years of World War II Navy service in the Pacific, he attended Michigan State University under the GI Bill. On graduating in 1949, he returned to Weirton in the sales department. Later he accepted a position at Shenango Steel, an independent company in Farrell, Pennsylvania, and in 1954 moved to Columbus, Ohio.

During this time, McConnell noticed that the major steel producers were busy building larger mills and concentrating on large tonnage orders, and that interest in filling specialized orders was waning. Observing a growing need for custom steel processing services, he moved into this promising niche. In early 1955 McConnell set up business with a desk and phone in his basement in the Columbus suburb of Worthington, Ohio. Even before incorporation, he had landed an order from a thermometer company for a load of steel, which he could obtain from his old employer Weirton Steel for $1,800. McConnell had $1,200 cash on hand and figured Weirton would offer the customary 30-day payment terms. Weirton refused, however, to offer credit to his new venture, and he had to rush to his bank for a $600 loan on his 1952 Oldsmobile to close the deal.

By June 1955, The Worthington Steel Company was incorporated. It ended its first year with five employees, $350,000 in sales, and a $14,000 profit. The company had advanced from mere brokerage to rudimentary processing in rented quarters, with a slitting machine to cut the steel coils into specified widths. Four years later it moved into its first, 16,000-square-foot plant in Columbus.

From this simple start, Worthington rapidly expanded its capabilities so that it could, in McConnell's words, "do nearly everything with steel except actually melt it to prepare it for the customer's use." This included processing to the exact gauge, width, length, and shape, as well as providing the precise finish, temper (degree of hardness), and other characteristics desired by the customer. Thus, McConnell stated, "Worthington occupies a unique niche between the integrated mills, which concentrate on large, standard orders, and the metal service centers, which generally have limited processing capabilities."

DIVERSIFYING AS WORTHINGTON INDUSTRIES

Gearing up for further expansion, Worthington went public in October 1968, selling 150,000 shares at $7.50 each. In its first year as a public company, the fiscal year ending in May 1969, Worthington reported sales of $21 million and net earnings of $460,000. McConnell had quickly grown the company into an established steel processor but was worried about its exposure to the cyclical nature of the industry. He therefore sought to diversify into related fields, taking the first step in 1971 with the purchase of the small, unprofitable pressure cylinder business of Lennox Industries. This operation became profitable the first year under the Worthington banner, and, before the decade was over, Worthington Cylinders had become the leader in low-pressure cylinders, such as propane tanks for barbecue grills. Also in 1971, to signal its newly diversified nature, the company changed its name from Worthington Steel to Worthington Industries, Inc. The founding steel processing operations fell under the Worthington Industries parent company umbrella as a division, alongside Worthington Cylinders.

The period between 1972 and 1974 was a boom period for the steel industry, with Worthington reaping the benefits in the form of rapidly escalating sales and earnings. Much of the profits were plowed back in the company in the form of new plant construction and further acquisitions. The 1972 purchase of a steel processing operation in Chicago was followed up with the 1975 acquisition of a steel processing firm that operated a plant in Rock Hill, South Carolina. Later, in 1976, Worthington completed construction of a 113,000-square-foot steel pickling and processing facility in Monroe, Ohio. This plant extended the company's processing capabilities into pickling, a chemical process to remove the surface oxide that developed on steel during hot rolling. During fiscal 1976, Worthington's sales surpassed the $100 million mark for the first time.

Another diversification step was taken in 1978 through the purchase of U-Brand Corporation, which

KEY DATES

1955: John H. McConnell incorporates The Worthington Steel Company in Worthington, Ohio, as a steel processing concern.
1968: Company goes public.
1971: Company diversifies with purchase of pressure cylinder business of Lennox Industries; company name is changed to Worthington Industries, Inc.
1993: John P. McConnell succeeds his father as CEO of Worthington Industries.
1996: Worthington acquires Dietrich Industries, Inc., producer of metal framing products for the construction industries.
1999: Divestment program is completed, narrowing firm's focus to value-added steel processing and steel-related niche markets.
2009: Amid global economic downturn, Worthington suffers full-year net loss for first time in its history.

made malleable iron, plastic, and steel pipe fittings, sold through hardware and plumbing supply stores. While U-Brand generally showed moderate profits, Worthington eventually came to regard the U-Brand product lines and marketing approach as too unlike its other lines, and sold the unit to Mueller Brass Company. The following year Worthington purchased Advanced Coating Technology, Inc., which specialized in architectural reflective glass, a process that involved applying a steel coating to glass. As with U-Brand, Worthington later sold this operation.

FURTHER ACQUISITIONS IN THE EIGHTIES

More significant was the company's 1980 merger with Buckeye International, Inc., which allowed steel processor Worthington to enter two other business segments: plastic and metal custom products and steel castings. Molded plastic products, sold mostly to automakers, included items ranging from air conditioning louvers to dashboard assemblies, but also had applications in cellular phones, hand tools, appliances, and a wide variety of other products. Precision metal parts, similarly marketed primarily to automakers, included components of antilock brakes, power steering, and transmissions.

The primary attraction for Worthington, however, was Buckeye's position as one of the largest producers of steel castings. Worthington maintained the Buckeye name for the castings division of the business, which had applications in the production of couplers for freight cars and the increasingly profitable undercarriages for rapid transit cars.

Besides Buckeye, two 1980 acquisitions added further specialized skills to the steel castings division, Capital Die, Tool and Machine Company and I. H. Schlezinger & Sons. Capital Die designed and built specialized machinery in its tool and die plant, while marketing its services to outside customers. I. H. Schlezinger was a processor of recyclable metals. In 1984 Worthington acquired National Rolling Mills of Malvern, Pennsylvania, which was most prominently the producer of steel grids used in suspended ceiling systems. Four years later, Worthington Cylinders ventured outside the United States for the first time via the acquisition of the Canadian firm Metal Flo Corporation, based in Guelph, Ontario. Metal Flo, which was subsequently renamed Worthington Cylinders of Canada, produced large-capacity propane and acetylene cylinders for portable heating and cooking, welding, and brazing.

In the meantime, Worthington entered into the first of a series of joint ventures in 1986 when it teamed with U.S. Steel to form Worthington Specialty Processing in Jackson, Michigan, already the site of a Worthington steel processing plant. This operation processed wide sheet steel for such uses as outer door panels in cars and appliances. Worthington entered several other joint ventures in the late 1980s. It teamed with two Japanese companies, Nissen Chemical Industry and Sumitomo Corporation, in 1988 to form London Industries, Inc., based in London, Ohio, which made molded plastic parts for Honda and a number of other foreign companies with U.S. production facilities. Worthington Industries ended the 1980s with record sales for fiscal 1989 of $939 million.

UNIQUE CORPORATE CULTURE

McConnell credited much of the company's success to the depth and competence of Worthington management, most of which was developed internally. Donald H. Malenick, who started as a slitting machine operator in 1959 and worked his way up through the ranks, became president and COO in 1976 and would retain that position for the next 23 years. In addition to the strength of its management, observers also cited the firm's unique corporate culture as another key to its success.

Anchored by the company's "golden rule" and strong emphasis on motivation, Worthington stressed a commitment to communication and recognition of good work, both financially and with other forms of encouragement. John H. McConnell admitted to having little use for unions, regarding them as the result of managements that fail to meet workers' needs. By contrast, Worthington was built on a philosophy of partnership and teamwork extending to all employees.

From its inception, Worthington regularly paid all workers cash bonuses based on tonnage shipped. In 1966, to stress the importance of customer service and quell any temptation to sacrifice quality in order to rush shipments, the incentive basis was shifted to pretax profits. At the same time, the production line workers were put on salary, just like office employees. The incentive plan provided workers with 40 percent or more of their annual pay. Under a separate plan, the incentive portion for managers often topped 60 percent.

Worthington also offered a high degree of job security. It avoided layoffs during major downturns by shifting people to other parts of the company, or assigning tasks such as painting, sweeping, and repairing equipment. The incentive and salary plans were not extended to the few unionized plants Worthington picked up in acquisitions. In several such plants, employees voted to decertify the unions in order to gain the team benefits. Over the years, the effectiveness of Worthington's employee policies was repeatedly cited by commentators and financial analysts, and the firm also won a spot on various "best companies to work for" lists.

CONTINUED GROWTH IN THE NINETIES

Worthington Industries began the 1990s suffering recessionary setbacks in 1990 and 1991, when sales and earnings were down. Sales and profits recovered in fiscal 1992 and grew steadily thereafter, with the firm by 1995 reporting earnings of $116.7 million on revenues of $1.48 billion. In the midst of the recession that began the decade, Worthington in 1990 completed construction of a new, $30 million steel processing and pickling plant in Portage, Indiana, in what at the time amounted to the firm's largest single capital expenditure in its history. The 450,000-square-foot plant in Portage replaced the facility in Chicago that had been purchased in 1972.

The early 1990s were also an important period in the executive ranks, as the founder's son, John P. McConnell, who had joined the company in 1975, was named in 1992 to the position of vice chairman, with responsibility for development and oversight of emerging business opportunities. Early the following year, he

succeeded his father as CEO of Worthington, with the elder McConnell remaining on as chairman of the board. Steeped in his father's strategic and managerial philosophies, John P. McConnell vowed to continue to build on his father's successes. He noted that he expected Worthington's earnings and revenues to grow at an annual rate of 15 percent, and that he planned to maintain Worthington's unique corporate culture.

A source of major growth for the company around this time was in cylinders and other equipment used to recover and recycle refrigeration gases. By federal law, these chemical refrigerants were required to be reclaimed during repair or replacement of air conditioning and refrigeration systems. Other promising new lines included cylinder kits for helium party balloons as well as compressed air tanks. In 1991 a 140,000-square-foot plant was opened in Jefferson, Ohio, that extended the company's cylinder product line to large cylinders that could store fuel for homes situated away from gas lines. The acquisition in early 1992 of Alabama-based North American Cylinders, Inc., moved Worthington into acetylene cylinders (important in welding) and high-pressure tanks.

Also in 1992, Worthington transferred the ceiling grid business it had gained through the acquisition of National Rolling Mills into a joint venture with floor and ceiling products leader Armstrong World Industries, Inc., forming the Worthington Armstrong Venture, or WAVE. In 1994 Worthington gained its first manufacturing asset in Europe when the WAVE venture opened a plant in Valenciennes, France, to manufacture steel tracks for acoustic ceiling tiles. Worthington officials considered partnering an effective method of lowering the risk of entering foreign markets, and this strategy was evident in another 1994 development that provided the company with its first foothold in Mexico. Worthington joined with Mexican steel producer Hylsa S.A. de C.V. to create a joint venture called Acerex S.A. de C.V., which was charged with building a $24 million steel processing plant in Monterrey. In addition to serving as an entrée into the Mexican market, this venture also provided Worthington with a hub from which to serve the southwestern United States.

Worthington also entered into discussions with U.S. Steel about a possible joint venture to establish a minimill to produce flat-rolled steel and hot-rolled coil, which could lower Worthington's costs and lessen its dependence on suppliers by supplying some of the steel for its processing plants. After extensive investigation, however, the company resolved instead to purchase steel from a minimill being built in Delta, Ohio, by the North Star and BHP steel companies. In May 1995 Worthington announced plans to build a $65 million steel processing plant near the mill, with projected output of $250 million. This plant, Worthington's 11th steel processing facility in the United States, began slitting and pickling operations late in 1996 and then started up its hot dipped galvanizing line the following April.

Also in 1996, John H. McConnell retired from his position as chairman, a post his son assumed in addition to his CEO duties. The company founder nonetheless retained a seat on the board of directors, and the title of chairman emeritus, until 2002. He died six years later. During his retirement, McConnell encapsulated his business philosophy in a book titled *Our Golden Rule*, which was published in 2006. He was also the majority owner of the Columbus Blue Jackets, a National Hockey League team founded in 2000 that was the first major league sports team for McConnell's adopted hometown.

LATE-CENTURY ACQUISITIONS, CAPITAL PROJECTS, AND DIVESTMENTS

Starting in 1996, John P. McConnell led Worthington through a phase of heavy investment in the form of acquisitions and capital projects while also pursuing additional joint ventures. Two significant acquisitions expanded Worthington into business sectors related to its steel-based core. In February 1996 the company purchased Dietrich Industries, Inc., for $146 million in cash and the assumption of $30 million in debt. Founded in 1959 and based in Pittsburgh, Dietrich was the largest producer of galvanized metal framing products for commercial and residential construction in the United States. At the time of the takeover, Dietrich employed 1,500 people at 18 facilities in 15 states, and it was generating annual sales of $285 million.

In its second significant acquisition of this period, Worthington in February 1997 bought the Gerstenslager Company, a leading producer of aftermarket automotive and commercial truck body panels, for $113 million in stock. Gerstenslager was founded in 1860 as a carriage factory in rural Marshallville, Ohio, later moved to the north-central Ohio town of Wooster, and by the 1990s specialized in stamping, assembling, priming, packaging, and shipping such vehicle components as fenders, doors, and hoods. When Worthington acquired the firm, its annual revenues amounted to $120 million.

As Worthington was acquiring related lines of business at home, the WAVE joint venture in the late 1990s expanded around the world, acquiring an existing facility in Spain and opening new facilities in China and England as well as in Las Vegas, Nevada, and Benton Harbor, Michigan. In 1998 Worthington opened its largest facility so far, a 750,000-square-foot steel processing plant located in Decatur, Alabama, adjacent to a steel minimill operated by Trico Steel Company. This plant had the capacity to process more than one million tons of steel per year.

In the late 1990s Worthington's cylinder division, already generating around $300 million in sales per year, expanded further. In addition to entering into a joint venture in Brazil focusing on the production of propane tanks, Worthington aggressively expanded in Europe. In 1998 it acquired the Austrian firm Jos. Heiser vormals J. Winter's Sohn GmbH, Europe's leading producer of high-pressure cylinders, including for such uses as cutting and welding tools, medical oxygen containers, fire extinguishers, and scuba gear. Worthington followed up the Heiser deal with two 1999 deals, acquiring a majority interest in Gastec spol. a.r.o., the leading pressure cylinder manufacturer in the Czech Republic, and purchasing outright the Portuguese company Metalurgica Progresso de Vale de Cambra, Lda., producer of small and medium-sized liquefied petroleum gas cylinders used in heating and industrial applications.

Between 1992 and 1998 Worthington Industries spent about $1 billion on the aforementioned capital projects and acquisitions, the vast majority of which involved its core operations in value-added steel processing and steel-related niche markets, such as cylinders and metal framing. The company's managers decided it would be best for Worthington to narrow its focus to these core areas by jettisoning three units that had largely evolved out of the 1980 acquisition of Buckeye International. These units, Worthington Custom Plastics, Worthington Precision Metals, and Buckeye Steel Castings, accounted for about 26 percent of the firm's fiscal 1997 revenues of $1.91 billion. By the end of the fiscal year ending in May 1999, Worthington had sold the units in piecemeal fashion for aggregate proceeds of $224 million.

As the divestment program neared its completion, Worthington reorganized its steel processing operations. In place of a decentralized structure in which its 11 wholly owned plants and three joint-venture plants operated independently of one another, the company created a centralized management structure organized into geographically based business units with a national sales force organized along product lines. During fiscal 2000, the first full year following the completion of the divestment program and the implementation of the reorganization, Worthington posted profits of $94.2 million on sales of $1.96 billion. In April 2000, in a move intended to signal the beginning of a new era at Worthington Industries, the company unveiled a new corporate logo. That same month, trading in the company's stock switched from the NASDAQ to the New York Stock Exchange.

RESTRUCTURING AMID A DOWNTURN

The U.S. steel industry was already in a cyclical downturn when the overall U.S. economy fell into recession in 2001, sending a number of major U.S. integrated steelmakers into bankruptcy. Worthington fared better thanks to its more specialized steel operations and its diversification into related fields. Sales, nevertheless, dropped in both the 2001 and 2002 fiscal years, totaling just $1.74 billion the latter year. Profits fell sharply in fiscal 2001 to $35.6 million. Worthington responded to the downturn with a restructuring launched in January 2002.

Six unprofitable or marginally profitable plants were shut down, including the steel processing facilities in Malvern, Pennsylvania, and Jackson, Michigan; a metal framing operation in Fredericksburg, Virginia; a Worthington Cylinders plant in Claremore, Oklahoma; and the cylinder joint-venture operation in Brazil, which had been operating two plants. About 500 employees, comprising 7 percent of the global workforce, were laid off, and Worthington recorded restructuring charges of $64.6 million, which cut the net income for fiscal 2002 to just $6.5 million.

As Worthington's business began recovering in fiscal 2003, the firm returned to growth mode and completed its first acquisition since 1999. In July 2002 Worthington acquired Unimast Incorporated for $114.7 million plus $9.3 million in assumed debt. Unimast was the second-largest producer of steel framing products in the United States, trailing only Dietrich. The subsequent integration of Unimast into Dietrich resulted in some redundancies and led to the closure of three plants. At this time, Worthington also continued to expand Worthington Steelpac Systems, LLC, a subsidiary launched in 2000 that manufactured steel pallets and other steel shipping products.

After a year of record sales and near-record profits in fiscal 2004, Worthington Industries enjoyed its best year ever in 2005, earning $179.4 million in profits on sales of $3.08 billion. Even while enjoying this strong recovery, the company continued to rationalize its operations, most notably by selling most of the assets of its underperforming steel processing plant in Decatur, Alabama, to Nucor Corporation in August 2004 for $80.4 million. That same year the company moved into the Canadian metal framing market for the first time through a joint venture, and it acquired the propane and specialty gas cylinder business of Western Industries,

Inc., for $65.1 million. In the latter deal, Worthington Cylinders gained two facilities in Wisconsin that produced disposable cylinders for hand torches, camping stoves, portable heaters, and tabletop grills. Worthington in 2004 also bought out the minority partner in its pressure cylinder venture in the Czech Republic.

In 2006 Worthington sold its stake in the Mexican steel processing joint venture that had been formed in 1994, recording a pretax gain of $27 million. Just a year later, however, Worthington returned to Mexico via a new joint venture with Inverzer, S.A. de C.V., that within a few years was operating steel processing plants in the Mexican cities of León, Queretaro, and Monterrey. Back home, meanwhile, the company acquired Precision Specialty Metals, Inc., in August 2006 for $31.7 million, gaining a stainless steel processing plant in Los Angeles that Worthington also began using as a base on the West Coast from which to offer other steel processing products and services.

FIRST YEAR IN THE RED

As the commercial and residential construction markets in the United States began struggling, Worthington in September 2007 announced plans to shutter metal framing plants in East Chicago, Indiana; Phoenix, Arizona; Rock Hill, South Carolina; and Wildwood, Florida. A manufacturing plant in Montreal was also closed, but Worthington continued to operate a distribution center on the site. Worthington was forced to make additional cutbacks once the economy fell deeply into recession in 2008 given that two of the key industries the firm served, the automotive and construction sectors, were hit particularly hard.

Late in 2008 the closure of three more plants was announced, including a steel processing facility in Louisville, Kentucky, and metal framing facilities in Renton, Washington, and Lunenburg, Massachusetts. Operations were suspended at two other metal framing plants. These cutbacks resulted in a 20 percent reduction in the company workforce, from 8,000 to 6,400. Goodwill impairment and restructuring charges totaling $140 million pretax sent Worthington into the first full-year net loss in its history for the fiscal year ending in May 2009. The loss amounted to $108.2 million, while the 2009 sales total of $2.63 billion represented a 14 percent drop from the previous year.

The first six months of fiscal 2010 showed signs of recovery as demand for Worthington's products and services began rising in the automotive, agricultural equipment, and infrastructure markets. Although sales were down sharply from the previous year, the company managed to post a net profit of $29.9 million for this six-month period. In a further restructuring move, Worthington in late 2009 closed down its metal framing plant in Joliet, Illinois. At the same time, however, a strong balance sheet enabled Worthington to remain alert to opportunities for expansion. In February 2010, for instance, the company purchased the steel processing division of Gibralter Industries, Inc., gaining a plant in Cleveland, Ohio, that supplied the metal used to make Canadian coins and also produced steel products for a number of automakers. Worthington was likely to pursue additional strategic acquisitions of a similar nature during the economic recovery.

Henry R. Hecht
Updated, Paula Kepos; David E. Salamie

PRINCIPAL SUBSIDIARIES

The Worthington Steel Company; Dietrich Industries, Inc.; Worthington Cylinder Corporation; The Gerstenslager Company; Worthington Integrated Building Systems, LLC; Worthington Steelpac Systems, LLC.

PRINCIPAL COMPETITORS

AK Steel Holding Corporation; Nucor Corporation; Reliance Steel & Aluminum Co.; Ryerson Inc.; Shiloh Industries, Inc.; Steel Technologies Inc.; United States Steel Corporation.

FURTHER READING

Basralian, Joseph, "If It Ain't Broke," *Financial World*, March 28, 1995, pp. 60+.

Gearino, Dan, "Double Whammy Takes a Toll: Troubles of Automakers, Commercial Builders Hurt Worthington Industries," *Columbus (Ohio) Dispatch*, March 1, 2009, p. 1D.

———, "Worthington Industries Reports First Yearly Loss," *Columbus (Ohio) Dispatch*, July 16, 2009, p. 12A.

Geer, John F., Jr., "Cyclical Lite: Worthington Industries Is Just a Steel Company. Not." *Financial World*, March 25, 1996, pp. 44+.

Matthews, Tom, "Staying the Course: Worthington Industries to Stick with Strategy of Diversifying as It Turns 50," *Columbus (Ohio) Dispatch*, June 3, 2005, p. 1H.

McConnell, John H., "*... And We've Only Scratched the Surface": The Growth Story of Worthington Industries*, New York: Newcomen Society in North America, 1981, 20 p.

———, *Our Golden Rule*, Columbus, OH: Franklin University Press, 2004, 161 p.

Petry, Corinna, "Worthington Sees Rising Steel Volume," *American Metal Market*, January 8, 2010, p. 7.

Rodengen, Jeffrey L., *The Legend of Worthington Industries*, 2nd edition, Fort Lauderdale, FL: Write Stuff Enterprises, 2003, 168 p.

Rudnitsky, Howard, "Pumping Steel," *Forbes*, January 1, 1996, p. 154.

———, "You Have to Trust the Workforce," *Forbes*, July 19, 1993, pp. 78+.

Wilson, Paul, "Quiet Contributor: Worthington Industries' Cylinder Division Profits from Steady Growth," *Columbus (Ohio) Dispatch*, November 29, 2006, p. 1D.

Winter, Ralph E., "Worthington Expects Growth in Market Share: Steel Processor Is Focusing on Customer Relations to Prosper in Downturn," *Wall Street Journal*, August 7, 2001, p. B7D.

Wolf, Barnet D., "Forging His Own Way: John P. McConnell Steering Worthington Industries Past Storms Dad Has Faced Before," *Columbus (Ohio) Dispatch*, September 24, 2000, p. 1H.

Zipser, Andy, "Nerves of Steel," *Barron's*, February 24, 1992, pp. 46–47.

Zabar's and Company Inc.

2245 Broadway
New York, New York 10024
U.S.A.
Telephone: (212) 787-2000
Fax: (212) 580-4477
Web site: http://www.zabars.com

Private Company
Incorporated: 1934
Employees: 250
Sales: $50 million (2008 est.)
NAICS: 445110 Supermarkets and Other Grocery (Except Convenience) Stores

■ ■ ■

Zabar's and Company Inc. is a New York City institution where celebrities and everyday people mix and shop for gourmet and kosher foods as well as housewares. The family-owned retailer operates a crowded Upper West Side store at the corner of 80th Street and Broadway, a 20,000-square-foot rabbit warren of departments, as well as an online and catalog business. Zabar's offers a fish counter that specializes in smoked fish, tuna and seafood salad, gefilte fish, and other delicacies. Zabar's is also known for caviar, packaged under its own private label.

Other offerings include cheeses from around the world, coffees and teas, bagels and breads, cakes and cookies, gourmet candy, dried fruit, nuts, deli meats, sausages and franks, entrees for reheating, preserves and fruit spreads, spices, oils, and sauces. Many of Zabar's

items are packaged in gift baskets and crates. The store includes a mezzanine where Zabar's sells coffee and tea makers, cookware, and assorted houseware items. Zabar's also offers catering and operates a small corner café with a separate entrance. All told, the store serves about 40,000 customers each week.

FOUNDER IMMIGRATES TO THE UNITED STATES: 1923

Zabar's was founded by Louis Zabar and his wife, Lillian Teit Zabar. They were raised in the same shtetl (a Jewish village) in the Ukraine, where Zabar was born in 1901. He learned the rudiments of commerce from his father who dealt in dried fruits and nuts and by the time he was a young man was playing an important part in the business. The elder Zabar was murdered in a pogrom, a periodic persecution of the Jewish population in Eastern Europe that if not officially sanctioned was met with a blind eye by the government. Louis Zabar fled the country and came to the United States through Canada in 1923, settling in Brooklyn. Lillian Zabar had preceded him, initially living with relatives in Philadelphia before coming to New York City where she was reunited with Louis and they were married. By this time, he was renting a stall to sell produce at a public market in Brooklyn.

STORE MOVES: 1941

It was in 1934 that Louis and Lillian Zabar moved to Manhattan's Upper West Side after learning of an appetizer counter available for rent at a large store, Daitch

Dairy, known for its cheese. Here Louis Zabar began to sell smoked fish and build a reputation for offering the highest-quality items at a fair price. A few years later the couple bought the store when the owner decided to sell. They sold fish on one side of the store, cheese on the other, and offered groceries in the back. The store was located in the heart of an affluent Jewish community and did well despite the lean years of the Great Depression. As the economy picked up with military spending while the United States prepared for possible war, which became a reality in late 1941, the Zabars relocated their store a few doors down to its current site in 1941, resulting in Zabar's Super Market, but simply known as Zabar's.

With business booming, Louis Zabar opened other grocery stores in Manhattan, mostly on upper Broadway. In 1949 he became ill, and in March 1950 he died in Miami Beach, Florida, at the age of 50. According to his obituary in the *New York Times* he owned 10 grocery stores, but other sources place the number at five. In any event, his passing at such an early age caught the family off-guard.

The youngest of three sons, Eli, was in second grade, while the middle son, Stanley, was attending college at the University of Pennsylvania. The eldest was Saul, who was enrolled at the University of Kansas with the goal of becoming a doctor when his father's health faltered. He dropped out and returned home to help his mother run the family business, although he expected to resume his school in a year or two. Instead, he never left the store. Stanley would work at Zabar's as well, focusing on administrative duties and finances, but for a time left to practice law.

Saul Zabar was not comfortable running several grocery stores. "It was like having five separate children with separate personalities, sales and bookkeeping," he told the *New York Times*. "I wanted to do one thing and do it well. I wanted to take care of it in a way that it survives and becomes famous." He consolidated the operations into a single location, but the man who played a key role in making Zabar's famous was someone who Louis Zabar had originally hired to sort soda bottles and sweep the floors at one of his grocery stores: Murray Klein.

MURRAY KLEIN JOINS ZABAR'S: 1950

Klein was born in a Ukrainian shtetl in 1923. His family was shattered by World War II. While his parents and five siblings were interned in Nazi concentration camps, where they ultimately died, Klein was away at trade school. He was sent to a Soviet labor camp, from which he eventually escaped and joined a Jewish guerrilla movement that helped to smuggle arms into Palestine. After becoming a political prisoner in Italy, he conducted a hunger strike, forcing his release to a displaced-persons camp in Rome, where he lived from 1945 to 1950 and ran his own bread business. With the help of a cousin he made his way to New York and found work with Louis Zabar before his death.

Klein became a manager for Saul Zabar but left in the 1950s to start his own hardware and housewares store in Manhattan. He was lured back to Zabar's but left several times before buying out Lillian's share of the business in 1960 to become a one-third partner with Saul and Stanley Zabar. "Murray was really the founder of Zabar's as it exists today," Saul Zabar maintained in *It Happened in Manhattan,* an oral history published in 2001. "He had a sense of humor; he liked to talk to celebrities. There was always something smart, but not offensive, coming out of his mouth. Murray was able to put everything together."

CUSTOMERS DEVELOPING MORE SOPHISTICATED TASTES

With Klein providing management, Saul Zabar was able to concentrate on buying fish and cheese. To complement the fish, Zabar's carried excellent bread, and Saul Zabar soon developed an interest in coffee. In the mid-1960s he devoted about a year learning the intricacies of coffee while attending daily two-house roasting and cupping sessions at White Coffee Corporation in Long Island City. In time, he became an expert and was able to order exotic blends for White to produce and Zabar's to sell. The 1960s was also a time when the rising popularity of jet airliners resulted in an increasing number of Americans vacationing overseas and led to something of a food revolution. Residents of the Upper West Side were especially interested in pursuing the latest food fads. It was during this period that Stanley Zabar became more actively involved in the business, helping to buy exotic European cheeses and breads, olive oils, pastas, and other items.

Klein also put his knowledge of the housewares business to use in providing the necessary cooking utensils required by Zabar's new breed of customers, described by author David Kamp as "a more worldly, affluent, educated, Upper West Side intellectual, New Yorker-reading, PBS-tote-bag-toting shopper." Because space was limited, Klein hung the wares from the ceiling, requiring a stepladder be pulled out to help customers make a purchase. It was worth the time, however. Klein would soon be bragging how he was making $1 million a year from the ceiling alone. Moreover, people who did not shop at Zabar's came in to buy housewares, often sampled the food, and became regular customers.

The youngest of the Zabar brothers, Eli, was also working for the business at night in the 1960s while attending Columbia University during the day. He became increasingly frustrated, however, with his brothers' unwillingness to make him a partner. In 1973 he struck out on his own, setting up his own Upper East Side deli, E.A.T., which became an instant hit and established Eli Zabar as an epicurean force in his own right.

To keep pace with sales, Zabar's acquired adjacent property to expand the store and by 1975 had created the present-day footprint. Zabar's also launched a mail-order business in the early 1980s. In 1981, having exhausted its ability to expand horizontally, Zabar grew vertically, creating a mezzanine for housewares, which no longer had to be hung from the ceiling. By this time Klein had grown the housewares business to about $1.5 million in annual revenues by clever buying that allowed him to offer low prices, resulting in strong sales, and an ability to purchase in volume. He also garnered a good deal of publicity in 1975 when he became involved in a flap with Cuisinarts Inc. after Zabar's began selling the company's French-made food processor for $135 when other stores charged $190. In just two days Klein sold 200 processors, prompting Cuisinarts to sever Zabar's

supply. Klein handed out about 1,000 rain checks to customers and sued Cuisinarts. In late 1977 Zabar's reached a settlement with the company and Klein was able to honor the rain checks by offering a plastic-base model of the processor, along with a coffee grinder and five pounds of coffee, for $135.

BATTLE OF BELUGA: 1983

Klein was combative by nature and enjoyed taking out newspaper ads to boast about Zabar's beating Macy's and Bloomingdale's on food and cookware prices. In the early 1980s he baited the Macy's department store food buyer into a discount food fight that escalated into the Caviar Wars ("the Battle of Beluga") of New York City lore. The first volleys were fired in 1983 over the price of Pommery mustard, which Klein cut and Macy's answered in kind. Lindt chocolate bars became fodder for the growing confrontation, as did other products. "Blood will run in the streets," Klein told the press, relishing the attention and the fight. The conflict then reached a head during the Christmas season when Macy's and Zabar's drew swords over the same brand of 14-ounce tins of Beluga caviar, which Macy's initially put on sale at $149. Klein countered with a lower price. The two sides undercut one another until Macy's began selling caviar at cost, $129. Refusing to be defeated, Klein lowered Zabar's price to $119.95, losing money on each sale. While on first blush the caviar war appeared to be a matter of pride overwhelming fiscal sense, the cost of it served Zabar's well in the long run. Not only did the store receive publicity it could never afford to buy, Zabar's established itself as a place to purchase caviar not just gefilte fish. Whatever amount of money Klein lost in the short run during the Battle of Beluga was more than compensated by caviar sales in the years that followed.

Klein was not above fighting with his partners as well. For a time, he fell out with the Zabar brothers over how to run the business, and in 1985 rumors circulated that Zabar's was for sale. Bear, Stearns & Company was hired to find a buyer as Klein claimed that he was ready to retire. Eventually the partners sat down and ironed out their problems and the talk of selling Zabar's died down. Their differences flared up again in 1992 when Klein sued the Zabar brothers over a demand that they buy him out for $6 million. In October 1994 an agreement was reached and Klein was bought out. He retired, leaving behind a company that was generating about $40 million in annual sales. Klein passed away in 2007 at the age of 84.

With Saul Zabar taking the lead, Zabar's maintained its place in New York's food world into the new century. The competition that Zabar's had helped to spawn, such as Balducci's and Dean & Deluca, had long since been sold by their founding families to corporations. The Zabar family expressed no interest in opening other stores, licensing the name or franchising the concept, let alone selling the business. Instead, they were content to run their Upper West Side fiefdom. They did, however, add a café with its own entrance on the corner where customers could take out Zabar's fare or enjoy it at one of the nook's few tables. Zabar's also supplemented its catalog business with online sales, increasing annual revenues to $50 million by 2009. Although Saul Zabar was 80 years of age and Stanley Zabar was in his late 70s, another generation of the family was involved in running the business. Thus, the Zabar's tradition in New York City would apparently continue for many years to come.

Ed Dinger

PRINCIPAL DEPARTMENTS

Coffee & Tea; Fish Counter; Cheese; Gift Baskets & Boxes; Housewares; Catering; Catalog.

PRINCIPAL COMPETITORS

Citarella; Dean & DeLuca, Inc.; Williams-Sonoma, Inc.

FURTHER READING

Chan, Sewell, "Remembering Murray Klein, 84, Former Co-Owner of Zabar's," *New York Times,* December 6, 2007.

Collins, Glenn, "Behind Zabar's Counters, 3 Feuding Partners," *New York Times,* March 16, 1985.

Fabricant, Florence, "As Demand Grows, Food Shops Expand," *New York Times,* November 25, 1981.

Frommer, Myrna Katz, and Harvey Frommer, *It Happened in Manhattan,* New York: Berkley Publishing Group, 2001, 312 p.

Gray, Christopher, "Streetscapes/Zabar's, Broadway between 80th and 81st Street," *New York Times,* December 2, 2009.

Kelley, Tina, "A Lifetime amid the Lox and Rugelach," *New York Times,* May 31, 2008.

Miller, Bryan, "At Zabar's, a Realignment at the Top," *New York Times,* October 20, 1994.

Moskin, Julia, "Murray Klein, Who Helped Build Zabar's into Food Destination, Dies at 84," *New York Times,* December 7, 2007.

Neerman, Marilyn, "Housewares Is Gaining on Herring at Zabar's," *Discount Store News,* May 30, 1983, p. 1.

Plueneke, Geraldine, "The Brothers Zabar," *Edible Manhattan,* January 2009.

Stout, David, "Lillian Zabar, Co-Founder of Quintessential Deli," *New York Times,* December 23, 1995.

Cumulative Index to Companies

Pediatric Services of America, Inc., 31 356–58
Pediatrix Medical Group, Inc., 61 282–85
Peebles Inc., 16 411–13; 43 296–99 (upd.)
Peek & Cloppenburg KG, 46 342–45
Peet's Coffee & Tea, Inc., 38 338–40; 100 333–37 (upd.)
Peg Perego SpA, 88 300–03
Pegasus Solutions, Inc., 75 315–18
Pei Cobb Freed & Partners Architects LLP, 57 280–82
Pelican Products, Inc., 86 331–34
Pelikan Holding AG, 92 296–300
Pella Corporation, 12 384–86; 39 322–25 (upd.); 89 349–53 (upd.)
Pemco Aviation Group Inc., 54 283–86
PEMEX *see* Petróleos Mexicanos.
Penaflor S.A., 66 252–54
Penauille Polyservices SA, 49 318–21
Pendleton Grain Growers Inc., 64 305–08
Pendleton Woolen Mills, Inc., 42 275–78
Pendragon, PLC, 109 441–45
Penford Corporation, 55 296–99
Pengrowth Energy Trust, 95 323–26
The Penguin Group, 100 338–42
The Peninsular and Oriental Steam Navigation Company, V 490–93; 38 341–46 (upd.)
Peninsular and Oriental Steam Navigation Company (Bovis Division), I 588–89 *see also* DP World.
Penn Engineering & Manufacturing Corp., 28 349–51
Penn National Gaming, Inc., 33 327–29; 109 446–50 (upd.)
Penn Traffic Company, 13 393–95
Penn Virginia Corporation, 85 324–27
Penney's *see* J.C. Penney Company, Inc.
Pennington Seed Inc., 98 301–04
Pennon Group Plc, 45 338–41
Pennsylvania Blue Shield, III 325–27 *see also* Highmark Inc.
Pennsylvania Power & Light Company, V 693–94
Pennwalt Corporation, I 382–84
PennWell Corporation, 55 300–03
Pennzoil-Quaker State Company, IV 488–90; 20 418–22 (upd.); 50 350–55 (upd.)
Penske Corporation, V 494–95; 19 292–94 (upd.); 84 305–309 (upd.)
Pentair, Inc., 7 419–21; 26 361–64 (upd.); 81 281–87 (upd.)
Pentax Corporation, 78 301–05
Pentech International, Inc., 29 372–74
The Pentland Group plc, 20 423–25; 100 343–47 (upd.)
Penton Media, Inc., 27 360–62
Penzeys Spices, Inc., 79 314–16
People Express Airlines Inc., I 117–18
Peoples Energy Corporation, 6 543–44
People's United Financial Inc. , 106 349–52

PeopleSoft Inc., 14 381–83; 33 330–33 (upd.) *see also* Oracle Corp.
The Pep Boys—Manny, Moe & Jack, 11 391–93; 36 361–64 (upd.); 81 288–94 (upd.)
PEPCO *see* Potomac Electric Power Co.
Pepper *see* J. W. Pepper and Son Inc.
The Pepper Construction Group, LLC, 111 385–88
Pepper Hamilton LLP, 43 300–03
Pepperidge Farm, Incorporated, 81 295–300
The Pepsi Bottling Group, Inc., 40 350–53
PepsiAmericas, Inc., 67 297–300 (upd.)
PepsiCo, Inc., I 276–79; 10 450–54 (upd.); 38 347–54 (upd.); 93 333–44 (upd.)
Pequiven *see* Petroquímica de Venezuela S.A.
Perdigao SA, 52 276–79
Perdue Farms Inc., 7 422–24; 23 375–78 (upd.)
Perfetti Van Melle S.p.A., 72 270–73
Performance Food Group, 31 359–62; 96 329–34 (upd.)
Perini Corporation, 8 418–21; 82 274–79 (upd.)
PerkinElmer, Inc., 7 425–27; 78 306–10 (upd.)
Perkins & Marie Callender's Inc., 107 345–51 (upd.)
Perkins Coie LLP, 56 268–70
Perkins Family Restaurants, L.P., 22 417–19
Perkins Foods Holdings Ltd., 87 371–374
Perma-Fix Environmental Services, Inc., 99 338–341
Pernod Ricard S.A., I 280–81; 21 399–401 (upd.); 72 274–77 (upd.)
Perot Systems Corporation, 29 375–78
Perrigo Company, 12 387–89; 59 330–34 (upd.)
Perry Ellis International Inc., 41 291–94; 106 353–58 (upd.)
Perry's Ice Cream Company Inc., 90 326–29
The Perseus Books Group, 91 375–78
Perstorp AB, I 385–87; 51 289–92 (upd.)
Pertamina, IV 491–93; 56 271–74 (upd.)
Perusahaan Otomobil Nasional Bhd., 62 266–68
Pescanova S.A., 81 301–04
Pet Incorporated, 7 428–31
Petco Animal Supplies, Inc., 29 379–81; 74 231–34 (upd.)
Peter Kiewit Sons' Inc., 8 422–24
Peter Pan Bus Lines Inc., 106 359–63
Peter Piper, Inc., 70 217–19
Peterbilt Motors Company, 89 354–57
Petersen Publishing Company, 21 402–04
Peterson American Corporation, 55 304–06
Pete's Brewing Company, 22 420–22

Petit Bateau, 95 327–31
Petland Inc., 110 363–66
PetMed Express, Inc., 81 305–08
Petrie Stores Corporation, 8 425–27
Petro-Canada, IV 494–96; 99 342–349 (upd.)
Petrobrás *see* Petróleo Brasileiro S.A.
Petrobras Energia Participaciones S.A., 72 278–81
Petroecuador *see* Petróleos del Ecuador.
Petrof spol. S.R.O., 107 352–56
Petrofac Ltd., 95 332–35
PetroFina S.A., IV 497–500; 26 365–69 (upd.)
Petrogal *see* Petróleos de Portugal.
Petrohawk Energy Corporation, 79 317–20
Petróleo Brasileiro S.A., IV 501–03
Petróleos de Portugal S.A., IV 504–06
Petróleos de Venezuela S.A., IV 507–09; 74 235–39 (upd.)
Petróleos del Ecuador, IV 510–11
Petróleos Mexicanos (PEMEX), IV 512–14; 19 295–98 (upd.); 104 373–78 (upd.)
Petroleum Development Oman LLC, IV 515–16; 98 305–09 (upd.)
Petroleum Helicopters, Inc., 35 334–36
Petroliam Nasional Bhd (Petronas), 56 275–79 (upd.)
Petrolite Corporation, 15 350–52 *see also* Baker Hughes Inc.
Petromex *see* Petróleos de Mexico S.A.
Petron Corporation, 58 270–72
Petronas, IV 517–20 *see also* Petroliam Nasional Bhd.
Petroplus Holdings AG, 108 381–84
Petrossian Inc., 54 287–89
Petry Media Corporation, 102 326–29
PETsMART, Inc., 14 384–86; 41 295–98 (upd.)
Peugeot S.A., I 187–88 *see also* PSA Peugeot Citroen S.A.
The Pew Charitable Trusts, 35 337–40
Pez Candy, Inc., 38 355–57
The Pfaltzgraff Co. *see* Susquehanna Pfaltzgraff Co.
Pfizer Inc., I 661–63; 9 402–05 (upd.); 38 358–67 (upd.); 79 321–33 (upd.)
PFSweb, Inc., 73 254–56
PG&E Corporation, 26 370–73 (upd.)
PGA *see* The Professional Golfers' Association.
Phaidon Press Ltd., 98 310–14
Phantom Fireworks *see* B.J. Alan Co., Inc.
Phar-Mor Inc., 12 390–92
Pharmacia & Upjohn Inc., I 664–65; 25 374–78 (upd.) *see also* Pfizer Inc.
Pharmion Corporation, 91 379–82
Phat Fashions LLC, 49 322–24
Phelps Dodge Corporation, IV 176–79; 28 352–57 (upd.); 75 319–25 (upd.)
PHH Arval, V 496–97; 53 274–76 (upd.)
PHI, Inc., 80 282–86 (upd.)
Philadelphia Eagles, 37 305–08
Philadelphia Electric Company, V 695–97 *see also* Exelon Corp.

Southern New England Telecommunications Corporation, 6 338–40

Southern Pacific Transportation Company, V 516–18 *see also* Union Pacific Corp.

Southern Peru Copper Corporation, 40 411–13

Southern Poverty Law Center, Inc., 74 312–15

Southern Progress Corporation, 102 388–92

Southern States Cooperative Incorporated, 36 440–42

Southern Sun Hotel Interest (Pty) Ltd., 106 435–39

Southern Union Company, 27 424–26

Southern Wine and Spirits of America, Inc., 84 371–375

The Southland Corporation, II 660–61; 7 490–92 (upd.) *see also* 7–Eleven, Inc.

Southtrust Corporation, 11 455–57 *see also* Wachovia Corp.

Southwest Airlines Co., 6 119–21; 24 452–55 (upd.); 71 343–47 (upd.)

Southwest Gas Corporation, 19 410–12

Southwest Water Company, 47 370–73

Southwestern Bell Corporation, V 328–30 *see also* SBC Communications Inc.

Southwestern Electric Power Co., 21 468–70

Southwestern Public Service Company, 6 579–81

Southwire Company, Inc., 8 478–80; 23 444–47 (upd.)

Souza Cruz S.A., 65 322–24

Sovereign Bancorp, Inc., 103 392–95

Sovran Self Storage, Inc., 66 299–301

SP Alpargatas *see* Sao Paulo Alpargatas S.A.

Spacehab, Inc., 37 364–66

Spacelabs Medical, Inc., 71 348–50

Spadel S.A./NV, 113 363–67

Spaghetti Warehouse, Inc., 25 436–38

Spago *see* The Wolfgang Puck Food Company, Inc.

Spangler Candy Company, 44 392–95

Spanish Broadcasting System, Inc., 41 383–86

Spansion Inc., 80 352–55

Spanx, Inc., 89 423–27

Spar Aerospace Limited, 32 435–37

Spar Handelsgesellschaft mbH, 35 398–401; 103 396–400 (upd.)

Spark Networks, Inc., 91 437–40

Spartan Motors Inc., 14 457–59

Spartan Stores Inc., 8 481–82; 66 302–05 (upd.)

Spartech Corporation, 19 413–15; 76 329–32 (upd.)

Sparton Corporation, 18 492–95

Spear & Jackson, Inc., 73 320–23

Spear, Leeds & Kellogg, 66 306–09

Special Olympics, Inc., 93 410–14

Specialist Computer Holdings Ltd., 80 356–59

Specialized Bicycle Components Inc., 50 445–48

Specialty Coatings Inc., 8 483–84

Specialty Equipment Companies, Inc., 25 439–42

Specialty Products & Insulation Co., 59 381–83

Spec's Music, Inc., 19 416–18 *see also* Camelot Music, Inc.

Specsavers Optical Group Ltd., 104 428–31

Spector Photo Group N.V., 82 344–47

Spectrum Brands, Inc., 109 514–20 (upd.)

Spectrum Control, Inc., 67 355–57

Spectrum Organic Products, Inc., 68 346–49

Spee-Dee Delivery Service, Inc., 93 415–18

SpeeDee Oil Change and Tune-Up, 25 443–47

Speedway Motorsports, Inc., 32 438–41; 112 396–400 (upd.)

Speedy Hire plc, 84 376–379

Speidel Inc., 96 404–07

Speizman Industries, Inc., 44 396–98

Spelling Entertainment, 14 460–62; 35 402–04 (upd.)

Spencer Stuart and Associates, Inc., 14 463–65 *see also* SSI (U.S.), Inc.

Sperian Protection S.A., 104 432–36

Spherion Corporation, 52 316–18

Spicy Pickle Franchising, Inc., 105 434–37

Spie *see* Amec Spie S.A.

Spiegel, Inc., 10 489–91; 27 427–31 (upd.)

SPIEGEL-Verlag Rudolf Augstein GmbH & Co. KG, 44 399–402

Spin Master, Ltd., 61 335–38

Spinnaker Exploration Company, 72 334–36

Spirax-Sarco Engineering plc, 59 384–86

Spirit Airlines, Inc., 31 419–21

Sport Chalet, Inc., 16 454–56; 94 402–06 (upd.)

Sport Supply Group, Inc., 23 448–50; 106 440–45 (upd.)

Sportmart, Inc., 15 469–71 *see also* Gart Sports Co.

Sports & Recreation, Inc., 17 453–55

The Sports Authority, Inc., 16 457–59; 43 385–88 (upd.)

The Sports Club Company, 25 448–51

The Sportsman's Guide, Inc., 36 443–46

Springs Global US, Inc., V 378–79; 19 419–22 (upd.); 90 378–83 (upd.)

Sprint Nextel Corporation, 9 478–80; 46 373–76 (upd.); 110 427–33 (upd.)

SPS Technologies, Inc., 30 428–30

SPSS Inc., 64 360–63

SPX Corporation, 10 492–95; 47 374–79 (upd.); 103 401–09 (upd.)

Spyglass Entertainment Group, LLC, 91 441–44

SQM *see* Sociedad Química y Minera de Chile S.A.

Square D, 90 384–89

Square Enix Holdings Co., Ltd., 101 454–57

Squibb Corporation, I 695–97 *see also* Bristol-Myers Squibb Co.

SR Teleperformance S.A., 86 365–68

SRA International, Inc., 77 400–03

SRAM Corporation, 65 325–27

SRC Holdings Corporation, 67 358–60

SRI International, Inc., 57 333–36

SSA *see* Stevedoring Services of America Inc.

SSAB Svenskt Stål AB, 89 428–31

Ssangyong Cement Industrial Co., Ltd., III 747–50; 61 339–43 (upd.)

SSI (U.S.), Inc., 103 410–14 (upd.)

SSL International plc, 49 378–81

SSOE Inc., 76 333–35

St Ives plc, 34 393–95

St. *see under* Saint

St. James's Place Capital, plc, 71 324–26

The St. Joe Company, 31 422–25; 98 368–73 (upd.)

St. Joe Paper Company, 8 485–88

St. John Knits, Inc., 14 466–68

St. Jude Medical, Inc., 11 458–61; 43 347–52 (upd.); 97 350–58 (upd.)

St. Louis Music, Inc., 48 351–54

St. Luke's-Roosevelt Hospital Center *see* Continuum Health Partners, Inc.

St. Mary Land & Exploration Company, 63 345–47

St. Paul Bank for Cooperatives, 8 489–90

The St. Paul Travelers Companies, Inc., III 355–57; 22 492–95 (upd.); 79 362–69 (upd.)

STAAR Surgical Company, 57 337–39

The Stabler Companies Inc., 78 352–55

Stafford Group, 110 434–38

Stage Stores, Inc., 24 456–59; 82 348–52 (upd.)

Stagecoach Group plc, 30 431–33; 104 437–41 (upd.)

Stanadyne Automotive Corporation, 37 367–70

StanCorp Financial Group, Inc., 56 345–48

Standard Candy Company Inc., 86 369–72

Standard Chartered plc, II 357–59; 48 371–74 (upd.)

Standard Commercial Corporation, 13 490–92; 62 333–37 (upd.)

Standard Federal Bank, 9 481–83

Standard Life Assurance Company, III 358–61

Standard Microsystems Corporation, 11 462–64

Standard Motor Products, Inc., 40 414–17

Standard Pacific Corporation, 52 319–22

The Standard Register Company, 15 472–74; 93 419–25 (upd.)

The Topaz Group, Inc., 62 369–71
Topco Associates LLC, 60 302–04
Topcon Corporation, 84 406–409
Toppan Printing Co., Ltd., IV 679–81;
 58 340–44 (upd.)
The Topps Company, Inc., 13 518–20;
 34 446–49 (upd.); 83 400–406 (upd.)
Tops Appliance City, Inc., 17 487–89
Tops Markets LLC, 60 305–07
Toray Industries, Inc., V 383–86; 51
 375–79 (upd.)
Torchmark Corporation, 9 506–08; 33
 405–08 (upd.)
Toresco Enterprises, Inc., 84 410–413
The Toro Company, 7 534–36; 26
 492–95 (upd.); 77 440–45 (upd.)
Toromont Industries, Ltd., 21 499–501
The Toronto-Dominion Bank, II
 375–77; 49 395–99 (upd.)
Toronto Maple Leafs *see* Maple Leaf
 Sports & Entertainment Ltd.
Toronto Raptors *see* Maple Leaf Sports &
 Entertainment Ltd.
The Torrington Company, 13 521–24
 see also Timken Co.
Torstar Corporation, 29 470–73 *see also*
 Harlequin Enterprises Ltd.
Tosco Corporation, 7 537–39 *see also*
 ConocoPhillips.
Toshiba Corporation, I 533–35; 12
 483–86 (upd.); 40 435–40 (upd.); 99
 453–461 (upd.)
Tosoh Corporation, 70 327–30
Total Compagnie Française des Pétroles
 S.A., IV 557–61 *see also* Total Fina Elf
 S.A.
Total Entertainment Restaurant
 Corporation, 46 427–29
Total Fina Elf S.A., 50 478–86 (upd.)
TOTAL S.A., 24 492–97 (upd.)
Total System Services, Inc., 18 516–18
The Tote *see* Horserace Totalisator Board
 (The Tote)
Totem Resources Corporation, 9
 509–11
TOTO LTD., III 755–56; 28 464–66
 (upd.)
Tottenham Hotspur PLC, 81 392–95
Touchstone Films *see* The Walt Disney
 Co.
TouchTunes Music Corporation, 97
 424–28
Toupargel-Agrigel S.A., 76 354–56
Touristik Union International GmbH.
 and Company K.G., II 163–65 *see*
 also Preussag AG.
TOUSA *see* Technical Olympic USA, Inc.
Touton S.A., 92 380–383
Tower Air, Inc., 28 467–69
Tower Automotive, Inc., 24 498–500
Towers Perrin, 32 458–60
Town & Country Corporation, 19
 451–53
Town Pump Inc., 113 434–37
Town Sports International, Inc., 46
 430–33
Townsends, Inc., 64 385–87

Toy Biz, Inc., 18 519–21 *see also* Marvel
 Entertainment, Inc.
Toymax International, Inc., 29 474–76
Toyo Sash Co., Ltd., III 757–58
Toyo Seikan Kaisha Ltd., I 615–16
Toyoda Automatic Loom Works, Ltd.,
 III 636–39
Toyota Motor Corporation, I 203–05;
 11 528–31 (upd.); 38 458–62 (upd.);
 100 415–22 (upd.)
Toys "R" Us, Inc., V 203–06; 18
 522–25 (upd.); 57 370–75 (upd.);
 110 463–71 (upd.)
TPG N.V., 64 388–91 (upd.)
TPI Composites, Inc., 112 435–38
Tracor Inc., 17 490–92
Tractebel S.A., 20 491–93 *see also* Suez
 Lyonnaise des Eaux;
 SUEZ-TRACTEBEL S.A.
Tractor Supply Company, 57 376–78
Trader Classified Media N.V., 57
 379–82
Trader Joe's Company, 13 525–27; 50
 487–90 (upd.)
TradeStation Group, Inc., 83 407–410
Traffix, Inc., 61 374–76
Trailer Bridge, Inc., 41 397–99
Trammell Crow Company, 8 532–34;
 57 383–87 (upd.)
Trane, 78 402–05
Trans-Lux Corporation, 51 380–83
Trans World Airlines, Inc., I 125–27; 12
 487–90 (upd.); 35 424–29 (upd.)
Trans World Entertainment
 Corporation, 24 501–03; 68 374–77
 (upd.)
Transaction Systems Architects, Inc., 29
 477–79; 82 397–402 (upd.)
TransAlta Utilities Corporation, 6
 585–87
Transamerica—An AEGON Company, I
 536–38; 13 528–30 (upd.); 41
 400–03 (upd.)
Transammonia Group, 95 425–28
Transatlantic Holdings, Inc., 11 532–33
TransBrasil S/A Linhas Aéreas, 31
 443–45
TransCanada Corporation, V 737–38;
 93 438–45 (upd.)
Transco Energy Company, V 739–40 *see*
 also The Williams Companies.
Transiciel SA, 48 400–02
Transitions Optical, Inc., 83 411–415
Transmedia Network Inc., 20 494–97 *see*
 also Rewards Network Inc.
TransMontaigne Inc., 28 470–72
Transneft *see* Oil Transporting Joint Stock
 Company Transneft
Transnet Ltd., 6 433–35
Transocean Sedco Forex Inc., 45 417–19
Transport Corporation of America, Inc.,
 49 400–03
Transportes Aéreas Centro-Americanos *see*
 Grupo TACA.
Transportes Aéreos Militares Ecuatorianos
 see TAME (Transportes Aéreos Militares
 Ecuatorianos)

Transportes Aereos Portugueses, S.A., 6
 125–27 *see also* TAP—Air Portugal
 Transportes Aéreos Portugueses S.A.
TransPro, Inc., 71 356–59
The Tranzonic Companies, 15 500–02;
 37 392–95 (upd.)
Travel Ports of America, Inc., 17
 493–95
TravelCenters of America LLC, 108
 496–500
Travelers Corporation, III 387–90 *see*
 also Citigroup Inc.
Travelocity.com LP, 46 434–37; 113
 438–42 (upd.)
Travelzoo Inc., 79 419–22
Travis Boats & Motors, Inc., 37 396–98
Travis Perkins plc, 34 450–52
TRC Companies, Inc., 32 461–64
Treadco, Inc., 19 454–56
Treasure Chest Advertising Company,
 Inc., 32 465–67
Tredegar Corporation, 52 349–51
Tree of Life, Inc., 29 480–82; 107
 441–44 (upd.)
Tree Top, Inc., 76 357–59
TreeHouse Foods, Inc., 79 423–26
Trek Bicycle Corporation, 16 493–95;
 78 406–10 (upd.)
Trelleborg AB, 93 455–64
Trend-Lines, Inc., 22 516–18
Trend Micro Inc., 97 429–32
Trendwest Resorts, Inc., 33 409–11 *see*
 also Jeld-Wen, Inc.
Trex Company, Inc., 71 360–62
Tri-State Generation and Transmission
 Association, Inc., 103 455–59
Tri Valley Growers, 32 468–71
Triarc Companies, Inc., 8 535–37; 34
 453–57 (upd.)
Tribune Company, IV 682–84; 22
 519–23 (upd.); 63 389–95 (upd.)
Trico Marine Services, Inc., 89 450–53
Trico Products Corporation, 15 503–05
Tridel Enterprises Inc., 9 512–13
Trident Seafoods Corporation, 56
 359–61
Trigano S.A., 102 426–29
Trigen Energy Corporation, 42 386–89
Trilon Financial Corporation, II 456–57
TriMas Corp., 11 534–36
Trimble Navigation Limited, 40 441–43
Trina Solar Limited, 103 460–64
Trinchero Family Estates, 107 445–50
 (upd.)
Třinecké Železárny A.S., 92 384–87
Trinity Industries, Incorporated, 7
 540–41
Trinity Mirror plc, 49 404–10 (upd.)
TRINOVA Corporation, III 640–42
TriPath Imaging, Inc., 77 446–49
Triple Five Group Ltd., 49 411–15
Triple P N.V., 26 496–99
Tripwire, Inc., 97 433–36
TriQuint Semiconductor, Inc., 63
 396–99
Trisko Jewelry Sculptures, Ltd., 57
 388–90
Triton Energy Corporation, 11 537–39

Veit Companies, 43 440–42; 92 398–402 (upd.)

Velcro Industries N.V., 19 476–78; 72 361–64 (upd.)

Velocity Express Corporation, 49 438–41; 94 441–46 (upd.)

Velux A/S, 86 412–15

Venator Group Inc., 35 444–49 (upd.) *see also* Foot Locker Inc.

Vencor, Inc., 16 515–17

Vendex International N.V., 13 544–46 *see also* Koninklijke Vendex KBB N.V. (Royal Vendex KBB N.V.).

Vendôme Luxury Group plc, 27 487–89

Venetian Casino Resort, LLC, 47 427–29

Ventana Medical Systems, Inc., 75 392–94

Ventura Foods LLC, 90 420–23

Venture Stores Inc., 12 507–09

Veolia Environnement, SA, 109 566–71

VeraSun Energy Corporation, 87 447–450

Verbatim Corporation, 14 533–35; 74 371–74 (upd.)

Vereinigte Elektrizitätswerke Westfalen AG, IV V 744–47

Veridian Corporation, 54 395–97

VeriFone, Inc., 18 541–44; 76 368–71 (upd.)

Verint Systems Inc., 73 370–72

VeriSign, Inc., 47 430–34

Veritas Software Corporation, 45 427–31

Verity Inc., 68 388–91

Verizon Communications Inc., 43 443–49 (upd.); 78 432–40 (upd.)

Verlagsgruppe Georg von Holtzbrinck GmbH, 35 450–53

Verlagsgruppe Weltbild GmbH, 98 441–46

Vermeer Manufacturing Company, 17 507–10

The Vermont Country Store, 93 478–82

Vermont Pure Holdings, Ltd., 51 394–96

The Vermont Teddy Bear Co., Inc., 36 500–02

Versace *see* Gianni Versace SpA.

Vertex Pharmaceuticals Incorporated, 83 440–443

Vertis Communications, 84 418–421

Vertrue Inc., 77 469–72

Vestas Wind Systems A/S, 73 373–75

Vestey Group Ltd., 95 433–37

Veuve Clicquot Ponsardin SCS, 98 447–51

VEW AG, 39 412–15

VF Corporation, V 390–92; 17 511–14 (upd.); 54 398–404 (upd.)

VHA Inc., 53 345–47

Viacom Inc., 7 560–62; 23 500–03 (upd.); 67 367–71 (upd.) *see also* Paramount Pictures Corp.

Viad Corp., 73 376–78

Viag AG, IV 229–32 *see also* E.On AG.

ViaSat, Inc., 54 405–08

Viasoft Inc., 27 490–93; 59 27

VIASYS Healthcare, Inc., 52 389–91

Viasystems Group, Inc., 67 372–74

Viatech Continental Can Company, Inc., 25 512–15 (upd.)

Vicarious Visions, Inc., 108 529–32

Vicat S.A., 70 341–43

Vickers plc, 27 494–97

Vicon Industries, Inc., 44 440–42

VICORP Restaurants, Inc., 12 510–12; 48 412–15 (upd.)

Victor Company of Japan, Limited, II 118–19; 26 511–13 (upd.); 83 444–449 (upd.)

Victoria Coach Station Ltd.*see* London Regional Transport.

Victoria Group, III 399–401; 44 443–46 (upd.)

Victorinox AG, 21 515–17; 74 375–78 (upd.)

Victory Refrigeration, Inc., 82 403–06

Vicunha Têxtil S.A., 78 441–44

Videojet Technologies, Inc., 90 424–27

Vidrala S.A., 67 375–77

Viel & Cie, 76 372–74

Vienna Sausage Manufacturing Co., 14 536–37

Viessmann Werke GmbH & Co., 37 411–14

Viewpoint International, Inc., 66 354–56

ViewSonic Corporation, 72 365–67

Viking Office Products, Inc., 10 544–46 *see also* Office Depot, Inc.

Viking Range Corporation, 66 357–59

Viking Yacht Company, 96 446–49

Village Roadshow Ltd., 58 356–59

Village Super Market, Inc., 7 563–64

Village Voice Media, 38 476–79

Villeroy & Boch AG, 37 415–18

Vilmorin Clause et Cie, 70 344–46

Vilter Manufacturing, LLC, 105 475–79

Vin & Spirit AB, 31 458–61 *see also* V&S Vin & Sprit AB.

Viña Concha y Toro S.A., 45 432–34

Vinci S.A., 27 54; 43 450–52; 113 455–59 (upd.)

Vincor International Inc., 50 518–21

Vinmonopolet A/S, 100 434–37

Vinson & Elkins L.L.P., 30 481–83

Vintage Petroleum, Inc., 42 421–23

Vinton Studios, 63 420–22

Vion Food Group NV, 85 438–41

Virbac Corporation, 74 379–81

Virco Manufacturing Corporation, 17 515–17

Virgin Group Ltd., 12 513–15; 32 491–96 (upd.); 89 479–86 (upd.)

Virginia Dare Extract Company, Inc., 94 447–50

Viridian Group plc, 64 402–04

Visa Inc., 9 536–38; 26 514–17 (upd.); 104 464–69 (upd.)

Viscofan S.A., 70 347–49

Vishay Intertechnology, Inc., 21 518–21; 80 401–06 (upd.)

Vision Service Plan Inc., 77 473–76

Viskase Companies, Inc., 55 379–81

Vista Bakery, Inc., 56 365–68

Vista Chemical Company, I 402–03

Vistana, Inc., 22 537–39

VistaPrint Limited, 87 451–454

Visteon Corporation, 109 572–76

VISX, Incorporated, 30 484–86

Vita Food Products Inc., 99 478–481

Vita Plus Corporation, 60 315–17

Vital Images, Inc., 85 442–45

Vitalink Pharmacy Services, Inc., 15 522–24

Vitamin Shoppe Industries, Inc., 60 318–20

Vitasoy International Holdings Ltd., 94 451–54

Viterra Inc., 105 480–83

Vitesse Semiconductor Corporation, 32 497–500

Vitro Corp., 10 547–48

Vitro Corporativo S.A. de C.V., 34 490–92

Vivarte SA, 54 409–12 (upd.)

Vivartia S.A., 82 407–10

Vivendi, 46 438–41 (upd.); 112 462–68 (upd.)

Vivra, Inc., 18 545–47 *see also* Gambro AB.

Vizio, Inc., 100 438–41

Vlasic Foods International Inc., 25 516–19

VLSI Technology, Inc., 16 518–20

VMware, Inc., 90 428–31

VNU N.V., 27 498–501

VNUS Medical Technologies, Inc., 103 485–88

Vocento, 94 455–58

Vodacom Group Pty. Ltd., 106 481–85

Vodafone Group Plc, 11 547–48; 36 503–06 (upd.); 75 395–99 (upd.)

voestalpine AG, IV 233–35; 57 399–403 (upd.)

Voith Sulzer Papiermaschinen GmbH *see* J.M. Voith AG.

Volcan Compañia Minera S.A.A., 92 403–06

Volcom, Inc., 77 477–80

Volga-Dnepr Group, 82 411–14

Volkert and Associates, Inc., 98 452–55

Volkswagen Aktiengesellschaft, I 206–08; 11 549–51 (upd.); 32 501–05 (upd.); 111 519–25 (upd.)

Volt Information Sciences Inc., 26 518–21

Volunteers of America, Inc., 66 360–62

Von Maur Inc., 64 405–08

Vonage Holdings Corp., 81 415–18

The Vons Companies, Inc., 7 569–71; 28 510–13 (upd.); 103 489–95 (upd.)

Vontobel Holding AG, 96 450–53

Voortman Cookies Limited, 103 496–99

Vornado Realty Trust, 20 508–10; 112 469–74 (upd.)

Vorwerk & Co. KG, 27 502–04; 112 475–79 (upd.)

Vosper Thornycroft Holding plc, 41 410–12

Vossloh AG, 53 348–52

Votorantim Participaçoes S.A., 76 375–78

Index to Industries

Aerospace

Agribusiness & Farming

Airlines

Flight Options, LLC, 75
Flying Boat, Inc. (Chalk's Ocean
 Airways), 56
Frontier Airlines Holdings Inc., 22; 84
 (upd.)
Garuda Indonesia, 6
Gol Linhas Aéreas Inteligentes S.A., 73
Groupe Air France, 6
Grupo Aeroportuario del Pacífico, S.A. de
 C.V., 85
Grupo TACA, 38
Gulf Air Company, 56
Hawaiian Holdings, Inc., 9; 22 (upd.); 96
 (upd.)
Hawker Siddeley Group Public Limited
 Company, III
Hong Kong Dragon Airlines Ltd., 66
Iberia Líneas Aéreas de España S.A., 6; 36
 (upd.); 91 (upd.)
Icelandair, 52
Indian Airlines Ltd., 46
International Airline Support Group, Inc.,
 55
IranAir, 81
Japan Airlines Corporation, I; 32 (upd.);
 110 (upd.)
Jersey European Airways (UK) Ltd., 61
Jet Airways (India) Private Limited, 65
JetBlue Airways Corporation, 44
Kenmore Air Harbor Inc., 65
Kenya Airways Limited, 89
Kitty Hawk, Inc., 22
Kiwi International Airlines Inc., 20
KLM Royal Dutch Airlines, 104 (upd.)
Koninklijke Luchtvaart Maatschappij,
 N.V. (KLM Royal Dutch Airlines), I;
 28 (upd.)
Korean Air Lines Co., Ltd., 6; 27 (upd.);
 114 (upd.)
Kuwait Airways Corporation, 68
Lan Chile S.A., 31
Lauda Air Luftfahrt AG, 48
Lloyd Aéreo Boliviano S.A., 95
Loganair Ltd., 68
LOT Polish Airlines (Polskie Linie
 Lotnicze S.A.), 33
LTU Group Holding GmbH, 37
Malév Plc, 24
Malaysian Airlines System Berhad, 6; 29
 (upd.); 97 (upd.)
Mesa Air Group, Inc., 11; 32 (upd.); 77
 (upd.)
Mesaba Holdings, Inc., 28
Middle East Airlines - Air Liban S.A.L.,
 79
Midway Airlines Corporation, 33
Midwest Air Group, Inc., 35; 85 (upd.)
MN Airlines LLC, 104
NetJets Inc., 96 (upd.)
Northwest Airlines Corporation, I; 6
 (upd.); 26 (upd.); 74 (upd.)
Offshore Logistics, Inc., 37
Pakistan International Airlines
 Corporation, 46
Pan American World Airways, Inc., I; 12
 (upd.)
Panalpina World Transport (Holding)
 Ltd., 47

People Express Airlines, Inc., I
Petroleum Helicopters, Inc., 35
PHI, Inc., 80 (upd.)
Philippine Airlines, Inc., 6; 23 (upd.)
Pinnacle Airlines Corp., 73
Preussag AG, 42 (upd.)
Qantas Airways Ltd., 6; 24 (upd.); 68
 (upd.)
Qatar Airways Company Q.C.S.C., 87
Reno Air Inc., 23
Royal Brunei Airlines Sdn Bhd, 99
Royal Nepal Airline Corporation, 41
Ryanair Holdings plc, 35
SAA (Pty) Ltd., 28
Sabena S.A./N.V., 33
SAS Group, The, 34 (upd.)
Saudi Arabian Airlines, 6; 27 (upd.)
Scandinavian Airlines System, I
Sikorsky Aircraft Corporation, 24; 104
 (upd.)
Singapore Airlines Limited, 6; 27 (upd.);
 83 (upd.)
SkyWest, Inc., 25
Société d'Exploitation AOM Air Liberté
 SA (AirLib), 53
Société Luxembourgeoise de Navigation
 Aérienne S.A., 64
Société Tunisienne de l'Air-Tunisair, 49
Southwest Airlines Co., 6; 24 (upd.); 71
 (upd.)
Spirit Airlines, Inc., 31
Sterling European Airlines A/S, 70
Sun Country Airlines, 30
Swiss Air Transport Company, Ltd., I
Swiss International Air Lines Ltd., 48
TAM Linhas Aéreas S.A., 68
TAME (Transportes Aéreos Militares
 Ecuatorianos), 100
TAP—Air Portugal Transportes Aéreos
 Portugueses S.A., 46
TAROM S.A., 64
Texas Air Corporation, I
Thai Airways International Public
 Company Limited, 6; 27 (upd.)
Tower Air, Inc., 28
Trans World Airlines, Inc., I; 12 (upd.);
 35 (upd.)
TransBrasil S/A Linhas Aéreas, 31
Transportes Aereos Portugueses, S.A., 6
Turkish Airlines Inc. (Türk Hava Yollari
 A.O.), 72
UAL Corporation, 34 (upd.); 107 (upd.)
United Airlines, I; 6 (upd.)
US Airways Group, Inc., I; 6 (upd.); 28
 (upd.); 52 (upd.); 110 (upd.)
Uzbekistan Airways National Air
 Company, 99
VARIG S.A. (Viação Aérea
 Rio-Grandense), 6; 29 (upd.)
Virgin Group Ltd., 12; 32 (upd.); 89
 (upd.)
Volga-Dnepr Group, 82
Vueling Airlines S.A., 97
WestJet Airlines Ltd., 38

Automotive

AB Volvo, I; 7 (upd.); 26 (upd.); 67
 (upd.)

Accubuilt, Inc., 74
Actia Group S.A., 107
Adam Opel AG, 7; 21 (upd.); 61 (upd.)
ADESA, Inc., 71
Advance Auto Parts, Inc., 57
Aftermarket Technology Corp., 83
Aisin Seiki Co., Ltd., III; 48 (upd.)
Alamo Rent A Car, Inc., 6; 24 (upd.); 84
 (upd.)
Alfa Romeo, 13; 36 (upd.)
Alvis Plc, 47
America's Car-Mart, Inc., 64
American Axle & Manufacturing
 Holdings, Inc., 67
American Motors Corporation, I
Amerigon Incorporated, 97
Andretti Green Racing, 106
Applied Power Inc., 9; 32 (upd.)
Arnold Clark Automobiles Ltd., 60
ArvinMeritor, Inc., 8; 54 (upd.)
Asbury Automotive Group Inc., 60
ASC, Inc., 55
Autobacs Seven Company Ltd., 76
Autocam Corporation, 51
Autoliv, Inc., 65
Automobiles Citroen, 7
Automobili Lamborghini Holding S.p.A.,
 13; 34 (upd.); 91 (upd.)
AutoNation, Inc., 50
AutoTrader.com, L.L.C., 91
AVTOVAZ Joint Stock Company, 65
Bajaj Auto Limited, 39
Bayerische Motoren Werke AG, I; 11
 (upd.); 38 (upd.); 108 (upd.)
Behr GmbH & Co. KG, 72
Belron International Ltd., 76
Bendix Corporation, I
Blue Bird Corporation, 35
BorgWarner Inc., III; 14; 32 (upd.); 85
 (upd.)
Brose Fahrzeugteile GmbH & Company
 KG, 84
Budd Company, The, 8
Bugatti Automobiles S.A.S., 94
Caffyns PLC, 105
Canadian Tire Corporation, Limited, 71
 (upd.)
Cardone Industries Inc., 92
CarMax, Inc., 55
CARQUEST Corporation, 29
Caterpillar Inc., III; 15 (upd.); 63 (upd.)
Checker Motors Corp., 89
China Automotive Systems Inc., 87
China FAW Group Corporation, 105
Chrysler Corporation, I; 11 (upd.)
Collins Industries, Inc., 33
Commercial Vehicle Group, Inc., 81
CNH Global N.V., 38 (upd.); 99 (upd.)
Consorcio G Grupo Dina, S.A. de C.V.,
 36
Crown Equipment Corporation, 15; 93
 (upd.)
CSK Auto Corporation, 38
Cummins Engine Company, Inc., I; 12
 (upd.); 40 (upd.)
Custom Chrome, Inc., 16; 74 (upd.)
Daihatsu Motor Company, Ltd., 7; 21
 (upd.)

Beverages

Bio-Technology

Mycogen Corporation, 21
Nektar Therapeutics, 91
New Brunswick Scientific Co., Inc., 45
Omrix Biopharmaceuticals, Inc., 95
Pacific Ethanol, Inc., 81
Pharmion Corporation, 91
Qiagen N.V., 39
Quintiles Transnational Corporation, 21
RTI Biologics, Inc., 96
Seminis, Inc., 29
Senomyx, Inc., 83
Serologicals Corporation, 63
Sigma-Aldrich Corporation, I; 36 (upd.); 93 (upd.)
Starkey Laboratories, Inc., 52
STERIS Corporation, 29
Stratagene Corporation, 70
Talecris Biotherapeutics Holdings Corp., 114
Tanox, Inc., 77
TECHNE Corporation, 52
TriPath Imaging, Inc., 77
Viterra Inc., 105
Waters Corporation, 43
Whatman plc, 46
Wilmar International Ltd., 108
Wisconsin Alumni Research Foundation, 65
Wyeth, 50 (upd.)

Chemicals

A. Schulman, Inc., 8; 49 (upd.)
Aceto Corp., 38
Air Products and Chemicals, Inc., I; 10 (upd.); 74 (upd.)
Airgas, Inc., 54
Akzo Nobel N.V., 13; 41 (upd.); 112 (upd.)
Albaugh, Inc., 105
Albemarle Corporation, 59
AlliedSignal Inc., 9; 22 (upd.)
ALTANA AG, 87
American Cyanamid, I; 8 (upd.)
American Vanguard Corporation, 47
Arab Potash Company, 85
Arch Chemicals Inc. 78
ARCO Chemical Company, 10
Arkema S.A., 100
Asahi Denka Kogyo KK, 64
Atanor S.A., 62
Atochem S.A., I
Avantium Technologies BV, 79
Avecia Group PLC, 63
Azelis Group, 100
Baker Hughes Incorporated, III; 22 (upd.); 57 (upd.)
Balchem Corporation, 42
BASF SE, I; 18 (upd.); 50 (upd.); 108 (upd.)
Bayer A.G., I; 13 (upd.); 41 (upd.)
Betz Laboratories, Inc., I; 10 (upd.)
BFGoodrich Company, The, 19 (upd.)
BOC Group plc, I; 25 (upd.); 78 (upd.)
BorsodChem Zrt., 113
Braskem S.A., 108
Brenntag Holding GmbH & Co. KG, 8; 23 (upd.); 101 (upd.)
Burmah Castrol PLC, 30 (upd.)

Cabot Corporation, 8; 29 (upd.); 91 (upd.)
Calgon Carbon Corporation, 73
Caliper Life Sciences, Inc., 70
Calumet Specialty Products Partners, L.P., 106
Cambrex Corporation, 16
Catalytica Energy Systems, Inc., 44
Celanese Corporation, I; 109 (upd.)
Celanese Mexicana, S.A. de C.V., 54
CF Industries Holdings, Inc., 99
Chemcentral Corporation, 8
Chemi-Trol Chemical Co., 16
Chemtura Corporation, 91 (upd.)
China Petroleum & Chemical Corporation (Sinopec Corp.), 109
Church & Dwight Co., Inc., 29
Ciba-Geigy Ltd., I; 8 (upd.)
Clorox Company, The, III; 22 (upd.); 81 (upd.)
Croda International Plc, 45
Crompton Corporation, 9; 36 (upd.)
Cytec Industries Inc., 27
Degussa-Hüls AG, 32 (upd.)
DeKalb Genetics Corporation, 17
Dexter Corporation, The, I; 12 (upd.)
Dionex Corporation, 46
Dow Chemical Company, The, I; 8 (upd.); 50 (upd.); 114 (upd.)
DSM N.V., I; 56 (upd.)
Dynaction S.A., 67
E.I. du Pont de Nemours & Company, I; 8 (upd.); 26 (upd.)
Eastman Chemical Company, 14; 38 (upd.)
Ecolab Inc., I; 13 (upd.); 34 (upd.); 85 (upd.)
Eka Chemicals AB, 92
Elementis plc, 40 (upd.)
Engelhard Corporation, 72 (upd.)
English China Clays Ltd., 15 (upd.); 40 (upd.)
Enterprise Rent-A-Car Company, 69 (upd.)
Equistar Chemicals, LP, 71
Ercros S.A., 80
ERLY Industries Inc., 17
Ethyl Corporation, I; 10 (upd.)
Evonik Industries AG, 111 (upd.)
Ferro Corporation, 8; 56 (upd.)
Firmenich International S.A., 60
First Mississippi Corporation, 8
FMC Corporation, 89 (upd.)
Formosa Plastics Corporation, 14; 58 (upd.)
Fort James Corporation, 22 (upd.)
Fuchs Petrolub AG, 102
G.A.F., I
General Chemical Group Inc., The, 37
Georgia Gulf Corporation, 9; 61 (upd.)
Givaudan SA, 43
Great Lakes Chemical Corporation, I; 14 (upd.)
GROWMARK, Inc., 88
Guerbet Group, 46
H.B. Fuller Company, 8; 32 (upd.); 75 (upd.)
Hauser, Inc., 46

Hawkins Chemical, Inc., 16
Henkel KGaA, III; 34 (upd.); 95 (upd.)
Hercules Inc., I; 22 (upd.); 66 (upd.)
Hillyard, Inc., 114
Hoechst A.G., I; 18 (upd.)
Hoechst Celanese Corporation, 13
Huls A.G., I
Huntsman Corporation, 8; 98 (upd.)
Ikonics Corporation, 99
IMC Fertilizer Group, Inc., 8
Imperial Chemical Industries PLC, I; 50 (upd.)
Inergy L.P., 110
International Flavors & Fragrances Inc., 9; 38 (upd.)
Israel Chemicals Ltd., 55
KBR Inc., 106 (upd.)
Kemira Oyj, 70
KMG Chemicals, Inc., 101
Koppers Industries, Inc., I; 26 (upd.)
Kwizda Holding GmbH, 102 (upd.)
L'Air Liquide SA, I; 47 (upd.)
Lawter International Inc., 14
LeaRonal, Inc., 23
Loctite Corporation, 30 (upd.)
Loos & Dilworth, Inc., 100
Lonza Group Ltd., 73
Lubrizol Corporation, The, I; 30 (upd.); 83 (upd.)
LyondellBasell Industries Holdings N.V., 45 (upd.); 109 (upd.)
M.A. Hanna Company, 8
MacDermid Incorporated, 32
Makhteshim-Agan Industries Ltd., 85
Mallinckrodt Group Inc., 19
MBC Holding Company, 40
Melamine Chemicals, Inc., 27
Methanex Corporation, 40
Mexichem, S.A.B. de C.V., 99
Minerals Technologies Inc., 52 (upd.)
Mississippi Chemical Corporation, 39
Mitsubishi Chemical Corporation, I; 56 (upd.)
Mitsui Petrochemical Industries, Ltd., 9
Monsanto Company, I; 9 (upd.); 29 (upd.)
Montedison SpA, I
Morton International Inc., I; 9 (upd.); 80 (upd.)
Mosaic Company, The, 91
Nagase & Company, Ltd., 8
Nalco Holding Company, I; 12 (upd.); 89 (upd.)
National Distillers and Chemical Corporation, I
National Sanitary Supply Co., 16
National Starch and Chemical Company, 49
NCH Corporation, 8
Nippon Soda Co., Ltd., 85
Nisshin Seifun Group Inc., 66 (upd.)
NL Industries, Inc., 10
Nobel Industries AB, 9
NOF Corporation, 72
North American Galvanizing & Coatings, Inc., 99
Novacor Chemicals Ltd., 12
Nufarm Ltd., 87

Conglomerates

Construction

Education & Training

Electrical & Electronics

Engineering & Management Services

Entertainment & Leisure

Financial Services: Banks

Financial Services: Excluding Banks

Food Products

Food Services, Retailers, & Restaurants

Health, Personal & Medical Care Products

VHA Inc., 53
VIASYS Healthcare, Inc., 52
Vion Food Group NV, 85
VISX, Incorporated, 30
Vitamin Shoppe Industries, Inc., 60
VNUS Medical Technologies, Inc., 103
Wahl Clipper Corporation, 86
Water Pik Technologies, Inc., 34; 83
  (upd.)
Weider Nutrition International, Inc., 29
Weleda AG 78
Wella AG, III; 48 (upd.)
West Pharmaceutical Services, Inc., 42
Wright Medical Group, Inc., 61
Wyeth, 50 (upd.)
Zila, Inc., 46
Zimmer Holdings, Inc., 45

Health Care Services

Acadian Ambulance & Air Med Services,
  Inc., 39
Adventist Health, 53
Advocat Inc., 46
Allied Healthcare Products, Inc., 24
Almost Family, Inc., 93
Alterra Healthcare Corporation, 42
Alticor Inc., 71 (upd.)
Amedisys, Inc., 53; 106 (upd.)
American Diabetes Association, 109
American Healthways, Inc., 65
American Medical Alert Corporation, 103
American Medical International, Inc., III
American Medical Response, Inc., 39
AMERIGROUP Corporation, 69
AmeriSource Health Corporation, 37
  (upd.)
Amil Participações S.A., 105
AmSurg Corporation, 48
Andrews Institute, The, 99
Applied Bioscience International, Inc., 10
Ardent Health Services LLC, 114
Ascension Health, 114
Assisted Living Concepts, Inc., 43
ATC Healthcare Inc., 64
Baptist Health Care Corporation, 82
Beverly Enterprises, Inc., III; 16 (upd.)
Bon Secours Health System, Inc., 24
Bravo Health Insurance Company, Inc.,
  107
Brookdale Senior Living, 91
C.R. Bard Inc., 9; 65 (upd.)
Cancer Treatment Centers of America,
  Inc., 85
Capital Senior Living Corporation, 75
Caremark Rx, Inc., 10; 54 (upd.)
Catholic Health Initiatives, 91
Children's Comprehensive Services, Inc.,
  42
Children's Healthcare of Atlanta Inc., 101
Children's Hospitals and Clinics, Inc., 54
Chindex International, Inc., 101
Chronimed Inc., 26
The Cleveland Clinic Foundation, 112
COBE Laboratories, Inc., 13
Colorado MEDtech, Inc., 48
Columbia/HCA Healthcare Corporation,
  15
Community Health Systems, Inc., 71

Community Psychiatric Centers, 15
CompDent Corporation, 22
CompHealth Inc., 25
Comprehensive Care Corporation, 15
Continental Medical Systems, Inc., 10
Continucare Corporation, 101
Continuum Health Partners, Inc., 60
Coventry Health Care, Inc., 59
Craig Hospital, 99
Cross Country Healthcare, Inc., 105
CVS Caremark Corporation, 45 (upd.);
  108 (upd.)
Cystic Fibrosis Foundation, 93
DaVita Inc., 73
Erickson Retirement Communities, 57
Express Scripts, Inc., 17; 109 (upd.)
Extendicare Health Services, Inc., 6
Eye Care Centers of America, Inc., 69
FHP International Corporation, 6
Fresenius AG, 56
Genesis Health Ventures, Inc., 18
Gentiva Health Services, Inc., 79
GranCare, Inc., 14
Group Health Cooperative, 41
Grupo Ángeles Servicios de Salud, S.A. de
  C.V., 84
Haemonetics Corporation, 20
Hamot Health Foundation, 91
Hazelden Foundation, 28
HCA, Inc., 35 (upd.); 111 (upd.)
Health Care & Retirement Corporation,
  22
Health Management Associates, Inc., 56
Health Net, Inc., 109 (upd.)
Health Risk Management, Inc., 24
Health Systems International, Inc., 11
HealthSouth Corporation, 14; 33 (upd.)
Henry Ford Health System, 84
Highmark Inc., 27
Hillhaven Corporation, The, 14
Holiday Retirement Corp., 87
Hologic, Inc., 106
Hooper Holmes, Inc., 22
Hospital Central Services, Inc., 56
Hospital Corporation of America, III
Howard Hughes Medical Institute, 39
Humana Inc., III; 24 (upd.); 101 (upd.)
IASIS Healthcare Corporation, 112
Intermountain Health Care, Inc., 27
Jenny Craig, Inc., 10; 29 (upd.); 92
  (upd.)
Kinetic Concepts, Inc. (KCI), 20
LabOne, Inc., 48
Laboratory Corporation of America
  Holdings, 42 (upd.)
LCA-Vision, Inc., 85
Legacy Health System, 114
Life Care Centers of America Inc., 76
Lifeline Systems, Inc., 53
LifePoint Hospitals, Inc., 69
Lincare Holdings Inc., 43
Manor Care, Inc., 6; 25 (upd.)
Marshfield Clinic Inc., 82
Matria Healthcare, Inc., 17
Maxicare Health Plans, Inc., III; 25 (upd.)
Mayo Foundation, 9; 34 (upd.)
McBride plc, 82
McKesson Corporation, 108 (upd.)

Medical Management International, Inc.,
  65
Medical Staffing Network Holdings, Inc.,
  89
Memorial Sloan-Kettering Cancer Center,
  57
Merge Healthcare, 85
Merit Medical Systems, Inc., 29
MeritCare Health System, 88
Mount Sinai Medical Center, 112
Myriad Genetics, Inc., 95
National Health Laboratories
  Incorporated, 11
National Jewish Health, 101
National Medical Enterprises, Inc., III
National Research Corporation, 87
New York City Health and Hospitals
  Corporation, 60
New York Health Care, Inc., 72
NewYork-Presbyterian Hospital, 59
NovaCare, Inc., 11
NSF International, 72
Omnicare, Inc., 111 (upd.)
Option Care Inc., 48
OrthoSynetics Inc., 35; 107 (upd.)
Oxford Health Plans, Inc., 16
PacifiCare Health Systems, Inc., 11
Palomar Medical Technologies, Inc., 22
Pediatric Services of America, Inc., 31
Pediatrix Medical Group, Inc., 61
PHP Healthcare Corporation, 22
PhyCor, Inc., 36
PolyMedica Corporation, 77
Primedex Health Systems, Inc., 25
Providence Health System, 90
Providence Service Corporation, The, 64
Psychemedics Corporation, 89
Psychiatric Solutions, Inc., 68
Quest Diagnostics Inc., 26; 106 (upd.)
Radiation Therapy Services, Inc., 85
RehabCare Group, Inc., 114
Ramsay Youth Services, Inc., 41
Renal Care Group, Inc., 72
Res-Care, Inc., 29
Response Oncology, Inc., 27
Rural/Metro Corporation, 28
Sabratek Corporation, 29
St. Jude Children's Research Hospital,
  Inc., 114
St. Jude Medical, Inc., 11; 43 (upd.); 97
  (upd.)
Salick Health Care, Inc., 53
Scripps Research Institute, The, 76
Select Medical Corporation, 65
Shriners Hospitals for Children, 69
Sierra Health Services, Inc., 15
Sisters of Charity of Leavenworth Health
  System, 105
Smith & Nephew plc, 41 (upd.)
Sports Club Company, The, 25
SSL International plc, 49
Stericycle Inc., 33
Sun Healthcare Group Inc., 25
Sunrise Senior Living, Inc., 81
SwedishAmerican Health System, 51
Tenet Healthcare Corporation, 55 (upd.);
  112 (upd.)
Twinlab Corporation, 34

Rocky Mountain Chocolate Factory, Inc., 73

Rolta India Ltd., 90

RSA Security Inc., 46

RWD Technologies, Inc., 76

SABRE Group Holdings, Inc., 26

SafeNet Inc., 101

Sage Group, The, 43

salesforce.com, Inc., 79

Santa Cruz Operation, Inc., The, 38

SAP AG, 16; 43 (upd.)

SAS Institute Inc., 10; 78 (upd.)

Satyam Computer Services Ltd., 85

SBS Technologies, Inc., 25

SCB Computer Technology, Inc., 29

Schawk, Inc., 24

Scientific Learning Corporation, 95

SCO Group Inc., The, 78

SDL PLC, 67

SeaChange International, Inc., 79

Seagate Technology, 8; 34 (upd.); 105 (upd.)

Siebel Systems, Inc., 38

Sierra On-Line, Inc., 15; 41 (upd.)

SilverPlatter Information Inc., 23

SINA Corporation, 69

SkillSoft Public Limited Company, 81

SmartForce PLC, 43

Smith Micro Software, Inc., 112

Softbank Corp., 13; 38 (upd.); 77 (upd.)

Sonic Solutions, Inc., 81

SonicWALL, Inc., 87

Spark Networks, Inc., 91

Specialist Computer Holdings Ltd., 80

SPSS Inc., 64

Square Enix Holdings Co., Ltd., 101

SRA International, Inc., 77

Standard Microsystems Corporation, 11

STC PLC, III

Steria SA, 49

Sterling Software, Inc., 11

Storage Technology Corporation, 6

Stratus Computer, Inc., 10

StreamServe Inc., 113

Sun Microsystems, Inc., 7; 30 (upd.); 91 (upd.)

SunGard Data Systems Inc., 11

Sybase, Inc., 10; 27 (upd.)

Sykes Enterprises, Inc., 45

Symantec Corporation, 10; 82 (upd.)

Symbol Technologies, Inc., 15

Synchronoss Technologies, Inc., 95

SYNNEX Corporation, 73

Synopsys, Inc., 11; 69 (upd.)

Syntel, Inc., 92

System Software Associates, Inc., 10

Systems & Computer Technology Corp., 19

T-Online International AG, 61

TALX Corporation, 92

Tandem Computers, Inc., 6

TechTarget, Inc., 99

TenFold Corporation, 35

Terra Lycos, Inc., 43

Terremark Worldwide, Inc., 99

Thomson Corporation, The, 34 (upd.); 77 (upd.)

ThoughtWorks Inc., 90

3Com Corporation, 11; 34 (upd.); 106 (upd.)

3DO Company, The, 43

TIBCO Software Inc., 79

Timberline Software Corporation, 15

TomTom N.V., 81

TradeStation Group, Inc., 83

Traffix, Inc., 61

Transaction Systems Architects, Inc., 29; 82 (upd.)

Transiciel SA, 48

Trend Micro Inc., 97

Triple P N.V., 26

Tripwire, Inc., 97

TriZetto Group, Inc., The, 83

Tucows Inc. 78

Ubisoft Entertainment S.A., 41; 106 (upd.)

Unica Corporation, 77

Unilog SA, 42

Unisys Corporation, III; 6 (upd.); 36 (upd.); 112 (upd.)

United Business Media plc, 52 (upd.)

United Internet AG, 99

United Online, Inc., 71 (upd.)

United Press International, Inc., 73 (upd.)

UUNET, 38

VASCO Data Security International, Inc., 79

Verbatim Corporation, 14; 74 (upd.)

Veridian Corporation, 54

VeriFone Holdings, Inc., 18; 76 (upd.)

Verint Systems Inc., 73

VeriSign, Inc., 47

Veritas Software Corporation, 45

Verity Inc., 68

Viasoft Inc., 27

Vital Images, Inc., 85

VMware, Inc., 90

Volt Information Sciences Inc., 26

Wanadoo S.A., 75

Wang Laboratories, Inc., III; 6 (upd.)

Weather Central Inc., 100

WebMD Corporation, 65

WebEx Communications, Inc., 81

West Group, 34 (upd.)

Westcon Group, Inc., 67

Western Digital Corporation, 25; 92 (upd.)

Wikimedia Foundation, Inc., 91

Wind River Systems, Inc., 37

Wipro Limited, 43; 106 (upd.)

Witness Systems, Inc., 87

Wolters Kluwer NV, 33 (upd.)

WordPerfect Corporation, 10

WSI Corporation, 102

Wyse Technology, Inc., 15

Xerox Corporation, III; 6 (upd.); 26 (upd.); 69 (upd.)

Xilinx, Inc., 16; 82 (upd.)

Yahoo! Inc., 27; 70 (upd.)

YouTube, Inc., 90

Zanett, Inc., 92

Zapata Corporation, 25

Ziff Davis Media Inc., 36 (upd.)

Zilog, Inc., 15; 72 (upd.)

Insurance

Admiral Group, PLC, 109

AEGON N.V., III; 50 (upd.)

Aetna Inc., III; 21 (upd.); 63 (upd.)

Aflac Incorporated, 10 (upd.); 38 (upd.); 109 (upd.)

Alexander & Alexander Services Inc., 10

Alfa Corporation, 60

Alleanza Assicurazioni S.p.A., 65

Alleghany Corporation, 10

Allianz AG, III; 15 (upd.); 57 (upd.)

Allmerica Financial Corporation, 63

Allstate Corporation, The, 10; 27 (upd.)

AMB Generali Holding AG, 51

American Family Corporation, III

American Financial Group Inc., III; 48 (upd.)

American General Corporation, III; 10 (upd.); 46 (upd.)

American International Group Inc., III; 15 (upd.); 47 (upd.); 109 (upd.)

American National Insurance Company, 8; 27 (upd.)

American Physicians Service Group, Inc., 114

American Premier Underwriters, Inc., 10

American Re Corporation, 10; 35 (upd.)

N.V. AMEV, III

AOK-Bundesverband (Federation of the AOK) 78

Aon Corporation, III; 45 (upd.); 113 (upd.)

Arthur J. Gallagher & Co., 73

Assicurazioni Generali S.p.A., III; 15 (upd.); 103 (upd.)

Assurances Générales de France, 63

Assured Guaranty Ltd., 93

Atlantic American Corporation, 44

Aviva PLC, 50 (upd.)

AXA Colonia Konzern AG, 27; 49 (upd.)

AXA Equitable Life Insurance Company, III; 105 (upd.)

AXA Group, 114 (upd.)

B.A.T. Industries PLC, 22 (upd.)

Baldwin & Lyons, Inc., 51

Bâloise-Holding, 40

Benfield Greig Group plc, 53

Berkshire Hathaway Inc., III; 18 (upd.); 42 (upd.); 89 (upd.)

Blue Cross and Blue Shield Association, 10

British United Provident Association Limited (BUPAL), 79

Brown & Brown, Inc., 41

Business Men's Assurance Company of America, 14

Capital Holding Corporation, III

Cathay Life Insurance Company Ltd., 108

Catholic Order of Foresters, 24; 97 (upd.)

China Life Insurance Company Limited, 65

ChoicePoint Inc., 65

Chubb Corporation, The, III; 14 (upd.); 37 (upd.); 113 (upd.)

CIGNA Corporation, III; 22 (upd.); 45 (upd.); 109 (upd.)

Cincinnati Financial Corporation, 16; 44 (upd.)

Tokio Marine and Fire Insurance Co., Ltd., The, III
Torchmark Corporation, 9; 33 (upd.)
Transatlantic Holdings, Inc., 11
Travelers Corporation, The, III
UICI, 33
Union des Assurances de Pans, III
United National Group, Ltd., 63
United Services Automobile Association, 109 (upd.)
Unitrin Inc., 16; 78 (upd.)
Universal American Corp., 111
UNUM Corp., 13
UnumProvident Corporation, 52 (upd.)
USAA, 10; 62 (upd.)
USF&G Corporation, III
UTG Inc., 100
Victoria Group, 44 (upd.)
VICTORIA Holding AG, III
Vision Service Plan Inc., 77
W.R. Berkley Corporation, 15; 74 (upd.)
Washington National Corporation, 12
Wawanesa Mutual Insurance Company, The, 68
WellCare Health Plans, Inc., 101
WellChoice, Inc., 67 (upd.)
WellPoint, Inc., 25; 103 (upd.)
Westfield Group, 69
White Mountains Insurance Group, Ltd., 48
Willis Group Holdings Ltd., 25; 100 (upd.)
Winterthur Group, III; 68 (upd.)
Yasuda Fire and Marine Insurance Company, Limited, The, III
Yasuda Mutual Life Insurance Company, The, III; 39 (upd.)
Zurich Financial Services, 42 (upd.); 93 (upd.)
Zürich Versicherungs-Gesellschaft, III

Legal Services

Akin, Gump, Strauss, Hauer & Feld, L.L.P., 33
American Bar Association, 35
American Lawyer Media Holdings, Inc., 32
Amnesty International, 50
Andrews Kurth, LLP, 71
Arnold & Porter, 35
Baker & Daniels LLP, 88
Baker & Hostetler LLP, 40
Baker & McKenzie, 10; 42 (upd.)
Baker and Botts, L.L.P., 28
Bingham Dana LLP, 43
Brobeck, Phleger & Harrison, LLP, 31
Cadwalader, Wickersham & Taft, 32
Chadbourne & Parke, 36
Cleary, Gottlieb, Steen & Hamilton, 35
Clifford Chance LLP, 38
Coudert Brothers, 30
Covington & Burling, 40
CRA International, Inc., 93
Cravath, Swaine & Moore, 43
Davis Polk & Wardwell, 36
Debevoise & Plimpton, 39
Dechert, 43
Dewey Ballantine LLP, 48

DLA Piper, 106
Dorsey & Whitney LLP, 47
Drinker, Biddle and Reath L.L.P., 92
Faegre & Benson LLP, 97
Fenwick & West LLP, 34
Fish & Neave, 54
Foley & Lardner, 28
Fried, Frank, Harris, Shriver & Jacobson, 35
Fulbright & Jaworski L.L.P., 47
Gibson, Dunn & Crutcher LLP, 36
Greenberg Traurig, LLP, 65
Heller, Ehrman, White & McAuliffe, 41
Hildebrandt International, 29
Hogan & Hartson L.L.P., 44
Holland & Knight LLP, 60
Holme Roberts & Owen LLP, 28
Hughes Hubbard & Reed LLP, 44
Hunton & Williams, 35
Jenkens & Gilchrist, P.C., 65
Jones, Day, Reavis & Pogue, 33
Kelley Drye & Warren LLP, 40
King & Spalding, 23
Kirkland & Ellis LLP, 65
Lambda Legal Defense and Education Fund, Inc., 106
Latham & Watkins, 33
LeBoeuf, Lamb, Greene & MacRae, L.L.P., 29
LECG Corporation, 93
Legal Aid Society, The, 48
Mayer, Brown, Rowe & Maw, 47
Milbank, Tweed, Hadley & McCloy, 27
Morgan, Lewis & Bockius LLP, 29
Morrison & Foerster LLP 78
O'Melveny & Myers, 37
Oppenheimer Wolff & Donnelly LLP, 71
Orrick, Herrington and Sutcliffe LLP, 76
Patton Boggs LLP, 71
Paul, Hastings, Janofsky & Walker LLP, 27
Paul, Weiss, Rifkind, Wharton & Garrison, 47
Pepper Hamilton LLP, 43
Perkins Coie LLP, 56
Phillips Lytle LLP, 102
Pillsbury Madison & Sutro LLP, 29
Pre-Paid Legal Services, Inc., 20
Proskauer Rose LLP, 47
Quinn Emanuel Urquhart Oliver & Hedges, LLP, 99
Robins, Kaplan, Miller & Ciresi L.L.P., 89
Ropes & Gray, 40
Saul Ewing LLP, 74
Seyfarth Shaw LLP, 93
Shearman & Sterling, 32
Sidley Austin Brown & Wood, 40
Simpson Thacher & Bartlett, 39
Skadden, Arps, Slate, Meagher & Flom, 18
Slaughter and May, 112
Snell & Wilmer L.L.P., 28
Sonnenschein Nath and Rosenthal LLP, 102
Southern Poverty Law Center, Inc., 74
Stroock & Stroock & Lavan LLP, 40
Sullivan & Cromwell, 26
Troutman Sanders L.L.P., 79

Vinson & Elkins L.L.P., 30
Wachtell, Lipton, Rosen & Katz, 47
Weil, Gotshal & Manges LLP, 55
White & Case LLP, 35
Williams & Connolly LLP, 47
Willkie Farr & Gallagher LLP, 95
Wilmer Cutler Pickering Hale and Dorr L.L.P., 109
Wilson Sonsini Goodrich & Rosati, 34
Winston & Strawn, 35
Womble Carlyle Sandridge & Rice, PLLC, 52

Manufacturing

A.O. Smith Corporation, 11; 40 (upd.); 93 (upd.)
A.T. Cross Company, 17; 49 (upd.)
A.W. Faber-Castell Unternehmensverwaltung GmbH & Co., 51
AAF-McQuay Incorporated, 26
Aalborg Industries A/S, 90
ACCO World Corporation, 7; 51 (upd.)
Acme United Corporation, 70
Acme-Cleveland Corp., 13
Acuity Brands, Inc., 90
Adolf Würth GmbH & Co. KG, 49
AEP Industries, Inc., 36
Aga Foodservice Group PLC, 73
Agfa Gevaert Group N.V., 59
Ahlstrom Corporation, 53
Aktiebolaget Electrolux, 22 (upd.)
Albert Trostel and Sons Company, 113
Alfa Laval AB, III; 64 (upd.)
Alliance Laundry Holdings LLC, 102
Allied Defense Group, Inc., The, 65
Allied Products Corporation, 21
Alltrista Corporation, 30
ALSTOM, 108
Alvis Plc, 47
American Cast Iron Pipe Company, 50
American Equipment Company, Inc., 104
American Homestar Corporation, 18; 41 (upd.)
American Locker Group Incorporated, 34
American Seating Company 78
American Tourister, Inc., 16
American Woodmark Corporation, 31
Amerock Corporation, 53
Ameron International Corporation, 67
AMETEK, Inc., 9; 114 (upd.)
Ampacet Corporation, 67
Anchor Hocking Glassware, 13
Andreas Stihl AG & Co. KG, 16; 59 (upd.)
Andritz AG, 51
Applica Incorporated, 43 (upd.)
Applied Films Corporation, 48
Applied Materials, Inc., 10; 46 (upd.)
AptarGroup, Inc., 69
Arc International, 76
Arçelik A.S., 100
Arctic Cat Inc., 16; 40 (upd.); 96 (upd.)
AREVA NP, 90 (upd.)
Ariens Company, 48
Aristotle Corporation, The, 62
Armor All Products Corp., 16

Materials

Mining & Metals

Nonprofit & Philanthropic Organizations

Paper & Forestry

Personal Services

Randstad Holding nv, 113 (upd.)
Regis Corporation, 18; 70 (upd.)
Rollins, Inc., 11; 104 (upd.)
Rosenbluth International Inc., 14
Screen Actors Guild, 72
Segway LLC, 48
Service Corporation International, 6; 51 (upd.)
Shutterfly, Inc., 98
Snapfish, 83
SOS Staffing Services, 25
Spark Networks, Inc., 91
Stewart Enterprises, Inc., 20
Supercuts Inc., 26
Town & Country Corporation, 19
24 Hour Fitness Worldwide, Inc., 71
UAW (International Union, United Automobile, Aerospace and Agricultural Implement Workers of America), 72
Weight Watchers International Inc., 12; 33 (upd.); 73 (upd.)
Yak Pak, 108
York Group, Inc., The, 50
YTB International, Inc., 108

Petroleum

Abraxas Petroleum Corporation, 89
Abu Dhabi National Oil Company, IV; 45 (upd.); 114 (upd.)
Adani Enterprises Ltd., 97
Aegean Marine Petroleum Network Inc., 89
Agland, Inc., 110
Agway, Inc., 21 (upd.)
Alberta Energy Company Ltd., 16; 43 (upd.)
Alon Israel Oil Company Ltd., 104
Amerada Hess Corporation, IV; 21 (upd.); 55 (upd.)
Amoco Corporation, IV; 14 (upd.)
Anadarko Petroleum Corporation, 10; 52 (upd.); 106 (upd.)
ANR Pipeline Co., 17
Anschutz Corp., 12
Apache Corporation, 10; 32 (upd.); 89 (upd.)
Aral AG, 62
Arctic Slope Regional Corporation, 38
Arena Resources, Inc., 97
Ashland Inc., 19; 50 (upd.)
Ashland Oil, Inc., IV
Atlantic Richfield Company, IV; 31 (upd.)
Atwood Oceanics, Inc., 100
Aventine Renewable Energy Holdings, Inc., 89
Badger State Ethanol, LLC, 83
Baker Hughes Incorporated, 22 (upd.); 57 (upd.)
Basic Earth Science Systems, Inc., 101
Belco Oil & Gas Corp., 40
Benton Oil and Gas Company, 47
Berry Petroleum Company, 47
BG Products Inc., 96
Bharat Petroleum Corporation Limited, 109
BHP Billiton, 67 (upd.)
Bill Barrett Corporation, 71
BJ Services Company, 25

Blue Rhino Corporation, 56
Blue Sun Energy, Inc., 108
Boardwalk Pipeline Partners, LP, 87
Bolt Technology Corporation, 99
Boots & Coots International Well Control, Inc., 79
BP p.l.c., 45 (upd.); 103 (upd.)
Brigham Exploration Company, 75
British Petroleum Company plc, The, IV; 7 (upd.); 21 (upd.)
British-Borneo Oil & Gas PLC, 34
Broken Hill Proprietary Company Ltd., 22 (upd.)
Bronco Drilling Company, Inc., 89
Burlington Resources Inc., 10
Burmah Castrol PLC, IV; 30 (upd.)
Callon Petroleum Company, 47
Caltex Petroleum Corporation, 19
Calumet Specialty Products Partners, L.P., 106
CAMAC International Corporation, 106
Cano Petroleum Inc., 97
Carrizo Oil & Gas, Inc., 97
Chevron Corporation, IV; 19 (upd.); 47 (upd.); 103 (upd.)
Chiles Offshore Corporation, 9
China National Petroleum Corporation, 46; 108 (upd.)
China Petroleum & Chemical Corporation (Sinopec Corp.), 109
Chinese Petroleum Corporation, IV; 31 (upd.)
Cimarex Energy Co., 81
CITGO Petroleum Corporation, IV; 31 (upd.)
Clayton Williams Energy, Inc., 87
Coastal Corporation, The, IV; 31 (upd.)
Compañia Española de Petróleos S.A. (Cepsa), IV; 56 (upd.)
Compton Petroleum Corporation, 103
Comstock Resources, Inc., 47
Conoco Inc., IV; 16 (upd.)
ConocoPhillips, 63 (upd.)
CONSOL Energy Inc., 59
Continental Resources, Inc., 89
Cooper Cameron Corporation, 20 (upd.); 58 (upd.)
Cosmo Oil Co., Ltd., IV; 53 (upd.)
Crown Central Petroleum Corporation, 7
Daniel Measurement and Control, Inc., 16; 74 (upd.)
DeepTech International Inc., 21
Den Norse Stats Oljeselskap AS, IV
Denbury Resources, Inc., 67
Deutsche BP Aktiengesellschaft, 7
Devon Energy Corporation, 61
Diamond Shamrock, Inc., IV
Distrigaz S.A., 82
DOF ASA, 110
Double Eagle Petroleum Co., 114
Dril-Quip, Inc., 81
Duvernay Oil Corp., 83
Dyneff S.A., 98
Dynegy Inc., 49 (upd.)
E.On AG, 50 (upd.)
Edge Petroleum Corporation, 67
Egyptian General Petroleum Corporation, IV; 51 (upd.)

El Paso Corporation, 66 (upd.)
Elf Aquitaine SA, 21 (upd.)
Empresa Colombiana de Petróleos, IV
Enbridge Inc., 43
EnCana Corporation, 109
Encore Acquisition Company, 73
Energen Corporation, 21; 97 (upd.)
ENI S.p.A., 69 (upd.)
Enron Corporation, 19
ENSCO International Incorporated, 57
Ente Nazionale Idrocarburi, IV
Enterprise GP Holdings L.P., 109
Enterprise Oil PLC, 11; 50 (upd.)
Entreprise Nationale Sonatrach, IV
EOG Resources, 106
Equitable Resources, Inc., 54 (upd.)
Ergon, Inc., 95
Exxon Mobil Corporation, IV; 7 (upd.); 32 (upd.); 67 (upd.)
F.L. Roberts & Company, Inc., 113
Ferrellgas Partners, L.P., 35; 107 (upd.)
FINA, Inc., 7
Fluxys SA, 101
Flying J Inc., 19
Flotek Industries Inc., 93
Forest Oil Corporation, 19; 91 (upd.)
Galp Energia SGPS S.A., 98
GDF SUEZ, 109 (upd.)
General Sekiyu K.K., IV
GeoResources, Inc., 101
Giant Industries, Inc., 19; 61 (upd.)
Global Industries, Ltd., 37
Global Marine Inc., 9
GlobalSantaFe Corporation, 48 (upd.)
Grant Prideco, Inc., 57
Grey Wolf, Inc., 43
Gulf Island Fabrication, Inc., 44
Halliburton Company, III; 25 (upd.); 55 (upd.)
Hanover Compressor Company, 59
Hawkeye Holdings LLC, 89
Helix Energy Solutions Group, Inc., 81
Hellenic Petroleum SA, 64
Helmerich & Payne, Inc., 18
Holly Corporation, 12; 111 (upd.)
Hunt Consolidated, Inc., 7; 27 (upd.)
Hunting plc 78
Hurricane Hydrocarbons Ltd., 54
Husky Energy Inc., 47
Idemitsu Kosan Co., Ltd., 49 (upd.)
Idemitsu Kosan K.K., IV
Imperial Oil Limited, IV; 25 (upd.)
Indian Oil Corporation Ltd., IV; 48 (upd.); 95 (upd.); 113 (upd.)
INPEX Holdings Inc., 97
Input/Output, Inc., 73
Iogen Corporation, 81
Ipiranga S.A., 67
KBR Inc., 106 (upd.)
Kanematsu Corporation, IV; 24 (upd.); 102 (upd.)
Kerr-McGee Corporation, IV; 22 (upd.); 68 (upd.)
Kinder Morgan, Inc., 45; 111 (upd.)
King Ranch, Inc., 14
Knot, Inc., The, 74
Koch Industries, Inc., IV; 20 (upd.), 77 (upd.)

Publishing & Printing

Retail & Wholesale

Rubber & Tires

Textiles & Apparel

Stone Manufacturing Company, 14; 43 (upd.)
Stride Rite Corporation, 8; 37 (upd.); 86 (upd.)
Stussy, Inc., 55
Sun Sportswear, Inc., 17
Superior Uniform Group, Inc., 30
Swank, Inc., 17; 84 (upd.)
Tag-It Pacific, Inc., 85
Talbots, Inc., The, 11; 31 (upd.); 88 (upd.)
Tamfelt Oyj Abp, 62
Tarrant Apparel Group, 62
Ted Baker plc, 86
Teijin Limited, V
Thanulux Public Company Limited, 86
Thomaston Mills, Inc., 27
Tilley Endurables, Inc., 67
Timberland Company, The, 13; 54 (upd.); 111 (upd.)
Truworths International Ltd., 107
Tommy Bahama Group, Inc., 108
Tommy Hilfiger Corporation, 20; 53 (upd.)
Too, Inc., 61
Toray Industries, Inc., V; 51 (upd.)
True Religion Apparel, Inc., 79
Tultex Corporation, 13
Tumi, Inc., 112
Under Armour Performance Apparel, 61
Unifi, Inc., 12; 62 (upd.)
United Merchants & Manufacturers, Inc., 13
United Retail Group Inc., 33
Unitika Ltd., V; 53 (upd.)
Umbro plc, 88
Van de Velde S.A./NV, 102
Vans, Inc., 16; 47 (upd.)
Varsity Spirit Corp., 15
VF Corporation, V; 17 (upd.); 54 (upd.)
Vicunha Têxtil S.A. 78
Volcom, Inc., 77
Vulcabras S.A., 103
Walton Monroe Mills, Inc., 8
Warnaco Group Inc., The, 12; 46 (upd.)
Wellco Enterprises, Inc., 84
Wellman, Inc., 8; 52 (upd.)
West Point-Pepperell, Inc., 8
WestPoint Stevens Inc., 16
Weyco Group, Incorporated, 32
Williamson-Dickie Manufacturing Company, 14; 45 (upd.)
Wolverine World Wide, Inc., 16; 59 (upd.)
Woolrich Inc., 62
Zara International, Inc., 83

Tobacco

Altadis S.A., 72 (upd.)
Altria Group Inc., 109 (upd.)
American Brands, Inc., V
B.A.T. Industries PLC, 22 (upd.)
British American Tobacco PLC, 50 (upd.); 114 (upd.)
Brooke Group Ltd., 15
Brown & Williamson Tobacco Corporation, 14; 33 (upd.)
Culbro Corporation, 15

Dibrell Brothers, Incorporated, 12
DIMON Inc., 27
800-JR Cigar, Inc., 27
Gallaher Group Plc, V; 19 (upd.); 49 (upd.)
General Cigar Holdings, Inc., 66 (upd.)
Holt's Cigar Holdings, Inc., 42
House of Prince A/S, 80
Imasco Limited, V
Imperial Tobacco Group PLC, 50
Japan Tobacco Inc., V; 46 (upd.)
KT&G Corporation, 62
Lorillard, Inc., 112
Nobleza Piccardo SAICF, 64
North Atlantic Trading Company Inc., 65
Philip Morris Companies Inc., V; 18 (upd.)
PT Gudang Garam Tbk, 103
R.J. Reynolds Tobacco Holdings, Inc., 30 (upd.)
RJR Nabisco Holdings Corp., V
Rothmans UK Holdings Limited, V; 19 (upd.)
Seita, 23
Souza Cruz S.A., 65
Standard Commercial Corporation, 13; 62 (upd.)
Swedish Match AB, 12; 39 (upd.); 92 (upd.)
Swisher International Group Inc., 23
Tabacalera, S.A., V; 17 (upd.)
Taiwan Tobacco & Liquor Corporation, 75
Universal Corporation, V; 48 (upd.)
UST Inc., 9; 50 (upd.)
Vector Group Ltd., 35 (upd.)

Transport Services

ABC Rail Products Corporation, 18
Abertis Infraestructuras, S.A., 65
Adams Express Company, The, 86
Aegean Marine Petroleum Network Inc., 89
Aéroports de Paris, 33
Air Express International Corporation, 13
Air Partner PLC, 93
Air T, Inc., 86
Airborne Freight Corporation, 6; 34 (upd.)
Alamo Rent A Car, Inc., 6; 24 (upd.); 84 (upd.)
Alaska Railroad Corporation, 60
Alexander & Baldwin, Inc., 10, 40 (upd.)
Allied Worldwide, Inc., 49
AMCOL International Corporation, 59 (upd.)
AMERCO, 6; 67 (upd.)
American Classic Voyages Company, 27
American Commercial Lines Inc., 99
American President Companies Ltd., 6
Anderson Trucking Service, Inc., 75
Anschutz Corp., 12
APL Limited, 61 (upd.)
Aqua Alliance Inc., 32 (upd.)
Arlington Tankers Ltd., 101
Arriva PLC, 69
Atlas Van Lines Inc., 14; 106 (upd.)
Attica Enterprises S.A., 64

Austal Limited, 75
Avis Group Holdings, Inc., 75 (upd.)
Avis Rent A Car, Inc., 6; 22 (upd.)
Avondale Industries, 7; 41 (upd.)
BAA plc, 10
BAE Systems Ship Repair, 73
Bekins Company, 15
Belships ASA, 113
Bénéteau SA, 55
Berliner Verkehrsbetriebe (BVG), 58
Bollinger Shipyards, Inc., 61
Boyd Bros. Transportation Inc., 39
Brambles Industries Limited, 42
Brink's Company, The, 58 (upd.)
British Railways Board, V
Broken Hill Proprietary Company Ltd., 22 (upd.)
Buckeye Partners, L.P., 70
Budget Group, Inc., 25
Budget Rent a Car Corporation, 9
Burlington Northern Santa Fe Corporation, V; 27 (upd.); 111 (upd.)
C.H. Robinson Worldwide, Inc., 40 (upd.)
Canadian National Railway Company, 71 (upd.)
Canadian National Railway System, 6
Canadian Pacific Railway Limited, V; 45 (upd.); 95 (upd.)
Cannon Express, Inc., 53
Carey International, Inc., 26
Carlson Companies, Inc., 6; 22 (upd.); 87 (upd.)
Carver Boat Corporation LLC, 88
Carolina Freight Corporation, 6
Cascade General, Inc., 65
Celadon Group Inc., 30
Central Japan Railway Company, 43
Chantiers Jeanneau S.A., 96
Chargeurs International, 6; 21 (upd.)
CHC Helicopter Corporation, 67
CHEP Pty. Ltd., 80
Chicago and North Western Holdings Corporation, 6
Chicago Transit Authority, 108
Christian Salvesen Plc, 45
Coach USA, Inc., 24; 55 (upd.)
Coles Express Inc., 15
Compagnie Générale Maritime et Financière, 6
Compagnie Maritime Belge S.A., 95
Compañia Sud Americana de Vapores S.A., 100
Con-way Inc., 101
Conrad Industries, Inc., 58
Consolidated Delivery & Logistics, Inc., 24
Consolidated Freightways Corporation, V; 21 (upd.); 48 (upd.)
Consolidated Rail Corporation, V
Correos y Telegrafos S.A., 80
CR England, Inc., 63
Crete Carrier Corporation, 95
Crowley Maritime Corporation, 6; 28 (upd.)
CSX Corporation, V; 22 (upd.); 79 (upd.)
Ctrip.com International Ltd., 97
Dachser GmbH & Co. KG, 88

Danaos Corporation, 91
Danzas Group, V; 40 (upd.)
Dart Group PLC, 77
Deutsche Bahn AG, V; 46 (upd.)
Deutsche Post AG, 108 (upd.)
DHL Worldwide Network S.A./N.V., 6; 24 (upd.); 69 (upd.)
Diana Shipping Inc., 95
Dollar Thrifty Automotive Group, Inc., 25
Dot Foods, Inc., 69
DP World, 81
DryShips Inc., 95
East Japan Railway Company, V; 66 (upd.)
EGL, Inc., 59
Eitzen Group, 107
Electric Boat Corporation, 86
Emery Air Freight Corporation, 6
Emery Worldwide Airlines, Inc., 25 (upd.)
Enterprise Rent-A-Car Company, 6
Estes Express Lines, Inc., 86
Eurotunnel Group, 37 (upd.)
EVA Airways Corporation, 51
Evergreen International Aviation, Inc., 53
Evergreen Marine Corporation (Taiwan) Ltd., 13; 50 (upd.)
Executive Jet, Inc., 36
Exel plc, 51 (upd.)
Expeditors International of Washington Inc., 17; 78 (upd.)
Federal Express Corporation, V
FedEx Corporation, 18 (upd.); 42 (upd.); 109 (upd.)
Ferretti Group SpA, 90
Ferrovie Dello Stato Societa Di Trasporti e Servizi S.p.A., 105
FirstGroup plc, 89
Forward Air Corporation, 75
Fountain Powerboats Industries, Inc., 28
Four Winns Boats LLC, 96
FreightCar America, Inc., 101
Fritz Companies, Inc., 12
Frontline Ltd., 45
Frozen Food Express Industries, Inc., 20; 98 (upd.)
Garuda Indonesia, 58 (upd.)
GATX Corporation, 6; 25 (upd.)
GE Capital Aviation Services, 36
Gefco SA, 54
General Maritime Corporation, 59
Genesee & Wyoming Inc., 27
Genmar Holdings, Inc., 45
Geodis S.A., 67
Go-Ahead Group Plc, The, 28
Greenbrier Companies, The, 19
Greyhound Lines, Inc., 32 (upd.)
Groupe Bourbon S.A., 60
Grupo Aeroportuario del Centro Norte, S.A.B. de C.V., 97
Grupo Aeroportuario del Pacífico, S.A. de C.V., 85
Grupo TMM, S.A. de C.V., 50
Grupo Transportación Ferroviaria Mexicana, S.A. de C.V., 47
Gulf Agency Company Ltd. 78
GulfMark Offshore, Inc., 49
Hanjin Shipping Co., Ltd., 50

Hankyu Corporation, V; 23 (upd.)
Hapag-Lloyd AG, 6; 97 (upd.)
Harland and Wolff Holdings plc, 19
Harmon Industries, Inc., 25
Harper Group Inc., 17
Heartland Express, Inc., 18
Hertz Corporation, The, 9; 33 (upd.); 101 (upd.)
Holberg Industries, Inc., 36
Horizon Lines, Inc., 98
Hornbeck Offshore Services, Inc., 101
Hospitality Worldwide Services, Inc., 26
Hub Group, Inc., 38
Hvide Marine Incorporated, 22
Illinois Central Corporation, 11
Ingalls Shipbuilding, Inc., 12
International Shipholding Corporation, Inc., 27
J.B. Hunt Transport Services Inc., 12
J Lauritzen A/S, 90
Jack B. Kelley, Inc., 102
John Menzies plc, 39
Kansas City Southern Industries, Inc., 6; 26 (upd.)
Kansas City Southern Railway Company, The, 92
Kawasaki Kisen Kaisha, Ltd., V; 56 (upd.)
Keio Corporation, V; 96 (upd.)
Keolis SA, 51
Kinki Nippon Railway Company Ltd., V
Kirby Corporation, 18; 66 (upd.)
Knight Transportation, Inc., 64
Koninklijke Nedlloyd Groep N.V., 6
Kuehne & Nagel International AG, V; 53 (upd.)
La Poste, V; 47 (upd.); 109 (upd.)
Laidlaw International, Inc., 80
Landstar System, Inc., 63
Leaseway Transportation Corp., 12
Localiza Rent a Car S.A., 111
Loma Negra C.I.A.S.A., 95
London Regional Transport, 6
Long Island Rail Road Company, The, 68
Lynden Incorporated, 91
Maine Central Railroad Company, 16
Mammoet Transport B.V., 26
MAN Aktiengesellschaft, III
Marten Transport, Ltd., 84
Martz Group, 56
MasterCraft Boat Company, Inc., 90
Mayflower Group Inc., 6
Mercury Air Group, Inc., 20
Mersey Docks and Harbour Company, The, 30
Metropolitan Transportation Authority, 35
Miller Industries, Inc., 26
Mitsui O.S.K. Lines Ltd., V; 96 (upd.)
Moran Towing Corporation, Inc., 15
Morgan Group, Inc., The, 46
Morris Travel Services L.L.C., 26
Motor Cargo Industries, Inc., 35
National Car Rental System, Inc., 10
National Express Group PLC, 50
National Railroad Passenger Corporation (Amtrak), 22; 66 (upd.)
Newport News Shipbuilding Inc., 13; 38 (upd.)
Neptune Orient Lines Limited, 47

NFC plc, 6
Nippon Express Company, Ltd., V; 64 (upd.)
Nippon Yusen Kabushiki Kaisha (NYK), V; 72 (upd.)
Norfolk Southern Corporation, V; 29 (upd.); 75 (upd.)
Oak Harbor Freight Lines, Inc., 53
Ocean Group plc, 6
Odakyu Electric Railway Co., Ltd., V; 68 (upd.)
Odfjell SE, 101
Odyssey Marine Exploration, Inc., 91
Oglebay Norton Company, 17
Old Dominion Freight Line, Inc., 57
OMI Corporation, 59
Oppenheimer Group, The, 76
Oshkosh Corporation, 7; 98 (upd.)
Österreichische Bundesbahnen GmbH, 6
OTR Express, Inc., 25
Overnite Corporation, 14; 58 (upd.)
Overseas Shipholding Group, Inc., 11
Pacer International, Inc., 54
Pacific Basin Shipping Ltd., 86
Patriot Transportation Holding, Inc., 91
Peninsular and Oriental Steam Navigation Company, The, V; 38 (upd.)
Penske Corporation, V; 19 (upd.); 84 (upd.)
Peter Pan Bus Lines Inc., 106
PHH Arval, V; 53 (upd.)
Pilot Air Freight Corp., 67
Plantation Pipe Line Company, 68
PODS Enterprises Inc., 103
Polar Air Cargo Inc., 60
Port Authority of New York and New Jersey, The, 48
Port Imperial Ferry Corporation, 70
Post Office Group, V
Poste Italiane S.p.A., 108
Preston Corporation, 6
RailTex, Inc., 20
Railtrack Group PLC, 50
REpower Systems AG, 101
Réseau Ferré de France, 66
Roadway Express, Inc., V; 25 (upd.)
Rodriguez Group S.A., 90
Rock-It Cargo USA, Inc., 86
Royal Olympic Cruise Lines Inc., 52
Royal Vopak NV, 41
Russian Railways Joint Stock Co., 93
Ryder System, Inc., V; 24 (upd.)
Saia, Inc., 98
Santa Fe Pacific Corporation, V
Schenker-Rhenus AG, 6
Schneider National, Inc., 36; 77 (upd.)
Sea Ray Boats Inc., 96
Seaboard Corporation, 36; 85 (upd.)
SEACOR Holdings Inc., 83
Securicor Plc, 45
Seibu Railway Company Ltd., V; 74 (upd.)
Seino Transportation Company, Ltd., 6
Simon Transportation Services Inc., 27
Skeeter Products Inc., 96
Smithway Motor Xpress Corporation, 39
Société Nationale des Chemins de Fer Français, V; 57 (upd.)

Utilities

Geographic Index

Albania
Albtelecom Sh. a, 111

Algeria
Sonatrach, IV; 65 (upd.)

Argentina
Acindar Industria Argentina de Aceros
    S.A., 87
Adecoagro LLC, 101
Aerolíneas Argentinas S.A., 33; 69 (upd.)
Alpargatas S.A.I.C., 87
Aluar Aluminio Argentino S.A.I.C., 74
Arcor S.A.I.C., 66
Atanor S.A., 62
Coto Centro Integral de Comercializacion
    S.A., 66
Cresud S.A.C.I.F. y A., 63
Grupo Clarín S.A., 67
Grupo Financiero Galicia S.A., 63
IRSA Inversiones y Representaciones S.A.,
    63
Ledesma Sociedad Anónima Agrícola
    Industrial, 62
Loma Negra C.I.A.S.A., 95
Mastellone Hermanos S.A., 101
Molinos Río de la Plata S.A., 61
Nobleza Piccardo SAICF, 64
Penaflor S.A., 66
Petrobras Energia Participaciones S.A., 72
Quilmes Industrial (QUINSA) S.A., 67
Renault Argentina S.A., 67
SanCor Cooperativas Unidas Ltda., 101
Sideco Americana S.A., 67
Siderar S.A.I.C., 66
Telecom Argentina S.A., 63
Telefónica de Argentina S.A., 61
YPF Sociedad Anonima, IV

Australia
ABC Learning Centres Ltd., 93
Amcor Limited, IV; 19 (upd.), 78 (upd.)
Ansell Ltd., 60 (upd.)
Aquarius Platinum Ltd., 63
Aristocrat Leisure Limited, 54
Arnott's Ltd., 66
Austal Limited, 75
Australia and New Zealand Banking
    Group Limited, II; 52 (upd.)
AWB Ltd., 56
BHP Billiton, 67 (upd.)
Billabong International Limited, 44; 112
    (upd.)
Blundstone Pty Ltd., 76
Bond Corporation Holdings Limited, 10
Boral Limited, III; 43 (upd.); 103 (upd.)
Brambles Industries Limited, 42
Broken Hill Proprietary Company Ltd.,
    IV; 22 (upd.)
Burns, Philp & Company Ltd., 63
Carlton and United Breweries Ltd., I
Cochlear Ltd., 77
Coles Group Limited, V; 20 (upd.); 85
    (upd.)
Colorado Group Ltd., 107
Commonwealth Bank of Australia Ltd.,
    109
CRA Limited, IV; 85 (upd.)
CSL Limited, 112
CSR Limited, III; 28 (upd.)
David Jones Ltd., 60
Elders IXL Ltd., I
Fairfax Media Ltd., 94 (upd.)
Foster's Group Limited, 7; 21 (upd.); 50
    (upd.); 111 (upd.)
Goodman Fielder Ltd., 52
Harvey Norman Holdings Ltd., 56

Hills Industries Ltd., 104
Holden Ltd., 62
James Hardie Industries N.V., 56
John Fairfax Holdings Limited, 7
Lend Lease Corporation Limited, IV; 17
    (upd.); 52 (upd.)
Lion Nathan Limited, 54
Lonely Planet Publications Pty Ltd., 55
Macquarie Bank Ltd., 69
McPherson's Ltd., 66
Metcash Trading Ltd., 58
MYOB Ltd., 86
National Australia Bank Ltd., 111
News Corporation Limited, IV; 7 (upd.);
    46 (upd.)
Nufarm Ltd., 87
Orica Ltd., 112
Pacific Dunlop Limited, 10
Pioneer International Limited, III
PMP Ltd., 72
Publishing and Broadcasting Limited, 54
Qantas Airways Ltd., 6; 24 (upd.); 68
    (upd.)
Repco Corporation Ltd., 74
Ridley Corporation Ltd., 62
Rinker Group Ltd., 65
Rural Press Ltd., 74
Santos Ltd., 81
Sims Metal Management, Ltd., 109
Smorgon Steel Group Ltd., 62
Southcorp Limited, 54
Suncorp-Metway Ltd., 91
TABCORP Holdings Limited, 44
Telecom Australia, 6
Telstra Corporation Limited, 50
Village Roadshow Ltd., 58
Washington H. Soul Pattinson and
    Company Limited, 112
Wesfarmers Limited, 109

Ghana

Greece

Goldstar Co., Ltd., 12
Hanjin Shipping Co., Ltd., 50
Hankook Tire Company Ltd., 105
Hanwha Group, 62
Hite Brewery Company Ltd., 97
Hotel Shilla Company Ltd., 110
Hynix Semiconductor Company Ltd., 111
Hyundai Group, III; 7 (upd.); 56 (upd.)
Kia Motors Corporation, 12; 29 (upd.)
Kookmin Bank, 58
Korea Electric Power Corporation
  (Kepco), 56
Korea Gas Corporation, 114
Korean Air Lines Co., Ltd., 6; 27 (upd.);
  114 (upd.)
KT&G Corporation, 62
Kumho Tire Company Ltd., 105
LG Corporation, 94 (upd.)
Lotte Confectionery Company Ltd., 76
Lotte Shopping Company Ltd., 110
Lucky-Goldstar, II
Pohang Iron and Steel Company Ltd., IV
POSCO, 57 (upd.)
Samick Musical Instruments Co., Ltd., 56
Samsung Electronics Co., Ltd., I; 41
  (upd.); 108 (upd.)
SK Group, 88
Ssangyong Cement Industrial Co., Ltd.,
  III; 61 (upd.)
Tong Yang Cement Corporation, 62
Young Chang Co. Ltd., 107

Spain

Abengoa S.A., 73
Abertis Infraestructuras, S.A., 65
Acciona S.A., 81
Adolfo Dominguez S.A., 72
Altadis S.A., 72 (upd.)
Áreas S.A., 104
Banco Bilbao Vizcaya Argentaria S.A., II;
  48 (upd.)
Banco Central, II
Banco do Brasil S.A., II
Banco Santander, S.A., 36 (upd.); 111
  (upd.)
Baron de Ley S.A., 74
Campofrío Alimentación S.A, 59
Chupa Chups S.A., 38
Codere S.A., 110
Compañia Española de Petróleos S.A.
  (Cepsa), IV; 56 (upd.)
Cortefiel S.A., 64
Correos y Telegrafos S.A., 80
Dogi International Fabrics S.A., 52
El Corte Inglés Group, V; 26 (upd.)
ENDESA S.A., V; 46 (upd.)
Ercros S.A., 80
Federico Paternina S.A., 69
Freixenet S.A., 71
Gas Natural SDG S.A., 69
Grupo Dragados SA, 55
Grupo Eroski, 64
Grupo Ferrovial, S.A., 40
Grupo Ficosa International, 90
Grupo Leche Pascual S.A., 59
Grupo Lladró S.A., 52
Grupo Planeta, 94
Iberdrola, S.A., 49

Iberia Líneas Aéreas de España S.A., 6; 36
  (upd.); 91 (upd.)
Industria de Diseño Textil S.A., 64
Instituto Nacional de Industria, I
La Seda de Barcelona S.A., 100
Loewe S.A., 104
Mapfre S.A., 109
Mecalux S.A., 74
Miquel y Costas Miquel S.A., 68
Mondragón Corporación Cooperativa,
  101
NH Hoteles S.A. 79
Nutrexpa S.A., 92
Obrascon Huarte Lain S.A., 76
Paradores de Turismo de Espana S.A., 73
Pescanova S.A., 81
Puig Beauty and Fashion Group S.L., 60
Real Madrid C.F., 73
Repsol-YPF S.A., IV; 16 (upd.); 40 (upd.)
Sol Meliá S.A., 71
Tabacalera, S.A., V; 17 (upd.)
Telefónica S.A., V; 46 (upd.); 108 (upd.)
TelePizza S.A., 33
Television Española, S.A., 7
Terra Lycos, Inc., 43
Unión Fenosa, S.A., 51
Uralita S.A., 96
Vidrala S.A., 67
Viscofan S.A., 70
Vocento, 94
Vueling Airlines S.A., 97
Zara International, Inc., 83
Zed Group, 93

Sweden

Axel Johnson Group, I
AB Volvo, I; 7 (upd.); 26 (upd.); 67
  (upd.)
Aktiebolaget Electrolux, 22 (upd.)
Aktiebolaget SKF, III; 38 (upd.); 89
  (upd.)
Alfa Laval AB, III; 64 (upd.)
Assa Abloy AB, 112
Astra AB, I; 20 (upd.)
Atlas Copco AB, III; 28 (upd.); 85 (upd.)
Autoliv, Inc., 65
Billerud AB, 100
Boliden AB, 80
Bonnier AB, 52
BRIO AB, 24; 103 (upd.)
Cardo AB, 53
Cloetta Fazer AB, 70
D. Carnegie & Co. AB, 98
Electrolux AB, III; 53 (upd.)
Eka Chemicals AB, 92
FöreningsSparbanken AB, 69
Gambro AB, 49
Gunnebo AB, 53
H&M Hennes & Mauritz AB, 98 (upd.)
Hennes & Mauritz AB, 29
Hexagon AB, 78
Hilding Anders AB, 102
Holmen AB, 52 (upd.); 111 (upd.)
ICA AB, II
Investor AB, 63
KappAhl Holding AB, 107
Kooperativa Förbundet, 99
Mo och Domsjö AB, IV

Modern Times Group AB, 36
NetCom Systems AB, 26
Nilson Group AB, 113
Nobel Industries AB, 9
Nobia AB, 103
Nordea AB, 40
Observer AB, 55
Perstorp AB, I; 51 (upd.)
Saab Automobile AB, I; 11 (upd.); 32
  (upd.); 83 (upd.)
Sandvik AB, IV; 32 (upd.); 77 (upd.)
Sapa AB, 84
SAS Group, The, 34 (upd.)
Scandinavian Airlines System, I
Scania AB, 112
Securitas AB, 42; 112 (upd.)
Skandia Insurance Company, Ltd., 50
Skandinaviska Enskilda Banken AB, II; 56
  (upd.)
Skanska AB, 38; 110 (upd.)
SSAB Svenskt Stål AB, 89
Stora Kopparbergs Bergslags AB, IV
Sveaskog AB, 93
Svenska Cellulosa Aktiebolaget SCA, IV;
  28 (upd.); 85 (upd.)
Svenska Handelsbanken AB, II; 50 (upd.)
Svenska Spel AB, 107
Sveriges Riksbank, 96
Swedish Match AB, 12; 39 (upd.); 92
  (upd.)
Swedish Telecom, V
Systembolaget AB, 113
Telefonaktiebolaget LM Ericsson, V; 46
  (upd.)
TeliaSonera AB, 57 (upd.)
Trelleborg AB, 93
Vattenfall AB, 57
V&S Vin & Sprit AB, 91 (upd.)
Vin & Spirit AB, 31

Switzerland

ABB ASEA Brown Boveri Ltd., II; 22
  (upd.)
ABB Ltd., 65 (upd.)
Actelion Ltd., 83
Adecco S.A., 36 (upd.)
Adia S.A., 6
AMAG Group, 102
Arthur Andersen & Company, Société
  Coopérative, 10
Aryzta AG, 112 (upd.)
Ascom AG, 9
Bâloise-Holding, 40
Barry Callebaut AG, 29; 71 (upd.)
Benninger AG, 107
Bernina Holding AG, 47
Bodum Design Group AG, 47
Bon Appetit Holding AG, 48
Charles Vögele Holding AG, 82
Chocoladefabriken Lindt & Sprüngli AG,
  27
Chocolat Frey AG, 102
Ciba-Geigy Ltd., I; 8 (upd.)
Compagnie Financiere Richemont AG, 50
Conzzeta Holding, 80
Coop Schweiz Genossenschaftsverband, 48
Credit Suisse Group, II; 21 (upd.); 59
  (upd.)

Taiwan

Thailand

Trinidad and Tobago

Tunisia

Turkey

Ukraine

United Arab Emirates

United Kingdom

United States

McCormick & Company, Incorporated, 7; 27 (upd.)
McCormick & Schmick's Seafood Restaurants, Inc., 71
McCoy Corporation, 58
McDATA Corporation, 75
McDermott International, Inc., III; 37 (upd.)
McDonald's Corporation, II; 7 (upd.); 26 (upd.); 63 (upd.)
McDonnell Douglas Corporation, I; 11 (upd.)
McGrath RentCorp, 91
McGraw-Hill Companies, Inc., The, IV; 18 (upd.); 51 (upd.)
MCI WorldCom, Inc., V; 27 (upd.)
McIlhenny Company, 20
McJunkin Corporation, 63
McKee Foods Corporation, 7; 27 (upd.)
McKesson Corporation, I; 12; 47 (upd.); 108 (upd.)
McKinsey & Company, Inc., 9
McLanahan Corporation, 104
McLane Company, Inc., 13
McLeodUSA Incorporated, 32
McMenamins Pubs and Breweries, 65
McMurry, Inc., 105
McNaughton Apparel Group, Inc., 92 (upd.)
MCN Corporation, 6
MCSi, Inc., 41
McWane Corporation, 55
MDU Resources Group, Inc., 7; 42 (upd.); 114 (upd.)
Mead & Hunt Inc., 113
Mead Corporation, The, IV; 19 (upd.)
Mead Data Central, Inc., 10
Mead Johnson & Company, 84
Meade Instruments Corporation, 41
Meadowcraft, Inc., 29; 100 (upd.)
MeadWestvaco Corporation, 76 (upd.)
Measurement Specialties, Inc., 71
Mecklermedia Corporation, 24
Medarex, Inc., 85
Medco Containment Services Inc., 9
MEDecision, Inc., 95
Media Arts Group, Inc., 42
Media General, Inc., 7; 38 (upd.)
Media Sciences International, Inc., 104
Mediacom Communications Corporation, 69
MediaNews Group, Inc., 70
Medicine Shoppe International, Inc., 102
Medical Action Industries Inc., 101
Medical Information Technology Inc., 64
Medical Management International, Inc., 65
Medical Staffing Network Holdings, Inc., 89
Medicis Pharmaceutical Corporation, 59
Medifast, Inc., 97
MedImmune, Inc., 35
Medis Technologies Ltd., 77
Meditrust, 11
Medline Industries, Inc., 61
Medtronic, Inc., 8; 30 (upd.); 67 (upd.)
Medusa Corporation, 24
Megafoods Stores Inc., 13

Meguiar's, Inc., 99
Meier & Frank Co., 23
Meijer, Inc., 7; 27 (upd.); 101 (upd.)
Mel Farr Automotive Group, 20
Melaleuca Inc., 31
Melamine Chemicals, Inc., 27
Mellon Bank Corporation, II
Mellon Financial Corporation, 44 (upd.)
Mellon-Stuart Company, I
Melting Pot Restaurants, Inc., The, 74
Melville Corporation, V
Melvin Simon and Associates, Inc., 8
MEMC Electronic Materials, Inc., 81
Memorial Sloan-Kettering Cancer Center, 57
Memry Corporation, 72
Men's Wearhouse, Inc., The, 17; 48 (upd.)
Menard, Inc., 34; 104 (upd.)
Menasha Corporation, 8; 59 (upd.)
Mendocino Brewing Company, Inc., 60
Mentholatum Company Inc., The, 32
Mentor Corporation, 26
Mentor Graphics Corporation, 11
Mercantile Bankshares Corp., 11
Mercantile Stores Company, Inc., V; 19 (upd.)
Mercer International Inc., 64
Merchants Company, The, 102
Merck & Co., Inc., I; 11 (upd.); 34 (upd.); 95 (upd.)
Mercury Air Group, Inc., 20
Mercury General Corporation, 25
Mercury Interactive Corporation, 59
Mercury Marine Group, 68
Meredith Corporation, 11; 29 (upd.); 74 (upd.)
Merge Healthcare, 85
Merial Ltd., 102
Meridian Bancorp, Inc., 11
Meridian Gold, Incorporated, 47
Merillat Industries Inc., 13
Merillat Industries, LLC, 69 (upd.)
Merisant Worldwide, Inc., 70
Merisel, Inc., 12
Merit Energy Company, 114
Merit Medical Systems, Inc., 29
MeritCare Health System, 88
Meritage Corporation, 26
Merix Corporation, 36; 75 (upd.)
Merkle Inc., 114
Merrell Dow, Inc., I; 9 (upd.)
Merriam-Webster Inc., 70
Merrill Corporation, 18; 47 (upd.)
Merrill Lynch & Co., Inc., II; 13 (upd.); 40 (upd.)
Merry-Go-Round Enterprises, Inc., 8
Mervyn's California, 10; 39 (upd.)
Mesa Air Group, Inc., 11; 32 (upd.); 77 (upd.)
Mesaba Holdings, Inc., 28
Mestek Inc., 10
Metal Management, Inc., 92
Metalico Inc., 97
Metatec International, Inc., 47
Metavante Corporation, 100
Meteor Industries Inc., 33
Methode Electronics, Inc., 13

Metris Companies Inc., 56
Metro Information Services, Inc., 36
Metro-Goldwyn-Mayer Inc., 25 (upd.); 84 (upd.)
Metrocall, Inc., 41
Metromedia Company, 7; 14; 61 (upd.)
Metropolitan Baseball Club Inc., 39
Metropolitan Financial Corporation, 13
Metropolitan Life Insurance Company, III; 52 (upd.)
Metropolitan Museum of Art, The, 55
Metropolitan Opera Association, Inc., 40
Metropolitan Transportation Authority, 35
Mexican Restaurants, Inc., 41
Meyer Natural Angus L.L.C., 112
MFS Communications Company, Inc., 11
MGA Entertainment, Inc., 95
MGIC Investment Corp., 52
MGM MIRAGE, 17; 98 (upd.)
MGM/UA Communications Company, II
Miami Herald Media Company, 92
Miami Subs Corporation, 108
Michael Anthony Jewelers, Inc., 24
Michael Baker Corporation, 14; 51 (upd.)
Michael C. Fina Co., Inc., 52
Michael Foods, Inc., 25
Michaels Stores, Inc., 17; 71 (upd.)
Michigan Bell Telephone Co., 14
Michigan National Corporation, 11
Michigan Sporting Goods Distributors, Inc., 72
Micrel, Incorporated, 77
Micro Warehouse, Inc., 16
MicroAge, Inc., 16
Microdot Inc., 8
Micron Technology, Inc., 11; 29 (upd.)
Micros Systems, Inc., 18
Microsemi Corporation, 94
Microsoft Corporation, 6; 27 (upd.); 63 (upd.)
MicroStrategy Incorporated, 87
Mid-America Apartment Communities, Inc., 85
Mid-America Dairymen, Inc., 7
Midas Inc., 10; 56 (upd.)
Middleby Corporation, The, 22; 104 (upd.)
Middlesex Water Company, 45
Middleton Doll Company, The, 53
Midland Company, The, 65
Midway Airlines Corporation, 33
Midway Games, Inc., 25; 102 (upd.)
Midwest Air Group, Inc., 35; 85 (upd.)
Midwest Grain Products, Inc., 49
Midwest Resources Inc., 6
Mikasa, Inc., 28
Mike-Sell's Inc., 15
Mikohn Gaming Corporation, 39
Milacron, Inc., 53 (upd.)
Milbank, Tweed, Hadley & McCloy, 27
Miles Laboratories, I
Millennium Pharmaceuticals, Inc., 47
Miller Brewing Company, I; 12 (upd.)
Miller Industries, Inc., 26
Miller Publishing Group, LLC, 57
Milliken & Co., V; 17 (upd.); 82 (upd.)
Milliman USA, 66
Millipore Corporation, 25; 84 (upd.)